THE
NORTH CAROLINA
GAZETTEER

D0062658

THE
NORTH CAROLINA
GAZETTEER

by WILLIAM S. POWELL

THE UNIVERSITY OF NORTH CAROLINA PRESS
CHAPEL HILL

98 97 96 95 94   13 12 11 10 9

For

my mother
and in memory of
my father

Who from summer to summer took
me on vacation trips from one
end of North Carolina to the other.
I cannot remember when I did not
know and love the coast, the
mountains, and many special places
in between.

PREFACE

The North Carolina Gazetteer is a geographical dictionary in which an attempt has been made to list all of the geographic features of the state in one alphabet. It is current and it is historical as well. Many features and places that no longer exist are included; many towns and counties for which plans were made but which never materialized are also included. Some names appearing on old maps may have been imaginary, but many of them also appear in this gazetteer.

Each entry is located according to the county in which it is found. I have not felt obliged to keep entries uniform. The altitude of a place, the date of incorporation of a city or town, may appear in the beginning of one entry and at the end of another. Some entries may appear more complete than others. I have included whatever information I could find. If there is no comment on the origin or meaning of a name, it is because the information was not available. In some cases, however, resort to an unabridged dictionary may suggest the meaning of many names.

Names of former post offices have been included only when the name was more than a convenience for delivering mail. If a post office name was attached to a community, it probably will appear. In the days before rural free delivery, however, hundreds of post offices existed in private homes or in stores. When a postmaster died or retired, the post office would be moved to the home or the store of the new postmaster, and frequently this meant that it would be in another county. The post office name was nothing more than a means of distributing mail. Lists of post offices will be found in postal directories. I do not consider them of importance in a gazetteer.

HOW THE GAZETTEER DEVELOPED

In 1951, when I was a member of the staff of the State Department of Archives and History, I read an interesting manuscript journal kept in the early eighteenth century by a British merchant who visited North

Carolina seeking a suitable location for a retail store. He mentioned several people with whom he talked and a number of creeks and small communities. The journal was unsigned, the people it mentioned were obscure, and the place names are no longer shown on maps. I returned the journal to its proper box and gave up my hopes of editing it for publication.

A few months later a commercial airplane exploded over eastern North Carolina, and a small community whose name appeared on no maps of the state suddenly was in newspaper headlines throughout the United States. At about the same time the name of a mountain in western North Carolina appeared in the state newspapers for some reason that I no longer remember, perhaps it was mentioned in a syndicated feature story on moonshiners. My attempts to locate the mountain on maps or in books was fruitless.

As a member of the Archives staff and later at the North Carolina Collection in Chapel Hill, I realized how futile it was to search for the names of small communities, streams, and other geographical features in any logical manner. No national gazetteer lists them. Many maps, even county maps, do not name them.

It was to meet such needs as this that I began the compilation of a North Carolina gazetteer some fifteen years ago. I cannot recall the circumstances of its beginning. For more than thirty years I have maintained an organized card file of notes on subjects of historical and bibliographical interest to me, and at first I simply dropped possible gazetteer entries into this file. Somewhere along the way the idea for a more serious use of these cards developed, and I began to think about how to proceed.

In response to a request from a patron directed to the North Carolina Collection for information concerning townships in the state, I compiled an alphabetical list of all townships. I do not think that such a list had been compiled previously. It was made from census reports in which townships are listed only by county. Entered on cards, this list soon became a part of the developing gazetteer file.

A request for information concerning the colonial parishes of eighteenth-century North Carolina led me to examine the laws creating counties and parishes. A list of parishes was the result, and this also was soon incorporated into my file.

Piecemeal work would accomplish little and might even be wasted, so I decided to approach the problem of compiling a gazetteer county by county. With a manageable unit, I undertook to gain some experience and to work out some standards. I began with Iredell County, where I grew up, and with Johnston County, where I was born. My personal knowledge of the face of the land in these counties was helpful in attempting to work out a plan for writing descriptions from information shown on maps. I next undertook an unfamiliar county—Alamance, the first in the alphabet and also conveniently nearby so that I could easily visit with map and note card in hand for an on-the-scene comparison.

Since soil survey maps are available for nearly all of the counties and

show a large amount of detailed information, they became the basic map
with which I worked. Although rather uniform in the amount and type of
information shown, their chief drawback is that they have appeared
sporadically from the early twentieth century until 1967. I supplemented
them with large county maps prepared by the State Highway Commission,
and for the county whose soil survey map was quite old, the highway map
was of great importance. These two maps were used in compiling the basic
entries for each county. Supplementary entries were prepared from such
diverse sources as the reports of the United States Board on Geographic
Names, county histories, geological surveys, lists of post offices, lists of
streams compiled by the North Carolina Department of Water Resources,
entries in *The North Carolina Guide,* and other general printed works.
Federal and state reports listing altitudes were combed for supplementary
information. Inscriptions of historical markers along the highways of the
state frequently provided additional facts. When I happened to be travel-
ing in the state, I made notes for entries on named communities, streams,
and other features as I encountered them.

During this period the county remained the basic unit by which I
worked. Cards containing entries for each county were filed in alphabetical
order by county. In 1960 I sought out men and women who were authorities on local history and geography in each county and asked that each
examine my file for the particular county. Many new entries resulted from
their contributions, but many were also eliminated. The problem of the
changing of county lines through the years, as well as the creation of new
counties from old, meant that I had not always properly located geographic
features. Many errors were corrected.

When the cards were returned to me from the counties, they were
microfilmed in their original county arrangement for security purposes and
to provide a means of checking them in this order at a later date if that
became necessary. The cards for all of the counties were then filed in one
alphabet. At this stage it became possible to combine entries for streams
flowing through one or more counties and for mountains that cross county
lines. Many duplications and errors were discovered and eliminated.

At this time historical maps were examined and entries were made show-
ing the earliest appearance of a name, changes in name which could be
determined from maps, and the names of features that no longer appear on
modern maps. Although the state is inadequately covered by United States
Geological Survey and Army Map Service maps, they were also examined
at this stage of the development of the gazetteer. They were not a major
source of information, however, because to take detailed information from
those that were available would have produced an unbalanced coverage of
the state. Nevertheless, the place names (streams and communities, for
example) which seemed to be of Indian origin and suggested early settlement were included because of their particular interest to historians, folk-
lorists, geologists, and botanists. These were included in the gazetteer as
they were discovered by chance while comparing soil survey and state

highway maps with geological survey or army map service maps. It is hoped that this arbitrary decision will not make use of the gazetteer difficult.

TERMS

Numerous generic terms form a part of the specific name of many geographic features in North Carolina. A few of them will be unfamiliar to some readers, but reference to a dictionary will provide definitions of most. Among these might be considered *bald, butt* or *butte, cove* (both in the mountains and along the bank of a stream or the ocean), *face* (generally an exposed rock surface on a mountain), *flat* (often any level place in the mountains), *hollow* (in the sense of a valley or mountain cove), *knob, lead* (which may be unique to North Carolina and for which I have been unable to get an entirely satisfactory definition, although it seems to be a mountain term for a lesser mountain or spur "leading" off the larger mountain), *pocosin* (a swamp or boggy place that may also run or flow as a stream), *run* (generally an eastern term to be equated with creek or branch), *spur, stamp* (in the mountains, apparently a place devoid of trees), and *top*.

The term *brook* occurs only three times in the gazetteer; *creek* and *branch* are the forms used for small streams. The term *village* apparently was used a few times before the Civil War, but in a very loose way, and it is not used today as applied to a municipality. All municipalities are incorporated either as cities or as towns, and I have attempted to use the proper term in the descriptions. Apparently the term *city* was first used in North Carolina in the laws of 1881. Unincorporated places dignified by a name are described simply as communities.

A number of general entries have been made which may be found useful. They include Coastal Plain, fall line, General Assembly (listing the places at which the legislature has met), geographic center, Mountain Region, Piedmont, thermal belt, and Welsh Tract, among numerous others.

ALPHABETIZING, SPELLING, AND ABBREVIATIONS

The gazetteer is arranged in straight alphabetical order by name whether the name consists of one word or more. The generic term is considered in this arrangement to be part of the name, as Collett Creek, Collett Ridge. Collinstown follows Collins Mountain because *t* follows *m*. The fact that Collinstown is one word and Collins Mountain two is not considered. In the case of duplicate names (Grassy Branch, for example) the arrangement under the name is alphabetical by county: Grassy Branch in Buncombe County will precede Grassy Branch in Cleveland County. If there were a community named Grassy Branch, it would follow all of the entries for *branches* of that name. The feature described by the generic name is listed before all other uses of the name: all mountains named Black Mountain are entered ahead of the town named Black Mountain. In alphabetizing I have followed the commonsense practice of arranging all Mc's and Mac's as though they were Mac. This, of course, puts Macedonia,

Mackerel, and Macon among the Mac's, but the advantages of such an arrangement are obvious. Words with irregular or unexpected spellings are interfiled alphabetically as though they were spelled correctly, for example Thorofare is entered as though it were spelled Thoroughfare.

An effort has been made to use the spelling preferred at or near the feature described. When obvious errors have been made in recent years by mapmakers in Raleigh, New York, or Chicago, I have followed the local usage, often with mention of the error. Sometimes historical precedent for a different form than that used on modern maps is so strong that I have commented on it.

Few abbreviations have been used. Alt.—altitude; approx.—approximate or approximately; inc.—incorporated; n—north; s—south; e—east; w—west; ne—northeast; etc.

MAPS

Throughout the gazetteer, references will be found to early usage of names or locations of features on certain maps. Further information on these maps will be found in William P. Cumming, *The Southeast in Early Maps* (Chapel Hill: The University of North Carolina Press, 1962) or in standard bibliographies of American maps available in most libraries of the state. A number of the maps cited have been reproduced in facsimile by the State Department of Archives and History, Raleigh.

The maps that I have most often cited are: White (1585), DeBry's engraving of White (1590), Velasco (1611), Smith (1624), Comberford (1657), Ogilby (1671), Hack (1684), Moll (1729), Moseley (1733), Collet (1770), Price (1808), and MacRae (1833). The gazetteer may be found to be virtually an index to these maps. In addition, many other maps are cited in occasional entries.

OTHER SOURCES

The need for a reference book such as this has been recognized for many years. *The Peoples Press* (Salem) for March 7, 1856, and *The American Advocate* (Kinston) for September 11, 1856, contained an advertisement in which William D. Cooke of Raleigh sought information for a North Carolina gazetteer. He asked for lists of post offices by county with distance and direction of each from the "county town," the names of rivers and creeks with the direction in which they flowed, the names and locations of mills and factories, the schools and colleges with the number of teachers and pupils, and the churches and their denominations. There is no evidence that Cooke's interest in the subject ever produced a book.

North Carolina entries in national gazetteers have always been brief and limited. The first publication to do more than list the counties and the larger cities and rivers was *How They Began: The Story of North Carolina County, Town, and Other Place Names,* compiled by workers of the WPA Writers' Program and published in New York in 1941 under the sponsorship of the State Department of Conservation and Development. Long out of print, it contained only seventy-three pages and numerous errors.

A useful source for information on counties and county seats is D. L. Corbitt's *The Formation of the North Carolina Counties* (Raleigh: State Department of Archives and History, 1950). Based on the laws of North Carolina and on the published *Colonial* and *State Records,* it contains detailed information on both the formation of the counties and on the subsequent changes in their boundaries. A new printing of this work with errata sheets is now being planned.

CORRECTIONS

In a work such as this, opportunities for error abound. I can only hope that I have avoided careless errors. Poor judgment may account for some, but in the face of conflicting evidence I have often had to make arbitrary decisions. Many possible entries have been omitted simply because I was uncertain of the reliability of the information. I am maintaining a file of such entries with the hope that additional information may come to light to answer my questions.

I will be grateful for information on which to base corrections as well as information that may lead to new entries. Correspondence on this subject may be addressed to the North Carolina Collection, University of North Carolina, Chapel Hill.

WILLIAM S. POWELL

Chapel Hill
March 30, 1968

ACKNOWLEDGMENTS

For assistance in many phases of the compilation of this gazetteer my greatest indebtedness is to George Stevenson, Jr., and to my wife, Virginia Waldrop Powell. With tireless devotion to the project, they have compiled long lists of entries from assorted sources. My special thanks go to George Stevenson for his careful work in comparing numerous historic maps with contemporary maps and preparing notes on early locations of geographic features and the changes in name that can best be discovered by this process. From published lists of altitudes, post offices, streams, and many shorter lists of various kinds, my wife prepared and interfiled hundreds of cards.

Two grants from the University Research Council made it possible for me to have the services at various times of four student assistants: George M. Beasley III, James A. Chesnutt III, William H. Salling, Jr., and George Stevenson, Jr. I am grateful to the University Research Council for its generosity and to these young men for the personal interest they took in their work. Without them the gazetteer would have been delayed many years.

Individuals throughout the state willingly answered my questions about specific places; others, hearing of the gazetteer, voluntarily contributed information. My indebtedness to them is great and my regret is sincere that I cannot acknowledge their contributions by name simply because they were so numerous.

Those on whom I called frequently for specific help include: C. Ritchie Bell, for botanical information; Sanford Boswell; Richard Bryson, especially for the preparation of the county maps; Myra Champion; Fred Coker; D. L. Corbitt; Christopher Crittenden; L. Polk Denmark; Louise McG. Hall; U. T. Holmes, for translations of foreign words, particularly Gaelic; Thomas Hyatt; Roy Johnson; J. O. Kilmartin, for information from the files of the United States Board on Geographic Names; Mrs. Pattie B. Mc-

Intyre; Elizabeth McPherson; Mrs. Elizabeth Merritt; Thomas C. Parra-
more; Mrs. Mary J. Rogers; Bill Sharpe; Frederick Symmes: Gary Trawick;
Mae Tucker; and Mrs. Elizabeth Wilborn. They responded with enthu-
siasm to all of my pleas for assistance.

Hardly a state or municipal agency escaped my persistent search for
facts, and many private business concerns fared little better. County agricultural agents, registrars of deeds, mayors, city and town clerks, as well
as postmasters displayed admirable civic spirit in their attempts to furnish
me with the information I sought. The office of the Secretary of State, the
State Highway Commission, the Department of Conservation and Development, and especially the staffs of the State Department of Archives and
History and of the State Library were generous with the time they devoted
in replying to my letters and telephone calls. Chambers of Commerce
throughout the state and the North Carolina League of Municipalities in
Raleigh willingly supplied data and showed not the least sign of annoyance
at my repeated requests for their services. To many members of the staff
of the Institute of Government in Chapel Hill I am deeply indebted for
information and advice, but especially to the director, John Sanders, and to
Marion Benfield, a former staff member. At my request they asked a team of
researchers working through all of the Session Laws of North Carolina for
another purpose, to record also the date of incorporation of municipalities.
This information, I feel, is a valuable part of the gazetteer. Officials of the
Carolina Power & Light Company, Duke Power Company, and the Virginia
Electric and Power Company proved to be generous sources for geographical facts as did officials of the railroads operating in the state. Attorneys and
surveyors in many counties came forward with information they had
gleaned from years of experience in working with local records. Editors of
every newspaper in the state came to my aid. They published many "letters
to the editor" in my desperate attempts to find persons with specific information.

At a critical stage in the preparation of the North Carolina gazetteer, I
sent the file of county entries to one or more knowledgeable persons in each
county. To these people my debt is great. They added much new information and saved me from many errors. Those errors which remain, however, should in no wise be considered the fault of anyone but me. In all
fairness it must be pointed out that for various reasons based on editorial
policy I could not always accept the advice offered me.

Without the help of the following North Carolinians this work would be
less complete and less accurate:

ALAMANCE COUNTY	*Howard White*
ALEXANDER COUNTY	*Charles E. Echerd*
	Homer M. Keever
	J. P. Lentz
ALLEGHANY COUNTY	*J. K. Doughton*
ANSON COUNTY	*Mary Louise Medley*

ASHE COUNTY	*Colonel A. L. Fletcher*
	Mrs. Jesse A. Reeves
AVERY COUNTY	*Horton Cooper*
BEAUFORT COUNTY	*Mrs. Pauline Worthy*
BERTIE COUNTY	*Dr. W. P. Jacocks*
BLADEN COUNTY	*Mrs. Carl C. Campbell*
BRUNSWICK COUNTY	*Cornelius Thomas*
BUNCOMBE COUNTY	*D. Hiden Ramsey*
	Colonel Paul A. Rockwell
BURKE COUNTY	*Dr. Edward W. Phifer*
CABARRUS COUNTY	*Eugenia Lore*
	Harold Nash
CALDWELL COUNTY	*James B. Dula*
	Allan L. Poe
CAMDEN COUNTY	*Jesse F. Pugh*
CARTERET COUNTY	*Tucker Littleton*
	F. C. Salisbury
CASWELL COUNTY	*H. G. Jones*
CATAWBA COUNTY	*Mrs. J. M. Ballard*
	Dr. J. E. Hodges
CHATHAM COUNTY	*Wade Barber*
	John H. London
	Lawrence F. London
CHEROKEE COUNTY	*John C. Christie*
CHOWAN COUNTY	*Elizabeth Vann Moore*
CLAY COUNTY	*Mrs. J. Walter Moore*
CLEVELAND COUNTY	*Mrs. O. Max Gardner*
COLUMBUS COUNTY	*Jim High*
CRAVEN COUNTY	*Rose B. Carraway*
	Elizabeth Moore
CUMBERLAND COUNTY	*Frank H. Jeter*
CURRITUCK COUNTY	*Dudley W. Bagley*
DARE COUNTY	*David Stick*
DAVIDSON COUNTY	*Wade H. Phillips*
	M. Jewell Sink
DAVIE COUNTY	*Flossie Martin*
DUPLIN COUNTY	*Mrs. Fred D. Hamrick, Jr.*
	Mrs. Christine W. Williams
DURHAM COUNTY	*A. B. Markham*
EDGECOMBE COUNTY	*Mabrey Bass, Jr.*
FORSYTH COUNTY	*Mary C. Wiley*
FRANKLIN COUNTY	*Hamilton H. Hobgood*
	Phil R. Inscoe
GASTON COUNTY	*Brice T. Dickson*
GATES COUNTY	*William T. Cross*
	Mrs. O. C. Turner

GRAHAM COUNTY	*W. M. Sherrill*
GRANVILLE COUNTY	*Claude A. Renn*
GREENE COUNTY	*Charles R. Holloman*
GUILFORD COUNTY	*James G. W. MacLamroc*
HALIFAX COUNTY	*Mrs. Quentin Gregory*
HARNETT COUNTY	*Malcolm Fowler*
HAYWOOD COUNTY	*Hiram C. Wilburn*
HENDERSON COUNTY	*Mrs. Sadie S. Patton*
HERTFORD COUNTY	*Mrs. W. D. Boone*
HOKE COUNTY	*Mrs. Kate B. Covington*
	Admiral A. M. Patterson
HYDE COUNTY	*Tommie Gaylord*
IREDELL COUNTY	*Homer M. Keever*
	Mrs. W. B. Knox
JACKSON COUNTY	*J. R. Buchanan*
JOHNSTON COUNTY	*Mrs. W. B. Beasley*
	T. J. Lassiter
JONES COUNTY	*John D. Larkins, Jr.*
	Tucker Littleton
LEE COUNTY	*Paul J. Barringer*
LENOIR COUNTY	*Charles R. Holloman*
LINCOLN COUNTY	*Mrs. Joseph Graham*
MC DOWELL COUNTY	*Ruth M. Greenlee*
MACON COUNTY	*Thomas A. Henson*
	Weimar Jones
	Lake V. Shope
MADISON COUNTY	*Mrs. J. B. Tweed*
MARTIN COUNTY	*R. H. Goodmon*
MECKLENBURG COUNTY	*Charles R. Brockmann*
MITCHELL COUNTY	*Jason B. Deyton*
MONTGOMERY COUNTY	*Colonel Jeffery F. Stanback*
MOORE COUNTY	*R. E. Wicker*
NASH COUNTY	*L. S. Inscoe*
NEW HANOVER COUNTY	*Louis T. Moore*
NORTHAMPTON COUNTY	*Mrs. Nancy Froelich*
ONSLOW COUNTY	*J. Parsons Brown*
	Tucker Littleton
ORANGE COUNTY	*L. J. Phipps*
PAMLICO COUNTY	*Dallas Mallison*
PASQUOTANK COUNTY	*L. S. Blades, Jr.*
PENDER COUNTY	*Clifton L. Moore*
PERQUIMANS COUNTY	*Mrs. J. Emmett Winslow*
PERSON COUNTY	*R. B. Griffin*
PITT COUNTY	*D. L. Corbitt*

POLK COUNTY	*Alan T. Calhoun*
	Mrs. Sadie S. Patton
RANDOLPH COUNTY	*Cleveland Thayer*
RICHMOND COUNTY	*Isaac S. London*
ROBESON COUNTY	*Penn Gray*
ROCKINGHAM COUNTY	*Mrs. Bettie Sue Gardner*
	Mrs. S. R. Prince
ROWAN COUNTY	*William D. Kizzah*
RUTHERFORD COUNTY	*Mrs. Fred D. Hamrick, Jr.*
SAMPSON COUNTY	*Mrs. Taft Bass*
SCOTLAND COUNTY	*A. B. Gibson*
STANLY COUNTY	*Fred T. Morgan*
STOKES COUNTY	*Mrs. Grace T. Rodenbough*
	L. H. van Noppen
SURRY COUNTY	*J. S. Gentry*
SWAIN COUNTY	*Kelly E. Bennett*
TRANSYLVANIA COUNTY	*O. H. Orr*
TYRRELL COUNTY	*Sara L. Taft*
UNION COUNTY	*S. Glen Hawfield*
	W. S. Tarlton
VANCE COUNTY	*S. T. Peace*
WAKE COUNTY	*Christopher Crittenden*
	Mrs. Mary J. Rogers
	Mrs. Louis Woodward
WARREN COUNTY	*J. Edward Allen*
WASHINGTON COUNTY	*Mrs. Tom Grier*
	Mrs. L. E. Hassell
WATAUGA COUNTY	*D. J. Whitener*
WAYNE COUNTY	*Mrs. E. Charles Powell*
	Mrs. S. R. Prince
WILKES COUNTY	*Johnson J. Hayes*
	Allan L. Poe
	T. E. Story
WILSON COUNTY	*Hugh B. Johnston, Jr.*
YADKIN COUNTY	*William Rutledge*
YANCEY COUNTY	*H. Grady Bailey*

For help with the tremendous task of alphabetizing some 20,000 cards, I am grateful to Mrs. Elizabeth Merritt, George Stevenson, Jr., Mrs. Pattie B. McIntyre, Mrs. Archibald Henderson, Miss Florence Blakely, Miss Mary L. Thornton, Mrs. Jane C. Bahnsen, and to my mother-in-law, Mrs. John B. Hill, my sons, John and Charles, and my wife Virginia.

It is with a real sense of loss that I must say that a number of people with whom I have worked on the North Carolina gazetteer have died. I miss their friendship, and their knowledge of local history is also a loss to the state and to their home communities.

Finally it remains my pleasure to acknowledge sincere appreciation to the Z. Smith Reynolds Foundation of Winston-Salem and to the University Research Council for generous grants to The University of North Carolina Press which made possible the publication of this book.

THE
NORTH CAROLINA
GAZETTEER

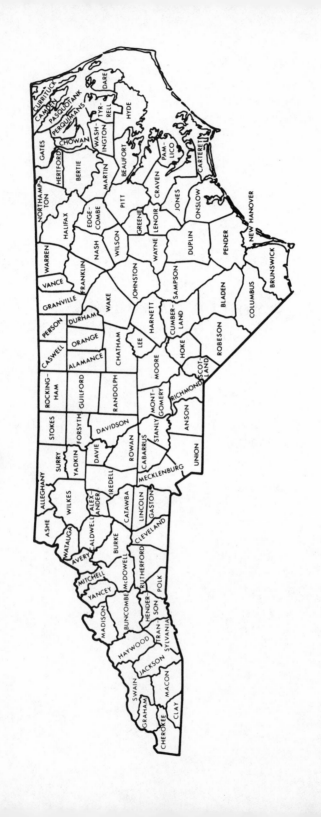

A

Aaron. *See* Montezuma.

Aaron. *See* Hood Swamp.

Aaron Branch rises in n Mitchell County and flows se into Bean Creek.

Aaron Creek rises in ne Cherokee County and flows nw into Taylor Creek.

Aaron Duff. *See* Iron Duff.

Aarons Corner, community in n Stokes County. Named for a church.

Aarons Creek rises in nw Granville County and flows ne into Virginia where it enters Dan River.

Aaron Swamp rises in w Robeson County and flows s into Ashpole Swamp.

Abbots Island. *See* Croatoan Island.

Abbot Top, mountain in central Cherokee County between Hiwassee River and West Prong Grape Creek.

Abbottsburg, town in sw Bladen County. Inc. 1903. Alt. approx. 99. Named for Joseph C. Abbott (1825-81), president of the Cape Fear Building Company here.

Abbotts Creek rises in ne Davidson County and flows sw into Yadkin River. Appears as Abbots Creek on the Collet map, 1770.

Abbott's Creek rises in n Wake County and flows ne into Neuse River.

Abbotts Creek, community in ne Davidson County. A Primitive Baptist Church was founded here in 1756. General Nathanael Greene camped here in February, 1781, before the Battle of Guilford Court House.

Abbotts Creek Township, ne Davidson. County.

Abbotts Creek Township, se Forsyth County.

Abbotts Township, sw Bladen County.

Abbs Creek rises in n Jackson County and flows s into Caney Fork.

Abe Creek rises in s Macon County and flows se into West Fork Overflow Creek.

Abel Bay, sw Hyde County in the mouth of Pungo River.

Abel's Creek rises in North River Pocosin in s Camden County and flows e into North River.

Aberdeen, town in s Moore County Inc.

1893. Known as Blue's Crossing until renamed in 1887 for the seaport in Scotland. Produces carpets, hosiery, textiles, furniture, and canned foods. Alt. 339.

Aberdeen Creek rises in s Moore County and flows sw into Lumber River. Known as Devil's Gut Creek or Devils Creek until early in the twentieth century.

Aberly, community in e Onslow County.

Abernethy, community in w Iredell County.

Abernethy Creek rises in sw Gaston County and flows ne and se in an arc into Crowders Creek.

Abes Mountain, sw Cleveland County near Broad River. Alt. 950.

Abier Creek rises in se Burke County and flows n into Henry Fork.

Abigails Islands appear on the Smith map, 1624, as the cluster of islands in Pamlico Sound off s Hyde County between Rose Bay and Swanquarter Bay. Now Bell, Great, Judith, Marsh, and Swanquarter Islands, *which see.*

Abingdon Creek rises in sw Caldwell County and flows se into Lower Creek. Sometimes called Greasy Creek. Originally Aventon Creek for Aventon Sherrill, early settler.

Abner, community in n Montgomery County.

Abraham Bay, small bay in the mouth of Turnagain Bay in n Carteret County.

Abraham's Plains, former district in ne Granville County. It had 62 heads of families in 1790 at the time of the first census. Took its name from the home of Col. Samuel Smith who had fought in the battle at Abraham's Plains at Quebec, Canada.

Abrams Branch rises in s Transylvania County and flows ne into French Broad River.

Abshers, community in n Wilkes County between Harris Creek and Middle Prong Roaring River.

Academy Crossroads. *See* Nahunta.

Acconeechy. *See* Hillsborough.

Ace Enloe Ridge, ne Swain County in Great

Smoky Mountains National Park, a short spur of Hughes Ridge.

Acme, town in ne Columbus County on Livingston Creek. Known originally as Livingston for the creek. Inc. 1905 as Cronly and named for local landowner; name changed to Acme, 1911, for Acme Manufacturing Company, producer of fertilizer. Produces fertilizer and paper. Alt. 37.

Acorn, community on Jones Pond e Gates County. Sometimes also known as Acorn Hill.

Acorn Hill. See Acorn.

Acre, community in n central Beaufort County. Long Acre appears on the Collet map, 1770, as a ridge in the Dismal Swamp of ne Beaufort and s Washington counties. It supported a post road from Plymouth to Bath. It is called Long Acre on various maps until Kerr, 1882, where it is marked "Long Acre Ridge." Long Acre community grew up at the s end of the ridge and a post office here from 1883 to 1907 was called Acresville. By 1917 it was called Acre from the railroad name and the ridge was no longer recorded on maps. Alt. 32.

Acresville. See Acre.

Acton, community between Enka and Sulphur Springs, central Buncombe County.

Adake, community in w Caldwell County on Wilsons Creek.

Adams, community in central Watauga County.

Adams Branch rises in n Cleveland County and flows se into Knob Creek.

Adams Branch rises in s central Transylvania County and flows s into French Broad River.

Adams Creek rises in central Cabarrus County and flows se into Dutch Buffalo Creek. Named for John Adam Blackwelder, an early settler.

Adams Creek rises in central Carteret County and flows n into Craven County where it enters Neuse River. A canal connecting the headwaters of Adams Creek with Newport River provides access between Newport and Neuse rivers for the Intracoastal Waterway. For a part of its course Adams Creek forms the boundary between Carteret and Craven counties.

Adams Creek rises in e Swain County and flows s between Cooper Creek and Owl Branch into Oconaluftee River.

Adams Crossroads, community in w Wake County between Brier Creek and Sycamore Creek.

Adams Hollow, in nw Swain County extends s on a tributary of Ekaneetlee Creek to Grill Cove.

Adams Mountain, w Caldwell County, Alt. 1,500.

Adams Point, point of land in e Beaufort County on Pamlico River near the mouth of Pungo River. Appears on the Moseley map, 1733.

Adams Store, community in n Halifax County.

Adams Store. See Adamsville.

Adamsville, former community in central Wayne County on the e edge of Goldsboro. At one time known as Adams Store. Now within the corporate limits of Goldsboro.

Addie, community in n Jackson County, on Scotts Creek. Located about 3 mi. ne of town of Sylva. Alt. 2,249.

Addor, town in s Moore County. Inc. 1881 as Keyser; named for an officer of the Raleigh and Augusta Airline Railroad. During World War I the name became unpopular because of the similarity to "Kaiser." Name changed in October, 1918, to Addor in honor of Felix Addor, local resident, who had been killed on the troopship S. S. Leviathan in March. Long inactive in municipal affairs.

Adkin Branch rises in n Lenoir County and flows se through the city of Kinston into Neuse River. Named for Robert Atkins who had land grants here in 1729.

Adkins, community in n Yancey County.

Adkins Branch rises in n Buncombe County and flows nw into Madison County where it enters Ivy River.

Adkins Falls, rapids in Cape Fear River in central Harnett County e of the town of Lillington, and near the confluence of Buies Creek with the river. Mentioned as early as 1819 in a survey of the rivers of North Carolina.

Adley, community in s Wilkes County on the s side of Yadkin River. The home of Captain John Brown in which the Wilkes County government was organized in March, 1778, is across the river. The W. Kerr Scott Dam is here.

Ad Tate Knob, on Utah Mountain in central Haywood County.

Advalorem Branch rises in n Swain County

between Jumpup Ridge and Bald Ridge and flows se into Forney Creek.

Advance, town in e Davie County. Known as Shady Grove as early as 1816. When a post office was est. in 1877 a new name was required because there was already a Shady Grove post office in the state. Named because local citizens expected progress with the addition of a post office to their community—it would advance. Inc. 1893. Alt. 810.

Affinity. *See* Marietta.

Afton, community in sw Warren County between Lees Branch and the head of Richneck Creek. Post office est. 1872, but discontinued in 1919.

Afton Run, stream, rises in n Cabarrus County and flows s into Coddle Creek. Also appears in early documents as Ashton Run and Astin's Run.

Aggie Run is formed in nw Beaufort County by the junction of Old Ford Swamp and Snoad Branch. It flows s into Tranters Creek.

Agiqua. *See* French Broad River.

Aho, community in s Watauga County near the heads of Stony Branch, Moore Branch, and Buffalo Creek. It is said that a group of men gathered to select a name for the community but being unable to agree on a name, decided that the next word spoken by any one of them would be accepted. After a long silence B. B. Dougherty arose, stretched, and said "Aho!"

Ahoskie, town in s Hertford County. Post office as early as 1828 named Ahosky Ridge. Inc. 1893. Name of Indian origin, spelled Ahostsky and Ahostskey as early as 1719. Produces apparel, lumber and wooden containers. Alt. 59.

Ahoskie Creek rises in se Northampton County and flows ne into Hertford County where it enters Ahoskie Swamp.

Ahoskie Swamp rises in s Hertford County and flows se and ne into Bear Swamp. Appears as Ahotskey Swamp on the Collet map, 1770.

Ahosky Township, s Hertford County.

Ahosky Ridge. *See* Ahoskie.

Ahostsky, Ahostskey, Ahotskey. *See* Ahoskie.

Aiken Branch rises in nw Swain County and flows se into Lake Cheoah.

Aiken Mill Creek rises in s Transylvania County and flows n into French Broad River.

Aiken Mountain, s Transylvania County between Aiken Creek and Carson Creek.

Airbellows, former community in s Alleghany County, now an entrance to the Blue Ridge Parkway. Alt. 3,800.

Air Bellows Gap on the Alleghany-Wilkes County line. An early road across the Blue Ridge Mountains passed through this gap. Alt. 3,744.

Airlie, community in w Halifax County.

Airlie, community in e New Hanover County on the n side of Bradleys Creek.

Akwetiyi, a spot on Tuckasegee River in nw Jackson County, about 1 mi. nw of town of Dillsboro, and between mouth of Dicks Creek and mouth of Laurel Branch. According to Indian tradition there was a dangerous water monster in the river here. The meaning of the name is lost.

Alamance, community in w Alamance County. A post office est. here as early as 1828; cotton mill built in 1837 by E. M. Holt. Alt. 454. Post office name for many years was Allemance.

Alamance Battleground State Historic Site, w central Alamance County. Markers and a museum on the 40-acre site tell the story of the battle on May 16, 1771, in which the North Carolina militia under Gov. William Tryon defeated the Regulators.

Alamance Church, community in se Guilford County. Second Ulster Scots Presbyterian Church in Guilford County, founded in second half of 18th century.

Alamance County was formed in 1849 from Orange County. Located in the central part of the state, it is bounded by Orange, Chatham, Randolph, Guilford, and Caswell counties. Named for Great Alamance Creek, *which see*, or the Battle of Alamance, May 16, 1771. The name appears as Aramancy River in the writings of William Byrd, 1728. Area: 434 sq. mi. County seat: Graham with an elevation of 656 ft. Townships are Nos. 1-13, formerly Patterson, Coble, Boon Station, Morton, Faucette, Graham, Albright, Newlin, Thompson, Melville, Pleasant Grove, Burlington, and Haw River. Produces wheat, oats, corn, tobacco, poultry, dairy and beef cattle, textiles, hosiery, electronics, paper boxes, apparel, furniture, crushed stone, prophyllite, and bricks.

Alamance Creek. *See* Great Alamance Creek.

Alarka, community in s Swain County on Yalaka Creek from which it takes its name.

Alarka. *See also* Yalaka.

Albans, community in ne Union County.

The Albemarle, or the **Albemarle Section,** a term applied to ne North Carolina. This was the location of the first county, Albemarle County, *which see.*

Albemarle, city and county seat in n central Stanly County. Alt. 505. Post office opened here as Smith's Store in 1826; name changed to Albemarle, 1841. Inc. 1857. Named for George Monck (1608-79), Duke of Albemarle, one of the original Lords Proprietors of Carolina in 1663.

Albemarle Beach, nw Washington County on Albemarle Sound, w of the town of Mackeys. Formerly known as Reas Beach.

Albemarle City Lake, central Stanly County on Long Creek. Formed in 1915. Covers 75 acres; maximum depth 40 ft. Fishing, swimming, boating.

Albemarle County was est. in 1664 in the ne portion of the Lords Proprietors' new province of Carolina covering a poorly defined 1,600 sq. mi. The first governor of the County was appointed in October, 1664, and it soon also had a legislature and courts. By 1668 it was divided into Chowan, Currituck, Pasquotank, and Perquimans precincts. The County ceased to exist as a unit of government in Carolina in 1689 when Governor Seth Sothel departed. The next governor had his commission for "that part of our province of Carolina that lyes north and east of Cape feare," which was basically the whole of modern North Carolina.

Albemarle River. *See* Albemarle Sound.

Albemarle Section. *See* The Albemarle.

Albemarle Sound, ne North Carolina, separated from the Atlantic Ocean by a part of the Outer Banks. Approx. 52 mi. long

and 5 to 14 mi. wide. Max. depth 25 ft. Sea level; fresh water not affected by tide. Waters from the Chowan and Roanoke rivers enter the Sound on the west; it drains into Roanoke, Croatan, and Pamlico Sounds. Explored by Ralph Lane, 1586; known as Sea of Rawnocke (Roanoke Sea) in 1609. Appears as Roanoke Sound on the Comberford map, 1657. Known briefly in 1663 as Carolina River and appears as Albemarle River on the Locke map, 1671, and the Blome map, 1672. The John Barnwell map of about 1722 was one of the first to use the name Albemarle Sound. First permanent settlements in North Carolina were made along its n shore. Named after 1663 for George Monck, Duke of Albemarle, one of the Lords Proprietors of Carolina. *See also* Weapemeoc.

Albemarle Township. *See* North Albemarle Township; South Albemarle Township.

Albert Mountain, s Macon County between Bearpen Gap and the head of Hurricane Creek. Alt. 5,207.

Albertson, community in ne Duplin County. Post office est. here as early as 1828.

Albertson Township, ne Duplin County.

Alberty. *See* Fairview.

Albright Township, former township in s central Alamance County, now township number 7.

Albright Township, nw Chatham County.

Albrittons, community in w Lenoir County.

Alder Branch, community in s Camden County. Alt. 10. Probably named for the alder bush which grows in profusion in the vicinity. The branch, called Cross Branch in colonial days, connects a swamp which drains into Pasquotank River to another swamp which drains into North River.

Aldridge Creek rises in sw Person County and flows se into South Flat River.

Alert, community in n Franklin County. Alt. 300. Settled about 1900. Name chosen by first postmaster, Thomas D. Farrow.

Alexander, town in n Buncombe County on French Broad River. Settled about 1828; inc. 1905 but long inactive in municipal affairs. Named for James Mitchell Alexander who built and operated a stagecoach tavern here. Alt. 1,791.

Alexander Branch rises in n Buncombe County near Lovelace Gap and flows nw into Paint Fork.

Alexander County was formed in 1847 from Iredell, Caldwell, and Wilkes counties. Located in the w central section of the state, it is bounded by Iredell, Catawba, Caldwell, and Wilkes counties. It was named for William Julius Alexander (1797-1857), member of the General Assembly from Mecklenburg County and Speaker of the House of Commons. Area: 259 sq. mi. County seat: Taylorsville with an elevation of 1,247 ft. Townships are Ellendale, Gwaltneys, Little River, Millers, Sharpes, Sugar Loaf, Taylorsville, and Wittenburg. Produces wheat, oats, dairy livestock, textiles, furniture, paper boxes, and sand.

Alexander Knob. See Jess Knob.

Alexander Mills, town in s Rutherford County. Inc. 1925. Named for textile mill est. by J. F. Alexander.

Alexandriana. See Croft.

Alexis, town in n Gaston County. Inc. 1899, but long inactive in municipal affairs. Formerly known as Alex's Cross Roads for a man named Alexander who owned land here.

Alex's Creek. See Grants Creek.

Alex's Cross Roads. See Alexis.

Alfordston, town authorized to be laid off and incorporated 1793, on land of Thomas Matthews. Site approx. one mi. s of Carthage, central Moore County. The town was never laid off.

Alfordsville, community in w Robeson County. A post office as early as 1822.

Alfordsville Township, sw Robeson County.

Alfred, community in se Beaufort County. Settled about 1910 and named for Fred R. Alfred, large landowner. Alt. 25.

Alfred Creek rises in ne Cherokee County and flows nw into Taylor Creek.

Alkalithia Springs. See All Healing Springs.

Allan Branch rises in n Yancey County and flows e into Nolichucky River.

Allan Creek rises in s Duplin County and flows s into Island Creek.

Allan Creek rises in n Madison County and flows se into Little Laurel Creek.

Allanstand, community in n Madison County on Martin Creek. In the days when stock was driven to market a drover's station or stand was operated here by a man named Allen.

Allbone Branch rises in w Clay County and flows sw into Hiwassee River.

Alleghany County was formed in 1859 from Ashe County. In the nw part of the state, it is bounded by the state of Virginia and by Surry, Wilkes, and Ashe counties. The name is a corruption of the Delaware Indian name for the Allegheny and Ohio rivers and is said to have meant "a fine stream." Area: 230 sq. mi. County seat: Sparta with an elevation of 2,939 ft. Townships are Cherry Lane, Cranberry, Gap Civil, Glade Creek, Piney Creek, Prathers Creek, and Whitehead. Produces corn, dairy products, livestock, textiles, apparel, crushed stone. There are manganese and granite deposits in the county.

Alleghany Township, s Davidson County.

Allegheny, community n Madison County on Shelton Laurel Creek.

Allegheny Mountains. See Appalachian Mountains.

Allemance. See Alamance.

Allen, community in ne Mecklenburg County.

Allen Branch rises in n Cherokee County and flows se into Davis Creek.

Allen Branch rises in ne Cherokee County and flows s into Junaluska Creek.

Allen Branch rises in central Henderson County and flows nw into Clear Creek.

Allen Branch rises in n Macon County and flows w into Burningtown Creek.

Allen Branch. See Bill Allen Branch.

Allen Creek rises in se Brunswick County and flows ne into McKenzie Pond (which see) which is drained by Lilliput Creek. Named for Eleazer Allen (1692-1750) founder of Lilliput Plantation. Name appears on the MacRae map, 1833. See also Lilliput Creek.

Allen Creek rises in s Catawba County and flows nw into Maiden Creek.

Allen Creek rises in s Haywood County and flows ne into Richland Creek. Named for Allen family, pioneer settlers in Haywood County, approx. 1812.

Allendale Township, se Hoke County.

Allen Gap, n Cherokee County near the headwaters of Allen Branch.

Allen Mountain, ne Buncombe County.

Allen Mountain, in s Macon County between Ball Creek and Coweeta Creek.

Allens Branch rises in n Jackson County and flows se into Scott Creek.

Allens Branch rises in e Orange County and flows ne into New Hope Creek.

Allens Creek rises in e Haywood County and flows nw into Pigeon River. Named for Allen family, pioneer settlers in Haywood County, approx. 1812.

Allen's Creek. See Lilliput.

Allens Crossroads, community in s Granville County.

Allen's Crossroads, community in sw Johnston County.

Allen's Fall. See Ramseur.

Allens Level, community in s Person County.

Allensville, community in e Person County. Formerly known as Trilby.

Allensville Township, e central Person County.

Allenton, community in e Robeson County. Alt. 131. Settled about 1868. Named for W. H. Allen, trainmaster. Bear Bay, post office one mile east, abandoned with the development of Allenton.

Allenton, former town in se Stanly County on Pee Dee River. Laid off in 1-acre lots on an 85-acre tract on the lands of William and James Allen and John Davison in 1799. A post office as early as 1822; Allenton ferry operated here into the twentieth century. Site now under waters of Lake Tillery.

Allents Cove Branch rises in e Transylvania County and flows n into Crab Creek.

All Healing Springs, community in w Alexander County. Springs discovered 1882 by Milt Milstead and developed as a resort which was popular as late as 1911. Named for supposed healing qualities of water; known also as Alkalithia Springs. Alt. 1,225.

All Healing Springs, community in sw Gaston County near the ne slope of Crowders Mountain. A health resort flourished here in the late nineteenth and early twentieth centuries because of the mineral springs.

All Healing Springs. See Crumpler.

Alliance, community in n Pamlico County, in the center of an area which produces potatoes and tobacco. Settled in the 1890's and named for the Farmers Alliance movement. Former railroad station here was known as West Alliance.

Alliby Creek. See Ellerbee Creek.

Alligator, farming and grazing community in ne Tyrrell County on the Big Savanna near Alligator Creek.

Alligator Bay, swamp in nw Brunswick County. A part of Green Swamp (which see).

Alligator Bay, in s Onslow County at the e end of Stump Sound.

Alligator Creek, a tidal stream on Eagles Island in e Brunswick County. It flows s into the Cape Fear River.

Alligator Creek rises in e central Camden County and flows e into North River.

Alligator Creek rises in central Pamlico County and flows n into Bay River.

Alligator Creek rises in n Tyrrell County and flows se and ne into the mouth of Alligator River. Appears on the Moseley map, 1733.

Alligator Dismal Swamp. See Great Alegator Dismal Swamp.

Alligator Lake, a natural lake in n Hyde County, 3½ mi. in diameter, almost a perfect circle. Not shown on the Collet map, 1770, or the Mouzon map, 1775; a map in The Political Magazine (Nov., 1780) shows an enlarged area at the head of Alligator River. Not until 1812, on a map published in Boston, is the lake clearly shown. Within a few years it was being labeled Alligator Lake on maps. The lake is filled by swamp drainage; its two outlets are the New Lake Fork of Alligator River and a drainage ditch leading into Pungo River. Alligator Lake, known locally as New Lake, covers approx. 6,000 acres and is 6 to 7 ft. at its deepest.

Alligator River rises in central Hyde County and flows e and n to the Hyde-Tyrrell County line, se to the Dare-Tyrrell County line, and n into Albemarle Sound. In part, the Intracoastal Waterway follows the Alligator River. Appears as Layn Flu[ve] on the Smith map, 1624, undoubtedly named for Ralph Lane, governor of the first Roanoke colony. Appears as Alligator River on the Ogilby map, 1671.

Alligator River Bridge. See East Lake Landing: Sandy Point.

Alligator Swamp rises in nw Brunswick County and flows n into Juniper Creek.

Alligator Township, ne Tyrrell County.

Alligoods, community in central Beaufort County. Alt. 37.

Allison, community in w central Caswell County. A post office was operated here during the approx. period 1880-1909.

Allison Creek rises in s Macon County and flows ne into Cartoogechaye Creek.

Allison Creek rises in s central Transylvania County, just south of Elk Lodge Mountain and flows se into French Broad River.

Allman Branch rises in n Buncombe County and flows nw into Madison County where it enters French Broad River.

Allman Branch rises in s Madison County and flows nw into French Broad River.

Allmon Branch rises in ne Cherokee County and flows se into Morris Creek.

Allmon Creek rises in n Cherokee County in the Snowbird Mountains and flows s into Hyatt Creek.

Allreds, community in ne Montgomery County.

Alma. See Daystrom.

Almond, community in w Swain County on Little Tennessee River. Inc. 1905 but no longer active in municipal affairs. Named for Bud Almond, donor of original town site. Alt. 1,613.

Almond Township, w Stanly County.

Alspaugh, community in central Forsyth County.

Alston, community in central Warren County. Post office est. here in 1903, but discontinued in 1918.

Altamahaw, community in w Alamance County on Haw River. Founded about 1860 with the establishment of a cotton gin here. Now the site of several textile mills. The community of Ossipee lies directly south. Name of Indian origin, meaning unknown.

Altamont, community in s Avery County. Name means high mountain.

Altamont Township, s Avery County.

Altapass, community in se Mitchell County on Little Rose Creek. Alt. 2,623.

Alto. See Lasker.

Alton, community in s central Union County.

Alum Knob, between Caney Fork and Tuckasegee River in central Jackson County.

Alum Knob, n Madison County between Alum Ridge and Shelton Laurel Creek.

Alum Ridge, nw Madison County parallel to Pounding Mill Branch.

Alum Spring, mineral waters in w Onslow County near Southwest Creek.

Aman's Store. See Verona.

Amantha, community on Cover Creek in w Watauga County. Settled 1870. First known as McBrides Mill for A. J. McBride, first postmaster. Name later changed to honor Amantha Combs, local resident.

Amelia, community in nw Alleghany County.

Ames Turnout. See Wingate.

Amherst, community in s central Caldwell County. Site of Amherst Academy in 19th century, named by Robert Logan Patton, principal, for Amherst College in Massachusetts, of which he was a graduate.

Amherst. See Roberson Store.

Amity Hill, community in s Iredell County.

Ammon, community in nw Bladen County.

Ammon Bottom, e Cherokee County between Elliott Branch and Piper Branch.

Ammon Knob on the Cherokee-Clay County line in the Valley River Mountains.

Ammons Branch rises in se Macon County and flows se into Chattooga River.

Ammons Branch rises in se Macon County and flows sw into Cullasaja River.

Ammons Branch rises in e Macon County and flow sw into Rabbit Creek.

Ammons Branch rises in s Madison County and flows w into Walnut Creek.

Ammons Branch rises in w Swain County and flows e into Little Tennessee River.

Ammons Knob, s Macon County between the head of Hayes Mill Creek and Nickajack Creek. Alt. 3,916.

Amos Creek rises in nw Caldwell County and flows s into Mulberry Creek. Probably named for Amos Green, a nineteenth-century resident of the area.

Amos Creek rises in ne Madison County and flows sw into Spillcorn Creek.

Amos Mill Pond. See Weldons Mill Pond.

Amos Plott Balsam. See Water Rock Knob.

Amour. See Armour.

Amy, community in n central Ashe County.

Añadales Chase, an otherwise unidentified designation appearing on the Smith map, 1624, shown between what is now Tar and Roanoke rivers, nw of the head of Pungo River, probably in what is now n Pitt and Martin counties.

Anderson, community in s central Caswell County, known earlier as Anderson's

Store. A post office was operated here during the approx. period 1820-1905.

Anderson Branch rises in w Clay County and flows nw into Hiwassee River.

Anderson Branch rises in s Graham County and flows ne into Tulula Creek.

Anderson Branch rises in sw Macon County and flows ne into Lowery Creek.

Anderson Branch rises in sw Madison County and flows ne into French Board River.

Anderson Cove, the valley through which Shelton Branch flows in n Buncombe County.

Anderson Cove Branch rises in w Madison County and flows nw into Puncheon Camp Branch.

Anderson Creek rises in s Cabarrus County and flows e into Rocky River. Appears on the MacRae map, 1833.

Anderson Creek rises in a bend of Hiwassee River below the Hiwassee Dam in western Cherokee County and flows sw into Hiwassee River.

Anderson Creek rises in s Craven County and flows e into the mouth of Slocum Creek.

Anderson Creek rises in s Harnett County and flows se into Little River. Named for Thomas Anderson, an early settler.

Anderson Creek rises in e Haywood County and flows ne into Burnett Creek.

Anderson Creek rises in n Lincoln County and flows se into Killian Creek.

Anderson Creek Township, s Harnett County.

Anderson Mountain, se Catawba County. Alt. 1,547.

Anderson Mountain, e Haywood County between the headwaters of Stamey Cove Branch and Sally Haines Branch.

Andersons Crossroads, community in n Halifax County.

Anderson's Mountain, ne Lincoln County. Also known as Little Mountain.

Anderson's Store. *See* Anderson.

Anderson Swamp Creek rises in central Vance County and flows n into Kerr Reservoir.

Anderson Township, s central Caswell County.

Andreas Branch rises in n central Swain County and flows w into Noland Creek.

Andrews, town in ne Cherokee County. Inc. 1905. First known as Valley Town, a name still applied to an adjacent community. Renamed for A. B. Andrews (1841-1915), leader in the development

of the Western North Carolina Railroad. Alt. 1,825. Produces textiles and apparel.

Andrews Bald, in Great Smoky Mountains National Park in n Swain County between Forney Creek and Salola Branch. Alt. 5,860.

Andrews Geyser, sw McDowell County, in Horseshoe Bend of the Southern Railway, was constructed in the 1880's, restored in 1911, as a tribute to Col. Alexander Boyd Andrews, builder of the Western North Carolina Railroad into Asheville. Water from a higher mountain lake about 2 mi. away is piped to the site. Natural pressure forces the water upward in a 100-ft. jet from the center of a stone fountain. Owned and maintained by the Southern Railway. Formerly passenger trains stopped here for 20 minutes to enable those interested to visit the site.

Andy, community in n Polk County on the head of Bullin Creek.

Andy Branch rises in nw Haywood County, in Great Smoky Mountains, and flows about 2 miles se to join Woody Branch, which then joins Conrad Creek to form Little Cataloochee Creek. Named for Andy Bennett, a former homeowner in the area.

Andy Gap, s Macon County between Cedar Cliff Mountain and Mulberry Gap.

Angelico Gap, sw Cherokee County at the sw end of Angelico Mountain.

Angelico Mountain, sw Cherokee County extending ne from Angelico Gap to Bowmans Gap. *See also* Rocky Face.

Angeline, community in n Henderson County between McDowell Creek and North Fork.

Angel Mountain, sw Macon County between Bryson Branch and Moore Creek.

Angier, town in n Harnett County. Inc. 1901. Named for Colonel John C. Angier, one of the town's founders. Produces apparel. Alt. 301.

Anglin Branch rises in w Yancey County and flows se into Jacks Creek. Named for Manon Anglin, an early settler.

Anglin Knob, central Yancey County near the head of Bailey Branch.

Angola, community in w Onslow County.

Angola. *See* Maple Hill.

Angola Bay, pocosin in s Puplin and n Pender counties. Angola Bay Game Preserve here is maintained by the N. C. Wildlife Resources Commission; bear, deer, and other wildlife abound. *See also* Holly Shelter Bay.

Angola Creek rises in Angola Bay in ne Pender County and flows s into Holly Shelter Creek.

Annandale, community in se Pender County. Alt. 44.

Annie Mountain, e Henderson County s of Bradley Mountain. Alt. 2,731.

Ann Mountain, on a branch of Cabin Creek in s Henderson County.

Anson County was formed in 1750 from Bladen County. In the s central section of the state, it is bounded by the state of South Carolina and by Union, Stanly, and Richmond counties. It was named for George Anson, Lord Anson (1697-1762), a British admiral who, for a number of years, was assigned to protect the commerce of the Carolina coast from pirates. Area: 536 sq. mi. County seat: Wadesboro with an elevation of 423 ft. Townships are Ansonville, Burnsville, Gulledge, Lanesboro, Lilesville, Morven, Wadesboro, and White Store. Produces oats, corn, milo, cotton, broilers, turkeys, hosiery, textiles, and wooden boxes. Sand, gravel, and crushed stone are also produced, and there are deposits of granite, sandstone, and shale for brick.

Ansonville, town in n central Anson County. Alt. 324. Settled 1844, named in 1857 for the county. Inc. 1885. Carolina Female College, 1850-1867, est. by local planters, later operated by the Methodist Church, was here. Building torn down, 1949.

Ansonville Township, n central Anson County.

Anthony Bolick Branch rises in nw Caldwell County on nw slopes of Rocky Knob and flows w into Johns River.

Anthony Branch rises in n Swain County and flows s into Proctor Creek.

Anthony Branch. See Auntery Branch.

Anthony Creek rises in e Avery County and flows se into Caldwell County where it enters Johns River.

Anthony Creek rises in central Catawba County and flows sw into Clark Creek.

Anthony Creek rises in s central Gaston County, about two miles se of community of South Gastonia, and flows n through Robinwood Lake to empty into Catawba Creek.

Anthony Mountain, s central Avery County.

Anthony's Creek rises in nw Caldwell County and se Avery County and flows se into Johns River.

Antioch, community in s Hoke County on Raft Swamp.

Antioch Township, s Hoke County.

Antioch Township, e Wilkes County.

Antone. See Concord.

Apalachia Lake, nw Cherokee County, on Hiwassee River at the Tennessee state line. Formed by Tennessee Valley Authority dam completed in 1943. Covers 1,123 acres, max. dept. 120 ft., approx. 10 mi. long.

Apex, town in w Wake County on the head of Beaver Creek. Inc. 1873. Named because it was supposed to be the highest point on the railroad between Richmond, Va., and Jacksonville, Fla. When first settled, the area was an important producer of turpentine and rosin. The town now produces apparel, plywood, and chemicals.

Appalachian Creek rises in nw Rutherford County and flows ne into Broad River.

Appalachian Mountains include all of the e mountains of the United States from Alabama to northern Maine. The name was given by Spaniards under De Soto in 1539 for the Apalachee Indians whose name meant "people on the other side" (of a river presumably). In North Carolina the Blue Ridge, Black Mountains, and Great Smoky Mountains are a part of the Appalachian Mountains. At one time both Appalachian and Allegheny were names applied to the range from Georgia to New York, but a study by Arnold Guyot, "On the Appalachian Mountain System," published in 1861, firmly established the present name. See also, Mountain Region.

Appalachian Trail, a marked footpath extending approx. 2,050 miles from Maine to Georgia. In North Carolina approx. 70 of the 200 miles within the state cross the crest of the Great Smoky Mountains. The highest point on the trail is Clingmans Dome with an alt. of 6,642 ft. Proposed in 1921 and completed in 1937, this has been described as the longest marked footpath in the world.

Appie, community in n Greene County. Named about 1907 for Mrs. Appie (Apelia?) Bynum, local resident.

Apple Grove, community in nw Ashe County. Alt. 3,137.

Appletree Branch rises in w Macon County and flows se into Nantahala River.

Appletree Branch rises in nw Macon County and flows sw into Queens Creek.

Appletree Swamp rises in ne Wayne County and flows se into Nahunta Swamp in Greene County. The name appears in local records prior to 1750.

Aquadale, community in s Stanly County. Inc. 1943; charter repealed 1945. Named by local resident: *aqua,* "water" *dale,* "valley." Many springs in the area.

Aquascogoc appears on the White map, 1585, as an Indian village near the head of Pungo River estuary not far from either modern Scranton in Hyde County or Belhaven in Beaufort County.

Aquascog River. See Whipping Creek.

Aquone, community in w Macon County on Nantahala River. Alt. 2,950. Settled on the site of Fort Scott, one of the stockades at which Cherokee Indians were collected before being removed to Oklahoma, 1838. Name believed to be a corruption of *egwanul'ti,* "by the river."

Arabia, a nickname applied about 1860 to the desolate Outer Banks of North Carolina.

Arabia, community in se Hoke County.

Aramancy River. See Great Alamance Creek.

Aramuskeet, described in 1758 as a part of Hyde County. "That Part of the County is a Peninsula, or rather an Island for three Parts of the Year, and can be entered by foot Passengers only in the Height of Summer, and that with great Difficulty for several Miles together. It was formerly an Indian Settlement, and there are at present about 12 Families of Indians, who live dispersed among the Whites, and dress and live like them, but they have still one whom they call the King among them." See also Aromuskek Marshes, Lake Mattamuskeet.

Arapahoe, town in s Pamlico County, inc. 1920. Post office est. 1886 said to have been named for a local race horse.

Ararat, community in e Surry County on Ararat River. Named for the river. Alt. 898.

Ararat River rises in Virginia and flows s across Surry County into Yadkin River.

Appears on the Collet map, 1770. Named for the Biblical Mount Ararat.

Arba, community in s Greene County. Named for the Biblical name Kirjatharba (Joshua 14:15).

Arbuckle, community in e Yancey County between North Toe and South Toe rivers near their junction. A former post office, Dobag [Doe Bag], served the area.

Arcadia, community in n Davidson County.

Arcadia Township, nw Davidson County.

Archdale, town in se Cleveland County. Alt. 943. Settled in the eighteenth century and named for Quaker John Archdale, governor of Carolina, 1694-1696.

Archdale, town in nw Randolph County. Settled about 1786 by Quakers. Inc. 1874 as Bush Hill; named from the fact that the area was originally covered with a growth of low bushes. Name changed to Archdale, 1887, in honor of John Archdale (1642?-1717), a Quaker, one of the Lords Proprietors of Carolina, and governor, 1694-1696. Original post office was ½ mi. from present site and named Bloomington until moved to Bush Hill in 1865. Archdale is now a residential suburb of High Point.

Archdale County was formed before 1696 "on Pampticoe River without the Bounds of the County of Albemarle." It was named for John Archdale (1642?-1717), governor of Carolina, 1694-96. The Precinct of Pampticoe was a part of Archdale County in 1696 at which time it became the County of Bath. The name of Archdale County was changed to Craven, *which see,* about 1712.

Archdale Precinct was formed from Bath County on December 3, 1705, and named in honor John Archdale (1642?-1717), Governor of Carolina, 1694-1696. The name was changed about 1712 to Craven County, *which see.*

Archer Lodge, community in n Johnston County.

Arch Hill, a mountain in n Macon County between Tellico Creek and Bird Branch.

Archies Creek rises in ne Surry County and flows e into Stokes County where it enters Dan River.

Archies Knob, nw Stokes County near Dan River.

Archie's Point, point ot land extending from Bogue Banks into Bogue Sound, sw Carteret County. Named for Archibald Smith. Sometimes also called Point of Woods.

Arch Ridge, se Clay County extends s in arc from Vineyard Mountain to Shooting Creek.

Arcola, community in se Warren County e of Fishing Creek. Post office est. here in 1849, but discontinued in 1919.

Arden, town in s Buncombe County. Settled about 1840. Inc. 1883 but long inactive in municipal affairs. Known first as Shufordsville. Renamed for the Forest of Arden in Shakespeare's play, "As You Like It." Alt. 2,225.

Ardulusa, community on Rockfish Creek in s Cumberland County.

Arenuse Creek consists of two branches, both rising in central Camden County and flowing generally sw into Pasquotank River. The branches come together in such a fashion that they seem to form an arrow nose. This fact was noted by the Indians and the white settlers merely translated their word for "arrownose" when they gave the creek its present name. The present name appears in records as early as 1694. To distinguish between the two branches, local inhabitants sometimes refer to First Milldam (nearest the county seat) and Second Milldam since watermills existed on each.

Argo, former town in n Nash County on Short Swamp Branch. Inc. 1889. Nearby Argo Gold Mine worked from about 1850 until about 1920. Both town and mine are now abandoned.

Argura, community in e central Jackson County on Gladie Creek. Alt. 3,291.

Argyle, former community on Little Rockfish Creek in ne Hoke County. Site now within the Fort Bragg Military Reservation. Named for Argyll, Scotland.

Arington Branch rises in n Madison County and flows sw into West Fork [Bull Creek].

Arlington, community in w Harnett County between the Cape Fear River and Upper Little River.

Arlington, town in ne Mecklenburg County on Clear Creek. Inc. 1930, but long inactive in municipal affairs.

Arlington, town in nw Yadkin County. Chartered 1893; long inactive in municipal affairs and rechartered 1930.

Arlington. See Coinjock.

Arlington Branch rises in s Swain County and flows nw into Tuckasegee River.

The Arm, an extension of Big Bald mountain, on the Madison-Yancey County, N. C.–Unicoi County, Tenn., line.

Armour, community in ne Columbus County. Named Amour (French, *love*) for the Love family in the area, but through the years the spelling became changed.

Armstrong, former community in nw McDowell County on Threemile Creek. With the establishment of Little Switzerland *which see,* two miles nw, this community began to decline.

Armstrong Branch rises in s Lincoln County and flows ne into Dellinger Branch.

Armstrong Creek rises in nw McDowell County and flows e into North Fork [Catawba River].

Arnold, community in w Davidson County near the headwaters of Swearing Creek.

Arnold Branch rises in e Macon County and flows sw into Cullasaja River.

Arnold Knob, se Mitchell County between North Toe River and Rose Creek.

Arnt, formerly a small community and site of Arnt Ferry over the Catawba River, ne Catawba County. Site now covered by waters of Lookout Shoals Lake.

Aromuskek Marshes appear on the Ogilby map, 1671, in the e section of present Hyde County between Lake Mattamuskeet and Pamlico Sound. *See also* Aramuskeet.

Arp Gap, w Cherokee County between Bowman Gap and Wolfpen Gap. Alt. approx. 2,750.

Arrowhead Branch rises in w Macon County and flows sw into Nantahala Lake.

Arrowwood Creek rises in w Macon County and flows se into Wayah Creek.

Arrwood Mill, community in e Cherokee County on Slow Creek.

Artesia, community in central Columbus County.

Arthur. See Bell-Arthur.

Arthurs Creek rises in nw Northampton County and flows s into Roanoke River.

Arthur Township, w central Pitt County, formerly known as Beaver Dam Township.

Art Stewart Ridge, w Graham County n of Wright Creek and parallel to it. Named for an early settler who came from Georgia.

Arturs Knob, e Mitchell County between Snow Creek and Bear Creek. Alt. 3,695. Named for Arthur ("Artur") McFalls (died 1839), who fought as a Tory at the Battle of King's Mountain in 1780 but afterwards joined the Americans. He lived alone for many years on this mountain. Sometimes erroneously called "Otters Knob."

Arundells Island. *See* Croatamung.

Asa Cove, s Macon County between Messer Ridge and Betty Creek.

Asahel Creek rises in ne Davidson County and flows se into Abbotts Creek.

Asbury, community in ne Montgomery County. Alt. 624. Auman's Hill post office est. here, 1850. Name of the community changed to Asbury in 1887 for a local Methodist Church.

Asbury, community in nw Stokes County between Dan River and Big Creek. Alt. 1,279.

Asbury, community in w Wake County on the head of Richland Creek. Settled 1900. Named by its founder, Calvin Bridgers, for Asbury, England. Alt. 484.

Asbury Mountain, ne Alexander County. Alt. 1,820. Probably named for local Asbury family which settled near the head of Snow Creek. Locally known as Big Mountain.

Asey Hole, deep section of White Oak River in e Onslow County near the mouth of Freemans Creek. Named for an old man, Asa Moore, who fell into the river here.

Asgini Ridge, nw Swain County extending as a short spur se from the Great Smoky Mountain ridge centering near lat. 35° 32' 50" N., long. 83° 46' 20" W.

Ash, community in w Brunswick County.

Ash Bearpen Knob, sw Watauga County on the head of Moodys Mill Creek.

Ashbee Harbor, a bay on the w shore of Roanoke Island, e Dare County, in the waters of Croatan Sound.

Ash Branch rises in w Jackson County and flows ne into Tuckasegee River.

Ash Cove, ne Cherokee County in the Snowbird Mountains.

Ash Cove Creek rises in ne Cherokee County and flows sw into Gipp Creek.

Asheboro, town and county seat, central Randolph County. Inc. 1796. Named for Samuel Ashe (1725-1813), governor of North Carolina, 1795-1798. Produces hosiery, apparel, textiles, automatic blankets, wooden staves, batteries, furniture, toys, and shoes. Alt. 879.

Asheboro West, unincorporated outskirts of Asheboro, central Randolph County. A portion of this area was taken into the town of Asheboro late in 1960 after the census had been taken.

Asheboro South, unincorporated outskirts of Asheboro, central Randolph County.

Asheboro Township, central Randolph County.

Ashe County was formed in 1799 from Wilkes County. In the nw section of the state, it is bounded by the states of Tennessee and Virginia, and by Alleghany, Wilkes, and Watauga counties. It was named for Samuel Ashe (1725-1813), a Revolutionary patriot, superior court judge, and governor of the state (1795-98). Area: 427 sq. mi. County seat: Jefferson with an elevation of 2,900 ft. Townships are Chestnut Hill, Clifton, Creston, Elk, Grassy Creek, Helton, Horse Creek, Hurricane, Jefferson, Laurel, North Fork, Obids, Oldfields, Peak Creek, Pine Swamp, Piney Creek, Pond Mountain, Walnut Hill, and West Jefferson. Produces corn, tobacco, dairy livestock, chemicals, textiles, hosiery, furniture, electronics. There is a tobacco market and a cheese plant in West Jefferson. Copper and mica are mineral products and the county has a potential for the production of stone, iron ore, and gem stones.

Ashe Creek rises in e Pender County in Holly Shelter Bay and flows w into Northeast Cape Fear River. Appears as Ashes Mill on the Price map, 1808, and as Ashe's Mill Creek on the MacRae map, 1833. Exeter, *which see*, was nearby.

Ashe Gap, on the Mitchell County, N. C.-Carter County, Tenn., line.

Ashes Creek. *See* Upper Broad Creek.

Ashe's Island, s Onslow County in Stump Sound on the s side of Spicers Bay, a tidal marsh and coastal beach island approx. 1¼ mi. long. Named for John Baptista Ashe (1748-1802).

Ashe's Mill Creek. *See* Ashe Creek; Exeter.

Asheville, city and county seat, central Buncombe County on French Broad River. Settled about 1792; inc. 1797. First called Morristown, probably for William Morrison who cast the deciding vote as one of the commissioners to select a site for the courthouse in 1792. Named Asheville in 1797 for Samuel Ashe, Governor of North Carolina (1795-98). As the city grew, its boundaries were extended to take in a number of adjacent inc. towns including Kenilworth, Biltmore, Montford, Ramoth (or Woolsey), Sunset Park, Victoria, and West Asheville. A health and tourist resort. Alt. 2,216. Asheville-Biltmore College is here. Industry: publishing, hosiery, glass products, dairy products, apparel, baby foods, electronics, furniture, textiles, handicrafts, metalwork.

Asheville Township, central Buncombe County.

Ash Flat Branch rises in s Macon County and flows n into Allison Creek.

Ashford, community in n McDowell County on North Fork [Catawba River]. Alt. 1,762.

Ash Knob, central Clay County between Downing and Licklog creeks.

Ashland, community in w Ashe County. Est. 1886 and known as Solitude until 1914 when the name was changed to Ashland for the county. Alt. approx. 3,000.

Ashland, community in sw Caswell County. A post office was operated here during the approx. period 1870-1905.

Ashley Branch rises in s Buncombe County and flows ne into French Broad River.

Ashley Heights, community in w Hoke County. Alt. 438.

Ashmont, community in w Hoke County.

Ashpole. *See* Fairmont.

Ashpole Swamp, s Robeson County between Ashpole Swamp (stream) and Lumber River.

Ashpole Swamp rises in w Robeson County and flows se and sw into South Carolina.

Ashton, community in s Pender County. Named for a member of the Ashe family who was a railroad official.

Ashton Run. *See* Afton Run.

Ashturn Branch rises in ne Cherokee County and flows n into Junaluska Creek.

Ashwood, s Bladen County, was the home of William Bartram, uncle of the naturalist of the same name. The naturalist lived here 1761-65, and 1770-72. It was called Ashwood by John Baptista Ashe, a previous owner, as early as 1731. It was on the right bank of Cape Fear River, approx. 5 mi. ne of Council. Only a

cellar excavation and some chimney brick remain to mark the site.

Ashwood, community in s Pamlico County. Named for the wood burned by a railroad which formerly ran through the community.

Ashworth Creek rises in se Buncombe County near Henderson County line and flows nw into Cane Creek.

Ashworth Creek rises in sw Cleveland County and flows n into Broad River.

Askew. *See* Union.

Askew Ridge, s Avery County.

Askewville, town in central Bertie County. Settled in 1890's, named for local family. Alt. 64. Inc. 1951.

Askins, community in ne Craven County. Named for Alec Askins on whose land a former post office was built. Alt. 18. *See also* Ernul.

Askins Creek, a cove on the Pamlico County side of s Hatteras Island, s Dare County, below the community of Avon.

Aspen, community in e Warren County. Post office est. here in 1908, but discontinued in 1915.

Aspen Grove. *See* Wittys Crossroads.

Assembly. For a reference to places at which the assembly is known to have met, *see* General Assembly.

Assembly Lake, se Buncombe County at Ridgecrest, Baptist assembly grounds, on a tributary of Swannanoa River.

Astin's Run. *See* Afton Run.

Atherton. *See* Jackson.

Athlone. *See* Bowlens Creek.

Atkin River. *See* Yadkin River.

Atkins Bank. *See* Kinston.

Atkinson, town in w Pender County. Laid out on the lands of W. H. Lewis in 1883 (the year after a station had been established here on the railroad) and known as Lewis. Inc. 1909 as Atkinson, named for an engineer whose work helped the completion of the railroad. Alt. 65.

Atkinson Pond, approx. 1 mi. long, on Moccasin Creek in se Johnston County.

Atlantic, town in ne Carteret County, incorporated 1905, but not now active in municipal affairs. Alt. 15. Settled about 1740; called Hunting Quarters until 1890.

Atlantic Beach, town on the e end of Bogue Banks on the Atlantic Ocean. Inc. 1937.

Atlantic Ocean forms the e boundary of North Carolina. The state has a shore line of 328 miles.

Atlantic Township, on Core Sound in e Carteret County. Formerly known as Hunting Quarters Township.

Atlantic Township, ne Dare County on the Outer Banks.

Atoah Creek rises in s Graham County and flows ne into Long Creek.

Atoah Gap, in s Graham County between Eller Cove and the headwaters of Atoah Creek.

Attakulla. See Mount Mitchell.

Atwell Township, sw Rowan County.

Atwood, community in s Forsyth County.

Auberry, community in w Clay County on Hiwassee River.

Auburn, community in e Wake County. Alt. 340.

Augerhole Branch rises in w Swain County and flows sw into Fontana Lake.

Aughburn. See Ogburn.

Aulander, town in nw Bertie County. In existence before the Civil War as Harmon's Crossroads. Inc. as Aulander in 1885. Alt. 73. The intended name was Orlando, but a phonetic spelling was used to distinguish it from Orlando, Fla. Another story is that a local sawmill operator, Andrew J. Dunning, had the town named for himself, i.e. "Ole Ander."

Aumans Crossroads, community in s Randolph County.

Auman's Hill. See Asbury.

Auntery Branch, also known as Anthony Branch, rises in se Graham County and flows sw into Tulula Creek. Named for Jack Anthony.

Aurelian Springs, community in w Halifax County. Named aurelian (golden) because the water from the seven springs here was believed to be a cure-all. A popular recreation area of the late nineteenth century.

Aurora, town in se Beaufort County. Alt. 25. Inc. 1880. Named for a former county newspaper, Aurora Borealis. Originally a free Negro settlement called Betty Town existed here.

Ausbon, community in w Washington County. Alt. 41. Named for C. V. M. Ausbon, Clerk of Superior Court, 1906-1942.

Austin, community in ne Wilkes County near the headwaters of Little Elkin River.

Austin Creek rises in n central Caldwell County and flows s into Warrior Creek.

Named for Thomas J. Austin who settled nearby during the Civil War.

Austin Creek rises in e Wake County and flows sw into Smiths Creek. Shown on 1870 map as Millstone Creek.

Austin Mountain, w Yancey County near the head of Dryspring Branch.

Auston Branch rises in s Madison County and flows s into Morrow Branch.

Autreys Creek Township. See Otter Creek Township.

Autryville, town in w Sampson County. Settled about 1888; inc. 1891. Named for James L. Autry who erected stores and established a trading center here. Alt. 108.

Avalon, former community in w Rockingham County. Built about 1889 as a mill village on the Mayo River. On June 11, 1911, the mill was destroyed by fire and soon afterwards the sixty or so houses in Avalon, a Moravian church, school, and company store were moved on horse-drawn rollers to Mayodan, about two miles west.

Avalon Beach, area of extensive real estate development n of Wright Memorial in e Dare County. Once known as Moore's Shore.

Aventon, community in n Nash County on the head of Crooked Swamp. Named for the Avent family which settled there about 1738; descendants still live on the original grant. A post office, Aventsville, opened here prior to 1828; Aventon post office operated from 1900 to about 1910. Alt. 175.

Avents Creek rises in n Harnett County and flows sw into Cape Fear River.

Aventsville. See Aventon.

Averasboro, formerly a town on the Cape Fear River in se Harnett County. Provided for by legislative act in 1791, to be laid off on land owned by Alexander Avera and called Averasburg. Site of a gristmill about 1740 and soon afterwards of other public buildings. Site of Confederate attack on Sherman's Army, March 15, 1865. Town began to decline soon after Civil War and by 1888 was practically abandoned. Site, one mile s of Erwin, is marked by grove of large oak and beech trees.

Averasboro Township, se Harnett County.

Averton Creek. See Abingdon Creek.

Avery County was formed in 1911 from Mitchell, Watauga, and Caldwell counties. In the nw section of the state, it is bounded by the state of Tennessee, and by Watauga, Caldwell, Burke, McDowell, and Mitchell counties. It was named for Colonel Waightstill Avery (1741-1821), Revolutionary soldier and attorney general of North Carolina. Area: 247 sq. mi. County seat: Newland with an elevation of 3,589. Townships are Altamont, Banner Elk, Beech Mountain, Cranberry, Linville, Roaring Gap, Toe River, Wilson's Creek. Produces corn, dairy and beef cattle, textiles, kaolin, iron, sand and gravel. There are also deposits of olivine and asbestos in the county.

Avery Creek rises in s Buncombe County and flows e into French Broad River.

Avery Creek rises in n Transylvania County and flows se into Davidson River.

Avery Creek, community in s Buncombe County on the e limit of Pisgah National Forest.

Avery Creek Township, sw Buncombe County.

Averys Bald. See Big Yellow Mountain.

Avilla, community in w Alexander County on Middle Little River.

Avoca, community in e Bertie County on the site of Avoca Plantation, part of the old Duckenfield estate. Name comes from the phrase "sweet vale of Avoca" in Thomas Moore's poem The Meeting of the Waters. See also Black Walnut Point.

Avon, community on Hatteras Island, se Dare County. Post office est. in 1873 as Kinnakeet. Post office renamed Avon in 1883. Alt. 3.

Avondale, community in se Rutherford County on Second Broad River between the communities of Caroleen on the north and Henrietta on the south.

Axe Ridge, in s Graham County, extends n from Panther Cove to Little Snowbird Creek.

Axtell, community in w Warren County between Long Branch and Phoebes Creek. Alt. 400. Settled during the Revolutionary War and first named Old Shatter, a corruption of Chateau. Shatter Muster Ground, used during the Civil War, was located here. The post office which was located here from 1885 until 1904 was named Shatter. Name changed in 1890 for famous race horse.

Aycock, community in n Wayne County and s Wilson County between Great Swamp and Aycock Swamp.

Aycock Creek rises in s Granville County and flows ne into Tar River.

Aycock Crossing, community in sw Wilson County.

Aycock Millpond, in n Wayne County on Great Swamp. Formerly known as Sassers Millpond for the original owners, but now named for present owners. Maximum depth 12 ft.; area covered, 30 acres. Fishing and boating open to the public.

Aycock Swamp rises in n Wayne County and flows ne into Wilson County where it enters Turners Swamp.

Aycocks Pond, sw Warren County on Lees Branch.

Ayden, town in s Pitt County. Inc. 1891. Name changed to Harriston in 1895 but changed back to Ayden in 1899. Alt. 64. Produces canned foods.

Ayden Branch rises in n Swain County and flows s into Beech Flats Prong.

Ayden Township, sw Pitt County.

Aydlett, community on the w shore of Currituck Sound in central Currituck County. Probably named for first postmaster, around 1909.

Ayersville, community in nw Rockingham County.

Ayles Creek rises in e Yancey County and flows ne into Little Crabtree Creek.

Ayr, former community in w Rutherford County near Lake Lure. Site of a pre-Civil War tannery which made saddles for the army during the war. A Scotsman, Francis Reynolds, operated the tannery and named the community for his native town. Post office est. here 1880, closed 1911. Only one house remains of the former thriving community.

Azalea, community in central Buncombe County, e of Asheville. Known as Gudger's Ford until renamed for the flowering shrub. Alt. 2,052.

B

Babbit's Pond. *See* Parrish's Pond.

Bacchus, community in e Yancey County.

Bachelor, community in se Craven County on Clubfoot Creek.

Bachelor Creek rises in Great Dover Swamp in ne Jones County, flows ne into central Craven County and then turns to flow se for approx. 3 mi. along the w border of Hog Island before entering Neuse River approx. 3½ mi. nw of town of New Bern. Approx. 14 mi. long . Appears as Batchellors Creek on the Moseley map, 1733. Formerly called Batchelder Creek. Named for Edward Batchelor.

Bachelor Creek rises in s Randolph County and flows e into Richland Creek. Named for a wild stallion that is reported to have roamed through this section. People called him "Bachelor."

Bachelor's Delight Swamp rises in n Onslow County and flows sw into New River. Mentioned in local records as early as 1744.

Back Bay, a bay formed by the encircling islands of Hog Island in ne Carteret County.

Back Creek rises in w Alamance County and flows se into Great Alamance Creek.

Back Creek rises in e Beaufort County and flows sw into Bath Creek.

Back Creek rises in se Craven County and flows nw on the Craven-Carteret County line into Adams Creek.

Back Creek, an inlet of North Landing River, ne Currituck County. It forms the n boundary of Mackay Island.

Back Creek rises in central Iredell County a short distance sw of Statesville and flows sw into Third Creek.

Back Creek rises in se Iredell County and flows ne into w Rowan County. It joins Withrow Creek to form North Second Creek. Appears as South Fork [Second Creek] on the Collet map, 1770.

Back Creek rises in w Orange County and flows sw into Alamance County where it enters Haw River. Appears on the Moseley map, 1733, as Buffalo Creek.

Back Creek rises in se Mecklenburg County and flows e into sw Cabarrus County to join Rocky River. So called because it appears to back into Rocky River rather than flow into it. Shown as Buck Creek on Kerr map, 1882, and as Black Creek on recent state highway maps.

Back Creek rises in central Randolph County and flows sw into Caraway Creek. This creek is dammed about five mi. w of Asheboro, creating a 250 acre lake which is the chief water supply of Asheboro Township.

Back Creek Mountain, central Randolph County w of Asheboro. One of the principle mountains of the Uwharrie range.

Back Creek Township, w central Randolph County.

Back Lake, a small lake on the mainland of Dare County e of the community of Lake Worth on Stumpy Point Bay.

Back Landing, in nw Tyrrell County on Scuppernong River. *See also* Newport.

Back Landing Creek rises in the highlands of Indian Island, se Camden County, and flows se into North River.

Back Marsh rises in n Duplin County and flows sw into Northeast Cape Fear River.

Back Sound, a sound between Shackleford Banks and Harkers Island in se Carteret County.

Back Swamp rises in nw Nash County and flows se into Big Peachtree Creek.

Back Swamp rises in nw Onslow County and flows sw into Duplin County where it enters Cypress Creek.

Back Swamp rises in w Robeson County and flows se into Lumber River in central Robeson County.

Back Swamp Township, central Robeson County.

Bad Branch rises in e Macon County and flows sw into Big Creek.

Bad Creek rises in sw Jackson County and flows se into South Carolina where it enters Chattooga River.

Bad Creek rises in n Mitchell County and flows se into Big Rock Creek.

Bad Fork rises in nw Henderson County and flows s into Wash Creek.

Bad Fork rises in nw McDowell County on the north slopes of Woods Mountain and flows ne approx. 2 mi. into Armstrong Creek.

Badin, community in ne Stanly County on Baldin Lake. Alt. 400. Est. 1913 by Adrien Badin, French industrialist who operated aluminum reduction plant here. Aluminum Company of America plant here since 1915.

Badin Lake on Yadkin River in Montgomery and Stanly counties. Covers 5,973 acres; max. depth 40 ft. Built 1917 by Carolina Aluminum Company to generate hydroelectricity and for recreation. Also referred to as Narrows Reservoir.

Bad Knob, in n Mitchell County between Aaron Branch and Big Ridge.

Bagley, community in ne Johnston County. Named for local family.

Bagley Academy Branch rises in ne Warren County and flows n into Little Stonehouse Creek.

Bahama (ba-hay-ma), community in n Durham County. Settled about 1880. Originally called Balltown until renamed. Bahama coined from the first two letters of the names of three prominent families-Ball, Harris, and Mangum. For a time in the nineteenth century, the post office name was Hunkadora. Alt. 507.

Bailey, community in w Mitchell County on Sams Branch.

Bailey, town in sw Nash County. Settled about 1860. Inc. 1908 as Baileys, named for Joe Bailey, an early settler; now known as Bailey. Alt. 233.

Bailey. See Center.

Bailey Branch rises in e Madison County and flows s into Gabriels Creek.

Bailey Branch rises in e Madison County and flows s into Middle Fork.

Bailey Branch rises in s Madison County and flows n into French Broad River.

Bailey Branch rises in central Yancey County and flows sw into Pine Swamp Branch. Named for M. A. Bailey who owned a large tract of land through which it flowed.

Bailey Branch rises in n Yancey County and flows ne into Pigpen Creek. Named for John and Charles Bailey, early settlers.

Bailey Branch rises in n Yancey County and flows se into Jacks Creek.

Bailey Branch rises in w central Yancey County on se slopes of Roland Knob and flows s into Cane River.

Bailey Cove, n central Yancey County near the head of Star Branch.

Bailey Creek rises in se Beaufort County and flows e into South Creek.

Bailey Hill, n Yancey County, extends nw from Locust Rough Mountain to Jacks Creek. Early settlers named Bailey are buried here and the site is reserved for a burying ground.

Bailey Meadows, in e Mitchell County between Sparks Ridge and Beaver Creek.

Bailey Mountain, e Yancey County between Browns Creek and South Toe River.

Bailey Ridge, s Madison County, extends ne from Bull Creek to Gabriels Creek.

Baileys. See Bailey.

Bailey's Camp, community in nw Caldwell County.

Bailey's Fork rises in s central Burke County and flows n into Silver Creek.

Bailey Township, se Nash County.

Bain, community in e Davidson County near the headwaters of Beaverdam Creek.

Baines Mountain, in s Swain County between Little Yalaka Creek and De Hart Branch.

Bairds Creek rises in w central Watauga County and flows sw into Watauga River.

Bairds Creek. See Beards Creek.

Baird's Forge. See Granite Falls.

Baker. See Drexel.

Baker Creek rises in w central Yancey County and flows n into Cane River. Named for Sidney Baker, an early settler.

Baker Gap, on the Watauga County, North Carolina-Johnson County, Tennessee line in the Stone Mountains.

Baker Island, a sandy island approx. 2 mi. long, in the Roanoke River, nw Northampton County. Called Eaton Island on the Price map, 1808, and Lashleys Island on the MacRae map, 1833.

Baker Mill. See Wheeler Creek.

Baker Mountain, w Catawba County. Alt. 1,812.

Bakers, community in w central Union County.

Bakers. See Ca-Vel.

Bakers Branch rises in n Madison County and flows ne into Spillcorn Creek.

Bakers Creek rises in n Catawba County and flows s into Lyle Creek.

Bakers Creek. See Mud Creek.

Bakers Crossroads, community in s Franklin County.

Bakers Crossroads, community in central Rockingham County.

Bakers Lake, a natural lake in nw Bladen County, approx. 1½ mi. long. Formerly known as Wilkinson's Lake.

Bakers Ridge, w Alleghany County.

Bakers Swamp rises in n Washington County and flows ne into Kendricks Creek.

Bakersville, town and county seat, in central Mitchell County on Cane Creek. Alt. 2,457. Settled prior to 1857 and named for David Baker who settled on a grant which he had at this site in 1797. During the latter part of the Civil War and until 1868 known as Davis, apparently in honor of Confederate President Jefferson Davis, Inc. 1868.

Bakersville Township, central Mitchell County.

Baker Swamp rises in e Cumberland County and flows sw into Reese Creek.

Balconce Branch rises in w Lee County and flows nw into Little Pocket Creek.

The Bald, a peak in nw Watauga County in the Stone Mountains.

Bald Beach, island on Atlantic Ocean in sw Brunswick County.

Bald Branch rises in sw Madison County and flows n into Spring Creek.

Bald Branch rises in n Swain County and flows se into Noland Creek.

Bald Branch rises in s Swain County between Rattlesnake Ridge and De Hart Bald and flows w into Wesser Creek.

Bald Cove, on the head of Cove Creek in e Haywood County.

Bald Creek rises in n Cherokee County and flows sw into Davis Creek.

Bald Creek in e Haywood County and flows sw into Crabtree Creek.

Bald Creek rises in e Pamlico County and flows ne into Bay River.

Bald Creek rises in w Yancey County and flows e into Cane River .

Bald Creek, community in w Yancey County on the stream of the same name. Alt. 2,576.

Bald Fork rises near Bald Knob in nw Buncombe County and flows sw into Sandymush Creek.

Bald Gap, w Haywood County in the Great Smoky Mountains National Park, between Canadian Top and Bald Top, near lat. 35° 39′ N., long., 83° 06′ 22″ W.

Bald Ground Mountain, nw Burke County. Alt. 4,100.

Bald Head. *See* Smith Island.

Baldhead Creek, a tidal waterway extending from just inside the outer coast of Smith Island in Brunswick County in a northwesterly direction into the Cape Fear River. Also known as Lighthouse Creek.

Bald Knob, peak at the e end of Peach Bottom Mountain, n Alleghany County. Alt. 3,653.

Bald Knob, peak on Newfound Mountain on Buncombe-Haywood County line near the headwaters of Bald Fork.

Bald Knob, on the Buncombe-Yancey County line between Swannanoa Gap and Pinnacle. Alt. 5,400-5,420.

Bald Knob, n Buncombe County nw of Cherry Log Gap.

Bald Knob, e Caldwell County. Alt. 1,727.

Bald Knob, on Haywood-Madison County line.

Bald Knob on the Jackson-Transylvania County line. Alt. 4,824. Part of Tennessee Ridge, *which see.*

Bald Knob, central Surry County.

Bald Knob, w Transylvania County between Johnnies Creek and Bee Tree Fork.

Bald Knob, w Yadkin County between Dobbins Creek and South Deep Creek.

Bald Knob, e Yancey County near the head of Plum Branch.

Bald Knob Creek rises in n Cleveland County and flows se into Little Knob Creek.

Bald Knob Mountain, w Alexander County. Alt. 1,887.

Bald Knob Ridge, s Yancey County between Left Prong South Toe River and Right Prong South Toe River.

Bald Mountain, on the Alexander-Wilkes County line.

Bald Mountain, central Avery County.

Bald Mountain, on Grassy Ridge near the Avery-Mitchell County line. Known also as Grassy Ridge Bald.

Bald Mountain, s Davidson County on Yadkin River.

Bald Mountain, n Jackson County between Blackrock Ridge and Sheepback Mountain. Alt. 5,400.

Bald Mountain, sw Jackson County between Flat Creek and Mill Creek. Alt. 4,050.

Bald Mountain, se Orange County about four miles nw of town of Carrboro. Alt. 762.

Bald Mountain, e Watauga County on South Fork New River.

Bald Mountain, community in nw Yancey County on Bald Mountain Creek.

Bald Mountain. See Rumbling Bald Mountain.

Bald Mountain Creek rises in central Avery County and flows ne into Banner Elk Creek.

Bald Mountain Creek rises in nw Yancey County and flows ne into Cane River.

Bald Mountain Falls, in Yadkin River opposite Bald Mountain in s Davidson County. Mentioned as early as 1819 in a survey of the rivers of North Carolina.

Bald Mountains, in Haywood, Madison, and Yancey counties, N. C., and Cocke, Greene, and Unicoi counties, Tenn., forming the common boundary line of N. C. and Tenn. from the Pigeon River, near lat. 36° 04′ 20″ N., long. 82° 24′ 30″ W., to the Nolichucky River, near lat. 35° 46′ 15″ N., long. 83° 04′ 50″ W. On 25 of 40 miscellaneous maps, 1795-1930, the section of these mountains between Pigeon River and the French Broad River bears no name; and the names on 15 maps vary between Iron, Great Iron, Smoky, and Great Smoky. There is also some recent usage of Max Patch.

Bald Mountain Township, ne Watauga County.

Bald of Humpback Mountain, s Mitchell County at the head of Rose Creek.

Bald Point, peninsula extending from s Hatteras Island, s Dare County, into Pamlico Sound.

Bald Ridge, central Avery County.

Bald Ridge, n Swain County between Slab Camp Branch and Advalorem Branch.

Bald Rock, mountain on the Jackson-Transylvania County line at the head of Tucker Creek. Alt. 4,150. Part of Tennessee Ridge, which see.

Bald Rock Mountain, s Jackson County, bordered on sw by Fairfield Lake and on n and w by Trays Island Creek. Alt. 4,232.

Bald Spot Mountain. See Gregory Bald.

Bald Spring Branch rises in n Clay County and flows sw into Fires Creek.

Bald Top, alt. 3,960, in Great Smoky Mountains National Park, w Haywood County, between Little Davidson Branch and Coggins Branch near lat. 35° 39′ N., long. 83° 06′ 30″ W.

Bald Top Mountain, n Henderson County between Clear Creek and Kyles Creek. Named by William Mills, first known white settler of the county.

Baldwin, community in sw Ashe County.

Named for family of early setlers. Alt. 3,100.

Baldwin Cove, s Buncombe County n of Baldwin Gap.

Baldwin Cove, on Burningtown Creek in central Macon County.

Baldwin Gap, on the Ashe County, N. C.-Johnson County, Tenn., line. Alt. 3,762.

Baldwin Gap, s Buncombe County, between Busbee and Butler Mountains. Alt. 3,076.

Baldwin Gap, s Buncombe County, between Stradley and Scott Mountains.

Baldwin Gap, n Henderson County between Rich Mountain and Hightop.

Baldwin Swamp rises in central Pitt County and flows se into Moyes Run.

Baldwin Township, ne Chatham County.

Bales Creek rises in sw Anson County and flows e into Deadfall Creek.

Balfour, community in central Henderson County adjoining Hendersonville on the north. Alt. 2,125. Railroad name is Smyth. Named for Captain William Balfour Troy who operated a rock quarry here in 1880 and was agent for the newly opened railroad. Produces surgical supplies.

Balfours, community in central Randolph County adjacent to Asheboro on the north, formerly known as North Asheboro. Named for an abandoned community of the same name in west central Randolph County, sw of Asheboro, which was the home of Colonel Andrew Balfour, Revolutionary patriot. Spero, formerly a community in its own right, is now considered to be a part of Balfours.

Bal-Gra, home of Thomas Pollock, President of the Council and acting governor, 1712-14 and 1722. Located in e Bertie County on the n side of Salmon Creek with its junction with Chowan River and Albemarle Sound. The brick house, named for the Pollock home in Renfrow County, Scotland, is no longer standing.

Ball, community in nw Ashe County. Formerly a post office.

Ballard, community in n Martin County, named for the plantation of John Bryant located near here in 1734. The first court in Martin County met in this community on the lands of John Griffin, 1774.

Ballard Cove, n Buncombe County south of Horse Gap.

Ballard Cove, the valley through which Ballard Creek flows in sw Buncombe County.

Ballard Creek rises in e Buncombe County and flows se into Cane Creek.

Ballard Creek rises in sw Buncombe County near Fork Mountain and flows n into Glady Fork.

Ballard Creek rises in n Lincoln County and flows se into Anderson Creek.

Ballard Crossroads, community in sw Gates County.

Ballard Gap, Swannanoa Mountains, s Buncombe County e of Face Rock peak.

Ballard Gap, e Transylvania County between Fodderstack Mountain and Pine Mountain.

Ballards Crossroads, community in w Pitt County.

Ballast Bank, the point of land in the mouth of South Fork Creek at Scuppernong River, w Tyrrell County.

Ballast Pit, stony area about 1 mi. square, e central Anson County. Worked commercially for construction material.

Ballast Point, peninsula from e Roanoke Island extending into Roanoke Sound's of Shallowbag Bay, e Dare County.

Ball Creek rises in s Macon County and flows ne into Coweeta Creek.

Ballentine's Mills, community in s Wake County.

Ball Gap, s Buncombe County, nw of Ball Mountain.

Ball Hill. See Intelligence.

Ball Island, small tidal marsh island in the Bay River estuary, e Pamlico County. A target for practice bombing by Marine air corps.

Ball Mountain, s Buncombe County.

Ballou Hill, community near Balsam on Jones Creek in ne Jackson County.

Ball Pocosin, e Lenoir County between Vine Swamp and Southwest Creek.

Balls Creek rises in e Catawba County and flows e into Catawba River.

Balls Creek Camp Ground, e Catawba County. Est. 1853, and trustees inc. 1861. Methodist. Camp meetings held here annually, last week in August.

Balls Mountain, s Orange County at the head of Mountain Creek.

Balls' Point, point of land extending from w Carteret County into White Oak River.

Balltown. See Bahama.

Balm, community in ne Avery County.

Balsam, town in ne Jackson County. Inc. in 1951 but not active in municipal affairs. Named for Balsam Mountains. Has highest standard gauge railroad e of Rocky Mountains. Alt. 3,315.

Balsam Branch rises in ne Swain County and flows se into Raven Fork.

Balsam Cone, mountain in s Yancey County between the head of Timber Creek and the head of Middle Creek. Alt. 6,611.

Balsam Cone. See Mount Craig.

Balsam Corner, mountain on the Haywood-Swain County line. In Great Smoky Mountains National Park near lat. 35° 40′ 17″ N., long. 83° 10′ 55″ W., near a sharp bend in the county line, hence the name. Alt. 6,020.

Balsam Corner Creek rises in ne Swain County in the Great Smoky Mountains National Park and flows sw into Straight Fork Raven Creek.

Balsam Gap, on the Buncombe-Yancey County line w of Walker Knob, near the s end of Bear Wallow Stand Ridge. The Blue Ridge Parkway passes through this gap. Alt. 5,320.

Balsam Gap, at the head of Richland Creek in w Haywood County. This is the lowest gap in the Balsam Mountain. Through it passed a prominent aboriginal Indian trail; a highway and railroad also pass through it now. Alt. 3,347.

Balsam Grove, community in w Transylvania County on North Fork French Broad River.

Balsam High Top, mountain on the Haywood-Swain County line between Beech Gap and Laurel Gap in Great Smoky Mountains National Park. Alt. 5,688.

Balsam Mountain, on the Haywood-Swain-Jackson County line, centering near lat. 35° 35′ N., long. 83° 12′ W. Tricorner Knob (which see) is at its junction with the main divide of the Great Smoky Mountains. Also known as Chiltoskie Ridge in Swain County. See also Richland Balsam.

Balsam Ridge, extends e from Huckleberry Knob to Winding Knob in w Haywood County.

Balsam Ridge, ne Swain County in the Great Smoky Mountains National Park, a short spur extending sw from Hughes Ridge.

Baltic, community in w Duplin County. Alt. 146.

Baltimore, community in e Davie County. Alt. 828. Site of a community store from the 1880's.

Baltimore, community in e Yadkin County between Forbush and Logan creeks. Named for a local church. A former post office here was named Tracadia.

Baltimore Branch rises in w Madison County and flows nw into Spring Creek.

Baltimore Landing, a clearing and landing for small boats on the Cashie River in se Bertie County. In use in the 1890's.

Bamboo, community in s Watauga County on Sawpit Branch.

Bandana, community in w Mitchell County on Toe River. Alt. 2,331. Name said to have been given after a railroad brakeman left a bandana tied to a laurel bush to mark the location of a station.

Bandana Hollow, central Mitchell County on a tributary of Toe River.

Bandy, community in e Catawba County. Named for pioneer Bandy family.

Bandy Cove Mountain, nw Burke County. Alt. 2,747.

Bandy Township, se Catawba County. Named for George Bandy, Virginian, who settled in Lincoln County, 1783.

Banjo Branch rises in central Avery County and flows s into North Toe River.

Banjo Branch rises in se Mitchell County and flows sw into North Toe River about one mi. e of Spruce Pine. Formerly known as Christ Branch; named changed after 1939.

Banjo Fork rises in e Beaufort County and flows nw into Pungo Creek.

Bank Mountain, n Henderson County between Garren Mountain and Kyles Creek.

Bank Point extends from se Pasquotank County into Pasquotank River on the s shore of Little Flatty Creek.

Banks, community in s Wake County.

Banks Branch rises in w Hertford County and flows ne into Meherrin River.

Banks Channel, a channel through a mass of tidal marsh islands in the extreme w end of Bogue Sound in sw Carteret County.

Banks Channel in Topsail Sound, s Pender County, near New Topsail Inlet.

Banks Creek rises in s Yancey County and flows nw into Price Creek.

Banner Branch rises in n Stokes County and flows sw into Snow Creek.

Banner Elk, town in ne Avery County on Elk River at the mouth of Shawneehaw Creek. Alt. 3,710. Inc. 1891 as Shawneehaw; reincorporated 1911 as Banner Elk. First settlers said to have arrived at the site about 1825. Named for the Banner family, early settlers on the Elk River. Lees-McRae Junior College is here.

Banner Elk Creek rises in e Avery County and flows n into Elk River.

Banner Elk Township, ne Avery County.

Bannerman's or Bannerman's Bridge, community in e Pender County on Northeast Cape Fear River. Est. prior to the Revolution, but now largely abandoned.

Banner's Store. See East Bend.

Bannertown, community in ne Surry County.

Banner Township, s Johnston County.

Banton Creek rises in ne Washington County and flows ne into Bull Bay; a portion of it forms the boundary with Tyrrell County. Sometimes erroneously called Bunton Creek.

Baptist Church Township, former township in central Cabarrus County. Now township number 11. In 1945 a part of this township was annexed to Concord, coextensive with Concord township.

Barbacue Creek. See Barbecue Swamp.

Bar Banks. See Bear Banks.

Barbecue Swamp rises in ne Bertie County and flows ne into Hertford County where it enters Chinkapin Creek.

Barbecue Swamp rises in w Harnett County and flows ne into Upper Little River. Named by Red Neill McNeill about 1750. Mists rising from the stream early in the morning reminded him of smoke rising from barbecue pits he had seen in the West Indies. In a fit of culinary nostalgia he named the stream Barbecue. Appears as Barbacue Creek on the Collet map, 1770.

Barbecue Township, sw Harnett County.

Barber, community in w Rowan County. Two lines of the railroad cross here, hence sometimes called Barber's Junction. Named either for W. P. Barber from whom the railroad purchased land for the station or for R. L. Barber, first postmaster. Alt. 752.

Barber Creek rises in central Pitt County and flows se into Tar River.

Barber Junction. See Barber.

Barclaysville, community in ne Harnett County. Once the center of the great Barclay-Barbee naval stores industry.

Barco, community in central Currituck County. Named for first postmaster. See also Coinjock.

Barden Inlet, a passage between Core Banks and Shackleford Banks n of Cape Lookout se Carteret County. Named for Graham Arthur Barden, a Congressman from North Carolina. Formerly known as Bardens Inlet, Lookout Bight Channel, and The Drain.

Barden Pond, w Duplin County on a tributary of Rockfish Creek.

Bardins Bay, a sand filled bay in w Cleveland County.

Bare Banks. *See* Bear Banks.

Bareford Swamp rises in w Bladen County and flows sw through Hesters Pond into Crawley Swamp.

Barefoot's Mill Pond. *See* Contentnea Lake.

Barfields. *See* Tuscarora Beach.

Bargaw Creek. *See* Burgaw Creek.

Barham, community in ne Wake County.

Barium Springs, community and former health resort in s Iredell County. Known by the Indians as Poison Springs; developed in the 1880's as Linsters Springs. Post office name changed from Poison Springs to Barium Springs in 1889. Named for springs which contain barium salts and other minerals. Presbyterian Orphans Home est. here, 1890-1891.

Barker Butt, e Swain County on Hickory Mountain.

Barker Creek rises in nw Graham County and flows ne into Cheoah River.

Barker Heights, community in central Henderson County s of Hendersonville. The Hendersonville Airport is here.

Barker Road Gap, on the Cherokee-Graham County line.

Barkers Bridge. *See* Stella.

Barkers Creek is formed by junction of West Fork and Middle Fork in w Jackson County and flows ne into Tuckasegee River.

Barkers Creek rises in s Macon County and flows s into Rabun County, Georgia, where it enters Betty Creek.

Barkers Creek, community in nw Jackson County. Alt. 1,901.

Barkers Creek Township, nw Jackson County.

Barker-Ten Mile, community in ne Robeson County. Named for Barker Methodist Church and Ten Mile Baptist Church. A prosperous farming center.

Barlowes, community in se Pender County on Bishop Creek. A former post office here was known as Sloop Point, *which see.*

Barnard, community in central Madison County on French Broad River at the mouth of Brush Creek. Alt. 1,534. Barnard's Station post office est. as early as 1830. Named for Job Barnard who settled here by 1794.

Barnards Creek rises in central New Hanover County and flows w into Cape Fear River.

Barnardsville, town in n Buncombe County near the junction of North Fork Ivy Creek and Dillingham Creek. Inc. 1959 A post office as early as 1882. Alt. 2,250. Produces wearing apparel.

Barn Branch rises in s Haywood County and flows n into Jonathans Creek.

Barnes Branch rises in n Haywood County and flows se into Big Creek.

Barnes Branch rises n in Madison County and flows w into Big Laurel Creek.

Barnes Creek rises in central Cleveland County and flows nw and sw in an arc into First Broad River.

Barnes Creek rises in sw Gates County and flows se into Chowan River.

Barnes Creek rises in s Randolph County and flows sw into Montgomery County where it enters Uwharrie River.

Barnes Crossroads, community in n Johnston County.

Barnes Store, community in w Wilson County. Named for Elias G. Barnes. A post office, 1877-1907.

Barnesville, community in s Robeson County. Alt. 125. Settled 1898. Named for R. R. Barnes who gave land for the right-of-way for a railroad, now abandoned.

Barnett Branch rises in central Cherokee County and flows sw into Slow Creek.

Barnett Branch rises in n Mitchell County and flows w into Big Rock Creek.

Barnett Branch rises in n Transylvania County and flows se into South Fork Mills River.

Barnett Branch rises in n Yancey County and flows sw into Unicoi County, Tenn., where it enters Spivey Creek.

Barnett Creek rises in e Clay County and flows ne into Buck Creek.

Barnett Creek rises in sw Currituck County and flows w into North River.

Barnett Knob, on the Jackson-Swain County line near the head of Pigeon Creek.

Barnett Mountain, central Madison County between Brush and Walnut creeks.

Barnetts Pond. *See* Loch Lily.

Barney Slue in the waters of Pamlico Sound, n of Hatteras Inlet, s Dare County.

Barns Creek. *See* Bartrams Creek.

Barnwell Mountain, on the Buncombe-Henderson County line.

Barnwell Mountain, ne Henderson County 1½ mi. sw of community of Bat Cave. Alt. approx. 2,700.

Barr Banks. *See* Bear Banks.

Barr Creek rises in sw Iredell County and flows s into Davidson Creek.

Barren Head. See Smith Island.

Barren Inlet. See Mason Inlet.

Barrett, community in ne Alleghany County.

Barrett Branch rises in se Clay County and flows nw into Right Fork [Eagle Creek] which is also sometimes known as Dave Barrett Creek.

Barrett Cove, n Buncombe County between Chestnut Knob and Reems Creek.

Barrett Mountain, sw Alexander County. Alt. 1,950. Named for Jonathan Barrett, pioneer settler who laid out road from Fort Dobbs to Quaker Meadows.

Barriers Mill, community on Dutch Buffalo Creek in e Cabarrus County.

Barringer Township, se Iredell County. Named for a Civil War muster ground.

Barris Creek rises in central Beaufort County and flows e into Pamlico River.

Barrows Mill Pond, w Northampton County on Gumberry Swamp. Approx. 1 mi. long. Appears as Jones Mill on the Collet map, 1770; known as Wheeler's Mill by 1833, and more recently by its present name. Boyhood home of Willie and Allen Jones, Revolutionary leaders, was here.

Barry Bay, a small bay in ne Carteret County, w of Core Sound, and s of Cedar Island and Thorofare Bay into which it empties.

Barshavia Creek. See Bechewa Creek.

Bart Branch rises in n Jackson County and flows sw into Scott Creek.

Bart Branch rises in w Transylvania County on Brushy Mountain and flows sw into Shoal Creek.

Bartlett. See Bluebutton.

Bartlett Creek rises in nw McDowell County and flows se into O'Dear Creek.

Bartlett Mountain, central Buncombe County se of Swan Mountain.

Bartleys Island, narrow sandy strip approx. 2¾ mi. long beside French Broad River, w Madison County.

Barton Creek Township, nw Wake County.

Bartonsville, community in ne Hertford County. Named for local Barton family before the Civil War.

Bartrams Creek rises in sw Carteret County and flows s into Bogue Sound. Also known in recent years as Barns Creek. Named probably for William Bartram

Bartrams Lake. See White Lake.

Basal Creek rises in sw Wake County and flows se and then ne through Mills Pond and into Sunset Lake where it joins Middle Creek.

The Basin, a body of water at the s tip of New Hanover County. The Cape Fear River on the w is separated from the Basin by a dam; New Inlet on the Atlantic Ocean side permits access from Onslow Bay. The Brunswick–New Hanover County line divides The Basin near its center.

Basin Creek rises in s Alleghany County and flows s through Doughton Park in n Wilkes County to join Lovelace Creek in forming Middle Prong Roaring River.

Basnight, community in w central Washington County midway between towns of Roper and Plymouth. Locally called Macedonia.

Basnights Ditch rises in s Tyrrell County and flows ne into The Frying Pan.

Bass. See Keener.

Bass Ferry. See West Point.

Bass Lake, s Watauga County on Stringfellow Branch in Moses H. Cone Memorial Park, which see. Formerly known as Cone Lake, it was formed before 1908. Covers 22 acres with a max. depth of 30 ft. On the Blue Ridge Parkway.

Bass Mountain, peak in the Cane Creek Mountains, s Alamance County.

Bass's Crossroads. See Momeyer.

Bat Cave, community in ne Henderson County on Broad River. Alt. 1,250. Named for a nearby cave inhabited by bats and rare animals. The cave is preserved as a natural area.

Batchelder Creek. See Bachelor Creek.

Batchellors Creek. See Bachelor Creek.

Batchelor Bay, formed at the mouth of the Roanoke and Cashie rivers, e Bertie County, at the head of Albemarle Sound.

Bateman Branch rises in nw Macon County and flows sw into Whiteoak Creek.

Bateman Gap, nw Macon County between Batey Branch and Bateman Branch.

Bates Branch rises in s Macon County and flows se into Little Tennessee River.

Bates Creek rises in central Cherokee County between Bates and Fain Mountains and flows sw into Hiwassee River.

Bates Gap, s Macon County between Fulcher Branch and Hickory Knoll Creek.

Bates Mountain, central Cherokee County extends from Hiwassee River to Blackwell Mountain.

Bates Mountain, at the head of Bates Branch in s Macon County.

Bates Ridge, s Macon County between Bristle Ridge and Hickory Knoll Creek.

Batey Branch rises in nw Macon County and flows s into Cold Springs Creek.

Bat Fork rises in se Henderson County and flows nw into Mud Creek.

Bath, town in central Beaufort County at junction of Bath and Back Creeks. Alt. 9. Settled 1690. Inc. 1705, o.s. The oldest town in North Carolina and was the county seat from 1696 to 1785 when it was changed to Washington. Probably named for Bath County in which it was originally located. Bath is now a State Historic Site and a number of restored buildings are open to the public. St. Thomas Church here, the oldest church in North Carolina, was built in 1734. The colonial assembly met here in 1744 and 1752.

Bath County, formed in 1696 from the territory s of Albemarle Sound, was named in honor in John Granville, Earl of Bath, one of the Lords Proprietors. On December 3, 1705, the territory was divided into Archdale, Pamptecough, and Wickham precincts. Bath County was not abolished with the creation of these precincts but continued to be referred to in records as late as 1724. As the precincts increased in importance, eventually becoming counties themselves, the parent county lost its identity.

Bath Creek rises in central Beaufort County and flows s into Pamlico River.

Bathsheba Creek. *See* Bechewa Creek.

Bath Township, e central Beaufort County.

Baton, community in s Caldwell County.

Bats Grave. *See* Batts Island.

Batson Creek rises in s Transylvania County and flows n into Carson Creek.

Battery Bolles. *See* Fort Fisher.

Battery Island, a tidal marsh island in the Cape Fear River opposite Southport, se Brunswick County.

Battis Point. *See* Wades Point.

Battleboro, town in ne Nash and sw Edgecombe counties. Inc. 1872. Had its origin about 1840 as a railroad depot in a rich agricultural area. The station was named for James and Joseph Battle, stockholders in the Wilmington and Raleigh Railroad. Produces lumber. Alt. 131.

Battle Branch rises in central Davidson County and flows sw into Abbotts Creek.

Battle Branch rises in e Macon County and flows s into Ellijay Creek.

Battle Branch rises in s Macon County and flows se into North Fork [Skeenah Creek].

Battle Cove, e Swain County between Falls Branch and Fishtrap Branch.

Battle Creek rises in s Swain County and flows ne into Yalaka Creek.

Battle Creek. *See* Johnsons Mill Creek.

Battleground, former community in central Guilford County, now within the limits of the city of Greensboro. Site of Battle of Guilford Courthouse, March 15, 1781.

Battle Run Brook rises in e Catawba County and flows se into North Fork Mountain Creek.

Battles Falls, in Cape Fear River in n Harnett County along a rock outcrop between the confluence of Camels Creek and Fish Creek with the river. The n end of these rapids, near Camels Creek, is called Battles Upper Falls; the s end, near Fish Creek, is called Battles Lower Falls. Mentioned as early as 1819 in a survey of the major rivers of North Carolina.

Batts Crossroads, community in ne Wilson County. Named for John Batts before the middle of the nineteenth century.

Batts Grave. *See* Batts Island.

Batts House, the home of Nathaniel Batts, first known permanent white settler in North Carolina, was built as early as 1655 and stood between Roanoke River and Salmon Creek, e Bertie County, facing Albemarle Sound.

Batts Island, former island in Albemarle Sound near the mouth of the Yeopim River sw Perquimans County. Named for Nathaniell Batts, who acquired property in the area September 24, 1660. It is mentioned in local records as early as 1694. In 1749 it was 40 acres in area and had houses and orchards on it; by 1756 it had been reduced to 27 acres. Early in the twentieth century it was a camp site for fishermen, but in recent years had been reduced to a mud flat with a few dead trees. A hurricane in the 1950's completely destroyed the island. Appears as Heroits Island probably for Thomas Hariot (1560-1621), on the Smith map, 1624; as Hariots Island on the Comberford map, 1657; and as Bats Grave on the Moseley map, 1733 and the Collet map, 1770.

Baucoms, community in n central Union County on the head of Watson Creek.

Baughn Mountain, w Rockingham County e

of the Mayo River and n of the Dan River near the junction of the two. Alt. approx. 1,200.

Baum Creek rises in sw Roanoke Island, Dare County, and flows sw into Oyster Creek.

Baum Point, extends from n Roanoke Island into Roanoke Sound, Dare County.

Bawdy Creek rises in e Johnston County and flows se into Neuse River.

Bawdy Swamp rises in central Johnston County and flows se into Bawdy Creek.

Baxter, community in e Henderson County on Tumblebug Creek.

Baxter Branch rises in n Madison County and flows se into White Rock Branch.

Baxter Creek rises in s Davie County and flows se approx. 2 mi. into Bear Creek.

Baxter Creek rises in n Haywood County near lat. 35° 43' N., long. 83° 06' 40" W., and flows nw into Big Creek. Named for Steven Baxter, a long-time resident and woodcutter in the area. Now in the Great Smoky Mountains National Park.

Bay. See Bull's Bay.

The Bay. See Turnagain Bay.

Bayboro, town and county seat, central Pamlico County on Bay River. Named for the river, which see. Became the county seat in 1876 succeeding Vandemere. Inc. 1881. Alt. 8.5.

Bay Branch rises in sw Beaufort County and flows e into Chocowinity Creek.

Baybush Swamp, a fine sandy loam swamp in n Craven County.

Bay City, community in Bay City Pocosin, n Pamlico County. Established in the early twentieth century as a farming community by out-of-state developers. Now produces grain.

Bay City Pocosin, muck-filled area approx. 12 mi. wide in n Pamlico and s Beaufort counties.

Bay Creek, a tidal creek on Smith Island in Brunswick County which extends from its junction with Cape Creek first se and then ne to flow into Buzzard Bay.

The Bay Creek. See Turnagain Creek.

Bayleaf, community in n central Wake County.

Bayley. See Shawboro.

Baymarsh Thorofare, waterway between Sheep Island and Portsmouth Island, e Carteret County.

Baymeade, community in ne New Hanover County.

Baynes, community in s Caswell County.

Bay River rises in n Pamlico County and flows ne for approx. 16 mi. into the Neuse River. Named for the bay tree which flourishes in the vicinity. Appears on the Moseley map, 1733.

Bay River Point, peninsula off e Pamlico County extending into Bay River estuary.

Bays. See Carolina Bays.

Baysden Mill Pond, in sw Onslow County on Cypress Creek. Covers approx. 10 acres; maximum depth 10 feet.

Bay Shore Park, town in s Carteret County on Bogue Sound. Incorporated 1959.

Bayside. See Bayview.

Bay Swamp, e Pender County, drains nw into Holly Shelter Bay.

Bayview, community on Pamlico River, central Beaufort County. Known earlier as Bayside.

Beach Branch rises in ne Cherokee County and flows se into Right Fork Webb Creek.

Beach Creek rises in s Clay County and flows sw into Brasstown Creek.

Beach Springs, community in w Perquimans County.

Beach Top, s Clay County near the headwaters of Beach Creek and Long Branch.

Beacon Height, mountain in e Avery County.

Beacon Island, in Pamlico Sound, ne Carteret County, is situated between Wallace Channel and Blair Channel leading through Ocracoke Inlet, and is approx. 1,200 ft. long. Name derived from two large beacons on the island formerly used by pilots guiding ships through the channels. Jonathan Price, writing in 1795, says a "fort" was built on the s end of the island in 1794-95 pursuant to an act of Congress. Appears on the Moseley map, 1733.

Beacon Island Road. See Wallace Channel.

Beacon Island Shoal, in Pamlico Sound in ne Carteret County, obstructing passage through Ocracoke Inlet. Located between Beacon Island and Wallace Channel. Appears on the Moseley map, 1733.

Beal's Knob, n Clay County near the Cherokee County line. Alt. 5,000-5,100.

Beals Mill Pond, e Northampton County on a tributary of Potecasi Creek.

Beaman Run, the s part of Howell Swamp, in n Greene County, which flows sw into Contentnea Creek. Named for the Beaman family which settled in the vicinity about the time of the Revolution.

Beamans Crossroads, community in n Sampson County between Old Mill Swamp and Marsh Swamp.

Beam Mill, community in e Cleveland County on Magness Creek. Alt. 1,001.

Bean Creek is formed in n Mitchell County by the junction of Right Fork Bean Creek and Left Fork Bean Creek. It flows se into Big Rock Creek.

Bean Shoals, a succession of rocks and loose stones in Yadkin River on Surry-Yadkin County line, approx. 1 mi. s of the confluence of Ararat River. The shoals measure two miles in length. The communities of Shoals (Surry County) and Bean Shoals (Yadkin County) are nearby. Mentioned as early as 1819 in a survey of the rivers of North Carolina.

Beantown Creek rises in central Haywood County and flows se and ne into Jonathans Creek.

Bear Banks, coastal beach in se Onslow County on the Atlantic Ocean between Bogue and Bear inlets. Mentioned in local records as early as 1713; also spelled Bare, Bar, and Barr. Known also as Bear Beach and Heady's Beach for Daniel Heady and four generations of his descendants who owned the area. The Banks are approx. 3½ mi. long.

Bear Bay. *See* Allenton.

Bear Beach. *See* Bear Banks.

Bear Branch rises in ne Cherokee County and flows nw into Junaluska Creek.

Bear Branch rises in central Columbus County and flows se into Waccamaw River. Schulkens Pond (*which see*) is on this branch.

Bear Branch rises in n Craven County and flows sw into Swift Creek.

Bear Branch rises in w Haywood County near lat. 35° 36′ N., long. 83° 10′ 50″ W., and flows e to join Horse Creek in forming Rough Creek.

Bear Branch rises in n Haywood County and flows nw into Cold Springs Creek.

Bear Branch rises in nw Henderson County and flows sw into Wash Creek.

Bear Branch rises in s Lee County and flows e into Crane Creek.

Bear Branch rises in e Madison County and flows n into Callahan Branch.

Bear Branch rises in s Madison County and flows ne into Spring Creek.

Bear Branch rises in w Madison County and flows e into Spring Creek.

Bear Branch rises in w Nash County and flows se into Sapony Creek.

Bear Branch rises in w Watauga County and flows nw into Buckeye Creek.

Bear Branch rises in se Wilson County and flows sw into Toisnot Swamp. Approx. 3 miles long.

Bearcamp Creek rises in sw Transylvania County and flows se into South Carolina and into Toxaway River.

Bear Cove, in w Macon County at the head of Wayah Creek.

Bear Creek rises in e Ashe County and flows nw into South Fork New River.

Bear Creek rises in w Beaufort County and flows n into Tar River.

Bear Creek rises in ne Cabarrus County and flows se into Stanly County where it enters Big Bear Creek.

Bear Creek rises in sw Chatham County and flows se and ne into Rocky River.

Bear Creek rises in s Cleveland County and flows sw into Shoal Creek.

Bear Creek rises in w Davie County and flows se approx. 14 mi. into South Yadkin River. Daniel Boone and his father, Squire Boone, and other members of the family owned land along this stream. Daniel Boone killed many bears along the creek, hence its name. The Bear Creek watershed is about 15,000 acres in area.

Bear Creek rises in e Franklin County and flows se into Nash County where it enters Back Swamp.

Bear Creek rises in nw Graham County and flows ne into Cheoah River.

Bear Creek rises in se Graham County and flows sw into Tulula Creek.

Bear Creek rises in central Jackson County and flows ne into Bear Creek Lake on Tuckasegee River. *See also* Bear Creek Lake.

Bear Creek rises in s Madison County and flows nw into French Broad River.

Bear Creek rises in central Mitchell County and flows s into North Toe River.

Bear Creek rises in e Onslow County and flows se into Brown's Sound. Appears on the Moseley map, 1733. Known earlier as Deep Creek.

Bear Creek rises in ne Pamlico County and flows se into Bay River. *See also* Mesic.

Bear Creek rises in e Pitt County and flows e into Tar River. Appears on the Collet map, 1770.

Bear Creek rises in s Randolph County and flows se into Moore County where it flows se then ne into Deep River.

Bear Creek rises in s Surry County and flows se into Fisher River.

Bear Creek rises in central Swain County in the Great Smoky Mountains National Park and flows se into Forney Creek.

Bear Creek rises in e Wayne County and flows se on the Wayne-Greene County line into nw Lenoir County and se into Neuse River. The name appears in local records as early as 1742.

Bear Creek, community in sw Chatham County. Known as Richmond until 1895. Alt. 473.

Bear Creek, community in se Graham County at the mouth of Bear Creek.

Bear Creek. See Warrior Creek.

Bear Creek Lake, central Jackson County on Tuckasegee River. Formed in 1954 as a reservoir for Nantahala Power and Light Company. Covers 476 acres with a max. depth of 195 ft. Shoreline is 13.5 mi. Used for generating hydroelectric power. Named for Bear Creek which feeds it. Also receives the waters of Sols, Flat, and Robinson creeks. Famous for bass and trout fishing. Alt. 2,560.

Bear Creek Township, sw Chatham County.

Beard, community in ne Cumberland County.

Beard Cove, central Buncombe County, between Beard Mountain and Gooch Peak in the Elk Mountains.

Beard Creek rises in s Pamlico County and flows s into Neuse River. Appears on the Moseley map, 1733. Local tradition attempts to associate the origin of the name with Blackbeard, the early eighteenth century pirate.

Beard Mountain, central Buncombe County in the Elk Mountains.

Beards Creek, community in s Pamlico County on Beard Creek (which see) and Neuse River, where a recreational area has been developed. Settled prior to 1750; a post office operated here from 1878 to 1914 as Bairds Creek.

Bearford Bay, a marshy bay in sw Duplin County.

Bear Gap, s Clay County on Chunky Gal Mountain.

Bear Gap, s Yancey County between Blue Sea Creek and Beech Nursery Creek.

Beargarden Pocosin, central Greene County. Named because it was a favorite haunt of bears and numerous flowering plants grow there. Yellow jasmine and honeysuckle were so fragrant that they could be smelled a mile or so away downwind.

Beargrass, town in s Martin County on a tributary of Beargrass Swamp. Settled

about 1828. Inc. 1909, but inactive in municipal affairs until 1961 when the General Assembly appointed new officers. Alt. 65.

Bear Grass Creek rises in central Craven County and flows s into Trent River s of New Bern.

Beargrass Swamp rises in s Martin County and flows w into Turkey Swamp.

Beargrass Township, s central Martin County.

Bearhead Creek rises in e Onslow County and flows nw into Wallace Creek.

Bear Inlet, se Onslow County, through which Brown's Sound drains into the Atlantic Ocean. Mentioned in local records as early as 1713, and appears on the Moseley map, 1733. Following the Spanish alarm of 1747 Bear Inlet Fort was constructed here.

Bear Island, not now indentifiable, appears on the Moseley map, 1733, in Bogue Sound, s Carteret County, w of Dog Island.

Bear Island, a sand island in the w section of Angola Bay, n Pender County.

Bear Knob, on the Cherokee-Graham County line.

Bear Knob, sw Macon County between Little Indian Creek and Nantahala River.

Bear Marsh Branch rises in nw Duplin County and flows sw into Merritt Mill Pond and Goshen Swamp.

Bearmeat Branch rises in se Swain County and flows sw into Yalaka Creek.

Bear Mountain, s Jackson County between Doubletop Mountain and Glassy Rock Creek. Alt. 4,650.

Bearpaw, community in w Cherokee County at the mouth of Bearpaw Creek.

Bearpaw Creek rises in w Cherokee County and flows sw and se into Hiwassee River.

Bearpen Branch rises in s Haywood County and flows w into Allen Creek.

Bearpen Branch rises in w Jackson County and flows ne into Dodgen Creek.

Bear Pen Branch rises in n Madison County and flows sw into Little Laurel Creek.

Bearpen Branch rises in n Swain County and flows se into Little Jonas Creek.

Bearpen Branch rises in n Swain County on Noland Ridge and flows se into Left Fork [Deep Creek].

Bear Pen Branch rises in n Transylvania County and flows ne into South Fork Mills River.

Bearpen Creek rises in s Macon County and flows w into Nantahala River.

Bearpen Creek rises in w Macon County and flows sw into Wine Spring Creek.

Bearpen Creek rises in n Madison County and flows s into Chimney Creek.

Bearpen Creek rises in ne Mitchell County and flows sw into Laurel Creek.

Bearpen Creek rises in n Swain County and flows s into Noland Creek.

Bearpen Gap, n central Avery County.

Bearpen Gap, sw Avery County near the Mitchell County line.

Bearpen Gap, ne Buncombe County w of Bearpen Knob.

Bearpen Gap, n Cherokee County near the headwaters of Slickrock Branch.

Bearpen Gap, n Cherokee County in the Unicoi Mountains between Chestnut Mountain and Hangover Top.

Bear Pen Gap, n Clay County between Tuni Creek and the Cherokee County line.

Bearpen Gap, on the Clay-Macon County line.

Bearpen Gap, n central Graham County on Cables Cove Creek.

Bearpen Gap, on the Jackson-Haywood County line between Spot Knob and Rough Butt. Alt. 2,872.

Bearpen Gap, s Macon County at the head of Shope Fork.

Bearpen Gap, w Macon County between Locust Tree Gap and Ray Branch.

Bearpen Gap, nw Swain County between Cable Branch and Fontana Lake.

Bearpen Gap, n Swain County between Laurel Branch and Bearpen Creek.

Bear Pen Islands Swamp, n central Brunswick County. A part of Green Swamp.

Bearpen Knob, ne Buncombe County between Beartree and Bearpen gaps.

Bearpen Knob, peak in s Jackson County bordered on nw by Chattooga River. Southern slope is head for Scotsman Creek. Also called Bearpen Mountain. Alt. 4,300.

Bearpen Mountain on the Jackson-Transylvania County line between Sassafras Mountain and Horsepasture River. Alt. 4,025.

Bearpen Mountain, se Macon County between Little Bearpen Mountain and Saltrock Branch.

Bearpen Mountain, s Macon County between Bearpen Creek and Steeltrap Knob.

Bearpen Mountain, n Madison County parallel to Former Camp Branch.

Bear Pen Ridge, se Clay County.

Bearpen Ridge, s Haywood County, between Daniels Cove and Correll Branch.

Bearpen Ridge, w Haywood County between Bearpen Branch and Caldwell Fork.

Bearpen Ridge, n Madison County between Hickeys Fork and Rock Branch.

Bearpen Ridge, ne Mitchell County between Laurel Creek and Bearpen Creek.

Bearpen Ridge, n Swain County in Great Smoky Mountains National Park, a short spur of Noland Ridge extending se.

Bearpen Ridge, sw Yancey County between Sodom Branch and Indian Creek.

Bearpen Rock, a mountain in w Avery County.

Bear Pocosin, ne Sampson County s of Youngs Swamp and e of Six Runs Creek.

Bear Point extends into Pamlico Sound from e Hyde County.

Bear Point, se Tyrrell County, extends from the mainland into Alligator River.

Bearpond, community in s Vance County, named for a local tradition of a celebrated bear hunt here. In 1785 a practical joke was played on Zeke Brown to put an end to his tall tales of bear killing. A mock bear hunt was arranged at the present site of Bearpond in which a local citizen, Jake Sims, dressed in bear skins and gave Brown such a scare he left the county for "Orrapeake." The community is now known locally as Buena Vista, after the plantation of Dr. Robert Christian Pritchard (b. 1812) in nearby s Warren County.

Bear Poplar, community in w Rowan County. Known first as Rocky Mount; present name adopted in 1878 when a post office was established. Name came from the nearby location of a poplar tree in which Capt. Thomas Cowan, Revolutionary hero, treed a bear in the late eighteenth century.

Bear Ridge, mountain in w Avery County.

Bear Ridge between Cashie Branch and Licklog Creek in n Jackson County.

Bear Ridge, s Yancey County between Blue Sea Creek and Beech Nursery Creek.

Bear Rock Branch rises in s Yancey County and flows se into South Toe River.

Bearskin, community in w central Sampson County near Bearskin Swamp.

Bearskin Creek rises in n Granville County and flows n into Grassy Creek.

Bearskin Creek rises in w Union County and flows e through the city of Monroe into Richardson Creek.

Bearskin Swamp rises in w central Sampson

County and flows sw into Little Coharie Creek.

Bear Swamp is formed in s Hertford County by the junction of Horse Swamp and Flat Swamp and flows e into Ahoskie Creek.

Bear Swamp, e Chowan and w Perquinmans counties. Covers about ⅚ of Chowan County but is gradually being drained to provide farm land as it produces good grain.

Bear Swamp rises in nw Duplin County and flows ne into Goshen Swamp.

Bear Swamp rises in w Halifax County and flows sw into Little Fishing Creek.

Bear Swamp rises in central Northampton County and flows se into Urahaw Swamp.

Bear Swamp rises in w Robeson County and flows se into Lumber River.

Bear Swamp Creek rises in n Franklin County and flows sw into Tar River.

Beartown Mountain, on the Carter (Tennessee)-Mitchell County line. Alt. 5,481.

Beartown Ridge, ne Mitchell County between Beartown Mountain and Big Rock Creek.

Beartrail Ridge Gap, on the Haywood-Jackson County line.

Beartrap Knob, s Haywood County between Raven Hollow and Possum Hollow.

Beartrap Ridge, s Haywood County between Big Beartrap Branch and Raven Hollow.

Beartree Creek rises in e Chatham County and flows se into New Hope Creek.

Beartree Gap, ne Buncombe County between Snowball Mountain and Bearpen Knob.

Bearwallow, community in ne Henderson County. Named by William Mills, pioneer settler, because of a nearby much-frequented bear wallow.

Bearwallow Bald, peak in n Swain County in Great Smoky Mountains National Park on Welch Ridge. Alt. 4,954.

Bearwallow Branch rises in Buncombe County and flows ne into Carter Creek.

Bear Wallow Branch rises in ne Madison County and flows sw into Foster Creek.

Bearwallow Branch rises in ne Swain County and flows sw into Bradley Fork.

Bearwallow Brook rises in n Transylvania County and flows se into South Fork Mills River.

Bearwallow Creek rises in e Jackson County and flows sw into Piney Mountain Creek.

Bearwallow Creek rises in nw Mitchell County and flows sw into Pigeonroost Creek.

Bearwallow Creek rises in sw Transylvania County and flows se into Toxaway River.

Bearwallow Creek rises in e Yancey County and flows n into Little Crabtree Creek.

Bearwallow Gap, se Buncombe County se of Bearwallow Mountain.

Bear Wallow Gap, ne Haywood County on the head of Wesley Creek.

Bearwallow Gap, nw Mitchell County on Bearwallow Creek.

Bear Wallow Knob, s Yancey County between Hurricane Gap and Ogle Gap. Alt. 5,085.

Bear Wallow Knob s Yancey County at the eastern end of Bear Wallow Ridge.

Bearwallow Mountain, on the Buncombe-Henderson County line. Alt. 4,249.

Bearwallow Ridge, n Jackson County between Cherry Orchard Branch and Rough Branch.

Bearwallow Ridge, n Swain County extends ne from the confluence of Proctor Creek and Hazel Creek to Proctor Ridge.

Bear Wallow Ridge, s Yancey County between Middle Fork and Grassy Knob Branch.

Bear Wallow Stand Ridge, s Yancey County between Raven Fork and Blue Sea Creek.

Bearwell Pocosin, se Lenoir County between Joshua Creek and Trent River. Probably a corruption of the family name Burwell. Thomas Burwell was living in the vicinity about 1750.

Beasley, community in n Washington County. Known locally as Holly Neck.

Beasley Bay, in Currituck Sound between Jarvis Channel and Currituck Banks in e Currituck County.

Beasley Branch rises in w Gates County and flows se into Run of Swamp.

Beasley Branch rises in s Transylvania County and flows se into Cherryfield Creek.

Beasley Creek rises in ne Macon County and flows sw into Cowee Creek.

Beasley Creek rises in w Transylvania County and flows s into West Fork French Broad River.

Beasley Gap, s Macon County between Mulberry Creek and Commissioner Creek.

Beasleys Creek rises on the Pender-Onslow County line and flows se into Stump Sound in s Onslow County. Appears on the Collet map, 1770.

Beasleys Mill Pond, on Millers Creek in w Duplin County.

Beason Creek rises in se Cleveland County and flows se into Buffalo Creek.

Beatie's Ford. *See* Beattie's Ford.

Beaton Branch rises in s Buncombe County and flows n into Bent Creek.

Beattie's Ford across the Catawba River, Lincoln-Mecklenburg counties near the Iredell County line. Named for John Beatty who owned land in the area as early as 1749. A post office named Beatie's Ford existed in this vicinity from as early as 1822 until 1882. A part of the British army, in pursuit of Gen. Nathanael Greene, crossed the river here on February 1, 1781. The site is now under the waters of Lake Norman.

Beatty Branch rises in central McDowell County and flows se into Paxton Creek.

Beattys Mill Pond in e Bladen County on Lake Creek.

Beaty Spring Knob, s Haywood County on the head of Inman Branch.

Beaucatcher Mountain, central Buncombe County, in e Asheville. Alt. approx. 3,200. About 1850 James W. Patton erected a summer house or arbor here, and it became quite popular with courting couples. Hence the name.

Beaufort, town and county seat in s central Carteret County. Laid out in 1715 and settled soon afterwards. Inc. 1723. Named for Henry Somerset (1684-1714), Duke of Beaufort, one of the Lords Proprietors of Carolina. Built on the site of an Indian village, Wareiock, said to have meant "Fish Town" or "Fishing Village," the town was first called Fishtown. Fish meal is a leading product of Beaufort today. Alt. 9.

Beaufort (BOE-furt) County was first called Pamptecough Precinct when it was formed in 1705 from Bath County; the name was changed to Beaufort about 1712 to honor Henry Somerset, Duke of Beaufort (1684-1714), who in 1709 became one of the Lords Proprietors. Located in the e part of the state, it is bounded by Craven, Hyde, Martin, Pitt, Pamlico, and Washington counties. Area: 957 sq. mi. County seat: Washington with an elevation of 11 ft. Townships are Bath, Long Acre, Chocowinity, Pantego, Richland, Washington. Produces tobacco, corn, soybeans, hogs, canned sea food, lumber, textiles, apparel, and phosphate.

Beaufort Inlet, s central Carteret County, from the Atlantic Ocean into Bogue Sound, between Bogue Banks on the west and Shackleford Banks on the east. Appears as Topsail Inlet on the de Graffenried map (French text), 1711, and was later known as Old Topsail Inlet.

Beaufort Township, on Taylors Creek and Beaufort Inlet in central Carteret County. For a time called township number 4.

Beautancus, community in n Duplin County near Bear Marsh Branch.

Beauty Spot, mountain on the Mitchell County, N. C.-Unicoi County, Tenn., line. Alt. 4,254.

Beauty Spot Gap, on the Mitchell County, N. C.-Unicoi County, Tenn., line.

Beaux, community in n Wilkes County near Mulberry Creek.

Beaver Branch rises in ne Wayne County and flows se into Nahunta Swamp in w Greene County. The name dates from colonial times.

Beaver Creek rises in s central Ashe County and flows se into South Fork New River.

Beaver Creek rises in ne Cabarrus County and flows s into Dutch Buffalo Creek about two miles n of town of Mount Pleasant.

Beaver Creek rises in ne Caldwell County and flows n into Wilkes County where it enters into Yadkin River.

Beaver Creek, about 13 mi. long, rises on the ne slope of Vaughn Hill in the Fort Bragg Military Reservation, nw Cumberland County, and flows e, then s into Little Rockfish Creek.

Beaver Creek rises in ne Cherokee County and flows se into Valley River.

Beaver Creek rises in e Forsyth County and flows ne into Reedy Fork Creek in nw Guilford County.

Beaver Creek rises in w Guilford County and flows w into Alamance County where it enters Great Alamance Creek.

Beaver Creek rises in sw Harnett County near the junction of Harnett-Lee-Moore County lines and flows sw then se into Moore County where it enters Crains Creek.

Beaver Creek rises in e Hoke County and flows se into Rockfish Creek.

Beaver Creek rises in nw Jones and e Lenoir counties and flows e into Trent River.

Beaver Creek rises in e Mitchell County and flows se into North Toe River.

Beaver Creek rises in e central Surry County and flows sw into Fisher River.

Beaver Creek rises in n central Wake County and flows sw into Neuse River almost directly opposite the mouth of Reedy Spring Branch.

Beaver Creek rises in w Wake County and flows sw into e Chatham County where it enters New Hope Creek.

Beaver Creek rises in sw Wilkes County near the Alexander County line in the Brushy Mountains and flows n into Yadkin River.

Beaver Creek, community in s central Ashe County. Alt. approx. 2,990.

Beaver Creek. See Cumberland.

Beaver Creek Pond. See Beaver Lake.

Beaver Creek Township, sw Wilkes County.

Beaver Creek Township, n Jones County.

Beaverdam, community in sw Buncombe County on Beaverdam Creek ne of Long Mountain.

Beaverdam. See Marshville.

Beaverdam Bald on the Cherokee County, N.C.-Monroe County, Tenn., line in the Unicoi Mountains. Alt. 4,280.

Beaverdam Bay, in ne Bladen County.

Beaverdam Bay, sw Bladen County.

Beaverdam Bay, a section of Green Swamp, central Brunswick County.

Beaver Dam Branch rises in e Brunswick County and flows e into Cape Fear River.

Beaverdam Branch rises in ne Franklin County and flows ne into Sandy Creek.

Beaverdam Branch rises in e Johnston County and flows se into Wayne County where it enters Neuse River.

Beaverdam Branch rises in w Johnston County and flows e into Middle Creek.

Beaverdam Branch rises in s Jones County and flows n into Mill Run.

Beaverdam Branch rises in sw Mecklenburg County and flows sw into Catawba River.

Beaverdam Branch rises in sw Nash County and flows se into Turkey Creek.

Beaverdam Branch rises in w Nash County and flows e into Big Peachtree Creek.

Beaver Dam Branch of Hunting Creek rises n of Calahaln in w Davie County and flows s into Hunting Creek.

Beaver Dam Brook rises in s Catawba County and flows sw into South Fork Catawba River.

Beaverdam Brook rises in Magnolia in w Duplin County and flows ne into Maxwell Creek.

Beaverdam Creek rises in se Bladen County and flows ne into Waymans Creek in Columbus County.

Beaverdam Creek is formed in the Elk Mountains, central Buncombe County, by the junction of Webb Cove Creek and Linn Cove Creek. It flows w into French Broad River.

Beaver Dam Creek rises in se Brunswick County and flows s into Cape Fear River.

Beaverdam Creek rises in sw Buncombe County near the Henderson County line and flows n into South Hominy Creek.

Beaverdam Creek rises in n central Cherokee County and flows sw into Hiwassee River.

Beaverdam Creek rises in central Cleveland County and flows s into First Broad River.

Beaverdam Creek rises in se Cumberland County and flows se into South River.

Beaverdam Creek rises in se Davidson County and flows s into Badin Lake on Yadkin River in nw Montgomery County.

Beaverdam Creek rises in w Davidson County and flows se into Swearing Creek.

Beaverdam Creek rises in w Duplin County and flows e into Maxwell Creek.

Beaverdam Creek rises in e Jones County and flows s into Trent River.

Beaverdam Creek rises in nw Gaston County and flows ne into South Fork Catawba River.

Beaverdam Creek rises in n Gates County and flows nw into Virginia where it enters Somerton Creek.

Beaverdam Creek rises in s Granville County and flows sw into Wake County where it enters Neuse River.

Beaverdam Creek rises in sw Granville County and flows s into Neuse River in nw Wake County.

Beverdam Creek rises in e Haywood County at Beaverdam Gap and flows sw into Pigeon River.

Beaverdam Creek rises in s Martin County and flows n into Conoho Creek.

Beaverdam Creek rises in s Nash County and flows ne into Toisnot Swamp.

Beaverdam Creek rises in n Richmond County and flows sw into Rocky Fork Creek.

Beaverdam Creek rises in w Rowan County and flows ne into Withrow Creek.

Beaverdam Creek rises in n Surry County and flows se into Little Fisher River.

Beaverdam Creek rises in e Union County and flows ne into Lanes Creek.

Beaverdam Creek rises in e Wake County and flows w into Neuse River.

Beaverdam Creek rises in central Wake County in the nw side of the city of Raleigh and flows ne into Crabtree Creek.

Beaverdam Creek rises in central Wake County and flows se into Neuse River.

Beaverdam Creek rises in se Wake County and flows se into Moccasin Creek.

Beaverdam Creek rises in n Watauga County and flows sw into Watauga River.

Beaverdam Creek rises in w Wayne County and flows se then ne into Thoroughfare Swamp.

Beaverdam Dismal, a swampy area in nw Sampson County between the heads of Little Coharie Creek and Beaverdam Swamp.

Beaverdam Gap, sw Buncombe County in Newfound Mountain.

Beaverdam Gap, on the Buncombe-Henderson County line w of Ferrin Knob.

Beaverdam Gap, n Cherokee County at the headwaters of Beaverdam and Cook creeks.

Beaverdam Gap, on the head of Beaverdam Creek in e Haywood County.

Beaverdam Gap, nw Henderson County on the nw end of Trace Ridge. Alt. 3,500.

Beaverdam Pocosin, nw Bertie County.

Beaverdam Ridge, w Watauga County extends nw from Watauga River, w of Cove Creek and se of Ward Hollow.

Beaverdam Run, rises in s Greene County and flows se in an arc into Contentnea Creek.

Beaverdam Swamp rises in central Beaufort County and flows w into Broad Creek.

Beaverdam Swamp rises in nw Bertie County and flows e into Loosing Swamp which becomes Stony Creek.

Beaver Dam Swamp rises in e central Brunswick County and flows s into Town Creek.

Beaverdam Swamp rises in w Columbus County and flows se to join Gum Swamp in forming Monie Swamp.

Beaverdam Swamp rises in ne Craven County and flows s into Little Swift Creek.

Beaverdam Swamp rises in n central Halifax County and flows se into Beech Swamp. Appears on the Collet map, 1770.

Beaverdam Swamp rises in s Lenoir County and flows ne into Trent River. Appears in local records as early as 1720.

Beaverdam Swamp rises in n Nash County and flows ne into Fishing Creek.

Beaverdam Swamp rises in e central Sampson County and flows se into Six Runs Creek.

Beaverdam Swamp rises in n Sampson County and flows sw into Great Coharie Creek.

Beaverdam Swamp rises in nw Sampson County and flows sw into Mingo Swamp.

Beaverdam Swamp rises in w Wayne County and flows se into Neuse River.

Beaverdam Swamp. See Nahunta Swamp.

Beaverdam Swamp Canal rises in s Harnett County and flows s into Cape Fear River.

Beaverdam Township, n Cherokee County.

Beaver Dam Township, se Cumberland County.

Beaverdam Township, e Haywood County.

Beaverdam Township, e Richmond County.

Beaverdam Township, n Watauga County.

Beaver Dam Township. See Arthur township.

Beaver Gap, s Cherokee County n of Sheep Knob.

Beaver Island Creek rises in e Stokes County and flows e into Rockingham County where it turns s to flow into Dan River.

Beaver Island Township, e Stokes County.

Beaver Lake, in the city of Asheville near its n limits, central Buncombe County. On Beaverdam Creek. Constructed as part of real estate development.

Beaver Lake, formed by a dam on Beaver Creek w Cumberland County. Approx. 1 mi. long. Sometimes also known as Beaver Creek Pond.

Beaverpond Creek rises in nw Northampton County and flows ne into Virginia where it turns se to flow back into Northampton County. It again turns ne to flow back into Virginia where it enters Fontaine Creek. It appears on the map of the North Carolina-Virginia line prepared by William Byrd in 1728.

Beaver Store, community in e Wayne County between Exum Mill Branch and The Slough.

Bechewa Creek rises in w Forsyth County and flows sw into Yadkin River. Appeared as Bathsheba Creek on Collet map, 1770, and as Barshavia Creek on MacRae map, 1833.

Beckham Mill Pond. See South Lake.

Beck Mountain, a granite formation in sw Chatham County.

Beckon Mill. See South Lake.

Becks Bald, peak on Hughes Ridge, n Swain

County in Great Smoky Mountains National Park. Alt. 5,022.

Becks Branch rises in ne Swain County in Great Smoky Mountains National Park and flows s into Oconaluftee River.

Beck Springs. See Bennett.

Beckwith, community in e Beaufort County.

Beddingfield Creek rises in e Wake County and flows se into Johnston County where it turns n and flows into Neuse River.

Bedford County. A bill was introduced in the Assembly on November 23, 1768, to create Bedford County and Trinity Parish from parts of Rowan and Orange counties, but the bill was rejected on December 1. The Bethabara Diary (Records of the Moravians, I, 381) for December 18, however, reports that a county by this name was established "last year" in "Lord Granville's part of the Province." Another bill to erect a Bedford County and St. John Parish from the upper part of Tyrrell and the lower part of Halifax counties was considered on November 6, 1769, but it was not passed. The name probably was intended to honor John Russell, Duke of Bedford (1710-71), Lord President of the Council, 1763-65.

Bee Branch rises in n Buncombe County near Rattlesnake Ridge and flows sw into Reems Creek.

Bee Branch rises in nw Buncombe County near Potato Knob and flows ne into Willow Creek.

Bee Branch rises in e Haywood County and flows w into East Fork Pigeon River.

Bee Branch rises in nw Henderson County and flows se into Big Creek.

Bee Branch rises in central Madison County between Red Hill Knob and Lisenbee Ridge and flows sw into Ammons Branch.

Bee Branch rises in e Mitchell County and flows w into Stagger Weed Creek.

Bee Branch rises in central Yancey County and flows sw into Cane River.

Bee Branch rises in n Yancey County and flows ne into Toe River.

Beebranch Mountain, central Yancey County near the head of Bee Branch.

Beech, community in n Buncombe County near the junction of Maney Branch and Reems Creek. Alt. 2,413. Named for large grove of beech trees in the vicinity.

Beech Bottom, community in w Avery County.

Beech Branch rises in e Nash County and flows se into w Edgecombe County and se into Tar River.

Beech Cove Branch rises in w Macon County and flows w into Natahala River.

Beech Creek rises in sw Cherokee County and flows ne into Hiwassee River.

Beech Creek rises in se Clay County and flows sw into Towns County, Georgia, where it enters Tallulah River.

Beech Creek rises in e Graham County and flows w into Sweetwater Creek.

Beech Creek rises in n Granville County and flows ne into Jonathan Creek.

Beech Creek rises in w Haywood County near lat. 35° 39' 30" N., long. 83° 11' 30" W., on e slope of Balsam High Top, and flows se to join Falling Creek in forming Palmer Creek.

Beech Creek rises in n Mitchell County and flows se into Big Rock Creek.

Beech Creek rises in sw Watauga County and forms a part of the Avery-Watauga County boundary. It flows nw into Watauga River.

Beech Creek, community in n Avery County. A post office est. here about 1850.

Beech Creek, community in w Watauga County.

Beech Creek. See Beech Swamp.

Beechertown, community in nw Macon County on Nantahala River. A large hydroelectric power development is here.

Beechflat Creek rises in e Jackson County and flows sw into Mull Creek.

Beech Flats Prong rises in n Swain County in Great Smoky Mountains National Park at Luftee Gap and flows se to join Kephart Prong in forming Oconaluftee River.

Beech Gap, se Clay County between Scaly Ridge and Fairfield Ridge.

Beech Gap, on the Clay-Macon County line.

Beech Gap, on the Haywood-Swain County line between Ledge Bald and Balsam High Top in the Great Smoky Mountains National Park. Formerly known as Big Swag Gap. Alt. approx. 5,060.

Beech Gap, on the Haywood-Transylvania County line between Tanasee Bald and Devils Court House.

Beech Gap. See Black Mountain Gap.

Beech Glen, community in e Madison County on Little Ivy Creek. Alt, 2,105.

Beechgrove, community in nw Washington County.

Beech Knob, e central Avery County. Alt. 5,067.

Beech Knob, on the Haywood-Transylvania County line. Alt. 5,160-5,180.

Beech Knob, on the Jackson-Haywood County line.

Beech Mountain, on the Avery-Watauga County line. Peak in Avery County. Alt. 5,506.

Beech Mountain, n Yancey County between Bent Creek and Little Creek.

Beech Mountain. See Bucks Peak.

Beech Mountain Township, n Avery County.

Beech Nursery Creek rises in s Yancey County and flows nw into Cane River.

Beech Nursery Gap, s Yancey County between Beech Nursery Creek and Big Pine Mountain.

Beechnut Gap, on the Swain County, N.C.-Sevier County, Tenn., line in Great Smoky Mountains National Park.

Beech Ridge, nw Haywood County between Seven Mile Ridge and the head of Big Creek.

Beech Ridge, between Lost Bottom Branch and Beech Creek in w Haywood County, Great Smoky Mountains National Park. It is a spur of Balsam Mountain extending se from Balsam High Top.

Beech Spring Gap, s Haywood County between Shining Rock and Dog Loser Knob.

Beech Swamp rises in central Halifax County and flows se into Fishing Creek. Appears as Rogers Creek on the Moseley Map, 1733, and as Beech Creek on the Collet map, 1770.

Bee Cove Lead extends ne from Yellow Creek to Bee Cove Knob in n Graham County.

Bee Cove Knob, n Graham County on the ne end of Bee Cove Lead.

Bee Creek rises in central Graham County and flows nw into Yellow Creek.

Bee Creek rises in w Mitchell County and flows s into Big Rock Creek.

Beef Market Top, ne Jackson County on Grassy Ridge. Alt. 5,040. Said to have been named (1) because deserters from the Confederate army, hiding in the area, stole and slaughtered cattle here, or (2) because a young man killed cattle here which belonged to the father of his sweetheart when he was forbidden by her father to see her again.

Bee Gap, at sw end of Sassafrass Ridge in sw Graham County.

Bee Gum Branch rises in n Swain County and flows se into Hazel Creek.

Bee Gum Branch rises in n central Swain County in Great Smoky Mountains National Park and flows sw into Forney Creek.

Bee Island Bay, swamp in w central Brunswick County. A part of Green Swamp.

Bee Knob, at the head of West Buffalo Creek in w Graham County.

Bee Knob, n Swain County in Great Smoky Mountains National Park on Pilot Ridge. Alt. 4,300.

Bee Log, community in n Yancey County on Bald Mountain Creek. Named when a fallen tree in the vicinity was discovered to contain bees and honey.

Bee Mountain, sw Caldwell County between the headwaters of Husbands and Abingdon creeks.

Bee Ridge, central Buncombe County ne of Busbee Reservoir.

Bee Ridge, in South Mountains in s Burke County.

Bee Ridge, e Mitchell County between Bee Branch and Stony Valley.

Bee Ridge, n Swain County w of Forney Creek parallel to Welch Branch.

Bee Ridge, e Yancey County, extends ne parallel to Dobag Creek.

Bee Rock Creek rises in nw McDowell County and flows e into Armstrong Creek.

Beer Rice Gap, on the Madison County, N.C.–Unioci County, Tenn., line.

Bee Stump Branch rises in s Yancey County and flows n into South Toe River.

Beetree Branch rises in ne Cherokee County and flows nw into Valley River.

Bee Tree Branch rises in n Wilkes County and flows s into Mulberry Creek.

Bee Tree Canal, w Tyrrell County, flows ne from Lake Phelps to a tributary of Scuppernong River. Dug by slave labor to drain swamplands for cultivation.

Beetree Creek rises in ne Buncombe County and flows sw into Swannanoa River. An early settlement west of the Blue Ridge Mountains was est. here in 1785.

Bee Tree Creek rises in s Jackson County and flows s into Cedar Creek.

Beetree Creek rises in e Madison County and flows sw into East Fork [Bull Creek].

Beetree Creek rises in e Mitchell County and flows sw into Little Rock Creek.

Beetree Creek rises in n Swain County in Great Smoky Mountains National Park and flows sw into Right Fork Deep Creek.

Bee Tree Creek rises in s Watauga County and flows ne into Boone Fork.

Bee Tree Fork rises in nw Transylvania County and flows se into North Fork French Broad River.

Bee Tree Mountain. See Craggy Knob.

Beetree Reservoir on Beetree Creek, ne Buncombe County. Alt. 2,669. This 55-

acre lake is a part of the water system of the city of Asheville.

Beetree Ridge extends se from Candler Knob to Big Creek in nw Henderson County.

Beetree Ridge, e Mitchell County between Reuben Creek and Beetree Creek.

Beetree Ridge, n Swain County in Great Smoky Mountains National Park, a spur extending sw from Thomas Ridge.

Bee Tree Ridge, n Watauga County extends sw, w of Laurel Branch.

Belcross, community in central Camden County named for Bell family.

Belew Creek, community in ne Forsyth County. A post office was here as early as 1831. Originally est. as Belews Creek Mill.

Belews Creek rises in e Forsyth County and flows ne across the se edge of Stokes County and into the Dan River on the Stokes–Rockingham County line. This creek rises independently of East and West Belews Creeks, both of which flow into it. Belews Creek appears on Collet map, 1770.

Belews Creek Township, ne Forsyth County.

Belfast, community in central Wayne County. Named by John Robinson, native of Ireland, for his wife's birthplace, Belfast, Ireland. Formerly called Scottsville.

Belford, community in nw Nash County near the Franklin County line. Named by David Sills, who settled here in 1798, for his home in n England. A post office established here as early as 1822.

Belgrade, community in ne Onslow County. Thousands of tons of limestone marl, used in building road foundations and in concrete, are shipped from here annually.

Belgrade. See Bonarva.

Belhaven, town in e Beaufort County on Pungo River and Pantego Creek. Alt. 4. Settled about 1890; inc. 1899. Named from the two words, belle and haven, meaning beautiful harbor. See also Aquascogoc.

Bellair, community in central Craven County.

Bellamy, crossroads community in e Robeson County. Alt. 108. Settled about 1910. Named for John D. Bellamy (1854-1932), division counsel for the Seaboard Air Line Railroad. Bellamy station, now abandoned, was two miles south.

Bellamys Lake, about ¾ mi. long, on Rocky Swamp near its confluence with Fishing Creek, sw Halifax County.

Bell–Arthur, town in w Pitt County. Settled about 1907. Inc. 1907 as Arthur; named for L. C. Arthur, local landowner and farmer. Name changed to Bell–Arthur, 1933. Alt. 79.

Bell Bay in the mainland of sw Hyde County on Pamlico Sound immediately w of Rose Bay. Known as Jasper's Creek in the 18th century. The courthouse for Hyde County was located on Jasper's Creek in 1791-92.

Bell Branch rises in s central Brunswick County and flows w into Shallotte Creek.

Bell Branch rises in ne Buncombe County and flows se into Beetree Creek.

Bell Collar Cove, on Shining Creek in s Haywood County.

Bellcollar Gap, on the Graham-Swain County line between Little Bald and Cheoah Bald.

Bell Coney Mountain, on the e end of Lizzy Mountain in central Jackson County. Alt. 4,349.

Bell Cove, site of early settlement on the e end of Bogue Banks, s Carteret County. Name is taken from the fact that a bell in the local church was rung for services. Storms drove out early settlers until settlement of Salter Path, which see.

Bell Creek rises in sw Anson County and flows s into Deadfall Creek.

Bell Creek rises in central Carteret County and flows sw into Core Creek.

Bell Creek rises in n Cherokee County and flows se into Garreck Creek.

Bellemont, community in w central Alamance County, est. as a mill village prior to 1900.

Bellevedere Pond, n Wayne County in a tributary of Nahunta Swamp.

Bellfont. See Russellborough.

Bell Island, a peninsula extending from the e mainland of Currituck County into Coinjock Bay and Currituck Sound. Formerly separated from the mainland and called Willowbies Island on the Ogilby map, 1671, in honor of Peregrine Bertie, Lord Willoughby de Eresby (1555-1601), thought to have been a subscriber to the Roanoke voyage of 1585. On the Collet map, 1770, and subsequent maps until MacRae, 1833, the name Betts Island is used. It is now 1½ mi. long and ½ mi. wide. See also Bell's Island.

Bell Island, peninsula which extends from the s mainland of Hyde County into Pamlico Sound between Swanquarter Bay and Rose Bay. *See also* Abigails Islands.

Bell Island. *See* Pittmans Island.

Bell Knob, on the Clay-Macon County line.

Bellows Bay, at the n end of Currituck Sound and mouth of North Landing River, extends into the s tip of MacKay Island in ne Currituck County.

Bell Mountain, s Cherokee County between Raminger and Cane creeks.

Bell Mountain, w Henderson County between Little Willow Creek and South Fork.

Bell Point, peninsula off n Pamlico County extending into Bay River.

Bell River is formed in s Alexander County where Glade Creek enters Lower Little River. It flows s approx. 1½ mi. into Catawba River. Local usage applies this name to Lower Little River s from a point about midway between the mouths of Muddy Fork and Spring creeks where N. C. Route 90 crosses Lower Little River.

Bells Branch rises in central Hertford County and flows se and ne into Potecasi Creek.

Bells Corners. *See* Newport.

Bells Creek rises in n Richmond County and flows se into Rocky Fork Creek.

Bells Cross Roads, community in sw Iredell County. A post office named Fallstown was est. here by 1828 but ceased operation many years ago.

Bells Crossroads, community in nw Pitt County.

Bells Ferry appears on the Moseley map, 1733, across Lockwoods Folly River on the Brunswick, N. C.-Charleston, S. C., road in New Hanover Precinct of Clarendon County. The site is in what is now s central Brunswick County.

Bell's Ferry. *See* Grifton.

Bells Ferry. *See* Mackeys Ferry.

Bells Island, a marshy island in Core Sound about 1 mi. e of Marshallberg in se Carteret County. Formerly known as Great Marsh.

Bell's Island, a real estate development, e Currituck County on Bell Island, *which see.* The 1967 General Assembly passed an act under which, by a vote of the residents, Bell's Island may be inc. as a town by resolution of the county commissioners.

Bells Point, the s end of Bells Island, on the w side of Core Sound about 1 mi. e of Marshallberg in s Carteret County. For-

merly known as Bell Point, Bell's Point, and Great Marsh Point.

Bell Swamp rises in e Onslow County and flows se and ne into Queens Creek. Probably named for George Bell who owned land here as early as 1713.

Bell Swamp, community in e central Brunswick County.

Bell Swamp Creek rises in e central Brunswick County and flows e into Rices Creek.

Belltown, community in central Granville County.

Bell View, community in s Cherokee County.

Bellvue Mountain, central Avery County.

Belmont, city in e Gaston County. Site of cotton mills in late nineteenth century. Named Garibaldi in the 1870's for the man who built the railroad water tank here. Incorporated as Belmont, 1895. Named for August Belmont (1853-1924), New York banker and financier. Roman Catholic St. Mary's College opened here in 1878, chartered 1886, renamed Belmont Abbey College, 1913. Also home of Sacred Heart Junior College. Produces textiles and hosiery. Alt. 685.

Belmont, community in e Nash County. North Carolina Wesleyan College established here, 1956 (address: Rocky Mount).

Belmont Mountain, n Henderson County between Clear Creek and Featherston Creek.

Belmont-South Rosemary, community on the w outskirts of Roanoke Rapids, n Halifax County.

Belva, community in n Madison County on Shelton Laurel Creek. Alt. 1,689.

Belvidere, community in w Perquimans County on the Perquimans River. Settled by Quakers early in the eighteenth century. The Moseley map, 1733, shows "G. Newby's Ferry" at about this site; appears as Newbes Bridge on the Collet map, 1770. A post office, Newby's Bridge, est. here, 1827; changed to Belvidere, 1861.

Belvidere Township, n Perquimans County.

Belville, highly developed plantation of 8,000 acres, of which 1,700 were cleared, in Currituck and Pasquotank counties. Flourished 1757-1777. Located on North River, with wharf and shipyard. Owned wholly or in large part by Thomas Macknight. Numerous buildings were scattered throughout the area connected by roads. Canals drained much of the land.

Belvoir Township, nw Pitt County.

Belvoir Township, n central Sampson County.

Belwood, community in ne Cleveland County. Alt. 990.

Bems Creek rises in w Halifax County and flows se into Little Fishing Creek.

Benaja, community in s Rockingham County. Alt. 687. Named for the creek.

Benaja Creek rises in ne Guilford County and flows ne into Rockingham County where it enters Haw River. Original name was Benajar. Believed to have been named for the tropical ben tree plus *ajar* in the sense of "out of place."

Ben Bolen Creek rises in sw Ashe County and flows w into Three Top Creek.

Bench Mountain, e Macon County between Caler Fork and Mica City Creek.

Bench Mountain, sw Watauga County, extends ne from White Rocks along the head of Spice Bottom Creek.

Ben Cove Branch rises in e Jackson County and flows se into Sols Creek.

Ben Creek rises in n Macon County and flows nw into Cold Spring Creek.

Benge, community in s Ashe County near Benge Gap on the Wilkes County line.

Benge Gap, on the Ashe-Wilkes County line.

Bengle Creek. *See* Wolfpen Creek.

Benham, community in ne Wilkes County between Little Elkin River and Elkin River.

Ben Johnson Lake on Eno River, central Orange County. Formed 1955. Covers 15 acres; maximum depth 12 ft. Source of water for town of Hillsborough. Known as Hillsboro Lake prior to February, 1956.

Bennett, town in sw Chatham County. Inc. 1915. Named for J. M. Bennett, superintendent of Southern Railway. Earlier known as Beck Springs and Beck Mountain. Was a terminus of Bonlee and Western Railroad, now abandoned. Alt. 250.

Bennett, community in nw Pamlico County.

Bennett Branch rises in se Haywood County and flows nw into East Fork Pigeon River.

Bennett Branch rises in w Haywood County in Great Smoky Mountains National Park and flows w in Cataloochee Creek. Named for Bennett family who lived in the area.

Bennett Branch rises in n Transylvania County near Bennett Gap and flows se into Cherry Cove Branch.

Bennett Gap, on the Haywood-Transylvania County line on Pisgah Ridge between Cherry Gap and Green Knob. Alt. approx. 4,420.

Bennett Gap, n Transylvania County between Lookingglass Creek and Avery Creek. Alt. 3,516.

Bennett Knob, n Transylvania County on Seniard Ridge s of Big Bear Pen Branch.

Bennetts, community se Anson County. Alt. 251.

Bennetts Creek is formed by the junction of Duke Swamp, Harrell Swamp, and Raynor Swamp in central Gates County. It flows sw and se into Chowan River. Named for Richard Bennett, Governor of Virginia, 1652-1655. Appears on the Ogilby map, 1671.

Bennetts Creek Landing. *See* Gatesville.

Bennetts Millpond, on Rockyhock Creek in central Chowan County. Formed about 1856. 2 mi. long and ⅓ mi. wide, centering near lat. 36° 09' 10" N., long. 76° 39' 40" W. Covers approx. 50 acres. Max. depth, 6 to 8 ft. Probably named for William Bennett (d. 1785), an early owner of the site.

Bennies Branch rises in s Macon County and flows ne into Turtle Pond Creek.

Benn Knob, Mountain on Burke-Cleveland County line. Part of South Mountains. Alt. 2,894.

Benny Cove extends nw from Benny Ridge to Vengeance Creek in ne Cherokee County.

Benny Ridge, mountain in Valley River Mountains between Kimsey Cove and Horse Ridge, ne Cherokee County.

Bensalem, community in w Moore County on the head of Dry Creek. A Presbyterian Church here was organized in 1813. Former names were Caledonia (a post office as early as 1830) and Bigoak (a post office in 1882).

Bensalem Township, w Moore County.

Bensborough. *See* Falkland.

Bens Creek rises in e Warren County and flows se into Little Fishing Creek. Mentioned in local records as early as 1764.

Benson, town in sw Johnston County. Inc. 1887 and named for M. C. Benson, pioneer settler and landowner. Alt. 245. Produces lumber and apparel.

Benson Creek rises in n Surry County and flows se into Stewart Creek.

Bens Ridge, sw Buncombe County, w of Ripshin Mountain.

Bens Ridge, se Watauga County extends se between Dugger Creek and the head of Flat Branch.

Bent Creek rises near Bent Creek Gap, s Buncombe County and flows ne into French Broad River.

Bent Creek rises in ne Cherokee County and flows nw into Valley River.

Bent Creek is formed in n Yancey County by the junction of Left Prong Bent Creek and Right Prong Bent Creek. It flows se approx. 1/10 mi. into Cane River.

Bent Creek, community in n Yancey County on Cane River near the mouth of Bent Creek.

Bent Creek Experimental Forest, s Buncombe County, a part of Pisgah National Forest.

Bent Creek Gap, s Buncombe County near the headwaters of Bent Creek. Alt. 3,270.

Bent Fork Gap, at the head of Bad Fork in nw Henderson County.

Bent Knee Knob, on the head of Stevens Creek, n Haywood County, near lat. 35° 38' 05" N., long. 83° 02' 30" W., in Great Smoky Mountains National Park. Alt. 4,000.

Bent Knob, central Mitchell County between Ellis Mountain and Toe River.

Bentley, community in s central Alexander County.

Bent Mountain, sw Buncombe County w of Piney Mountain.

Benton Branch rises in sw Caswell County and flows sw into Stoney Creek.

Benton Branch rises in e Lenoir County and flows ne into Dailys Creek. Probably named for Francis Benton who was living in the vicinity as early as 1760.

Benton Crossroads. See Fairview.

Benton Heights, town in central Union County. Incorporated 1913. Merged with city of Monroe in 1945. Alt. 595.

Bentonville, community in s Johnston County.

Bentonville Battlefield, state historic site, s Johnston County. Scene of Civil War battle, March 19-20, 1865, at which Confederates under Gen. Joseph E. Johnston checked the advance of Federals under Gen. William T. Sherman. Bloodiest battle ever fought on North Carolina soil.

Bentonville Township, se Johnston County.

Bent Ridge, sw Avery County.

Bent Ridge, s Mitchell County in a bend of North Toe River.

Benvenue, community in e Nash County between Horn Beam Swamp and Compass Creek. Took its name from the plantation of Benjamin Hickman Bunn, which was named about 1890 for Ben Venue, a small mountain in Perthshire, Scotland.

Berea, community in w Granville County. Alt. 475. Settled prior to 1870.

Bergaw Creek. See Burgaw Creek.

Berkeley County, est. prior to 1691 by the Lords Proprietors of Carolina in what is now e South Carolina. Named for John Berkeley (ca. 1607-78), Baron Berkeley of Stratton, one of the original eight Lords Proprietors.

Berkeley Parish, Church of England, Perquimans County, was est. in 1701, coextensive with the county. In 1767 it was composed of 900 white taxable "inhabitants in midling Circumstances." The parish as a unit of local administration was abolished in 1776 with the adoption of the state constitution and the disestablishment of the Church of England.

Berkeley Precinct. See Perquimans County.

Berlin. See Bina.

Bermuda Island in the waters of Kitty Hawk Bay, n Dare County.

Bernal Branch rises in w Johnston County and flows se into Hannah Creek.

Bernice, community in ne Ashe County.

Berry. See Graham.

Berry Creek rises in e Macon County and flows nw into Corbin Creek.

Berry Gap, on the Jackson-Macon County line.

Berryhill Township, former township in sw Mecklenburg County. Now township number 2.

Berry Mill, community in e Macon County on Watauga Creek.

Berry Mountain, s Madison County between Dan Payne Mountain and Doctor Mountain.

Berry Mountains, two adjacent mountains in se Gaston County on South Fork Catawba River.

Berrys Gap, sw Buncombe County between Long and Young Pisgah Mountains.

Berryville. See Hickory.

Bert Creek rises in se Graham County and flows sw by Bert Creek Lead into Tulula Creek. Named for Bert Wiggins.

Bert Creek Lead, se Graham County between Franks Creek and Bert Creek.

Bertha, community on w shore of Currituck Sound in central Currituck County.

Bertie, former town in se Bertie County. Inc. 1939 and merged with the town of Windsor in 1959. Known earlier as Rosemont.

Bertie (BURR-tee) County was formed in 1722 from Chowan County. Located in the ne section of the state, it is bounded by Albemarle Sound, Chowan River, and Washington, Martin, Halifax, Northampton, and Hertford counties. Area: 721 sq. mi. Named for James Bertie (1673-1735) who held a proprietary share of North Carolina. His brother Henry (1675-1735) appears as a Proprietor in 1728 and it has often been said that the county was named for both men. County seat: Windsor with an alt. of 10 ft. Townships are Colerain, Indian Woods, Merry Hill, Mitchells, Roxobel, Snake Bite, Whites, Windsor, and Woodville. Site of the home of Nathaniell Batts, first known permanent white settler in North Carolina, which was built by 1655. Produces tobacco, corn, soybeans, peanuts, cotton, hogs, sweet potatoes, and lumber. See also Society Parish.

Berwick, community in w central Bladen County.

Bessemer City, town in w Gaston County. Incorporated 1893. Named for Sir Henry Bessemer (1813-1898), discoverer of process for making steel from cast iron. Iron ore had been found in the vicinity and there were hopes that steel mills might be est. here. Produces textiles, machinery, and chemicals. Alt. 912.

Bessie, community on the head of Flat Creek in sw Jackson County.

Best, community in e Wayne County. Named for Henry Best who had a grant of land here in 1743. Alt. 126.

Best. See Biltmore.

Beta, community in n Jackson County on Scott Creek. Alt. 2,145.

Bethabara. See Old Town.

Bethania, town in w Forsyth County on Muddy Creek. Settled 1759, inc. 1839, but not now active in municipal affairs. Named by the Moravians, whose second or "new town" it was, for the Biblical town of Bethany. Refugees during the French and Indian War found protection within the Bethania stockade and many of them remained to build homes there. Alt. 789.

Bethania Township, nw Forsyth County.

Bethany, community in n Davidson County. Settled in late eighteenth century by Germans and called Fredericktown. Later known as Possumtown. In 1861 a new church was built and named Bethany, a name soon applied to the community.

Bethany, community in e central Iredell County named for Bethany Presbyterian Church organized here in 1775. Ebenezer Academy, building still standing, operated here 1822-1857.

Bethany, community in sw Rockingham County. A post office est. here as early as 1822.

Bethany. See Milwaukee.

Bethany Township, central Iredell County.

Bethel, community in nw Caswell County.

Bethel, community on Peter Cove Branch in s Haywood County.

Bethel, community in sw Hoke County.

Bethel, community in s Perquimans County.

Bethel, town in n Pitt County. Settled before the Civil War. Inc. 1873. Named for Bethel Methodist Church. Alt. 69.

Bethel, community in nw Watauga County on Rube Creek.

Bethel, community in w Wayne County near Bear Creek.

Bethel. See Harrellsville.

Bethel. See Whortonsville.

Bethel Church Township, a former township in s Cabarrus County. Now township number 10.

Bethel Creek rises in sw Perquimans County and flows se into Yeopim River.

Bethel Hill, community in n Person County.

Bethel Township, w central Bladen County.

Bethel Township, sw Perquimans County.

Bethel Township, n Pitt County.

Bethesda, community in se Durham County.

Bethlehem, community in s Hertford County.

Bethlehem. See Redland.

Betsey Gap, on Madison-Haywood County line. Alt. 5,895.

Betsy Branch rises in central Jackson County and flows nw into Trout Creek.

Betsy Ridge, n McDowell County, extends s from Woods Mountain.

Bett Brook rises in s Catawba County and flows se into Clark Creek.

Bettie community in e Carteret County on e side of North River.

Bettie McGee's Creek rises in w Randolph

County and flows sw into Uwharrie River. Said to have been named for the second wife of William Bell, first sheriff of the county. She is said to have nursed wounded soldiers at the Battle of Guilford Court House during the Revolution.

Bettis Branch rises in n Cherokee County and flows s and sw into Valley River.

Bettis Branch rises in n Haywood County near lat. 35° 42′ 54″ N., long. 83° 97′ W., in Great Smoky Mountains National Park, and flows nw into Big Creek.

Betts Branch rises in central Swain County and flows sw into Deep Creek.

Betts Island. See Bell Island.

Betty Branch rises in w Clay County and flows s into Hiwassee River.

Betty Branch rises in nw Henderson County and flows se into Boylston Creek.

Betty Branch rises in w Jackson County and flows ne into Savannah Creek.

Betty Creek rises in s Macon County and flows se into Rabun County, Georgia, where it joins Darnell Creek to form Little Tennessee River.

Betty Creek Gap, at the head of Betty Creek in s Macon County.

Betty Gap, w Jackson County near the head of Betty Branch. Alt. 3,000.

Betty Noland Cliff, between Norton Branch and the head of Ammons Branch in se Macon County.

Betty Town. See Aurora.

Beulah, community in sw Hyde County.

Beulah, community in e central Polk County.

Beulah, community in central Sampson County.

Beulah Township, ne Johnston County.

Beulaville, town in e Duplin County. Alt. 95. Inc. 1915. Produces apparel.

Bevins Branch rises in se Cherokee County and flows se and ne into Brendle Branch.

Bev Jones Crossroads, community in s Wake County s of Swift Creek.

Bewes Ordinary appears on the Collet map, 1770, apparently in what is now w Guilford County s of the community of Colfax e of Deep River and near Sandy Ridge Church.

Biddie Toe Creek rises in w Nash County and flows ne into Tar River.

Biddleville, community in central Mecklenburg County.

Big Abrams Gap, mountain gap on the Swain County, N. C.-Blount County, Tenn., line in the Great Smoky Mountains National Park.

Big Alamance Creek rises in se Guilford County and flows ne to join Little Alamance Creek in forming Great Alamance Creek, *which see.*

Big Andy Ridge, ne Buncombe County between Little Andy Creek and Walker Branch. See also Point Misery.

Big Arm Creek rises in n Johnston County and flows sw into Marks Creek.

Big Bald, on the Avery-Mitchell County line. Sometimes called Penland Yellow or Big Yellow.

Big Bald, on the Haywood-Swain County line, a peak on Balsam Mountain, 2½ mi. sw of Balsam Corner.

Big Bald, on the Haywood-Transylvania County line between Flat Laurel Gap and Frying Pan Mountain. Alt. 5,340.

Big Bald, on the Yancey County, N. C.-Unicoi County, Tenn., line. Peak in Yancey County is at the n end of Hensley Ridge. Alt. 5,516. Known by the Indians as Sasseenohla, "white man." Previously called Grier Bald for David Grier, spurned lover of the daughter of Col. David Vance. He lived here from 1802 until 1834 when he was killed for having killed a hunter who "trespassed" on the mountain. Much of the mountain is covered by mounds ranging from the size of a football to a bushel basket which emit a hollow sound when struck. Scientists theorize that the mounds are the rotted roots of balsam and spruce trees blown over by a tornado centuries ago. *See also,* The Arm.

Big Bald Branch rises in w Haywood County and flows nw into Caldwell Fork.

Big Bald Mountain, on the Ashe-Watauga County line e of Long Hope Creek.

Big Bald Mountain, on the Avery-Mitchell County line.

Big Bay, e central Bladen County.

Big Bay, sw Bladen County. See also Delightful Plains.

Big Bay, a section of Little Green Swamp, nw Brunswick County.

Big Bay, central Columbus County filled with fine sandy loam.

Big Bay, a loam filled bay in sw Columbus County.

Big Beach, a section of outer beach in sw Brunswick County between Holdens Beach and Shallotte Inlet.

Big Bear Creek rises in nw Stanly County and flows se into Long Creek.

Big Bear Pen Branch rises in n Transylvania

County and flows e into Lookingglass Creek.

Big Beartrail Ridge, s Haywood County, between Right Hand Prong and Little Beartrap Branch.

Big Beartrap Branch rises in s Haywood County and flows e into Middle Fork.

Big Bearwallow Creek rises in central Transylvania County and flows s into North Fork French Broad River.

Big Beaverdam Creek rises in se Sampson County and flows e into Duplin County where it enters Rockfish Creek.

Big Bend, a turn in Pigeon River in n Haywood County near the mouths of Groundhog Creek and Skiffley Creek.

Big Black Pine Ridge, w Watauga County extends nw to the Avery-Watauga County line n of Grassy Gap Branch.

Big Branch rises in se Alexander County and flows se into Elk Shoal Creek.

Big Branch rises in w Avery County and flows sw into Roaring Creek.

Big Branch rises in w Avery County and flows ne into Horse Creek.

Big Branch rises in ne Brunswick County and flows e into Cape Fear River.

Big Branch rises near Potato Knob in ne Buncombe County and flows s into Right Fork.

Big Branch rises in s Columbus County and flows sw into Grissett Swamp.

Big Branch rises in nw Cumberland County and flows se into Beaver Creek.

Big Branch rises in se Duplin County and flows w into Muddy Creek.

Big Branch rises in s Franklin County and flows ne into Cedar Creek.

Big Branch, swamp in s Gates County which drains e into Cole Creek.

Big Branch rises in e Granville County and flows s into Gibbs Creek.

Big Branch rises in w Harnett County and flows se into Barbecue Swamp.

Big Branch rises in nw Haywood County and flows se into Big Creek.

Big Branch rises in n Haywood County and flows nw into Big Creek.

Big Branch rises in central Haywood County and flows ne into Pigeon River.

Big Branch rises in s Haywood County and flows ne into Little East Fork Pigeon River.

Big Branch rises in central Haywood County and flows w into Pigeon River.

Big Branch rises in n Macon County and flows nw into Cold Spring Creek.

Big Branch rises in e Madison County and flows s into Little Ivy Creek.

Big Branch rises in s Madison County and flows ne into Robert Branch.

Big Branch rises in n Mitchell County and flows e into Right Fork Bean Creek.

Big Branch rises in sw Nash County and flows sw into Turkey Creek.

Big Branch rises in s Randolph County and flows sw into Little River.

Big Branch rises in ne Swain County and flows se into Enloe Creek.

Big Branch rises in e Transylvania County near Shuford Mountain and flows sw into Little Mountain.

Big Branch rises in s Transylvania County and flows sw into East Fork French Broad River.

Big Branch rises in ne Wake County and flows se into Little River.

Big Branch rises in w Wake County and flows se into Little Whiteoak Creek.

Big Branch rises in w Wake County and flows s into Whiteoak Creek.

Big Branch rises in e Wake County and flows n into Walnut Creek.

Big Branch rises in e Warren County and flows sw to join Walkers Creek in forming Little Fishing Creek.

Big Branch rises in w Wilson County and flows s into Contentnea Creek. Known earlier as Johnson's Branch.

Big Branch rises in e Yancey County and flows se and ne into Crabtree Creek.

Big Branch. *See* Mill Branch.

Big Buckeye Cove, se Haywood County on the head of East Fork Pigeon River.

Big Buffalo Creek rises in central Lee County and flows nw into Deep River.

Big Bugaboo Creek rises in ne Wilkes County and flows s into Yadkin River.

Big Butt, on the Buncombe-Yancey County line between Flat Spring Knob and Little Butt.

Big Butt, s Macon County between Mooney Gap and Bearpen Gap.

Big Butt, on the Madison County, N. C.-Greene County, Tenn., line. Alt. 4,836.

Big Butt Creek rises in ne Buncombe County and flows nw into Straight Creek.

Big Butte, mountain on the Buncombe-Yancey County line sw of Flat Springs Gap. Alt. 6,001. Formerly known as Wilson Knob Mountain. Also called Yeates Knob.

Big Butte Mountain, w Avery County.

Big Butt Mountain, w Haywood County in the Great Smoky Mountains National

Park. On Mount Sterling Ridge near lat. 35° 40' 20" N., long. 83° 10' 10" W.

Big Butt Mountain, peak of Newfound Mountain on the Buncombe-Haywood County line. Alt. 4,744.

Big Cataloochee Mountain, w Haywood County in Great Smoky Mountains National Park. A Balsam Mountain peak, alt. 6,122, near lat. 35° 40' 25" N., long. 83° 10' 27" W. Known briefly in the 1890's as Nibb's Knob when a member of the U. S. Geological Survey party attempted to name the peak for himself.

Big Chestnut Bald, mountain on the Swain County, N. C.-Sevier County, Tenn., line in the Great Smoky Mountains National Park. Alt. 4,970.

Big Chinquapin Branch. *See* Chinquapin Branch.

Big Colly Bay, ne Bladen County, approx. 5½ mi. long. Colly Creek rises here. Probably named from the obsolete adjective, colly, meaning grimy or coal-black.

Big Cove, ne Buncombe County s of Chestnut Cove Ridge.

Big Cove, sw Buncombe County near the headwaters of Webb Branch.

Big Cove, at the head of Big Cove Branch in the Snowbird Mountains, ne Cherokee County.

Big Cove lies between Ramp Cove Branch and Vengeance Creek in the Valley River Mountains, ne Cherokee County.

Big Cove, e Haywood County on Cove Field Branch.

Big Cove, e Haywood County between Bobs Ridge and Roland Ridge. Little Creek flows through this cove.

Big Cove, w Jackson County between Tatham Creek and Savannah Creek.

Big Cove, ne Swain County on Raven Fork, just n of the community of Swayney. Alt. 2,452.

Big Cove ne Transylvania County e of Cat Ridge.

Big Cove Branch rises in ne Cherokee County and flows sw into Dan Holland Creek.

Big Crabtree Creek rises in se Yancey County and flows n on the Mitchell-Yancey County line into North Toe River.

Big Craggy, mountain on the McDowell-Yancey County line near the head of Big Lost Cove Creek.

Big Craggy. *See* Craggy Dome.

Big Creek rises in n Carteret County and flows ne into South River.

Big Creek rises in e Cumberland County and flows ne and se into South River on the Cumberland-Sampson County line.

Big Creek rises in s Haywood County and flows e into West Fork Pigeon River.

Big Creek rises in w Haywood County near lat. 35° 42' 05" N., long. 83° 14' 50" W., and flows ne into Pigeon River.

Big Creek rises in nw Henderson County and flows ne where it joins Fletcher Creek to form North Fork.

Big Creek rises in e Macon County and flows sw into Lake Sequoyah.

Big Creek rises in se Macon County and flows sw into Rabun County, Georgia, where it enters Overflow Creek.

Big Creek rises in n Madison County and flows s into Shelton Laurel Creek.

Big Creek rises in e Montgomery County and flows nw into Little River.

Big Creek rises in ne Surry County and flows se into Stokes County where it enters Dan River.

Big Creek rises in sw Swain County and flows n into Silvermine Creek.

Big Creek rises in n Yancey County and flows ne and se into Cane River.

Big Creek Township, nw Stokes County.

Big Cypress Swamp rises in s Columbus County and flows s to join Monie Swamp in forming Seven Creeks.

Big Dam Branch rises in n Cherokee County in the Snowbird Mountains and flows sw into Hyatt Creek.

Big Deserter Island, a land formation in s Duplin County surrounded by marsh.

Big Dismal, a pocosin at the head of Big Swamp, a stream in w Sampson County.

Big Dog Mountain, in se Macon County between Cullasaja River and Kettle Rock.

Big East Fork, a cove on Dry Branch in e Haywood County.

Big Elk Creek rises in ne Watauga County and flows se into South Fork New River at town of Todd.

Big Elk Mountain, s central Avery County.

Big Fall Creek. *See* Honeycutt Creek.

Big Falls on Stony Creek in central Alamance County near the confluence with Haw River. A post office by this name existed in the vicinity as early as 1882. *See also* Hopedale.

Big Falls, in Snowbird Creek in sw Graham County. In a series of two or three falls, water drops from approx. 25 to 60 feet.

The Big Falls. *See* High Falls.

Big Fat Gap, nw Graham County at the head of Bear Creek.

Big Flats, mountain peak in se Buncombe County w of Patton Gap in Swannanoa Mountains.

Big Flats Branch rises in n Swain County and flows sw into Bone Valley Creek.

Big Flatty Creek rises in s Pasquotank County and flows se into Albemarle Sound. Shown on the Hack map, 1684 as Flatt Creek, on the Moseley map, 1733, and the Collet map, 1770, as Flatty Creek.

Big Fork Knob, peak on Big Fork Ridge, ne Buncombe County.

Big Fork Ridge, ne Buncombe County between Mineral and Carter creeks.

Big Fork Ridge, w Haywood County in Great Smoky Mountains National Park, extending ne from Cataloochee Balsam; a Balsam Mountain summit between Rough Fork and Caldwell Fork. Center near lat. 35° 35′ 40″ N., long. 83° 07′ 30″ W.

Big Fork Ridge, n Swain County, extends ne in a horseshoe shape from between Pilkey Creek and the head of West Fork [Chambers Creek] to Welch Ridge and se between West Fork and North Fork to their junction forming Chambers Creek.

Big Fork Ridge, s Yancey County between Cane River and Cattail Creek.

Big Garland Gap, n Graham County between Sawyer Creek and Stecoah Creek at the sw end of Hogback Mountain.

Biggerstaff Branch rises in se Mitchell County and flows sw into Beaver Creek.

Big Gooseberry Ridge, e Jackson County between Frady Creek and Chastine Creek.

Big Governors Creek rises in e Moore County and flows nw into Deep River on the Moore-Lee County line. Called Millstone Creek in a 1748 grant to Governor Gabriel Johnston. Named for Johnston who owned 7,000 acres n of the creek. Appears as Governors Creek on the Collet map, 1770.

Big Grassy Creek rises in e central Avery County and flows sw into Linville River.

Big Green Mountain, se Jackson County between Little Green Mountain and Panthertown Creek. Alt. 4,100.

Big Grill Ridge, nw Swain County in Great Smoky Mountains National Park extending se from Devils Tater Patch.

Big Harris Creek rises in central Cleveland County and flows se into First Broad River.

Big Haw Mountain, central Avery County.

Big Head Branch rises in ne Swain County and flows se into Straight Fork.

Big Hogback Creek rises in se Jackson County and flows sw into Horsepasture River.

Big Horse Creek rises in sw Grayson County, Virginia, and flows se into n central Ashe County where it enters North Fork New River.

Big Indian Creek rises in sw Macon County and flows n into Nantahala River.

Big Island in Green Swamp, central Brunswick County.

Big Island, off the w shore of s Hatteras Island in the waters of Pamlico Sound, s Dare County.

Big Island, a land formation in e Duplin County surrounded by swamp.

Big Island in Yadkin River, Rowan-Davidson counties, Area: 100 acres. Trading Ford, which see, was located at the e end of Big Island. See also Island Borough.

Big Island, 50-acre sandy island in Yadkin River, ne Yadkin County.

Big Ivy Creek. See North Fork Ivy Creek.

Big Island lies off the sw shore of Roanoke Island, Dare County, in the waters of Croatan Sound.

Big Junction, a mountain on the Graham County, N. C.-Monroe County, Tenn., line.

Big Juniper Creek rises in w Moore County and flows ne into McLendons Creek.

Big Kennedy Creek rises in s Yadkin County and flows s into Iredell County. It enters Flat Rock Creek ne of Houstonville.

Big Kinnakeet Coast Guard Station, se Hatteras Island in Dare County. First est. as lifesaving station in 1878-79. Lifesaving Service and Revenue Cutter Service joined to form United States Coast Guard in 1915. Now decommissioned.

Big Kitchens Knob, se Clay County at the nw end of Big Kitchens Ridge.

Big Kitchens Ridge, se Clay County between Sassafras Branch and Holden Cove.

Big Knob, on Snowbird Creek in sw Graham County.

Big Knob, on Haywood-Madison County line.

Big Knob, nw Henderson County between Queen Creek and Davie Mountain.

Big Knob, on the n end of Big Ridge in s Jackson County.

Big Knob, n Madison County on the ne end of Bearpen Ridge.

Big Knob, e Madison County on the head of Bear Branch.

Big Knob, s Watauga County on the head of Buffalo Creek.

The Big Lake, formed by a large rock dam on Long Creek, w Surry County. Covers approx. 30 acres; max. depth 35 ft. Privately owned by the Reynolds family of Winston-Salem.

Big Laurel, peak in se Clay County on the nw end of Little Kitchens Ridge.

Big Laurel, community in n Madison County on Spillcorn Creek. Alt. 2,034.

Big Laurel, community in se Swain County on the head of Yalaka Creek.

Big Laurel Branch rises in s Macon County and flows nw into Kilby Creek.

Big Laurel Creek, rises in nw Ashe County and flows se into North Fork New River.

Big Laurel Creek rises in e Madison County and flows w into French Broad River.

Big Laurel Creek rises in w Macon County and flows nw into Whiteoak Creek.

Big Laurel Gap, on the McDowell-Yancey County line near the head of Neals Creek. Alt. approx. 3,700.

Big Laurel Mountain, on the McDowell-Yancey County line.

Big Laurel Township, former township in n central Madison County, now township number 10.

Big Lick, community in sw Stanly County. Inc. 1879; charter repealed 1919. Named because salt in the ground attracted deer and buffalo. See also, Oakboro.

Big Lick Creek rises in e central Durham County and flows ne into Neuse River.

Big Lick Township, s central Stanly County.

Big Lost Cove Creek rises in s Yancey County and flows n into South Toe River.

Big Marsh Swamp rises in Hoke County and flows se into Robeson County where it joins Gallberry Swamp to form Big Swamp.

Big Meadow Creek rises in w Stanly County and flows w into se Cabarrus County where it enters Rocky River.

Big Meadows, loamy section between Balls Mountain and Blackwood Mountain, on the head of Old Field Creek in s Orange County.

Big Milksick Knob, on the Clay-Macon line.

Big Mooney Branch rises in s Macon County and flows sw into Kilby Creek.

Big Mountain. See Asbury Mountain.

Big Mountain Branch rises in w Transylvania County and flows sw into North Fork French Broad River.

Big Mountain Creek rises in s Montgomery

County and flows sw into Richmond County where it enters Pee Dee River.

Big Mountain Gap, central Transylvania County in Big Mountain Ridge, Pisgah National Forest. Alt. approx. 3,060.

Big Mountain Ridge, central Transylvania County, extends about two mi. in a north-south direction. Bounded on the n by Three Forks Mountain. The Ridge is a part of Pisgah National Forest.

Bigoak. See Bensalem.

Big Oak Gap, w Macon County on Fire Gap Ridge.

Big Peachtree Bald, in the Valley River Mountains on the Cherokee-Clay County line.

Big Peachtree Creek rises in e Franklin County and flows se into Nash County where it is joined by Little Peachtree Creek to form Stony Creek.

Big Pine, community on Big Pine Creek in s Madison County. Alt. 2,500. Post office, Big Pine Creek, est. prior to 1882.

Big Pine Creek rises in ne Alleghany County and flows w into Brush Creek.

Big Pine Creek is formed in s Madison County by the junction of North Fork and South Fork and flows ne into French Broad River opposite Barnard.

Big Pine Creek Township, former township in sw Madison County. Now township number 12.

Big Pine Fishing Gut, a water filled defile adjoining the Neuse River in e Durham County.

Big Pine Mountain, s Yancey County between Beech Nursery Creek and Big Poplar Creek.

Big Pine Ridge, s Clay County between Rocking Chair Branch and Pounding Creek.

Big Pine Ridge, n Transylvania County extends se between Jumping Branch and Pounding Mill Branch.

Big Piney Branch rises in ne Buncombe County and flows se into Flat Creek.

Big Piney Ridge, ne Buncombe County between Big Piney Branch and Little Piney Branch.

Big Pisgah, See Mount Pisgah.

Big Pisgah Mountain, w Transylvania County between Panthertail Mountain and West Fork French Broad River.

Big Pocosin, a sand and swamp pocosin in ne Craven County and s Beaufort County.

Big Pocosin, sand and swamp area covering approx. 150 sq. mi. in sw Beaufort and ne Craven counties. Includes Reedy and

Blount pocosins in its n and nw edges. Drained by many tributaries into Neuse River at the sw end and into Pamlico River at the ne end.

Big Pond Branch rises in central Columbus County and flows sw into Beaverdam Swamp.

Big Poplar Creek rises in s Yancey County and flows ne into Sugar Camp Creek.

Big Porpoise Bay, in Pamlico Sound on the e side of Goose Creek Island, ne Pamlico County.

Big Raft Swamp rises in s Hoke County and flows se into Robeson County where it enters Lumber River.

Big Rattlesnake Branch rises in ne Buncombe County and flows s into Swannanoa River.

Big Ridge, w Haywood County, Great Smoky Mountains National Park. A short spur of Big Fork Ridge extending se near lat. 35° 34′ 50″ N., long, 83° 08′ W.

Big Ridge extends se between Horse Cove and Middle Fork in nw Henderson County.

Big Ridge, central Jackson County extends se between West Fork Tuckasegee River and Tuckasegee River.

Big Ridge, central Mitchell County between Rebel Creek and Snow Creek.

Big Ridge, n Mitchell County between Pigeonroost Creek and Bean Creek.

Big Ridge, se Yancey County parallel to Roaring Fork.

Big Ridge, w Watauga County, extends se from n of Beech Creek.

Big Ridge, community in s Jackson County near Lake Thorpe.

Big Ridge. See Pups Ridge.

Big Ridge Mine, on the head of Deep Gap Creek, s Haywood County. An old source of feldspar and mica operated most recently during World War II.

Big Roan Ridge, w Avery County.

Big Rock Creek rises in n Mitchell County and flows sw into Toe River.

Big Rocky Branch rises in n Madison County and flows se into White Rock Branch.

Big Rocky Creek. See Patterson Creek.

Big Rough Knob, e central Avery County.

Big Sandy Creek rises in ne Wilkes County and flows sw into East Prong Roaring River.

Big Savanna, n Tyrrell Countty, is a slough extending ne in an arc north of Mills Ridge from near the community of Levels to Alligator Creek.

Big Savannah or **Burgaw Savannah,** central and nw Pender County. Originally covered over 2,000 acres, lying between 50 and 60 ft. above sea level. A flat, treeless area, surrounded by pine woods. Water table generally at or close to the surface. In recent years much of the Big Savannah has been drained and taken into cultivation. By 1960 only between 400 and 500 acres remained. Noted for the large variety of wild flowers which grow among the grasses.

Big Scaly, peak in se Clay County at the ne end of Scaly Ridge. Alt, 5,070.

Big Shoal Branch rises in sw Macon County and flows e into Big Indian Creek.

Big Shoeheel Creek rises in n Scotland County and flows s through w Robeson County into South Carolina where it enters Little Pee Dee River. See also Maxton for an explanation of the name Shoeheel.

Big Snowball Mountain. See Snowball Mountain.

Big Spring Branch rises in w Haywood County and flows se into Jonathans Creek.

Big Spring Branch rises in Forest City in s central Rutherford County and flows ne into Second Broad River.

Big Spring Branch rises in ne Rutherford County and flows se into Cleveland County where it enters Hinton Creek.

Big Spring Creek rises in e Mitchell County and flows s into Hawk Creek.

Bigspring Gap, s Macon County at the head of Pinnacle Branch.

Big Spring Gap, e Mitchell County at the head of Big Spring Creek.

Big Spruce Ridge, w Haywood County, Great Smoky Mountains National Park, extends se from Cataloochee Balsam; a Balsam Mountain peak between Straight Creek and Caldwell Fork, center near lat. 35° 34′ 30″ N., long. 83° 08′ 40″ W.

Big Stamp, a peak in the Valley River Mountains on the Cherokee-Clay County line.

Big Stamp Knob, on the Cherokee-Clay County line.

Big Stonehouse Creek. See Stonehouse Creek.

Big Swag, peak of Round Mountain Ridge in nw Swain County in Great Smoky Mountains National Park. Alt. 3,685.

Big Swag Branch rises in central Jackson County and flows n into Bear Creek.

Big Swag Gap. See Beech Gap.

Big Swamp rises in nw Brunswick County and flows sw into Juniper Creek for a distance of several miles; it forms a part of the boundary between Brunswick and Columbus counties.

Big Swamp is formed in e Robeson County by the junction of Big Marsh Swamp and Gallberry Swamp. It flows sw into Lumber River. Its e high water line forms the boundary between Bladen and Robeson counties and a part of the Cumberland-Robeson County line.

Big Swamp rises in w Sampson County and flows s into South River.

Big Tom, peak in Mount Mitchell State Park, s Yancey County. One of two peaks known as Black Brothers until 1947 when renamed in honor of Thomas ("Big Tom") David Wilson (1825-1909), fabulous bear hunter and guide who found the body of Dr. Elisha Mitchell, July 7, 1857, after he lost his life on Mount Mitchell. Known earlier as Hairy Bear Mountain.

Big Tomahawk Creek rises in s Sampson County and flows s to join Little Tomahawk Creek to form Tomahawk Creek.

Big Troublesome Creek. See Troublesome Creek.

Big Warrior Mountain, s Polk County, w of town of Tryon. Named for Big Wayah ("wolf") chief of the Cherokee Indians. Alt. 2,466.

Big White Oak Creek rises in w Wake County and flows s and sw into Chatham County where it enters New Hope River.

Big White Pocosin, sandy pocosin in se Cumberland County.

Big Witch Creek rises in n Jackson County and flows sw into Wrights Creek.

Big Witch Gap, on the Jackson-Swain County line near the head of Moody Branch.

Big Yellow. See Big Bald.

Big Yellow Bald Mountain, w Avery County.

Big Yellow Mountain at the Avery-Mitchell County, N. C., and Carter County, Tenn., junction. Alt. approx. 5,600. Known also as Bright Yellow Mountain and Averys Bald. See also Rose Ridge.

Bilboa, community in s Durham County nead the head of Northeast Creek. Named for the Bilbo family which lived in the vicinity in the early nineteenth century before moving to Mississippi. Alt. 401.

Bilesville. See New London.

Bill Allen Branch rises in e central Yancey County and flows n into Little Crabtree Creek. Named for Bill Allen, an early settler who raised a large family here.

Bill Branch rises in central Catawba County and flows sw into Clark Creek.

Bill Cole Mountain, n Buncombe County between Bradley and Gentry gaps. Alt. 3,284. See also Morgan Ridge.

Bill Cove, e Haywood County between Poplar Cove and James Branch.

Bill Davenport Branch rises in se Mitchell County and flows s into North Toe River.

Billet's Bridge. See Shiloh.

Bill Holt Mountains, a short range in the Cane Creek Mountains, s Alamance County.

Billie Top, a peak on Holland Mountain on the Buncombe-Haywood County line between Newfound Gap and Grassy Top.

Bill Moore Creek rises in s Buncombe County near Stradley Mountain and flows n into Hominy Creek. Enka Lake is on Bill Moore Creek.

Bills Branch rises in w Haywood County and flows sw into Evans Creek.

Bills Creek rises in nw Rutherford County and flows e into Cove Creek. Named for the Rev. William (Billy) Logan, whose brick house still stands nearby.

Bills Creek, community in w Rutherford County on the stream of the same name.

Bills Knob, n Haywood County on the eastern end of Cedar Cliff.

Bills Mountain, e Henderson County near Henderson Creek.

Bills Mountain, nw Rutherford County between Bills Creek and Broad River. Alt. approx. 2,450. Named for the Rev. William (Billy) Logan.

Bill Wray Gap, s central Yancey County at the sw end of Callaway Mountain.

Billy Branch rises in n Transylvania County and flows sw into South Fork Mills River.

Billy Cabin Ridge, in se Macon County between Big Creek and Cullasaja River.

Billy Cove, valley in se Buncombe County nw of Billy Cove and Billy Cove Knob.

Billy Cove, s Swain County between De Hart Creek and Marr Branch.

Billy Cove Gap, s Buncombe County between Billy Cove Knob and Hickory Top.

Billy Cove Knob, s Buncombe County, sw of Billy Cove Gap.

Billy's Branch rises in central Carteret County and flows w into Black Creek.

Billys Creek rises in n Franklin County and flows ne into Tar River.

Billy's Creek flows between tidal marsh islands in the mouth of White Oak River in e Onslow County. Named for Billy (William) Russell.

Billy Top, n Haywood County on the head of Laurel Branch.

Biltmore, former town in central Buncombe County. Inc. 1893 but since 1929 within the corporate limits of Asheville. Named for the Biltmore Estate, *which see.* Alt. 1,994. Known as Best as early as 1882 when a post office existed here, named for William J. Best, one of the owners of the Western North Carolina Railroad. *See also* South Biltmore.

Biltmore Estate, central Buncombe County on the s outskirts of Asheville. Built for George W. Vanderbilt (1863-1914); the name combines the last part of his family name with *more*, an old English word for rolling, upland country. The house, in the style of a French chateau, was formally opened in 1895 after 5 years of construction. Handsomely furnished, surrounded by lovely formal gardens and with adjoining forests, farms and dairy lands, the estate is now open to the public.

Biltmore Forest, a part of the Biltmore estate in s Buncombe County, approx. 11,000 acres along the Swannanoa and French Broad rivers. Alt. approx. 2,000-2,300. Est. 1890 on land largely cut over; planting continued until about 1911. Gifford Pinchot, the first trained American forester, planned and directed the work. In 1898 Carl A. Schenck founded the Biltmore School of Forestry here, the first such school in the New World. *See also* Carl Alwin Schenck Forest.

Biltmore Forest, town in central Buncombe County, sw of Asheville. Inc, 1923 and named for the experimental forest est. on the Vanderbilt estate. Alt. 2,050.

Bina, community in n central Ashe County. First known as Berlin but name changed during World War I.

Bingham Branch rises in e Alamance County in the n outskirts of Mebane and flows nw into Mill Creek.

Bingham Heights, community in central Buncombe County ne of Emma. Site of Bingham School, 1889-1923, and residence of Col. Robert Bingham.

Bingham Township, sw Orange County.

Birch, community in sw Cherokee County on Beech Creek.

Birch Branch. *See* Birch Creek.

Birch Cove, the valley through which Chairmaker Branch flows in central Clay County.

Birch Creek rises in central Pender County and flows sw into Rileys Creek. Now often referred to locally as Birch Branch.

Birchfield Branch rises in nw Swain County and flows se into Fontana Lake.

Birchfield Creek rises in w Avery County and flows se into North Toe River.

Birch Fork Creek rises in n Rockingham County and flows e into Wolf Island Creek.

Birch Knob, central Clay County at the se end of Birch Cove.

Birch Spring Gap, n Cherokee County in the Snowbird Mountains.

Birch Spring Gap, nw Swain County in Great Smoky Mountains National Park on Twentymile Ridge.

Bird Branch rises in n Macon County and flows n into Little Tennessee River.

Bird Creek rises in se Buncombe County and flows ne into McDowell County where it enters Crooked Creek.

Bird Creek rises in s Haywood County and flows e into West Fork Pigeon River.

Bird Creek rises in w Mitchell County and flows se into Pigeonroost Creek.

Bird Island on the Atlantic Ocean, sw Brunswick County. The w tip of the island is in South Carolina.

Bird Islands, approximately a dozen small islands on Clam Shoal, in the waters of Pamlico Sound, s Dare County, off the s part of Hatteras Island.

Bird Rock Falls, w Transylvania County on North Fork French Broad River just below where it is formed by junction of Indian Creek and Shoal Creek. Alt. approx. 2,720.

Birdstand Mountain, s Haywood County between Little East Fork Pigeon River and West Fork Pigeon River.

Birdtown, community in e Swain County on Oconaluftee River. Probably named for the Bird Clan, *In-a-cheese-quah,* one of the original seven clans of the Cherokee. Bird Town is one of the five townships of the Qualla Reservation, *which see.* Alt. 1,900. *See also* Oconaluftee River.

Biscoe, town in e Montgomery County. Alt. 609. Inc. 1901. Known as Filo until 1895 when it was renamed for Major Henry Biscoe, lumber commission merchant. Produces textiles.

Biscoe Township, e Montgomery County.

Bishop, community in ne Brunswick County.

Bishop Creek rises in se Pender County and flows s into Topsail Sound.

Bishops Cross, a community in e Beaufort County. Alt. 12. Perhaps named for the interesting figure, somewhat like a Bishop's staff, formed by former railroad intersection and two highways which crossed it.

Bissett Mill Pond, s Nash County on Beaverdam Creek. About ¾ mi. long.

Bixby, community in e Davie County. The first train on that portion of the track ran in 1891. From 1881 to at least 1889 the community was known as Chaplin's Stand. Named by a railroad conductor after he observed a large stock of Bixby Shoe Polish in the community store. Alt. 835.

Bizzell Millpond, e Wayne County on Walnut Creek. This was the site of the Dobbs County courthouse, jail, and stocks from sometime after 1758 until 1779. After the formation of Wayne County in 1779 the county court met variously on Little River. The old courthouse, jail, and stocks were sold to Col. William McKinne. The McKinne heirs sold the property to Elijah Bizzell of Duplin County who moved here and erected a mill in 1839.

Black Ankle, community in n Cleveland County.

Black Ankle, derisive name for an area in s central Randolph County. Named because bootleggers operating there during Prohibition would start fires over a large area when they were operating a still so that officers of the law cound not find the still. They were said to have "black ankles" from walking through the ashes of old fires to start new ones.

Black Ankle, a strip of deep fertile soil across the s portion of Robeson County. Named for the fact that a plowman's ankles would be black after plowing in this soil.

Black Bald, s Macon County at the head of Dry Branch. Alt. approx. 5,100.

Black Balsam Knob, s Haywood County between the headwaters of Yellowstone Prong and Flat Laurel Creek.

Black Branch rises in e Clay County and flows sw into Buck Creek.

Black Branch rises in sw Duplin County and flows ne into Rockfish Creek.

Black Branch rises in e Hoke County and flows s into Beaver Creek.

Black Brothers, former name of two peaks approx. 1 mi. n of Mount Mitchell, s Yancey County. Renamed Mount Craig and Big Tom, which see, in 1947.

Blackburn, community in sw Catawba County. Alt. 1,000.

Blackburn Knob, s Watauga County between Middle Fork [of South Fork New River] and Matney Branch.

Black Camp Gap on the Haywood-Swain County line near the head of Bunches Creek in Great Smoky Mountains National Park on Balsam Mountain. A loghouse camp was built here for the use of cattle rangers and hunters. A forest fire partially burned the camp, burning off the bark and charring the logs of the cabins. Later campers lodging here got themselves black from contact with the burnt logs, hence the name Black Camp. Alt. 4,492.

Black Creek rises in e Carteret County and flows s into Newport River. Sometimes called Black River.

Black Creek rises in sw Columbus County and flows sw into Lake Tabor, which see.

Black Creek rises in e Hoke County and flows s into Puppy Creek.

Black Creek rises in e Rutherford County, sw of Hollis, and flows se into Hinton Creek.

Black Creek rises in s Wake County and flows se into Johnston County where it enters Neuse River.

Black Creek rises in w central Wake County and flows ne into Crabtree Creek.

Black Creek rises in sw Wilson County and flows e into Contentnea Creek.

Black Creek, town in s Wilson County named for nearby stream. Alt. 120. Est. 1840 as a station and post office on the Wilmington and Weldon Railroad. Inc. 1870.

Black Creek. See Back Creek.

Black Creek Swamp appears on the Collet map, 1770, as a fork of East Mingo Branch, which see, lying completely in modern Harnett County between Black River and East Mingo Branch. This particular fork is no longer named on maps.

Black Creek Township, s Wilson County.

Black Dome. See Mount Mitchell.

Black Fields, an area of black, poorly drained soil in e Washington County, covering an area of approx. six square miles, w of the community of Scuppernong. Mentioned as early as 1868 in local records.

Black Fox Ridge, s central Burke County.

Black Gap, on the Clay-Macon County line. Alt. 3,841.

Black Gut Creek rises in nw Northampton County and flows s into Roanoke River.

Blackjack, community in e Pitt County.

Black Jack Branch rises in e Union County

and flows e into w Anson County and into Brown Creek.

Blackjack Mountain, w Henderson County at the head of Little Mud Creek.

Black Jack Mountain, w Randolph County just w of Caraway Mountain in a close group with Slick Rock, Vineyard, and Prickly Pear mountains.

Black Jack Township, w central Richmond County.

Black Knob, se Buncombe County sw of High Windy peak. Alt. 4,240.

Black Lake, a natural lake in e central Bladen County with a maximum depth of 71 feet and covering 1,418 acres. Fishing, boating, and swimming. Owned by State of North Carolina.

Blackman Crossroads, community in s Johnston County.

Blackman's Landing. See Coniott Landing.

Black Mine, former gold mine in w Union County near the town of Indian Trail.

Black Mingle Pocosin, n Gates County.

Black Mingo. See East Mingo Branch.

Black Mountain, n central Alleghany County. Formerly known as Carson Mountain.

Black Mountain, a peak on the se end of Laurel Mountain in nw Henderson County. Alt. 3,952.

Black Mountain, n Jackson County extends ne from Tuckasegee River between Parker Knob and Fern Mountain.

Black Mountain, w Jackson County on the head of Cagle Branch.

Black Mountain on the Jackson-Haywood County line. An attempt was made to change this name to Browning Peak in honor of R. Getty Browning, State Highway location engineer, but it has not been accepted locally. Alt. 6,275.

Black Mountain, at the head of Black Mountain Branch in s Macon County. Alt. 3,735.

Black Mountain, sw Randolph County s of Mill Creek.

Black Mountain, ne Rutherford County at the head of Brier Creek. Alt. 2,614.

Black Mountain, n Transylvania County between Clawhammer Cove and Bear Pen Branch.

Black Mountain. See Mount Chapman.

Black Mountain. See Mount Hardy.

Black Mountain, town in se Buncombe County. Inc. 1893. Known earlier as Grey Eagle. Named for the Black Mountain range by S. Dougherty in whose home the first post office was est. Alt. 2,395.

Summer resort. Produces lumber. Black Mountain College operated nearby, 1933-56.

Black Mountain Branch rises in s Macon County and flows ne into South Fork [Skeenah Creek].

Black Mountain Gap, about .2 mi. nw of Bald Knob, between the Black Mountain on the n and the Blue Ridge on the s on the Buncombe-Yancey County line. Lat. 35° 43' N., long. 82° 16' 45" W. Known originally as Beech Gap, later as Swannanoa Gap, and finally since 1949 by its present name. Alt. approx. 5,200.

Black Mountain Gap. See Mount Hardy Gap.

Black Mountain Natural Area in Pisgah National Forest, Yancey County. Covers 1,405 acres, the watershed of Middle Creek, a tributary of the South Toe River on the e slope of Mt. Mitchell. This area was set aside from all commercial use on October 22, 1932, and reserved for scientific study.

Black Mountains, range extending from the Buncombe-Yancey County line ne to the head of Bowlens Creek in s central Yancey County. Among the peaks are Mount Mitchell, Clingmans Dome, Potato Knob, and Mount Craig. Named for the dark green foliage of Fraser's fir which covers the top and sides. Known by the Cherokee Indians as *See-noh-ya,* "dark," or "night." See also Appalachian Mountains.

Black Mountain Township, e central Buncombe County.

Blacknel, community in n Lee County. Named for Tom Blacknal, a free Negro. This is primarily a Negro community centered around an old church.

Black Knob, e Transylvania County, about 1½ mi. w of Cascade Lake. Alt. approx. 3,220.

Black Pine Ridge, n Madison County between Dry Creek and Mill Creek.

Black Ridge, s Yancey County between Lower Creek and Camp Creek.

Black River rises in n Harnett County and flows se across the county into e Cumberland County where, at the Cumberland-Sampson County line, it joins East Mingo Branch to form South River.

Black River, formed in s Sampson County by the junction of Six Runs Creek and Coharie River. It flows s on the Bladen-Sampson County line, the Bladen-Pender County line, and into w Pender County where it turns se to flow into Cape Fear River at the New Hanover County line. Approx. 30 mi. long. Appears as Black or Swampy River on the Moseley map, 1733.

Black River. See Ivanhoe.

Black River Township, ne Cumberland County.

Black River Township, ne Harnett County.

Black Rock, a peak in se Jackson County between Rye Mountain and Little Green Mountain. Alt. 4,500.

Black Rock, community and fishery in e Bertie County. Site of Black Rock plantation, home of Thomas Pollock, Jr.

Blackrock Branch rises in se Macon County and flows sw into Big Creek.

Blackrock Creek rises in n Jackson County and flows nw into Soco Creek.

Blackrock Gap, s Macon County between Dryman Fork and Ball Creek.

Blackrock Knob, e Swain County in Yalaka Mountains near the head of Piney Wood Creek. Alt. 4,364.

Blackrock Mountain, n Jackson County on the n end of Blackrock Ridge on Plott Balsams. Alt. 6,100.

Blackrock Mountain, on the Jackson-Macon County line between Hamburg Gap and Buck Gap.

Blackrock Mountain, on the Jackson-Macon County line, between Granite City formations and Wildcat Gap.

Blackrock Ridge in n Jackson County extends n from Scott Creek to Soco Creek.

Blacksnake Branch rises in n Transylvania County and flows se into Turkey Creek.

Blackstock Branch rises in n Buncombe County and flows nw into Madison County where it enters Ivy River.

Blackstock Knob, on the Buncombe-Yancey County line between Balsam and Rainbow gaps. Alt. 6,325. Probably named for a surveyor, Nehemiah Blackstock, who worked in the vicinity in 1845.

Blackstone, community in ne Caldwell County. Named by Col. George N. Folk, who conducted a law school here after the Civil War, for Sir William Blackstone (1723-80), English jurist.

Black Swamp rises in w Bladen County and flows w into Big Swamp in Robeson County. Bryants Pond is on Black Swamp.

Black Swamp, se tip of Camden County.

Black Swamp rises in n Nash County and flows se into Beaverdam Swamp.

Black Swamp, w Pitt County, drains se into Little Contentnea Creek.

Black Swamp Creek rises in se Jones County and flows s into White Oak River.

Black Walnut Point, e Bertie County on Chowan River between Avoca and Scotch Hall plantations.

Blackwalnut Swamp rises in e Bertie County and flows e into Chowan River.

Blackwater River rises in Virginia and flows sw into North Carolina where it joins the Nottoway River a short distance s of the Virginia line on the Hertford-Gates County line to form the Chowan River. The name appears on the Comberford map, 1657.

Blackwater Run rises in s Rowan County and flows s into n Cabarrus County where it enters Dutch Buffalo Creek. The last Indians in Cabarrus County lived along this stream.

Blackwell, community in nw Caswell County. A post office was operated here during the approx. period 1830-1909. A tobacco factory also formerly existed here.

Blackwell Gap, central Cherokee County near the middle of Bates Mountain.

Blackwell Mountain, a peak on Bates Mountain, central Cherokee County.

Blackwell Ridge, sw Macon County between Long Branch and Curtis Creek.

Blackwood, community in s Orange County. Alt. 487.

Blackwood Creek rises in central Gaston County near the sw limits of West Gastonia and flows s into Crowders Creek.

Blackwood Mountain, s Orange County between Mountain Creek and Old Field Creek.

Bladenboro, town in sw Bladen County. Inc. 1903. Alt. 111. Named for the county. Produces textiles. See also West Bladenboro.

Bladenboro Township, sw Bladen County.

Bladen County was formed in 1734 from New Hanover County. Located in the se section of the state, it is bounded by Sampson, Pender, Columbus, Robeson, and Cumberland counties. It was named for Martin Bladen (1680-1746), English soldier and politician who was Commissioner of Trade and Plantations, 1717-46. Area: 891 sq. mi. County seat: Elizabethtown with an elevation of 121 ft. Townships are Abbotts, Bethel, Bladenboro, Brown Marsh, Carvers Creek, Central, Colly, Cypress Creek, Elizabethtown, French's Creek, Hollow, Lake Creek, Turnbull, White Oak, and Whites Creek. Produces tobacco, corn, soybeans, oats, peanuts, hogs, dairy livestock, textiles, apparel, boats, and sand for concrete.

Bladen Lakes State Forest in Bladen County covers 35,875 acres of which 1,000 acres around Jones, Singletary and Salters lakes are reserved for park purposes and in which no cutting is done. Named for the lakes included in the area. Objectives: to build up the growing stock of timber on over-cut and previously badly burned areas, to utilize all the resources of the area including game, forestry demonstration, and recreation. Acquired by the State of North Carolina from the federal government in 1939.

Blades, community in e Craven County on Clubfoot Creek.

Blaine, community in nw Montgomery County. Known as Post Oak prior to 1884 when it was renamed in honor of James G. Blaine (1830-93), Republican nominee for president.

Blaine Branch rises in central Macon County and flows ne into Cartoogechaye Creek.

Blaine Knob, s Macon County between Jones Creek and North Fork [Skeenah Creek].

Blair Channel, in Carteret and Hyde counties, a navigable lane in Ocracoke Inlet running n and s between Wallace Channel and Teaches Hole. Appears on the Price survey of Ocracoke Inlet, 1795, as Ship Channel.

Blair Creek rises in s Clay County and flows ne into Hiwassee River.

Blair Fork rises in central Caldwell County and flows s and sw into Lower Creek.

Blakeley County. On November 28, 1817, the General Assembly attempted to create a county by this name from a portion of Rowan County. It was intended to honor the War of 1812 naval hero, Johnston Blakely (1781-1814).

Blakeleyville, town authorized to be est. and laid off on the lands of Andrew Polk on Little Creek in nw Anson County in 1817. Probably named for Captain Johnston

Blakely, North Carolina naval hero who lost his life at sea in the War of 1812. There is no evidence that the town was est. nor is it known whether there was any connection with the nearby community of Blakely in Montgomery County.

Blakely, former community in w Montgomery on Pee Dee River at the mouth of Island Creek. A post office as late as 1822, but abandoned shortly afterwards as a result of the depression of 1819. See also Blakeleyville.

Blakely, former town in nw Northampton County on the e side of Roanoke River. Inc. 1832-33. To be laid off on 200 acres of land owned by John D. Amis. Named for Johnston Blakely (1781-1814), hero of the War of 1812. Was terminal point in 1833 of the Petersburg Railroad, the first railroad in North Carolina. Town declined as Weldon, just across the river in Halifax County, flourished.

Blakely's Depot. See Garysburg.

Blake Mountain, s Buncombe County n of Skyland.

Blake Mountain, on the Henderson-Polk County line.

Blanch, community in n Caswell County on Dan River. Named for Miss Blanche Moore, niece of D. G. Watkins, who owned the land on which the community developed beginning about 1875. Alt. 750.

Bland Branch rises in s Duplin County and flows se into Allan Creek.

Bland Crossroads, community in w Lenoir County.

Blankenship Creek rises in s Yancey County and flows nw into Price Creek.

Blanket Bottom Creek. See Blanket Creek.

Blanket Creek rises in sw Forsyth County and flows sw into Yadkin River. Appears as Linviles Creek on the Collet map, 1770; called Blanket Bottom Creek in Moravian records of 1778; and appears as Clements Creek on the MacRae map, 1833.

Blanton Branch rises in n Jackson County and flows n into Ochre Creek.

Blantyre, community in e Transylvania County near the mouth of Gash Creek. Named by C. H. Boswell, railway construction engineer, for his birthplace near Glasgow, Scotland.

Blazed Creek rises in ne Macon County and flows sw into Beasley Creek.

Blazed Gap, on the Macon-Swain County line.

Bledsoe Creek rises near Fender Mountain

in w Alleghany County and flows se into
Little River.
Blennerhassett Island, s Madison County in
the French Broad River opposite Mar-
shall. This sandy island, approx. ¼ mi.
long, was probably named for the island
in the Ohio River below Parkersburg, W.
Va., where Harman Blennerhassett and
Aaron Burr plotted in 1805-06 to seize an
empire in the West.
Blevin Branch rises in n Buncombe County
and flows se and w into Panther Branch.
Blevine Knob, w Yancey County between
Edney Branch and Cane River.
Blevins Branch rises in n Mitchell County
and flows w into Big Rock Creek.
Blevins Creek rises in central Avery County
and flows nw into Cranberry Creek.
Blevins Creek, community in central Avery
County.
Blevins Crossroads, community in ne Alle-
ghany County.
Blevins Ridge, n central Avery County.
Blewett Falls Lake, on the Pee Dee River in
Anson and Richmond counties. Rocking-
ham Power Co. began development of
falls for hydroelectric power, 1907-08;
Carolina Power and Light Co. took over,
1926. A dam 1,470 ft. long now impounds
a lake 9.4 mi. long covering 2,500 acres.
Named for William Bluit or Blewett
(1719-1810), native of England, who
owned land here in 1758. Falls, now
under the lake, were 8 or 9 feet over a
distance of about 1,000 ft.
Blewing Creek. See Blue Creek.
Bloat Springs Landing on Cape Fear River
in central Bladen County.
Blockade Branch rises in w Macon County
and flows ne into Choga Creek.
Blockade Shoal lies off the nw shore of Roanoke Island, e Dare County, in the waters
of Croatan Sound.
Blockers, Blockersville. See Stedman.
Block House Creek rises in South Carolina
and flows ne into Polk County where it
enters Pacolet River.
Blockhouse Mountain, nw Swain County in
Great Smoky Mountains National Park on
Jenkins Trail Ridge near lat. 35° 33' N.,
long. 83° 42' 35" W. Alt. 5,425.
Blockhouse Ridge, nw Swain County in
Great Smoky Mountains National Park, a
spur of Jenkins Trail Ridge extending se
from Blockhouse Mountain near lat. 35°
32' 40" N., long. 83° 41' 15" W.
Blood Camp Ridge, central Avery County.

Blood Creek rises in sw Wilkes County and
flows n into W. Kerr Scott Reservoir.
Bloodrun Creek rises in w Chatham County
and flows sw into Brush Creek. Local tradition says that a "hot skirmish" occurred
between a small band of Whigs and
Tories during the Revolutionary War.
Each side, not wishing to reveal its losses,
buried its dead secretly. One of the sites
selected as a burying ground was near this
small stream, and it was given its present
name to commemorate the shedding of
blood in battle.
Bloody Bluff, s Sampson County overlooking Black River.
Bloody Fork rises in n Yancey County and
flows nw into Cane River.
Bloody Rock, near Cullasaja, e Macon
County. A blood-colored liquid oozing
from the granite rock is said by legend to
mark the site where a young man of the
community was murdered by a jealous
rival for the affections of a local lass.
Bloomery Swamp is formed by the junction
of Millstone and Juniper creeks in nw
Wilson County. It flows se into Con-
tentnea Creek. Known prior to 1782 as
Great Swamp.
Bloomingdale, community in s Robeson
County.
Bloomington, community in w Stanly County. Probably named for an early operator
of a cotton gin.
Bloomington. See Archdale.
Blossie Creek, waterway off Roanoke Bay,
separating Off Island from Bodie Island,
e Dare County.
Blossom Swamp rises in s Pender County
and flows ne into Trumpeters Swamp.
Probably named for Samuel Blossom, a
Portuguese emigrant who operated a ferry
across the Northeast Cape Fear River in
the late nineteenth and early twentieth
century.
Blossomtown, community in central Macon
County on a tributary of Cartoogechaye
Creek.
Blount Pocosin, the n section of Big Pocosin
in sw Beaufort County.
Blounts Creek rises in Big Pocosin, s Beau-
fort County and flows n approx. 10 mi.
into Pamlico River. Appears as Slade
Creek on the Collet map, 1770.
Blounts Creek rises in central Cumberland
County and flows se into Little Cross
Creek.
Blounts Creek, community in s Beaufort

County approx. 2 mi. from the source of the stream for which it is named. A post office est, here about 1894.

Blounts Ford. See Grifton.

Blountsville, former town in nw Martin County on the Roanoke River. Inc. 1785 on the lands of Whitmel Hill (1743-97) near Hamilton, but probably never developed. A post office, Clark's Store, existed here as early as 1822 and as late as 1831.

Blowing Rock, town in s Watauga and n Caldwell counties near the head of Yadkin River. First settled in 1870; inc. 1889. Named for a peculiar rock formation rising above the Johns River valley which creates a current of air that returns to the sender light articles thrown over the void. Known as Ohlanto by the Indians and the subject of many legends. In 1927 the communities of Green Park (which see) and Mayview Park were annexed. Fort Rollins, used in the Civil War, was located here, Alt. 3,586.

Blowing Rock Township, s Watauga County.

Blowing Spring, w Swain County near Nantahala Gorge; its waters fall into Nantahala River.

The Blue Banks, high marl bank along the Contentnea Creek below Edwards Bridge, Greene-Pitt County. The name comes from the distinctive color of the formation. The banks are on both sides of the creek but are more prominent on the Pitt County side.

Blue Branch rises in n Buncombe County and flows w into French Broad River.

Bluebutton, community in s central Camden County, named for the plantation of Stephen Richardson located here in 1722, in turn named for the small periwinkle (Vinca minor) commonly called bluebutton and native to this area. This community was the gathering point, in 1840, for families in the area beginning on their w migration. From 1908-1929 the post office name of Bluebutton was Bartlett, named for a local family.

Blue Creek rises in e Caldwell County and flows ne into Kings Creek.

Blue Creek rises in n Granville County and flows ne into Little Grassy Creek. For a possible source of the name see Blue Wing Creek.

Blue Creek rises in w Onslow County and flows se into New River. Mentioned in local records as early as 1744.

Bluefield, community in s central Bladen County. Named for John Blue.

Blue Gap, sw Buncombe County, e of Thompson Knob.

Blue Mud Creek is formed in n Warren County by the junction of Terrapin and Malones creeks; it flows n into Smith Creek.

Blue Ridge, community in e Henderson County. Alt. 2,270.

Blue Ridge or **Blue Ridge Mountains** is the name applied to the e portion of the Appalachian Mountains, which see, extending from a few miles north of Harpers Ferry, W. Va., to n Georgia. The average elevation is from 2,000 to 4,000 ft. The highest peaks of the Blue Ridge are in the Black Mountains of North Carolina, which see. The name comes from the hazy blue appearance of the mountains. The Cherokee Indians knew this section of the mountains as Sa-koh-na-gas, "blue."

Blue Ridge Cove Creek rises in s Yancey County and flows n into South Toe River.

Blue Ridge Gap, s Transylvania County in Blue Ridge Mountains near the head of Toxaway Creek.

Blue Ridge Island, a sandy elevation in the middle of Angola Bay in s Duplin and n Pender counties.

Blue Ridge Parkway, an elongated park with a scenic motorway following the crest of the Blue Ridge Mountains from Shenandoah National Park in Virginia to the Great Smoky Mountains National Park in North Carolina and Tennessee. It averages more than 3,000 ft, above sea level. There are a number of wayside parks, marked historic sites (including cabins and farm buildings), a mineral museum, scenic overlooks, and other points of interest along the way. The Parkway was begun in 1936 and when completed will extend 469 mi. It enters North Carolina in ne Alleghany County and extends sw for 252.1 mi. Portions of the route have not yet been completed.

Blue Ridge Pinnacle. See Pinnacle.

Blue Ridge Township, e Henderson County.

Blue Ridge Township, se Watauga County.

Blue Rock Branch rises in e Yancey County and flows w into South Toe River.

Blue Rock Knob, se Buncombe County ne of Little Pisgah Mountain.

Bluerock Knob, e Yancey County near the head of George Fork. Alt. 4,859.

Blue Rock Knob, e Yancey County between Blue Rock Branch and Sevenmile Ridge.

Blue Sea Creek rises in s Yancey County and flows nw into Beech Nursery Creek.

Blue Sea Falls on Blue Sea Creek, s Yancey County in Pisgah National Forest.

Blue's Crossing. See Aberdeen.

Blue's Mountain, an elevation in n Hoke County on the Fort Bragg Military Reservation. Named for the Blue family, former owners.

Blues Pond, w Scotland County on Joes Creek. Covers 30 acres. Formed prior to 1909 and known earlier as Gibsons Millpond.

Blue Springs Township, sw Hoke County. A part of Robeson County until 1911.

Blue Valley, joined valleys of East Fork Overflow Creek and West Fork Overflow Creek in se Macon County.

Bluewing, community in nw Granville County.

Blue Wing Creek rises in e Person County and flows ne into Hyco Creek in Virginia. It was mentioned in 1728 by William Byrd. The bluewing was a small duck regarded as a delicacy.

Bluewing Mine, copper mine on branch of Aarons Creek in nw Granville County. First operated 1898-1900, but opened again for a short time during World War I.

Bluff, community in w Madison County on Meadow Fork. Alt. 2,150.

Bluff Branch rises in n Clay County and flows sw into Tusquitee Creek.

Bluff Mountain, sw Ashe County. Alt. 5,073.

Bluff Mountain, w Madison County near the head of Hickory Ridge Branch. Alt. 4,640.

Bluff Park. See Doughton Park.

Bluff Point, s Chowan County, approx. 8½ mi. se of Edenton, extends into Albemarle Sound. Mentioned in local records from the early eighteenth century; appears on the Moseley map, 1733.

Bluff Point extends from the s mainland of Hyde County into Pamlico Sound between East Bluff Bay and West Bluff Bay. Appears as Machapunga Bluff on the Moseley map, 1733.

Bluff Point extends from e Onslow County into White Oak River.

Bluff Point extends from se Pasquotank County into the Pasquotank River on the n shore of Little Flatty Creek.

The Bluffs, rough, rocky mountain peaks in sw Alleghany County e of the Blue Ridge Parkway near Doughton Park, which see.

Bluff Shoal formed by the merging waters of the Albemarle and Pamlico Sounds extends from Bluff Point on the s mainland of Hyde County to Royal Shoal on the Carteret-Hyde County line. The name appears as early as the Mouzon map, 1775.

Bly Gap, s Clay County. The Appalachian Trail passes through this gap just n of the Georgia line.

Blythe Branch rises in e Transylvania County and flows sw into Lydia Creek.

Blythe Mill Creek rises in nw Henderson County and flows se into French Broad River.

Blythe Mountain, w Henderson County on Little Willow Creek.

Board Camp Creek rises in n Swain County in Great Smoky Mountains National Park below Broad Camp Gap and flows w into Forney Creek.

Board Camp Gap, n Swain County on Forney Ridge, in Great Smoky Mountains National Park.

Board Cove Branch rises in ne Swain County and flows n into Bunches Creek.

Board Gap, on Drymans Branch in s Macon County.

Boardman, town in nw Columbus County on Lumber River. Inc. 1891 as Hub; name changed in 1899 to honor prominent American Baptist clergyman, George Dana Boardman (1828-1903). Long inactive in municipal affairs.

Boardtree Creek rises in s Macon County and flows se into Poplar Cove Creek.

Boathouse Creek rises in w Carteret County and flows sw into White Oak River.

Boat Island, e Onslow County just inside Bogue Inlet. Named because early fishermen pulled boats up here.

Boatman Branch rises in n Franklin County and flows se into Sandy Creek.

Bobbitt, community in se Vance County near Lynch Creek.

Bob Creek rises in n Cherokee County and flows sw into Tellico River.

Bob Branch rises in ne Cherokee County and flows sw into Beaver Creek approx. 150 yds. before the latter stream enters Valley River.

Bob Branch rises in w central Clay County and flows s parallel to and east of Graveyard Ridge into Hiwassee River.

Bob Branch rises in n Randolph County and flows ne into Muddy Creek.

Bob Creek rises in ne Pender County and flows s into Angola Creek.

Bob's Cove, site of early settlement on e

end of Bogue Banks, s Carteret County. Storms drove out early settlers until settlement of Salter Path, *which see.*

Bobs Creek rises in e Yancey County and flows nw into South Toe River.

Bob's Knob, s Burke County. Alt. 2,000.

Bob's Ridge, e Haywood County between Big East Fork and Big Cove.

Bob Whites Corner, community in s Pasquotank County.

Boby Cove, between Laurel Mountain and Big Creek in nw Henderson County.

Boddies Mill Pond, w Nash County on Stony Creek. Covers more than 100 acres; maximum depth 15 feet. Owned by Braswell Milling Company and furnishes power for corn mill.

Bodie Island, one of the Outer Banks, e Dare County. N boundary was formerly New Inlet, now the area around Kitty Hawk. Bounded on the s by Oregon Inlet. Mentioned by John Lawson in 1700. Appears on the Moll map, 1729. Cow Island and Duggs Island, also shown on the Moll map, are now joined with and are a part of Bodie Island. *See also* Etacrewac.

Boger City, community in central Lincoln County. Named for Robert Boger who est. a textile mill here. Previously known as Goodson's Store and Goodsonville.

Boggan, community in central Anson County. Alt. 306. Probably named for Patrick Boggan, pioneer settler. *See* Wadesboro.

Bogue, community in w Carteret County. Site of auxillary air base for Cherry Point Marine Air Station.

Bogue. *See* Swansboro.

Bogue Banks, a barrier beach in s Carteret County, forming one of the Outer Banks. It is 25 mi. long and from one-half to two miles wide. Fort Macon is at the e end; the towns of Atlantic Beach, Salter Path, and Emerald Isle are on the Bogue Banks. The name appears on the Moseley map, 1733. Josiah Bogue settled in the vicinity in the early eighteenth century. Named for him or for the family.

Bogue Inlet, an inlet from the Atlantic Ocean into Bogue Sound, between Dudley's Island, e Onslow County, and Bogue Banks, sw Carteret County. White Oak River enters the Atlantic Ocean through this inlet. Shown on the de Graffenried map (French text), 1711.

Bogue Sound extends from the sw end of Carteret County along its southern edge to the se section of the county at Beaufort

and Morehead City. The Sound drains into the Atlantic Ocean through Beaufort Inlet, *which see.*

Bogue Swamp rises in n central Columbus County and flows se into Waccamaw River.

Bogue Township, central Columbus County.

Boiling Springs, town in sw Cleveland County. Alt. 990. Inc. 1911 and took its name from a boiling spring, known since the days of the Cherokee Indians. Site of Gardner-Webb Junior College, an outgrowth of a high school est. here in 1905.

Boiling Springs, community in n Cherokee County on Hanging Dog Creek.

Boiling Springs Lake, town in se Brunswick County, inc. 1961.

Boiling Springs Township, former township in sw Cleveland County, now township number 2.

Bold Branch rises in n Henderson County and flows se into Clear Creek.

Bolden Branch rises in ne Cherokee County and flows nw into Junaluska Creek.

Bold Run Branch rises in s Franklin County and flows sw into Wake County where it enters New Light Creek.

Bolick Branch. *See* Anthony Bolick Branch.

Bolin Creek rises in se Orange County on the s slope of Bald Mountain and flows se, just n of the town of Chapel Hill, to join Booker Creek in forming Little Creek. Appears as Bollings Creek on a map of Chapel Hill made in 1792 by John Daniel. The Bolling family settled in Orange County in the eighteenth century.

Bolin Knob, mountain at junction of Burke-McDowell-Rutherford County line. Alt. approx. 2,200. Named for a family living in the area by the late eighteenth century.

Bolivia, town in e central Brunswick County. Settled in the late 19th century and inc. in 1911. Alt. 40. County seat located nearby 1978.

Bollens Run rises in s Granville County and flows s into Tar River.

Bollers Knob, central Henderson County at the head of Findley Creek.

Bolling, community in n Halifax County a short distance w of Roanoke Rapids.

Bolling Creek. *See* Bolin Creek.

Bolton, town in nw Coumbus County. Settled 1889. Inc. 1915. Named for Bolton Lumber Company. Alt. 66.

Bolton Township, e Columbus County.

Bonaparte Landing, sw Brunswick County on the Intracoastal Waterway.

Bonarva, plantation of the Pettigrew family

in se Washington County and w Tyrrell County. Of the various plantation houses of the Pettigrew family, two were on Bonarva. Belgrade, in Washington County, was built about 1796 and is still standing; it was named for the earlier Pettigrew house on Harveys Neck in Perquimans County. Magnolia was built in Tyrrell County, the site of the greater portion of the Pettigrew lands. ,Scotch Hall was the Pettigrew home in Bertie County. Belgrade is now a part of the Pettigrew State Park, *which see.*

Bonarva Canal, w Tyrrell County, flows from Lake Phelps ne into Old Canal. Known also as Magnolia Canal. Dug during Ante-Bellum era with slave labor to drain swamplands for cultivation.

Bond Creek rises in se Beaufort County and flows n into the mouth of South Creek at Pamlico River.

Bonds Ferry. *See* Pamlico River.

Bone Camp Branch rises in s Madison County and flows sw into Bull Creek.

Bones Creek rises in nw Cumberland County and flows se and s into Little Rockfish Creek.

Bone Valley, nw Swain County in Great Smoky Mountains National Park. Named after an early settler found the bleached bones of his long lost cows here.

Bone Valley Creek, formed in nw Swain County in Great Smoky Mountains National Park by the junction of Roaring Creek and Defeat Branch. It flows s into Hazel Creek.

Boney Mill Pond, on Paget Branch in s Duplin County.

Bonlee, community in sw Chatham County. Est, 1894 and first known as Dunlap's Mill; in 1898 renamed Causey for Joshua Causey, local resident. Renamed Bonlee in 1910, supposedly for a brand of cloth. Inc. 1913; charter repealed 1936. Alt. 526.

Bonner Bay, waterway in e Pamlico County between the mouth of Spring Creek and Bay River.

Bonner Bridge. *See* Oregon Inlet.

Bonnerton, community in se Beaufort County.

Bonnets Points appears on the Moseley map, 1733, from what is now se Brunswick County extending into Cape Fear River between Elizabeth River and Dutchmans Creek.

Bonnie Doone, community in central Cumberland County nw of Fayetteville near

limits of the Fort Bragg Military Reservation. Inc. 1941; charter repealed 1953.

Bonsal, community in sw Wake County on the head of Tom Jack Creek. Settled 1900. Inc. 1907; charter repealed 1917. Named for the railroad engineer who drove the first train through here. Alt. 305.

Booker Creek rises in se Orange County and flows through Eastwood Lake to join Bolin Creek just e of town of Chapel Hill to form Little Creek.

Boogertown, community in s Gaston County at the n end of Jackson Knob, about 3 mi. s of Gastonia.

Boomer, community in s Wilkes County on Warrior Creek by which name it was known until renamed for "Boomer" Matheson, local postmaster.

Boomer Branch rises in n Swain County and flows se into Proctor Creek.

Boomer Inn Branch rises in s Haywood County and flows e into Right Hand Prong [of Pigeon River].

Boomer Township, sw Wilkes County.

Boone, town and county seat, central Watauga County. Inc. 1871. Named for Daniel Boone (1734-1820) who, according to tradition, camped here while on a hunting trip. Home of Appalachian State University. The outdoor drama, "Horn in the West," by Kermit Hunter has been produced here each summer since 1952. Produces electronics components, apparel, canned foods, wood products, and shoes. Alt. 3,266.

Boone Branch rises in n Clay County and flows se into Tuni Creek.

Boone Camp Branch rises in e Watauga County and flows se into Elk Creek.

Boone Cove Gap, on the Madison County, N. C.,-Unicoi County, Tenn., line.

Boone Creek rises in s Watauga County and flows ne into Flannery Fork [of South Fork River].

Boone Fork rises in s Watauga County and flows ne and n into Watauga River.

Boone Ridge, w Yancey County between Wolf Branch and Shepherd Branch.

Boone's Cave, on a high bluff overlooking the Yadkin River in w Davidson County is traditionally said to have been occupied by Daniel Boone. It is near Horseshoe Neck *(which see),* and a park is maintained near the cave by local citizens.

Boones Crossroads, community in sw Northampton County.

Boone's Fork, stream, rises in nw Caldwell

County and flows w into Mulberry Creek.
Named for Jesse Boone, pre-Revolutionary settler and nephew of Daniel Boone.

Boones Gap, sw Wilkes County near the
headwaters of Warrior Creek. Named for
the explorer, Daniel Boone (1734-1820).

Boones Mill Pond, w Northampton County
on Gumberry Swamp. Covers 100 acres;
mix. depth 20 ft. An engagement occurred here during the Civil War on July
29, 1864.

Boone Township, w Davidson County,
named for Daniel Boone who is said to
have lived in a cabin along the banks of
the Yadkin River in this area.

Boone Township, central Watauga County.

Boonford, community in e Yancey County
on North Toe River. Named for Daniel
Boone who is said to have forded the
river here.

Boon Hill Township, se Johnston County.
See also Princeton.

Boons Ferry appears on the Collet map,
1770, as being on the Meherrin River between ne Northampton County and nw
Hertford County. By 1802 it had ceased
operation, and by 1833 Boone Bridge
existed at the site. A bridge still crosses
the river here.

Boons Fork, community in central Northampton County.

Boon Station, community in w central
Alamance County.

Boon Station Township, former township in
w central Alamance County, now township number 3.

Boonville, town in n Yadkin County. Inc.
1895. Named for Daniel Boone (1734-
1820) who is said to have camped at the
site. Produces textiles and processed grain.

Boonville Township, nw Yadkin County.

Bordensville. *See* Mill Creek.

Border Creek rises in e Linclon County and
flows se into Catawba River.

Boring Creek rises in s Transylvania County
and flows nw into East Fork French
Broad River.

Boring Mill Branch rises in s Buncombe
County and flows se into French Broad
River.

The Borough, sw Pender County on Black
River near the mouth of Moores Creek, a
shipping point for goods sent by water.
Dates from prior to the Revolution.
Apparently this is the site authorized to
be laid off in 1798 for the town of Par-
kersborough on the land of Hardy Parker.
It is not known whether the town was

actually established. The remains of an
old wharf may still be seen a short distance from the bank of the river. A fishing camp is now operated at the site and
three old roads through the woods con-
verge at the wharf site.

Bosley. *See* Wardville.

Bost Creek rises in se Cabarrus County and
flows se into Rocky River.

Bostic, town in central Rutherford County
between Second Broad River and Puzzle
Creek. Alt. 923. Inc. 1893. Named for
George T. Bostic, first mayor.

Bosts Mills, community in se Cabarrus
County on Rocky River, former site of
grist and saw mills.

Boswell, community in central Buncombe
County w of Asheville near Deaver View.

Boteler Peak, ne Vineyard Mountain, e
Clay County. Alt. 4,500.

Bottom, community in n Surry County on
Beaverdam Creek.

Bottomless Pools in Pool Creek, sw Rutherford County at Lake Lure. Formed by
whirlpool action of the rushing water in
weaker sections of the huge granite rock
over which it flows. Three pools now exist
and a fourth is apparently being formed.
In 1947 a geologist who studied them reported that the pools may vary in age
100,000 to a million years.

Boulding Creek rises in central Granville
County and flows se into Fishing Creek.

Boushell, community in e central Wake
County.

Bowden Mountain, e Davidson County between the headwaters of Flat Swamp
Creek and Fourmile Branch.

Bowden Pond, on the head of Bear Swamp
in w Duplin County.

Bowdens, town in nw Duplin County. Alt.
167. Settled prior to 1872, inc. 1911.
Named for Captain James Bowden who
owned land in the vicinity. Railroad
name is Bowden.

Bowditch, community in e Yancey County
on Ayles Creek.

Boween River rises in s Cleveland County
and flows sw into South Carolina where
it enters Broad River.

Bowen Point, a point of land on the w side
of the mouth of Shallotte River. The
channel of the Intracoastal Waterway
cuts through this point.

Bowers Creek rises in s Swain County and
flows nw into Yalaka Creek.

Bowers Gap, on the Avery-Watauga County
line se of Shawneehaw Creek.

Bower's Store. *See* Sparta.

Bowies Falls. *See* Buies Falls.

Bowlens Creek rises in s Yancey County and flows nw into Cane River.

Bowlens Creek, community in central Yancey County. Formerly known as Athlone.

Bowlens Pyramid, peak in s central Yancey County between Jumpoff Gap and the head of George Fork. Alt. 4,908. The northernmost peak in the Black Mountains.

Bowling Green Creek rises in nw Mitchell County and flows se into Hollow Poplar Creek.

Bowman Bluff, an elevation in w Henderson County overlooking French Broad River. Named because it was an Indian lookout site.

Bowman Gap, sw Cherokee County between Angelico Mountain and Pack Mountain. Alt. approx. 3,215.

Bowman Gap, n Yancey County between the head of Shoal Creek and Bailey Hill.

Bowmans Bluff, community in w Henderson County near the mouth of Willow Creek. Settled about 1875-80.

Bowan's Crossing. *See* Icard.

Bowans Gap, sw Cherokee County at the ne end of Angelico Mountain.

Bowmore, community in s Hoke County.

Box, P[ort]. *See* P[ort] Box.

Box Creek rises in n central Rutherford County at Camel Knob and flows s into Second Broad River.

Boyd Branch rises near Little Hickory Top in s Buncombe County and flows se into Bent Creek.

Boyd Creek rises in central Alamance County and flows s into Haw River.

Boyden, community in se Surry County on Yadkin River. Alt. 771.

Boyd Mountain, nw Buncombe County between Cherry and Wade gaps.

Boyds Crossroads, community in e Pitt County.

Boyd's Ferry. *See* Grimesland.

Boyd Township, ne Transylvania County.

Boyette, town in sw Wilson County. Inc. 1887 as Silverboro; name changed 1897 to honor first mayor, Nathan Boyette. Long inactive in municipal affairs.

Boyles' Store. *See* Dalton.

Boylston, community in nw Henderson County. Site of numerous unsuccessful attempts to mine gold. Named for Revolutionary soldier.

Boylston Creek rises in ne Transylvania County and flows ne into Henderson County where it enters French Broad River.

Boza Creek rises in nw Rockingham County and flows sw into Mayo River.

Bracebridge Hall, home of Elias Carr, governor 1893-97, stands five miles se of Pinetops, s Edgecombe County.

Brachcoast Swamp, pocosin in e Cumberland County drained by Reese Creek. One of the Carolina Bays, *which see.*

Brack Branch rises in s Madison County and flows se into Big Pine Creek.

Bracken Mountain, a ridge approx. 1½ mi. long in w Transylvania County south of and parallel to the headwaters of Tucker Creek. Named for a large coarse fern growing here.

Brackens Creek rises in two forks in central Transylvania County; one flows ne and the other se to join. The creek then flows e into Nicholson Creek.

Bracketts Creek rises in s Rutherford County and flows se into Floyds Creek.

Brackett Township, se McDowell County.

Braden Mountain, e Cherokee County, extends from the headwaters of Lamb Branch on the s to Slow Creek on the n, due w of Indian Grave Gap.

Bradey Branch rises in ne Cherokee County and flows se into Valley River.

Bradford Mountain, s Caldwell County. Alt. 1,313. Named for Bennet Bradford, eighteenth century settler who is buried on its slopes.

Bradford Mountain, se Transylvania County in Blue Ridge Mountains.

Bradley Branch rises in s Macon County and flows se into Norton Branch.

Bradley Butt, e Macon County between Fall Branch and Mica City Creek.

Bradley Creek rises in central New Hanover County and flows se into Greenville Sound.

Bradley Creek rises in n Macon County and flows sw into Little Tennessee River.

Bradley Creek rises in ne Transylvania County and flows se into South Fork in Pisgah National Forest. Site of early iron works; a forge was operated here during the Civil War.

Bradley Creek rises in s Transylvania County and flows sw into East Fork French Broad River.

Bradley Fork formed in ne Swain County in Great Smoky Mountains National Park by the junction of Chasm Prong and Gulf Prong. It flows se into Oconaluftee River.

Bradley Gap, w Avery County.

Bradley Gap, n Buncombe County between Bruce Knob and Bill Cole Mountain.

Bradley Mountain, e Henderson County between Little Hungry River and Hungry River, Alt. 2,731.

Bradley's Store. See Kipling.

Bradshaw Branch rises in s Lincoln County and flows sw into Leepers Creek.

Bradshaws Millpond in s Sampson County drains sw into Black River.

Bradshaw Township, nw Mitchell County.

Bragg Crossroads, community in s Granville County.

Bragtown, former community in central Durham County n of the city of Durham, now within the limits of the latter. Also spelled Braggtown.

Branchs Store, community in n Duplin County.

Branchville. See Manson.

Brandle Branch rises in se Cherokee County and flows se into Little Brasstown Creek.

Brandon, community in n Ashe County. Alt. approx. 2,850.

Brand Swamp rises in n Wilson County and flows se into Cattail Swamp. Named for Benjamin Brand.

Brandy Creek rises in w Franklin County and flows ne into Cedar Creek.

Brandy Gap, in nw Mitchell County at the head of Right Fork [Pigeonroost Creek].

Brank Cove, the valley through which Brank Cove Branch flows in n Buncombe County, w of Thurz Mountain.

Brank Cove Branch rises near Brittain Mountain in n Buncombe County and flows nw into Flat Creek.

Brank Mountain, n Buncombe County between Pink Fox Cove and Little Middle Mountain.

Branon, community in s central Yadkin County near South Deep Creek.

Branson Creek rises in central Onslow County and flows e into New River.

Brant Island, a tidal marsh island approx. ½ mi. long in Pamlico Sound, ne Pamlico County, off Goose Creek Island.

Brantley Island, a neck of land in sw Brunswick County between Saucepan Creek and the Intracoastal Waterway.

Brassfield, community in s Durham County. Named for a local family. Formerly known as Flemington; name changed prior to 1865.

Brassfield Township, se Granville County.

Brasstown, community in sw Clay County on Ledford Branch. Alt. 1,650. Reputedly named from a confusion of two Cherokee

words of similar sound but different meaning—itse'yi, "a place made green with vegetation," and untsai'yi, "brass." The John C. Campbell Folk School, on a 175-acre farm, is here.

Brasstown Creek rises in s Clay County and flows nw to the Cherokee-Clay County line which it forms for a short distance before flowing into Hiwassee River.

Brasstown Gap, s Clay County on the headwaters of Beach Creek.

Brasstown Knob, n Jackson County on Coward Mountain.

Brasstown Township, se Clay County.

Braswell, community in nw Columbus County.

Braswells Crossroads, community in s Halifax County.

Brave Mountain, on the n end of Buck Mountain in w Haywood County.

Bray. See Riddle.

Brazel Creek rises in s Wake County and flows ne into Sunset Lake.

Breakneck Ridge, e central Avery County.

Breakneck Ridge, ne Swain County in Great Smoky Mountains National Park, a spur extending w from Hyatt Ridge.

Breedlove Branch rises in ne Swain County and flows s into Bulldie Creek.

Brendletown, community in e Macon County on Coon Creek.

Brett Bay in the waters of Core Sound, ne Carteret County. Formerly known as Britts Bay.

Brevard, town and county seat, central Transylvania County. Est. as county seat 1861 or 1862; Inc. 1889. Named for Ephriam Brevard (1744-81), teacher, secretary of the convention which drew up the Mecklenburg Resolves of May 31, 1775, and Revolutionary surgeon. Home of Brevard College, founded 1853 as Rutherford College, which see, merged in 1934 with Weaver College and took its present name. Transylvania Music Camp, begun in 1936, is here. Noted tourist area. Produces chemicals, textiles, and leather products. Alt. 2,230.

Brevard Station. See Stanley.

Brevard Township, central Transylvania County.

Brewer Branch rises in w Swain County and flows s into Tuckasegee River.

Brewers, community in n Wilkes County near Double Creek. Alt. 1,450.

Briar Branch rises in se Buncombe County and flows ne into Wolfpit Branch.

Briar Creek rises in se Durham County and

flows s into Wake County and into Stirrup Iron Creek.

Briar Patch Branch rises in n Madison County and flows sw into Culvin Creek.

Briarpatch Ridge, s Mitchell County between Middle Fork Grassy Creek and
East Fork Grassy Creek.

Briary Creek rises in sw Henderson County
and flows sw into Transylvania County
where it enters Reasonover Creek.

Briary Knob, e Haywood County on the
head of Pisgah Creek.

Brice Creek rises in s Craven County and
flows nw into Trent River. Appears on
the Moseley map, 1733.

Brice Creek Pocosin, sw Craven County.

Brick Church, community in se Guilford
County. First German Calvinist (German
Reformed) church in Guilford County.

Brickhaven, community in Chatham County.
Center of brick manufacturing.

Brickhouse. *See* Savages Crossroads.

Brickhouse Point, e Pasquotank County extends into the Pasquotank River s of
Davis Bay.

Brick Kiln Branch rises in ne Onslow County and flows se into White Oak River.

Brickle Inn. *See* Union.

[Brickle's Ferry]. *See* Brittle's Ferry.

Brick Mill. *See* Hunsucker.

Bricks, community in n Edgecombe County.
Named for Joseph Keasbey Brick in whose
honor an agricultural, industrial and nor-
mal school for Negroes was est. here in
1895 by Mrs. Julia Elma Brewster Brick.

Brickton, community in n Henderson County. Site of large brick manufacturing
plant.

Bridal Veil Falls, se Macon County on Cullasaja River. Water falls 120 ft. *See also*
Cullasaja River.

Bridal Veil Falls, e Transylvania County on
Little River between the mouth of Rea-
sonover Creek and the mouth of Tom
Creek. Height of the falls is 50 ft.

Bridge Branch rises in n Macon County and
flows se into Burningtown Creek.

Bridge Creek rises in s Scotland County and
flows s to join Leiths Creek in forming
the Little Pee Dee River.

Bridge Creek rises in n Swain County and
flows se into Deep Creek.

Bridge Creek rises in central Craven County
and flows s into Trent River.

Bridge Falls, se Haywood County on West
Fork of Pigeon River. In a series of falls,
water drops between 300 and 400 ft.

Named because a bridge crosses the river
at the top of the falls.

Bridgers Creek rises in s Northampton County and flows w into Roanoke River. Appears as Bridges Creek on the Moseley
map, 1733. Pulhams Ferry, according to
the Collet map, 1770, was operated across
the Roanoke River at the mouth of
Bridgers Creek. By 1808 and as late as
1833 the ferry was known as Pollock's
Ferry, and in 1862 it was known as
Devereux's Ferry.

Bridgersville, town in e Wilson County. Inc.
1925, but long inactive in municipal
affairs. Named for John F. Bridgers. Post
office operated here 1889-1895.

Bridges Camp Gap, on the Haywood-Transylvania County line.

Bridges Creek rises in e Montgomery County and flows nw into Little River.

Bridges Creek. *See* Bridgers Creek.

Bridgeton, town in central Craven County.
Settled about 1900. Inc. 1907. Named for
the bridge across the Neuse River which
connects it with New Bern. Alt. 8.

Bridgewater, community in w Burke County
on the Catawba River. Originally the
name of the plantation of John Rutherford who named it for Francis Egerton
(1736-1803), Earl of Bridgewater, inland
navigation expert and canal builder.

Bridgewater Reservoir. *See* Lake James.

Bridle Creek rises in w Warren County and
flows e into Fishing Creek. A bridge
across the creek is mentioned in local
records as early as 1765.

Bridle Creek, former plantation house in w
Warren County approx. 3 mi. sw of War-
renton. Two Confederate major generals,
Matthew Whitaker Ransom and Robert
Ransom, brothers, were born here. Only
ruined foundations now mark the site.

Bridle Ridge extends se from Yancey County into nw McDowell County between
Bee Rock and Cow creeks.

Brief, community in n Union County between Red Creek and Duck Creek.

Brier Creek rises in nw Cleveland County
and flows sw and s into Rutherford County where it enters First Broad River.

Brier Creek rises in nw Columbus County
and flows nw into Big Swamp in Robeson
County.

Brier Creek rises in central Mecklenburg
County and flows sw into Little Sugar
Creek.

Brier Creek rises in w Wake County and
flows s into Stirrup Iron Creek.

Brier Creek rises in s Wilkes County in the Brushy Mountains and flows ne into Yadkin River.

Brier Creek, community in s Wilkes County. Brier Creek Baptist Church here est. in the eighteenth century. A post office by this name served the community from about 1822 until 1882.

Brier Knob, on Swain County, N. C.-Blount County, Tenn., line in Great Smoky Mountains National Park near lat. 35° 34′ 15″ N., long. 83° 40′ 48″ W. Alt. 5,225.

Brier Lick Gap, on Swain County, N. C.-Blount County, Tenn. line in Great Smoky Mountains National Park, near lat. 35° 32′ 00″ N., long. 83° 49′ 42″ W.

Brier Ridge, n Jackson County between Licklog Creek and Dark Cabin Creek.

Briertown Mountain, sw Swain County extends ne beside Nantahala Gorge.

Briery Bay, a loam filled bay in s Columbus County.

Briery Hall Point, a point of land in central Dare County near the nw end of South Lake and its junction with Alligator River.

Brier Ridge, n Yancey County e of Coxe Branch.

Briery Run rises in n Lenoir County and flows e into Stonyton Creek.

Briery Swamp rises in n Pitt County and flows se into Tranters Creek.

Briggs Hollow, valley in central Avery County.

Bright, community in n Polk County on Lake Adger, Green River.

Brights Creek rises in nw Polk County and flows se into Green River.

Brights Mill Creek. See Mill Creek.

Brightwater Branch rises in w Henderson County near Jumpoff Mountain and flows n into Shaw Creek.

Bright Yellow Mountain. See Big Yellow Mountain.

Brigman Hollow, n Madison County on a branch of Rocky Branch.

Brim, community in ne Surry County near Archies Creek.

Brindletown, community in sw Burke County. In the heart of the former gold mining area of the county. A post office as early as 1830. A former township by this name was abolished in 1885 and merged with Silver Creek Township.

Brinkleyville, community in w Halifax County. Named for Joseph Brinkley who settled here in 1767. A post office as early as 1822.

Brinkleyville Township, sw Halifax County.

Brinkly. See Delco.

Bristle Ridge, s Macon County between Bates Ridge and Little Tennessee River.

Bristol, community in n Ashe County. Post office in late nineteenth century.

Bristol Branch rises in n Clay County and flows s into Tusquitee Creek.

Bristol's Mill Creek rises in n central Burke County and flows s into Lower Creek at Chesterfield. Formerly known as White's Mill Creek, Bullinger's Mill Creek, and Kincaid's Mill Creek.

Bristow, community in nw Mecklenburg County.

Brittain. See Westminster.

Brittain Cove, n Buncombe County on the s side of Brittain Mountain.

Brittain Cove, se Buncombe County.

Brittain Mountain, n Buncombe County, sw of Watershed Ridge.

Brittain Store, community in central Burke County.

Britten Creek rises in nw Polk County and flows se approx. 5½ mi. into Green River. Sometimes known as Bullin Creek.

Brittle Ordinary. See Union.

Brittle's Ferry appears on the Collet map, 1770, just above Winton on Chowan River, e Hertford County. This is probably a corruption of the prominent Hertford County name of Brickle.

Britton Creek rises in ne Cherokee County and flows s and sw into Valley River. Panther Den Falls (which see) are on Britton Creek n of Andrews.

Britton Creek rises in central Henderson County and flows se into Mud Creek.

Britton Mountain, s Buncombe County. Alt. 2,530.

Brittons Creek rises in nw Bertie County and flows w and s into Roanoke River.

Brittons Crossroads or Store. See Roxobel.

Britts Bay. See Brett Bay.

Britts Store, community in n Hertford County.

Britts Township, se Robeson County.

Broadbay Township, s Forsyth County. Named for Broadbay, Massachusetts, now Waldsboro, Maine, the early home of the first settlers of Friedland, a community in the township. See also Friedland.

Broad Branch rises in n Mitchell County and flows w into Big Fork Creek.

Broad Creek, fed by several canals from the Dismal Swamp in n Beaufort County, flows s and e into Pantego Creek.

Broad Creek rises in w Beaufort County and flows s into Pamlico River.

Broad Creek, a canal in se Bertie County connecting two sides of a loop in the Roanoke River.

Broad Creek rises in se Bertie County and flows e in Cashie River.

Broad Creek rises in the North River Pocosin of s Camden County and flows e into North River. Appears on the Collet map, 1770.

Broad Creek rises in w Carteret County and flows se into Bogue Sound. Appears on the Moseley map, 1733.

Broad Creek, stream in Nelson Bay, cuts into mainland in ne Carteret County.

Broad Creek, a bay near the nw end of South Lake, central Dare County.

Broad Creek, a tidal creek in the waters of Roanoke Sound on e Roanoke Island in e Dare County.

Broad Creek rises in se Macon County and flows se into Clear Creek.

Broad Creek rises in e Pamlico County and flows e into Neuse River estuary. Appears on the Moseley map, 1733. Known locally as Lower Broad Creek.

Broad Creek Point, peninsula on the e shore of Roanoke Island, e Dare County, extending se into Roanoke Sound and Broad Creek.

Broad Creek. See Scranton Creek.

Broad Inlet appears on the Moseley map, 1733, in the beach barrier of e New Hanover County between the present Masonboro and Moore Inlet.

Broadneck Swamp, se Bertie County. Named from its location in a neck of the Roanoke River. See also Town Swamp.

Broad River rises in se Buncombe County, flows se across ne Henderson County into w Rutherford County, se to the Polk-Rutherford County line where it is joined by Green River, se and ne into Cleveland County, and se into South Carolina where it joins Saluda River at Columbia to form the Congaree River. Sometimes known locally as Rocky Broad River and Main Broad River. Known by the Indians as Ess-ee-daw. See also Hickory Nut Gorge. Lake Lure is on Broad River. Appears on the Collet map, 1770.

Broad River Township, se Buncombe County. Formerly in McDowell County but annexed to Buncombe County by legislative act in 1925.

Broad Run rises in e Pitt County and flows se into Tar River.

Broad Swamp, w Beaufort County, is the lower course of Hall Swamp. It flows s into Pamlico River.

Broadway, town in e Lee County. Inc. 1907. Settled in the 1870's and named for a broad, level opening in the vast pine forest which covered the area.

Broadway Gap, s Macon County between Little Scaly Mountain and Fork Mountain.

Brock, community in n Graham County on Sawyer Creek.

Brock Knob, on French Broad River in w Henderson County.

Brodie, former community in s Warren County on Shocco Creek. A post office was est. here in 1879; apparently the community died out after it was discontinued in 1913.

Brogden, community in s Wayne County.

Brogden Township, s Wayne County. Named for the family of Curtis Hooks Brogden (1816-1901), governor of North Carolina and a native of the county.

Brokeleg Branch rises in ne Cherokee County and flows s into Gipp Creek.

Broke Yoke Gap, on Graham-Swain County line between Tyre Knob and Peachtree Gap.

Bromine-Arsenic Springs. See Crumpler.

Brompton, central Bladen County on Cape Fear River, 4 mi. n of Elizabethtown. Started as a home by Governor Gabriel Johnston (1699-1752) but not completed. Evidence remains of unfinished building.

Brook Branch rises in w Jackson County and flows se into Greens Creek.

Brook Cove, community in se Stokes County.

Brookford, town in w Catawba County, on Henry Fork at site of former Hanging Rock Bridge. Inc. 1907. Alt. 1,000. Named for parts of the name of joint owners of a local mill, Holbrook and Shuford.

Brookride, community in ne Watauga County.

Brooks Branch rises near Potato Knob in sw Buncombe County and flows se into Newfound Creek.

Brooks Cove, the valley through which South Hominy Creek flows in sw Buncombe County.

Brooks Cove, sw Buncombe County near the headwaters of Little Pole Creek.

Brooks Cove, e Cherokee County on the headwaters of Messer Branch.

Brooks Cove. See Welch Cove.

Brooks Creek rises in e Hertford County and flows se into Wiccacon River.

Brooks Crossroads, community in w Yadkin County, Alt. 1,072.

Brooksdale, community in central Person County. Named for the Brooks family, local landowners and merchants.

Brooks Gap, on the Buncombe-Haywood County line near the headwaters of South Hominy Creek.

Brooks Gap, central Graham County on Santeetlah Lake.

Brooks Knob, on the Surry-Wilkes County line.

Brooks Point, off the n shore of Hatteras Island, opposite Cape Hatteras and extending into the waters of Pamlico Sound, s Dare County.

Brookston, community in e Vance County. Post office est. in 1882.

Broomfield Swamp Creek rises in se Beaufort County and flows e into South Creek.

Broom Straw Mountain, e Madison County between Paint Fork and Crooked Creek.

Browders Branch rises in n Columbus County and flows sw into West Prong Creek.

Brower's Mill (or Mills), former community and post office on Fork Creek in se Randolph County. A post office existed here as early as 1831, when Alfred Brower was postmaster, and as recent as 1910. The name appears on a map of 1919, but apparently is not found after that date.

Brower Township, se Randolph County.

Brown Branch rises in sw Beaufort County and flows sw into Chocowinity Creek.

Brown Branch rises in n Buncombe County near Carter Mountain and flows sw into Ivy Creek.

Brown Branch rises in s Buncombe County and flows sw into Fourmile Branch.

Brown Branch rises in e Watauga County and flows nw into South Fork New River.

Brown Branch rises in s Watauga County and flows se into Middle Fork [of South Fork New River].

Brown Cove, e Haywood County between Medford Cove and Sorrells Cove.

Brown Creek rises in South Carolina and flows ne through the se corner of Union County and into Anson County where it enters Pee Dee River in n central Anson County.

Brown Creek rises in n Carteret County and flows n into Neuse River.

Brown Creek rises in ne Cherokee County and flows n and nw into Valley River.

Brown Creek rises in e Macon County and flows w into Watauga Creek.

Brown Creek rises in e Pamlico County and flows s into Broad Creek.

Brown Creek rises in w Transylvania County and flows se into Parker Creek.

Brown Creek, community in se Union County.

Brown Fork Gap, at the e end of Cheoah Mountains in e central Graham County at the head of Sawyer Creek.

Brown Gap, on the Haywood County, N. C.-Cocke County, Tenn., line. The Appalachian Trail passes here and Pounding Mill Branch rises a short distance e.

Brown Gap, e Macon County between Corbin Creek and Brown Creek.

Brown Gap, at the head of Henson Branch in se Macon County.

Browning Branch rises in s Haywood County and flows nw into Richland Creek.

Browning Peak. See Black Mountain (Jackson-Haywood County line).

Brown Marsh Station. See Clarkton.

Brown Marsh Swamp rises in sw Bladen County and flows se into Columbus County where its name is changed to Red Hill Swamp. Appears as Brown Meadow on the Moseley map, 1733, See also Brown Meadow.

Brown Marsh Township, s central Bladen County.

Brown Meadow appears on the Collet map, 1770, in what is now Columbus County, nw of the headwaters of White Marsh. See also Brown Marsh Swamp.

Brown Mountain, central Alleghany County.

Brown Mountain, s Buncombe County e of Skyland.

Brown Mountain, on the Burke-Caldwell County line, approx. 1½ mi. w of Wilson Creek. Alt. 2,725. Noted for mysterious lights, known since 1833 in many popular legends. Many explanations have been offered for the lights, burning marsh gas, foxfire, and light refraction by the atmosphere of train, automobile or city lights, among them.

Brown Mountain, w Jackson County on the head of Cullowhee Creek.

Brown Mountain, community in w central Stokes County.

Brown Mountain Beach, a bathing beach in Wilson Creek in w Caldwell County.

Brown Ridge, n Avery County.

Browns Creek rises in central Bladen County and flows e into the Cape Fear River. Appears as Earthquake Branch on the Moseley map, 1733.

Browns Creek rises in e Yancey County and flows e into South Toe River.

Brown's Creek. *See* Browns Swamp.

Brown's Crossroads, community in nw Randolph County. The old county seat town of Johnstonville *(which see)* was here.

Browns Ford in the Yadkin River, sw Wilkes County. Named for Captain John Brown, Revolutionary soldier, who lived nearby and in whose home the first county government was organized in 1778. A bridge was built here after 1900, and a modern highway bridge now is at the site.

Browns Inlet, se Onslow County between the n end of Onslow Beach and Bear Inlet. Appears on the Moseley map, 1733.

Brown's Island, s Carteret County, approx. 1½ mi. long, n of the e end of Harkers Island and separated from it by Westmouth Bay and Eastmouth Bay.

Brown's Island, a coastal beach island approx. 3 mi. long, on the Atlantic Ocean in se Onslow County. Now within the limits of Camp Lejeune. It lies between Brown's Inlet and Bear Inlet. Sometimes referred to locally by an older name, Shacklefoot Island.

Browns Knob, sw Buncombe County between Billy Cove and Sheep Rock. Alt. 3,760.

Browns Landing, United States Lock Number 2 on Cape Fear River in central Bladen County.

Browns Mill Creek rises in s Transylvania County and flows ne into French Broad River.

Browns Mountain, sw Wilkes County between Yadkin River and Long Fork of Beaver Creek. Named for James Brown, eighteenth-century resident who lived at its foot. Alt. 2,075. Joins Jerry Mountain in ne Caldwell County.

Browns Siding. *See* Vaughn.

Brown's Sound, s Onslow County. Largely tidal marsh, it lies between Brown's Island and Onslow Beach and the mainland and extends from Bear Inlet to New River Inlet. It empties into the Atlantic Ocean through Bear Inlet, Brown's Inlet, and New River Inlet. Now within the limits of Camp Lejeune.

Brown's Store. *See* Locust Hill.

Browns Summit, community in n Guilford County. Alt. 805. Land here acquired by Jesse Brown, 1858. Named for him in 1863 when Richmond and Danville Railroad was built because the Brown farm was the highest point on the line.

Browns Swamp rises in e Cumberland County and flows se into Big Creek.

Browns Swamp rises in se Onslow County and flows sw into Turpentine Creek. Appears in local records as Brown's Creek as early as 1744.

Browns Turnout. *See* Vaughn.

Brownsville, community in ne Granville County on Grassy Creek. A post office as early as 1822.

Browntown, former town in ne Davidson County. Inc. 1843, at the junction of the Fayetteville to Salem and the Greensboro to Salisbury roads. A center of trade and furniture making until one of the roads was changed in 1859. The coming of the railroad brought a decline to the town and after the Civil War it was abandoned. Many of the people moved to what became High Point.

Browntown, community in s Greene County. Named for the fact that it was a community of mulattoes. Settled prior to 1890.

Bruce, community in w Pitt County. Cottendale, the plantation of the Cotten family (Sallie Southall C., Bruce Cotten, and others) is nearby.

Bruce Knob, n Buncombe County between Wolfpen Gap and Middle Mountain.

Bruce Knob, central Macon County between the head of Wallace Creek and Carson Cove.

Bruce Ridge, e Clay County between Glade Branch and Cold Spring Branch.

Bruce's Crossroads. *See* Summerfield.

Bruce Township, nw Guilford County named for Charles Bruce, early settler, Revolutionary soldier and founder of Bruce's Crossroad, now Summerfield.

Brumleys Creek rises in ne Caldwell County and flows se into Lower Creek approx. 3 mi. w of Lenoir.

Brummett Creek rises in w Mitchell County and flows sw into Toe River.

Brummett Creek, community in w Mitchell County. A post office existed here in the 1880's.

Brunswick, former town in se Brunswick County on Cape Fear River, now a State Historic Site. A museum contains artifacts and many building sites have been excavated. Settled about 1725 and inc. in 1745. Named for King George I, Duke of Brunswick and Lunenberg. First abandoned about 1776, but two or three families moved back after the Revolution. By

1830 the town was totally in ruins. During the Civil War Fort St. Philip (named for St. Philips Church here but also known as Fort Anderson) was constructed over a part of the site. Brunswick was the county seat 1764-79. Several colonial governors resided here.

Brunswick, town in central Columbus County. Inc. 1925.

Brunswick County was formed in 1764 from New Hanover and Bladen counties. In the se section of the state, it is bounded by the Atlantic Ocean, South Carolina, Columbus, Pender, and New Hanover counties, and Cape Fear River. Named for the town of Brunswick, *which see.* Area: 907 sq. mi. County seat in rural setting near Bolivia. Townships are Lockwood Folly, Northwest, Shallotte, Smithville, Town Creek, and Waccamaw. Produces corn, soybeans, oats, hogs, beef cattle, fishmeal, lumber, fertilizer, and processed sea food.

Brunswick River, ne Brunswick County, extends s from Cape Fear River along the w side of Eagles Island and empties into Cape Fear River. Approx. 5 mi. long. This undoubtedly is the Hilton's River discovered by William Hilton in 1663 and described by him in an account published the next year.

Brush Creek is formed in e Alleghany County by the waters of Laurel Branch, Little Pine, and Little Glade Creeks. It flows n into Little River.

Brush Creek rises in se Buncombe County near Bearwallow Mountain and flows nw into Cane Creek.

Brush Creek rises in w Chatham County and flows sw into Randolph County where it enters Deep River.

Brush Creek rises in nw Cherokee County and flows sw and se into Shuler Creek.

Brush Creek rises in w Guilford County and flows ne into Reedy Fork Creek.

Brush Creek rises in e Macon County and flows w into Cullasaja River.

Brush Creek rises in central Madison County and flows se into French Broad River.

Brush Creek rises in s Swain County and flows w into Little Tennessee River.

Brush Creek rises in ne Yancey County and flows n into Toe River.

Brushcreek, community in w Chatham County on Little Brush Creek.

Brush Creek Township, e Yancey County.

Brush Fence Ridge, on the Buncombe-Yancey County line between Point Misery and Balsam Gap.

Brush Fork rises in sw Ashe County and flows ne into North Fork New River.

Brush Fork Creek rises in central Anson County and flows s into Reedy Fork Creek.

Brush Mountain, w Randolph County.

Brush Mountain, nw Rockingham County by the Mayo River. Probably named form the fact that it is very rocky and supports little vegetation.

Brushy Branch rises in s Macon County and flows ne into Wayah Creek.

Brushy Branch rises in n Swain County and flows sw into Walker Creek.

Brushy Branch rises in n Transylvania County and flows ne into South Fork Mills River.

Brushy Creek rises in s Avery County and flows sw into North Toe River.

Brushy Creek rises in w Cleveland County and flows se into First Broad River.

Brushy Creek rises in central Forsyth County ne of the city of Winston-Salem near Smith Reynolds Airport, and flows s on the e side of Winston-Salem into Middle Fork.

Brushy Creek rises in s Mitchell County and flows nw into Crabtree Creek.

Brushy Creek rises in e Rutherford County and flows se into Cleveland County where it enters First Broad River.

Brushy Creek rises in central Transylvania County and flows se into Tucker Creek.

Brushy Face, mountain in se Macon County between Horseshoe Mountain and Sassafras Knob.

Brushy Fork rises in n Davidson County and flows s into Abbotts Creek.

Brushy Fork rises in central Watauga County and flows nw into Cove Creek.

Brushy Fork, community in w central Watauga County. Formerly known as Hagaman.

Brushy Fork Branch rises in ne Craven County and flows sw into Little Swift Creek.

Brushy Fork Branch rises in e central Forsyth County and flows s and sw into Salem Creek near the e limits of Winston-Salem.

Brushy Fork Creek rises in w Jackson County and flows ne into Greens Creek.

Brushy Fork Creek rises in w Stokes County and flows se into Town Fork Creek.

Brushy Fork Mountain, w Jackson County between Savannah Creek and Brushy Fork.

Brushy Fork Township, w central Watauga County.

Brushy Gap, ne Swain County in Great Smoky Mountains National Park on Shiltoskie Ridge.

Brushy Head Mountain, ne Cherokee County between Graybeard Creek and Valley River.

Brushy Knob, ne Buncombe County near the headwaters of Walker Branch.

Brushy Mountain, ne Buncombe County near Beetree Reservoir.

Brushy Mountain, se Buncombe County se of Dutchman Mountain.

Brushy Mountain, n Haywood County between Mount Sterling Creek and Dogwood Flats Creek. Alt. approx. 5,600.

Brushy Mountain, s Jackson County between Scotsman Creek and Fowler Creek.

Brushy Mountain, w Polk County, ne of town of Saluda.

Brushy Mountain extends se in w Transylvania County from Gloucester Gap to Tarkiln Branch.

Brushy Mountain. *See* Gilbreath.

Brushy Mountain, a low range extending across s Wilkes, n Alexander, and into e Caldwell County. Sometimes also described as crossing Yadkin and Surry counties, with isolated Pilot Mountain included as the e peak. Pore's Knob in Wilkes County, the highest peak, is 2,680 ft.; Hibriten Mountain in Caldwell County is 2,265. Shown on the 1755 ed. of the Fry-Jefferson map.

Brushy Mountain Township, s Wilkes County.

Brushy Ridge, central Buncombe County sw of Wolf Branch.

Brushy Ridge, ne Buncombe County between Sugar Fork and Laurel Branch.

Brushy Ridge, nw Burke County. Alt. 3,600.

Brushy Ridge extends ne between Bear Branch and Bad Fork in nw Henderson County.

Brushy Ridge, e Macon County between

Little Salt Rock Creek and the head of Wildcat Creek.

Brushy Ridge, s Macon County between Rock Branch and Falls Branch.

Brushy Ridge, w Madison County between Maple Spring Branch and Meadow Fork.

Brushy Ridge, se Polk County on the South Carolina line.

Brushy Ridge Branch rises in w Transylvania County and flows sw into Cathey's Creek.

Bryan, community in e Pitt County.

Bryan Creek rises in central Pitt County and flows se into Tar River.

Bryant Branch rises in n Davie County near Pino and flows se approx. 4 mi. into Dutchmans Creek. Named for the Bryant family which settled in the area prior to 1752.

Bryant Mountain, sw Cherokee County between Wolf Creek and Hothouse Branch.

Bryant Mountain, central Watauga County n of Howard Creek.

Bryantown, community in s Northampton County.

Bryan Township, w Surry County.

Bryants Pond, nw Bladen County on Reedy Meadow Creek and Black Swamp. Formed by a dam built about 1860 to create a millpond. Fishing, swimming, and boating.

Bryant Swamp rises in Big Bay in sw Bladen County and flows w into Robeson County where it enters Big Swamp.

Bryson Branch rises in ne Cherokee County and flows se into Morris Creek.

Bryson Branch rises in ne Cherokee County and flows sw into Valley River.

Bryson Branch rises in s Jackson County and flows se one mi. to empty into Scotsman Creek.

Bryson Branch rises in e Macon County and flows ne into Cullasaja River.

Bryson Branch rises in e Macon County and flows se into Joe Creek.

Bryson Branch rises in w Macon County w of Panther Knob and flows sw into Nantahala River.

Bryson Branch rises in central Swain County and flows se through Bryson City into Tuckasegee River.

Bryson City, town and county seat in central Swain County on Tuckasegee River. Alt. 1,736. Inc. 1887 as Charleston. Name changed to Bryson City in 1889 by act of General Assembly; named in honor of Capt. Thaddeus Dillard Bryson (1829-

90), one of the founders of the town of Charleston.

Bryson Cove, on a tributary of Cowee Creek in n Macon County.

Bryson Creek rises in e Translyvania County and flows se into w Henderson County where it enters French Broad River.

Bryson Knob, e Macon County between Mashburn Branch and Cullasaja River.

Bryson Lead, nw Cherokee County, parallel to Shular Creek and nw of Chestnut Orchard Ridge, Nin Ridge, and Groundhog Ridge.

Bryson Mountain, n Henderson County between Sitton Creek and Foster Creek.

Bubble Branch rises in w Jackson County and flows se into West Fork Tuckasegee River.

Bubbling Springs Branch rises in s Haywood County and flows n into West Fork Pigeon River.

Buby Gap, on the Jackson-Macon County line.

Buchanan Branch rises in sw Clay County and flows sw into Brasstown Creek.

Buchanan Falls on Pee Dee River on the Anson-Richmond County line about 1½ mi. n of the South Carolina line.

Buchanan Ferry. *See* Diggs Ferry.

Buchanan Hollow, e Mitchell County between Mine Hill and Sandy Branch.

Buchanan's Pond, nw Scotland County on a tributary of Gum Swamp Creek. Formed in 1950 and named for owner, D. M. Buchanan. Covers 23 acres; maximum depth 12 ft. Fishing, swimming, boating.

Buck, community in s Wilkes County near Millers Creek.

Buck Branch rises in e Duplin County and flows sw into Little Limestone Creek.

Buck Branch rises in s Durham County and flows sw into Burden Creek.

Buck Branch rises in w Edgecombe County and flows ne into Tar River.

Buck Branch rises in s central Rutherford County nw of Forest City and flows ne into Second Broad River.

Buck Branch rises in s Wake County and flows s into Swift Creek.

Buck Branch rises in central Wilson County and flows approx. 3 mi. s into Toisnot Swamp, *which see.* Known as Buckhorn Branch as early as 1754.

Buck Cove, e Haywood County on the head of Thickety Creek.

Buck Cove Mountain, e Haywood County between Buck Cove and Rice Cove.

Buck Creek rises in north central Carteret County and flows w into South River.

Buck Creek rises in se Clay County and flows nw and ne into Nantahala River.

Buck Creek, a tidal marsh creek in s Hyde County, flows sw into Juniper Bay.

Buck Creek rises in w McDowell County and flows se into Catawba River. Buck Creek Falls are on this stream near its head.

Buck Creek rises in e Macon County and flows nw into Cullasaja River.

Buck Creek. *See* Back Creek.

Buck Creek. *See* McLendons Creek.

Buck Creek Falls. *See* Buck Creek.

Buck Creek Gap on the McDowell-Yancey County line between Horse Trail Gap and Hazlenut Gap. Alt. approx. 3,200.

Buckeye Branch rises in e Haywood County and flows se into Bald Creek.

Buckeye Branch rises in ne Swain County and flows se into Raven Fork.

Buckeye Cove, ne Buncombe County on the w side of North Fork [Swannanoa River].

Buckeye Cove, s Buncombe County s of Potato Knob.

Buckeye Cove on the Cherokee County, N. C.-Polk County, Tenn., line between Rocky Ford and Potato creeks.

Buckeye Cove, e Haywood County on the head of Cove Creek.

Buckeye Cove, e Haywood County on the head of Murray Branch.

Buckeye Cove, nw Haywood County on the head of Big Creek.

Buckeye Cove Creek rises in ne Buncombe County and flows nw into North Fork Ivy Creek.

Buckeye Creek rises at Buckeye Spring on the Avery-Watauga County line and flows nw and n into Beech Creek.

Buckeye Creek rises in s Haywood County and flows nw to join Haywood Gap Stream in forming Middle Prong [West Fork Pigeon River].

Buckeye Creek rises in s Macon County and flows sw into Tessentee Creek.

Buckeye Gap, on the Avery-Mitchell County line.

Buckeye Gap, on the Haywood-Jackson County line.

Buckeye Gap on Swain County, N. C.-Sevier County, Tenn., line, in Great Smoky Mountains National Park near lat. 35° 34' 43" N., long. 83° 36' 05" W.

Buckeye Gap, central Watauga County s of Norris Branch.

Buckeye Knob, e Haywood County between the head of Bald Creek and the head of Cove Creek.

Buckeye Knob, central Watauga County on the w slope of Rich Mountain.

Buckeye Knob, n Watauga County between the forks of Fork Ridge.

Buckeye Mountain, a peak in the Swannanoa Mountains, s Buncombe County between Cedar Cliff and Face Rock.

Buckeye Ridge, w Madison County between Max Patch Mountain and Roaring Fork Mountain.

Buckeye Spring, on the Avery-Watauga County line. Source of Buckeye Creek.

Buck Forest, mountain, e Transylvania County between Laurel and Tom creeks.

Buck Gap, on the Buncombe-McDowell County line, s of Sourwood Gap.

Buck Gap, on the Jackson-Macon County line. Alt. 3,950.

Buck Gap, s Macon County between Wolf Gap and the head of Evans Creek.

Buck Gap, on Swain County, N. C.-Blount County, Tenn. line in Great Smoky Mountains National Park near lat. 35° 32' 03" N., long. 83° 49' 20" W.

Buckhead Creek rises in central Cumberland County and flows s into Little Rockfish Creek.

Buckhead Swamp rises in se Bladen County and flows s into Columbus County, where it enters Slap Swamp.

Buck Hill, mountain peak in sw Avery County.

Buckhill Branch rises in w Duplin County and flows sw into Buster Hall Branch.

Buck Hill Gap, w Avery County.

Buck Hollow Mountain, ne Rutherford County at the head of Duncans Creek.

Buckhorn, community in w Orange County.

Buckhorn. *See* Como.

Buckhorn Bald, n Swain County in Great Smoky Mountains National Park on Forney Ridge, Alt. 4,829.

Buckhorn Branch rises in ne Cherokee County in Swag Cove on Buckhorn Ridge and flows nw into Vengeance Creek.

Buckhorn Branch rises in se Granville County and flows s into Wake County where it enters New Light Creek. Approx. 4 mi. long.

Buckhorn Branch rises in se Orange County and flows se into Bolin Creek.

Buckhorn Branch rises in n Swain County and flows w into Forney Creek.

Buckhorn Branch rises in w Wilson County and flows n into Contentnea Creek.

Buckhorn Branch. *See* Buck Branch.

Buckhorn Creek rises in nw Cherokee County and flows sw into Copper Creek.

Buckhorn Creek rises in sw Gates County and flows se into Chowan River.

Buckhorn Creek rises in n Hertford County and flows e into Chowan River.

Buckhorn Creek rises in e Transylvania County and flows s into Little River.

Buckhorn Creek rises in sw Wake County and flows sw into se Chatham County where it enters Buckhorn Lake on the Cape Fear River.

Buckhorn Crossroads, community in w Wilson County south of Contentnea Creek and w of Buckhorn Branch.

Buckhorn Falls, in Cape Fear River at the junction of Chatham, Harnett, and Lee counties. Mentioned as early as 1819 in a survey of the major rivers of North Carolina. Since 1908 the site of a power generating plant of Carolina Power and Light Co. Navigation locks built here as early as 1805; iron ore mined nearby during the Civil War.

Buckhorn Gap, se Macon County.

Buckhorn Gap, n Transylvania County between the head of Avery Creek and Rich Mountain.

Buckhorn Iron Furnace. *See* Cokesbury.

Buckhorn Knob, n Caldwell County. Named by Bryson Coffey about 1870 for a big pair of antlers which he found there. Alt. approx. 1,500.

Buckhorn Lake, se Chatham and ne Lee counties on Cape Fear River. Formed by a dam constructed in 1907, the lake covers 400 acres with a max. depth of 21 ft. Used to generate hydroelectric power.

Buckhorn Mountain, s Macon County between Buckhorn Gap and Cullasaja River.

Buckhorn Ridge, ne Cherokee County in the Valley River Mountains.

Buckhorn Ridge, e Swain County between First Hurricane Branch and Second Hurricane Branch.

Buckhorn Swamp rises in ne Robeson County and flows se into Gallberry Swamp.

Buckhorn Township, nw Harnett County.

Buckhorn Township, sw Wake County.

Buckingham Mountain, sw Alamance County.

Buck Island, a tidal marsh island, about one-half mile square, in North River, sw Currituck County.

Buck Island is a raised area of land surrounded by swamp in Mon Swamp in se Tyrrell County.

Buck Knob, central Cherokee County between Hiwassee River and West Prong Grape Creek. Alt. 2,584.

Buck Knob, w Cherokee County between Shular Creek and Caney Branch.

Buck Knob between Wayehutta Creek and Cane Creek in n Jackson County.

Buck Knob, s Jackson County on the head of Frolictown Creek.

Buck Knob, w Jackson County on the head of Little Pine Creek.

Buck Knob, w Jackson County between Wilson Creek and Tilley Creek.

Buck Knob, w Haywood County, Great Smoky Mountains National Park, near lat. 35° 33′ N., long. 83° 08′ 12″ W.

Buck Knob, on Laurel Creek in w Henderson County.

Buck Knob, sw Macon County at the head of Allison Creek.

Buckland, community in n central Gates County. Alt. 32. Settled prior to 1711. Named for home of Cole family in Virginia.

Buckland Mill Branch rises in n Gates County and flows sw where it joins Hacklan Branch to form Cole Creek. Formerly known as Knotty Pine Creek.

Buckleberry Pocosin, se Bertie County.

Buckle Creek rises in sw Bladen County and flows se into Pender County where it enters Lyon Creek.

Bucklesberry Pocosin, nw Lenoir County. Mentioned in local records as early as 1780. Camp Blackjack (named for the blackoak, commonly called blackjack oak), a Civil War training camp on the railroad near La Grange, was in this vicinity.

Buckle Swamp rises in se Bladen County and flows se into Pender County where it enters Lyon Creek.

Buck Marsh rises in se Wayne County and flows se into Duplin County where it enters Buck Run.

Buck Mountain, w Haywood County between Fie Creek and Evans Creek.

Buck Mountain, w Lee County. Several very rocky hills, one of which is quite steep, in an area of 3 or 4 acres.

Buck Mountain, w Macon County between Wayah Creek and Camp Branch.

Buck Mountain, w Montgomery County between Cedar Creek and Bundle Mountain.

Buck Mountain, sw Polk County between Pacolet River and Cove Creek.

Buck Mountain, n Surry County between Fulcher Mountain and Round Peak Mountain.

Buck Mountain in sw Transylvania County extends se between the headwaters of Thompson River and Whitewater River.

Buckner, community in e Madison County on Middle Fork. Alt. 2,400. Named for pioneer settler.

Buckner. See Colon.

Buckner Branch rises in n Buncombe County near Wildcat Mountain and flows nw into Ivy Creek.

Buckner Branch rises in e central Madison County and flows nw into Big Laurel Creek.

Buckner Branch rises in s central Swain County and flows ne into Tuckasegee River 1½ mi. w of Bryson City.

Buckner's Knob. See Craggy Pinnacle.

Buck Quarter Creek rises in ne Orange County and flows s into Eno River. It is mentioned in land grants as early as 1750. Sometimes called Buck Water Creek.

Buck Ridge, n Avery County.

Buck Ridge, sw Avery County.

Buck Ridge, se Buncombe County between Rocky Fork and Ellison Branch.

Buck Ridge n Haywood County on Chestnut Branch.

Buck Ridge, e Mitchell County between Gouges Creek and Jackson Branch.

Buck Ridge, s Watauga County, extends se from Sawpit Branch parallel to Days Creek.

Buck Ridge, ne Yancey County between Green Mountain and Brush Creek.

Buck Run rises in ne Duplin County and flows sw into Northeast Cape Fear River.

Bucks Corner, community in w Carteret County n of Pettiver's Creek.

Buck Shoal, in French Broad River in n Henderson County. Named because deer formerly fed on moss growing here. Bill Nye (1850-96), American humorist, lived here from about 1880 until his death.

Buck Shoals, community in sw Yadkin County on North Hunting Creek. Named for the herds of deer which once gathered in the shoals of the creek.

Buck Shoals Township, sw Yadkin County.

Buckskin Branch rises in central Duplin County and flows se into Grove Creek.

Bucks Knob, e Madison County near the head of East Fork [Bull Creek].

Bucks Peak, se Alleghany County and ne Wilkes County. Appears on maps also as Buck Mountain and State Highway maps as Beech Mountain.

Buck Spring, e Haywood County, springs

forming in part the headwaters of Pisgah Creek.

Buck Spring, ne Warren County between Hubquarter Creek and Stonehouse Creek. Formerly the plantation of Nathaniel Macon (1758-1837), Member of Congress (1791-1828) and Speaker of the U.S. House of Representatives. The farm community in this area bore this name when a post office was established here in 1901. The plantation buildings have been purchased by Warren County.

Buck Spring Gap, on the Haywood-Transylvania County line on Pisgah Ridge just s of Little Pisgah Mountain at the head of Pisgah Creek. Alt. 4,980.

Buck Swamp rises in s Wayne County and flows nw into Thoroughfare Swamp.

Buck Swamp Township, nw Wayne County.

Buck Water Creek. *See* Buck Quarter Creek.

Buck Water Mountain, e Macon County between Little Buck Creek and Katie Creek.

Buckwheat Knob, n Transylvania County on the head of Avery Creek.

Buddy Gap, s Macon County between Coweeta Creek and Little Tennessee River.

Budget Falls, in Yadkin River in se Surry County, w of the junction of Ararat River. Mentioned as early as 1819 in a survey of the rivers of North Carolina.

Bud Lowe Gap, s Wilkes County near the head of Rocky Creek.

Bud Ridge, s Buncombe County e of Billy Cove.

Buena Vista, community in n central Bertie County.

Buena Vista, community in s Buncombe County e of Biltmore Forest. Inc. 1891; charter repealed 1903.

Buena Vista, sw Warren County near the Franklin County line, was formerly the home, office, and tavern of Dr. Robert Christian Pritchard. The main house built in 1848 is now in poor condition. *See also* Bearpond.

Buffalo, community in ne Cherokee County at the mouth of Gipps Creek.

Buffalo, community in ne Stokes County near the head of Buffalo Creek.

Buffalo Branch rises in w Johnston County and flows s into Middle Creek.

Buffalo City, community on the mainland, w Dare County. Settled 1888. Named for Buffalo City Mills, former sawmill here. Alt. 10.

Buffalo Cove, community in n Caldwell County. Named for the cove in which many buffalo were killed. Settled late eighteenth century.

Buffalo Branch rises in w Warren County and flows s into Shocco Creek. Mentioned in local records as early as 1764.

Buffalo Creek rises in nw Anson County and flows e into Pee Dee River.

Buffalo Creek rises near Bluff Mountain in se Ashe County and flows ne into North Fork New River.

Buffalo Creek rises in n Caldwell County and flows s into Yadkin River.

Buffalo Creek rises in n Cleveland County and flows sw through Cleveland County into South Carolina where it enters Broad River.

Buffalo Creek rises in nw Cleveland County and flows sw into Rutherford County where it enters Brier Creek.

Buffalo Creek rises in ne Davie County and flows sw approx. 3 mi. into Dutchman Creek about 4 mi. from its mouth in the Horseshoe of Yadkin River.

Buffalo Creek rises in n Forsyth County and flows ne into s Stokes County where it enters Town Fork Creek.

Buffalo Creek rises in central Franklin County and flows sw into Tar River.

Buffalo Creek rises in nw Franklin County and flows ne into Tar River.

Buffalo Creek rises in n Franklin County and flows se into Sandy Creek.

Buffalo Creek, formed by the junction of North Buffalo Creek and South Buffalo Creek in ne Guilford County. It flows ne into Reedy Fork Creek. Named after 1755 but before 1758.

Buffalo Creek rises in sw Harnett County and flows s into e Moore County (formerly Hoke County) where it enters Little River.

Buffalo Creek rises in w Hoke County and flows sw into Lumber River.

Buffalo Creek rises in w Moore County and flows ne into Deep River.

Buffalo Creek rises in ne Orange County and flows se into Durham County where it enters North Fork Little River.

Buffalo Creek rises in n Richmond County and flows sw into Little River.

Buffalo Creek rises in n Rockingham County and flows se into Dan River.

Buffalo Creek rises in nw Rutherford County and flows s into Broad River.

Buffalo Creek rises in ne Stokes County and flows ne into Rockingham County where it enters Mayo River.

Buffalo Creek rises in s Union County and

flows sw into South Carolina where it enters Lynches Creek.

Buffalo Creek rises in s Vance County and flows s into Tar River. Water-ground corn meal is produced commercially on this creek.

Buffalo Creek rises in e Wake County and flows se into Johnston County where it enters Little River.

Buffalo Branch rises in s Wake County and flows s into w Johnston County where it enters Middle Creek.

Buffalo Creek rises in s Warren County and flows s into Fishing Creek.

Buffalo Creek rises in s Watauga County and flows se into Caldwell County.

Buffalo Creek. *See* Back Creek.

Buffalo Creek. *See* Irish Buffalo Creek.

Buffalo Creek (town). *See* Warrensville.

Buffalo Island, swampy land formation on Potecasi Creek in central Hertford County.

Buffalo Knob, a stony elevation on the Cleveland-Lincoln County line.

Buffalo Lake, w Harnett County on the headwaters of Reedys Swamp. Approx. ½ mi. long. Alt. 293.

Buffalo Race Path. *See* Bute County.

Buffalo Shoals Creek rises in w Iredell County and flows s into Catawba River.

Buff Creek rises in n Jackson County and flows s into Scott Creek.

Buffeys Branch rises in s Transylvania County and flows sw into East Fork French Broad River.

Buford. *See* Canton.

Buford Township, s central Union County.

Buggs Island Lake. *See* Kerr Reservoir.

Bug Hill, community in se Columbus County.

Bug Hill Township, se Columbus County.

Buie, community in n Robeson County. Inc. 1909. Charter repealed, 1947, though previously long inactive in municipal affairs. Railroad name is Buies.

Buies. *See* Buie.

Buies Creek rises in ne Harnett County and flows sw into Cape Fear River. Known as Archie Buie's Creek on early maps of the region.

Buies Creek, community in e central Harnett County. Settled in the latter part of the nineteenth century. Inc. 1903; charter repealed 1967. Campbell College is here. Alt. 210.

Buies Falls, rapids in Cape Fear River in central Harnett County at the junction of Buies Creek with the river. Called Bowies

Falls by Hamilton Fulton in his 1819 survey of the rivers of North Carolina.

Buies Pond, n Robeson County on a branch of Richland Swamp. Covers approx. 150 acres with a max. depth of 10 to 12 ft.

Buladean, community in n Mitchell County on Big Rock Creek. Known first as Magnetic City for its location near large deposits of magnetic iron ore. Present name said to have been the name of the daughter of the first postmaster, Beulah Dean.

Bull Bay, nw Tyrrell County and ne Washington County, formed by the Scuppernong River estuary in Albemarle Sound. Surface area approx, 10,000 acres; max. depth, 14 ft.

Bull Branch rises in ne Bertie County and flows sw into Chinkapin Swamp.

Bull Branch rises in ne Burke County and flows sw into Linville River.

Bull Branch rises in w Robeson County and flows s into Little Pee Dee River.

Bull Branch is formed in ne Pender County by the junction of Bullhead Branch and Bull Tail Branch. It flows se into Moores Creek.

Bull Branch rises in e Union County and flows nw into Richardson Creek.

Bull Branch. *See* Millers Creek.

Bull Cove, se Clay County between Bear Pen and Fairfield ridges.

Bull Cove, sw Macon County on a tributary of Big Indian Creek.

Bull Creek rises in n Buncombe County near Bull Mountain and flows s into Swannanoa River. The last buffalo seen in the county was killed by the first white settler in this vicinity, Joseph Rice.

Bull Creek is formed in s Madison County by the junction of East Fork and West Fork and flows s into Ivy River.

Bull Creek rises in ne Washington County and flows ne into Bull Bay.

Bull Creek Township, former township in s central Madison County, now township number 3.

Bull Creek Gap, n Madison County between Big Laurel Creek and the head of West Fork [Bull Creek].

Bulldie Creek rises in ne Swain County and flows se into Raven Fork.

Bulldie Ridge, ne Swain County in Great Smoky Mountains National Park, a spur extending ne from Katalsta Ridge.

Bullfrog Creek rises in central Currituck County in Great Swamp and flows s into North River.

Bull Gap, n Buncombe County at the w end of Bull Mountain. Alt. 3,177.

Bullhead, community in w Greene County s of Nahunta Swamp near the Wayne County line. Settled as early as 1769. During the Revolution, as British soldiers approached, a ferocious bull was turned loose to frighten them. Soldiers, however, killed the bull, cut off his head, and placed it on a fence post.

Bullhead Branch rises in ne Pender County and flows s to join Bull Tail Branch in forming Bull Branch.

Bullhead Creek rises in s Alleghany County and flows s into Wilkes County where it enters East Prong Roaring River.

Bullhead Gap, ne Buncombe County between Craggy Dome and Bullhead Mountain.

Bullhead Mountain, ne Buncombe County in the Great Craggy Mountains. Named for its resemblance to a bull's head. Alt. 5,958.

Bullhead Mountain, se Alleghany County near Blue Ridge Parkway. Alt. 3,784-3,800.

Bullhead Ridge, ne Buncombe County between Waterfall and Peach Orchard creeks.

Bull Head Township, nw Greene County.

Bull Hill, community in sw Northampton County.

Bull Hill Mill Pond, sw Northampton County on Wheeler Creek. Covers approx. 400 acres; max. depth 12 ft. Partly a natural lake but enlarged by a dam on the creek. Originally known as Lake Witheranna.

Bullin Creek. See Britten Creek.

Bullinger's Mill Creek. See Briston's Mill Creek.

Bullinger Mountain, e Caldwell County. Alt. 1,595. Probably named for Henry Bullinger, eighteenth-century settler.

Bull Mountain, n Buncombe County between Lane Pinnacle and Bull Gap. See also Lane Pinnacle.

Bull Mountain, s Watauga County s of Sims Creek and e of Laurel Creek.

Bullock, community in ne Granville County. Settled about 1750. Alt. 429.

Bullpen Cove, se Haywood County on East Fork Pigeon River.

Bull Point, ne Washington County, extends into Bull Bay from the n shore of Bull Creek estuary.

Bull Pocosin, n Sampson County bounded on the s by Goshen Swamp, on the w by Ward Swamp and Craddock Swamp, and on the n by Kill Swamp.

Bull Ruffin Mountain, se Watauga County. Alt. approx. 4,100.

Bull Run Creek rises in s Guilford County and flows sw into East Prong Deep River.

Bull Run Creek rises in e central Surry County and flows se into Ararat River.

Bull's Bay, community in nw Tyrrell County. Called Bay when a post office was here. It is on Bull Bay.

Bullscrape Gap, central Avery County. Alt. 3,882. A salt lick here once attracted cattle; bulls scraped the ground with hooves, pawing before charging one another in combat. See also Montezuma.

Bull Tail Branch rises in ne Pender County and flows s to join Bullhead Branch in forming Bull Branch.

Bulltail Swamp rises in se Sampson County and flows se into Duplin County where it enters Doctors Creek.

Bumgardner Branch rises in n Swain County and flows sw into Deep Creek.

Bumgardner Ridge, n Swain County in Great Smoky Mountains National Park, a spur extending sw from Sunkota Ridge.

Bumgarner Branch rises in n Jackson County approx. 2 mi. se of Sylva and flows sw 1½ mi. into Mill Creek.

Bumgarner Gap, n Wilkes County between North Fork Reddies River and Burke Mountain. Named for Daniel Bumgarner, early nineteenth-century resident.

Bumgartner Mountain, peak in South Mountains on Burke-Rutherford County line.

Bumplanding Creek rises in sw Currituck County and flows w into North River.

Buna Ridge, e Madison County parallel to Holland Branch.

Bunches Bald, on the Jackson-Swain County line near the head of Madcap Branch.

Bunches Creek rises in ne Swain County in Great Smoky Mountains National Park and flows s, w, and nw into Raven Fork.

Buncombe County was formed in 1791 from Burke and Rutherford counties. Located in the w section of the state, it is bounded by McDowell, Henderson, Haywood, Madison, and Yancey counties. Named for Colonel Edward Buncombe (1742-78), a Revolutionary soldier. Area: 770 sq. mi. County seat: Asheville with an elevation of 2,216 ft. Townships are Asheville, Avery Creek, Black Mountain, Broad River, Fairview, Flat Creek, French Broad, Ivy, Leicester, Limestone, Lower Hominy, Reems Creek, Sandy Mush, Swannanoa, Upper Hominy. Produces tobacco, corn, apples, dairy livestock, broilers, hosiery, glass products, dairy products, apparel, electronics, baby foods, textiles, furniture, lumber, and crushed stone.

Buncombe Hall, the home of Col. Edward Buncombe of the Continental line, who was captured at Germantown and died a prisoner in 1778. Stood one mile w of Roper, nw Washington County.

Buncombe Horse Range Ridge, s Yancey County between South Fork Upper Creek and Right Prong South Toe River.

Bundle Mountain, n Montgomery County between Buck Mountain and Morris Mountain.

Bunn, town in s Franklin County. Alt. 295. Settled about 1909, inc. 1913. Named for Green Bunn, local resident.

Bunnlevel, community in s Harnett County. Est. in 1904 or 1905 around railroad depot. Originally called Bunn's Level after a local resident's flat plot of land. Inc. 1921 as "Bunlevel," but recently inactive in municipal affairs. Authorized by General Assembly in 1961 to est. municipal government if approved by vote but this was defeated.

Bunton Creek. See Banton Creek.

Bunton Island lies off the sw shore of Roanoke Island, e Dare County, in the waters of Croatan Sound.

Bunyan, community in w Beaufort County. Alt. 14. A post office was est. here prior to 1882.

Burch, community in s Surry County. Alt. 881. A former post office here was named Rusk.

Burden, community in nw Bertie County.

Burden Creek rises in s Durham County and flows sw into Northeast Creek.

Burden Branch rises in w Wayne County and flows sw into Moccasin Swamp.

Burdett, community in ne Mecklenburg County.

Burd Gap, sw Macon County at the head of Anderson Branch.

Burgaw, town and county seat, central Pender County. When the county was formed in 1875 it was directed that the place chosen as a county seat should be named Cowan, but an act of 1877 directed that it should be named Stanford. Burgaw was chosen and an act of the General Assembly of 1879 changed the name of "Stanford" to Burgaw and inc. the town. Burgaw appears on maps as early as 1861. See Burgaw Creek for early uses of the name. Alt. 49.

Burgaw Creek rises in s Graham County and flows ne into Long Creek.

Burgaw Creek rises in central Pender County ne of the town of Burgaw and flows se into Northeast Cape Fear River. Appears on the Collet map, 1770, as Bargaw Creek, and on the Mouzon map, 1775, as Bergaw Creek. Burgaw Plantation in the vicinity appears in records of 1764.

Burgaw Savannah. See Big Savannah.

Burgaw Township, central Pender County.

Burger Mountain, w Cherokee County between Shoal Creek and Apalachia Lake.

Burgess, community in n side of Harveys Neck in s Perquimans County.

Burgin Cove, se Buncombe County between Black Mountain and Ridgecrest.

Burgin Cove Branch rises in se Yancey County and flows nw into Three Forks Creek.

Burgoin Gap, e Macon County between Rough Knob and Moses Branch.

Burke County was formed in 1777 from Rowan County. Located in the w central section of the state, it is bounded by Catawba, Cleveland, Rutherford, McDowell, Avery, and Caldwell counties. It was named for Dr Thomas Burke (1747-83), member of the Continental Congress and governor of North Carolina. Area: 517 sq. mi. County seat: Morganton with an elevation of 1,182 ft. Townships are Drexel, Icard, Jonas Ridge, Linville, Lovelady, Lower Creek, Lower Fork, Morganton, Quaker Meadow, Silver Creek, Smoky Creek, Upper Creek, and Upper Fork. Produces corn, soybeans, oats, wheat, poultry, dairy products, hosiery, apparel, textiles, furniture, sand, gravel, and mica.

Burkemont, mountain peak in the South Mountains of s Burke County.

Burkemont, community in s Burke County near the headwaters of Bailey's Fork.

Burke Mountain, n Wilkes County extending n between North Fork Reddies River and Mulberry Creek. Probably named for James Burke (died 1776), pioneer settler.

Burkes Creek rises in s Caswell County and flows ne into Pinson Creek.

Burl Branch rises in e Cherokee County and flows s and se into Peachtree Creek.

Burleson Bald, sw Avery County.

Burleson Branch rises in ne Buncombe County and flows sw into North Fork Ivy Creek.

Burleson Branch rises in central Yancey County and flows n into Cane River.

Burlington, city in central Alamance County. About 1851 the North Carolina Railroad built its repair shops here and the name Company Shops was applied to the community until 1887 when a list of names suggested by local citizens was referred to a committee for decision. Burlington is said to have been suggested by Katherine Scales, daughter of the governor. Burlington was inc. 1893. Railroad shops moved to Spencer in 1896. A Civil War training camp was est. at Company Shops. Alt. 658. Produces textiles, hosiery, electronics, and paper boxes.

Burlington Crossroads, community in s Hoke County.

Burlington Township, former township in central Alamance County, now township number 12

Burl Mountain, w Henderson County between French Broad River and Johnsons Mill Creek.

Burl Mountain, n central Transylvania County between King Creek and Southern Mountain.

Burnett Bear Pen Ridge, s Yancey County near the head of Big Lost Cove Creek.

Burnett Cove, e Haywood County on Burnett Creek.

Burnett Creek rises in e Haywood County and flows nw into East Fork Pigeon River.

Burnett Reservoir, ne Buncombe County on North Fork [Swannanoa River] w of Walkertown. A part of the Asheville water system.

Burnett Siding, community in s Haywood County on West Fork Pigeon River.

Burney, community in nw Bladen County.

Burney Mountain, on the Buncombe-Henderson County line.

Burningtown, community in central Macon County on Burningtown Creek.

Burningtown Bald, n Macon County between Copper Bald and Burningtown Gap. Alt. 5,115.

Burningtown Creek rises in w Macon County and flows ne and nw into Little Tennessee River.

Burningtown Falls, in Downes Branch in central Macon County.

Burningtown Gap, n Macon County at the head of Burningtown Creek. Alt. approx. 3,700.

Burningtown Township, n central Macon County.

Burns Creek rises in w Henderson County and flows se into French Broad River.

Burns Gap, sw Cherokee County near the headwaters of Shoal Creek.

Burns Mountain, central Mitchell County between Bandana Hollow and Snow Creek. Appears as Burns Mountain on maps but is known locally as Burnt Mountain.

Burnsville, community in nw Anson County. Area setled by 1753; known as Burnsville by 1836. Probably named for Walter Burns who operated an early tavern here.

Burnsville, town and county seat, central Yancey County. Alt. 2,817. Est. 1833 at the creation of the county. Named for Otway Burns (1775-1850), privateer of the War of 1812 and later member of the General Assembly. Although he was an easterner he supported the political ambitions of the westerners around the time Yancey County was created. Burnsville was chartered in 1857 but repealed in 1921; rechartered 1922. Produces hosiery, carpets, textiles, and minerals.

Burnsville Township, nw Anson County.

Burnsville Township, central Yancey County.

Burnt Branch rises in ne Cherokee County and flows nw into Valley River.

Burntcabin Creek rises in e Clay County and flows s into Shooting Creek.

Burnt Cabin Gap in se Jackson County between Panthertown Creek and Little Hogback Mountain.

Burnt Chimney. *See* Forest City.

Burnt Coat Branch rises in ne Duplin County and flows sw into Northeast Cape Fear River.

Burnt Coat Swamp rises in w central Halifax County and flows sw into Beech Swamp. Appears on the Collet map, 1770.

Burnt Mill Creek rises in Bear Swamp, se Chowan County, and flows se on the Chowan-Perquimans County line into Yeopim River. The Collet map, 1770, shows Mingo Mill on the headwaters of Yeopim River; the present name appears in local records as early as 1800.

Burnt Mills, community in n central Camden County. Tradition says watermills were destroyed by fire in the vicinity, hence the name. Last mill there discontinued about 1910, but water still flows down the mill race.

Burnt Mountain, e Transylvania County on the head of McCrary Branch.

Burnt Mountain. See Burns Mountain.

Burnt Ordinary, formerly an inn on the post road in what is now n central Warren County, about ¾ mi. ne of the present town of Macon. Appears on the Collet map, 1770. The correct name for the inn is thought to have been Burnet Ordinary.

Burnt Pocosin, n Sampson County between Little Coharie Creek and Sevenmile Swamp.

Burnt Ridge, e Yancey County between the head of Browns Creek and the head of Shuford Creek.

Burnt Rock Ridge follows the course of Sassafras Creek in sw Graham County.

Burnt Shanty Branch rises in ne Cherokee County and flows s into Valley River.

Burntshirt Mountain, ne Henderson County.

Burnt Shop. See Melville.

Burnt Spruce Ridge, n Swain County in Great Smoky Mountains National Park, a short spur extending se from Noland Ridge near lat. 35° 32' 30" N., long. 83° 26' 20" W.

Burnt Stocking Branch rises in e Johnston County and flows se into Little Creek. Mentioned in local records as early as 1779.

Burnt Swamp rises in w Robeson County and flows se into Richland Swamp.

Burnt Swamp Township, central Robeson County.

Burnt Tavern. See Clarksville.

Burnt Timber Branch rises in e central Avery County and flows s into Wilson Creek.

Burris Creek rises in w Surry County and flows e and ne into Fisher River.

Burr Mountain, n Buncombe County between Dillingham Creek and North Fork Ivy Creek.

Burrtown. See Erwinsville.

Bursted Rock Creek rises in s Transylvania County and flows nw into East Fork French Broad River.

Burt, community in sw Wake County.

Burthen Channel flows through a mass of tidal marsh island in the extreme w end of Bogue Sound in sw Carteret County. Probably originally known as Borden Channel for William Borden who owned the neighboring section of Bogue Banks and a plantation on the mainland. The local pronounciation of Borden is Burden and from Burden the name Burthen derived.

Burton, community in e Durham County. Alt. 300.

Burton Creek rises in e Pamlico County and flows s into Broad Creek.

Busbee, community in s Buncombe County. Named for the nearby mountain.

Busbee Mountain, s Buncombe County near the headwaters of Robinson Creek. Named for one Busby, Indian fighter and hunter, whose cabin was on its slopes.

Bush Arbor, community in s Caswell County.

Bush Creek rises in s Avery County and flows sw into North Toe River.

Bush Creek rises in ne Chatham County and flows ne into Overcup Creek.

Bush Creek rises in e Lee County and flows ne into Cape Fear River.

Bush Creek rises in n Randolph County and flows sw into Deep River.

Bush Hill. See Archdale.

Bushnell, former town in w Swain County on Tuckasegee River. Inc. 1913. Site now under the backwaters of Fontana Lake.

Bushy Fork rises in sw Person County and flows ne into South Flat River.

Bushy Fork, community in sw Person County.

Bushy Fork Township, sw Person County.

Bushy Ridge w Jackson County between Hog Cove Branch and Sassafras Branch.

Busick, community in ne Guilford County. Alt. approx. 850.

Busick, community in se Yancey County on Three Forks Creek. Post office serving the community in the late nineteenth century was named Three Forks.

Bussels Creek rises in s Wilkes County and flows ne into Hunting Creek.

Buster Hall Branch rises in w Duplin County and flows s into Stewarts Creek.

Bute County, formed from Granville County in 1764; named in honor of John Stuart

(1713-92), Earl of Bute, who until his resignation in 1763 had been First Lord of the Treasury. The county was divided in 1779 to form Franklin and Warren counties. The courthouse was ordered to be built on Jethro Sumner's land at a place called Buffalo Race Path; the site is in Warren County approx. 6 mi. se of Warrenton. *See also* St. John's Parish, Granville County.

Butler. *See* Oakland.

Butler Creek rises in w Surry County and flows se into North Fork Mitchell River.

Butler Gap, e Yancey County near the head of Long Branch.

Butler Island, ne Tyrrell County in the mouth of Alligator Creek.

Butler Knob, peak in the South Mountains, s Burke County. Alt. 2,062.

Butler Mountain, s Buncombe County between Baldwin Gap and Chestnut Mountain.

Butler Mountain, se Henderson County.

Butlers, community in central Bertie County.

Butlers Crossroads, community in s central Sampson County.

Butner, community in sw Granville County. State hospital, training school, factories, are here. Camp Butner, *which see,* activated 1942, closed 1946, named for Major General Henry Wolfe Butner (1875-1937), was here. *See also* Hampton; Knap of Reeds. Produces textiles, hosiery.

Butte Mountain, n Caldwell County on Little Kings Creek. Alt. 2,500.

Butte Mountain, e Madison County between Holland Branch and Middle Fork.

Butter Gap, w Transylvania County between Stone Mountain and Cedar Rock Creek.

Buttermilk Creek rises in s Caswell County and flows se into Alamance County where it enters Haw River.

Buttermilk Mountain, on Bradley Creek in nw Henderson County.

Butters, community in w Bladen County. Butters Lumber Company was located here. Alt. 111.

Butterwood Creek, rises in nw Halifax County and flows sw into Bear Swamp.

Butterwood Township, w central Halifax County.

Butt Mountain, w Henderson County in Great Smoky Mountains National Park, a spur extending se from Big Butt Mountain on Mt. Sterling Ridge, near lat. 35° 39' 20" N., long. 83° 09' 10" W.

Butt Mountain, se Henderson County.

Button Bay, a loam filled bay in n Columbus County.

Button Branch rises in nw Columbus County and flows sw into Dunn Swamp.

Buxton, community on Hatteras Island, se Dare County. One of the most thickly populated sections of the Outer Banks. Formerly known as The Cape (for Cape Hatteras), but the post office was changed to Buxton, 1882. Named for Judge Ralph P. Buxton (1826-1900).

Buxton, plantation house in s Warren County s of the community of Inez, and the home of John Buxton Williams, a local planter. The house, built in 1850, is still standing.

Buxton Woods. *See* Hatteras Woods.

Buzzard Bay, an inlet of the Cape Fear River and the Atlantic Ocean (through Corncake Inlet), in the n part of Smith Island, Brunswick County.

Buzzard Bay, in South River near site of former Lukens community, n central Carteret County.

Buzzard Bay, on the sound side of n Bodie Island in e Dare County; opposite the town of Kill Devil Hills and on s coast of Colington Island. *See also* Colington Island.

Buzzard Branch rises in n Franklin County and flows ne into Sandy Creek.

Buzzard Knob, s Buncombe County nw of Hickory Top.

Buzzard Knob, sw Buncombe County w of Stony Fork community.

Buzzard Knob, sw Macon County at the sw end of Horse Ridge.

Buzzard Knob, s Macon County between Nickajack Creek and Stansfield Branch.

Buzzard Point, a large neck of marsh land on the Roanoke River, se Halifax County.

Buzzard Rock, peak in central Buncombe County between Roaring Gap and Sassafras Gap.

Buzzard Rock, peak between Wildcat cliffs and Blackrock Mountain on the Jackson-Macon County line.

Buzzard Rock, peak on Sevenmile Ridge, e Yancey County near the head of Murphy Branch.

Buzzard Roost, mountain in South Mountains in s Burke County.

Buzzard Roost, peak in n Haywood County w of Pigeon River near Big Bend.

Buzzard Roost, a mountain on the Cherokee-Graham County line at the n end of Hanging Dog Mountain. Alt. 4,081.

Buzzardroost Mountain, central Swain County between Middle Peachtree Creek and Canebrake Branch.

Buzzard Roost Ridge, n Macon County parallel to Mason Branch.

Buzzards' Rocks, near Shulls Mill s Watauga County.

Byers Branch rises in central Clay County and flows sw into Shooting Creek.

Byers Creek rises in e Henderson County and flows sw into Lewis Creek.

Byers Creek rises in n Henderson County and flows sw into Mud Creek.

Byers Creek rises in sw Iredell County and flows s into Davidson Creek.

Byers Mountain, n Henderson County on Byers Creek.

Bynum, community in n Chatham County on Haw River. Named for the Bynum family which est. a cotton mill here. Alt. 322.

Bynum Mill Creek rises in s Edgecombe County and flows ne into Town Creek.

Byrd Pond. s Harnett County on Stewarts Creek. Approx. ½ mi. long.

Byrds Branch rises in n Yancey County and flows se into Jacks Creek.

Byrds Creek rises in s Person County and flows ne into South Flat River.

Byrdsville, community in ne Columbus County.

C

Cabarrus, community in s Cabarrus County.

Cabarrus County was formed in 1792 from Mecklenburg County. Located in the s central section of the state, it is bounded by Stanly, Union, Mecklenburg, Iredell, and Rowan counties. It was named for Stephen Cabarrus (1754-1808), member of the General Assembly and speaker of the House of Commons. Area: 360 sq. mi. County seat: Concord with an elevation of 704 ft. Townships are Nos. 1-12, formerly Rocky River, Poplar Tent, Odell School, Kannapolis, Mount Gilead, Watts Cross Roads, Earnhardts, Mount Pleasant, Smiths, Bethel Church, Baptist Church, and Concord. Reed Gold mine in the county was the site of the first authentic discovery of gold in North Carolina, 1799. Produces wheat, oats, corn, cotton, poultry, dairy products, textiles, hosiery, apparel.

Cabbage Branch rises in n central Anson County and flows s into Brown Creek.

Cabbage Inlet appears on the Moseley map, 1733, in the barrier beach of e New Hanover County between what is now Masonboro Sound and Myrtle Sound. It was still open in 1775 but closed by 1808.

Cabe Branch rises in s Swain County and flows nw into Little Tennessee River.

Cabin, community in e Duplin County on Cabin Creek.

Cabin Branch rises in nw Anson County and flows se into Brown Creek.

Cabin Branch rises in ne Bertie County and flows sw into Chinkapin Swamp. A Cabin Creek is mentioned in local records as early as 1723.

Cabin Branch rises in central Durham County and flows e into Little River.

Cabin Branch rises in w Hoke County and flows ne into Rockfish Creek. Now within the Fort Bragg Military Reservation.

Cabin Branch rises in s Pitt County and flows se into Cow Swamp.

Cabin Branch rises in ne Swain County and flows sw into Bradley Fork.

Cabin Branch rises in e central Wake County and flows w into Marsh Creek near its junction with Crabtree Creek.

Cabin Branch rises in n Wilson County and flows se into Rocky Ford Branch.

Cabin Branch rises in n Wilson County and flows approx. 3 mi. s into Bloomery Swamp.

Cabin Cove, se Buncombe County, e of Garren Mountain.

Cabin Creek rises in se Davidson County and flows sw into Yadkin River.

Cabin Creek rises in e Duplin County and flows s into Limestone Creek.

Cabin Creek rises in s Henderson County and flows se into Green River.

Cabin Creek rises in ne Jackson County and flows sw into Dark Ridge Creek.

Cabin Creek rises in e Macon County and flows sw into Rabbit Creek.

Cabin Creek rises in e Montgomery County and flows ne into Moore County and into Bear Creek.

Cabin Creek. See Candor.

Cabin Ridge Plantation, the home of Col. Thomas Lee of Lees Mills (now Roper, which see), used as the first courthouse for Washington County; county court met here from 1800 until sometime in 1801.

Cabin Swamp, community in central Tyrrell County near Second Creek.

Cabin Branch rises in w Swain County and flows se into Hazel Creek.

Cable Gap, ne Graham County at the head of Panther Creek.

Cable Gap, n Graham County at the e end of Yellow Mountain between the headwaters of Yellow Creek and Cables Cove Creek.

Cable Creek rises in central Randolph County and flows sw and nw into Back Creek.

Cables Cove Creek rises in n central Graham County and flows n into Fontana Lake.

Cabo de Trafalgar. See Cape Fear.

Cadon Branch rises in s Macon County and flows sw into Tessentee Creek.

Cadon Gap, s Macon County at the head of Whiterock Branch.

Cadwell Creek rises in Virginia and flows sw into n Stokes County. Turning slightly to the nw, it flows back into Virginia.

Caesar Austin Branch rises in central Clay County and flows se into Tusquitee Creek. Named for a Negro who lived on the branch.

Caesars Branch rises in n Franklin County and flows ne into Little Shocco Creek.

Caesar Swamp rises in w Sampson County and flows se into Little Coharie Creek.

Caffey Gap, s Watauga County on the head of Laurel Creek.

Cagle Branch rises in w Jackson County and flows se into Savannah Creek.

Cahaba, community in sw Bertie County.

Cahoogue Creek rises in se Craven County approx. 3 mi. nw of North Harlowe and flows approx. 3½ mi. nw into Hancock Creek.

Cahoon Point extends from e Onslow County into White Oak River. Named for John Cahoon, early settler.

Caintuck Township. See Canetuck Township.

Cairo, community in se Anson County. Center of rich farming land. Named for Cairo, Egypt, also center of rich farming land.

Cairo, community in s Wake County. Named for the city in Egypt.

Cajahs Mountain, s Caldwell County. Alt. 1,342. Said to have been named for a man named Micajah who was hanged here.

Calabash, community in sw Brunswick County. Settled prior to 1880. Original name was Pea Landing. Changed to Calabash in 1880 for the gourds that hung outside wells in the vicinity. Noted for its sea food restaurants.

Calabash Creek rises in sw Brunswick County and flows w into South Carolina where it enters Little River.

Calahaln, community in w Davie County. Probably named for William Callahan (or his descendants) who was in the area as early as 1778. Post office est. here 1858.

Calahaln Mountain, w Davie County. Signs of excavations made on the mountain are said to be the result of Indians digging for gold.

Calahaln Township, w Davie County.

Cal Cove, s Graham County between Willie Knob and Little Snowbird Creek.

Caldwell, community in ne Orange County.

Caldwell Branch rises in sw Madison County and flows w into Spring Creek.

Caldwell County was formed in 1841 from Burke and Wilkes counties. Located in the w central section of the state, it is bounded by Alexander, Catawba, Burke, Avery, Watauga, and Wilkes counties. It was named for Joseph Caldwell (1773-1835), first president of the University of North Carolina. Area: 480 sq. mi. County seat: Lenoir with an elevation of 1,182 ft. Townships are Globe, Judson, Johns River, King's Creek, Lenoir, Little River, Lovelady, Lower Creek, Mulberry, North Catawba, Patterson, Wilson Creek, and Yadkin Valley. Produces poultry, dairy products, hogs, furniture, apparel, textiles, hosiery, mirrors, pianos, and gravel.

Caldwell Creek rises in s Cabarrus County and flows n into Reedy Creek. Named for family of David Caldwell (d. about 1780).

Caldwell Fork rises in w Haywood County in Great Smoky Mountains National Park and flows ne to join Palmer Creek in forming Cataloochee Creek.

Caldwell, community in n Mecklenburg County between towns of Cornelius and Huntersville. Named for Dr. Joseph Caldwell (1773-1835), president of the University of North Carolina. 1804-1812, 1816-1835.

Caldwell Township, se Catawba County. Named in 1868 for Caldwell family, who were large landowners.

Caleb Branch rises in w Carteret County and flows w into Hadnot Creek.

Caleb's Creek rises in e Onslow County and flows ne into White Oak River.

Caledonia, North Carolina State Prison farm on the Roanoke River, e Halifax County. It consists of 3,700 acres. Named for an early plantation here. Believed to have been settled by Highland Scots in the 1720's. Dikes were built along the river to control flooding. The plantation was later owned by Samuel Johnston of Edenton. Numerous Indian relics have been found here.

Caledonia Creek rises in sw Pender County and flows s into Black River.

Caledonia. See Bensalem.

Caler Cove, at the head of Caler Cove Branch in n Macon County.

Caler Cove Branch rises in n Macon County and flows s into Little Tennessee River.

Caler Fork rises in e Macon County and flows sw into Cowee Creek.

Caler Knob, on Macon-Swain County line near the head of Gibby Branch.

Cales Creek rises in nw Catreret County and flows sw into White Oak River.

Calf Branch rises on Fort Bragg Military Reservation in n Hoke County and flows sw into Rockfish Creek.

Calf Creek rises in sw Beaufort County and flows n into Pamlico River.

Calfpen Gap, ne Graham County.

Calhoun, community in e Transylvania County between Little River and McCall Branch.

Calhoun Branch rises in w Cherokee County and flows s into Hiwassee River.

Calhoun Branch rises in nw Swain County and flows s into Desolation Branch.

Calhoun Branch rises in w Swain County and flows sw into Fontana Lake.

Calhoun Island, formerly a 15-acre island in Little Tennessee River in ne Graham County. Now under the waters of Fontana Lake.

Calico, community in s Pitt County. Named for the fact that a local store, owned by Henry Venters and his father, sold more calico cloth than any other store in Pitt County. This store also housed the local post office.

Calico Bay, a loam-filled bay in sw Duplin County.

Calico Creek rises in central Carteret County and flows e and se into the mouth of Newport River. An English ship, loaded with calico, is said to have wrecked near Beaufort in a storm. Afterwards pieces of calico were found draped over bushes growing along this creek.

California, community in central Hertford County on the head of Mill Branch.

California, community in ne Madison County. A post office, California Creek, est. here prior to 1882.

California, community in w Pitt County.

California Branch rises in n Cabarrus County and flows n into Rowan County where it enters South Second Creek.

California Creek rises in e Madison County and flows s to join Paint Fork in forming Little Ivy Creek.

California Gap, s Macon County between Gold Mine Branch and California Ridge.

California Knob, central Surry County.

California Ridge, s Macon County between California Gap and Henderson Mountain.

California Township. See Falkland Township.

Call, community in s Wilkes County on Mill Creek. Named for a local family.

Callaghan Creek rises in central Dare County on the mainland and flows e into Croatan Sound.

Callahan, community in n Granville County.

Callahan Branch rises in e Madison County and flows ne into Laurel Creek.

Callahan. See also Calahaln.

Callaway Mountain, central Yancey County parallel to Cane River.

Callisons, community in central Pamlico County.

Call Millpond, s Wilkes County on Fishing Creek. Covers two acres; maximum depth 12 ft. A grain mill and a sawmill are operated here.

Caltolina, former lumbering community in

e Person and w Granville counties. A 1,300-acre tract belonging to the John Pomfret Webb family and later to the Calton family, from which the name was developed. About 1919 the tract was divided into 15 farms.

Calvander, community in se Orange County. Formed from the name of Calvin Andrews who operated Andrews' Academy here. The post office was first known as Faucette. Andrews' wife was Elizabeth Faucette.

Calvert, community in s Transylvania County between Calloway Creek and French Broad River.

Calvin. See Carbon City.

Calypso, town in nw Duplin County. Settled about 1890, inc. 1913. Alt. 167. Named for the sea nymph in Homer's *Odyssey.* Produces lumber.

Calypso Community Pond, on the head of Dicks Branch in nw Duplin County.

Cam Branch rises in n Duplin County and flows e into Northeast Cape Fear River.

Cambridge. See Ostwalt.

Camden, uninc. county seat in w central Camden County. Known as Plank Bridge as early as 1740; inc. as Jonesborough, 1792. As early as 1840 the name Camden was being used. From the end of the Revolution until about 1830 this was a port of entry for customs collection. Alt. 10.

Camden County was formed in 1777 from Pasquotank County. Located in the ne section of the state, it is bounded by the state of Virginia, Albemarle Sound, and Pasquotank, Gates, and Currituck counties. It was named for Sir Charles Pratt, Earl of Camden (1716-94), English jurist and political leader who opposed taxation of the American colonies and believed the Stamp Act to be unconstitutional. Area: 308 sq. mi. County seat: Camden with an elevation of 10 ft. Townships are Court House, Shiloh, and South Mills. Produces corn, soybeans, Irish potatoes, and hogs.

Camden Point, the se tip of Camden County

which extends into the Albemarle Sound. See also Poquoson Point.

Camel Field, cove in n Buncombe County between North Knob and Reems Creek.

Camel Hump Knob, a peak in the Great Smoky Mountains National Park on the line between Haywood County, N. C., and Cocke County, Tenn., near lat. 35° 43' 33" N., long. 83° 13' W. Alt. 5,200-5,250.

Camel Knob, n Rutherford County n of Camp Creek. Alt. 2,124.

Camels Creek rises in w Harnett County and flows ne into Cape Fear River. Named for "Surveyor John" Campbell who settled along its banks about 1770.

Cameron, town in e Moore County. Inc. 1876 and named for a civil engineer who surveyed the Raleigh and Augusta Airline Railroad. Alt. 304.

Camerons Hill. See Johnsonville.

Camerer Ridge, on the Haywood County, N. C.-Cocke County, Tenn., line in the Great Smoky Mountains National Park, extends ne from Low Gap to Mount Camerer, thence e approx. 2½ mi. to the valley of Pigeon River. Named in honor of A. B. Camerer, formerly of the U.S. Department of Interior, who was active in promoting the Park.

Camp Alamance, Civil War training camp near Company Shops, now Burlington, central Alamance County.

Campania, an estate of 19,000 acres in Currituck, Pasquotank, and Perquimans counties, owned by Thomas Macknight. Being developed at the time of the Revolutionary War.

Camp Ashe, a Civil War training camp in New Hanover County, described in contemporary records as being "12 miles from Wilmington."

Camp Bay, a bay in central Columbus County filled with fine sand.

Camp Beauregard, Civil War training camp in w Warren County near the community of Ridgeway.

Campbell, community in n Stokes County near the head of Little Creek.

Campbell Creek rises in se Beaufort County and flows e to join Upper Spring Creek in forming Goose Creek.

Campbell Creek rises in s Graham County and flows ne into Tulula Creek.

Campbell Creek is formed in w Haywood County by the junction of East and West Forks and flows ne into Jonathans Creek.

Campbell Gap, central Macon County between Iotla Branch and Iotla Creek.

Campbell Island, e Brunswick County on the Cape Fear River. Once known as Crane Island. Named for William Campbell (1745-81), a general in the Revolution.

Campbells Creek rises in e Mecklenburg County and flows s into McAlpine Creek.

Campbell's Creek, community in se Beaufort County in the center of an Irish potato growing area. Prosphate deposits exist in the vicinity.

Campbell's Crossroads. See Semora.

Campbells Falls, rapids in Cape Fear River in se Harnett County near the confluence of Juniper Creek with the river. Mentioned as early as 1819 in a survey of the rivers of North Carolina.

Campbell's Mill on Waterhole Swamp. See Pembroke.

Campbellton. See Fayetteville.

Camp Blackjack. See Bucklesberry Pocosin.

Camp Branch rises in w Avery County and flows s into Horse Creek.

Camp Branch rises in se Buncombe County and flows nw into Swannanoa River.

Camp Branch rises in ne Clay County and flows se into Clear Creek.

Camp Branch rises in e Durham County near the Wake County line and flows ne into Lick Creek.

Camp Branch rises in s Haywood County and flows nw into Browing Branch.

Camp Branch rises in n Haywood County and flows sw into Pigeon River.

Camp Branch rises in w Macon County and flows se into Wayah Creek.

Camp Branch rises in nw Macon County and flows sw into Nantahala River.

Camp Branch rises in nw Surry County and flows sw into Fisher River.

Camp Branch rises in e Swain County and flows ne into Connelly Creek.

Camp Branch rises in s Wake County and flows s into Middle Creek.

Camp Branch rises in e Watauga County and flows ne into Elk Creek.

Camp Branch rises in n central Wilkes County and flows ne into Roaring River.

Camp Branch, community n central Brunswick County.

Camp Branch Falls, 360-ft. waterfalls on the Nantahala River, Clay-Macon County line.

Camp Butner, former army post in Durham, Granville, and Person counties. Est. 1942; closed 1946. Infantry training center, convalescent hospital, and reassignment center. Named for Major General Henry Wolfe Butner (1875-1937), native of Surry County. See also Butner.

Campcall, community in central Cleveland County on Little Harris Creek.

Camp Campbell, a Civil War training camp near Kinston in e Lenoir County.

Camp Canal, Civil War training camp in Carteret County, probably at or near Morehead City.

Camp Chronicle, a World War I training camp located on the w side of present S. Linwood Street, Gastonia, central Gaston County. Operated in connection with an artillery range at the foot of Crowders Mountain. Named for Major William Chronicle, killed at the Battle of Kings Mountain, 1780.

Camp Clingman, former Confederate camp in Asheville (French Broad Ave. near Philip St.), central Buncombe County. Named for Thomas L. Clingman, U.S. Senator and Brigadier General in the Confederate Army.

Camp Crabtree, Civil War training camp located approx. 3 mi. n of Raleigh on "Crabtree," plantation of Kimbrough Jones, Sr.

Camp Creek rises in n Burke County and flows nw into Avery County where it enters Linville River. Named for three brothers, Everette, Howard, and Arthur Camp, of Chicago, who were railroad constructors in the vicinity.

Camp Creek rises in se corner of Burke County and flows ne into Jacob Fork.

Camp Creek rises in se Burke County and flows se into Catawaba County where it enters Jacob Fork.

Camp Creek rises in w Cherokee County and flows nw and ne into Apalachia Lake.

Camp Creek rises in sw Cleveland County and flows n into Broad River.

Camp Creek rises in se Henderson County and flows ne into Polk County where it enters Green River.

Camp Creek rises in e Jackson County and flows sw into Tanasee Creek.

Camp Creek rises in nw Jackson County and flows sw into Tuckasegee River.

Camp Creek rises in w Johnston County and flows s into Black Creek.

Camp Creek rises in s McDowell County and flows sw into Rutherford County where it continues sw and then turns se to enter Second Broad River.

Camp Creek rises in s Person County and

flows se across the ne corner of Durham County into Granville County where it enters Knap of Reeds Creek.

Camp Creek rises in w Stokes County and flows ne into Cascade Creek.

Camp Creek rises in sw Surry County and flows se and ne into Mitchell River.

Camp Creek rises in s Yancey County and flows se into South Toe River.

Camp Creek Bald, on Madison County, N. C.-Greene County, Tenn., line. Alt. 4,844.

Camp Creek Mountain, s central Avery County.

Camp Creek Township, n central Rutherford County.

Camp Davis, a Civil War training camp near Wilmington, w New Hanover County.

Camp Davis, World War II anti-aircraft training base at Holly Ridge, s Onslow County. Opened April, 1941, and attained a maximum of 60,000 men and women; closed October, 1944. Reopened briefly in the summer of 1945 as an Air Force convalescent hopsital and redistribution station. Named for Maj. Gen. Richmond Pearson Davis (1866-1937), a native of North Carolina.

Camp Fisher, Civil War training camp near High Point, sw Guilford County.

Camp Gap, nw Macon County at the head of Camp Branch.

Camp Greene, World War I training camp, 6,000 acres in area, est. July, 1917, named for General Nathanael Greene, was located in Charlotte, Mecklenburg County.

Camp Grier Lake, w McDowell County on a tributary of Mill Creek; $\%_{10}$ mi. long, about 1 mi. nw of Old Fort. A summer camp is operated here by the Presbyterian Church. Formerly known as Lake Refuge.

The Campground, sw Gates County approx. 3 mi. nw of Gatesville, the site of religious camp meetings from the 1820's until the present century. Popular with the people from Hertford, Bertie, and Chowan counties. An artesian well at the site supplied water.

Campground Gap, on the Buncombe-Yancey County line between Campground Knob and Rocky Knob.

Campground Knob, on Buncombe-Yancey County line between Sugartree Gap and Campground Gap.

Camp Hebron, s Watauga County on Boone Fork, operated for girls.

Camp Hill, a Civil War training camp described as being near Garysburg in Northampton County. It was also referred to as a "camp of instruction."

Camping Creek rises in sw Franklin County and flows ne into Cedar Creek.

Camping Fork rises in n Mitchell County and flows sw into Right Fork Bean Creek.

Camping Island Creek rises in central Stokes County and flows ne between Hanging Rock and Flat Shoal Mountain into Dan River.

Camp Jeter, former Confederate camp in Asheville (Cherry Street-Flint Street section), central Buncombe County.

Camp Johnston, a Civil War training camp in the vicinity of Kinston, named for General Joseph E. Johnston.

Camp Knob, n Cleveland County between Cove and Cox creeks.

Camp Lamb, a Civil War training camp near Wilmington, w New Hanover County.

Camp Lejeune, Marine base in s Onslow County on both sides of New River, adjacent to Jacksonville. Construction began in 1942. Known first as New River Marine Base; later named for Major General John A. Lejeune (1867-1942), World War I Marine Commandant. The base covers 173 sq. mi., of which 26,000 acres are under water. Onslow Beach, a part of the base, is used for amphibious assault training.

Camp Mackall, World War II training camp, the second largest Airborne training center in the nation. Site in e Richmond and nw Scotland counties. See also Hoffman.

Camp Macon. See Macon.

Camp Mangum, Civil War training camp in central Wake County about three mi. w of Raleigh.

Camp Mason, Civil War training camp near Graham, central Alamance County.

Camp Mason, Civil War training camp near Goldsboro in central Wayne County.

Camp Mountain, e Jackson County between Tanasee Creek and the Transylvania County line.

Camp Patton, Civil War training camp in Asheville (East Chestnut Street east of Charlotte Street), central Buncombe County. Probably named for Capt. Thomas W. Patton, who served with distinction in the Confederate Army. The camp was probably on land which he owned, as his home was nearby.

Camp Point at the nw tip of the largest island in the Hog Island group, ne Carteret County. Earlier known as Whale Camp Point and was the site of an early settlement.

Camp Polk, World War I tank camp of 1,600 acres located in Raleigh and named for William Polk, Revolutionary War colonel.

Camp Ridge, mountain in w Avery County.

Camprock Branch rises in s Macon County and flows se into Shope Fork.

Camp Springs, community in sw Caswell County. Believed to have been named because Cornwallis' troops camped here during the American Revolution.

Camps Store. See Gaston.

Camp Swamp rises in s Columbus County and flows se into Horry County, S. C., where it enters Buck Creek.

Camp Tuscarora, Boy Scout camp and lake in s Wayne County s of Sleepy Creek.

Camp Two Branch rises in s Haywood County and flows nw into Middle Prong.

Camp Vance, a Civil War training Camp near Sulphur Springs, central Buncombe County. Named for Col. Robert B. Vance of the 29th N.C. Regiment which trained here.

Camp Vance, central Burke County, site of camp for state troops, 1861-1864, named for Colonel Zebulon B. Vance, War Governor. Raided by Federal troops in 1864.

Camp Whiting, a Civil War training camp at Wilmington, w New Hanover County.

Camp Wilson, See Vaughan's Springs.

Camp Wyatt, a Civil War training camp in s New Hanover County about 2 mi. n of Fort Fisher. Named for Henry Lawson Wyatt, first North Carolina soldier killed in action in the Civil War, at Bethel Church, June 10, 1861.

Canada Township, se Jackson County.

Cana, community in n Davie County. Made a post office in 1875 and named for James H. Cain, first postmaster.

Canadian Top, peak in w Haywood County, Great Smoky Mountains National Park, near lat. 35° 38' 55" N., long. 83° 06' 13" W.

Canal A, in central Washington County, drains ne from East Dismal Swamp into Main Canal.

Canal B, in central Washington County, drains ne from East Dismal Swamp into Main Canal.

Canal Gut rises in sw Bertie County and flows s into Roanoke River.

Canal Swamp rises in e Northampton County and flows se into Hertford County where it enters Potecasi Creek.

Canby, community in s Montgomery County on Thickety Creek.

Candle Branch rises in w Forsyth County and flows sw into Yadkin River.

Candler, community in sw Buncombe County at the junction of South Hominy and Hominy creeks. Alt. 2,108. Named for George Candler, an early settler.

Candler Knob, on Buncombe-Henderson County line, sw of Cutthroat Gap. Alt. 4,548.

Candor, town in e Montgomery County. Alt. 729. Inc. 1891. Named by three local merchants who envisioned a "town of frankness and sincerity." Post office est. as Cabin Creek in 1873; name changed in 1885.

Candy Creek rises in ne Guilford County and flows n into Rockingham County where it enters Haw River. Known as Kenady's Branch and as Kanady Creek prior to 1800, named for an early settler.

Cane Bottom, community in n Yancey County on Nolichucky River.

Canebrake Branch rises in w central Swain County and flows s into Tuckasegee River.

Cane Brake Creek rises in s Rutherford County and flows s into Broad River.

Cane Branch rises in Angola Bay, n Pender County, and flows se into Holly Shelter Creek.

Cane Branch rises in e Yancey County and flows n into Little Crabtree Creek.

Cane Creek rises in sw Alamance County and flows e into Haw River. Cane Creek Friends (Quaker) Meeting House was established along its banks in 1751. Named for canebrakes on the banks of the stream.

Cane Creek rises in se Buncombe County near Cane Creek Gap and flows sw into Henderson County where it enters French Broad River.

Cane Creek rises in s Cherokee County and flows ne into Nottely River.

Cane Creek rises in n Jackson County and flows sw into Tuckasegee River.

Cane Creek rises in sw Jackson County and flows se into Chattooga River.

Cane Creek rises in se McDowell County and flows s into Rutherford County where it turns sw to flow into Second Broad River.

Cane Creek rises in w McDowell County and flows ne into Catawba River.

Cane Creek rises in se Macon County and flows se into Chattooga River

Cane Creek rises in e Mitchell County and flows w into Toe River.

Cane Creek, rises in w Orange County and flows sw into Haw River.

Cane Creek rises in sw Person County and flows e into the Hyco River.

Cane Creek rises in w Rutherford County and flows ne into Lake Lure.

Cane Creek rises in s Union County and flows sw into Catawba River in South Carolina.

Cane Creek rises in n Wilkes County and flows se into North Prong Roaring River.

Cane Creek. See Crane Creek.

Cane Creek Gap, se Buncombe County near the headwaters of Cane Creek.

Cane Creek Mountains, s Alamance County. Among the named peaks are Huronian Mountain and Stafford Hill. Alt. approx. 1,033.

Cane Creek Township, e Mitchell County.

Canedy Gap, w Cherokee County at the se end of Chestnut Gap Mountain.

Canedy Mountain, w Cherokee County s of Canedy Gap between Shoal and Bearpaw creeks.

Cane Island, sandy island approx. ¼ mi. long, in French Broad River, w Madison County.

Cane Mountain, between Foster Creek and McDowell Creek in nw Henderson County.

Cane Mountain extends from Cane River in n Yancey County ne to the junction of Toe and Cane Rivers.

Cane River rises in the Black Mountains of s Yancey County and meanders n to join Toe River on the Mitchell-Yancey County line to form Nolichucky River.

Cane River, community in w central Yancey County.

Cane River Gap, on Buncombe-Yancey County line, se of Ivy Gap. Also known as Little Cane River Gap.

Cane River Gap, sw Yancey County near the head of Elk Fork.

Cane River Township, nw Yancey County.

Canetuck, community in sw Pender County on Buckle Creek.

Canetuck Township, sw Pender County, formerly Caintuck.

Caney Bottom Creek rises in n Transylvania County and flows se into Cove Creek.

Caney Branch rises in w Cherokee County and flows se and sw into Hiwasee River.

Caney Branch rises in se McDowell County on the e slopes of Witness Rock Ridge and flows ne about 2 mi. into Armstrong Creek.

Caney Fork, stream is formed in ne Jackson County by the junction of Piney Mountain Creek and Rough Butt Creek, and flows sw into Tuckasegee River.

Caney Fork Bald, on Haywood-Jackson County line nw of Lone Bald. Alt. 5,926.

Caney Fork Branch rises in s Madison County and flows nw into Robert Branch.

Caney Fork Township, e central Jackson County.

Caney Lead extends ne from Hangover Lead to Cheoah River in nw Graham County.

Canie Creek rises in central Buncombe County and flows se into Hominy Creek.

Cannon, community in w Henderson County. Settled soon after the Revolutionary War.

Cannon Branch rises in n Avery County and flows e into Buckeye Creek.

Cannon Branch rises in s Watauga County and flows sw into Boone Fork.

Cannon Creek rises in e Transylvania County and flows se into Buckhorn Creek.

Cannon Gap, n Avery County near the head of Cannon Creek.

Cannon Gap, in s Watagua County on the head of Payne Branch.

Cannon Lake, fed by several small streams in sw Rowan County. Covers 100 acres. Owned by Cannon Mills, Kannapolis, and used as a source of water for the mills and community.

Cannons Crossroads, community in central Pitt County.

Cannon's Ferry, community on the Chowan River in nw Chowan County.

Cannon Swamp rises in central Pitt County and flows se into Moyes Run.

Canoe Creek rises in w Burke County and flows se into Catawba River in central Burke County.

Cansadie Top, central Haywood County between Shook Gap and Jolly Gap.

Canterbury Creek. See Southwest Creek.

Canto, community in nw Buncombe County near the Madison County line.

Canton, town in e Haywood County. Inc. 1889 as Buford. Name changed to Pigeon River in 1891 and to Canton in 1893.

Named for Canton, Ohio, source of the steel used in the bridge being built across Pigeon River. Produces paper. Alt. 2,609.

Cantrell Creek rises in n Transylvania County and flows se into South Fork Mills River.

Cantrell Creek rises in s Transylvania County and flows n into French Broad River.

Cantrell Mountain, w Henderson County between North Fork and South Fork.

Cantrell Top, nw Cherokee County.

The Cape. See Buxton.

Cape Amidas. See Cape Hatteras.

Cape Carteret, town in sw Carteret County on Bogue Sound. Inc. 1959.

Cape Creek, a tidal creek on Smith Island in se Brunswick County rising about 1 mi. n of Cape Fear just inside the outer beach and extending nw to the main outlet on the w shore of Smith Island.

Cape Fair. See Cape Fear.

Cape Fear, the southernmost tip of Smith Island, s Brunswick County, at the mouth of Cape Fear River in the Atlantic Ocean. Discovered by Verrazzano in 1524. Appears as *Promontorium tremendum* on the DeBry map, 1590, and as Cape of Feare on the Molyneux map, 1592. The name apparently originated in 1585 when the *Tiger* en route to Roanoke Island, was nearly wrecked "on a breache called the Cape of Feare." John White had a similar experience and mentioned the name again in 1587. Spanish maps of the same period mark this Cabo de Trafalgar. At a later time when it was desirable to attract colonists to the Carolina region, the name Cape Fair was substituted but not permanently accepted.

Cape Fear, community in central Harnett County near the n bank of Cape Fear River.

Cape Feare. See Cape Lookout.

Cape Fear River is formed by the junction of Deep and Haw rivers on the Chatham-Lee County line. It flows se along the Chatham-Lee County line and through Harnett County, s through Cumberland, se through Bladen, and along the Columbus-Pender, Brunswick-Pender, and Brunswick-New Hanover County lines into the Atlantic Ocean. It had a succession of names after it was first discovered by Europeans. Spanish explorers in 1526 named it Rio Jordan; an English colony in 1664 named it Charles River; between 1664 and 1667 when Clarendon County existed

in the area, it was known as Clarendon River. It appears as Clarendon River on the Ogilby map, 1671; as "C. Fear R. or Clarendon R." on the Gascoyne map, 1682; as Cape Fear River on the Barnwell map, 1722; as Clarendon River on the Moll map, 1729; and as Cape Fear River on the Moseley map, 1733, and thereafter on others.

Cape Fear Section, a term applied to se North Carolina along the Cape Fear River. Appears as Pine Plains on the Ogilby map, 1671.

Cape Fear Township, se Chatham County.

Cape Fear Township, former township in e Lee County, now township number 3.

Cape Fear Township, n New Hanover County.

Cape Hatteras, the easternmost point in North Carolina, is at the s tip of Hatteras Island, se Dare County. Diamond Shoals, extending into the Atlantic Ocean se from the Cape, reach to the Gulf Stream at the noted "graveyard of the Atlantic." Called Cape Saint John on the Velasco map, 1611; Cape Amidas on the Smith map, 1624; and its present name on Ogilby's map, 1671. The word Hatteras apparently is an English rendition of the Algonquian Indian expression of "there is less vegetation." The sixteenth century Indian village of Croatoan may have been located here. See also various entries under Hatteras; Diamond Shoals.

Cape Hatteras National Seashore Recreational Area, est. 1953, consists of the s part of Bodie Island, and most of Ocracoke and Hatteras Islands except the settled areas. Camp sites provided. Maritime Museum near Buxton. On the Outer Banks of se Dare and Hyde counties.

Cape Hatteras Woods. See Hatteras Woods.

Cape Kenrick in the sixteenth and early seventeenth centuries extended into the Atlantic Ocean from Hatteras Island in e Dare County between the communities of Rodanthe and Salvo. It appears on the Velasco map, 1611. It disappeared later in the seventeenth century either through erosion or in a storm. Wimble Shoals, *which see*, are now at the site. Kenrick is believed to be derived from the Algonquian Indian word for "sinking-down-sand."

Capella, community in w Stokes County between Quaker Gap and East Prong Yadkin River.

Cape Lookout, the southernmost tip of Core

Banks in se Carteret County. A lighthouse, coast guard station, and a few
summer cottages are here. The DeBry
map, 1590, marks this "Promontorium
tremendum." On the Velasco map, 1611,
it is Cape Feare. On the Ogilby map,
1671, it appears as Cape Lookout.

**Cape Lookout National Seashore Recrea-
tional Area** authorized to be est. by U. S.
Congress, 1966, on Core Banks, Portsmouth Island, and Shackleford Banks, on
the Outer Banks of e Carteret County.
Area will contain approx. 16,400 acres.
Land is presently (1967) being acquired
through state, federal, and foundation
funds. It will be similar to Cape Hatteras
National Seashore Recreational Area,
which see.

Cape Lookout Shoals, in the Atlantic Ocean
off Cape Lookout *(which see),* se Carteret
County.

Capelsie, community in s Montgomery
County on Little River. Named for Capel
family, owners of a cotton mill established
here about 1870.

Cape of Feare. *See* Cape Fear.

Cape Point, the extreme tip of land at Cape
Hatteras, extends into the Atlantic Ocean,
se Dare County.

Capernium, community in sw Forsyth
County.

Cape Saint John. *See* Cape Hatteras.

Capital. *See* Edenton, George City, New
Bern, Raleigh.

Capps Hill, community in n Mecklenburg
County on the head of Stuarts Creek.

Caraleigh, former community in central
Wake County now within the city of
Raleigh.

Caraway Creek rises in nw Randolph County
and flows s into Uwharrie River near
town of Farmer. Appears on the Collet
map, 1770. Traditionally an Indian name,
probably a survival of Keyauwee, the
name of an Indian tribe which inhabited
the area when white men first entered it.
See also Keeauwee.

Caraway Mountain, w Randolph County between Black Creek and Caraway Creek,
(which see). Appears on the Collet map,
1770, as a name applied to all of the
small mountains here between the Uwharrie and Deep rivers.

Carbon City, community in w central Burke
County. Formerly known as Calvin but
renamed following the construction of
the Great Lakes Carbon Company plant
at the site.

Carbonton, community in s Chatham County
on Deep River at the junction of the
Chatham-Lee-Moore County lines. Named
by Mrs. Peter Evans, daughter of Gov.
John Motley Morehead, for the element
carbon, a constituent of coal which was
thought to be abundant in the vicinity.
Alt. 260.

Cardenas, community in s Wake County.

Careening Point, extended into North River
estuary of Carteret County from the mainland, on Moseley map, 1733. The name
has fallen into disuse, though the point
still exists.

Carl Alwin Schenck Forest, central Wake
County, approx. 3 mi. w of North Carolina
State University. Covers 300 acres. Est.
1937 and afterwards named in honor of
Dr. Schenck (1865-1955) who, in 1898,
founded the first forestry school in the
United States at Biltmore Forest, *which
see.* The school was closed in 1912. The
Schenck Forest, owned and operated by
the School of Forest Resources, N. C.
State University, is used for demonstra-
tion, research, and forest genetics. Dr.
Schenck's ashes are scattered in the
Forest.

Carlile Island. *See* Colington Island.

Carlos, community in n Cumberland County.

Carlton. *See* Carroll.

Carmen, community in n Madison County
on Shelton Laurel Creek.

Carolana, a province proposed to be established in America and named in the charter of King Charles I to Sir Robert Heath,
October 30, 1629. The province was to
extend from 31° to 36° n latitude along
the Atlantic Ocean and presumably w to
the Pacific Ocean. No settlements were
made, and the charter was considered
vacated in 1663 when Carolina was
granted to eight Lords Proprietors by
King Charles II. *See also* County of Norfolk.

Carolarns Islands, presumably the Outer
Banks, *which see,* named in the charter of
King Charles I to Sir Robert Heath,
October 30, 1629.

Caroleen, community in se Rutherford
County on Second Broad River. Alt. 805.
Named in honor of Caroline, wife of
Simpson B. Tanner, Sr., industrialist. The
Post Office Department ruled that Caro-
line was too similar to Carolina to be ac-
ceptable, so the name Caroleen was
selected instead. The communities of
Avondale and Henrietta lie directly s.

Carolina was named by King Charles II of England in his own honor in the charter which he granted in 1663 to eight Lords Proprietors. It was applied to the region between Florida and the Virginia colony and extending from the Atlantic to the Pacific Ocean. *See also* Carolana.

Carolina, community in central Alamance on Haw River. A textile mill est. here prior to 1901.

Carolina Bays, oval-shaped lakes, swamps, pocosins, savannahs, and peat beds in se North Carolina, e South Carolina and ne Georgia. Several explanations have been advanced as to the origin of the Carolina Bays, but the most generally accepted one is that they were formed thousands of years ago by a shower of meteorites. White Lake, Jones Lake, Singletary Lake, and Lake Waccamaw are Carolina Bays. There also are numerous others, many of which no longer contain water.

Carolina Beach, town in se New Hanover County on the Atlantic Ocean. Alt. 5. Settled about 1885; inc. 1925. Sugar Loaf, a former community at or near this site, was the scene of an engagement between Confederate and Union forces after the capitulation of Fort Fisher, January 15, 1865.

Carolina Beach Inlet, se New Hanover County, an artificially created inlet from the Atlantic Ocean through the barrier bar about 2.5 mi. n of the town of Carolina Beach. A dredged channel extends from the inlet to the Intracoastal Waterway

Carolina City, laid out in 1855, s central Carteret County, by Carolina City Land Company to be terminal point of Atlantic and North Carolina Railroad. Opening of Morehead City on adjacent land to the e and the coming of the Civil War brought about its death. Union army camped at the site for three years and afterwards the State Guard trained here for a time.

Carolina Power Lake, nw Person and ne Caswell counties on Hyco River. Formed in 1964 by the construction of Hyco Dam by Carolina Power and Light Company to condense turbine exhaust steam at its electric generating plant here. The lake is approx. 10 mi. long and covers 3,750 acres. It is also used for public recreation. Sometimes referred to as Roxboro Lake and as Hyco Lake.

Carolina River. *See* Albemarle Sound.

Carolina Shoal Beach, extreme s tip of the mainland of New Hanover County between the Atlantic Ocean and the Cape Fear River.

Carolina Township, ne Pitt County.

Carolina Island. *See* Conine Island.

Caroon Point, a point extending from mainland of n Dare County, near Mashoes, into Albemarle Sound.

Carpenter, community in w Wake County settled 1865. Named for first settler, William Carpenter. Alt. 325.

Carpenter Knob, in n Cleveland County between Poundingmill and Knob creeks. Alt. 1,619.

Carpenter Branch rises in w Haywood County and flows s into Jonathans Creek.

Carpenters Branch rises in s Macon County and flows n into Allison Creek.

Carpenters Knob, w Lincoln County. Alt. 1,500.

Carr, community in nw Orange County.

Carraway Creek rises in s central Wayne County and flows nw approx. 5 mi. into Neuse River. First known as Michael's Creek for the owner of surrounding land, Michael Rosher. Land sold to John Carraway in 1743 and the name of the creek changed.

Carrboro, town in se Orange County immediately w of Chapel Hill. Alt. 500. Settled 1898. Inc. 1911 as Venable; named for Francis P. Venable (1856-1934), president of the University of North Carolina. Changed to Carrboro, 1913, for Julian S. Carr (1845-1924), who est. a mill here. Produces textiles.

Carrell Knob on the Cherokee-Clay County line in the Valley River Mountains.

Carringer Gap, n Graham County between Yellow Creek and Cochran Creek.

Carrol Knob, s Macon County between Jones Creek and the head of North Fork Coweeta Creek.

Carroll, community in w Duplin County. Railroad name is Carlton.

Carroll Branch rises in w Clay County on the e slope of Carroll Knob and flows s into Carroll Lake near lat. 35° 03' 45" N., long. 83° 54' 53" W., in Nantahala National Forest.

Carrol Gap, near the se base of Carroll Mountain, w Clay County between the headwaters of Sweetwater and Qualls creeks, near lat. 35° 02' 45" N., long. 83° 51' 20" W.

Carroll Gap, e Watauga County on the head of Long Branch.

Carroll Knob, on the Cherokee-Clay County line, at the sw end of Valley River Mountains, Nantahala National Forest. Alt. 2,540.

Carroll Lake, a spring-fed lake in w Clay County, n of Hiwassee River, formed about 1920. Covers 30 acres; max. depth 20 ft. Privately owned. Named for John C. Carroll, first owner.

Carroll Mountain, w Clay County, s of Hiwassee River and n of Qualls Creek. *See also* Jim Carroll Top.

Carrolls Branch rises in se Moore County and flows e into Mill Creek.

Carroll's Creek rises in n Burke County and flows s into Johns River.

Carrot Island, a marshy island about 1.5 mi. long, se of Beaufort in s Carteret County and separated from the mainland by Taylor Creek. Formerly Cart Island.

Carrs Creek rises in s Lee County and flows s into Little River.

Carr's Mount, community in central Anson County on n outskirts of Wadesboro. Alt. 445. Site of a silk mill in the early twentieth century. Other mills operated here from early nineteenth century and early fair grounds and racetrack were here.

Carrs Township ne Greene County. Named for the Carr family, prominent in the area from a time prior to 1804.

Carr Township, e Durham County.

Carson, community in central Catawba County. Alt. 1,000.

Carson Cove, on a tributary of Iotla Creek in central Macon County.

Carson Creek rises in s Transylvania County and flows nw into French Broad River.

Carson Mountain, n Buncombe County n of Wildcat Knob.

Carson Mountain, n Rutherford County, extends ne between Cane Creek and Lookadoo Mountain.

Carson Mountain. *See* Black Mountain.

Carson's Creek, community in se Transylvania County near the South Carolina line.

Carter, community in ne Buncombe County near the junction of Mineral and Carter creeks.

Carter, community in s Gates County.

Carter Branch rises in n Macon County and flows sw into Little Tennessee River.

Carter Cove, the valley through which Beaverdam Creek flows in sw Buncombe County.

Carter Cove, the valley through which

Carter Cove Creek flows in central Buncombe County.

Carter Cove, s Clay County near Brasstown Gap.

Carter Cove, community in s Clay County in the cove of the same name.

Carter Cove Creek rises in the Elk Mountains, central Buncombe County and flows sw into Beaverdam Creek.

Carter Creek rises in the Great Craggy Mountains, ne Buncombe County and flows generally nw to join Mineral Creek in forming Stony Creek.

Carteret, a town inc. 1723 to be laid out on the ne side of Roanoke Island, then Bertie, later Tyrrell, and now e Dare County. An act of 1715, without naming the town, had also attempted to encourage its establishment. A few lots may have been sold by 1733 when it was referred to as "Roanoak Town." but it never developed as planned.

Carteret County was formed in 1722 from Craven County. Located in the e section of the state, it is bounded by the Atlantic Ocean, by Onslow, Jones, and Craven counties, and by Neuse River and Pamlico Sound. Bogue and Core Sounds separate the outer banks from the mainland of the county. It was named for John Carteret (1690-1763), afterwards Earl Granville, one of the Lords Proprietors. Area: 1,063 sq. mi. (532, land; 531, water). County seat: Beaufort with an elevation of 9 ft. Townships are Beaufort, Cedar Island, Davis, Harkers Island, Merrimon, Harlowe, Marshallburg, Morehead, Newport, Portsmouth, Smyrna, Straits, and White Oak. Produces corn, soybeans, cabbage, sweet potatoes, Irish potatoes, hogs, apparel, fishmeal, and ships.

Carteret Precinct, Albemarle County, formed by 1681, composed of present Currituck, Pasquotank, and Camden counties.

Carteret Township, former township of ne Carteret County. Previously a part of Straits Township, now largely Merrimon Township.

Carter Gap, on the Clay-Macon County line.

Carter Mill Ridge, n Madison County between Big Creek and Mill Creek.

Carter Mountain, n Buncombe County near the Madison County line.

Carter Pond, s Wayne County in Yellow Swamp.

Carters Creek rises in ne Davie County near Hillsdale and flows 3 mi. se into Yadkin River. Formerly known as Linville Creek.

Carters Falls, sw Surry County on the Yadkin River near Elkin.

Carters Mills, community in n Moore County on Bear Creek. Named for S. M. Carter in whose home the post office was first opened. A mill here was est. about 1790 by Nicholas Nall, who also had a tavern here on the old Salem-Cross Creek road.

Carters Mountain extends nw in northern Wilkes County between North Prong Roaring River and Middle Prong Roaring River.

Carters Ridge, s Mitchell County between Grassy Creek and North Toe River.

Cartersville, community in s Duplin County.

Carter Top on the n end of Rich Mountain in nw Jackson County.

Carthage, town and county seat, central Moore County. Authorized to be laid off and inc. 1796. Name changed to Fagansville in 1806 for Richardson Fagin, Sheriff of Moore County, 1785-1787, and on whose land the town was located; changed back to Carthage, 1818. Produces textiles. Alt. 575.

Carthage Township, central Moore County.

Cart Island. See Carrot Island.

Cartledge Creek rises in central Richmond County on w edge of town of Ellerbe, and flows sw into Pee Dee River. Named for Edmund Cartledge who owned land in the vicinity prior to 1758.

Cartoogechaye Creek rises in s Macon County and flows ne into Little Tennessee River. The name is believed to be the Cherokee Indian word for "corn fields."

Cartoogechaye Township, w Macon County

Cartwheel Branch rises in e Onslow County and flows ne into Holland Mill Creek.

Carver Creek rises in nw Clay County and flows sw into Hiwassee River.

Carver Creek rises in n Cumberland County and flows se into Cape Fear River.

Carver Gap, nw Clay County in Tusquitee Mountains.

Carver Knob, s Madison County between Morrow Branch and Worley Cove.

Carver Mountain between Cope Creek and Blanton Branch in n central Jackson County. Alt. 3,600.

Carvers, community in se Bladen County.

Carvers Branch rises in s Mitchell County and flows sw into East Fork Crabtree Creek.

Carvers Creek rises in se Bladen County and flows e into Cape Fear River. Appears as Livingswood Creek on the Collet map of 1770.

Carvers Creek rises in n Cumberland County and flows se into Cape Fear River.

Carvers Creek, community in n Cumberland County.

Carvers Creek Township in se Bladen County.

Carvers Creek Township, n central Cumberland County.

Carvers Falls on Carver Creek, central Cumberland County approx. 7 mi. ne of Fayetteville, at the junction of the forks of Carver Creek near its mouth in the Cape Fear River.

Carvers Gap, on the Mitchell County, N.C.-Carter County, Tenn., line.

Carvers Gap Creek rises in e Mitchell County and flows se into Fall Creek.

Cary, town in w Wake County, settled about 1863 as the site of Frank Page's lumber operations and known as Page's Turnout or Page's Tavern. Later, when the railroad was built, it became Page's Siding. Inc. 1871 as Carey; named for Senator Samuel Fenton Carey (1814-1900) of Ohio, a Prohibition leader. The spelling became Cary as early as 1899.

Cary Branch rises in sw Wake County and flows sw into Buckhorn Creek.

Cary Creek rises in w Wake County and flows sw into Chatham County where it enters Whiteoak Creek.

Cary Flat Branch rises in e central Avery County and flows s into Wilson Creek.

Cary Township, w central Wake County.

Casar, town in n Cleveland County. Settled about 1870, inc. 1903, but long inactive in municipal affairs. Alt. 1,145. Intended to be named for Julius Caesar but an error was made in the spelling.

Casar Township, former township in nw Cleveland County, now township number 11.

Cascade Branch rises in n Madison County and flows se into Spring Creek.

Cascade Creek rises in s Virginia and flows se into Rockingham County where it enters Dan River.

Cascade Creek rises in w central Stokes County and flows nw into Dan River. Named for the falls in the creek. Mentioned by William Byrd in 1728.

Cascade Falls in Cascade Creek, w central Stokes County in Hanging Rock State Park. From a high rock precipice, water falls some 200 ft. in an "Upper Cascade" and then falls another 60 ft. in a "Lower Cascade." The falls are s of Tories Den.

Cascade Lake in e Transylvania County in Little River. Covers 150 acres and has maximum depth of 75 ft. Used for hydroelectric power and recreation.

Cascoponung River. See Scuppernong River.

Case Camp Ridge in n Transylvania County extends e in an arc from Pisgah Ridge to Case Ridge Gap.

Case Cove, the valley through which Wise Branch flows in sw Buncombe County.

Case Ridge Gap in n Transylvania County at the e end of Case Camp Ridge.

Casey Bay on Pamlico Sound side of Portsmouth Island w of community of Portsmouth, e Carteret County.

Casey Branch rises in sw Polk County and flows ne into Cove Creek.

Casey Island in Pamlico Sound, off Portsmouth Island, e Carteret County.

Cash Corner No. 2, community in s Pamlico County se of Arapahoe. Named because a store at the crossroads here sold goods cheaper for cash than on credit. See also Hollyville.

Cash Creek rises in w Henderson County and flows se into French Broad River.

Cashie Branch rises in n Jackson County and flows nw into Scott Creek.

Cashie Neck, swampy region of se Bertie County between the Roanoke and Cashie rivers opposite Plymouth.

Cashie River rises in nw Bertie County and flows se into Batchelor Bay and Albemarle Sound. One of the few rivers in the state to have its complete course in one county, Cashie was originally named Kesiah, the present name being a gradual corruption. See also Connaritsa.

Cashiers, town in s Jackson County beside Cashiers Lake. Inc. 1927. Post office est. 1839 as Cashiers Valley; named changed to Cashiers in 1881. The origin of the name is uncertain, but there are many stories, some concerning a horse named Cash which grazed here. Other stories concern a hermit named Cashiers who lived here.

Cashiers Lake, an artificial lake in s Jackson County formed in 1922 on Chattooga River. Covers 30 acres with a maximum depth of 50 feet. Used for fishing, boating and power. Named for nearby town of Cashiers.

Cashiers Township, s Jackson County.

Cashiers Valley. See Cashiers.

Cashoke Creek rises in se Bertie County and flows se into Cashie River.

Cason Old Field, community in s central Anson County. Named for local family.

Castalia, town in nw Nash County. Settled about 1850 and had a high school in 1853. Named about 1853 by David S. Richardson, local schoolmaster and native of Cornish, N. H., for Castalian Springs (of Greek mythology) located near Mt. Parnassus. Alt. 319.

Castalia Township, nw Nash County.

The Castle, an island of approx. $\frac{1}{10}$ acre in the Pamlico River, w Beaufort County, about 350 yards off shore from the town of Washington.

Castle Creek rises in n Person County and flows n into Hyco River.

Castle Dobbs. See Russellborough.

Castle Hayne, community in n New Hanover County. Est. by 1861 and known as Spring Garden for a number of years. Appears as such on the Colton map, 1861, and on other maps through the 1870's. By 1882 (Kerr map) it was called Castle Hayne. Named for Captain Roger Haynes who built a "castle" nearby prior to the Revolutionary War. Originally Castle Haynes but shortened to Castle Hayne by the railroad and later adopted by the post office. A 6,000-acre agricultural colony est. here by Hugh MacRae in the early twentieth century included a number of Dutch families. Produces commercial flowers and bulbs, vegetables, and chemicals. Alt. 20.

Castle Tryon. See Russellborough.

Castle of Thundertontrenck. See Lenox Castle.

Castletons Creek. See Raccoon Creek.

Castoria, community in n central Greene County. A noted pre-Civil War plantation house of this name still exists here and gave its name to the community. Probably named for Castor, one of the Greek mythological Dioscuri twins.

Casville, community in w Caswell County. Known as Dove's Crossroads until about 1962.

Caswell, community in n Jones County. Alt. 46.

Caswell. *See* Kinston.

Caswell. *See* Point Caswell.

Caswell Beach, the s beach front on Oak Island, se Brunswick County.

Caswell Branch rises in sw Warren County and flows s into Shocco Creek.

Caswell County was formed in 1777 from Orange County. In the n central section of the state, it is bounded by the state of Virginia and by Person, Orange, Alamance, and Rockingham counties. It was named for Richard Caswell (1729-89), member of the first Continental Congress, Major General in the Revolutionary War, and first governor of the state of North Carolina. Area: 435 sq. mi. County seat: Yanceyville with an elevation of 619 ft. Townships are Anderson, Dan River, Hightowers, Leasburg, Locust Hill, Milton, Pelham, Stony Creek, Yanceyville. Produces wheat, oats, corn, tobacco, livestock, hogs, textiles, lumber, crushed stone, and sand.

Caswell Court House. *See* Yanceyville.

Caswell Distirict, one of the districts into which Caswell County was divided at the time of the 1790 census. It contained 201 heads of families.

Caswells Branch. *See* Poorhouse Run.

Caswells Landing. *See* Hookerton.

Caswell Township, w Pender County.

Cataloochee, community on Cataloochee Creek in w Haywood County. Now almost entirely in the Great Smoky Mountains National Park. Alt. 2,620. Pop. formerly around 250, now 12 to 15. Cataloochee is a white man's corruption of the Indian word *gad-a-lu-sti*, a descriptive exclamation which means "standing in a row." It is what the Indians saw from Cove Creek Gap—timber standing up on the distant mountains near the head of the watershed.

Cataloochee Balsam, mountain on the Haywood-Swain County line between Horse Creek Gap and Pauls Gap. Alt. 5,940.

Cataloochee Creek is formed in w Haywood County by the junction of Caldwell Fork and Palmer Creek. It flows se and e into Waterville Lake on Pigeon River.

Cataloochee Divide, w Haywood County, Great Smoky Mountains National Park, extending ne from Whim Knob. It forms the e boundary of the Park for more than 10 mi. It also marks the Cataloochee Creek and Johnson Creek drainage line.

Cataloochee Township, ne Haywood County.

Catawba, town in e Catawba County on the Catawba River. Inc. 1893. Alt. 834. Post office first est. as Chestnut Grove in nearby Iredell County but the name was changed to Catawba Station when it was moved to e Catawba County in 1859. Became Catawba in 1877.

Catawba County was formed in 1842 from Lincoln County. Located in the w central section of the state, it is bounded by Iredell, Lincoln, Burke, Caldwell, and Alexander counties. It was named for the Catawba Indians who once inhabited the region. Area: 412 sq. mi. County seat: Newton with an elevation of 996 ft. Townships are Bandy, Caldwell, Catawba, Clines, Hickory, Jacobs Fork, Mountain Creek, and Newton. Produces wheat, oats, corn, dairy products, hogs, livestock, hosiery, furniture, textiles, electronics, fabricated metals, lumber, paper boxes, crushed stone, and brick.

Catawba Creek rises in central Gaston County, within the limits of Gastonia, and flows se into South Carolina where it enters the Catawba River near the state line.

Catawba Falls on the headwaters of Catawba River in sw McDowell County near Ridgecrest. Water falls in a continuous spray down five levels of rock. Sometimes called Rocky Glen for one of the upper falls where water plunges over a ledge 200 ft. high.

Catawba Lake. *See* Lake Wylie.

Catawba Land. *See* Piedmont.

Catawba River rises in the Blue Ridge Mountains in sw McDowell County near the Buncombe-McDowell County line. It flows ne through McDowell and e through Burke County; forms successively the Caldwell-Catawba, Alexander-Catawba, Iredell-Catawba, Iredell-Lincoln, Mecklenburg-Lincoln, and Mecklenburg-Gaston County lines. It enters South Carolina about 21 mi. w of Charlotte and flows s to join Big Wateree Creek in Wateree Pond to form the Wateree River about 20 mi. above Camden. From its headwaters to the South Carolina line it flows approx. 150 mi. Catawba was an Indian word which may have meant "people of the river banks" or "people of the river (Catawba) with broken banks." For some of the named fords across the river see also Beattie's, Cowan's, Island, Sherrills, Tools, and Tuckaseege.

Catawba Springs, community in n Catawba County. Former resort, popular in late eighteenth and early nineteenth centuries. Est. as Elliott Springs on June 10, 1859, and became White Sulphur Springs on August 1, 1860. The Sparkling Catawba Springs Company was inc. in 1869 to erect buildings and open and est. the mineral springs. Became Sparkling Catawba Springs in 1877.

Catawba Springs, popular pre-Civil War resort on Killian Creek, e Lincoln County. Owned by Captain John Reid, Revolutionary soldier, and known first as Reid's Springs.

Catawba Springs Township, e Lincoln County.

Catawba Station. See Catawba.

Catawba Township, e Catawba County. Name changed in 1879 from Hamilton Township.

Catawba Vale. See Old Fort.

Cat Creek rises in e Macon County and flows nw into Rabbit Creek.

Cateechee Branch rises in e central Transylvania County and flows se into French Broad River.

Caterpillar Creek, rises in se Alamance County and flows se into Orange County where it enters Cane Creek.

Cates Creek, rises in central Orange County and flows ne into Eno River.

Catfield Point, s Onslow County in Stones Bay.

Catfish Lake, a natural lake in Croatan National Forest, e Jones and sw Craven counties. Covers 950 acres with a max.

depth of 4 to 5 ft. It is in the Lakes Pocosin, which see.

Catfish Point, in e Tyrrell County, extends from the mainland into Alligator River.

Cat Gap, central Transylvania County near the head of King Creek.

Catharine Creek rises in e Hertford County and flows n into Chowan River. Undoubtedly a corruption of Cautaking, Catokinge, or Cataking, an Indian village of the sixteenth century located in this area. The Indian name probably meant "at the land that pushes" or "bulges out," as if into the river.

Catharine Lake, a natural lake in nw Onslow County. Covers approx. 45 acres with a max. depth of 15 ft. Alt. 17. A community by this name existed as early as 1861 but the lake itself apparently is not shown on early maps. Local tradition says that it was named by John Avirette for his fiancee, Catharine Cole. Another source relates that it was named for the Cothran family in the vicinity.

Catherine Creek is formed on the Gates-Chowan County line by the junction of Trotman and Warwick creeks and flows sw into Chowan River. Appears on the Collet map, 1770, as Catharines Creek.

Cathey Cove, s Haywood County on a tributary of Little East Fork Pigeon River.

Cathey Creek rises in nw Mecklenburg County and flows w into Davidson Creek.

Cathey Gap, e Haywood County between Rocky Knob and Pressly Mountain.

Cathey Gap in the middle of Wolf Mountain, e Jackson County.

Cathey Ridge, s Haywood County between Cathey Cove and Hemlock Branch.

Cathey's, community in w Rowan County. Named for George Cathey who had a grant of land here in 1750.

Catheys Creek rises in n Rutherford County and flows se into Second Broad River.

Catheys Creek rises in w Transylvania County and flows se into French Broad River.

Catheys Creek, community in central Transylvania County, centered on Limekiln Branch approx. 1 mi. nw of French Broad River. Named for Joseph Cathey (1803-74), one of the first settlers in the area. Alt. approx. 2,160.

Cathey's Creek. See Kerr Creek; Sloans Creek.

Catheys Creek Falls located on Catheys Creek in central Transylvania County, between King Mountain and Kagle Mountain. Falls are 40 ft. high. Alt. approx. 2,520.

Catheys Creek Township, central Transylvania County.

Cathey's Fort. See Woodlawn.

Cat Island, a small island in sw Carteret County in Bogue Sound.

Cat Pen Branch rises in w Madison County and flows s into Roaring Fork.

Cat Pen Gap, n Transylvania County between Cat Gap and Horse Cove.

Cat Point, central Onslow County in Farnell Bay.

Cat Ridge, ne Transylvania County n of McCall Mountain.

Catskill Creek. See Catskin Creek.

Catskin Creek rises in s Pender County and flows sw into Merricks Creek. Formerly Catskill Creek until corrupted by local usage into the present name.

Cat Square, crossroads community in nw Lincoln County. Named after unwanted cats and kittens were left there on several occasions.

Catstair Branch rises in ne Cherokee County and flows nw into Ashturn Branch.

The Catstairs, a very rough and steep trail followed by wildcats from one mountain to another near the head of West Fork Overflow Creek in s Macon County. See also Winding Stairs, for another use of this name.

Cattail Bay, a loam filled bay in central Columbus County.

Cattail Branch rises in n Wilson County near Cliftonsville and flows s approx. 1 mi. into Toisnot Swamp.

Cattail Creek rises in central Granville County and flows sw into Tar River.

Cat Tail Creek rises in n Johnston County and flows se into Little River.

Cattail Creek is formed in s Yancey County by the junction of North Fork Cattail Creek and South Fork Cattail Creek. It flows nw into Cane River.

Cattail Peak, s Yancey County between Balsam Cone and Potato Hill in the Black Mountains. Alt. 6,583.

Cattail Swamp rises in n central Wilson County and flows e into Town Creek.

Causey. See Bonlee.

Cavanaugh Ditch, a drain in s Duplin County to carry the waters of Kenan Pocosin into Northeast Cape Fear River.

Ca-Vel, community in central Person County. Post office est. 1948. Formerly known as Bakers. Produces textiles.

The Caves, natural subterranean caves in

nw Rutherford County between Broad River and Buffalo Creek in Rumbling Bald Mountain, which see.

Cawcaw Bay, shallow muck area about 5 mi. long and about 2 mi. wide near sw edge of Green Swamp, sw Brunswick County.

Cawcaw Swamp rises in Cawcaw Bay, sw Brunswick County and flows sw into Waccamaw River.

Cecils Harbor appears on the Smith map, 1624, applied to the three bays in s Hyde County now called Rose Bay, Swanquarter Bay, and Juniper Bay. Perhaps named for William Cecil, Lord Burleigh (1520-98) or Robert Cecil, first Earl of Salisbury (1563?-1612).

Cecil Township, s Haywood County.

Cedar Bay, formed by waters of Neuse River and the n tip of Carteret County.

Cedar Bay in the waters of Currituck Sound on the nw side of Church Island in central Currituck County.

Cedar Bay off the sw shore of Roanoke Island, e Dare County, in the waters of Croatan Sound.

Cedar Bay Point, a point on the s shore of the Neuse River about 4 mi. upstream from its mouth and n of the entrance to Cedar Bay in ne Carteret County.

Cedar Branch rises in central Columbus County and flows e into Soules Swamp.

Cedar Branch rises in se Wilson County and flows s approx. 3½ mi. into Black Creek.

Cedar Cliff, community in se Alamance County on Haw River. A post office est. here as early as 1882.

Cedar Cliff, peak in the Great Craggy Mountains, ne Buncombe County, between Eagle Rock Cove and Wolf Branch. Alt. 4,400.

Cedar Cliff, peak in the Swannanoa Mountains, s Buncombe County. Alt. 3,846.

Cedar Cliff, e Haywood County between Panther Creek and Rust Fork.

Cedar Cliff, n Haywood County extends eastward from Snowbird Creek to Bills Knob.

Cedar Cliff, on Jackson-Swain County line near junction of Chestnut Cove Creek with Connelly Creek in e Swain County.

Cedar Cliff on the Jackson-Swain County line.

Cedar Cliff, at the head of Shepherd Creek in n Macon County.

Cedar Cliff, s Macon County between Buckeye Creek and Hickory Knoll Creek.

Cedar Cliff Knob, ne Buncombe County w of Sheepwallow Knob.

Cedar Cliff Lake, central Jackson County on Tuckasegee River, 14 mi. s of Sylva. Covers 121 acres; max. depth 150 ft. Dam constructed 1952; used to generate hydroelectric power for Nantahala Power and Light Company. Named for Cedar Cliff Mountain at the upper end of the lake. Alt. 2,330.

Cedar Cliff Mountain, on Buncombe-Rutherford County line between Harris View and Cedar Knob. Alt., 3,829.

Cedar Cliff Mountain, central Jackson County between Niggerskull Creek and Gladie Creek.

Cedar Cliff Mountain, s Macon County between Andy Gap and Buddy Gap. Alt. 4,824.

Cedar Cliff Ridge, n Macon County at the head of Shepherd Creek.

Cedar Cliff Ridge, ne Macon County parallel to Huckleberry Creek.

Cedar Cliffs at the s end of Cullowhee Mountain in w Jackson County.

Cedar Cove, w Graham County between Cedar Top and Santeetlah Creek.

Cedar Creek rises in e Anson County and flows n into Pee Dee River.

Cedar Creek rises in se Buncombe County and flows se into Rutherford County where it enters Cove Creek.

Cedar Creek rises in se Caldwell County on the slopes of Hibriten Mountain and flows e into Upper Little River at Cedar Valley.

Cedar Creek rises in n Carteret County and flows sw into Adams Creek.

Cedar Creek rises in s Cumberland County and flows sw into Cape Fear River.

Cedar Creek rises in w Franklin County and flows se into Tar River.

Cedar Creek rises in s Granville County and flows sw into Robertson Creek.

Cedar Creek rises in w Harnett County and flows ne into Cape Fear River.

Cedar Creek rises in s Jackson County and flows w into Lake Thorpe.

Cedar Creek rises in se Rowan County and flows ne for about three miles into Yadkin River.

Cedar Creek rises in s Stanly County and flows se and ne into Lake Tillery.

Cedar Creek rises in n Wake County and flows ne into Neuse River.

Cedar Creek rises in s Yadkin County and flows s into Davie County where it turns se to enter Dutchmans Creek. Approx. 13 mi. long.

Cedar Creek, community in s Cumberland County on the stream of the same name. Appears as Terebinthe on the Kerr map, 1882.

Cedar Creek Township, e central Cumberland County.

Cedar Falls, community in central Randolph County on Deep River. Inc. 1899; charter repealed 1901. Once known as Everett's Mill, for Colonel Benjamin Everett. The first cotton mill in the county, Sapona Cotton Mill, was built here in 1836.

Cedar Fork rises in ne Wake County and flows e into Little River at Mitchells Millpond. Also known as Cedar Prong of Little River.

Cedar Fork, community in e Duplin County.

Cedar Forks, community in w Northhampton County.

Cedar Fork Township, former township in se Durham County. Combined with Patterson township to form Triangle township.

Cedar Fork Township, w Wake County.

Cedar Grove, community in nw Orange County. A post office est. here as early as 1828.

Cedar Grove Township, nw Orange County.

Cedar Hammock, an island in Bogue Sound, sw Carteret County.

Cedar Hill, community in n Anson County.

Cedar Inlet, an inlet about midway Core Banks in e Carteret County, on Outer Banks.

Cedar Island, large island in ne Carteret County between West Bay and Core Sound. Appears on Moll map, 1729.

Cedar Island, a small island in Bogue Sound, s Carteret County.

Cedar Island, a two-acre uninhabited tidal marsh island in Cedar Island Bay on the w side of Church Island, central Currituck County.

Cedar Island, in the waters of Roanoke Sound off the sw tip of Bodie Island, e Dare County.

Cedar Island, tidal marsh island approx. ½ mi. long in n Pamlico County. Appears on the Lawson map, 1709, and the Moseley map, 1733.

Cedar Island, community on the island of the same name, ne Carteret County.

Cedar Island. See Smith Island.

Cedar Island Bay, approx. 4 mi. long and 1½ mi. wide, in ne Carteret County.

Bounded by Cedar Island, Back Bay, and Core Sound.

Cedar Island Bay in the waters of Currituck Sound on the w side of Church Island in central Currituck County. Named for the small tidal marsh island in the Bay.

Cedar Island Point, ne Carteret County; most e point of Cedar Island, on s side of entrance from Core Sound into Cedar Island Bay.

Cedar Island Township, on Pamlico and Core Sounds of ne Carteret County, formerly a part of Hunting Quarters (now Atlantic) Township.

Cedar Knob, on Buncombe-Rutherford County line, s of Cedar Cliff.

Cedar Knob, e Macon County between the head of Indian Camp Branch and Walnut Creek.

Cedar Knob, w Madison County between Granger Mountain and Friezeland Creek.

Cedar Lodge, community in e Davidson County. Named for the home of John W. Thomas, founder of Thomasville, who lived here 1825-52. A nineteenth century post office serving the community was Fair Grove, a name by which the community is also sometimes known.

Cedar Mountain, a peak in the South Mountains, s Burke County Alt. 2,160.

Cedar Mountain, sw Polk County. Alt. 2,200.

Cedar Mountain, community in se Transylvania County on Walker Creek near its junction with Little River, approx. 7 mi. se of town of Brevard. Includes former community of Loftis.

Cedar Point, point of land in sw Carteret County extending into the mouth of White Oak River and Bogue Sound. Appears on the Moseley map, 1733.

Cedar Point, a point extending from the n mainland of Carteret County into Neuse River.

Cedar Point, point of land on the w shore of Bodie Island in the waters of Roanoke Sound, a short distance n of Oregon Inlet, e Dare County.

Cedar Point, in s Onslow County extends into n Howards Bay.

Cedar Point, community in sw Carteret County.

Cedar Point Mountain, w Rockingham County near Mayo River.

Cedar Prong of Little River. See Cedar Fork.

Cedar Rock, e Transylvania County between Buck Forest and Little River.

Cedar Rock, community in e central Caldwell County, named for cedar trees growing from a rock formation.

Cedar Rock, community in e Franklin County.

Cedar Rock Creek rises in w Transylvania County near Cedar Rock Mountain and flows n into Davidson River.

Cedar Rock Creek rises in w Transylvania County near Cedar Rock Mountain and flows sw into Catheys Creek.

Cedar Rock Mountain, w Randolph County.

Cedar Rock Mountain, n central Transylvania County between Sandy Gap and Butter Gap. Alt. 4,056.

Cedar Rock Township, former township in e Franklin County, now township number 8.

Cedar Run. See Vashti.

Cedar Run Creek rises in ne Alexander County and flows s into South Yadkin River. This is considered to be the head stream of South Yadkin River.

Cedar Swamp Creek rises in central Carteret County and flows ne into Newport River.

Cedar Top, mountain in w Graham County between Hooper Mill Creek and Hooper Cove. Alt. approx. 4,000.

Cedar Valley, community in s Caldwell County on Upper Little River.

Cefare, community in nw Wilson County between Turkey Creek and Marsh Swamp. Named for Cefare Bissett. A post office existed here 1899-1904.

Ceffo, community in w Person County.

Celia Creek rises in sw Caldwell County and flows se into Husbands Creek. Originally named Sealeys Creek for George Sealey, eighteenth-century settler.

Celo, community in e Yancey County on Browns Creek. Alt. 2,735. Named for nearby Celo Knob.

Celo Knob, e Yancey County near the head of Browns Creek. Alt. 6,326.

Celo Ridge, e Yancey County between Ayles and Browns creeks. Named for the Indian word seeloo, "corn."

Cemetery Branch rises in central Wake County within the limits of Raleigh and flows n into Pigeon House Branch.

Center, community in w Davie County. Est. in the 1820's as a camp meeting ground. A post office established here operated under the name Selena in 1889-1890; changed to Bailey, 1890-1902. Community retains original name, however.

Center, community in w Yadkin County e of Cranberry Creek.

Center, community in central Yadkin County. A late nineteenth century post office here was named Chestnut Ridge.

Center Grove Township, n central Guilford County.

Center of North Carolina. See Geographic center.

Center Township, central Chatham County.

Center Township, se Stanly County.

Centerville, community in ne Franklin County. Alt. 300. Settled about 1882. Named because of its central position between Warrenton, Louisburg, and Littleton.

Centerville. See Kelly.

Central Falls, community on Deep River, central Randolph County. Long the site of one or more textile mills. Named for minor falls on the river, now obliterated by dams constructed for water power.

Central Township, central Bladen County.

Centre, community in s Guilford County. Named for Centre Friends Meeting, begun in 1757.

Centre Hill, town in e Chowan County. Inc. 1935 but no longer active in muncipal affairs. A post office est. here in 1886 was first known as Centre Hill but was renamed for James N. Tyner (1826-1904), a former Postmaster General. Tyner is still the post office name.

Cerro Gordo, town in w Columbus County. Inc. 1874 and named for the Mexican battleground where General Winfield Scott, in 1847, was victorious. In Spanish the name means "big hill." Alt. 95.

Cerro Gordo Township, w Columbus County.

Chacandepeco. See Chancandepeco Inlet.

Chadbourn, town in n Columbus County. Inc. 1883. Named for a family of lumber merchants. Produces lumber and textiles. Alt. 105.

Chadbourn Township, w central Columbus County.

Chadwick Acres, town in s Onslow County on Chadwick Bay. Inc. 1961. Planned for development as a resort area. Covers 308 acres.

Chadwick Bay, se Carteret County, the mouth of Chadwick Creek. Named for Samuel Chadwick, eighteenth century whaler who lived in the vicinity.

Chadwick Bay, in s Onslow County in New River.

Chadwick Creek rises in s Carteret County

and flows s into Chadwick Bay. Appears as Larler Creek on the Collet map, 1770.

Chadwick Creek rises in ne Pamlico County and flows se into Bay River.

Chainshot Island, ne Carteret County in Core Sound, midway between Hog Island and Harbor Island. Named for a kind of shot consisting of two balls or half balls united by a short chain, formerly used in naval warfare to cut a ship's rigging or to sweep its decks. Named as early as the Moseley map, 1733. See also Hunting Quarter Sound.

Chairmaker Branch rises in central Clay County and flows nw into Tusquitee Creek.

Chairman, community in ne Brunswick County.

Chalk Creek rises in n Rutherford County and flows sw into Cove Creek.

Chalk Mountain, s Mitchell County between Brushy Creek and North Toe River. Alt. 3,558.

Chalk Mountain. See Toms Mountain.

Chalybeate (ka-lib-e-ate) community in n Harnett County. Settled 1760. Named for nearby springs containing salts of iron. Former health resort. Alt. 175.

Chambers, community in sw Burke County.

Chambers Branch rises in e Haywood County on Chambers Mountain and flows s into Pigeon River.

Chambersburg Township, se Iredell County. Named for local Chambers family.

Chambers Cove, s Haywood County on a tributary of West Prong Pigeon River.

Chambers Creek rises in w Cherokee County and flows sw into Hiwassee Lake.

Chambers Creek rises in n Swain County and flows sw into Fontana Lake.

Chambers Creek Gap, n Swain County on Welch Ridge near the head of Bear Creek. Named for John Chambers, an early settler.

Chambers Mountain, e Haywood County extends ne from the head of Long Branch to the head of Rogers Cove Creek.

Champion, community in sw Wilkes County near South Prong Lewis Fork Creek.

Chancandepeco Inlet from the Atlantic Ocean into Pamlico Sound through Hatteras Island n of Cape Hatteras, se Dare County. It opened prior to 1585 and closed prior to 1657. Appears as Chacandepeco on the Velasco map, 1611. The name is possibly a Spanish spelling for an Algonquian Indian word meaning "it dips and disappears as shallows."

Chandler Creek rises in e Madison County and flows se into California Creek.

Chandler Knob, n Madison County near the head of Revere Creek.

Chaney Creek rises in central Onslow County and flows sw into New River.

Chapanoke, community in e Perquimans County. Named for an Indian village, Chepanoc, the site of which probably is on Wade Point, Pasquotank County. The name apparently was an Indian word for "land of the dead" ["cemetery"?]. Alt. 15.

Chapel Branch rises in sw Hertford County and flows nw into Cutawhiskie Swamp. See also St. Johns (community).

Chapel Branch rises in w Beaufort County and flows n into Bear Creek.

Chapel Creek rises se of the town of Chapel Hill, se Orange County and flows se into Morgan Creek.

Chapel Creek rises in n Pamlico County and flows s into Bay River.

Chapel Creek rises in s Pasquotank County and flows se into Big Flatty Creek.

Chapel Hill, town in se Orange County, seat of the University of North Carolina which opened January 16, 1795. A committee to lay out the town was authorized by the trustees of the University on December 8, 1792, and lots were first sold on October 12, 1793. Appears on the Samuel Lewis map published in Carey's atlas in 1795. Inc. 1819. Named for the Church of England New Hope Chapel which once stood at the crossroads on this wooded hill. Alt. 501.

Chapel Hill Township, se Orange County.

Chapel Swamp, nw Tyrrell County on the w side of Scuppernong River. Named for St. Paul's Church which stood in the vicinity in the eighteenth century.

Chaplin's Stand. See Bixby.

Chapman, community in n Alexander County.

Chapmans Creek rises in central Surry County and flows se into Fisher River.

Chappel Creek appears on the Moseley map, 1733, rising in e Beaufort Precinct and flowing e into Machapungo River. This probably is either modern Jordan or Satterthwaite Creek.

Chappels Creek rises in s Person County and flows s into North Flat River.

Chappel Swamp, n Washington County on the head of Whites Creek, drains nw into Kendricks Creek.

Charity, community in s Duplin County.

Charity, community in n central Yadkin County. Named for Charity Baptist Church.

Charles, community in n central Iredell County.

Charles Creek rises in ne Mitchell County and flows sw into Little Rock Creek.

Charles Creek rises in w Transylvania County and flows se into Catheys Creek.

Charles Creek. See Muddy Creek.

Charles River. See Cape Fear River.

Charleston, community in se Halifax County.

Charleston. See Bryson City; Waughtown.

Charleston Township, e Swain County. Enlarged between 1934-1940 with the establishment of Great Smoky Mountains National Park to include the e part of Forneys Creek Township and all of Oconalufty Township.

Charles Town, center of a colony from Charlestowne, Massachusetts, est. in 1662 under the leadership of William Hilton, on Town Creek, e Brunswick County. Abandoned in 1663. In 1664 a colony from Barbados under the leadership of Sir John Yeamans occupied the site, but they abandoned it in 1665. New Town on the Ogilby map, 1671, apparently was intended to designate this settlement. See also Clarendon County.

Charley Bald, a peak at the n end of Charley Ridge on Rich Mountain in e Jackson County. Alt. 5,530.

Charley Branch rises in w Madison County and flows se into Spring Creek.

Charley Branch rises in w Swain County and flows se into Wiggins Creek.

Charley Creek rises in e Jackson County and flows s into Wolf Creek.

Charley Knob on the s end of Charley Ridge in e Jackson County.

Charley Ridge, e Jackson between Gage Creek and Charley Creek.

Charlie Creek rises in n Yancey County and flows s into Little Creek.

Charlie Ridge, n Buncombe County, w of Brittain Mountain.

Charlies Bunion Mountain, on Swain County, N.C.-Sevier County, Tenn., line, in Great Smoky Mountains National Park. Alt. 5,375. So named because Charles Connor remarked to George Masa that the peak looked "like a bunion on Old Smoky's foot."

Charlies Island, a land formation in s Duplin County which is surrounded by swamp.

Charlies Ridge, on the Avery-Mitchell County line between Wolf Ridge and Spear Tops.

Charlone Creek. *See* Shelton Creek.

Charlotte, city and county seat, central Mecklenburg County. Settled about 1750; inc. 1768. Named for Charlotte Sophia of Mecklenburg-Strelitz (1744-1818), queen of George III. Appears as Charlottesburgh on the Collet map, 1770. Home of University of North Carolina at Charlotte, George Washington Carver College, Queens College, Johnson C. Smith University, and Central Piedmont Community College. Produces fabricated metals, textiles, dairy and bakery products, industrial machinery, canned foods, paper products, hosiery, processed meat, primary metals, aircraft. parts, apparel, furniture, electronic components, boxes, and chemicals. Alt. 795.

Charlotte Branch rises in w Madison County and flows ne into Spring Branch.

Charlotte Cove, n Cherokee County between Moss Branch and Little Dam Branch.

Charlotte Crossing. *See* Claremont.

Charlottesburgh. *See* Charlotte.

Charlotte Township, former township in central Mecklenburg County, now township number 1.

Chasm Prong rises in n Swain County in Great Smoky Mountains National Park and flows e to join Gulf Prong in forming Bradley Fork.

Chasteen Creek rises in ne Swain County in Great Smoky Mountains National Park and flows sw into Bradley Fork.

Chasteen Mountain, sw Clay County between Trout Cove Branch and Greasy Creek.

Chastine Creek rises in e Jackson County and flows s into Caney Fork.

Chatham. *See* Pittsboro.

Chatham County was formed in 1771 from Orange County. Located in the central section of the state, it is bounded by Wake, Harnett, Lee, Moore, Randolph, Alamance, Orange, and Durham counties.

It was named for William Pitt, Earl of Chatham (1708-78), who vigorously opposed the harsh measures taken in England with regard to the American colonies in 1774-75 and who advocated cessation of hostilities in 1777. Area: 707 sq. mi. County seat: Pittsboro with an elevation of 409 ft. Townships are Albright, Baldwin, Bear Creek, Cape Fear, Center, Gulf, Hadley, Haw River, Hickory Mountain, Matthew, New Hope, Oakland, and William. Produces wheat, oats, corn, livestock, poultry, furniture, textiles, hosiery, crushed stone, and clay for brick. *See also* Pitt County.

Chattooga Ridge in s Jackson County extends se in an arc from Little Terrapin Mountain to Heddie Mountain. The name is a variation of the Cherokee word *chatawga*, "chicken."

Chattooga River rises in sw Jackson County and flows s to the Jackson-Macon County line which it forms for a short distance before flowing into South Carolina where it enters Savannah River.

Chattoka, a Tuscarora Indian village appearing on the Lawson map, 1709, and the Moll map, 1729, between the Neuse and Trent rivers, central Craven County. The name meant "where the fish are taken out." When the Tuscarora Indians moved to New York they took this name with them and it has survived as Chautauqua.

Chatuge Lake, se Clay County on Hiwassee River. Created 1942 by a dam in the river at the mouth of Shooting Creek. Lake about 10 mi. long, covers over 8,000 acres; max. depth 144 ft. Forms a holding reservoir in the T.V.A. system. Used for power, boating, swimming, fishing.

Chawanoac, an Indian village near the junction of the present Chowan-Gates-Hertford County lines on the Chowan River. Appears on the White map, 1585. *See also* Chowan.

Cheathamville. *See* Manson.

Cheaves Mill, formerly a homestead and mill in sw Vance County located approx. a mile upstream from the mouth of Tabb Creek, below the junction of Long Creek. Appears on the Collet map, 1770.

Cheecods Creek. *See* Chicod Creek.

Cheek Creek rises in se Montgomery County and flows sw into Richmond County where it enters Little River.

Cheek Creek Township, s central Montgomery County.

Cheek Mountain, grass covered peak in the Peach Bottom Mountain range, w central Alleghany County.

Cheeks, community in se Randolph County on Deep River.

Cheeks Crossroads, community in w Orange County.

Cheeks Township, w central Orange County.

Cheeohwa. See Cheoah.

Cheeweo, a Tuscarora Indian village, appears on the Moseley map, 1733, on the Roanoke River. Site probably near the present town of Williamston in n central Martin County.

Cheney Bay, s Carteret County lying between Turner Creek and North River Thorofare.

Cheoah, community in e central Graham County on Sweetwater Creek. Alt. 2,300. Named for the Indian word *tsiyahi* or *cheeohwa* meaning "otter."

Cheoah Bald, on the Graham-Swain County line between Bellcollar Gap and Sassafras Gap. Alt. 5,062.

Cheoah Branch rises in nw Swain County and flows sw into Fontana Lake.

Cheoah Mountains extend across central Graham County e in an arc from the headwaters of Gladdens Creek to the headwaters of Sawyer Creek.

Cheoah River is formed in central Graham County by the junction of Sweetwater and Tulula creeks. It flows nw into Little Tennessee River at Cheoah Dam. Santeetlah Lake is on Cheoah River.

Cheoah Township, s Graham County. See also Qualla Reservation.

Cheoah Valley. See Robbinsville.

Chepanuu, two Indian villages of the Weapemeoc tribe shown on the DeBry map, 1590, in what is now sw Pasquotank County on the Little River estuary.

Cheraw, community in central Caldwell County, named for the Cheraw (or Saura) Indians which formerly roamed the area.

Cherokee, town in e Swain County on Oconaluftee River. Alt. 1,955. The name Cherokee probably is from the Muskogee Indian word *tciloki* meaning "people of a different speech." The outdoor drama, "Unto These Hills," by Kermit Hunter has been produced here each summer since 1950.

Cherokee County was formed in 1839 from Macon County. Located in the w section of the state, it is bounded by the states of Georgia and Tennessee and by Graham, Swain, Macon, and Clay counties. It was named for the Cherokee Indians, some of whom still live in the region. Area: 467 sq. mi. County seat: Murphy with an elevation of 1,535 ft. Townships are Beaverdam, Hot House, Murphy, Notla, Shoal Creek, and Valley Town. Produces corn, poultry, dairy products, livestock, hogs, textiles, apparel, lumber, marble, talc, and crushed stone.

Cherokee Creek rises in se Rutherford County and flows n into Second Broad River.

Cherokee Gap, on Jackson-Swain County line near Oconaluftee River.

Cherokee Indian Reservation. See Qualla Reservation.

Cherry, town in e Washington County on Scuppernong River. Inc. 1907. A post office from 1898 until 1908.

Cherry, community in e Wayne County between Nahunta Swamp and The Slough, settled prior to 1833. Name is a corruption of the former name, Sherard, by which it appears on the MacRae map, 1833, or Sherards Crossroads, as it was known as recently as 1915. Named for a local family which settled in the area in the eighteenth century.

Cherry Branch rises in nw Macon County and flows nw into Otter Creek.

Cherry Branch rises in n Swain County and flows w into Forney Creek.

Cherry Cove, s Haywood County on the head of Cherry Cove Creek.

Cherry Cove, sw Macon County at the head of Allison Creek.

Cherry Cove Branch rises in s Clay County and flows nw into Hothouse Branch.

Cherry Cove Branch rises in n Transylvania County and flows ne into Looking Glass Creek.

Cherry Cove Creek rises in s Haywood County and flows ne into Allen Creek.

Cherry Creek rises in n Haywood County and flows s into Cold Springs Creek.

Cherry Creek rises in central Henderson County and flows w into Mud Creek.

Cherry Creek rises in n Swain County and flows s into Right Fork.

Cherryfield, coummnity in s Transylvania County between Morgan Mill Creek and Cherryfield Creek. Alt. 2,180.

Cherryfield Creek rises in w Transylvania County on s slopes of Three Forks Mountain and flows se into French Broad River.

Cherry Flats, e Haywood County on the head of Cove Creek.

Cherry Gap, on the Buncombe-Haywood County line between Grassy Gap and Boyd Mountain.

Cherry Gap, on the Haywood-Transylvania County line on Pisgah Ridge s of Bennett Gap.

Cherry Gap, on the Mitchell County, N.C.-Unicoi County, Tenn., line.

Cherry Gap, n Swain County near the nw end of Pilot Ridge, between North Fork [Chambers Creek] and Bear Creek.

Cherry Gap, w Watauga County w of Pond Branch.

Cherry Gap Branch rises in w Jackson County and flows w into Cullowhee Creek.

Cherry Glade, community in nw Pasquotank County.

Cherry Grove, community in sw Caswell County.

Cherry Grove, community in sw Columbus County.

Cherry Hill, plantation in s Warren County near the community of Inez, the home of George W. Alston. The house built in 1852 is still standing.

Cherry Knob, on Cullowhee Mountain in w Jackson County.

Cherry Knob, nw Swain County, in Great Smoky Mountains National Park on the w side of Jenkins Trail Ridge, and at the ne end of Big Fork Ridge. Alt. 4,420.

Cherry Lane, community in se Alleghany County, settled about 1838, and named for cherry tree bordered lane leading to home of Frank Bryan. Alt. 2,810.

Cherry Lane Township, se Alleghany County.

Cherry Log Gap, n Buncombe County, between Bald Knob and Little Snowball Mountain.

Cherry Log Ridge, s Yancey County between Left Prong South Toe River and Hemphill Creek.

Cherry Mountain, s Clay County extends ne in an arc from Joe Knob. See also Davie Mountain; Joe Knob.

Cherry Mountain, mountain range in e Rutherford County. Called Flint Hill prior to the Civil War when flint for rifles was obtained here. Acquired the name Cherry Mountain after the war when Amos Owens, Confederate veteran, made corn liquor and "cherry bounce" (from cherry trees growing here). See also Sweezy Mountain.

Cherry Mountain, s Yancey County between Middle Fork [Upper Creek] and South Fork [Upper Creek.]

Cherry Orchard Branch rises in n Jackson County and flows nw into Hornbuckle Creek.

Cherry Point, a point of land extending into the Neuse River near the mouth of Hancock Creek in se Craven County.

Cherry Point Marine Air Station, se Craven County on Neuse River. Begun in July, 1941; opened March, 1942. On 12,000 acres, it has been called the largest Marine air station in the world. The Overhaul and Repair Department of the U. S. Marine Air Corps here is the largest industrial defense plant in the state. A small community, Cherry Point, existed here prior to the est. of the station. The town of Havelock is adjacent.

Cherry Pond, a marsh in central Duplin County.

Cherry Ridge Landing, s Tyrrell County on Alligator River approx. 2 mi. e of its confluence with Northwest Fork [Alligator River]. The Indian village Tramaskecooc, which see, was at or near this site.

Cherry Run rises in w Beaufort County and flows· sw into Tranters Creek.

Cherryville, town in nw Gaston County. Post office est. here in 1847 as White Pines. Named changed to Cherryville in 1865; inc. 1872. Named for a row of cherry trees planted along an old rail fence parallel to the post road. Produces textiles. Alt. 971.

Cherryville Township, nw Gaston County.

Chesquau Branch rises in w Swain County and flows s into Fontana Lake.

Chesson, community in n central Washington County.

Chester Branch rises in s Jackson County and flows s into Fowler Creek.

Chesterfield, community in n central Burke County. Formerly known as Hoodsville.

Chesters Creek rises in w Carteret County and flows se into White Oak River.

Chestnut Bald on the Haywood-Transylvania County line between Devils Court House and Silvermine Bald. Alt. 6,040.

Chestnut Branch rises in n Clay County and flows ne into Tuni Creek.

Chestnut Branch rises in n Haywood County, near lat. 35° 45′ 15″ N., long. 83° 09′ 45″ W., and flows e into Big Creek.

Chestnut Branch rises in n Mitchell County and flows e into Left Fork Bean Creek.

Chestnut Branch rises in e Watauga County and flows ne into Elk Creek.

Chestnut Branch rises in ne Yancey County and flows ne into Toe River.

Chestnut Cove, the valley through which Chestnut Cove Branch flows in ne Buncombe County.

Chestnut Cove, s Buncombe County, sw of Truckwheel Mountain.

Chestnut Cove, e Swain County between Deep Gap and Camp Branch.

Chestnut Cove Branch rises in ne Buncombe County near Middle Mountain and flows w through Chestnut Cove into North Fork [Swannanoa River].

Chestnut Cove Creek rises in nw Haywood County and flows se into Big Creek.

Chestnut Cove Creek rises in e Swain County and flows ne into Connelly Creek.

Chestnut Cove Gap, s Buncombe County near Chestnut Cove.

Chestnut Cove Knob, on the Jackson-Macon County line.

Chestnut Cove Ridge, ne Buncombe County between Chestnut Cove and Big Cove.

Chestnut Creek rises in nw Transylvania County and flows s into Court House Creek.

Chestnut Creek rises near Candler Knob on the Buncombe-Henderson County line and flows n into Stony Fork.

Chestnut Crossroads. See Macon.

Chestnut Flat, a relatively level area in n Buncombe County near Coles Cove.

Chestnut Flat Cove, s Haywood County on Little East Fork Pigeon River.

Chestnut Flat Ridge, central Haywood County parallel to Laurel Branch.

Chestnut Flats, a relatively level area in se Buncombe County ne of Blue Rock Knob.

Chestnut Flats, a relatively level valley in ne Cherokee County near the head of Alfred Creek in the Valley River Mountains.

Chestnut Flats, central Haywood County on Chestnut Flat Ridge.

Chestnut Gap, on Buncombe-Madison County line between Little Sandy Mush Bald and North Fork Gap.

Chestnut Gap, on the Jackson-Macon County line.

Chestnut Gap, in w Macon County at the head of Pierce Creek.

Chestnut Gap Mountain, w Cherokee County extending se from Shoal Creek to Canedy Gap.

Chestnut Grove, community in sw Stokes County.

Chestnut Grove. See Catawba.

Chestnut Hill, community in ne Ashe County.

Chestnut Hill, former town in e central Rowan County immediately s of Salisbury and now a part of that city. Inc. 1863.

Chestnut Hill Township, ne Ashe County.

Chestnut Knob, n Buncombe County between Brank Mountain and Windy Gap.

Chestnut Knob, on the Graham County, N. C.-Monroe County, Tenn., line.

Chestnut Knob, w Macon County between Roaring Fork Creek and Jarrett Creek.

Chestnut Knob, ne Rutherford County.

Chestnut Knob n central Transylvania County near the head of Shutin Branch. Alt. approx. 3,860.

Chestnut Knob, n Yancey County on Sugarloaf Mountain.

Chestnut Knob, s Yancey County near South Fork Upper Creek.

Chestnut Log Branch rises in central Cherokee County and flows s into Pace Branch.

Chestnut Log Gap, n Graham County between Tuskeegee Creek and Sawyer Creek.

Chestnut Log Spring Gap, on the Madison County, N. C.-Greene County, Tenn., line.

Chestnut Mountain, s Buncombe County, s of Minehole Gap.

Chestnut Mountain, at the junction of Avery-Burke-Caldwell County lines. Alt. 3,173.

Chestnut Mountain, n central Caldwell County. Alt. 2,555.

Chestnut Mountain, s Caldwell County. Alt. 1,760.

Chestnut Mountain, n Cherokee County in the Unicoi Mountains. See also Hawk Knob.

Chestnut Mountain, e Haywood County between Burnett Cove and Hominy Creek.

Chestnut Mountain, central Jackson County between Shoal Creek and Little Trout Creek.

Chestnut Mountain, se Jackson County between Laurel Knob and Bald Rock Mountain. Alt. approx. 4,160.

Chestnut Mountain, se Macon County between Big Creek and the head of Cane Creek.

Chestnut Mountain, s Macon County between Rattlesnake Ridge and the head of Nichols Branch.

Chestnut Mountain, on the Madison-Yancey County line. Alt. 3,749.

Chestnut Mountain, s Polk County between Round Mountain and Tryon Mountain. Alt. approx. 2,100.

Chestnut Mountain, n Transylvania County on the head of Grogan Creek. Alt. approx. 3,700.

Chestnut Mountain, sw Transylvania County between Toxaway River and Horsepasture River. Alt. approx. 2,820.

Chestnut Mountain, w Transylvania County between North Fork Flat Creek and Morton Creek. Alt. approx. 3,340.

Chestnut Mountain, e central Watauga County s of the community of Meat Camp extends se from South Fork New River. Alt. approx. 3,520.

Chestnut Mountain, n Wilkes County between Mulberry Creek and Herald Mountain.

Chestnut Mountain, ne Yancey County between the head of Chestnut Creek and Brush Creek.

Chestnut Oak Flats, level valley in w Avery County.

Chestnut Oak Ridge, w Avery County.

Chestnut Orchard Branch rises in n Haywood County and flows sw into Groundhog Creek.

Chestnut Orchard Branch rises in w Macon County and flows n into Choga Creek.

Chestnut Orchard Ridge, nw Cherokee County extending se from Bryson Lead to Turkey Pen Hollow and Copper Creek.

Chestnut Ridge, n central Avery County.

Chestnut Ridge, n Buncombe County between Reems Creek and Main Creek.

Chestnut Ridge, on the Cleveland-Gaston County line.

Chestnut Ridge, a high strip of ground in Big Pocosin in sw Gates County.

Chestnut Ridge, e Haywood County between Ugly Creek and Shining Creek.

Chestnut Ridge, se Haywood County between East Fork Pigeon River and the Haywood County line.

Chestnut Ridge, e Jackson County between Rough Fork Creek and Piney Mountain Creek.

Chestnut Ridge, nw McDowell County between Threemile and Cox creeks.

Chestnut Ridge, sw Macon County between Little Lyman Branch and Devils Prong.

Chestnut Ridge, se Macon County, extends s from Cullasaja River to Dog Mountain.

Chestnut Ridge, ne Mitchell County between Feeding Ridge and Bearpen Creek.

Chestnut Ridge, ne Surry County between Rutledge Creek and the head of Big Creek.

Chestnut Ridge, n Swain County in Great Smoky Mountains National Park extends sw from Little Chestnut Bald between Desolation Branch and Defeat Branch.

Chestnut Ridge, nw Yancey County near the head of Little Creek.

Chestnut Ridge. See Center.

Chestnut Ridge Creek rises in e Jackson County and flows sw into Piney Mountain Creek.

Chestnut Stamp Knob, n Clay County at the ne end of Evans Ridge.

Chestnut Top, on Buncombe-Henderson County line. Alt. 3,069.

Chestnutwood Ridge, w Avery County.

Chetola Lake, s Watauga County on Middle Fork [of South Fork New River] n of town of Blowing Rock. Formed by a dam constructed in 1920; also fed by Stringfellow Branch. Covers 15 acres with a max. depth of 20 ft.

Chicamacomico Banks, the name commonly given to Pea Island in e Dare County. The name appears on John Lawson's map, 1709, as Chickinnaccomac. A portion of the word is believed to be derived from an Algonquian word for "sinking-down-sand."

Chicamacomico Coast Guard Station, in the community of Rodanthe on n Hatteras Island in e Dare County. Est. in 1874 as Lifesaving Station. Lifesaving Service and Revenue Cutter Service joined to form United States Coast Guard in 1915. Decommissioned, 1954.

Chickasaw Knobs, n Henderson County near Clear Creek. Alt. 2,686.

Chickehauk. See Kitty Hawk.

Chickinacommock. See New Inlet.

Chickinnaccomac. See Chicamacomico.

Chickorack River. See South Creek.

Chicod. See Simpson.

Chicod Creek rises in w Beaufort County and flows nw into Pitt County where it enters Tar River. Appears as Cheecods Creek on the Collet map, 1770.

Chicod Township, se Pitt County.

Chicora, a name applied to the Carolina coastal area, probably from the Cape Fear River to the Savannah River, explored by the Spaniard Louis Vázques de Ayllón in 1526.

Chiking Indian Fort, referred to in grants made in 1730 for land in what is now Greene County. It was located 3 to 4 mi. downstream from Hookerton, se Greene County, on the n side of Contentnea Creek, approx. ¾ mi. above the mouth of Polecat Branch.

Childsburgh. *See* Hillsborough.

Chiltoes Mountain, on Haywood-Swain County line in Great Smoky Mountains National Park. Located at ne end of Balsam Mountain near lat. 35° 35′ 56″ N., long. 83° 11′ 09″ W. Alt. 5,888.

Chiltoskie Ridge. *See* Balsam Mountain.

Chimney Creek rises in n Madison County and flows e into Big Creek.

Chimney End Ridge, e Mitchell County between Reuben Creek and Powers Branch.

Chimney Knob, s Macon County between Carpenters Branch and Jones Creek.

Chimney Mountain, nw Burke County. Alt. 3,657. Known by the Cherokee Indians as Connatara.

Chimney Rock, a resort community in w Rutherford County s of Broad River. Named for nearby granite monolith rising 225 feet from the shoulder of Chimney Rock Mountain and overlooking Hickory Nut Gorge (*see* Hickory Nut Gap) and Lake Lure. Alt. 1,050. A post office by this name existed here as early as 1843. The corporate limits of the town of Lake Lure are indefinite, but apparently Chimney Rock itself lies within the bounds of that town.

Chimney Rock Mountain, w Rutherford County.

Chimney Rock Township, w Rutherford County.

Chimney Top, peak on Piney Mountain, w central Polk County. Ostin Creek rises here. Alt. 1,500.

Chimneytop Mountain in s Jackson County one mi. e of Hampton Lake and s of Rocky Mountain. Alt. 4,618. Known by the Cherokee Indians as *Kayoo-lanta,* "a chimney."

China Creek rises in s Watauga County about 1 mi. w of town of Blowing Rock, and flows s into Thunderhole Creek in n Caldwell County.

China Grove, town in s Rowan County. Post office est. here in 1823; name changed to

Luthersville in 1846, but in 1849 it was changed back to China Grove. Named for chinaberry trees growing here. Inc. 1889. Alt. 867.

China Grove Township, s Rowan County.

Chinkapin Creek rises in ne Bertie County and flows ne into Hertford County where it turns n to enter Wiccacon River. Appears on the Moseley map, 1733.

Chinkapin Creek rises in n Union County and flows se into Stewarts Creek.

Chinquapin, community in se Duplin County, one mi. e of Northeast Cape Fear River. Name is an Algonquian Indian word for a kind of small chestnut. Produces tobacco, corn, and poultry.

Chinquapin Branch rises in e Haywood County and flows sw into Pisgah Creek.

Chinquapin Branch rises in w Jones County and flows e 4½ mi. to empty into Trent River. Also known as Big Chinquapin Branch.

Chinquapin Creek rises in w Stokes County and flows sw into Surry County where it enters Toms Creek.

Chinquapin Creek rises in s Yadkin County and flows s into n Davie County where it turns sw to flow into Dutchmans Creek.

Chinquapin Cross Roads. *See* Courtney.

Chinquapin Mountain, s Macon County between East Fork Overflow Creek and Little Scaly Mountain.

Chinquapin Mountain, central Transylvania County between Gladys Branch and Country Club Lake.

Chinquapin Ridge, high ground in Pantego Swamp, e Beaufort County.

Chinquapin Ridge, a loamy section in n Pitt County between Great Swamp and Gum Pond (swamp).

Chinquapin Township, w Jones County.

Chip, community in ne Craven County.

Chip, community in s Montgomery County between Thickety Creek and Little River.

Chisholm's Store. *See* Pekin.

Chiska Creek rises in w central Bertie County and flows e into Cashie River. Hills Mill on this creek is shown on the Collet map, 1770, but apparently not on later maps.

Chisman, community in se Stokes County.

Chockeyotte, town in n Halifax County. Inc. in 1901.

Chockoyotte Creek rises in n Halifax County and flows se into Roanoke River. Name believed to be a Tuscarora Indian word. A very fine stone aqueduct, part of the pre-Civil War Roanoke Navigation

Canal, remains over this creek. It appears as Chocolate Creek on the Collet map, 1770.

Chocolate Creek rises in se Guilford County and flows ne into Stinking Quarter Creek.

Chocolate Creek. See Chockoyotte Creek.

Chocolate Drop. See Foster Mountain.

Chocowinity, town in w Beaufort County. Known as Godleys Crossroads until renamed for nearby creek. Inc. 1917; charter repealed 1947; reinc. 1959. Railroad station name is Marsden, named in 1917 for Marsden J. Perry, a railroad official. Alt. 35.

Chocowinity Bay formed by the mouth of Chocowinity Creek in Pamlico River, w Beaufort County.

Chocowinity Creek rises in sw Beaufort County and flows n into Chocowinity Bay and Pamlico River. Called Worsley Creek on the Collet map, 1770; by 1808 (Price's map) it was called by its present name, though MacRae's map in 1833 called it Chocowinity Swamp. The name is said to be Indian in origin and to mean "fish from many waters."

Chocowinity Swamp. See Chocowinity Creek.

Chocowinity Township, sw Beaufort County.

Choffington, traditional site of the first courthouse of Cumberland County located at the mouth of Little River, near the present site of Linden in the n part of the county. The courthouse appears to have been here from 1755 until it was moved to Campbellton in 1765. The name may be derived from the old English word "chuff," meaning a rustic or rude, coarse fellow and may have been applied by people of English descent to . the recently-arrived Scots.

Choga Creek rises in w Macon County and flows ne into Nantahala Lake.

Choggy Butte Mountain in e Jackson County on the head of Mull Creek.

Chokeberry Branch rises in n Swain County and flows w into Forney Creek.

Choowatic Creek rises in se Bertie County and flows e into Roquist Creek.

Choratuck Inlet. See Currituck Inlet.

Chowan, an Indian town, shown on the Moseley map, 1733, as lying in the s central part of the present Gates County between Bennetts Creek and Trotman Creek.

Chowan Beach, pleasure beach on Chowan River, s of the mouth of Meherrin River, on the e border of Hertford County. First named Mount Gallant for John Gallant who operated a ferry here about 1720. See also Mount Gallant for another place of the same name. Known as Mount Zion in the latter half of the eighteenth century.

Chowan County was formed by 1668 as Shaftesbury Precinct of Albemarle County. Renamed Chowan Precinct about 1681. Located in the ne section of the state, it is bounded by Albemarle Sound, Chowan River, and Bertie, Hertford, Gates, and Perquimans counties. It was named for the Chowan River. Area: 234 sq. mi. County seat: Edenton with an elevation of 16 ft. Townships are Nos. 1- 4, formerly Edenton, Middle, Upper, and Yeopim. Produces corn, soybeans, peanuts, cotton, hogs, textiles, lumber, processed seafood.

Chowan River is formed on the Hertford-Gates County line a short distance s of the Virginia state line by the junction of the Nottoway and Blackwater rivers. It flows se on the Hertford-Gates and Bertie-Chowan County lines into Albemarle Sound. Named for the Chowanoc tribe of Indians who lived in the area. The word is a variant of the Algonquian *sorwán*, "south." It may have derived from *sowán-ohke*, "south country." The river was referred to by the Roanoke explorers, 1584-85, but given no specific name except as the location of the tribe. Appears as Choan River on the Comberford map, 1657.

Chowanoke. See Croatoan Island.

Chrissawn Knob, se Yancey County on South Toe River near the mouth of Rock Creek.

Christ Branch. See Banjo Branch.

Christ-Church Parish. See Craven Parish.

Christian Creek rises in se Buncombe County and flows nw into Swannanoa River.

Christie Ford. See Murphy.

Chronicle, community in se Catawba County. Est. 1857. Named for Major William

Chronicle, killed at Battle of Kings Mountain. Alt. 1,048.

Chuckle, community in n Wilkes County near East Prong Roaring River.

Chum Creek rises in ne Rutherford County and flows s into Duncans Creek.

Chunky Gal Mountain, se Clay County, extending se from Riley Knob to Big Laurel. Alt. 4,600-4,986. Named by slim Indian maidens who delighted in the capture (by her father) of a chunky Indian lass who had run away to marry a young brave against her family's wishes.

Chunky Pipe Creek rises in central Durham County and flows e into Little Lick Creek.

Chunn Cove, central Buncombe County near the headwaters of Ross Creek.

Chunn Cove Creek. See Ross Creek.

Church Branch rises in central Clay County and flows s between Matlock Creek and Moores Branch into Tusquitee Creek.

Churchill, community in ne Warren County. Post office est. here in 1884, but discontinued in 1905.

Church Island, a peninsula in e Currituck County extending into Currituck Sound. Coinjock Bay lies between its w shore and the mainland of the county. It is 5 mi. long, 1 mi. wide. Shown as Emperors Island on the Comberford map, 1657, and as White Island on the Ogilby map, 1671, Church Island on the Moseley map, 1733. The w portion of the penisula is known as Piney Island.

Churchland, community in w Davidson County.

Cid, community in e Davidson County. Est. 1885. Named for (a) Sidney Muffley, superintendent of silver mine nearby, or (b) Cid, Scotland, by miners who came from there.

Cilley. See German's Hill.

Cindy Branch rises in central Cherokee County and flows se into Morgan Creek.

Cindy Edwards Branch rises in sw Beaufort County and flows w into Chocowinity Creek.

Cipo River. See Pamlico River.

Cisco Cove, central Buncombe County, s of Cisco Mountain.

Cisco Mountain, central Buncombe County between Piney Mountain and Randall Gap.

Citron, community in sw Alleghany County. Known as City until some time after 1918.

Citte Weeks Branch, stream about 3 mi. long, rises in w Carteret County and flows w into White Oak River. Also known as Godfrey Branch. Named for Citte Weeks.

City. See Citron.

Clabber Branch rises in sw Clay County and flows se into Pinelog Creek.

Clam Shoal in the waters of Pamlico Sound, s Dare County, off the s part of Hatteras Island. Bird Islands are on Clam Shoal.

Clanpit Cove, on Burningtown Creek in central Macon County.

Claremont, town in ne Catawba County. The earliest name was Charlotte Crossing; later Setzer's Depot. Changed to Claremont in 1892. Inc. 1893. Alt. 969. Named for Clare Sigmon, daughter of Jones Sigmon, an early settler. Produces furniture.

Clarendon, community e Brunswick County.

Clarendon, community in sw Columbus County. Inc. 1907 as a town; charter repealed, 1921.

Clarendon County, one of 3 counties (Albemarle and Craven being the others) set up in 1664 by the Lords Proprietors of Carolina. It embraced the territory around the mouth of Cape Fear River (then known as Charles River). Named for Edward Hyde (1609-74), Earl of Clarendon, one of the Lords Proprietors. See also Charles Town, a settlement which existed in this part of the colony, 1662-65.

Clarendon River. See Cape Fear River.

Clargeons Creek. See Yeopim Creek.

Clarissa, community in e Mitchell County on Cane Creek.

Clark, community in w Haywood County.

Clark Branch rises near Yellow Mountain in nw Buncombe County and flows se into Sandy Mush Creek.

Clark Branch rises in n central Buncombe County and flows nw into Flat Creek.

Clark Branch rises in w Swain County and flows se into Fontana Lake.

Clark Creek rises in n Catawba County and flows se and sw through Catawba County into Lincoln County where it enters South Fork Catawba River.

Clark Creek on Goose Creek Island, ne Pamlico County, flows nw between Mouse Harbor on the e and Pamlico River on the w.

Clark Creek rises in s Watauga County and flows n into Dutch Creek.

Clarke Creek rises in ne Mecklenburg County and flows se into w Cabarrus County where it enters Rocky River. Named for

a family of early settlers, one of whom
was scalped by Indians.

Clark Gap, between Cunningham Mountain
and Couch Mountain in n Henderson
County.

Clark Point, point of land extending into
Goose Creek, se Beaufort County.

Clarks, community in central Craven County. Alt. 31.

Clarks. See Salvo.

Clarks Bay, a small bay in the waters of
Pamlico Sound off n Hatteras Island, e
Dare County, s of Salvo.

Clarks Branch rises in a small pond in s central Brunswick County and flows s into
Lockwoods Folly River.

Clarks Creek is formed in n Mecklenburg
County by the junction of North Prong
and South Prong. It flows e into Cabarrus
County where it enters Rocky River.

Clarks Creek rises in w Montgomery County
and flows sw into Pee Dee River.

Clarks Island, a small tidal marsh island off
the se tip of Eagles Island in the Cape
Fear River, ne Brunswick County.

Clarks Little River. See Upper Little River.

Clarks Mountain, e central Anson County.
Alt. approx. 525.

Clarks Store. See Blountsville.

Clarksville, community in nw Davie County.
It was in this neighborhood that John
Pinchback operated Burnt Tavern or
Pinchback's Tavern after 1797. Before
the Civil War the stage from Salem to
Statesville stopped here for the night.
Hinton Rowan Helper (1829-1909), author
of The Impending Crisis (1857), was born
nearby on a farm on Bear Creek. A post
office operated here from 1855 until 1869.

Clarksville. See Salvo.

Clarksville Township, nw Davie County.

Clarkton, town in s Bladen County. Alt. 93.
Inc. 1901. Known earlier as Brown Marsh
Station and Dalton. Renamed after 1863
for John Hector Clark (1821-98).

Clawhammer Cove in n Transylvania County extends s from Clawhammer Mountain
to Avery Creek.

Clawhammer Creek rises in n Transylvania
County and flows e into South Fork Mills
River.

Clawhammer Mountain in n Transylvania
County between Clawhammer Cove and
Clawhammer Creek.

Clay, community in e Granville County.

Clay. See Linville.

Clay County was formed in 1861 from Cherokee County. In the w section of the
state, it is bounded by the state of
Georgia and by Cherokee and Macon
counties. It was named for Henry Clay
(1777-1852). Area: 219 sq. mi. County
seat: Hayesville with an elevation of
1,893 ft. Townships are Brasstown, Hayesville, Hiwassee, Shooting Creek, Sweetwater, and Tusquittee. Produces corn,
poultry, lumber, and apparel.

Claypole Branch rises in s Transylvania
County and flows ne into Middle Fork
French Broad River.

Clayroot, community in se Pitt County.

Clayroot Swamp rises in se Pitt County and
flows sw and se into Swift Creek. For a
part of its course it forms the boundary
between Craven and Pitt counties.

Clayton, town in nw Johnston County. Inc.
1869. Known previously as Stallings Station. Named for a local school, Clayton
Academy, or for Senator John M. Clayton
(1796-1856) of Delaware, co-author of the
Clayton-Bulwer Treaty of 1850 with
Great Britain. Alt. 345. Produces textiles
and apparel.

Clayton Bay, swamp nw Brunswick County.
A part of Green Swamp.

Clayton Branch rises in se Cherokee County
and flows nw into Little Brasstown Creek.

Clayton Creek rises in s Buncombe County
and flows ne into French Broad River.

Clayton Hall. See Rocky Point.

Clayton Township, nw Johnston County.

Clear Branch rises in n central Avery County and flows ne into Elk River.

Clear Branch rises in se Buncombe County
and flows sw into Broad River.

Clear Branch rises in Green Swamp in e
central Columbus County and flows se
into Big Swamp. For a little over 2 mi. it
forms a part of the boundary between
Brunswick and Columbus counties.

Clear Branch rises in e Columbus County
and flows se on the Brunswick-Columbus
County line into Honey Island Swamp.

Clear Branch rises in nw Macon County and flows s into Queens Creek.

Clear Branch rises in sw Macon County and flows ne into Lowery Creek.

Clear Branch rises in s Madison County and flows ne into Little Sandymush Creek.

Clear Branch rises in e Watauga County and flows se into Elk Creek.

Clear Creek rises in s Avery County near Doe Hill Mountain and flows sw into North Toe River.

Clear Creek rises in w Avery County near Little Buck Hill and flows s into North Toe River.

Clear Creek rises in sw Burke County and flows n into Silver Creek.

Clear Creek rises in ne Clay County and flows ne into Nantahala River.

Clear Creek rises in e Henderson County and flows sw into Mud Creek. Known by the Cherokee Indians as Os-quee-ha-ha.

Clear Creek rises in w McDowell County and flows se into Catawba River.

Clear Creek rises in se Macon County and flows se into Georgia where it enters West Fork [Chatooga River].

Clear Creek rises in e Mecklenburg and flows e into s Cabarrus County and then sw into n Union County where it enters Rocky River at coincident corners of Cabarrus, Stanly and Union counties. Formerly known as Red Creek.

Clear Creek rises in Greenville County, S. C., and flows ne into Transylvania County where it enters Little River.

Clear Creek rises in se Yancey County and flows w into South Toe River.

Clear Creek, community in s Carbarrus County.

Clear Creek Ridge, s Yancey County extends ne from South Toe River to East Branch.

Clear Creek Township, former township in e Mecklenburg County, now township number 6.

Clear Creek Township, ne Henderson County.

Clear Pond, natural lake in se Brunswick County. Maximum depth 12 feet, 2 acres in area.

Clear Run, community in s Sampson County on Black River.

Clear Run Swamp rises in se Sampson County and flows sw into Black River.

Cleaveland County. See Cleveland County.

Clegg, community in s Durham County.

Cleghorn Creek rises in w central Rutherford County and flows sw into Broad River. The name occurs in deeds as early as 1764; perhaps named for John Cleghorn, pioneer settler.

Cleghorn Mountain, n Rutherford County at the head of Catheys Creek.

Clement, community in w Sampson County near Jones Swamp.

Clements Creek. See Blanket Creek.

Clemmons, town in sw Forsyth County. Known as Clemmonstown as early as 1816; inc. 1824 as Clemmonsville but later known simply as Clemmons. Alt. 792. No longer active in municipal affairs. Named for Peter Clemmons who moved here from Delaware in 1777. Clemmons was the author of *Poor Peter's Call to His Children*, printed in Salisbury in 1812.

Clemmonsville Township, sw Forsyth County.

Clems Beech Ridge, e Jackson County between Oak Ridge Creek and Chestnut Ridge Creek.

Cleveland, town in w Rowan County. Inc. 1883 as Third Creek; name changed in 1887 to honor Grover Cleveland (1837-1908), President of the United States. Alt. 788.

Cleveland County was formed in 1841 from Rutherford and Lincoln counties. Cleaveland was originally used but the present spelling was adopted in 1887. In the sw section of the state, it is bounded by the state of South Carolina and by Rutherford, Burke, Lincoln, and Gaston counties. It was named for Colonel Benjamin Cleaveland (1738-1806), noted partisan leader of the western frontier and one of the heroes of the Battle of King's Mountain. Area: 466 sq. mi. County seat: Shelby with an elevation of 85 ft. Townships are Nos. 1-11, formerly River, Boiling Springs, Rippys, Kings Mountain, Warlick, Shelby, Sandy Run, Polkville, Double Shoals, Knob Creek, and Casar. Produces wheat, oats, corn, dairy products, hogs, livestock, poultry, textiles, bakery products, hosiery, limestone, and mica.

Cleveland Mills, inc. 1877 as a town between Lawndale and Casar in n central
Cleveland County. No longer in existence.

Cleveland Township, w Johnston County.

Cleveland Township, nw Rowan County.

Clifdale, community in w Cumberland
County. Formerly known as Clifton. Alt.
237.

Cliff Branch rises in n Swain County and
flows ne into Oconaluftee River.

Cliffield Mountain, on the Polk-Henderson
County line.

Cliffs. See Rhodhiss.

Cliffside, community in se Rutherford County on Second Broad River. Founded by
Raleigh B. Haynes who est. a textile mill
here. High Shoals, former community in
this vicinity, was a post office as early as
1828.

Cliffside Lake, at the junction of South
Skitty Branch and Skitty Creek in se
Macon County.

Cliffs of the Neuse State Park, se Wayne
County. Est. 1945 on 355 acres given to
the state by the Weil family of Goldsboro
and others. Cliffs 90 ft. above the Neuse
River are an unusual geological feature in
this section of the state. Galax, laurel and
other mountain plants grow here. It is a
scenic and recreational park with a nature
museum, trails, etc. Swimming and fishing. Address: Route 2, Seven Springs.

Clifton, community in central Ashe County.
Alt. approx. 2,900.

Clifton. See Clifdale.

Cliftons Pond, on Crooked Creek in sw
Franklin County. Formed about 1890.
Covers approx. 55 acres. Maximum depth
16 feet. Named for owners.

Clifton Township, nw Ashe County.

Cliftonville, community in n Wilson County
near the head of Cattail Branch. Named
for Clifton Parker. Post office, 1895-1902.

Climax, community in se Guilford County.
Alt. 824. Est. 1853. Named for its location on highground.

Clinchcross, community in e McDowell
County. Probably named for the nearby
Clinchfield Railroad.

Cline Creek rises in central Catawba County and flows sw into Clark Creek.

Cline Mine, former copper and gold mine
near the community of Watts Crossroads,
ne Cabarrus County, approx. 8 mi. ne of
Concord. Last worked about 1901-02 but
more recently explored by the U. S.

Bureau of Mines and by the Tennessee
Copper Company.

Clines Township, n Catawba County.

Clingman, community in e Wilkes County
near West Swan Creek. Named for Congressman Thomas L. Clingman (1812-97).
Known also as Frog Level.

Clingman Mine Branch rises in n Avery
County and flows e into Buckeye Creek
on the Avery-Watauga County line.

Clingmans Creek rises in n Swain County
near Clingmans Dome and flows se into
Noland Creek.

Clingmans Dome, mountain on the Swain
County, N. C.-Sevier County, Tenn., line
in Great Smoky Mountains National Park.
Named approx. 1860 by Prof. Arnold
Guyot for Thomas L. Clingman (1812-97),
member of the party which first measured
it in 1858. Clingman was a soldier, mountain climber, geologist, Congressman and
Senator from North Carolina. Alt. 6,642,
the highest point in the park. A 45-ft.
observation tower has been built at the
peak. Known to the Indians as Ku-wa-hi
meaning "mulberry place." Early settlers
called it Smoky Dome.

Clinton, former town in se Davie County
(then Rowan) at the junction of South
Yadkin and North Yadkin rivers. Inc.
1818 by Yadkin Navigation Co. Some
100 lots were sold before a panic in 1819
stopped work at the site. A post office
existed here in 1822 but the town was
abandoned soon afterwards.

Clinton, town and county seat central Sampson County. Authorized to be laid out,
1818; inc. 1822. Courthouse est. here
about 1784 on land owned by Richard
Clinton (1721-96), for whom the town
was later named. Alt. 158.

Clinton Township, former township in central Sampson County now divided into
North Clinton and South Clinton townships.

Clio, community in e central Iredell County.
Site of Clio's Nursery, a classical school
established in 1778 by the Rev. James
Hall (1744-1826). His attempt to make
the sciences a part of academic training
was the first in North Carolina.

Clontz Branch rises in w Haywood County
and flows nw into Caldwell Fork.

Closs, community in e Lenoir County. A
post office from 1888 to 1905.

Cloudiand, community in ne Mitchell County on ne Roan Mountain.

Clover Branch rises in nw Madison County and flows n into French Broad River.

Cloverdale, community in n Henderson County.

Clover Garden, former community in sw Orange County near Haw River. A post office was established here as early as 1822. Clover Garden Methodist Church is here.

Clubfoot Canal, about 2½ mi. long extending from the head of Clubfoot Creek to the head of Harlowe Creek, n Carteret County and n Craven County, affording a waterway from the Neuse River to Newport River. Planned 1797; completed about 1828.

Clubfoot Creek rises near the Carteret-Craven county line and flows n into Neuse River. A canal connects this stream with Harlowe Creek in central Carteret County, affording a waterway from the Neuse River to Newport River. Appears on the Moseley map, 1733. The Indian name for this stream was Irisquoque.

Club Gap, n Transylvania County at the sw end of Rich Mountain.

Club Lake, se Macon County on Monger Creek.

Clun Seat, a 10,000-acre estate in se Warren County between Great Fishing and Shocco creeks, granted to Edward Moseley in 1728, and after his death in 1749 sold by his sons to Joseph Montfort. Mentioned in local records as late as 1765. Probably named for the Clun River or the town of Clun in England.

Clyde, town in central Haywood County. Inc. 1889. Named for a member of a firm of railroad construction engineers. Known previously as Lower Pigeon. Alt. 2,539.

Clyde Township, central Haywood County.

Coakley, town in e Edgecombe County, inc. 1903 but not now active in municipal affairs.

Coalglen, community in s Chatham County on Deep River. Known earlier as Farmville. Site of former Carolina Coal Mine from which the name is derived.

Coalville, community in ne Cherokee County in Nantahala National Forest.

Coastal Plain, e North Carolina, extends inland from 100 to 150 mi. from the Atlantic Ocean to the fall line of the rivers. This western limit extends from Northampton and Halifax counties on the n in a sw direction through Anson County on the s. In altitude the area ranges from sea level to approx. 500 ft. Generally the soil is sand and black loam. See also Tidewater Area.

Coats, town in e Harnett County. Inc. 1905 and named for Elder Tom Coats. Previously known as Troyville for a Fayetteville lawyer. Alt. 314.

Cobb Bluff, s central Cherokee County on the Nottely River at the mouth of Moccasin Creek.

Cobb Creek rises in nw Yadkin County and flows ne into Martin Creek.

Cobb Point, e Pasquotank County extends into the Pasquotank River between Forbes Bay and Davis Bay.

Cobbs Creek rises in e Caswell County and flows ne into Person County where it enters North Hyco Creek.

Cobbs Crossroads, community in n Wilson County near Town Creek.

Cobb's Shop, community in w Caswell County.

Cobb Town, community in s Edgecombe County.

Cobin Branch rises in the Cane Creek Mountains, s Alamance County, and flows nw into Rock Creek.

Coble Township, former township in sw Alamance County, now township number 2.

Coburn, community in sw Buncombe County.

Coburn Knob, n central Swain County in Great Smoky Mountains National Park near the head of Lands Creek. Alt. 4,370.

Coburn's, community in nw Union County.

Cochran Branch rises in s Swain County and flows ne into Tuckasegee River.

Cochran Creek rises in central Graham County and flows w into Cheoah River.

Cochrane Cove, on Burningtown Creek in central Macon County.

Cockerne Ferry. See Colerain.

Cockey Township, former township in sw Edgecombe County, now township number 13.

Cockey Swamp rises in ne Nash County and flows se into sw Edgecombe County where it enters Town Creek.

Cockle Point, peninsula extending from e Pamlico County into Neuse River.

Cockrells Crossroads, community in central Nash County.

Cod Camp Creek rises in sw Cumberland County and flows se on the Cumberland-Robeson County line before entering

Robeson County where it flows into Gallberry Swamp.

Coddle Creek rises along the Rowan-Iredell
County line and flows s through Cabarrus
County into Rocky River. Appears on the
Collet map, 1770, as Codle Creek.

Coddle Creek, community in nw Cabarrus
county.

Coddle Creek Township, se Iredell County.

Cody Branch rises in central Graham County and flows nw into Yellow Creek.

Cody Creek rises in w central Surry County
and flows se into Fisher River.

Cody Gap, central Graham County at the
head of Cody Branch.

Coefield Branch rises in ne Cherokee County and flows ne into McClellan Creek.

Coefield Creek rises in ne Cherokee County
and flows nw into Radder Creek.

Coenjock. *See* Coinjock.

Coffee Branch rises in e Haywood County
and flows n into Garden Creek.

Coffee Creek rises in w Caldwell County e
of Rocky Knob and flows se into Mulberry Creek.

Coffee Creek, a tidal creek in n central
Carteret County which flows into South
River.

Coffee Ridge, n Haywood County parallel
to Laurel Creek.

Coffey Branch rises in w Mecklenburg County and flows s into Sugar Creek.

Coffey Cove, central Cherokee County between Mason Branch and Rhea Branch.

Cofield, community in e Hertford County.

Coggins Bend, n Macon County, in Little
Tennessee River.

Coggins Branch rises in w Haywood County,
Great Smoky Mountains National Park,
near lat. 35° 39' 08" N., long. 83° 06'
12" W., and flows ne into Little Cataloochee Creek.

Coglin Creek rises in s Onslow County and
flows w into New River.

Cognac (cog-nack), community in e Richmond County. Settled about 1890 and
first known as Eighty-Nine Mile Siding for
its distance from Raleigh. Renamed for
the town in France or the brandy produced there. Alt. 400.

Coharie River is formed in s Sampson County by the junction of Little Coharie and
Great Coharie creeks and flows se for
approx. 6 mi. to join Six Runs Creek in
forming Black River.

Cohary Swamp. *See* Great Coharie Creek.

Coinjock, community in s central Currituck

County. Inc. 1893 as Arlington but dis-
solved by court order, March, 1894, because of technical inaccuracy in description of the boundary. A post office here
was called Coenjock as early as 1830, the
same name used by Bishop Thomas Coke
in writing of a visit here in 1785. On
Intracoastal Waterway. Originally located
where Barco is today; moved s when
Albemarle Canal was built to this point at
which a bridge crossed the canal. Other
early spellings were Cornjack and Cowenjock. Alt. 5.

Coinjock Bay in the waters of Currituck
Sound, central Currituck County, between Church Island and the mainland.

Cokesbury, community in n Harnett County.
Early center of Methodism in Cape Fear
area. Named for Thomas Coke (1747-
1814) and Francis Asbury (1745-1816),
Methodist bishops. Nearby Buckhorn
Iron Furnace operated during Civil War
and until 1873.

Cokesbury, community in e Vance County
on the head of Rocky Branch, named for
the Methodist Bishops Coke and Asbury.

Cokey Swamp rises in se Nash County and
flows se into w Edgecombe County where
it enters Town Creek. Tiancok, an Indian
village (*which see*) appears here on the
Comberford map, 1657. Tyancoka Creek
appears on the Collet map, 1770, at this
location, and the spelling Tincoco and
Tiancoco are used on other maps. *See
also* Redmans Old Field.

Cokey Township. *See* Edgecombe County.

Colbert Creek rises in s Yancey County and
flows se into South Toe River.

Colbert Ridge, s Yancey County between
Locust Creek and Colbert Creek.

Coldass Creek rises in nw Caldwell County
and flows e into Johns River. Both this
and Pinchgut Creek were named by two
men hunting in the area. They followed
a stream until it came to a fork. There
they separated, each following one of the
forks, and agreed to meet later and name
each stream according to their feelings
toward it. One man carried the food and
the other the sleeping equipment. They
became lost, but finally met the next day
when they gave the two names to the
creeks. Sometimes shown as Cold Water
Creek on modern maps.

Cold Branch rises in central Clay County
and flows nw into Tusquitee Creek.

Cold Branch rises in w Graham County and flows se into Santeetlah Creek.

Cold Camp Creek rises on the Cumberland-Robeson County line and flows se into Gallberry Swamp.

Cold Creek rises in e Haywood County and flows ne into East Fork Pigeon River.

Cold Creek rises in e Jackson County and flows sw into Tanasee Creek.

Cold Knob, on Buncombe-Henderson County line between Bent Creek Gap and Pine Mountain.

Cold Mountain, on Avery-Burke County line. Alt. 3,830.

Cold Mountain, in s Haywood County, is parallel to Little East Fork Pigeon River. Alt. 6,030. According to Cherokee legend some children played on a large rock at the foot of this mountain and their footprints are said to be there still. Their name for the mountain was Da-tsu-la-gun-yi, meaning "where they made tracks."

Cold Mountain on the Jackson-Transylvania County line w of Panthertail Mountain. Alt. 4,500.

Cold Mountain Branch rises in s Transylvania County and flows ne into East Fork French Broad River.

Coldside Mountain in s Jackson County between Heddie Mountain and Terrapin Mountain.

Cold Spring, community is nw Burke County.

Coldspring Branch rises in e Cherokee County and flows nw into Peachtree Creek.

Coldspring Branch rises in ne Cherokee County and flows nw into Vengeance Creek.

Cold Spring Branch rises in e Clay County and flows sw into Shooting Creek.

Cold Spring Branch rises in n Clay County and flows se into Long Branch.

Cold Spring Branch rises in s Haywood County and flows nw into Shiny Creek.

Cold Spring Branch rises in n Madison County and flows ne into Allan Creek.

Cold Spring Branch rises in se Swain County and flows nw into Yalaka Creek.

Coldspring Branch rises in nw Swain County and flows se into Lost Cove Creek.

Coldspring Branch rises in w Swain County and flows w and nw into Hazel Creek.

Cold Spring Creek rises in n Burke County and flows s into Carroll's Creek.

Cold Spring Creek rises in n Macon County and flows sw into Whiteoak Creek.

Coldspring Gap, on Cherokee-Graham County line in e end of Unicoi Mountains.

Cold Spring Gap on the Jackson-Transylvania County line.

Cold Spring Gap, n Swain County in Great Smoky Mountains National Park near the head of Bear Creek. Called in Cherokee A-ha-lu-na, meaning "ambushed," or U-ni-ha-lu-na, meaning "where they watched." Cherokees are said to have ambushed a large party of invading Iroquois, slaying all but one. His ears were cut off, as was the custom, and he was sent home to take the news to his people.

Cold Spring Knob, nw Graham County in the middle of Hangover Lead.

Cold Spring Knob, s Haywood County on Lickstone Ridge. Alt. 5,920-5,960.

Cold Spring Knob, on the Swain County, N. C.-Sevier County, Tenn., line in Great Smoky Mountains National Park at the junction of Miry Ridge and the main divide of the Great Smoky Mountains. Alt. 5,240. Named for the spring of cold water near the summit.

Coldspring Mountain, on the Madison County, N. C.-Greene County, Tenn., line.

Cold Springs Creek rises in n Haywood County and flows sw into Pigeon River.

Coldwater Creek rises in s Rowan County and flows s into Cabarrus County where it enters Rocky River. Appears on the Collet map, 1770.

Cold Water Creek. See Coldass Creek.

Cole Cove, s Buncombe County between Pine Mountain and Fannie Ridge.

Cole Creek, formed by junction of Hacklan Branch and Buckland Mill Branch in w Gates County. Flows s through Lilleys Millpond and empties into Sarem Creek. Formerly known as Sarem Creek.

Cole Creek rises on the e side of Rendezvous Mountain, w Wilkes County, and flows s aprox. 3 mi. into North Prong Lewis Fork Creek.

Cole Gap, sw Cherokee County at the sw end of Damons Mountain.

Cole Gap, se Macon County w of Houston Branch and approx. 3 mi. n of town of Highlands.

Cole Gap Mountain, w central Stokes County between Indian and Neatman creeks.

Coleman Creek rises in s Clay County and flows e into Hyatt Mill Creek.

Coleman Branch rises in w Johnston County and flows sw into Black Creek.

Coleman Gap, se Cherokee County at the headwaters of John Mason Branch.

Cole Mountain, e Macon County at the head of Houston Branch.

Cole Mountain Gap, at the head of Skitty Creek in e Macon County. Alt. 4,100.

Colerain, town in ne Bertie County. Settled by 1700; inc. 1794. Named by its founder, John Campbell, for his home town of Coleraine, County Londonderry, Ireland. The post office, est. here in 1818, dropped the final letter of the name in the mid-nineteenth century. Cockerne Ferry across the Chowan River n of the site of Colerain appears on the Collet map, 1770, but it apparently ceased operation by 1808.

Colerain Township, ne Bertie County.

Coleridge, community in e Randolph County on Deep River. Originally known as Foust's Mill. A cotton mill est. here in 1883. Named for James A. Cole, local storekeeper.

Coleridge Township, e central Randolph County.

Colers Ordinary. See Ridgeway.

Coles Cove, the valley through which Coles Creek flows in n Buncombe County.

Coles Creek rises in n Buncombe County near Watershed Ridge and flows nw into Flat Creek.

Coleville, community in n Stokes County near Cadwell Creek. A post office here in the late nineteenth century was Colesville.

Coleman Gap, on the Clay-Macon County line. The Appalachian Trail passes through this gap.

Colesville. See Coleville.

Coley Gap, w Madison County between Puncheon Camp Branch and Divide Mountain.

Coleys Branch rises in n Gaston County and flows ne into South Fork Catawba River.

Coleys Crossroads. See Vicksboro.

Colfax, community in w Guilford County. Alt. 972. Named for Schuyler Colfax (1823-85), vice president of the United States (1869-73).

Colfax Township, e Rutherford County. Named for Schuyler Colfax (1823-85), vice president of the United States.

Colington, scattered fishing community on Colington Island, ne Dare County.

Colington Creek, a waterway between Kitty Hawk Bay and Buzzard Bay; e of Colington Island and separating it from n Bodie Island, in e Dare County.

Colington Island, in Roanoke Sound, ne Dare County. About 2 mi. from n to s and from e to w, it is separated from Bodie Island by Colington Creek. Named for Sir John Colleton (1608-66), one of the Lords Proprietors to whom it was granted in 1663. Settled by the winter of 1664-65. Earlier known as Carlile Island in honor of Christopher Carleill, stepson of Sir Francis Walsingham, who accompanied Sir Francis Drake on his 1586 Florida-Virginia expedition as his lieutenant general. Appears as Carlile Island on the Ogilby map, 1671, and as Colleton Island on both the Blome map, 1672, and the Moseley map, 1733. The Collet map, 1770, and the Mouzon map, 1775, have Collintons Island.

Colington Island Shoal lies off the nw tip of Roanoke Island, Dare County, in the waters of Albemarle and Croatan Sounds.

Colkins Neck, a sandy area about 2 mi. long and 1 mi. wide, almost surrounded by tidal marsh, sw Brunswick County along the South Carolina line.

Colleton County, est. prior to 1691 by the Lords Proprietors of Carolina in what is now se South Carolina. Named for Landgrave James Colleton who resided in the area and served as "governor" from 1686 until 1690.

Colleton Island. See Colington Island.

Collett Camp Branch rises in n Clay County and flows sw into Long Branch.

Collett Creek rises in ne Cherokee County and flows nw into Tatham Creek.

Collett Ridge, ne Cherokee County in the Valley River Mountains.

Collettsville, town in w Caldwell County on Johns River. Inc. 1897 but no longer active in municipal affairs. Named for James H. Collet on whose land the town was laid out. Settled as early as 1837, when post office was est.

Collie Swamp rises in w Martin County and flows s into Tranters Creek. Appears as Huskanaw Swamp on the Price map, 1808, and the MacRae map, 1833.

Collins Canal. See Somerset Canal.

Collins Creek rises in s Orange County and flows sw into Chatham County where it enters Haw River.

Collins Creek rises in ne Rutherford County and flows s into North Fork.

Collins Creek rises in n Swain County in Great Smoky Mountains National Park and flows ne into Oconaluftee River.

Collins Crossroads. *See* Hollemans Crossroads.

Collins Gap, on the Swain County, N. C.-Sevier County, Tenn. line in the Great Smoky Mountains National Park. Alt. 5,720.

Collins Mountain, w central Swain County on the nw end of Jackson Line Mountain.

Collinstown, community in n Stokes County n of Dan River.

Collinsville, community in s Polk County on Hughes Creek. Settled about 1875. Named for Thomas G. Collins, local planter.

Collinwood, former community in w Swain County on Little Tennessee River, the site is now under the waters of Fontana Lake.

Colly, community in ne Bladen County.

Colly Creek rises in Big Colly Bay in ne Bladen County and flows se into Pender County where it enters Black River.

Colly Swamp, an arm of Big Colly Bay in ne Bladen County.

Colly Township, e central Bladen County.

Colmans Gap, central Haywood County on the head of Big Branch.

Colon, community in n Lee County. Coal from Egypt mine formerly delivered to the Seaboard Railroad here; now the center of a large gas-fired brick industry. Post office est. in 1891 as Buckner, changed to Colon in 1892.

Colson's Mill. *See* Coulson Ordinary.

Colt Creek rises in se Henderson County and flows ne into Polk County where it enters Pacolet River.

Columbia, town and county seat in n Tyrrell County on Scuppernong River. Alt. 10. Originated as a trading post, Shallop's Landing; inc. 1793 as Elizabeth Town. Name changed to Columbia in 1801. Became county seat in 1802. Name is poetic appelation for the United States. Produces lumber.

Columbia. *See* Ramseur.

Columbia Township, ne Pender County.

Columbia Township, e central Randolph County.

Columbia Township, n central Tyrrell County.

Columbus, town and county seat, s Polk County, on the head of Whiteoak Creek. Inc. 1857. Named for Dr. Columbus Mills, State legislator who was instrumental in the formation of the county. Alt. 1,145.

Columbus, town authorized to be est. on the lands of Jesse Nixon, ne Randolph County, in 1812. Apparently the town was never laid out. A post office at the proposed site on Sandy Creek in 1828 was called Nixon's.

Columbus County was formed in 1808 from Brunswick and Bladen counties. Located in the se section of the state, it is bounded by the state of South Carolina and by Robeson, Bladen, Pender, and Brunswick counties. It was named for Christopher Columbus. Area: 954 sq. mi. County seat: Whiteville with an elevation of 59 ft. Townships are Bogue, Bolton, Bug Hill, Cerro Gordo, Chadbourn, Fair Bluff, Lees, Ransom, South Williams, Tatums, Waccamaw, Welch Creek, Western Prong, Whiteville, and Williams. Produces tobacco, corn, soybeans, oats, peanuts, pecans, cotton, poultry, livestock, hogs, fertilizer, paper, lumber, textiles, and apparel. Produce markets are at Chadbourn and Tabor City.

Columbus Township, s central Polk County.

Colvard Creek rises in n Cherokee County on Hanging Dog Mountain and flows se into Valley River.

Colvard Creek rises in ne Cherokee County and flows ne and nw into Gumflats Creek.

Colvin Creek rises in ne Madison County and flows sw into Spillcorn Creek.

Colvins Creek rises in w Pender County and flows se into Black River.

Combs Knob, n Wilkes County between Big Sandy Creek and Little Sandy Creek. Named for George Combs, a Revolutionary soldier, who lived nearby.

Comet, community in n central Ashe County.

Comfort, community in s Jones County. A post office existed here as early as 1828.

Commissary Branch rises in s Transylvania County and flows nw into Little River.

Commissary Hill, s Yancey County approx. 9/10 mile se of Mount Mitchell. Alt. 5,780. Named for a commissary located here by the Carolina Spruce Lumber Company during lumbering operations in the early 1900's.

Commissary Ridge, s Yancey County between Mount Mitchell and Commissary Hill.

Commissioner Gap, s Macon County between Rich Knob and Commissioners Creek.

Commissioners Creek rises in s Macon County and flows se into Little Tennessee River. Perhaps named in honor of the commissioners who determined the North Carolina-Georgia state line in 1819.

Como, town in n Hertford County. First known as Buckhorn. Post office est. in 1883 was named Como for Lake Como in Italy. Inc. 1967.

Company Shops. See Burlington.

Compass Bald Mountain, ne Clay County at the head of Compass Creek. Alt. 3,296.

Compass Creek rises in n Clay County between Julie Ridge and Deadline Ridge and flows s into Tusquitee Creek. Received its name when Robert Henry, a surveyor and Revolutionary War veteran, dropped his compass in the stream as he was crossing it.

Compass Creek, rises in central Nash County and flows se into Edgecombe County to enter Tar River 1 mi. e of Edgecombe-Nash County line.

Complex, community in se Davidson County.

Conaby Creek rises in w Washington County s of the town of Plymouth and flows ne into Roanoke River. Appears as Conalis Creek on the Collet map, 1770, and as Conaly Creek on maps as recent as the 1932 soil survey map. Shown as Coneby Creek on the MacRae map, 1833, and referred to as Conoby Creek in Doc. No. 259, House of Representatives, 63d Congress, 1st Session, 1913.

Conalis Creek. See Conaby Creek.

Conaly Creek. See Conaby Creek.

Concord, city and county seat, central Cabarrus County. Inc. 1798, alt. 704. Named for the harmonious settlement of a dispute over the site for the town. Home of Barber-Scotia College. Produces textiles, hosiery, and poultry products.

Concord, community in sw Duplin County.

Concord, community in nw Person County.

Concord, community in w Sampson County between Bearskin Swamp and Great Coharie Creek.

Concord, community in s central Yancey County on Cane River. Two former communities, Antone and Dellingers, are now considered to be a part of Concord.

Concord. See Seaboard.

Concord Lake, n Carbarrus County on the e edge of Kannapolis. Formed in 1926 by a dam on Patterson Branch. Covers 85 acres with a max. depth of 25 ft. Owned by the city of Concord and used for fishing and as a municipal water source.

Concord Mountain, s Buncombe County, sw of Fairview Gap.

Concord North, uninc. outskirts of the city of Concord, central Cabarrus County.

Concord Township, former township in central Cabarrus County, now township number 12. In 1945 parts of townships number 4, 5, and 11 (Cooks Cross Roads, Mount Gilead, and Baptist Church) were added to this township.

Concord Township, w central Iredell County. Named for Concord Presbyterian Church, near its center, est. 1775.

Concord Township, w central Randolph County.

Coneat. See Coniott Landing.

Coneby Creek. See Conaby Creek.

Coneghta. See Conetoe.

Cone Lake. See Bass Lake.

Cone Memorial Park. See Moses H. Cone Memorial Park.

Conetoe, town in se Edgecombe County, inc. 1887. Known earlier as Warren's Station. Named for nearby Conetoe Creek. Produces tobacco, cotton, peanuts. Alt. 49.

Conetoe Creek rises in e Edgecombe County and flows s where it forms a part of the Edgecombe-Pitt County line. It then flows s and sw into Tar River in Pitt County. The Collet map, 1770, shows Great Coneghta Pocosin as a swampy area on the w side of present-day Conetoe Creek in Edgecombe County. The name appears in county records as early as 1745.

Coney Creek rises in se Caswell County near Ridgeville and flows n into North Hyco Creek. Coney is an old name for rabbit.

Coneyhoe Creek. See Conoho Creek.

Confederate Memorial Forest, in Pisgah National Forest along the Haywood-Transylvania County line on the West Fork Pigeon River and the Blue Ridge Parkway. Dedicated July 12, 1942. Sponsored by the N. C. United Daughters of the Confederacy, the forest contain 125 acres planted with 125,000 red spruce and balsam trees.

Cong Branch rises in w Sampson County and flows s into Little Coharie Creek.

Congleton, community in ne Pitt County at the head of Great Branch. Inc. 1885 as Keelsville with members of both the Congleton and Keel families appointed temporary officers. The name, however, was not adopted nor was a municipal government continued.

Congo, community in w Wilkes County between Lewis Fork Creek and Fishdam Creek.

Conine Bend in the Roanoke River, s Bertie County, at the w mouth of Conine Creek.

Conine Creek, s Bertie County, is a canal connecting two bends in the Roanoke River and creating Conine Island.

Conine Island, s Bertie County, formed in a bend of the Roanoke River by Conine Creek which cuts across a neck formed by the river. Appears as Caroline Island on the Collet map, 1770. *See also* Purchase Islands.

Coniott Creek rises in sw Bertie County and flows se into Roanoke River. The name is a Tuscarora Indian word meaning "making cloth."

Coniott Landing, on the Roanoke River in se Bertie County, at the mouth of Coniott Creek. Possibly the site of the extinct town, Wimberly, which was inc. in 1752. One Joseph Wimberly petitioned to operate a ferry across the Roanoke River at "Coneat," and the town was built on his land. Site has also been known as Blackman's Landing. Blackman and Wimberly families were owners of large tracts of land in the county.

Conley Branch rises in n McDowell County and flows approx. 2 mi. se into North Fork [Catawba River] near Sevier.

Conley Branch rises in w Macon County and flows sw into Jarrett Creek.

Conley Ridge, s Macon County between Wheatfield Branch and Stillhouse Branch.

Connaritsa, community in nw Bertie County. The name Conneritsat appears in local records as early as 1729 with reference to the location of a bridge across Cashie River.

Connaritsa Pocosin, nw Bertie County.

Connaritsa Swamp rises in nw Bertie County in Connaritsa Pocosin and flows se into Cashie River.

Connatara. *See* Chimney Mountain.

Connelly Creek rises in se Swain County and flows nw into Tuckasegee River.

Connelly Mountain, e Swain County between Chestnut Cove Creek and Improvement Creek.

Connelly Springs, town in e central Burke County on Island Creek approx. 2 mi. e of town of Valdese. Settled before the Civil War and named Happy Home. Later, the Connelly family developed a resort here around mineral springs. Named for Mrs. William L. Connelly. Inc. 1920 but not now active in municipal affairs. Alt. 1,195.

Conner Mill Branch rises in central Haywood County and flows n into Pigeon River.

Connestee Falls in s Transylvania County in Carson Creek. Said to have been named for Indian Princess Connestee.

Connor, community in w Wilson County near Turkey Creek. Post office, 1890-1904.

Conoby Creek. *See* Conaby Creek.

Conoconary Creek. *See* Conoconnara Swamp.

Conoconnara Swamp rises in central Halifax County and flows ne into Roanoke River. It appears as Conoconary Creek on the Collet map, 1770. The 2,500-acre plantation of Thomas Pollock, Sr., Conoconnara, was located here in 1721. Before the American Revolution a Church of England chapel stood near the banks of this stream.

Conoconnara Township, e Halifax County.

Conoho. *See* Oak City.

Conoho Bend, in the Roanoke River at the mouth of Conoho Creek in n Martin County.

Conoho Creek rises in nw Martin County and flows se into Roanoke River. Appears as Coneyhoe Creek on the Collet map, 1770. The headwaters of Conoho Creek are called Fort Branch on the Collet map.

Conover, town in central Catawba County. Settled 1871. Inc. 1877. Alt. 1,060. Said to have been named by Mrs. John Seitz, local resident, for Canova, the Italian sculptor whose statue of Washington was destroyed by the fire that leveled the capitol in Raleigh in 1831. Produces furniture, lumber, and textiles.

Conoway Knob on the McDowell-Rutherford County line. Alt. 2,144.

Conrad Branch rises in nw Haywood County on the n side of Cooks Knob and flows ne approx. 1½ mi to join Woody Branch in forming Little Cataloochee Creek.

Conrad Hill, former site of a gold mine, central Davidson County near Holly Grove community.

Conrad Hill Township, e central Davidson County.

Contara. See Whitewater Falls.

Contaroga. See Whitewater Falls.

Contentnea, town in central Greene County on Contentnea Creek. Inc. 1877, but long inactive in municipal affairs. Named for the Tuscarora Indian village of Cotechney (meaning "thief" or "rogue") which was located 3 or 4 mi. upstream.

Contentnea Creek is formed in w Wilson County by the junction of Moccasin and Turkey creeks. It flows se into Greene County, across the county and onto the Lenoir-Pitt County line which it follows into Neuse River. Formerly known as Great Contentnea Creek, it is referred to in the De Graffenried account of the founding of New Bern, 1709-10. Appears as Great Cotecktney Creek on the Collet map, 1770. Cotechney was an Indian village on the creek banks in present Greene County. Other eighteenth century references to this stream use the name Quotankney Creek. See also Moccasin River.

Contentnea Lake, central Wilson County on Contentnea Creek. Formed 1773. Covers 450 acres; max. depth 15 ft. First known as Cobb's Mill Pond (1773); later as Hadley's Mill Pond (named for Thomas Hadley), Barefoot's Mill Pond (1863), Wiggins Pond (1886), David Daniel's Pond (1897). Acquired by Wilson Power and Light Co., 1904.

Contentnea Neck Township, ne Lenoir County.

Contentnea Township. See Winterville.

Conway, town in e Northampton County. Settled about 1835 and known first as Martin's Crossroads; later, by the early 1880's, as Kirby; and finally as Conway, to honor the wife of an officer of the railroad. Inc. 1913. Alt. 105.

Conway Creek. See Little Fishing Creek.

Conwell, community in se Northampton County on the e limits of Rich Square.

Cook Branch rises in e Graham County and flows ne into Rock Creek.

Cook Branch rises in n Madison County and flows s into Big Laurel Creek.

Cook Branch rises in n Mitchell County and flows s into Little Rock Creek.

Cook Branch rises in s Watauga County and flows ne into Pounding Mill Creek.

Cook Creek rises in central Cherokee County near Beaverdam Gap and flows se into Hanging Dog Creek. See also Kilby Cove.

Cook Creek rises in n Cherokee County and flows sw into Garreck Creek.

Cook Creek. See Island Creek.

Cook Gap, s Watauga County between the head of Laurel Branch and the head of Flannery Creek. Alt. 3,349.

Cook Mountain, nw Buncombe County between Sugar Creek and North Turkey Creek, s of Earlies Gap.

Cooks Creek, w Haywood County in Great Smoky Mountains National Park, rises near lat. 35° 40' 30" N., long. 83° 09' 38" W., and flows se into Pretty Hollow Creek.

Cooks Creek rises in central Surry County and flows sw into Fisher River.

Cooks Crossing, community in n Cabarrus County.

Cooks Cross Roads Township, former township in nw Cabarrus County, now township number 4. Formerly also known as Kannapolis Township.

Cooks Knob, w Haywood County, Great Smoky Mountains National Park, near lat. 35° 39' 28" N., long. 83° 08' 42" W., on Indian Ridge between Short Bung (ridge) and Davidson Branch.

Cooks Wall Mountain, w Stokes County at the head of Indian Creek.

Cooktown, community in n Mitchell County on Holison Creek.

Cooleemee, community in s Davie County on the South Yadkin River. Site of former Fisher's Ford. Cotton mill est. here and named for Cooleeme Plantation, which see. Post office est. 1900. Produces textiles. Alt. 840.

Cooleemee Plantation, e Davie County overlooking the Yadkin River. Land purchased by the Hairston family in 1817; plantation house, with four wings in the form of a cross from a central hall, begun in 1850, completed in 1854. Still owned by the Hairston family. Origin of the name unknown, but legend says that Revolutionary War Major Peter Hairston had fought the Creek Indians in Florida; he returned home with a young Indian captive who could remember only one word of his native tongue, the word Cooleemee, believed to mean "place where the white oak grows."

Coolers Knob Mountain, w Randolph County between Cedar Rock Mountain and Brush Mountain.

Cooley Creek rises in central Franklin County and flows ne into Neal Gut.

Coollyconch Mountain, a sandy loam elevation in nw Cumberland County on the Fort Bragg Military Reservation.

Cool Run, community in sw Brunswick County.

Cool Spring, community in e central Iredell County. Began with a store and hotel in the 1850's. An academy here in the 1870's became a high school at the turn of the century.

Cool Spring. See Creswell.

Cool Spring Branch rises in se Union County and flows n into Lanes Creek.

Cool Spring Precinct. See Scuppernong Township.

Cool Spring Township, e central Iredell County.

Cool Springs Township, se Rutherford County.

Coombs Fork, community in w Jones County.

Coon Creek rises in e Granville County and flows s into Fishing Creek.

Coon Creek rises in e Macon County and flows sw into Watauga Creek.

Coon Hollow, s Haywood County on a tributary of Middle Prong.

Coon Mountain, n central Alexander County. Alt. 1,520.

Coontree Branch rises in n Transylvania County near Coontree Mountain and flows s into Davidson River.

Coontree Mountain, n Transylvania County on the head of Coontree Branch.

Cooper, community in ne Cherokee County.

Cooper, community in ne Cumberland County on South River.

Cooper. See Swannanoa.

Cooper Branch rises in w Mitchell County and flows s into Toe River.

Cooper Creek rises in n Swain County in Great Smoky Mountains National Park and flows sw into Tuckasegee River.

Cooper Gap, n Yancey County between Peterson Ridge and the head of Sampson Branch.

Cooper Gap Township, n Polk County.

Cooper Knob, at the sw end of Franks Creek Lead in s Graham County.

Cooper Mountain, w central Swain County, a spur running sw from Jackson Line Mountain.

Coopers Branch rises in n central Avery County and flows nw into Cranberry Creek.

Coopers Township, s central Nash County.

Coopertown, community in s Nash County between Little Sapony Creek and Sapony Creek. Known also as Deans Community.

Coor Millpond, w Wayne County on Beaverdam Swamp. A mill here was owned by Ollin Coor, sheriff of Wayne County in 1848.

Coot Cove, w Swain County between the forks of Pilkey Creek.

Cope Branch rises in nw Swain County and flows s into Haw Gap Branch.

Cope Creek rises in n central Jackson County on the sw slope of Carver Mountain and flows w approx. 4 mi. into Scott Creek on the e limits of Sylva.

Cope Knob, on the Jackson-Macon County line.

Copeland, community in s Surry County near the head of East Double Creek.

Copeland Creek rises in w Ashe County and flows se into North Fork New River.

Cope Mountain, n Jackson County between Soapstone Creek and Scott Creek.

Coppedge Crossroads, community in e Franklin County.

Copperas Bald, mountain in w Avery County.

Copperas Mountain, ne Buncombe County at the nw end of Big Fork Ridge.

Copperas Rock, peak in n Transylvania County on Mills River.

Copper Bald, n Macon County at the head of Big Branch. Alt. 5,249.

Copper Creek rises in n Cherokee County between Groundhog Ridge and Copper Ridge and flows se into Beaverdam Creek.

Copper Gap, on the Swain County, N. C.-Sevier County, Tenn., line in Great Smoky Mountains National Park between Eagle Rock and Mount Sequoyah.

Copper Knob, n Macon County between Rhinehardt Creek and Younce Creek.

Copper Mine Branch rises in central Clay County and flows se into Pounding Creek.

Copper Mine Branch rises in Forest City, s central Rutherford County, and flows se into Broad River.

Coppermine Creek rises in e Jackson County and flows se into Mull Creek.

Copper Mine Creek rises in n Lee County and flows se into Hughes Creek. Named for a copper mine operated near its head. On a knoll near its junction with Hughes Creek many broken Indian arrowheads have been found. Since no perfect arrowheads have been found it has been suggested that they were made at this site.

Copper Mines, former community in nw Alleghany County. Copper mines operated here during the Civil War. Post office continued into the twentieth century.

Copper Neck, w Chowan County s of the mouth of Rockyhock Creek. The name is a corruption of Cowpen Neck, the name of a plantation owned in 1747 by Charles West.

Copper Ridge, nw Cherokee County extends ne from Nin Ridge.

Copper Swamp rises in e Martin County and flows w into Gardners Creek.

Cora, community in s Caldwell County. Named for daughter of Albert G. Corpening. Alt. 1,224.

Corani River. See New River.

Coranine River. See Newport River.

Coranine Sound. See Core Sound.

Corapeake, community in ne Gates County. settled late seventeenth or early eighteenth century. Known as Orapeake until a post office was est. and the Post Office Department made a mistake in the spelling. Alt. 44. See also Bearpond.

Corapeake Swamp rises in n Gates County and flows se into Hamburg Ditch in the Dismal Swamp. Appears as Orapeak Creek on the Moseley map, 1733. The lower course of the stream is called Elm Swamp on the Moseley map but Loosen Swamp on the Collet map, 1770. Later maps, until as recently as 1929, use the name Orapeake Swamp.

Corbett, community in se Caswell County. Named about 1880 for J. C. and Calvin Corbett who operated a store here. Alt. 800.

Corbetts Ferry. See Ivanhoe.

Corbin Creek rises in e Macon County and flows sw into Cat Creek.

Corbin Knob, on the Jackson-Macon County line. Alt. 4,445.

Corbin Mountain, on the Henderson County, N. C.-Greenville County, S. C., line.

Corbinton. See Hillsborough.

Cordova, community in sw Richmond County on the Pee Dee River. A post office, Steeles Mill, existed here as early as 1828, and this is still the name of the railroad station. Cordova post office est. 1899. Produces textiles.

Corduroy Swamp rises in n Northampton County and flows e and ne to join Rogers Swamp in forming Kirbys Creek.

Core Banks, outer barrier beach extending from Cape Lookout to Swash Inlet, along the se side of Core Sound, e Carteret County. Named for Core Indians. Velasco map, 1611, shows the name Endesoakes at the ne end of Core Banks; the Smith map, 1624, shows the name Salvage Island. Including Portsmouth Island, the Core Banks are approx. 44 mi. long. See also Cape Lookout National Seashore Recreational Area.

Core Beach, a portion of Core Banks (which see) in e Carteret County between Core Sound and the Atlantic Ocean. It lies just s of Portsmouth Island.

Core Creek originally rose in central Carteret County and flowed s into Newport River. Dredging and the cutting of a canal now make Core Creek a connecting link between the waters of Neuse and Newport rivers.

Core Point, s side of Pamlico River central Beaufort County. Named for Coree Indians.

Core Sound, a body of water between the mainland and the Outer Banks extending from Cape Lookout to Pamlico Sound in e Carteret County. Named for the Coranine or Coree Indians who lived in the area. The name Corenines appears here on the Comberford map, 1657. The Moll map, 1729, shows Coranine Sound, and the Moseley map, 1773, has Core Sound.

Corinth, community in sw Catawba County.

Corinth, community in se Chatham County. Named for Corinth, Greece, when the Classic Revival was in vogue.

Corinth, community in se Granville County.

Cornatzer, community in central Davie County. Named for local family. Alt. 777.

Corncake Inlet, se Brunswick County from Onslow Bay in the Atlantic Ocean into Buzzard Bay and Cape Fear River n of Smith Island.

Corncob Island, w Bogue Sound, sw Carteret County.

Corncob Mountain extends ne between Seniard Creek and Sitton Creek in nw Henderson County.

Corn Crib Point, se Carteret County, extends into Jarrett Bay se of the community of Davis.

Corndack Creek rises in e Moore County and flows s into Little River. Originally known as Cuidreach Creek, it was named for the Cuidreach McDonald family. Early English mapmakers could only translate its Gaelic pronunciation as Corn-dack.

Cornelius, town in n Mecklenburg County. Est. in 1893 as Liverpool. Inc. in 1905 and renamed Cornelius in honor of Joe B. Cornelius, principal stockholder in a local mill. Produces textiles. Alt. 833.

Cornelius Creek rises in s Iredell County and flows sw into Catawba River.

Corner Knob, on the Jackson-Macon County line.

Corner Rock Creek rises in ne Buncombe County and flows w to join Walker Branch in forming Dillingham Creek.

Cornet Branch rises in se Macon County and flows se into Clear Creek.

Cornet Knob, se Macon County between Tom Branch and Cornet Branch.

Cornett Branch rises in nw Watauga County and flows se into Rube Creek.

Cornjack. See Coinjock.

Cornwall, community in n Granville County.

Cornwell Branch rises in e Cherokee County and flows se into Snead Branch.

Corolla, community on Currituck Banks, e Currituck County. Known as Currituck Beach until 1895 when a post office was est. here and named Corolla. Whales Head Club built here in the 1920's is now used as a summer school for boys. A lighthouse here, the last major one constructed on the Outer Banks, was first lighted December 1, 1875.

Correll Branch rises in w Haywood County, Great Smoky Mountains National Park, near lat. 35° 42' 05" N., long. 83° 07' 06" W., and flows se into Little Cataloochee Creek. This stream has also been known as North Prong.

Corundum, community in e Clay County on Barnett Branch.

Corundum Hill, e Macon County between Lickskillet Branch and Crows Branch. Named for the mineral found here.

Corys Store, community in s Martin County on Smithwick Creek.

Cosby Knob, on the Haywood County, N. C.-Cocke County, Tenn., line, Great Smoky Mountains National Park, on the Great Smoky Mountains divide near lat. 35° 43' 47" N., long. 83° 11' 12" W. Alt. 5,145.

Cosma, community in sw Wake County.

Costin, community in w Pender County on Moores Creek, formerly called Costins Store.

Costins Store. See Costin.

Cotan. See Seco.

Cotechney. See Snow Hill.

Cottage Point e Pasquotank County, extends into the Pasquotank River within limits of Elizabeth City.

Cottendale. See Bruce.

Cotten's Cross Roads. See Roxobel.

Cotton Creek rises in e Montgomery County and flows e into Moore County where it enters Cabin Creek.

Cotton Grove, community in s central Davidson County.

Cotton Grove Township, w central Davidson County.

Cotton Hammock, e Carteret County between community of Stacy and Piney Point.

Cotton Patch, former community on Pigeon River in n Haywood County. A number of years ago a resident planted a small patch of cotton here, and his wife used it to weave cloth. The patch is now grown over and the place abandoned, but the name persists.

Cotton Patch Bay, an arm of Big Colly Bay in ne Bladen County.

Cotton's Crossing. See Tuscarora Beach.

Cottonville, community in s Stanly County. Named prior to the Civil War because of great amount of cotton grown in the vicinity.

Cottrell Hill, community in e Caldwell County on Zacks Fork. Named for William Cottrell who settled here shortly before the Civil War.

Couches Creek rises in ne Swain County in Great Smoky Mountains National Park and flows se into Oconaluftee River.

Couch Mountain, n Henderson County between Clark Gap and Rich Mountain.

Couch Mountain, e Orange County on the head of Little Creek.

Coulson Ordinary appears on the Collet map, 1770, on the Pee Dee River in what is now se Stanly County, e of the town of Norwood. At Colson's Mill nearby Colonel William Lee Davidson's Whig militia defeated Colonel Samuel Bryan's Tories in July, 1780.

Council, town in s Bladen County. Alt. 64. Inc. 1905. Named for industrialist K. Clyde Council (1886?-1951). Also called Council Station because of depot on railroad.

Council Gap, w central Watauga County near the head of Bairds Creek.

Council Mill Pond, s Bladen County 14 mi. se of county seat, an artificial pond on

Friar Swamp owned by Clyde Council estate. Fishing. Not open to the public.

Council Station. *See* Council.

Counterfeit Branch rises in n Haywood County and flows sw into Pigeon River.

Country Line Creek rises in se Rockingham County and flows ne across Caswell County into Virginia where it enters Dan River ne of Milton. Mentioned in local records as early as 1754. Named from the eighteenth century custom of calling the North Carolina-Virginia line the "country line."

County Line Gap on the Caldwell-Wilkes County line.

County Line Ridge on the Caldwell-Wilkes County line.

County of Norfolk was created in 1636 by authorities in Virginia to give Henry Frederick Howard, Lord Maltravers, a specific area for his proposed settlement. Maltravers in 1632 acquired the Heath grant (*see* Carolana). This new county extended from about the site of present Suffolk, Va., to New Bern, N. C. It was into this area that the earliest settlers of what is now North Carolina began to move from Virginia. The County of Norfolk was soon divided into Upper Norfolk and Lower Norfolk counties, with the latter containing the region which later became a part of North Carolina.

Court House Bald, se Clay County on the se end of Ravenrock Ridge.

Court House Bay, s Onslow County in New River. The county's first courthouse was on the banks of New River here, 1734-1735.

Court House Creek rises in nw Transylvania County and flows se into North Fork French Broad River.

Court House Falls, nw Transylvania County in Court House Creek.

Courthouse Knob, n peak of Richland Mountains in n Buncombe County near lat. 35° 41' N., long. 82° 27' 30" W.

Courthouse Township, central Camden County.

Courtney, community in s Yadkin County. Formerly known as Chinquapin Cross Roads. Named for Courtney Baptist Church, organized here in 1832. A late nineteenth century post office serving this community was named Cross Roads Church.

Cove, community in e Haywod County on Cove Creek.

Cove Branch rises in s Transylvania County

and flows ne into East Fork French Broad River.

Cove City, town in w Craven County. Alt. 48. Settled, 1859. Inc., 1907. Known earlier as Cove Creek.

Cove Creek rises in n Cleveland County and flows se into Ward Creek.

Cove Creek rises in Great Dover Swamp, w Craven County and flows ne into Neuse River. Appears as Core Creek on the Moseley map, 1733, and as Moon Creek on the Collet map, 1770.

Cove Creek rises in central Haywood County and flows ne into Jonathans Creek.

Cove Creek rises in e Haywood County and flows w into Fines Creek.

Cove Creek rises in se Henderson County and flows ne into Polk County where it enters Green River.

Cove Creek rises in s McDowell County and flows sw into Rutherford County where it enters Broad River.

Cove Creek rises in nw Transylvania County and flows se into Davidson River.

Cove Creek rises in n Watauga County and flows sw into Watauga River.

Cove Creek, community in central Haywood County on Jonathans Creek. Post office from late nineteenth century until mid-twentieth century.

Cove Creek Gap, central Haywood County, Great Smoky Mountains National Park, near lat. 35° 37' 52" N., long. 83° 02' 50" W., at the head of Winding Stair Branch. Alt. 4,071.

Cove Creek Ridge, central Watauga County forms a semicircle just sw of Buckeye Knob.

Cove Creek Township, w central Watauga County.

Cove Field Branch rises in sw Haywood County and flows ne into Allen Creek.

Covefield Branch rises in se Macon County and flows se into Clear Creek.

Cove Field Ridge, sw Haywood County parallel to Cove Field Branch.

Cove Gap, on the Alexander-Wilkes County line s of Pores Knob.

Covington, community in nw Richmond County. A post office was est. here as early as 1830.

Covington Mountain, nw Cleveland County on Brier Creek. Alt. 2,038.

Cowan. *See* Burgaw.

Cowan Cove, the valley through which the upper course of Smith Mill Creek flows in central Buncombe County.

Cowan Knob on the w end of Lizzy Mountain in central Jackson County.

Cowan's Ford, over Catawba River at the Lincoln-Mecklenburg County line, now under the waters of Lake Norman. Cornwallis, pursuing Gen. Nathanael Greene, crossed the Catawba here after a sharp fight on February 1, 1781, in which Gen. William Lee Davidson was slain.

Coward Bald, peak at ne end of Coward Mountain in e Jackson County. Alt. 5,200.

Coward Lake formed in 1950 in central Jackson County on Norton Creek. Covers 1 acre and has maximum depth of 10 feet. Used for fishing. Not open to the public.

Coward Creek, a small tidal stream flowing e through the swampy part of Oak Island into Molassas Creek in se Brunswick County.

Coward Mountain extends from Moses Creek in central Jackson County ne to Coward Bald.

Cowarts, community in central Jackson County on Caney Fork.

Cow Bog Branch rises in central Columbus County and flows se into Waccamaw River.

Cow Branch rises in nw Columbus County and flows sw into Porter Swamp.

Cow Branch rises in n Burke County and flows n into Avery County where it enters Linville River.

Cow Branch rises in w Jackson County and flows s into Middle Creek.

Cow Branch rises in sw Wilson County and flows e into Robin Branch.

Cow Branch rises in w Wilson County and flows s into Contentnea Creek.

Cow Camp Branch rises in central Avery County and flows n into North Toe River.

Cow Camp Creek rises in central Avery County and flows n into Kentucky Creek.

Cow Camp Gap, near head of Cow Camp Creek in central Avery County.

Cow Creek rises in the highlands of Garrenton's Island in e Camden County and flows e into North River.

Cow Creek rises in nw McDowell County and flows se into Armstrong Creek.

Cowee, chief town of the Middle Cherokees, destroyed during the American Revolution. The mound on which the council house stood is a short distance nw of Franklin in central Macon County. The name is believed to have meant "place of the Deer Clan." Also spelled Keowee.

Cowee Bald, on the Jackson-Macon County line. Alt. 5,085.

Cowee Creek rises in n Macon County and flows sw into Little Tennessee River.

Cowee Gap, on the Jackson-Macon County line.

Cowee Mountains, a range of mountains in se Swain, e Macon, and w Jackson counties. The Jackson-Macon County line follows the peak of the ridge.

Coweeta, community in sw Macon County between the Nantahala Mountains and Little Tennessee River, near Otto. Alt. 2,875. U.S. Forest Service hydrologic laboratory is located here. Older residents and old records use the spelling Coweta. Federal officials have arbitrarily adopted the spelling Coweeta and it now appears on maps and official records.

Coweeta Creek rises in s Macon County and flows ne into Little Tennessee River.

Coweeta Gap, s Macon County between Carrol Knob and Black Mountain.

Cowee Township, ne Macon County.

Cowee Tunnel. See Dillsboro.

Cowenjock. See Coinjock.

Coweta. See Coweeta.

Cowford Swamp rises in sw Robeson County and flows ne into Ashpole Swamp.

Cow Gallus Creek rises in e Pamlico County and flows e into Long Creek.

Cowhead Creek rises in se Onslow County and flows sw into Frenchs Creek.

Cow Hole Branch rises in n Duplin County and flows s into Goshen Swamp.

Cowhorn Swamp rises in n Onslow County and flows sw into New River.

Cow Island, higher ground surrounded by swamp, s Duplin County.

Cow Island. See Bodie Island.

Cowl Cove, on a tributary of Clear Branch in sw Macon County.

Cowlick Branch rises in w Edgecombe County and flows nw into Tar River.

Cowmire Branch rises in central Cherokee County and flows s into Colvard Creek.

Cowpen Island, a point of land extending from Core Banks into Core Sound in se Carteret County.

Cowpen Neck. See Copper Neck.

Cowpen Top, peak on Whiteoak Mountain in n Haywood County.

Cowper's Hill. See Maxton.

Cow Pond Branch rises in nw Craven County and flows s into Neuse River.

Cowrock Mountain, s Jackson County between Logan Creek and Long Branch. Alt. 4,240.

Cowstamp Mountain, e Swain County between Long Creek and Hickorynut Branch.

Cow Swamp rises in s Pitt County and flows ne into Chicod Creek.

Cox Branch rises in w Jackson County and flows e into Cullowhee Creek.

Cox Branch rises in e Translyvania County and flows sw into Cascade Lake.

Coxcomb Mountain, on the Buncombe-Yancey County line between Rocky Knob and Ogle Meadows. Alt. 5,443.

Cox Creek rises in n Cleveland County and flows se into Ward Creek.

Cox Creek rises in n Henderson County and flows se into Clear Creek.

Cox Creek rises in nw McDowell County and flows s into Armstrong Creek.

Cox Creek Gap, n Yancey County between the head of North Cox Creek and South Cox Creek.

Coxe Branch rises in n Yancey County and flows se into Little Creek.

Coxe's Store. *See* Newton Grove.

Cox Knob, e Yancey County between the forks of Long Branch and Crabtree Creek.

Cox Mill. *See* Mill Grove.

Cox Millpond, on the Johnston-Wayne County line on Mill Branch, just before its confluence with Mill Creek. Named for an early Quaker family of Wayne County.

Cox Point extends from e Onslow County into White Oak River.

Coxsborough, town authorized to be laid off in 1797 at or near Cox's Mill, e central Randolph County at the junction of Mill Creek and Deep River. Warehouses for inspection of agricultural products were to be est. here in connection with navigation up and down Deep River. Apparently the town was never set. *See also* Cox's Mill.

Cox's Falls, formerly rapids in Neuse River in sw Wayne County, but now submerged by Goldsboro Cooling Pond. Mentioned as early as 1819 in a survey of the rivers of North Carolina.

Cox's Knob, e Caldwell County. Alt. 2,430. Probably named for Matthew Cox, eighteenth-century settler.

Cox's Mill, former mill on Deep River, e central Randolph County. Was headquarters of David Fanning, noted leader of N. C. Tories, 1781-1782. Appears on the Collet map, 1770. *See also* Coxsborough; Mill Creek.

Cox Store, community in e Polk County be-

tween Whiteoak Creek and Green River. Alt. 868.

Coxville, community in s Pitt County.

Cozad Branch rises in ne Cherokee County and flows se into Morris Creek.

Cozad Gap, ne Cherokee County in the Snowbird Mountains.

Cozart, community in sw Granville County. Alt. 332.

Crab Creek rises in e Alleghany County and flows nw into Little River.

Crab Creek rises in w Henderson County and flows w into e Transylvania County and nw into Little River aprox. 2 mi. n of Cascade Lake.

Crab Creek Township, w Henderson County.

Craborchard Creek rises in sw Watauga County near Avery County line, and flows e into Dutch Creek. Also known as Orchard Creek.

Crab Orchard Fields, an open section in e Haywood County between Crabtree Bald and Gudger Knob.

Crab Orchard Township, former township in e central Mecklenburg County, now township number 7.

Crab Point, a point of the mainland in central Carteret County extending into waters of Newport River.

Crab Point Bay in Newport River, Carteret County, near mouth of Calico Creek n of Morehead City.

Crab Point Thorofare, a channel running between Newport Marshes and the mainland in central Carteret County.

Crabtree, community in e Haywood County. Alt. 2,659. Settled about 1809. Named for the creek.

Crabtree Bald, e Haywood County at sw end of Crab Orchard Fields. Alt. 5,320-5,360.

Crabtree Creek rises in n Franklin County and flows ne into Richland Creek.

Crabtree Creek rises in e Haywood County and flows sw into Pigeon River.

Crabtree Creek rises in w Wake County and flows ne and se into Neuse River e of Raleigh. Appears on the Collet map, 1770.

Crabtree Creek State Park. *See* Umstead State Park.

Crabtree Falls, on Long Branch in sw Mitchell County near Big Crabtree Creek.

Crabtree Gap, e Haywood County on the head of Rogers Cove Creek.

Crabtree Mountain, sw Mitchell County at the head of Roaring Branch. Alt. 3,960.

Crabtree Township, e central Haywood County.

Crabtree Township, e Yancey County.

Craddock Swamp rises in n Sampson County and flows sw into Ward Swamp.

Craggy, community in central Buncombe County on the w bank of French Broad River s of Elk Mountain. Alt. 1,944.

Craggy Dome, peak in Great Graggy Mountains, ne Buncombe County. Formerly known as Big Craggy. Alt. 6,080-6,100.

Craggy Gardens, a 675-acre area in ne Buncombe County n of Craggy Knob. Noted for its native purple rhododendrom which blooms in mid-June.

Craggy Knob, peak in Great Craggy Mountains, ne Buncombe County. Sometimes shown on old maps as Bee Tree Mountain or High Top of Bee Tree. Alt. 5,600-5,700.

Craggy Pinnacle, peak in the Great Craggy Mountains, ne Buncombe County. Appears in early records and on old maps as Buckner's Knob. Alt. 5,900-6,000.

Cragnola Gap, at the head of Cabin Creek in s Henderson County.

Craig Mountain, s Macon County near the heads of Mulberry Creek and Waterloo Branch.

Craig's Creek rises in w Caldwell County and flows e into Wilson's Creek.

Craigs Point extends into the e side of Sulliers Bay in se Onslow County.

Crains Creek, name applied to the lower course of Dunhams Creek (*which see*) in e Moore County. It flows se into Little River. Named for the Crain family which settled along its banks before 1750.

Crains Creek rises in s Lee County and flows s into Moore County where it joins Dry Fork Branch to form Whiteoak Creek. Crains Creek and Whiteoak Creek together were formerly known as North Fork Crains Creek and Little Crains Creek.

Cramerton, town in se Gaston County on South Fork Catawba River. Est. 1906 when a mill was constructed by J. H. Mayes. Known as Mayesworth until purchased by Cramerton Mills, Inc., founded by Stuart W. Cramer (1868-1940). Inc. 1967. Produces textiles. Alt. 633.

Cranberry, community in n central Avery County. Alt. 3,202. A post office est. here in 1850 as Cranberry Forge; discontinued for a brief period following the Civil War. Named changed to Cranberry after 1882. Named for cranberries which grew abundantly nearby. Cranberry Iron Mine, *which see,* was here.

Cranberry Creek is formed in e Ashe County by the junction of Piney Fork and Mulberry creeks and flows nw into South Fork New River.

Cranberry Creek rises in w Avery County and flows nw into Elk River.

Cranberry Creek rises in n Jackson County and flows sw into Hornbuckle Creek.

Cranberry Creek rises in se Watauga County and flows n into s Ashe County where it enters South Fork [New River].

Cranberry Creek rises in w Yadkin County and flows se into South Deep Creek.

Cranberry Gap, central Avery County between Minneapolis and Cranberry. Alt. 3,500.

Cranberry Iron Mine, surface iron mines in n central Avery County. Believed to have been worked by Cherokee Indians. Discovered by white settlers in 1781; worked from 1826 to the present, but most actively from 1865 to 1930. Supplied iron to the Confederacy. See also Cranberry.

Cranberry Island, high ground in n Tyrrell County surrounded by peatlands n of community of Levels.

Cranberry Knob, nw Burke County. Alt. 4,223.

Cranberry Ridge, n Jackson County between Cranberry Creek and Hornbuckle Creek.

Cranberry Township, sw Alleghany County.

Cranberry Township, w Avery County.

Crane Branch rises in central Madison County and flows n into Revere Creek.

Crane Creek rises in s Cherokee County and flows sw into Nottely River.

Crane Creek rises in s Sampson County and flows s into Six Runs Creek.

Crane Creek rises in s Wilkes County and flows ne into Rocky Creek.

Crane Creek rises in s Rowan County and flows ne into High Rock Lake (Yadkin River). Mentioned in local records as early as 1728. Appears on the Collet map, 1770, as Cane Creek, but as Crane Creek on the Price map, 1808. Crane Creek has three tributaries, all called Crane Creek; one of them is sometimes called Town Creek near Salisbury, however.

Crane Creek. See Crains Creek. This stream in Lee and Moore counties has been variously spelled Crane, Crane's and Crains.

Crane Island. See Campbell Island.

Crane Ponds, a cluster of half a dozen small natural lakes in nw Onslow County. Apparently first named on Bache's U. S. Coast Survey map, 1865.

Cranes Island. See Eagles Island.

Crane(y) Island. *See* Harkers Island.

Cransford Cove, w Macon County at the head of Wayah Creek.

Craters Mill, community in s Forsyth County.

Craven, community in e Rowan County.

Craven County, one of three counties (Albemarle and Clarendon being the others) set up in 1664 by the Lords Proprietors of Carolina. Its territory embraced what later became South Carolina. The Ashley River settlement, Charles Town (Charleston), was est. in 1670.

Craven County was formed in 1705 as Archdale Precinct of Bath County, although there is evidence that an Archdale County, *which see,* existed as early as 1696. The name was changed to Craven County about 1712. Located in the e section of the state, it is bounded by Carteret, Jones, Lenoir, Pitt, Beaufort, and Pamlico counties. It has been said that the county was named for William, Earl of Craven (1606-97), one of the original Lords Proprietors and longest lived of the eight. More likely, however, it was named for his grandnephew, William, Lord Craven (who inherited his title and interest in Carolina, and who died the year before the name of the county was changed from Archdale to Craven), or for the third William, Lord Craven, one of the Proprietors at the time the change in the name of the county was made. Area: 785 sq. mi. County seat: New Bern with an elevation of 12 ft. Townships are Nos. 1-3, 5-9. All of former Township No. 4 was included in Pamlico County when it was created in 1872. Produces tobacco, corn, soybeans, peanuts, hogs, dairy products, processed meat, lumber, boats, and apparel.

Craven Gap, central Buncombe County between Rice Knob and Peach Knob in the Elk Mountains.

Craven Parish, Church of England, Craven County, est. 1715, coextensive with the county. By 1741 it was being called Christ-Church Parish. In 1767 there were 1,378 white taxables in the parish. The parish as a unit of local administration was abolished in 1776 with the adoption of the state constitution and the disestablishment of the Church of England. Christ Church Parish of the Episcopal Church, however, still functions in New Bern.

Crawford. *See* Currituck; Danbury.

Crawford Branch rises in ne Cherokee County and flows nw into Collett Creek.

Crawford Branch rises in central Clay County and formerly flowed s into Licklog Creek. It now flows into Chatuge Lake and a part of its former course is now partially covered by it.

Crawford Branch rises in w Henderson County and flows ne into Boylston Creek.

Crawford Branch rises in central Macon County and flows se and ne into Little Tennesee River.

Crawford Creek rises in s Clay County and flows se through Wright Cove into Brasstown Creek.

Crawford Creek rises in e Haywood County and flows ne into East Fork Pigeon River.

Crawford Creek Gap, s Haywood County on the head of Crawford Creek.

Crawford Gap, n Haywood County on the ne end of Hurricane Mountain.

Crawford Mountain, sw Orange County on Cane Creek.

Crawford Township, w central Currituck County. *See also* Currituck.

Crawley Creek rises in e Moore County and flows n into Big Governors Creek.

Crawley Creek rises in n Rutherford County and flows se into Camp Creek.

Crawley Swamp rises in w Bladen County and flows w into Robeson County where it enters Big Swamp.

Creasman Branch rises in s Buncombe County and flows e into Wesley Creek.

Creedmoor, town in s Granville County. Inc. 1895 as Creedmore; reinc. 1905 as Creedmoor. Appears as Creedmoor in an atlas of 1887. Said to have been called "Need More" in the earliest days of the community but with its growth a more dignified name was desired. Creedmoor evolved as an antic in semantics. Produces apparel.

Creedmoor Lake, se Granville County on Ledge Creek. Formed in 1939 as a source of water for the town of Creedmoor. Covers 100 acres. Max. depth, 30 ft.

Creeds Hill Coast Guard Station, formerly on s Hatteras Island, se Dare County.

First formed as a lifesaving station in 1878-79, it became a Coast Guard Station in 1915, but has since been deactivated. The building here is now privately owned.

Creed's Hills. See Frisco.

Creek, community in s Warren County on Fishing Creek. Settled prior to 1800. Post office located here 1883-1930.

Creeksville, community in central Northampton County on Potecasi Creek.

Creeping Swamp rises in sw Beaufort County and flows sw into Clayroot Swamp. For a part of its course it forms the Beaufort-Pitt and the Craven-Pitt County line.

Cremo, community in n central Bertie County.

Crenshaw's Branch rises in central Wake County and flows ne into Neuse River.

Crescent, community in s Rowan County.

Cressville. See Creswell.

Crestmont, former community in nw Haywood County on Big Creek near lat. 35° 45' N., long 83° 06' 37" W. A saw-milling community, the site is now in the Great Smoky Mountains National Park. It was inc. in 1913 but the charter was repealed in the same year.

Creston, community in w central Ashe County. Alt. approx. 2,850. Post office est. 1830 as North Fork; changed to Creston, 1882. Named from its location near the crest of the mountains.

Creston Township, sw Ashe County.

Creswell, town in e Washington County, n of Scuppernong River. Alt. 6. Known as Cool Spring as early as 1826 when a post office by that name was est. here. This name was used locally as late as 1895. When William Atkinson became postmaster in 1874, the post office name was changed to Cressville in honor of John A. J. Creswell, U. S. Postmaster General. Inc. 1874 as Cressville; named changed to Creswell in 1885.

Cribs Creek rises in nw Anson County and flows n into Rocky River.

Cricket, community in central Wilkes County. Est. 1888 and named by the post office department.

Cricket Hill, a man-made island in w Bogue Sound, s Carteret County .

Cricket Swamp rises in e central Bertie County and flows s into Eastmont Swamp. Probably named for John Crickett who owned land in this area as early as 1729.

Crims Crossroads. See Grimes Crossroads.

Crisp, community in s Edgecombe County.

Crisp Creek rises in w Martin County and flows sw into sw Edgecombe County. It then flows se and forms a portion of the Edgecombe-Pitt County line before entering Conetoe Creek.

Croaker Channel, w Carteret County in White Oak River. Named from a species of fish. Formerly one of two channels used to reach Swansboro in the days of sailing vessels. Boats coming up Bogue Sound used Croaker Channel while those approaching from the Atlantic Ocean used Ship (or West) Channel. Croaker Channel is now almost filled with sand.

Croatamung, an island shown on White's map, 1585, in what is now a part of Currituck Banks in e Currituck County. Smith, 1624, calls it Arundells Island; Comberford, 1657, makes it Lucks Island. As the latter is what the n boundary of the Carolina territory granted to the Lords Proprietors in 1663. See also Lucks Island.

Croatan, community in e Craven County. Settled about 1800. Alt. 28.

Croatan National Forest, in parts of Carteret, Craven, and Jones counties. Est. 1933. Covers 294,610 acres. Includes the Croatan Cooperative Wildlife Management Area. Headquarters are in New Bern.

Croatan Sound connects Albemarle and Pamlico Sounds between Roanoke Island and the mainland of Dare County. Appears as Occam (Algonquian Indian, akāmi, "the opposite shore") on White's map, 1590, and as The Narrows on the Moseley map, 1733.

Croatan Township, central Dare County on the mainland.

Croatoan Island, a name applied by John White on his map of 1585, to the s portion of Hatteras Island (Dare County) and a portion of Ocracoke Island (Hyde County). Hatteras Inlet, now dividing this portion of the Outer Banks into two islands, was opened in 1846. Ralph Lane, governor of the first Roanoke colony, named the island "My Lord Admirals Iland" in honor of Lord Howard of Effingham, created Lord High Admiral in 1585. By 1657 Comberford showed the island as "Chowanoke." Smith, in 1624, had called it Abbots Island. The name Croatoan was derived from the Indian village which was on the present Cape Hatteras. (Krō-ōtän, "talk town," indicating the chief's residence.) *See also* Portsmouth Island.

Croft, community in n Mecklenburg County. A post office here, Alexandriana, was est. in the home of Joseph McKnitt Alexander as early as 1822 and continued until as recent as 1882. By 1896 the name Croft was in use.

Cromarties Bridge. *See* Hickory Grove Crossroads.

Cromartys Ferry. *See* Hickory Grove Crossroads.

Cromwell Canal, a stream, rises in s Edgecombe County and flows sw into Tar River.

Cronly. *See* Acme.

Crooked Branch rises in s Richmond County and flows s into South Carolina where it enters Lightwood Knot Creek.

Crooked Creek rises in e Beaufort County and flows s into Pungo River.

Crooked Creek rises in se Buncombe County and flows ne into McDowell County where it enters Catawba River.

Crooked Creek rises in Sanderlin's Swamp in central Camden County and flows e through the North River Pocosin into North River.

Crooked Creek rises in w Durham County and flows se into Eno River.

Crooked Creek rises in sw Franklin County and flows se and ne into Tar River.

Crooked Creek rises in nw Jackson County and flows sw into Tuckasegee River.

Crooked Creek rises in s Lincoln County and flows sw into Leepers Creek.

Crooked Creek rises in e Madison County and flows sw into Middle Fork.

Crooked Creek rises in n Stokes County and flows ne into Virginia where it enters Mayo River.

Crooked Creek is formed in n Union County by the junction of North Fork Crooked Creek and South Fork Crooked Creek. It flows ne into Rocky River.

Crooked Creek. *See* Fork Creek.

Crooked Creek Township, sw McDowell County.

Crooked Fork rises in nw Granville County and flows se in an arc into Aarons Creek.

Crooked Run rises in n Cleveland County and flows se into First Broad River.

Crooked Run rises in w Granville County and flows s into Tar River.

Crooked Run rises in central Jones County and flows n into Trent River.

Crooked Run rises in w Vance County and flows ne into Kerr Reservoir.

Crooked Run Creek rises in s Stokes County and flows sw into n Forsyth County where it flows back nw into Stokes County again and into Little Yadkin River.

Crooked Swamp rises in n Nash County and flows se then ne into Fishing Creek.

Cross Branch rises in s Columbus County and flows sw into Horry County, S. C., where it enters Buck Creek.

Cross Branch. *See* Alder Branch.

Cross Canal drains water from nw Camden County (Dismal Swamp) to the e into Dismal Swamp Canal.

Cross Canal. *See* Hamburg Ditch.

Cross Creek rises in n Cumberland County and flows se through Lake Wood and Fayetteville into Cape Fear River. So named because early settlers found that Cross Creek and Little Cross Creek crossed. *See also* Fayetteville.

Cross Creek, colonial trading center in central Cumberland County on Cape Fear River begun about 1760. Appears as Crosscreek on both the Collet map, 1770, and the Mouzon map, 1775. Consolidated with Campbellton, approx. 1¼ mi. away, in 1778. In 1783 the name was changed to Fayetteville, *which see.*

Cross Creek Township, central Cumberland County. Co-extensive with the city of Fayetteville.

Cross Hill, former community near Carthage, central Moore County. Here, at Alexander Morrison's home, Tories gathered before going to the Battle of Moores Creek Bridge, February 27, 1776.

Crossing Knob, w Watauga County w of a bend in Watauga River.

Cross Knob, n Buncombe County between Chestnut Ridge and Rattlesnake Ridge.

Cross Landing, community in w Tyrrell County e of Scuppernong River.

Cross Millpond. *See* Hunters Millpond.

Cross Mountain on the Buncombe-McDowell County line. Alt. approx. 3,600.

Crossnore, town in s Avery County. Alt. 3,546. Inc. 1925. Settled about 1838 and named for George Crossnore, general store keeper. Crossnore School, founded in 1911 by Dr. Mary Martin Sloop, has trained countless mountain children.

Cross Roads. *See* Maysville.

Cross Roads Church. *See* Courtney.

Cross Roads Township, s central Martin County.

Crossroads Township, central Wilson County.

Cross Swamp, rises in e Columbus County and flows se into Waccamaw River.

Crossway, community in s Scotland County on Lytch's Pond.

Crouse, town in s Lincoln County. Settled about 1840. Inc. 1907. Named for W. L. Crouse, a physician who built the first house in the community.

Crow Branch rises in s Jackson County and flows ne into Whitewater River.

Crow Branch rises in se Orange County about 2 mi. n of town of Chapel Hill and flows e into Booker Creek.

Crow Creek rises in s Macon County and flows ne into Cullasaja River.

Crow Creek rises in sw Randolph County and flows se into Montgomery County where it enters Uwharrie River.

Crowder Mountain Township, sw Gaston County.

Crowders, community in s Gaston County. Nineteenth century post office here was known as Crowder's Creek. Alt. 775.

Crowders Creek rises in sw Gaston County and flows ne and se into South Carolina where it enters Catawba River.

Crowders Mountain, sw Gaston County. Named for Ulrich Crowder, an early settler who soon moved away. Some action against Tories took place here during the Revolution. Alt. 1,624. *See also* All Healing Springs.

Crowells, community in central Halifax County between Tillery and Enfield. Named for two brothers, Edward and Joseph Crowell, who settled here about 1730.

Crowells Springs, community in e Stanly County on Mountain Creek.

Crow Hill, point of land w of Straits, e Carteret County, extending into North River.

Crow Island appears on the Collet map, 1770, and it existed as late as 1833. In Currituck Sound, ne Currituck County, it was se of Knotts Island and barred the soundside of New Currituck Inlet until the inlet closed. After 1833 Crow Island began disintegrating so that by 1861 it was only a mass of tidal marsh islands.

Crown Stream, community in s Pender County. An abandoned railroad station nearby was named Richards.

Crozier Branch rises in se Mecklenburg County and flows e into Carbarrus County where it enters Ready Creek.

Crumpler, community in ne Ashe County on North Fork New River in bluegrass country. Named for Major Thomas Newton Crumpler who died of wounds received in the Civil War on July 18, 1862.

Thompson's Bromine-Arsenic Springs nearby discovered in 1885; hotel and cottages built in 1887. This and nearby All Healing Springs made the region a popular resort in the late nineteenth and early twentieth century.

Cruse, community in e Haywood County on East Fork Pigeon River. Est. 1885 and named by first postmaster who had just read *Robinson Crusoe.* Alt. 2,900.

Crusoe Island. *See* River View Community.

Crutchfield, community in sw Surry County on Yadkin River. Alt. 872.

Crutchfields Falls, rapids in Yadkin River, w Surry County near the mouth of Fishers River, s of the community of Crutchfield. The rapids comprise a fall of 4 ft. over a distance of approx. ¼ mi. Mentioned as early as 1819 in a survey of the rivers of the state.

Crystal Lake, e Moore County on Shaddock's Creek, at the community of Lakeview. Formed in 1855 when Duncan Blue constructed a dam here; enlarged about 1908. Covers approx. 100 acres. Used for fishing, swimming, and boating.

Cuba, former community in n Rutherford County on Gilkey Creek. Post office from 1850 until 1906. Site of a cotton gin, mill, store, and other buildings; market for cherry bark and herbs. Land here recently sold for its timber.

Cub Branch rises in e Jackson County and flows se into Charley Creek.

Cub Creek rises in e central Burke County and flows se into Henry Fork.

Cub Creek rises in ne Davie County and flows sw into Cedar Creek.

Cub Creek rises in central Durham County flows n into Eno River. Once called Cub Island Creek.

Cub Creek rises in w Granville County and flows ne into Tar River.

Cub Creek rises in n Mitchell County and flows sw into Cane Creek.

Cub Creek rises in ne Chatham County and flows ne and se into sw Durham County where it enters Morgan Creek.

Cub Creek rises in e Rutherford County and flows ne into First Broad River.

Cub Creek rises in s Wilkes County and flows n into Yadkin River.

Cub Island Creek. *See* Cub Creek.

Cuccoowink Creek. *See* Dawson Creek.

Cucklemaker Swamp rises in n central Bertie County and flows s into Hoggard Mill Creek.

Cucklers Creek. *See* Cuckolds Creek.

Cuckolds Creek rises in e Beaufort County

and flows w into Pantego Creek. In recent years, perhaps because of the meaning of the word cuckold, the name Cucklers has been applied to this creek.

Cucumber Creek rises on Noah's Mountain, s Alamance County and flows s into Wells Creek.

Cucumber Creek. *See* Rock Hole Creek.

Cudda Bum, a creek, rises in ne Davidson County and flows s into Abbotts Creek. Named for Cuddahy Crouch who lived nearby. "Bum" was his favorite expression, and when Cuddahy Creek was dammed for a mill he began to speak of it as "a bum creek." From Cuddahy's Bum Creek the name Cudda Bum evolved.

Cuidreach Creek. *See* Corndack Creek.

Culberson, town in sw Cherokee County on South Fork Rapier Mill Creek. Inc. 1911. Named for Henry Culberson who donated the site for the town and the post office. Alt. 1,618.

Culbert Branch rises in ne Cherokee County and flows nw into Junaluska Creek.

Culbert Ridge, n Yancey County between Hensley Branch and Bald Mountain Creek.

Culbreth, community in w Granville County.

Cullasaja, community in e Macon County on Cullasaja River. Once known as Sugar Town. The Cherokee word, *Kul-say-gee,* meant "sugar" or "sweet."

Cullasaja Branch rises in s Swain County and flows ne into Yalaka Creek.

Cullasaja Falls. *See* Cullasaja River.

Cullasaja River rises in se Macon County and flows nw into Little Tennessee River. Bridal Veil, Dry, and Lower Cullasaja Falls, *which see,* are on this river. Moses Ashley Curtis, writing from Franklin on September 2, 1829, said that the "Falls of Sugar Town Creek" are "very imposing —nearly as high as Linville."

Culler. *See* Pinnacle.

Cullie Creek rises in n central Carteret County and flows nw into Cedar Creek. It is a very short stream.

Cullowhee, community in w central Jackson County on Tuckasegee River. Originally named Kullaughee Valley, an Indian word meaning "place of the lilies." Name changed to Painter, for the first postmaster, when a post office was est. here in 1882. Renamed Cullowhee about 1900. Home of Western Carolina University, founded in 1889. Alt. 2,066.

Cullowhee Creek rises in w Jackson County and flows n into Tuckasegee River.

Cullowhee Gap, on the Jackson-Macon County line.

Cullowhee Mountain, w Jackson County extends n from Hunter Jim Creek to Webster Creek. Alt. 4,411.

Cullowhee Township, w central Jackson County.

Cumberland, town in w Cumberland County. Settled 1850. Known as Beaver Creek for the stream on which it is located, until 1889 when it was inc. Long inactive in municipal affairs. Alt. 125.

Cumberland County was formed in 1754 from Bladen County. Located in the se section of the state, it is bounded by Sampson, Bladen, Robeson, Hoke, Harnett, and Moore counties. It was named for William Augustus, Duke of Cumberland (1721-65), second son of George II, who was commander of English troops at the Battle of Culloden in 1746 in which Scottish Highlanders were defeated. His extreme severity earned him the nickname of "The Butcher." It is ironic that the county named for him should have been settled by Scottish Highlanders. Area: 662 sq. mi. County seat: Fayetteville with an elevation of 107 ft. Townships are Beaver Dam, Black River, Carvers Creek, Cedar Creek, Cross Creek, Eastover, Grays Creek, Manchester, Pearces Mill, Rockfish, Seventy-first. Produces tobacco, corn, soybeans, wheat, oats, cotton, poultry, bakery products, textiles, dairy products, machinery, and lumber: *See also* Fayette County; Choffington.

Cumberland Gap, central Cherokee County near the junction of Rose and Dockery creeks.

Cumberland Knob, nw Surry County. Alt. 2,885. The Blue Ridge Parkway crosses here, and Cumberland Knob Recreation Area with picnic grounds and hiking trails is here. Said to have been named by Dr. Thomas Walker, a Virginia explorer, for his patron, the Duke of Cumberland, in the 1750's.

Cummins Creek rises in ne Onslow County and flows se into Grants Creek.

Cumnock, community in nw Lee County. The Egypt coal mine here, operated at intervals from 1855 until 1928, supplied coal for Confederate blockade-runners. The community was named Egypt because large crops of corn produced in the area brought in buyers from the outside as in the Biblical story of Joseph. Post office name changed to Cumnock in 1895 for an official of the mine. Alt. 259.

Cundiff Creek rises in s Surry County and flows se into Yadkin River.

Cunningham, community in nw Person County. Named for John W. Cunningham, local landowner and planter. Post office, Cunningham's Store, est. as early as 1822.

Cunningham Creek rises in s Macon County and flows ne into Shope Fork.

Cunningham Mill. See Monroeton.

Cunningham Mountain, n Henderson County between Fletcher Branch and Clark Gap.

Cunningham Township, nw Person County.

Curl Tail Creek rises in nw Stanly County and flows ne in an arc into Riles Creek. Named for its meandering course. Known in 1903 as Fraley Branch.

Currie, community in sw Pender County. Alt. 33. Settled about 1888. Named for John H. Currie, a director of the Cape Fear & Yadkin Valley Railroad. Battle of Moores Creek Bridge, February 27, 1776, the first battle of the Revolution in North Carolina, was fought nearby. Moores Creek National Military Park, a 30-acre tract with numerous historical monuments and a museum, is at the site.

Curries Branch rises in n Columbus County and flows s into West Prong Creek.

Currituck, community and county seat, central Currituck County. Mentioned in local records as early as 1755. In 1822 a commission was appointed to purchase 20 acres around the courthouse, if local citizens voted approval, to lay out a town to be named Crawford. This action was defeated. Alt. 8.

Currituck Banks, or North Banks of Currituck, in e Currituck County, one of the Outer Banks, extends s from Virginia to Bodie Island in e Dare County. All or a part of Currituck Banks is shown as Lucks Island on the Comberford map, 1657. See also Lucks Island; Croatamung; Point Bacon; Goade Island.

Currituck Beach. See Corolla.

Currituck County was formed by 1681 as a precinct to Albemarle County. Located in the ne section of the state, it is bounded by the Atlantic Ocean, Albemarle Sound, Camden County, and the state of Virginia. The name is traditionally said to be an Indian word for wild geese, Coratank. Area: 469 sq. mi. County seat: Currituck with an alt. of 8 ft. Townships are Crawford, Fruitville, Moyock, and Poplar Branch. Produces Irish potatoes, sweet potatoes, corn, soybeans, hogs, and lumber. See also Farmington.

Currituck Creek rises in se Hertford County and flows se into Bertie County where it enters Chowan River.

Currituck Inlet, an inlet through what is now Currituck Banks, e Currituck County, shown on the Comberford map, 1657, as Choratuck Inlet. Closed by a storm in 1828. See also Denniss Island.

Currituck Narrows. See Poplar Branch.

Currituck Parish, Church of England, Currituck County, coextensive with the county, est. 1715. In 1767 the parish had 400 white taxables. The parish as a unit of local administration was abolished in 1776 with the adoption of the state constitution and the disestablishment of the Church of England.

Currituck Point extends from the sw mainland of Hyde County into the mouth of Pungo River.

Currituck Sound, the body of water between Currituck Banks on the e and the mainland of Currituck County on the w and from Knotts Island on the n to Powells Point on the s. Approx. 30 mi. long and 4 mi. wide at the maximum. It appears on the Moseley map, 1733. See also Titepano.

Currituck Township, w Hyde County.

Curtis Cove, s Haywood County. A tributary of West Fork Pigeon River flows through the cove.

Curtis Creek rises in n central Avery County and flows n into Elk River.

Curtis Creek rises near Doubletop Mountain on the Buncombe-Haywood County line and flows sw into Hominy Creek.

Curtis Creek rises in w McDowell County and flows se into Catawba River.

Curtis Creek rises in sw Macon County and flows sw into Nantahala River.

Curtiss Knob, s Macon County at the head of Piney Knob Creek.

Cuscopang River. *See* Scuppernong River.

Cushing Branch rises in n Henderson County and flows nw into Cane Creek. Also known as Cushion Creek.

Cushion Creek. *See* Cushing Branch.

Cutawhiskie Swamp rises in se Northampton County and flows ne into Hertford County where it enters Livermans Mill Pond on Potecasi Creek. Named for an Indian village mentioned in local records (with various spellings) as early as 1718.

Cut Laurel Gap, in Stone Mountains, w Ashe County on the Tennessee state line. Named because early settlers encountered such a thick "rhododendron hell" here that they had to cut a tunnel through it for a mile or more. Alt. 3,746.

Cutoff Island, e Dare County, in the waters of Roanoke Sound off the sw tip of Bodie Island.

Cut-off Ridge, n Jackson County extends n from Scott Creek.

Cutshall Branch rises in n Madison County and flows w into Shelton Laurel Creek.

Cutshalltown, community in n Madison County on a tributary of Shelton Laurel Creek.

Cutthroat Gap, on the Buncombe-Henderson County line betwen Candler Knob and Stony Bald. Alt. approx. 4,200.

Cuwhiffle Swamp rises in se Sampson County near Delway and flows nw into Six Runs Creek. The name may be derived through faulty pronunciation from the Gaelic *Culmhutar* (*pron.* kulvútar), "smuggler" or "mutineer." *See also* Quewhiffle.

Cwareunoc, an Indian village shown on the De Bry map, 1590, as being on Bogue Sound, s Carteret County.

Cycle, community in w Yadkin County on Dobbins Creek. Known first as Pea Ridge. Post office est. about 1913 and named Cycle from the fact that the patrons it served lived in a circle from the post office. Post office name gradually replaced the older name.

Cynthia Branch rises in n Yancey County and flows w into Cane River.

Cypress Branch rises in central Columbus County and flows ne into White Marsh.

Cypress Creek rises in Cypress Creek Bay in ne Bladen County and flows s and e into South River.

Cypress Creek rises in central Columbus County and flows n into White Marsh.

Cypress Creek rises in e Franklin County and flows s into Tar River. Appears on the Collet map, 1770, as Cyprus Creek.

Cypress Creek rises in sw Harnett County and flows sw into Hoke County where it enters Crane Creek.

Cypress Creek rises in n Northampton County and flows ne into Virginia where it enters Meherrin River. Appears on the map of the North Carolina-Virginia line run by William Byrd and others, 1728, and on the Moseley map, 1733.

Cypress Creek rises in w Onslow County and flows sw into Duplin County where it flows nw and ne into Cape Fear River.

Cypress Creek rises in n Onslow County and flows n into Jones County where it enters Trent River. Appears on the Collet map, 1770.

Cypress Creek. *See* Goodwin Creek.

Cypress Creek, community in ne Bladen County.

Cypress Creek, community in se Duplin County.

Cypress Creek Bay, ne Bladen County.

Cypress Creek Bay, a muck-loam filled bay in central Columbus County.

Cypress Creek Township, ne Bladen County.

Cypress Creek Township, se Duplin County.

Cypress Creek Township, former township in se Franklin County, now township number 9.

Cypress Creek Township, s Jones County.

Cypress Point, a point of land extending from the mainland of w Dare County, s of Mill Tail Creek, into Alligator River.

Cypress Run rises in se Beaufort County and flows e into South Creek.

Cypress Swamp rises in w Gates County and flows sw into Taylor Millpond.

Cypress Swamp rises in w Onslow County and flows se into Sandy Run Swamp.

Cypress Swamp. *See* Goodwin Creek.

Cyprett's Bridge (Ceputt's, Cipritz, Cyprits, Cypretz), former bridge over New Hope Creek in ne Chatham County on the road from New Bern by Raleigh to Pittsboro. It was selected in 1793 from seven suggested sites within fifteen miles of which the University of North Carolina was to be located. Later called Prince's Bridge, *which see.*

Cyrus, community in w Onslow County on Harris Creek.

D

Dabbs, community in s central Caswell County.

Dabney, community in w Vance County.

Dabney Township, w Vance County.

Dads Top, mountain peak n of Twelve O'clock Top on the Buncombe-Haywood County line.

Dailys Creek rises in w Lenoir County and flows ne into Neuse River. Probably named for John Dailey who settled here about 1800.

Dalkeith, plantation house in se Warren County near Arcola. Built in 1824 by Jack Burgess, and still used as a dwelling.

Dallas, town in central Gaston County. Authorized to be laid out as county seat by act creating the county, 1846. It remained the county seat until 1909 when Gastonia was selected by popular vote. Inc. 1863. Named for George M. Dallas (1792-1864), vice president of the United States at the time the county was created. This area received postal service as early as 1817 from Hoylesville post office, named for Andrew Hoyle, first postmaster, and located 3 mi. e of site of Dallas. This post office was moved to Dallas in 1848 to become Dallas post office.

Dallas Township, n central Gaston County.

Da-loh-no-geh. See Yellow Mountain.

Dalton, community in sw Stokes County. Alt. 785. A post office here in the early nineteenth century was known as Boyles' Store.

Dalton. See Clarkton.

Dalton Branch rises in nw Swain County in Great Smoky Mountains National Park and flows se into Moore Springs Branch.

Dalton Creek rises in e Macon County and flows ne into Caler Fork.

Dalton Gap, on the Swain County, N. C.-Blount County, Tenn., line in Great Smoky Mountains National Park between Sheep Wallow Knob and Parsons Bald. Alt. 2,955.

Dalton Ridge, nw Swain County in Great Smoky Mountains National Park extending nw from the head of Judy Branch to Sheep Wallow Knob.

Dam Creek rises in s Pasquotank County and flows e into Big Flatty Creek.

Damons Mountain, sw Cherokee County extends from Cole Gap ne to Dickey Branch.

Dana, community in e Henderson County. A post office was est. here between 1890 and 1894 expressly to serve the Hadley Hotel; named for Dana Hadley, son of the owner of the hotel. Apple growing and packing center.

Danbury, town and county seat, central Stokes County on the Dan River. Replaced Germantown as the county seat in 1849 when the county was divided to form Forsyth County. Inc. 1957. Called simply "county town of Stokes" from about 1849 until 1851 when it was given the name Crawford in honor of the wife of John Hill, long-time clerk of court and member of Congress. Changed to Danbury in 1852 for name of plantation of Governor Alexander Martin (1738-1807) near the mouth of Jacobs Creek on the Dan River in Rockingham County. Martin was governor when Stokes County was created. Alt. 825. See also Intelligence.

Danbury Township, central Stokes County.

Danbury Creek rises in sw Stokes County and flows w into Little Yadkin River.

Dandy, community in nw Ashe County. Alt. 3,455.

Danes Creek rises in n Macon County and flows se into Younce Creek.

Dan Gap, s Macon County between Henderson Mountain and Little Fishhawk Mountain.

Dan Holland Creek rises in ne Cherokee County and flows se into Valley River.

Daniel Boone's Cave. See Boone's Cave.

Daniel Boone Wildlife Management Area, part of Pisgah National Forest in nw Burke County.

Daniel Ridge in nw Transylvania County between Shuck Ridge Creek and Daniel Ridge Creek.

Daniel Ridge Creek rises in nw Transylvania County and flows se into Right Fork Davidson River.

Daniels Cove, s Haywood County on Shining Creek.

Daniels Creek rises in w Harnett County and flows ne into Cape Fear River. The name is a corruption of Donnelys; named for Arthur Donnely who settled on its banks in 1750. Earlier known as McPhersons Creek.

Daniels Gap, on the Ashe-Wilkes County line.

Daniels Marshes. See Roanoke Marshes.

Daniels-Rhyne, textile community ir central Lincoln County sw of Lincolnton Originally two separate communities. Daniels named for Daniel Warlick, pioneer settler. Rhyne named for founder of local mill.

Daniel Swash waterway through a group of unnamed tidal marsh islands in Pamlico Sound just off Portsmouth Island, e Carteret County.

Daniel Town, community in s Rutherford County. Named for Leonard N. Daniel who operated a store here, owned adjacent land, and built several houses.

Dan Payne Mountain, s Madison County at the head of Caney Fork Branch.

Dan River rises in s Patrick County, Virginia, and flows se into Stokes County. It flows se and ne into Rockingham County and back into Virginia. It dips back into North Carolina on the Caswell-Rockingham County line and into n Caswell County after which it flows ne in Virginia into the Kerr Reservoir (which see) on Roanoke River. Mentioned by William Byrd in 1728. Probably an Indian name.

Dan River Township, n central Caswell County.

Dans Creek rises in ne Columbus County and flows se and e into Livingston Creek.

Dans Creek rises in ne Swain County and flows sw into Straight Fork.

Dan Sisk Gap, s Burke County in South Mountains.

Dans Knob, e Madison County between Beetree Creek and East Fork [Bull Creek].

Danson's Manor. See Shiloh.

Danton, town authorized to be est. in 1803 on the lands of Thomas Rivers on the n side of Dan River, Stokes County. Apparently the town was never developed.

Danville. See Leaksville.

Danville. See Startown.

Dan Weeks Point, a point of land extending into White Oak River, sw Carteret County.

Darb Branch rises in n Transylvania County and flows ne into Bradley Creek.

Darby, community in w Wilkes County on Elk Creek. Named for Darby Hendrix, eighteenth-century pioneer landowner.

Dardens, community in ne Martin County. A post office known as Davis' Store served this area from about 1828 to 1846. Named Dardens for local family, one of whom, Col. James G. Darden, was a personal friend of Warren G. Harding from as early as 1917 and later, as an oil man, was involved in the Teapot Dome affair. Alt. 46.

Dare County was formed in 1870 from Currituck, Tyrrell, and Hyde counties. Located in the ne section of the state, it is bounded by the Atlantic Ocean; Pamlico, Croatan, and Albemarle Sounds; and Hyde and Tyrrell counties. It was named for Virginia Dare, born August 18, 1587, on Roanoke Island in the county, who was the first child of English parents to be born in America. Area: 1,246 sq. mi. (388, land; 858, water). County seat: Manteo with an elevation of 12 ft. Townships are Atlantic, Croatan, East Lake, Hatteras, Kennekeet, and Nags Head. Produces scuppernongs, figs, poultry, processed sea food, and lumber.

Darham Creek. See Durham Creek.

Dark Branch rises in central Duplin County and flows se into Northeast Cape Fear River.

Dark Branch rises in central Swain County and flows sw into Yalaka Creek.

Dark Cove, extends nw from Big Butte Mountain to West Cove in e Haywood County.

Dark Mountain, n Montgomery County near Barnes Creek.

Dark Prong rises in s Haywood County and flows e into East Fork Pigeon River.

Dark Ridge, mountain in n Avery County.

Dark Ridge, ne Jackson County between Dark Ridge Creek and Cabin Creek.

Dark Ridge, community in n Avery County.

Dark Ridge Creek rises in n Avery County and flows w into Tennessee where it enters Elk River.

Dark Ridge Creek rises in ne Jackson County and flows nw into Scott Creek.

Darkridge Gap, mountain gap in n Avery County.

Darlington, community in central Halifax County.

Darnell, community in nw Wilkes County on a tributary of North Fork Reddies River. Named for Abdiel Darnell who settled in this vicinity shortly after 1800.

Dasemunkepeuc. See Manns Harbor.

Dashoga Ridge, ne Swain County in Great Smoky Mountains National Park. Its center is near lat. 35° 40' 40" N., long. 83° 14' 55" W.

Da-tsu-la-gun-yi. See Cold Mountain.

Dave Barrett Creek. See Right Fork [Eagle Creek].

Dave Bellew Top, peak in sw Cherokee County between Wolf Creek and Hot House Creek.

Davenport Branch rises in e Clay County and flows sw into Buck Creek.

Davenport Branch rises in s Clay County and flows se into Hiwassee River.

Davenport Forks, community in ne Washington County s of Deep Creek.

Davenport Gap, a windgap in the Great Smoky Mountains where the North Carolina-Tennessee boundary crosses the ne boundary of Great Smoky Mountains National Park, Haywood County, N. C., and Cocke County, Tenn., near lat. 35° 46' 30" N., long. 83° 6' 30" W. Named in honor of Col. William Davenport, who in 1821 marked a stone on the "north side of Cataloochee Turnpike Road" as the starting point of his survey of the Tennessee-North Carolina state line.

Daveport Mountain, w Henderson County between Johnsons Mill Creek and Shaw Creek.

Dave Rock in w Transylvania County e of Bart Branch.

Davers Island. See Harkers Island.

David Daniel Pond. See Contentnea Lake.

Davids Creek rises in e Stanly County and flows se into Cedar Creek.

Davidson, town in n Mecklenburg County. Inc. 1879 as Davidson College; name changed, 1891. Davison College founded here, 1837, named for General William Lee Davidson (1746-81), Revolutionary hero killed at the Battle of Cowan's Ford. Produces asbestos products. Alt. 826.

Davidson Branch rises in w Haywood County and flows s into Palmer Creek.

Davidson College. See Davidson.

Davidson County was formed in 1822 from Rowan County. Located in the central section of the state, it is bounded by Randolph, Montgomery, Rowan, Davie, Forsyth, and Guilford counties. It was named for General William Lee Davidson (1746-81), who was killed at the Battle of Cowans Ford on the Catawba River during the Revolutionary War. Area: 560 sq. mi. County seat: Lexington with an elevation of 810 ft. Townships are Abbotts Creek, Alleghany, Arcadia, Boone, Conrad Hill, Cotton Grove, Emmons, Hampton, Healing Springs, Jackson Hill, Lexington, Midway, Reedy Creek, Silver Hill, Thomasville, Tyro, and Yadkin College. Produces wheat, oats, corn, tobacco, poultry, eggs, dairy products, hogs, livestock, frozen foods, textiles, hosiery, furniture, apparel, lumber, concrete pipe, batteries, lumber, slate, flagstone, and shale for brick.

Davidson County, now in Tennessee, was created in 1783 and named in honor of General William Lee Davidson (1746-81). Nashville (now the capital of Tennessee) became the county seat. This was a part of the territory ceded by North Carolina in 1789 to the Federal government. For further information see D. L. Corbitt, The Formation of North Carolina Counties.

Davidson Creek rises in s Iredell County and flows sw into Mecklenburg County where it enters Catawba River. Probably named for George Davidson who owned 500 acres on the creek in 1778.

Davidson Gap, se of Robinson Rough on the Buncombe-Madison County line.

Davidson Gap, w Haywood County, Great Smoky Mountains National Park, near lat. 35° 39' 08" N., long. 83° 06' 07" W., between Bald Top and Cooks Knob.

Davidson River rises in w Transylvania County and flows se into French Broad River.

Davidson River, community. See Pisgah Forest.

Davidson's Fort. *See* Old Fort.

Davidson Township, sw Iredell County. Named for a local family.

Davidsonville, community in s Cherokee County on Moccasin Creek.

Davids Point, a projection of n Hatteras Island into Pamlico Sound, e Dare County. Lies e of Great Island and s of the community of Waves.

Davie, community in central Henderson County. Alt. 2,214.

Davie Academy. *See* Kappa.

Davie Branch rises in nw Henderson County and flows ne into North Fork.

Davie County was formed in 1836 from Rowan County. Located in the central section of the state, it is bounded by Davidson, Rowan, Iredell, Yadkin, and Forsyth counties. It was named for William Richardson Davie (1756-1820), distinguished Revolutionary soldier, member of the Federal Convention of 1787, governor of North Carolina, minister to France, and one of the founders of the University of North Carolina. Area: 264 sq. mi. County seat: Mocksville with an elevation of 866 ft. Townships are Calahaln, Clarksville, Farmington, Fulton, Jerusalem, Mocksville, and Shady Grove. Produces corn, wheat, oats, dairy products, livestock, hogs, apparel, furniture, chemicals, and textiles.

Davie Crossroads, community in s Davie County at the crossing of U. S. Highway 601 and N. C. Highway 801. Est. 1911-1915 when a garage and store opened here. Locally now familiarly called Greasy Corner. Alt. approx. 740.

Davie Mountain, s Clay County at the sw end of Cherry Mountain. Alt. 2,958.

Davie Mountain, nw Henderson County near Davie Branch.

Davis, community on Core Sound in e Carteret County, on Davis Shore.

Davis. *See* Bakersville.

Davis Bald, on the Macon-Swain County line near the head of Little Laurel Creek. Alt. approx. 4,500.

Davis Bay, e Pasquotank County between Cobb Point and Brickhouse Point on the Pasquotank River.

Davis Branch rises in w Madison County and flows s into French Broad River.

Davis Branch rises in s central Swain County and flows sw into Yalaka Creek.

Davis Cove Branch rises in w Madison County and flows e into Spring Creek.

Davis Creek rises in se Brunswick County and flows sw into tidal marshes which drain into the Atlantic Ocean through Lockwoods Folly Inlet.

Davis Creek rises in n Cherokee County and flows sw and se into Hanging Dog Creek.

Davis Creek rises in s Swain County and flows w into Sawmill Creek.

Davis Ford, former ford over Rocky River, Anson-Stanly County line, at the mouth of Richardson Creek. John Davis owned a plantation in this vicinity. Richard Lane Ordinary is shown at approx. this site on the Collet map, 1770.

Davis Gap, mountain gap in s central Swain County on the head of Davis Branch.

Davis Island in Core Sound at the s end of Davis Shore, e Carteret County. Named for William Davis who settled here in 1715.

Davis Landing on Pungo River, e Beaufort County.

Davis Mill Pond on Trotters Creek, w Lenoir County. Formed about 1850. Covers 60 acres; max. depth 12 ft.

Davis Mill Pond. *See* Pages Lake.

Davis Shore, e shore of a peninsula in e Carteret County extending into Core Sound.

Davis Slough, e Dare County in the waters of Pamlico Sound sw of Oregon Inlet.

Davis' Store. *See* Dardens.

Davistown, former community in s Edgecombe County. Now merely a railroad crossing.

Davis Township, on Core Sound in e Carteret County.

Davis White Sulphur Springs, former resort in e Alexander County. Flourished from about 1883 until early twentieth century. Known also as Sulphur Springs. Davis family operated gristmill here both before and after the site was popular as a summer resort.

Dawson, community in s Halifax County. A post office as early as 1830.

Dawson, community in n Lenoir County. Named for a local family. Formerly a depot on the Hines Lumber Company railroad from Kinston to Snow Hill. A center for shipping logs and cotton many years ago. A school was operated in this vicinity as early as 1793. The Industrial Christian College was operated here from 1906 until about 1921.

Dawson Creek rises in s Pamlico County and flows se into Neuse River. Appears on the Moseley map, 1733. Named for Richard Dawson who purchased land here in 1706. Prior to 1706 the creek was known as Cuccoowink Creek. *See also* Janeiro.

Day Book, community in ne Yancey County on Jacks Creek. Alt. 2,350. Post office est. about 1815 and named for a book in which names were recorded of settlers moving west. Another version of the traditional origin of the name is that it came from a time book kept for employees of a local lumber company.

Daylo, community in nw Wilkes County on Middle Fork Reddies River. Est. 1924 by E. N. Vannoy, a merchant, and named for a brand of flashlights which he sold.

Days Creek rises in s Watauga County and flows nw into East Fork [of South Fork New River].

Days Crossroads, community in n Halifax County.

Day's Gap. *See* Hugh Day's Gap.

Daystrom, community in w Robeson County. Alt. 179. Known first as Alma for the Alma Lumber Company which operated here. Name changed about 1950 when Daystrom Laminates, a furniture division of Daystrom, Incorporated, began operations here.

Dead Backwater, a sluggish body of water that flows only at high tide between Bird Island and the mainland of Colkins Neck extending from inside Mad Inlet to Bonaparte Creek in sw Brunswick County.

Deaden Top, peak in central Cherokee County between Hiwassee River and West Prong Grape Creek.

Deadfall Creek rises in sw Anson County and flows ne and s into South Carolina where it enters Thompson Creek.

Deadline Ridge, central Clay County, extends n from Tusquitee Creek to Chestnut Branch.

Deals. *See* Wash Woods.

Deals Branch rises in nw Swain County and flows s into Lake Cheoah.

Deals Creek rises in n Rowan County and flows ne into Yadkin River.

Deals Gap, mountain gap on the Swain County, N. C.-Blount County, Tenn., line, in Great Smoky Mountains National Park. Alt. 1,957.

Dealsville, community in w Alexander County. Alt. 1,150. Named for local family which operated a store and leather tannery.

Dean, community in e Macon County on Lake Emory.

Dean Island, a sandy island approx. ½ mi. long in Little Tennessee River in n Macon County.

Deans Community. *See* Coopertown.

De Armond Bald, mountain in nw Swain County on Jenkins Trail Ridge in Great Smoky Mountains National Park. Alt. 5,100.

De Armond Ridge, nw Swain County in Great Smoky Mountains, a short spur extending southwest from De Armond Bald on Jenkins Trail Ridge.

Deavers Mill Pond, on Poley Swamp in n Duplin County. Alt. 106.

Deaver View, community in central Buncombe County.

Deaver View Mountain, central Buncombe County. Alt. 3,130.

DeBerry's Mill Pond, ne Northampton County on Kirbys Creek. Covers approx. 100 acres; max. depth 10 ft.

Debruhls. *See* Rhems.

Debs Knob, s Wilkes County near the head of East Prong Cub Creek. Probably named for Deborah Riddle, a nineteenth century resident of the area.

Deck Hill, peak in s Watauga County between Flannery Fork [South Fork New River] and Payne Branch.

Deep Bay, s Hyde County between Bell Island and Judith Island.

Deep Bay, a bay on the se shore of South Lake, central Dare County.

Deep Bottom, stream, rises in w Washington County and flows nw into Welch Creek. Mentioned in local records as early as 1868.

Deep Bottom Branch rises in n Jones County and flows s into Beaver Creek.

Deep Branch rises in ne Cherokee County and flows se into Valley River.

Deep Cove, a channel separating Judith Island and Swanquarter Island in Pamlico Sound in s Hyde County.

Deep Creek rises in n central Alamance County and flows sw into Stony Creek.

Deep Creek rises in sw Anson County and flows s into Deadfall Creek.

Deep Creek rises in e Carteret County and flows s into North River.

Deep Creek rises in n central Carteret County and flows s into Newport River.

Deep Creek rises in central Currituck County in Maple Swamp and flows sw into North River.

Deep Creek rises in w Graham County and flows ne into Cheoah River.

Deep Creek rises in se Halifax County and flows s into ne Edgecombe County from where it flows sw into Fishing Creek.

Deep Creek rises in n Halifax County and flows ne into Roanoke River. Appears as Great Creek on the Collet map, 1770, a name which is still sometimes applied to it.

Deep Creek rises in s Halifax County and flows se into Fishing Creek in n Edgecombe County. It appears on the Collet map, 1770.

Deep Creek rises in e Hertford County and flows ne into Chowan River.

Deep Creek rises in Fort Bragg Military Reservation in ne Hoke County and flows ne into Little River.

Deep Creek rises in sw Moore County and flows s into Lumber River.

Deep Creek rises in nw Northampton County and flows se into Roanoke River. Appears as Falling Run on the MacRae map, 1833; name changed after 1862.

Deep Creek rises in central Person County and flows se into Durham County where it enters Flat River.

Deep Creek rises in Sevier County, Tenn., and flows s through central and e Swain County into Tuckasegee River.

Deep Creek rises in n Washington County and flows ne into Bull Bay.

Deep Creek is formed in s Yadkin County by the junction of North Deep Creek and South Deep Creek. It flows se into Yadkin River. Appears as Fifth Creek on the Collet map, 1770.

Deep Creek. See Bear Creek.

Deep Creek. See Indian Creek.

Deep Creek, community in sw Anson County. A post office operated here for a brief time about 1882.

Deep Creek, former Township ne Edgecombe County. Now township number 4.

Deep Creek Gap, mountain gap n Swain County on Fork Ridge in Great Smoky Mountains National Park.

Deep Creek Township, sw Yadkin County.

Deep Creek Township. See Edgecombe County.

Deep Cut. See Eufola.

Deep Ford Creek rises in w Transylvania County and flows e and ne into Toxaway River.

Deep Gap, mountain gap in Bullhead Mountain, se Alleghany County.

Deep Gap, mountain gap in Firescald Mountain, w Avery County.

Deep Gap, at nw end of Firescald Ridge in sw Graham County.

Deep Gap, central Graham County in Cheoah Mountains at the head of East Buffalo Creek.

Deep Gap, w Haywood County between Strawberry Knob and Maggie Spring Gap.

Deep Gap, s Haywood County between Deep Gap Cove and Hickory Flat Cove.

Deep Gap, s Haywood County on Shining Rock Ledge.

Deep Gap, s Haywood County on the head of Deep Gap Creek.

Deep Gap, on the head of Plott Creek in w Haywood County.

Deep Gap, on the Henderson-Polk County line.

Deep Gap, s Jackson County on the head of Frolictown Creek.

Deep Gap, on Jackson-Haywood County line.

Deep Gap, e Jackson County between Snaggy Bald and Lynn Gap.

Deep Gap, n Jackson County between Parker Knob and Steep Mountain.

Deep Gap, on the McDowell-Yancey County line between Glass Rock Knob and Green Knob.

Deep Gap, e Macon County between Round Mountain and Panther Mountain.

Deep Gap, on the Clay-Macon County line.

Deep Gap, n Madison County at the nw end of Brigman Hollow.

Deep Gap, on Big Ridge in n Mitchell County.

Deep Gap, w Polk County on Harm Creek.

Deep Gap, e Swain County between Deep Gap Branch and Connelly Mountain.

Deep Gap, nw Swain County between Haw Gap Branch and Mill Branch, on Forrester Ridge.

Deep Gap, se Swain County between the head of Bowers Creek and Yalaka Creek.

Deep Gap, w Swain County between the head of Rowan Branch and Pilkey Creek.

Deep Gap, w Transylvania County on the head of Laurel Fork Davidson River.

Deep Gap, n Transylvania County on the head of Brushy Branch.

Deep Gap, e Watauga County 12 mi. e of Boone. Alt. 4,500.

Deep Gap, s Yancey County near the head of Colbert Creek.

Deep Gap, w Yancey County between Possumtrot and Horton creeks.

Deep Gap, community in e Watauga County on Deep Gap Creek. Post Office est. 1894 as Yuma. Name changed about 1920.

Deep Gap Branch rises in e Swain County and flows ne into Chestnut Cove Creek.

Deep Gap Cove, s Haywood County on a tributary of Little East Fork Pigeon River.

Deep Gap Creek rises in s Haywood County and flows nw into Allen Creek.

Deep Gap Creek rises in e Watauga County near Laxon and flows ne into se Ashe County where it enters South Fork New River. Once known as Gap Creek.

Deep Gap Mountain, e Graham County extends ne from Dry Creek.

Deep Gully, rises on Craven-Jones County line and flows se into Trent River.

Deep Gully, a canal on the Jones-Craven County line which flows se into Trent River.

Deep Gully Creek rises in n Onslow County and flows sw into Mill Creek.

Deep Hole Point. See Marshallberg.

Deep Inlet appears on the Price map, 1808, in e New Hanover County just n of the present Masonboro Inlet. Deep Inlet closed after 1838 but before 1861.

Deeplow Gap, n Swain County on the e slope of Thomas Ridge in Great Smoky Mountains National Park.

Deep Point, point of land extending into Alligator River, e of junction of Intracoastal Waterway and Alligator River, n Hyde County.

Deep River is formed in sw Guilford County at High Point Lake by the junction of East Fork Deep River and West Fork Deep River. It flows se through Randolph County, across the ne edge of Moore County, and forms a part of the Chatham-Lee County line. It joins Haw River in se Chatham County to form Cape Fear River. The junction of Haw and Deep rivers was one of six sites suggested in 1788 for the location of the state capital.

Deep River Township, former township in n Lee County. Now township number 4.

Deep River Township, w Guilford County.

Deep River Township, ne Moore County.

Deep Run, a stream fed by several canals in e Beaufort County, flows w into Broad Creek.

Deep Run rises in w Onslow County and flows se into Southwest Creek.

Deep Run, town in sw Lenoir County. Inc. 1925. Est. in the 1880's when Ira D. Sparrow and Ike Stroud opened a turpentine distillery and built several stores at the site. A Baptist Church erected here about 1850 is still in use. For a time the place was nicknamed "Red Town" because a number of the earliest houses were painted red.

Deep Run, rises in sw Lenoir County and flows ne into Southwest Creek.

Deep Run Swamp rises in e Martin County and flows nw into Gardners Creek.

Deep Swamp Branch rises in se Hertford County and flows ne into Chowan River.

Deep Water Point appears on the Moseley map, 1733, in what is now Brunswick County between Elizabeth River and Walden Creek e of the present town of Southport. Appeared as late as 1851-53 on navigation charts. See also Walkersburg.

Deer Branch rises in ne Franklin County and flows e into Sandy Creek.

Deer Branch rises in n Yancey County and flows se into Big Branch.

Deer Creek, a creek in Core Sound, near Core Banks, in e Carteret County.

Deer Creek rises in sw Carteret County and flows s two mi. into Bogue Sound.

Deer Creek rises in nw Haywood County and flows se into Big Creek.

Deer Creek Gap on the line between Haywood County, N. C., and Cocke County, Tenn., Great Smoky Mountains National Park, near lat. 35° 43′ 04″ N., long. 83° 15′ W.

Deerfield, community in s Watauga County near East Fork [of South Fork New River].

Deer Gap, s Macon County between High Knob and Rich Knob.

Deer Island, se Onslow County w of Swansboro in the mouth of Hawkins Slough. Formerly 3 acres, but now considerably reduced. The name is coming to be applied to the nearby peninsula between Swansboro and The Hammock.

Deer Lick Branch rises in s Mitchell County and flows n into East Fork Crabtree Creek.

Deerlick Gap, on the McDowell-Mitchell County line.

Deerlick Knob, in e Macon County between

Corbin Creek and the head of Laurel Creek.

Deerlick Ridge extends e from West Buffalo Creek to Snowbird Creek in s Graham County.

Deerlick Ridge, e Haywood County between Rice Cove Creek and Rough Creek.

Deer Mountain, s Yancey County between Winter Star Ridge and the head of Locust Creek. Alt. 6,212.

Deer Park Mountain, w Madison County between Ferry Branch and Spring Creek.

Deerplay Gap, on the Avery-Mitchell County line.

Deer Pond Branch rises in n Granville County and flows ne into Spewmarrow Creek.

Deer Ridge, n Yancey County parallel to Deer Creek.

Deerstand Creek rises in nw McDowell County on the s slope of Woods Mountain and flows s into Slim Creek.

Defeat Branch rises in n Swain County in Great Smoky Mountains National Park and flows sw to join Roaring Creek in forming Bone Valley Creek. Named after an early hunter here had his shoes burned in the camp fire while he slept during a snow storm.

Defeat Knob, on the Cherokee-Clay County line in the Valley River Mountains.

Dehart, community in n Wilkes County near North Prong Roaring River.

De Hart Bald, in s Swain County on the head of Licklog Creek.

De Hart Branch rises in s Swain County and flows sw into Yalaka Creek.

De Hart Branch rises in s Swain County between Bearpen Ridge and Rattlesnake Ridge and flows w into Wesser Creek.

De Hart Creek rises in s Swain County and flows sw into Little Tennessee River.

Delco, town in ne Columbus County. The site was first known as Brinkly when it was a stop on the Wilmington, Columbia & Augusta Rail Road. Inc. 1913 as New Berlin when Hugh MacRae of Wilmington attempted to attract German colonists to work surrounding farm lands. In 1918, during World War I, the name was changed to Pershing in honor of General John Pershing. After about six months, for some reason now unknown, it became necessary to change the name. Delco was chosen because the Delco Light Plant Company had just installed a lighting system in the local high school. Alt. 50.

Delight. *See* Lattimore.

Delightful Plains is shown on the Moseley map, 1733, as extending from the present Big Bay of Bladen County se and parallel with the present Brown Marsh Swamp.

Dellaplane, community in s Wilkes County between Brier Creek and Fishing Creek. Col. John Bryan (1753-1842) settled here about 1803.

Dellinger Branch rises in s Lincoln County and flows se into Leepers Creek.

Dellinger Hollow, in e Mitchell County between Long Ridge and the Avery-Mitchell County line.

Dellingers. *See* Concord.

Dellview, town in nw Gaston County. Inc. 1925 by three Dellinger brothers who operated a large chicken farm at the site. They wanted better protection from stray dogs than was provided by the county. By incorporating their farm as a town they could enact and enforce a town ordinance against stray dogs. About 1930 fire destroyed the chicken business and by 1967 only a single member of the family was living in the "town."

Dellwood, community in central Haywood County on Jonathans Creek. Alt. 2,771.

Delmar, community in central Halifax County between Halifax and Enfield.

Del Mar Beach, se Pender County on the Atlantic Ocean side of Topsail Island.

Delmont, community in s Henderson County on Little Mud Creek.

Deloach Branch rises in central Edgecombe County and flows sw into Cokey Swamp.

DeLoatche's Mill Pond, central Northampton County on Potecasi Creek.

De Lozier Gap, n Swain County on Welch Ridge near the head of West Fork [Chambers Creek].

Delway, community in se Sampson County on the head of Cuwhiffle Swamp.

Delta, community in e Stokes County.

Democrat, community in n Buncombe County near the junction of Sugar and Ivy creeks. Alt. 2,119.

Democrat, community on the Madison-Yancey County line on Middle Creek.

Denim, former community in central Guilford County, now within the limits of the city of Greensboro. Est. 1895 and named for the cloth made by the local mill.

Denis Creek, a tidal creek rising in the n part of Oak Island in Brunswick County and flowing e into Elizabeth River.

Denneysville. *See* New Castle.

Dennis, community in n Forsyth County. Formerly known as Salem Chapel.

Dennis, community in n Polk County.

Dennis Creek rises in s Watauga County and flows se into Caldwell County.

Dennis Crossroads, community in w Wake County between Jim Branch and Buckhorn Creek.

Dennis Mountain, w Montgomery County between Walker Mountain and Dutchmans Creek.

Denniss Island, formerly an island in present Currituck Banks, e Currituck County. It was separated from Currituck Banks by Currituck Inlet on the n and Musketo Inlet on the s, both of which are now closed. Shown on Comberford map, 1657. See also Currituck Inlet; Musketo Inlet.

Denny, community in w Wilkes County on Elk Creek. Named in the early twentieth century for John A. Denny, a local citizen.

Dennys Store, community in e Person County.

Denson Creek rises in n Montgomery County and flows se into Little River.

Denton, town in se Davidson County. Inc. 1907. Known as Finch's Crossroads prior to 1875. Post office est. 1878 and name changed to Denton at the recommendation of Samuel Moses Peacock who had been reading about the town of the same name in Texas and who became the first postmaster. Produces furniture, hosiery, and textiles.

Denton Gap, on the Graham County, N. C.-Monroe County, Tenn., line.

Dentons, community in s Graham County on Little Snowbird Creek.

Denver, town in ne Lincoln County. Inc. 1877. Settled about 1770 and known as Dry Pond, for an adjacent swampy area; in 1873, it was renamed by D. Matt Thompson, school principal, for the capital of Colorado then being considered for admission to the Union.

Deppe, community in ne Onslow County. Named for Nelson R. Deppe of Pennsylvania who established a lumber mill at the site.

Derby, community in ne Richmond County.

Derham Creek. See Durham Creek.

Derita, community in central Mecklenburg County. Named for Derita Lewis, a friend of Amos L. Rumple, first postmaster when post office est. in 1882. Alt. 812.

DeRossett Creek rises in Angola Bay, n Pender County and flows sw into Northeast Cape Fear River. Named for the DeRossett family, early settlers.

Derreberry Branch rises in ne Cherokee County and flows nw into Puett Creek.

Derreberry Gap, ne Cherokee County in the Valley River Mountains.

The Desert, a term sometimes applied locally to that part of the Dismal Swamp which lies in Camden and Currituck counties. See Dismal Swamp.

The Desert, a pocosin in n Robeson County between Big Raft Swamp and Big Marsh Swamp. Oval shaped and presumed to be one of the Carolina Bays, which see. Covers 1,200 acres; water depth varies from 6 inches to 4 feet, but one spot is said to be bottomless. Game abounds here, especially deer.

Deserta Arenosa. See Sandhills.

Deserta Montana. See Sandhills.

Deserter Island, a land formation in s Duplin County surrounded by swamp.

Desolation Branch rises in nw Swain County in Great Smoky Mountains National Park and flows sw into Roaring Creek. It was named after some early hunters were thoroughly soaked in a cold rain here.

Deuces Quarter. See Jews Quarter Island.

Devenport. See River Neck.

Devereux's Ferry. See Bridgers Creek.

Devil Den Ridge, n Macon County between Matlock Creek and Wests Branch.

Devil Knob, e Madison County on Laurel Creek.

Devils Court House, sw Jackson County, is a northern ridge or extention of Whiteside Mountain, which see.

Devils Courthouse, a mountain of jagged black rock in nw Transylvania County near the Haywood County line. Located s of the Blue Ridge Parkway from which a spectacular overlook affords a fine view of the mountain. Named for its sinister appearance. Alt. 5,740.

Devils Court House Ridge, n Swain County in Great Smoky Mountains National Park, a short spur extending south from Mount Buckley.

Devil's Cradle Creek rises in n Franklin County and flows se into Flatrock Creek.

Devils Creek rises in nw Yancey County and flows ne into Nolichucky River.

Devils Creek Gap, nw Yancey County near the head of Devils Creek.

Devils Den, ridge in s Yancey County extending s between Little Mountain Creek and Long Arm Ridge.

Devil's Den. See Pilot Mountain.

Devils Elbow, a sharp bend in the Cashie

River, se Bertie County. Appears on the Collet map, 1770.

Devils Elbow Landing on Pungo River, e Beaufort County.

Devils Fork rises in e Henderson County and flows w into Mud Creek.

Devils Fork Gap on the Madison County, N. C.-Unicoi County, Tenn., line.

Devils Garden on the Alexander-Wilkes County line on the Blue Ridge Parkway. Alt. 3,428. A rough, rocky area in which rattlesnakes and copperheads are commonly found.

Devils Garden, a strip of rough stony land beside another strip of steep eroded land, se Buncombe County between Trantham Creek and Laurel Branch.

Devils Gut, stream in ne Martin County connecting a bend in the Roanoke River. Mentioned in local records as early as 1729 and shown on the Collet map, 1770.

Devils Head, w Rutherford County, a natural rock formation suggestive of the devil's head, near Chimney Rock.

Devil's Kitchin, pocosin in n Pender County adjacent to Stag Park tract.

Devils Nest, peak in n Mitchell County on Big Ridge.

Devils Prong rises in sw Macon County and flows n into Kimsey Creek.

Devils Race Patch, peak in nw Swain County in Great Smoky Mountains National Park on Jenkins Trail Ridge. Alt. approx. 5,160.

Devils Shoals Ford, former ford across the Catawba River, s Caldwell and ne Burke County. Site now under the waters of Lake Hickory.

Devils Tater Patch, peak on the Swain County, N. C.-Blount County, Tenn., line in Great Smoky Mountains National Park. Alt. 4,752.

Devil's Tramping Ground, w Chatham County, ten miles south of Siler City, a circular path about 40 ft. in diameter which old timers say has "always" been here. Legend says the Devil comes here at night to walk in a circle while he plots against the good and thinks up new forms of evil. No vegetation has grown in the path.

Devotion, community in w Surry County on Mitchell River.

Dewberrie, community in nw Warren County. Post office here from 1900 until 1905.

Deweese, community in nw Cabarrus County.

Deweese Township, former township, ne Mecklenburg County. Now township number 9.

Deweese Creek rises in w Macon County and flows ne into Burningtown Creek.

Deweese Township, former township in nw Cabarrus County. Now township number 3. Formerly also known as Odell School Township, which see.

Dewey Pier, landing in n Tyrrell County on Albemarle Sound w of Ship Point.

Dewitt, community in e Henderson County on Henderson Creek.

Dews Creek rises in e central Brunswick County and flows north into Town Creek.

Dew's Mill. See Silver Lake.

Dexter, community in e Granville County.

Dial Creek rises in n Durham County and flows s into Flat River.

Diamond City, former community near the e end of Shackleford Banks, s Carteret County. Named for the diamond-shaped design painted on the Cape Lookout Lighthouse. Site of whaling operations in the 18th and 19th centuries. Several storms in the early 20th century caused the residents to begin moving to Harker's Island, Morehead City, Beaufort, and elsewhere.

Diamond Creek rises in w Transylvania County and flows se into North Fork French Broad River.

Diamond Grove, community in n Northampton County. A post office was est. here as early as 1828.

Diamond Hill, community and former post office, nw Anson County. So called simply as a "fancy name."

Diamond Shoals, a series of three shoals extending se from Cape Hatteras (which see) into the Atlantic Ocean off se Dare County. Nearest the Cape is Hatteras Shoals; Inner Diamond Shoal is in the middle, and Outer Diamond Shoal extends farthest into the Atlantic. The channel between Hatteras Shoals and Inner Diamond Shoal is Hatteras Slough; Diamond Slough is the channel between the two Diamond Shoals. At this point warm Gulf Stream waters collide with cold arctic waters from the north causing a constant turbulence in the Atlantic. This is the "graveyard of the Atlantic." Appears as Sholes of Hatteras on the Moll map, 1729.

Diamond Slough. See Diamond Shoals.

Diamond Valley, in w Macon County between Chestnut Gap and Dicks Creek.

Dick Branch rises in n Buncombe County and flows sw into Flat Creek.

Dick Branch rises in central Cherokee County in Dick Cove and flows se into Morgan Creek.

Dick Cove, central Cherokee County at the headwaters of Dick Branch.

Dickens, community in e Franklin County. Alt. 250. Settled about 1892. Named for T. H. Dickens, first postmaster.

Dickens Creek rises in w Granville County and flows sw into Knap of Reeds Creek.

Dickerson, community in e Granville County. Named for A. J. Dickerson who gave land for the railroad right-of-way and depot.

Dickey Branch rises in sw Cherokee County and flows se into Nottely River.

Dickey Mountain, sw Cherokee County extends ne from Rapier Mill Creek to Dickey Branch.

Dickey Top, peak on Dickey Mountain, sw Cherokee County.

Dick Green Branch rises in s Watauga County and flows n into Middle Fork [South Fork New River]. Named for a farmer in the area.

Dickinson Clear-water Branch rises in ne Brunswick County and flows e into the Cape Fear River.

Dickinson's Branch rises in s Wilson County and flows e into Contentnea Creek.

Dicks. See Randleman.

Dicks Branch rises in n Haywood County and flows ne into Pigeon River.

Dicks Branch rises in nw Duplin County and flows s into Goshen Swamp.

Dicks Branch rises in w Johnston County and flows s into Black Creek.

Dicks Branch rises in nw Warren County and flows nw in an arc into ne Vance County where it enters Kerr Reservoir.

Dicks Creek formed in n Jackson County by the junction of West Fork and East Fork and flows sw into Tuckaseege River.

Dicks Creek rises in w Macon County and flows ne into Nantahala River.

Dicks Creek rises in se Mitchell County and flows se into North Toe River.

Dicks Creek rises in e Onslow County and flows ne into Queens Creek.

Dicks Gap, s Yancey County between South Toe River and Three Forks Creek.

Dicks Knob, s Madison County at the head of Little Pine Creek.

Dicks Mountain, a peak in the Peach Bottom Mountain range, w central Alleghany County.

Dickson Creek rises in central Jackson County and flows nw into West Fork Tuckasegee River.

Die Bend, a bend in the Nottely River in sw Cherokee County downstream from the mouth of Walker Mill Creek.

Diggs, community in sw Richmond County.

Diggs Ferry over the Pee Dee River about two miles n of the South Carolina line. Formerly known as the Buchanan Ferry.

Dillard, community in e Stokes County.

Dillard Creek rises in ne Chowan County and flows sw into Chowan River. The Sixth Report of the U. S. Geographic Board in 1933 announced the decision that this stream should henceforth be known as Indian Creek, but the ruling seems to have been ignored locally. Appears as Indian Town Creek on the Moseley map, 1733.

Dillard Top, peak on the Cherokee-Graham County line in the Unicoi Mountains.

Diller Branch rises in s Cleveland County and flows ne into Broad River.

Dillingham, community in ne Buncombe County on Dillingham Creek.

Dillingham Creek is formed in ne Buncombe County by the junction of Corner Rock Creek and Walker Branch. It flows nw to join North Fork Ivy Creek to form Ivy Creek.

Dill Knob, se Buncombe County. Alt. approx. 3,790.

Dillon Ridge extends ne and supports a school and a few houses in the middle of swamplands in n Tyrrell County. Alt. 14. Site of commercial timber operations.

Dills Branch rises in n Jackson County and flows s into Scotts Creek. Named for Allen B. Dills.

Dillsboro, town in n Jackson County on the Tuckasegee River. Inc. 1889 and named for William A. Dills, founder of the town and member of the General Assembly, 1889-91. Post office first est. here as Cowee Tunnel in the home of Dills whose wife was postmistress. Known as Webster Station from 1882 until 1889.

Dillsboro Township, nw Jackson County.

Dills Creek rises in s Rutherford County and flows s into Broad River.

Dills Creek rises in n Jackson County and flows se into Fisher Creek.

Dills Gap, w Jackson County between Black Mountain and Tuckasegee River.

Dills Knob, e Macon County between Buzzard Knob and Cullasaja River.

Dimmette, community in e Wilkes County near the headwaters of Little Elkin River.

Dimond City. *See* Dymond City.

Dimsdale, community in n Polk County between Bullin Creek and Walnut Creek.

Dina Branch rises in s Haywood County and flows ne into North Fork.

Dinah Landing, on Upper Goose Creek, central Beaufort County.

Dingle Creek rises in s Buncombe County and flows w into French Broad River.

Dinkin Branch rises in n Cherokee County and flows sw into Owl Creek.

Dipping Vat Creek rises in e Pamlico County and flows se into Long Creek.

Dirty Britches Creek. *See* Shit-Britches Creek.

Dirty John Creek rises in w Macon County and flows sw into Jarrett Creek.

Dish Knob, ne McDowell County near the Burke County line. Alt. 1,800.

Dismal Bay, sand filled bay in s Sampson County north of Keiths Bay. *See also* Carolina Bays.

Dismal Branch rises in s Johnston County and flows se into Johnson Swamp.

Dismal Branch rises in Little Dismal Swamp, sw Johnston County, and flows sw into Mingo Swamp.

Dismal Cove, sw Macon County at the head of Pat Stable Branch.

Dismal Creek rises in w Henderson County and flows nw into Crab Creek.

Dismal Mountain, e Jackson County, extends ne from Tuckasegee River to Neddie Creek.

Dismal Swamp, marsh, lake, and cypress-filled area approx. 30 mi. long and 10 mi. wide, largely in se Virginia, but partially in Gates, Pasquotank, Camden, and Currituck counties. Appears on the Dudley map, 1647, as "Terra Bassa" (low land), and on the Comberford map, 1657, as "a swampy wilderness." Present name might have been known as early as 1715, when the term "dismal swamp" was applied to the Pasquotank County area by John Talbot in a letter to John Urmston, SPG missionary to the colony. Shown on the Moseley map, 1733, as Great Dismal Swamp (the name it is sometimes called today), and as Dismal Swamp on the Mitchell map, 1755. George Washington initiated surveys in 1763 for a canal. The Intracoastal Waterway now passes through the swamp. Also called The Desert, in North Carolina.

Dismal Swamp Canal connects the waters of Elizabeth River in Virginia with those of the Pasquotank River. It flows from the state line through nw Camden County. The Intracoastal Waterway is routed through the Canal, and there are locks on the western borders of South Mills.

Dismal Township, nw Sampson County.

District of Washington in the western territory of North Carolina which is now Tennessee developed from the Watauga Settlement, *which see*, and was recognized by North Carolina in 1776. Delegates attended the Provincial Congress at Halifax in November, 1776. The District was the second place in America to be named for George Washington. In 1777 Washington County was formed from the District and Jonesboro became the county seat. This was a part of the area ceded by North Carolina in 1789 to the Federal government. *See also* Franklin.

The Ditch, waterway from Pamlico River to Goose Creek, e Beaufort County. It separates Reeds Hammock from the mainland.

Ditch Branch rises in s Wake County and flows s into w Johnston County where it enters Middle Creek.

Ditch Creek in ne Pamlico County connects Jones Bay with the Bay River estuary.

Divide Mountain, w Madison County between Rector Branch and Rocky Branch.

Dividing Ridge, s Avery County.

Dividing Ridge, in ne Henderson County between Burntshirt Mountain and the Buncombe-Henderson County line.

Dividing Ridge in n Transylvania County extends se from the head of Thompson Creek to Funneltop Mountain.

Dividing Ridge, w Wilkes County between Lewis Fork Creek and Stony Fork Creek.

Dix Creek rises near Dix Creek Gap in sw Buncombe County and flows ne into Newfound Creek.

Dix Creek rises in s Haywood County and flows n into East Fork Pigeon River.

Dix Creek Gap, sw Buncombe County between Suther Knob and Hayes Top.

Dixie, community in w Mecklenburg County.

Dixie, community in s central Wilson County.

Dixon, community in s Onslow County.

Dixon Branch rises in se Cleveland County and flows sw into South Carolina where it enters Kings Creek.

Dixon Creek, a short stream in n central

Carteret County flowing n into South River.

Dixon Creek rises in the w part of Goose Creek Island, ne Pamlico County, and flows w into Goose Creek.

Dixon Gap, n Cleveland County. Alt. 943.

Dixon Mine, former gold mine in s Yadkin County between Courtney and the head of Roby Creek.

Dixon Mountain, w Madison County between Little Creek and Meadow Fork.

Dixon Point, in s Onslow County extends into Stump Sound from the mainland.

Dixons Store, community in ne Person County.

Dobag. See Arbuckle; Doe Bag Creek.

Dobbersville, community in sw Wayne County near the Sampson County line.

Dobbin Creek rises in nw Yadkin County and flows s into North Hunting Creek.

Dobbins Mill Pond, central Yadkin County on North Deep Creek, covers approx. 25 acres. Max. depth 30 ft. Formed 1936 by Nelson Dobbins. Used for fishing, boating, irrigation, water skiing.

Dobbs County, formed from Johnston County in 1758, was named in honor of Arthur Dobbs (1689-1765), governor of North Carolina, 1754-1765. Wayne County was formed from Dobbs in 1779, portions of it were added to other counties, and the remainder was divided into Glasgow and Lenoir counties in 1791. Walnut Creek was the county seat until 1779, and Kingston (Kinston) from 1779 to 1791. See also Bizzell Millpond; St. Patrick's Parish.

Dobbs Parish, Rowan County, was est. in 1755 to consist of the Wachovia (which see) section of the county settled by the Unitas Fratrum (United Brethren) or Moravians. The parish as a unit of local administration was abolished in 1776 with the adoption of the state constitution. The area included in Dobbs Parish is now largely in Forsyth County. See also St. Luke's Parish.

Dobson, town and county seat, central Surry County. Est. 1851 as county seat after the county had been divided. Inc. 1891. Named (1) for William Dobson, local justice of the peace in 1776, or (2) for William P. Dobson, member of the General Assembly in 1814. Surry Community College, est. 1966, is located here. Alt. 1,265.

Dobson Branch rises in central Macon County and flows ne into Cartoogechaye Creek.

Dobson Branch rises in e Mitchell County and flows nw into Sugartree Branch.

Dobson Hill, community in s Graham County on Snowbird Creek.

Dobson Knob, e McDowell County.

Dobson Mount, mountain in central Macon County between Patton Mountain and the head of McKee Branch. Alt. approx. 3,500.

Dobson Mountain, s Jackson County between Little Hogback Creek and Long Branch.

Dobson Ridge between the forks of Wrights Creek and Big Witch Creek in n Jackson County.

Dobson's Crossroads. See Kernersville.

Dobson Township, central Surry County.

Doby Creek rises in n Mecklenburg County and flows ne into Mallard Creek.

Dock Branch rises in n Buncombe County near the Madison County line and flows se into Whittemore Creek.

Dockery, community in n Wilkes County near Middle Prong Roaring River.

Dockery Creek rises in central Cherokee County and flows se into Hanging Dog Creek.

Dockerys Store, community in w Richmond County. A post office existed here as early as 1828.

Doc Stewart Ridge extends ne from Little Huckleberry Knob to Santeetlah Creek in w Graham County. Named for an early settler.

Doctor Branch rises in ne Cherokee County and flows s into Valley River.

Doctor Mountain, s Madison County at the head of Bear Creek.

Doctors Creek rises in se Sampson County and flows e along the Duplin-Pender County line into Rockfish Creek.

Dodgen Creek rises in w Jackson County and flows ne into Cullowhee Creek.

Dodgen Ridge, e Jackson County between Gladie Creek and Sols Creek.

Dodgetown, community in e Stokes County.

Dodging Hill, e Henderson County between Bat Fork and Green River.

Dodson Store. See Gilreath.

Dodsons Creek, formerly a separate stream in n Vance County, but its entire course now lies under the waters of Kerr Reservoir.

Dodson Crossroads, community in s Orange County.

Doe Bag Creek rises in e Yancey County and flows ne into Toe River. Sometimes spelled Dobag.

Doe Branch rises in e Jackson County and flows ne into Tuckasegee River.

Doe Branch rises in w Madison County and flows ne into French Broad River.

Doe Branch, community in w Madison County. First settler moved here from Tennessee in 1824.

Doe Creek rises in n central Carteret County and flows w into South River.

Doe Hill Mountain, s Avery County. Alt. 4,217.

Doe Knob, e Clay County between Buck Creek and Johnson Branch.

Doe Knob, peak on Swain County, N. C.-Blount County, Tenn., line, in Great Smoky Mountains National Park. Alt. 4,520.

Dogback Mountain, part of Linville Mountain, lies on Burke-McDowell County line.

Dogback Mountain, on the Jackson-Macon County line. Alt. 4,950.

Dog Branch rises in central Alleghany County and flows se into Little River.

Dog Branch rises in central Martin County and flows se into Ready Branch.

Dog Cove, e Swain County on the head of Wesser Creek between Middle Ridge and Odear Cove.

Dog Creek rises in e Ashe County and flows se into South Fork New River.

Dog Creek rises in w Henderson County and flows sw into Boylston Creek.

Doggett Gap, s Madison County at the head of Friezeland Creek.

Doggett Knob, s Madison County at the head of Walnut Cove Branch.

Dog Island, formerly a single island in Bogue Sound near Bogue Banks, s Carteret County. Appears on the Moseley map, 1733. Now three small islands.

Dog Loser Knob, s Haywood County between Beech Spring Gap and Old Butt Knob.

Dog Mountain, se Macon County at the s end of Chestnut Ridge. Alt. approx. 4,000.

Dog Ridge Mountain, n Madison County in a bend of Big Laurel Creek.

Dogs' Ears, rock formation near Shulls Mill s Watauga County.

Dogville Crossroads. See Hassell.

Dogwood Branch rises in s Virginia and flows se into Northampton County where it enters Pea Hill Creek.

Dogwood Flats, e Mitchell County between Beaver Creek and Gouges Creek.

Dogwood Flats, community in n Haywood County on Dogwood Flats Creek.

Dogwood Flats Creek rises in n Haywood County and flows ne into Mount Sterling Creek.

Dogwood Gap, w Madison County at the head of Georgia Branch.

Dogwood Ridge, high ground in s Washington County in East Dismal Swamp. Length from western to eastern extremity approx. 2½ miles. Soloman Sawyer's plantation, known by this name, was located here as early as 1742.

Dogwood Stump Mountain, in s Burke County between Jacob Fork and White-oak Creek. Alt. 2,546.

Dolly Gut, gully cut by stream in central Craven County. Stream rises in central Craven County and flows ne into Neuse River just s of Greens Thorofare.

Dome, community in se Buncombe County near the junction of Flat Creek and Broad River.

Donahues Creek rises in n Caldwell County and flows s into Yadkin River.. Named for Henry Donahue who died in 1775 and is buried nearby.

Donaldson Branch rises in se Cherokee County and flows se into Brasstown Creek.

Donaldson Creek rises in e Person County and flows nw into Maho Creek.

Donegal County. In 1749 a bill was introduced in the House of the General Assembly to erect the "upper part of New Hanover County" into Donegal County, but the bill was not passed. The parish would have been called St. Colomb. It would have been named for Donegal County, Northern Ireland.

Donnelys Creek. See Daniels Creek.

Donnoha, community in nw Forsyth County on Yadkin River. An Indian village was at or near this place which is named for Donnahee, an Indian chief. The name was given in 1889 or 1890 by Dr. Samuel Martin of Winston, a descendant of the chief, who accompanied the surveying party which laid out the road from Winston to Wilkesboro and which passes through Donnoha. Richmond, former seat of Surry County, 1774-89, and which was destroyed in 1830 by a cyclone, was nearby. Alt. 757.

Donoho Creek rises in s Bladen County and flows e into Cape Fear River. Named for David Donoho who had a grant of land here in 1727.

Doolie, community in sw Iredell County. Takes its name from a local Baptist Church.

Doolittle Mill Pond, n Northampton County

on Paddys Delight Creek. Covers approx. 75 acres. Max. depth 10 ft.

Doomas Creek. See Dumas Creek.

Dora, community in w Lincoln County.

Dora. See Midstate Mill; Red Springs.

Dora Mills. See Midstate Mill.

Dora's Island, se Onslow County, in the mouth of Queens Creek.

Dorithea Creek. See Muddy Creek.

Dorsey, former community in w Swain County on Tuckasegee River. Site now under waters of Fontana Lake.

Dortches, community in e Nash County near the head of Horn Beam Swamp. Settled about 1890. Named for local family. Alt. 120.

Dosier, community in w Forsyth County.

Doster, community in s central Union County.

Dothan, community in s Columbus County.

Dotmond, community in ne Caswell County.

Dotson Branch rises in central Haywood County and flows ne into Pigeon River.

Double Branch rises in w Forsyth County and flows s into Panther Creek.

Double Branch rises in nw Northampton County and flows se into Black Gut Creek.

Double Branch rises in w Transylvania County and flows se into Parker Creek.

Double Creek rises in w Person County and flows nw into South Hyco Creek.

Double Creek is formed in s Surry County by the junction of East Double Creek and West Double Creek. It flows s approx. ¼ mi. into Yadkin River.

Double Creek rises in n Wilkes County and flows sw into Middle Prong Roaring River.

Double Gap, w Haywood County, Great Smoky Mountains National Park, on Cataloochee Divide near lat. 35° 34' 17" N., long. 83° 06' W.

Double Gap Branch rises in w Haywood County and flows nw into Caldwell Fork.

Double Gap Ridge, w Haywood County, Great Smoky Mountains National Park, a short spur of Cataloochee Divide, extending nw near lat. 35° 34' 45" N., long. 83° 06' 12" W.

Double Head, a mountain on the Buncombe-Henderson County line. Also known as Double Knob. Alt. 3,399.

Doublehead Creek rises in w Avery County and flows se into North Toe River.

Doublehead Gap, w Avery County.

Double Knob on the head of Slatten Creek in central Jackson County.

Double Knob Mountain in s Jackson County on the head of Packs Creek. Alt. 4,412.

Double Knob. See Double Head.

Double Knobs, mountain peak in n central Avery County.

Double Knobs, two adjacent peaks south of Lenoir in se Caldwell County. Alt. over 1,200.

Double Knobs, twin peaks in central Clay County near Downing Creek.

Double Shoals, community in central Cleveland County between Big Harris Creek and First Broad River. Settled in the nineteenth century and named for two shoals in the nearby river. Alt. 995.

Double Shoals Township, former township in e central Cleveland County, now township number 9.

Doubleside Gap, e Haywood County between Long Branch and West Cove.

Double Spring Gap, s Haywood County on Lickstone Ridge. Alt. 4,000.

Double Spring Gap, on Swain County, N. C.-Sevier County, Tenn., line in Great Smoky Mountains National Park e of Silers Bald. Alt. approx. 5,520.

Double Springs Gap, s Transylvania County on the head of Morgan Mill Creek.

Double Top, mountain on the Buncombe-Henderson County line n of Dads Top.

Double Top, mountain at the s end of Rich Mountain in nw Jackson County.

Doubletop Branch rises in s Macon County and flows nw into Hickory Knoll Creek.

Doubletop Creek rises in n Jackson County and flows ne into Dark Ridge Creek.

Doubletop Fields, grassy pastureland in s Macon County between Buckeye Creek and Hickory Knoll Creek. An early settler cleared land atop the mountain on which he settled as well as on the next mountain, hence the name.

Doubletop Mountain, on the Haywood-Buncombe County line.

Double Top Mountain, central Jackson County between Johns Creek and Niggerskull Creek. Alt. 5,481.

Doubletop Mountain, n Jackson County on the head of Cashie Branch.

Doubletop Mountain, s Macon County between Dryman Fork and Mulberry Gap.

Doughton, community in ne Wilkes County on Elkin River.

Doughton. See Sherwood.

Doughton Mountain, peak in the Peach Bottom Mountain range, n central Alleghany County. Alt. 3,650.

Doughton Park, s Alleghany and n Wilkes

counties, a Blue Ridge Parkway recreation area on Basin Creek. Covers approx. 7,000 acres. Est. about 1935 as Bluff Park; renamed to honor Congressman Robert L. Doughton (1863-1954), who worked for the establishment of the Parkway. A high, rolling bluegrass area terminates here in precipitous bluffs, and stands of magnificent rhododendron bloom in May and June. Wild Cat Rock is nearby. See also The Bluffs.

Douglas Ordinary. See St. Johns.

Dover, town in nw Craven County. Settled, 1879, but the place name dates from as early as 1749 when Francis Stringer owned a plantation here called Dover, probably named for the city in England. Inc. 1901. Alt. 63.

Dover, community in nw Moore County on Wolf Creek.

Dover Crossroads. See Gum Swamp,

Dover Knob, s Macon County between Penson Knob and Norton Branch.

Dovers Branch rises in se Yancey County and flows nw into Three Forks Creek.

Dover Branch rises in se Yancey County and flows ne into Crabtree Creek.

Dover Ridge, se Yancey County between Dover Branch and Crabtree Creek.

Dove's Crossroads. See Casville.

Dowdle Branch rises in s Macon County and flows se into Little Tennessee River.

Dowdle Knob, s Macon County between Little Tennessee River and Porter Cove.

Dowellton, central Yadkin County approx. 1¼ mi. west of the present courthouse in the vicinity of modern Harmony Grove Church, was the site of the first court held for the new county in 1851.

Downes Branch rises in central Macon County and flows n into Burningtown Creek.

Downing Creek rises in central Clay County and flows se through Holden Cove into Hiwassee River.

Downs Mountain, s Macon County between Mulberry Creek and Norton Branch.

Downsville, community in e Caldwell County. Named for Downs family, two members of which were postmasters here following the Civil War.

Dowry Island, about ¼ mi. long is in Chowan River on the Gates-Hertford County line.

Dowtins Creek. See Duncans Creek.

Draco, community in e Caldwell County on the headwaters of Middle Little River.

The Drain. See Barden Inlet.

The Drain, a cove on the w shore of Hat-

teras Island in the waters of Pamlico Sound, s Dare County, n of the site of the former Little Kinnakeet Coast Guard Station.

Drakes Crossroads, community in central Northampton County.

Dram Tree Point extends from Eagles Island, w New Hanover County, into Cape Fear River. Named for an old moss-covered cypress tree which stood here; it is said that out-going mariners, in passing this point, had a drink to the success of their voyage. To those inward bound it was a welcome signal that port was near.

Draper, former town in n Rockingham County on Dan River. Named for William F. Draper, founder of local mills. Est. 1905; inc. 1945; merged with Leaksville and Spray in 1967 to form Eden, which see.

Draughn, community in n Edgecombe County.

Dresden, community in central Ashe County. Alt. approx. 2,800.

Drew, community in w central Bertie County. Est. about 1900 and named for a local family.

Drewry, community in e Vance County. Alt. 453. Settled in 1860 and named by G. W. Morrow, president of the Clarksville Railroad for his father, Drewry Morrow.

Drexel, town in central Burke County. Inc. 1913. Alt. 1,192. Named for the Drexel family of Philadelphia. Originally known as Baker. A large furniture manufacturing plant is located here.

Drexel Township, e central Burke County.

Drift Branch rises in w Haywood County and flows se into Richland Creek.

Drift Falls in sw Transylvania County in Horsepasture River just upstream from High Falls.

Drip Off Creek rises in nw Iredell County and flows s into Rocky Creek.

Drivers Store, community in e Wilson County near Whiteoak Swamp.

Driving Creek rises in w Nash County and flows sw into Turkey Creek.

Drowned Bay, mucky swamp, sw Brunswick County.

Drowning Creek rises in e central Burke County and flows ne into Catawba River.

Drowning Creek rises on the Montgomery-Moore County line and flows se across Moore County. At the Moore-Richmond County line it joins Naked Creek to form Lumber River.

Drowning Creek Mountains extend from ne Burke County into nw Catawba County.

Drug Store, community in w Johnston County.

Druid, community in n Madison County.

Druid Hills, community in central Henderson County adjoining Hendersonville on the north. Alt. 1,788.

Drum Creek rises in the s part of Goose Creek Island, ne Pamlico County, and flows s into Jones Bay.

Drum Hill, community in n Gates County. Alt. 79. Settled about 1890.

Drum Inlet between Portsmouth Island on the ne and Core Banks on the sw in e Carteret County. Water from Pamlico and Core Sounds drains into the Atlantic Ocean through this inlet. Also known as Whalebone Inlet. Named for a species of fish. An inlet in this area appears on the de Graffenried map (French text), 1711, as Drum Passage. Another Drum Inlet appears on the Moseley map, 1733, now commonly referred to as Old Drum Inlet. The inlet shown on the Moseley map closed in the late eighteenth century.

Drummersville, community in n Duplin County.

Drummond's Point, se tip of Chowan County extending into the mouth of Yeopim River. Named before 1700 for William Drummond (d. 1677), first governor of Albemarle under the Lords Proprietors. Appears on the Moseley map, 1733. Site of one of the largest early seine fisheries on Albermarle Sound.

Drum Pasage. See Drum Inlet.

Drum Point, point on mainland of ne Carteret County extending into mouth of Nelson Bay.

Drums Crossroads. See Drumsville.

Drumsville, community in se Catawba County, formerly Drums Crossroads. Alt. 946.

Dry Branch rises in ne Buncombe County and flows se into Right Fork [Swannanoa River].

Dry Branch rises in e Haywood County and flows e into East Fork Pigeon River.

Dry Branch rises in n Haywood County and flows s into Groundhog Creek.

Dry Branch rises in central Hoke County and flows ne into Rockfish Creek.

Dry Branch rises in n Macon County and flows sw into Cold Spring Creek.

Dry Branch rises in e Mitchell County and flows s into Cane Creek.

Dry Creek rises in w Alamance County and flows e into Haw River.

Dry Creek rises in n Chatham County and flows ne into Haw River.

Dry Creek, an intermittant stream, rises in e Durham County and flows ne into Ellerbe Creek.

Dry Creek, rises in ne Durham County and flows s into Lake Michie.

Dry Creek rises in e Graham County and flows n into Stecoah Creek.

Dry Creek rises in n Harnett County and flows s into Cape Fear River.

Dry Creek rises in n Madison County and flows sw into Big Creek.

Dry Creek rises in w Moore County and flows ne into Cabin Creek.

Dry Creek rises in n Rockingham County and flows e into Cascade Creek.

Dry Creek rises in ne Wake County and flows ne into Moccasin Creek.

Dry Falls, waterfall in Cullasaja River, se Macon County, nw of Highlands. Water drops approx. 75 ft. from a protruding ledge making it possible to walk behind it without getting wet, hence the name. See also Cullasaja River.

Dry Ford, n Union County in Rocky River.

Dry Fork rises in w Lee County and flows ne into Pocket Creek.

Dry Fork Branch rises in s Lee County and flows sw into Moore County where it joins Crains Creek to form Whiteoak Creek.

Dry Gap Ridge, n Haywood County parallel to Skiffley Creek.

Dry Lake, ne Surry County. Formed in 1937 by the construction of a dam across a dry hollow into which a small unnamed stream was diverted. Covers approx. 8 acres; max. depth 15 ft. Municipal water supply for Mount Airy.

Dryman Fork rises in s Macon County and flows ne into Coweeta Creek.

Dryman Mountain, central Buncombe County nw of Asheville.

Drymans Branch rises in s Macon County and flows w into Middle Creek.

Dry Mountain, peak on Newfound Mountain on the Buncombe-Haywood County line s of Haywood Gap.

Dry Pocosin, a muck-filled pocosin in e Duplin County.

Dry Pond. See Denver.

Dry Pond Gap, s Watauga County between the heads of Storey Creek, Buffalo Creek, and Joe Creek.

Dry Pond Ridge, w Madison County be-

tween Mountain Island Branch and Raccoon Branch.

Dry Sand Shoal. See Vera Cruz Shoal.

Drysborough, former town in central Craven
County. Inc. 1806, and referred to in the
session laws until as late as 1847. The
site is now within the limits of New Bern
and is that part of the town which lies
n of Queen Street.

Dry Sluice Gap, mountain gap on the Swain
County, N. C.,-Sevier County, Tenn., line
in Great Smoky Mountains National Park.
Alt. 5,375.

Drys Mill, community in ne Cabarrus
County.

Dryspring Branch rises in w Yancey County
and flows nw into Banks Creek.

Dry Wells Township, sw Nash County.
Created 1903 by act of General Assembly.

Duart, community in nw Bladen County.

Dublin, town in nw Bladen County. Alt.
approx. 130. Inc. 1913.

Dublin. See Royal.

Dublin Creek rises in w Carteret County
and flows sw into White Oak River.

Duck, community near the s end of the
North Banks in ne Dare County. Situated
next to Currituck Sound. Named for wild
ducks in the area. Alt. 10.

Duck Branch rises near Cross Mountain on
the Buncombe-McDowell County line and
flows sw into Broad River.

Duck Branch rises in central Mitchell County and flows s into Mine Creek.

Duck Branch rises in se Mitchell County
and flows s into Rose Cree.

Duck Creek rises in central Beaufort County and flows s into Pamlico River. Appears
on the Collet map, 1770.

Duck Creek rises in ne Caldwell County and
flows se into Alexander County where it
enters Middle Little River.

Duck Creek, a short stream in n central
Carteret County, flows e into South River.

Duck Creek rises in e Craven County and
flows sw into Neuse River.

Duck Creek rises in s Iredell County east of
Barium Springs and flows ne into Third
Creek.

Duck Creek rises in se Onslow County and
flows n into Farnell Bay. Mentioned in
local records as early as 1744.

Duck Creek rises in w Person County and
flows nw into South Hyco Creek.

Duck Creek rises in n Union County and
flows se into Goose Creek.

Duck Creek, community in se Onslow County on Mirey Branch.

Duckenfield estate. See Avoca.

Ducker Creek rises near Ducker Mountain
in s Buncombe County and flows sw into
French Broad River.

Ducker Mountain, s Buncombe County.

Duckettsville. See Roper.

Duckett Top, w Madison County between
Meadow Fork and Spring Creek.

Duck Island, in Roanoke Sound at the s end
of Bodie Island in e Dare County.

Duckmill Branch rises in n Madison County
and flows se into Shelton Laurel Creek.

Duck Mountain, s Macon County between
Saltrock Gap and Middle Creek.

Duck Pond Swamp, pocosin in e central
Cumberland County drained by Reese
Creek. One of the Carolina Bays, which
see.

Dude Branch rises in w Haywood County,
Great Smoky Mountains National Park,
near lat. 35° 41' 45" N., long. 83° 07'
08" W., and flows se into Correll Branch.

Dudley, town in s Wayne County. Settled
in 1837. Inc. 1897; charter repealed 1899.
Re-incorporated 1903. Named for E. B.
Dudley, governor of North Carolina (1836-
1841), and president of Wilmington and
Raleigh Railroad. Alt. 185.

Dudley Shoals, community on Upper Little
River in se Caldwell County.

Dudley's Island, e Onslow County in the
mouth of White Oak River at Bogue
Inlet.

Duel Hill. See Marshall.

Duffs Creek rises in sw Duplin County and
flows s into Rockfish Creek.

Duges Island, e Carteret County in Core
Sound near Core Banks.

Dugger Creek rises in se Watauga County
and flows se into Wilkes County where it
enters Elk Creek at Darby. Appears in
eighteenth century records as Julius Duggar's Rock House Creek.

Dugar Mountain, se Watauga County between Mast Knob and Little Dugger
Mountain. Alt. 3,700.

Duggs Island. See Bodie Island.

Duharts Creek rises in central Gaston County and flows se into South Fork Catawba
River.

Duke. See Erwin.

Duke Forest, w Durham and e Orange
counties, consists of a total of 7,241 acres
in five main units. Est. in 1931, it is

owned by Duke University and used for demonstration, an experimental forest, and an outdoor laboratory for students in forestry. There are recreational areas and provisions for picnickers, hikers, and horseback riders.

Duke Hall. See Halls.

Duke Power Park, state park in s Iredell County on Lake Norman. Contains 1,328 acres with six miles of shoreline. Boating, camping, and recreational facilities.

Dukes, community in nw Nash County. Named for the Rev. G. W. Duke, local resident.

Dukes Crossroads, community in e Beaufort County.

Dukes Crossroads. See Epsom.

Duke Swamp rises in n Gates County and flows s to join Raynor Swamp and Harrell Swamp to form Bennetts Creek.

Duke Township, se Harnett County. Named for the former community, Duke, now Erwin.

Dukeville, community in e Rowan County on High Rock Lake. Named by A. W. Hicks, editor of the *Spencer News* for James B. Duke.

Dukie Halls Crossing. See Halls.

Dula Knob, s Mitchell County between Middle Fork Grassy Creek and East Fork Grassy Creek.

Dula Springs, community in n Buncombe County on Little Flat Creek e of Weaverville.

Dula Town, a community of Negroes in s central Caldwell County. Named for Alfred Dula who gave 400 acres of land to his freed slaves. At the close of the Civil War he also gave a horse, wagon, and cow to each family among his former slaves.

Dumas Creek rises in n Montgomery County and flows se into Denson Creek. Named for Dumas family, early settlers. Appears on recent maps as Doomas Creek.

Dumplin Creek, a short stream in n central Carteret County, flows w into Adams Creek.

Dunbars Landing, in nw Tyrrell County on the n side of Scuppernong River.

Duncan, community in n Harnett County. Alt. 430.

Duncan Creek rises in e Transylvania County and flows sw into Little River.

Duncan Mountain, se Transylvania County s of Duncan Creek.

Duncans Creek rises in ne Rutherford County and flows se into Cleveland County where it enters First Broad River.

Duncans Creek rises in ne Rutherford County and flows w into Broad River.

Duncans Creek rises in central Warren County and flows e into Walkers Creek. At one time called Dowtins Creek.

Duncans Creek, community in ne Rutherford County. Post office est. here 1829.

Duncans Creek Township, ne Rutherford County.

Dundarrach, town in s Hoke County. Inc. 1911.

Dunfields Creek rises in n central Cumberland County and flows sw into Cape Fear River.

Dunhams Creek rises in e central Moore County and flows se. A short distance above the mouth of Herds Creek it becomes Crains Creek, *(which see)*. Named for Joseph Dunham who settled along its banks in 1760.

Dunlap's Mill. See Bonlee.

Dunmoor Branch rises in e central Bertie County and flows n into Cricket Swamp.

Dunn, town in se Harnett County. First known as Tearshirt and later as Lucknow. Renamed Dunn in 1886 for Bennett R. Dunn, construction engineer of the Atlantic Coast Line Railroad. Inc. 1887. Produces apparel, canned foods, lumber, and candy. Alt. 214.

Dunn Creek rises in s Transylvania County and flows nw into French Broad River.

Dunn Mountain, s Rowan County s of Crane Creek and ne of the town of Granite Quarry. Alt. approx. 1,000. Named for John Dunn, early attorney and clerk of Rowan County court.

Dunns Creek rises near Brushy Mountain in w Transylvania County and flows ne into Catheys Creek.

Dunns Rock, peak in ne Transylvania County s of French Broad River.

Dunns Rock Township, se Transylvania County.

Dunnsville. See Neuse Crossroads.

Dunn Swamp rises in nw Columbus County and flows nw into Porter Swamp.

Dunn Township, former township in se Franklin County, now township number 1.

Dunsmore, community in sw Buncombe County on Stony Fork.

Dunsmore Cove, valley of Dunsmore Cove Branch, se Buncombe County near Ridgecrest.

Dunsmore Cove Branch rises near the McDowell County line in se Buncombe County and flows nw into Swannanoa River.

Dunsmore Mountain, sw Buncombe County. Alt. 2,700.

Duplin (DOO-plin) County was formed in 1750 from New Hanover County. Located in the e section of the state, it is bounded by Jones, Onslow, Pender, Sampson, Wayne, and Lenoir counties. It was named for Thomas Hay (1710-87), Lord Duplin, member of the Board of Trade and Plantations. Area: 823 sq mi. County seat: Kenansville with an elevation of 127 ft. Townships are Albertson, Cypress Creek, Faison, Glisson, Island Creek, Kenansville, Limestone, Magnolia, Rockfish, Rose Hill, Smith, Warsaw, and Wolfescrape. Produces tobacco, corn, cotton, strawberries, cucumbers, miscellaneous vegetables, lumber, poultry, textiles, and apparel.

Duplin Court House. *See* Kenansville.

Duplin Roads. *See* Wallace.

Dupree Crossroads, community in nw Pitt County.

Durant Island, about 5 m. long from e to w and 3 mi. n to s at the widest, in Albemarle Sound, n Dare County. Appears on the Moseley map, 1733.

Durant Point, peninsula extending from the s part of Hatteras Island, s Dare County, into Pamlico Sound, n of Sandy Bay.

Durants Neck, peninsula extending into Albemarle Sound between Perquimans and Little rivers, e Perquimans County. Site of the home of George Durant (1632-1694), pioneer settler in the Albemarle about 1662. Appears as Point Durant on the Hack map, 1684, and as Durants Point on the Moseley map, 1733.

Durants Neck, community on Durants Neck peninsula, e Perquimans County. Formerly known as New Hope; a post office by this name was est. by 1820.

Durants Point, point of land extending into Pungo River from w Hyde County, opposite Belhaven in e Beaufort County.

Durants Point. *See* Durants Neck.

Durgantown. *See* Vanceboro.

Durgy Mine, former gold and copper mine

in e Person County. Operated late nineteenth century and until about 1920. At its peak operation, approx. 500 persons were employed in the mine.

Durham, city and county seat, central Durham County. A post office est. here in 1851 was named Durhamsville; changed to Durham in 1855. Named for Dr. Bartlett Snipes Durham (1822-58), donor of land for the railroad station. Inc. 1866. Center of tobacco manufacturing. Home of Duke University and North Carolina College. In addition to tobacco products, also produces drugs, bricks, grain products, dairy products, apparel, textiles, hosiery, commercial printing, furniture, corrugated boxes, and industrial machinery. Alt. 406. *See also* Prattsburg.

Durham Branch rises in central Swain County and flows se into Deep Creek.

Durham County was formed in 1881 from Orange and Wake counties. Located in the central section of the state, it is bounded by Wake, Chatham, Orange, Person, and Granville counties. It was named for the town of Durham, *which see*. Area: 300 sq mi. The county seat is Durham with an elevation of 406 ft. Townships are Carr, Durham, Lebanon, Mangum, Oak Grove, and Triangle. Produces tobacco, corn, wheat, oats, broilers, eggs, hogs, cigarettes and other tobacco products, drugs, bricks, textiles, apparel, hosiery, corrugated boxes, industrial machinery, and commercial printing.

Durham Creek rises in ne Craven County and flows se on the Craven-Pamlico County line into Upper Broad Creek.

Durham Creek rises in nw Pamlico County and flows n into Beaufort County where it enters Pamlico River. Named for Richard Durham who acquired land near its mouth in 1706. Appears in local records as early as 1715 as Dereham's Creek and by 1770 it was being called Derham and Darham Creek. Appears on the MacRae map, 1833, as Derham Creek. The garrison which gave Garrison Point *(which see)* its name was located on Durham's land.

Durham Township, central Durham County.

Dusty Hill, community in central Northampton County.

Dutch Buffalo Creek rises near Organ and Lowerstone churches in se Rowan County and flows se through Cabarrus County into Rocky River. Named for the "Pennsylvania Dutch" (German, *Deutsch*) who settled here. *See also* Irish Buffalo Creek.

Dutch Cove, e Haywood County on the head of Dutch Cove Creek.

Dutch Cove Creek rises in e Haywood County and flows nw into Hominy Creek.

Dutch Creek rises in sw Watauga County on n slope of Hanging Rock and flows ne into Watauga River.

Dutch Creek Falls, sw Watauga County on Dutch Creek approx. ½ mi. upstream from the mouth of Pigeonroost Creek. Falls are 85 ft. high and make a perpendicular descent over moss and lichen-covered rock. Also known as Marianna Falls.

Dutch District. *See* Dutchville Township.

Dutchman Creek rises in se Brunswick County and flows se into the Cape Fear River.

Dutchman Creek rises in s central Wake County and flows ne into Swift Creek.

Dutchman Mountain, peak in w Randolph County.

Dutchman Ridge, mountain peak on the Buncombe-McDowell County line.

Dutchmans Creek, formed in ne Gaston County by the junction of Leepers Creek and Killians Creek, flows se into Catawba River.

Dutchmans Creek rises in w Montgomery County and flows sw into Island Creek.

Dutchmans Creek, approx. 30 mi. long, rises in s Yadkin County and flows s into ne Iredell County and then se across Davie County into Yadkin River near the Horseshoe. Appears on the Collet map, 1770.

Dutch Second Creek. *See* South Second Creek.

Dutchville Township, sw Granville County. A nineteenth century post office in this part of the county was called Dutchville, and in 1790 there was a Dutch District which had 76 heads of families reported in the census for that year.

Dyeleaf Creek rises on the s side of Spring Mountain in ne Buncombe County and flows w through Laughter Cove into Cane Creek. Named for Sweet Leaf or Horsesugar (*Symplocos tinctoria*), the leaves and bark of which yield a yellow dye.

Dyeleaf Mountain, se Buncombe County between Cane and Garren creeks.

Dyer Knob, in w Watauga County n of Rush Branch and e of Beaverdam Creek. Alt. approx. 3,300.

Dykers Creek rises in w Davidson County and flows into Yadkin River.

Dymond City, former community in se Martin County in Great Swamp. A post office by this name existed in 1882. Appears as Dimond City on the Kerr map, 1882, located near the head of Deep Run Swamp.

Dysartsville, community in se McDowell County. Alt. 1,262. Named for the Dysart family, early settlers. One Capt. Dysart served in the Revolutionary War.

Dysartville Township, se McDowell County.

E

Eads Gap, se Buncombe County between Chestnut Flats and Garren Mountain.

Eagle Branch. *See* Spread Eagle Branch.

Eagle Cliff, ne Mitchell County between Fork Mountain and Roan Mountain.

Eagle Creek is formed in se Clay County by the junction of Left Fork and Right Fork and flows nw into Shooting Creek. Known also as Eagle Fork Creek.

Eagle Creek is formed in nw Swain County

in the Great Smoky Mountains National Park by the junction of Gunna Creek and Tub-Mill Creek. It flows sw into Fontana Lake. Named from the fact that a nest of eagles was found near its head.

Eagle Falls, a low falls on Dan River, w central Rockingham County. Land adjacent was granted to Charles Galloway in 1745, and early county courts were held on his property. Eagle Falls plantation here, occupied by the Galloway family for many years, later passed to descendants named Carter. The house is now used for farm storage. *See also* Jackson.

Eagle Fork Creek. *See* Eagle Creek.

Eagle Gap, w Cherokee County between Fowler Bend and Hiwassee Dam.

Eagle Knob, in central Graham County between Sweetwater Creek and Mountain Creek.

Eagle Knob on the Jackson-Macon County line. Alt. 4,500.

Eagle Mills, community in ne Iredell County. Mill operated by the Eagle family here burned by Stoneman's raiders, 1865, later rebuilt. A grain mill is now operated on Hunting Creek at the site.

Eagle Mills Township, ne Iredell County.

Eaglenest Branch rises in e Transylvania County near Black Knob and flows ne into Little River.

Eaglenest Creek rises in w Haywood County and flows se into Richland Creek.

Eaglenest Mountain, w Haywood County on the head of Eaglenest Creek.

Eaglenest Ridge, w Haywood County extends e from Rattlesnake Knob to Eaglenest Mountain.

Eagle Rock, mountain on Swain County, N. C.-Sevier County, Tenn., line between Pecks Corner and Copper Gap. Alt. 5,950-6,000.

Eagle Rock, town in e Wake County. A printing press operated here as early as 1854. Named for a rock on which an eagle fell when shot by Thomas Richard Debnum, around whose home the town developed. Inc. 1911 when lumber industry thrived here. Not now active in municipal affairs. Alt. 326.

Eagle Rock Creek rises in Great Craggy Mountains, ne Buncombe County, and flows sw into Beetree Reservoir.

Eagle Rock Cove, valley of Eagle Rock Creek, ne Buncombe County.

Eagles Island, a group of swampy islands in w New Hanover County between the Cape Fear and Brunswick rivers opposite Wilmington. Named for Joseph and Richard Eagle, eighteenth century settlers in the vicinity. *See also* Dram Tree Point. Appears as Cranes Island on the Ogilby map, 1671.

Eagle Springs, community in w Moore County. Settled about 1890. There is a mineral spring here and probably named for the Eagle family which settled in the vicinity in the eighteenth century. Alt. 668.

Eagle Swamp rises in n Lenoir County and flows se into Contentnea Creek.

Eagleton Point, point of land extending nw from Colington Island into the waters of Kitty Hawk Bay, n Dare County. Also known as North Point and Eggleston Point.

Eagletown, community in se Northampton County, an early Quaker settlement.

Eakers Corner, community on Stoney Run in w Cleveland County.

Earl, town in s Cleveland County. Inc. 1889, but long inactive in municipal affairs. Named for Abel Earl, local landowner. Alt. 925. Produces manufactured fibers.

Earleys, community in s Hertford County. Alt. 65.

Earlies Gap, nw Buncombe County between Cook and Robinson Mountains.

Earl Mountain, ne Rutherford County between the head of Duncans Creek and South Creek.

Earnhardts Township, former township in ne Cabarrus County. Now township number 7. In 1945 a part of this township was annexed to Concord, coextensive with Concord township. In 1940 this township was listed as Reed Misenhiemers.

Earpsboro, community in n Johnston County near Little River.

Earthquake Branch. *See* Browns Creek.

Easonburg, community in se Nash County, on n side of Tar River.

Eason Crossroads, community in central Gates County.

Eason Millpond, w Pitt County on Kitten Creek.

East Arcadia, community in se Bladen County. Known originally as Marlville, for local marl beds.

Eastatoe Creek rises in ne Pickens County, South Carolina, in the Blue Ridge Mountains and flows n into s Transylvania County, North Carolina, and ne into Middle Fork French Broad River.

Eastatoe Gap, s Transylvania County between Shoal Creek and Eastatoe Creek. Alt. 2,686.

Eastatoe Township, s central Transylvania County.

East Bay, in n Piney Island e of Rattan Bay, ne Carteret County. Approx. ¾ mi. long and ½ mi. wide.

East Belews Creek rises in e Forsyth County and flows n into Belews Creek.

East Bend, town in ne Yadkin County between Logan Creek and Yadkin River. Known as Banner's Store for a local merchant, Martin Banner, until the name was changed about 1849 for a nearby east bend in Yadkin River. Inc. 1887.

East Bend Township, ne Yadkin County.

East Bluff Bay, s Hyde County in Pamlico Sound e of Bluff Point.

East Branch rises in s Pitt County and flows s into Swift Creek.

East Branch rises in se Yancey County and flows n into Little Whiteoak Creek.

East Branch Chicod Creek formed in w Beaufort County by the junction of Juniper and Harding Swamps. It flows nw into Pitt County where it enters Chicod Creek.

Eastbrook, community in ne Brunswick County.

East Buffalo Creek rises in central Graham County and flows sw into Santeetlah Lake.

East Buies Creek rises in ne Harnett County and flows sw into Buies Creek. It appears as Hugh McCrarey's Creek on early maps of the region and later as Hugh's Creek.

East Creek rises in central Currituck County and flows sw into North River.

East Dismal Swamp, a 20,000 acre area of peat and muck swamp extending ne from n Beaufort County across s and e Washington County into w Tyrrell County. *See also* Dogwood Ridge; New Lands.

East Double Creek rises in s Surry County and flows s to join West Double Creek in forming Double Creek.

Eastern Channel, a tidal waterway in s Brunswick County extending w from Montgomery Slough to Lockwoods Folly Inlet.

Eastern Channel, a tidal waterway in sw Brunswick County extending e from Tibbs Inlet inside Hales Beach for about 3 mi.

East Fayetteville, unincorporated outskirts of city of Fayetteville, central Cumberland County, 1½ mi. e of Market House.

East Flat Rock, former town in central Henderson County. Alt. 2,214. Inc. 1926; charter repealed by local action 1948, and by act of the General Assembly, 1949. Railroad name is Flat Rock, *which see.* Est. as a commercial adjunct to the residential community of Flat Rock. Produces textiles.

East Fork, community in s Transylvania County.

East Fork [Barkers Creek] rises in w Jackson County and flows n to join West Fork in forming Barkers Creek.

East Fork [Bull Creek] rises in e Madison County and flows sw to join West Fork in forming Bull Creek.

East Fork [Campbell Creek] rises in w Haywood County and flows n into Campbell Creek.

East Fork Chattooga River rises in s Jackson County and flows s into South Carolina where it enters Chattooga River.

East Fork [Cove Creek] rises in w Watauga County and flows s into Cove Creek.

East Fork Crabtree Creek rises in s Mitchell County and flows nw into Crabtree Creek.

East Fork Creek rises in e Beaufort County and flows s into Pamlico River.

East Fork Deep River rises in w Guilford County and flows se into High Point Lake where it joins West Fork Deep River to form Deep River.

East Fork [Dicks Creek] rises in n Jackson County and flows sw to join West Fork in forming Dicks Creek.

East Fork French Broad River rises in s Transylvania County and flows sw and nw into French Broad River.

East Fork Gap, e Haywood County on the head of Garden Creek.

East Fork [Goose Creek] rises in n Pamlico County and flows sw into Goose Creek.

East Fork Grassy Creek rises in s Mitchell County and flows nw to join Middle Fork Grassy Creek in forming Grassy Creek.

East Fork [Jenkins Creek] rises in n Jackson County and flows sw to join West Fork in forming Jenkins Creek.

East Fork [Kirkland Creek] rises in s Swain County and flows nw to join West Fork [Kirkland Creek] in forming Kirkland Creek.

East Fork Lake in central Jackson County on Tuckasegee River. Formed in 1955 to be a reservoir for Nantahala Power and Light Company. Combines with Wolf Creek Lake (*which see*) to generate hydroelectric power. Covers 40 acres with maximum depth of 120 ft. Shoreline is 3.2 mi. Named for East Fork of Tuckasegee River, an old name for this part of Tuckasegee River.

East Fork [Moses Creek] rises in n Jackson County and flows sw to join West Fork in forming Moses Creek.

East Fork Overflow Creek rises in se Macon County and flows sw to join West Fork Overflow Creek in forming Overflow Creek.

East Fork Pigeon River rises in sw Haywood County near the Transylvania County line and flows n to join West Fork Pigeon

River in forming Pigeon River. Known by the Cherokee Indians as Junietta.

East Fork [Savannah Creek] rises in w Jackson County and flows nw into Savannah Creek.

East Fork Shut-in Creek rises in w Madison County and flows nw to join West Fork Shut-in Creek in forming Shut-in Creek.

East Fork [of South Fork New River] rises in s Watauga County and flows nw to join Middle Fork and Flannery Fork in forming South Fork New River approx. 2 mi. se of town of Boone.

East Fork [South River], a short stream at the headwaters of South River in n central Carteret County.

East Fork Township, s Haywood County.

East Fork Twelvemile Creek rises in w Union County and flows sw to join West Fork in forming Twelvemile Creek.

East Franklin, community in central Macon County.

East Fruitland. See Pores Knob.

East Gastonia, unincorporated outskirts of city of Gastonia, central Gaston County.

Eastham Creek rises near the center of Goose Creek Island, ne Pamlico County, and flows nw into Goose Creek.

East Howellsville Township, e Robeson County.

East Kings Mountain, former town in w Gaston County on the Cleveland County line. Inc. 1907. By a vote of the people it was transferred to Cleveland County in 1915. Became a part of Kings Mountain (which see) in 1923.

East Lake, a lake on the mainland of n Dare County, empties into the mouth of Alligator River.

East Lake, community on the mainland of nw Dare County, on South Lake. Settled about 1790. Alt. 10.

East Lake Landing, nw Dare County on Alligator River. State-operated free ferry from this point to Sandy Point in ne Tyrrell County now replaced by the Lindsay C. Warren Bridge, 2.83 mi. long and opened in May, 1962; named for Lindsay C. Warren (b. 1889), former U. S. Congressman and Comptroller-General.

East Lake Township, nw Dare County mainland.

Eastland, community in w Caswell County. A post office was operated here during the approx. period 1880-1905.

East Laport, community in n Jackson County on Tuckasegee River. Developed at the site of an eighteenth-century French trading post which the French considered to be an east gate or door *(la porte)* to the Cherokee country. Alt. 2,186.

East Laurinburg, town in s Scotland County. Inc. 1903 as Scotland Village; name changed 1909.

East Lumberton, former town in e central Robeson County. Inc. 1901. Charter repealed, 1953. Now a part of Lumberton. Was a mill-owned village until 1949-1950 when houses were sold to individuals.

Eastman Creek rises in n Carteret County and flows w into South River.

East Mingo Branch rises in sw Johnston County and flows south to join Black River in forming South River on the Cumberland-Sampson County line. For a part of its course it forms the boundary between Johnston and Harnett counties and between Harnett and Sampson counties. Sometimes also known as Mingo Swamp. Appears as Black Mingo on the Collet map, 1770. Mingo was an Indian word for a treacherous person. It was also a frequently used name for slaves, appearing as such as early as 1680 in Albemarle County. See also Black Creek Swamp.

East Monbo, now covered by waters of Lake Norman, but formerly a community on the Catawba River in w Iredell County. A cotton mill was established here in the late nineteenth century and named Mont Beau by its owners. The natives soon corrupted the name to Monbo, and since it was on the east side of the river it became East Monbo (there being another mill on the west side of the river in Catawba County). East Monbo was long a popular picnic and swimming site.

Eastmost River is formed in se Bertie County by the junction of Middle River and a branch of Roanoke River near its mouth. It flows ne into Batchelor Bay.

Eastmost Swamp rises in e central Bertie County and flows s into Salmon Creek.

Eastmouth Bay, in the waters of Core Sound between the two large islands comprising Harkers Island in se Carteret County.

East Nelson Creek rises in ne Cherokee County and flows se into Valley River.

Eastover Township, e central Cumberland County.

East Prong rises in central Burke County and flows w into Sandy Run Creek.

East Prong rises in w Carteret County and flows sw into Sanders Creek.

East Prong Cub Creek rises in s Wilkes County and flows nw into Cub Creek at the eastern outskirts of Wilkesboro. Originally known as Little Cub Creek.

East Prong Deep River rises in w Guilford County and flows se into Deep River.

East Prong [Hickory Fork] rises in n Madison County and flows sw into Hickory Fork.

East Prong Little Yadkin River rises in w Stokes County and flows sw to join West Prong Little Yadkin River in forming Little Yadkin River.

East Prong Moon Creek rises in w Caswell County and flows ne into Moon Creek.

East Prong Roaring River rises in ne Wilkes County and flows se into Roaring River.

East Ridge, e Watauga County extends se between Mary Simmons Ridge and Clear Branch.

East Rockingham, unincorporated outskirts of town of Rockingham, w Richmond County.

East Sanford Township, former township in central Lee County. Now township number 5.

East Spencer, town in e Rowan County. Originated as Southern City (along the route of the Southern Railway), a real estate development by John S. Henderson and others. Inc. 1901. The town of Spencer is to the sw. "Spring Hill," plantation of Maxwell Chambers, was here.

East Swan Creek rises in w Yadkin County and flows nw into Wilkes County where it joins West Swan Creek in forming Swan Creek.

East Wilmington, unincorporated outskirts of the city of Wilmington, w New Hanover County.

Eastwood, community in s Moore County. Named for J. B. Eastwood, lumberman, who established a store here about 1912.

Eastwood Lake, s Orange County in ne Chapel Hill. Formed in 1937 by a dam on Booker Creek. Approx. ¾ mi. long, covering 58 acres with a maximum depth of about 20 ft. Now the center of a residential area.

Easy Hill, community in ne Brunswick County.

Easy Ridge, n Swain County in Great Smoky Mountains National Park, a short spur extending ne from Noland Divide.

Easy Ridge Gap, s Swain County on the head of First Hurricane Branch.

Easy Street, Negro community in n Sampson County. Named from the fact that it was easy to purchase illegal liquor here.

Eaton Island. See Baker Island.

Eatons Ferry, in ne Warren County on Roanoke River, was privately owned and operated as early as about 1770, appeared on the Price map, 1808. It was purchased by the state in 1935 and operated until January, 1962, when a bridge over Gaston Lake was opened.

Eaves Creek rises in n Franklin County and flows se into Lynch Creek.

Ebenezer, community in central Cherokee County at the junction of Dockery and Hanging Dog Creek.

Ebenezer, community in e Gaston County.

Eby Creek rises in s Transylvania County and flows sw into Little River.

Echo, crossroads community in sw Robeson County.

Echota Mission, n Jackson County, maintained by Holston Conference of Methodist Church for Cherokee Indians about 1840-1885. School est. 1850. Missionary's house still stands.

Ecola, former community in w Swain County, site now under the waters of Fontana Lake.

Ecusta. See Pisgah Forest.

Edam, community in nw Wilson County.

Eden, town in n Rockingham County on Dan and Smith rivers. Formed in 1967 by the merger of Leaksville, Draper, and Spray, which see. Named for William Byrd's estate here, Land of Eden, which see.

Edenhouse, community in e Bertie County on the Chowan River. Site of Eden House, home of Charles Eden, governor 1714-22 and Gabriel Johnston, governor 1732-52.

Edenhouse Point, point of land extending into Chowan River, e Bertie County. Location of an early seine fishery.

Edens Pond. See Watsons Pond.

Edenton, town and county seat, s Chowan County, on Albemarle Sound. Settled by 1710 and known by the Indians as the Town on Matecomack Creek. Town authorized to be laid off here in 1712 and the first lot sold in 1714. Known as the Town on Queen Anne's Creek from 1715 until 1722 when it was inc. as Edenton in honor of Charles Eden (1673-1722), governor, who had just died. Edenton was the capital of the colony from 1722 until 1743, and a building was provided for the assembly by 1733 (and perhaps as early as 1725), though the assembly met here 1722-36 and 1740-43. The Edenton Tea Party on Oct. 25, 1774, is the earliest known instance of political activity by American women. Alt. 16. Processes peanuts and seafood; produces textiles, veneer, seed, fertilizer, and lumber. See also St. Paul's Parish.

Edenton District at the time of the 1790 Census was composed of Bertie, Camden, Chowan, Currituck, Gates, Hertford, Pasquotank, Perquimans, and Tyrrell counties and the town of Edenton.

Edenton Township, former township in s Chowan County, now township number 1. For voting purposes the township is divided into East Edenton and West Edenton.

Edenton Bay, s Chowan County in Albemarle Sound. Formed by the mouth of Pembroke Creek. Covers approx. 4,000 acres.

Edgar, community in n Randolph County.

Edgecombe, community in se Pender County.

Edgecombe, Parish of, Church of England, Edgecombe County, later Halifax, est. 1741 with the creation of Edgecombe County. Coextensive with the county. In 1756 the parish was divided creating St. Mary's Parish in the south, the Parish of Edgecombe remaining in the north. With the creation of Halifax County in 1758 the Parish of Edgecombe became coextensive with the new county. St. Mary's Parish was coextensive with Edgecombe County. Edgecombe Parish in 1767 had 1,500 white taxables. The parish as a unit of local administration was abolished in 1776 with the adoption of the state constitution and the disestablishment of the Church of England. The spelling "Edgcomb" was generally used for the name of this parish in local records.

Edgecombe County was formed in 1741 from Bertie County. Located in the e section of the state, it is bounded by Martin,

Pitt, Wilson, Nash, and Halifax counties. It was named for Richard Edgecumbe (1680-1758), afterwards first Baron Edgecumbe, a member of Parliament, lord of the treasury, and holder of other political offices. Area: 511 sq. mi. County seat: Tarboro with an elevation of 71 ft. Townships are Nos. 1-14, formerly Tarboro, Lower Conetoe, Upper Conetoe, Deep Creek, Lower Fishing Creek, Upper Fishing Creek, Swift Creek, Sparta, Otter Creek, Lower Town Creek, Walnut Creek, Rocky Mount, Cokey, and Upper Town Creek. Produces tobacco, corn, soybeans, peanuts, cotton, hogs, livestock, textiles, lumber, toys, paper products, machinery, fabricated metals, and furniture.

Edgemont, community in w Caldwell County.

Edgewater, community in central Beaufort County on the n bank of Pamlico River.

Edgewater, community in s central Carteret County, nw of Morehead City. Alt. 19 ft. Formerly named Morehead Bluffs.

Edgewood, community in e Caswell County.

Edinburg, former town in sw Montgomery County. Inc. 1807 at the store of and on the land of John Billingsly. A post office was here as early as 1828 and as recently as 1882. Site now abandoned. Named for the city in Scotland by local residents of Scottish descent.

Edith, community in se Catawba County. Alt. 1,050.

Edith Lake, s Henderson County on Green River. Approx. 1½ mi. long.

Edmonds, community in ne Alleghany County and Virginia.

Edney Branch rises in w Yancey County and flows s into Cane River.

Edneyville, community in e Henderson County. Named for the Reverend Samuel Edney, Methodist minister who served as postmaster and magistrate. A post office as early as 1830. Alt. 2,247.

Edneyville Township, ne Henderson County.

Ed Top, peak in n Haywood County on the head of Laurel Branch.

Edward, town in se Beaufort County. Alt. 25. Inc. 1889 as Edwards' Mill but long inactive in municipal affairs. Named for Josephus Edwards who built a mill on nearby Durham Creek about 1868.

Edward Cove, s Haywood County on a tributary of Bird Creek.

Edward Jones Creek. See Little Turnbull Creek.

Edwards Branch rises in n Macon County and flows se into Daves Creek.

Edwards Branch rises in n Mitchell County and flows s into Little Rock Creek.

Edwards Bridge, community in e Greene County on Contentnea Creek. Bridge by this name over the creek as early as the 1850's.

Edwards Creek rises in se Macon County and flows se into Big Creek.

Edwards Crossroads, community in n Alleghany County. Alt. approx. 2,800.

Edwards Crossroads, community in central Northampton County.

Edwards' Mill. See Edward.

Edwards Mountain, peak in the Peach Bottom Mountain range, central Alleghany County. Alt. approx. 3,400.

Edwards Mountain, ne Chatham County.

Edwards Pocosin, s Northampton County between Lily Pond Creek and Quarter Swamp.

Edwards Township, e Wilkes County.

Efland, community in w Orange County. Alt. 658.

Eggleston Point. See Eagleton Point.

Egg Shoal, in the waters of Pamlico Sound, s Dare County, off the s part of Hatteras Island.

Eggtown, community in nw Anson County.

Egypt. See Cumnock.

Egypt Land, a name applied to the s portion of Vance County because of its reputation at one time as a land of slaves and corn.

Egypt Township, n Yancey County.

Eight-foot Ditch, canal in nw Pasquotank which drains ne into Shepherd Ditch.

Eighty-Nine Mile Siding. See Cognac.

Ekaneetlee Creek rises in nw Swain County in Great Smoky Mountains National Park and flows se into Eagle Creek.

Ekaneetlee Gap, on the Swain County, N. C.-Blount County, Tenn., line in the Great Smoky Mountains National Park. Alt. 3,852.

Ela, community in e Swain County on Tuckasegee River. Name is a Cherokee word meaning "earth." Alt. 1,830.

Elah or Eliah, community in northeastern Brunswick about 2 mi. sw of Leland. Settled prior to 1882. Inc. 1903 as Myrtle to meet the requirement that whiskey stills could be operated only in incorporated towns. Charter repealed, 1905. Took name Elah from local Elah Baptist Church.

Ela Lake, on Oconaluftee River in e Swain

County. Covers 20 acres, max. depth 15 ft. Formed in 1925. Owned by the Aluminum Company of America and used to generate electric power. Formerly known as Onitalooga Lake.

Elams, community in ne Warren County between Walker Creek and Lizard Creek. Settled in 1880 and named for James Elam, local resident. Alt. 400.

Elbaville, community in e Davie County. Name derived from the first syllables of names of two local families—Ellis and Bailey. Post office est. 1870. Alt. approx. 808.

Elberon, community in s Warren County between Lees Branch and Buffalo Branch. Post office est. here in 1897, but discontinued in 1954.

Elberta, community in w Moore County. A peach growing center named for the Elberta peach. Alt. approx. 661.

Elbethel, community in se Cleveland County. Named for El Bethel Methodist Church.

Elbow Branch rises in n Swain County and flows nw into Hazel Creek.

Elbow Creek rises in nw Cherokee County and flows s into Shuler Creek.

Elbow Landing on Pungo River, e Beaufort County.

Elbow Ridge, n Swain County in Great Smoky Mountains National Park, a short spur extending w from Welch Ridge between Elbow Branch and Hazel Creek.

Elder Branch rises in central Duplin County and flows se into Maxwell Creek.

Eldorado, community in nw Montgomery County. Formerly a center of gold mines of varying productivity named for a legendary South American king who owned much gold. A post office in the late nineteenth century. Now a residential community for people employed in Denton, High Point, and Thomasville.

Eldorado Township, nw Montgomery County.

Eldora Township, e central Surry County.

Eleanors Crossroads, community in central Gates County.

Elease, community in s Cumberland County.

Eleazer, community in sw Randolph County on Uwharrie River.

Elevation Township, sw Johnston County. Named from the fact that it is in a hilly section of the county.

Elf, community in s Clay County on Chatuge Lake.

Elgin, plantation house in central Warren County. Built in 1832 and named by a Scottish immigrant, Peter Mitchel, for his native city, Elgin, county seat of Elginshire (or Moray County). The house is still used as a dwelling.

Elise. See Robbins.

Elliott Cove, n Swain County between Sunkota Ridge and Deep Creek.

Elisha, community in s Pasquotank County.

Elisha Creek, approx. 5 mi. long, rises in central Davie County and flows se into Dutchmans Creek. Appears in local records, 1815, as "Lisha, formerly called Licking Creek."

Elizabeth City, city and county seat, e Pasquotank County on Pasquotank River. Settled in 1790; inc. as Redding in 1793. In 1794 named changed from "Reading" to Elizabethtown; became Elizabeth City in 1801. Probably named for Elizabeth Tooley, wife of Adam Tooley on whose land the town was est. Elizabeth City State Teachers College and College of the Albermarle are here. Produces textiles, ships, lumber, hosiery, apparel, paper boxes, and industrial machinery. Alt. 12.

Elizabeth City Township, e central Pasquotank County.

Elizabeth River rises in se Brunswick County and flows e into the Cape Fear River.

Elizabethtown, town and county seat, central Bladen County. Alt. 121. Est. 1773, chartered 1843, and inc. 1895. Named either for Queen Elizabeth I of England or for the sweetheart of Isaac Jones on whose land the town was laid out. In the Battle of Elizabethtown, August 27, 1781, Whigs broke Tory power in Bladen County by driving them into Tory Hole, a deep ravine along the banks of Cape Fear River here.

Elizabeth Town. See Columbia.

Elizabethtown. See Elizabeth City.

Elizabethtown Township in central Bladen County.

Elk Branch rises in e Mitchell County and flows s into Cane Creek.

Elk Creek rises in w Alleghany County and flows n into New River.

Elk Creek rises in s central Ashe County and flows s into South Fork New River on the Ashe-Watauga County line.

Elk Creek rises in ne Stokes County and flows s into Dan River.

Elk Creek rises in e Watauga County and flows e and se into Wilkes County where it enters Yadkin River.

Elk Creek rises in e Watauga County and flows se into w Wilkes County where it enters Yadkin River.

Elk Creek, community in w central Alleghany County.

Elk Fork rises in sw Yancey County and flows ne into Little Creek.

Elk Hollow Branch rises in w Avery County and flows e into Roaring Creek.

Elk Hollow Ridge, w Avery County.

Elkin, town in sw Surry County on Yadkin River near the mouth of Elkin River. Alt. 947. Inc. 1889. Named for the river. Immediately s, separated by Yadkin River, is the town of Jonesville in Yadkin County. Produces woolen goods.

Elkin River rises in ne Wilkes County and flows se across the sw corner of Surry County and into Yadkin River on the Surry-Yadkin County line near the town of Elkin. Appears on the Collet map, 1770.

Elkinsville. See Elkton.

Elkin Township, sw Surry County.

Elk Knob, n Graham County between Tuskeegee Creek and Sawyer Creek.

Elk Knob, n Watauga County near the head of Hoskin Fork.

Elkland. See Todd.

Elk Lodge Mountain, s central Transylvania County between Allison Creek and Lamb Creek.

Elk Marsh. See Marsh Swamp.

Elk Mountain, community in central Buncombe County w of Woodfin. Alt. 1,950.

Elk Mountains, central Buncombe County ne of Asheville, extend from Peach Knob to Roaring Gap. Alt. 3,149-3,190.

Elk Park, town in nw Avery County. Inc. 1885. First county court held here while the courthouse at Newland was under construction. Named for elk which once roamed this region. Alt. 3,182.

Elk Ridge extends s from Bluff Mountain in sw Ashe County.

Elk Ridge, s Watauga County extends northeastward between Dutch Creek and Clark Creek.

Elk Ridge, w Wilkes County between Elk Creek and Stony Fork Creek.

Elk River rises in ne Avery County near Banner Elk and flows w into Tennessee where it enters Watauga River. For most of its course it flows in a deep gorge.

Elk River Falls in Elk River, nw Avery County, a drop of about 85 ft., and for the next four miles downstream there is a fall of about 100 ft. per mile.

Elks Crossroads. See Todd.

Elk Shoal, community in w Yancey County on Cane River. A nineteenth century post office serving the community was named Wampler.

Elk Shoal Creek rises in w Yancey County and flows e into Cane River.

Elk Shoals, former community in e Alexander County near headwaters of Elk Shoals Creek. Post office est. here in 1858 was discontinued in 1901 with postal service being offered the community from Stony Point. Named for shoals in creek at which elk crossed.

Elk Shoals Creek rises in se Alexander County and flows s and sw into Catawba River. The name occurs in local records as early as 1760, and the stream is shown on the Collet map, 1770.

Elk Shoals Creek rises in n Catawba County and flows se into Catawba River.

Elk Spur, central Avery County.

Elk Spur, n Wilkes County near Little Sandy Creek.

Elkton, community in s Bladen County. Alt. 90.

Elkton Swamp rises in s Bladen County and flows s into Brown Marsh Swamp.

Elk Township, s Ashe County.

Elk Township, se Watauga County.

Elk Township, sw Wilkes County.

Elkville, community in sw Wilkes County on Yadkin River. Alt. 1,200.

Elk Wallow Creek rises in w Yancey County and flows se into Bald Creek.

Elk Wallow Knob, on the Madison-Yancey County line near the head of Elk Wallow Creek. Alt. approx. 4,600.

Elkwallow Knob, nw Mitchell County between Leatherman Fork and Bearwallow Creek.

Elkwood. See Weaverville.

Elk X Roads. See Todd.

Elk Wallow Gap, central Buncombe County in Elk Mountains.

Ell Branch rises in s Jackson County and flows se into Robinson Creek.

Ellenboro, town in e Rutherford County. Alt. 1,046. Founded 1886; inc. 1889. Said to have been named for Ellen Robinson, daughter of the president (or engineer) of the Carolina Central Railroad. Robinson gave a bell to the school here with his daughter's name engraved inside. May have been named by Burwell Blanton Byers, owner of much local property, for himself and his wife, Ellen—Ellenburwell, which later became Ellenboro.

Ellenburwell. See Ellenboro.

Ellendale, community in w Alexander County. Formerly known as Ellendale Chalybeat Springs, a summer resort. Named for Ellen Reid, daughter of the owner of the spring.

Ellendale Township, w Alexander County.

Eller, community in n Davidson County. Alt. 902. Named for one Eller who settled in the vicinity about 1753. Also known locally as Midway from its position between Lexington and Winston-Salem.

Ellerbe, town in n central Richmond County. Scottish settlers in the eighteenth century had a fair at this site each May and November and it came to be known as The Fair Grounds. After W. T. Ellerbe developed a popular watering place at nearby Ellerbe Springs the present name began to be applied. Incorporated 1911. Produces hosiery.

Ellerbee Creek rises in w Durham County about 2 mi. w of Durham and flows e and ne about 11 mi. into Neuse River. Known earlier as Alliby Creek and Elliby Creek.

Eller Branch rises in n Buncombe County and flows nw into Madison County where it enters Ivy River.

Eller Cove, n Buncombe County between Little Davis and Lydie Mountains.

Eller Cove, n Buncombe County between McDairies Ridge and Greenfield Ridge.

Eller Cove, s Graham County between Horse Range Ridge and Atoah Gap.

Elliby Creek. See Ellerbee Creek.

Ellicott Mountain, s Jackson County near the head of East Fork Chattooga River. Alt. 3,800. Named for Andrew Ellicott (1745-1820), who surveyed the North Carolina-Georgia state line in 1813.

Ellicott Rock on the e side of Chattooga River in sw Jackson County at the North Carolina-South Carolina-Georgia state line. A granite boulder indicating this junction was marked in 1813 by and named for Andrew Ellicott (1754-1820), surveyor.

Ellijay, community in e Macon County on Ellijay Creek. Alt 2,200. Name is from a Cherokee word meaning "verdant earth."

Ellijay Creek rises in e Macon County and flows sw into Cullasaja River.

Ellijay Township, e central Macon County.

Ellingtons Creek rises in nw Warren County and flows ne into Smiths Creek.

Elliott, community in e Sampson County. Alt. 137. A post office was opened here in

1886 but it closed about 1940. Named for Dr. Elliott Lee of Clinton. An early stop on the railroad here was known as Summit. The community is at the site of "Mount Pleasant," the plantation of James Faison.

Elliott Branch rises in e Cherokee County and flows s into Peachtree Creek.

Elliott Springs. See Catawba Springs.

Ellisboro, community in w Rockingham County. Alt. 829.

Ellis Creek in nw Bladen County drains s from Suggs Mill Pond, which see, into Cape Fear River.

Ellis Creek rises in s Davidson County and flows w into Yadkin River.

Ellis Cross Roads, community in ne Rowan County. Settled about 1885.

Ellis Lake, a natural lake in Croatan National Forest, s Craven and n Carteret counties. Covers 1,500 acres. Maximum depth, 4 to 5 feet. Named for the Ellis family which lived on its shores many years ago. One of several lakes in Lakes Pocosin.

Ellis Mountain, central Mitchell County between Rebel Creek and Toe River.

Ellison Branch rises in se Buncombe County and flows s into Cane Creek.

Ellison Branch rises in n Watauga County and flows w into Cove Creek.

Ellison Creek rises in sw Forsyth County and flows sw into Yadkin River.

Ellis Store, community in se Bertie County.

Elm City, town in n Wilson County. Alt. 131. Inc. 1873 as Toisnot and post office est. here succeeding nearby post office at Joyner's which see. Named changed to Elm City, 1891; back to Toisnot in 1895; and again to Elm City in 1913.

Elmira Crossroads, community in se Pitt County.

Elmore, community in s central Scotland County formerly called Elmores Crossroads.

Elmore Branch rises in e Macon County and flows s into Rabbit Creek.

Elmores Crossroads, community in se Gaston County.

Elmores Crossroads. See Elmore.

Elm Swamp. See Corapeake Swamp.

Elmwood, community in se Bertie County on Salmon Creek. Named for an early plantation at the site. Was early waiting place for the ferry across the creek to Edenton and beyond.

Elmwood, community in e central Iredell

County. Alt. 836. Named for elm trees in the vicinity.

Elon College, town in w Alamance County. Inc. 1893. Formerly known as Mill Point for a freight depot for shipping mill products manufactured nearby. Elon College, a four-year coeducational institution, opened here in 1890. Its name comes from the Hebrew word for oak and was selected because of the large oak trees at the site. Alt. 716.

Elrod, community in w Robeson County.

Elrod Branch rises in s Watauga County and flows nw into Middle Fork [South Fork New River].

Elroy Store, community in e Wayne County near the head of Walnut Creek.

El-see-toss. See Mount Pisgah.

Elsworth Creek rises in e Davie County and flows sw into Dutchmans Creek.

Elwell Ferry, across Cape Fear River in se Bladen County.

Emaline Gap, s Macon County between Everett Mountain and Brush Creek.

Emandell, community in sw Washington County w of Van Swamp. Since the 1950's the name has not generally appeared on maps of the county.

Embro, community in central Warren County n of Reedy Creek. A post office est. here in 1889 was discontinued in 1921.

Emerald Isle, town on Bogue Banks, se Carteret County. Inc. 1957. Located on the Atlantic Ocean, it is a resort town.

Emerson, community in s Bladen County. Alt. 104. Railroad name, Portersville.

Emerson, community in sw Columbus County.

Emerson Branch rises in nw tip of Cabarrus County where it forms a part of the headwaters of Coddle Creek.

Emit, community in n Johnston County on Little River. See also Flower Hill.

Emma, community in central Buncombe County w of Asheville. Alt. 2,075.

Emma Branch rises in central Buncombe County near Dryman Mountain and flows se through the community of Emma into Smith Mill Creek.

Emmons Mine, former gold mine in e Davidson County about 5 mi. n of Denton. In 1855 a large gold nugget ("123 pennyweights") was picked up in the vicinity.

Emmons Township, e central Davidson County.

Emperor Landing, sw Chowan County in the mouth of Chowan River. Probably named for Emperor Moseley, early land-owner here.

Emperors Island. See Church Island.

Encas, community in e Wilson County.

Endesokes. See Core Banks.

Endicott Branch rises in nw Surry County and flows se into Fisher River.

Endy, community in w Stanly County. Named for Arch Eudy who, in 1899, applied for the establishment of a post office here. The Post Office Department misread his name and assigned the name Endy instead of the requested Eudy.

Endy Township, central Stanly County.

Energy. See Siler City.

Enfield, town in s Halifax County. The county seat of Edgecombe County was here from 1745 until the formation of Halifax in 1759; the first Halifax court met here, but Halifax (town) was afterwards the county seat. Inc. 1861. Named probably for the town of Enfield, Middlesex, England. Known originally as Huckleberry Swamp. Alt. 111.

Enfield Township, s Halifax County.

Engagement Hill, a sand dune a short distance n of Nags Head, Bodie Island, e Dare County. A favorite spot for visits by young couples vacationing at Nags Head in former days.

Engelhard, community in e Hyde County on Far Creek. Alt. 2. Inc. 1874; charter revoked 1967. Named for Joseph A. Engelhard (1832-79), publisher of the *Wilmington Daily Journal,* 1861-1870. Known earlier as Far Creek.

Engine Gap, ne Mitchell County near the Tennessee state line.

English, community in e Madison County at the head of Puncheon Fork Creek. Named for an early settler.

English Branch rises in e Madison County and flows se into Puncheon Fork Creek.

English Branch rises near Chalk Mountain in s Mitchell County and flows se into North Toe River. Named for Isaac English, an early settler.

English Branch rises in w Yancey County and flows se into Jacks Creek.

English Knob, e Mitchell County between Beaver Creek and Gouges Creek.

English Town, community in n Pender County.

Enka, community in central Buncombe County. Alt. 2,060. Home of the American Enka Corporation, est. 1929. The name is from the letters N and K taken from the firm's official name: Nederland-

sche Kunstzyde Fabricken. Produces textiles and chemicals.

Enka Lake, central Buncombe County on Bill Moore Creek. Covers 40 acres; max. depth 40 ft. Owned by American Enka Corp. as a source of water for rayon manufacturing. Formed 1928.

Enloe Creek rises in ne Swain County in Great Smoky Mountains National Park and flows se into Raven Fork Creek.

Enloe Ridge, ne Swain County in Great Smoky Mountains National Park, a short spur extending e from Hughes Ridge.

Ennetts Point, w Carteret County, extending into Bogue Sound w of the mouth of Deer Creek. Named for the Ennett family.

Ennice, community in e Alleghany County. Named for Ennice Higgins, daughter of the first postmaster, 1883.

Enno. See Hollemans Crosroads.

Enoch Canal, e Washington County, extends ne from Lake Phelps to Mall Creek.

Enoch Mill Creek rises in s Sampson County and flows se into Black River.

Enochville, town in sw Rowan County. Inc. 1877. Named for St. Enoch's Evangelical Lutheran Church. Long inactive in municipial affairs.

Enola, community in s Burke County. Name is "alone" spelled backwards.

Enon, community in e Yadkin County between Logan Creek and Yadkin River.

Enon Mountain in e Transylvania County west of Lydia Creek.

Eno River rises in n Orange County and flows se across the county into w Durham County where it flows e to join Flat River in forming the Neuse River. Appears on the Moseley map, 1733. The name probably is from the Tuscarora Indian word *e-eno*, "a great way; far off."

Enos Plotts Balsam Mountain, w Haywood County, about 5 mi. w of Waynesville. Alt. 6,097. Known by the Cherokee Indians as Sunneehaw. See also Plott Balsam.

Eno Township, e central Orange County.

Ens Creek. See South Fork.

Enterprise, community in n Davidson County. Name chosen to suggest the nature of the inhabitants.

Enterprise, community in e Warren County between Stonehouse Creek and Little Stonehouse Creek.

Enterprise, former community s of town of Mount Olive in s Wayne County. Now within town limits of Mount Olive.

Entwistle, community in central Richmond County.

Ephesus, community in s Davie County. Named in 1890 when a post office was est. here in Miles A. Foster's store.

Ephraim Branch rises in n Haywood County and flows sw into Groundhog Creek.

Ephriam Hensley Mountain, n Madison County between Rick Branch and Big Creek.

Ephriam Place, mountain on the Unicoi County, Tenn.-Mitchell County, N. C., line.

Epping Forest, an eighteenth-century community and census district in sw Vance County. The community was located near the present town of Kittrell. In 1790 the district had 65 heads of families.

Epps Springs, community in central Swain County on Tuckasegee River. Alt. 1,662.

Epsom, community in e Vance County and n Franklin County. Known as Dukes Crossroads in 1881. When a post office was est. here the name Duke was rejected because there was another post office by that name. According to tradition the present name was suggested by Dr. Bennett P. Alston who noticed a stock of Epsom salts in the local store.

Erastus, community in w Jackson County on Little Piney Creek.

Erect, community in se Randolph County. Name suggested to post office department in the 1870's by C. M. Tysor, local merchant, to compliment the posture of his neighbor, Tom Bray.

Erlanger, former community in central Davidson County. Est. 1914, and named for founder of local mill. Alt. 806. Now within the limits of Lexington.

Ernul, community in ne Craven County. Alt. 25. Settled about 1888. Named for James and Freeman Ernul, residents. Post Office est. 1919 from one previously at Askins.

Ervinsville. See Erwinsville.

Ervintown, community in nw Onslow County on the w limits of Richlands. Named for the numerous Ervins living here.

Erwin, town in se Harnett County. Est. about 1902 with the construction here of Erwin Cotton Mills. First known as Duke for the Duke family of Durham. Name changed to Erwin about 1925 for William Allen Erwin (1856-1932), operator of the local mill. Inc. 1967. Produces textiles. Alt. 195.

Erwinsville, also known as Ervinsville, a former town in sw Cleveland County (then Rutherford County). Inc. 1808; previously inc. as Burrtown in 1800. Located near the mouth of First Broad River and the South Carolina line, e of Ellis Ferry. In 1800 the General Asembly authorized 50 acres here to be laid out and sold in lots. Post office est. 1813, active until 1882. Town site later abandoned.

Eskota, community in s Yancey County on Cane River. Alt. 3,101.

Eskridge Cove, the valley through which Eskridge Cove Branch flows in se Buncombe County.

Eskridge Cove Branch rises in se Buncombe County near Lookoff Gap and flows nw into Swannanoa River.

Esmeralda, community in nw Rutherford County on Broad River.

Ess-ee-daw. See Broad River.

Essex, town in sw Halifax County. Inc. 1891 but long inactive in municipal affairs. Prior to 1860 this was the center of a settlement of free Negroes.

Essex Island. See Etacrewac.

Estatoe, community in s Mitchell County on Brushy Creek. Named for the daughter of an Indian chief.

Estatoe. See Rosman.

Estatoe River. See Toe River.

Estelle, community in ne Caswell County. A post office was operated here during the approx. period 1880-1905.

Estes Branch rises in n Swain County and flows sw into Indian Creek.

Etacrewac, appears on the White maps, 1585 and 1590, as an island which today would be bounded on the n by the community of Duck on the North Banks and on the s by a point on Bodie Island opposite Broad Creek Point on Roanoke Island, e Dare County. The name appears to have been Algonquian Indian for "ever-green-ground." See also Bodie Island; North Banks. The Smith map, 1624, appears to apply the name Essex Island here.

Ether, community in ne Montgomery County. Known as Freeman's Cross Roads prior to the establishment of a post office here when it was named by Dr. F. E. Asbury, local physician.

Etheridge Creek rises in se Halifax County and flows se on the Halifax-Edgecombe County line into Etheridge Swamp.

Etheridge's Branch, rises in nw Wilson County and flows s and se into Contentnea Creek.

Etheridge Swamp receives the waters of Etheridge Creek on the Halifax-Edgecombe County line and flows se into Conoho Creek in Martin County.

Ethram Boney Bay, a large sandy loam marsh in s Duplin County.

Etna, community in n Macon County on Lakey Creek.

Etowah, community in w Henderson County. Alt. 2,101. The name comes from the Cherokee word I'tawa or Et-toh-wah, an unidentified kind of tree.

Eubanks, community in s Orange County.

Euchulla Cove, w Swain County between Wiggins Creek and Nantahala River.

Eufola, community in w Iredell County on Southern Railway. Alt. 788. Prior to 1903 known as Deep Cut and the railroad station was Plotts. May have been named for the Eufaula or Yufala Indian tribe in Georgia.

Eupeptic Springs, community and former resort (1860's-1870's) in nw Iredell County. Known as Powder Springs prior to development as a resort by Dr. John Ford, who renamed it Eupeptic (good digestion).

Eure, town in w Gates County. Alt. 22. Inc. 1915 but no longer active in municipal affairs.

Eureka, community in central Moore County. Originally centered about Eureka Farm Life School, est. about 1915. In 1920, James Rogers McConnell Hospital was built here; later moved to Pinehurst and now known as Moore Memorial Hospital. McConnell lost his life in World War I, serving in the Lafayette Escadrille.

Eureka, town in ne Wayne County near the head of Watery Branch. Inc. 1879 as Saul's Cross Roads; name changed 1901.

Eurins Creek rises in e central Stokes County and flows se into Rockingham County where it enters Dan River. Perhaps a variant of the older forms Hewins, Hewings, and Hughens.

Eury Lake, central Montgomery County on Little River, approx. 8 mi. s of Troy. Constructed about 1914 by S. J. and W. G. Smitherman and J. C. Hurley to provide electric power. Covers 80 acres with a shoreline of approx. 3 mi. Later owned by Carolina Power and Light Company but sold in 1962 to the Montgomery County Hunt Club, Inc. Known as Hurley Lake until 1916 when the present name came into use.

Euto. See New Salem.

Evans, community in sw Chatham County.

Evans Branch rises in central Clay County and flows sw into Johnson Mill Creek.

Evans Branch rises in w Haywood County and flows s into Jonathans Creek.

Evans Creek rises in s Macon County and flows nw into Tessentee Creek.

Evansdale, community in s Wilson County. Post office, 1908-1910. Named for one Evans who operated a sawmill at the site.

Evans Gap, w Swain County between Greasy Branch and Flat Branch.

Evans Knob, se Buncombe County s of Jobs Peak near the McDowell County line.

Evans Knob, w Swain County between Fishtrap Branch and Tuckasegee River. Alt. 2,481.

Evans Mountain, w Henderson County at the head of South Fork.

Evans Ridge, n Clay County, extends ne from Shearer Creek to Chestnut Stamp Knob.

Evan's Store Crossroad. See Winnabow.

Everett Creek rises in s Onslow County and flows e and n into New River.

Everett Mountain, s Macon County between Buck Creek and Emaline Gap.

Everetts, town in w Martin County. Settled about 1877. Inc. 1891 as Everitts; reincorporated 1893 as Everetts. Named for local family; S. F. and J. A. Everetts were commissioners of the town when incorporated. Alt. 66.

Everetts Creek rises in s New Hanover County and flows e into Myrtle Sound.

Everett's Crossroad, community in central Beaufort County.

Everetts Mill. See Cedar Falls.

Everetts Mill Pond, approx. 1 mi. long, in sw Richmond County on Marks Creek.

Evergreen, town in nw Columbus County. Settled 1870; inc. 1907. Named for surrounding pine forest. Alt. 104.

Evergreen Island, Pamlico Sound just off the central section of Portsmouth Island, e Carteret County.

Evergreen Slough inlet into e end of Portsmouth Island on Pamlico Sound side, e Carteret County.

Everitts. See Everetts.

Everittsville, former community near Dudley in s Wayne County. Prior to the Civil War a group of plantation owners built homes together here and went out daily to tend their nearby plantations. There were schools and churches, and in 1851 a post office, but not stores or other businesses. Named for Joseph Everitt, early settler. Only a cemetery remains to mark the site.

Ewart, community in n Mitchell County on Big Rock Creek.

Ewing, community in w Wake County.

Excelsior. *See* Rutherford College.

Exeter, former town in e Pender County on the e side of Northeast Cape Fear River on a high sandy bluff between Sand Hill Cove and Jumping Run. Flourished from about 1740 to 1790. Inc. 1754 as New Exeter, for Exeter, England, but it seems generally to have been known as Exeter. Appears on the Collet map, 1770, as Exeter. Began to decline as South Washington (*which see*) grew in importance after 1790 but appears on the Purcell map, 1792. Rutherfords Mill (later Ashe's Mill) was located nearby in the nineteenth century. In 1781, during the Revolution, British Major Sir James Henry Craig constructed field fortifications here which are still visible. Headquarters of the Holly Shelter State Game Management Area now occupy the approximate site.

Exum, community in nw Brunswick County.

Exum Mill Branch rises in e Wayne County and flows e and ne into The Slough. Named for early settlers who had a mill on this stream in the late eighteenth century.

Exum Store, community in ne Wayne County between Turner Swamp and Ivy Swamp.

Exway, community in n Richmond County on the Montgomery County line. A crossroads community, the name X-Way was recommended to the post office department when a post office was about to be est. The name was accepted but the spelling was altered.

Ezzell Mill Pond. *See* McLamb Mill Pond.

F

Face Rock, peak in the Swannanoa Mountains, s Buncombe County, between Ballard Gap and Buckey Mountain.

Face Rock, peak at the w end of Bearwallow Mountain on the Buncombe-Henderson County line.

Factor Branch rises in central Haywood County and flows ne into Lake Junaluska. Name for a 'factory" which once stood nearby. This was a large warehouse where plants and herbs were collected, graded, dried, and packed for shipment.

Factory Branch rises in w Macon County and flows sw into Nantahala River.

Factory Branch. *See* Factor Branch.

Fagansville. *See* Carthage.

Faggart Mine. *See* Nash Mine.

Faggarts, community in central Cabarrus County.

Faggarts Township. *See* Watts Cross Roads Township.

Faggs Creek rises in n Stokes County and flows s into Dan River.

Fain Cove, e Cherokee County through which a short tributary of Slow Creek flows.

Fain Mountain, central Cherokee County extends ne from Laurel Creek.

Fair Bluff, town in w Columbus County on a bluff overlooking Lumber River. Authorized to be laid off on the lands of John Wooton at Fair Bluff in 1807 and to be known as Wootonton. The authorized name apparently was not adopted as Fair Bluff appears on the Price map, 1808, and on the MacRae map, 1833. Reinc. in 1873 as Fair Bluff. Alt. 69.

Fair Bluff Township, w Columbus County.

Fairfax, community in nw Swain County on Lake Cheoah.

Fairfield, town on the n shore of Lake Mattamuskeet in central Hyde County. Alt. 3. Inc. 1885. Said to have been named for "fair fields" of crops grown on adjacent reclaimed swampland.

Fairfield, community in e Union County between Richardson Creek and Niggerhead Creek.

Fairfield Falls, s Jackson County on Trays Island Creek, near n edge of Fairfield Lake. Alt. approx. 3,200.

Fairfield Lake, s Jackson County on Trays Island Creek formed in 1910. Covers 100 acres and has maximum depth of 40 ft. Used for fishing, swimming, boating and as a power source. Not open to the public. *See also* Fairfield Falls.

Fairfield Ridge, se Clay County between Scaly Ridge and Bear Pen Ridge.

Fairfield Township, n central Hyde County.

The Fair Grounds. *See* Ellerbe.

Fair Grove. *See* Cedar Lodge.

Fairmont, town in s Robeson County. Known first as Ashpole for nearby Ashpole Swamp. Inc. 1899 as Union City; name changed to Ashpole, 1901; and to Fairmont, 1907. Largest North Carolina Border Belt tobacco market.

Fairmont. See Southmont.

Fairmont Township, s Robeson County.

Fair Mountain, s Watauga County on the head of Laurel Creek.

Fairntosh, community in n Durham County. Named for the plantation of Duncan Cameron (1777-1853); house built 1802 still stands. Former post office here was named Stagville. Alt. 284.

Fairplains, community in central Wilkes County near Long Branch.

Fairport, community in e Granville County.

Fairview, community in se Buncombe County.

Fairview, community in nw Macon County on Queens Creek.

Fairview, community in s Surry County. Alt. 1,109. Formerly known as Fairview Crossroads and earlier as Alberty.

Fairview, community in n Union County between Crooked Creek and Goose Creek. Formerly known as Benton Crossroads.

Fairview Gap, s Buncombe County ne of Concord Mountain.

Fairview Township, se Buncombe County.

Faison, town in nw Duplin County. Est. as Faison's Depot about 1833 on the land of Henry Faison. Inc. as Faison's Depot in 1872 through the efforts of Elias Faison, landowner and stockholder in the Wilmington and Raleigh Railroad. Received postal service from nearby Wrightsville as early as 1822. Fruit and vegetable market; produces cucumber pickles. Alt. 166.

Faisons Old Tavern, community in central Northampton County between Corduroy and Wildcat Swamps. Named for a tavern operated here by the Faison family. The community of Odamsville, which had a post office as early as 1830, is traditionally said to have been the predecessor of Faisons Old Tavern.

Faison Township, nw Duplin County.

Faith, town in s Rowan County. Inc. 1903. Named for a granite quarry opened here by J. T. Wyatt who lacked experience in quarrying but went ahead with his work "on faith."

Falcon, town in ne Cumberland County on Mingo Swamp. Alt. 125. Known as Starling's Bridge from as early as 1863 until 1893 when a post office was established here. Inc. 1913. When a name was being sought for the post office, it is said that J. A. Culbreth glanced at a box of Falcon pens on the shelf of a country store and said, "Name it Falcon."

Falkland, town in w Pitt County. Post office est. here in 1813 as Bensborough, changed to Falkland in 1838. Inc. 1887. Said to have been named for Falkland, Scotland, long the home of Scottish kings; or may have been named for the Falkland Islands which the British had long claimed but only finally occupied a few years before Bensborough was changed to Falkland. Alt. 76.

Falkland Township, nw Pitt County. Formerly named California township.

Fall Branch rises in central Alamance County and flows ne into Haw River.

Fall Branch rises in central Avery County at Bellvue Mountain and flows sw into North Toe River.

Fall Branch rises in central Avery County near Big Elk Mountain and flows s into Plumtree Creek.

Fall Branch rises in w Avery County near Big Yellow Bald Mountain and flows s into Roaring Creek.

Fall Branch rises in central Avery County near Blood Camp Ridge and flows sw into North Toe River.

Fall Branch rises in ne Buncombe County and flows se into North Fork [Swannanoa River].

Fall Branch rises in e Cherokee County and flows se and sw into Hiwassee River.

Fall Branch rises in n Haywood County and flows nw into Cold Springs Creek.

Fall Branch rises in w Macon County and flows ne into Burningtown Creek.

Fall Branch rises in e Macon County and flows nw into Mica City Creek.

Fall Branch rises in w Madison County and flows s into Roaring Fork.

Fall Branch rises in e Wake County and flows e into Little River.

Fall Branch rises in s Yancey County and flows nw into Big Lost Cove Creek.

Fallcliff, community in w Jackson County on Cullowhee Creek.

Fall Creek rises in e Mitchell County and flows s into Little Rock Creek.

Fall Creek rises in e Haywood County and flows sw into Crabtree Creek.

Fall Creek rises in e Lee County and flows ne into Cape Fear River.

Fall Creek rises in sw Polk County and flows ne into Pacolet River.

Fall Creek rises in n Yadkin County and flows nw into Yadkin River.

Fall Creek. See Honeycutt Creek.

Fall Creek Township, ne Yadkin County.

Falling Branch rises in n Franklin County and flows sw into Tooles Creek.

Falling Creek rises in nw Catawba County and flows ne into Catawba River.

Falling Creek rises in sw Greene County and flows se across Lenoir County into Neuse River. Appears in local records as early as 1730-1735.

Falling Creek rises in ne Sampson County and flows ne into w Wayne County where it enters Beaverdam Creek. See also Thoroughfare Swamp.

Falling Creek rises in e Richmond County and flows w into Hitchcock Creek.

Falling Creek, community in n Lenoir County on the stream of the same name. The Croom family operated a store here early in the nineteenth century and it was the location of a free public school in 1840.

Falling Creek. See Thoroughfare Swamp.

Falling Creek Township, central Lenoir County.

Falling Hollow sw Watauga County on the head of Watauga River.

Falling Rock Creek rises in w Haywood County, Great Smoky Mountains National Park, near lat. 35° 36' 56" N., long. 83° 10' 40" W. Flows ne to join Beech Creek in forming Palmer Creek. Named when an overhanging rock cliff on a stream where hunters, fishermen and others camped, fell when heated by a big camp fire. One person was killed and others injured.

Falling Run. See Deep Creek.

Falling Water Branch rises in s Yancey County and flows w into Cane River.

Fall line, the dividing line between coastal plain and piedmont North Carolina where the soft sedimentary soils of the coastal plains meet the hard rocks of the piedmont. It often is marked in streams by falls and rapids. The fall line runs w of Wilson and e of Sanford in an irregular progression north and south.

Fall Ridge, s Watauga County extends s in Watauga Township, causes a bend in Boone Fork.

Falls, community in n Wake County on Neuse River. See also Falls of the Neuse.

Falls Branch rises in s Macon County and flows s into Rabun County, Georgia, where it enters Barkers Creek.

Falls Branch rises in s Macon County and flows s into North Fork Coweeta Creek.

Falls Branch rises in e Macon County and flows s into North Prong Ellijay Creek.

Falls Branch rises in se Swain County and flows n into Yalaka Creek.

Falls Branch rises in e Swain County and flows nw into Tuckasegee River.

Falls Creek rises in n Avery County and flows w into Elk River.

Falls Creek rises in sw Chatham County and flows s into Moore County where it enters Deep River.

Falls Creek rises in n Cumberland County and flows ne into Carver Creek. Named for the falls just downstream from its junction with Carver Creek.

Falls of Gouges Creek, e Mitchell County.

Falls of the Neuse, rapids in Neuse River n Wake County near the community of Falls. Name appears on the Price map, 1808.

Fallston, town in ne Cleveland County. Settled 1885. Inc. 1893, but long inactive in municipal affairs. Alt. 950. Named for John Z. Falls, sheriff of the county when the town was incorporated.

Fallstown. See Bells Cross Roads.

Fallstown Township, sw Iredell County.

False Gap, on the Swain County, N. C.-Sevier County, Tenn., line in the Great Smoky Mountains National Park between The Sawteeth and Laurel Top.

Fancy Hill. See Loray.

Fannie Ridge, extends ne from the Henderson County line into s Buncombe County between Cole Cove and Reed Cove.

Faraby Island, a narrow sandy loam island about 1 mi. long, in the mouth of North Landing River, ne Currituck County. Sometimes called Ferebee's Island.

Far Creek rises in e Hyde County near Engelhard and flows se into Pamlico Sound. Appears as Gibbs Creek on the Collet map, 1770, and as recently as 1833 on other maps. In 1862 it was called Fur Creek and by 1882, Far Creek.

Far Creek. See Engelhard.

Farley Branch rises in n Graham County and flows e into Little Tennessee River.

Farley Cove follows the se course of a small stream flowing into Santeetlah Lake in w central Graham County.

Farlow Gap, nw Transylvania County between Klesee Creek and Shuck Ridge Creek. Alt. 4,559.

Farmer, town in w Randolph County. Inc. 1897, but long inactive in municipal affairs. In center of a rich farming community.

Farmer Branch rises in s Haywood County and flows nw into Richland Creek.

Farmer's Branch rises in w central Wilson County and flows s into Toisnot Swamp. Named prior to 1770 for Isaac Farmer, Sr.

Farmers Creek rises in n Yadkin County and flows n into Yadkin River.

Farmers Store, community in nw Ashe County.

Farmers Turnout. See Maco.

Farmer Top, central Cherokee County s of Hiwassee River and nw of Murphy.

Farmer Top, central Cherokee County near the headwaters of Dockery and Rose creeks.

Farmington, community in n Davie County. As early as 1805 former residents of Currituck County began to move into this area. [Two hurricanes in 1830 and another one in 1839 caused extensive crop damage in the Currituck County area; the population of the county dropped from 7,655 in 1830 to 6,703 in 1840.] This was known as Little Currituck until 1837 when a post office was est. and named Farmington for the fertile farming land here. Alt. 758.

Farmington Township, ne Davie County.

Farmville, town in w Pitt County. Settled about 1850 and known as New Town prior to 1872 when it was inc. as Farmville from the fact that it was in the center of rich farming land. Produces building materials. Alt. 86.

Farmville. See Coalglen.

Farmville Township, w Pitt County.

Farnell Bay, central Onslow County, is formed by an indentation of the e bank of New River, se of Hadnot Point.

Farnell Point, central Onslow County on the mouth of Wallace Creek.

Farner Branch rises in n Cherokee County and flows w into Cook Creek.

Faro, community in ne Wayne County near the head of Beaver Branch.

Farrar, former town in central Edgecombe County on the sw limits of Tarboro and now wholly within Tarboro. The name West Tarboro was changed to Hilma in 1893 when it was inc. Name changed from Hilma to Farrar, 1899, probably for O. C. Farrar who purchased land in Tarboro for a cotton mill. Charter repealed, 1909.

Farrars Island in the Cape Fear River at the junction of the Chatham, Harnett, and Lee County lines, nw of Buckhorn Falls. Approx. 1½ mi. long. Mentioned as early as 1819 in a survey of the rivers of the state.

Farrington, community in ne Chatham County. Named for local Fearrington family at the time of the construction of the Durham and Southern Railroad.

Fate Puett Cove, e Cherokee County on the headwaters of Burl Branch, se of Indian Grave Gap.

Faucette. See Calvander

Faucette Township, former township in n central Alamance County. Now township number 5.

Faucetts Store, community in nw Halifax County.

Faucett Township, central Halifax County.

Faulk, community in se Union County.

Faulkner Creek rises in ne Surry County and flows sw into Ararat River. Probably named for William Faulkner, an eighteenth-century resident of the county.

Faust, community in e Madison County on Big Laurel Creek.

Fawn Branch rises near Burl Mountain in n central Transylvania County and flows se into King Creek.

Fawn Mountain, e Yancey County between Blue Rock Branch and a bend in South Toe River.

Fax Creek rises in n Graham County and flows ne into Little Tennessee River.

Fayette County was formed in July, 1784, when an act of the General Assembly divided Cumberland County into Fayette and Moore counties. It was intended to honor Marquis de Lafayette (1757-1834), who visited the United States that year. Fayette County retained the courthouse in Fayetteville. In October of the same year the act was amended to retain the name Cumberland for the county.

Fayette District at the time of the 1790 census was composed of Anson, Cumberland, Moore, Richmond, Robeson, and Sampson counties and the town of Fayetteville.

Fayetteville, city and county seat, central Cumberland County, at the head of navigation on the Cape Fear River. The first settlement at the site was about 1730. Inc. 1762 as Campbellton, named for Farquhard Campbell. In 1778 Campbellton, and the adjacent trading center of Cross Creek, *which see,* were consolidated as Lower and Upper Campbellton, respectively. Name changed to Fayetteville in 1783 in honor of Marquis de Lafayette (1757-1834), who assisted the Americans during the Revolutionary War. The legislature met here 1786, 1788-90, 1793-94. Location of Fayetteville State Teachers College and the North Carolina Methodist College. Produces textiles, dairy products, bakery products, machinery, lumber, and bottled carbonated drinks. Alt. 107. Fort Bragg, *which see*, is nearby.

Featherston Creek rises in n Henderson County and flows sw into Mud Creek.

Fed Cove, on a tributary of Caler Fork in e Macon County.

Federal Point projects from the s tip of New Hanover County between Cape Fear River and the Atlantic Ocean.

Federal Point Township, s New Hanover County.

Fed Gap, e Macon County between Fed Cove and Mason Mountain.

Feds Branch rises in n Yancey County and flows s into Cane River.

Fee Branch rises in s Yancey County and flows se into Rock Creek.

Feeding Ridge, n Mitchell County between Cook Branch and Gouges Creek.

Feezor, community in s Davidson County. Named for local family.

Felts, community in se Wilkes County. Named for a local family.

Fender Mountain, peak in the Peach Bottom Mountain range, w Alleghany County. Alt. approx. 3,600.

Fenix, community in w Cumberland County.

Fentress. *See* Pleasant Garden.

Fentress Township, s central Guilford County. Named for Frederick Fentriss.

Ferebee's Island. *See* Faraby Island.

Ferguson, community in w Wilkes County on Yadkin River. Named for Captain Lindsay C. Ferguson, a nineteenth-century resident.

Ferguson Hill, central Yancey County between Pine Swamp Branch, Cane River, and Bowlens Creek.

Ferguson Peak, on the Buncombe-Henderson County line, se of Hickory Nut Gap.

Fern Knob, n Swain County in Great Smoky Mountains National Park on Suli Ridge between Jonas Creek and Huggins Creek. Alt. 3,780.

Fern Mountain, n Jackson County on the ne end of Black Mountain. Alt. 5,200.

Fernside, community in central New Hanover County. Est. 1908 and named for Fernside Fertilizer plant. Alt. 15.

Ferrells Creek rises in s Orange County and flows s into Chatham County where it enters Haw River.

Ferrell's Springs Branch rises in ne Wake County and flows se into Upper Barton's Creek.

Ferrells Township, sw Nash County.

Ferrin Knob, on the Buncombe-Henderson County line between Beaverdam and Long gaps.

Ferry, community in s Rutherford County formerly known as Ferry Store.

Ferry Branch rises in w Madison County and flows ne into French Broad River.

Fetner, community in w Wake County.

Few, community in s Durham County. Formerly known as Oyama, the name of a Japanese city given the community when a railroad station opened here about 1904. The name was changed after the attack on Pearl Harbor, December 7, 1941, to honor Dr. William P. Few (1867-1940), first president of Duke University.

Fiars Creek. *See* Fires Creek.

Fiddler Creek rises in s Forsyth County and flows sw into South Fork. Named for Fidler or Fiedler family living in the vicinity by 1777. Appears as James Creek on Collet map, 1770.

Fiddlers Run rises in central Burke County and flows n into Sandy Run Creek.

Fie Creek rises in w Haywood County and flows s into Jonathans Creek.

Field Branch rises in w Hoke County on Fort Bragg Military Reservation and flows e into Rockfish Creek. Earlier known as Old Field Branch. Leslies Mill Pond, now drained, was formerly on this creek.

Fields, community in nw Lenoir County. Alt. 111. Named for a local family.

Fieldsboro. *See* Walstonburg.

Fie Top Mountain, w Haywood County. Alt. 5,040-5,060. A ski run is now maintained here.

Fifth Creek rises in n central Iredell County and flows e into South Yadkin River. A portion of this stream in the Bethany Community is known as Five Mile Branch. It is the fifth creek in a series of creeks crossed by early settlers from Salisbury.

Fifth Creek. *See* Deep Creek.

Fig, community in w central Ashe County. Alt. approx. 2,880.

Figure Eight Island, e New Hanover and Pender counties between Middle Sound and the Atlantic Ocean and extending from Mason Inlet on the s to Rich Inlet on the n. In 1965 work was begun to develop the island as a resort beach. A

260-foot causeway and a bridge over the Intracoastal Waterway connect it with the mainland.

Fillie Gap, ne Buncombe County e of Mc-Kinney Gap.

Filmore, community in w Wilson County.

Filo. See Biscoe.

Finch Cove, e Haywood County on Rush Fork.

Fincher Mountain, central Haywood County on the head of McElroy Branch.

Fincher's Branch rises in ne Orange County and flows s into Buck Quarter Creek. It was named for Jonathan Fincher who acquired land in the vicinity in 1755.

Finchs Crossroad. See Denton.

Finch's Mill Pond, w Wilson County on Bloomery Swamp. Formed 1875 and named for owner. Covers 30 acres; max. depth, 10 ft. Fishing, boating. Finch Mill post office, 1898-1901.

Findley Creek rises in central Henderson County and flows ne and s into Perry Creek.

Fines Creek rises in ne Haywood County and sw into Waterville Lake on Pigeon River. Named for a scout who was killed in 1783 when he and others were chasing some Indians who had stolen their horses.

Fines Creek, community in n Haywood County on the creek of the same name. Settled about 1850.

Fines Creek Gap, ne Haywood County on the head of Fines Creek. Alt. 3,948.

Fines Creek Township, ne Haywood County.

Finger, community in w Stanly County.

Finley, community on the upper waters of the Yadkin River in n Caldwell County Named for Finley P. Curtis who was active in securing the first post office for the community.

Fire Gap Ridge, w Macon County between Roaring Fork Creek and Jarrett Creek.

Firescald Branch rises in w Avery County and flows s into Henson Creek.

Firescald Branch rises in w Yancey County and flows se into Big Creek.

Firescald Creek rises in n McDowell County on the sw slope of Betsy Ridge and flows sw into Slim Creek.

Fire Scald Knob, se Alleghany County about three miles se of Bullhead Mountain.

Firescald Mountain, w Avery County.

Firescald Mountain, w Yancey County between Simms Fork and Elk Wallow Creek. Alt. 4,840.

Firescald Ridge, n Graham County extends

ne from Bearpen Gap to Little Tennessee River.

Firescald Ridge extends se from Deep Gap to Snowbird Creek in sw Graham County.

Fire Scald Ridge, s Haywood County between West Hollow and West Fork Pigeon River.

Firescald Ridge, n Jackson County between Blackrock Creek and Shut-in Creek.

Firescald Ridge, sw Macon County between Park Creek and Pat Stable Branch.

Firescald Ridge, n Swain County in Great Smoky Mountains National Park, a spur of Welch Ridge extending se between Jonas Creek and Little Jonas Creek.

Fires Creek rises in n Clay County and flows sw into Hiwasseee River. Appears as Fiars Creek in the 1861 law establishing the county.

First Broad River rises in e Rutherford County and flows se into Cleveland County. There it flows se and sw into Broad River. Appears on the Collet map, 1770, as Sandy River.

First Gum Swamp. See Gum Swamp.

First Hurricane Branch rises in s Swain County and flows sw into Yalaka Creek.

First Potts Creek rises in w Davidson County and flows se into High Rock Lake on Yadkin River. Appears on the Collet map, 1770, as Potts Creek.

Fish Creek rises in e Guilford County and flows ne across the nw corner of Alamance County into Caswell County where it enters Buttermilk Creek.

Fish Creek rises in w Harnett County and flows ne into Cape Fear River.

Fishcreek. See Mamers.

Fishdam Creek rises in w Wilkes County and flows se into Yadkin River. Known as Fish Trap Creek until the 1960's when the spillway of one of the flood control dams in connection with the W. Kerr Scott Dam emptied into it and the name was changed.

Fisher Creek rises in n Jackson County and flows s into Scott Creek.

Fisher Lake, on a tributary of Watkins Creek in s Macon County.

Fisherman Bay, e Pamlico County, in the Bay River estuary.

Fisherman Islands, two small tidal marsh islands, e Pamlico County, in the Bay River estuary se of Bay Point.

Fishermare Branch rises in n Cherokee County on Fishermare Ridge and flows s into Hyatt Creek.

Fishermare Ridge, n Cherokee County in the Snowbird Mountains.

Fisher Peak, mountain on the Surry County, N. C.-Carroll County, Va., line. Alt. 3,609.

Fisher River rises in Virginia and flows s into Surry County and se across the county into Yadkin River. Appears on the Collet map, 1770.

Fiser's Ford. See Cooleemee.

Fisher Swamp rises in ne Craven County and flows sw into Little Swift Creek.

Fisherville, community in s Forsyth County.

Fishhawk Mountain, s Macon County between Little Fishhawk Mountain and Wolf Rock. Alt. 4,684.

Fish Hawk Point, ne Carteret County extending into Rumley Bay.

Fishing Branch rises in n Person County and flows nw into Marlowe Creek.

Fishing Creek rises in e Granville County and flows s into Tar River.

Fishing Creek rises in nw New Hanover County and flows ne into Cape Fear River. See also Longs Island.

Fishing Creek rises in s Wilkes County in the Brushy Mountains and flows ne into Yadkin River.

Fishing Creek rises in e Vance County and flows ne in Vance and Warren counties, and se and s in Warren County, to the Franklin-Warren, Halifax-Nash, and Halifax-Edgecombe County lines to a point approx. 7 mi. n of Tarboro from where it flows s to enter Tar River. It appears as Great Fishing Creek on the Moseley map, 1733, and on the Collet map, 1770.

Fishing Creek District. See Fishing Creek Town.

Fishing Creek Township, e central Granville County. A Fishing Creek District had 59 heads of families in 1790.

Fishing Creek Township, se Warren County.

Fishing Creek Township, former township in central Wilkes County, now a part of Wilkesboro Township.

Fishprong Branch rises in e Clay County and flows se into Barnett Creek.

Fish Ridge, n Haywood County extends s beside Morgan Creek.

Fishton, community in w Polk County on Green River.

Fishtown. See Beaufort.

Fishtrap Branch rises in e Swain County and flows ne into Tuckasegee River.

Fish Trap Creek. See Fishdam Creek.

Fitch, community in s Caswell County, formerly known as Fitch's Store. A post office was operated here during the approx. period 1870-1920.

Fitches Knob, se Wilkes County. Alt. 1,850.

Fites Creek rises in e Gaston County and flows se into Catawba River.

Fitts, community in n central Warren County. Post office est. in 1895, but discontinued in 1905. Named for the first postmaster, Edward F. Fitts.

Five Comb Branch rises in ne Cherokee County and flows se and sw into Valley River.

Five Forks, community in n Person County.

Five Forks, community in sw Stokes County. A post office by this name existed in the late nineteenth century.

Five Forks, community in n Warren County s of Gaston Lake and e of Jordans Creek. Settled about 1880. Alt. 400.

Five Forks, community in n Yadkin County.

Fivemile Branch rises in central Columbus County, flows se then n into Cedar Branch.

Five Mile Branch. See Fifth Creek.

Five Mile Creek rises in e Robeson County and flows sw into Saddletree Swamp.

Five Points, community in ne Cabarrus County.

Five Points, community in w Hoke County.

Flag Branch rises in se Union County and flows ne into Rays Fork.

Flannery Fork [of South Fork New River] rises in Moses H. Cone Memorial Park approx. 2 mi. nw of town of Blowing Rock, s Watauga County, and flows w into Trout Lake and then ne to join East Fork and Middle Fork in forming South Fork New River approx. 2 mi. se of town of Boone.

Flat Branch rises in w Brunswick County and flows s into Wet Ash Swamp.

Flat Branch rises near Lookoff Gap in se Buncombe County and flows se into Rocky Fork.

Flat Branch rises in ne Cherokee County and flows s into Valley River.

Flat Branch rises in ne Cherokee County and flows nw into Collett Creek.

Flat Branch rises in nw Gates County and flows se through Jones Swamp into Hacklan Branch.

Flat Branch rises in n Haywood County and flows nw into Laurel Creek.

Flat Branch rises in s Mecklenburg County and flows sw into Sixmile Creek.

Flat Branch rises in w Mitchell County and flows sw into Nolichucky River.

Flat Branch rises in w Surry County and flows e into Fisher River.

Flat Branch rises in w Swain County and flows nw into Tuckasegee River.

Flat Branch rises in s Watauga County and flows se into Buffalo Branch.

Flat Branch rises in se Watauga County and flows ne into Laurel Fork.

Flat Branch, community in e Gates County.

Flat Branch. See Sweetwater Creek.

Flat Branch Gap, on the Jackson-Macon County line.

Flat Creek rises in se Buncombe County and flows se into Broad River. Appears as Upper Flat Creek on recent State Highway Commission maps.

Flat Creek rises in n Buncombe County near Watershed Ridge and flows sw into French Broad River.

Flat Creek rises in ne Buncombe County and flows sw through Montreat into Swannanoa River.

Flat Creek rises in e Granville County and flows ne into Vance County where it enters Nutbush Creek.

Flat Creek rises on the Fort Bragg Military Reservation in n Hoke County and flows ne into Little River.

Flat Creek rises in s Jackson County and flows n into Bear Creek Lake on the Tuckasegee River.

Flat Creek rises in sw Jackson County and flows n into Mill Creek.

Flat Creek rises in se Rowan County and flows e approx. 4½ mi. into Yadkin River. Known also as Flat Swamp Creek.

Flat Creek rises in ne Swain County in Great Smoky Mountains National Park and flows se into Bunches Creek.

Flat Creek formed in s Transylvania County by the junction of South Fork and North Fork and flows ne into West Fork French Broad River.

Flat Creek rises in w Vance County and flows ne into Kerr Reservoir.

Flat Creek, community in n Buncombe County. Alt. 2,161.

Flat Creek Bald, ne Swain County in Great Smoky Mountains National Park on the n end of Overlook Ridge. Alt. 5,240.

Flat Creek Falls, se Buncombe County on Flat Creek.

Flat Creek Township, n central Buncombe County.

Flat Fork Creek rises in central Anson County and flows n into Brown Creek.

Flat Gap, e central Burke County.

Flat Gap, w Haywood County on Eaglenest Ridge.

Flat Gap, on the Jackson-Haywood County line.

Flat Knob, n Macon County at the head of Rhinehart Creek.

Flat Land Branch rises in e central Avery County and flows s into Wilson Creek.

Flat Laurel Creek rises in s Haywood County and flows nw into West Fork Pigeon River.

Flat Laurel Gap, on the Haywood-Transylvania County line between Big Bald and Little Bald Mountain.

Flat Mountain, s Jackson County between East Fork Chattooga River and Whitewater River. Also called Flattop Mountain. Alt. 3,931.

Flat Mountain, se Macon County between Cullasaja River and Big Creek.

Flat River is formed in s Person County by the junction of North Flat River and South Flat River. It flows se into n Durham County and se across the county to join Eno River in forming Neuse River. Appears on the Moseley map, 1733.

Flat River Township, s central Person County.

Flat Rock, mountain in e central Avery County.

Flat Rock, residential community adjacent to East Flat Rock, which see, central Henderson County. Alt. 2,207. A post office as early as 1830. Named for a smooth outcropping of granite which was a Cherokee Indian ceremonial ground centuries ago.

Flat Rock, community in w Stokes County.

Flat Rock, community in ne Surry County. Named for a nearby open-faced granite quarry, the largest in the world, at which work was begun in 1889.

Flat Rock Branch rises in n Nash County and flows ne into Swift Creek.

Flatrock Creek rises in n Franklin County and flows se into Sandy Creek.

Flat Rock Creek rises in sw Wilkes County and flows se through the corner of Yadkin County and into Iredell County where it enters Hunting Creek. Sometimes known locally as North Hunting Creek.

Flats, a tourist resort and community in se Macon County near the head of Middle Creek. It is on an elevation which extends se from Middle Creek in Macon County into Rabun County, Georgia.

Flat Shoal Creek rises in s central Stokes County and flows ne into Dan River.

Flat Shoal Mountain, central Stokes County parallel to Flat Shoal Creek.

Flat Shoals, community in s central Stokes County.

Flat Springs, sw Yancey County at the head of Indian Fork.

Flat Springs Creek rises in Tennessee and flows e into n Avery County where it enters Beech Creek.

Flat Springs Gap, on the Buncombe-Yancey County line between Flat Springs Knob and Big Butt.

Flat Springs Knob, on the Buncombe-Yancey County line ne of Flat Springs Gap at lat. 35° 47' 30" N., long. 82° 20' 30" W. Alt. 5,700-5,800. Sometimes also known as Flattop.

Flats Township, s central Macon County.

Flat Swamp rises in s Hertford County and flows se to join Horse Swamp in forming Bear Swamp.

Flat Swamp rises in n Jones County and flows s into Rattlesnake Branch.

Flat Swamp rises in w Martin County and flows se into Tranters Creek.

Flat Swamp rises in sw Onslow County and flows nw into Pender County where it enters Shaking Creek.

Flat Swamp Creek rises in e central Bertie County and flows sw into Hoggard Mill Creek. Flat Swamp is mentioned in local records as early as 1724.

Flat Swamp Creek rises in e Davidson County and flows sw into Yadkin River.

Flat Swamp Creek. See Flat Creek.

Flat Swamp Mountain, a long mountain in s Davidson and e Rowan counties through which the Yadkin River cut a channel. Geologists have expressed the belief that the mountain is the remnant of ancient lava flow.

Flatt Creek. See Big Flatty Creek.

Flat Top, peak on Flat Top Mountain, se Buncombe County, between Lookoff Gap and High Hickory Knob in Swannanoa Mountains.

Flat Top, mountain knob in central Caldwell County.

Flattop, peak in n Yancey County n of Big Creek. Alt. approx. 4,807.

Flattop. See Flat Springs Knob.

Flattop Branch rises in s Watauga County at the sw end of Flattop Mountain and flows se into Middle Fork [of South Fork New River].

Flattop Cliffs. See Flattop Mountain.

Flattop Creek rises in e central Avery County and flows n into Banner Elk Creek.

Flattop Mountain, e Avery County. Alt. approx. 5,050. Known also as Flattop Cliffs.

Flat Top Mountain, se Buncombe County between Trantham Creek and Flat Branch.

Flattop Mountain, s Watauga County, nw of Blowing Rock. Alt. 4,568.

Flattop Mountain, n Yancey County, extends ne from the head of Deer Creek to Nolichucky River.

Flattop Mountain. See Flat Mountain.

Flattop Mountain Branch rises in nw Yancey County and flows w into Tennessee where it enters Spivey Creek.

Flatt's Creek. See Salmon Creek.

Flatty Creek. See Big Flatty Creek.

Flatwood Gap, nw Macon County. Alt. 1,475.

The Flatwoods, level land at the head of Shoal Creek in sw Henderson County.

Flax Creek rises in sw Cherokee County and flows se into Persimmon Creek.

Flay, community in w Lincoln County.

Fleaback Mountain, s Clay County between Needmore Branch and Hothouse Branch. Alt. 3,165.

Flea Branch rises in e Madison County and flows s into Laurel Creek.

Flea Mountain, central Cherokee County between Dockery and Cook creeks.

Fleetwood, community in s Ashe County.

Fleetwood Point, extends from mainland of ne Dare County into Croatan Sound.

Fleming's Creek. See Raymonds Creek.

Flemington. See Brassfield.

Flemington. See Lake Waccamaw (town).

Fletcher, community in n Henderson County. Alt. 2,112. Named for Dr. George W. Fletcher, popular country doctor and surgeon during the Civil War. Est. about 1883 after the railroad was completed. With the development of Fletcher, Shufordville, approx. 2 mi. n, declined and the post office there was transferred to Fletcher and the name changed. Produces textiles.

Fletcher Branch rises in n Henderson County and flows nw into Cane Creek.

Fletcher Creek rises in nw Henderson County and flows se where it joins Big Creek to form North Fork.

Fletcher Knob, w Caldwell County. Named for Reuben Fletcher, Revolutionary soldier.

Flint, community in w Wake County.

Flint Gap, nw Cherokee County in the Unicoi Mountains.

Flint Gap, ne Graham County between Meetinghouse Mountain and Little Tennessee River.

Flint Hill, se Cleveland County between Jolly Mountain and Sandy Run Creek.

Flint Hill, community in n Montgomery County.

Flint Hill, community in w Randolph County.

Flint Hill, community in e Yadkin County near Yadkin River. A late nineteenth century post office here was named Shore. Inc. 1903 as Shore by A. E. Shore and others for the legal manufacturing of whiskey. Charter repealed 1911. Present name adopted prior to 1924.

Flint Hill. See Cherry Mountain.

Flint Hill. See Scottville.

Flint Hill Creek rises in e Rutherford County and flows ne into Cleveland County where it enters Hinton Creek.

Flint Knob, se Buncombe County between Miner and Sam gaps.

Flint Level Branch rises in w Madison County and flows sw into French Broad River.

Flint Rock Gap, n Macon County near the head of Sugar Cove Creek.

Flint Spring Branch rises in n Clay County and flows se into Fires Creek.

Flinty. See Newdale.

Flinty Gap on the McDowell-Yancey County line between Green Knob and Big Craggy.

Floral College, community in nw Robeson County. Alt. 193. Named for a woman's college which operated here from 1841 until 1878. One of the earliest colleges for women in the South, it was named for the wild flowers growing in profusion in the area.

Florence, community in e Pamlico County on Bald Creek. Known earlier as Spring Creek; named for Florence, wife of Stanley Martin, first postmaster.

Flounder Slue Rock, two small islands in Pamlico Sound, ne Carteret County n of Portsmouth Island. In 1795 these islands were called Flounder Rocks.

Flower Cove, s Swain County on the head of Marr Branch.

Flower Gap, s Haywood County between Nigger Springs and Dina Branch.

Flower Hill, worn down remains of an ancient mountain, n Johnston County between Emit community and Moccasin Creek. Rhododendron flourishes here.

Flower Knob, s Haywood County on the head of Little East Fork Pigeon River.

Flowers Gap, at the head of Coon Creek in e Macon County.

Flowers Swamp rises in e Robeson County and flows sw into Lumber River.

Flows Store, community in s Cabarrus County, named for Daniel W. Flowe who opened a store here in 1881. Flowe's store, closed about 1925, still stands.

Floyds Creek rises in s Rutherford County and flows s into Broad River.

Flynn Ridge, s Yancey County between Setrock Creek and Whiteside Branch.

Fodderstack Mountain, nw Buncombe County between South Turkey and North Turkey creeks.

Fodderstack Mountain, se Macon County between Rich Gap and Satulah Mountain.

Fodderstack Mountain, e Transylvania County between Lydia Creek and French Broad River.

Fodderstack Mountain. See Terrapin Mountain.

Folkstone, community in s Onslow County. Alt. 69. Believed to have been named by a retired sea captain for his native town in England.

Folly Creek rises in w Henderson County and flows nw into Little Willow Creek.

Folly Fork, community in ne Gates County. Folly post office est. prior to 1828. Frequently in the seventeenth and eighteenth centuries the word Folly was used in the sense of the French folie, "delight," or "favorite abode," and it formed a part of the name of English estates.

Folly Swamp rises in ne Gates County and flows e into Dismal Swamp.

Fontana, former community in nw Swain County, est. 1902 by employees of Montvale Lumber Co. The site is now covered by the waters of Fontana Lake, which see. Said to have been named by Mrs. George Leidy Wood, wife of an official of the lumber company, because it was "a short word, musical, easy to spell" and it reminded her of "the waterfalls that looked like fountains, leaping from ledge to ledge" in the nearby forest.

Fontana Lake, n Graham and w and central Swain counties, on Little Tennessee River and its tributaries. Forms the s boundary of the Great Smoky Mountains National Park. Dam begun in 1941, completed in 1945, forms the lake, largest of the Tennessee Valley Authority system. Max. depth 480 ft. The lake, 30 mi. long, has a shoreline of 248 mi., and covers 10,530 acres at full lake. Provides flood control, electric power, and recreation facilities. The dam here is the highest in e America and the fourth highest in the world. Alt. 1,710. *See also* Fontana and Fontana Village.

Fontana Village, resort community in n Graham County in Welch Cove near Fontana Lake. Alt. 1,800. Built in 1941 as a construction village for the employees of Fontana Dam. After the dam was completed it was leased to a private corporation for development as a resort. *See also* Welch Cove.

Fontcal. *See* Wagram.

Fontena, formerly the plantation of the Baker family, located between Little Fishing Creek and Reedy Creek near the community of Grove Hill, s Warren County. The plantation house, no longer standing, was built in 1790 by Judge Blake Baker, Attorney General of North Carolina in 1794. In 1816 the library at Fontena was described as the finest in the state.

Fonville, community in s Harnett County.

Footsville, community in s Yadkin County near South Deep Creek. Known first as Footville.

Forbes, community in w Mitchell County on Toe River. Alt. 2,185.

Forbes Bay, e Pasquotank County between Cottage Point and Cobb Point on the Pasquotank River.

Forbes Millpond, central Pitt County on Greens Mill Run.

Forbush, community in central Yadkin County on Logan Creek.

Forbush Creek rises in n Yadkin County and flows se into Logan Creek.

Forbush Township, se Yadkin County.

Ford Creek rises in se Granville County and flows ne into western Franklin County where it enters Tar River.

Forest, community in central Craven County.

Forest City, town in s central Rutherford County. Alt. 869. Inc. 1877 as Burnt Chimney; named changed to Forest City in 1887 in honor of Forest Davis, lumber merchant.

Forest Grove, community in n Watauga County on Forest Grove Creek.

Forest Grove Creek rises in n Watauga County and flows sw into Beaverdam Creek.

Forest Hill, former town in central Carbarrus County. Inc. 1887 but now a part of

the city of Concord. Began as a mill settlement in the 1850's and named McDonalds Mill. Later known as Odell Mill, Locke Mills, and now the site of Randolph Mill.

Forestville, community in ne Wake County s of the town of Wake Forest. Inc. 1879; charter repealed 1915.

Forge Knob, on the Swain County, N. C.-Blount County, Tenn., line in Great Smoky Mountains National Park between Rich Gap and Buck Gap.

Forge Mountain, nw Henderson County between South Fork Mills River and Boylston Creek in Pisgah National Forest. Alt. 3,280. Granted to Philip Sitton about 1806 as a "forge bounty" where he manufactured iron for many years. Adjoining it was the Gillespie gun works where the famous long guns were fashioned from Sitton's iron.

Fork, town in se Davie County. Inc. 1895 as Fork Church, but long inactive in municipal affairs. Developed around Fork Baptist Church, organized in 1793. Alt. 824.

Fork Branch rises in ne Onslow County and flows ne into White Oak River.

Fork Branch rises in n Watauga County on Fork Ridge and flows sw into Little Beaverdam Creek.

Fork Church. *See* Fork.

Fork Creek rises in s Avery County and flows s into Three Mile Creek.

Fork Creek rises in s Randolph County and flows se into Deep River. Appears as Crooked Creek on the Collet map, 1770; as Pork Creek (perhaps a typographical error) on the Price map, 1808; and as Fork Creek on the MacRae map, 1833.

Forked Mountain, on the Henderson-Transylvania County line.

Forked Ridge, ne Buncombe County, sw of Slaty Branch.

Forked Ridge, on the Henderson-Transylvania County line.

Forked Ridge in w Watauga County extends nw between Grassy Gap and Beech Creek.

Forked Tree Mountain, ne Buncombe County between Burleson Branch and North Fork Ivy Creek.

Fork Legged Mountain, e Madison County at the head of California Creek.

Fork Mountain, central Avery County.

Fork Mountain, sw Buncombe County near the headwaters of Ballard Creek.

Fork Mountain, ne Buncombe County between Left Fork Creek and Beetree Creek.

Fork Mountain, n Caldwell County. Alt. 2,000. Named for its position near a fork in the Yadkin River.

Fork Mountain, w Haywood County, Great Smoky Mountains National Park, near lat. 35° 40' 14" N., long. 83° 07' W., on e slope of Indian Ridge.

Fork Mountain, e Haywood County between Pisgah Creek and Reed Creek.

Fork Mountain, nw Haywood County n of Conrad Branch in Great Smoky Mountains National Park. Alt. approx. 4,000.

Fork Mountain, s Macon County between Piney Knob Fork and Turtle Pond Creek.

Fork Mountain, n Macon and s Swain counties, parallel to Poplar Cove.

Fork Mountain, s Madison County. Alt. approx. 3,560.

Fork Mountain, n Mitchell County between Little Rock Creek and Roan Mountain. Alt. approx. 4,500. Named because, to an early settler, its three peaks resembled the tines of a fork.

Fork Mountain, n Rutherford County between Camp and Cane creeks. Alt. approx. 1,750.

Fork Mountain, s Swain County between Yalaka Creek and Bowers Creek.

Fork Mountain Branch rises in central Avery County and flows s into North Toe River.

Fork Mountain Township, central Mitchell County.

Fork Point, point of land at the mouth of Bond Creek in se Beaufort County at Pamlico River.

Fork Point a peninsula in w Beaufort County between Chocowinity Bay and Pamlico River.

Fork Point Island in Chocowinity Bay, w Beaufort County. Approx. ⅒ mi. long.

Fork Ridge, ne Cherokee County in the Snowbird Mountains.

Fork Ridge extends from central Cherokee County ne into n Cherokee County between Davis and Bald creeks.

Fork Ridge, n Clay County, extends ne between Little Fires Creek and Bald Spring Branch.

Fork Ridge, n Graham County between Oldfield Gap and Little Tennessee River.

Fork Ridge, w Graham County between Squally Creek and Hooper Mill Creek.

Fork Ridge, s Haywood County extends from the head of West Fork Pigeon River to the mouth of Middle Prong.

Fork Ridge, n Jackson County between Jones Knob and Yellow Face.

Fork Ridge, central Jackson County between Trout Creek and Mill Creek.

Fork Ridge, extends ne from Rattlesnake Ridge in ne Jackson County to Campbell Creek in w Haywood County.

Fork Ridge, w Jackson County between Dodgen Creek and Whiterock Creek.

Fork Ridge between North Fork and Plott Balsams in n Jackson County.

Fork Ridge, s Macon County between Shope Fork and Henson Creek.

Fork Ridge, s Macon County at the head of Peeks Creek.

Fork Ridge, n Mitchell County between Grassy Creek and Big Rock Creek.

Fork Ridge, n Mitchell County between Right Fork and Pigeonroost Creek.

Fork Ridge, n Swain County in Great Smoky Mountains National Park, a spur extending se from Mt. Collins.

Fork Ridge, n Swain County extends sw from Thomas Ridge between Left Fork and Right Fork to their confluence to form Indian Creek.

Fork Ridge, nw Watauga County. Begins near head of Little Beaverdam Creek at State Line Gap and extends s, branching sw and se to form an inverted Y. Highest point is about 4,300.

Fork Ridge, n Yancey County parallel to Hensley Branch.

Fork Ridge, s Yancey County between Middle Fork Rock Creek and North Fork Rock Creek.

Fork River Bald on the Haywood-Transylvania County line at the nw end of Fork River Ridge.

Fork River Ridge, nw Transylvania County extends se from Fork River Bald between Daniel Ridge Creek and Right Fork Davidson River.

Forks of Ivy, community on the Buncombe-Madison County line on Ivy Creek. Named from the fact that it is near the junction of Ivy and Little Ivy creeks. Alt. 1,978.

Forks of the Pigeon. See Canton.

Forks of Tar River. See Washington.

Fork Swamp rises in sw Beaufort County in Reedy Pocoson and flows s into Craven County where it enters Palmetta Swamp. Named because an adjacent road forks— one road leading to Pinetown and the other to Washington.

Fork Swamp rises in central Pitt County and flows s into East Branch.

Fork Township, se Warren County.

Fork Township, w Wayne County. Named for location in fork of Neuse and Little rivers. Designation has remain unchanged since first listed in 1838.

Former Camp Branch rises in n Madison County and flows s into Big Laurel Creek.

Forney, former community in w Swain County on Tuckasegee River at the mouth of Forney Creek. Alt. 1,537. The site is now under the waters of Fontana Lake.

Forney Creek rises in e Lincoln County and flows se into Killian Creek. Named for Jacob Forney, pioneer settler of about 1750

Forney Creek rises in n Swain County in the Great Smoky Mountains National Park and flows sw and s into Tuckasegee River.

Forney Ridge, n Swain County in Great Smoky Mountains National Park, a lofty spur extending sw from Clingmans Dome between Forney Creek and Noland Creek.

Forneys Creek Township, nw Swain County.

Forrester Ridge, nw Swain County in Great Smoky Mountains National Park extends se from Blockhouse Mountain to the confluence of Haw Gap Branch and Hazel Creek.

Forshee, community in s Rockingham County between Troublesome Creek and Little Troublesome Creek.

Forsyth County was formed in 1849 from Stokes County. In the central part of the state, it is bounded by Guilford, Davidson, Davie, Yadkin, and Stokes counties. It was named for Colonel Benjamin Forsythe (ca. 1760-1814), a native of Stokes County who was killed on the Canadian frontier in the War of 1812. Area: 424 sq. mi. County seat: Winston-Salem with an elevation of 858 ft. Townships are Abbotts Creek, Belews Creek, Bethania, Broadbay, Clemmonsville, Kernersville, Lewisville, Middle Fork, Old Richmond, Old Town, Salem Chapel, South Forks, Vienna, and Winston. Produces tobacco,

wheat, oats, corn, poultry, dairy products, livestock, hogs, cigarettes and other tobacco products, hosiery, textiles, bakery products, machinery, fabricated metals, furniture, processed meats, corrugated boxes, apparel, lumber, and crushed stone. See also Dobbs Parish; Wachovia.

Forsyth Creek rises in e central McDowell County and flows se into Lake James on the Catawba River.

Fort Anderson. See Brunswick.

Fort Barnwell, community in nw Craven County. Alt. 40. Settled about 1800. Named for Fort Barnwell, constructed by Colonel John Barnwell of South Carolina in a campaign against the Tuscarora Indians in April, 1712. Remains of the fort are on a bluff overlooking the Neuse River, 2 mi. ne of the community.

Fort Bartow, Civil War fort on Roanoke Island, Dare County.

Fort Benjamin, Civil War fort on the Newport River, e Carteret County, opposite town of Newport.

Fort Bragg Military Reservation, nw Cumberland, e Hoke and Moore, and s Harnett counties. Est. 1918 as Camp Bragg, a U.S. Field Artillery training center; name changed to Fort Bragg in 1922. Named for General Braxton Bragg (1817-76), Confederate commander. Alt. 110. Area, 200 sq. mi. Now headquarters for airborne troops. Reached an all-time peak of 104,000 men just prior to the North African invasion in World War II. Pope Air Force Base is on the Reservation.

Fort Branch rises in nw Bertie County and flows n into Hertford County where it enters Ahoskie Creek.

Fort Branch. See Conoho Creek.

Fort Branch, a Confederate fort at Rainbow Banks, nw Martin County. Built to prevent Union gunboats from going up the Roanoke River to Weldon to attack the railroad bridge. Earthworks remain.

Fort Butler Mountain, s Cherokee County s of Right Prong Martin Creek and w of Martin Creek. Named for the fort near the present town of Murphy (which see) where Gen. Winfield Scott, in command of U.S. forces, gathered the Cherokee Indians before moving them west in 1838.

Fort Caswell on the se tip of Oak Island in se Brunswick County. Begun by United States in 1826; seized by North Carolina troops in 1861 and abandoned by Confederates in 1865. Used also in Spanish-American and World Wars. Well preserved remains now in Baptist summer camp area.

Fort Clark, Civil War fort on Cape Hatteras, a mile up the beach from Hatteras Inlet. It was laid out by William Beaverhout Thompson and construction started about July, 1861.

Fort Creek rises in ne Caldwell County, e of Fort Defiance, and flows n into Yadkin River.

Fort Creek rises in w Franklin County and flows n into Tar River.

Fort Defiance, ne Caldwell County. Home of William Lenoir, leader in Revolutionary War and public affairs, built 1788-92, stands on site of frontier Fort Defiance.

Fort Dobbs, built 1755-56 to protect western counties from Indians. Site in n central Iredell County, 4½ mi. n of Statesville w of U.S. highway 21.

Fort Dobbs. See Fort Macon.

Fort Fisher, state historic site and former Confederate fort, at the s tip of New Hanover County. Construction begun in April, 1861, under direction of Capt. Charles P. Bolles who was soon transferred. The first section of the fort was named Battery Bolles. Upon completion, the fort, constructed of sand, palmetto logs, and railroad iron, was named for Capt. Charles F. Fisher (1816-1861), who had been killed at the Battle of First Manassas while commanding North Carolina troops. Fort Fisher controlled the Cape Fear River and kept the port of Wilmington open. The fort was bombarded from the sea on December 23-25, 1864, and January 12-13, 1865. It fell on January 15. During World War II the site was used in connection with coastal defense. Restoration of the Civil War fort and development as a state historic site was begun in 1960. Museum opened 1965.

Fort Fisher Junction, community in s New Hanover County. Prior to 1957 when the name was changed by the County Commissioners, the community was known as Monkey Junction because the owner of a store here once owned a great many monkeys.

Fort Hamby, a name applied to a log house fortified in 1865 at the end of the Civil War by deserters from the Union Army. Named for a woman, apparently of evil repute, who formerly owned the house. Located in sw Wilkes County near the mouth of Lewis Fork Creek in Yadkin River, it provided refuge for a band of armed men who robbed and murdered the residents of several counties. A group of local citizens, including a number of former Confederate soldiers, attacked the "fort," set it on fire, and captured a number of the men. Some were shot during the attack and others were tried and sentenced to prison.

Fort Hampton. See Fort Macon.

Fort Hembree. See Hayesville.

Fort Hill, former Confederate batteries on the Pamlico River, e central Beaufort County, which enabled Gen. D. H. Hill's forces to besiege Washington in the spring of 1863.

Fort Hill, a Civil War fort "near Hill's Point" in Buncombe County. The exact location cannot now be determined.

Fortin Island, the westernmost of a small group of islands in Core Sound, about 3 mi. se of community of Davis, se Carteret County.

Fortiscue Creek rises in sw Hyde County near Beulah and flows nw into Pungo River.

Fort Island, a large sandy area in Big Pocosin in sw Gates County about 1 mi. n of Chowan River. Named for George Fort.

Fort Johnston was located at the present town of Southport, se Brunswick County. Built 1748-64 and named for Gov. Gabriel Johnston (1699-1752); burned by Whigs 1775. Rebuilt by United States government 1794-1809. Seized by Confederate forces in 1861 and used in the Civil War. Only the officers' quarters remain.

Fort Lamb, small battery below Fort Anderson on Price Creek in se Brunswick County. Named for Colonel William Lamb (1835-1909) of Fort Fisher.

Fort Landing, ne Tyrrell County at the mouth of Alligator Creek. Believed to be the oldest settlement in Tyrrell County but date unknown. Said to have been named for an old fort that stood near the Alligator Creek landing. The Price map, 1808, shows Warington at this approx. location. Appears as Port Landing on the MacRae map, 1833, but as Fort Landing on subsequent maps.

Fort Lane, a Civil War fort, was located three mi. se of New Bern in Craven County.

Fort McFadden. *See* Mountain Creek.

Fort McGaughey. *See* Westminster.

Fort Macon, built 1826-1834, on the e end of Bogue Banks, s Carteret County to protect Beaufort Inlet. Replaced the earlier Fort Hampton and Fort Dobbs. Now a state park, est. 1924, on 390 acres. Historical museum maintained inside the brick fort; swimming, fishing, hiking, nature study. Scene of Civil War battle.

Fort Macon Village, part of the Cherry Point Housing Area in se Craven County. *See also* Cherry Point.

Fort Raleigh, ne shore of Roanoke Island, e Dare County. The remains of the earthen fort, constructed in 1585 by Ralph Lane's colony, were reconstructed in 1950 by the National Park Service after extensive archaeological study. Appears on the Collet map, 1770. The Fort Raleigh National Historic Site and the Waterside Theatre at which Paul Green's drama, *The Lost Colony* has been presented in the summer since 1937, are here. An Elizabethan Garden maintained by the North Carolina garden clubs and a museum are also nearby.

Fort Rollins. *See* Blowing Rock.

Fort Run, stream, rises in w Greene County and flows ne into Contentnea Creek. Named from the fact that an early eighteenth century Tuscarora Indian fort was located nearby. John Lawson was killed near the head of this stream in 1711.

Fort St. Philip. *See* Brunswick.

Fort Shaw, former fort on the beach of Oak Island in se Brunswick County. Used to protect Confederate blockade-runners moving in close to shore.

Fort Thompson, Civil War fort, site five mi. se of New Bern on Neuse River in Craven County.

Fort Totten, one of the forts built around New Bern by Union forces after they took the town in March 1862. Located in s central Craven County.

Foscoe, community in sw Watauga County on Watauga River. Alt. 2,969.

Foster Cove, n Graham County between Carringer Gap and Bee Creek.

Foster Creek rises in ne Madison County and flows sw into Big Laurel Creek.

Foster Creek Township, former township in n central Madison County, now township number 16.

Foster Knob, s Macon County between Ash Flat Branch and Rockyface Mountain.

Foster Mill Creek rises near Hogback Mountain in nw Henderson County and flows se into Mills River.

Foster Mountain, central Polk County n of Columbus. Also called Chocolate Drop. Alt. 1,500.

Foster Ridge, s Macon County, parallel to Ash Flat Branch.

Foster's Mill Creek. *See* Sweeten Creek.

Foundery Branch rises in central Granville County and flows se into Fishing Creek.

Fountain, community in se Duplin County.

Fountain, town in w Pitt County. Settled about 1900 and first known as Reba for the sister of Henry Clark Bridgers, founder of the East Carolina Railway. When a post office was established the name had to be changed as another Reba already existed in the state. Inc. 1903; named for Robert Almon Fountain (1878-1962), local merchant.

Fountain Fork, community in e Edgecombe County.

Fountain Hill, community in w Anson and e Union counties.

Fountain Hill, community in n Lenoir County on Contentnea Creek. Named for a local family, the first member of which, Francis Fountain, settled in this vicinity prior to 1769.

Fountain Park, community on Hickory Nut Creek in ne Henderson County.

Fountainshead, town inc. 1818 and authorized to be laid out in Anson County on the lands of John and James Permenter, 11 mi. e of Wadesboro. This would have been on or near the Pee Dee River; no evidence exists that the town was est. *See also* Permetter Creek.

Fountain Township, w Pitt County.

Four Corners, community in nw Davie County. In 1924-1925 a gasoline station and a grocery store were built at the rural crossroads here and given this name by the owners.

Four Diamond Ridge, mountain in ne Avery County.

Four Forks, community in central Pasquotank County.

Fourmile Branch rises in s Buncombe County and flows nw into French Broad River ½ mi. s of The Lagoon.

Fourmile Branch rises in central Davidson County and flows s into Flat Swamp Creek.

Fourmile Creek rises in se Mecklenburg County and flows sw into McAlpine Creek.

Four Oaks, town in w Johnston County. Settled about 1885; inc. 1889. Named for four oaks growing from the stump of a tree that had been cut down in an opossum hunt in the yard of K. L. Barbour, first to build a house here. Alt. 208.

Fourth Creek, rises in w Iredell County and flows e into Rowan County where Third and Fourth creeks join before entering South Yadkin River. It is the fourth creek in a series of creeks crossed by early settlers from Salisbury. The name appears on the Collet map, 1770. A settlement on this creek about 1750 later became the city of Statesville, which grew up around Fourth Creek (Presbyterian) Church.

Fourway, community in s Greene County. Community took the name of a filling station built here in the late 1920's or early 1930's.

Foust's Creek. See Moulder Branch.

Foust's Mill. See Coleridge.

Fowler Bend, formerly a sharp bend in Hiwasee River in w central Cherokee County, now a peninsula extending into Hiwassee Lake.

Fowler Cove, in n Swain County on the head of North Fork [Chambers Creek].

Fowler Creek rises in sw Jackson County between Terrapin Mountain and Coldside Mountain and flows s 4 mi. into Chattooga River at the county line.

Fowlers Mill Creek rises in e Wake County and flows e into Little River.

Fox Branch rises in s Madison County and flows nw into Ivy River.

Fox Branch rises in nw Swain County and flows se into Lake Cheoah.

Fox Cabin Gap on the Madison County, N. C.-Greene County, Tenn., line.

Fox Creek rises in n Franklin County and flows sw into Tar River.

Fox Creek rises in w Granville County and flows s into Shelton Creek.

Fox Creek rises in e Madison County and flows s into Laurel Creek.

Fox Creek rises in w Yancey County and flows se into Bald Creek.

Foxes Island, central Harnett County, in Cape Fear River nw of Lillington. Mentioned in Fulton's survey of North Carolina rivers in 1819 and appears on the MacRae map, 1833. A series of low falls or rapids here, known as Fox Island Falls,

drop between 5 and 10 ft. over a distance of about a quarter of a mile.

Fox Gap, nw Swain County in Great Smoky Mountains National Park on Twentymile Ridge between the head of Fox Branch and Hamilton Hollow.

Fox Grape Branch rises in ne Brunswick County and flows w into Columbus County where it enters Dams Creek.

Fox Island Falls. See Foxes Island.

Fox Knob, nw Yadkin County at the ne end of the Brushy Mountains. Alt. 1,590. Also known as Star Peak.

Fox Mountain, central Polk County, ne of Columbus. Alt. 1,500.

Fox's Mountain, nw Iredell County. Named for Fox family, owners in twentieth century. Formerly known as Shumaker Mountain for early settlers. On the s side of Fox's Mountain there has been constructed "an authentic Western town" called Love Valley.

Foxtown Mountain, w Madison County between Baltimore Branch and Spring Creek.

Foys Creek rises in s Pender County and flows s into Topsail Sound.

Fradey Mountain, s Buncombe County between Ducker and Blake Mountains.

Frady Creek rises in e Jackson County and flows se into Chastine Creek.

Fraley Branch. See Curl Tail Creek.

Francisco, community in n Stokes County between Big Creek and Dan River.

Francis Cove, in s Haywood County on the head of Raccoon Creek.

Francktown. See Franktown.

Frank, community in w Avery County. Said to have been named prior to 1901 for a post office official.

Franklin, a state organized in December, 1784, in what had been the western territory of North Carolina. The area had been ceded by the state to the Federal government briefly, but the act of cession was repealed. During this period residents of the area organized the State of Franklin, and it was not until 1789 that North Carolina was able to re-establish jurisdiction over the area, the State of Franklin having collapsed the previous year. The area was again (and finally) ceded in 1789 and the State of Tennessee, admitted to the Union in 1796, was formed from it. See also Watauga Settlement; District of Washington.

Franklin, town and county seat in central Macon County on Little Tennessee River.

Alt. 2,113. Settled prior to 1828; inc. 1855. Named for Jesse Franklin (1760-1823), Governor of North Carolina, 1820-21. A mound here marks the site of the old Cherokee town, Nikwasi. A council of Sir Alexander Cuming with the Indians here led to a treaty in 1730. Produces textiles and lumber.

Franklin, community in n Rowan County est. about 1828 as Franklinville, named for Benjamin Franklin. Named changed to Franklin in 1884.

Franklin Branch rises in w Caldwell County and flows s into Johns River near the town of Collettsville.

Franklin County was formed in 1779 from Bute, which see, when that county was divided to form Franklin and Warren counties. Located in the ne section of the state, it is bounded by Nash, Wake, Granville, Vance, and Warren counties. It was named for Benjamin Franklin (1706-90). Area: 494 sq. mi. County seat: Louisburg with an elevation of 280 ft. Townships are Nos. 1-10, formerly Dunn, Harris, Youngsville, Franklinton, Hayesville, Sandy Creek, Gold Mine, Cedar Rock, Cypress Creek, and Louisburg. Produces corn, wheat, oats, tobacco, cotton, dairy products, hogs, livestock, textiles, apparel, furniture, lumber, and fabricated metals.

Franklin Gap, sw Cherokee Countty s of Franklin Mountain.

Franklin Mountain, sw Cherokee County between Hothouse Branch and Wolf Creek.

Franklin Spring, former resort in nw Person County. Flourished in the early twentieth century. Mineral water bottled and sold.

Franklinsville. See Franklinville.

Franklinsville Township, e central Randolph County.

Franklinton, town in w Franklin County. Alt. 432. Est. in 1839 as Franklin Depot on land of Shemuel Kearney. Name changed to Franklinton in 1842 when it was incorporated. Produces textiles.

Franklinton Township, former township in

w Franklin County, now township number 4.

Franklin Township, central Macon County.

Franklin Township, ne Rowan County.

Franklin Township, s Sampson County.

Franklin Township, nw Surry County.

Franklinville, town in e Randolph County on Deep River. Inc. 1847 as Franklinsville. Named in honor of Jesse Franklin (1760-1832), governor of North Carolina, 1820-1821. Site acquired in 1801 by Christian Morris who built a gristmill here; purchased in 1820 by Elisha Coffin who, with others, built a cotton mill here in 1838.

Franklinville. See Franklin.

Frank Mountain, s Henderson County near the South Carolina state line. Formerly known as Gau Mountain.

Franks Creek rises in e Graham County and flows sw between Franks Creek Lead and Bert Creek Lead into Tulula Creek.

Franks Creek Lead follows the course of Franks Creek in e Graham County.

Franks Ferry. See Mill Creek.

Franktown, community in nw Onslow County between Jenkins Swamp and Juniper Swamp. Formerly called Francktown for the Franck family which owned much land in the area.

Frankum Branch rises in s Cherokee County on Poor House Mountain and flows se into Ricks Branch.

Frankum's Creek rises in nw Caldwell County and flows s into Mulberry Creek.

Fray Creek. See Fryes Creek.

Frazier Creek rises in e central Forsyth County and flows sw into Brush Fork Branch e of Winston-Salem.

Fraziers. See Progress.

Fraziers Creek on the w end of Bogue Banks, sw Carteret County, flows w into Bogue Inlet.

Fraziers Crossroads, community in s Hertford County.

Frederick, community in sw Beaufort County. Settled 1908 and named for Frederick H. von Eberstein, local farmer.

Frederick, community in w Wilson County. Post office, 1894-1895.

Fredericktown. See Bethany.

Freedom Hill. See Princeville.

Freeland, community in nw Brunswick County.

Freeman, community in ne Columbus County. Believed to have been named for free Negroes living in the area before the Civil War.

Freeman Branch rises in ne Cherokee County and flows s into Beaver Creek.

Freeman Creek rises in s Henderson County and flows se into Edith Lake.

Freeman Knob, n Cherokee County in the Unicoi Mountains.

Freeman's Channel, in the tidal marshes of Brown's Sound in s Onslow County.

Freemans Creek rises in e Onslow County and flows ne into White Oak River.

Freeman's Cross Roads. See Ether.

Freemans Township. See Youngsville Township.

Freemason Creek rises in s Caldwell and flows s into Catawba River.

Fremont, town in n Wayne County. Inc. in 1867 as Nahunta; name changed in 1869. Settled prior to 1830 and known as Narhantes and Torhunta. Named Fremont in honor of Col. S. L. Fremont, chief engineer of Wilmington and Weldon Railroad. Birthplace of Gov. Charles B. Aycock (1859-1912) one mile s, has been restored as a State Historic Site. Alt. 152.

French Branch rises in central Jones County and flows n into Trent River.

French Broad River is formed in s Transylvania County near Rosman by the junction of North Fork and West Fork. It flows ne in Transylvania and into Henderson County where it turns nw to flow through Buncombe and Madison counties into Tennessee. From the state line it flows w 102 mi. to join Holston River near Knoxville to form Tennessee River. One of the Cherokee names was Tah-kee-os-tee, "racing waters." Others, frequently for only a part of the river, were Poe-li-co, Agiqua, and Zillicoah. Known by the English at first as Broad River and appears as such on the De Brahm manuscript map of Indian Nations in the Southern Department, 1766. By 1776 the present name was in use. Named because much of the territory which it drained w of the Blue Ridge was held by the French in the eighteenth century.

French Broad Township, nw Buncombe County.

Frenchmans Creek. See Frenchs Creek.

Frenchs Creek rises in se Bladen County and flows s into Cape Fear River.

Frenchs Creek rises in se Onslow County and flows nw into New River opposite Rhodes Point. Appears as Frenchmans Creek in local records as early as 1744. Took its name from the fact that Alex-

ander Nicola, a Frenchman, settled near its mouth.

Frenchs Creek Township, se Bladen County.

Fresh Pond Hill, a sand hill near Wash Woods, 4 mi. s of the Virginia state line, on Currituck Banks, ne Currituck County.

Friars Cove, se Buncombe County between High Hickory Ridge and Eskridge Cove.

Friar Swamp rises in se Bladen County and flows s into Columbus County where it enters Buckhead Swamp. Council Mill Pond is on Friar Swamp.

Friar Swamp rises in n Columbus County and flows sw into Lake Waccamaw.

Friday Shoals in South Fork Catawba River, n Gaston County near Hardin. Named for Captain Nicholas Friday who settled here about 1760. The court for newly-established Lincoln County met at his house in 1783 and 1784.

Freidland, community in s Forsyth County. Settled 1770 by Moravian families from Broadbay, Mass., now Waldsboro, Maine. Name, in German, means "land of fruit."

Friendship, community in w Duplin County.

Friendship, community in w Guilford County, est. 1833. Alt. 893. Named for a Friends (Quaker) meeting house.

Friendship, community in sw Wake County. Settled about 1800, and named for a church previously est. here. Also known as Jordans. Alt. 350.

Friendship, community in ne Yadkin County near Yadkin River.

Friendship Township, w central Guilford County.

Fries Creek rises in nw Forsyth County and flows sw into Yadkin River.

Friezeland Creek rises in s Madison County and flows nw into Spring Creek.

Frisbee Branch rises in s Swain County and flows sw into De Hart Branch.

Frisco, community on Hatteras Island sw of Buxton, se Dare County. Known first as Trent, but post office est. in 1898 was named Frisco, perhaps to avoid confusion with Trenton, Jones County. In 1795 three sand dunes known as Stowe's Hills were described here. Later the name Creed's Hill was applied to a single large sand dune s of Frisco.

Frog Creek rises in n Rutherford County and flows s into Camp Creek.

Frog Level, community in w central Pitt County. Alt. 81.

Frog Level. See Clingman.

Frog Level. See Oakland.

Frog Level Swamp, sw Bertie County.

Frog Mountain, on Lower Trail Ridge in sw Macon County.

Frog Pond, community in e Cherokee County n of Peachtree.

Frogsboro, community in e Caswell County.

Frohock Mill. See Grants Creek; Macay's Mill.

Frohock Sawmill appears on the Collet map, 1770, as being near the mouth of Hunting Creek in present w Davie County. Undoubtedly owned by John Frohock (d. 1772), colonial official.

Frolictown Creek rises in se Jackson County and flows ne into Panthertown Creek.

Frost Mill Creek rises in n Davie County and flows e into Dutchmans Creek. Formerly known as Sweet Creek, and as such appears in numerous early local records.

Frost's Iron Works, former community in sw Stokes County. A post office in 1830; iron foundry flourished here about 1850-1860.

Frosty Knob, mountain in w central Buncombe County. Alt. 4,576.

Frozen Creek rises in s Transylvania County and flows sw then se into Toxaway Creek.

Frozenhead Ridge, w Watauga County extends se from the head of East Fork [Cove Creek] to Cove Creek, s of George Gap Branch.

Frozen Knob on the Madison County, N. C.-Unicoi County, Tenn., line.

Frozen Knob in s Transylvania County e of Frozen Creek.

Frozen Lake, s Transylvania County on Frozen Creek.

Fruitland, community in n Henderson County on Kyles Creek. Named for large quantity of fruit produced in the vicinity.

Fruitland. See Pores Knob.

Fruit Ridge, community in central Columbus County between Whiteville and Chadbourn.

Fruitville Township, ne Currituck County.

Fry, former community in w Swain County on Nantahala River. Site now under the waters of Fontana Lake.

Fryes Creek rises in n Davidson County and flows nw into Muddy Creek. Appears on the Collet map, 1770, as Fray Creek.

The Frying Pan, in e Tyrrell County, is a large body of water roughly shaped like a frying pan. It flows se into Alligator River. Appears on the Collet map, 1770.

Fryingpan Bend, in Roanoke River in n Martin County.

Frying Pan Creek, a bay on the n side of Pamlico River, e Beaufort County.

Fryingpan Gap, on the Haywood-Transylvania County line. Said to be so named because a frying pan was left here at a common camping ground for the use of all comers.

Frying Pan Landing, e Tyrrell County on The Frying Pan.

Fryingpan Mountain in Haywood and Transylvania counties. Part of Pisgah Ridge, n of Beech Knob in Pisgah National Forest.

Frying Pan Shoals, in the Atlantic Ocean immediately off Cape Fear, the s tip of New Hanover County. Appears on the Collet map, 1770.

Fry Mountain, in e Swain County at the ne end of Buckhorn Ridge.

Fuda Creek rises in se Mecklenburg County and flows ne into Cabarrus County where it enters Back Creek. Said locally to be named for a Scottish word, sometimes spelled "foody," meaning "slightly crazy."

Fulbright Cove, central Haywood County, one mile n of Lake Junaluska.

Fulcher Branch rises in s Macon County and flows w into Little Tennessee River.

Fulcher Landing, s Onslow County on New River, now the principal landing at the community of Sneads Ferry, which see.

Fulcher Mountain, n Surry County between Fisher River and Buck Mountain.

Fulchers Creek, a stream about 1 mi. long flowing se into Core Sound about midway between Nelson Bay and Brett Bay, in e Carteret County.

Fulchertown, community in s Macon County on Fulcher Branch.

Fulford, community in sw Brunswick County.

Fulford Point, peninsula extending off the nw side of Goose Creek Island into Goose Creek estuary, ne Pamlico County.

Fulk Creek rises in se Stokes County and flows se into Dan River.

Fullard Creek rises in s Onslow County and flows se into Chadwick Bay. Named for Thomas Fulwood or Fullwood, an early settler. Mentioned in local records as early as 1748.

Fuller's Creek rises in sw Caswell County and flows n into Moon Creek.

Fullwood or Fullwood's Store. See Matthews.

Fulp, community in n Forsyth County and s Stokes County.

Fulp Creek rises in ne Forsyth County and flows n into Redbank Creek.

Fulton, presently a small community in e Davie County on the Yadkin River. Inc.

1819, but active only a short time in municipal affairs, if at all. Site laid off in town lots when attempts were made to improve navigation on the Yadkin River. Post office est. 1822. Probably name for Hamilton Fulton (d. 1834), State Engineer, who was employed in connection with many internal improvement projects. A native of England, Fulton arrived in North Carolina in July, 1819.

Fulton Township, se Davie County.

Funnel Top, a peak in w central Graham County between Santeetlah Gap and Santeetlah Lake. Alt. approx. 3,200.

Funneltop Mountain in n Transylvania County between Billy Branch and Shooting Ridge.

Funston, community in e central Brunswick County.

Fuquay Springs. See Fuquay-Varina.

Fuquay-Varina, town in sw Wake County

n of Harnett County line. Settled prior to 1860. Inc. 1909 as Fuquay Springs, taking its name from David and Stephen Fuquay, early settlers. In 1963 merged with nearby town of Varina (which see) and assumed its present name. Produces tobacco, electronics equipment, apparel, dairy products. Alt. 350.

Furches, community on the Alleghany-Ashe County line.

Furches, community in e Ashe County.

Fur Creek. See Far Creek.

Furniss Mine, adjoins the Phoenix Mine property in e Cabarrus County about 8 miles se of city of Concord. Former gold mine (late 1800's). Extensive underground exploration in 1954-56 for tungsten, by Carolina Tungsten Mining Company.

Furr City. See Oakboro.

Furrs, community in se Cabarrus County.

Furr Township, sw Stanly County.

Futches Creek rises in ne New Hanover County and flows se into Topsail Sound.

G

Gabby Branch rises in n Cherokee County and flows sw into Colvard Creek.

Gabes Branch rises in s Nash County and flows ne into Henry Branch. Mentioned in local records as early as 1779.

Gabes Mountain Branch rises in e central Avery County and flows s into Wilson Creek.

Gabourel's Bluff was a name applied to an area on the w side of Cape Fear River in present ne Brunswick County. At one time it was the property of Joshua Gabourel, attorney and Justice of the Peace in New Hanover County in 1736. Known as Partridge's Bluff prior to 1735.

Gabriels Creek rises in e Madison County and flows sw into Ivy River.

Gadd Creek rises in w Polk County and flows s into Green River.

Gaddis Branch rises in s Haywood County and flows n into Jonathans Creek.

Gaddysville, community in sw Robeson County.

Gaddy's Wild Goose Refuge, n central Anson County near Ansonville. Est. 1934 by Lockhart Gaddy when nine geese were offered winter protection and food. Thousands of geese now winter here.

Gaddy Township, s Robeson County.

Gage Bald on Rich Mountain in e Jackson County on the head of Gage Creek. Alt. 5,800.

Gage Creek rises in e Jackson County and flows se into Wolf Creek.

Gailors Hammock. See Gaylords Island.

Galamore Branch rises in ne Swain County and flows s into Raven Fork.

Galatia, community in n Northampton County.

Galbreath Creek rises in e Swain County and flows s into Tuckasegee River.

Gale Creek rises in nw Pamlico County and flows se into Bay River. A part of the Intracoastal Waterway.

Gales Creek rises in w Carteret County and flows s into Bogue Sound. Appears on the Moseley map, 1733. Probably named for Christopher Gale (1680-1734).

Gallagans, community in n Madison County.

Gallant Point, a point of land in s Carteret County extending into the mouth of Newport River. Separated from Beaufort by Town Creek.

Gallants Channel in the mouth of Newport River, central Carteret County. Named for John Galland, an early settler, but in pronunciation the d became a t.

Gallatin. *See* Graham.

Gallberry Swamp rises on the Cumberland-Robeson County line and flows se to join Big Marsh Swamp in forming Big Swamp.

Galloway, community in s Transylvania County on Toxaway Creek.

Galloway Creek rises in s Transylvania County and flows se into French Broad River.

Galloway Creek. *See* West Prong [of Glady Fork].

Galloway Crossroads, community in e Pitt County.

Galloway Mountain, s Clay County between Shooting Creek and the Georgia line.

The Gallows Branch rises in Salisbury, e Rowan County, and flows w into Grant Creek. Named from the fact that the early site of public hangings for Rowan County was nearby.

Gambrick Branch rises in nw Burke County and flows e into Linville River.

Gamewell, community in sw Caldwell County. Alt. 1,078. Named for Gamewell Tuttle, a Methodist circuit rider who was in this area about 1840.

Gander Mountain. *See* Mount Bolus.

Ganders Fork, community in e Duplin County.

Gannaway, community in sw Caswell County. A post office was operated here during the approx. period 1890-1905.

Gant Inlet. *See* Gunt Inlet.

Gap, community in w Stokes County at the head of East Prong Little Yadkin River.

Gap Bay, boggy area on the Pender-Sampson County line se of Newtons Crosroads. *See also* Carolina Bays.

Gap Civil Township, n central Alleghany County. Local training camps were located here during the first part of the Civil War. *See also* Sparta.

Gap Creek rises in s Buncombe County and flows e ino Cane Creek.

Gap Creek, community in s Ashe County. In time past copper has been mined in the vicinity.

Gap Creek. *See* Deep Gap Creek.

Gap Point, se Hyde County, extends into Pamlico Sound from the se end of Ocracoke Island.

Gapway Swamp rises in sw Columbus County and flows nw into South Carolina where it enters Lumber River.

Garbacon Creek, rises in n Carteret County and flows n into Neuse River.

Gar Creek rises in w Mecklenburg County and flows sw into Catawba River.

Garden City, community in central New Hanover County. Alt. 15. Settled about 1912. Named for natural beauty of area.

Garden City. *See* Pleasant Garden.

Garden Creek rises in e Haywood County and flows ne into Pigeon River. One of the earliest settlements in the county was at a wide bottom on this stream which still is known by its earliest name—Garden Farm.

Garden Creek rises in n Wilkes County in Doughton Park and flows e into East Prong Roaring River.

Garden Farm. *See* Garden Creek.

Garden Hill, former community in s Guilford County s of Sedgefield near Groometown. Site of Gardiner Hill Gold Mine. Both the community and the mine were deserted after the 1849 gold rush in California.

Garden Township, e Wilson County. Named for Jack Gardner, prominent local merchant in the mid-nineteenth century.

Gardner's Branch rises in e Wilson County and flows n into Town Creek.

Gardners Creek rises in e Martin County and flows ne into Devils Gut.

Gardnerville, community in s Pitt Couny.

Gargales Creek. *See* Muddy Creek.

Gar Gut rises in e Beaufort County and flows s into Pamlico River.

Garland, town in sw Sampson County. Settled about 1888; inc. 1907. Named for Augustus Hill Garland (1832-99), Attorney General of the United States, 1885-89. Known earlier as Sloan's Crossing. Alt. 137.

Garland Creek rises in sw Cherokee County and flows se into Rapier Mill Creek.

Garland Gap, central Mitchell County on Pumpkin Patch Mountain.

Garlington's Island, a spur of high land containing approx. 250 acres extending from the center of Camden County through North River Pocosin to a point on Crooked Creek two miles from North River. Named because it was the site of the home of Captain James S. Garlington (1765?-1822?), commander of two companies raised for service in the War of 1812. Sometimes also known as Garrenton's Island.

Garner, town in s Wake County. Settled about 1800. Inc. 1883 as Garner's Station, named for founder, H. C. Garner. Charter repealed 1891; reincorporated in 1905 as Garner.

Garner Branch rises in e Davidson County a short distance n of Denton and flows s into Yadkin River.

Garner Cove, s Haywood County on the head of Raccoon Creek.

Garner's Station. See Garner.

Garners Store, community on the Randolph-Moore County line.

Garreck Creek rises in n Cherokee County and flows se and sw into Beaverdam Creek.

Garren Branch. See Gerren Branch.

Garren Creek rises in se Buncombe County and flows nw into Cane Creek.

Garren Mountain, se Buncombe County sw of Dyeleaf Mountain.

Garren Mountain, n Henderson County between Bank Mountain and Sand Flat Mountain.

Garrenton's Island. See Garlington's Island.

Garrett Creek rises in central Haywood County and flows nw into Jonathans Creek. Named for W. G. B. Garrett (ca. 1845-1925), who owned land and had a ranger's cabin here.

Garretts Gap, w Haywood County, Great Smoky Mountains National Park, near lat. 35° 32' 55" N., long. 83° 08' 25" W. on Cataloochee Divide.

Garringer Branch rises in se Cherokee County and flows se into Little Brasstown Creek.

Garr Island in the waters of Pamlico Sound off the n tip of Pea Island, e Dare County.

Garrison Branch rises in w Macon County and flows sw into Nantahala Lake.

Garrison Point, point of land on the s side of Pamlico River, central Beaufort County, near the mouth of Durham Creek. Named because a fort or garrison was erected here in 1711 during the Tuscarora Indian War. See also Durham Creek.

Garysburg, town in w Northampton County. Inc. 1891. Known as Garys in 1833 but changed to Garysburg after the post office here received that name in 1838. Alt. 145. Peebles Tavern and Blakely's Depot were nearby communities in the early nineteenth century, but they were supplanted by Garysburg.

Gash Creek rises in e Transylvania County and flows se into French Broad River.

Gashes Creek rises in central Buncombe County and flows nw into Swannanoa River.

Gasters Creek rises in s Lee County and flows se into Little River.

Gaston, former town in nw Northampton County on Roanoke River. It developed as the n terminus of the Raleigh and Gaston Railroad, chartered 1835 and completed 1840. The town began to decline after 1865 when the bridge across the Roanoke River was burned. Named for Judge William Gaston (1778-1844). The site is now under the waters of Roanoke Rapids Lake. The modern community of Thelma, across the river, is approx. s of the site. See also South Gaston.

Gaston, town in nw Northampton County on Roanoke River. Inc. 1949 at which time the name was changed from Camp's Store. Named for the township and for the old town of Gaston, the site of which is about 5 mi. w.

Gaston County was formed in 1846 from Lincoln County. Located in the sw section of the state, it is bounded by the state of South Carolina and by Cleveland, Lincoln, and Mecklenburg counties. It was named for William Gaston (1778-1844), a member of Congress and a judge of the Supreme Court of North Carolina. Area: 363 sq. mi. County seat: Gastonia with an elevation of 825 ft. Townships are Cherryville, Crowell Mountain, Dallas, Gastonia, River Bend, and South Point. Produces corn, wheat, oats, cotton, poultry, eggs, dairy products, hogs, livestock, textiles, hosiery, machinery, corrugated boxes, chemicals, motor vehicle parts, zippers, crushed stone, mica, and sand.

Gastonia, city and county seat, central Gaston County. Inc. 1877 and named for the county in which it was located. Replaced Dallas as the county seat, 1909. Produces textiles, hosiery, machinery, corrugated boxes, electronic components, apparel, and motor vehicle parts. Gaston College, est. 1964, is here. Alt. 825.

Gastonia Township, s central Gaston County.

Gaston Lake, formed on Roanoke River about eight mi. upstream from the city of

Roanoke Rapids, and extends along the
Halifax-Northampton County line nw into
ne Warren County and into Virginia. Gaston Dam, 3,600 ft. wide and 105 ft. high,
was completed in 1963 by Virginia Electric and Power Company, and lies on the
upstream end of the Roanoke Rapids Lake.
Gaston Lake is 34 mi. long, with maximum
width of 1.3 miles; covers 20,300 acres,
with a shoreline of 350 mi. and a max.
depth of 97 ft. Used for generation of
hydroelectric power and recreation.

Gaston Township, nw Northampton County.

Gates, community in n Gates County. Alt.
73.

Gates County was formed in 1779 from
Chowan, Hertford, and Perquimans counties. Located in the ne section of the state,
it is bounded by Camden, Pasquotank,
Perquimans, Chowan, and Hertford counties, and the state of Virginia. It was
named for General Horatio Gates (1728?-
1806), commander of Revolutionary forces
which defeated Burgoyne at Saratoga,
October, 1777. Area: 349 sq. mi. County
seat: Gatesville with an elevation of 40 ft.
Townships are Gatesville, Hall, Haslett,
Holly Grove, Hunters Mill, Mintonsville,
and Reynoldson. This area was explored
in 1622 by John Pory, who came down
from Jamestown, Va. Produces peanuts,
corn, soybeans, cotton, hogs, and lumber.

Gates Courthouse. See Gatesville.

Gatesville, town and county seat in central
Gates County. Alt. 40. Inc. 1830. Known
originally as Bennetts Creek Landing, and
as Gates Courthouse from 1779 until 1830.

Gatesville Township, central Gates County.

Gatewood, community in nw Caswell County, named for J. M. Gatewood, local
resident. A post office was operated here
during the approx. period 1880-1905.

Gath. See White Cross.

Gatlington, community in nw Gates County on Chowan River. Beach here is a
popular picnic area and boat races are
held on the river. Prior to the Civil War,
known as Lumberton and center for the
manufacture of barrel staves and sawed
lumber to be shipped down the river.

Gau Mountain. See Frank Mountain.

Gay, community in w Jackson County on
Savannah Creek.

Gaylord, community in e Beaufort County.

Gaylords Hammock. See Gaylords Island.

Gaylords Island, high ground in Pantego
Swamp, e Beaufort County. Known as
Gaylords Hammock (also spelled Gailors
Hammock) as early as 1754.

Gaylors Branch rises in w Transylvania
County between Indian Creek and Shoal
Creek, and flows s about one mi. to
empty into Indian Creek just above its
junction with Shoal Creek.

Gela, community in n Granville County. Alt.
483.

Gem Creek rises in w Jackson County and
flows se into Little Pine Creek.

General Assembly has met in the following
places, which see. Bath, Edenton, Fayetteville, Halifax, Halls Creek, Hillsborough,
Little River, New Bern, Perquimans
County, Raleigh, Smithfield, Tarboro,
Wake Court House (Raleigh), and Wilmington. It may also have met at other
places but many records of the seventeenth and eighteenth centuries have not
survived.

Genlee, community in s Durham County.
Formerly known as Togo, the name of a
Japanese city given the community when
a railroad station opened here about 1904.
The name was changed after the attack
on Pearl Harbor, December 7, 1941, to
honor General Robert E. Lee. Produces
brick.

Genoa, community in s central Wayne County. Named for the birthplace of Columbus,
Genoa, Italy.

Gentry Branch rises in n Buncombe County
and flows nw into Adkins Branch.

Gentry Gap, n Buncombe County between
Bill Cole and Lankford Mountains.

Gentrys Store, community in n Person
County.

Geographic center of North Carolina has
been determined by the Geological Survey, U.S. Department of the Interior, to
be in Chatham County, ten miles nw of
Sanford. See also Gulf.

George, community in e Northampton Coun-
ty, approx. 1 mi. sw of Woodland.
Named for a local citizen, George Harri-
son Parker. Former post office was
George; railroad station was Woodland
Station.

George Branch rises on the Buncombe-Haywood County line near Grassy Top and flows se into Hominy Creek.

George Branch rises in w central Watauga County and flows sw into Brushy Fork.

George City, proposed provincial capital in what is now ne Lenoir County near Kinston. Authorized to be laid out in 1758 at Tower Hill (*which see*), but its establishment was not approved by officials in London. The name was intended to honor King George II.

George Creek rises in s Cherokee County and flows ne into Martin Creek.

George Fork rises in e Yancey County and flows n into Little Crabtree Creek.

George Gap, w Watauga County on the head of George Gap Branch.

George Gap Branch rises in w Watauga County and flows se into Cove Creek.

George Ira Creek rises in w Haywood County and flows ne into Woody Creek.

George Martin Branch rises in e Cherokee County and flows nw into Valley River.

George Orr Mountain in e Transylvania County extends ne from the head of Boylston Creek to Bryson Creek. Named for first clerk of court in Transylvania County.

Georges Branch rises in n Swain County and flows sw into Indian Creek.

Georgetown, Negro community in ne Davidson County between forks of Spurgeon and Abbotts creeks.

Georgetown, community in e Lenoir County near Kinston. Takes its name from the George City, *which see.*

George Town, planned and begun in 1786 by George Hazard between Bear Creek and Queens Creek in se Onslow County. It did not prosper and was soon abandoned

Georgeville, community in se Cabarrus County, at junction of Dutch Buffalo Creek and Rocky River. Named for George Shinn; formerly known as Shinnville. *See also* Reed Mine.

Georgia Branch rises in w Madison County and flows e into Spring Creek.

German's Hill, a ridge in ne Caldwell County on which was formerly located a small community (post office name Cilley). Named for Wellborn German who lived here until 1848.

Germanton, community in s Stokes and n Forsyth counties. Alt. 662. Inc. 1790; charter repealed 1895. County seat of Stokes County from the creation of the

county until 1849 when it was divided to form Forsyth County.

Germantown, town in sw Hyde County. Inc. 1791. Named for German Bernard on whose land the town was laid off. County seat from about 1792 until 1820.

Germany Cove, in central Haywood County on a tributary of Hemphill Creek.

Gerren Branch rises in s Transylvania County and flows se into Glady Fork. Also spelled Garren Branch.

Gerren Creek rises in s Transylvania County and flows ne into East Fork French Broad River.

Gerton, community in ne Henderson County.

Gethsemane, community in n Edgecombe County.

Ghents Creek rises in n Person County and flows ne into Hyco River.

Ghio, community in se Richmond County. Named in the 1860's for a German engineer employed by the railroad.

Ghock Fork, rises in e Richmond County and flows nw into Hitchcock Creek.

Ghormley Mountain extends ne from Thompson Branch to Quinn Creek in w Cherokee County.

Ghoul's Fork rises in central Carteret County and flows sw into Black Creek.

Gibbs Branch rises in nw Jackson County and flows w into Oconaluftee River.

Gibbs Creek rises in e Granville County and flows se into Tar River.

Gibbs Creek. See Far Creek.

Gibbs Lake, marsh in se Duplin County.

Gibbs Mountain, e Yancey County on the head of Shuford Creek. Alt. 6,224. Named for the Rev. Billy Gibbs, a circuit rider.

Gibbs Point, point of land extending into Pamlico Sound from s Hatteras Island n of the community of Avon, s Dare County. Probably named for Henry Gibbs who had a grant of land on Hatteras Island in 1716.

Gibbs Point extends into Pamlico Sound from the e mainland of Hyde County.

Gibbs Point, peninsula extending into the mouth of North Landing River, ne Currituck County. A nearby community is known as Gibbs Woods. This was the site of the home of Capt. John Gibbs who, in 1690, claimed to be governor of Albemarle. The Moseley map, 1733, shows this as Gover. Gibbs's Point.

Gibbs Woods, community near Gibbs Point in ne Currituck County. *See also* Gibbs Point.

Gibbton, community in central Pamlico County on Trent River.

Gibby Branch rises in w Macon County and flows e into Choga Creek.

Gibby Branch rises in s Swain County and flows nw into Brush Creek.

Gibby Branch rises in s central Swain County and flows se into Bucknor Branch.

Gibraltar, former comunity in central Union County between Richardson's and Crooked creeks. Appears on the Shaffer map, 1886. Later known as Polk Mountain but no longer recognized as a community.

Gibson, town in w Scotland County. Post office est. here 1846 and named for Noah Gibson, storekeeper and first postmaster. Inc. 1899. Alt. 255.

Gibson Branch rises in e Haywood County and flows sw into Wesley Creek.

Gibson Cove in nw Jackson County between Gibson Knob and Tuckasegee River.

Gibson Cove, s Swain County east of Wesser Creek.

Gibson Cove Branch rises in central Macon County and flows se into Cartoogechaye Creek.

Gibson Knob, nw Jackson County between Gibson Cove and Peggy Gap.

Gibson Knob, central Macon County between Gibson Ridge and Mint Branch.

Gibson Millpond. See Blues Pond.

Gibson Pond, e central Richmond County on Ghock Fork.

Gibson Ridge, central Macon County between Wallace Branch and Gibson Cove Branch.

Gibson Ridge, se Swain County extends n from Peaks Bald between Jones Creek and Little Laurel Creek.

Gibsonville, town in e Guilford and w Alamance counties. Alt. 728. Est. 1855 and inc. 1871. Named for Joseph Gibson (1785-1857), local land and slave owner who also was active in contracting and grading for the North Carolina Railroad. A station est. about a mile n of his home was named for him and became the town. Produces textiles, apparel, and hosiery.

Giddensville, community in ne Sampson County on the w edge of Bear Pocosin.

Gideon Swamp rises in n Nash County and flows se into Sandy Creek.

Giesky Creek rises in s Clay County and flows nw into Shooting Creek.

Gilberts Creek rises in s Stanly County and flows s into Rocky River.

Gilbert Town, former county seat of Rutherford County, 1781-85. Site, now abandoned, is a short distance n of Rutherfordton in the center of the county on Hollands Creek. Named for William Gilbert, owner of the land.

Gilead, community in sw Beaufort County.

Gilead Ridge, mountain ridge in South Mountains that form Burke-Cleveland County line.

Giles Creek rises in n Franklin County and flows sw into Tooles Creek.

Giles Creek rises in se Rockingham County and flows sw into Haw River.

Gilkey, community in n Rutherford County. Formerly known as Millwood until renamed for a local family.

Gilkey Creek rises in n Rutherford County and flows se into Mill Creek.

Gilkey Township, central Rutherford County.

Gill, community in s Vance County, named for a local family.

Gillam Gap, on the Ashe-Wilkes County line.

Gill Branch rises in n Buncombe County near Weaverville and flows sw into Reems Creek.

Gillburg, community in s Vance County on the head of Gills Little Mill Creek.

Gillespie Gap on the McDowell-Mitchell County line. Alt. 2,800. Troops en route to the Battle of Kings Mountain passed through here on September 29, 1780. The State Mineral Museum is located on the Blue Ridge Parkway here on the Mitchell County side of the gap.

Gillett, former community in s Onslow County e of Stones Bay. Abandoned 1941 with the establishment of Camp Lejeune Marine Base.

Gilletts Creek rises in se Onslow County and flows se into Brown's Sound. Also known locally as Old Woman's Swamp from the fact that an elderly woman was drowned here many years ago. Now within the Camp Lejeune Marine Base. Mentioned in local records as early as 1744.

Gilliams Creek rises in n Vance County and flows nw into Island Creek Reservoir.

Gillikin Creek rises in e Carteret County and flows w into North Leopard Creek.

Gillis Station. See Parkton.

Gill Mountain, s Wilkes County extending ne from Morris Knob to Owen Knob.

Gills Knob, n Caldwell County. Alt. 2,000. Probably named for Gilbert Cottrell, eighteenth-century settler in the vicinity.

Gills Little Mill Creek rises in s Vance County and flows s into n Franklin County where it enters Lynch Creek.

Gilmer Township, central Guilford County.

Gilmore Swamp rises in ne Sampson County and flows se into Six Runs Creek.

Gilreath, community in s Wilkes County on North Rocky Creek. Formerly known as Brushy Mountain and as Dodson Store. Old Gilreath, another community is located approx. 3 mi. nw.

Gin, community in n Cumberland County.

Gin Branch rises in central Nash County and flows s into Sapony Creek.

Gingerberry, high ground in Murphy Bay, e Bladen County.

Gingercake Creek rises in nw Burke County and flows se, e, and ne into Steels Creek.

Gingercake Mountain, nw tip of Burke County on Jonas Ridge. Alt. 4,120. A summer residential community, Gingercake Acres, is here.

Gipps Creek rises in ne Cherokee County and flows sw into Valley River.

Gladden Ridge, w Madison County parallel to Raccoon Branch.

Gladdens Creek rises in central Graham County and flows w into Cheoah River.

The Glade, a relatively level area on Newfound Mountain on the Buncombe-Haywood County line between Grassy Gap and Beaverdam Gap.

The Glade, loamy marsh in se Duplin County.

Glade Branch rises in e Clay County and flows ne into Buck Creek.

Glade Creek rises in central Alexander County and flows s into Lower Little River to form Bell River, *which see.*

Glade Creek rises in s central Alleghany County and flows n into Little River.

Glade Creek rises in se Buncombe County and flows se into Broad River.

Glade Creek rises in se Macon County and flows ne into Chatooga River.

Glade Creek rises in ne Transylvania County and flows se into French Broad River.

Glade Creek, community in e Alleghany County.

Glade Creek Township, ne Alleghany County.

Glade Gap, e Clay County near Glade Branch.

Glade Mountain, nw Buncombe County e of Cherry Gap.

Glade Mountain, e Haywood County between head of Thickcty Creek and head of Willow Creek. Peaks are Goat Rock, Wines Top, and Point Lookout.

Glade Mountain, at the head of Glade Creek in se Macon County.

Glades Creek rises in s McDowell County and flows n into Catawba River.

Glade Top, on the Buncombe-Haywood County line.

Glade Valley, community in se Alleghany County. Glade Valley High School here operated under direction of Presbyterian Church.

Gladie Creek rises in e Jackson County and flows sw into Tuckasegee River.

Gladis, community in e Mecklenburg County.

Gladstone. See Misenheimer.

Glady, community in sw Buncombe County on South Hominy Creek.

Glady Branch rises in w Swain County and flows s into Tuckasegee River.

Glady Fork rises on the Buncombe-Henderson County line n of Glady Fork Gap and flows nw into South Hominy Creek.

Glady Fork, formed in s Transylvania County by the confluence of West Prong and South Prong. It flows n into East Fork French Broad River.

Glady Fork Gap, on the Buncombe-Henderson County line.

Gladys Branch rises in central Transylvania County and flows sw into Spanish Oak Branch.

Gladys Fork Gap, at the head of Fletcher Creek in nw Henderson County.

Glasgow County, formed in 1791 from Dobbs County, was named in honor of James Glasgow, Secretary of State of North Carolina from 1777 until 1798. The name was changed to Greene (*which see*) in 1799 when it became publicly known that Glasgow was involved in land frauds. Glasgow died in Tennessee in 1820.

Glass, community in n Cabarrus County. Named for Peter Glass, an early German settler.

Glassmine Branch rises in ne Buncombe County and flows sw into North Fork [Swannanoa River].

Glassmine Gap, on Little Bald Mountain, sw Macon County.

Glassmine Mountain, w Transylvania County between Lamance and Beasley creeks. Named from the fact that isinglass (mica) was mined in the vicinity.

Glassmine Ridge, ne Buncombe County between Sugarhouse Cove and Corner Rock Creek.

Glass Rock Knob, on the McDowell-Yancey County line.

Glassy Rock, mountain in se Henderson County overlooking Flat Rock community. During the Civil War renegades hid here and money and other valuables which they concealed in the caves here were later found. Also a point on the "underground railroad" for escaping slaves.

Glassy Rock Creek rises in s Jackson County and flows s into Webb Lake.

Glassy Rock Mountain on the se end of Glassy Rock Ridge, s Jackson County. Alt. approx. 4,500.

Glassy Rock Ridge, s Jackson County between Rattlesnake Knob and Glassy Rock Mountain.

Glen Alpine, town in sw Burke County. Inc. 1883. Alt. 1,206. First known as Turkey Tail because of an old tree root which resembled a turkey's tail. Later called Sigmonsburg for a local storekeeper, and finally given its present name when the railroad was built.

Glen Ayre, community in e Mitchell County on Little Green Creek. A late nineteenth century post office here was known as Little Rock Creek.

Glen Burnie Falls on New Years Creek, w edge of town of Blowing Rock in s Watauga County. Height 75 feet. Part of Blowing Rock recreation area since 1906.

Glenburnie Gardens, residential area about 3 mi. n of New Bern, central Craven County.

Glencannon Falls, e central Transylvania County in Williamson Creek.

Glencoe, community in central Alamance County. Site of textile mills.

Glen Cove, the valley through which Glen Cove Branch flows in se Buncombe County.

Glen Cove Branch rises in se Buncombe County and flows nw into Swannanoa River.

Glendale Springs, community in se Ashe County. Alt. 2,850.

Glendon, community in ne Moore County. Named for E. F. Glenn, owner of the town site. A pyrophyllite open cut mine and processing plant are operated here. Alt. 301.

Glen Falls, on East Fork Overflow Creek in se Macon County. Water drops about 75 feet.

Glenfield, community in s Greene County. Tyndal's College, located nearby, was established about 1913, abandoned about

1929. Founded by James Tyndal and son, John, prominent Baptists. The community was settled prior to 1890.

Glenhaven, community in central Beaufort County on the n bank of Pamlico River.

Glen Mary Falls in New Years Creek, w edge of town of Blowing Rock in s Watauga County. Height 100 ft. Part of Blowing Rock recreation area since 1906.

Glenn, community in nw Ashe County. Alt. approx. 3,500.

Glenn. *See* University.

Glenn Bald, mountain peak in s Buncombe County between Lance Mountain and Shut-in Ridge. Alt. 2,703.

Glenn Gap, on the Monroe County, Tenn.-Graham County, N. C., line.

Glenn Mountain in s Person County near Flat River.

Glenola, community in n Randolph County. Alt. approx. 793.

Glen Raven, community in w Alamance County. Alt. 701. Named by John Q. Gant (1847-1930), who est. first mill at the site. He first chose Glendale, but the name was rejected because it was already a post office name in the state. He kept the "Glen," however, and added Raven because of his fondness for hunting crows.

Glenville, town in s Jackson County between Thorpe Reservoir and Glassy Rock Ridge. Inc. 1891. Alt. approx. 3,560.

Glenville Lake. *See* Lake Thorpe.

Glenwood, former community in central Guilford County now within Greensboro city limits.

Glenwood, community in s McDowell County. Inc. 1909; ceased to be active in municipal affairs in 1927; charter repealed 1945. A post office here for a time was known as Nealsville.

Glenwood Township, se McDowell County.

Gliden, community in n Chowan County. Alt. 38.

Glisson Township, n central Duplin County.

Globe, community in nw Caldwell County. Alt. 1,325. Settled about 1775 and named because the area cleared by the settlers was practically round. Globe Academy operated here from 1882 until it was washed away in a flood in 1916.

Globe Mountains, a range of mountains extending across nw Caldwell County on the e side of Johns River. Alt. from 1,500 to 3,283.

Globe Township, nw Caldwell County.

Gloucester, town authorized to be laid off

in 1754 on 50 acres of land owned by John Jenkins on the s side of the Pee Dee River in Anson County. No evidence exists that the town was ever established.

Gloucester, community in e Carteret County. Alt. 10. Settled about 1800 and named for the city in Massachusetts.

Gloucester District, one of the districts into which Caswell County was divided at the time of the 1790 census. It contained 211 heads of families.

Gloucester Gap, a low gap at the heads of Shoal Creek and Long Branch nw of Rich Mountain, n Henderson County.

Gloucester Township, nw Transylvania County.

Glover Creek rises in ne Carteret County and flows s into Styron Bay between Sealevel and Atlantic.

Glovers Crossroads, community in ne Bertie County.

Gnat Ridge, in se Macon County between Henson Branch and Brooks Creek.

Gneiss, community in e Macon County on Cullasaja River. Alt. 2,115. Named for gneiss, a laminated or foliated metamorphic rock found in the vicinity.

G. Newby's Ferry. See Belvidere.

Goade Island, a name applied on the Smith map, 1624, to the s extremity of Currituck Banks, e Currituck County.

Goat Bald, w Macon County between Bearpen Creek and Wine Spring Creek.

Goat Island, s central Carteret County in Bogue Sound off Morehead City.

Goat Island, e Pasquotank County n of Elizabeth City in the Pasquotank River.

Goat Knob, s Jackson County s of Coldside Mountain near Chester Branch.

Goat Knob, on the Jackson-Macon County line.

Goat Neck, community in ne Tyrrell County ne of Fort Landing.

Goat Rock, e Haywood County on Glade Mountain. Alt. approx. 4,450.

Goatrock Ridge, in central Haywood County, extends e from Jonathans Creek to Snakeden Top.

Gobble Creek rises in w Davidson County and flows nw into Yadkin River.

Godfrey Branch. See Citte Weeks Branch.

Godfrey Creek rises in s Pender County and flows w into Harrisons Creek.

Godleys Crossroads. See Chocowinity.

Godley Store, community in se Beaufort County.

Godwin, town in ne Cumberland County. Settled 1877. Inc. 1905. Named for Issac

W. Godwin, who gave the railroad right-of-way. Alt. 156.

Godwins, community in s Johnston County.

Godwin's Branch rises in e Wilson County and flows se into Whiteoak Swamp.

Goff's Swamp. See Goss Swamp.

Goins Creek rises in Virginia and flows s into Surry County where it enters Stewart Creek.

Gold, former community in nw Burke County on Canoe Creek.

Gold Branch rises in s Cherokee County and flows sw into Nottely River.

Golden. See Golden Valley.

Golden Creek rises in s central Avery County and flows se into Linville River.

Goldengrove. See Kenansville.

Golden Ridge, n Madison County between Rocky Branch and Hurricane Creek.

Golden Valley, community in ne Rutherford County on the head of First Broad River. A post office, Golden, est. here as early as 1835. Large tracts of timber exist in the area; although worked by a lumber company many years ago there are said to be stands of virgin timber remaining in this wild country because it was too difficult to get it out.

Golden Valley Township, ne Rutherford County.

Gold Hill, community in sw Rockingham County.

Gold Hill, community in central Rutherford County.

Gold Hill, town in s Rowan County. Gold was discovered here in 1824 and the community soon developed. Inc. 1859; reincorporated, 1874, but long inactive in municipal affairs. Extensive mining operations carried on here over a long period of years. Alt. 764.

Gold Hill Township, se Rowan County.

Goldmine Branch rises near Forge Mountain on the Henderson-Transylvania County line and flows ne into Boylston Creek.

Gold Mine Branch rises in n Graham County and flows e into Cheoah River.

Gold Mine Branch rises in s Macon County and flows e into Cullasaja River.

Goldmine Branch rises in w Swain County and flows s into Tuckasegee River.

Goldmine Branch rises in s Watauga County and flows w into Middle Fork [of South Fork New River].

Gold Mine Township, former township in ne Franklin County, now township number 7.

Gold Park Lake, on an unnamed stream in s

central Wayne County. Formed by an artificial dam in 1940; maximum depth ten
feet; area 20 acres. Swimming facilities;
open to public. First named Woodland
Lake; name changed in 1954 to present
name, based on name of county seat,
Goldsboro.

Gold Pit Creek rises in w Macon County
and flows nw into Cold Spring Creek.

Gold Point, town in w Martin County on
Collie Swamp. Settled about 1871. Inc.
1899 as Goldpoint, but long inactive in
municipal affairs; reincorported 1957 as
Gold Point. Originally called Long Town.
Alt. 74.

Gold Rock, community in ne Nash County
on Swift Creek. Inc. 1875 as Whitaker's
Mills, but long inactive in municipal
affairs. Henry W. Whitaker was appointed
first mayor. Present name selected about
1890 by R. R. Gay, postmaster, when a
post office was established here and it was
necesary to avoid confusion with nearby
Whitakers. Alt. 110.

Goldsboro, city and county seat, central
Wayne County e of Neuse River where it
is joined by Little River. Inc. 1847; became county seat in 1850, succeeding
town of Waynesboro (which see). Named
for Major Matthew Tilghman Golds-
borough, native of Maryland, assistant
engineer for Wilmington and Weldon
Railroad. Includes former community of
Adamsville (which see). Produces textiles,
electronic components, primary metals,
leather products, bakery products, tobacco, furniture, lumber, cottonseed oil,
machinery, dairy products, and processed
grain. Alt. 111. Seymour Johnson Air
Base, est. 1942, is here.

Goldsboro Cooling Pond, in w central Wayne
County, about five miles w of county seat.
Formed in 1961 to cover 575 acres with
maximum depth of 15 ft., and a shoreline
of 4.6 mi. Used to provide supplementary
cooling for the Goldsboro Steam Electric
Generating Plant, and named for same.
Lies in a looping meander of Neuse River
(though its water level is as much as 22 ft.
above that of the river) and its water
covers the site of an old Quaker meeting
house. The upper meander loop forms an
area known as Quaker Neck; the lower
meander loop was known as The Roundabout in the 1830's.

Goldsboro Township, central Wayne County.

Goldspring Gap, s Macon County between
Wolfpen Gap and Pickens Nose.

Goldston, town in s Chatham County. Settled about 1885; inc. 1907. Named for
Joseph Goldston on whose land the town
developed. Alt. 424.

Gold Valley Crossroads, community in w
Nash County.

Goldview Knob, central Buncombe County,
sw of Beard Mountain.

Gooch Gap, on the McDowell-Mitchell
County line.

Gooch Peak, central Buncombe County in
the w part of the Elk Mountains.

Goode Creek rises in se Rutherford County
and flows s into Broad River.

Goodings Creek. See Goodwin Creek.

Goodluck, community in n Henderson County on Hooper Creek.

Goodman, community in nw Anson County.
Named for local family; J. C. Goodman,
Civil War veteran, established a tannery
here soon after the war.

Goodman Branch rises in e central Brunswick County and flows s into Town Creek.

Goodman Branch rises in n Union County
and flows se into Richardson Creek.

Goodmans Island, in se Bertie County between the mouth of Cashie River and
Eastmost River. Irregularly shaped, it
measures approx. 1¼ mi. in width and
length from its most distant points. See
also Purchase Islands.

Goodman Swamp rises in nw Bladen County
and flows sw into Robeson County where
it enters Big Swamp.

Goodman Swamp rises in s Nansemond
County, Virginia, and flows s into Gates
County where it enters Duke Swamp.

Goodson's Store. See Boger City.

Goodsonville. See Boger City.

Good Spring Branch rises in w Haywood
County and flows se into Pretty Hollow
Creek.

Goodwin Creek rises in w Perquimans County and flows e into Perquimans River.
Named for Caleb Goodwin who operated
a mill on the creek about 1820. Appears
as Cypress Swamp on the Moseley map,
1733, and generally known as Cypress
Creek until renamed for the miller. Appears as Goodings Creek on the 1905 soil
survey map.

Goodwin Forest, central Moore County, a
tract of 1,122 acres owned by James L.
Goodwin (d. 1967) from 1930 until his
death when it was given to North Carolina State University for use in education,
research, and recreation. Net proceeds are
used for scholarships in the School of

Forest Resources. Both pine and hardwoods grow in the forest.

Goodwin Hills, community on n Cedar Island in ne Carteret County.

Goodwin Mill Pond, approx. 1½ mi. long, on Goodwin Creek, w Perquimans County.

Goose Bay, off the se end of the largest island in the Hog Island group, ne Carteret County.

Goose Bay Point at the s tip of the largest island in the Hog Island group, ne Carteret County.

Goose Branch rises in e Nash County and flows se into Tar River.

Goosecastle Point, neck of land extending from n end of Church Island into Currituck Sound in central Currituck County.

Goose Creek rises in w Carteret County and flows 3 mi. s into Bogue Sound. Appears on the Moseley map, 1733.

Goose Creek formerly rose in s Clay County and flowed nw into Hiwassee River. Its course is now covered by the waters of Chatuge Lake.

Goose Creek rises in e Gates County and flows se and e into Dismal Swamp.

Goose Creek rises in se Hertford County and flows se into Chowan River.

Goose Creek rises in e Mecklenburg County and flows se into Union County where it turns ne to enter Rocky River.

Goose Creek rises in e Onslow County and flows se into Sanders Creek. Mentioned in local records as early as 1744.

Goose Creek, forming a part of the boundary between Beaufort and Pamlico counties, is formed on the county line by the junction of Campbell and Upper Spring creeks. It flows n into Pamlico River. The Intracoastal Waterway connects Goose Creek and Jones Bay.

Goose Creek rises in w Pamlico County and flows sw into Neuse River. Appears on the Moseley map, 1733.

Goose Creek rises in e Swain County and flows se into Oconaluftee River.

Goose Creek rises in e Tyrrell County and flows e into Alligator River. Appears on the Collet map, 1770.

Goose Creek Island, the ne neck of Pamlico County cut off from the mainland by the Intracoastal Waterway. Near the end of the nineteenth century a Goose Creek Island post office served this area. The North Carolina Wildlife Resources Commission maintains the Goose Creek Wildlife Management Area of 5,865 acres w of the Intracoastal Waterway in Beaufort

and Pamlico counties. See also Greens Land.

Goose Creek Township, n Union County.

Goose Island, in Core Sound near Core Banks in e Carteret County.

Goose Neck Creek rises in n Granville County and flows e into Kerr Reservoir.

Goose Nest. See Oak City.

Goose Nest Township, nw Martin County. See also Oak City.

Goose Pond, community in ne Bertie County. Named for the goose pond on a local plantation owned by the Holley family.

Gordens Island. See Wococon Island.

Gordons Mountain, sw Anson County near the head of Lick Creek. Alt. 400-500 ft.

Gordonton, community in e Davidson County. Earlier known as Gordontown.

Gordonton, comunity in sw Person County. A post office as early as 1830.

Gordontown, town authorized to be established in 1824 on the lands of James Gordon on Cribs Creek, nw Anson County but there is no evidence that the town was laid out.

The Gorge. See Linville Gorge.

Gorman, community in e Durham County.

Gorvas Island, an island of uncertain identity shown on the Moll map, 1729, within the bounds of present Currituck County.

Goshen, community in w Granville County. The home of General Thomas Person (1733-1800) was here. A Goshen District in 1790 had 67 heads of families.

Goshen, community in ne Sampson County at the head of Goshen Swamp.

Goshen, former community in sw Wilkes County on Yadkin River. The site is now a part of the W. Kerr Scott Reservoir.

Goshen Branch rises in s Watauga County and flows ne into Storey Branch.

Goshen District. See Goshen.

Goshen Hill, s Watauga County between Raccoon Branch and Goshen Branch.

Goshen Swamp rises in ne Sampson County and flows se into Duplin County where it continues se until it enters Northeast Cape Fear River. Appears on the Collet map, 1770. Holley's Mill is also shown on the Collet map as being near the headwaters of this stream.

Goss Swamp rises in se Wilson County and flows sw into Toisnot Swamp. Known earlier as Goff's Swamp.

Gouches Branch rises in sw Buncombe County near Bert Mountain and flows ne into Newfound Creek.

Gouge Branch rises n of Gouge Mountain

in se Mitchell County and flows nw into Toe River.

Gouge Knob, central Mitchell County at the head of Rebel Creek.

Gouge Mountain, se Mitchell County.

Gouges Creek rises in e Mitchell County and flows se into North Toe River.

Gouges Creek rises in n Mitchell County and flows s into Little Rock Creek.

Goulds, community in sw Wilkes County on Yadkin River at the mouth of Stony Fork Creek. Named for Andy Gould who operated a mill on Stony Fork Creek.

Goulds Fork, rises in sw Anson County and flows n into Brown Creek.

Gourdvine Creek rises in e Union County and flows nw into Richardson's Creek.

Gover. Gibbs's Point. *See* Gibbs Point.

Governors Creek. *See* Big Governors Creek; Crawley Creek.

Governors Island, loamy section in e Swain County on Tuckasegee River extending se from the mouth of Galbreath Creek to the mouth of Johnson Branch.

Governors Island, community in e Swain County on Johnson Branch. Takes its name from an adjoining loamy area on the Tuckasegee River.

Gowans Cove, nw Cherokee County through which an unnamed stream flows into Shuler Creek.

Gow-ta-no. *See* Neuse River.

Grable Branch rises in central Macon County and flows n into Owenby Branch.

Grabtown, community in sw Bertie County.

Grabur Heights, community in central Alamance County.

Grade, community in nw Alexander County. Alt. approx. 975.

Gradys, community in se Wayne County near Buck Marsh.

Grady Township, sw Pender County.

Gragg, community in ne Avery County. Probably named for John Gragg, Revolutionary soldier (buried at Montezuma) or for Gragg Prong (*which see*) probably also named for him.

Gragg Prong, stream, rises in e central Avery County and flows s into Lost Cove Creek.

Graggs Fork, rises in nw Caldwell County and flows s into Anthonys Creek.

Graham, city and county seat, central Alamance County. Laid out in 1849 at the formation of the county to serve as county seat. Inc. 1851. Named for William A. Graham, governor, 1845-49. In the act providing for the town it was first named

Gallatin, then Montgomery, Berry, and finally Graham as chosen by Representative Giles Mebane who introduced the bill to create Alamance County. Alt. 656. Produces textiles, hosiery, and primary metals.

Graham Branch rises in e Cherokee County and flows se into Slow Creek.

Graham Branch rises in n Granville County and flows nw into Little Grass Creek.

Graham County was formed in 1872 from Cherokee County. Located in the w section of the state, it is bounded by the state of Tennessee, and by Cherokee and Swain counties. It was named for William A. Graham (1804-75), United States Senator, governor of North Carolina, Secretary of the Navy, and Confederate Senator. Area: 299 sq. mi. County seat: Robbinsville with an elevation of 2,150 ft. Townships are Cheoah, Stecoah, and Yellow Creek. Produces poultry, livestock, dairy products, carpets, and lumber.

Graham Creek rises in central Transylvania County and flows ne into Nicholson Creek.

Graham Mountain, on the Buncombe-Henderson County line.

Graham Top, central Cherokee County near the headwaters of Cook Creek.

Graham Township, former township in central Alamance County. Now township number 6.

Graingers, town in ne Lenoir County. Alt. 74. Inc. 1925. Named for Jesse Grainger on whose plantation it developed after a railroad station was est. here.

Grampian Hills, a range of hills about 3 mi. long in s Orange County, running sw and ne. Named for the Grampian Hills, natural boundary between Scottish Highlands and Scottish Lowlands in Scotland.

Granburys Crossroads. *See* Roxobel.

Grandfather, community in sw Watauga County on Watauga River.

Grandfather Mountain, at junction of Avery, Caldwell, and Watauga counties. Alt. 5,964. Privately owned travel attraction. "Mile High Swinging Bridge" connects two peaks. Annual "Singing on the Mountain" and "Gathering of the Scottish Clans" are held. Named from the fact that, when viewed from a distance, the outline of the mountain against the sky suggests the profile of an old man. Highest point in the Blue Ridge. Called *Tanawha* by the Cherokee Indians meaning "a fabulous hawk or eagle."

Grandmother Creek rises in e central Avery County near Grandmother Gap and flows sw into Linville River.

Grandmother Gap, e Avery County.

Grandmother Mountain, e Avery County. Alt. 4,696.

Grandmother Ridge, e central Avery County.

Grandin, former town in ne Caldwell County. Inc. 1913 on the lands of the Grandin Lumber Co. Long inactive in municipal affairs and now a ghost town.

Grandview, community in central Cherokee County at the junction of Davis and Hanging Dog creeks.

Grand View, community in e Watauga County s of Laxon Creek.

Grandy, community in s Currituck County on the e side of North River. Post office est. in late 1890's. Named for Caleb Grandy, first postmaster.

Grange. See Little River.

Granger Branch rises in sw Madison County and flows nw into Spring Creek.

Granger Mountain, w Madison County between Foxtown Mountain and Spring Creek.

Granite City, a formation of granite cliffs s of Devils Court House area, between Blackrock Mountain and Chattooga River on the Jackson-Macon County line.

Granite Falls, a 35-ft. waterfall in Gunpowder Creek, se Caldwell County. Known first as Falls of Gunpowder. Baird's Forge or Baird Iron Works est. here, 1795, by Maj. Andrew Baird.

Granite Falls, town in se Caldwell County. Inc. 1863. Takes its name from the waterfalls of the same name (*which see*) a short distance ne of the town. A former post office serving the community was Baird's Forge; renamed Lovelady in 1824; and Granite Falls in 1887. Produces textiles and pianos. Alt. 1,213.

Granite Quarry, town in s Rowan County. Inc. 1901 as Woodside; named changed in 1905 for local quarries. Post office est. as Woodside, 1891; named changed to Granite Quarry, 1902.

Granny Branch rises in n central Wayne County and flows ne into The Slough.

Granny Cove Branch rises in ne Buncombe County and flows se through Granny Cove into North Fork [Swannanoa River].

Granny Green Mountain, s Macon County between Lowery Creek and Allison Creek.

Granny Mountain, w Haywood County between Johnson Gap and Jonathans Creek.

Granny Squirrel Branch rises in ne Cherokee County and flows ne into Valley River.

Granston Lake. See White Lake.

Grant Branch rises in central Northampton County and flows se into Urahaw Swamp.

Grantham, community in sw Wayne County between Beaverdam Creek and Neuse River. Formerly called Grantham's Store.

Granthams, community in e Craven County.

Grantham's Store. See Grantham.

Grantham Township, sw Wayne County. Named for Grantham family, eighteenth century settlers of the area.

Grant Knob, n Macon County between Mouse Mountain and Devil Den Ridge.

Grants. See Grantsboro.

Grantsboro, community in w Pamlico County. Named for an early settler. Alt. 20. Railroad name is Grants.

Grants Creek rises in ne Onslow County and flows ne into White Oak River. Named for an early settler, Alexander Grant. A 1730 reference to this stream in local records calls it Alex's Creek. Known by present name since 1744.

Grants Creek rises in s Rowan County and flows ne into Yadkin River. Named because the earliest known grants of land in this area were along this stream. Frohock Mill on Grants Creek appears on the Collet map, 1770.

Grant Township, e central Randolph County.

Grantville, community in e Madison County.

Granville County was formed in 1746 from Edgecombe. Located in the ne section of the state it is bounded by Vance, Franklin, Wake, Durham, and Person counties and by the state of Virginia. It was named for

John Carteret, Earl Granville (1690-1763), owner of the Granville District, *which see,* in which the new county was located. Area: 543 sq. mi. County seat: Oxford with an elevation of 476 ft. Townships are Brassfield, Dutchville, Fishing Creek, Oak Hill, Oxford, Salem, Sassafras Fork, Tally Ho, and Walnut Grove. Produces tobacco, corn, wheat, poultry, livestock, hogs, dairy products, textiles, hosiery, lumber, and apparel.

Granville District was the portion of North Carolina allotted to John Carteret, Earl Granville (1690-1763), one of the Lords Proprietors who refused to sell his interest in North Carolina to the Crown in 1729. The upper half of present day North Carolina was included in the District which extended from the Virginia boundary to 35° 34', a strip sixty miles wide. The southern line was run from the coast to Bath in 1744, to Haw River in 1746, and to Rocky River in 1766. The District was lost to the Granville estate at the time of the American Revolution.

Granville Parish, Church of England, Granville County, est. in 1758 in the w part of the county, when St. John's Parish (est. 1746 with the formation of the county and coextensive with it) was divided. After St. John's Parish in the e became Bute County in 1764, Granville Parish was coextensive with Granville County. In 1767 there were 1,022 white taxables in the parish. The parish as a unit of local administration was abolished in 1776 with the adoption of the state constitution and the disestablishment of the Church of England. *See also* St. John's Parish.

Grape Branch rises in ne Duplin County and flows sw into Northeast Cape Fear River.

Grape Branch rises in s Jones County and flows se into White Oak River.

Grape Branch rises in se Nash County and flows ne into Tar River.

Grape Cove, s Swain County between Mica Knob and Marr Branch.

Grape Creek rises in central Cherokee County and flows se and sw into Hiwassee River.

Grape Creek rises in Great Dover Swamp, n Jones County, and flows ne into Craven County where it enters Cove Creek.

Grape Creek, community in central Cherokee County near the mouth of Hanging Dog Creek.

Grapevine Bay, se Tyrrell County in Alligator River.

Grapevine Landing, se Tyrrell County on Grapevine Bay.

Grapevine Ridge, e Madison County between West Fork [Bull Creek] and Beetree Creek.

Grapevine Township, former township in central Madison County, now township number 14.

Graphiteville, community in w McDowell County. Alt. 2,037.

Grass Branch rises in n central Ashe County and flows s into Windfall Creek.

Grass Land Ridge, s Madison County between South Fork [Big Pine Creek] and Little Pine Creek. Alt. 3,884.

Grassy Bald, mountain on the Haywood-Jackson County line. Alt. 5,613.

Grassy Branch rises in central Buncombe County and flows s into Swannanoa River.

Grassy Branch rises in se Buncombe County and flows ne into Rock Creek.

Grassy Branch rises in w Cleveland County and flows ne into First Broad River.

Grassy Branch rises in central Haywood County and flows nw into Pigeon River.

Grassy Branch rises in nw Macon County and flows sw into Queens Creek.

Grassy Branch rises in w central Swain County and flows sw into Yalaka Creek.

Grassy Branch rises in se Swain County and flows n into Connelly Creek.

Grassy Branch rises in e Swain County and flows nw into Raven Fork.

Grassy Camp Creek rises in sw Jackson County and flows ne into Norton Creek.

Grassy Cove Gap, s Haywood County between Grassy Cove Ridge and Little Buckeye Cove.

Grassy Cove Ridge, s Haywood County, extends e from Grassy Cove Top to Grassy Cove Gap.

Grassy Cove Top, s Haywood County on the s end of Shining Rock Ledge.

Grassy Creek rises in n Alexander County and flows s and w into Lower Little River.

Grassy Creek rises in s Ashe County and flows s approx. 4 mi. into South Fork New River near the Watauga County line.

Grassy Creek rises in Grayson County, Va., and flows se into Ashe County where it enters North Fork New River.

Grassy Creek rises in se Buncombe County and flows sw into Henderson County where it enters Broad River.

Grassy Creek rises in w Granville County and flows ne into Kerr Reservoir.

Grassy Creek rises in sw Henderson County and flows w into Transylvania County where it enters Little River.

Grassy Creek rises in w Jackson County and flows se into West Fork Tuckasegee River.

Grassy Creek rises in w Madison County and flows ne into French Broad River.

Grassy Creek rises in s Mitchell County and flows n into North Toe River.

Grassy Creek rises in ne Moore County and flows ne into Deep River. Appears in local records as early as 1747 and on the MacRae map, 1833.

Grassy Creek rises in e Surry County and flows s into Yadkin River. Appears on the Collet map, 1770.

Grassy Creek rises in e Transylvania County and flows w into Little River.

Grassy Creek rises in n Union County and flows ne into Rocky River.

Grassy Creek rises in e Watauga County and flows se into South Fork New River.

Grassy Creek, community in ne Ashe County. Settled about 1788.

Grassy Creek, community in n Granville County. A church here was est. in 1755.

Grassy Creek Township, ne Ashe County.

Grassy Creek Township, s Mitchell County.

Grassy Gap, on the Buncombe-Haywood County line on Newfound Mountain.

Grassy Gap, n Cherokee County in the Unicoi Mountains.

Grassy Gap, se Clay County on Chunky Gal Mountain.

Grassy Gap, on Graham-Swain County line between Grassy Top and Tyre Knob.

Grassy Gap, n Mitchell County between Grassy Knob and Right Fork Bean Creek.

Grassy Gap, sw Swain County between Silvermine Gap and Briertown Mountain.

Grassy Gap Branch rises in w Watauga County and flows nw into Buckeye Creek on the Avery-Watauga County line.

Grassy Islands, several islands in Pee Dee River n of Blewett Falls Lake on the Anson-Richmond County line. Shown on the Price map, 1808 and the MacRae map, 1833.

Grassy Knob, n Buncombe County between Salton Gap and Frosty Knob.

Grassy Knob, nw Buncombe County, ne of High Knob.

Grassy Knob, s Buncombe County.

Grassy Knob, central Caldwell County.

Grassy Knob, n Haywood County between Pigeon River and Wilkins Creek.

Grassy Knob, w Haywood County on Eaglenest Ridge.

Grassy Knob, nw Iredell County. Now tree-covered, but apparently grassland when first discovered by settlers. The first Baptist church in the county was organized at its base in 1789, and an old Masonic lodge exists in the community nearby.

Grassy Knob, s Jackson County between Round Mountain and Whitewater River.

Grassy Knob on the Jackson-Macon County line.

Grassy Knob, a peak on Grassy Mountain on the McDowell-Mitchell County line. Alt. approx. 2,020.

Grassy Knob, central Macon County at the head of Poindexter Branch.

Grassy Knob, n Madison County between Shelton Laurel Creek and Spillcorn Creek.

Grassy Knob, n Mitchell County between Grassy Gap and Rich Branch.

Grassy Knob, central Watauga County on the e slope of Rich Mountain.

Grassy Knob, w Yancey County between Price and Banks creeks.

Grassy Knob Branch rises in s Yancey County and flows se into Upper Creek.

Grassy Knob Ridge, s Yancey County, between Lower Creek and Grassy Knob Branch.

Grassy Knobs, s Macon County between Rattlesnake Ridge and Middle Creek.

Grassy Lot Gap, n Transylvania County between Thompson Creek and Bradley Creek. Alt. 3,358.

Grassy Mountain, sw Henderson County near Grassy Creek. Alt. 3,678.

Grassy Mountain on the McDowell-Rutherford County line.

Grassy Point, e Beaufort County, on Pungo River.

Grassy Ridge, on the Avery-Mitchell County line.

Grassy Ridge Bald, on the Avery-Mitchell County line. Alt. 6,200-6,300.

Grassy Ridge Bald. See Bald Mountain.

Grassy Ridge Branch rises in s Haywood County and flows nw into Middle Prong.

Grassy Top on the Cherokee County, N. C.-Monroe County, Tenn., line in the Unicoi Mountains. Alt. 4,979.

Grassy Top, on the Graham-Swain County line between The Jump-up and Grassy Gap.

Grassy Top, peak on Holland Mountain on Haywood-Buncombe County line.

Gravel Creek rises in s Buncombe County and flows se into Cane Creek.

Gravel Knob on the Madison County, N. C.-Greene County, Tenn., line.

Gravelly Hill. *See* Hickory Grove Crossroads.

Graves Ferry appears on the Moseley map, 1733, over the Neuse River near the mouth of Bachelor Creek, s Craven County. The road from Bath to Wilmington crosses here. A 1901 map shows Nelsons Old Ferry at this site.

Graveyard Cove in White Oak River, w Carteret County, a short distance n of the community of Stella. Named for nearby cemetery.

Graveyard Creek rises in s Mitchell County and flows ne into Grassy Creek.

Graveyard Mountain, n McDowell County between North Fork [Catawba River] and Woodlawn. Alt. approx. 2,250.

Graveyard Ridge, w central Clay County in the Tusquitee Mountains, runs n and s along the Hiwassee River.

Graveyard Ridge, s Haywood County, between Yellowstone Prong and Dark Prong. A flat area here has numerous mounds resembling graves. They have been dug into but no human remains found. It has been decided that a hurricane or windstorm perhaps 500 to 1,000 years ago uprooted many trees. Through the years the old root stumps and trees rotted out, leaving only the dirt mound. There is a slight depression beside each mound which is the hole from which the stumps came.

Graybeal, community in w Ashe County. Alt. approx. 3,000.

Graybeard Creek rises in ne Cherokee County and flows w into Vengeance Creek s of Brushy Head Mountain.

Graybeard Mountain, on the Buncombe-McDowell County line. Alt. 5,360-5,400.

Gray Camp Branch rises in nw Haywood County and flows se into Big Creek.

Gray Gap, s Macon County between The Pinnacle and Tessentee Creek.

Grays Branch rises in sw Caswell County and flows se into Stony Creek.

Grays Branch rises in n Columbus County and flows sw into Pinelog Swamp.

Grays Chapel, community in ne Randolph County. Named for a local family. A post office est. here as early as 1882.

Grays Creek rises in s Cumberland County and flows se in an arc into Cape Fear River.

Grays Creek rises in sw Rutherford County and flows w into Broad River.

Grays Creek rises in e Wilkes County and flows ne into Yadkin River. Named for

James Gray, pre-Revolutionary settler here.

Grays Creek, community in s central Cumberland County approx. 6 mi. s of city of Fayetteville.

Grays Creek Township, sw Cumberland County.

Grays Landing. *See* Windsor.

Grays Mill appears on the Collet map, 1770, near the mouth of Sawyers Creek, w Camden County.

Grays Mountain, s Randolph County between Needhams Mountain and Pond Mountain.

Grayson, community in nw Ashe County.

Gray's Point, central Onslow County in s Farnell Bay.

Gray Swamp, s Pasquotank County between Little Flatty Creek and Big Flatty Creek.

Gray Wolf Creek rises in n Swain County in Great Smoky Mountains National Park and flows sw into Forney Creek.

Greasy Branch rises in w Madison County and flows e into Spring Creek.

Greasy Branch rises in w central Swain County and flows sw into Little Tennessee River.

Greasy Corner. *See* Davie Crossroads.

Greasy Cove, nw Buncombe County, se of Rogers Gap.

Greasy Cove Prong rises in se Haywood County and flows e into East Fork Pigeon River.

Greasy Creek rises in ne Alexander County and flows e into South Yadkin River.

Greasy Creek rises in sw Clay County and flows sw into Brasstown Creek.

Greasy Creek rises in central Clay County in Winchester Cove and flows nw into Tusquitee Creek.

Greasy Creek rises in n Mitchell County and flows s into Big Rock Creek.

Greasy Creek. *See* Abingdon Creek.

Greasy Mountain, sw Wilkes County between Long Fork of Beaver Creek and Beaver Creek.

Great Alamance Creek is formed by the junction of Little Alamance and Big Alamance creeks in e Guilford County and flows e across Alamance County where it enters Haw River. Appears as Aramancy River on the Moseley map, 1733. Called Aramanchy River by William Byrd, 1728.

Great Alegator Dismal Swamp appears on the Collet map, 1770, as the large swampy area in much of present Tyrrell, Dare, and n Hyde counties.

Great Branch rises in e Beaufort County and flows e into Pungo River.

Great Branch rises in s Nash County and flows e into Tar River.

Great Branch rises in ne Pitt County and flows se into Meadow Branch.

Great Coharie Creek rises in n Sampson County and flows s to join Little Coharie Creek in forming Coharie River. Appears as Cohary Swamp on the Collet map, 1770.

Great Coneghta Pocosin. See Conetoe Creek.

Great Contentnea Creek. See Contentnea Creek.

Great Coteckney Creek. See Contentnea Creek.

Great Craggy Mountains, range in ne Buncombe County extending s from Balsam Gap to the Swannanoa River. Alt. 3,332. Known by the Cherokee Indians as *Sunnatee*, "morning."

Great Creek rises in North River Pocosin in s Camden County and flows e into North River.

Great Creek, tidal creek in Jarrett Bay, se Carteret County.

Great Creek. See Deep Creek; Smith Creek.

Great Dismal Swamp. See Dismal Swamp.

Great Ditch, waterway between two of the e islands in the Hog Island group, ne Carteret County.

Great Dover Swamp, located in ne Jones County and sw Craven County, drains sw into Trent River and its tributaries. Mill Branch, Moseley Creek, Bachelor Creek, Grape Creek, Rollover Creek, and Cove Creek rise in Great Dover Swamp.

Great Elliby. See Upper Bartons Creek.

Great Falls on the Yadkin River a short distance s of The Narrows on the Montgomery-Stanly County line.

Great Falls. See Roanoke Rapids.

The Great Falls. See High Falls.

Great Fishing Creek. See Fishing Creek.

Great Hammock Swash, lies between Core Beach and Core Banks (on the sound side) in e Carteret County.

Great Hogback, mountain on Jackson-Transylvania County line. Alt. 4,785.

Great Iron Mountain. See Bald Mountain; Great Smoky Mountians.

Great Island, in se Bertie County between Cashie River and Middle River, and formed in part by the Thoroughfare. The largest of a group of nine islands, it measures approx. 4¾ mi. long and 2½ mi. wide. See also Purchace Islands.

Great Island, approx. 200 acres of high land located in North River Pocosin, e Camden County, about two miles e of Alder Branch and near the headwaters of Hunting Creek. No longer inhabited, but at one time as many as eight families lived here.

Great Island, in Core Sound near Core Banks in e Carteret County.

Great Island, a small marshy island in the Neuse River in se Craven County.

Great Island, in the waters of Pamlico Sound off the w coast of Hatteras Island, e Dare County, sw of the community of Waves.

Great Island, s Hyde County in Pamlico Sound, 25-30 acres in area. Appears as Gul Island on the Collet map, 1770. See also Abigails Islands.

Great Island, ne Tyrrell County in the mouth of Alligator Creek.

Great Island Bay, in Core Sound against the Core Banks, e Carteret County.

Great Lake, a natural lake in Croatan National Forest, s Craven County. Covers approx. 2,600 acres. Max. depth 4 to 5 ft. One of several lakes in Lakes Pocosin.

Great Lick Creek. See Lick Creek.

Great Marsh, tidal marsh covering the w portion of Knotts Island, ne Currituck County.

Great Marsh. See Bells Island.

Great Marsh Point. See Bells Point.

Great Mountain, ne Henderson County.

Great Neck Landing, e Onslow County on Queens Creek. In recent years the name Reed's Landing has come to be used.

Great Pee Dee River. See Pee Dee River.

Great Pisgah. See Mount Pisgah.

Great Pond, in the nw part of Hog Island, on the s side of Pamlico Sound, ne Carteret County.

Great Sandy Run Pocosin, w Onslow County between Shelter Swamp and Sandy Run Swamp.

Great Shell Rock. See North Rock.

Great Smoky Mountains are a part of the Appalachian Mountains, *which see*, and they lie along the North Carolina-Tennessee state line. Clingmans Dome at 6,642 ft., is the highest peak. The first written reference to the name Smoky is probably that found in the act of cession, passed in 1789 by the General Assembly of North Carolina, which, in describing the boundary of North Carolina and what is now Tennessee, stated. ". . . thence along the highest ridge of the said mountain to the place where it is called Great Iron or

Smoky Mountain." *See also* Bald Mountains.

Great Smoky Mountains National Park lies in portions of Haywood and Swain counties, N. C., and Blount, Cocke, and Sevier counties, Tenn. Establishment authorized by Congress in 1926, the culmination of activity for this purpose beginning in the 1880's. Administered by the National Park Service since 1931. Contains approx. 461,000 acres. Has campgrounds, museums, restorations, nature trails and other features of interest including a variety of wild animals, birds, and plants. Clingmans Dome, alt. 6,642, is the highest point in the Park and it has an observation tower.

Great Swamp in Beaufort, Martin, and Washington counties between the Roanoke and Pamlico Rivers.

Great Swamp, swamp lands covering most of central Currituck County and extending into e Camden County.

Great Swamp rises in e Johnston County, flows ne across nw Wayne County, and into s Wilson County where it enters Black Creek.

Great Swamp rises in Grindle Pocosin in n Pitt County and flows s into Johnsons Mill Run.

Great Swamp rises in n Tyrrell County and flows n into Albemarle Sound.

Great Swamp. *See* Bloomery Swamp; Starkeys Creek.

Great Swamp Branch. *See* Hall Swamp.

Great Swamp Township, nw Wayne County.

Great White Marsh. *See* White Marsh.

Greenback, community in n central Warren County. Post office est. 1884, but discontinued in 1907.

Green Banks Landing on Cape Fear River, ne Brunswick County.

Greenbrier Knob. *See* Mount Davis.

Green Cove, valley of Nichols Branch in s Macon County.

Green Cove, community on Green Cove Creek in e Mitchell County. Site of a large commercial apple orchard.

Green Cove Creek rises in e Mitchell County and flows nw into Cane Creek.

Green Creek rises in s Haywood County and flows n into West Fork Pigeon River.

Green Creek rises in e Jackson County and flows nw into Panthertown Creek.

Green Creek rises in sw Jackson County on the s slope of Whiteside Mountain and flows se into Chattooga River.

Green Creek rises in e Mitchell County and flows w into Little Rock Creek.

Green Creek rises in e Pamlico County and flows s into Broad Creek.

Green Creek rises in ne Rockingham County and flows n into Wolf Island Creek.

Greene Channel in the sw end of Topsail Sound, s Pender County.

Greene County was formed in 1799 when the name of Glasgow County, *which see,* was changed to Greene. Located in the e section of the state, it is bounded by Pitt, Lenoir, Wayne, and Wilson counties. It was named for General Nathanael Greene (1742-86), outstanding Revolutionary War leader whose action at the Battle of Guilford Courthouse saved North Carolina from the British and led to the American victory at Yorktown. Area: 269 sq. mi. County seat: Snow Hill with an elevation of 74 ft. Townships are Bull Head, Carrs, Hookerton, Jason, Olds, Ormonds, Shine, Snow Hill, and Speights Bridge. Produces tobacco, corn, cotton, poultry, hogs, lumber, and textiles. *See also* St. Patrick's Parish.

Greene County, now in Tennessee, was created in 1783 and named in honor of General Nathanael Greene (1742-86). Greeneville became the county seat. This was a part of the territory ceded by North Carolina in 1789 to the Federal government. For further information *see* D. L. Corbitt, *The Formation of North Carolina Counties.*

Greene Ridge, n Madison County between Big Creek and Dry Creek.

Greenesville. *See* Greenville.

Greene Township, se Guilford County. Named for General Nathanael Greene.

Greenevills Rode. *See* Port Granvil.

Greenfield Lake, a natural lake now within the limits of city of Wilmington, w New Hanover County. Covers 125 acres; max. depth 12 ft. Mentioned by name in the will of Dr. Samuel Green, original owner, about 1760. A municipal park and garden surround the lake.

Greenfield Ridge, n Buncombe County between Eller Cove and Rattlesnake Ridge.

Green Gap, in central Graham County at the head of Mountain Creek.

Green Gap, on Yellow Creek Mountains in n Graham County s of Fontana Village.

Green Gap, e Haywood County between Cove Creek and Fines Creek.

Green Hill, community in w Rutherford County between Maple and Mountain creeks.

Green Hill, an eighteenth-century community in w Washington County on Conaby Creek, e of the town of Plymouth. The community declined as Plymouth, on the Roanoke River grew in importance as a port town.

Green Hill, s Watauga County n of the community of Green Park.

Green Hill Place, home of Major Green Hill (1741-1826) in central Franklin County, 1 mi. e of Louisburg. Site of the first annual conference of the Methodist Episcopal Church, 1785.

Green Hill Township, w Rutherford County.

Green Island, in the waters of Pamlico Sound off the n tip of Pea Island, e Dare County.

Green Knob, s Haywood County in the middle of Fork Ridge.

Green Knob on the Haywood-Transylvania County line between Bennett Gap and Pisgah Ridge. Alt. 5,150.

Green Knob, on the McDowell-Yancey County line between Deep Gap and Flinty Gap. Alt. 5,070.

Greenland Creek rises in se Jackson County and flows nw to join Panthertown Creek to form Tuckasegee River.

Greenlee, community in s central McDowell County on Catawba River. Settled before the Revolution.

Green Level, community in w Wake County on head of Whiteoak Creek, est. before 1865.

Green Mountain, a peak of Linville Mountain on the Burke-McDowell County line.

Green Mountain, a range extending from central into ne Caldwell County. Alt. from 2,000 to 2,330. Indian name was *Oawahua.* Indian Grave Gap here is the site of Indian burials. Indians lived on the top of the range.

Green Mountain, n Henderson County between Kyles Creek and Piney Mountain.

Green Mountain, n Jackson County between Hornbuckle Creek and Open Branch.

Green Mountain extends n in ne Yancey County from near the head of Shoal Creek to Toe River. Alt. approx. 4,500.

Green Mountain, community in n Yancey County on Toe River. Alt. 4,990.

Green Mountain Branch rises in s Watauga County and flows sw into Boone Fork.

Green Mountain Gap, n central Yancey County between Phillips Knob and Three Quarters Creek.

Green Mountain Knob, s Watauga County s of Martin Knob.

Green Mountain Township, ne Yancey County.

Green Oak Creek rises in e Pender County and flows sw into Northeast Cape Fear River.

Green Park, former community in n Caldwell County, now within the limits of Blowing Rock, *which see.* Named for the Green family, descendants of Richard Green who settled here in the late eighteenth century.

Green Point, ne Carteret County at mouth of Lewis Creek on e side of Cedar Island.

Green Point, ne Carteret County on w side of central Cedar Island, extending into West Bay.

Green Pond. *See* Highs Crossroads.

Green Ridge, s Haywood County between Tom Creek and Green Creek.

Green River rises in sw Henderson County and flows ne into Polk County where it turns se to enter Broad River on the Polk-Rutherford County line. Lake Summit in Henderson County and Lake Adger in Polk County are on Green River. A bridge across the Green River gorge in se Henderson County is 225 ft. above the river. It is the highest bridge in the state and probably the highest in the se United States.

Green River, community in e Polk County between Mill Creek and Whiteoak Creek.

Green River Township, s Henderson County.

Green River Gap on the Henderson-Transylvania County line. Alt. 2,700. Green River rises nearby.

Greensboro, city and county seat, central Guilford County. Alt. 838. Est. 1808 and inc. 1810. Named for General Nathanael Greene (1742-86), American leader at nearby Battle of Guilford Courthouse, 1781. Produces textiles, hosiery, apparel, fabricated metals, paper boxes, dairy products, tobacco, chemicals, electronics, and baked goods. The University of North Carolina at Greensboro, Bennett College for Women, Greensboro College, Guilford

College, and North Carolina Agricultural and Technical University are located here.

Greens Branch rises in n Columbus County and flows se into West Prong Creek.

Greens Creek rises in w Jackson County and flows e into Savannah Creek.

Greens Creek rises in se Pamlico County and flows e into Neuse River. Appears as Powel's Creek on the Lawson map, 1709. Soon afterwards it came to be known as Farnifold Green's Creek for Furnifold Green who had a grant for 1,700 acres here in 1707. Green was killed by the Tuscarora Indians in 1714.

Greens Creek, community in w Jackson County on Savannah Creek. Alt. 2,120.

Greens Creek Township, w Jackson County.

Greens Creek Township, se Polk County.

Greens Fork, community in central Gates County.

Greens Gap, on the Jackson-Macon County line.

Green's Ferry. *See* Spring Bank.

Green's Grove. *See* Washburns Store.

Greens Land is the name applied on the Ogilby map of 1671 to that part of present-day Pamlico County which lies between the Pamlico and Bay rivers.

Greens Millpond, w central Gates County on Cole Creek. Covers approx. 30 acres; max. depth 8 ft. Formerly known as Lilleys Millpond.

Greens Mill Run rises in central Pitt County and flows ne into Tar River. Approx. 6½ mi. long. Perhaps the same stream as Rock Creek on the Moseley map, 1733, and the Collet map, 1770.

Greens Creek rises in se Polk County and flows ne into Whiteoak Creek.

Greens Point, a projection of n Hatteras Island into Pamlico Sound, e Dare County, beside the community of Rodanthe.

Greens Store, community in se Rutherford County.

Greens Thorofare, a channel of water separated from the main body of Neuse River, and bypassing a curve in the river in n Craven County. Name appears in local records as early as 1819. Land in this area was included in a 1707 grant to Furnifold Green, killed by the Tuscarora Indians in 1714.

Greenstreet Mountain, n Wilkes County parallel to East Prong Roaring River. Named for a local family.

Green Swamp, nw Brunswick and e Columbus counties, an area of approx. 140 sq. mi. of peat and muck timberland. In 1795

the state of N. C. granted 170,120 acres here to Benjamin Rowell, William Collins, and Stephen Williams. *See also* River View Community.

Green Swamp, n Pender County between Angola Bay and Northeast Cape Fear River drains sw into Northeast Cape Fear River.

Green Top, mountain peak in sw Buncombe County between Rich Knob and Yellow Gap.

Green Valley, the valley through which Round Hill Branch flows in nw Buncombe County.

Green Valley, community in w Ashe County.

Greenville, city and county seat, central Pitt County on Tar River. Inc. 1771 as Martinsborough, named for Josiah Martin (1737-86), last royal governor of North Carolina, serving from 1771 to 1775. Name changed in 1786 to Greensville in honor of Nathanael Greene (1742-86), Revolutionary general. With the passage of time the name came to be spelled as it is today. East Carolina University, begun in 1908, is located here. Produces tobacco, lumber, textiles, batteries, bakery products, and boats. Alt. 64.

Greenville Sound, e New Hanover County between Middle Sound on the n and Masonboro Sound on the s.

Greenville Township, central Pitt County.

Greenwood Township, former township in s Lee County, now township number 1.

Greenwood Township, e Moore County.

Greer Branch rises in nw Swain County in Great Smoky Mountains National Park and flows sw into Twentymile Creek.

Greer Branch rises in s Watauga County and flows e into Middle Fork [South Fork New River].

Greer Creek rises in s central Henderson County and flows nw into Mud Creek.

Greer Creek. *See* South Fork.

Greer Knob, nw Swain County in Great Smoky Mountains National Park on Twentymile Ridge between Greer Branch and Proctor Sang Branch. Alt. 4,463.

Gregg Branch rises in central Buncombe County near Jack Gap and flows se into Beetree Creek.

Gregory, community in w Currituck County. Alt. 9.

Gregory Bald, peak on the Swain County, N. C.-Blount County, Tenn., line in Great Smoky Mountains National Park between Parsons Bald and Rich Gap. Alt. 4,948. Known earlier as Bald Spot Mountain.

Gregory Branch rises in e Cherokee County and flows nw into Pipes Branch.

Gregory Branch rises in nw Haywood County and flows se into Big Creek.

Gregory Crossroads, community in nw Onslow Couny near New River.

Gresham's Lake in central Wake County, on Perry Creek, ne of city of Raleigh. Formed in 1939, to cover 100 acres with a maximum depth of 30 ft. Named for owner, S. T. Gresham. Used for boating and fishing.

Gretna Green, community in w Halifax County.

Grey Eagle. *See* Black Mountain.

Greystone, community in e Vance County. Alt. 493. Settled in 1880 and named for gray granite once mined here in large quantities.

Grice Branch rises in se Buncombe County and flows sw into Broad River.

Grier Bald. *See* Big Bald.

Griffins Crossroads, community in e Chatham County.

Griffins Township, se Martin County.

Griffins Township, nw Nash County.

Griffinsville *See* Marshville.

Griffith, community in s Mecklenburg County.

Griffith Branch rises in w Mitchell County and flows s into Brummett Creek.

Griffith's Mill Pond. *See* Worrells Mill Pond.

Griffton. *See* Grifton.

Grifton, town in s Pitt and n Lenoir counties. Known as Peter's Ferry as early as 1756 when Hugh McAden stopped here; in 1764 it was called Blount's Ford; and in the mid-nineteenth century was called Bell's Ferry for the ferry operated by Warren Bell. Inc. in 1883 as Bell's Ferry. Name changed to Griffton in 1889 to honor C. M. A. Griffin, local merchant. Griffton soon came to be spelled Grifton. Produces apparel. Alt. 28.

Grifton Township, s Pitt County. Created after 1950.

Griggs Branch rises in ne Cherokee County and flows sw between Fork Ridge and Old Mattie Ridge into Welch Mill Creek.

Grill Cove, nw Swain County in Great Smoky Mountains National Park on Ekaneetlee Creek.

Grimes Crossroads, community in ne Forsyth County. Also known as Crims Crossroads.

Grimesland, town in e Pitt County. The first settlement here in the eighteenth century was known as Boyd's Ferry, a name which it retained until after 1880. (Boyd's Ferry across the Tar River, ¼ mile ne of the town, continued to operate until after 1909.) For a short while it was called Mt. Calvert, and in 1885 the post office was named Nelsonville. In 1887 the name was changed to Grimesland in honor of J. Bryan Grimes (1828-1880), Confederate general. Inc. 1893. Alt. 36.

Grimesland Township, e Pitt County. Created after 1950.

Grimes Millpond, in e Pitt County, drains into Chicod Creek.

Grimshawes, community on the head of the Chattooga River in s Jackson County. Named for the first postmaster, Thomas Grimshawe, Sr.

Grindle Creek rises in n Pitt County and flows se into Tar River. Probably named for the fish, *amiatus calva,* sometimes commonly known as grindle.

Grindle Pocosin, n Pitt County.

Grindool. *See* Whitehurst.

Grindstone Branch rises in central Anson County and flows n into Goulds Fork.

Grindstone Knob, e Macon County at the head of Indian Camp Creek.

Grindstone Knob, e Macon County between Ellijay Creek and Walnut Creek.

Grindstone Ridge, nw Henderson County near Bradley Creek.

Grinnel Hill, community in n Tyrrell County near town of Columbia.

Grinnell Creek, swampy lowgrounds of se Bertie County between Broad Creek and Middle River.

Grinnel Slough, stream and swamp in s Pitt County between Contentnea and Swift creeks and bordered on the s by Neuse River. The stream flows nw into Contentnea Creek.

Grissettown, community in sw Brunswick County.

Grissett Swamp rises in sw Columbus County and flows se into Monie Swamp.

Grissom, community in se Granville County.

Grist Mountain, e Davidson County between Flat Swamp Creek and Lick Creek.

Grists, community in w Columbus County.

Grogan Creek rises in n Transylvania County and flows ne into Davidson River.

Grogansville, town in nw Rockingham County Inc. 1889 at W. P. Grogan's store, but apparently never functioned as a municipality.

Grog Creek rises in e Rutherford County and flows s into Cleveland County where it enters Sandy Run Creek.

Grog Creek rises in s Rutherford County and flows w into Broad River.

Groometown, community in s Guilford County. Named for local family.

Gross Mine, former gold mine in s Yadkin County on Harmon Creek.

Groundhog Branch rises in s Watauga County and flows se into Yadkin Creek.

Groundhog Creek rises in n Haywood County and flows sw into Pigeon River.

Groundhog Ridge, nw Cherokee County in the Unicoi Mountains.

Groundnut Creek rises in nw Lenoir County and flows se into Moseley Creek. Named for the groundnut or peanut. Groundnut Swamp appears in local records as early as 1750-60.

Grove Creek rises in central Duplin County and flows e into Northeast Cape Fear River. Appears on the Collet map, 1770, as Grove Swamp.

Grove Hill, community in s Warren County e of Buffalo Creek and s of Reedy Creek. Settled prior to 1800; post office est. 1828 but discontinued in 1954. During 1840, the post office name was temporarily changed to Owens Store. *See also* Fontena.

Grovemont, community in se Buncombe County n of Swannanoa.

Grovemont. *See* Kenansville.

Grover, town in s Cleveland County. Inc. 1885. Alt. 877. Named for Grover Cleveland (1837-1908), President of the United States, 1885-89, 1893-97. Produces textiles.

Grovestone, community in se Buncombe County between Swannanoa and Black Mountain.

Grove Swamp. *See* Grove Creek.

Grove Township, e Harnett County. Named for Congressman William Barry Grove (1764-1818), of Fayetteville.

Gudger. *See* Newfoundland.

Gudger Knob, e Haywood County on the ne end of Crab Orchard Fields.

Gudger's Ford. *See* Azalea.

Guerrant Springs. *See* Oregon Hill.

Guffy Branch rises in s Wake County and flows s into Ditch Branch.

Guide, community in s Columbus County.

Guilders Creek rises in n central Yancey County on n slopes of Rocky Knob and Phillips Knob and flows nw into Jacks Creek.

Guilford, community in s central Beaufort County.

Guilford, community in w central Guilford County. Named for the county.

Guilford College, town in w central Guilford County. Quaker settlement founded 1750 and known as New Garden. Boarding school opened 1837; renamed Guilford College in 1889 at which time the community name also was changed. Chartered 1895. The college is now within the limits of the city of Greensboro. Alt. 939.

Guilford County was formed in 1771 from Rowan and Orange counties. Located in the n central section of the state, it is bounded by Alamance, Randolph, Davidson, Forsyth, and Rockingham counties. It was named for Francis North, first Earl of Guilford (1704-90), member of Parliament and intimate personal friend of George III and Queen Charlotte. Area: 652 sq. mi. County seat: Greensboro with an elevation of 838 ft. Townships are Bruce, Center Grove, Deep River, Fentress, Friendship, Gilmer, Greene, High Point, Jamestown, Jefferson, Madison, Monroe, Morehead, Oak Ridge, Rock Creek, Sumner, and Washington. Produces tobacco, corn, wheat, oats, poultry, eggs, dairy products, livestock, hogs, textiles, hosiery, apparel, paper boxes, baked goods, cigarettes, toys, lumber, chemicals, and corrugated boxes.

Guilford Courthouse, former county seat, central Guilford County. Est. 1774; chartered as Martinville *(which see)*, 1785; abandoned 1808. Battle here on March 15, 1781, between American General Nathanael Greene and British General Lord Charles Cornwallis; site now a National Military Park.

Guinea Mill Run, a stream, rises in n Currituck County and flows se into Tull Creek. A part of Dismal Swamp drains into Guinea Mill Run.

Gulden Creek rises in se Craven County and flows nw into Clubfoot Creek.

Gulf, town in s central Chatham County. Inc. 1913 but long inactive in municipal affairs. Early nineteenth-century center of trade and coal mining. Alt. 275. The geographic center of the state, *which see*, is nearby.

Gulf Branch rises in nw Burke County and flows sw into Linville River.

Gulf Branch rises in s Macon County and flows n into Big Laurel Branch.

Gulf Creek rises in se Chatham County and flows sw into Cape Fear River.

Gulf Prong rises in ne Swain County and flows s to join Chasm Prong in forming Bradley Fork.

Gulf Stream is a warm current in the Atlantic Ocean which flows out of the Gulf of Mexico along the e coast of the United States and e in the North Atlantic toward Europe. Along the coast of North Carolina it approaches Cape Hatteras and gives that part of the state a milder winter than would otherwise be the case. Winter temperatures of the surface waters here are approx. 63° while summer temperatures are about 80°. The Gulf Stream was first described by Benjamin Franklin, and it appears on a map prepared for him in 1770 by Timothy Folger.

Gulf Township, sw Chatham County.

Gul Island. *See* Great Island.

Gulledge Township, s central Anson County.

Gulley's Mill, community in s Wake County.

Gull Island, a tiny island in sw Carteret County in Bogue Sound.

Gull Island Bay on the w shore of Hatteras Island in the waters of Pamlico Sound, s Dare County opposite Gull Island.

Gull Shoal, a small island in Pamlico Sound off the w shore of Hatteras Island, se Dare County. The name appears in local records as early as 1794 as "Gull Shore."

Gull Shore. *See* Gull Shoal.

Gull Rock, community in e Hyde County on Wyesocking Bay. A former post office here was Gulrock.

Gulrock. *See* Gull Rock.

Gumberry, community in n central Northampton County. Settled about 1882. Alt. 134. Name probably derived from fruit of a tree described by John Lawson (d. 1712) as a type of black gum (*Nyssa Ogeche?*), the berries of which were used by the Indians in making soup and in cooking peas and beans.

Gumberry Swamp rises in w Northampton County and flows s to join Lily Pond Creek in forming Wheeler Creek. For origin of name, *see* Gumberry.

Gum Branch rises in sw Gates County and flows ne into Taylor Millpond.

Gum Branch rises in w Hoke County and flows se into Rockfish Creek.

Gum Branch rises in w Mecklenburg County and flows w into Long Creek.

Gum Branch rises in se Wilson County and flows nw into Whiteoak Swamp.

Gum Branch, community in n Onslow County between Cowhorn Swamp and Bachelors Swamp. Mentioned in local records as early as 1748.

Gum Corner, community in w Currituck County.

Gum Creek rises in e Stanly County and flows se into Cedar Creek.

Gumflats Creek rises in ne Cherokee County and flows nw into Taylor Creek.

Gum Fork, rises in n Lee County and flows ne into Hughes Creek.

Gum Forks, community in nw Northampton County.

Gum Lake, ne Nash County on Beaverdam Swamp.

Gumlog Creek rises in Union County, Georgia, and flows ne into Clay County where it enters Brasstown Creek.

Gum Log Creek rises in s Union County and flows se into Lanes Creek.

Gum Neck, community in s Tyrrell County on a canal which flows se into Alligator River.

Gum Neck Creek, commonly called Gum Neck Landing, rises in se Tyrrell County and flows s into Alligator River. Appears as Landing Creek on the Collet map, 1770.

Gum Neck Landing. *See* Gum Neck Creek.

Gum Neck Township, s Tyrrell County.

Gum Pond, a swamp in Grindle Pocosin in n Pitt County.

Gumstand Gap, n Transylvania County on Seniard Ridge.

Gum Swamp, se Beaufort and nw Pamlico counties.

Gum Swamp rises in w Columbus County and flows se to join Beaverdam Swamp in forming Monie Swamp.

Gum Swamp rises in e Duplin County and flows sw into Limestone Creek.

Gum Swamp rises in s Hoke County and flows se into Robeson County where it enters Lumber River.

Gum Swamp rises in nw Jones County, w of the town of Dover, and flows nw into Craven County where it enters Tracey Swamp. Formerly both were known as Gum Swamp. Two Civil War engagements took place on Gum Swamp, one on April 28 and the other on May 22,

1863. The first engagement is called by various names—Wise's Crossroads, Dover Crossroads, and First Gum Swamp.

Gum Swamp rises in se Martin County and flows s into Beaufort County where it enters Latham Creek.

Gum Swamp rises in ne Pender County and flows s into Angola Creek.

Gum Swamp rises in w Pitt County and flows se into Swift Creek.

Gum Swamp rises in n Tyrrell County and flows ne into Albemarle Sound.

Gum Swamp Creek rises in n Lenoir County and flows sw into Falling Creek. Name appears in local records dating from before the Revolution. Named for sweetgum trees in the area and sometimes locally called Swee'gum Swamp.

Gum Swamp Creek rises in e Richmond County and nw Scotland County and flows s across Scotland County into South Carolina where it enters Little Pee Dee River.

Gum Swamp Run rises in se Beaufort County in Gum Swamp and flows w into South Creek.

Gumtree, community in n Davidson County, named for a gum tree (cut down about 1948) at the junction of the Thomasville and Lexington roads to Winston-Salem.

Gun Creek rises in w central Alamance County and flows se into Great Alamance Creek.

Gunlock Ridge, w Swain County between Hickory Cove and Hazel Creek.

Gunna Creek rises in nw Swain County and flows sw to join Tub-Mill Creek in Great Smoky Mountains National Park to form Eagle Creek.

Gunpowder Creek rises in central Caldwell County and flows se into Catawba River.

Gunt, Gun, or Gant Inlet from the Atlantic Ocean into Pamlico Sound through Bodie Island opened prior to 1733 and closed in the 1770's. Appears as Gun Inlet on the Moseley map, 1733.

Gunter Branch rises in n Madison County and flows sw into Big Laurel Creek.

Gunter Fork rises on the e slope of Luftee Knob, w Haywood County in the Great Smoky Mountains National Park, and flows ne into Big Creek.

Gunter Gap, on the Jackson-Swain County line near the head of Connelly Creek in se Swain County.

Gunter Knob, s Madison County at the head of Simmons Branch.

Guntertown, community in n Madison County on Barnes Creek.

Gupton, community in Franklin County. Alt. 300. Settled about 1898. Named for J. E. Gupton, local landowner.

Gurley Store, community in w Wayne County between Little River and Nahunta Swamp.

Gurleys Store, community in e central Rutherford County between Heaveners and Robinson creeks.

Gusher Knob, mountain in sw Avery County. A plant here for processing fine china clay is perhaps the most modern of its type in the world.

The Gut, central Craven County, a channel extending between Bachelor Creek and Neuse River forming the n boundary of Hog Island. Approx. one mi. long.

Gutches Creek rises in n Mitchell County and flows s into Little Rock Creek.

Guthrie, community in e Forsyth County. In 1858 Jackson Guthries and two other men from Virginia settled here and began growing tobacco.

Guthrie Point, extends from the mainland of sw Carteret County into Bogue Sound.

Gutter Branch rises in w Mecklenburg County and flows w into Long Creek.

Guy Knob, s Macon County between Mashburn Branch and Hayes Mill Creek.

Guyton, community in w Bladen County.

Gwaltneys Township, ne Alexander County.

Gwinns Millpond, se Richmond and w Scotland counties on Joes Creek. Covers 75 acres; maximum depth 10 ft. Formed prior to 1909.

H

Haas Creek rises in s Catawba County and flows s into Pott Creek.

Hachers Run rises in central Granville County and flows se into Foundery Branch. It appears as Hatches Run on the Collet map, 1770.

Hack Gap Knob, n Madison County on Colvin Creek.

Hackett, community in w Watauga County.

Hacklan Branch rises in n Gates County and flows s where it is joined by Buckland Mill Branch to form Cole Creek.

Hackney, community in sw Beaufort County.

Haddocks Crossroads, community in s Pitt County.

Hadley, community in e Duplin County approx. 3 mi. e of town of Beulaville.

Hadleys Mill, community in central Chatham County on Landum Creek. An early nineteenth-century post office was here. Old mill still standing but not in use.

Hadley's Mill Pond. See Contentnea Lake.

Hadley Township, nw Chatham County.

Hadnot Creek rises in w Carteret County and flows about 5 mi. sw into White Oak River. Named for an early settler.

Hadnot Point, in central Onslow County at the junction of Wallace Creek and New River. The headquarters and hospital of Camp Lejeune Marine Base are here. Said to have been named for Charles Hadnot, an early settler.

Hagaman, community in n central Caldwell County. Named for Hagaman family, large land owners in the vicinity.

Hagaman. See Brushy Fork.

Hagan Creek rises in s Surry County and flows se into Yadkin River.

Hagan Fork rises in central Catawba County and flows ne into McLin Creek.

Hagers Mountain, n Person County between Fishing Branch and Mitchell Creek.

Haines Cove, e Haywood County between Conner Mill Branch and Anderson Mountain.

Haines Eyebrow, peak in nw McDowell County near the head of Buck Creek.

Hairston, town in se Stokes County. Inc. 1793 as Hairstonborough, but long inactive in municipal affairs.

Hairy Bear. See Big Tom.

Halcher Swamp, rises in central Edgecombe County and flows nw into Harts Mill Run.

Halcombville, a town authorized in 1816 to be laid off on the lands of George D. Halcomb and Peter Dowel in Surry County. There is no evidence that the town was actually established.

Hale Cove, n Buncombe County between Frosty Knob and Paint Fork.

Hales Beach, a section of outer beach in sw Brunswick County extending from Shallotte Inlet to Tubbs Inlet.

Half Acre Ridge, w Haywood County, Great Smoky Mountains National Park, a short spur extending nw from Cataloochee Divide, near lat. 35° 37' 45" N., long. 83° 04' 15" W., between Den Branch and Winding Stair Branch.

Half Moon, community in n Onslow County between Bachelors Delight Swamp and Half Moon Creek.

Half-Moon Bay, w Carteret County in White Oak River between Terrapin Run and Hill's Bay. Named from the adjacent channel.

Half Moon Branch rises in nw Craven County and flows ne into Neuse River. Appears in local records as early as 1770. See also Cove Creek.

Half-Moon Channel in White Oak River, w Carteret and e Onslow counties. In recent years this channel has gradually filled in and is no longer the main channel of the river.

Half Moon Creek rises in n Onslow County and flows w into New River. Appears as Half Moon Swamp in local records as early as 1744.

Half Moon Swamp. See Half Moon Creek.

Halfway Point, the southernmost point of Mackay Island, ne Currituck County. A name given by old steamboat men, but no one now knows why.

Halifax, town and county seat, n Halifax County on Roanoke River. Authorized to be laid out, 1757; inc. 1760. Named for George Montagu, second Earl of Halifax (1716-71), who was president of the Board of Trade at the time the town was est. Alt. 135. The legislature met here in 1779 until 1781. See also Enfield.

Halifax County was formed in 1758 from Edgecombe County. Located in the ne section of the state, it is bounded by Bertie, Martin, Edgecombe, Nash, Warren, and Northampton counties. It was named for George Montagu, second Earl of Halifax (1716-71), president of the Board of Trade and Plantations, called the "Father of the Colonies" for his success in extending American commerce. Area: 724 sq. mi. County seat: Halifax with an elevation of 135 ft. Townships are Brinkleyville, Butterwood, Coconnara, Enfield, Faucett, Halifax, Littleton, Palmyra, Roanoke Rapids, Roseneath, Scotland Neck, and Weldon. Produces peanuts, corn, oats, soybeans, tobacco, cotton, poultry, hogs, livestock, dairy products, textiles, paper, lumber, apparel, and sand. *See also* Roanoke County.

Halifax District at the time of the 1790 census was composed of Caswell, Chatham, Granville, Orange, Randolph, and Wake counties.

Halifax Township, e Halifax County.

Hall, community on Scotts Creek in n Jackson County.

Hallback Mountain, s Yancey County approx. one mile w of Mount Mitchell. Alt. 6,300-6,400.

Hall Creek rises in sw tip of Burke County and flows n into Silver Creek.

Hallison. *See* Parkwood.

Hall Knob, sw Burke County. Alt. approx. 1,850.

Hall Mountain, n Macon County in a bend of Little Tennessee River.

Hallow. *See* Mount Airy.

Hallowing Point, extends from the mainland of central Craven County at New Bern into the Neuse-Trent River estuary opposite Union Point. Appears on the Lawson map, 1709, and the Moll map, 1729.

Hall Pocosin, n Gates County.

Hall Pond, near the head of Little Beaverdam Creek in w Duplin County.

Hall Point, extends from mainland of ne Carteret County into mouth of Thorofare Bay.

Halls, community in s Hertford County. Also known as Duke Hall or Dukie Hall's Crossing.

Hallsboro, town in central Columbus County. Settled 1888; inc. 1889, but long inactive in municipal affairs. Named for family of original settler. Produces lumber. Alt. 66.

Hallsborough was authorized to be laid out in se Surry County at the junction of Little Yadkin and Yadkin rivers in 1809 on the land of John Hall. There is no evidence that such a town was ever laid out.

Hallsborough. *See* Hallsville.

Hall's Branch rises in e Wake County and flows sw into Little River below Moore's Mill.

Hall's Creek rises in e Onslow County and flows sw into Queens Creek. Named for early settlers Edward or Thomas Hall. Also known as Hotel Creek.

Halls Creek rises in w Pasquotank County and flows sw into Little River. First North Carolina Assembly met on the banks of this creek in 1665.

Halls Crossroads, community in s Franklin County.

Halls Ferry. *See* Siloam.

Halls Ferry Junction, community in n Stanly County. Named for the fact that railroad passengers changed trains here for the ferry over Yadkin River.

Halls Ford, s Swain County in Little Tennessee River at Horseshoe Bend.

Hall's Gut, a drain in e central Hertford County which empties into Chowan River.

Halls Harbor, a natural harbor in the s waters of Currituck Sound in s Currituck County.

Halls Knob, sw Cherokee County between the headwaters of Beech Creek and Nottely River.

Halls Marsh Branch rises in n Duplin County and flows s into Goshen Swamp.

Halls Mills, community in n Wilkes County on Mulberry Creek.

Halls Mill Creek rises in n Wilkes County and flows sw into Mulberry Creek.

Halls Point, s Onslow County, extends into New River.

Halls Township, n central Sampson County.

Hallsville, community on Northeast Cape Fear River near the mouth of Limestone Creek, central Duplin County. Authorized to be laid out in 1818 on the lands of William Hall, Sr., and sons, and named Hallsborough. Post office est. as early as 1828.

Hall Swamp, community in w Beaufort County.

Hall Top, central Haywood County on Chestnut Flat Ridge.

Hall Township, w Gates County. Formerly known as Scratch Hall Township; origin of name unknown.

Hambey Bend, a bend in Hiwassee River, w Cherokee County, near the mouth of Anderson Creek below Hiwassee Dam.

Hambton Creek rises in s Cherokee County and flows nw into Hiwassee River.

Hamburg Ditch flows through Dismal Swamp in ne Gates County connecting Corapeake Swamp with Cross Canal in nw Camden County. Both canals were known as Cross Canal in 1808 and as White Oak Spring Canal in 1833.

Hamburg Gap, on the Jackson-Macon County line n of Yellow Mountain.

Hamburg Mountain, n Buncombe County e of Weaverville. Alt. 2,910. Traditionally the site of neutral hunting grounds used by Cherokee and Catawba Indians.

Hamburg Township, sw Jackson County.

Hamby Branch rises in e central Cabarrus County and flows s into Rocky River.

Hamby Mountain, w Wilkes County between Smithies Creek and North Prong Lewis Fork Creek. Probably named for William Hamby, an eighteenth century settler on North Prong Lewis Fork Creek.

Hambys Creek rises in e Davidson County and flows sw and nw into Rich Fork Creek.

Hamer, community in n central Caswell County. A post office was operated here during the approx. period 1880-1905.

Hamer Creek rises in sw Montgomery County and flows se into Richmond County where it enters Little River.

Hamilton, town in n Martin County on Roanoke River. Known as Milton prior to 1804 when the name was changed to Hamilton and the town inc. Probably named for Alexander Hamilton (1757-1804). Also in 1804 the polling place at nearby Hogtown, which see, was combined with that at Hamliton. Produces textiles.

Hamilton Creek. See Washington Creek.

Hamilton Hollow, valley in nw Swain County between Fox Gap and Twentymile Creek.

Hamilton Lakes, former town in central Guilford County est. by Alfred M. Scales. Inc. 1925; merged with city of Greensboro 1945.

Hamiltons Crossroads, community in e Union County e of Niggerhead Creek and w of Gourdvine Creek.

Hamiltons Old Field, former community in central Rutherford County three miles n of present Rutherfordton. In 1862 residents claimed to have been the first to nominate Zebulon B. Vance for governor.

Hamilton Township, nw Martin County.

Hamilton Township. See Catawba Township.

Hamlet, town in s Richmond County. Settled about 1875. Inc. 1897. Named by John Shortridge, local citizen, for the word then descriptive of its size. An important railroad center with maintenance shops, hump classification yard, and other facilities. Produces dairy products, apparel and furniture. Alt. 349.

Hamlins Shoals, rapids in Roanoke River, nw Halifax County, extending from the mouth of Stonehouse Creek to Tucker Island. The name appears on the MacRae map, 1833. See also Tucker Island.

Hammer Branch rises in n Swain County in Great Smoky Mountains National Park and flows se into Deep Creek.

Hammers Millpond in w Robeson and sw Scotland counties on Little Pee Dee River.

The Hammock, e bank of the mouth of Queens Creek in se Onslow County. Called Starkey's Hammock in the 1790's when it was owned by Edward Starkey. North Carolina Negro teachers hold summer meetings here.

Hammond Mountain, s Henderson County between Mill Creek and Cabin Creek. Alt. 2,978.

Hammonds Creek rises in central Bladen County and flows ne into Cape Fear River. Appears on the Moseley map, 1733.

Hampstead, community in se Pender County. Alt. 56.

Hampton, former community in sw Granville County near Durham-Granville County line dating from the nineteenth century. The site now lies within the Butner area. See also Butner.

Hampton. See Ruth.

Hampton Bay. See Pettivers Bay.

Hampton Branch rises in nw Macon County and flows s into Partridge Creek.

Hampton Branch rises in e Madison County and flows sw into Puncheon Fork Creek.

Hampton Branch rises in n Yancey County and flows ne into Mine Fork Creek.

Hampton Lake in s Jackson County on Fowler Creek at High Hampton Estate, about 1 mi. e of town of Cashiers. Was formed in 1918 and today covers 24 acres with a maximum depth of 25 feet. Used for recreation.

Hampton Lodge, community on n end of Church Island in central Currituck County.

Hampton Township, nw Davidson County.

Hamptonville, town in s Yadkin County near South Deep Creek. Settled about 1738; chartered 1818, but long inactive in municipal affairs. Named for Hampton family, early settlers who came from England.

Hamrick, community in se Yancey County on South Toe River.

Hams Crossroads, community in e Pitt County.

Hancock Bay, e Carteret County between Tusk Creek and Middens Creek.

Hancock Creek rises in s Craven County and flows n into Neuse River. Now within the limits of Cherry Point Marine Air Station. Appears as Handcocks Creek on the Moseley map, 1733. See also Hancock Town.

Hancock Point, w Carteret County, extending into White Oak River.

Hancock Town, appears on the Moseley map, 1733, as Handcocks Town, in present Craven County. It was the Tuscarora Indian village of the famous King Hancock who participated in the 1710 attack on New Bern.

Hancock Village, part of Cherry Point Housing Area in se Craven County. See also Cherry Point.

Handpole Branch rises in central Avery County and flows n into Kentucky Creek.

Handy, community in se Davidson County. Named when a post office was est.; residents formerly received their mail at Jackson Hill, 3 mi. w, and wanted a post office that would be "handy" for them.

Handy Gap, n Wilkes County on Carters Mountain. Named for local family.

Hanes or Hanestown, former community in s Forsyth County. Named for Hanes family which est. a mill village here. Now within the corporate limits of Winston-Salem. Alt. 887.

Haney Creek rises in s Yancey County and flows e into Elk Fork.

Hanging Bluff. See Hanging Rock State Park.

Hanging Dog, community in nw Cherokee County.

Hanging Dog Creek rises in n Cherokee County on Hanging Dog Mountain and flows sw into Hiwassee River. It was named because an Indian's hunting dog became hung in a mass of jammed logs and vines in the flooded creek.

Hanging Dog Gap, n Cherokee County in the n end of Hanging Dog Mountain.

Hanging Dog Mountain extends from central Cherokee County ne into the Snowbird Mountains in sw Graham County. Named peaks include Buzzard Roost, High Peak, and Rocky Knob.

Hanging Rock on the Avery-Watauga County line at the sw end of Hanging Rock Ridge. Alt. 5,237. Known by the Cherokee Indians as Yonah-wayah, "bear's paw."

Hanging Rock, e Mitchell County between Hanging Rock Branch and Gouges Creek.

Hanging Rock Branch rises in e Mitchell County and flows sw into Beaver Creek.

Hanging Rock Ridge extends ne from Hanging Rock on the Avery-Watauga County line between Dutch Creek and Watauga River to Townsend Gap in s Watauga County.

Hanging Rock State Park, central Stokes County in the Sauratown Mountain range, named for a natural rock formation. Contains 3,865 acres. Est. 1935. Scenic, recreational; vacation cabins, tent and trailer camping; picnicking, swimming, boating, fishing, hiking, and nature study. Lookout tower. See also Cascade Falls; Moores Knob; Tories Den. Appears as Hanging Bluff on the Kerr map, 1882.

Hangman Branch rises in Drowned Bay, sw Brunswick County and flows s into Calabash Creek.

Hangover Creek rises in w Graham County in Saddle Tree Gap and flows nw into Slickrock Creek.

Hangover Lead, nw Graham County, extends nw from Saddle Tree Gap to Cold Spring Knob, and ne from Cold Spring Knob to Yellowhammer Gap.

Hangover Mountain, w Graham County near the Tennessee line. Alt. approx. 5,180.

Hankins, community in e central McDowell County.

Hanks Branch rises in e Davidson County and flows e into Hunts Fork.

Hanlon Mountain, nw Buncombe County, e of Fodderstack Mountain. Alt. 3,197.

Hannah Branch rises in e Yancey County and flows w into South Toe River.

Hannah Creek rises in w Johnston County and flows se into Mill Creek.

Hannah Mountain, s Macon County between Mulberry Gap and Norton Branch.

Hanrahan, community in sw Pitt County.

The Hanted Pond. See Jumping Run.

Haoe (hey-yo), mountain in w Graham County near the Tennessee line. Alt. 5,249. Named after John Stratton, Sr., pioneer settler, climbed the mountain and looked into Tennessee and shouted "Hey-yo." He then turned toward North Carolina and repeated the shout.

Haoe Lead, w Graham County between Saddle Tree Gap and Rock Creek Knob.

Haoe Trail encircles Joyce Kilmer Memorial Forest in w Graham County and leads through the center of the forest following the main course of Little Santeetlah Creek.

Hap Mountain, sw Madison County. Alt. 4,072.

Happy Hill, s Macon County between High Holly and Pipetrack Gap.

Happy Home. See Connelly Springs; Rutherford College.

Happy Top, s Cherokee County s of Nottely River and w of Laudermilk Bend.

Happy Valley, the valley of the upper Yadkin River in n central Caldwell County between the town of Patterson and the Wilkes County line. It was the site of the homes of numerous prominent early settlers.

Harbinger, community on s tip of Currituck County. Named for a steamboat which once docked here.

Harbon Cove, e Haywood County on Bald Creek.

Harbor Channel, s Carteret County in Bogue Sound between Morehead City and Sugar Loaf Island.

Harbor Island, ne Carteret County in Core Sound, midway between Chainshot Island and Wainwright Island. Appears on the Moseley map, 1733. Once horseshoe-shaped, but storms have caused erosion and much of it is now washed away. The site of fishermen's huts and anchorage. See also Hunting Quarter Sound.

Harbor Island, e New Hanover County w of Wrightsville Beach. A test site is operated here by North Carolina State University to determine the relative amounts of corrosive growths on construction reinforcements used in a coastal environment.

Hardbargain Branch rises in ne Rutherford County and flows se into First Broad River.

Hardee Creek rises in s Pitt County and flows n into Tar River.

Hardin, community in ne Cherokee County nw of Andrews.

Hardin, town in n Gaston County on South Fork Catawba River. Inc. 1887 as Hardin and in 1897 as town of Hardin Cotton Mills. Prior to 1887 that portion of the town on the n side of the river was known as Worth and this is still the railroad name. Long inactive in municipal affairs. Alt. 679.

Hardin Creek rises in central Watauga County and flows se into South Fork New River.

Harding Swamp rises in w Beaufort County and flows w to join Juniper Swamp in forming East Branch Chicod Creek.

Mentioned in local records as early as 1750.

Hardison Mill Creek rises in s Martin County and flows nw into Statons Pond on Sweetwater Creek.

Hard Ridge, s Haywood County, extends ne in an arc from the head of Gaddis Branch to Factor Branch.

Hardscrabble Branch rises in w Yancey County and flows ne into Cane River. Named by early settlers who found the soil here to be so unproductive that they had a "hard scrabble" to make a living.

Hard Slate Gap, w Graham County between Hooper Mill Creek and Snowbird Creek.

Hardy, community in w Johnston County.

Hardy Creek, a short stream in n central Carteret County, flowing e into South River.

Hardy Creek rises in s Stanly County and flows s into Rocky River.

Hardy Mill Branch rises in w Johnston County and flows ne into Black Creek.

Hardy Store, community in e Wayne County near West Bear Creek. Named for a family living in the area since before the Revolution.

Hares Branch rises in w Hertford County and flows ne into Worrell Mill Pond.

Hares Creek rises in s Graham County and flows ne into Tulula Creek. Named for Jim Hare, early Negro resident of the area.

Hares Crossroads, community in n Johnston County.

Hare's Mill Pond, e Hertford County near the mouth of Deep Creek. Formed about 1736. Covers approx. 75 acres. Maximum depth 10 feet.

Hare Snipe Creek rises in nw Wake County and flows se into Crabtree Creek.

Hargetts Store, community in w Jones County.

Hargrove. See Providence.

Hargrove Crossroads, community in ne Sampson County.

Hariots Island. See Batts Island.

Harkers Island, se Carteret County between The Straits and Back Sound, approx. 5 mi. long and 1 mi. wide. Granted to Thomas Sparrow, March 21, 1714; later sold to Ebenezer Harker, Sept. 15, 1730. Known as Craney Island until 1783 when three brothers, Zachary, James, and Ebenezer Harker, who owned the island, divided it among themselves. In 1957 the entire island was inc. as the town of Harkers Island. Appears as Davers

Island on the Smith map, 1624, and as Crane Island on the Moseley map, 1733. On the latter map, the name Harker appears to denote the owner.

Harkers Island Township, on Back Sound, The Straits, and the Atlantic Ocean in s Carteret County. Believed to have been home of Indian Manteo who befriended the Roanoke colonists, 1587.

Harley, community in w Wilkes County on South Prong Lewis Fork Creek. Named for Harley Thompson, nineteenth century resident.

Harley Branch rises in e Haywood County and flows sw into East Fork Pigeon River.

Harlowe, community in n central Carteret County on Harlowe Creek.

Harlowe Canal. *See* Clubfoot Canal.

Harlowe Creek rises in central Carteret County and flows s into Newport River. A canal connects this creek with Clubfoot Creek, affording a waterway from the Neuse River to Newport River.

Harlowe Township, on Newport River and Core Creek, n central Carteret County, formed from a part of Newport Township in 1917.

Harm Creek rises in e Henderson County and flows e into Polk County where it enters Brights Creek.

Harmiller Gap, n Yancey County near the head of Howell Branch.

Harmon, community in nw Wilkes County near the head of North Fork Reddies River.

Harmon Creek rises in s Yadkin County and flows ne into South Deep Creek.

Harmon Den Mountain, n Haywood County between Cold Springs Creek and Tom Hall Branch.

Harmon Gap, n Avery County.

Harmon Knob, n Watauga County s and w of Norris Fork.

Harmon's Crossroads. *See* Aulander.

Harmony, town in ne Iredell County. Originally known as Harmony Hill because of the "protracted" or "harmony" meetings held here from about 1850. Inc. 1874 as Harmony Hill Camp Ground; name changed to Harmony in 1927. A late nineteenth-century academy here became the first high school in the county, 1907. Alt. 993.

Harmony Hill Camp Ground. *See* Harmony.

Harnet Cove, sw Buncombe County, sw of Yellow Gap.

Harnett, community in s Harnett County. Gravel deposits are now worked here.

Harnett County was formed in 1855 from Cumberland County. Located in the e section of the state, it is bounded by Chatham, Cumberland, Hoke, Moore, Lee, Wake, and Johnston counties. It was named for Cornelius Harnett (1723-81), Revolutionary patriot, president of the Provincial Council, the Council of Safety, and delegate to the Continental Congress. Area: 607 sq. mi. County seat: Lillington with an elevation of 325 ft. Townships are Anderson Creek, Averasboro, Barbecue, Black River, Buckhorn, Duke, Grove, Hectors Creek, Johnsonville, Lillington, Neills Creek, Stewarts Creek, and Upper Little River. Produces tobacco, corn, wheat, oats, soybeans, cotton, sweet potatoes, poultry, hogs, livestock, apparel, canned foods, candy, lumber, textiles, sand, and gravel.

Harnett Township, e New Hanover County.

Harold. *See* South Creek.

Harper Branch rises in central Jones County and flows e into Mill Run.

Harper Creek is formed in se Avery County by the junction of North Harper and South Harper creeks. It flows e into Caldwell where it enters Wilsons Creek.

Harper Creek rises in n Henderson County and flows se into Clear Creek.

Harpers Crossroads, community in sw Chatham County e of Beck Mountain.

Harrells, town largely in se Sampson County although a small area of the inc. limits lies in sw Duplin County. Appears as Harrells Store on the Morse-Breese map, 1843. Inc. 1943 as Harrells Store; name changed to Harrells, 1955. Alt. 88.

Harrells Bay, swamp in sw Duplin County.

Harrells Quarter, community in se Bertie County.

Harrellsville, town in se Hertford County on Wiccacon River. Inc. 1883. Post office est. here in 1827 as Bethel. Name changed to Harrellsville in 1847 to honor Abner Harrell.

Harrellsville Township, se Hertford County.

Harrell Swamp rises in e Gates County and flows sw to join Duke Swamp and Raynor Swamp in forming Bennetts Creek.

Harrell Township, n central Mitchell County.

Harrelson Branch rises in n Duplin County and flows e into Northeast Cape Fear River.

Harrelsonville, community in central Columbus County.

Harricane, community in n Wake County. For a long time the area was notorious for its distillers. The name came from a hurricane which struck the section over a century ago, causing extensive damage.

Harrington, community in w Harnett County. Cornwallis camped here en route to Wilmington following the Battle of Guilford Courthouse. A post office was est. here as early as 1837. John McLean Harrington edited and published a handwritten newspaper here, 1858-60.

Harris, community in s Moore County between Big Juniper Creek and McLendons Creek.

Harris, community in s Rutherford County. Est. about 1909 when the Carolina, Clinchfield and Ohio Railway built a station here. Post office est. 1912 as Orenburg since there was another post office named Harris in the state. In 1914 the first Harris post office closed, and the name was then taken by the former Orenburg post office. Named for a local family.

Harris Branch rises in w Yancey County and flows s into Lickskillet Branch.

Harrisburg, community in sw Cabarrus County. First Known as Harris' Depot. Alt. 610.

Harris Burgh appears on the Collet map, 1770. It was the location of the Granville County courthouse for various periods between 1746 and 1764 and was located between Hachers Run and Fishing Creek, se of the present town of Oxford. Harris Burgh was named for Sherwood Harris, a citizen of the community. In 1778 it was described by James Iredell as containing "half a dozen straggling houses, and is a burlesque upon a town." It continued to exist, however, until Oxford was made the county seat in 1811.

Harris Creek rises in s Avery County and flows w into North Toe River.

Harris Creek rises in ne Cherokee County and flows nw into Valley River.

Harris Creek rises in n McDowell County and flows e into Tom Creek.

Harris Creek rises in w Onslow County and flows e into Southwest Creek.

Harris Creek rises in n Wilkes County and flows se into Double Creek.

Harris Crossroads, community in s Franklin County.

Harris Crossroads, community in w Vance County on the head of Crooked Run.

Harris Depot. See Harrisburg.

Harris Gap, w Jackson County between West Fork [Barkers Creek] and Nation Creek.

Harris Lake, se Macon County on Satulah Branch.

Harris Landing, community and landing on Chowan River, w Chowan County. Also known as Tynch Town.

Harris Millpond, s Martin County on Beargrass Swamp.

Harris Millpond, w Pitt County on Tyson Creek.

Harris Mill Run rises in w central Pitt County and flows ne into Tar River.

Harris Mountain on the McDowell-Rutherford County line. Named for John W. Harris, one of the commissioners who surveyed the line between the two counties about 1845.

Harris Mountain. See Shumont Mountain.

Harrison Branch rises in s Watauga County and flows n into Hodges Creek.

Harrison Gap, on the Monroe County, Tenn.-Graham County, N. C., line.

Harrison Gap, s Macon County at the head of Lowery Creek.

Harrison's, former community in s Mecklenburg County, was visited by George Washington, May 28, 1791. Harrison Methodist Church here was organized about 1785 and named for Harrison Hood, donor of the site. With the development of Pineville, 3 mi. w, after 1873, Harrison's began to decline.

Harrisons Creek rises in s Cumberland County and flows s into Bladen County where it enters Cape Fear River.

Harrisons Creek rises in s Pender County and flows nw into Merricks Creek. Named for Charles Harrison who owned property in the vicinity as early as 1739.

Harrisons Crossroads, community in central Rockingham County.

Harris Swamp Branch rises in e central Brunswick County and flows e into Mills Creek.

Harriston. See Ayden.

Harris Top, sw Cherokee County on Pack Mountain between Pack Top and Signal Pole Hill. Alt. approx. 2,815.

Harris Top, peak on Payne Mountain in sw Cherokee County.

Harris Township, former township in s Franklin County, now township number 2.

Harris Township, n Stanly County.

Harris View, mountain peak in se Buncombe County near the Rutherford County line.

Harrisville, community in s Montgomery County.

Harrold Mountain. See Herald Mountain.

Harry M. Wright Nature Preserves, se Macon County near Highlands, approx. 50 acres in 5 tracts owned and preserved by the Nature Conservancy, Washington, D. C. Contains trees and shrubs including virgin hemlock. Named for the former owner who donated the natural area.

Harrys Branch rises in sw Duplin County. near Bearford Bay and flows sw into Rockfish Creek.

Harshaw Bottom, a sandy strip along the Hiwassee River in e Cherokee County.

Harshaw Branch rises in se Cherokee County on Poor House Mountain and flows se into Hambton Creek.

Harshaw Gap, central Cherokee County near a bend in West Prong Grape Creek before it flows into Grape Creek.

Hart Branch rises in e Transylvania County and flows ne into Little River.

Hartford. See Hertford.

Hartland, community in w Caldwell County. Formerly known as Tuttles Cross Roads for Andrew Hull Tuttle, early nineteenth-century merchant here.

Hartleys Creek rises in w Davidson County and flows nw into Yadkin River.

Hartman, community in central Stokes County.

Hartsboro, community in central Edgecombe County.

Hartsease. See Heartsease.

Harts Mill Run, rises in central Edgecombe County and flows ne into Tar River.

Hartsville, community in ne Wake County.

Harvard, community in s Yancey County.

Harvel Bay, sand filled bay in se Sampson County at the head of Clear Run Swamp. See also Carolina Bays.

Harvey. See Harveys Neck.

Harveys Neck, peninsula in e Perquimans County extending into Albemarle Sound between Perquimans and Yeopim rivers. Home of John Harvey (d. about 1679),

colonial governor, and Thomas Harvey (d. 1699), governor, 1694-1699. Appears simply as Harvey on the Hack map, 1684.

Harveytown, former community n of Kinston in e Lenoir County. Now within the corporate limits of Kinston. Grew up following the Civil War when Amos Harvey and his son, Lemuel, rented property here to Negroes who moved into town from surrounding plantations.

Harwells Island, silty clay island in Roanoke River, in nw Northampton County, sw of the community of Vultare. Appears as Jones Island on the Price map, 1808, but as Harwells Island on the MacRae map, 1833.

Haslett Tonwship, n central Gates County.

Hassell, town in w Martin County. Settled about 1878 and known as Dogville Crossroads until inc. in 1903. Named for Primitive Baptist Elder Sylvester Hassell (1842-1928). Alt. 78.

Hastings Corner, community in e central Camden County. Named for the Hastings family which settled here about 1700.

Hasty, town in s Scotland County. Inc. 1889, but long inactive in municipal affairs. Named for a family which owned land here when a railroad flag stop was est. Alt. 197.

Hatchell's Point. See Windmill Point.

Hatches Run. See Hachers Run.

Hatch Point, in s Onslow County, extends into New River. Probably named for Lemuel Hatch, who owned property in the vicinity in 1760.

Hatorask. See Hatteras Island.

Hatrask. See Hatteras Island.

Hatorask Inlet from the Atlantic Ocean into Roanoke Sound through Bodie Island opened prior to 1585 and closed prior to 1657. The site was a short distance n of the present Oregon Inlet, e Dare County. At various times Hatorask Inlet was also known as Port Fernando and under other spellings of Hatorask.

Hattaway Mountain, e Stanly County between Little Mountain Creek and Sugarloaf Mountain.

Hatteras, town near the s end of Hatteras Island, se Dare County. Inc. 1931, but no longer active in municipal affairs. The name apparently is an English rendition of the Algonquian Indian expression of "there is less vegetation." Post Office est. 1858. Alt. 10.

Hatteras Bight, a cove in the Atlantic Ocean, off the s shore of Hatteras Island at Cape Hatteras, s Dare County.

Hatteras Inlet, an inlet from the Atlantic Ocean into Pamlico Sound lies between Hatteras Island, s Dare County, on the n, and Ocracoke Island, s Hyde County, on the s. It was opened in 1846. Previously was closer to Ocracoke Inlet and closed in 1760-70. From 1760-70 to 1846, Cape Hatteras was joined to Ocracoke Island.

Hatteras Island, one of the Outer Banks of e Dare County extending from Hatteras Inlet on the s to New Inlet and Pea Island on the n. Appears as Hatrask on the White map, 1585, though at that time the name was not applied to as much of the Island as today. The name appears as Hattorask, though misplaced, on the Comberford map, 1657. Smith's map, 1624, calls it Hertfords Island, while the Moseley map, 1733, gives it its present name. See also, Croatoan Island; Paquiac.

Hatteras Shoals. See Diamond Shoals.

Hatteras Slough. See Diamond Shoals.

Hatteras Township, s Dare County on the Outer Banks.

Hatteras Woods, a heavily wooded area, eight mi. in length n of Cape Hatteras in se Dare County. Also known as Cape Hatteras Woods or Buxton Woods.

Hatters Branch rises in ne Wake County and flows sw into Smiths Creek.

Hattie, community in w Watauga County, named for Hattie Farthing.

Hatton Island. See Isle Hatton.

Haulover Point, a peninsula extending w into Albemarle Sound from the n mainland of Dare County. It is near the e tip of Durant Island.

Haunty Branch rises in s central Transylvania County and flows nw into French Broad River.

Havelock, town in se Craven County on Slocum Creek. Settled prior to 1857 and named in that year when the Atlantic and North Carolina Railroad from Goldsboro to Morehead City reached this point. Honors Sir Henry Havelock (1795-1857), British Major General and noted Baptist layman, who dramatically relieved British forces garrisoned at Lucknow, India, on September 25, 1857. Alt. 24. Cherry Point Marine Corps Air Station, which see, is adjacent.

Haw Branch rises in central Avery County and flows n into North Toe River.

Haw Branch rises in nw Beaufort County and flows sw into Tranters Creek.

Haw Branch rises in n Buncombe County near Cherry Log Gap and flows n into Dillingham Creek.

Haw Branch rises in sw Nash County and flows s into Turkey Creek.

Haw Branch, community in nw Onslow County on New River.

Hawbranch, community in ne Moore County. Also spelled Haw Branch.

Haw Cove, sw Avery County.

Haw Creek rises in central Buncombe County and flows sw into Swannanoa River. Named in 1860 for the black haw bushes growing along its banks.

Haw Creek rises in w Orange County and flows sw into Alamance County where it enters Haw River. Appears as Jumping Run on the Moseley map, 1733.

Hawes Mill Creek. See Haw Mill Creek.

Haw Fields, name given by traders in the early eighteenth century to the region occupied by Saxapahaw and Sissipahaw Indians between the Haw and Eno rivers in what is now Alamance and Orange counties. The Indians had left by the time the first white settlers arrived, and they called the region "Haw old fields," a name mentioned in 1728 by William Byrd. Haw Fields was used in 1736 in connection with a land grant here. Edward Moseley patented 10,000 acres of land in the region on November 6, 1728.

Haw Gap, central Avery County.

Haw Gap, nw Swain County on Jenkins Trail Ridge in the Great Smoky Mountains National Park.

Haw Gap Branch rises in nw Swain County in Great Smoky Mountains National Park and flows se across the park boundary for a distance of 4.5 mi. into Hazel Creek.

Hawk, community in e Mitchell County at the junction of Right Fork [Cane Creek] and Left Fork [Cane Creek]. A late nineteenth-century post office here was known as Hawk Mine.

Hawkbill Creek rises in ne Buncombe County and flows ne into Mineral Creek.

Hawkbill Gap, ne Buncombe County between Hawkbill Rock and Snowball Mountain.

Hawkbill Rock, prominent rock mass in ne Buncombe County near lat. 35° 42' 30" N., long. 82° 24' 45" W. in Pisgah National Forest. When viewed from the valley below the rock has the appearance of a hawk's bill.

Hawk Branch, n Yancey County is formed by the junction of South Fork Hawk Creek and Middle Fork Hawk Creek and flows w into Cane River. Sometimes known locally as Hog Branch.

Hawk Branch, community in n Yancey County between Middle Fork Hawk Branch and South Fork Hawk Branch.

Hawk Creek rises in e Mitchell County and flows sw into Left Fork [Cane Creek.]

Hawk Mine. See Hawk.

Hawk Mountain, e Mitchell County between Big Spring Gap and Little Yellow Mountain. Alt. approx. 5,450.

Hawkins Bay, off the n end of Huggins Island in the mouth of White Oak River, se Onslow County. Named for Bazel Hawkins.

Hawkins Branch rises in s Pender County and flows sw into Northeast Cape Fear River.

Hawkins Branch rises in e Transylvania County and flows se into Little River.

Hawkins Branch rises in n Washington County and drains w into Chappel Swamp.

Hawkins County, now in Tennessee, was created in 1787 and named in honor of Benjamin Hawkins (1754-1816). Rogersville became the county seat. This was a part of the territory ceded by North Carolina in 1789 to the Federal government. For further information see D. L. Corbitt, The Formation of North Carolina Counties.

Hawkins Island, in the e end of Brown's Sound, s Onslow County.

Hawkins Knob, e Jackson County, near Caney Fork between Chastine Creek and Mull Creek.

Hawkins Mill Creek rises in n Stokes County and flows sw into Snow Creek.

Hawkins Slough, channel among the tidal marsh islands in White Oak River, w of Swansboro, e Onslow County. Named for Bazel Hawkins, but in recent years has begun to be called Ward's Creek.

Hawk Knob, n Cherokee County on nw end of Chestnut Mountain in the Unicoi Mountains.

Hawk Knob, n Swain County in Great Smoky Mountains National Park on Welch Ridge. Alt. 4,940.

Hawk Mountain, w Transylvania County on Toxaway River.

Haw Knob, on Jess Ridge in n Buncombe County near lat. 35° 44′ N., long. 82° 27′ W. Known as Rocky Knob until 1932

when the name was changed to eliminate duplication of names in the same vicinity.

Haw Knob, on the Monroe County, Tenn.-Graham County, N. C., line. Alt. 5,472.

Hawk Ridge, n Swain County in Great Smoky Mountains National Park, a short spur extending w from Welch Ridge between Huggins Branch and Elbow Branch.

Hawksbill Mountain, nw Burke County near the se end of Jonas Ridge. Alt. 4,020. Known by the Cherokee Indians as Nokassa.

Hawkside, community in n Onslow County.

Haw Mill Creek rises in w Pender County and flows s into Black River. Formerly called Hawes Mill Creek.

Hawns, town chartered in 1749 to be laid out on 36 acres in Northampton County at the plantation of Samuel Jordan on the n side of Roanoke River. "Lots of half an acre each with convenient streets and squares" were authorized but apparently never laid off. The name came from the title of one of the Lords Proprietors, Baron Carteret of Hawnes and Earl Granville. See also Granville District.

Haw Patch, a level area below the peak of Fork Mountain in n Mitchell County.

Haw Pocosin, nw Bertie County.

Hawra, community in sw Wilson County near the head of Lee Swamp. Post office, 1898-1903.

Haw Ridge, ne Mitchell County parallel to Holder Creek.

Haw River rises in ne Forsyth County and flows ne and se through Guilford and Rockingham counties and across Alamance and Chatham counties to join Deep River on the Chatham-Lee County line to form Cape Fear River. It is approx. 130 mi. in length. In 1709 John Lawson called this the Hau River and said that it was named for the Sissipahau Indians who lived along its banks. Appears as Saxapahaw River on the Moseley map, 1733, but by its present name on the Collet map, 1770. The junction of Deep and Haw rivers was one of six sites suggested in 1788 for the location of the state capital.

Haw River, community in e Alamance County on Haw River. Founded by descendants of Adam Trollinger, a German immigrant who settled here in 1747. His son, Jacob, built a gristmill at the site and for many years it was known as Trollinger's Crossing or Ford. Alt. 539. Produces textiles.

Haw River Township, former township in

central Alamance County. Now township number 13.

Haw River Township, se Chatham County.

Hawshore Mountain, s central Avery County.

Haws Run rises in w Onslow County and flows e into Southwest Creek.

Hawtree Creek rises in n central Warren County and flows n into Virginia where it enters Roanoke River. Appears on the Moseley map, 1733.

Hawtree Township, n Warren County.

Haydon Top, s Cherokee County s of Murphy.

Hayes Branch rises in central Watauga County and flows s into Laurel Creek.

Hayes Cove, sw Buncombe County w of Bent Mountain.

Hayes Gap, n Cherokee County in Hanging Dog Mountain.

Hayes Mill Creek rises in s Macon County and flows w into Little Tennessee River.

Hayes Mountain, se Wilkes County near the Alexander County line.

Hayes Ridge, e Swain County between Williams Branch and Wesser Creek.

Hayes Run rises in s Madison County and flows sw into French Broad River.

Hayes Top, sw Buncombe County, nw of Dix Creek Gap.

Hayesville, town and county seat, central Clay County on Hiwassee River. Alt. 1,893. Inc. 1891. Named for George W. Hayes (1804-64), a member of the General Assembly who was instrumental in the formation of the county. Fort Hembree, ¾ mi. nw, was one of the forts at which Gen. Winfield Scott, in command of U.S. forces, gathered the Cherokee Indians before moving them w in 1838. Produces lumber, apparel.

Hayesville or Haysville Township, former township in nw Franklin County, now township number 5.

Hayesville Township, sw Clay County.

Hay Meadow, community in n central Wilkes County on Bee Tree Branch.

Hay Meadow Creek rises in n Wilkes County and flows s into Mulberry Creek.

Hayne, community in w Sampson County. Alt. 153.

Haynes Knob, n Haywood County between Crawford Gap and Wesley Creek. Alt. approx. 3,500.

Haynes Pond on Mingo Swamp on the Harnett-Sampson County line. A little more than ½ mi. in length.

Hays, community in n central Wilkes Coun-

ty between Hay Meadow Creek and the head of Camp Branch. A former post office est. here in. the 1890's was named for the first postmaster, Paulina Hays Elledge.

Hays Knob, sw Cherokee County between Wildcat Cove and Potato Creek.

Hays Mill Creek rises in central Cherokee County and flows se into Valley River.

Haystack Marshes. See Newport Marshes.

Haystack Point, point of land on the n shore of Pungo River, e Beaufort County.

Hayward Creek rises in w Craven County and flows e and sw into Trent River. Appears in early records as Haywood Creek and in the nineteenth century as both Hayward and Samuel Creek.

Haywood, town in se Chatham County on Deep River. Inc. 1796 as Lyons; name changed to Haywoodsborough in 1797, and to Haywood in 1800. Long inactive in municipal affairs. Named for John Haywood (1755-1827), state treasurer. Moncure is now immediately to the nw of Haywood.

Haywood County was formed in 1808 from Buncombe County. Located in the w section of the state, it is bounded by the state of Tennessee and by Madison, Buncombe, Transylvania, Jackson, and Swain counties. It was named for John Haywood (1755-1827), state treasurer from 1787 to 1827. Area: 544 sq. mi. County seat: Waynesville with an elevation of 2,635 ft. Townships are Beaverdam, Cataloochee, Cecil, Clyde, Crabtree, East Fork, Fines Creek, Iron Duff, Ivy Hill, Jonathans Creeks, Pigeon, Waynesville, and White Oak. Produces apples, corn, dairy products, livestock, hogs, poultry, paper, rubber goods, shoes, leather, textiles, furniture, sand, and gravel.

Haywood Gap, in Newfound Mountain on the Buncombe-Haywood County line between Rocky Knob and Dry Mountain.

Haywood Gap, on the Haywood-Jackson County line. Alt. 5,225.

Haywood Gap Stream rises in s Haywood

County at Sweetwater Spring and flows
ne to join Buckeye Creek in forming
Middle Prong [West Fork Pigeon River].

Hazanet Knob, central Graham County in
the Cheoah Mountains at the head of
Cochran Creek.

Hazel, former town in central Buncombe
County at or near West Asheville. Inc.
1891 but soon became inactive in municipal affairs. A part of the site is now in
the city limits of Asheville.

Hazel Creek rises in n Swain County on
the sw slope of Silers Bald in the Great
Smoky Mountains National Park and flows
sw into Fontana Lake. It was named for
a patch of hazelnut bushes near its mouth.

Hazel Dell, community in e central Caldwell
County. Formerly a post office.

Hazel Hollow, w Jackson County, between
Mince Branch and Dicks Creek.

Hazel Knob on the Cherokee County, N. C.-
Monroe County, Tenn., line in the Unicoi
Mountains.

Hazelnut Gap on the McDowell-Yancey
County line between Buck Creek Gap and
Horse Gap.

Hazelton, community in n Gates County.

Hazel Top, peak in central Haywood County on the nw end of Teaberry Ridge.

Hazelwood, former town in s Haywood
County adjacent to Waynesville. Inc.
1905. In 1953 it became a part of Waynesville. Named for hazelnuts growing in the
vicinity. Alt. 2,713. *See also* Waynesville.

Headquarters Mountain, se Avery County.
Alt. 4,135.

Heady Mountain, s Jackson County at s end
of Chattooga Ridge. Also spelled Heddie
Mountain.

Heady's Beach. *See* Bear Banks.

Healing Springs, community and springs in
s Davidson County between Flat Swamp
and Lick Creek at n end of Flat Swamp
Mountain.

Healing Springs Township, s Davidson
County.

Healthy Plain, community in w Wilson
County.

Heartline Creek. *See* North Fork Tar River.

Hearts Delight Pocosin, nw Bertie County.

Heartsease, community in central Edgecombe County about 8 mi. nw of Tarboro.
Named by Richard Hart who built his
home here. Appears as Hartsease on U.S.
Geological Survey map, 1903.

Heath Mill Run rises in n Jones County and
flows s into Beaver Creek.

Heathsville, community in w central Halifax County.

Heaton, community on Elk River, n Avery
County. Alt. approx. 3,500. Named for the
Rev. James M. Heaton of Tennessee who
came to w North Carolina in 1882.

Heaveners Creek rises in e Rutherford County and flows w into Robinson Creek.

Hebo Mountain on the Haywood-Madison
County line. Alt. 4,300-4,368.

Hebron, community in s Mecklenburg
County.

Hebron Mountain, w Henderson County between Cantrell Mountain and North Fork.
Alt. 2,966.

Heck Creek rises in central Madison County
and flows sw into Walnut Creek.

Hector Creek rises in s Harnett County and
flows s on the Moore-Cumberland County
line into Little River. Named for Hector
McNeill, an early settler.

Hector Creek rises in sw Wake County and
flows sw through n Harnett County into
Cape Fear River. Named for Hector Mc-
Neill who settled along its banks, 1740.

Hector Creek Township, n Harnett County.

Heddie Mountain. *See* Heady Mountain.

Hedgecock, community in s Guilford County.

Hedricks Island, a narrow island of sand,
approx. 1 mi. long, in Yadkin River, w
Davidson County.

Heffner Gap, on the McDowell-Mitchell
County line.

Heidelburg Ferry appears on the Moseley
map, 1733, on New River in what is now
s Onslow County, serving the Bath-
New Bern-Wilmington road.

Heights of Gowerie, high bank overlooking
Yadkin River, e Rowan County. Site of
the home of Albert Torrence (1752-1825)
and from which Cornwallis cannonaded
forces of Gen. Nathanael Greene, 1781.

Heighwaree. *See* Uwharrie Mountains.

Heintooga Bald, ne Swain County in Great
Smoky Mountains National Park on Overlook Ridge. Alt. 5,240.

Heintooga Creek rises in ne Swain County
in Great Smoky Mountains National Park
and flows sw into Bunches Creek.

Heintooga Ridge, nw Swain County in Great
Smoky Mountains National Park between
Heintooga Creek and Redman Creek.

Heldermans, former community in s Lincoln
County on the opposite side of Leepers
Creek from the community of Mariposa,
but now a part of Mariposa.

Helena. *See* Timberlake.

Helens Crossroads, community in s Pitt
County.

Hell Pocosin, a loam filled pocosin in nw

Onslow County between Purgatory Pocosin and the head of New River.

Hell's Half Acre. See Providence.

Hell Swamp, e Beaufort County n of Pungo Creek.

Hell Swamp, central Duplin County between North Prong Horse Branch and West Prong Horse Branch.

Helron, community in central Granville County.

Helton, community in n Ashe County. Alt. 2,600. Site of iron forges, 1807-1857.

Helton Creek rises in n central Ashe County and flows se into North Fork New River.

Helton Township, ne Ashe County.

Hembys Bridge, community in w Union County.

Hemlock, community in w Ashe County.

Hemlock Branch rises in s Haywood County and flows ne into Little East Fork Pigeon River.

Hemlock Knob, peak on the Swain County, N. C.-Sevier County, Tenn., line in the Great Smoky Mountains National Park between Mount Davis and Cold Spring Knob.

Hemmed Island, a 75-acre island covered with hardwoods in the Tar River, central Edgecombe County.

Hemp. See Robbins.

Hemphill Bald, w Haywood County, Great Smoky Mountains National Park, on Cataloochee Divide, near lat. 35° 33′ 50″ N., long. 83° 06′ 11″ W. Alt. 5,573.

Hemphill Creek rises in central Haywood County and flows e into Jonathans Creek. Named for an early settler in area.

Hemphill Creek rises in s Yancey County and flows ne into South Toe River.

Hemphill Knob, central Buncombe County s of Lake Craig.

Hemphill Mountain, n Buncombe County between Pink Fox Cove and Pennix Cove.

Hemphill Spring, s Yancey County. Former resort on the old Mount Mitchell toll road operated by Graybeal family and used for a time during the construction of the Blue Ridge Parkway.

Hemp Patch Branch rises in s Macon County and flows sw into Big Mooney Branch.

Henderson, city and county seat, s central Vance County. Alt. 513. Inc. 1841 and named for Leonard Henderson (1773-1833), Chief Justice of N. C. Supreme Court from 1829 to 1833. Originally settled in 1789 when Samuel Reavis and his sons, Lewis, Samuel, Jr., and Whitfield built a house here. Referred to as Lone-

some Valley by a later settler, William Evans, who was homesick for Virginia. Produces textiles, hosiery, minerals, tobacco, glass products, and pickles.

Henderson, former town in w Montgomery County at the junction of Yadkin and Uwharrie rivers. Inc. 1794; "re-surveyed" in 1813. Was the site of the courthouse from soon after the establishment of the town until about 1816. By the 1850's Henderson was no longer being shown on maps of the state. See also Tindallsville.

Henderson Branch rises in e Haywood County and flows ne into Burnett Creek.

Henderson County was formed in 1838 from Buncombe County. Located in the w section of the state, it is bounded by the state of South Carolina and by Transylvania, Haywood, Buncombe, McDowell, Rutherford, and Polk counties. It was named for Leonard Henderson (1773-1833), Chief Justice of the N.C. Supreme Court. Area: 382 sq. mi. County seat: Hendersonville with an elevation of 2,146 ft. Townships are Blue Ridge, Clear Creek, Crab Creek, Edneyville, Green River, Hendersonville, Hoopers Creek, and Mills River. Produces apples, corn, miscellaneous fruits and vegetables, dairy products, livestock, hogs, poultry, eggs, surgical supplies, textiles, electronics, hosiery, limestone, granite, and clay.

Henderson Creek rises in e Henderson County and flows nw into Clear Creek.

Henderson Mountain, s Macon County between Fork Ridge and California Ridge.

Henderson Shoals. See McAdenville.

Henderson Township, central Vance County.

Hendersonville, town and county seat, central Henderson County. Alt. 2,146. Authorized to be laid out, 1840; inc. 1847. Named for Leonard Henderson (1773-1833), Chief Justice of the North Carolina Supreme Court, 1829-1833. Produces electronics components, hosiery, textiles, and apparel.

Hendersonville Township, central Henderson County.

Hendricks Creek rises in central Edgecombe County and flows se through Tarboro into Tar River.

Hendrix, community in w Wilkes County on Stony Fork Creek.

Hen Mountain, central Caldwell County. Alt. 2,020. Formerly known as Turkey Hen Mountain. A nearby peak, Hibriten Mountain, was formerly known as Turkey Cock Mountain.

Henrico, community in nw Northampton County.

Henrietta, former community in s Edgecombe County. Now merely a railroad crossing.

Henrietta, community in se Rutherford County on Second Broad River. Founded 1887 by Simpson B. Tanner, Sr., with the establishment of Henrietta Mills. Named for Tanner's mother-in-law, Henrietta McRae Spencer.

Henry, community in nw Lincoln County.

Henry Branch rises in w Nash County and flows se into Sapony Creek. Mentioned in local records as early as 1779.

Henry Branch rises near Black Mountain in n Transylvania County and flows sw into Avery Creek.

Henry Creek rises in n Jackson County and flows s into Buff Creek.

Henry Fork rises in s Burke County and flows ne and e into Catawba County where it joins Jacob Fork to form South Fork Catawba River. Named for the pioneer settler Heinrich Weidner or Henry Whitener.

Henry Knob, central Haywood County between Big Spring Branch and Jonathans Creek.

Henry Mountain, s Transylvania County between Paxton Creek and Cantrell Creek.

Henry River, community in e Burke County.

Hensley Branch rises in n Madison County near Big Knob and flows se on the w side of Ephriam Hensley Mountain into Shelton Laurel Creek.

Hensley Branch rises in n Yancey County and flows ne into Bald Mountain Creek.

Hensley Ridge, n McDowell County, extends e from Betsy Ridge, Alt. approx. 2,300.

Hensley Ridge, nw Yancey County between Bald Mountain Creek and Jim Creek.

Henson Branch rises in se Macon County and flows se into Clear Creek.

Henson Cove, e Haywood County on Garden Creek.

Henson Creek rises in w Avery County and flows se into North Toe River.

Henson Creek rises in s Macon County and flows ne into Shope Fork.

Henson Gap, se Macon County between Henson Branch and Brooks Creek.

Henson Ridge, n Jackson County between Locust Creek and Cane Creek.

Hepco, former community on Waterville Lake (in Pigeon River), central Haywood County. Alt. 2,298. Was site of Haywood Electric Power Company development and the name came from the initials of the company. Now abandoned.

Herald Mountain, n Wilkes County between the head of Bee Tree Branch and Cane Creek. Named for the Harrold family, early settlers on Bee Tree Branch.

Herbert C. Bonner Bridge. See Oregon Inlet.

Herbert Stamp, peak in ne Clay County between Tipton Branch and Tate Branch.

Herbin's Creek rises in se Rockingham County and flows sw into Haw River. Known as High Rock Creek as early as 1754; renamed about 1800 for John and William Herbin, local landowners.

Herds Creek rises in e Moore County and flows s into Crains Creek. Named for Charles Herd, who settled at its mouth about 1760.

Heriots Island. See Batts Island.

Herrells, community in nw Mitchell County.

Herren Cove, the valley through which the e tributary of Pole Creek flows in sw Buncombe County.

Herring or Herrings Crossroads, community in n central Sampson County on the head of Merkle Swamp.

Herring Pond, stream rises in n Carteret County and flows n into Neuse River.

Herring Run rises in central Beaufort County and flows s into Runyon Creek.

Herring's Chapel, community in sw Pender County on the e side of Long Creek.

Herring Shoal Island, small island, about ½ mi. in diameter, off the s end of Bodie Island in Roanoke Sound, e Dare County.

Herrings Township, n central Sampson County.

Herring Swamp rises in n Duplin County and flows se into Marsh Branch.

Herrin Knob, on the Haywood-Jackson County line.

Herron Cove, n Buncombe County sw of Little Davis Mountain.

Hertford, town and county seat, central Perquimans County on Perquimans River. Inc. 1758. Named for the town of Hertford in England. Appears as Hartford on the Collet map, 1770. First known as Phelps Point for Jonathan Phelps on whose land it was est.; appears in local records as early as 1701. Produces apparel. Alt. 15.

Hertford County was formed in 1759 from Chowan, Bertie, and Northampton counties. Located in the ne section of the state, it is bounded by Gates, Chowan, Bertie, and Northampton counties and the state of Virginia. It was named for Francis Seymour Conway (1719-94), Earl (afterwards Marquis) of Hertford, a Lord of the Bed Chamber and Knight of the Garter. Area: 361 sq. mi. County seat: Winton with an elevation of 45 ft. Townships are Ahoskie, Harrellsville, Maneys Neck, Murfreesboro, St. Johns, and Winton. Produces peanuts, tobacco, corn, soybeans, hogs, livestock, apparel, lumber, wooden containers, aluminum castings.

Hertfords Island. See Hatteras Island.

Hertford Township, w central Perquimans County.

Hester, community in s Granville County. Named for Henry M. Hester, donor of the railroad right-of-way and station site. Alt. 384.

Hesters Pond, w Bladen County on Bareford Swamp. Covers between 75 and 80 acres; max. depth, 8 ft. at the dam.

Hestertown, community in se Robeson County on Lumber River.

Hetherly Height, high ground in se Henderson County.

Hewins Creek. See Eurins Creek.

Hewitt, community in sw Swain County. Named for Frank R. Hewitt, talc mine operator. Alt. 1,878.

Hewitt Gap, in sw Swain County on Nantahala Gorge.

Hewlets Creek rises in central New Hanover County and flows se into Masonboro Sound.

Hexlena, community in n central Bertie County. Inc. 1899; charter repealed 1905.

Hiawatha. See Watha.

Hibbard Mountain, w Cherokee County extends ne from Bearpaw Creek.

Hibriten Mountain, central Caldwell County in the Brushy Mountains. Alt. 2,265. Formerly known as Turkey Cock Mountain, but renamed in honor of Brighton, England, by Miss Emma Baker who came here from England to teach school. See also Hen Mountain; Brushy Mountains.

Hickleberry Mountain, w Stokes County at the head of Town Fork Creek.

Hickman's Creek rises in se Caldwell County and flows s into Upper Little River.

Hickmans Crossroads, community in sw Brunswick County.

Hickory, city in nw Catawba County. Alt. 1,163. Inc. 1863 as Hickory Tavern. Named for a log tavern built at the site in the 1850's. Name changed to Hickory, 1873. West Hickory, inc. as Berryville in 1895 is now within the limits of Hickory. Highland, inc. 1905, whose charter was repealed in 1931, is also now a part of Hickory. Highland was named for Highland Academy located within its limits. Lenoir Rhyne College now occupies site of former Highland Academy. Produces hosiery, textiles, furniture, electronics, fabricated metals, primary metals and lumber.

Hickory, community in ne Nash County between Beaverdam Swamp and Fishing Creek. Sometimes also known as Pittmans Store.

Hickory Basin, a depression in e Graham County at the head of Shell Stand Creek.

Hickory Bearpen Mountain, e Madison County between Roaring Fork and Little Creek.

Hickory Bottom, sandy valley in nw Swain County between Pinnacle Ridge and Hazel Creek.

Hickory Bottom Branch rises in n McDowell County and flows s into Armstrong Creek near Woodlawn.

Hickory Branch rises in n central Avery County and flows s to join Whitehead Creek before flowing into Elk River.

Hickory Branch rises in sw Cherokee County and flows se into Persimmon Creek.

Hickory Branch rises in w Macon County and flows se into Dicks Creek.

Hickory Cove, w Swain County between Sandy Gap Branch and Gunlock Ridge.

Hickory Cove, w Swain County between Watia Creek and Jake Branch.

Hickory Cove, s Swain County extends ne between Marr Branch and Brush Creek.

Hickory Cove Creek rises in nw Clay County and flows sw into Rock House Creek.

Hickory Creek rises in se Caldwell County and flows s into Upper Little River.

Hickory Creek rises in e Cleveland County and flows sw into First Broad River.

Hickory Creek rises in s Guilford County and flows s into Deep River. Appears on the Collet map, 1770.

Hickory Creek rises in ne Stokes County and flows e into Rockingham County where it enters Mayo River.

Hickory Crossroads, community in e Johnston County.

Hickory Cross Roads, community in n Perquimans County.

Hickory East, uninc. outskirts of city of Hickory, nw Catawba County.

Hickory Flat Branch rises in n Swain County and flows s into Oconaluftee River.

Hickory Flat Branch rises in w central Swain County and flows sw into Tuckasegee River.

Hickory Flat Cove, s Haywood County on a tributary of West Fork Pigeon River.

Hickory Flat Creek rises near Mine Mountain in n Transylvania County and flows sw into East Fork French Broad River.

Hickory Flats, e Mitchell County between Beaver Creek and Gouges Creek.

Hickory Fork rises in n Madison County and flows se into Shelton Laurel Creek.

Hickory Gap, near the junction of the Buncombe-Madison-Yancey County lines. Alt. approx. 3,550.

Hickory Gap, s Graham County between Little Snowbird Creek and Teeseteska Ridge.

Hickory Gap, s Macon County between Rector Knob and Bennies Branch.

Hickory Grove, community in sw Chatham County.

Hickory Grove, community in e Mecklenburg County. A post office was est. here as early as 1828.

Hickory Grove, community in e Wake County.

Hickory Grove. See Wilson.

Hickory Grove Crossroads, community in e Bladen County on South River. Stewarts Ferry appears on the river here on the Price map, 1808. The MacRae map, 1833, shows Cromartys Ferry here, while the soil survey map, 1914, shows Cromarties Bridge across the river and the community of Gravel Hill a short distance w. Gravelly Hill had appeared on the Colton map, 1861, and on various other

maps through Kerr's in 1882. Gravelly Hill post office was here as early as 1828, but by 1906 it was Gravelhill. The present name occurs first apparently on the Geological Survey map, 1954.

Hickory Hill. See Lawrence.

Hickory Knob, at the junction of the Alexander, Caldwell, and Wilkes County lines.

Hickory Knob, sw Burke County.

Hickory Knob on the Cherokee-Macon County line.

Hickory Knob, e Macon County between Laurel Creek and North Prong Ellijay Creek.

Hickory Knob, n Transylvania County between Presley Branch and South Prong Turkey Creek.

Hickory Knob Mountain at junction of Alexander, Caldwell, and Wilkes counties. Alt. 2,635.

Hickory Knoll Creek rises in s Macon County and flows sw into Little Tennessee River.

Hickory Log Branch rises in n Madison County and flows se into Shelton Laurel Creek.

Hickory Mountain, w Chatham County, approx. five miles east of Siler City.

Hickory Mountain on the Henderson-Transylvania County line n of Hooker Creek.

Hickory Mountain Township, w central Chatham County.

Hickory North, unincorporated outskirts of city of Hickory nw Catawba County.

Hickory Nut Branch rises in central Avery County and flows s into North Toe River.

Hickorynut Branch rises in e Swain County on Yalaka Mountains near Hickorynut Knob and flows s into Una Creek.

Hickory Nut Creek rises in ne Henderson County and flows se into Broad River.

Hickory Nut Falls on Broad River near Chimney Rock, w Rutherford County. 400 ft. high.

Hickory Nut Gap, central Avery County.

Hickorynut Gap on the Buncombe-Henderson County line between Tater Knob and Ferguson Peak. Alt. 2,878. Originally known as Sherrill's Gap. One of two gaps (the other being Swannanoa Gap) through which early settlers and travellers from the east reached the Asheville plateau. It is believed that De Soto passed through this gap in 1540.

Hickory Nut Gap, nw Swain County on Long Hungry Ridge in the Great Smoky Mountains National Park.

Hickory Nut Gorge, w Rutherford County,

through which Broad River flows. A good view of the Gorge may be had from atop Chimney Rock.

Hickorynut Knob, e Swain County on Yalaka Mountains near the head of Hickorynut Branch.

Hickory Nut Mountain, in sw Burke County. Alt. 2,512.

Hickory Nut Mountain, central Jackson County extends n from Slatten Creek to Tuckasegee River.

Hickorynut Mountain, in e Swain County between Second Hurricane Branch and Hickorynut Branch.

Hickorynut Mountains, a long ridge, s McDowell County between Crooked Creek and Cove Creek.

Hickory Point, se Beaufort County, on the s side of Pamlico River at the mouth of South Creek.

Hickory Point extends from sw Carteret County into Hills Bay.

Hickory Ridge, in n Haywood County between Rube Rock Branch and Chestnut Orchard Branch.

Hickory Ridge Branch rises in w Madison County and flows s into Roaring Fork.

Hickory Run rises in w Onslow County and flows ne into Southwest Creek.

Hickory Springs. See Mount Vernon Springs.

Hickory Spur, peak, w Madison County between Levy Branch and French Broad River.

Hickory Tavern. See Hickory.

Hickory Top, s Buncombe County between Billy Cove Gap and Little Hickory Top.

Hickory Township, w Catawba County. Was Hickory Tavern Township prior to 1876.

Hicks Branch rises in ne Cherokee County and flows se into Junaluska Creek.

Hicks Branch rises in n Haywood County and flows ne into Pigeon River.

Hicks Branch rises in w Macon County and flows n into Nantahala Lake.

Hicks Creek rises in s Iredell County w of Troutman and flows s into Catawba River.

Hicks Crossroads, community in nw Mecklenburg County.

Hicks Crossroads, community in nw Vance County n of Flat Creek.

Hicks Grove, community in s Rutherford County s of Broad River.

Hicks Pond, in n Warren County on Mill Creek.

Hickstown, former town in central Durham County. Inc. 1887 on property of W. H. and Ella Hicks; charter repealed 1889.

Site is now within the corporate limits of the city of Durham.

Hicootomony River. See Hyco River.

Hiddenite, community in e central Alexander County. Named for William Earl Hidden (1853-1918), mineralogist of New York, who prospected in the area about 1880. Mines nearby produced the gem, hiddenite, found only in North Carolina. Inc. 1913; charter repealed 1919. Known as White Plains prior to the arrival of Hidden and so appears on a map of 1871. Alt. 1,140. Produces poultry.

Hide Pond, a muck-filled slough in se Duplin County.

Hidetown, community in e Graham County on Stecoah Creek.

Higdon Branch rises in e Macon County and flows nw into Ellijay Creek.

Higdon Mountain, e Macon County at the head of Higdon Branch. Alt. 4,045.

Higdonville, community in e Macon County on Battle Branch.

Higgens Island, formerly a 10-acre island in Little Tennessee River in ne Graham County. Now under the waters of Fontana Lake.

Higgins, community in n central Yancey County on Cane River. Alt. 2,390. Named for John Higgins, early settler and father of a large family.

Higgins Creek rises in w Yancey County and flows nw into Cane River.

Higgins Knob, w Yancey County between Langford Branch and Higgins Creek.

Higgins Township, central McDowell County.

Highfall Branch rises in central Cherokee County and flows se into Morgan Creek.

Highfall Branch rises in central Cherokee County and flows n into Valley River.

High Falls, in Little River in e Transylvania County s of the mouth of Grassy Creek. Height of the falls is 50 feet.

High Falls, n Transylvania County in South Fork Mills River. Height of the falls is 30 ft.

High Falls, se Transylvania County in Little River near Cedar Mountain. Height of the falls is 75 ft.

High Falls, in Horsepasture River in sw Transylvania County between Drift Falls and Stairway Falls. Height of falls is 150 ft.

High Falls, community in n Moore County on Deep River. William England built a mill here about 1790. Originally known as The Great Falls and The Big Falls, for a 15 ft. waterfall in the river. The community of Prosperity, approx. one mi. e, was settled about 1862 but by 1941 had been almost completely abandoned in favor of High Falls. Prosperity was named from the fact that it was in the center of a prosperous farming section.

High Falls of the Tuckasegee. *See* Tuckasegee Falls.

High Hampton Estate, se Jackson County on the w edge of Hampton Lake. Estate named for General Wade Hampton, Confederate officer and governor of South Carolina, who had a home here. It is now a private recreation area and resort. High Hampton Inn and Country Club are here. Alt. 3,524.

High Hickory Knob, se Buncombe County between Patton Gap and Flat Top in the Swannanoa Mountains.

High Hickory Ridge, se Buncombe County n of High Hickory Knob.

High Hill, community in n Hertford County.

High Hill Inlet between Whalebone Island in Pamlico Sound and Portsmouth Island in e Carteret County.

The High Hills, sand dunes on Portsmouth Island about 1 mi. ne of Drum Inlet, e Carteret County.

High Holly, a mountain in s Macon County between Kinley Mountain and Middle Creek.

High Knob, n Buncombe County between High Swan and Rich Knob peaks.

High Knob, nw Buncombe County between Robinson Mountain and Grassy Knob.

High Knob, ne Buncombe County w of Pigpen Knob.

High Knob, mountain in Wilson Ridge in nw Caldwell County. Alt. 2,686.

High Knob, s Macon County between Deer Gap and Beasley Gap.

High Knob, n Madison County at the head of Duckmill Branch.

High Knob, e Mitchell County between Ivy Knob and Lightwood Mountain.

High Knob, e Mitchell County between Little Bald and Stagger Weed Creek.

High Knob, n central Transylvania County at the e end of Shutin Ridge.

High Knob, s Yancey County near the head of Banks Creek.

High Knob, sw Yancey County on Wilson Ridge.

Highland. *See* Hickory.

Highland Falls, in the headwaters of Cullasaja River in se Macon County.

Highland Lake, central Henderson County on King Creek. Constructed about 1906. Covers 20 acres; maximum depth 20 feet. A summer camp owned by the Roman Catholic Church. Alt. 2,117.

Highland Ridge, ne Swain County in Great Smoky Mountains National Park, a spur extending se from Katalsta Ridge between Enloe Creek and Raven Fork.

Highlands, town in se Macon County. Alt. 3,838, the highest town in the state. Laid out as a summer resort in 1875 by Samuel T. Kelsey and Charles Hutchinson of Kansas. It is said that they chose the site from a map when they discovered that a line drawn on it from Chicago to Savannah crossed another line at this point drawn from Baltimore to New Orleans. Inc. 1879. Named for its high elevation. Highlands has an average yearly precipitation of 79 in., the greatest of any place east of the Rocky Mountains. *See also* Horse Cove. Highlands Biological Station est. here 1927, a non-profit research and field training center for the study of plants and animals.

Highlands Township, se Macon County.

High Laurel Branch rises in w Macon County and flows w into Nantahala Lake.

High Lonesome Mountain, se Jackson County between Fowler Creek and Ellicott Mountain.

High Mountain, ne Rutherford County between Oakey Mountain and Silver Creek Knob.

High Peak, on the Buncombe-Henderson County line.

High Peak, central Burke County. Alt. 2,184.

High Peak on the Burke-Rutherford County line in the South Mountains. Alt. approx. 2,720.

High Peak, ne Cherokee County on the head of Tom Thumb Creek in the Snowbird Mountains. Alt. approx. 3,800.

High Peak, n Cherokee County on Hanging Dog Mountain. Also known as High Top. Alt. 4,053.

High Peak, se Watauga County between Joes Creek and Triplett Creek.

Highpeak, mountain on the Henderson-Transylvania County line.

High Peak, n Yancey County between the heads of Seng Branch and Bailey Branch. Alt. approx. 4,400.

High Peak, w Yancey County near the head of Wolf Branch.

High Peak, community in se Burke County

approx. 5 mi. se of Morganton at foot of South Mountains.

High Pinnacle, central Buncombe County nw of Elk Wallow Gap in the Elk Mountains.

High Point, s peak of Deaver View Mountain in central Buncombe County.

High Point, peak in w Jackson County between Nation Creek and Rocky Branch.

High Point, city in sw Guilford County. Alt. 940. Laid out in 1853 and inc. 1859. Named for the fact that it was the highest point on the North Carolina Railroad. Produces textiles, hosiery, furniture, baked goods, apparel, corrugated boxes, fabricated metals, toys, lumber, and chemicals. An important furniture market is operated here. Home of High Point College. See also Browntown.

High Point Lake in sw Guilford County is formed at the junction of East Fork Deep River and West Fork Deep River where Deep River is formed. The lake was created by a dam constructed in 1928 and is named for and owned by the city of High Point. Max. depth 20 ft.; area, 150 acres.

High Point Township, sw Guilford County. Named for the town.

High Ridge, w Madison County between Davis Branch and Murray Branch.

High Rock, mountain in central Madison County between Hunter Creek and Brush Creek at the n end of High Rock Ridge. Alt. 3,555.

High Rock, community in s Davidson County on Yadkin River. Alt. 584.

High Rock, former community and post office in se Rockingham County on Haw River. Mentioned in local records as early as 1754; mill operated here from as early as 1752 until the 1920's when the dam was broken. Gov. William Tryon camped here, 1771; Generals Cornwallis and Greene camped here during the Revolution. The name survives as applied to a local farm; handsome brick house here built about 1807.

High Rock Creek. See Herbin's Creek.

High Rock Lake, on Yadkin River in Davidson and Rowan counties. Formed in 1927 by a dam in the river constructed for the Carolina Aluminum Company. Covers approx. 18,000 acres. Maximum depth 60 to 70 ft. Named because the dam is built from one high rock to another above the bed of the river.

High Rock Lake on Steel Creek in s Tran-

sylvania County. Covers 15 acres and has maximum depth of 15 ft.

High Rock Ridge, central Madison County between Brush Creek and Walnut Creek.

High Rock Ridge, n Swain County in Great Smoky Mountains National Park, a spur extending w from Welch Ridge between Cold Spring Branch and Hazel Creek.

High Rock Wildlife Management Area on High Rock Lake in sw Davidson County. Operated by State of North Carolina on privately owned land. Principal wildlife are deer, turkey, and quail.

High Rocks, peak in n Swain County in Great Smoky Mountains National Park on Welch Ridge. Alt. 5,188.

High Rocks, peak in n Yancey County at the ne end of Chestnut Ridge.

Highs Crossroads, community in s Nash County near Bissett Mill Pond. It is now known also as Green Pond community.

High Shoals, community on South Fork Catawba River in n Gaston County. Settled about 1750. Named for high rocky shoal in the river. Alt. 724.

High Shoals. See Cliffside.

High Shoals Branch rises in s Madison County and flows e into Little Pine Creek.

High Shoals Township, se Rutherford County. Named for a series of shoals in Second Broad River. See also Cliffside.

Highsmith, community in s Pender County on Mill Creek. Named for the Highsmith family which operated a large farm and sawmill at the site.

High Swan, peak at the n end of Swan Mountain in central Buncombe County.

High Top, se Buncombe County in the Blue Ridge Mountains between High Windy and Lakey Knob.

High Top, sw Buncombe County ne of Stony Knob.

High Top, n Graham County on the e end of Yellow Creek Mountains.

High Top, s Haywood County at the head of Big Branch.

High Top, central Haywood County between Messer Branch and Sugar Cove.

Hightop, n Henderson County between Baldwin Gap and Terry Gap. Alt. 3,482.

High Top, w Jackson County at the head of Brook Branch.

High Top, s Macon County between Low Gap and Pine Knob.

High Top. See High Peak.

High Top of Bee Tree. See Craggy Knob.

Hightower Gap, s Swain County between Licklog Creek and Wiggins Creek.

Hightower Township, se Caswell County.

Hightowers, community in se Caswell County, named for Daniel Hightower, who moved here from Virginia about 1795. A post office was operated here during the approx. period 1830-1930.

Hightsville, community in w New Hanover County, north of Wilmington, on Smiths Creek.

High Windy, peak in se Buncombe County between Black Knob and High Top.

Hildebran, town in e Burke County, inc. 1899. Alt. 1,149. Named for J. A. Hildebran, lumber merchant. Produces textiles and hosiery.

Hildebran Creek rises in central Catawba County sw of Conover and flows s into Clark Creek.

Hill Forest, n Durham County. Contains 1,400 acres. The original tract of 275 acres was donated by George Watts Hill of Durham to North Carolina State College in 1929. He later assisted in financing additional purchases of land to bring the forest to its present area. Named for the original donor. The Sophomore class of the School of Forest Resources spends ten weeks in summer camp here doing surveying and all phases of forestry such as timber cruising, dendrology, stand improvement, and mensuration. The camp is equipped with classrooms, dormitory, dining hall, and all necessary facilities.

Hillgrit, community in n Henderson County.

Hill Hollow, n Mitchell County on a tributary of Spring Creek.

Hilliards Mill. See Tippetts Mill Pond.

Hilliardston, community in n Nash County on Swift Creek. Settled about 1780. Named for John Hilliard, one of the first settlers. Alt. 200.

Hills Bay in White Oak River, w Carteret County. Named for Edward Hill who owned the adjacent land and Cedar Point Plantation here before and during the Civil War.

Hillsboro Store, formerly a community in e Wayne County between Hills Pond and Bear Creek.

Hillsborough, town and county seat, central Orange County, on Eno River. Alt. 543. The Indian town of Acconeech (also Occaneechi), mentioned by Lawson appears on the Moseley map, 1733, at approx. this site on Eno River. After white occupation in 1754 the site came to be known as Corbinton for Francis Corbin, colonial official. Inc. as Childsburgh, 1759, in honor of Thomas Childs, Attorney General of the province. Name changed to Hillsborough in 1766 in honor of Wills Hill, Earl of Hillsborough (1718-93), president of the Board of Trade and Plantations and Secretary of State for the Colonies. The spelling later changed unofficially to Hillsboro but the original spelling was restored in 1965. Produces textiles and furniture. The legislature met here in 1778, 1782-84.

Hillsborough District was composed of Caswell, Chatham, Granville, Orange, Randolph, and Wake counties at the time of the 1790 census.

Hillsborough Lake. See Ben Johnson Lake.

Hillsborough Township, central Orange County.

Hill's Bridge, nineteenth-century span across Potecasi Creek, n Hertford County, between Murfreesboro and Winton. Site of a Civil War skirmish, 1863. U. S. Highway 158 now crosses at or near this site.

Hills Creek rises in sw Beaufort County and flows n into Pamlico River.

Hills Creek rises in e Rutherford County and flows sw into Second Broad River.

Hills Creek rises in n Scotland County and flows ne into Lumber River.

Hills Crossroads, community in e Halifax County. Settled prior to 1830.

Hillsdale, community in n Guilford County.

Hillsdale, community in ne Davie County. Alt. 807.

Hillside Branch rises in s Watauga County and flows se into Buffalo Branch.

Hills Mill. See Chiska Creek.

Hills Point, sw Beaufort County on the s side of Pamlico River.

Hill's Point. See Fort Hill.

Hills Pond, e Wayne County on the head of West Bear Creek.

Hill's Rock, a landing in sw Carteret County on the mainland side of Bogue Sound. Named for Edward Hill on whose plantation it was located in the middle of the nineteenth century. Also known as White Rock.

Hills Store, community in e Lincoln County.

Hill Top, community in sw Guilford County.

Hilma. See Farrar.

Hiltons River. See Brunswick River.

Hines Crossroads, community in n Halifax County. Named for Peter Hines, an early settler, a part of whose home still stands here.

Hinklesville. See Welcome.

Hinshaw, community in w Yadkin County.

A former post office serving the community was named Randolph.

Hinson, community in w Washington County. Alt. 43.

Hinsons Crossroads, community in w Columbus County.

Hinton Creek rises in e Rutherford County and flows e into Cleveland County where it enters First Broad River.

Hinton's Branch rises in e central Wake County and flows ne into Beaverdam Creek.

Hinton's Quarter, former site of Johnston County courthouse, nw Johnston County, e of Clayton on the s side of Neuse River. Probably named for John Hinton who owned much land in this area. A courthouse was est. here in 1759 or 1760 and remained until 1771 when it was removed to Smithfield, *which see,* after the formation of Wake County. Gov. William Tryon, on May 3, 1771, at Smith's Ferry a short distance e, reviewed troops from Wilmington and New Bern enroute to suppress the Regulators. The site is now an open field.

Hipps Ridge, nw Cherokee County extends ne parallel to Wolf Ridge.

Hirams Hill, a sandhill on Bogue Banks, sw Carteret County. Site of former community. Named for Hiram Moore.

Hitchcock Creek rises in e Richmond County and flows sw into Pee Dee River.

Hiwassee Dam, resort community covering 547 acres in w Cherokee County. Privately owned. Originally served as site of construction camp from 1936 to 1940 when Hiwassee Dam was being built on Hiwassee River. Alt. 1,375.

Hiwassee Lake, nw Cherokee County, formed at the completion of Hiwassee Dam in 1940 on Hiwassee River. Approx. 20 mi. long, covering 6,120 acres with a max. depth of 250 ft. Owned by Tennessee Valley Authority and used for flood control, power generation, and recreation.

Hiwassee Lake State Park, former state park in western Cherokee County containing 834 acres. Est. 1948; lease from Tennessee Valley Authority terminated on December 31, 1952, and it ceased to exist as a state park. Was operated as a scenic and recreational area and provided fishing and nature study; had vacation cabins.

Hiwassee River rises in Towns County, Georgia, and flows nw into Clay County, through Lake Chatuge, and nw and w across the Cherokee-Clay County line; nw in Cherokee County through Hiwassee Lake and Apalachia Lake, and into Tennessee where it enters Tennessee River approx. 30 mi. w of Athens, Tenn. Named for the Cherokee word *ayuhwá-si*, "a meadow."

Hiwassee Township, s central Clay County.

Hobart. See Piney.

Hobbsville, community in s Gates County. Alt. 40.

Hobbton, community in n Sampson County near Wards Swamp. A post office was est. here as early as 1882.

Hobby Branch rises in se Alamance County and flows s into Haw River.

The Hobby Hole, a deep hole in Contentnea Creek approx. 3 mi. below Ruffin's (formerly Peacock's) Bridge se of Stantonsburg on the Greene-Wilson County line. Traditionally reputed to be "bottomless." Its max. depth in 1923 was only 58 ft; by 1955, it had largely filled up.

Hobgood, town in s Halifax County. Inc. 1891. Named for Franklin P. Hobgood (1847-1924), educator and president of Oxford College. Alt. 91.

Hobson Branch rises in n Buncombe County and flows nw into Ivy Creek.

Hobson Creek rises in n Mitchell County and flows s into Little Rock Creek.

Hobucken, community on s Goose Creek Island, ne Pamlico County. Originally known as Jones Bay; renamed for Hoboken, New Jersey, to which large shipments of Irish potatoes were formerly made. See also Secotaoc.

Hockiday Ridge, w Watauga County extends ne from Watauga River to Rush Branch.

Hocutts Crossroads, community in n Johnston County.

Hodges Creek rises in se Buncombe County and flows ne into McDowell County where it enters Crooked Creek.

Hodges Creek rises in se Hertford County and flows se into Chowan River.

Hodges Creek rises in s central Watauga County and flows e into Flannery Fork [of South Fork New River].

Hodges Gap, s central Watauga County between Laurel Creek and Hodges Creek.

Hodges Gap, community in s central Watauga County on Hodges Creek.

Hodges Gap Mountain, s Watauga County, 1 mi. sw of town of Boone. Alt. 3,376.

Hodges Mill Creek rises in e Wake County and flows w into Neuse River.

Hodgetown, community in e Watauga County s of Camp Branch and w of Elk Creek.

Hodgins Pond, s Hoke County on Raft Swamp, formed in 1871 and named for Henry Hodgins. Covers 100 acres. Max. depth 8 ft.

Hoe Swamp rises in n Sampson County and flows se into Six Runs Creek.

Hoffman, town in e Richmond County. Settled in the mid-1870's with the construction of the Raleigh and Augusta Air Line Railroad. Inc. 1899 and reincorporated in 1913. Named for Richard C. Hoffman (1839-1926), president of the railroad. Post office est. here 1878. During World War II Camp Mackall was adjacent to Hoffman on the e in Richmond and Scotland counties.

Hoflers Fork, community in e Gates County.

Hofmann Forest, Onslow and Jones counties, contains 78,000 acres. Est. in 1934 by the North Carolina Forestry Foundation. Named for Dr. Julius V. Hofmann (1882-1965) who est. the forest program at North Carolina State College in 1929 and was director of the Division of Forestry when he retired in 1948. Used as a demonstration forest by the School of Forest Resources of North Carolina State University.

Hogan Branch rises in ne Cherokee County and flows s into Junaluska Creek.

Hogan Branch rises in se Clay County between Kimsey Bald and Marbleyard Ridge and flows sw into Buck Creek.

Hogan Creek rises in se Orange County and flows se through Hogan's Lake and into Bolin Creek.

Hogan Ridge, e Clay County between Hogan Branch and Black Branch.

Hogans Creek rises in nw Caswell County and flows ne into Dan River.

Hogan's Lake, se Orange County, 2½ mi. nw of town of Carrboro. Alt. 488. Formed in 1930 by H. C. Hogan and named for his family. Covers 17 acres with a max. depth of 15 feet. For private recreation.

Hogback Gap, w Swain County between Cabe Branch and De Hart Creek.

Hogback Knob, w Henderson County. Alt. 3,020.

Hogback Mountain, nw Henderson County at the head of Foster Mill Creek.

Hogback Mountain, n Graham County between Stecoah Creek and Sawyer Creek, extending ne from Big Garland Gap to Wildcat Gap. Alt. 5,200.

Hogback Mountain on the Jackson-Macon County line. Alt. 4,950.

Hogback Mountain, e Macon County between Walnut and Buck creeks.

Hog Back Mountain, ne Madison County between Bear Wallow Branch and Peter Cove Creek.

Hogback Mountain, w Madison County between Spring Creek and Meadow Fork.

Hogback Ridge, s Buncombe County between Redmans Cove and Buckeye Cove.

Hogback Township, sw Transylvania County.

Hogback Valley, community in w Transylvania County near Lake Toxaway.

Hog Branch rises in nw Ashe County and flows s into Big Laurel Creek.

Hog Branch rises in w Orange County and flows s into Cane Creek.

Hog Branch. See Hawk Branch.

Hog Camp Branch rises in s Watauga County and flows se into Rockhouse Creek.

Hog Cane Branch rises in w Jackson County and flows n into Savannah Creek.

Hogeye Branch rises in nw Buncombe County and flows ne into Sandymush Creek.

Hoggard Mill Creek rises in central Bertie County and flows sw into Cashie River. Appears as Wills Quarter Creek on the Collet map, 1770, a name which was in use as late as 1882.

Hoggard's Mill, 2 mi. n of Windsor in se Bertie County on Hoggard Mill Creek. The large pond here was the site of Lockhart Mill according to the Collet map, 1770. The surrounding community was known as Wolfington and was the county seat from 1722 until it was moved to Windsor in 1774. By 1833 the site bore its present name. See also Hoggard Mill Creek.

Hoggard Swamp, s Hertford County. Wiccacon River rises here.

Hogg's Folly, name formerly applied to a tract of land in w New Hanover County adjoining Wilmington on the n. John Hogg, in the eighteenth century, by means of a ditch, enclosed a tract of land on which he intended to establish a market garden. Evidently failure of the project produced the name.

Hog Hill, se Catawba County. Named from the fact that early settlers branded their hogs and let them roam here until fall when they were taken home to be fattened.

Hog Island, swampy island in central Craven County formed by Neuse River on the e and Bachelor Creek and The Gut on the w. Formerly known as Leaches Island for George M. Leach who owned the island in 1804, and so appears on the Price map, 1808, the MacRae map, 1833, and the U.S. Coast Survey map, 1865. Approx. 3½ mi. long and 1 mi. wide at its widest point.

Hog Island, ne Carteret County, group of islands between Back Bay and Pamlico Sound. Site of early settlement. See also Whale Camp Point. Appears as Hog Island on Moseley map, 1733.

Hog Island in Pamlico Sound near Hog Island Point on the e mainland of Hyde County.

Hog Island. See Lake Bay.

Hog Island Bay, name erroneously given to Cedar Island Bay, ne Carteret County, on the 1935 Soil Survey map.

Hog Island Narrows, ne Carteret County, connecting Cedar Island Bay with Back Bay.

Hog Island Point, s point of Hog Island in ne Carteret County.

Hog Island Point extends off the e mainland of Hyde County into Pamlico Sound.

Hog Island Swamp, sw Sampson County, s of Little Coharie Creek.

Hogjaw Gap, n Cherokee County.

Hoglot Branch rises in s Macon County and flows ne into Bates Branch.

Hogpen Bay, in the waters of Core Sound extending into Core Banks in se Carteret County.

Hogpen Branch rises in sw Buncombe County near Hogpen Gap and flows nw into Glady Fork.

Hogpen Branch rises in ne Cherokee County and flows nw into Taylor Creek.

Hogpen Branch rises in sw Johnston County and flows n into Mills Creek.

Hogpen Creek rises in se Rutherford County and flows ne into Second Broad River.

Hogpen Gap, sw Buncombe County s of Young Pisgah Mountain.

Hogpen Gap, ne Cherokee County in the Valley River Mountains. Alt. 2,353.

Hogpen Gap, central Cherokee County between West Prong Grape Creek and Grape Creek.

Hogpen Mountain, nw Rutherford County. Alt. approx. 1,900.

Hog Point, a point of land in n Carteret County extending into the waters of Turnagain Bay.

Hog Quarter. See Spot.

Hogsed Cove, se Clay County through which Eagle Creek flows.

Hogs Falls, rapids in Neuse River in s Wayne County in The Roundabout. Mentioned

as early as 1818 in a survey of the rivers of North Carolina.

Hogshead Creek rises in e Transylvania County and flows nw into French Broad River.

Hog Swamp rises in s Robeson County and flows s into Ashpole Swamp.

Hogtown, former town in n Martin County on Roanoke River about 1 mile se of Hamilton, which see. Appears on the Collet map, 1770, and on the Price map, 1808. In 1804, however, the polling place at Hogtown was moved to Hamilton, and the former place began to decline. Probably named for the local Hogg family.

Ho-Ho Village, a modern community on the mainland side of Bogue Sound, sw Carteret County, between Bogue and Morehead City.

Hoke, community in sw Washington County. Alt. 41. Known as Long Ridge from about 1857 until about 1900. The post office name was changed to Hoke in 1900 in honor of R. F. Hoke (1837-1912), the Confederate general who forced the evacuation of the Federal troops from the occupied towns of Plymouth and Washington in 1864.

Hoke County was formed in 1911 from Cumberland and Robeson counties. Located in the se section of the state, it is bounded by Cumberland, Robeson, Scotland, Moore, and Harnett counties. It was named for Robert F. Hoke (1837-1912), of Lincoln County, a major general in the Confederate army. Area: 382 sq. mi. County seat: Raeford with an elevation of 262 ft. Townships are Allendale, Antioch, Blue Springs, McLauchlin, Quewhiffle, Raeford, and Stonewall. Produces tobacco, corn, wheat, oats, soybeans, cotton, turkeys, livestock, hogs, watermelons, and textiles.

Holberts Cove, community in w Polk County, w of Miller Mountain.

Holcombe, community in ne Madison County.

Holcombe Branch rises in e Madison County and flows nw into Little Ivy Creek.

Holcombe Cove, the valley through which Moore Creek flows in sw Buncombe County.

Holden Beach, a section of outer beach in s Brunswick County w of Lockwoods Folly Inlet and e of Big Beach. Approx. 3½ mi. long. A summer resort with cottages is here.

Holden Cove, se Clay County between Big Kitchens and Little Kitchens ridges.

Holden Cove, valley in central Clay County through which Downing Creek flows.

Holden's Crossroads, community in e Wilson County n of White Oak Swamp. Named for W. T. Holden, local landowner.

Holder Branch rises in w Duplin County and flows sw into Maxwell Creek.

Holder Creek rises in ne Mitchell County and flows se into Charles Creek.

Holiday Island, approx. 2 mi. long, in the Chowan River, nw Chowan County. Formerly about 150 acres, but now only about 40 to 50. Appears on the Collet map, 1770, as Holladay Island.

Holiday Lake. See Pages Lake.

Holland, community in s Wake County. Est. 1900. Named for J. C. Holland. Alt. 411.

Holland Branch rises in e Madison County and flows se into Middle Fork.

Holland Branch rises in e Onslow County and flows n into Holland Mill Creek.

Holland Creek rises in s Rutherford County and flows ne into Second Broad River.

Holland Gap, e Haywood County on Glade Mountain.

Holland Mill Creek rises in e Onslow County and flows into White Oak River. Also called Holland's Creek.

Holland Mountain extends from near Canton in e Haywood County to Hooker Gap in sw Buncombe County. Its peak is known as The Pinnacle.

Hollands, community in n Pitt County on Conetoe Creek.

Hollands Creek rises in w Chatham County and flows se into Rocky River.

Hollands Creek rises in n central Rutherford County and flows se into Catheys Creek. Named for James Holland, member of the first Board of Trustees of the University of North Carolina. Gilbert Town, former county seat, was on this creek.

Holland's Creek. See Holland Mill Creek.

Hollands Crossroads, community in nw Wayne County n of Nahunta Swamp.

Holland's Point extends from e Onslow County into Queens Creek.

Hollands Sein Hole, a shallow place in Northeast Cape Fear River in central Duplin County suitable for seining.

Hollemans Crossroads, community in sw Wake County between Whiteoak Creek and Cary Branch. Known in late 1800's as Enno, and in early 1900's as Collins Crossroads.

Holley Branch rises in se Mitchell County and flows se into North Toe River.

Holley's Mill. See Goshen Swamp.

Hollis, community in e Rutherford County on Hinton Creek.

Hollister, community in w Halifax County.

Hollow. See Mount Airy.

Holloway Branch rises in w Macon County and flows nw into Whiteoak Creek.

Holloway Mines, copper mines on Aarons Creek in nw Granville County. Operated from shortly prior to 1900 to about 1910 and again briefly during World War I.

Holloway Ridge, nw Yancey County between Patsy Creek and Riddle Branch.

Holloway Township, ne Person County.

Hollow Ground Swamp, in central Tyrrell County. See also Long Island.

Hollow Poplar. See Poplar.

Hollow Poplar Creek rises in nw Mitchell County and flows sw into Nolichucky River.

Hollow Rock, former rock cave on Deep River in se Chatham County near Moncure. Said to have been used for shelter by Indians. Destroyed in 1957 for gravel for road construction.

Hollow Township, nw Bladen County.

Holly Bottom Branch rises at Wildcat Spring, n Haywood County, and flows se into Groundhog Creek.

Holly Branch rises in se Macon County and flows ne into Cane Creek.

Holly Grove, community in n central Bertie County.

Holly Grove, community in central Davidson County. See also Conrad Hill.

Holly Grove, community in ne Gates County.

Holly Grove, community in w Richmond County.

Holly Grove Township, ne Gates County.

Holly Meadow Branch rises in central Cabarrus County and flows s into Coddle Creek.

Holly Neck. See Beasley.

Holly Point, peninsula extending from w Goose Creek Island, ne Pamlico County, into Gooose Creek at the mouth of Dixon Creek.

Holly Ridge, a raised strip of ground in Dismal Swamp in se Gates County.

Holly Ridge, town in s Onslow County. Alt. 66. Est. about 1890 as a wood station on the railroad. Inc. 1941. Named for a slight elevation here on which holly formerly grew; at Holly Shelter Bay about 1 mi. s was Sages Ordinary (dating from the Revolution) at which George Washington spent the night, April 23, 1791. See also Camp Davis.

Holly Shelter Bay, a pocosin in e Pender County bounded on the ne by Shaken Creek, on the w by Northeast Cape Fear River, and on the s by Trumpeter Swamp. It is about 10 mi. long and 7 mi. wide. Appears as Holly Schelter Precoson on the Collet map, 1770 (although mistakenly applied to Angola Bay), and on the Price map, 1808. Holly Shelter Wildlife Management Area, 48,470 acres, is operated here by the N. C. Wildlife Resources Commission; bear and deer abound.

Holly Shelter Creek receives the waters of Angola, Shaken, and Moores creeks, Cane Branch, and other streams in ne Pender County and flows w approx. 30 mi. into Northeast Cape Fear River. Called Shelter River in a 1913 report by the U.S. Chief of Engineers. Appears as Holly Schelter Creek on the Collet map, 1770.

Holly Springs community in e Carteret County on Newport River.

Holly Springs, community in w Henderson County between Boylston and Brock creeks.

Holly Springs, community in s Rutherford County, former resort with a hotel.

Holly Springs, town in s Wake County. Settled 1826. Inc. 1877. Named for holly trees growing near a spring in the vicinity. Alt. 350.

Holly Springs, community in n Yadkin County between Smithtown and Yadkin River.

Holly Springs Township, sw Wake County.

Holly Township, ne Pender County.

Hollyville, town in ne Pamlico County adjoining Vandemere. Inc. 1907 but long inactive in municipal affairs. Named for local holly trees. Known more recently as Cash Corner. See also Cash Corner No. 2.

Hollywood Ridge, community in n central Caldwell County on a ridge parallel to and s of Yadkin River.

Holman, community in w Davie County near the headwaters of Bear Creek. Settled about 1786 and named for Holman family.

Holmes Point, on the w side of New River in central Onslow County. Formerly known as Little Ragged Point.

Holsclaw's Creek rises in e Caldwell County and flows e into Duck Creek.

Holt Knob, se Macon County between Monger Creek and Mill Creek.

Holt Lake, central Johnston County on Black Creek. Original dam constructed prior to 1911; present dam, downstream from first, built in early 1920's. Covers approx. 400 acres; max. depth 25 ft.

Holy Swamp rises in central Robeson County and flows se into Big Raft Swamp.

Homing Creek rises in e Wake County and flows se into Little River.

Hominy, community in sw Buncombe County. Alt. 2,097.

Hominy Creek rises in e Haywood County and flows generally e into central Buncombe County where it enters French Broad River. Said to have been visited by a South Carolina hunting party before the Revolution and given this name because they ate hominy for supper here the first night.

Hominy Gap, e Haywood County. Alt. 2,678. The highway between Canton and Asheville passes through this gap.

Hominy Heights, former community in central Wilson County just west of and named for Hominy Swamp, now within the limits of the city of Wilson. Known earlier as White's Store. Captain William White operated a store here as early as 1812.

Hominy Swamp rises in w central Wilson County and flows se into Contentnea Creek. Appears in local records as early as 1764. Said to have been named for a hominy mill operated on its waters by that date.

Honeycut Cove, near the n end of the Elk Mountains, central Buncombe County, e of Jump Cove.

Honeycutt, community in w Mitchell County on Big Rock Creek.

Honeycutt Branch rises in n Mitchell County and flows s into Cane Creek.

Honeycutt Creek rises in n central Wake County and flows ne into Neuse River. Formerly called Fall Creek and Big Fall Creek.

Honeycutt Mine, former gold mine on Little Buffalo Creek, ne Cabarrus County.

Honeycutts Township, central Sampson County.

Honey Hill, town in central Columbus County. Inc. 1895, but long inactive in municipal affairs.

Honey Island Swamp rises in w Brunswick and e Columbus counties and flows sw along the Brunswick-Columbus County line through Green Swamp into Juniper Creek.

Honey Pond, community w central Brunswick County.

Honey Pot Swamp rises in central Gates County and flows s into Bennetts Creek.

Honolulu, community in n Craven County.

Hood Creek rises in ne Brunswick County and flows n into Cape Fear River.

Hood Gap, e Haywood County at the ne end of Buck Cove.

Hoods or **Hoods Crossroads,** community in e Mecklenburg County. Morning Star Lutheran Church organized here in 1775.

Hoods Pond, e Wake County in Marks Creek.

Hoodsville. *See* Chesterfield.

Hood Swamp, community in e Wayne County near West Bear Creek. Formerly called Aaron for Aaron Parks (d. 1845) a local farmer and lay religious leader. Renamed for local Free Will Baptist church of which Parks was a member. Name has appeared in nineteenth century records as Wood Swamp.

Hoof Inn, an early nineteenth-century tavern in w Washington County, located on what is now the Plymouth-Pinetown road, approx. midway between Ausbon and Hinson.

Hooker, community in e Alleghany County. Alt. approx. 2,600.

Hooker Creek rises in w Henderson County and flows sw into e Transylvania County and into Little River.

Hooker Gap, sw Buncombe County at the e end of Holland Mountain.

Hookers Knob, e Madison County between Jarvis Mountains and Gabriels Creek.

Hookerton, town in se Greene County on Contentnea Creek. Alt. 75. Inc. as Hookerton, 1817, on the lands of William Hooker. Known as Caswells Landing prior to the Revolution for Benjamin Caswell, brother of Governor Richard Caswell. Several early nineteenth century academies flourished here, and a public library was est. in 1817.

Hookerton Township, s Greene County.

Hooks Branch rises in w Johnston County and flows s into Black Creek.

Hooper Bald, w Graham County between McGuires community and Huckleberry Knob. Alt. 5,429. Named for Enos Hooper who moved to Graham from Jackson County and had a farm in the valley below the mountain.

Hooper Branch rises in s Graham County and flows nw into Snowbird Creek.

Hooper Branch rises in n Lincoln County and flows se into Anderson Creek.

Hooper County was authorized to be est. from Robeson and Richmond counties in 1851 provided the people in the territory voted for its erection. The vote was against the new county. It was to have been named in honor of William Hooper, one of the signers of the Declaration of Independence.

Hooper Cove, w Graham County between Cedar Top and Rattler Ford.

Hooper Creek rises in n Henderson County and flows w into Cane Creek.

Hooper Creek rises in s Polk County and flows se into South Carolina where it enters Pacolet River.

Hooper Knob, central Jackson County between Moses Creek and Wayehutta Creek. Alt. 3,719.

Hooper Mill Creek rises in w Graham County and flows se and n into Santeetlah Lake.

Hoopers Creek Township, n Henderson County.

Hoophole Landing, e Beaufort County on Pungo River. A small community adjoining the landing bears the same name.

Hoop Pole Creek, a waterway between several small islands near the e end of Bogue Banks, s Carteret County in Bogue Sound.

Hootentown. *See* Wootentown.

Hoot Owl Cove, nw Jackson County on Shoal Creek.

Hootowl Hollow, sw Mitchell County parallel to Roaring Branch.

Hoots Millpond, e Wilkes County on Little Elkin River. Grain and sawmill operated here by the Hoots family.

Hoover Hill, community in w Randolph County. A post office was est. here as early as 1882. In the early twentieth century a prosperous gold mine was operated here. Ancestors of President Herbert Hoover are buried in the vicinity.

Hoover Meadow, se Yancey County between the sw end of Dovers Ridge and Sevenmile Ridge.

Hop Creek rises in nw Catawba County and flows se into Jacob Fork.

Hope. See Trinity.

Hopedale, community in central Alamance County on Stony Creek at Big Falls, *which see.* Produces textiles.

Hope Mills, town in sw Cumberland County. Known as Rockfish before the Civil War. Inc. as Hope Mills, 1891, when mills were built. Produces textiles. Alt. 117.

Hope Valley Forest, n Chatham and s Durham counties, contains 1,735 acres. Est. in 1941 when the U.S. government conveyed a rehabilitation camp area to North Carolina State College. Now owned and operated by the School of Forestery of N. C. State University for demonstration and research.

Hopewell, community in nw Mecklenburg County, It developed around Hopewell Presbyterian Church, organized 1762.

Hopewell, community in e Rutherford County. Named for a local church.

Hopewell Branch rises in central Madison County and flows sw into French Broad River.

Hopis Branch rises in w Madison County and flows s into Meadow Fork.

Hopkins, community in n Ashe County.

Hopkins, community in e Wake County.

Hopkins Mine, former gold mine in ne Cabarrus County on Beaver Creek.

Hop Mountain, sw Madison County, a peak on Spring Creek Mountain. Alt. 4,072.

Hopper's Ford. See Worthville.

Horace, community in e Henderson County between Little Hungry and Hungry rivers.

Horn Beam Swamp rises in e Nash County and flows se into Edgecombe County where it enters Compass Creek.

Hornblower Point, s Chowan County, extends from e side of Edenton Bay into Albemarle Sound. A railroad bridge across the sound extends from this point to the mouth of Kendricks Creek in n Washington County. Now a part of Edenton Naval Air Station property. Shown as Moseleys Point on the Collet map, 1770; as Hornblow's Point on the MacRae map, 1833; and as Skinner's Point on the Price map, 1808, and on the Kerr map, 1882. Named for the Horniblow family which owned property here.

Hornbuckle Creek rises in n Jackson County and flows nw into Soco Creek.

Hornbuckle Ridge, w Jackson County between Sassafras Branch and Grassy Knob.

Horn Camp Swamp rises in s Robeson County and flows sw into Ashpole Swamp.

Horne Creek rises in se Surry County and flows se into Yadkin River.

Horner, community in e Granville County.

Hornes Bay, a sand filled bay in w Columbus County. See Carolina Bays.

Hornet Swamp rises in w Sampson County and flows w into Little Coharie Creek.

Horneyhead Mountain in central Jackson County on the ne end of Niggerskull Mountain. Alt. 4,060.

Horniblow. See Hornblower Point.

Hornpipe Creek rises in s Lenoir County and flows nw into Southwest Creek. The name appears in local records dating from before the Revolution.

Horns Branch rises in s Surry County and flows ne into King Creek.

Horn's Branch rises in w Wilson County and flows w into Shepherd's Branch.

Horn Swamp. See Sandy Run.

Hornytown, community in ne Davidson County at the head of Abbotts Creek.

Horsebone Gap on the Haywood-Jackson County line on the main Balsam Range. The Blue Ridge Parkway passes through or near this gap. Named from the fact that a horse, turned out to graze in this area, died and his bones lay bleaching in the sun for a number of years.

Horse Branch rises in sw Beaufort County and flows ne into Chocowinity Creek.

Horse Branch rises in w Lenoir County and flows se into Southwest Creek. The name appears in local records dating from before the Revolution.

Horse Branch rises in n Madison County and flows se into Shelton Laurel Creek.

Horse Branch rises in n Pender County and flows sw into Long Creek. Named for adjacent high ground to which wild horses retreated in time of flood in pre-Revolutionary days.

Horsebranch, community in central Pender County on Horse Branch.

Horse Cove, w Graham County between Little Santeetlah Creek and Rock Creek Knob.

Horse Cove, nw Henderson County between Beetree Ridge and Big Ridge.

Horse Cove, se Macon County, through which Edwards and Blackrock creeks flow. A post office by this name served the area in the late nineteenth century. Woodrow Wilson, in a letter written from Horse Cove on July 30, 1879, reported that he spent a part of the summer here with his mother and other relatives. John R. Thompson rented summer homes and furnished meals for visitors from New Orleans, Charleston, and other coastal cities. Highlands, *which see*, was being developed nearby at about this time.

Horse Cove, w central Swain County extends e from Noland Creek between Andreas Branch and Massie Gap.

Horse Cove, n Transylvania County extends ne from Cat Pen Gap to Davidson River.

Horse Cove Branch rises in n Macon County and flows ne into Burningtown Creek.

Horse Cove Ridge, w Graham County, forms the sw watershed of Little Santeetlah Creek and the sw boundary of Joyce Kilmer Memorial Forest.

Horse Creek rises in sw Grayson County, Va., and flows se into n central Ashe County where it enters North Fork New River.

Horse Creek rises in w Avery County and flows e into North Toe River.

Horse Creek rises in nw Durham County and flows s into North Fork Little River.

Horse Creek rises in w Franklin County and flows sw into n Wake County where it enters Neuse River. Appears on the Collet map, 1770.

Horse Creek, w Haywood County, Great Smoky Mountains National Park, rises near lat. 35° 35' 17" N., long. 83° 10' 40" W., and flows ne to join Bear Branch in forming Rough Creek.

Horse Creek rises on Fort Bragg Military Reservation in n Hoke County and flows ne into Little River.

Horse Creek rises in s Moore County near town of Pinehurst and flows s into Deep Creek.

Horse Creek rises in w central Polk County and flows s into Pacolet River.

Horse Creek rises in Cherokee County, S. C., and flows ne into Rutherford County where it enters Broad River.

Horse Creek rises in s Stanly County and flows ne into Long Creek.

Horse Creek Gap on the Haywood-Swain County line on Balsam Mountain between Chiltoes Mountain and Cataloochee Balsam. Alt. 5,575.

Horse Creek Ridge, w Avery County.

Horse Creek Township, nw Ashe County.

Horse Fork rises in nw Catawba County and flows n into Catawba River.

Horsefork Mountain, e Haywood County

extends ne from Fall Creek to Grassy Gap.

Horse Gap on the Ashe-Wilkes County line.

Horse Gap, n Buncombe County between Sheep Knob and Ray Knob.

Horse Gap on the McDowell-Yancey County line near the head of Left Prong Three Forks Creek.

Horse Gap, n Transylvania County between Laurel Brook and Cantrell Creek.

Horse Island, a long, narrow tidal marsh island se of Beaufort in s Carteret County.

Horse Island in Core Sound, ne Carteret County. Ruins of a club house exist on the island, and two persons are said to have been murdered here. Fishermen claim to have seen ghosts on the island.

Horse Knob, n Transylvania County at the nw end of Huckleberry Ridge near the head of South Prong Turkey Creek.

Horselot Cove, central Clay County, s of Evans Ridge.

Horse Mountain on the McDowell-Yancey County line.

Horse Mountain Gap, s Burke County. Alt. 2,018.

Horsepasture River rises in s Jackson County and flows se across sw Transylvania County into South Carolina where it enters the Toxaway River.

Horse Pen Bay, swamp in nw Brunswick County. A part of Green Swamp.

Horsepen Bay, a small pocosin near the head of Horse Branch, *which see*, n Pender County.

Horse Pen Branch rises in sw Bladen County and flows w into Horse Pen Swamp.

Horsepen Branch rises in s Greene County and flows se into Rainbow Creek. The name appears in local records prior to the Revolution.

Horsepen Branch rises in s Warren County and flows se into Shocco Creek.

Horse Pen Creek rises in s central Bladen County and flows se into Brown Marsh Swamp.

Horsepen Creek rises in nw Columbus County on the Columbus-Robeson-Bladen County lines and flows w into Big Swamp.

Horsepen Creek rises in w Guilford County and flows ne into Reedy Fork Creek.

Horse Pen Mountain, at the head of Cabin Creek in s Henderson County.

Horsepen Pocosin, a sandy pocosin in sw Gates County. Alt. 28.

Horsepen Point, se Carteret County, extends from Core Banks into Core Sound.

Horsepen Point, on Ocracoke Island near

the community of Ocracoke, se Hyde County.

Horse Pen Ridge, w Haywood County, Great Smoky Mountains National Park, a spur extending nw from Cataloochee Divide, center near lat. 35° 35′ 40″ N., long. 83° 05′ 07″ W.

Horsepen Swamp rises in nw Beaufort County and flows sw into Tranters Creek.

Horse Pen Swamp rises in sw Bladen County and flows w into Robeson County where it enters Big Swamp.

Horsepen Swamp rises in w Pitt County and flows se into Swift Creek.

Horse Pool appears on the Moseley map, 1733, in what is now e Gates County in the w edge of the Dismal Swamp.

Horse Range Ridge, s Graham County extends se from Little Snowbird Creek to Old Billy Top.

Horse Ridge, n Avery County.

Horse Ridge, s Burke County in the South Mountains. Alt. 2,800.

Horse Ridge, ne Cherokee County in the Valley River Mountains.

Horse Ridge, sw Macon County between Siler Bald Branch and Factory Branch.

Horse Ridge, ne Swain County in Great Smoky Mountains National Park, extending sw from Balsam Mountain between Stillwell Creek and Left Fork [Deep Creek].

Horse Ridge, nw Watauga County extends n between Rube Creek and Little Beaverdam Creek.

Horse Ridge, n Yancey County between Seng Branch and Cynthia Branch.

Horse Ridge. *See* Balsam Mountain.

Horse Run rises in e Duplin County and flows se into Cabin Creek.

Horse's Creek rises in s Moore County and flows sw into Deep Creek.

Horse's Creek rises in w Moore County and flows nw into Dry Creek.

The Horseshoe, bend in Nantahala River, w Macon County.

The Horseshoe, a ridge parallel to a deep bend in Hazel Creek, w Swain County.

Horseshoe, community in nw Camden County, settled shortly after 1700 and formerly known as Newfoundland.

Horse Shoe, community in w Henderson County. Named for its situation on a sharp bend in French Broad River. Alt. 2,083.

Horseshoe Bend, in nw Swain County, is a bend in Eagle Creek at the sw end of Big Fork Ridge.

Horseshoe Bend, w Swain County in Little Tennessee River.

Horseshoe Bend. *See* Andrews Geyser.

Horse Shoe Mountain, w Henderson County between Johnsons Mill Creek and French Broad River. Alt. 2,775.

Horseshoe Mountain, se Macon County at the head of Brooks Creek.

Horseshoe Neck, a sharp bend in the Yadkin River in w Davidson and e Davie counties. The neck of land formed by the bend is in Davidson County. Appears on the Collet map, 1770, as Horse-shoe. *See also* Boone's Cave.

Horseshoe Ridge, s Swain County between Dark Branch and Davis Branch.

Horseshoe Rock, peak on the sw end of Wolf Mountain, e Jackson County.

Horse Swamp rises in s Hertford County and flows se and ne to join Flat Swamp in forming Bear Swamp.

Horse Swamp rises in e Onslow County and flows nw into Little Northeast Creek.

Horse Swamp Pocosin, e Onslow County between Queens Creek and Little Northeast Creek.

Horse Swamp rises in s Robeson County and flows sw into Aaron Swamp.

Horse Trail Gap on the McDowell-Yancey County line near the head of Roaring Fork.

Horse Trough Mountain, w Montgomery County near Woodrun Creek.

Horsetrough Ridge, ne Swain County in Great Smoky Mountains National Park, a spur extending sw from Overlook Ridge between Heintooga Creek and Selma Creek.

Horseway Swamp rises in e Pitt County and flows ne into Beaufort County where it enters Chicod Creek.

Horton Bay, n central Carteret County, behind Horton Point near the mouth of South River.

Horton Branch rises in n Cherokee County and flows sw into Beaverdam Creek.

Horton Branch rises in s Watauga County and flows se into Joe Creek.

Horton Creek rises in w Yancey County and flows e into Indian Creek.

Horton Hill, n Yancey County between Bee Branch and Sidney Hill.

Horton Knob, n Macon County between Allen Branch and Rose Creek.

Horton Point, n central Carteret County, on e shore of South River near its mouth.

Hoskin Fork rises in nw Watauga County

and flows n into sw Ashe County where it enters North Fork New River.

Hoskins Point. *See* Palmetto Point.

Hosley Branch. *See* Hostler Branch.

Hostler Branch rises in w Caswell County and flows e into Country Line Creek. Appears as Hosley Branch on early maps of the county.

Hotel. *See* Woodville.

Hotel Creek. *See* Hall's Creek.

Hothouse, community in sw Cherokee County on Persimmon Creek.

Hothouse Branch rises in sw Cherokee County and flows se into Hot House Creek. Named from the fact that the Indians had "hot houses" in which heated stones were placed for "sweat baths" to refresh fatigued warriors and hunters.

Hothouse Branch rises in s Clay County and flows nw into Shooting Creek.

Hot House Branch rises in central Hertford County and flows nw into Potecasi Creek.

Hot House Creek rises in sw Cherokee County and flows sw into Fannin County, Georgia, where it enters Ocoee River.

Hot House Township, sw Cherokee County.

Hot Springs, town in w Madison County on French Broad River. Named for thermal springs in the town, discovered in 1778; a health resort since 1800. Name changed from Warm Springs, 1886; inc. 1889. Alt. 1,332. An internment camp for Germans during World War I was here. Produces textiles. Spaightville, *which see,* inc. 1802, may have been at this site.

Hot Springs Mountain, w Madison County parallel to Mountain Island Branch.

Hot Springs Township, former township in nw Madison County, now township number 9.

House, community in central Pitt County, approx. 1 mile n of Greenville.

House Creek rises in central Wake County just w of city of Raleigh, and flows ne into Crabtree Creek.

House Creek Township, central Wake County.

House of Passage. *See* Old Town.

House's Mill Pond, n Sampson County on Sevenmile Swamp. A mill est. here in 1812 by William House still grinds corn.

Houston, community in sw Union County. Alt. 666.

Houston Branch rises in e Macon County and flows sw into Big Creek.

Houston Gap, e Mitchell County between Little Bear Creek and Beaver Creek.

Houston Knob, e Macon County between Moss Branch and Walnut Creek.

Houston Knob, w Yancey County between Possumtrot Creek and Indian Creek.

Houston Ridge, central Avery County.

Houstonville, community in ne Iredell County.

Howard Branch rises in s Macon County and flows n into Dryman Fork.

Howard Creek rises in n Watauga County and flows se into South Fork New River.

Howard Creek, community 3 mi. n of Boone in central Watauga County.

Howard Gap, s Macon County between Middle Creek and Norton Branch.

Howard Gap, w Polk County between Warrior Mountain and Miller Mountain. Named for Captain Thomas Howard, whose men, led by Skyuka, defeated Cherokee Indians here in 1776. *See also* Skyuka Mountain.

Howard Knob, mountain in central Watauga County about ½ mi. n of town of Boone. Named during Revolutionary War when a Loyalist, Benjamin Howard, fled from American patriots to a cave on this mountain. There is no record of his discovery. Alt. 4,420. *See also* Sampson's Chimney.

Howard Reef, in Pamlico Sound, se Hyde County, approx. 1 nautical mi. n of Ocracoke Island, and is approx. 1¾ mi. long and over ½ mi. wide.

Howards Bay, s Onslow County in New River between Cedar Point and Sulliers Bay.

Howards Creek. *See* Indian Creek.

Howards Creek Township, w central Lincoln County.

Howard's Knob Gap, central Watauga County. Alt. 3,679.

Howard Swamp rises in s Robeson County and flows sw into Indian Swamp.

Howell Branch rises in n Yancey County and flows s into Big Creek.

Howell Creek rises in central Wayne County and flows se into Stony Creek.

Howells Point, a small neck of land on the e side of Lockwoods Folly River just n of the channel of the Intracoastal Waterway in s Brunswick County.

Howell Swamp, rises in n Greene County and flows sw into Beaman Run. Named for the Howell family living in the vicinity as early as 1769.

Howes Point, se Brunswick County on Cape Fear River. Now within the bounds of Sunny Point ammunition depot. Birthplace of General Robert Howe (1732-86).

Howes Point, e New Hanover County, extends from the mainland into the n waters of Middle Sound.

Howie Mine, former gold mine in w Union County s of East Fork Twelvemile Creek.

Howland Creek rises in e Carteret County and flows approx. 2.2 mi. se into Jarrett Bay.

Howlett Creek rises in e Granville County and flows n into Little Island Creek.

Howsers Creek rises in central Gaston County and flows e into South Fork Catawba River.

Hoyles Creek rises in s Lincoln County and flows sw into n Gaston County where it turns se to flow into South Fork Catawba River.

Hoyles Store, community in s Lincoln County between Rockdam Creek and Leonard Fork. The Hoylesville post office which existed in 1822 may have been at or near this community. *See also* Dallas.

Hoylesville. *See* Dallas.

Hoyts Stop, a short channel running into the Banks Channel in w Carteret County. Named for Hoyt Tootle, a Negro fisherman who stopped the channel for fish.

Hub. *See* Boardman.

Hubbard, former community in w Swain County on Little Tennessee River. The site is now covered by the waters of Fontana Lake.

Hubert, community in e Onslow County on Bell Swamp.

Huble Creek. *See* Hubquarter Creek.

Hubquarter Creek rises in ne Warren County and flows ne into Gaston Lake. Appears as Huble Creek on the Collet map, 1770, but with its present name on the Price map, 1808.

Huckleberry Branch rises in sw Wilson County and flows n into Black Creek.

Huckleberry Creek rises in ne Macon County and flows s into Beasley Creek.

Huckleberry Gap, n Madison County between White Rock Branch and Chimney Creek.

Huckleberry Knob, w Graham County between Hooper Bald and Little Huckleberry Knob. Alt. approx. 5,570.

Huckleberry Knob, w Haywood County between Deep Gap and Murray Gap.

Huckleberry Knob, n Madison County between Huckleberry Gap and White Oak Gap.

Huckleberry Mountain, n Henderson County between Rattlesnake Knob and Kyles Creek. Alt. 2,959.

Huckleberry Mountain, ne Rutherford County between Pot Branch and North Fork. Alt. 2,108.

Huckleberry Mountain Artists' Colony. *See* Huckleberry Ridge.

Huckleberry Patch, mountain in sw Watauga County at the head of Boone Fork.

Huckleberry Ridge, s Henderson County between Cabin Creek and Rush Mountain. Cited in early county records as Whortleberry Mountain. Formerly a Girl Scout Camp and in recent years an artists' and writers' summer retreat known as Huckleberry Mountain Artists' Colony.

Huckleberry Ridge, ne Macon County between Blazed Creek and Huckleberry Creek.

Huckleberry Ridge, n Madison County parallel to Rock Branch.

Huckleberry Ridge, n Pender County, a sandy area on the sw side of Angola Bay.

Huckleberry Ridge, n Transylvania County extends se beside South Prong Turkey Creek.

Huckleberry Springs, community in w Durham County a short distance nw of the city of Durham. Formerly a popular picnic site because of the excellent spring water.

Huckleberry Swamp. *See* Enfield.

Hudson, town in s Caldwell County. Settled in the late nineteenth century and known as Sardis for a local Baptist Church. Inc. 1905 and named for David Hudson, the founder. Produces textiles and furniture. Alt. 1,264.

Hudson Spring, community in nw Anson County on Richardson Creek.

Hudson Township, se Caldwell County.

Huey Gap, central Haywood County on the head of Dotson Branch.

Huff Island, se Bertie County between Middle River and Roanoke River. Measures approx. 4½ mi. long and 1 mi. wide. *See also* Purchace Islands.

Huff Island, a sandy island approx. ¼ mi. long in French Broad River, w Madison County.

Huffmans Creek rises in n Davidson County and flows sw into Reedy Creek.

Huffmantown, community in nw Onslow County between Mill Swamp and Purgatory Pocosin.

Huggins Bay, a loam filled bay in sw Columbus County. *See also* Carolina Bays.

Huggins Branch rises in n Swain County and flows nw into Hazel Creek.

Huggins Creek rises in sw Columbus County and flows s into South Carolina where it enters Jordan Swamp.

Huggins Creek rises in n Swain County in the Great Smoky Mountains National Park and flows sw into Forney Creek.

Huggins Hell, thicket of rhododendron and laurel covering between four and five hundred acres in n Swain County in Great Smoky Mountains National Park. Named for Irving Huggins, early settler, who was trapped here for several days while herding cattle.

Huggins Island, e Onslow County between Dudley's Island and Swansboro in White Oak River. Named for Luke Huggins. Appears as Stones Island on the Moseley map, 1733. A fort or battery erected here by Confederate forces was designed to protect Bogue Inlet and West Channel from the Union fleet; it was destroyed in 1862.

Huggins Ridge, n Swain County in Great Smoky Mountains National Park, a short spur extending nw from Welch Ridge between Sawbrier Ridge and Huggins Branch.

Hugh Day's Gap, ne Caldwell and w Wilkes counties. Alt. 1,687. Named for Hugh Day, a hatter in the area in the early nineteenth century.

Hughes, community in central Avery County.

Hughes Branch rises in e Macon County and flows sw into Watauga Creek.

Hughes Branch rises in n Mitchell County and flows se into Bean Creek.

Hughes Branch rises in central Swain County and flows n into Tuckasegee River.

Hughes Creek rises in n Lee County and flows e into Lick Creek.

Hughes Creek rises in nw Mitchell County and flows sw into Hollow Poplar Creek.

Hughes Creek rises in s Polk County and flows se into South Carolina where it enters Pacolet River.

Hughes Creek appears on the Collet map, 1770, apparently rising in what is now ne Yadkin County n of East Bend and flowing ne into Yadkin River.

Hughes Gap, w Mitchell County at the head of Cooper Branch.

Hughes Gap, on the Carter County, Tenn.-Mitchell County, N. C., line.

Hughes Knob, w Jackson County between Bearpen Creek and Jim Creek.

Hughes Ridge, e Avery County.

Hughes Ridge, ne Swain County in Great Smoky Mountains National Park, extends approx. 11 mi. s from Pecks Corner.

Hughes Ridge, n Yancey County between Lottie Creek and Little Creek.

Hughes Ridge Branch rises in e Avery County and flows e into Rockhouse Creek.

Hugh's Creek. See East Buies Creek.

Hugo, community in n Lenoir County. The name may have been given in honor of the French author, Victor Hugo, by someone connected with a pre-Civil War school.

Huitt Bay, swamp in s central Brunswick County, a part of Green Swamp.

Hull Branch rises in se Avery County and flows e into South Harper Creek.

Hulls Crossroads, community in w Lincoln County.

Hulme Hill (hull hill), a low ridge in n central Caldwell County on the n side of Yadkin River. Named for Major William Hulme, planter and legislator, who settled here in 1807.

Humpback Mountain on the Avery-McDowell County line at the e end of Dividing Ridge. Alt. approx. 4,200. Known by the Cherokee Indians as Konnasoga.

Humphrey, community in se Duplin County.

Hump Mountain, w Avery County. Alt. 5,587.

Hungry Creek rises in e Haywood County and flows nw into East Fork Pigeon River.

Hungry Mountain, e Henderson County at the head of Hungry River. Alt. 3,006.

Hungry Neck. See Kelly.

Hungry River rises in e Henderson County and flows sw into Green River.

Hunkadora. See Bahama.

Hunsucker, community in sw Scotland County. Formerly known as Brick Mill.

Hunsucker's Store. See Star.

Huntdale, community in w Mitchell County on Toe River. Alt. 2,058.

Hunter Branch rises in n central Haywood County and flows n into Stevens Creek.

Hunter Branch rises in s Madison County and flows s into Ivy River.

Hunter Creek rises in central Madison County between Watershed Mountain and High Rock and flows se into Walnut Creek.

Hunter Jim Creek rises in w Jackson County and flows se into West Fork Tuckasegee River.

Hunters Bridge, community in central Beaufort County on Bath Creek.

Hunters Creek rises at Great Lake in sw Craven County and flows sw along the Carteret-Jones County line into White Oak River. Named for the Hunter family, early settlers.

Hunters Millpond, built prior to 1720 at the junction of Raynor Swamp and Harrell Swamp at the head of Bennetts Creek, e Gates County, was destroyed about 1922 when a new highway was built. It was about 1 mi. long. Known in later years as Cross Millpond.

Hunters Mill Township, e central Gates County.

Huntersville, town in n Mecklenburg County. Inc. 1873. Known previously as Hunter's Depot. Named for Robert Hunter, local resident about 1860. Alt. 814.

Huntersville. See Mount Holly.

Huntersville. See Murphy.

Huntersville Township, former township in ne Mecklenburg County, now township number 15.

Hunting Branch rises in Cane Creek Mountains in s Alamance County and flows s into Cane Creek.

Hunting Branch rises in n Northampton County and flows se into Corduroy Swamp.

Hunting Creek rises in central Burke County and flows n through Morganton into Catawba River.

Hunting Creek rises in North River Pocosin, s Camden County and flows e into North River.

Hunting Creek rises in n Rutherford County and flows s into Robinson Creek.

Hunting Creek rises in s Wilkes County in the Brushy Mountains and flows se through ne Iredell and w Davie counties into South Yadkin River. See also Flat Rock Creek; Frohock Sawmill.

Hunting Creek, community in s Wilkes County on Hunting Creek.

Hunting Island, an island in Bogue Sound in sw Carteret County.

Hunting Island Creek rises in w Carteret County and flows s into Bogue Inlet.

Hunting Quarter Inlet appears on the Moseley map, 1733, in Core Banks of Carteret County. It was opened and closed in the 1730's.

Hunting Quarter Sound appears on the Moseley map, 1733, as the water now forming the n end of Core Sound in ne Carteret County. Four small islands extending se from the present Hog Island separated this sound from Pamlico Sound. Three of the four islands were named: Chainshot, Harbour, and Shell.

Hunting Quarters Township, former township in e Carteret County. Cedar Island Township was formed from a part of Hunting Quarters and the remainder is now Atlantic Township. This area was formerly a summer camp of the Core Indians.

Hunting Run rises in n Pitt County and flows se into Grindle Creek.

Huntsboro, community in e Granville County.

Huntsborough, town authorized in 1814 to be laid off on the lands of Jonathan Hunt "on the waters of Little Ivey" in what was then Buncombe but is now Madison County. This town apparently did not materialize.

Hunts Branch rises in central Transylvania County and flows se into Tucker Creek.

Hunts Fork rises in e Davidson County and flows se into Rich Fork Creek.

Hunts Pond. See Lake View.

Hunt's Store. See New Castle.

Huntsville, town in se Yadkin County near Yadkin River. Chartered 1792 by Charles Hunt of Salisbury who sold lots here. Thomas L. Clingman, United States Senator and Confederate General, born here. Town rechartered 1822 but long inactive in municipal affairs.

Huntsville Mountains, a ridge in s McDowell County near Glenwood. Extensive gold mining operations were carried on here from the mid-nineteenth century until 1909.

Huntsville Township, sw Rockingham County.

Hurdle Mills, community in sw Person County.

Hurdle Ridge, a strip of high ground in the Dismal Swamp, se Gates County.

Hurley Lake. See Eury Lake.

Huronian Mountain, a peak in the Cane Creek Mountains, s Alamance County.

Hurrah Ridge, s Macon County between West Fork Overflow Creek and Abe Creek.

Hurricane Branch rises in nw Ashe County and flows ne into Horse Creek.

Hurricane Branch rises in ne Cherokee County and flows s into Welch Mill Creek.

Hurricane Branch rises in nw Swain County and flows s into Ekaneetlee Creek.

Hurricane Cove, e Graham County on the headwaters of Panther Creek.

Hurricane Creek rises in central Clay County and flows nw into Tusquitee Creek.

Hurricane Creek rises in n Haywood County and flows sw into Pigeon River.

Hurricane Creek rises in sw Jackson County and flows ne into Lake Thorpe.

Hurricane Creek rises in s Macon County and flows w into Nantahala River.

Hurricane Creek rises in w Macon County and flows w into Jarrett Creek.

Hurricane Creek rises in n Madison County and flows se into Big Laurel Creek.

Hurricane Creek rises in central Wake County and flows s into Crabtree Creek.

Hurricane Gap, central Cherokee County between Hiwassee River and West Prong Grape Creek.

Hurricane Gap on the Madison County, N. C.-Greene County, Tenn., line.

Hurricane Gap, s Yancey County between the head of Falling Water Branch and South Fork Cattail Creek.

Hurricane Mountain, n Haywood County, extends ne from the head of Toms Branch to the head of Morgan Creek.

Hurricane Mountain, w central Swain County between Laurel Branch and Tuckasegee River.

Hurricane Ridge, n Haywood County, extends ne between Hurricane Creek and Cold Springs Creek.

Hurricane Ridge, n Mitchell County parallel to Big Branch.

Hurricane Ridge, nw Swain County, a short spur extending w from Big Grill Ridge.

Hurricane Ridge. See Rose Ridge.

Hurricane Top, mountain in sw Macon County between Clear Branch and Rocky Cove.

Hurricane Township, ne Ashe County.

Hurst Beach. See Onslow Beach.

Hurts Creek rises in n Montgomery County and flows sw into Denson Creek.

Husbands Creek rises in sw Caldwell County and flows s into Lower Creek. Named for Veazey Husband, locally noted Tory who lived in the vicinity.

Husk, community in nw Ashe County. Railroad name is Nella. Post office est. here in 1915.

Huskanaw Swamp. See Collie Swamp.

Huskey Creek rises in n Swain County and flows s into Beech Flats Prong.

Hyatt Bald, ne Swain County in Great Smoky Mountains National Park on Hyatt Ridge. Alt. 5,153.

Hyatt Branch rises in w Swain County and flows sw into Goldmine Branch.

Hyatt Cove, nw Jackson County at the head of Shoal Creek.

Hyatt Creek rises in n Cherokee County in the Snowbird Mountains and flows se into Valley River.

Hyatt Creek rises in sw Haywood County and flows e into Richland Creek.

Hyatt Creek rises in ne Swain County on Hyatt Ridge near Hyatt Bald and flows s into Straight Fork.

Hyatt Creek, community in sw Haywood County on Hyatt Creek.

Hyatt Mill Creek rises in s Clay County and flows ne into Hiwassee River.

Hyatt Ridge, ne Swain County in Great Smoky Mountains National Park, a spur extending se from Dashoga Ridge with its center near lat. 35° 39' 35" N., long. 83° 13' 58" W. See also, McGee Spring.

Hyco Lake. See Carolina Power Lake.

Hyco River is formed in nw Person County by the junction of North Hyco and South Hyco creeks. It flows ne into Virginia where it enters Dan River. In 1728 William Byrd referred to this stream as "Hicootomony, or Turkey-Buzzard River, from the great number of those unsavoury Birds that roost on the tall Trees growing near its banks." Appears on the Moseley map, 1733, as Hyco-ote. Hyco Dam, completed in 1964, now impounds its waters to form Carolina Power Lake.

Hyco-ote. See Hyco River.

Hycotee, community in e central Caswell County. A post office was operated here during the approx. period 1880-1905.

Hyde County was formed in 1705 as Wickham Precinct, which see, of Bath County. The name was changed to Hyde about 1712. Located in the e section of the state, it is bounded by Pamlico Sound, by Beaufort, Washington, Tyrrell, and Dare counties, and (on the Outer Banks) by the Atlantic Ocean and Dare and Carteret

counties. Named for Governor Edward
Hyde who died in 1712. Area: 1,364 sq.
mi. (634, land; 730 water). County seat:
Swan Quarter with an elevation of 10 ft.
Townships are Currituck, Fairfield, Lake
Landing, Mattamuskeet, Ocracoke, and
Swan Quarter. Produces soybeans, corn,
hogs, livestock, dairy products, lumber,
and wooden boxes. See also Woodstock
Point; Aramuskeet.

Hyde Islands, formerly two islands with a
total of 10 acres in Little Tennessee River
in ne Graham County. Now under the
waters of Fontana Lake.

Hydeland, community in s Hyde County, s
of Lake Mattamuskeet near the head of
Juniper Bay.

Hyde Mill Creek rises in s Graham County
and flows ne into Tulula Creek.

Hyde Parish, Church of England, Hyde
County, est. 1715, coextensive with the
county. By 1767 the parish was being
called St. George's and in that year had
441 white taxables. The parish as a unit
of local administration was abolished in
1776 with the adoption of the state constitution and the disestablishment of the
Church of England.

Hyder Mountain, e Haywood County between Pigeon River and Long Branch.

Hydro, community in sw Montgomery
County on Pee Dee River at the dam
which forms Lake Tillery. Power generating plant is here.

Hymans, community in central Craven
County.

Hymans Ferry, former ferry across Roanoke
River, s Bertie County.

I

Icard, community in e Burke County. First
known as Bowman's Crossing. Alt. 1,172.

Icard Township, e Burke County.

Icaria, community in n Chowan County. Alt.
34.

Icemorlee. See West Monroe.

Ichley, community in n Orange County.

Icy Knob, on Burke-Rutherford County line.

Ida, community in w Scotland County.
Named for Ida Cotton Mills which in turn
were named for Ida Morgan, daughter of
Mark Morgan.

Idalia, community in se Beaufort County.

Idlewild, community in s Ashe County. Alt.
2,700.

Ijames Crossroads, community in w Davie
County. A Baptist Church built here in
1897 on land given by Cas Ijames was
known as Ijames Crossroads Church.

Ike Cove, s Haywood County on a tributary
of Little East Fork Pigeon River.

Ike Mountain, n Buncombe County w of
Dillingham.

Immer, community in n Montgomery County.

Improvement Cove, e Swain County between Middle Ridge and Connelly Mountain on Improvement Creek.

Improvement Creek rises in e Swain County and flows ne into Wesser Creek.

Inanda, former town in central Buncombe
County on French Broad River at the
mouth of Hominy Creek. Inc. 1893;
charter repealed 1901. A church at the
site still bears the name.

Inadu Knob, on Haywood County, N. C.
and Cooke County, Tenn., line, Great
Smoky Mountains National Park near lat.
35° 43' 37" N., long. 83° 14' 27" W.
Formerly Snake Knob, but to prevent
duplication within the Park the name was
changed to Inadu, the Indian word for
snake. Alt. 5,941.

Index, community in se Ashe County.

Indian Branch rises in e Haywood Co. and
flows se into Bald Creek.

Indian Camp Bay, an arm of Big Colly Bay,
in ne Bladen County.

Indian Camp Branch rises in n Buncombe
County near Jupiter and flows sw into
Shepherd Branch.

Indian Camp Branch rises in central Jackson
County and flows se into West Fork
[Moses Creek].

Indian Camp Branch rises in e Macon County and flows n into Ellijay Creek.

Indian Camp Branch rises in w Macon
County and flows sw into Wine Spring
Creek.

Indian Camp Branch rises in w Madison
County and flows se into Big Pine Creek.

Indian Camp Branch rises in w central Transylvania County and flows se into Kuykendall Creek.

Indian Camp Creek rises in n Macon County and flows se into Burningtown Creek.

Indian Camp Gap, n Jackson County near the heads of Allens Branch and Kitchin Branch.

Indian Camp Mountain, s Transylvania County in the Blue Ridge Mountains, e of Estatoe Creek.

Indian Creek rises in nw Bertie County and flows s into Roanoke River. This was the n boundary of the Tuscarora Indian property in Indian Woods Township. Mentioned in local records as early as 1723. Appears as Deep Creek on the Collet map, 1770. See also Resootskeh.

Indian Creek rises in sw Catawba County, flows se across w Lincoln County, dips briefly into nw Gaston County and flows ne back into Lincoln County where it enters South Fork Catawba River. Appears on the Collet map, 1770, as Howards Creek, but as Indian Creek on the Price map, 1808.

Indian Creek rises in s Chatham County and flows se into Deep River.

Indian Creek rises in s Cumberland County and flows s into Bladen County where it enters Harrisons Creek.

Indian Creek, waterway in ne Currituck County between Knotts Island and Mackay Island.

Indian Creek rises in w Hertford County and flows e into Livermans Mill Pond.

Indian Creek rises in n Jackson County and flows nw into Soco Creek.

Indian Creek rises in w Stokes County and flows ne into Cascade Creek.

Indian Creek, formed in n Swain County in Great Smoky Mountains National Park by the junction of Left Fork [Indian Creek] and Right Fork [Indian Creek]. It flows sw into Deep Creek.

Indian Creek rises in n Swain County and flows s into Noland Creek.

Indian Creek rises in w Transylvania County and flows s into Toxaway River.

Indian Creek rises in w Transylvania County and flows sw and se to join Shoal Creek in forming North Fork French Broad River.

Indian Creek rises in central Vance County and flows n into Kerr Reservoir.

Indian Creek rises in w Yancey County and flows n into Price Creek.

Indian Creek. See Dillard Creek; Town Creek.

Indian Ford, shallow rock formation in Contentnea Creek, central Wilson County,

½ mi. below Contentnea Lake. Mentioned in early records as "the falls" below which the stream is navigable by boat.

Indian Fork rises in sw Yancey County and flows se into Cane River.

Indian Gap, on Swain County, N. C.-Sevier County, Tenn., line near the head of Right Fork [Deep Creek]. Alt. 5,317.

Indian Grave Creek rises in central Davidson County and flows se into Swearing Creek.

Indian Grave Gap, ne Caldwell County in the Green Mountain range. See also Green Mountain.

Indian Grave Gap, sw Cherokee County near the headwaters of Hickey Branch.

Indian Grave Gap, ne Cherokee County in the Valley River Mountains.

Indian Grave Gap, on the Mitchell County, N. C.-Unicoi County, Tenn., line. Alt. approx. 3,100.

Indian Grave Gap, s Swain County between Brush Creek and Little Tennessee River.

Indian Grave Gap, w central Swain County on the head of Laurel Branch.

Indian Island in Pamlico River, se Beaufort County. Approx. 1¹⁄₁₀ mi. long and ³⁄₁₀ mi. wide.

Indian Island, approx. 500 acres of arable land in North River Pocosin, se Camden County, bounded on the e by North River. This formerly was a thickly settled community but it is now abandoned. Named from the large number of Indian artifacts found here.

Indian Knob, peak on Indian Ridge, w Haywood County near lat. 35° 40' 06" N., long. 83° 07' 43" W., in Great Smoky Mountains National Park. Alt. 5,120.

Indian Landing, e Beaufort County on Pungo River.

Indian Ridge, w Haywood County, Great Smoky Mountains National Park, a spur extending s from Mount Sterling Ridge, center near lat. 35° 40' N., long. 83° 07' 10" W.

Indian Ridge, sw Macon County between Big Indian Creek and Nantahala River.

Indian Ridge, w Swain County on a bend in Nantahala River now surrounded at the sw end by the backwaters of Fontana Lake.

Indian Rock or Indian Rock Tomb. See Pix Head Rock.

Indian Run rises in e Beaufort County in Pantego Swamp and flows e into Pungo River.

Indian Spring Branch rises in sw Buncombe

County near the Haywood County line and flows w into South Hominy Creek.

Indian Springs, community in s Wayne County near a tributary of Smith Millpond. Settled as early as 1829 and named for local springs traditionally used by Saponi Indians.

Indian Springs Township, se Wayne County. First listed on county tax records in 1838.

Indian Swamp rises in s Robeson County and flows s into Ashpole Swamp.

Indian Swamp rises on the Tyrrell-Washington County line and flows n into Banton Creek.

Indian Top, central Cherokee County between West Prong Grape Creek and Rose Creek.

Indiantown, community in e central Camden County. A post office was operated here from 1802 until 1939. Settled prior to 1697. In 1704 the Governor's Council ordered a reservation to be laid off for the Yeopim Indians, and it is from this reservation that the present name derives.

Indiantown, former community in w central Currituck County, approx. 5 mi. s of Shawboro. Appears in local records as early as 1764; a post office as early as 1822 and as recent as 1882. Currituck Seminary, burned during the Civil War, was here.

Indiantown Creek, a name sometimes applied to the upper course of North River *(which see)* in Camden County.

Indian Town Creek. *See* Dillard Creek.

Indian Trail, town in w Union County. Inc. 1907. Located between heads of North Fork Crooked Creek and South Fork Crooked Creek. Alt. 697.

Indian Wells, indicated on the Price map, 1808, and the MacRae map, 1833, as four wells on Cape Fear River in se Bladen County. Possibly these were natural artesian wells, common to this area.

Indian Well Swamp rises in s Pitt County and flows se into Clayroot Swamp.

Indian Woods, central Bertie County, a reservation set aside in 1717 for the Tuscarora Indians remaining in North Carolina after the war of 1711-13. These Indians later joined relatives in New York and the state sold this tract of land in 1828.

Indian Woods Township, sw Bertie County.

Indigo Branch rises in Horry County S. C., and flows nw into sw Brunswick County where it enters Cawcaw Swamp.

Inez, community in s Warren County, e of Shocco Creek. Post office est. here in 1890, but discontinued in 1938.

Ingalls, community in sw Avery County. Named for Senator John J. Ingalls (1833-1900), of Kansas. A nineteenth century post office serving this area was named Keenerville.

Ingles Cove, n Buncombe County n of Ingles Gap.

Ingles Field Gap, s Buncombe County between Little Hickory Top and Stradley Mountain.

Ingles Gap, n Buncombe County between Grassy Knob and Ravens Knob.

Ingleside, community in n Franklin County.

Ingles Ridge, n Buncombe County between Sugar Cove and Sawyer Cove.

Ingold, community in s Sampson County on the e side of Great Coharie Creek. Alt. 100. Settled about 1888. Inc. 1889; charter repealed 1895.

Ingraham Mountain, ne Buncombe County near Dillingham.

Ingram Branch rises in ne Cherokee County and flows ne into Worm Creek.

Ingram Branch rises in w Macon County and flows se into Nantahala Lake.

Ingrams Mountain, ne Anson County. Alt. approx. 525.

Ingrams Township, s central Johnston County.

Ink. *See* Newlife.

Inland Waterway. *See* Intracoastal Waterway.

Inman Branch rises in s Haywood Co. and flows se into West Fork Pigeon River.

Inner Diamond Shoal. *See* Diamond Shoals.

Institute, community in nw Lenoir County. Named for the Lenoir Collegiate Institute which operated here for a number of years after 1855. Some of the buildings of the institute are now used as residences.

Institute Branch rises in w Hertford County and flows ne into Worrell Mill Pond.

Institute Township, nw Lenoir County.

Intelligence, community in w Rockingham County. Known as Ball Hill until about 1920. Between 1850 and 1900 several tobacco factories flourished here. Named because the first modern school in rural Rockingham County was here. "Danbury," plantation home of Governor Alexander Martin (1740-1807), was nearby.

Intracoastal Waterway extends from Gloucester, Mass., to Key West, Fla., a distance of 1,950 miles of which 308 are in North Carolina. It passes through sounds, rivers, and canals. The depth of the Waterway is 12 ft., minimum width is 47 ft., and minimum vertical clearance is 80 ft. The oldest segment of the Waterway in North Carolina was begun in 1856 as a private enterprise. In 1873 control and maintenance of the network of coastal canals was taken over by the U.S. Corps of Engineers and work was expanded through the 1940's. Further improvements are still being made. Pleasure craft, towed barges, and small freight boats use the Intracoastal Waterway. Known familiarly as the Inland Waterway.

Invershiel, mountain resort in e Avery County near Grandfather Mountain. A village containing shops, a church, and other buildings is modeled after an old Scottish village. Named for the village in Scotland from which the MacRae family came, ancestors of the developers of the resort. Est. 1966.

Iotla Branch rises in n Macon County and flows se into Iotla Creek.

Iotla Creek rises in central Macon County and flows ne into Little Tennessee River.

Iotla Gap, central Macon County near the head of Iotla Creek.

Iowa Hill, e Mitchell County between Beaver Creek and North Toe River.

Iredell, community in sw Brunswick County.

Iredell County was formed in 1788 from Rowan County. Located in the central section of the state, it is bounded by Rowan, Cabarrus, Mecklenburg, Lincoln, Catawba, Alexander, Wilkes, Yadkin, and Davie counties. It was named for James Iredell (1751-99), Attorney General of North Carolina during the Revolution, and delegate from Edenton to the Constitutional Convention of 1788 where he advocated adoption of the Federal Constitution. Area: 594 sq. mi. County seat: Statesville with an elevation of 925 ft. Townships are Bethany, Chambersburg, Coddle Creek, Concord, Cool Spring, Davidson, Eagle Mills, Fallstown, New Hope, Olin, Sharpesburg, Shiloh, States-

ville, Turnersburg, and Union Grove. Produces wheat, oats, corn, poultry, eggs, dairy products, livestock, hogs, canned milk, textiles, apparel, furniture, pencil sharpeners, fabricated metal, flour, lumber, and machinery. *See also* York County.

Iredell House. *See* James Iredell House.

Iredell Station. *See* Loray.

Irena, community in central Clay County on Tusquitee Creek.

Irish Buffalo Creek rises in sw Rowan County and flows s into Cabarrus County where it enters Coldwater Creek. Called Buffalo Creek on the Collet map, 1770, but Irish Buffalo Creek on the Price map, 1808. Named for Scotch-Irish settlers. *See also* Dutch Buffalo Creek.

Irish Creek rises in w Burke County and flows se to join Upper Creek in forming Warrior Fork [Catawba River].

Irisquoque. *See* Clubfoot Creek.

Iron Duff, community in central Haywood County on Big Branch. Named for an early settler, Aaron MacDuff. Known as Aaron Duff until 1873 when a post office was est. An error in Washington resulted in the use of the name Iron Duff instead of Aaron Duff.

Iron Duff Township, central Haywood County.

Ironhill, community in s Columbus County.

Iron-Lithia Springs, former resort community in s Wilkes County near Old Gilreath. Buildings destroyed by fire about 1900. Alt. approx. 1,500.

Ironmonger Mountain, s central Burke County. Alt. 1,823.

Iron Mountain, nw Mitchell County at the head of Bearwallow Creek.

Iron Mountain Gap, on the Mitchell County, N. C.-Unicoi County, Tenn., line. Alt. 3,725.

Iron Mountains. *See* Unaka Mountains.

Iron Ore Ridge, n Buncombe County, extends sw from Jones Knob in the Elk Mountains.

Iron Station, town in s Lincoln County. Settled about 1789. Inc. 1909. Named from the fact that many iron mines and forges were operated within a radius of ten mi. between 1790 and 1880. Earlier known as Sharon.

Ironton Township, e central Lincoln County.

Irvin River. *See* Smith River.

Irvins Creek rises in e Mecklenburg County and flows sw into McAlpine Creek.

Irvins Crossroads, community in s Lenoir County.

Irvinsville, a town authorized in 1815 to be laid out in sw Cleveland County (then Rutherford County), located on Broad River opposite Quinn's Ferry. The town seems not to have developed as expected and the last mention of it apparently occurs in local records of 1828.

Irwin Creek rises in n Mecklenburg County and flows sw into Stewart Creek.

Isaac Creek rises in se Craven County and flows n into Adams Creek.

Isaac Hollow in w Watauga County extends se n of George Gap Branch.

Isaac Parlier's Creek. See Purlear Creek.

Isaac Walton Lake, formerly Water Works Lake, in w Person County on Storys Creek at the mouth of Satterfield Creek. Formed prior to 1928. Covers 213 acres. Maximum depth 25 ft. Owned by the town of Roxboro.

Isenhour, community in ne Stanly County. Grew up around Isenhour Brick Yard in early twentieth century.

Isenhour Mine, former gold mine in ne Cabarrus County, on Little Buffalo Creek.

Isinglass Creek rises in n Franklin County and flows ne into Little Shocco Creek.

Isinglass Ridge, s Graham County, extends se from Sassafras Ridge to Little Snowbird Creek. Named for isinglass or mica which is mined in the area.

Island Borough, former town in e Rowan County. Inc. and authorized to be laid out in 1795 on the Yadkin River. opposite the e end of Big Island, which see. Site is about 3 mi. ne of Spencer. Intended to promote navigation on the river, the town was to be built on land owned by Edward Yarborough. Little if any development took place at the site.

Island Branch Swamp connects Resolution Branch to Musselshell Creek in nw Jones County.

Island Creek rises in se Alexander County and flows s into Catawba River.

Island Creek rises in e Anson County and flows se into Pee Dee River.

Island Creek rises in e Burke County and flows n into Catawba River.

Island Creek rises in s Duplin County and flows se into Northeast Cape Fear River. Appears as Cook Creek on the Collet map, 1770; not shown on the Price map, 1808, but shown and named Island Creek on the MacRae map, 1833.

Island Creek, a channel of Chowan River flowing north of an unnamed island ¾ mi. long in western Gates County.

Island Creek rises in ne Granville County and flows n and ne along the Granville-Vance County line until it reaches the nw corner of Vance County where it enters Island Creek Reservoir.

Island Creek rises in e Jones County and flows n into Trent River. Appears on the Moseley map, 1733, which also shows Murfy's Ferry across the Trent River near the mouth of Island Creek.

Island Creek rises in w Montgomery County and flows n and nw into Pee Dee River.

Island Creek rises in n New Hanover County and flows nw forming the New Hanover-Pender County line before entering Northeast Cape Fear River.

Island Creek rises in se Rockingham County and flows ne into Caswell County where it enters Dan River.

Island Creek rises in sw Rutherford County and flows ne into Broad River.

Island Creek rises in sw Stanly County and flows s into Rocky River. Called Stillwater Creek on the Kerr map, 1882.

Island Creek. See Lillington Creek.

Island Creek District, formerly a census precinct in what is now nw Vance County approx. two miles w of the town of Williamsboro. By 1790, 107 heads of families had settled in this area.

Island Creek Reservoir, in the nw corner of Vance County, is fed by Island Creek and Little Island Creek. It is separated from Kerr Reservoir by a dike which prevented the flooding of nearby tungsten mines. Extends about 5 mi. along the Granville-Vance County line. Formed about 1952 after the completion of Kerr Reservoir.

Island Creek Township, s central Duplin County.

Island Ford, former passage over the Catawba River between Catawba and Iredell counties near the site of the dam which forms Lookout Shoals Lake, which see. Appears on maps of the Revolutionary period and on the Price map, 1808, as one of the northernmost fords over the river.

Island Ford, across Yadkin River in w Surry County near the community of Jonesville. Mentioned in local records as early as 1778.

Island Swamp rises in e Pitt County and flows ne into Chicod Creek.

Isle Hatton, an island in Pamlico Sound which cannot now be identified, appears on the Smith map, 1624.

Isothermal Belt. See Thermal Belt.

Ivanhoe, community in s Sampson County on Black River. Named in the 1880's for the hero in Sir Walter Scott's novel of the same name. Alt. 29. The Colton map, 1861, shows a community at this site named Black River. Corbetts Ferry here was taken by Gen. Richard Caswell on the eve of the Battle of Moores Creek Bridge. Corbetts Ferry appears on maps at this site through 1865. Black River Presbyterian Church est. here in 1740 occupies a building erected in 1859.

Ivestor Gap, s Haywood County, on the head of Little East Fork Pigeon River.

Ivestor Ridge, s Haywood County, between Grassy Cove Prong and Dark Prong.

Ivory Crossroads, community in e Franklin County.

Ivory Ridge, w Watauga County extends ne from Hockiday Ridge s of Rush Branch.

Ivory Swamp rises in n Wayne County and flows ne into Wilson County where it enters Contentnea Creek.

Ivy, community in e Madison County on Little Ivy Creek. Alt. 2,150. A post office existed here as early as 1828. Named by early settlers because of the abundance of laurel which they called ivy.

Ivy Creek is formed in n Buncombe County by the junction of North Fork Ivy Creek and Dillingham Creek, and flow w into Madison County (doubling back into Buncombe County at one point) where it joins Little Ivy Creek at the county line to form Ivy River.

Ivy Creek rises in n Northampton County and flows ne into Jordans Mill Pond on Cypress Creek.

Ivy Gap, on the Buncombe-Yancey County line nw of Cane River Gap.

Ivy Gap, w Haywood County, Great Smoky Mountains National Park, near lat. 35° 43′ 23″ N., long. 83° 05′ 10″ W.

Ivy Gap, on the Madison-Yancey County line near Fox Creek. Alt. approx. 3,140.

Ivy Gap, community in n Haywood County on Mt. Sterling Creek.

Ivy Gap, community in w Yancey County near the Madison County line.

Ivy Hill Township, w central Haywood County.

Ivy Knob, ne Buncombe County between Little Will Branch and North Fork Ivy Creek.

Ivy Knob, w Henderson County between Brock Mountain and Cash Creek.

Ivy Knob, e Mitchell County on Laurel Branch.

Ivy Ridge, nw Swain County in Great Smoky Mountains National Park, a short spur extending e from Big Grill Ridge.

Ivy River is formed on the Buncombe-Madison County line by the junction of Ivy Creek and Little Ivy Creek. It flows w through s Madison County into French Broad River, crossing back briefly into Buncombe County at three points.

Ivy Swamp rises in ne Wayne County and flows ne into Wilson County where it enters Contentnea Creek. Named for the Ivey family, early settlers.

Ivy Top, s Clay County near the headwaters of Webb Creek.

Ivy Township, nw Buncombe County.

J

Jack, community in ne Warren County. Post office est. here in 1901, but discontinued in 1905. Due to a shift in population, the community is dwindling, and the name is not widely known.

Jack Bradley Branch rises in n Swain County and flows s into Beech Flats Prong.

Jack Cabin Branch rises in s Jones County and flows nw into Trent River.

Jack Cove, nw Jackson County, formerly Schuler Cove. In 1956, on a 5,000 acre tract here, R. H. Kress est. the Jack Kress School and renamed Schuler Cove in honor of his late son. Operated as a trade school, there is a model farm and nursery; classes in forestry and various trades are conducted.

Jack Creek rises in central Beaufort County and flows e into Nevil Creek.

Jack Creek rises in e Beaufort County and flows nw into Pungo Creek.

Jack Creek rises in nw Jackson County and flows sw into Tuckasegee River.

Jackdaw, community in s central Stanly County.

Jacket Swamp rises in w central Halifax County and flows se into Burnt Coat Swamp.

Jackeye Creek rises in ne Brunswick County and flows ne approx. 5 mi. into Brunswick River.

Jack Gap, central Buncombe County between Pine Knob and Bartlett Mountain.

Jackie Branch rises in s Clay County and flows se into Shooting Creek.

Jackies Mill Branch rises in n Yancey County and flows se into Cane River.

Jack Island Swamp, w Duplin County on Nahunga Creek.

Jack Knob, e Macon County between Passmore Knob and Watauga Creek.

Jackrabbit Mountain, s Clay County. Now a peninsula in Chatuge Lake.

Jacks Bay, ne Carteret County on e side of Piney Island and adjacent to Long Bay.

Jacks Branch rises in w Anson County and flows se into Brown Creek.

Jacks Branch rises in s Graham County and flows s into Tulula Creek.

Jacks Branch rises in w Madison County and flows sw into French Broad River.

Jack's Branch rises in e central Wake County and flows se into Neuse River.

Jacks Creek rises in w central Yancey County and flows ne into Toe River.

Jacks Creek Township, ne Yancey County.

Jacks Fork, rises in s Greene County and flows n into Tyson Marsh.

Jacks Knob, s Jackson County bordered on the e by Scotsman Creek. Alt. approx. 3,440.

Jack Smith Creek rises in central Craven County sw of New Bern and flows ne into Neuse River. It forms a part of the limits of New Bern.

Jackson, town and county seat, central Northampton County. Alt. 131. Inc. 1873. Settled prior to 1741 and known as Potecase Bridge. Made county seat in 1741 and known as Northampton Court House until renamed Jackson in 1826, presumably for Andrew Jackson (1767-1845), recent unsuccessful Democratic candidate for President. In 1808 the General Assembly had authorized the county seat to be named Atherton, but this apparently was never done. It probably was intended to honor Major Jeptha Atherton, member of the Provincial Congress and of the General Assembly. Produces lumber.

Jackson, town authorized in 1818 to be laid off by Isaac Medley, Eustis Hunt, Gideon Johnston, John May, Sr., and Joseph Porter "on the north side of Dan river, at the Eagle falls in Rockingham county." The scheme for developing a town here

was proved to be a fraud in the case Morehead vs. Hunt, December, 1826. *See also* Eagle Falls.

Jackson, community in sw Union County between Waxhaw Creek and Cane Creek. President Andrew Jackson was born nearby.

Jackson Branch rises in central Cherokee County and flows se into Colvard Creek.

Jackson Branch rises in se Mitchell County and flows s into Middle Ridge Branch.

Jackson Corner, community in n Pasquotank County.

Jackson County was formed in 1851 from Haywood and Macon counties. Located in the w section of the state, it is bounded by the states of South Carolina and Georgia, and by Macon, Swain, Haywood, and Transylvania counties. It was named for Andrew Jackson (1767-1845), president of the United States. Area 499 sq. mi. County seat: Sylva with an elevation of 2,047 ft. Townships are Barkers Creek, Canada, Caney Fork, Cashiers, Cullowhee, Dillsboro, Greens Creek, Hamburg, Mountain, Qualla, River, Savannah, Scott Creek, Sylva, and Webster. Produces corn, dairy products, livestock, hogs, paper, textiles, mica, olivine, and crushed stone.

Jackson Creek rises in se Buncombe County and flows ne into McDowell County where it enters Crooked Creek.

Jackson Creek rises in nw Franklin County and flows n into Tar River.

Jackson Creek rises in central Granville County and flows e into Tar River.

Jackson Creek rises in w Moore County and flows s into Drowning Creek. Named for William Jackson, who settled on it about 1754.

Jackson Creek rises in w Randolph County and flows se into Uwharrie River.

Jackson Creek, community in w Randolph County.

Jackson Gap, on the McDowell-Mitchell County line.

Jackson Hamlet, a Negro community in s

Moore County between towns of Aberdeen and Pinehurst. Est. about 1899 and named for James Jackson, an original resident.

Jackson Hill, community in s Davidson County. Said to have been named because an admirer of Andrew Jackson raised a flagstaff here to celebrate Jackson's election to the Presidency, 1828. A post office as early as 1830.

Jackson Hill Township, s Davidson County.

Jackson Knob, se Gaston County, approx. one mi. sw of Boogertown. Alt. 1,080.

Jackson Knob, on the McDowell-Mitchell County line. Alt. 3,223.

Jackson Line Mountain, extends se from w central Swain County to Little Yalaka Creek in s part of the county.

Jackson's Corner, community in n Sampson County.

Jacksons Crossroads, community in central Duplin County.

Jacksons Pond, on Cypress Creek in e Franklin County. Formed 1885. Covers 65 acres; maximum depth 20 ft.

Jackson Springs, town in sw Moore County on Jackson Creek. Inc. 1921; named for William Jackson who settled nearby in 1754. The mineral spring, developed as a resort in the late nineteenth century, was patronized largely by wealthy cotton growers of North and South Carolina. The hotel here burned in 1932. Alt. 730.

Jacksons Store, crossroads community in central Lenoir County. Named for one Jackson, said to have been a Civil War veteran, who operated the store for many years prior to his death in the 1920's.

Jackson Swamp, e Beaufort County.

Jackson Swamp rises in e Robeson County and flows e into Big Swamp.

Jackson Township, s Nash County.

Jackson Township, central Northampton County.

Jackson Township, sw Union County.

Jacksonville, town authorized in 1818 to be laid off on the lands of Hezekiah Naylor and Maccajah Lassiter in Randolph County "on the road from Fayetteville to Salisbury." The exact location is not known, and the town probably was never developed.

Jacksonville, city and county seat, central Onslow County on New River. Alt. 23. A courthouse was constructed near here about 1757 at Wantland's Ferry. A new courthouse was constructed within ½ mi. of the old one about 1819 and the county

seat was called Onslow Court House. In 1843, the town of Jacksonville was authorized to be est. and inc. here, but it was not immediately done; the act containing this authority was re-enacted in 1849. Named for President Andrew Jackson (1767-1845). Produces lumber and apparel. Camp Lejeune is adjacent. See also Johnston.

Jacksonville Township, central Onslow County.

Jacks Swamp rises in n Northampton County and flows ne into Virginia where it enters Fountains Creek. Appears on the map of the North Carolina-Virginia line run by William Byrd and others, 1728.

Jack Swamp flourished as a community on the stream of that name in n Northampton County from about 1775, when a Quaker Meeting House was built there, until about 1812 by which time most of the people had moved to central North Carolina and to Ohio.

Jack Trail Mountain, w Madison County between Little Creek and Meadow Fork.

Jacob Branch rises in central Macon County and flows ne into Rocky Branch.

Jacob Branch rises in w Pitt County and flows se into Black Swamp.

Jacob Branch rises in w Robeson County and flows se into Lumber River.

Jacob Fork rises in s Burke County and flows ne into Catawba County where it joins Henry Fork to form South Fork Catawba River. Named for pioneer settler, Jacob Shuford.

Jacobs Creek rises in sw Rockingham County and flows ne into Dan River. "Danbury," the home of Governor Alexander Martin (1740-1807) was near its mouth. The Indian settlement, Upper Saura Town, was also nearby prior to 1710.

Jacob Creek rises in e central Stanly County and flows se into Pee Dee River.

Jacobs Fork Township, sw Catawba County.

Jacob's Gap, w Ashe County near the Tennessee state line. Named for an Indian youth said to have been killed by a white man.

Jacobs Knob, e Macon County between Lickskillet Branch and Cullasaja River.

Jacob Swamp rises in central Robeson County and flows se into Weatherspoon Cooling Pond. Approx. 7 mi. long.

Jacobs Swamp rises in s Nash County and flows se into Tar River.

Jacocks Landing. See Wellington.

Jady Branch rises in w Gates County and

flows sw into an unnamed swamp which flows se into Taylor Millpond.

Jake Branch rises in se Clay County and flows nw into Muskrat Branch.

Jake Branch rises in w Swain County and flows s into Nantahala River.

Jake Cove Branch rises in w Clay County and flows s into Fires Creek.

Jake Hollow, w Mitchell County on a tributary of Pigeonroost Creek.

Jake Ridge, se Clay County between Jake Branch and Muskrat Branch.

Jalong. See Longhurst.

James Branch rises in e Haywood Co. and flows nw into Cove Creek.

James Cathey's Creek. See Kerr Creek; Sloans Creek.

James City, community in central Craven County on Neuse River near its junction with Trent River approx. 1½ mi. s of city of New Bern. Alt. 10. Settled 1865. Named for Horace James, former Union chaplain, who supervised a freedmen's camp at the site.

James Creek rises in se Moore County and flows ne into Little River. Named for James McNeill, an early settler.

James Creek rises in ne Pamlico County on n Goose Creek Island and flows ne into Pamlico River.

James Creek. See Fiddler Creek.

James Iredell House, state historic site, in Edenton, s Chowan County. Approx. 2 acres. Est. 1951. The Iredell house, built about 1759, is included in the area and open to the public as a historical museum.

James Mill Creek. See Staffords Creek.

Jameston. See Jamesville.

Jamestown, town in sw Guilford County. Est. 1770 and named for James Mendenhall, an early settler whose first name was chosen in the Quaker fashion to avoid ostentation. Inc. 1881; charter repealed 1893; rechartered 1947. Produces corrugated boxes and textiles. Alt. 779.

James-Town. See Jamesville.

Jamestown Township, sw Guilford County.

Jamesville, town in e Martin County on Roanoke River. Inc. 1785 as James-Town; reincorporated 1832 as Jameston; name changed to Jamesville, 1855. Alt. 47.

Jamesville Township, ne Martin County.

Jane Cantrell Creek rises in s Transylvania County and flows nw into South Prong [of Glady Fork].

Janeiro, community in s Pamlico County on Dawson Creek, which see. Known as Dawson Creek until a post office was est. many years ago, since discontinued. Named by seafaring men of the community for Rio de Janeiro, Brazil.

Jane Knob, e Macon County between Brown Creek and Corbin Creek.

Jane Otter Branch rises in nw Macon County and flows nw into Otter Creek.

Jane's Bald, on the Mitchell County, N. C.-Carter County, Tenn., line. Said to have been named for a woman who lost her life here in a snowstorm but who saved her young child by covering it with her own body.

Japan, former community in ne Graham County on forks of Tobacco and Panther creeks. Est. about 1908 as a supply center for surrounding lumbering camps. Named for "Japan clover" (*Lespedeza striata*) growing in the area. During World War II local residents began calling it MacArthur, for General Douglas MacArthur, but the post office name was never changed. Innundated by waters of Fontana Lake, 1944.

Jarmantown, community in nw Onslow County between Hall Pocosin and the head of New River.

Jarrett Bald, w Macon County between Wine Spring Creek and High Laurel Branch.

Jarrett Bay extends ino the mainland of e Carteret County from Core Sound. It appears as Jarrets Creek on the Moseley map, 1733. Named for the Jarratt family.

Jarrett Creek rises in w McDowell County and flows se into Catawba River.

Jarrett Creek. See Moore Creek.

Jarrett Hollow, n Mitchell County, through which an unnamed tributary of Right Fork Bean Creek flows.

Jarrett Knob, w Macon County between Moore Creek and Tyler Branch. Alt. approx. 4,500.

Jarretts Creek rises in sw Rutherford County and flows sw into Broad River.

Jarrets Creek. See Jarrett Bay.

Jarrett's Gap, sw Macon County s of Moore Creek. Alt. 2,931.

Jarrett's Point, s Onslow County, extends into New River. Named for John Jarratt. Now within the limits of Camp Lejeune Marine Base.

Jarvins Mountain, se Buncombe County near the Rutherford County line between Stone and Weedy Mountains.

Jarvis Branch rises in e Madison County and flows se into California Creek.

Jarvisburg, community in sw Currituck County on North River. Settled prior to 1750. Named for the Jarvis family of which Governor Thomas J. Jarvis was a member. Alt. 15.

Jarvis Channel, se Currituck County in Currituck Sound.

Jarvis Mountain, e Madison County between Gabriels Creek and Sprinkle Branch.

Jason, town in sw Greene County. Inc. 1889, but long inactive in municipal affairs.

Jason Township, sw Greene County.

Jasper, community in central Craven County. Alt. 6. Settled about 1868. Named for local citizen, James Spear.

Jasperfield Branch rises in sw Madison County and flows nw into Spring Creek.

Jasper's Creek. See Bell Bay.

Jawbone Branch rises in nw Burke County and flows s into Steels Creek.

Jaynes Cove, central Haywood County on a tributary of Jonathans Creek.

Jean Guite Creek rises on the w side of the s end of the North Banks, ne Dare County, and flows n into Currituck Sound. Also known as Martins Point Creek.

Jefferson, town and county seat, central Ashe County. Inc. 1803 and named for Thomas Jefferson who was President of the United States at that time. Alt. 2,900. Produces chemicals and textiles.

Jefferson, town authorized to be laid out in Chatham County at Tyson's Mill on Deep River in 1796. Commissioners were appointed, but there is no evidence that the town was ever developed. A warehouse was to have been erected in the town for the inspection of tobacco, beef, pork, flour, and other commodities.

Jefferson, a proposed town in what is now sw Cleveland County. A law of 1799, slightly changed in 1800, authorized the establishment of a town in s Rutherford County between the Broad River and South Carolina. A building for a warehouse and for the inspection of tobacco was to be erected there. Commissioners were authorized to purchase 50 acres of land and to lay out the town. As late as July, 1803, the county court appointed a successor commissioner, but all plans for the town appear to have been abandoned when it was decided that the river could not be made navigable.

Jefferson Township, central Ashe County.

Jefferson Township, e central Guilford County.

Jenick Branch rises in ne Cherokee County and flows nw into Graybeard Creek.

Jenkins Branch rises in se Buncombe County and flows w into Rock Creek.

Jenkins Branch rises in s Swain County and flows nw into Tuckasegee River.

Jenkins Cove, ne Cherokee County. An unnamed stream flows nw in this cove.

Jenkins Cove, e Currituck County off the w side of Currituck Banks in Currituck Sound.

Jenkins Creek formed by junction of East Fork and West Fork in n Jackson County and flows sw into Soco Creek.

Jenkins Divide, n Jackson County between Big Witch Creek and Jenkins Creek.

Jenkins Swamp rises in n Onslow County and flows s into Cowhorn Swamp.

Jenkins Trail Ridge, nw Swain County in Great Smoky Mountains National Park, extending s across the park boundary from Thunderhead Mountain to Pickens Gap.

Jenks Branch rises in n Cherokee County at the foot of Jenks Knob and flows ne into Tipton Creek.

Jenks Knob on the Cherokee County, N. C.-Monroe County, Tenn., line in the Unicoi Mountains.

Jenney Knob, w Jackson County between Little Savannah Creek and Savannah Creek.

Jennie's Creek rises in central Wake County and flows s into Neuse River.

Jennie Wolf Creek. See Schene Wolf Creek.

Jennings, community in n Iredell County on Rocky Creek.

Jenny Branch rises in w Swain County and flows se into Tuckasegee River.

Jenny Lind, community in w Lenoir County, named for the Swedish singer (1820-1887) who, according to local legend, once sang beneath a tree here.

Jennys Gut rises in central Perquimans County and flows n into Racoon Creek.

Jericho, community in s Caswell County. A post office was operated here during the approx. period 1905-1920.

Jericho, community in s Davie County near the head of Baxter Creek. Named for the Jericho Church of Christ, est. here in 1872. A post office operated here for a short time after 1900 was known as Kurfees.

Jericho, former community in se Wayne County on the n side of Neuse River from Seven Springs (then Whitehall). Destroyed by Union forces during the battle of Whitehall on Dec. 16, 1862. Site now included in the corporate limits of Seven Springs, *which see.*

Jericho Run rises in e Lenoir County and flows ne into Stonyton Creek. The name appears in local records as early as the 1740's.

Jerome, community in nw Bladen County.

Jerome. See Micro.

Jerome Bog, a pocosin on the Bladen-Cumberland County line e of the community of Jerome. An almost perfect elliptical shape with its long axis running nw-se, it is an ancient lake now filled with peat. *See also* Carolina Bays.

Jerry. See Levels.

Jerry Bald, n Swain County in Great Smoky Mountains National Park at the ne end of Jerry Bald Ridge. Alt. 5,080.

Jerry Bald Ridge, n Swain County in Great Smoky Mountains National Park, a spur extending se from Andrews Bald on Forney Ridge between Mill Creek and Noland Creek.

Jerry Branch rises in w Transylvania County and flows sw into West Fork French Broad River.

Jerry Creek rises in w Avery County and flows e into Roaring River. Named for Jerry Hughes, an early settler.

Jerry Knob, central Haywood County between Jones Cove and Liner Cove.

Jerry Mountain, ne Caldwell County.

Jersey Settlement, former community on the e bank of Yadkin River near the present Linwood *(which see)* in w Davidson County, formerly Rowan. So called because settlers in the 1750's arrived from New Jersey. A post office by this name existed as late as 1830.

Jerusalem, former community in s Davie County. In 1815 a union church was organized here, erected on land given by Nicholas Click, and named New Jerusalem. By the 1830's a community was growing up around the church; a post office est. in 1850 was called Jerusalem. Church still active (Baptist), but the community has ceased to exist as such. Alt. 787.

Jerusalem Township, s Davie County.

Jessama, community in w central Beaufort County. Shown erroneously under the name Midway on recent federal maps.

Jesse Branch rises in sw Buncombe County near Rich Knob and flows nw into Beaverdam Creek.

Jesse Gap, n Buncombe County between Jess Ridge and Jess Knob.

Jesse Ridge, w Haywood County, Great Smoky Mountains National Park, center near lat. 35° 38′ 20″ N., long. 83° 06′ 50″ W., between Little Davidson Creek and Mossy Branch.

Jess Knob, n Buncombe County between Bald Knob and Jess Gap. Appears as Alexander Knob on recent State Highway Commission maps.

Jess Ridge, n Buncombe County extending nw from Jess Gap.

Jesses High Top, peak in the Swannanoa Mountains of se Buncombe County.

Jessie, community in s Cumberland County on Harrisons Creek.

Jester, community in ne Avery County.

Jeter, community in nw Rutherford County on Cedar Creek.

Jewel Branch rises in n central Alleghany County and flows se into Little River.

Jewel Hill. See Marshall.

Jews Quarter Island, a peninsula approx. 2½ mi. long, extending into the s waters of Currituck Sound from the mainland, se Currituck County. Presently owned by the Chatham family and used as a hunting lodge. Appears as Deuces Quarters on early maps.

Jim Branch rises in s Buncombe County and flows nw into Christian Creek.

Jim Branch rises in w Haywood Co. and flows nw into Rough Fork.

Jim Branch rises in sw Wake County and flows sw into Buckhorn Creek.

Jim Carroll Top, w Clay County, a peak of Carroll Mountain. Alt. 2,700.

Jim Creek rises near Stone Mountain in sw Henderson County and flows sw into Grassy Creek.

Jim Creek rises in n Yancey County and flows se into Bald Mountain Creek.

Jimmies Run rises in nw Northampton County and flows s into Roanoke River.

Jimmy Branch rises in n Buncombe County near Richland Mountain and flows w into Ox Creek.

Jimmy Gap, s Macon County between Bates Ridge and Hickory Knoll Creek.

Jim Ray Branch rises in n central Yancey County and flows s into Little Crabtree Creek.

Jims Beech Ridge, e Jackson County, between Bearwallow Creek and Chestnut Ridge Creek.

Jinnys Branch rises in sw Brunswick County and flows e and s into Shallotte Inlet.

Jinnys Branch, community in sw Brunswick County.

Joanna Bald, on the Cherokee-Graham County line near the head of Anderson Branch. Alt. 4,708.

Joanna Mountain, e Transylvania County e of Little River, between Grassy Creek and Briary Creek.

Jobs Cabin Township, w Wilkes County.

Jobs Peak, se Buncombe County near the McDowell County line, n of Evans Knob.

Jockey's Ridge, a sand dune 138 ft. high a short distance n of Nags Head, Bodie Island, e Dare County. It is the highest coastal sand dune on the Atlantic or Gulf coasts. Apparently indicated by a symbol but not named on the Mouzon map, 1775; the name was in use by 1851.

Joe, community in w Madison County on Meadow Fork. Alt. 2,649.

Joe Branch rises in sw Beaufort County and flows ne into Chocowinity Creek.

Joe Cove, valley in central Clay County through which Perry Creek flows.

Joe Creek rises in e Macon County and flows sw into Ellijay Creek.

Joe Knob, s Clay County on the sw end of Cherry Mountain.

Joel Branch rises in n central Transylvania County and flows e into Davidson River.

Joel Cove, e Clay County between Fishprong Branch and Buck Creek.

Joel Jackson Pond. See Williams Lake.

Joel Ridge, nw Rutherford County, extends e from the head of Buffalo Creek.

Joe Mountain, n Jackson County between North Fork and Scott Creek.

Joes Branch rises in s Vance County and flows sw into Ruin Creek.

Joes Creek rises in s Richmond County and flows se onto the Richmond-Scotland County line and se into Scotland County where it enters Gum Swamp Creek. See also Rochdale.

Joes Creek rises in s Watauga County and flows se into Caldwell County.

Joes Creek, community in w Scotland County.

Joes Fork, rises in s Moore County and flows ne into Nicks Creek.

Joe's Fork rises in s Watauga County and flows se into n Caldwell County where it enters Buffalo Creek.

Joes Island Creek rises in e Pasquotank County and flows e into Pasquotank River.

Joe White Mountain, w Caldwell County. Named for Major White, Revolutionary officer who lived on Johns River nearby.

Joe Young Ridge, s central Yancey County between Bowlens Creek and Bowlens Pyramid.

John Anders Ridge, on Buncombe-Madison County line extending sw from Moody Gap.

John Autrey Branch rises in s Yancey County and flows n into Rock Creek.

John Branch rises in sw Macon County and flows e into Little Indian Creek.

John Brown Branch rises in central Jackson County and flows w into Tuckasegee River.

John Green Bend, a bend in the Hiwassee River in w Cherokee County.

John H. Kerr Reservoir. See Kerr Reservoir.

John Ish High Top, a peak in w Cherokee County in a bend of Hiwassee River.

John Mason Branch rises in se Cherokee County and flows nw into Little Brasstown Creek.

John Newton Branch rises in central Cherokee County and flows s into Pace Branch.

Johnnies Creek rises in w Transylvania County and flows se into Tucker Creek.

John Reese Branch rises in central Clay County and flows w and nw into Downing Creek.

John Rock, mountain in nw Transylvania County between Cat Gap and Davidson River. Alt. approx. 3,220.

John Rock Branch rises in nw Transylvania County n of Cedar Rock Mountain and flows n on the w side of John Rock approx. one mi. into Cedar Rock Creek.

Johns, community in se Scotland County. Settled about 1875. Named for Captain James T. John, owner of land on which the railroad station was built. Alt. 179.

Johns Branch rises in w Graham County and flows se into Santeetlah Creek.

Johns Branch rises in sw Madison County and flows nw into Spring Creek.

Johns Camp Branch rises in e Mitchell County and flows se into Fall Creek.

Johns Cove, s Haywood County on Crawford Creek.

Johns Cove, nw Swain County between Twentymile Creek and Twentymile Ridge.

Johns Creek rises in central Jackson County and flows nw into Caney Fork.

Johns Knob, on the Graham County, N. C.-Monroe County, Tenn., line.

Johns Millpond, se Scotland County on Leiths Creek. Formed 1840. Covers 150 acres; maximum depth 15 ft.

Johnson Branch rises in e Clay County and flows nw into Davenport Branch.

Johnson Branch rises in w Haywood County and flows n into Campbell Creek.

Johnson Branch rises in w Macon County and flows e into Nantahala Lake.

Johnson Branch rises in n Madison County and flows w into Shelton Laurel Creek.

Johnson Branch rises in e Swain County and flows s into Tuckasegee River.

Johnson Branch rises in e Wayne County and flows ne into Exum Mill Branch.

Johnson Cove, se Buncombe County, e of Turkey Ridge.

Johnson Cove, e central Yancey County between Bowlens Creek and George Fork. Said to have been named for a yodeler who walked through the region yodeling.

Johnson Creek, a tidal creek in Core Sound, near the Core Banks, e Carteret County.

Johnson Creek rises in s Granville County and flows e into Tar River.

Johnson Creek rises in s Vance County and flows se into n Franklin County where it enters Lynch Creek.

Johnson Drainage Ditch rises s of Hendersonville in central Henderson County and flows ne into Bat Fork near its junction with Mud Creek.

Johnson Gap, n Graham County between tributaries of Sawyer Creek and Stecoah Creek.

Johnson Gap, near the nw end of the Henderson-Transylvania County line.

Johnson Gap, w Haywood County between Johnson Branch and Pine Tree Cove.

Johnson Knob, nw Henderson County, on Laurel Mountain between Sassafras Gap and Rich Gap Mountain. Alt. 5,540.

Johnson Mill Creek rises in n Clay County and flows sw into Tusquitee Creek.

Johnson Pond, n Harnett County, on West Buies Creek. Approx. ½ mi. long.

Johnson Pond. See Watsons Pond.

Johnson Ridge, n Clay County between Evans and Julie ridges. See also Matlock Bald.

Johnson's Branch. See Big Branch.

Johnsons Corner, community in nw Camden County. Named for Charlie Johnson who operated a store here following the Civil War.

Johnsons Creek rises in se Lincoln County and flows s into ne Gaston County where it enters Catawba River.

Johnsons Falls on the Yadkin River at Donnoha, ne Forsyth County. Fall of about four feet in ½ mi. A ledge of rock extends diagonally across the river over which the water falls in a straight plunge for two ft.

Johnsons Island, ne Currituck County off Currituck Banks.

Johnsons Mill Creek rises in w Henderson County and flows nw into Shaws Creek. Also known locally as Battle Creek.

Johnsons Mill Run rises in n Pitt County in Grindle Pocosin and flows s into Tar River.

Johnsons Mills, community in s Pitt County. A post office was est. here in 1882.

Johnsons Pond, s Wake County on Terrible Creek.

Johnsonville, community in sw Cherokee County at the mouth of Hothouse Branch.

Johnsonville, community in w Harnett County named for Samuel Johnson, early inn keeper here. Surrounding elevated lands first known as Mt. Pleasant by Highland Scots who settled here in the 1750's. Name changed later to Camerons Hill for Daniel Cameron who lived nearby. Afterwards changed to its present name. Flora MacDonald, Scottish heroine, lived here, 1774-1775. In a mound 4 mi. w are buried over 100 Indians, victims of a massacre shortly before the area was settled by Scots. The mound has been vandalized by the curious within recent years and is now sprinkled with bone fragments.

Johnsonville. See Traphill.

Johns River rises in n Caldwell County near the foot of Blowing Rock. Approx. 32 mi. long, it flows s, sw, and se across w Caldwell and into n Burke County where it enters Catawba River. Named for John Perkins, local Negro landowner.

Johns River Township, w Caldwell County.

Johns Swamp rises in se Bladen County and flows s into Colly Creek.

Johnston, former county seat in s Onslow County on New River. Inc. 1741; destroyed by a hurricane in September, 1752, and abandoned. Named for Gabriel Johnston (1699-1752), governor of North Carolina, 1734-52.

Johnston County was formed in 1746 from Craven County. Located in the e section of the state, it is bounded by Wilson,

Wayne, Sampson, Cumberland, Harnett, Wake, and Nash counties. It was named for Gabriel Johnston (1699-1752), governor of North Carolina, 1734-52. Area: 795 sq. mi. County seat: Smithfield with an elevation of 155 ft. Townships are Banner, Bentonville, Beulah, Boon Hill, Clayton, Cleveland, Elevation, Ingrams, Meadow, Micro, O'Neals, Pine Level, Pleasant Grove, Selma, Smithfield, Wilders, and Wilson's Mills. Produces tobacco, corn, soybeans, wheat, oats, cotton, poultry, eggs, hogs, livestock, dairy products, sweet potatoes, textiles, apparel, lumber, processed meat, furniture, chemicals, cottonseed oil, and crushed stone.

Johnston Court House. *See* Smithfield.

Johnston Swamp rises in s Johnston County and flows ne into Stone Creek.

Johnstonville, former town, est. 1788 in ne Randolph County as the county seat. Named for Governor Samuel Johnston (1733-1816), who was Chief Executive at the time. The town declined after 1796 when Asheboro was est. as the county seat in a more central location. The community of Brown's Crossroads is now here.

Johnstonville Township, sw Harnett County.

Johnstown, community in s Lincoln County on Indian Creek.

John Taylor Branch rises in w Madison County and flows e into Spring Creek.

John West Cove in ne Cherokee County. Named for an early settler who lived in the cove.

Jolly Branch rises in sw Cleveland County and flows s beside Jolly Mountain into Broad River.

Jolly Branch rises in se Orange County about 2 mi. n of town of Carrboro, and flows sw into Bolin Creek.

Jolly Gap, central Haywood County on the head of Dotson Branch.

Jolly Mountain, in sw Cleveland County on Broad River. Alt. approx. 925.

Jomeokee. *See* Pilot Mountain.

Jonas Creek rises in n Swain County in Great Smoky Mountains National Park and flows s into Forney Creek.

Jonas Ridge, mountain range in nw Burke County. Named for Jonas Braswell, an early settler who froze to death here.

Jonas Ridge, community in nw Burke County.

Jonas Ridge Township, n Burke County.

Jonathan Creek rises in nw Granville County and flows e into Goose Neck Creek.

Jonathan Crossroads, community in n Granville County.

Jonathans Creek rises in w Haywood County and flows ne across the county into Pigeon River.

Jonathans Creek Township, w central Haywood County. Named for Jonathan McPeters, one of the first white men to visit and settle in the area.

Jones, community in se Beaufort County.

Jones Bay, ne Pamlico County in Pamlico Sound on the s side of Goose Creek Island. *See also* Hobucken.

Jonesboro, former town in central Lee County a short distance se of Sanford. The courthouse was equidistant between the two towns. Jonesboro was settled about 1869 and inc. 1873. Named for L. C. Jones who built the railroad between Wilmington and Sanford. Merged with Sanford, 1947. The former town is now known as Jonesboro Heights in Sanford.

Jonesboro Township, former township in e central Lee County, now township number 2.

Jonesborough. *See* Camden.

Jones Branch rises in sw Buncombe County near Jones Mountain and flows w into Newfound Creek.

Jones Branch rises in ne Cherokee County and flows se into Ricket Branch.

Jones Branch rises in sw Cleveland County and flows n into Broad River.

Jones Branch rises in central Haywood Co. and flows nw into Pigeon River.

Jones Branch rises in w Madison County and flows ne into East Fork Shut-in Creek.

Jones Branch rises in nw Watauga County and flows s into Little Beaverdam Creek.

Jones Chapel, community in nw Martin County.

Jones County was formed in 1778 from Craven County. Located in the e section of the state, it is bounded by Carteret, Craven, Duplin, Lenoir, and Onslow counties. It was named for Willie Jones (1740-1801), Revolutionary leader, president of the Council of Safety, and later opponent of the adoption of the Constitution of the United States. The Lawson map, 1709, shows "Mr Jones 4000 Acres" at this location. The Moseley map, 1733, shows "Mr. Frederick Jones 7375 Acres." Area: 468 sq. mi. County seat: Trenton with an alt. of 28 ft. Township are Nos. 1-7, White Oak, Pollocksville, Trenton, Cypress Creek, Tuckahoe, Chinquapin, and Beaver Creek. Produces tobacco, corn, soybeans, hogs, livestock, lumber, marl, sand, and gravel.

Jones Cove, central Haywood County near the head of Jones Branch.

Jones Cove, central Macon County at the head of Jacob Branch.

Jones Cove Creek rises in central Buncombe County and flows sw through Jones Cove into Bull Creek.

Jones Creek is formed in se Anson County by the junction of North Fork Jones Creek and South Fork Jones Creek. It flows ne and s into Pee Dee River. During the Civil War a gun factory was operated on the bank of this stream and Jones Creek was the name of a post office in the vicinity for a time around 1882.

Jones Creek rises in sw Avery County and flows e into North Toe River.

Jones Creek rises in se Buncombe County and flows se into Broad River.

Jones Creek rises in ne Jackson County and flows w into Dark Ridge Creek.

Jones Creek rises in s Macon County and flows n into Cartoogechaye Creek.

Jones Creek rises in e Rockingham County and flows ne into Hogans Creek. Appears as Pruetts Fork in early records; known as Manly Mill Creek in the 1920's and more recently by its present name.

Jones Creek rises in ne Swain County and flows sw into Raven Fork.

Jones Creek rises in s Swain County and flows nw into Bowers Creek.

Jones Creek. See Lick Creek.

Jones' Folly. See Jones Knob.

Jones Gap, s Macon County between Cadon Gap and the head of Stephens Creek.

Jones Gap in the Blue Ridge Mountains on the Transylvania County, N.C.-Greenville County, S.C., line near Walker Creek.

Jones Island in White Oak River, w Carteret County, near the mouth of Pettivers Creek. Named for Robert Jones.

Jones Island. See Harwells Island.

Jones Island. See Pittmans Island.

Jones Knob, n Buncombe County, at the n

end of Iron Ore Ridge in the Elk Mountains.

Jones Knob, sw Cherokee County between Rocky Ford Creek and Shoal Creek.

Jones Knob on the Haywood-Jackson County line. Alt. 6,240-6,260. Formerly known as Jones' Folly because at a time when Dr. Elisha Mitchell and T. L. Clingman were disputing over the highest peak in the Southern Appalachians, a man named Jones came into the area and reported this to be the highest mountain. Upon questioning him, his friends discovered that he had not been near the top so they called it Jones' Folly. In the 1850's, Guyot tried to name this Mount Junaluska but the name did not stick.

Jones Knob, w Jackson County between Windy Gap and Poplar Cove Knob. Alt. approx. 4,140.

Jones Knob, s Macon County at the head of Whiterock Branch. Alt. 4,600.

Jones Lake, central Bladen County, one of the Carolina Bays, which see. Covers 224 acres; max. depth 8.7 ft. It is a part of Jones Lake State Park. Fishing, swimming, and boating. Known earlier as Woodwards Lake for Samuel Woodward, a local justice of the peace in 1734. Probably named for Isaac Jones who owned adjacent property a little later.

Jones Lake State Park, central Bladen County, 4 mi. n of Elizabethtown. Est. 1939; includes 2,000 acres. A scenic and recreational area with provisions for picnicking, swimming, fishing, camping, boating, hiking, and nature study. See also Jones Lake; Salters Lake.

Jones Mill appears on the Collet map, 1770. It was located near the mouth of the stream in sw Camden County now known as Portohonk Creek.

Jones Mill, community in e Cherokee County on Peachtree Creek.

Jones Mill. See Barrows Mill Pond.

Jones Mill. See Page's Mill.

Jones Mountain, central Buncombe County w of Wilson.

Jones Mountain, sw Buncombe County, ne of Rockyface Mountain.

Jones Pond, a natural lake in e Gates County fed by several small streams and emptying into the Dismal Swamp. It is about ¾ mi. long and 2 to 6 feet in depth.

Jones Pond, se Scotland County on Bridge Creek. Formed about 1810. Covers 75 acres, maximum depth 8 ft.

Jones Store, community in s Lenoir County.

Jones Swamp, w central Gates County drained by Flat Branch.

Jones Swamp rises in w Sampson County and flows sw into South River.

Jonesville, town in nw Yadkin County on the s side of Yadkin River. Est. about 1811 on the land of Richard Cunningham and Jesse Lester and named Martinsborough, probably for Gov. Alexander Martin of nearby Stokes County who died in 1807. Name changed to Jonesville for a local citizen, Hardy Jones, in 1815. Inc. 1852. Alt. 998.

Joppa, community in n Perquimans and s Gates counties.

Jordan Branch rises in w Gates County and flows nw into Lassiter Branch.

Jordan Branch rises in e Haywood County and flows nw into Fall Creek.

Jordan Creek rises in e Beaufort County and flows e into Pungo River. Appears on the Collet map, 1770. See also Chappel Creek.

Jordan Creek rises in s Caswell County and flows sw into n Alamance County where it enters Stony Creek.

Jordan Creek rises in central Granville County and flows se into Coon Creek.

Jordan Island in e Pasquotank County in Newbegun Creek near the community of Weeksville.

Jordan River. See Cape Fear River.

Jordans. See Friendship.

Jordans Creek rises in n Scotland County and flows se into Juniper Creek.

Jordans Creek rises in n Warren County and flows n into Sixpound Creek.

Jordans Landing on Roanoke River, s Bertie County. The house on the Jordan plantation here is one of the oldest in the county.

Jordans Mill Pond, n Northampton County on Cypress Creek. Ivy Creek also flows into Jordans Mill Pond. Covers approx. 135 acres with a max. depth of 12 ft. Named for an early owner.

Joshua Branch rises in s Transylvania County and flows ne into East Fork French Broad River.

Joshua Creek rises in se Lenoir County and flows se into Jones County where it enters Trent River. Probably the same as Joshua Foy's Creek which is mentioned in local records as early as 1763.

Joshua Foy's Creek. See Joshua Creek.

Joshua Lake on Gerren Creek in s Transylvania County. Covers 60 acres and has maximum depth of 70 ft.

Joshua Mountain, s Transylvania County between the head of Joshua Branch and Middle Fork French Broad River. Alt. 3,163.

Joy, community in nw Burke County.

Joyce Creek rises in Dismal Swamp, n Camden County and flows se and sw into Pasquotank River. Though slightly missplaced this probably is the Joys Fork shown on the Moseley map, 1733, and as Joy Creek on the Price map, 1808.

Joyce Kilmer Memorial Forest, w Graham County in Nantahala National Forest, was dedicated to poet Joyce Kilmer (1886-1918), author of Trees and Other Poems, on July 30, 1936. It contains 3,840 acres of virgin forest including poplar, hemlock, and oak and is one of the finest stands of its type in America. Little Santeetlah Creek flows through the forest.

Joycetown, community in se Caldwell County. An industrial center, named in 1947 by Regina Reid for Joyce Hogan, wife of James Hogan, owner of a manufacturing plant there. Seven or eight industrial plants are located here.

Joy Fork. See Joyce Creek.

Joyland, community in central Durham County on the outskirts of the city of Durham.

Joyner's, former town in n Wilson County. Site approx. one mile n of Elm City. Inc. 1870 on Wilmington and Weldon Railroad, now Seaboard Coast Line Railroad. Depot est. 1839; post office, 1846-1873. Declined after establishment of Toisnot, now Elm City, which see.

Joynes, community in n Wilkes County on East Prong Roaring River.

Jubilee, community in w Davidson County.

Judaculla Mountain, n Jackson County between Balsam and Willits. Judaculla (or Jutaculla) was a giant in Indian legend.

Judaculla Ridge, e Jackson County between Beechfat Creek and Mull Creek.

Judaculla Rock, central Jackson County 3½ mi. se of East Laport on Caney Fork. Large rock covered with well preserved Indian picture writing of unknown origin and meaning.

Judd Mountain, w Wilkes County between Lewis Fork Creek and South Fork Reddies River. Named for the Judd family which settled in the vicinity before 1778.

Judes Gap on the Polk-Rutherford County line.

Judges Quarter, community in s Hyde County.

Judith, community in n central Union County.

Judith Island, peninsula on Bell Island in s Hyde County. *See also* Abigails Islands.

Judkins Township, e Warren County.

Judson, former community in w Swain County on Little Tennessee River. Alt. 1,563. Site now under the waters of Fontana Lake.

Judson Lake in s Transylvania County drains n into Little River. Covers 8 acres and has maximum depth of 20 ft.

Judy Branch rises in nw Swain County and flows s into Lake Cheoah.

Jugtown, community in sw Buncombe County.

Jugtown, former community in sw Catawba County near the Lincoln County line. An area approx. 8 mi. square in which pottery was made from the early nineteenth century until recently. Jacob Weaver, German potter, began the work and used a secret color formula which he never shared with anyone else. Hilton family and others also worked here.

Jugtown, community in nw Moore County n of Bear Creek. Est. about 1920 by Jacques Busbee (1870-1947), an artist from Raleigh. Manufactured hand-turned pottery which has been widely distributed in the United States. Other potters, some of whom were trained by Busbee, work in the vicinity.

Jugtown Branch rises in sw Buncombe County near Jugtown an flows se into Pole Creek.

Julian, community in s Guilford and n Randolph counties. Alt. 772.

Julie Knob, n Clay County on Julie Ridge. Named for a Negro slave formerly owned by Robert Henry, who built her a house at the foot of the mountain when she was freed.

Julie Ridge, n Clay County between Deadline and Johnson ridges.

Julius Duggar's Rock House Creek. *See* Dugger Creek.

Julius Knob, n Yancey County, on Cane Mountain near the head of Sampson Branch. Alt. 3,931.

Jump and Run Branch rises in central Duplin County and flows sw into Northeast Cape Fear River.

Jump Cove, n Buncombe County, e of Iron Ore Ridge.

Jumping Branch rises in n Transylvania County and flows se into South Fork Mills River.

Jumping Creek rises in e Jones County and flows s into Trent River.

Jumping Off Place, peak in nw Wilkes County w of Middle Fork Reddies River. It is the steepest portion of the Blue Ridge Mountains in the county.

Jumping Run rises in e Burke County and flows n into Catawba River.

Jumping Run, a stream about 1 mi. long, rises in s Carteret County and flows e and then s into the n side of Bogue Sound about 4 mi. e of Broad Creek.

Jumping Run rises in s Franklin County and flows ne into Crooked Creek.

Jumping Run rises in central Franklin County and flows sw into Tar River.

Jumping Run rises on the Fort Bragg Military Reservation in ne Hoke County and flows ne into Little River.

Jumping Run rises in sw Johnston County and flows ne into Mill Creek.

Jumping Run rises in n Lenoir County and flows sw into Falling Creek. The woodland pond forming the headwaters of this stream has been called The Hanted Pond since 1730.

Jumping Run, rises in nw Nash County and flows n into Tumbling Run.

Jumping Run, rises in s New Hanover County and flows w into Greenfield Lake.

Jumping Run rises in se Onslow County and flows w into Frenchs Creek.

Jumping Run rises in e Pender County and flows w into Northeast Cape Fear River.

Jumping Run. *See* Haw Creek.

Jumping Run Creek rises in central Alexander County and flows sw into Glade Creek. Name appears in local records as early as 1790.

Jumping Run Creek formed in w Harnett County by the confluence of Reedys Swamp and McLeod Creek (*which see*) and flows se into n Cumberland County to enter Little River.

Jumping Swamp, rises in s Columbus County and flows ne and e into Grissett Swamp.

The Jump Off. *See* Mount Kephart.

Jumpoff Gap, s central Yancey County between Bowlens Creek and Bowlens Pyramid.

Jumpoff Mountain, w Henderson County between the headwaters of Brightwater Branch and North Fork. Alt. approx. 3,150.

Jumpoff Rock, w Henderson County on Jumpoff Mountain. Used by Indians as a post for sentinels to observe the approach of enemy up French Broad River valley.

During the 1920's a resort hotel was begun here but never completed.

Jump Run, a tidal inlet near the mouth of Middens Creek, e of the community of Smyrna in e Carteret County.

The Jump-up, peak on the Graham-Swain County line between Grassy Top and Swim Bald.

Jumpup Ridge, n Swain County in Great Smoky Mountains National Park, a spur extending se from Bald Ridge between Bear Creek and Advalorem Branch.

Junaluska Creek rises in ne Cherokee County and flows sw and nw into Valley River.

Junaluska Gap on the Cherokee-Macon County line in the Snowbird Mountains n of Rich Knob. Alt. 3,506.

Junaluska Mountain, sw Haywood County, about 5 mi. sw of Lake Junaluska. Alt. 5,071. Named to honor Junaluska, Cherokee chief who saved Andrew Jackson's life at the battle of Horseshoe Bend, 1812. Known for a time in the 1920's as North Eaglenest Mountain in connection with the promotion of a hotel here. *See also* Jones Knob.

Juneau, community in w Mecklenburg County.

Juney Whank Branch rises in n Swain County and flows se into Deep Creek.

Junietta. *See* East Fork Pigeon River.

Juniper Bay, s Hyde County in Pamlico Sound e of Marsh Island. Appears as New Mattamuskeet Creek on the Moseley map, 1733. *See also* Cecils Harbor.

Juniper Branch, rises in s Pitt County and flows ne into Chicod Creek.

Juniper Branch rises in s Wake County and flows s into Middle Creek.

Juniper Creek rises in Green Swamp in n central Brunswick County. It flows w and sw into Waccamaw River. For a distance of several mi. it forms a part of the boundary between Brunswick and Columbus counties.

Juniper Creek rises in e Harnett County and flows sw into Cape Fear River.

Juniper Creek rises on the Fort Bragg

Military Reservation in n Hoke County and flows s into Rockfish Creek.

Juniper Creek rises in s Lee County and flows ne into Little River.

Juniper Creek rises in s Nash County and flows e into nw Wilson County where it joins Millstone Creek to form Bloomery Swamp.

Juniper Creek rises in n Scotland County and flows se into Big Shoeheel Creek.

Juniper Creek rises in s Tyrrell County and flows ne into Northwest Fork [Alligator River.]

Juniper Run rises in se Johnston County and flows se into Mill Creek.

Juniper Swamp rises in w Beaufort County and flows w to join Harding Swamp in forming East Branch Chicod Creek.

Juniper Swamp rises in s Johnston County and flows se into Hannah Creek.

Juniper Swamp rises in n Onslow County and flows s into Cowhorn Swamp.

Juniper Swamp rises in sw Onslow County and flows nw into Pender County where it enters Shaking Creek.

Juno, community in central Buncombe County on Dix Creek.

Jupiter, town in n Buncombe County. Inc. 1895, but long inactive in municipal affairs.

Just, community in e Madison County on Terris Fork.

Justice, community in e Franklin County on Little Peachtree Creek. Alt. 261. Settled about 1873.

Justice Creek rises in e Mitchell County and flows e into Avery County where it enters North Toe River.

Justice Ridge, sw Buncombe County, n of Candler Heights.

Jutts Creek rises in se Graham County and flows n into Tulula Creek. Named for Jutt Colvard.

Jutts Creek, community in se Graham County.

Jutts Gap on the Cherokee-Graham County line in the Snowbird Mountains.

K

Kadar, community in s Wake County.

Kagle Branch rises in w central Transylvania County and flows s into Catheys Creek.

Kagle Mountain, central Transylvania County between Catheys Creek and Kuykendall Creek. Alt. 3,908.

Kaiser Lake, s Transylvania County at the head of Morgan Mill Creek. Covers two acres and has a maximum depth of 20 ft.

Kalamazoo, community in s Madison County.

Kalmia, community in se Mitchell County. A post office operated here from the late 1930's until the 1950's.

Kanady Creek. *See* Candy Creek.

Kanati Fork rises in n Swain County in Great Smoky Mountains National Park on the e slope of Nettle Creek Bald and flows ne into Beech Flats Prong.

Kannapolis, municipality in s Rowan and n Cabarrus counties. Alt. 765. It is the 17th largest uninc. community in the U. S. and the largest in N. C. James William Cannon bought 600 acres here along the Southern Railway tracks in 1905 where he built houses and a mill which began production in 1908. Cannon Mills are here. The name comes from a form of the family name plus *polis,* the Greek word for city. Produces textiles, towels, and apparel.

Kannapolis Township, former township in nw Cabarrus County, now township number 4. Once named Cooks Cross Roads Township.

Kanuga Lake, central Henderson County on Little Mud Creek. Formed about 1908. Covers 12 acres; maximum depth 20 feet. Summer camp owned by the Episcopal Church. Named for prehistoric Cherokee town, Ka-nu-ga, on the West Fork of Pigeon River in Haywood County. The Indian name traditionally meant "The Meeting Place of Many Peoples."

Kappa, community in w Davie County. In the 1870's known as Ketchie's Mill for a mill erected on Little Creek here at that time. Post office est. 1883 in the home of W. R. Ketchie, a Lutheran minister, who gave it the name Kappa, the Greek name for the letter *K.* Davie Academy opened here about 1908, and the name Davie Academy is also sometimes still used for the community.

Karrs Branch rises in sw Iredell County w of Troutman and flows sw into Hicks Creek.

Katalsta Ridge, ne Swain County in Great Smoky Mountains National Park, a spur extending s from Eagle Rock. Named for a daughter of Yonaguska, noted as a pottery maker.

Kate Gap on the Madison County, N. C.-Cocke County, Tenn., line.

Kate Knob, s Macon County between Pine Ridge and Jones Creek.

Katesville, community in central Franklin County. Settled 1888. Named for Mrs. Kate Griffin, donor of the site. Alt. 300.

Katie Creek rises in e Macon County and flows w into Walnut Creek.

Kawana, community in se Avery County.

Kaylors Knob, sw Burke County.

Kayoo-lanta. *See* Chimneytop Mountain.

Kays Crossroads, community in se Gates County.

Kearney, community in n Franklin County. Alt. 300. Named in 1894 for Charlie B. Kearney.

Kearney Creek rises in se Craven County and flows e into Adams Creek.

Keasler Branch rises in central Buncombe County near Craven Gap and flows se into Bull Creek.

Keeauwee, an Indian village, appears on the Moseley map, 1733. Site was on the trading path of the Cherokee and Catawba Indians to Virginia on Deep River in present nw Randolph County. *See also* Caraway Creek.

Keel Creek rises in se Hertford County and flows s approx. 3 mi. to enter Chowan River at the ne corner of Bertie County.

Keelsville. *See* Congleton.

Keene, community in s Durham County about 3 mi. s of the city of Durham. Site of the yards of the Norfolk and Southern Railroad.

Keener, community in n Sampson County at the head of Beaverdam Swamp. A post office here in the 1880's was named Bass.

Keener Creek rises in central Cherokee County and flows se into Marble Creek.

Keener Knob, e Macon County between the head of Crows Branch and Ledford Branch.

Keener Mountain, e Macon County between Long Branch and Brush Creek.

Keenerville. *See* Ingalls.

Keeters Store, community in central Halifax County.

Keeversville. *See* Plateau.

Keg Drive Branch rises in n Swain County and flows se into Left Fork [Deep Creek].

Keg Island, in the Cape Fear River, w New Hanover County, se of Campbell Island.

Kehukee, community in s Pasquotank County.

Kehukee Creek *See* Kehukee Swamp.

Kehukee Swamp rises in e Halifax County and flows sw into Roanoke River. Appears as Kehukee Creek on the Collet map, 1770.

Keith, community in w Pender County on Black River.

Keiths Bay, sand filled bay in s Sampson County on the head of Keiths Swamp. *See also* Carolina Bays.

Keiths Swamp rises in s Sampson County and flows se into Black River.

Kelford, town in nw Bertie County. Settled 1890; inc. 1893. Built on the land of Col. S. A. Norfleet whose home, Kelford, was named for a ford in Scotland. Alt. 88.

Keller Gap on the Watauga County, N. C.-Johnson County, Tenn., line in the Stone Mountains.

Kellogs Fork, community in e Gates County.

Kellum, community in n Onslow County.

Kellumtown, a community of Negroes in se Onslow County. Made up largely of people formerly living on land which became Camp Lejeune Marine Base.

Kelly, community in se Bladen County. Formerly known also as Centerville and as Hungry Neck.

Kelly Cove, n Macon County on a tributary of Burningtown Creek.

Kelly Creek rises in se Henderson County 1½ mi. sw of Saluda and flows se into Pacolet River. Lake Kelly, *which see,* is on Kelly Creek.

Kelly Mountain, s Transylvania County between Tower Creek and Cantrell Creek. Alt. approx. 2,980.

Kelly Ridge, n Macon County between Shope Cove and Kelly Cove.

Kellys Creek rises in s Pender County and flows w into Rileys Creek.

Kellys Pond on Southwest Creek in e Lenoir County. Formed in or prior to 1738 by a man named Marshall. Covers 312 acres; max. depth 10 ft.

Kelsey, community in nw Caldwell and sw Watauga counties near Boone Fork, 3 mi. w of Blowing Rock. Probably named for Samuel T. Kelsey who operated a nursery near here in the late nineteenth century. Also known as White's Spring.

Kelvyn Fork, creek rises in w Wake County and flows w into Brier Creek.

Kemps Mill, community in s Randolph County on Richland Creek.

Kems Branch rises in e Haywood Co. and flows n into Allens Creek.

Kenady's Branch. *See* Candy Creek.

Kenan Ditch, a drain in s Duplin County to carry the waters of Kenan Pocosin into Northeast Cape Fear River.

Kenan Pocosin, a large swamp in s Duplin County which is drained by ditches into Northeast Cape Fear River.

Kenansville, town and county seat, central Duplin County. Authorized to be laid out in 1816; inc. 1852. Alt. 127. Named for General James Kenan (1740-1810), member of Provincial Congress and Revolutionary officer. Site once known as Grovemont. "Goldengrove," plantation of Congressman James Gillespie, was at or near the site of Kenansville before it was laid out. Earlier Duplin Court House was approx. 2½ mi. w of present town of Warsaw on the Duplin-Sampson County line.

Kenansville Township, central Duplin County.

Kendall Beach, community on Neuse River in sw Pamlico County. Developed after World War I by a man named Kendall.

Kendrick Crossroad, community in sw Mecklenburg County.

Kendricks Creek rises in East Dismal Swamp, central Washington County and flows approx. 9 mi. n into Albemarle Sound. Formerly called Mackeys Creek. The part of Kendricks Creek which is south of the town of Roper is sometimes called Mill Creek locally.

Kenilworth, former town in central Buncombe County. Inc. 1891; became a part of Asheville, 1905.

Kenly, town in e Johnston County. Settled about 1875; inc. 1887. Named for J. I. Kenly, an official of the Atlantic Coast Line Railroad. Alt. 220.

Kennebec, community in s Wake County. Named for a county in Maine.

Kennedy Creek, central Beaufort County. A short but rather wide stream at the w limit of Washington. It flows south into Pamlico River.

Kennedy Creek rises in ne Cherokee County and flows ne and w into Worm Creek.

Kennedy Creek rises in n Mecklenburg County and flows s into Sugar Creek.

Kennedy Crossroads, community in s Wayne County w of Mount Olive.

Kennedy Falls, community in ne Cherokee County.

Kennedy Ford, ne Union County in Rocky River.

Kennedy Top, ne Cherokee County near the headwaters of Kennedy Creek.

Kennekeet Banks. *See* Kinnakeet Banks.

Kennekeet Township, e Dare County on the Outer Banks. Also spelled Kinnekeet.

Kenneth Branch rises in s Wake County and flows se into Neill Creek.

Kenneth Creek rises in s Wake County and flows s into Harnett County where it enters Neill Creek.

Kenricks Mounts or Kindrickers Mounts, sand dunes fixed by vegetation, shown on the White map, 1590, somewhat s of the present community of Rodanthe on Hatteras Island, e Dare County. They were presumably submerged with Cape Kenrick, *which see*.

Kenton Fork, community in n Granville County.

Kentucky Creek rises in central Avery County and flows s and w into North Toe River.

Keowee. *See* Cowee.

Kephart Prong rises in n Swain County in Great Smoky Mountains National Park on the e slope of Mount Kephart and flows se to join Beech Flats Prong in forming Oconaluftee River. Named for Horace Kephart (1862-1931), author and authority on campcraft, who is buried in Bryson City.

Kerners Crossroads. *See* Kernersville.

Kerners Mill Creek rises in e Forsyth County and flows w into Salem Lake.

Kernersville, town in e Forsyth County, inc. 1871. Site first settled in 1756 by Caleb Story, an Irishman. About 1770 it was purchased by William Dobson and came to be known as Dobson's Crossroads; Washington had breakfast at Dobson's tavern on June 2, 1791. In 1871 Joseph Kerner bought the property and the town which developed there took his name. Formerly Kerner's Crossroads. Home of Southern Pilgrim College (not accredited). Produces hosiery, textiles, and fabricated metals.

Kernersville Township, e Forsyth County.

Kernersville Water Reservoir on Kerners Mill Creek, e Forsyth County. Formed 1953. Covers 120 acres. Maximum depth 25 ft.

Kerr, community in s Sampson County. Settled about 1888. Named for John Daniel Kerr who influenced the location of the Cape Fear & Yadkin Valley Railroad on the e side of the Cape Fear River. Alt. 91.

Kerr Creek rises in w Rowan County and flows ne into Back Creek. Appears in early records as James Cathey's Creek, named about 1749 for an early settler. *See also* Millbridge.

Kerr Reservoir, formed in 1952 with the completion of John H. Kerr Dam on

Roanoke River in Virginia. Also fed by Dan River, Nutbush Creek, Island Creek, and many smaller tributaries, it extends into central Vance County, n Granville County, and nw Warren County. Normally it covers 48,900 acres, is 39 mi. long with a shoreline of 800 miles. Max. depth 99 ft. Used for hydroelectric power generation, flood control, municipal water supply, irrigation, and many forms of recreation. Named for Congressman John H. Kerr (1873-1958). Popularly known as Buggs Island Lake for an island in Roanoke River below the dam. The section of the Reservoir extending into Vance County on Nutbush Creek is sometimes known as Townsville Lake. The official name is John H. Kerr Reservoir.

Kershaw, community in s Pamlico County between Greens and Kershaw creeks.

Kershaw Creek rises in se Pamlico County and flows se into Greens Creek.

Kesiah River. *See* Cashie River.

Ketchie's Mill. *See* Kappa.

Kettle Rock, se Macon County between Big Dog Mountain and Chinquapin Mountain.

Keyser. *See* Addor.

Kick Shin Creek rises in central Surry County and flows e into Cody Creek.

Kidville, community in e Lincoln County.

Kies Mountain, s Randolph County.

Kilbart Slough, a short tidal creek in sw Brunswick County which joins the channel of the Intracoastal Waterway n of Hales Beach.

Kilby Branch rises in n Haywood County and flows se into Big Creek.

Kilby Branch rises in n Wilkes County and flows s into Reddies River. Named for William Kilby, colonial settler.

Kilby Cove, s Cherokee County. An unnamed stream flowing through this cove forms the headwaters of the e fork of Cook Creek.

Kilby Creek rises in sw Macon County and flows ne into Nantahala River.

Kilby Gap on the Alexander-Wilkes County line in the Brushy Mountains. Named for William Kilby, Jr., early nineteenth century resident of the area. Alt. 1,540.

Kilby Gap, sw Macon County on Kilby Creek.

Kildeer Mountain, w Cherokee County between Rocky Ford Creek and Shoal Creek.

Kilkenny, community in s Tyrrell County. *See also* Warbler.

Kilkenny Landing, s Tyrrell County on Alligator River.

Kill Devil Hills, town on n Bodie Island, e Dare County. Inc. 1953. There are numerous legends concerning the origin of the name, but among the earliest was one recorded in 1728 by William Byrd of Virginia. He reported that rum consumed in that part of Carolina was shipped from New England and was of such strength that a saying arose that "That thar rum is powerful enough to kill the devil." The name, marking a large sand dune appears first on the Price map, 1808. It was from Kill Devil Hill in 1903 that the Wright brothers made their first successful airplane flight. Alt. 11.

Kill Devil Hills Coast Guard Station, on n Bodie Island in e Dare County. First est. as a life-saving station in 1878-79. Lifesaving Service and Revenue Cutter Service joined to form United States Coast Guard in 1915.

Kill'em Swamp rises in se Hertford County and flows nw into Chinkapin Creek.

Killets Creek rises in central Moore County and flows n into McLendons Creek. Named For William Killet, who settled in the area about 1766.

Killian Branch rises near Killian Knob in central Buncombe County and flows se into Beaverdam Creek. Probably named for Daniel Killian, friend and host of Bishop Francis Asbury in his travels, 1803.

Killian Knob, central Buncombe County, near Gooch Peak n of Asheville.

Killian Knob, w Haywood County between Mitchell Cove and Riddle Cove.

Killians Creek rises in s Catawba County, flows s through e Lincoln County and into ne Gaston County where it joins Leepers Creek in forming Dutchmans Creek. Appears as Killings Creek on the Collet map, 1770.

Killings Creek. See Killians Creek.

Killpecker Ridge, nw Swain County in Great Smoky Mountains National Park, a spur extending se from Jenkins Trail Ridge.

Killquick. See Lawrence.

Kill Quick. See Quick.

Kill Swamp rises in n Sampson County and flows sw into Great Coharie Creek.

Kilmer Memorial Forest. See Joyce Kilmer Memorial Forest.

Kimesville, community in w Alamance and e Guilford counties. Settled about 1745; a mill here dates from about 1788. Named for pioneer German family in the area, Keim or Kime.

Kimsey Bald, on the Clay-Macon County line.

Kimsey Cove, ne Cherokee County in the Valley River Mountains. An unnamed stream flowing through the cove empties into Vengeance Creek.

Kimsey Cove, w Macon County at the head of Gibby Branch.

Kimsey Creek rises in s Buncombe County and flows sw into Henderson County where it enters Cane Creek. A large lime deposit along Kimsey Creek is now used for crushed stone.

Kimsey Creek rises in sw Macon County and flows ne into Nantahala River.

Kimsey Gap, s Macon County between Allison Creek and Jones Creek.

Kimsey Ridge, s Clay County, extends ne in an arc from Sweetwater Gap to Sweetwater Creek.

Kinack, a name appearing on the Ogilby map, 1671, for the land now in Craven County between Upper Broad Creek and Swift Creek.

Kincaids Mill Creek. See Bristol's Mill Creek.

Kind, community in sw Madison County.

Kindrickers Mounts. See Kenricks Mounts.

King, community in sw Stokes County. Alt. 1,115. Originally known as King's Cabin, for a double log cabin owned by Oscar King. The present name was adopted with the coming of the railroad.

King Blount's Town. See Ucohnerunt.

King Creek rises in s Henderson County and flows ne into Bat Fork.

King Creek rises in s Surry County and flows se into Fisher River.

King Creek rises in central Transylvania County and flows se into French Broad River.

King Mountain, s Henderson County n of the community of Zirconia.

King Mountain, sw Randolph County.

King Mountain, w central Transylvania County between Negro Prong and Catheys Creek.

Kings Bluff, United States Lock Number 1 on Cape Fear River, se Bladen County.

Kingsboro, community in central Edgecombe County. Alt. 113.

Kings Branch rises in s Mecklenburg County and flows s into Sugar Creek. Appears as Kings River on the Collet map, 1770.

King's Cabin. See King.

Kings Creek rises in nw Alleghany County and flows sw into South Fork New River.

Kings Creek rises in ne Caldwell County and flows n into Yadkin River. Has been known by this name since the colonial period, hence it probably honors King George III.

Kings Creek rises in se Cleveland County on Kings Mountain and flows se into South Carolina where it enters Broad River.

King Creek rises in ne Craven County and flows n into Neuse River.

Kings Creek rises in nw Guilford County and flows w into Forsyth County where it enters East Belews Creek.

Kings Creek rises in s Onslow County and flows se into Spicers Bay.

Kings Creek rises in s Vance County and flows s into n Franklin County where it enters Tar River.

Kings Creek, community in e Caldwell County.

Kings Creek Township, ne Caldwell County.

Kings Crossroads, community in nw Guilford County.

Kings Crossroads, community in w Pitt County.

Kingsdale, former town in se Robeson County near the head of Mill Swamp Creek. Inc. 1907, but long inactive in municipal affairs. Site of huge sawmill operations which cleared virgin longleaf pine timber in the region; operations ceased about 1918 and the site abandoned. Some mill foundations, machine parts, and railroad fill still visible.

Kings Island in the waters of Pamlico Sound, s Dare County, off Brooks Point, Hatteras Island.

Kings Mountain, a range about 3 mi. long in se Cleveland and sw Gaston counties, extending into South Carolina. The highest peak, The Pinnacle, is at the n end of the range, separated from the rest of the range by Sherrars Gap. The Revolutionary Battle of Kings Mountain, October 7, 1780, was fought a short distance s in South Carolina.

Kings Mountain, n Jackson County between Tuckasegee River and Cope Creek.

Kings Mountain, city in se Cleveland County. Inc. 1874. Alt. 995. Named for the mountain 7 mi. s. In 1923 East Kings Mountain (which see) became a part of Kings Mountain. Produces textiles, lumber, minerals, and hosiery.

Kings Mountain Township, former township in se Cleveland County, now township number 4.

Kings Point, peninsula extending from the mainland of ne Carteret County into Brett Bay.

Kings River. See Kings Branch.

Kingville, former Negro community in n central Stanly County, now a part of the city of Albemarle. Named for Dr. O. D. King, on whose land it was founded in 1890.

Kinley Mountain, s Macon County between High Holly and the Georgia state line.

Kinnakeet. See Avon.

Kinnakeet Banks, the name commonly given to the middle section of Hatteras Island in e Dare County extending s from Chicamacomico Banks to Hatteras Woods. Also spelled Kennekeet Banks.

Kinnekeet Township. See Kennekeet Township.

Kinsey, community in s Cherokee County on Nottely River. Alt. 1,609.

Kinston, city and county seat, e Lenoir County on Neuse River. Site granted to Robert Atkins in 1729 and came to be known as Atkins Bank. A chapel erected here about 1748, and a tobacco warehouse built about 1757. Inc. 1762 as Kingston in honor of King George III. Renamed Kinston, 1784, after the American Revolution. Name changed to Caswell in honor of Governor Richard Caswell in 1833, but changed back to Kinston the following year. Lenoir County Community College, est. 1966, is here. Alt. 44.

Kinston Township, e central Lenoir County.

Kipland. See Kipling.

Kipling, community in n central Harnett County. Known as Bradley's Store in late nineteenth century. Railroad time table of 1907 lists it as Kipland.

Kirby. See Conway.

Kirby Branch rises in nw Watauga County on the se prong of Fork Ridge and flows approx. 1½ mi. se into Cove Creek.

Kirby Grange, plantation of Christopher Gale, first Chief Justice of N. C., appointed in 1712, stood near Bath, central Beaufort County.

Kirby Knob, on the Jackson-Macon County line. Alt. 4,410.

Kirbys Creek is formed by the junction of Rogers Swamp and Corduroy Swamp in n Northampton County. It flows se and ne into Meherrin River which forms the Northampton-Hertford County line.

Kirby's Gap, nw Caldwell County. Alt. 1,789.

Kirby Township, ne Northampton County.

Kirkendall Creek. See South Prong [of Glady Fork].

Kirkland, community in ne New Hanover County.

Kirkland Creek rises in w Swain County and flows se into Fontana Lake.

Kirkland Creek, formed in s Swain County by the confluence of West Fork and East Fork, and flows ne into Tuckasegee River.

Kirkland Gap, n Graham County between Yellow and Fax creeks through which the Appalachian Trail passes.

Kirklin Creek rises in central Cherokee County and flows nw into Hiwassee River.

Kirkpatrick, former community in central Guilford County, now a part of the city of Greensboro.

Kitchen, community in n central Halifax County.

Kitchen Branch rises in ne Buncombe County near Sourwood Gap and flows sw through Montreat into Flat Creek.

Kitchin Branch rises in n Jackson County and flows se into Scott Creek.

Kit Creek rises in w Wake County and flows nw into Chatham County where it enters Northeast Creek.

Kits Knob, n Buncombe County, nw of Jones Knob in the Elk Mountains.

Kit Swamp, rises in n Craven County and flows sw into Little Swift Creek.

Kitten Creek rises in w Pitt County and flows ne into Otter Creek.

Kittrell, town in sw Vance County between Long Creek and Buffalo Creek. Alt. 372. Inc. 1885 and named for George Kittrell who gave land for a railway station here. An old Confederate cemetery is here. Nearby Kittrell's Springs (which see) is said to have been the first summer resort in the state. Before the incorporation of the town the community was known as Staunton. See also Epping Forest. Kittrell College, est. 1886, is here.

Kittrell's Springs, health resort, social and recreational center in the nineteenth century. Springs are ½ mi. w of the town of Kittrell, sw Vance County.

Kittrell Township, s Vance County.

Kitty Fork, community in n central Sampson County near Great Coharie Creek.

Kitty Hawk, community and summer resort in e Dare County, on the s boundary of the North Banks. Former site of the New Inlet. Settled before 1790. Name probably is a variation of an Indian place name as it appears on maps as early as 1738 as Chickehauk. At nearby Kill Devil Hill in 1903, the Wright Brothers made their first successful airplane flight. Alt. 9.

Kitty Hawk Bay, ne Dare County, at the e end of Albemarle Sound, which see. Bounded on the n by the s extremity of North Banks and on the s by Colington Island.

Kitty Hawk Woods, a real estate development in ne Dare County on Currituck Sound. The 1967 General Assembly passed an act under which, by a vote of the residents, Kitty Hawk Woods may be inc. as a town by a resolution of the county commissioners.

Klansoona. See Terrapin Mountain.

Klesee Creek rises in nw Transylvania County and flows sw into Court House Creek.

Knap of Reeds, former community in sw Granville County dating from the nineteenth century or earlier. The site is now within the Butner area. A Knap of Reeds District in 1790 had 77 heads of families at the time of the first census.

Knap of Reeds Creek rises in w Granville County and flows s into Neuse River on the Granville-Durham County line.

Knee Branch rises in s Hertford County and flows n into Ahoskie Swamp. Probably named from the cypress knees in the area.

Knightdale, town in e Wake County on the head of Poplar Creek. Chartered in 1927 and named for its founder, H. H. Knight. Alt. 318.

Knights Crossroads, community in w Halifax County.

Knights Crossroads, community in e Wake County.

Knobbs Creek rises in e central Pasquotank County and flows se into Pasquotank River at the n limits of Elizabeth City.

Knob Creek rises in n Cleveland County and flows sw into First Broad River.

Knob Creek rises in sw Jackson County and flows e into Norton Creek.

Knob Creek rises in nw Rutherford County and flows sw into Broad River.

Knobcreek, community in n Cleveland County on Knob Creek.

Knob Creek Township, former township in ne Cleveland County, now township number 10.

Knobs Township, nw Yadkin County.

Knotts Island, a peninsula in n Currituck County, approx. 5 by 3½ mi., extends into North Carolina from Princess Anne County, Virginia. Knotts Island Channel on the e connects Currituck Sound with Back Bay (in Virginia); North Landing River on the w rises in Virginia and flows past Knott Island into Currituck Sound. Appears as Knot Isle on the Comberford map, 1657. Probably named for James Knott or a member of his family. Knott held land in s Virginia as early as 1642. See also Mackay Island.

Knotts Island Channel, a waterway between Knotts Island and Currituck Banks, ne Currituck County. The Channel connects Currituck Sound in North Carolina with Back Bay in Virginia.

Knottville, community in e central Wilkes County between Rock and Mulberry creeks.

Knotty Pine Creek. See Buckland Mill Branch.

Kolasko. See Weatherman Bald.

Kona, community in w central Mitchell County near the junction of North Toe and South Toe rivers. The name is said to have been coined by R. M. Lawson, first dispatcher for the railroad, simply because it was a short, easily spelled and understood word.

Konnatoga. See Little Pisgah Mountain.

Koonasoga. See Humpback Mountain.

Koonces Bay on White Oak River, sw Carteret County, between Wire Point and Balls Point. Named for the Koonce family.

Kornegay, community in e Duplin County.

Kototine. See Little River.

Kross Keys, community in s Polk County. Settled about 1900. Named by Greenberry Sanders, first postmaster, because of key-like intersection of roads at this point.

Krunkleton Knob, s Burke County. Alt. 2,600.

Kuhns, community in w Carteret County. Named for William Kuhn, native of Germany and later a resident of the Stella community, who engaged in lumbering along the White Oak River.

Kullaughee Valley. See Cullowhee.

Kure Beach, town in se New Hanover County on the Atlantic Ocean. Inc. 1947. Named for the Kure family which first came here in 1867. Alt. 5.

Kurfees. See Jericho.

Ku-wa-hi. See Clingmans Dome.

Kuykendall Branch rises in n Buncombe County near the Madison County line and flows sw into French Broad River.

Kuykendall Creek rises in w central Transylvania County and flows se and sw into Catheys Creek.

Kyle, community in nw Macon County on Whiteoak Creek.

Kyles Creek rises in n Henderson County and flows se into Clear Creek.

L

Laboratory, community in s central Lincoln County. Named for Confederate drug manufactory operated under the direction of Dr. A. S. Piggott. A part of the original laboratory still stands.

Lackey, community in e Alexander County.

Lackey Mountain, e Alexander County. Alt. 1,430.

Lacky Crossroads, community in central Cleveland County e of Lawndale.

Lacys Creek rises in nw Chatham County and flows ne into Rocky River.

Ladd Branch rises in central Cherokee County and flows w into Parsons Branch.

Ladonia, community in nw Surry County on Fisher River.

LaGrange, town in nw Lenoir County. Known as Rantersville and Moseley Hall prior to 1869 when it was inc. as LaGrange after Lafayette's estate near Paris. Moseley Hall had been the plantation name given by Thomas Moseley of Vir-

ginia who settled here before the Revolution. William Dunn Moseley (1795-1863), first governor of the state of Florida, was born here. Produces trailers, tobacco trucks, and cotton gins. Alt. 113. See also Moseley County.

The Lagoon, s Buncombe County, separated from the French Broad River by a narrow strip of land s of city of Asheville near the Biltmore Estate.

Lake Adger in n central Polk County on Green River. Built by Blue Ridge Power Company in 1925, and known as Turners Lake for nearby Turners Shoals. Duke Power Company bought the hydroelectric plant and water rights in 1927 and later renamed the lake, possibly for John B. Adger who was active in power development on Broad River in South Carolina. Covers 438 acres with a max. depth of 86 ft. Used to generate hydroelectric power.

Lake Ashnoca, central Buncombe County on Ragsdale Creek. The property of the Asheville School for Boys, it covers 27 acres.

Lake Bay, community in se Moore County on Carrolls Branch. Formerly known as Hog Island.

Lake Benson in s Wake County on Swift Creek. Formed in 1925 and named Rands Mill Pond for owners. Later renamed for B. B. Benson, former Raleigh city councilman. Covers 490 acres and has maximum depth of 19 ft. Enlarged in 1951. Used as reservoir and fishing.

Lake Brandt, an artificial lake in central Guilford County on Reedy Fork Creek. Maximum depth 25 ft. 400 acres. Formed in 1920 and named for former Greensboro mayor Leon J. Brandt (1874-1920) Municipal water supply for Greensboro and owned by the city.

Lake Burlington, central Alamance County on Stony Creek. Formed 1910; enlarged 1961. Source of water for the city of Burlington. Covers 750 acres; 7½ mi. long with a 50 mi. shoreline. Fishing, boating, Known earlier as Stony Creek Lake.

Lake Charles on Crassy Creek, se Buncombe County.

Lake Cheoah, nw Graham and sw Swain counties. Formed 1928 by Aluminum Company of America in damming Little Tennessee River. Covers 648 acres. Max. depth 200 ft. Used for power, swimming, and boating. Alt. 1,276.

Lake Chub. See Loch Lily.

Lake Comfort, community on the s shore of Lake Mattamuskeet in central Hyde County.

Lake Craig, on Swannanoa River in central Buncombe County near the e boundary of Asheville. The Asheville Recreation Park is located near the dam. Named for Governor Locke Craig (1860-1925), whose home was nearby. The lake covers approx. 55 acres. Was a source of water for the city of Asheville prior to about 1903.

Lake Creek flows se from Black Lake into South River in e Bladen County.

Lake Creek Township in e Bladen County.

Lake Devin, central Granville County on Hachers Run, was formed in 1954 as a source of water for the town of Oxford. Covers 100 acres. Max. depth 40 ft. Named for former Chief Justice of the North Carolina Supreme Court, W. A. Devin, a resident of Oxford.

Lake Drain flows e from Singletary Lake in e Bladen County into Colly Creek.

Lake Eden, on a tributary of North Fork [Swannanoa River], e Buncombe County at the former site of Black Mountain College.

Lake Emory, on Little Tennessee River in central Macon County. Covers 200 acres. Maximum depth 20 feet. Formed 1925. Used by Nantahala Power & Light Company to generate electricity.

Lakefield, community in e Hoke County.

Lake Fisher, ne Cabarrus County. Formed in 1946 by a dam on Cold Water Creek. Covers 277 acres. Max. depth 30 ft. Named for L. A. Fisher, superintendent of Concord water and light department. Used for fishing and as a source of water for the city of Concord.

Lake Franklin, e Anson County, se of Lilesville. Covers approx. 5 acres. max. depth 25 ft. Formed 1908 when gravel was removed from the site. Named for the owner of the property from which the gravel was dug.

Lake Gresham in n central Wake County on Perry Creek. Formed in 1939. Covers 100 acres and has maximum depth of 30 ft. Used for recreation.

Lake Hickory on Catawba River. Alexander and Caldwell counties on the n, Burke and Catawba on the s. Formed by a dam constructed in 1928 by Duke Power Co. Covers 4,110 acres. Source of hydroelectric power; fishing, boating, swimming. Dam at the site of former Oxford Ford across the river; named for Samuel Oxford, pioneer settler who opened the ford. Alt. 829. Lake formerly known as Oxford Lake or Oxford Reservoir.

Lake Hunt, s Rockingham County. Covers approx. 175 acres. Max. depth 7 ft. Reidsville municipal recreation center is here. Named for the late George Hunt, mayor of Reidsville.

Lake James, on Catawba River, Burke and McDowell counties. Formed when Bridgewater Dam was built in 1916-1923, and formerly called Bridgewater Reservoir. Fed by North Fork [Catawba River], Linville River, and numerous smaller tributaries in addition to Catawba River. Owned by Duke Power Co. and named for James B. Duke (1856-1925). Covers 6,510 acres with a shoreline of 150 mi. Used for recreation and for generation of hydroelectric power.

Lake Johnson in s central Wake County on Walnut Creek. Covers 160 acres and has maximum depth of 18 ft. Owned by city of Raleigh. Used for fishing, boating and municipal water supply.

Lake Juanita. See Lake Louise.

Lake Junaluska, central Haywood County on Richland Creek. Formerly covered 250 acres, but silt has filled it until it is much smaller. Named for the Cherokee Indian chief, Junaluska (ca. 1758-1858). The lake covers the site of the former community of Tuscola which had a post office in the 1870's and 1880's.

Lake Junaluska, community in central Haywood County on the lake. Methodist assembly grounds and resort area. The assembly was inc. in 1909 and the community site selected soon afterwards. Alt. 2,584.

Lake Kawana, se Avery County on Linville River. Two acres in area; max. deptht 10 ft. Owned by Linville Resort and used for fishing, boating, swimming and sometimes in winter for ice skating. Also known as Linville Lake.

Lake Kelly, water supply reservoir in se Henderson Connty for town of Saluda. Located at the head of Kelly Creek.

Lake Kenilworth, central Buncombe County in the city of Asheville. Approx. ½ mi. long.

Lake Landing, community in e Hyde County on the se shore of Lake Mattamuskeet. The courthouse was here from about 1820 until 1836.

Lake Landing Township, e Hyde County.

Lake Lanier in s Polk County, N. C., and ne Greenville County, S. C., formed about 1916-18. Covers 127 acres with a max. depth of 70 ft. Named for poet Sidney Lanier (1842-81) who spent his last years in Polk County. Water rights belong to Southern Mercerizing Company. Used for recreation and for commercial purposes.

Lake Lee. See Lake Monroe.

Lake Logan, s Haywood County, on West Fork Pigeon River. Approx. 1½ mi. long and ¼ mi. wide. A water reservoir for Champion Paper and Fiber Company in Canton. Alt. 2,909.

Lake Louise, a 35-acre lake formed in 1927 in se Alleghany County, on the head-waters of Laurel Branch. It is owned by Roaring Gap, Inc., and open to stock holders and guests only for fishing, swimming, and boating.

Lake Louise, n Buncombe County in the town of Weaverville. Covers 6 acres; max. depth 50 ft. Fed by five underwater springs. Built before 1907 by Charles R. Moore and named Lake Juanita for Juanita Peace, a young girl who lived in the Moore home. At Moore's death the property was given to Weaver College and later to the town of Weaverville, when the name was changed to Lake Louise in honor of Mrs. Moore, the donor.

Lake Lure, w Rutherford County, on Broad River. Formed in 1928 as a part of a resort development; the dam is 104 ft. high. The lake covers 1,500 acres with a shore line of 27 miles. Used for recreation.

Lake Lure, town in w Rutherford County on the lake of the same name. Est. 1925; inc. 1927. Alt. 1,050. The town has an immense corporate limit situating it on Buffalo Creek, Broad River, and Pool Creek. The corporate limits are indefinite, but Chimney Rock apparently is included within the town.

Lake Mattamuskeet, central Hyde County, a natural lake covering approx. 30,000 acres. Alt. 3 ft. below sea level. Max. depth 5 ft. Discovered 1585 by Grenville's exploring party. Appears as Paquippe on the White map, 1585, for an Indian word meaning shallow (or dry) lake; as Paquike Lake on the Comberford map, 1657; and as Mattamuskeet Lake on the Moseley map, 1733. Present name from an Indian word Mata-mackya-t-wi, "it is a moving swamp" (or "quaky bog"). As early as 1789 efforts were made to drain the lake for farming purposes, and the most recent efforts at drainage came to an end in 1934. Now a wildlife refuge. See also Aramuskeet; Aromuskek Marshes; New Holland.

Lake Michael, w Orange County. Formed in 1953 as a municipal water supply for the town of Mebane. Covers 51 acres; max. depth 20 ft. Named for Arthur Michael, engineer for the town of Mebane at the time the lake was formed.

Lake Michie (Mick-e), reservoir for the city of Durham, about 4 mi. long, on Flat River, ne Durham County.

Lake Mirl, e central Wake County on Hodges Creek. Formed in 1940. Covers 5 acres with a max. depth of 10 ft. Open to the public for recreation.

Lake Monroe, central Union County s of Monroe. It is at the junction of Richardson and Little Richardson creeks. Formed in 1925 and known first as Lake Lee for the owners. Later acquired by city of

Monroe as a municipal water source. Covers 144 acres with a max. depth of 35 ft.

Lake Norman, on the Catawba River in Catawba, Iredell, Mecklenburg and Lincoln counties. Formed by the dam at Cowan's Ford, completed 1963. Covers 32,510 acres. Shore line approx. 520 mi. Hydroelectric plant of Duke Power Co. Named for Norman A. Cocke, retired president of the company. Alt. 760 *See* Duke Power Park.

Lake Palcoy, in central Haywood Co. near Lake Junaluska.

Lake Phelps, natural fresh water lake in e Washington County and w Tyrrell County, the bed of which is thought to have been formed by the impact of a meteor. The lake surface covers 16,600 acres, with a max. depth of 12 ft.; mean alt. 10 ft. Owned by the State of N. C. and included in the Pettigrew State Park *(which see).* Said to have been named for Josiah Phelps, one of a group of explorers who discovered it in 1775. Known for a while as Scuppernong Lake and appears as such on the Collet map, 1770. Used for fishing, swimming, and boating.

Lake Point, point of land on the sw tip of Durant Island, central Dare County.

Lake Raleigh, in central Wake County on Walnut Creek. Formed in 1900. Covers 72 acres and has maximum depth of 25 ft. Used as municipal water supply.

Lake Refuge. *See* Camp Brier Lake.

Lakers Creek. *See* Raccoon Creek.

Lake Run flows s from Little Singletary Lake, ne Bladen County, into Ellis Creek.

Lake Santeetlah. *See* Santeetlah Lake.

Lake Sapphire, central Transylvania County on Allison Creek approx. 1½ mi. n of town of Brevard. Covers 3 acres with a max. depth of 30 ft. Used for recreation. *See also* Sapphire Lake.

Lake Scuppernong. *See* Lake Phelps.

Lake Sequoyah, se Macon County at the head of Cullasaja River. Formed about 1920. Covers approx. 150 acres with a max. depth of 40 ft. Owned by the town of Highlands and used as a source of power and for swimming, fishing, boating, and skating. Named for Sequoyah (1770?-1843), Indian teacher.

Lakes Pocosin, a mucky slough in the sw corner of Craven County and extending into nw Carteret and e Jones counties. Ellis Lake, Great Lake, Little Lake, and Long Lake in Craven County, and Catfish Lake in Jones and Craven counties are located in the pocosin.

Lake Summit, s Henderson County on Green River. Formed in 1920 as a source of power. Covers 350 acres with a max. depth of 100 ft. A textile mill is now operated here and there are many summer homes along the shores of the lake.

Lake Susan, ne Buncombe County, formed by a dam on Flat Creek in Montreat.

Lake Tabor, s Columbus County, formed by a dam on Grissett Swamp. Covers 8 acres with a max. depth of 15 ft. Known as Spiveys Pond in the early twentieth century when it was used to provide waterpower to operate a grist mill. The dam broke in 1950. The site was purchased by the Tabor City Recreation Department, the dam rebuilt, and the name changed in 1955.

Lake Tahoma, w McDowell County on Buck Creek and Little Buck Creek. Formed about 1927 by J. Q. Gilkey of Marion. The name, an Indian word believed to mean "mountain lake of the gods," was suggested by Mary Hudgins of Marion. Covers approx. 500 acres; max. depth 30 to 40 ft. Owned by Lake Tahoma, Inc., a land-holding corporation.

Lake Thorpe, an irregular-shaped reservoir in w Jackson County formed in 1941 by a dam on the West Fork of Tuckasegee River. Originally known as Glenville Lake for the nearby community; renamed in 1951 for J.E.S. Thorpe, former president of Nantahala Power and Light Company. Also known for a time as Thorpe Reservoir. Covers 1,462 acres with a maximum depth of 135 ft. Used to generate hydroelectric power and for recreation. Alt. 3,492.

Lake Tillery on Pee Dee River in Montgomery and Stanly counties. Formed in 1928. Covers 5,260 acres with a shore line of 104 mi. and a max. depth of 89 ft. Owned by Carolina Power and Light Company and used for generating hydroelectric power, boating, swimming, and fishing. Originally named Norwood Lake for nearby town of Norwood. Renamed for former president of the company, Paul A. Tillery (1880-1933).

Lake Tomahawk, se Buncombe County on Tomahawk Branch.

Lake Toxaway, resort community in w Transylvania County on Toxaway River. The original Toxaway Inn, built in 1901, became a popular resort for the wealthy.

The lake, formed in 1903, covered 540 acres with a shoreline of 15 mi. and a max depth of 50 feet. The dam was destroyed in a storm in 1916 but was rebuilt in 1961. The lake now covers 900 acres, the largest privately owned lake in w North Carolina, and is surrounded by homes. There is also a golf course and an airport in the community. The name is derived from the Cherokee word *Tortzoo-whah*, "redbird."

Lake Trojan, s central Wake County on a tributary of Swift Creek. Formed about 1900 and called Yates Mill Pond for the owner of the mill. Name changed in the 1950's. Covers 20 acres with a max. depth of 15 ft. Owned by North Carolina Equipment Company. Used as a source of power, for fishing and swimming. Not open to the public.

Lake View, pond on Flatrock Creek in n Franklin County. Formed 1890. Known as Hunts Pond until 1931. Covers 10 acres; max. depth 12 ft.

Lakeview, community in e Moore County on Crystal Lake. Alt. 300.

Lake Waccamaw, a natural lake in ne Columbus County, 5 mi. long, 3 mi. wide. Surrounding area drains into the lake; appears on Moseley map, 1733. Named for local tribe of Indians.

Lake Waccamaw, town in n Columbus County on the n shore of Lake Waccamaw. Known as Flemington from as early as 1853 until about 1885 when the present name came into use. Inc. 1911. Alt. 62.

Lake Wheeler, s Wake County on Swift Creek. Formed in 1957. Covers 540 acres with a max. depth of 30 ft. Named for Fred B. Wheeler, former mayor of Raleigh. Used as a recreation area and as a source of water for the city of Raleigh.

Lake William, on Little Rockfish Creek due w of city of Fayetteville in w Cumberland County near county line. Approx. ¾ mi. long.

Lake Witheranna. See Bull Hill Mill Pond.

Lake Wood, lake approx. 1 mi. long on Cross Creek, nw Cumberland County. Covers approx. 20 acres. Max. depth, 20 ft. Fishing, swimming.

Lakewood. See Tuxedo.

Lake Worth, small community on the mainland of Dare County on the w shore of Stumpy Point Bay.

Lake Wylie on the Catawba River in Gaston and Mecklenburg counties is formed by a dam constructed in 1924-1926 in South Carolina. Most of the lake, which covers 12,455 acres with a shore line of 325 mi., is in South Carolina. Known as Catawba Lake until 1960 when it was renamed Lake Wylie for Dr. Walker Gill Wylie (1848-1923), friend and associate of James B. Duke. Site of Duke Power Co. hydroelectric plant.

Lakey Creek rises in n Macon County and flows sw into Little Tennessee River.

Lakey Gap, se Buncombe County in Blue Ridge Mountains. Alt. 3,028.

Lakey Knob, se Buncombe County between Lakey Gap and High Top.

Lamance Creek rises in w central Transylvania County approx. 2 mi. s of the community of Balsam Grove and flows se into North Fork French Broad River.

Lamance Creek Falls on Lamance Creek in w central Transylvania County. Falls are 18 ft. high. Sometimes known as Lemon Creek Falls.

Lamb Branch rises in e Cherokee County and flows sw into Peachtree Creek.

Lamb Creek rises in central Transylvania County s of Shutin Ridge and flows e and then s into Allison Creek on w edge of community of Pisgah Forest.

Lambert, community in w Stanly County. Named for local family.

Lambert Branch rises in e Swain County and flows se into Oconaluftee River.

Lambert Cove, w Macon County on a tributary of Nantahala River.

Lambert Fork Creek rises in nw Alexander County and flows se into Lower Little River. Named for Alexander Lambert, early Scottish settler.

Lambert Point, peninsula extending from n Pamlico County into Bay River.

Lambeth. See Monticello.

Lamb Knob, w Madison County between East Fork Shut-in Creek and Stony Spur.

Lamb Mountain, e Henderson County between Lewis Creek and Mills Gap.

Lamb Mountain, s Macon County between Buck Creek and Cullasaja River. Alt. approx. 4,600.

Lambo Creek rises in central Transylvania County and flows s into French Broad River.

Lambsburg, community in n Surry County. Also known as Piper Gap.

Lambs Corner, community in w Camden County, named for local family.

Lamm's, community in n Wilson County s of Bloomery Swamp. Post office, 1895-1906. Named for Thomas Ruffin Lamm.

Lamm's Crossroads, community in w Wilson County s of Contentnea Creek. Named for Haywood Lamm.

Lamms Mill Pond on Moccasin Creek on the Johnston-Nash County line. Approx. ½ mi. long. A mill last operated here about 1930.

Lancaster, commumnity in w Edgecombe County.

Lancaster Crossroads, community in w Nash County, between Back Swamp and Peach-tree Creek.

Lancaster Store, community in e Wayne County between The Slough and West Bear Creek.

Lance Creek rises in sw Watauga County, flows s to Camp Yonahlosee, then flows in a nw arc into Watauga River. About 4 mi. long.

Lance Mountain, s Buncombe County e of Reynolds Gap.

Landgrave Smith's Island. See Smith Island.

Landing Creek. See Gum Neck Creek.

Landing Ridge, a ridge of higher ground in Big Pocosin, sw Gates County.

Landis, town in sw Rowan County. Inc. 1901. Named for Judge Kenesaw Mountain Landis (1866-1944), who imposed a 29-million dollar fine on Standard Oil Company at the time the community was searching for a name. Landis Northeast is a community on the outskirts of the town.

Land of Eden, former 20,000-acre estate of William Byrd (1674-1744) along the Dan River, n Rockingham County, which he purchased in 1733. Named because of its Garden of Eden qualities. An additional 6,000 acres were granted to Byrd's son in 1742. Purchased from the younger Byrd by the Farley family in 1755 and by 1769 it had been divided into farms and plantations. The town of Eden, formed in 1967 by the merger of Leaksville, Spray, and Draper, took its name from Byrd's estate.

Landrum Creek rises in central Chatham County and flows se into Rocky River.

Lands Creek rises in n central Swain County and flows sw into Tuckasegee River.

Lane Pinnacle, n Buncombe County at the e end of Bull Mountain. Alt. 5,277. Named for the owner, Charles Lane, who, in the first quarter of the nineteenth century, operated an iron forge on Reems Creek. He obtained some of his ore from this mountain.

Lane River. See Alligator River.

Lanesboro, commmunity in w Anson County on Lanes Creek. A post office existed here as early as 1828 and as recently as 1882. Now sometimes known as Old Lanesboro.

Lanesboro Township, w central Anson County.

Lane's Creek, community in se Union County.

Lanes Creek rises in s Union County and flows e and ne into w Anson County and ne into Rocky River.

Lanes Creek Township, se Union County.

Lane's Ferry, community in s central Pender County on Northeast Cape Fear River. The river is now bridged, but a ferry was operated here for most of the nineteenth century and into the twentieth. Named for Levin Lane, large landowner of the vicinity. See also Rocky Point.

Lanes Store, community in n Rutherford County on Cane Creek.

Lane Swamp rises in ne Nash County and flows se into Swift Creek.

Langford Branch rises in w Yancey County and flows nw into Cane River.

Langs Mill Run rises in e Wilson and s Edgecombe counties and flows se into Pitt County where it enters Black Swamp.

Langston, community in e central Wayne County, e of Stony Creek. Named for Langston family which received land grants in this area as early as 1758.

Lanier Crossroads, community in se Duplin County.

Laniers Creek rises in w Randolph County and flows e into Uwharrie River.

Lanier Swamp rises in e Martin County and flows nw into Gardners Creek.

Lankford Mountain, n Buncombe County w of Bill Cole Mountain.

Lanning Branch rises near Lanning Ridge in nw Transylvania County and flows sw into Right Fork Davidson River.

Lanning Ridge in nw Transylvania County extends south from Seniard Mountain.

Lansing, town in nw Ashe County. Inc. 1928. Produces electronics.

Lanvale, community ne Brunswick County.

Lapland. See Marshall.

Largo, former plantation in sw Warren County. The plantation house was built in 1790 by Hugh Johnson, and subsequently sold to Peter R. Davis, an early merchant of Warrenton (fl.1800-1841).

Lark Knob, in ne Macon County between Beasley Creek and Mica City Creek.

Larler Creek. See Chadwick Creek.

Larry Brush Branch rises in nw Macon County and flows se into Cold Spring Creek.

Lash. *See* Walnut Cove.

Lashleys Island. *See* Baker Island.

Lasker, town in central Northampton County. Inc. 1895; named for Hezekiah Lasker, railroad conductor. Earlier known as Alto.

Lassiter, community in ne Wake County. Settled 1875. Named for its founder, C. J. Lassiter. Alt. 300.

Lassiter Branch rises in w Gates County and flows nw into Somerton Creek.

Lassiter Mill Lake, artificial lake in sw Forsyth County on Blanket Creek, formed in 1935. Built for a mill dam by Lassiter family. Covers 50 acres and has max. depth of 20 ft. Not open to the public.

Lassiters Creek rises in n Nash County and flows s into Stony Creek.

Lassiters Crossroad, community in central Northampton County.

Lassiters Mill Pond on Crabtree Creek in central Wake County within nw city limits of Raleigh. Present dam built in 1907-08 by Miss Mary Lassiter, and pond named for her. A mill built on this site in 1778 by Issac Hunter burned about 1823.

Lassiters Mills, community and former post office, se Randolph County on Uwharrie River. Mill built in 1845 on the w side of the river was moved to the e side in 1925.

Latham, community in nw Beaufort County.

Latham Creek rises in nw Beaufort County and flows se into Old Ford Swamp.

Lattimore, town in w Cleveland County. Settled in 1880 and a post office named Delight est. here in 1885. Inc. 1899 as Lattimore, named for Audley M. Lattimore, Confederate veteran and first postmaster. Alt. 945.

Lauada, community in s Swain County on Pole Bridge Branch.

Laudermilk Bend, a bend in Nottely River, s Cherokee County, above Cobb Bluff.

Laughlins Creek rises in s Caswell County and flows se into Alamance County where it enters Buttermilk Creek.

Laughter Cove, se Buncombe County between Spring and Garren Mountains. Named for a family of notorious moonshiners that lived in the cove in the first half of the twentieth century.

Laughton Point extends from the mainland

of central Carteret County into Newport River.

The Launch, a narrow inlet between Tull Bay and the mouth of North Landing River in ne Currituck County. Appears on the Collet map, 1770. Site of shipbuilding operations from colonial times until the present, hence the name.

Laure Branch rises in s Clay County and flows n into Shooting Creek.

Laurel, community in n Franklin County.

Laurel, community in n Madison County on Big Laurel Creek.

Laurel Bottoms, valley in se Avery County along the Linville River, n of the town of Linville.

Laurel Branch rises in se Alleghany County and flows sw then ne into Brush Creek.

Laurel Branch rises in w Avery County and flows sw into Roaring Creek.

Laurel Branch rises in se Buncombe County near Flat Top Mountain and flows s into Cane Creek.

Laurel Branch rises in se Buncombe County and flows sw into Broad River.

Laurel Branch rises in ne Buncombe County in the Great Craggy Mountains and flows se into North Fork [Swannanoa River].

Laurel Branch rises in s Buncombe County and flows se into Bent Creek.

Laurel Branch rises in s Cherokee County and flows nw into Nottely River.

Laurel Branch rises in ne Cherokee County on Brushy Head Mountain and flows nw into Burnt Branch.

Laurel Branch rises in n Haywood County on e slopes of Cowpen Top and flows ne into Waterville Lake.

Laurel Branch rises in n Haywood County on s slopes of Ed Top and flows sw into se part of Waterville Lake.

Laurel Branch rises in n central Haywood County s of Chestnut Flat Ridge and flows e to join Pigeon River opposite Solray Gap.

Laurel Branch rises in s Haywood County e of Cold Spring Knob and flows e into West Fork Pigeon River 1½ mi. s of Lake Logan dam.

Laurel Branch rises in n Henderson County and flows se into Bold Branch.

Laurel Branch rises in w Jackson County and flows n into Tuckasegee River.

Laurel Branch rises in w Macon County and flows nw into Rowlin Creek.

Laurel Branch rises in s Macon County and flows ne into Cullasaja River.

Laurel Branch rises in w Macon County and flows se into Nantahala Lake.

Laurel Branch rises in e Mitchell County and flows s into Cane Creek.

Laurel Branch rises in n Swain County and flows sw then e into Noland Creek.

Laurel Branch rises in nw Swain County and flows se into Tub-Mill Creek.

Laurel Branch rises in w central Swain County and flows ne into Tuckasegee River.

Laurel Branch rises in w Swain County and flows w into Fontanna Lake near the confluence of Hazel Creek.

Laurel Branch rises in s Transylvania County and flows sw into East Fork French Broad River.

Laurel Branch rises in w Transylvania County and flows ne into West Fork French Broad River.

Laurel Branch rises in w Transylvania County and flows w into North Fork French Broad River.

Laurel Branch rises in n Watauga County and flows se into Cove Creek.

Laurel Branch rises in s Watauga County and flows nw into Sawpit Branch.

Laurel Branch rises in s central Yancey County and flows w into Cane River.

Laurel Branch rises in s Yancey County and flows ne into South Toe River.

Laurel Branch rises in sw Yancey County and flows e into Cane River.

Laurel Brook rises in n Transylvania County and flows se into South Fork Mills River.

Laurel Creek rises in nw Ashe County and flows se into North Fork New River.

Laurel Creek rises in se Burke County and flows se parallel to Prospect Ridge into Henry Fork.

Laurel Creek rises in central Cherokee County near Fain Mountain and flows sw into Hiwassee River.

Laurel Creek rises in w Cherokee County and flows ne into Apalachia Lake.

Laurel Creek rises in se Durham County and flows ne into Lick Creek.

Laurel Creek rises in n Haywood County and flows nw into Big Creek.

Laurel Creek rises in e Macon County and flows s into Ellijay Creek.

Laurel Creek rises in ne Mitchell County and flows s into Little Rock Creek.

Laurel Creek rises in e Transylvania County and flows ne into Cascade Lake (Little River).

Laurel Creek rises in ne Transylvania County and flows se into Henderson County where it enters South Fork.

Laurel Creek rises in sw Transylvania County and flows s into Whitewater River.

Laurel Creek rises in nw Wake County near Little Laurel Creek and flows ne into Big Lick Creek.

Laurel Creek rises in s Watauga County and flows n into Boone Fork.

Laurel Creek rises in w Watauga County and flows ne into Watauga River.

Laurel Creek Falls in w Watauga County on Laurel Creek just before its confluence with Watauga River.

Laurel Creek Township, w Watauga County.

Laurel Fork rises in central Buncombe County and flows n into Reems Creek.

Laurel Fork rises in s Watauga County and flows ne and se into Elk Creek.

Laurel Fork Creek rises in sw Alleghany and se Ashe counties and flows n to join Meadow Fork Creek in forming Mulberry Creek.

Laurel Fork Creek rises in s Henderson County and flows ne into Green River.

Laurel Fork [Davidson River] rises in w Transylvania County and flows e into Davidson River.

Laurel Gap, in Locust Ridge, ne Buncombe County.

Laurel Gap, on the Haywood-Swain County line, Great Smoky Mountains National Park on Balsam Mountain between Balsam High Top and Balsam Corner, near lat. 35° 39' 55" N., long. 83° 11' 15" W. Alt. approx. 5,400.

Laurel Gap, between Rocky Knob and Glade Ridge in e Haywood Co.

Laurel Gap, on the Jackson-Macon County line.

Laurel Gap, in n Transylvania County between Rich Mountain and Poundingstone Mountain.

Laurel Gap Branch rises in ne Swain County and flows sw into Balsam Corner Creek.

Laurel Hill, community in sw Buncombe County near Beaverdam.

Laurel Hill, community in nw Lincoln County.

Laurel Hill, community in w Scotland County. Named for Presbyterian Church est. here 1793, and in turn named for laurel growing on the elevated site. A post office est. here as early as 1822. Alt. 250.

Laurel Hills, rugged terrain s of Chapel Hill, se Orange County.

Laurel Hill Township, w central Scotland County.

Laurel Knob, mountain between Double Knob Mountain and Cowrock Mountain in s Jackson County. Alt. approx. 4,300.

Laurel Knob, s Jackson County between Hurricane Creek and Hurricane Lake. Alt. 4,014.

Laurel Lake, se Buncombe County near Black Mountain.

Laurel Mountain extends se in an arc from Sassafras Gap to Yellow Gap in nw Henderson County.

Laurel Mountain, n Transylvania County between Cantrell Creek and Laurel Gap.

Laurel Mountain, se Yancey County near the head of Roaring Fork.

Laurel Park, town in central Henderson County adjoining Hendersonville on the latter's sw line. Inc. 1925.

Laurel Patch Bald, alt. 5,560-5,580, on Jackson-Haywood County line.

Laurel Point, extends from w Dare County n of Mill Tail Creek, into Alligator River.

Laurel Point, extends from ne Washington County into Albemarle Sound.

Laurel Ridge, n Buncombe County between Laurel Fork and Sugarcamp Fork.

Laurel Ridge, at the se end of Laurel Mountain in nw Henderson County.

Laurel Ridge on the Madison-Yancey County line n of Big Laurel Creek.

Laurel Ridge, w Mitchell County between Bird Creek and Pate Creek.

Laurel Ridge, in ne Mitchell County between Laurel Creek and Holder Creek.

Laurel Ridge, s Yancey County between Elk Fork and Cane River.

Laurel River rises in central Carteret County and flows e into Merrimon River.

Laurel Springs, community in sw Alleghany County. Settled about 1859 and named for a spring flowing from laurel-covered rocks. Alt. 2,822.

Laurel Spur on the Watauga-Wilkes County line e of Stony Fork Creek.

Laurelton, community in n Madison County on Foster Creek.

Laurel Top, peak on Graham County, N. C.-Monroe County, Tenn., line. Alt. approx. 5,325.

Laurel Top, peak on Swain County, N. C.-Sevier County, Tenn., line in Great Smoky Mountains National Park near the head of Gulf Prong. Alt. 5,900-5,950.

Laurel Township, w central Ashe County.

Laurenceville. See Lawrenceville.

Laurinburg, city and county seat, s Scotland County. Appears on maps as early as 1865. Inc. 1877 as Laurenburg; charter amended 1883 and name spelled Laurinburg. Named for McLaurin family, early Scottish settlers. Alt. 227. St. Andrews Presbyterian College, est. 1961, is located here.

Lawndale, town in central Cleveland County on First Broad River. Alt. 843. Settled in 1870, inc. 1903. Named for spreading green lawns of Major H. F. Schenck, owner of the local mills est. in 1888 and of the local power company.

Lawrence, town in ne Edgecombe County. Known as Killquick as early as 1837, the name by which it was chartered in 1883. Laid off in an area ½ mi. square from Richard H. Gatlin's "big new store." Name changed to Hickory Hill in 1885 and to Lawrence in 1889. Original Killquick charter repealed in 1893; chartered as Lawrence in 1901, but long inactive in municipal affairs.

Lawrence Run rises in w Pitt County and flows nw into Tyson Creek.

Lawrenceville, former town in w Montgomery County on Pee Dee River. Authorized to be laid out as the county seat, 1815; named Laurenceville, 1816. Post office name as early as 1822 was Lawrenceville. After Stanly County was formed from Montgomery in 1841, Lawrenceville was no longer in the center of the county and was soon replaced as the county seat by Troy. By 1860 it was no longer being shown on maps of the state. The site is now abandoned.

Laws, community in n Orange and s Person counties. Formerly known as Laws Store.

Lawson Creek rises in central Craven County and flows ne into Trent River.

Lawson Gant Lot, bald spot on Swain County, N. C.-Sevier County, Tenn., line near lat. 35° 32′ 45″ N., long. 83° 47′ 38″ W.

Lawson Gant Lot Branch rises in nw Swain County in Great Smoky Mountains National Park and flows se into Tub-Mill Creek.

Lawsonville, community in e Rockingham County between Lick Fork and Jones creeks. Named for Bobbie Lawson, early resident and subject of popular local legend. Lawson's Store post office was here as early as 1830. Site of several early tobacco factories and a carriage and wagon factory.

Lawsonville, community in n Stokes County. Alt. 1,179.

Laws Store. *See* Laws.

Lawyers Springs, w Anson County on a tributary of Brown Creek. So named because lawyers on the way to court used to stop here. Local tradition says a party of lawyers, spending the night here, froze to death on a snowy winter night.

Layn Flu. *See* Alligator River.

Laytown, community in ne Caldwell County. Named for Thomas Lay, eighteenth-century settler.

Laytown Creek rises in n Caldwell County and flows se into Yadkin River. Originally called Linville's Mill Creek.

Laxon, community in e Watauga County.

Laxon Creek rises in e Watauga County and flows nw into South Fork New River.

Leaches Island. *See* Hog Island.

Lead, community in s Henderson County on Green River.

Leading Ridge, n Mitchell County between Shepherd Knob and Big Rock Creek.

Lead Mine Ridge, w Madison County between Doe Branch and Rocky Branch.

Leaflet, community in w Harnett County near Upper Little River.

Leak Creek rises in n Davidson County and flows nw into s Forsyth County where it enters South Fork.

Leaksville, former town in n Rockingham County on Dan and Smith rivers. Alt. 700. Inc. 1874. Named for John Leak who owned a plantation here before 1797. A post office est. here in 1817. In 1793 the General Assembly directed that a town to be named Danville be laid out at this site as a tobacco inspection station; in 1797 commissioners were appointed "to build and improve the Town of Leaksville in accordance with the plan drawn up by Abraham Philips.' Phillips [*sic*] had been a member of the commission appointed in 1793 to lay out the town of Danville. In 1967 Leaksville was merged with Draper and Spray, *which see,* to form the town of Eden, *which see.*

Leaksville Township, n Rockingham County.

Leaman, community in n Moore County on Bear Creek.

Leander, community in nw Watauga County on Beaverdam Creek.

Leaper's Creek. *See* Leepers Creek.

Leasburg, town in e Caswell County. Inc. 1788 but long inactive in municipal affairs. Named for William and James Lea who owned part of the original site. Location of Caswell County courthouse from 1777 until 1791 when it was moved to the center of the county after Person County was formed from Caswell. Alt. 750.

Leasburg Township, e central Caswell County.

Leatherman, community on Shepherd Creek in n Macon County.

Leatherman Gap, on Macon-Swain County line between Leatherman Knob and Raven Mountain. Alt. 4,300.

Leatherman Knob, on Macon-Swain County line between Leatherman Gap and Shepherd Bald.

Leatherman Mountain, on the Macon-Swain County line.

Leathermans Fork rises in w Mitchell County and flows sw into Right Fork [Pigeonroost Creek].

Leatherwood Branch rises in w Clay County and flows se into Fires Creek.

Leatherwood Branch rises in n Haywood Co. and flows e into Big Creek.

Leatherwood Cove, central Haywood Co. just n of Lake Junaluska.

Leatherwood Mountain, ne Cherokee County s of Andrews.

Leatherwood Top, alt. 5,000-5,020, in w Haywood Co. between Walker Bald and Tritt Knob.

Leaventhorps View. *See* Shumont Mountain.

Lebanon Township, central Durham County.

Ledbetter, community in central Richmond County. Named for the family which est. a mill on Hitchcock Creek here about 1895.

Ledbetter Branch rises in ne Macon County on the slope of Tellico Ridge and flows n into Swain County where it enters Little Tennessee River.

Ledbetter Creek rises in sw Swain County on Cheoah Bald in Nantahala National Forest and flows s into Nantahala River.

Ledbetter Lake, central Richmond County on Hitchcock Creek at the community of Ledbetter (*which see*). Covers 800 acres.

Ledford Branch rises in s Cherokee County and flows nw into Nottely River.

Ledford Branch rises in sw Clay County and flows sw, nw, and sw again into Brasstown Creek.

Ledford Branch rises in e Macon County and flows se into Walnut Creek.

Ledford Creek rises in s Buncombe County and flows se into Bent Creek.

Ledford Creek. *See* Left Fork [Eagle Creek].

Ledford Gap, s Clay County near the headwaters of Hothouse Branch.

Ledge Bald on Haywood-Swain county line,

Great Smoky Mountains National Park, on Balsam Mountain near lat. 35° 38′ 35″ N., long. 83° 12′ 05″ W. Alt. 5,175.

Ledge Creek rises in sw Granville County, just nw of town of Stem, flows s through Creedmoor Lake w of town of Creedmoor, and empties into Neuse River at Durham-Wake County line. Appears as Ledge of Rocks Creek on the Collet map, 1770, and others.

Ledge Creek rises in ne Swain County in Great Smoky Mountains National Park and flows sw into Straight Fork [of Raven Fork].

Ledge Gap, on Haywood-Swain County line between Beech Gap and Pin Oak Gap.

Ledge of Rocks Creek. See Ledge Creek.

Ledger, community in central Mitchell County on Snow Creek. Said to have been named by the Post Office Department because of a report submitted in a ledger by a local resident named Phillips. His record of mail sent and received in the community through another post office resulted in the establishment of a post office here. The "Good Will" Free Library opened in Ledger in 1886 through the efforts of Charles Hallet Wing is said to have been the first free public library in the state and the third county library in the United States. See also Wing.

Lee Branch rises in w Macon County and flows sw into Nantahala Lake.

Leechville, town in e Beaufort County on Pungo River. Inc. 1834 and name changed from Lumberton. Reinc. 1899 but long inactive in muncipal affairs.

Lee County was formed in 1907 from Moore and Chatham counties. Located in the central section of the state, it is bounded by Harnett, Moore, and Chatham counties. It was named for General Robert E. Lee (1807-70). Area: 256 sq. mi. County seat: Sanford with an elevation of 375 ft. Townships are Nos. 1-7, formerly Greenwood, Jonesboro, Cape Fear, Deep River, East Sanford, West Sanford, and Pocket. Pro-

duces tobacco, corn, wheat, oats, dairy products, hogs, bricks, lumber, electronics, sheet metal, apparel, industrial machinery, furniture, sand, and gravel.

Lee Creek rises in central Buncombe County near Spivey Mountain and flows ne into French Broad River.

Lee Creek rises in s Macon County and flows e into Jones Creek.

Lee Mountain, e Haywood Co., extends ne between Bald Creek and Liner Creek.

Leepers Creek is formed by the junction of Sawmill and Lippard creeks in ne Lincoln County. It flows se into Gaston County where it joins Killians Creek to form Dutchmans Creek. Appears as Leapers Creek on the Collet map, 1770.

Lees Branch rises in w Warren County and flows se and sw into Shocco Creek.

Leesburg. See Willard.

Lees Creek rises in se Beaufort County and flows nw into Pamlico River. Appears on the Collet map, 1770.

Lees Creek rises in nw Northampton County and flows sw into Roanoke River.

Lees Landing, on Upper Broad Creek in w Pamlico County.

Lees Millpond, e Scotland County on Big Shoeheel Creek. Covers 50 acres; maximum depth 18 ft.

Lees Mills. See Roper.

Lees Mills Township, central Washington County, formed in 1868 but a voting precinct before that time.

Lees Point extends from w Carteret County into White Oak River.

Lees Township, se Columbus County.

Leesville, former community in s Robeson County between Hog Swamp and Oldfield Swamp. A post office existed here as early as 1828 and as recently as 1882. The name is still used in the county with reference to the general area.

Leesville, community in nw Wake County on head of Lower Bartons Creek. Named for John Lee, who first settled here about 1800. Alt. 300.

Leesville Township, nw Wake County.

Lee Swamp rises in sw Wilson County and flows se in an arc into Black Creek. Named for local family.

Left Fork rises in ne Buncombe County and flows se into Beetree Reservoir.

Left Fork Bean Creek rises in n Mitchell County and flows se to join Right Fork Bean Creek to form Bean Creek.

Left Fork Belews Creek. See West Belews Creek.

Left Fork [Cane Creek] rises in e Mitchell County and flows sw to join Right Fork [Cane Creek] to form Cane Creek.

Left Fork [Deep Creek] rises in n Swain County in Great Smoky Mountains National Park and flows se into Deep Creek.

Left Fork [Eagle Creek] rises in se Clay County and flows sw to join Right Fork in forming Eagle Creek. Known also as Ledford Creek.

Left Fork [Indian Creek] rises in n Swain County and flows sw into Right Fork [Indian Creek] to form Indian Creek.

Left Fork [of Raven Fork] rises in ne Swain County in Great Smoky Mountains National Park and flows s to join Right Fork and Middle Fork in forming Raven Fork [of Oconaluftee River].

Left Fork [Redman Creek] rises in ne Swain County and flows sw to join Right Fork [Redman Creek] in forming Redman Creek.

Left Fork [Swannanoa River] rises in ne Buncombe County and flows e into North Fork [Swannanoa River]. Often known locally as Left Hand Fork.

Left Fork Webb Creek rises in ne Cherokee County near Moody Stamp and flows se to join Right Fork Webb Creek in forming Webb Creek.

Left Hand Fork. See Left Fork [Swannanoa River].

Left Prong Bent Creek rises in n Yancey County and flows se to join Right Prong Bent Creek in forming Bent Creek.

Left Prong [Bridge Creek] rises in n central Swain County and flows ne into Bridge Creek.

Left Prong South Toe River has its origin at Pinnacle Spring, s Yancey County, and flows e to join Right Prong South Toe River in forming South Toe River.

Left Prong Three Forks Creek rises in se Yancey County and flows sw to join Right Prong in forming Three Forks Creek.

Legerwood, community in n central Caldwell County. Named for Samuel Legerwood Patterson (1850-1908), onetime State Commissioner of Agriculture, who gave his plantation, "Palmyra," for a farm school for boys here.

Leggett, town in n Edgecombe County, inc. 1895 and reinc. 1925 but not now active in municipal affairs. Post office name in late nineteenth century was Leggettsville.

Leggetts Crossroads, community in nw Beaufort County.

Leggettsville. See Leggett.

Legion Beach, a recreation and picnic area

on Albemarle Sound in n Tyrrell County 3 mi. e of Columbia. Owned by local American Legion Post. Boating, bathing, fishing.

Legislature. For a reference to places at which the legislature is known to have met, see General Assembly.

Leicester, community in nw Buncombe County. Inc. 1859; charter repealed 1905. Named for or by Leicester Chapman, a settler from Leicester, England. Alt. 2,090.

Leicester Township, w Buncombe County.

Leiths Creek rises in central Scotland County and flows se to join Bridge Creek to form the Little Pee Dee River.

Leland, community in nw Brunswick County.

Leman Gap, on Burke-Cleveland County line.

Lemley's Township, former township nw Mecklenburg County. Now township number 10.

Lemon Creek Falls. See Lamance Creek Falls.

Lemon Gap on the Madison County, N. C.-Cocke County, Tenn., line.

Lemon Springs, community in s Lee County. Was designated a railroad station in 1890. Named for mineral springs, owned by a man named Lemon, which were formerly a favorite picnic spot. Alt. 369.

Lena, community in s Cumberland County.

Lennon Crossroads, community in s central Brunswick County.

Lennon's Marsh. See Warwick Bay.

Lennon's Mill Pond. See Warwick Bay.

Lenoir, city and county seat, central Caldwell County. Laid out 1841, inc. 1851. Named in honor of General William Lenoir (1751-1839), a Revolutionary War leader. A nearby forerunner of Lenoir was Tucker's Barn, a small community which developed around a tavern and blacksmith shop operated by the Tucker family. Produces furniture, apparel, textiles, hosiery and mirrors. Alt. 1,182.

Lenoir Branch rises in central Macon County and flows s into Cartoogechaye Creek.

Lenoir (leh-NOR) County was formed in 1791 from Dobbs when it was divided to form Glasgow and Lenoir. Located in the e section of the state, it is bounded by Craven, Jones, Duplin, Wayne, Greene, and Pitt counties. It was named for William Lenoir (1751-1839), one of the heroes of the Battle of Kings Mountain. Area: 399 sq. mi. County seat: Kinston with an elevation of 44 ft. Townships are Contentnea Neck, Falling Creek, Institute, Kinston, Moseley Hall, Neuse, Pink Hill, Sand Hill, Southwest, Trent, Vance, and Woodington. Produces tobacco, corn, wheat, oats, soybeans, cotton, hogs, dairy products, livestock, chemicals, textiles, apparel, sand, and gravel. See also St. Patrick's Parish.

Lenoir Creek rises in s Haywood Co. and flows ne into East Fork Pigeon River.

Lenoir Township, s central Caldwell County.

Lenox Castle, former resort in se Rockingham County. A tavern, baths, store, and springs made this a popular spa; probably operated prior to 1800, but flourished from 1803 until after 1844. Named for John Lenox who advertised his tavern as "The Castle of Thundertontrenck" in 1804. A post office as late as 1882.

Lenox Point extends from the mainland of s Carteret County into North River Thorofare, e of the limits of Beaufort. Also once known as Titus Point.

Lenoxville, a proposed town chartered 1816, to be laid out on the lands of James McKinlay in s Carteret County e of Beaufort at present-day Lenox Point. Apparently it was never developed. A contemporary manuscript map of Lenoxville is in the North Carolina Collection at the University of North Carolina.

Lens Knob, w Surry County near Saddle Mountain Creek.

Lenzton, community in w Richmond County.

Leo. See Skinnersville.

Leon, community in e Duplin County.

Leonard Creek rises in central Davidson County and flows s into Abbotts Creek.

Leonard Creek rises in central Davie County near the town of Mocksville and flows e for approx. 4 mi. into Dutchmans Creek.

Leonard Fork rises in s Lincoln County and flows se into Indian Creek.

Leonards Crossroads, community in nw Columbus County.

Leonards Point, extends from n Washington County into Albemarle Sound.

Leonsburg, former town in w Hyde County between Germantown and Sladesville. Inc. 1833, but now only a rural community.

Leroy Creek rises in n central Avery County and flows ne into Elk River.

Lester, community in n Wilkes County between North Fork Reddies River and Mulberry Creek.

Letha, community in n Franklin County.

Letitia, community in sw Cherokee County.

Lettered Rock Ridge, nw Burke County. Alt. 3,100.

Level Cross, community and former post office, n Randolph County. Named for the level intersection of several roads here.

Levelcross, community in se Surry County. Named from the fact that two roads cross here in comparatively level country.

Level Cross Township, n central Randolph County.

Levels, community in n central Tyrrell County at the head of Riders Creek. Alt. approx. 4. Also called Riders Creek Community. Formerly received postal service from post office named Jerry, about 1 mi. sw of community.

Levingtons Creek. See Livingston Creek.

Levy Branch rises in w Madison County and flows nw into Big Pine Creek.

Lewarae, town in s Richmond County. Est. 1900; inc. 1905. No longer active in municipal affairs. Named from parts of the names of three local families: Leak, Wall, and MacRae.

Lewellyn Cove follows the course of a stream emptying into Little Tennessee River in n Graham County.

Lewis, community in e Granville County. Named for Howell Lewis, local plantation owner. Alt. 545.

Lewis. See Atkinson.

Lewis Branch rises in e central Brunswick County and flows n into Lewis Swamp.

Lewis Branch rises in nw Jackson County and flows ne into Tuckasegee River.

Lewis Branch rises in n Madison County and flows s into Big Laurel Creek.

Lewisburg, community in n Yancey County on Cane River at the mouth of Bald Mountain Creek. Alt. 2,288.

Lewis Canal, in central Washington County drains ne from East Dismal Swamp into Main Canal.

Lewis Creek, an inlet of Core Sound into se Cedar Island in ne Carteret County.

Lewis Creek, rises on se Core Banks and flows n into Core Sound in se Carteret County.

Lewis Creek rises in e Henderson County and flows nw into Clear Creek.

Lewis Creek rises in s Onslow County and flows ne into Morgan Bay. Mentioned in local records as early as 1744 as Lewis's Creek.

Lewis Creek rises in n Pender County and flows ne into Northeast Cape Fear River.

Lewis Crossroads, community in n Halifax County.

Lewis Fork, community in sw Wilkes County on South Prong Lewis Fork Creek. Lewis Fork Baptist Church here was organized in 1792.

Lewis Fork Creek is formed in sw Wilkes County by the junction of North Prong Lewis Fork Creek and South Prong Lewis Fork Creek and flows se approx. 3 mi. into W. Kerr Scott Reservoir. See also Fort Hamby.

Lewis Fork Township, sw Wilkes County.

Lewis Gap, central Buncombe County, n of Patton Mountain.

Lewis McDaires Knob, n Buncombe County on Lankford Mountain. See also McDaires Cove and Ridge.

Lewis Mountain, between Henderson Creek and Lewis Creek in e Henderson County.

Lewis Point, n Tyrrell County, extends from the mainland into Albemarle Sound w of Peartree Point.

Lewis's Creek. See Lewis Creek.

Lewis Swamp rises in e central Brunswick County and flows e to join Rattlesnake Branch in forming Town Creek.

Lewiston, town in nw Bertie County. Inc. 1881. Named for the Watson Lewis family. A previous post office here was known as Turner's Cross Roads. Alt. 50. See also Woodville.

Lewisville, former town in se Columbus County. Inc. 1885, but long inactive in municipal affairs. Two rural service stations now mark the site.

Lewisville, community in w Forsyth County. Named in honor of Lewis Lagenauer around whose home it developed.

Lewisville Township, sw Forsyth County.

Lewters Crossroads, community in ne Northampton County.

Lexine. See Washburns Store.

Lexington, city and county seat, central Davidson County. Inc. 1827. Named for the Battle of Lexington, April 19, 1775, in Massachusetts. Davidson County Community College, est. 1966, is here. Alt. 810. Produces dairy products, textiles, hosiery, lumber, furniture, apparel, and batteries.

Lexington Township, central Davidson County.

Liberia, community in s central Warren County s of Reedy Creek.

Liberty, town in ne Randolph County. Inc. 1889. Named for the nearby plantation of John Leak who settled here in 1807. Alt. 790.

Liberty, community in se Rowan County. Named for a local church.

Liberty Hill, former community in central Guilford County, now a part of Greensboro.

Liberty Knob, w Surry County near the head of Millers Creek.

Liberty Township, ne Randolph County.

Liberty Township, se Yadkin County.

The Lick. See Williamsboro.

Lick Creek rises in sw Anson County and flows n into Brown Creek.

Lick Creek rises in n Chatham County and flows n across the county line into Alamance County for a short distance before turning s again into Chatham County where it enters Terrell Creek.

Lick Creek rises in e Davidson County and flows sw into Yadkin River.

Lick Creek rises s Durham County and flows ne into Neuse River. Once known as Great Lick Creek.

Lick Creek rises in n Forsyth County and flows ne into s Stokes County where it enters Town Fork Creek. Probably named for a salt lick frequented by deer; the name appears in records as early as 1755.

Lick Creek rises in central Lee County and flows ne into Cape Fear River.

Lick Creek rises in e Montgomery County and flows ne into Cotton Creek.

Lick Creek rises in ne Orange County and flows ne into Person County where it enters Byrds Creek.

Lick Fork rises in n Forsyth County and flows sw into Mill Creek. Appears as Jones Creek on the Collet map, 1770; not named on subsequent maps until it appears as Little Lick Fork on MacRae map, 1833.

Lick Fork rises in n Gaston County and flows ne into s Lincoln County where it enters Mill Creek.

Lick Fork Creek rises in w Montgomery County and flows sw into Clarks Creek.

Lick Fork Creek rises in s Rockingham County and flows ne into Caswell County where it enters Hogans Creek.

Licking Branch rises in w Gates County and flows sw into Jady Branch.

Licking Creek. See Elisha Creek.

Licklog Branch rises in se Buncombe County and flows s into Rocky Fork.

Lick Log Creek rises in central Clay County and flows sw into Lake Chatuge. The name originated when the Davis family, early settlers, felled trees and cut notches in the logs to hold salt for their cattle.

Licklog Creek rises in s Jackson County on s slopes of Heady Mountain and flows s and w 1½ mi. to join Fowler Creek.

Licklog Creek rises in n Jackson County and flows nw into Scott Creek.

Lick Log Creek, community in s Clay County.

Licklog Gap, se Buncombe County in the Swannanoa Mountains between Lookoff Gap and Jesses High Top.

Licklog Gap, nw Burke County. Alt. 2,420.

Licklog Gap, on the Haywood-Jackson County line. Takes its name from a "licklog" formerly here—a log with boxes chopped into its upper side to hold salt for the cattle to lick.

Licklog Gap, in s Macon County between Grassy Knobs and Middle Creek.

Licklog Gap, in w Macon County at the head of Whiteoak Creek.

Lick Log Gap on the Madison County, N. C.-Greene County, Tenn., line.

Licklog Gap, n Swain County in the Great Smoky Mountains National Park between Hickory Cove and Right Fork [Cold Spring Branch], near lat. 35° 29' 05" N., long. 83° 39' 48" W.

Lick Meadow Branch rises in e Franklin County and flows ne into Redbud Creek.

Lick Mountain, s Caldwell County. Alt. 1,990.

Lick Mountain, w Montgomery County near Dutchmans Creek.

Lick Mountain, w Randolph County, sw of Jackson Creek.

Lick Ridge, in e Mitchell County between Honeycutt Branch and Young Cove Creek.

Lick Rock, on the Madison County, N. C.-Unicoi County, Tenn., line.

Lick Run rises in central Lincoln County and flows se into Leepers Creek.

Lickskillet, community in s Macon County between the head of Tessentee Creek and Piney Knob Fork. Named by hunters who left unwashed cooking utensils in camp and returned to find that they had been licked by dogs or other animals.

Lickskillet, community in s Warren County s of Shocco Creek.

Lickskillet Branch rises in w Yancey County and flows se into Bald Creek.

Lickstone Bald, on Lickstone Ridge in s Haywood County. Alt. 5,700. Named from the fact that salt was put on a large smooth rock for cattle.

Lickstone Mountain, on the Jackson-Haywood County line. Alt. 5,576.

Lickstone Ridge, extends ne from Soco Creek in n Jackson County to Wolfpen Mountain in s Haywood County.

Liddell, community in w Lenoir County.

Light, community in e Davidson County.

Light Gap, ne Buncombe County near Big Andy Ridge.

Light Ground Pocosin, a muck-filled area approx. 4 by 5 mi., w central Pamlico County.

Lighthouse Creek. See Baldhead Creek.

Lightwood Knot Creek rises in s Richmond County and flows s into South Carolina where it joins Beverly Creek to form Crooked Creek.

Lightwood Mountain, e Mitchell County at the head of Laurel Branch.

Liledoun, community in central Alexander County on Lower Little River. Produces textiles.

Liles Creek. See Lyle Creek.

Lilesville, town in e Anson County. Inc. 1874. A post office as early as 1828. Named for Nelson P. Liles, local merchant. Alt. 474.

Lilesville Township, e Anson County.

Lilleys Millpond. See Greens Millpond.

Lillian, community in n Wake County.

Lillie. See Lizzie.

Lillington, town and county seat on Cape Fear River, central Harnett County. Inc. 1859 and the name changed from Long Creek Village to Lillington in honor of the Revolutionary patroit, Alexander Lillington (1725-86). Alt. 325. Produces apparel. See also Summerville.

Lillington. See Long Creek.

Lillington County was authorized to be est. in 1859 from a portion of New Hanover County, provided that two-thirds of the qualified voters of Rocky Point Precinct approved. The act was not approved, but Pender County, which see, was later est. in approx. the same area.

Lillington Creek rises in e Pender County and flows sw into Northeast Cape Fear River. Named for General Alexander Lillington (1725-86), whose plantation was nearby. Appears as Island Creek on the Collet map, 1770; as Maxwell Creek on the Price map, 1808; and as Lillington's Mill Creek on the MacRae map, 1833.

Lillington's Mill Creek. *See* Lillington Creek.

Lillington Township, central Harnett County.

Lilliput, the plantation of Eleazer Allen (1692-1750), councillor, judge, receiver-general, and treasurer of North Carolina, was located on the n side of Lilliput Creek in e Brunswick County. Land granted to Allen, 1725, and he named the plantation for the imaginary country in Jonathan Swift's satire *Gulliver's Travels* (first published in 1726). Part of the 300-volume library at Lilliput was inherited by a daughter of James Hasell, and might have been incorporated into the remarkable Hasell library. Lilliput was purchased by Gov. William Tryon as a summer residence, and he still owned the property as late as 1784. Location of Lilliput is shown on the Moseley map, 1733, under the name of "E. Allen;" on the Collet map, 1770, as "Lilliput to the G.;" and on the Price map, 1808, as "Lilliput."

Lilliput Creek, e Brunswick County, flows e from McKenzie Pond into Cape Fear River. Named for a nearby plantation (*see* Lilliput). Shown as Allen's Creek on the MacRae map, 1833, and on the Colton map, 1861. Appears as Lilliput Creek on the 1865 U.S. Coast Survey map, and on the Kerr map, 1882.

Lilly, community in ne Camden County.

Lily Branch rises in central Mitchell County and flows sw into North Toe River.

Lily Pond Creek rises in w Northampton County and flows sw to join Gumberry Swamp in forming Wheeler Creek.

Lima, community in central Craven County.

Limekiln Branch rises in w central Transylvania County and flows se into French Broad River.

Limekiln Creek rises in w Gaston County and flows sw into Long Creek.

Limekiln Creek rises in n McDowell County and flows e through Woodlawn into North Fork [Catawba River].

Lime Rock, community in s Surry County on Yadkin River. Alt. 820.

Limestone Creek rises in e Duplin County and flows sw into Northeast Cape Fear River.

Limestone Creek rises in s Buncombe County and flows s into Merrill Cove Creek.

Limestone Township, s central Buncombe County. A post office named Limestone

existed in Buncombe County as early as 1828.

Limestone Township, se Duplin County.

Linbank, formerly a post office and community in s Vance County approx. 4 mi. s of the town of Henderson. The building used from 1829 until 1849 as a post office is still standing, and the name survives as the name of the local road on which the building stands.

Linches Creek. *See* Lynch Creek.

Lincoln County was formed in 1779 from Tryon County when it was divided to form Lincoln and Rutherford counties. Located in the sw section of the state, it is bounded by Mecklenburg, Gaston, Cleveland, Catawba, and Iredell counties. It was named for Benjamin Lincoln (1733-1810), distinguished general of the Revolution. Area: 309 sq. mi. County seat: Lincolnton with an elevation of 860 ft. Townships are Catawba Springs, Howards Creek, Ironton, Lincolnton, and North Brook. The Schenck-Warlick Mill, the first cotton mill in the South, was built about 1813 approx. one mile w of Lincolnton. Produces corn, wheat, oats, cotton, poultry, dairy products, livestock, hogs, textiles, furniture, machinery, hosiery, crushed stone, mica, sand, and amethyst.

Lincoln Hollow, valley in w Avery County between Teagues Ridge and Powdermill Creek.

Lincolnton, town and county seat, central Lincoln County. Inc. 1785. Name honors General Benjamin Lincoln (1733-1810), Revolutionary leader. The Battle of Ramsour's Mill, a Whig victory over the Tories, was fought June 20, 1780, at a site on the n outskirts of Lincolnton. Produces textiles, furniture, machinery, and hosiery. Alt. 860.

Lincolnton Township, central Lincoln County.

Lindell, community in w Greene County.

Linden, town in n Cumberland County. Settled about 1800. Inc. 1913 and named for a grove of linden trees nearby. Known as Little River Academy prior to 1910. Alt. 150. *See also* Choffington.

Linden Mountain, w Randolph County on Jackson Creek.

Lindley's Mill, on Cane Creek in s central Alamance County, a short distance w of Sutphin, was the site of a battle on Sept. 13, 1781, in which John Butler's Whigs failed to rescue Gov. Thomas Burke from David Fanning's Tories. The first grist-mill here was erected in 1756 by Thomas Lindley.

Lindsay C. Warren Bridge. *See* East Lake Landing; Sandy Point.

Lindscomb Branch rises in nw Brunswick County and flows w into Columbus County where it enters Livingston Creek. Sometimes known locally as Linksom Branch and believed to have been named originally Lynchum Branch.

Line, community in sw Rutherford County.

Lineberry, community in n Randolph County. Named for Captain Scott Lineberry, local resident.

Line Creek rises in s Buncombe County and flows ne into French Broad River. Forms the Buncombe-Henderson County boundary for approx. 1 mi.

Liner Cove, central Haywood County near Jerry Knob.

Liner Creek rises in e Haywood County and flows sw into Crabtree Creek.

Line Runner Lake in s Transylvania County on Gerren Creek. Covers 11 acres and has max. depth of 28 ft. Used for recreation.

Line Runner Ridge in s Transylvania County extends n in an arc from Blue Ridge Mountains to the head of Gerren Creek.

Linksom Branch. *See* Lindscomb Branch.

Linn Cove, the valley through which Linn Cove Creek flows in central Buncombe County.

Linn Cove Creek rises in Elk Mountains in central Buncombe County and flows sw to join Webb Cove Creek in forming Beaverdam Creek.

Linsters Springs. *See* Barium Springs.

Linviles Creek. *See* Blanket Creek.

Linville, town in e central Avery County on Linville River. Alt. 3,623. Summer resort. Post office est. 1883 as Clay, changed to Porcelain in 1885, and to Linville in 1888. Laid out by Samuel T. Kelsey of Kansas who had earlier (with Charles Hutchinson) laid out Highlands. Inc. 1891 but not now active in municipal affairs.

Linville Creek rises in e Davie County and flows ne into Yadkin River.

Linville Creek rises in central Watauga County and flows sw in an arc into Brushy Fork.

Linville Creek. *See* Carters Creek.

Linville Falls, nw Burke County on Linville River approx. 2 mi. s of the Avery-Burke County line. In 1876, there were two distinct falls, each approx. 35 ft. high. In early 1900's, lower ledge gave way so that now Upper Falls cascade over a smooth 12 ft. rock shelf, and then the water drops 90 ft. at Lower Falls into a rock-encircled pool at the head of Linville Gorge, the wildest gorge in eastern America. Reached by foot trail near the Blue Ridge Parkway. Named for William and John Linville, killed by Indians below the falls in 1766. According to Allen Poe, they were relatives of Daniel Boone's wife.

Linville Falls, community on Avery-Burke County line, near the nw tip of Burke County w of Linville River. Alt. 3,325. Named for falls on nearby river.

Linville Gorge, a narrow defile through which the Linville River flows in nw Burke County, extending from Linville Falls to Lake James. This is said to be the wildest gorge in the eastern United States. Linville Gorge "wild area" in Pisgah National Forest in Burke County, set aside on February 7, 1951, contains 7,655 acres preserved in their natural state. Foot trails make it accessible, but no other development is permitted. This is the only National Forest Wilderness Unit in the East. Cherokee Indians knew Linville River as *Eeseeoh*, "river of cliffs."

Linville Lake. *See* Lake Kawana.

Linville Mountain, e Avery County.

Linville River rises in e Avery County approx. 3 mi. sw of Grandfather Mountain. It flows sw in Avery and se and s in Burke County where it enters Lake James. Said to have been named for two brothers, relatives of Daniel Boone, who hunted along its banks between 1760 and 1766, and who were killed by Indians. Known by the Cherokee as *Eeseeoh*, "River of Cliffs." *See also* Linville Gorge.

Linville's Mill Creek. *See* Laytown Creek.

Linville Township, central Avery County.

Linville Township, w Burke County.

Linwood, community in w Davidson County in the former Jersey Settlement, *which see*. Alt. 659. Named by Dr. William

Rainey Holt (1798-1868) for his nearby plantation. Produces lumber.

Lippard Creek rises in s Catawba County and flows sw into Lincoln County where it joins Sawmill Creek to form Leepers Creek.

Lisbon, community in s central Bladen County. Was the plantation of Colonel John Slingsby, Tory commander at the Battle of Elizabethtown at which he was fatally wounded.

Lisbon, former community in s Sampson County at the junction of Six Runs Creek and Coharie River where Black River is formed. Authorized to be laid out on the land of Jesse Peacock in 1785 and named Lisburn, probably for the town of the same name in Northern Ireland, birthplace of Hugh Waddell (1734?-1773), colonial soldier. Authorized to be resurveyed in 1824 when it was called Lisbon. A post office est. here as early as 1833 and named Lisborne operated as Lisbon as late as 1882.

Lisbon Township, s central Sampson County.

Lisburn. See Lisbon.

Lisenbee Branch rises in n Madison County and flows s into Spillcorn Creek.

Lisenbee Ridge, central Madison County extends sw approx. 1½ mi. between Heck Creek and Bee Branch.

Lisenberry Mountain, ne Rutherford County between First Broad River and Duncans Creek. It is said that carpetbaggers lived in a cave here during the Reconstruction period following the Civil War.

Lisha. See Elisha Creek.

Listen Knob, peak in central Caldwell County about five miles ne of Lenoir. Named from the fact that foxhunters built fires on the top as they listened to their dogs running foxes.

Listers Corner, community in s Pasquotank County.

Litaker Township, s Rowan County.

Lithia Springs, community in central Lincoln County, a popular nineteenth century resort. General Robert F. Hoke (1837-1912) owned the springs and shipped bottled water from them.

Little Abrams Gap, Great Smoky Mountains National Park, on the Swain County, N. C.-Blount County, Tenn., line, near lat. 35° 33' 18" N., long. 83° 46' 34" W.

Little Alamance Creek rises in central Guilford County and flows ne to join Big Alamance Creek in forming Great Alamance Creek, *which see.*

Little Alamance Creek rises in w Alamance County and flows se into Great Alamance Creek.

Little Andy Creek rises in ne Buncombe County and flows w into Corner Rock Creek.

Little Andy Ridge, ne Buncombe County, n of Little Andy Creek and Big Andy Ridge.

Little Bald, on the Cherokee-Graham County line in the Snowbird Mountains.

Little Bald, se Clay County. Alt. 5,030.

Little Bald, e Graham County at the head of Franks Creek.

Little Bald, e Mitchell County between High Knob and Wiggins Cove.

Little Bald, on the Yancey County, N. C.-Unicoi County, Tenn., line. Alt. approx. 5,240.

Little Bald Branch rises in w Haywood County and flows ne into Caldwell Fork.

Little Bald Branch rises in sw Madison County and flows nw into Spring Creek.

Little Bald Knob, w Haywood County, Great Smoky Mountains National Park; on Cataloochee Divide between Sheepback Knob and Fie Creek, near lat. 35° 33' 05" N., long. 83° 07' 10" W.

Little Bald Mountain, on the Haywood-Transylvania County line on the Pisgah Ridge. Alt. 5,280-5,320.

Little Bald Mountain, sw Macon County, extends se from Runaway Knob to the head of Long Branch. Alt. 5,217.

Little Bald Mountain, on the Madison County, N. C.-Greene County, Tenn., line.

Little Bald Mountain. See Mount Squires.

Little Bald Rock Mountain, s Jackson County on e edge of Fairfield Lake and s of Bald Rock Mountain.

Little Bald Knob, on the Mitchell County, N. C.-Unicoi County, Tenn., line.

Little Balsam Gap, on the head of Plott Creek in w Haywood County.

Little Balsam Knob, on the head of Plott Creek in w Haywood County.

Little Bear Creek rises in ne Cabarrus County and flows sw into Dutch Buffalo Creek.

Little Bear Creek rises in s Mitchell County and flows sw into North Toe River.

Little Bear Creek rises in w central Stanly County and flows s into Long Creek.

Little Bearpen Gap, on the Jackson-Haywood County line.

Little Bearpen Mountain, se Macon County between Bearpen Mountain and Cullasaja River.

Little Beartrail Ridge, s Haywood County

between Little Beartrap Branch and Big Beartrap Branch.

Little Beartrap Branch rises in s Haywood County and flows ne into Middle Prong.

Little Bear Wallow Creek rises in w Transylvania County and flows sw into North Fork French Broad River.

Little Bearwallow Mountain, n Henderson County between Bearwallow Mountain and Hickory Nut Creek.

Little Beaver Creek rises in w Wake County and flows nw into e Chatham County where it enters Beaver Creek.

Little Beaverdam Creek rises in sw Duplin County and flows se into Big Beaverdam Creek.

Little Beaverdam Creek rises in nw Gaston County and flows ne into Beaverdam Creek.

Little Beaverdam Creek rises in se Granville County and flows sw into Wake County where it enters Beaverdam Creek.

Little Beaverdam Creek rises in nw Watauga County and flows sw into Beaverdam Creek.

Little Beaverdam Swamp rises in w Sampson County and flows sw into South River.

Little Bernal Branch rises in w Johnston County and flows se into Bernal Branch.

Little Black Creek rises in s Wake County and flows se into w Johnston County and where it enters Black Creek.

Little Bottom Branch rises in w Madison County and flows ne into Spring Creek.

Little Branch rises in w Haywood County and flows se into Winchester Creek.

Little Branch rises in n Johnston County and flows se into Swift Creek.

Little Branch rises in w Wake County and flows sw into Whiteoak Creek.

Little Brasstown Creek rises in s Cherokee County and flows ne into Brasstown Creek.

Little Brier Creek rises in w Wake County and flows sw into Brier Creek.

Little Brier Ridge, spur of Brier Ridge extending ne to Dark Ridge Creek in ne Jackson County.

Little Broad Creek rises in North River Pocosin in s Camden County and flows e into North River ½ mi. below the mouth of Broad Creek.

Little Brown Creek rises in sw Anson County and flows n into Brown Creek.

Little Brown Creek rises in se Union County and flows se into Brown Creek.

Little Browns Landing on Cape Fear River in central Bladen County.

Little Brush Creek rises in sw Chatham County and flows sw into Randolph County where it enters Brush Creek.

Little Brush Creek rises in ne Yancey County and flows nw into Brush Creek.

Little Brush Mountain, made up of a chain of five or six peaks in w Alexander and e Caldwell counties.

Little Brushy, peak at the s end of Brushy Mountain, ne Buncombe County.

Little Brushy Mount, a range of mountains in e Caldwell and w Alexander counties. Alts. from 1,850 to 1,890.

Little Buck Creek rises in nw Burke County and flows ne into Steele's Creek.

Little Buck Creek rises in se Clay County and flows sw into Buck Creek.

Little Buck Creek rises in nw McDowell County on the s slopes of Woods Mountain and flows se into Buck Creek and Lake Tahoma.

Little Buck Creek rises in e Macon County and flows sw into Buck Creek.

Little Buckeye Cove, se Haywood County on the head of East Prong Pigeon River.

Little Buck Hill, mountain in w Avery County.

Little Buckle Swamp rises in se Bladen County and flows se into Buckle Swamp.

Little Buck Mountain, on Alexander-Caldwell County line. Alt. 1,890.

Little Buffalo Creek rises in e Johnston County and flows se into Little River.

Little Buffalo Creek rises in central Lee County and flows n into Deep River.

Little Buffalo Creek rises in sw Lincoln County and flows sw into Cleveland County where it enters Buffalo Creek.

Little Buffalo Creek rises in nw Richmond County and flows sw into Buffalo Creek.

Little Buffalo Creek rises in s Rowan and n Cabarrus counties and flows sw into Dutch Buffalo Creek.

Little Buffalo Creek rises in s Vance County and flows sw into Buffalo Creek.

Little Buffalo Creek. See West Buffalo Creek.

Little Bugaboo Creek rises in n Wilkes County and flows se into Big Bugaboo Creek.

Little Butt Knob, on Buncombe-Yancey County line between Big Butt Knob and Point Misery. Alt. approx. 3,300.

Little Camp Creek rises in n Rutherford County and flows sw into Camp Creek.

Little Cane River Gap. See Cane River Gap.

Little Caraway Creek rises in nw Randolph County and flows s into Caraway Creek.

Little Cataloochee Creek, is formed in nw

Haywood County in Great Smoky Mountains National Park by the junction of Woody Branch and Conrad Branch. Flows e 2 mi. to empty into Cataloochee Creek.

Little Catawba River. See South Fork Catawba River.

Little Cawcaw Swamp rises in sw Brunswick County and flows w into Cawcaw Swamp at e limit of Thomas Bay.

Little Cedar Cliff, ne Buncombe County near Ingraham Mountain.

Little Cedar Mountain, s Buncombe County in the Swannanoa Mountains.

Little Celo Mountain, e Yancey County at the ne end of Celo Ridge.

Little Chestnut Bald, mountain peak in the Great Smoky Mountains National Park, on the Swain County, N. C.-Sevier County, Tenn., line, near lat. 35° 33′ 54″ N., long. 83° 38′ 30″ W. Alt. 5,042.

Little Chestnut Mountain, ne Burke County and sw Caldwell counties.

Little Chestnut Ridge, Great Smoky Mountains National Park, n Swain County, a short spur of Locust Ridge, near lat. 35° 32′ 50″ N., long. 83° 39′ 54″ W.

Little Chimney Knob, s Macon County between Chimney Knob and Kimsey Gap.

Little Chinquapin Branch rises in w Jones County and flows e, about 3½ mi. into Trent River.

Little Choga Creek rises in w Macon County and flows se into Nantahala Lake.

Little Coharie Creek rises in nw Sampson County and flows se to join Great Coharie Creek in forming Coharie River.

Little Coharie Township, w Sampson County.

Little Cokey Swamp, rises in w Edgecombe County and flows se into Cokey Swamp.

Little Cold Water Creek rises in n Cabarrus County and flows s into Cold Water Creek.

Little Colly Creek rises in e Bladen County and flows s into Colly Creek.

Little Contentnea Creek rises in se Wilson County and flows se on the Greene-Pitt County line into Pitt County, then back to the Pitt-Greene County line which it follows into Contentnea Creek. See also Contentnea Creek. Appears as Little Cotecktney Creek on the Collet map, 1770.

Little Cotecktney Creek. See Little Contentnea Creek.

Little Cove Creek, w Polk County flows ne and nw into Green River.

Little Crabtree Creek rises in central Yancey County and flows e into South Toe River.

Little Craggy Knob, ne Buncombe County between Sugar Fork and Left Fork.

Little Crains Creek. See Whiteoak Creek.

Little Creek appears on the Collet map, 1770, shown as flowing parallel to the present Broad Creek of Camden County, though south of it. The creek north of the present Broad Creek is probably intended as there is no parallel stream south of it.

Little Creek rises in sw Alamance County and flows n into Stinking Quarter Creek.

Little Creek rises in n Anson County and flows n into Rocky River.

Little Creek rises in se Anson County and flows s into Jones Creek.

Little Creek, e Beaufort County, an inlet of Pungo Creek near the junction with Pungo River.

Little Creek rises in se Beaufort County and flows nw into South Creek.

Little Creek rises in Black Swamp on the s tip of Camden County and flows n into North River.

Little Creek rises in s Carteret County and flows s into Newport River.

Little Creek rises in nw Cumberland County and flows n into Little River.

Little Creek rises in w Davie County and flows se approx. 6 mi. into South Yadkin River.

Little Creek rises in the sw section of Winston-Salem, central Forsyth County, and flows sw into Muddy Creek. Appears as Loar Creek on the Collet map, 1770; as Long Run on the Price map, 1808; and under its present name on the MacRae map, 1833.

Little Creek rises in s Franklin County and flows ne into Crooked Creek.

Little Creek rises in e Haywood County and flows sw into Bald Creek.

Little Creek rises in w Hoke County and flows sw into Lumber River.

Little Creek rises in e Johnston County and flows ne into Wilson County where it enters Contentnea Creek.

Little Creek rises in n Johnston County and flows se into Little River. Appears on the Collet map, 1770.

Little Creek rises in nw Johnston County and flows se into Swift Creek.

Little Creek rises in n Lincoln County and flows ne into Catawba River.

Little Creek rises in se Macon County and flows se into Big Creek.

Little Creek rises in ne Madison County and flows s into Big Laurel Creek.

Little Creek rises in sw Madison County and flows ne into Spring Creek.

Little Creek rises in w Madison County and flows e into Meadow Fork.

Little Creek rises in e central Moore County and flows nw into McLendons Creek.

Little Creek rises in se Moore County and flows s into Little River.

Little Creek rises in sw Nash County and flows sw into Moccasin Creek.

Little Creek is formed in se Orange County by the junction of Booker Creek and Bolin Creek; it flows e into sw Durham County where it flows se into New Hope Creek.

Little Creek rises in w Stanly County and flows sw into Big Bear Creek.

Little Creek rises in n Stokes County and flows sw into Peters Creek.

Little Creek rises in w Surry County and flows se into Snow Creek.

Little Creek rises in e Wake County and flows se into n Johnston County where it enters Moccasin Creek.

Little Creek rises in n Yancey County and flows se into Cane River.

Little Creek, community on Little Creek s of Sams Gap, ne Madison County. Alt. 2,892.

Little Creek Gap on the Haywood-Madison County line.

Little Creek Point, s Onslow County in New River.

Little Crooked Creek rises in sw McDowell County and flows e into Crooked Creek.

Little Cross Creek rises in n Cumberland County and flows se into Cross Creek. Early settlers found that Cross Creek and Little Cross Creek crossed.

Little Cub Creek. See East Prong Cub Creek.

Little Currituck. See Farmington.

Little Cypress Creek rises in e Franklin County and flows sw into Cypress Creek.

Little Cypress Creek rises in s Jones County and flows ne into Cypress Creek.

Littledals Ferry. See Mt. Gould.

Little Dam Branch rises in n Cherokee County on Hanging Dog Mountain and flows ne into Hyatt Creek.

Little Davidson Branch rises in w Haywood County and flows nw into Davidson Branch.

Little Davis Mountain, n Buncombe County in the Elk Mountains.

Little Deep Creek rises in n central Carteret County and flows s into Deep Creek.

Little Deep Creek rises in s Halifax County and flows se into Deep Creek.

Little Deep Creek rises in w Warren County and flows ne into Ellingtons Creek.

Little Dismal Swamp, nw Johnston County, drains into Dismal Branch.

Little Dugger Creek rises in se Watauga County and flows se into Wilkes County where it enters Dugger Creek.

Little Dugger Mountain, se Watauga County near the head of Little Dugger Creek.

Little Ease Creek, a bay on the n side of Pamlico River, e Beaufort County.

Little East Fork Pigeon River rises in s Haywood County and flows nw into West Fork Pigeon River.

Little Elk Creek rises in w Alleghany County and flows n into Elk Creek.

Little Elk Creek rises in sw Avery County and flows ne into Elk River.

Little Elkin River rises in ne Wilkes County and flows se into Yadkin River.

Little Elk Knob, n Graham County between Tuskeegee Creek and Sawyer Creek.

Little Elk Mountain, central Avery County.

Little Elk Ridge, central Avery County.

Little Elliby. See Upper Bartons Creek.

Little Fall Branch rises in n Haywood County and flows nw into Cold Springs Creek.

Little Fall Creek rises in n central Wake County e and flows ne into Fall Branch.

Littlefield, community in s Pitt County. Alt. 57.

Little Fires Creek rises in n Clay County and flows sw into Fires Creek.

Little Fisher River rises in n Surry County and flows se into Fisher River.

Little Fishhawk Mountain, s Macon County between Fishhawk Mountain and Whiterock Gap. Alt. 4,706.

Little Fishing Creek is formed in e central Warren County by the junction of Walkers Creek and Big Branch. It flows se into w Halifax County where it enters Fishing Creek on the Halifax-Nash County line. Appears as Conway Creek on the Moseley map, 1733, and as Little Fishing Creek on the Collet map, 1770.

Little Fishing Creek. See Mill Creek.

Little Flat Creek rises in n Buncombe County near Brittain Mountain and flows nw into Flat Creek.

Little Flatty Creek rises in se Pasquotank County and flows se into Pasquotank River.

Little Florida, artifical pond in nw Tyrrell County, formed in 1946 by the digging of sand from a farm to make a fill. Covers 3 acres; maximum depth 30 feet. Named by C. E. Liverman, former owner, for name of the farm. Owned by North Carolina

Highway Department. Open to public. Fishing, swimming.

Little Fodderstack Mountain, se Macon County at the head of Edwards Creek.

Little Fork rises in ne Buncombe County and flows nw into Right Fork. These are tributaries of Swannanoa River. Sometimes known locally as Little Right Hand Fork.

Little Fork Ridge, ne Buncombe County between Hawkbill and Mineral creeks.

Little Fork Ridge, w Haywood County between Big Fork Ridge and Woody Creek.

Little Fork Ridge, n Mitchell County between Left Fork Bean Creek and Right Fork Bean Creek.

Little Foster Creek rises in ne Madison County and flows s into Foster Creek.

Little Gap Creek rises in n Watauga County and flows n into Ashe County where it enters South Fork New River.

Little Glade Creek rises in se Alleghany County and flows n into Brush Creek.

Little Governors Creek rises on the Lee-Moore County line and flows nw into Big Governors Creek. Forms part of the Lee-Moore County line for its entire course. Named for Governor Gabriel Johnston who acquired land in the vicinity in 1748.

Little Grandfather Mountain on the Alleghany-Wilkes County line. Alt. 3,745.

Little Grassy Creek rises in n Granville County and flows n into Grassy Creek.

Little Green Creek rises in se Jackson County, n of Cold Mountain and flows 1½ mi. w into Tuckasegee River.

Little Green Mountain in se Jackson County between Big Green Mountain and Panthertown Creek. Alt. approx. 4,100.

Little Green Swamp, ne Brunswick County. Approx. 10 mi. square.

Little Grill Ridge in the Great Smoky Mountains National Park, w Swain County, a short spur from Big Grill Ridge, lat. 35° 32′ 38″ N., long. 83° 47′ 28″ W.

Little Gunpowder Creek rises in s Caldwell County and flows e into Gunpowder Creek.

Little Hamer Creek rises in s Montgomery County and flows s into Richmond County where it enters Hamer Creek.

Little Harris Creek rises in central Cleveland County and flows se into Big Harris Creek.

Little Haw Creek rises in e Alamance County and flows sw into Haw Creek.

Little Hawk Mountain, e Mitchell County between Hawk Creek and Long Hollow.

Little Haw Knob, on the Graham County,

N. C.-Monroe County, Tenn., line. Alt. 5,146.

Little Haw Mountain, central Avery County.

Little Helton Creek rises in n Ashe County and flows se into Helton Creek.

Little Hensley Branch rises in n Yancey County and flows ne into Cane River.

Little Hickory Creek rises in s Cleveland County and flows w into Hickory Creek.

Little Hickory Knob, n Transylvania County between Avery Creek and Thrift Cove Branch.

Little Hickory Top, s Buncombe County, sw of Ingles Field Gap.

Little Hogback Creek rises in se Jackson County and flows s into Horsepasture River.

Little Hogback Mountain, se Jackson County between Burnt Cabin Gap and Toxaway Mountain.

Little Hogback Mountain, on the Jackson-Macon County line.

Little Horse Creek rises near Pond Mountain in nw Ashe County and flows se into Horse Creek.

Little Horse Creek rises in w Avery County and flows se into North Toe River.

Little Hoyles Creek rises in n Gaston County and flows s into Hoyles Creek.

Little Hubquarter Creek rises in e Warren County and flows n into Hubquarter Creek.

Little Huckleberry Knob, w Graham County between Huckleberry Knob and Doc Stewart Ridge. Alt. approx. 5,380.

Little Hump Mountain, on the Avery County, N. C.-Carter County, Tenn., line.

Little Hungry River rises in e Henderson County and flows sw into Hungry River.

Little Hunting Creek rises in s Wilkes County and flows se into Hunting Creek.

Little Hurricane Creek rises in n Madison County and flows se into Big Laurel Creek.

Little Indian Creek rises in s Chatham County and flows e into Indian Creek.

Little Indian Creek rises in nw Lincoln County near the Catawba County line and flows se into Indian Creek.

Little Indian Creek rises in sw Macon County and flows ne into Nantahala River.

Little Inlet, former inlet from the Atlantic Ocean through Onslow Beach in s Onslow County. Appears on the Moseley map, 1733, and on the Mouzon map, 1775, where the maximum depth is shown to be 6 feet. Does not appear on the Price map, 1808, or on subsequent maps.

Little Island Creek rises in nw Vance County and flows n into Island Creek.

Little Ivy Creek is formed in w Madison County by the junction of California Creek and Paint Fork and flows sw to join Ivy Creek at the Buncombe-Madison County line in forming Ivy River.

Little Jacobs Creek rises in s Stanly County and flows se and ne into Jacobs Creek.

Little Jacob Swamp rises in central Robeson County and flows se into Jacob Swamp.

Little John Creek rises in se Craven County and flows nw into Hancock Creek.

Little Jonas Creek rises in n Swain County and flows se into Jonas Creek.

Little Juniper Creek rises in central Moore County and flows nw into Big Juniper Creek.

Little Juniper Creek rises in s Lee County and flows ne into Little River.

Little Kings Creek rises in ne Caldwell County and flows ne into Kings Creek.

Little Kinnekeet Coast Guard Station, decommissioned station on Hatteras Island, se Dare County. First est. as a lifesaving station in 1874. Lifesaving Service and Revenue Cutter Service joined to form U.S. Coast Guard in 1915.

Little Kitchens Ridge, se Clay County between Holden Cove and Tallulah River.

Little Knob, on Haywood-Swain County line.

Little Knob on the Madison County, N. C.-Greene County, Tenn., line.

Little Knob Creek rises in n Cleveland County and flows se into Knob Creek.

Little Lake, natural lake in Croatan National Forest, s Craven County. Covers approx. 500 acres. Max. depth 4 to 5 ft. One of several lakes in Lakes Pocosin.

Little Laurel Branch rises in se Mitchell County and flows s into North Toe River.

Little Laurel Creek, rises in w Ashe County and flows e into Big Laurel Creek.

Little Laurel Creek rises in w Macon County and flows ne into Whiteoak Creek.

Little Laurel Creek rises in n Madison County and flows sw and se into Shelton Laurel Creek.

Little Laurel Creek rises in se Swain County and flows ne into Yalaka Creek.

Little Laurel Creek rises in nw Wake County and flows w into Big Lick Creek.

Little Ledge Creek rises in s Granville County and flows s into Ledge Creek.

Little Lick Creek rises in s Durham County and flows ne into Neuse River.

Little Lick Creek rises in e Lee County and flows n into Lick Creek.

Little Lick Fork. See Lick Fork.

Little Limestone Creek rises in e Duplin County and flows se into Limestone Creek.

Little Long Creek rises in central Gaston County and flows se into Long Creek.

Little Long Mountain, sw Randolph County between King Mountain and Poison Fork.

Little Lost Cove Creek rises in e central Avery County and flows ne into Lost Cove Creek.

Little Lost Cove Creek rises in s Yancey County and flows nw into South Toe River.

Little Lyman Branch rises in sw Macon County and flows n into Kimsey Creek.

Little Manor, ne Warren County near the town of Littleton, home of William Person Little, state senator from Warren County (1804-1806). The house was built in 1780 and is still standing.

Little Marsh Swamp rises in s Hoke County and flows se into Robeson County where it enters Gallberry Swamp.

Little Matrimony Creek rises in n Rockingham County and flows e in an arc into Matrimony Creek, which see.

Little Meadow Creek rises in se Cabarrus County and flows sw into Rocky River.

Little Middle Mountain, n Buncombe County between Brank Mountain and Brittain Cove, 2½ mi. ne of town of Weaverville.

Little Middle Ridge, ne Madison County between Colvin and Amos creeks.

Little Mountain, se Clay County extending from Eagle Creek e to White Oak Stamp.

Little Mountain, s Haywood County on Plott Creek.

Little Mountain, between Hyatt Creek and Richland Creek, s Haywood County. It is an extended ridge approx. 1 mi. long.

Little Mountain, on Gash Creek in w Henderson County.

Little Mountain, community in e McDowell County.

Little Mountain, s Macon County between Coweeta Creek and Little Tennessee River.

Little Mountain, e Mitchell County between Green Cove Creek and Cane Creek.

Little Mountain, sw Polk County. Alt. 1,600.

Little Mountain, n Rutherford County at the head of Hunting Creek.

Little Mountain, w Surry County between Mitchell River and South Fork.

Little Mountain, ne Transylvania County between Silver Creek and Boylston Creek.

Little Mountain, sw Wilkes County near Yadkin River.

Little Mountain, s Yancey County, extends ne from Setrock Creek to John Autrey Branch.

Little Mountain. See Anderson's Mountain.

Little Mountain Creek rises in n Richmond County and flows sw into Big Mountain Creek.

Little Mountain Creek rises in ne Stanly County and flows se into Mountain Creek.

Little Mountain Creek rises in s Yancey County and flows se into South Toe River.

Little Mud Creek rises in w Henderson County and flows ne into Mud Creek.

Little Mulberry Creek, approx. 5 mi. long, rises in Pisgah National Forest, n Caldwell County, and flows first se then sw into Mulberry Creek.

Little Neatman Creek rises in s Stokes County and flows sw into Neatman Creek.

Little Nettle Branch rises in nw Haywood County and flows n into Big Creek.

Little New Mountain, central Buncombe County, e of Wilson.

Little Nigger Head, peak in n Clay County between Tusquitee Gap and Tuni Creek.

Little Northeast Creek rises in ne Onslow County and flows sw into Northeast Creek.

Little Nutbush Creek, former stream rising in n central Vance County and flowing ne into Nutbush Creek. Now submerged by Kerr Reservoir.

Little Panthertail Mountain, w Transylvania County between Panthertail Mountain and Indian Creek.

Little Paw Creek rises in w Mecklenburg County and flows w into Catawba River.

Little Peachtree Creek rises in e Franklin County and flows se into Nash County where it joins Big Peachtree Creek to form Stony Creek.

Little Pee Dee River is formed in se Scotland County by the junction of Bridge and Leiths creeks. It flows se across the w corner of Robeson County and into South Carolina where it enters Pee Dee River near its mouth.

Little Permetter Creek rises in n central Anson County and flows s into Permetter Creek, which see.

Little Persimmon Creek rises in e Cleveland County and flows nw into Persimmon Creek.

Little Peters Creek rises in Virginia and flows sw into Stokes County where it enters Peters Creek.

Little Pine Creek rises in e Alleghany County and flows sw into Brush Creek.

Little Pine Creek rises in w Jackson County and flows se into Pine Creek.

Little Pine Creek rises in s Madison County and flows ne into French Broad River.

Little Pine Creek Township, former township in s central Madison County, now township number 7.

Little Pine Gap, s Madison County on the sw end of Rocky Ridge.

Little Pine Mountain, n Avery County.

Little Piney Branch rises in ne Buncombe County and flows se into Flat Creek.

Little Piney Ridge, ne Buncombe County, sw of Little Piney Branch.

Little Piney Ridge, s Yancey County between Big Poplar Creek and Mitchell Creek.

Little Pinnacle, s Macon County between Pinnacle Branch and the head of Jones Creek.

Little Pisgah Mountain of Buncombe-Haywood-Henderson County lines e of Mount Pisgah. Alt. approx. 5,320.

Little Pisgah Mountain on the Buncombe-Henderson County line between the headwaters of Ashworth Creek and Blue Rock Knob. Alt. 4,412. Known as Konnatoga by the Cherokee Indians.

Little Pisgah Ridge, nw Henderson County, a part of Pisgah Ridge.

Little Plumtree Creek rises in central Avery County and flows s and w into Plumtree Creek.

Little Pocket Creek rises in w Lee County and flows ne into Pocket Creek.

Little Polecat Creek rises in n Randolph County and flows sw into Polecat Creek.

Little Pole Creek rises near Luther Knob in sw Buncombe County and flows s into Pole Creek.

Little Pond Branch rises in w Watauga County and flows nw into Pond Branch.

Little Porpoise Bay in Pamlico Sound on the e side of Goose Creek Island, ne Pamlico County.

Little Prong, community in nw Brunswick County.

Little Quankey Creek rises in n Halifax County and flows se into Quankey Creek.

Little Raft Swamp rises in s Hoke County and flows se into Raft Swamp in n Robeson County.

Little Ragged Point. See Holmes Point.

Little Rattlesnake Branch rises in ne Buncombe County and flows s into Swannanoa River.

Little Richardson Creek rises in s Union

County and flows n into Richardson Creek.

Little Richmond, community in s Surry County e of Snow Creek.

Little Rich Mountain, at the head of Queen Creek in nw Henderson County.

Little Rich Mountain on Transylvania County, N.C.-Greenville County, S.C., line near Wildcat Branch.

Little Ridge, w Haywood County, Great Smoky Mountains National Park, a short spur of Big Fork Ridge extending ne, center near lat. 35° 35′ 38″ N., long. 83° 08′ 28″ W.

Little Ridgepole Mountain, s Macon County between Big Laurel Branch and Betty Creek.

Little Right Hand Fork. See Little Fork.

Little River rises in sw Alleghany County and flows e and n into Virginia where it enters New River.

Little River rises in s Burke County and flows s into Jacob Fork.

Little River, formed in nw Durham County by the junction of North Fork Little River and South Fork Little River; it flows se into Eno River. Appears on the Moseley map, 1733.

Little River rises in sw Franklin County near the town of Youngsville and flows s across e Wake County, across ne Johnston County and into central Wayne County where it splits into 2 branches, each entering Neuse River sw of city of Goldsboro. Shown on Collet map, 1770.

Little River rises in sw Moore County and flows se across n Hoke County into Cumberland County and along the Cumberland-Harnett County line into the Cape Fear River. Appears on the Collet map, 1770. Known also as Lower Little River.

Little River, nw Northampton County, a part of the Roanoke River which flows on the n side of Tucker Island.

Little River rises in e Perquimans and w Pasquotank counties and flows se on the county line into Albemarle Sound. Appears on the Comberford map, 1657, as Yeopim River, but is correctly shown on the Ogilby map, 1671. In 1662, the Indians in the area seem to have known the river as Kototine. The legislature met at Little River in 1707, 1709, 1712, and 1716.

Little River rises in central Randolph County and flows s through Montgomery County into Richmond County where it enters Pee Dee River. Appears on the Collet map, 1770.

Little River rises in se Transylvania County and flows ne then nw into French Broad River.

Little River, community in w Alexander County. Alt. approx. 1,125.

Little River, community in e Transylvania County on Little River about two mi. n of Cascade Lake. Now includes community of Grange whose post office was est. in 1882. Alt. approx. 2,120.

Little River Academy. See Linden.

Little River Township, n Alexander County.

Little River Township, e Caldwell County.

Little River Township, e Moore County. Transferred from Hoke to Moore County, 1958.

Little River Township, ne Montgomery County.

Little River Township, ne Orange County.

Little River Township, se Transylvania County.

Little River Township, ne Wake County.

Little Roaring Creek rises in nw Avery County and flows e into Cranberry Creek.

Little Rock Branch rises in sw Macon County and flows sw into Nantahala River.

Little Rock Creek rises in e Mitchell County and flows sw into Big Rock Creek.

Little Rock Creek. See Glen Ayre.

Little Rock Creek Township, ne Mitchell County.

Little Rockfish Creek rises in Fort Bragg Military Reservation on the Cumberland-Hoke County line and flows se along the line to Lake William where it enters w Cumberland County and flows se to enter Rockfish Creek at town of Hope Mills.

Little Rockfish Creek rises in s Duplin County and flows s from Boney Mill Pond into Rockfish Creek on the Duplin-Pender County Line.

Little Rock Knob on the Mitchell County, N. C.-Carter County, Tenn., line. Alt. approx. 4, 920.

Little Rocky Creek. See Olin Creek.

Little Rocky Face, a peak in e Haywood County between the head of Garden Creek and the head of Harley Branch.

Little Rocky Knob, n Buncombe County ne of Razor Mountain.

Little Rocky Knob, nw Caldwell County on sw side of Rocky Knob. Alt. approx. 2,250.

Little Rocky Mountain, e Macon County on a tributary of Little Salt Rock Creek.

Little Rose Creek rises in se Mitchell County and flows nw into Rose Creek.

Little Ruin Creek rises in w Vance County and flows se into Ruin Creek.

Little Salt Rock Creek rises in e Macon County and flows nw into Wildcat Creek.

Little Sam Knob, s Haywood County between Bubbling Springs Branch and Flat Laurel Creek. Alt. 5,862.

Little Sandy Branch rises in s Stokes County and flows se into Town Fork Creek.

Little Sandy Creek rises in ne Wilkes County and flows s into East Prong Roaring River.

Little Sandy Gap, on the Buncombe-Madison County line e of Davidson Gap.

Little Sandy Mush Bald, peak on the Buncombe-Madison County line between Sandy Mush Bald and Chestnut Gap.

Little Sandymush Creek rises in s Madison County and flows e into Sandy Mush Creek.

Little Sandy Run Swamp rises in w Onslow County and flows se into Sandy Run Swamp.

Little Santeetlah Creek rises in w Graham County and flows se through the Joyce Kilmer Memorial Forest into Santeetlah Creek, which see.

Little Sapony Creek rises in w Nash County and flows se into Sapony Creek.

Little Savannah Creek rises in w Jackson County and flows nw into Savannah Creek.

Little Scaly Mountain, s Macon County between Abe Creek and Chinquapin Mountain. Alt. 4,200.

Little Shaddox Creek rises in n Lee County and flows e into Cape Fear River.

Little Sheep Cliffs, s Jackson County between Horsepasture River and Sheep Cliffs.

Little Shell Rock. See North Rock.

Little Shepherd Mountain, w Randolph County between Uwharrie River and Little Caraway Creek.

Little Shoal Creek rises in w Cherokee County and flows se into Shoal Creek.

Little Shocco Creek rises in e Vance County and flows se into Warren and onto the Franklin-Warren County line before entering Shocco Creek.

Little Shuckstack, mountain in Great Smoky Mountains National Park, nw Swain County, lat. 35° 29′ 26″ N., long. 83° 48′ 37″ W. Alt. 3,821.

Little Silver Creek rises in sw Burke County and flows ne into Silver Creek.

Little Singletary Lake, a natural lake in n Bladen County; approx. 1½ mi. long and ¾ mi. wide. Fishing. See also Carolina Bays.

Littles Mill, community in nw Richmond County on Little River. A post office was est. here prior to 1882.

Little Snowball Mountain, n Buncombe County between Cherry Log Gap and Snowball Gap. Alt. 4,824.

Little Snowbird Creek rises in s Graham County and flows ne and nw into Snowbird Creek.

Little Snow Creek rises in n Stokes County and flows se into Snow Creek.

Little Spivey Creek rises in n Yancey County and flows w into Tennessee where it enters Spivey Creek.

Little Spruce Ridge, w Haywood County, Great Smoky Mountains National Park, a spur extending ne from Cataloochee Divide, center near lat. 35° 33′ 35″ N., long. 83° 08′ 04″ W., between Little Bald Branch and Bearpen Branch.

Little Steeltrap Creek rises in n Swain County and flows sw into Forney Creek.

Little Stonehouse Creek rises in e Warren County and flows ne into Gaston Lake.

Little Stone Mountain, n Wilkes County on the w side of East Prong Roaring River.

Little Sugar Creek rises in central Mecklenburg County and flows sw into South Carolina where it enters Sugar Creek. Appears as Shugan Creek on the Collet map, 1770, but with its present name on the Price map, 1808.

Little Swamp, rises in e Columbus County and flows sw into Juniper Creek.

Little Swamp rises in s Nash County and flows se into Toisnot Swamp.

Little Swamp Branch rises in sw Johnston County and flows se into Mill Swamp Branch.

Little Swift Creek rises in ne Craven County and flows sw into Swift Creek.

Little Switzerland, community and summer resort in nw McDowell County on the head of Threemile Creek. Alt. 3,500. Founded in 1910 as a summer resort by Heriot Clarkson (1863-1942). Named because of the supposed resemblance of the mountains of the area to those of Switzerland. See also Armstrong.

Little Tennessee River is formed in Rabun County, Georgia, by the junction of Betty and Darnell creeks. It flows n and nw into Macon County and through Lake Emory; into Swain County and along the Graham-Swain County line through Fontana Lake and Lake Cheoah; and into Tennessee where it enters the Tennessee River. This river, discovered in 1540 by Hernando

De Soto, was the first tributary of the Mississippi River discovered by Europeans.

Little Terrapin Mountain, s Jackson County approx. 1½ mi. s of Hampton Lake, is bordered on the w by Fowler Creek. Alt. 3,900.

Little Timber Ridge, n Avery County.

Little Tomahawk Creek rises in w Forsyth County and flows se into Stewarts Creek. Some time prior to 1762 Stewarts Creek was known as Tomahawk Branch. *See also* Stewarts Creek.

Little Tomahawk Creek rises in s Sampson County and flows nw to join Big Tomahawk Creek in forming Tomahawk Creek.

Littleton, town in e Warren County and nw Halifax County. Alt. 389. Inc. 1877 and named for Little Manor *(which see).* Person Ordinary, the tavern owned by Thomas Person (1733-1800), Regulator, officer of the Continental Line, and state legislator, was located here and is shown on the Collet map, 1770. The tavern, which is still standing, was called Peterson Inn on the Price map, 1808. Littleton was mentioned by name in newspapers as early as 1823, and in 1831 a post office was est. here under the present name. The MacRae map, 1833, shows Littleton as an established community.

Littleton's Store, community in central Onslow County between Rocky Run and Mott Creek.

Little Town Creek rises in s Montgomery County and flows se into Town Creek.

Littletown Township, nw Halifax County.

Little Troublesome Creek is formed in central Rockingham County by the junction of two unnamed branches. One rises in the town of Reidsville and the other rises sw of the town. They join approx. 2 mi. s of Reidsville and flow se into Haw River.

Little Tuni Creek rises in n Clay County between Deadline Ridge and Tuni Creek and flows s into Tusquitee Creek.

Little Tuni Creek rises in w Macon County and flows n into Big Choga Creek.

Little Trout Creek rises in central Jackson County and flows n into Mill Creek.

Little Turnbull Creek rises in ne Bladen County and flows w into Turnbull Creek. Once known as Edward Jones Creek.

Little Uwharrie River rises in nw Randolph County and flows se into Uwharrie River.

Little Warrior Mountain, s Polk County, w of town of Tryon. The name is a corruption

of the Indian word *"wayah"* meaning "wolf."

Little Webb Creek rises in s Buncombe County and flows sw into Gap Creek.

Little Whiteoak Creek rises in w Wake County and flows sw into Whiteoak Creek.

Little Whiteoak Creek rises in e Yancey County and flows nw into South Toe River.

Little Whitewater Creek rises in s Jackson County and flows se to join Silver Run Creek in forming Whitewater River.

Little Will Branch rises in ne Buncombe County and flows sw into North Fork Ivy Creek.

Little Willow Creek rises in w Henderson County and flows ne into French Broad River. A legendary Cherokee route, "Willow Trail," followed the course of this stream.

Little Yadkin River is formed in sw Stokes County by the junction of East Prong Little Yadkin River and West Prong Little Yadkin River and flows s into Forsyth County where it enters Yadkin River.

Little Yalaka Creek rises in s Swain County and flows sw into Yalaka Creek.

Little Yellow Mountain on the Avery-Mitchell County line. Alt. 5,000-5,100.

Little Yellow Mountain, se Macon County between Brooks Creek and Monger Creek.

Liverman. *See* Newtown.

Liverman Creek rises in n Hertford County and flows se into Meherrin River.

Livermans Mill Pond, w Hertford County, 1½ mi. long, drains into Potecasi Creek.

Liverpool. *See* Cornelius.

Livingston. *See* Acme.

Livingston Creek rises in Green Swamp in n central Brunswick County and flows n across Columbus County where it enters the Cape Fear River. Appears as Levingtons Creek on maps as early as 1844.

Livingswood Creek. *See* Carvers Creek.

Lizard Creek rises in s Brunswick County, Virginia, and flows se into ne Warren County where it enters Gaston Lake.

Lizard Lick, crossroads community in e Wake County near town of Wendell. Named by a passing observer who saw many lizards sunning and "licking" themselves on a rail fence here.

Lizard Ridge, community in e central Caldwell County between Zacks Fork and Blair Fork.

Lizzards Creek rises in Virginia and flows se into n Halifax County where it enters Roanoke River.

Lizzie, community in central Greene County; a post office in the late nineteenth century. Said to have been known first as Lizzie's Store for the old lady who kept a store here. Also called Lillie during the 1890's.

Lizzie's Store. See Lizzie.

Lizzy Mountain, central Jackson County between Dickson Creek and Trout Creek.

Lloyd Cove, s Macon County e of Green Cove on a tributary of Tessentee Creek.

Lloyd Crossroads, community in se Hertford County.

Lloyds Meadows, an area of meadow land approx. 2 mi. long and 1 mi. wide, in e Onslow County at the head of Horse Swamp.

Loafers Glory, community in central Mitchell County on Cane Creek. Named about 1890 by Jonathan Burleson because men delighted in whiling away their time on the porch of the local general store.

Loar Creek. See Little Creek.

Lobelia, community in se Moore County.

Loch Lily, lake on Storys Creek, nw Person County. Formed prior to 1928 and known first as Barnetts Pond, later as Lake Chub, and finally by its present name. Covers 94 acres. Maximum depth 12 ft.

Locke Mills. See Forest Hill.

Locke Township, central Rowan County. Named for Gen. Matthew Locke (1730-1801), statesman and patriot, who lived here.

Locketts Island, a clay loam island approx. 1 mi. long in Roanoke River, w Northampton County.

Lockhart Mill. See Hoggard's Mill.

Lockport, community in se Chatham County on Deep River, w of Moncure. An earlier post office here was known as Lockville. Site of locks of Cape Fear and Deep River Navigation Co.; Carolina Power and Light Co. has a small power plant here now which uses the lock canal as a mill race. At Ramsey's Mill here, following the Battle of Guilford Court House in 1781, the British general, Lord Cornwallis, built a bridge over Deep River.

Locks Creek rises in e central Cumberland County and flows sw and s into Cape Fear River. See also Lords Creek.

Lockville. See Lockport.

Lockwoods Folly Inlet, the inlet between Holden Beach and Long Beach through which Lockwoods Folly River flows into Long Bay of the Atlantic Ocean, s central Brunswick County. Appears on the Ogilby map, 1671. The name is said to have been given because a man named Lockwood built a fine boat up Lockwoods Folly River but discovered that it was too large to float into the Atlantic through the inlet. He was forced to abandon his boat and it eventually fell to pieces. Frequently in the seventeenth century, however, the word Folly was used in the sense of the French folie, "delight," or "favorite abode," and it formed a part of the name of English estates. Lockwoods Folly River, which see, has been described as the second most beautiful river in North Carolina and it may have been the "delight" or "favorite abode" of an early settler named Lockwood. See also Longs Delight.

Lockwoods Folly River is formed in central Brunswick County by the junction of Pinch Gut Creek and Red Run and flows w and s through Lockwoods Folly Inlet, which see, into Long Bay of the Atlantic Ocean. This river has been described as perhaps the second most beautiful in the state after Waccamaw River.

Lockwoods Folly Township, s central Brunswick County.

Locust, town in sw Stanly County. Inc. 1905, but long inactive in municipal affairs. A post office, Locust Level, opened 1869; discontinued 1919. Re-established under present name, 1955. Named for large locust tree. Locust Level changed to Locust in 1894.

Locust Gap, ne Buncombe County between Rough Hew Ridge and Forney Creek.

Locust Cove Gap, e Graham County on the headwaters of Stecoah Creek.

Locust Creek rises in n Jackson County and flows sw into Tuckasegee River.

Locust Creek rises in e Yancey County and flows se into South Toe River.

Locust Gap, ne Buncombe County between Pigpen Cove and Sugarhouse Cove.

Locust Gap, ne Cherokee County at the end of Townhouse Ridge between Townhouse and Welch Mill creeks.

Locust Gap, on Jackson-Haywood County line.

Locust Gap, n Swain County on Locust Ridge near the head of Big Flats Branch.

Locust Gap on the Watauga County, N. C.-Johnson County, Tenn., line in the Stone Mountains.

Locust Grove, community in n Randolph County.

Locust Grove. *See* Satterwhite.

Locust Hill, community in w Caswell County. Named for locust trees in the vicinity. Known as Brown's Store from the early nineteenth century until the 1840's when the name was changed. Jethro Brown operated the store. Rose Hill, home of Bedford Brown, U.S. Senator, 1829-1840, state legislator, opponent of secession, 1860, stands here; built about 1802.

Locust Hill, home of William Eaton, w Vance County. Built between 1740-1743; served as an early religious center for the Episcopal Church, and the first Granville County Superior Court met here in 1746. Located approx. 3 mi. sw of the town of Henderson.

Locust Hill Township, w central Caswell County.

Locust Knob, s central Avery County.

Locust Knob, ne Buncombe County in the Great Craggy Mountains. Alt. approx. 5,480.

Locust Knob, n McDowell County, a part of Pompey Ridge between O'Dear Creek and Long Branch. Alt. approx. 2,650.

Locust Knob, central Mitchell County between Toe River and Pumpkin Patch Mountain.

Locust Knob in Great Smoky Mountains National Park, ne Swaia County on Heintooga Ridge, lat. 35° 33' 27" N., long. 83° 12' 08" W. Alt. 4,034.

Locust Level. *See* Locust.

Locust Licklog Gap, central Graham County in Cheoah Mountains between Hazanet Knob and Wauchecha Bald.

The Locust Mountain, on Burke-McDowell County line.

Locust Ridge, ne Buncombe County s of Staire Branch.

Locust Ridge on the Madison County, N. C.-Unicoi County, Tenn., line.

Locust Ridge in Great Smoky Mountains National Park, w Swain County extending s from Big Chestnut Bald.

Locust Ridge, e Yancey County between Whiteoak and Locust creeks.

Locust Rough Mountain, n Yancey County at the se end of Bailey Hill.

Locust Rough Ridge, w Yancey County between Simms Fork and Lickskillet Branch.

Locust Tree Branch rises in w Macon County and flows se into Wyah Creek.

Locust Tree Gap, w Macon County at the head of Locust Tree Branch.

Locust Tree Gap central Macon County between Bruce Knob and Wilkes Knob.

Loftins Crossroads, community in e Lenoir County. Named for the Loftin family which settled here.

Loftis, community. *See* Cedar Mountain.

Logan, community in n central Rutherford County. Named for a local storekeeper; the post office est. prior to 1882 but now discontinued was Logans Store.

Logan Creek rises in s Jackson County and flows s into Horsepasture River.

Logan Store Township, e Rutherford County.

Loggerhead Inlet from the Atlantic Ocean into Pamlico Sound through Hatteras Island n of the present community of Rodanthe, e Dare County. It opened prior to 1851 and closed in the late 1870's.

Loggy Branch rises in s Clay County and flows n into Right Fork.

Loggy Gap, mountain gap in central Avery County.

Loggy Knob, n Mitchell County between Bearwallow Creek and Waterfall Branch.

Loggy Ridge, n Swain County in Great Smoky Mountains National Park, at lat. 35° 33' N., long. 83° 32' 08" W.

Log Hollow Branch rises in n Transylvania County and flows se into Big Bear Pen Branch.

Log Shoal in the waters of Pamlico Sound, s Dare County, off the s part of Hatteras Island and e of Bird Islands.

Lola, community on Cedar Island in ne Carteret County.

Lomax, community in n Wilkes County between East Prong Roaring River and Big Bugaboo Creek in the center of a very good wheat and tobacco producing area.

Lona Creek rises in se Beaufort County and flows n into South Creek.

London Bald, on the Cherokee-Macon County line.

Lone Bald Mountain, on Haywood-Jackson County line. Originally Lone Balsam Mountain from the fact that a single large balsam tree stood on its crest. With the disappearance of the tree the name was shortened to Lone Bald. Alt. 5,880.

Lone Balsam Mountain. *See* Lone Bald Mountain.

Lone Hickory, community in s Yadkin County near South Deep Creek.

Lone Knob, n Madison County between Duckmill Branch and West Prong [Hickory Fork].

Lone Mountain, ne Rutherford County, between the heads of First Broad River and Cane Creek. Alt. approx. 1,650.

Lone Oak Channel, between Beasley Bay and Currituck Sound, e Currituck County.

Lone Pine Ridge, Great Smoky Mountains National Park, n Swain County, a short spur extending sw from Thomas Ridge, lat. 35° 31′ 15″ N., long. 83° 23′ 13″ W.

Lonesome Mountain, n Madison County on Big Laurel Creek.

Lonesome Valley. *See* Henderson.

Long Acre, an elevated area of clay loam extending s from the head of Conaby Creek in w Washington County to Pungo Creek, se of the community of Pinetown, in n central Beaufort County. The ridge is broken at the Tare-over in sw Washington County by Van Swamp. Appears on the Collet map, 1770. *See also* Tare-over.

Long Acre Township, n central Beaufort County. *See also* Acre.

Long Arm Mountain, nw Burke County. Alt. 4,350. Highest point in county.

Longarm Mountain, n Haywood County extends ne from the head of Dogwood Flats Creek to the head of Stinking Camp Creek.

Long Arm Ridge, s Yancey County, extends se between Devils Den and Laurel Branch.

Long Bay in the Atlantic Ocean off the se coast of North Carolina and ne South Carolina from Winyah Bay on the s to Cape Fear on the n. Appears on the Moseley map, 1733,

Long Bay, ne Carteret County between Cedar Island and Piney Island, s of West Bay.

Long Beach, a section of outer beach in se Brunswick County on the Atlantic Ocean w of Caswell Beach and e of Lockwoods Folly Inlet. Long Beach, a town here, was inc. 1955. A summer resort.

Long Bottoms, an area of approx. 50 acres of level old field land between two mountains in sw Graham County on Snowbird Creek.

Long Branch rises in se Alamance County and flows e into Mary's Creek.

Long Branch rises in nw Buncombe County near Graybeard Mountain and flows w into North Fork [Swannanoa River].

Long Branch rises in nw Buncombe County and flows se into Sandy Mush Creek.

Long Branch rises in ne Buncombe County and flows sw into Beetree Creek.

Long Branch rises in s Buncombe County and flows ne into Bent Creek.

Long Branch rises in ne Cherokee County and flows nw into Valley River.

Long Branch rises in sw Cherokee County and flows se into Hothouse Branch.

Long Branch rises in n Clay County and flows sw into Fires Creek.

Long Branch rises in n Clay County and flows sw into Tuni Creek.

Long Branch rises in s Clay County and flows se into Crawford Creek.

Long Branch rises in se Cleveland County and flows nw into Beason Creek.

Long Branch rises in sw Columbus County and flows ne into Porter Swamp.

Long Branch rises in s Duplin County and flows se into Cypress Creek.

Long Branch rises in s Durham County and flows sw into w Wake County where it enters Kit Creek.

Long Branch rises in central Franklin County and flows se into Tar River approx. 4 mi. se of town of Louisburg.

Long Branch rises in e Franklin County and flows sw into Cypress Creek.

Long Branch rises in se Graham County and flows w into Sweetwater Creek.

Long Branch rises in n Guilford County and flows sw into East Fork Deep River.

Long Branch rises in e Haywood County and flows sw into East Fork Pigeon River.

Long Branch rises in s Haywood County and flows ne into Cherry Cove Creek.

Long Branch rises in e Haywood County and flows sw into Beaverdam Creek.

Long Branch rises in e Haywood County and flows w into Pigeon River.

Long Branch rises in nw Henderson County and flows se into North Fork.

Long Branch rises in s Hertford County and flows se into Chinkapin Creek.

Long Branch rises in se Hertford County and flows sw into Kill'em Swamp.

Long Branch rises in e Jackson County and flows se into Charley Creek.

Long Branch rises in s Jackson County e of Cowrock Mountain and flows se to enter Trays Island Creek n of Fairfield Lake.

Long Branch rises in w Jackson County and flows sw into Tuckasegee River s of Hazel Hollow.

Long Branch rises on the s slopes of Jones Knob in w Jackson County and flows sw into Savannah Creek.

Long Branch rises in w Jackson County and flows ne into Cullowhee Creek.

Long Branch rises in n Johnston County and flows se into Little River.

Long Branch rises in ne Jones County and flows sw approx. 3 mi. into Trent River.

Long Branch rises in ne McDowell County and flows n into Pepper Creek.

Long Branch rises in n McDowell County on the s slope of Pompey Ridge and flows se into Armstrong Creek.

Long Branch rises in e Macon County and flows sw into Cullasaja River.

Long Branch rises in n Macon County and flows se into Lakey Creek.

Long Branch rises in n Macon County and flows n into Little Tennessee River.

Long Branch rises in nw Macon County and flows w into Whiteoak Creek.

Long Branch rises in sw Macon County and flows w into Nantahala River.

Long Branch rises in e Madison County and flows nw into Big Laurel Creek.

Long Branch rises in s Madison County and flows s into Ivy River.

Long Branch rises in w Madison County and flows e into Meadow Fork.

Long Branch rises in s Mitchell County and flows sw and w into Big Crabtree Creek.

Long Branch rises in sw Polk County and flows nw into Pacolet River.

Long Branch rises in central Randolph County and flows nw into Back Creek.

Long Branch rises in e Robeson County and flows se into Big Swamp.

Long Branch rises in ne Rutherford County and flows se into Cleveland County where it enters Duncans Creek.

Long Branch rises in sw Swain County and flows sw into Siles Branch approx. 1 mi. se of community of Almond.

Long Branch rises in n central Swain County and flows sw into Lands Creek.

Long Branch rises in ne Transylvania County and flows se into Sitton Creek.

Long Branch rises in w Transylvania County and flows se into North Fork French Broad River.

Long Branch rises in w Transylvania County and flows ne into Davidson River.

Long Branch rises near the e border of Vance County and flows ne into w Warren County where it enters Matthews Creek.

Long Branch rises in central Wake County and flows s into Marsh Creek.

Long Branch rises in s Warren County and flows e into Fishing Creek.

Long Branch rises in e Watauga County and flows s into Southwest Stony Fork Creek.

Long Branch rises in n Watauga County and flows sw into Cove Creek.

Long Branch rises in s Watauga County and

flows se into Caldwell County where it enters China Creek. Approx. 1 mi. long.

Long Branch rises in central Wilkes County and flows se into Mulberry Creek.

Long Branch rises in sw Wilson County and flows se into Black Creek.

Long Branch rises in e Yancey County and flows nw into South Toe River.

Long Branch rises in n Yancey County and flows ne into Pigpen Creek.

Long Branch rises in n Yancey County and flows ne into Cane River.

Long Branch, community in se Cleveland County.

Long Branch, community in s Robeson County.

Long Brook rises in s Catawba County and flows sw into Pinch Gut Creek.

Long Bunk, ridge in w Haywood County, in Great Smoky Mountains National Park, extending se from Mount Sterling Ridge with its center near lat. 35° 41' 10" N., long. 83° 06' 40" W. Lies between Andy Branch and Dude Creek.

Long Cove, n Swain County between Bearwallow Ridge and Long Cove Ridge.

Long Cove Ridge, Great Smoky Mountains National Park, n Swain County extending sw from Proctor Ridge, lat. 35° 33' 15" N., long. 83° 36' 25" W.

Long Creek rises in ne Catawba County and flows se and e into McLin Creek.

Long Creek rises in the town of Kings Mountain in se Cleveland County and flows se into Buffalo Creek.

Long Creek rises in se Craven County and flows n into Neuse River.

Long Creek rises in Great Swamp, central Currituck County and flows s into North River.

Long Creek rises in w Gaston County and flows e into South Fork Catawba River.

Long Creek rises in s Graham County and flows n into Santeetlah Lake.

Long Creek rises in s Martin County and flows ne into Hardison Mill Creek.

Long Creek rises in n Mecklenburg County and flows sw into Catawba River. Appears as Wis's Creek on the Collet map, 1770, but with its present name on the Price map, 1808.

Long Creek rises in e Pamlico County and flows e and n into Bonner Bay.

Long Creek rises in nw Pender County and flows se into Northeast Cape Fear River. Appears on the Moseley map, 1733.

Long Creek rises in s Rowan County and flows across the ne tip of Cabarrus Coun-

ty; it enters n Stanly County where it runs
the entire length of the county before
entering Rocky River on the border of
Stanly and Anson counties.

Long Creek rises in nw Stanly County and
flows se and sw into Rocky River. Appears
on the Collet map, 1770.

Long Creek rises in w Surry County and
flows se into Mitchell River.

Long Creek rises in e Swain County and
flows sw into Una Creek.

Long Creek rises in s Vance County and
flows s into Tabbs Creek.

Long Creek, community in s Pender County
on the stream of the same name. Alt. 50.
Formerly known as Lillington, but the
name was changed after the town of the
same name was est. in Harnett County
in 1859.

Long Creek Township, now township number 11, w central Mecklenburg County.

Long Creek Township, s central Pender
County.

Long Creek Village. See Lillington.

Long Drive Ridge, Great Smoky Mountains
National Park, n Swain County, extends
sw from Thomas Ridge, lat. 35° 33′ 25″
N., long. 83° 23′ 38″ W.

Long Fork of Beaver Creek rises in sw
Wilkes County and flows e into Beaver
Creek.

Long Gap, sw Buncombe County between
Rich Knob and Ferrin Knob.

Long Gap, on the Buncombe-McDowell
County line between Pot Cove Gap and
Sourwood Gap.

Long Hill Township, ne Surry County.

Long Hollow, at the head of Left Fork
[Cane Creek] in e Mitchell County.

Long Hope Creek rises in nw Watauga
County and flows n into sw Ashe County
where it enters Three Top Creek.

Long Hungry Ridge, nw Swain County,
Great Smoky Mountains National Park,
between Twentymile Creek and Moore
Springs Branch, lat. 35° 31′ 08″ N., long.
83° 50′ 57″ W.

Longhurst, community in central Person
County. Settled about 1890 and known
first as Jalong for J. A. Long, Sr., who
est. a cotton mill here. Post office est.
here in 1913; name changed to Longhurst
in 1936.

Long Island, a long, tidal marsh island in
sw Carteret County, in Bogue Sound.

Long Island, high ground in e central Tyrrell County at the ne end of Hollow
Ground Swamp.

Long Island, community in e Catawba County. Post office est. here about 1895. Former site now covered by waters of Cowan's Ford Dam. The post office and many
homes were moved to nearby higher
ground. Named for an island in the Catawba River. An earlier post office approx.
one mi. away was known as Shawnee.

Long Island, community in w Iredell County
on Catawba River.

Long John Mountain, central Henderson
County, extends from the nw limits of
Hendersonville almost to French Broad
River. Named for an early whisky distiller.

Long Lake, natural lake in Croatan National
Forest, s Craven County. Covers 1,100
acres. Max. depth 4 to 5 ft. One of several
lakes in Lakes Pocosin.

Long Level Mountain, w central Avery
County.

Long Level Mountain, e Mitchell County
between Rube Green Top and Dellinger
Hollow.

Long Levels, a rocky elevation approx. 1½
mi. long in e Haywood County between
the head of Silvers Cove Creek and Long
Levels Branch. Numerous other small unnamed streams rise here.

Long Levels Branch rises in e Haywood
County and flows se into Bald Creek.

Long Mountain, sw Buncombe County,
approx. 1¼ mi. long.

Long Mountain, w Madison County between
John Taylor Branch and Turkey Cove
Branch.

Long Mountain, w Montgomery County between Clarks Creek and Pee Dee River.

Long Mountain, s Randolph County e of
Poison Fork, a long level ridge.

Long Mountain, n Rutherford County on
Chalk Creek.

Long Mountain, ne Rutherford County between Molly Fork and the head of First
Broad River.

Long Mountain Branch rises in w Madison
County near Long Mountain and flows e
into Spring Creek.

Long Neck Point, peninsula extending from
w Goose Creek Island into Goose Creek
at the mouth of Upper Spring Creek, ne
Pamlico County.

Long Pine, community in sw Anson County.
Named for local Methodist Church est.
1791-95. A post office here in the 1880's.

Long Point, on s side of Pamlico River, se
Beaufort County.

Long Point, in ne Carteret County, a se

point of Cedar Island extending into the waters of Core Sound.

Long Point, a long narrow point of land extending off a tidal marsh island adjacent to Piney Island in the waters of Coinjock Bay, central Currituck County. The Intracoastal Waterway separates this small island from the parent island (Piney).

Long Point, peninsula extending se from a small tidal marsh island in Currituck Sound, s Currituck County. This island lies immediately s of Rattle Snake Island and e of Poplar Branch Bay.

Long Point, a peninsula extending from the mainland of central Dare County into East Lake.

Long Point, se extremity of North Banks in ne Dare County, between Kitty Hawk Bay and Currituck Sound. Long Point actually is separated from North Banks by very shallow water.

Long Point extends from the e mainland of Hyde County into Pamlico Sound.

Long Reach Sein Hole, a shallow place in Northeast Cape Fear River in central Duplin County suitable for seining.

Long Ridge, mountain in se Avery County.

Long Ridge, w Cherokee County, extends ne from Apalachia Dam on Hiwassee River. Named for its length.

Long Ridge, a sandy ridge extending from s Craven County below Great Lake into nw Carteret County.

Long Ridge, s Macon County between Barkers Creek and Commissioner Creek.

Long Ridge, Great Smoky Mountains National Park, ne Swain County, extending sw from Hughs Ridge, lat. 35° 37' N., long. 83° 19' W.

Long Ridge, s Tyrrell County, is a stretch of loam surrounded by peat extending se at the head of Southwest Fork [Alligator River].

Long Ridge, an elevated area of clay loam in n Washington County, extending s from the forks of Kendricks Creek to the edge of East Dismal Swamp. This was one of the sites of earliest settlement in Washington County. Appears on the Price map, 1808, and mentioned in local court records as early as 1718. *See also* Long Acre.

Long Ridge, w Watauga County n of Laurel Creek.

Long Ridge. *See* Hoke.

Long Run. *See* Little Creek.

Longs Delight appears on the Ogilby map, 1671, near the upper portion of the Cape Fear River. It was a name assigned prob-

ably for Capt. Anthony Long, member of an expedition led by Capt. William Hilton in 1663 to explore the lower Cape Fear region. *See also* Lockwoods Folly Inlet.

Long Shoal in the waters of Pamlico Sound off the se mainland of Dare County. The waters of Parched Corn Bay lie between it and the mainland.

Long Shoal Bay, the mouth of Long Shoal River in s Dare County.

Long Shoal Point extends from the mainland of s Dare County into Pamlico Sound. Appears on the Moseley map, 1733.

Long Shoal Point, ne Tyrrell County, extends from the mainland into the mouth of Alligator River near the mouth of Alligator Creek.

Long Shoal River rises in the s mainland of Dare County and flows se along the Dare-Hyde County line into Long Shoal Bay in Pamlico Sound. Appears on the Moseley map, 1733.

Long Shoals, community in s Buncombe County on French Broad River.

Longshoals, community in s Lincoln County on South Fork Catawba River. Settled prior to 1901. Named for shoals in the river at this point. Alt. 732.

Long Shoals Mill Pond, s Lincoln County on South Fork Catawba River. Formed 1901 to provide power for cotton mill. Covers 125 acres. Maximum depth 12 feet.

Long Shore Branch rises in e Ashe County and flows n into North Fork New River.

Longs Island, name applied on the Ogilby map, 1671, to the land now in nw New Hanover County between the Brunswick and Cape Fear rivers, n of Eagles Island. This peninsula was formerly an island when Fishing Creek flowed between the two rivers. *See also* Longs Delight.

Longs Store, community in w Person County.

Longs Store, community in n central Rutherford County.

Long's Store, community in n Union County.

Longtown, community in w Burke County.

Longtown, community in se Lincoln County.

Longtown, community in w Yadkin County on South Deep Creek.

Long Town. *See* Gold Point.

Longview, town in nw Catawba County w of Hickory. Inc. 1907. Earlier known as Penelope.

Longwood, community in sw Brunswick County.

Longwood Park, community on the outskirts of Hamlet, s Richmond County. Known also as Northeast Hamlet.

Lonnie Womble Creek rises in n Lee County and flows se into Cape Fear River.

Lookadoo Mountain, n Rutherford County between Carson Mountain and the head of Duncans Creek.

Looking Glass Creek rises in n Transylvania County e of Bennett Gap on the Haywood-Transylvania County line and flows s into Davidson River. Located in Pisgah National Forest.

Looking Glass Falls, n Transylvania County on Looking Glass Creek about ½ mi. upstream from its mouth on Davidson River. The falls are 85 ft. high. Located in Pisgah National Forest.

Looking Glass Rock, n Transylvania County on the se end of Seniard Ridge in Pisgah National Forest. Named because the huge rock face of the mountain glistens like a giant mirror.

Lookoff Gap, se Buncombe County near Flat Top in the Swannanoa Mountains.

Lookout Bight, a bay in the waters of the Atlantic Ocean, formed by the s end of Shackleford and Core Banks, in se Carteret County in connection with a stone breakwater started before World War 1 but never completed.

Lookout Bight Channel. See Barden Inlet.

Lookout Knob, ne Catawba County.

Lookout Knob, se Yancey County near the head of Roaring Fork.

Lookout Mountain, ne Buncombe County, se of Montreat.

Lookout Mountain, central Buncombe County between Woodfin and Asheville.

Lookout Point, the s tip of Cedar Island extending into the waters of Core Sound in ne Carteret County.

Lookout Shoals Lake on Catawba River, bounded by Iredell and Alexander counties on the n, Catawba County on the s. Formed by a dam constructed in 1915 by Duke Power Co. Covers 1,270 acres. Source of hydro-electric power; fishing, boating, camping. See also Island Ford.

Loose Mountain, w Caldwell County.

Loosen Swamp. See Corapeake Swamp.

Loosing Swamp rises in n central Bertie County and flows ne into Stony Creek. Mentioned in local records as early as 1725.

Loosing Swamp rises in n central Lenoir County and flows e for approx. 5 mi. into Stonyton Creek. The name appears in local records as early as 1744. It is believed to be derived from Lucerne, the Swiss city, and was given to the swamp by Swiss settlers who moved into the area from New Bern in the early eighteenth century. Also appears as Louson; Lousin; and Luzern.

Loray, community in w Iredell County. Grew up around Concord Church, est. 1775. Prior to 1903 when it was given its present name by Miss Ora Sharpe, it was known as Fancy Hill post office and Iredell Station on the railroad.

Lords Creek rises in n central Cumberland County and flows sw between Dunfields Creek and Locks Creek to empty into Cape Fear River e of the town of Fayetteville. The stream appears as both Lords Creek and Locks Creek (which see) on the Kerr map, 1882, but this error is corrected by the McDuffie map, 1884.

Lords Creek rises in s New Hanover County and flows w into the Cape Fear River. Named for the Lord family of Brunswick County.

Lost Bottom Creek, w Haywood County, Great Smoky Mountains National Park, rises near lat. 35° 40' N., long. 83° 11' 07" W., and flows se into Palmer Creek.

Lost Cove, n Jackson County between Lost Cove Branch and Lickstone Ridge.

Lost Cove, n Yancey County on a short unnamed stream which flows nw into Nolichucky River.

Lost Cove, community in n Yancey County on Nolichucky River.

Lost Cove Branch rises in n Jackson County and flows se into Soco Creek.

Lost Cove Creek rises in e central Avery County and flows e into Caldwell County where it enters Wilsons Creek.

Lost Cove Creek, Great Smoky Mountains National Park, rises in nw Swain County and flows se into Fontana Lake.

Lost Cove Ridge, se Avery County.

Lost Cove Ridge, s Yancey County, extends ne parallel to South Toe River between Little Lost Cove Creek and Big Lost Cove Creek.

Lost Knob, e Jackson County between Lynn Gap and Deep Gap.

Lost Ridge, n Watauga County extends ne of Forest Grove Creek.

Lottie Creek rises in nw Yancey County and flows se into Bald Mountain Creek.

Loudermilk Ridge, Great Smoky Mountains National Park, w Swain County, lat. 35° 28' 33" N., long. 83° 39' 48" W.

Louie Camp Branch rises in n Swain County and flows se into Bradley Fork.

Louisburg, town and county seat, central Franklin County, on Tar River. Alt. 280. Authorized to be laid out and named Lewisburg, 1779. Named for French King, Louis XVI, to whose court Benjamin Franklin (for whom the county was named) was then American representative. Both spellings occur in early records, the present form soon becoming the only one used. Home of Louisburg College. Produces lumber and fabricated metals.

Louisburg Township, former township in central Franklin County, now township number 10.

Louis Ray Knob, ne Buncombe County.

Louse Island, nw Washington County in the mouth of Roanoke River. In a cluster of marshy islands, Louse Island is one of the smallest, approx. 2,000 ft. long and 200 ft. wide and lies in the river between Rice Island and the mainland. *See also* Purchace Islands.

Lousin Swamp. *See* Loosing Swamp.

Louson Swamp. *See* Loosing Swamp.

Lousy Creek rises in n central Wilkes County and flows s into Reddies River.

Louzanla Islands, area of fine sandy loam surrounded by swamp in e Washington County, sw of the community of Scuppernong.

Love Joy, community in n Montgomery County. Formerly known as Queen and had a post office by this name as early as 1896.

Lovelace, community in se Wilkes County between Little Hunting Creek and Hunting Creek. Named for Archibald Lovelace, prominent early nineteenth century resident.

Lovelace Creek rises in s Alleghany County and flows s into Wilkes County where it joins Basin Creek to form Middle Prong Roaring River.

Lovelace Creek rises in n Rockingham County and flows ne into Wolf Island Creek.

Lovelace Gap, n Buncombe County between Lovelace Knob and Jess Knob.

Lovelace Knob, n Buncombe County nw of Lovelace Gap. Alt. 4,315.

Lovelace Township, se Wilkes County.

Lovelady Township, e central Burke County.

Lovelady Township, se Caldwell County. Named for a projected town, Lovelady, planned by Abner Summers before the Civil War. Lovelady post office served a rural area, but it later was moved and the name changed to Granite Falls, *(which see).*

Love Knob, w Watauga County at the n end of Ward Hollow.

Love Mountain, n Henderson County between Belmont Mountain and Clear Creek.

Lovers Leap, high point overlooking Hiwassee River in central Cherokee County.

Lovers Leap Ridge, n Madison County between Silvermine Branch and Pump Branch.

Loves Creek rises in w Chatham County and flows e into Rocky River.

Lovesfield, community in central Jackson County.

Loves Fish Lake, ne Surry County on Toms Creek. Covers 8 acres; max. depth 30 ft. Fishing. Named for J. B. Love, owner. Created 1949.

Loves Ford, n Union County in Rocky River.

Love's Level, community in n Union County.

Lovett Island, a small island in sw Carteret County in Bogue Sound. Apparently named for the family whose surname appears in the old records as Lovett, Lovitt, and Lovick. Thomas Lovett or Lovick was an early landowner in the county.

Love Valley. *See* Fox's Mountain.

Loviade Mountain, n Madison County between Wolf Branch and the head of Spillcorn Creek.

Lovill, community in central Watauga County on Brushy Fork. Named for Captain Edward F. Lovill of Boone. Alt. 3,112.

Lovills Creek, approx. 18 mi. long, rises in Virginia and flows s into Surry County where it enters Ararat River.

Lowell, town in central Gaston County. Settled about 1850 when Woodlawn Mill was built on South Fork River. First known as Wrights Station for William Wright, nearest resident. Inc. 1879 as Lowell because the construction of several textile mills here suggested the name of the textile center in Massachusetts. Alt. 770.

Lowe Mountain, w Randolph County between Taylors Creek and Caraway Creek. Named for Dan Lowe.

Lower Bartons Creek rises in nw Wake County at community of Leesville, and flows ne into Neuse River just e of mouth of Upper Bartons Creek, *which see.*

Lower Beaverdam Creek rises in w Scotland County and flows se into Gum Swamp Creek.

Lower Broad Creek. *See* Broad Creek.

Lower Campbellton. *See* Fayetteville.

Lower Coneto Township, former township in e central Edgecombe County, now township number 2.

Lower Creek rises in ne Caldwell County, flows sw across the county and into n Burke County where it enters Catawba River.

Lower Creek rises in s Transylvania County and flows sw into East Fork French Broad River.

Lower Creek rises in s Yancey County and flows se into South Toe River.

Lower Creek Township, n central Burke County.

Lower Creek Township, e central Caldwell County.

Lower Cullasaja Falls, se Macon County, nw of Highlands on Cullasaja River. Water falls a total of 310 ft. in ¼ mi. See also Cullasaja River.

Lower Double Branch rises in w Haywood County and flows se into Cataloochee Creek.

Lower Dowry Creek rises in e Beaufort County and flows approx. 2 mi. sw into Pungo River.

Lower Falls, on the Graham County, N. C.-Monroe County, Tenn., line on Slickrock Creek. Water drops 1,200 ft.

Lower Ferry on New River. See Sneads Ferry.

Lower Fishing Creek, former township in ne Edgecombe County, now township number 5.

Lower Fork Township, se Burke County.

Lower Grassy Branch rises in n Swain County and flows sw into Kephart Prong.

Lower Hominy Township, w central Buncombe County.

Lower Little River. See Little River.

Lower Little River rises in sw Moore County and flows e through Moore County, forms the n boundary of Fort Bragg Military Reservation in Hoke and Cumberland counties and in part along the Cumberland-Harnett County line to Cape Fear River.

Lower Norfolk County. See County of Norfolk.

Lower Pigeon. See Clyde.

Lower Sassafras Gap, Great Smoky Mountains National Park, n Swain County, on Noland Divide, near the head of Bridge Creek, lat. 35° 31′ 09″ N., long. 83° 27′ 15″ W.

Lower Saura Town, former Indian villiage in ne Rockingham County on Dan River. Site approx. 2 mi. e of Leaksville. Probably occupied by Saura Indians by the middle of the seventeenth century and abandoned in early eighteenth century. Saura or Sara meant "a place of tall grass or weeds." See also Upper Saura Town; Town Creek.

Lower Second Creek. See South Second Creek.

Lower Spring Creek rises in se Beaufort County and flows e into Goose Creek.

Lower Town Creek Township, former township in s Edgecombe County, now township number 10.

Lower Trail Ridge, se Macon County between Devils Prong and Little Indian Creek.

Lowery Creek rises in s Macon County and tween Devils Prong and Little Indian Creek.

Lowery Cove, n Buncombe County, nw of Thurz Mountain.

Lowery Creek rises in s Macon County and flows ne into Cartoogechaye Creek.

Lowery Knob, central Macon County between Dobson Branch and Salser Branch.

Lowery Mill Creek rises in n central Forsyth County and flows s and sw into Salem Lake.

Lowes Grove, community in s Durham County on w edge of Research Triangle Park.

Lowesville, community in se Lincoln County. Named for Lowe family.

Low Falls. See Cullasaja River.

Low Gap, w Avery County in Roan Mountain.

Low Gap, n Buncombe County at the se end of Ike Mountain.

Low Gap, on the Haywood County, N. C.-Cocke County, Tenn., line, Great Smoky Mountains National Park, near lat. 35° 44′ 16″ N., long. 83° 10′ 50″ W.

Low Gap, e Haywood County on Lee Mountain.

Low Gap, nw Haywood County on the head of Low Gap Branch.

Low Gap, between Rich Mountain and West Fork [Dicks Creek] in nw Jackson County.

Low Gap, s Macon County between High Top and McDowell Mountain.

Low Gap, on Macon-Swain County line near the head of Brush Creek.

Low Gap, on the Mitchell County, N. C.-Unicoi County, Tenn., line.

Low Gap, e Yancey County between Seven-mile Ridge and Crabtree Creek.

Low Gap, s central Yancey County between Bowlens Creek and Low Gap Hollow.

Lowgap, community in nw Surry County. Named from a nearby low gap in the Blue Ridge Mountains.

Low Gap, community in s central Yancey County.

Low Gap Branch rises in nw Haywood County and flows se into Big Creek.

Low Gap Hollow, s central Yancey County between Cane River and Bowlens Creek.

Low Gap Wildlife Pond, nw Surry County on North Fork Mitchell River. Covers 12 acres; max. depth 26 ft. Formed 1954 and owned by Low Gap Wildlife Club. Fishing.

Lowing Bald, sw Swain County near the head of Big Creek.

Lowland, community on w Goose Creek Island, ne Pamlico County. Processes seafood.

Loyal Creek. See Riles Creek.

Luart, community in central Harnett County.

Lucama, town in s Wilson County. Alt. 140. Known earlier as Lucas's Crossroads. Named about 1883, according to tradition, by Josephus Daniels, then editor of a newspaper in Wilson, for three friends LUcy, CArrie, and MAry Borden. Post office est. 1884. Inc. 1889.

Lucas Creek rises in se Bladen County and flows sw into Cape Fear River.

Lucia, community in ne Gaston County. Oak Grove, home of James Johnston, officer in the Revolution, member of the Provincial Congress, N. C. legislature, and Convention of 1788, is 2 mi. e. The house, built in 1782, still stands.

Luck, community in sw Madison County on Spring Creek.

Lucknow. See Dunn.

Lucks Island appears on the Comberford map, 1657, as the present Currituck Banks, e Currituck County. It was mentioned as the northern limits of Carolina in the charter granted in 1663 to the eight Lords Proprietors. See also Currituck Banks; Croatamung.

Lucy Branch rises in s Lenoir County and flows ne into Spring Branch.

Luftee Gap, Great Smoky Mountains, n Swain County, on Thomas Ridge, lat. 35° 36' 30" N., long. 83° 26' 23" W. Alt. approx. 5,200.

Luftee Knob on Haywood-Swain County line, Great Smoky Mountains National Park, near lat. 35° 41' 34" N., long. 83° 10' 30" W., between Balsam Corner and Mount Sterling Ridge. Alt. 6,216.

Lukens, former community in n Carteret County. Abandoned following a severe storm in 1933. Church, houses, and school moved across South River to the communities of South River and Merrimon. Named for the Lukens family.

Lul, community in e Wake County.

Lumbee River. See Lumber River.

Lumber Bridge across Cashie River in central Bertie County appears on the Collet map, 1770. The lumber bridge stood as late as 1833, and there is still a bridge across the river at this point.

Lumber Bridge, town in ne Robeson County. Alt. 192. Settled about 1776. Inc. 1891. Named for the wooden bridge across Little Marsh Swamp here.

Lumber Bridge Township, n Robeson County.

Lumber River is formed on the Moore-Richmond County line where Naked Creek enters Drowning Creek. It flows se along the Moore-Richmond and Hoke-Scotland County lines and for a short distance along the Robeson-Scotland County line. It then flows se, e, and s across Robeson County to the Columbus-Robeson County line which it follows into South Carolina. A short distance s of the state line Lumber River enters Little Pee Dee River. It is approx. 125 mi. long. Sometimes known locally as Lumbee River.

Lumbershed Marsh, a tidal marsh island in the w end of Bogue Sound, se Onslow County, between Dudleys Island and Cedar Point. Named from a lumbershed built here during a lumber industry boom.

Lumberton, city and county seat, e central Robeson County on Lumber River. Alt. 137. Inc. 1788. Laid out on Red Bluff Plantation, owned by John Willis. Named for Lumber River. East Lumberton and West Lumberton, which see, formerly incorporated municipalities, were made a part of the city of Lumberton in 1953.

Lumberton. See Gatlington.

Lumberton. See Leechville.

Lumberton Township, e central Robeson County.

Lump Mountain, n Rutherford County near the head of Chalk Creek.

Lumptown, community in central Madison County at the head of Revere Creek.

Lunday, community in w central Mitchell County on Toe River. Alt. 2,346.

Luneville. See Polkton.

Lupton, former community on the southern-most island in the Hog Island group, ne Carteret County. Named for Lupton family.

Lupton Lake in s Jackson County ne of Cashiers on Horsepasture River. Formed in 1924; covers 15 acres and has max. depth of 40 ft. Named for owner. Used for fishing, swimming, boating and as a power source. Open to the public.

Luther Branch rises in ne Cherokee County on Brushy Head Mountain and flows ne into Taylor Creek.

Luther Gap, sw Buncombe County between Luther Knob and Stony Knob.

Luther Knob, sw Buncombe County between Luther Gap and Dix Creek Gap.

Luthers, community in sw Buncombe County.

Luthersville. See China Grove.

Lutz Creek, a marsh creek in sw Currituck County, flows sw into North River.

Lyddies Creek rises in ne Mitchell County and flows nw into Big Rock Creek.

Lydia Creek rises in e Transylvania County and flows se into French Broad River.

Lydie Mountain, n Buncombe County in the Elk Mountains.

Lyle Creek rises in n Catawba County and flows se into Catawba River. Appears on Collet map, 1770, as Liles Creek.

Lyle Knob, e Macon County between Mason Mountain and the head of Thompson Branch. Alt. approx. 3,600.

Lyman, community in e Duplin County.

Lynch, community in sw Madison County.

Lynchburg, community in sw Lenoir County.

Lynch Cove, se Buncombe County, e of Sheep Ridge.

Lynch Creek rises in n Orange County and flows n into Caswell County where it enters North Hyco Creek.

Lynch Creek rises in s Vance County and flows s into Franklin County where it enters Tar River. Appears as Linches Creek on the Collet map, 1770. Said to have been named for a Major Lynch, sent to Bute County (now Franklin and War-ren) by Governor Tryon in 1768 to collect taxes, but who was hanged by a mob of Regulators on the bank of this stream. This action is said to have given rise to the term *lynch*.

Lynches Creek rises in s Union County and flows s into South Carolina where it enters Pee Dee River. Appears on the Collet map, 1770. Also sometimes known as Lynches River.

Lynches River. See Lynches Creek.

Lynchs Corner, community in n Pasquo-tank County.

Lynchum Branch. See Lindscomb Branch.

Lyndover, community in nw Durham County.

Lynesville. See Townsville.

Lynn, town in s Polk County on Skyuka Creek. Inc. 1911, but long inactive in mu-nicipal affairs. Named for Lynn McAboy, son of an early settler, Dr. L. R. McAboy. Alt. 1,500.

Lynn Branch rises in ne Swain County and flows ne into Straight Fork [of Raven Fork].

Lynn Cove, se Swain County extends n from Shepherd Bald to Yalaka Creek.

Lynn Gap, e Jackson County between Lost Knob and High Knob.

Lynn Gap, on the McDowell-Mitchell Coun-ty line.

Lynn Mountain, sw Catawba County. Alt. approx. 1,300. Believed to have been named for a pioneer settler. Sometimes also spelled Linn.

Lynn's Branch rises in nw Wake County and flows se into Sycamore Creek.

Lyon Branch rises in n Clay County and flows sw into Tusquitee Creek.

Lyon Creek. See Lyon Swamp Canal.

Lyons, community in sw Granville County. Alt. 346.

Lyons. See Haywood.

Lyons Creek rises in n Franklin County and flows ne into Devil's Cradle Creek.

Lyon Swamp, se Bladen County e of Cape Fear River.

Lyon Swamp Canal, se Bladen County, drains se from Lyon Swamp into sw Pen-der County where it is called Lyon Creek before emptying into Lyon Thorofare.

Lyon Thorofare, sw Pender County, con-nects Cape Fear River with Black River approx. 4 mi. above their natural junction. Approx. 3 mi. long.

Lytchs Millpond, s Scotland County on Gum Swamp Creek. Formed 1870. Covers 325 acres; max. depth 12 ft.

Lytle Cove, the valley through which Stepp Branch flows in se Buncombe County.

M

Mabel, community in n Watauga County on Cove Creek.

McAdams Creek rises in e Alamance County and flows w into Back Creek.

McAdenville, town in e Gaston County. First Known as Henderson Shoals, for Lawson Henderson, early Lincoln County official; later as Spring Shoals for a local land owner, Adam A. Springs, graduate of the University of North Carolina, 1798. Inc. 1883 as McAdenville. Named for Rufus Yancey McAden (1833-89), speaker of the N. C. House of Representatives in the stormy session of 1866, and local owner of mills. Alt. 600.

McAllister Creek rises in e Cabarrus County and flows s into Adams Creek.

McAlpine Creek rises in e Mecklenburg County and flows sw into South Carolina where it enters Sugar Creek.

McAlpine Mountain, s Henderson County at the head of King Creek.

McAlpin's Grove. See Rennert.

MacArthur. See Japan.

Macay's Mill, an early Rowan County landmark. It was used as a recruiting place for soldiers in the Revolution as well as a point of discharge. It was owned for many years by Judge Spruce Macay, who taught Andrew Jackson law in Salisbury. The mill, on Grants Creek in the se section of the county, was built by Thomas Frohock and later sold to Macay. The mill was used until World War I although the mill pond was drained about 1870 because of fever epidemics. Appears on the Collet map, 1770, as Frohock Mill.

McBrides Mill. See Amantha.

McBryde's Pond, sw Hoke County. Located on an unnamed stream which flows into Big Raft Swamp about 2 mi. nw of Antioch. Named for Thomas F. McBryde, owner.

McCain, community in w Hoke County. Formerly named Sanatorium because a state tuberculosis sanatorium is located here. Renamed McCain in 1948, in honor of Dr. Paul P. McCain, who died in 1946. Alt. 550.

McCall Branch rises in e Transylvania County and flows sw into Little River

McCall Gap, s Mitchell County between South Fork [Carvers Branch] and Middle Fork Grassy Creek.

McCall Mountain in n Transylvania County at the w end of Forge Mountain.

McCalls Mill Creek. See Staffords Creek.

McCampbell Knob, Great Smoky Mountains National Park, Swain County, N. C.-Blount County, Tenn. line. Lat. 35° 33' 53" N., long. 83° 45' 18" W.

McClellan Creek rises in ne Cherokee County and flows n into Tatham Creek.

Macclesfield, town in s Edgecombe County, inc. 1901 and named for Macclesfield, England, from which the ancestors of Henry Clark Bridgers, founder of East Carolina Railroad, had come. Alt. 100.

McClure Branch rises in s Lincoln County and flows ne into Leepers Creek.

McClure Cove, e Haywood County on Pigeon River.

McClure Creek rises in s Haywood County and flows ne into West Fork Pigeon River.

McClure Hicks Creek rises in nw Alamance County and flows s into Ridge Creek.

McClure Ridge, w Haywood County, Great Smoky Mountains National Park, a short spur extending nw from Cataloochee Divide, center near lat. 35° 34' 35" N., long. 83° 06' 52" W., between Big Bald Branch and Double Gap Branch.

McCollums Pond at the head of Big Creek in e Montgomery County.

McComb Branch rises in e Cherokee County and flows nw into Hiwassee River.

McConnell, community in n Moore County. Named for James McConnell (1888-1917), of the Lafayette Escadrille in World War I. His father, Judge McConnell, operated the railroad which ran from Cameron, via Carthage, and terminated at McConnell on the s side of Deep River, opposite High Falls. See also, Eureka.

McCoy Cove, e Buncombe County, ne of the town of Black Mountain.

McCoy Creek rises in e Anson County and flows se into Pee Dee River.

McCoys Mill Pond, e Robeson County in Big Swamp. Approx. 2 mi. long.

McCrarey's Creek. See East Buies Creek.

McCrary Branch rises in e Transylvania County and flows se into Little River.

McCronan Creek rises in w Craven County and flows ne into Neuse River.

McCullen, community in n Sampson County near Hoe Swamp.

McCuller, community in s Wake County. Settled 1800. Named for first settler, John McCullers. Alt. 300.

McCullers Branch rises in w Johnston County and flows se into Black Creek.

McCullers Pond, s Wake County on a tributary of Middle Creek. Covers four acres and has a max. depth of 20 ft. One of the oldest in the county.

McCullough Branch rises in s Mecklenburg County and flows se into Sugar Creek.

McDade, community in nw Orange County.

McDaires Cove, n Buncombe County on the nw side of McDaires Ridge. *See also* Lewis McDaires Knob.

McDaires Ridge, n Buncombe County, extends sw from Bald Knob to Reems Creek. *See also* Lewis McDaires Knob.

McDaniel, community in sw Sampson County.

McDaniel Bald, on the Cherokee-Graham County line in the Unicoi Mountains. Alt. 4,662.

McDaniels Township, sw Sampson County.

McDeeds Creek rises in se Moore County and flows ne to join Mill Creek in forming Shaddock's Creek. Formerly known as Shaddock's Creek.

McDonald Ridge, w Macon County between Jarrett Bald and Middle Ridge.

McDonalds, town in s Robeson County. Alt. 175. Inc. 1911. Named for Peter McDonald, a turpentine distiller whose business was largely responsible for the opening of a railroad station here.

McDonald's Mill. See Forest Hill.

McDowell Branch rises in central Macon County and flows se into Little Tennessee River.

McDowell County was fo..med in 1842 from Rutherford and Burke counties. Located in the w central section of the state, it is bounded by Burke, Rutherford, Henderson, Buncombe, Yancey, Mitchell, and Avery counties. It was named for Major Joseph McDowell (1758-96), of Pleasant Gardens, who fought at the Battle of Kings Mountain and was a member of Congress and of the commission to settle the North Carolina-Tennessee line. Area: 447 sq. mi. County seat: Marion with an elevation of 1,437 ft. Townships are Brackett, Crooked Creek, Dysartsville, Glenwood, Higgins, Marion, Montford Cove, Nebo, North Cove, and Old Fort. Produces corn, soybeans, dairy products, livestock, hogs, textiles, hosiery, furniture, paper boxes, limestone, and gravel.

McDowell Creek rises in n Henderson County and flows e and ne into French Broad River.

McDowell House. See Quaker Meadows.

McDowell Mountain, s Macon County between Middle Creek and Little Tennessee River.

McDowells, community in n Mecklenburg County.

McDowells Creek rises in n Mecklenburg County and flows sw into Mountain Island Lake on the Catawba River.

McDuffie Creek rises in e Hoke County and flows se into Puppy Creek.

Mace Branch rises in n McDowell County on the s slope of Stony Knob and flows se about 1½ mi. into Rag Creek.

Macedonia, community in s Cherokee County.

Macedonia, community in w Chowan County at the mouth of Rockyhock Creek. Named for local Baptist Church.

Macedonia, community in w Wake County between Swift Creek and Walnut Creek.

Macedonia, community in ne Yadkin County.

Macedonia. See Basnight.

McElroy Branch rises in central Haywood County and flows se into Factor Branch.

McElroy Cove, central Haywood County between Yates Cove and Toms Top.

McFarlan, town in se Anson County. Inc. 1885 as McFarland but the 1900 census used the name McFarlan. Named for Allan McFarland (1819-69), president of the Cheraw and Salisbury Railroad. Post office est. here in 1883 when the post office at nearby Sneedsboro was discontinued. Alt. 297.

McFarland, community in w Hoke County.

McGalliard Creek rises in central Burke County and flows n into Catawba River.

McGee Branch rises in ne Swain County and

flows se into Straight Fork [of Raven Fork].

McGees Creek rises in nw Franklin County and flows ne into Taylors Creek.

McGee Spring, Great Smoky Mountains National Park, ne Swain County, on w slope of Hyatt Ridge near summit at lat. 35° 38' 20" N., long. 83° 14' 20" W. Drains nw into Right Fork [of Raven Fork].

McGehees Mill, community in nw Person County on Hyco River. A post office here in the 1890's was known as Woodburn.

McGill Branch rises in s Gaston County and flows se into Crowders Creek.

McGinnis Crossroads, community in se Polk County.

McGinnis Mountain. See McInnis Mountain.

McGinty Creek, w Haywood County, Great Smoky Mountains National Park, rises on n slope of Big Cataloochee Knob, near lat. 35° 40' 30" N., long. 83° 10' 12" W., and flows ne into Swallow Fork Creek.

McGowan Creek rises in w Orange County and flows e into Eno River.

McGowans Crossroads, community in se Pitt County.

McGrady, community in n Wilkes County on Mulberry Creek. Alt. 1,459.

McHan Branch rises in e Swain County and flows s into Oconaluftee River.

McHan Cove, a small valley heading se of DeHart Bald, s Swain County, draining nw into the valley of Wesser Creek.

McHan Knob, s Swain County between Pole Bridge Branch and Yalaka Creek.

Machapounga River. See Pungo River.

Machapunga, Machapungo. See Pungo.

Machapunga Bluff. See Bluff Point.

McHargue Mountain, nw Iredell County.

Machelhe Island, marsh island about half a mile long in the Pasquotank River, w Camden County, opposite Elizabeth City. Probably named for the Macheel family living in the area as early as 1723.

Machine Branch rises in nw Cumberland County and flows n into Little River.

Machine Creek rises in e central Polk County and flows se into Whiteoak Creek.

Machpelah, community in se Lincoln County.

McInnis Mountain, sw Wilkes County between Warrior Creek and Beaver Creek. Named for McGinnis family.

McIntosh Branch rises in central Yancey County and flows s into Pine Swamp Branch.

McIntosh Creek rises in w Moore County and flows n into Big Governors Creek.

McIntyre Branch rises in n Mecklenburg County and flows nw into Long Creek.

McIver. See Williamsburg.

McKay Island, se Chatham County in Cape Fear River. Approx. ½ mi. long and containing 65 acres, the island once was 100 acres in area.

Mackay Island, a portion of sw Knotts Island, ne Currituck County. It is separated from Knotts Island by Indian Creek and Back Creek, an inlet of North Landing River. Approx. 2 mi. long and 2 mi. wide. Appears as Notts or Mackys Island on the Collet map, 1770.

McKee Branch, w Haywood County, Great Smoky Mountains National Park, rises near lat. 35° 35' 02" N., long. 83° 04' 50" W., and flows nw into Caldwell Fork.

McKee Branch rises in central Macon County and flows nw into Cartoogechaye Creek.

McKees Creek rises in e Mecklenburg County and flows ne into Reedy Creek in Cabarrus County.

McKenzie Pond, artificial pond in e Brunswick County. Formed approx. 1860; max. depth 10 ft., covers 50 acres. Fed by Allen Creek and drained by Lilliput Creek. (which see). Also spelled McKensie Pond.

Mackerel Mountain, on the Henderson County, N. C.-Greenville County, S. C., line. Alt. 3,031.

Mackey Mountain, w McDowell County. Alt. 3,994.

Mackeys, community in n Washington County w of the mouth of Kendricks Creek on Albemarle Sound. Alt. 8. Settled about 1765 near the s terminus of Mackeys Ferry, which see, named for Col. William Mackey, local landowner. Post office est. 1856 as Mackeys Ferry; name changed to Mackeys in 1913. Mackeys Ferry appears on the Collet map, 1770.

Mackeys Creek rises in w McDowell County and flows se into Catawba River.

Mackeys Creek. See Kendricks Creek.

Mackeys Ferry, formerly located at the present community of Mackeys in n Washington County, on Kendricks Creek. Shown as T. Bells Ferry on the Moseley map, 1733; purchased from Bell by Col. William Mackey in 1735 and was in continuous operation until 1938. At the time it was dismantled, the ferry operated between the town of Edenton in s Chowan County and the s shore of Albemarle Sound immediately n of the community of Pleasant Grove in n Washington County.

Mack Gap, w Jackson County on the head of Sutton Branch.

Mack Hill Gap, n Yancey County on Mc-Kinney Branch.

McKinney Branch rises in central Buncombe County and flows se into Smith Mill Creek.

McKinney Branch rises in n Buncombe County and flows nw into Ivy Creek.

McKinney Branch rises in Pisgah National Forest in nw Henderson County, and flows se into Boylston Creek.

McKinney Branch rises in n Yancey County and flows nw into Toe River.

McKinney Creek rises in sw Buncombe County near the Henderson County line and flows nw into Stony Fork.

McKinney Creek rises in se Polk County and flows se into Rutherford County where it enters Broad River.

McKinney Gap, ne Buncombe County near the headwaters of Whitaker Branch.

McKinney Gap on the McDowell-Mitchell County line near the se corner of Mitchell County.

McKinney Gap, e Mitchell County at the head of Bear Creek.

McKinney Gap, w Yancey County near the head of Elk Wallow Creek.

McKinney Lake, e Richmond County on Hitchcock Creek. Covers 65 acres.

McKinney Ridge, n central Mitchell County n of town of Bakersville and between Cub Creek and Honeycutt Branch.

McKoy, community in sw Johnston County and ne Sampson County.

Mack Perry Pond on Fowlers Creek, ne Wake County. Covers 38 acres, max. depth 20 ft. Used for fishing and irrigation.

Macks, community in w Johnston County.

Mack Williams Branch rises in w Yancey County and flows se into Jacks Creek.

McLamb Crossroads, community in n Sampson County.

McLamb Mill Pond, s Sampson County on Clear Run Swamp. Formed about 1800 and knows successively as Rackley Mill Pond, Ezzell Mill Pond, and since about 1949 by its present name. Covers approx. 75 acres; max. depth 14 ft.

McLauchlin Township, e Hoke County.

McLean Creek rises in s Harnett County and flows ne into Upper Little River. Named for Peter McLean who settled along its banks about 1760.

McLeans Branch rises in e Moore County and flows s into Thagards Pond on Little River.

McLeans Creek rises in nw Montgomery County and flows se into Uwharrie River.

McLeansville, community in e Guilford County. Named for a pioneer family of Ulster Scots who settled in this area.

McLendons Creek rises in w Moore County and flows ne into Deep River. From 1748-1754 known as Buck Creek. Named for Joel McLendon, who settled here about 1748.

McLeod, community in n Richmond County.

McLeod Creek rises in n Harnett County and flows s to join Reedys Swamp in forming Jumping Run Creek. The basin of this creek was once an inland sea, 30 mi. square. Its limestone bed, composed of fossilized shells, is 8 ft. thick.

McLeods Branch rises in s Moore County and flows n into Joes Fork.

McLin Creek rises in central Catawba County and flows ne into Lyle Creek.

McMilly Swamp rises in s Brunswick County and flows w into Shallotte River.

McMullen Creek rises in s Mecklenburg County and flows sw into McAlpine Creek.

McMurray Branch rises in Forest City, s central Rutherford County, and flows n into Broad River.

McNairs Millpond, central Scotland County on Juniper Creek. Formed 1830. Covers 50 acres; max. depth 15 ft.

McNeills Township, se Moore County.

McNeils Pond, se Hoke County on Beaver Creek. Built in 1870 by J. A. McNeil. Covers 100 acres. Max. depth 8 ft.

Maco, community in ne Brunswick County. Named Farmers Turnout in 1867, but about 1890 intended to be named Maraco for the MacRae Co. which developed land in the vicinity. The present name, easier to pronounce, came into use instead. Alt. 49. Site of the "Maco Light," an unidentified phenomenon which has been recurring frequently since a train wreck here in 1867. Traditionally, the light is the lantern of Joe Baldwin, a railroad conductor who was killed while attempting to prevent the wreck. The tradition was related to President Grover Cleveland who saw the light in 1889 and asked for an explanation.

Macon, town in n central Warren County on head of Sixpound Creek and Walkers Creek. Alt. 285. Settled in early 1800's and shown as Chestnut Crossroads on the MacRae map, 1833. Post office of Macon est. in 1839. Inc. in 1889; named for Nathaniel Macon, member of Congress,

1815-1828, and president of N. C. Constitutional Convention, 1835. A Civil War
training camp, Camp Macon, was located
here.

Macon County was formed in 1828 from
Haywood County. Located in the w section of the state, it is bounded by the state
of Georgia and by Clay, Cherokee, Swain,
and Jackson counties. It was named for
Nathaniel Macon (1758-1837), speaker of
the House of Representatives and United
States Senator. Area: 520 sq. mi. County
seat: Franklin with an elevation of 2,113
ft. Townships are Burningtown, Cartoogechaye, Cowee, Ellijay, Flats, Franklin,
Highlands, Millshoal, Nantahala, Smiths
Bridge, and Sugar Rock. Produces corn,
dairy products, livestock, hogs, textiles,
lumber, and mica.

McPhail Branch rises in n Sampson County
and flows e into Merkle Swamp.

McPhaul's Pond, located on Little Raft
Swamp in sw Hoke County. Named for
owner, Henry McPhaul.

McPherson Creek rises in nw Cumberland
County and flows n into Little River.

McPhersons Creek. See Daniels Creek.

McQueen's Store. See Plainview.

McQuires, community in w Graham County
between Queen Ridge and Hooper Bald.

McRae Canal. See Skinner Canal.

McWilliams Pond. See Monroes Millpond.

Madcap Branch rises in ne Swain County
and flows nw into Bunches Creek.

Mad Inlet, tidal waterway between Bald
Beach and Bird Island in sw Brunswick
County.

Madison, town in w Rockingham County at
the junction of Mayo and Dan rivers. Alt.
577. Authorized to be laid out in 1815;
settled 1818; inc. 1851. Named for James
Madison (1751-1836), President of the
United States when the town was authorized.

Madison County was formed in 1851 from
Buncombe and Yancey counties. Located
in the w section of the state, it is bounded
by Yancey, Buncombe, and Haywood
counties and the state of Tennessee. It
was named for James Madison (1751-
1836), fourth President of the United
States. Area: 456 sq. mi. County seat:
Marshall with an elevation of 1,650 ft.
Townships are Nos. 1-16, formerly Mar-
shall, Shelton Laurel, Bull Creek, Middle
Fork of Ivy, West Fork of Ivy, Sandy
Mush, Little Pine Creek, Spring Creek,
Hot Springs, Big Laurel, Upper Laurel,
Big Pine Creek, Meadow Fork of Spring
Creek, Grapevine, Mars Hill, and Foster
Creek. Produces tobacco, corn, dairy prod-
ucts, livestocks, textiles, and electronics.

Madison Township, ne Guilford County.
Named for President James Madison and
his wife Dolley Payne, said to have been
born at the Quaker settlement of New
Garden, now Guilford College.

Madison Township, nw Rockingham County.

Magazine Branch rises in central Cherokee
County and flows sw and se into Valley
River.

Maggie, community and resort center in
Maggie Valley, w Haywood County.
Named when the first post office was est.
in 1909, for Maggie Mae Setzer (later
Mrs. Ira Pylant of Hendersonville), daugh-
ter of the postmaster. Alt. 3,019.

Maggot Ridge, w Haywood County, Great
Smoky Mountains National Park, extends
n from Buck Knob on Cataloochee Divide,
center near lat. 35° 33' 45" N., long.
83° 08' 32" W. For origin of the name
see Maggot Spring Gap.

Maggot Spring Gap, w Haywood County,
Great Smoky Mountains National Park,
near lat. 35° 33' 08" N., long. 83° 07'
55" W. Named for a nearby spring used
by cattle rangers which had in it the larva
of some insect which resembled a maggot.

Magness Creek rises in e Cleveland County

and flows s, nw, and s into First Broad River.

Magnetic City. *See* Buladean.

Magnolia, town in w Duplin County. Alt. 108. Inc. 1855 as Stricklandsville to be laid out on the lands of Jesse Strickland. Name changed to Magnolia, 1857, for magnolia trees growing here.

Magnolia, old Pettigrew family plantation in w Tyrrell County on shores of Lake Phelps. Built in 1830 by Ebenezer Pettigrew. Birthplace of Confederate General J. J. Pettigrew. Now part of Pettigrew State Park, restored as a museum. Old plantation covered approx. 2,000 acres. The home was named Bonarva.

Magnolia Canal. *See* Bonarva Canal.

Magnolia Township, sw Duplin County.

Maho Creek rises in e Person County and flows n into Virginia where it enters Hyco River. Named Mayo River in 1728 by William Byrd and his "dividing line" survey party for William Mayo, one of the surveyors.

Mahogany Knob. *See* White Hurricane Knob.

Mahogany Rock, e of Blowing Rock, s Watauga County, on Blue Ridge Parkway. Alt. 3,425.

Mahogany Rock, small summer resort, in s Alleghany County.

Maiden, town in s central Catawba County. Alt. 891. Inc. 1883. Named for Maiden Creek on which it is located. Produces furniture, textiles.

Maiden Cane Creek rises in w Wilkes County and flows ne into Reddies River.

Maiden Creek rises in s Catawba County and flows approx. 7 mi. sw into Clark Creek. Named for profusion of maidencane *(Poaceae hemitomon)* found growing in the bottom land nearby when first seen by early settlers.

Maidenhair Falls, s Jackson County on Trays Island Creek, ½ mi. n of Fairfield Lake. Alt. 3,640.

Maidenhair Falls, se Transylvania County on Hogshead Creek 2 mi. se of Brevard. Water falls 50 ft.

Maiden Point, extends into Jones Bay, ne Pamlico County. Named because the shoreline drawn on a map has same conformation as a female breast.

Main Canal, extends nw from n central Washington County where it receives the waters drained from East Dismal Swamp by a system of canals and channels them into Kendricks Creek.

Main Channel, in Bogue Sound sw Carteret County leading s into Bogue Inlét.

Main Creek rises in ne Buncombe County and flows nw into Reems Creek.

Maine. *See* Oak Grove.

Majolica, community in n central Rowan County on Southern Railway. Alt. 713. It is said that while V. C. McBee, railroad superintendent, was considering a name for the termination of a siding here, his clerk, T. C. McNeely, brought in a green majolica pot filled with drinking water. McNeely suggested that the water be used for christening and that the place be named for the pot.

Major Hills, mountain in s Alamance County.

Makatoka, community in nw Brunswick County.

Makleyville, community in sw Hyde County on Pungo River near the mouth of Slade Creek.

Mallard Creek rises in n Mecklenburg County and flows e into Cabarrus County where it enters Rocky River. Though the name is slightly misplaced, it occurs on the Collet map, 1770.

Mallard Creek. *See* Town Creek.

Mallard Creek Township, former township in e central Mecklenburg County, now township number 8.

Mall Creek rises in e Washington County, receives drainage from Enoch Canal, and flows ne into Scuppernong River. First shown on the MacRae map, 1833.

Malloby's Branch rises in central Wake County and flows se into Beaverdam Creek.

Mallory Creek rises in e Brunswick County and flows e into Cape Fear River.

Malloys Pond. *See* Richmond Millpond.

Malmo, community in ne Brunswick County.

Malones Creek rises in w Warren County and flows nw into Blue Mud Creek.

Maltby, community in central Cherokee County, between the junction of Cindy Branch and Dick Branch. Alt. 1,611.

Mamers, community in w Harnett County. A short distance se was the pre-Civil War community and post office of Fishcreek. A muster ground for the county militia was here.

Mamie, farming community in s Currituck County on Albemarle Sound. Post office est. here in 1904 and named for Mamie Crank.

Manchester, town in nw Cumberland County on Little River. Inc. 1895, but long inactive in municipal affairs. Adjacent to Spring Lake.

Manchester Township, nw Cumberland County.

Maney Branch rises in n Buncombe County near Paint Fork Gap and flows sw into Reems Creek.

Maney Gap on the Madison-Yancey County line near the head of Indian Creek. Alt. 3,848.

Maney's Ferry. See Riddicksville.

Maneys Neck Township, n Hertford County.

Mangum, community in nw Richmond County.

Mangum Store, community in ne Durham County on Dry Creek, about 2 mi. n of Lake Michie.

Mangum Township, n Durham County.

Manly, community in s Moore County. Inc. 1879 as Manly Station and in 1899 as Manly; no town government was est. and the charter was repealed in 1955. Named for Charles Manly (1795-1871), governor of North Carolina, 1849-51. Alt. 444.

Manly Mill Creek. See Jones Creek.

Manly Station. See Manly.

Mannings Township, w Nash County.

Mann Point, on the w shore of n Bodie Island, in Roanoke Sound, between Kill Devil Hills and Nags Head, e Dare County.

Manns Harbor, community on the e shore of the mainland, central Dare County, on Croatan Sound. Settled in the early nineteenth century. Known earlier as Croatan. Named for a German sea Captain, Charles Mann, who harbored here during a fierce storm. He later returned with his wife and nine children to live. The Indian village of Dasemunkepeuc (Algonquian word meaning "where there is an extended land surface separated by water") was located approx. here and is shown on the White maps, 1585 and 1590, and on the Velasco map, 1611. Alt. 10.

Manor Branch rises in nw Buncombe County near Newfound Mountain and flows ne into Sandy Mush Creek.

Mansfield, community in s Carteret County w of Morehead City.

Manson, town in w Warren County near the head of Rocky Creek. Inc. 1874, but not now active in municipal affairs. Alt. 424. First known as Cheathamville; name changed to Branchville in 1858 because the Roanoke Valley Railway branch

joined the Raleigh and Gaston Railroad here. Name changed to Manson in 1859 in honor of Dr. O. F. Manson (1822-1888), local physician and later a Confederate surgeon.

Manteo, town and county seat, on n Roanoke Island, e Dare County. Settled 1865. Inc. 1899. Named for the Indian chief, Manteo, taken to England in 1584 by Philip Amadas and Arthur Barlowe, in the service of Walter Raleigh. Alt. 12. "The Lost Colony," an outdoor drama by Paul Green presented nearby each summer since 1937.

Manus, community in n Richmond County.

Maple, community in central Currituck County. Named for the Maple Leaf, a Federal transport which grounded on Currituck Beach with 101 Confederate prisoners during the Civil War. Alt. 7.

Maple, community in n central Washington County.

Maple Bald Creek rises in s Yancey County and flows se into Rock Creek.

Maple Branch rises in nw Beaufort County and flows sw into Tranters Creek.

Maple Branch rises in s Warren County and flows se into Fishing Creek.

Maple Camp Bald, s Yancey County on the head of Maple Bald Creek. Alt. 5,275.

Maple Camp Ridge, s Yancey County between Middle Creek and Maple Creek.

Maple Creek rises in ne Cleveland County and flows sw into First Broad River.

Maple Creek rises in s Nash County and flows se into Tar River.

Maple Creek rises in nw Rutherford County and flows se into Mountain Creek.

Maple Creek rises in s Yancey County and flows e in an arc into Rock Creek.

Maple Fork Branch rises in ne Northampton County and flows se and n to join a small unnamed stream which rises in Hertford County to form Turkey Creek.

Maple Gap, s Transylvania County in Blue Ridge Mountains near the head of Abrams Branch.

Maple Grove, community in nw Caldwell County near Staircase Mountain.

Maple Hill, community in ne Pender County on Moores Creek. Alt. 50. Named by a member of the Ashe family for the trees growing at the site. A post office as early as 1882. Angola, formerly considered to be a separate community (and with a post office as early as 1882), about 1½ mi. nw, is now considered to be within the Maple Hill community.

Maple Run rises in n Duplin County and flows ne into Goshen Swamp.

Maple Spring. See Mapleville.

Maple Spring Branch rises in w Madison County and flows ne into Meadow Fork.

Maple Spring Branch rises in e Union County and flows se into Beaverdam Creek.

Maple Spring Gap, on the Haywood-Madison County line. Alt. 4,050.

Maple Springs, community in s Swain County between the head of Siles Branch and the head of Tarkiln Branch.

Maple Springs, community in w Wilkes County on South Prong Lewis Fork Creek.

Maple Swamp, central Currituck County near the w shore of Currituck Sound.

Maple Swamp rises in n Edgecombe County and flows se into Fishing Creek.

Maple Swamp Creek rises in e central Burke County and flows se into Laurel Creek.

Mapleton, town in n Hertford County. Inc. 1901, but long inactive in municipal affairs.

Mapleville, community in central Franklin County. Alt. 350. Settled about 1877. Known first as Maple Spring because a maple tree grew by the spring which furnished water for a church here.

Maplewood, community in e Watauga County.

Maraco. See Maco.

Marasanico, apparently an Indian village, appears on the White map, 1585, located in what is now s Craven County on the Neuse River.

Marathon, former community in n New Hanover County near Castle Hayne. An agricultural colony of Greek farmers was est. here by Hugh MacRae of Wilmington in the early twentieth century, but it was not successful.

Maraton, village of the Moratuc Indian tribe, shown on the Smith map, 1624, as being on the Chowan River in present e Chowan County, downstream from Rockyhock Creek. The Comberford map, 1657, places the village farther upstream.

Marble, community in central Cherokee County. Inc. 1911; charter revoked June 22, 1939. Alt. 1,686. Named for deposits of marble in the vicinity.

Marble Creek rises in central Cherokee County and flows se into Valley River.

Marbleyard Ridge, se Clay County between Hogan Branch and Little Buck Creek.

Marcus, former community in w Swain County on Tuckasegee River. Site now under the waters of Fontana Lake.

Maready, community in se Duplin County.

Mare Branch rises in e Hertford County and flows s into Bertie County where it enters Keel Creek.

Mare Branch rises in s Lee County and flows e into Juniper Creek.

Mare Branch rises in w central Wilson County and flows ne into Contentnea Creek.

Margaret, community in e Franklin County. Named by C. P. Harris for his daughter. A post office prior to 1909.

Margaret Peak on the McDowell-Rutherford County line. Alt. 2,500.

Margaretsville, town in ne Northampton County. Appears on county maps as early as 1865; chartered 1885 as Margarettsville, but charter repealed 1891. Re-chartered as Margaretsville in 1895. Named for Mrs. Margaret Ridley, an early resident. Alt. 54. The railroad name is Margaret.

Marg Mountain, s Haywood County, between Camp Branch and Browning Branch.

Margrace, community in se Cleveland County.

Maria Creek rises in ne Carteret County and flows se into Core Sound.

Marianna Falls. See Dutch Creek Falls.

Maribel, community in n Pamlico County on Chapel Creek, known originally as Shoofly. At the establishment of a post office, long since discontinued, it was named by postmaster Fentress for his sweetheart in Georgia, a girl named Mary Belle.

Marietta, town in s Robeson County. Alt. 125. Settled about 1898. Inc 1911. Formerly known as Affinity until renamed by Augustus Marriel, a promoter of the Raleigh and Charleston Railroad whose line formerly ran through the town.

Marietta Township, s Robeson County.

Marines, former community in s Onslow County on New River. A post office as early as 1885. Abandoned 1941 with the development of Camp Lejeune.

Marion, city and county seat, central McDowell County. Alt. 1,437. Inc. 1844. Named for General Francis Marion (1732?-95), Revolutionary leader. East Marion and West Marion are adjacent unincorporated communities. Produces textiles, hosiery, furniture, and paper boxes.

Marion Township, w central McDowell County.

Mariposa, community in s Lincoln County on Leepers Creek. See also Heldermans.

Mark Creek. See Morgan Creek.

Markee's Creek. See Stewart's Town.

Mark Pine Bay, a muck filled bay in central Columbus County.

Marks Creek rises in n Johnston County and flows sw into Neuse River.

Marks Creek rises in se Richmond County and flows sw into Pee Dee River. Reference is made to a "Markees's Creek" in this vicinity in the act of 1799 incorporating Stewart's Town.

Marks Creek rises in e Wake County and flows s into Johnston County where it enters Neuse River.

Marks Creek Township, se Richmond County.

Marks Creek Township, e Wake County.

Marks Knob, Great Smoky Mountains National Park, ne Swain County on Dashoga Ridge. Lat. 35° 40' 47" N., long. 83° 14' 30" W. Alt. 6,140.

Marks Pond, se Harnett County, approx. ½ mi. long, on Buffalo Creek.

Marlboro, community in s Pender County.

Marlboro, town in w Pitt County immediately s of Farmville. Inc. 1875, but long inactive in municipal affairs. Alt. 82.

Marl Branch rises in w Hertford County and flows s into Potecasi Creek.

Marler, community in w Yadkin County.

Marley's Ford, former ford through Yadkin River w Wilkes County near the mouth of Stony Fork Creek. The site is now under the waters of W. Kerr Scott Reservoir.

Marlins Creek. See Sloans Creek.

Marlowe Creek rises in central Person County in the city of Roxboro and flows n into Hyco River.

Marl Pits, on the head of Stewarts Creek in w Duplin County. Abounds in fossils, sharks' teeth, and a few fossilized whale bones.

Marlville. See East Arcadia.

Marmaduke, community in s Warren County n of Fishing Creek. A post office was est. here in 1893, but discontinued in 1930.

Marr Branch rises in s Swain County and flows se into Brush Creek.

Marr Gap, central Cherokee County between Bates Creek and Hiwassee River.

Marrow Bone River. See Stony Creek.

Marrow Branch rises in central Haywood

County and flows ne into Pigeon River.

Marsden Creek rises in central Henderson County and flows nw into Mill Pond Creek.

Marsden. See Chocowinity.

Marshall, town and county seat, s Madison County on French Broad River. Authorized to be est. 1852; site still in dispute, 1855. Inc. 1863 and named for John Marshall (1755-1835), Chief Justice of the U. S. Supreme Court. Alt. 1,650. An early post office here, before the establishment of the county seat, was named Lapland. For a period before Marshall was laid out Jewel Hill (or Duel Hill), at present-day Walnut, was the seat of government. County court was held at Jewel Hill as late as the fall of 1859.

Marshallberg, community on the mainland of se Carteret County, approx. 8 mi. e of town of Beaufort. Settled about 1800. Named by Matthew Marshall, a rural mail carrier, for himself. Alt. 5. Formerly known as Deep Hole Point.

Marshallberg Township, s central Carteret County.

Marshall Ridge extends se from Turkey Knob to Clear Creek in n Henderson County.

Marshall Tavern. See Ridgeway.

Marshall Township, former township in s central Madison County, now township number 1.

Marsh Bay, a loam filled bay in s Columbus County.

Marshbourns Pond in e Wake County on Buffalo Creek.

Marsh Branch rises in central Duplin County and flows e into Grove Creek.

Marsh Creek rises in central Wake County and flows se into Crabtree Creek.

Mars Hill, town in w Madison County on Gabriels Creek. Inc. 1893; named for a hill in Athens, Greece. Alt. 2,300. Mars Hill College, est. 1856, is here. Produces electronic components.

Mars Hill Township, former township in se Madison County, now township number 15.

Marsh Island, a peninsula extending from the s mainland of Hyde County into Pamlico Sound between Swanquarter Bay and Juniper Bay. See also Abigails Islands.

Marsh Point extends from the s mainland of Hyde County into Rose Bay.

Marsh Swamp rises in n Halifax County and flows se into Beech Swamp. Appears as Elk Marsh on the Collet map, 1770, and with its present name on the Price map of 1808.

Marsh Swamp rises in n Sampson County and flows se into Great Coharie Creek.

Marsh Swamp rises in nw Wilson County and flows se into Contentnea Creek.

Marsh Township, sw Surry County.

Marshville, town in e Union County. Settled in 1874. Originally known as Beaverdam, for nearby Beaverdam Creek, and at this time centered aound a depot on the Central Carolina Railroad. Inc. 1877 as Griffinsville; name changed to Marshville in 1897 for the Marsh family which donated land for a school and church. Produces processed poultry, asbestos products, boxes, and staves.

Marshville Township, e Union County.

Marston, community in e Richmond County. Est. 1913. Named for Edgar L. Marston of New York, developer of local real estate. Alt. 431.

Martha, community and former post office, w Randolph County. Named for first postmistress, Mrs. Martha Ingram.

Martin Bay, e Pitt County in Tar River.

Martin Branch rises in nw Buncombe County and flows n into Turkey Creek.

Martin Branch rises in se Durham County and flows n into Lick Creek.

Martin Branch rises in n McDowell County and flows se approx. 1½ mi. into North Fork [Catawba River] near North Cove.

Martin Branch rises in n Madison County and flows sw into Little Laurel Creek.

Martin County was formed in 1774 from Halifax and Tyrrell counties. Located in the e section of the state, it is bounded by Washington, Beaufort, Pitt, Edgecombe, Halifax, and Bertie counties. It was named for Josiah Martin (1737-86), last royal governor of North Carolina, and very likely would have been changed as were some other counties named for late royal governors except for the popularity of Alexander Martin, governor in 1782-85 and 1789-92. Area: 482 sq. mi.

County seat: Williamston with an elevation of 60 ft. Townships are Beargrass, Cross Roads, Goose Nest, Griffins, Hamilton, Jamesville, Poplar Point, Robersonville, Williams, and Williamston. Produces tobacco, peanuts, corn, cotton, Irish potatoes, hogs, livestock, poultry, apparel, canned goods, chemicals, lumber, paper, and textiles.

Martin Cove, s Swain County on Yalaka Creek.

Martin Creek rises in w Avery County and flows e into Roaring Creek.

Martin Creek rises in ne Buncombe County and flows sw into North Fork Ivy Creek.

Martin Creek rises in. s Cherokee County and flows ne into Hiwassee River.

Martin Creek rises in n Haywood County on Hurricane Mountain and flows s into Fines Creek.

Martin Creek rises in n Rockingham County and flows ne into Virginia where it enters Smith River.

Martin Creek rises in se Stokes County and flows se into Town Fork Creek.

Martin Creek rises in nw Yadkin County and flows nw into Yadkin River.

Martin Knob, s Watauga County between Green Mountain Branch and Cannon Branch.

Martin Mill Creek rises in n central Forsyth County and flows s and sw to enter Lowery Mill Creek approx. 1 mi. before it flows into Salem Lake.

Martin Ridge, w Avery County.

Martinsborough. *See* Greenville.

Martin's Crossroads. *See* Conway.

Martins Gap, Great Smoky Mountains National Park, n Swain County, on Sunkota Ridge, lat. 35° 31' 10" N., long. 83° 24' 30" W.

Martins Mill, community on West Fork Little River in ne Montgomery County. A post office, Martin's Store, existed here as early as 1828. Named for Farquhardt Martin who had a store here, 1822-60. Dam at the mill site was washed out in 1927.

Martins Point, a projection in the s North Banks, ne Dare County, extending into Currituck Sound. Located at the mouth of Jean Guite Creek.

Martins Point Creek. *See* Jean Guite Creek.

Martin's Store. *See* Martins Mill.

Martinville, former town and county seat, central Guilford County, est. 1774 as Guilford Courthouse (*which see*) and chartered as Martinville, 1785. Named for Governor Alexander Martin (1740-1807). Abandoned 1808 with the establishment of Greensboro as county seat.

Marty's Ridge, nw Burke County. Alt. 3,625.

Marvin, community in w Union County.

Marvin. See Point Harbor.

Mary Branch rises in central Cherokee County and flows sw into Valley River.

Mary Branch rises in ne Cherokee County and flows sw into Stewart Branch.

Mary Gap, e Madison County at the head of Gabriels Creek.

Mary Gray Knob, between Rock Hollow Branch and Rogers Cove Creek in e Haywood County.

Mary Knob on the Haywood-Madison County line.

Mary Sander Creek, a tidal creek in s Currituck County, n of Poplar Branch Bay.

Marys Branch rises in w Avery County and flows e into Roaring Creek.

Mary's Creek rises in s Alamance County in the foothills of the Cane Creek Mountains and flows e into Haw River.

Marys Gap, e Haywood County between Rice Cove and Sassafras Knob.

Mary Simmons Ridge, e Watauga County extends s between Boone Camp Branch and East Ridge.

Masa Knob, peak on Swain County, N.C.-Sevier County, Tenn., line, Great Smoky Mountains National Park, about halfway between Mount Kephart and Charlies Bunion at lat. 35° 38′ 10″ N., long. 83° 22′ 40″ W. Alt. over 6,000 ft. Named for George Masa (died 1933), Japanese photographer whose extensive knowledge of the area, acquired through eighteen years' association with it, was recognized by his appointment as a member of the Nomenclature Committee for the first map of the Park.

Mascomenge, a village of the Weapemeoc Indians, shown on the White map, 1585, as being on what is now the s tip of Chowan County on Albemarle Sound.

Masequetuc, on the White map, 1585, village of the Weapemeoc tribe, probably situated on what is now the se tip of Pasquotank County. Variant spelling, Masquetuc.

Mashawatoc. See Mashoes.

Mashburn Branch rises in s Macon County and flows n into Cullasaja River.

Mashoes, community on the ne shore of the mainland of Dare County on Albemarle Sound. Legend relates that it is named for one Peter Michieux or Mashews who, with his family, was shipwrecked on a nearby beach in the eighteenth century. He was washed ashore with his wife and child clinging to him. When he regained consciousness, he found both were dead. The shock of this experience shattered his reason and some twenty years later he sat with his back to a cypress tree and died. His skeleton and a board on which he had rudely carved the account of his tragic experience were discovered some years later. The name, in spite of this legend, may be of Indian origin; John White's map, 1585 shows an Indian village named Mashawatoc on the eastern Virginia shore.

Mason Bay, n Pamlico County, in Bay River.

Masonboro, community in e New Hanover County on Masonboro Sound. Appears on the Collet map, 1770. Named because a number of zealous Masons in the late eighteenth century built houses here. A popular resort in the early and middle nineteenth century.

Masonboro Inlet, e New Hanover County, opposite the mouth of Hewlets Creek between the waters of Middle and Masonboro Sounds. Shole Inlet, on the Moseley map, 1733 (Shoal on the Mouzon map, 1775), was at this site, but closed after 1775. A new inlet nearby, Deep Inlet, opened by 1808 and closed after 1833. Masonboro Inlet opened by 1833 at the old Shole or Shoal Inlet site. Took its name from the resort community of Masonboro s of the mouth of Hewlets Creek.

Masonboro Township, central New Hanover County.

Masonboro Sound, e New Hanover County between Greenville Sound and Myrtle Sound.

Mason Branch rises in central Cherokee County near Mason Knob and flows se into Valley River.

Mason Branch rises in n Macon County and flows sw into Little Tennessee River.

Mason Branch rises in Swain County on Una Mountain and flows sw into Yalaka Creek.

Mason Creek rises in w central Transylvania County and flows se into Cherryfield Creek.

Mason Inlet, ne New Hanover County be-

tween Moore Inlet on the s and Rich
Inlet on the n. The waters of Topsail
Sound enter the Atlantic Ocean through
this inlet. Appears as Barren Inlet on the
Moseley map, 1733, and on other maps
as late as 1909; as Queen Inlet during
the period 1906-36.

Mason Knob, n Cherokee County.

Mason Mountain, n Macon County between
Mason Branch and Cowee Creek.

Mason Mountain, e Macon County between
Lyle Knob and Fed Gap.

Masons Cross, crossroads community in s
Scotland County.

Masontown, community in ne Carteret
County on Nelson Bay between the
mouths of Broad and Salter creeks.

Masquetuc. See Masequetuc.

Massey, community in w central Wake
County.

Massey Branch rises in e Beaufort County
and flows ne into Pungo Creek near
Yeatesville.

Massie Gap, w central Swain County between Horse Cove and the head of
Hickory Flat Branch.

Massy Creek rises in w central Rockingham County and flows n into Dan River.

Mast, community in n Watauga County on
Cove Creek. Alt. 2,670.

Mast Knob, se Watauga County nw of
Dugger Mountain.

Matakomak, a name appearing on the Ogilby map, 1671, to designate the territory
presently in Chowan County between
Yeopim River and Pembroke Creek.

Matchipungo. See Pungo.

Matecomack. See Edenton; Matakomak;
Queen Anne's Creek.

Matherson Branch rises in w Macon County
and flows se into Pine Branch.

Matherson Creek rises in ne Cherokee
County and flows ne into Worm Creek.

Mathis, community in se Forsyth County.
Named for a family which settled in the
vicinity as early as 1757.

Matkin, community in sw Caswell County.
Named in 1967 for a family long resident
in the area when a plant of Burlington
Industries was opened here. A name was
required for directing truck drivers to the
rural location.

Matlock Bald, n Clay County on the n end
of Johnson Ridge. Alt. 5,230.

Matlock Creek rises in n Clay County and
flows se between Johnson and Julie
ridges into Tusquitee Creek.

Matney, community in w Watauga County
on Craborchard Creek.

Matney Branch rises in s Watauga County
and flows n into East Fork [of South Fork
New River].

Matrimony Creek rises in nw Rockingham
County at the Virginia line and flows se
into Dan River. Named prior to 1728
when William Byrd recorded that it was
"call'd so by an unfortunate marry'd man,
because it was exceedingly noisy and
impetuous."

Mattacomack Creek. See Queen Anne's
Creek.

Mattamuskeet, former township in central
Hyde County, now reported as "Unorganized territory." Most of this area
is now owned by the Federal government
and is a fish and wildlife reservation.
Residents vote and list taxes in Lake
Landing township.

Mattamuskeet Lake. See Lake Mattamuskeet.

Matt Branch rises in nw Swain County and
flows se into Fontana Lake.

Matthews, town in se Mecklenburg County.
Inc. 1879. Known as Fullwood or Fullwood's Store from as early as 1825 when
a post office existed here until 1874 when
it was given its present name to honor an
official of the Central Carolina Railroad.
Produces textiles, electrical equipment,
pottery, and tools. Alt. 729.

Matthews Branch rises in w Haywood
County and flows s into Mossy Branch.

Matthews Creek rises in ne Duplin County
and flows sw into Northeast Cape Fear
River.

Matthews Creek rises in w Warren County
and flows ne into Fishing Creek.

Matthews Crossroads, community in w Nash
County near the headwaters of Pig
Basket Creek.

Matthews Cross Roads. See Siler City.

Matthews Township, w central Chatham
County.

Matt Mountain, nw Swain County between
Cable Branch and Fontana Lake.

Mattock Creek rises in n Macon County
and flows sw into Cowee Creek.

Maufin, town inc. in 1905, n Pitt County
on the n side of Grindle Creek. Apparently it was not developed as the
charter was repealed in 1911.

Mauls Point, small tip of land in w central
Beaufort County extending into Pamlico
River at the ne edge of Blounts Bay.
Named for Dr. Patrick Maule (d.1736),

but earlier known as Smiths Point for a family who lived here.

Mauls Swamp rises in n Craven County and flows sw into Swift Creek.

Mauney Cove, s Haywood County on the head of Mauney Cove Branch.

Mauney Cove Branch rises in central Haywood County and flows ne into Factor Branch.

Mauney Gap, central Graham County between Snowbird Creek and Long Creek.

Maury, town in e Greene County. Alt. 78. Est. late nineteenth century. Inc. 1911. Named for Matthew Fontaine Maury (1806-73), oceanographer.

Maw Point, peninsula in e Pamlico County extending into Pamlico Sound and forming the se side of Fisherman Bay.

Max Patch Mountain, w Madison County at the sw end of Buckeye Ridge. Alt. 4,629.

Maxton, town in w Robeson County on Big Shoeheel Creek. Alt. 197. Inc. 1874 as Shoe Heel; changed to Tilden in 1877 to honor Samuel J. Tilden (1814-86), Democratic nominee for President, 1876; to Quhele in 1879, probably from a form of the Gaelic word *Caoile*, "the narrow part of a stream"; to Shoe Heel in 1881 for the imagined meaning of Quhele; and to Maxton in 1887. Local tradition says that the area was long known as Mackstown because of the many people of Scottish descent living here whose names begin with Mc or Mac; this was changed to Maxton by postal authorities when the first post office was est. in 1866. An earlier post office serving the community was Cowper's Hill, est. 1815, a mile or so e of the present town. Carolina College operated here 1908-26; Presbyterian Junior College, 1929-60; and Carolina Military Academy is now here.

Maxton Township, w Robeson County.

Maxwell, community in ne Henderson County at the s end of Marshall Ridge.

Maxwell Branch rises in n Transylvania County and flows sw into Avery Creek.

Maxwell Creek rises in w Duplin County and flows se into Stocking Head Creek.

Maxwell Creek. See Lillington Creek.

Maxwells Mill Pond, on Burnt Coat Creek in ne Duplin County.

Mayapple Gap, between Doubletop Mountain and Thunder Struck Mountain in n Jackson County. Named for the herb (*Podophyllum peltatum*).

Mayberry Hollow, valley in n central

Avery County a short distance n of Cranberry.

May Branch rises in w Macon County and flows se into Nantahala Lake.

Mayesworth. See Cramerton.

Mayfield, community in ne Rockingham County.

Mayhew, community in sw Iredell County.

Mayhew Lake, a small body of water formed by a dam on New Years Creek w of Blowing Rock, s Watauga County.

Mayne Creek rises in w Cleveland County and flows sw into Sandy Run Creek.

Mayodan, town in w Rockingham County on Mayo River. Inc. 1899. Named for the Mayo River and the nearby Dan River. Alt. 594. See also Avalon.

Mayonia. See Whitakers.

Mayo River rises in s Henry County, Virginia, and flows s into Rockingham County in which it flows se into Dan River. Named for William Mayo who settled in Virginia about 1723 (d. 1744).

Mayos Crossroads, community in se Edgecombe County.

Mayo Township, nw Rockingham County.

Mays Crossroads, community in w Franklin County.

Maysville, town in s Jones County on White Oak River. Inc. 1897. A post office here as early as 1828 was known as Cross Roads. This appears to be the "Young's Cross Roads" which is mentioned frequently in official records of the Civil War. Alt. 41.

Mayview Hill, s Watauga County on the head of China Branch.

Mayview Lake in s Watauga County in the headwaters of Middle Fork [South Fork New River].

Mayview Park. See Blowing Rock.

Mazeppa, community in se Iredell County. Alt. 901.

Meadlock Mountain, n Mitchell County between the head of Honeycutt Branch and Young Cove Creek. Originally spelled Medlock.

The Meadow, a loamy swamp in sw Johnston County.

Meadow Branch rises in se Duplin County and flows se into Back Swamp.

Meadow Branch rises in nw Graham County and flows w into Cheoah River.

Meadow Branch rises in n Moore County and flows ne into Buffalo Creek.

Meadow Branch rises in se Nash County and flows s into Wilson County where it enters Bloomery Swamp.

Meadow Branch rises in s Orange County and flows sw into Chatham County where it enters Ferrells Creek.

Meadow Branch rises in ne Pitt County and flows se into Tranters Creek.

Meadow Branch rises in w Wilkes County and flows s into Cole Creek.

Meadow Creek rises in se Alamance County near the foot of Mount Willing and flows sw into Haw River.

Meadow Creek rises in w Chatham County and flows se into Rocky River.

Meadow Creek rises in s Randolph County and flows e into Fork Creek.

Meadow Creek rises in w Stokes County and flows se into Pinch Gut Branch.

Meadow Creek rises in e Watauga County and flows n into s Ashe County where it enters New River.

Meadow Fork rises in w Madison County and flows ne into Spring Creek.

Meadow Fork Creek rises in sw Alleghany County and flows sw into Ashe County where it joins Laurel Fork Creek to form Mulberry Creek.

Meadow Fork Gap on the Haywood-Madison County line.

Meadow Fork Mountain, w Madison County parallel to Meadow Fork.

Meadow Fork of Spring Creek Township, former township in se Madison County, now township number 13.

Meadow Gap, e Madison County between Beetree Creek and Long Branch.

Meadow Gap, Great Smoky Mountains National Park, nw Swain County, on Forrester Ridge, lat. 35° 33′ 43″ N., long. 83° 42′ 10″ W.

Meadow Mine, w Avery County. Mica was discovered about 1870 and this mine, still being worked, is said to have produced more mica than any other mine in history.

Meadows, community in central Stokes County between Flat Shoal Creek and the head of Zilphy Creek.

Meadows Store, community in w Madison County on Spring Creek.

Meadows Summit, former station on the Danville and Western Railroad, now the Carolina and Northwestern Railroad, n Rockingham County. The Tri-City Airport [Leaksville, Spray, and Draper, now Eden] is here now.

Meadows Township, s central Stokes County.

Meadow Township, s Johnston County.

Meads Corner, community in s Pasquotank County.

Mears Fork Creek rises in ne Guilford County and flows ne into Haw River near the Rockingham County line.

Meat Camp, community in n Watauga County on Meat Camp Creek.

Meat Camp Creek rises in ne Watauga County and flows se into South Fork New River. Named because early hunters had a camp here to which they took hides and salted meat.

Meat Camp Township, n central Watauga County.

Mebane, town in e Alamance and w Orange counties. Settled about 1854 and named for a local family. Inc. 1880 as Mebansville; name changed 1883. Mepern's [Mebane's?] Tavern in this vicinity was mentioned by Bishop Spangenberg in 1752. The Bingham School was here from 1865 to 1891. Produces bedding, furniture, textiles, and apparel. Alt. 678.

Mechanic, community in w Randolph County.

Mechanicks Hill. See Robbins.

Mechanicsville. See Robbins.

Mecklenburg County was formed in 1762 from Anson County. Located in the s central section of the state, it is bounded by the state of South Carolina and by Gaston, Lincoln, Iredell, Cabarrus, and Union counties. It was named for Princess Charlotte Sophia of Mecklenburg-Strelitz (1744-1818), who married George III in 1761. Area: 549 sq. mi. County seat: Charlotte with an elevation of 795 ft. Townships are Nos. 1-15, formerly Charlotte, Berryhill, Steele Creek, Sharon, Providence, Clear Creek, Crab Orchard, Mallard Creek, Dewees, Lemley, Long Creek, Paw Creek, Morning Star, Pineville, and Huntersville. Produces corn, wheat, oats, cotton, eggs, poultry, diary products, processed meat, baked goods, fabricated metals, textiles, industrial machinery, canned foods, paper products, chemicals, hosiery, apparel, furniture, aircraft parts, electronics, and asbestos products.

Medford Branch rises in s Haywood County and flows nw into Browning Branch.

Medford Cove, e Haywood County between Brown Cove and Chambers Branch.

Medlin, former community in nw Swain County now within the bounds of the Great Smoky Mountains National Park. Settled before 1886 and named for Marion Medlin, popular Baptist minister who lived in the vicinity. After the property was acquired for the National Park houses and stores were torn down and moved. Only local family cemeteries remain to mark the site.

Medlock Mountain. See Meadlock Mountain.

Medoc, community in w Halifax County between Brinkleyville and Ringwood. Named for nearby Medoc Mountain.

Medoc Mountain, a comparatively high hill on the e bank of Little Fishing Creek, w Halifax County. Named for a vineyard established here in the late nineteenth century and named for Médoc, France, which contains some of that country's most famous vineyards. "Rocky Hill," the summer home of Gov. Hutchins G. Burton (1774-1832), was nearby.

Medora, community in w Edgecombe County.

Meege Crossroads, community in n Chowan County. At one time a post office here was called Meege, which was the nickname of Mrs. Miles Elliott, wife of the postmaster.

Meetinghouse Branch rises in n central Sampson County and flows se into Great Coharie Creek.

Meeting House Branch rises in e central Wilson County and flows sw in an arc into Buck Branch. Name appears in local records as early as 1775.

Meetinghouse Mountain extends ne from Stecoah Creek to Little Tennessee River in ne Graham County.

Meeting of the Waters, creek in se Orange County rising just s of the town of Chapel Hill and flowing se into Morgan Creek.

Meherrin, community in ne Northampton County. An earlier community of this name is now known as Severn.

Meherrin Creek. See Potecasi Creek.

Meherrin River rises in Virginia and flows s into North Carolina where it forms the Hertford-Northampton County line for approx. 9 mi. after which it flows se across Hertford County into Chowan River. Appears as Pochike River on the Comberford map, 1657, and as Wayanock on the Hack map, 1684. Parker's Ferry has been operated across the Meherrin River near its mouth since the early years of the twentieth century.

Melrose, community in sw Polk County. A former post office serving the community was called Mimosa. Alt. 1,424.

Melrose Falls, sw Polk County on Big Fall Creek, a short distance w of town of Tryon.

Melton Branch rises in central Clay County and flows n into Perry Creek.

Melton Branch rises in n Mitchell County and flows e into Left Fork Bean Creek.

Melton Creek rises in ne Cherokee County and flows se and sw into Valley River.

Melton Mountain, n Rutherford County between Little and Carson Mountains.

Melville, community in e Alamance County. Settled about 1845 and known at first as Burnt Shop.

Melville Township, former township in e central Alamance County, now townships number 10 and 13.

Melvin Hill, community in se Polk County. Settled in late nineteenth century. Named for Thomas Melvin, first postmaster.

Melvin's Mill Pond, ne Bladen County on Little Turnbull Creek.

Memminger Creek rises in central Henderson County and flows ne into King Creek. Named for C. G. Memminger (1803-1888), Confederate Secretary of the Treasury, who had a summer home at Flat Rock in the county.

Menola, community in w Hertford County.

Mentso, marked as the central part of Pamlico Sound, present day Hyde County, on the White map, 1590, but apparently a place on the shore, as the name seems to come from an Indian word meaning "he cooks for the first time." This could be the name given a stopping place for eating on travels, perhaps the end of a day's journey in the direction from Roanoke Island.

Mequopen. See Second Creek.

Mercer, community in s Edgecombe County. Probably the location of Mercersville post office in 1828.

Mercers Mill Pond, a stream which rises in se Brunswick County and flows sw into tidal marshes which drain into the

Atlantic Ocean through Lockwoods Folly Inlet.

Mercersville. *See* Mercer.

Merchants Millpond, central Gates County on Bennets Creek. Formed about 1857 by Rufus Williams and known as Williams Millpond until about 1910 when it was sold. The new owner built a store there, hence the name. Approx. 3 mi. long. Maximum depth 8 feet. Sawmill and gristmill formerly operated here, but now a popular place for fishing.

Meredith Branch rises in n Yancey County and flows s into Cane River.

Meredith Township, central Wake County.

Merkle Bay, off the nw side of Cedar Island in ne Carteret County. Merkle is local pronunciation of myrtle.

Merkle Swamp rises in n Sampson County and flows se into Great Coharie Creek. Appears as Myrtle Swamp on the Kerr map, 1882.

Merricks Creek rises in s Pender County and flows nw and sw into Northeast Cape Fear River.

Merrill Cove, s Buncombe County e of Merrill Mountain.

Merrill Cove Creek rises in s Buncombe County and flows se into Cane Creek.

Merrill Creek rises near Black Knob in e Transylvania County and flows e into Cascade Lake [Little River].

Merrill Mountain, s Buncombe County between Robinson Creek and Merrill Cove.

Merrimon, community in n Carteret County.

Merrimon River rises in central Carteret County and flows s into North River.

Merrimon Township, n central Carteret County on Neuse and South rivers and Adams Creek. At one time a part of Straits and Smyrna townships. Previously also known as township number 9.

Merritt, community on Trent River in central Pamlico County. Originally known as Trent; renamed to honor Gen. Wesley Merritt (1834-1910), who captured Manila in 1898.

Merritt Mill Pond, on Bear Marsh Branch in n Duplin County.

Merry Hill, community in e central Bertie County. Named for the Webb family plantation of this name on which it developed. A post office was est. here by 1822. *See also* Society Parish.

Merry Hill Township, se Bertie County.

Merrymount. *See* Paschall.

Merry Oaks, town in se Chatham County.

Inc. 1901, but long inactive in municipal affairs. Named for grove of oaks in which Indians are said to have held tribal celebrations. Alt. 246.

Mertie, community in n Wilkes County between North Fork Reddies River and Burke Mountain.

Mesic, community in ne Pamlico County on Bear Creek. First known as Bear Creek; renamed for S. R. Messick, the second postmaster. Alt. 4.

Messer Branch rises in e Cherokee County and flows s into Slow Creek.

Messer Branch rises in central Haywood County and flows ne into Cove Creek.

Messer Branch rises in n Haywood County and flows ne into Teague Branch.

Messer Branch rises in s central Swain County and flows se into Bucknor Branch.

Messer Creek, w Haywood County, Great Smoky Mountains National Park, rises near lat. 35° 36′ 57″ N., long. 83° 36′ 57″ W., and flows e into Rough Fork. Formerly known as Sugar Fork but changed to honor Elijah Messer, an early settler on the stream.

Messer Ridge, s Macon County, extends se into Rabun County, Georgia.

Metackwem. *See* Metocuuem.

Metakquam. *See* Metocuuem.

Method, community in w central Wake County near the head of House Creek.

Metocuuem, an Indian village of either the Weapemoc or Chawanoac tribes located in what is now e Bertie County between the mouths of Chowan and Roanoke rivers near Albemarle Sound. Appears on the DeBry map, 1590; and on the Velasco map, 1611 as Metakquam. Variant spellings are Metackwem and Mettaquen. The name may have meant "big woods" or "trees".

Mettaquen. *See* Metocuuem.

Mewborn Crossroads, community in n Lenoir County. Named for the Mewborn family which settled here before the Revolution.

Miami. *See* Newtown.

Miami Mountain, se Buncombe County near the town of Black Mountain.

Mica City Creek rises in ne Macon County and flows sw into Cowee Creek.

Mica Knob, s Swain County between Whiteoak Branch and Grape Cove.

Micaville, community in e Yancey County near the junction of Ayles and Little

Crabtree creeks. Alt. 2,504. Named for mica mined in the vicinity.

Michael Branch rises in w Alamance County and flows s into Back Creek.

Michael's Creek. See Carraway Creek.

Michfield, community in s Randolph County. Said to have been named for a local resident, Mrs. Michfield Wright, or for the Michell family.

Micro, town in e Johnston County. Settled about 1890; inc. 1899 as Jerome. Named for Jerome Creech, local landowner. Named changed to Micro, meaning "small," in 1905 because of confusion with the community of Jerome in Bladen County. Alt. 192.

Micro Township, e central Johnston County.

Midas Spring, w central Mecklenburg County, nine mi. from Charlotte. Discovered 1812 by a slave. Since 1871 commercially bottled water, high in magnesium and calcium content, has been available. Spring is located on a 40-acre tract, Midas Park.

Middens Creek, a tidal creek about 1 mi. long near Smyrna, se Carteret County. It flows se into Core Sound. Named for Samuel Mittams or Middams.

Middle Bay in Pamlico Sound on se side of Goose Creek Island, ne Pamlico County.

Middleburg, town in e Vance County between Mill Creek and Fishing Creek. Alt. 489. Inc. 1880; named for the fact that it was midway between the terminals of the Raleigh and Gaston Railroad. According to tradition, the first medical school in North Carolina was established here in 1808 by Dr. Joseph Hawkins.

Middleburg-Nutbush Township, e Vance County. Two separate townships were merged in 1965.

Middle Cave, community in e Watauga County.

Middle Creek rises in w Cumberland County and flows se into Bones Creek.

Middle Creek rises in w Franklin County and flows ne into Tar River.

Middle Creek rises in e Hyde County at Middletown and flows se approx. 1¼ mi. into Pamlico Sound.

Middle Creek rises in s Macon County and flows sw and nw into Little Tennessee River.

Middle Creek rises in s Transylvania County se of Kelly Mountain, and flows sw through Rainbow Lake into East Fork French Broad River.

Middle Creek rises in sw Wake County se of the town of Apex, and flows se through Sunset Lake, continues across s Wake County and into central Johnston County where it enters Neuse River w of the town of Smithfield. Appears on the Collet map, 1770.

Middle Creek rises in s Yancey County and flows ne into South Toe River.

Middle Creek Falls, on Middle Creek s of Rattlesnake Ridge, s Macon County.

Middle Creek Township, s Wake County.

Middle Elk Ridge, central Avery County.

Middle Falls, in Snowbird Creek between Upper Falls and Big Falls in sw Graham County. Water drops approx. 50 feet.

Middle Fork rises in nw Henderson County and flows se into Fletcher Creek.

Middle Fork rises in sw Macon County and flows n into Kilby Creek.

Middle Fork rises in e Madison County and flows sw into Little Ivy Creek.

Middle Fork [Barkers Creek] rises in w Jackson County and flows ne to join West Fork in forming Barkers Creek.

Middle Fork French Broad River rises in s Transylvania County and flows nw into French Broad River.

Middle Fork [Grassy Creek] rises in s Mitchell County and flows ne to join East Fork [Grassy Creek] in forming Grassy Creek.

Middle Fork [Hawk Branch] rises in n Yancey County and flows sw to join South Fork [Hawk Branch] in forming Hawk Branch.

Middle Fork Little Horse Creek rises in nw Ashe County and flows e into Little Horse Creek.

Middle Fork [Lower Creek] rises in ne Caldwell County and flows sw into Zacks Fork.

Middle Fork Muddy Creek. See Salem Creek.

Middle Fork of Ivy Township, former township in e Madison County, now township number 4.

Middle Fork [of Raven Fork] rises in ne Swain County in Great Smoky Mountains National Park and flows sw to join Left Fork and Right Fork to form Raven Fork [of Oconaluftee River].

Middle Fork [Reddies River] rises in nw Wilkes County and flows se to join North Fork [Reddies River] in forming Reddies River.

Middle Fork Ridge, Great Smoky Mountains National Park, ne Swain County, a

spur extending sw from Dasohga Ridge,
lat. 35° 39' 15" N., long. 83° 15' 30" W.
Middle Fork [Rock Creek] rises in s Yancey
County and flows e to join North Fork
[Rock Creek] in forming Rock Creek.
Middle Fork [of South Fork New River]
rises in s Watauga County on e limits of
town of Blowing Rock and flows ne and
then n to join East Fork and Flannery
Fork in forming South Fork New River
approx. 2 mi. se of town of Boone.
Middle Fork Township, e central Forsyth
County.
Middle Fork [Upper Creek] rises in s
Yancey County and flows se to join
South Fork [Upper Creek] in forming
Upper Creek.
Middle Fourth Creek. See Morrison Creek.
Middle Ground, a former shoal between
Oak Island and Bald Head (Smith Island)
in se Brunswick County, appears on the
Collet map, 1770. It is called Sea Cattle
on the Prince map, 1808, but the shoal
had eroded and was practically gone by
1833 (MacRae map).
Middle Little River rises in e Caldwell
County and flows se into Alexander
County where it enters Lake Hickory,
Catawba River.
Middle Marshes, a group of tidal marsh
islands at the nw end of Back Sound in
se Carteret County.
Middle Mountain, n Buncombe County be-
tween Frosty Knob and Bruce Knob.
Middle Mountain, ne Buncombe County be-
tween Flat Creek and North Fork
[Swannanoa River].
Middle Mountain, e Mitchell County be-
tween Stony Valley and Soapstone
Branch.
Middle Mountain, s Transylvania County
between South Prong and the head of
East Fork French Broad River.
Middle Peachtree Creek rises in central
Swain County and flows s into Peachtree
Creek.
Middle Prong rises in ne Pamlico County on
the n side of Goose Creek Island and
flows n into Pamlico River.
Middle Prong of Little River. See Perry
Creek.
Middle Prong [Roaring River] is formed in
n Wilkes County by the junction of
Basin and Lovelace creeks. It flows se to
join North Prong [Roaring River] in form-
ing Roaring River.
Middle Prong [West Fork Pigeon River]
is formed in s Haywood County by the

junction of Haywood Gap Stream and
Buckeye Creek and flows n into West
Fork Pigeon River.
Middle Ridge, w Haywood County, Great
Smoky Mountains National Park, extends
se from Canadian Top, center near lat.
35° 38' 20" N., long, 83° 05' 35" W., be-
tween Upper Double Branch and Lower
Double Branch.
Middle Ridge, sw Macon County between
the head of Park Creek and Kimsey
Creek.
Middle Ridge, n Madison County between
Lisenbee Branch and Colvin Creek.
Middle Ridge, e Mitchell County between
Little Rock Creek and Green Creek.
Middle Ridge Branch rises in se Mitchell
County and flows s into Dicks Creek.
Middle Ridge, e Swain County between
Improvement Creek and Wesser Creek.
Middle Ridge, s Yancey County between
Middle Creek and Colbert Creek.
Middle River rises in Bertie County and
flows ne into Cashie River. Named from
the fact that along much of its course it
lies midway between Roanoke and
Cashie rivers.
Middlesex, town in sw Nash County, set-
tled about 1907. Inc. 1908. Named for
the English city. Produces apparel. Alt.
255.
Middle Sound, e New Hanover County be-
tween Topsail Sound on the n and Green-
ville Sound on the s.
Middle Swamp rises in s central Bladen
County and flows s and w into Elkton
Swamp.
Middle Swamp rises in se Brunswick County and flows sw into Lockwoods Folly
River.
Middle Swamp rises in n Gates County and
flows e into Duke Swamp.
Middle Swamp rises in n Greene County
and flows se on the Greene-Pitt County
line into Little Contentnea Creek.
Middleton Creek rises in se Chowan Coun-
ty and flows ne into Yeopim River.
Middle Top, w Haywood County between
Walker Bald and Germany Cove. Alt.
5,165.
Middletown, town in e Hyde County be-
tween Lake Mattamuskeet and Pamlico
Sound. Inc. 1787, but long inactive in
municipal affairs.
Middle Township, former township in central Chowan County, now township number 2.
Middle Trail Ridge, sw Macon County be-

tween Little Indian Creek and Nichols Branch.

Middle Watch Creek. *See* Salem Creek.

Midgett Island in the waters of Pamlico Sound off the w coast of Hatteras Island, e Dare County.

Midland, community in s Cabarrus County. Named this because it lies halfway between Charlotte and Norwood on the railroad.

Midstate Mill, community adjoining the w limits of Red Springs in n Robeson County. A textile mill est. here in the nineteenth century; now location of Amerotron textile mills. Known briefly as Dora or Dora Mills after that name ceased to be applied to what is now Red Springs, *which see*. Dora post office est. by 1882.

Midville, community in central Onslow County adjoining Jacksonville on the se.

Midway, community in s central Brunswick County.

Midway, community in w Robeson County. The former communities of Raemon or Raemont and Branchville are now considered to be a part of Midway community.

Midway, community in s Rockingham County.

Midway, former community in w Vance County located at the crossroads now approx. 1 mile sw of Hicks Crossroads. Appears on the MacRae map, 1833. So named because it was located approx. midway between Williamsboro and Oxford.

Midway. *See* Eller.

Midway. *See* Jessama.

Midway Park community in central Onslow County on the outskirts of Camp Lejeune Marine Base.

Midway Township, n central Davidson County.

Mike Branch rises in ne Cherokee County and flows se into Morris Creek.

Mikes Knob, s Madison County between Friezeland Creek and Little Pine Creek.

Mikes Mountain, n Rutherford County between the head of Catheys Creek and Second Broad River.

Milam, community in sw Ashe County.

Milburnie, pond in e central Wake County on Beaverdam Creek. Covers 50 acres and has maximum depth of 20 ft. Used for recreation. Named for the former community of Milburnie here. A post of-

fice in the nineteenth century served the community and a printing establishment was operated here.

Mildred, town in e Edgecombe County. Inc. 1887, but not now active in municipal affairs. Alt. 46.

Miles, community in se Alleghany County between Bucks Peak and Stone Mountain.

Miles, community in w Orange County.

Miles Gap, n Madison County between Cutshalltown and Shelton Laurel Creek.

Miles Point, s Camden County in the mouth of Pasquotank River. Named for Miles Jones who lived nearby approx. 1840-1860.

Milesville, community in s Caswell County. A post office was operated here during the approx. period 1880-1905.

Milk House Branch. *See* Tanyard Branch.

Milksick Cove, sw Buncombe County, the valley through which the w tributary of Pole Creek flows.

Milksick Cove, central Clay County near Chatuge Lake.

Milksick Cove, central Swain County extends s from Tuckasegee River.

Milksick Knob, s Macon County between Tommy Branch and Wayah Creek.

Milksick Ridge, w Jackson County between Pressley and Tilley creeks.

Millboro, community in n Randolph County.

Mill Branch rises in nw Bertie County and flows n into Hertford County where it enters Ahoskie Creek.

Mill Branch rises in ne Cherokee County and flows s into Valley River.

Mill Branch rises in ne Cherokee County and flows se into Valley River.

Mill Branch rises in e Cherokee County and flows sw into Peachtree Creek.

Mill Branch rises in e Clay County near Boteler Peak and flows se into Shooting Creek.

Mill Branch rises in e Clay County and flows nw into Perry Creek.

Mill Branch rises in Great Dover Swamp, w Craven County, and flows e into Cove Creek.

Mill Branch rises in sw Columbus County and flows e into Gum Swamp.

Mill Branch rises in s Duplin County and flows se into Pagets Branch.

Mill Branch rises in se Duplin County and flows sw into Cypress Creek.

Mill Branch rises in n Franklin County and flows s into Sandy Creek.

Mill Branch rises in central Hertford County and flows nw into Potecasi Creek.

Mill Branch rises in w Johnston County and flows s into Middle Creek.

Mill Branch rises on the Johnston-Wayne County line and flows ne into Mill Creek.

Mill Branch rises in w Jones County and flows se into Trent River.

Mill Branch rises in s Macon County and flows ne into Cunningham Creek.

Mill Branch rises in n Martin County and flows n into Conoho Creek.

Mill Branch rises in nw Swain County and flows se into Bone Valley Creek.

Mill Branch rises in w Swain County and flows sw into Fontana Lake.

Mill Branch rises in w Transylvania County and flows se into West Fork French Broad River.

Mill Branch rises in nw Wilson County and flows s into Contentnea Creek.

Mill Branch rises in s Wilson County and flows e into Contentnea Creek.

Mill Branch rises in w Wilson County and flows se into Shepherd's Branch. Apparently once known as Big Branch.

Mill Branch, community in sw Brunswick County.

Millbridge, community in w Rowan County. Named for the mill built in 1822 by Dr. Samuel Kerr and the nearby bridge over Kerr Creek.

Mill Brook rises in n central Wake County and flows se into Marsh Creek.

Millbrook, community in n central Wake County approx. 3 mi. n of the city of Raleigh. Settled prior to 1860 and named for the brook on which a gristmill was operated. Alt. 318.

Mill Cove, ne Currituck County formed by the waters of Knotts Island Channel which cuts into the eastern shore of Knotts Island.

Mill Creek rises in e Alamance County and flows w into Back Creek.

Mill Creek rises in ne Alamance County and flows s into Stag's Creek.

Mill Creek rises in ne Alexander County and flows s into South Yadkin River.

Mill Creek rises in s Anson County and flows ne into Pee Dee River.

Mill Creek rises in s Ashe County and flows s into South Fork New River.

Mill Creek rises in ne Brunswick County and flows se into Brunswick River.

Mill Creek rises in nw Cabarrus County and flows s into Coddle Creek. See also Mill Hill.

Mill Creek rises in se Caldwell County and flows s into Upper Little River on the Caldwell-Alexander County line.

Mill Creek rises at the foot of the Green Mountain range in central Caldwell County and flows se into Zacks Fork Creek. Named because several mills once were operated along its course.

Mill Creek rises in central Carteret County and flows s into the estuary of Newport River.

Mill Creek rises in e Carteret County and flows s and se into the headwaters of Newport River.

Mill Creek rises in w Cherokee County and flows w into Hiwassee River.

Mill Creek rises in s Clay County and flows ne into Hiwassee River.

Mill Creek rises in n Forsyth County and flows s into Muddy Creek.

Mill Creek rises in w Henderson County and flows sw into Crab Creek.

Mill Creek rises in ne Henderson County and flows se into Hickory Nut Creek.

Mill Creek rises in se Hoke County and flows ne into Rockfish Creek.

Mill Creek rises in central Hoke County and flows ne into Rockfish Creek.

Mill Creek rises in central Jackson County and flows nw into Trout Creek.

Mill Creek rises in n Jackson County and flows sw into Tuckasegee River.

Mill Creek rises in sw Jackson County and flows ne into Lake Thorpe.

Mill Creek rises in n Johnston County and flows s into Neuse River.

Mill Creek rises in s Johnston County and flows ne into Neuse River.

Mill Creek rises in s Jones County and flows n into Trent River. Appears on the Moseley map, 1733, which also shows Franks Ferry across the Trent River near the mouth of Mill Creek.

Mill Creek rises in w Lincoln County and flows se into Indian Creek.

Mill Creek rises in w McDowell County and flows se into Catawba River.

Mill Creek rises in se Macon County and flows ne into Mirror Lake.

Mill Creek rises in central Macon County and flows se into Cartoogechaye Creek.

Mill Creek rises in n Madison County and flows sw into Shelton Laurel Creek.

Mill Creek rises in se Moore County and flows e to join McDeeds Creek in forming Shaddock's Creek.

Mill Creek rises in w Moore County and flows ne into Cabin Creek. In 1754 it was originally called Smiths Mill Creek for "Sandhill" John Smith who had a mill here. Later called Tillis's Mill Creek for Richard Tillis who bought the mill from Smith; still later, Sowell's Mill Creek from another owner, a name by which it is also sometimes known today.

Mill Creek rises in central Onslow County and flows s into Stones Bay.

Mill Creek rises in e Onslow County and flows se into Bear Creek.

Mill Creek rises in n Onslow County and flows sw into New River.

Mill Creek rises in s Onslow County and flows s into Alligator Bay.

Mill Creek rises in s Pender County and flows n into Long Creek.

Mill Creek rises in s Pender County and flows se into Rileys Creek.

Mill Creek rises in e Perquimans County and flows sw into Perquimans River. Known originally as Vosses Creek, named for William Voss who owned land here before 1700. At the end of the nineteenth century it was called Brights Mill Creek for a local mill owner at that time. From this name the modern name derived.

Mill Creek rises in central Person County and flows ne into Maho Creek.

Mill Creek rises in w Person County and flows n into South Hyco Creek.

Mill Creek rises in central Randolph County and flows se into Deep River. Appears on the MacRae map, 1833, and apparently named for Cox's Mill, which see, located at its junction with Deep River.

Mill Creek rises in sw Randolph County and flows nw into Uwharrie River.

Mill Creek rises in n Rutherford County and flows se into Catheys Creek.

Mill Creek rises in w Sampson County and flows s into South River.

Mill Creek rises in s Stokes County and flows se into Town Fork Creek.

Mill Creek rises in w Surry County and flows se into Mitchell River.

Mill Creek rises in n Swain County in the Great Smoky Mountains National Park and flows sw into Noland Creek.

Mill Creek rises in s Transylvania County and flows nw into French Broad River.

Mill Creek rises near Middle Mountain in s Transylvania County and flows n into Little River.

Mill Creek rises in n Union County and flows se into Richardson Creek.

Mill Creek, former stream rising in e Vance County and flowing nw into Nutbush Creek, but now covered by Kerr Reservoir.

Mill Creek rises in nw Wake County and flows w into Big Lick Creek.

Mill Creek rises in w Wake County and flows n into Crabtree Creek.

Mill Creek rises in n Warren County and flows ne into Hawtree Creek.

Mill Creek rises in s Wilkes County and flows n into Fishing Creek near its junction with Yadkin River. Formerly known as Little Fishing Creek.

Mill Creek, community in e central Brunswick County.

Mill Creek, community in s central Carteret County at the mouth of Mill Creek on the n shore of Newport River. Formerly known as Bordensville for William Borden, an early Quaker settler who operated a shipyard here.

Mill Creek. See Kendricks Creek.

Mill Creek. See Mill Tail Creek.

Milledgeville. See Tuckertown.

Miller, community in e central Wayne County. Formerly known as Millers Station.

Miller Branch rises in e central Bertie County and flows n into Cricket Swamp.

Miller Branch rises in w Mitchell County and flows s into Brummett Creek.

Miller Branch rises in w Yancey County and flows s into Fox Creek.

Miller Cove, se Buncombe County near the headwaters of Broad River.

Miller Cove, sw Swain County on the n side of Nantahala Gorge.

Miller Creek rises in s Buncombe County and flows se into Tweed Creek.

Miller Gap, on the Ashe-Wilkes County line.

Miller Gap, central Avery County.

Miller Gap, central Haywood County on the head of Rabbitskin Branch.

Miller Hollow, w Macon County between Tom Bryan Cove and Deweese Creek.

Miller Mountain, central Buncombe County, sw of Spivey Gap.

Miller Mountain, se Buncombe County, e of Little Pisgah Mountain.

Miller Mountain, w Polk County between Howard Gap and Tryon Mountain. Alt. 2,500.

Millers Branch rises in n central Avery County and flows nw into Cranberry Creek.

Millers Creek rises in e Caldwell County and flows e into the headwaters of Upper Little River. Formerly known as Bull Branch.

Millers Creek rises in s Caldwell County and flows w into Lower Creek.

Millers Creek rises in w Duplin County and flows w into Stewarts Creek.

Millers Creek rises in w Surry County and flows se into Mitchell River.

Millers Creek rises in central Wilkes County and flows se into Yadkin River.

Millers Creek, community in central Wilkes County near the head of Millers Creek. Alt. 1,423.

Millers Landing, n Tyrrell County on Alligator Creek.

Miller's Point, a point of land extending into Pasquotank River in s Camden County. Named for Thomas Miller who was granted land here on January 1, 1694.

Millers Station. See Miller.

Millers Township, s Alexander County.

Millersville, community in s central Alexander County. Named for one Miller, owner of an antebellum cotton mill here.

Millford, former community in e Vance County at Southerland Millpond. Appears on the MacRae map, 1833, but the name was out of use by 1913.

Mill Fork rises in n Caldwell County and flows se into Yadkin River. Originally called South Fork of the Yadkin.

Mill Fork rises in sw Franklin County and flows sw into Wake County where it enters Horse Creek.

Mill Gap, n Macon County between Matlock Creek and Shepherd Creek.

Mill Grove, country home of Carl Propst in w Cabarrus County. Originally home of Robert Harris who ran a mill on nearby Rocky River. Later sold to Michael Cox and named Cox Mill.

Mill Grove, community about 2 mi. n of city of Durham in central Durham County.

Mill Hill, home built by Jacob Stirewalt in 1821, on Mill Creek in n Cabarrus County. Restored in 1938. Nearby creek dammed to provide power for a gristmill and tannery.

Millingport, community in w Stanly County.

Mill Knob, s Macon County between North Fork Coweeta Creek and Coweeta Creek.

Mill Knob, s Yancey County between Sodom Branch and Indian Creek.

Mill Landing, e Bertie County, on Salmon Creek. Site of a gristmill built in 1771 by George Ryan and operated for many years; ruins still exist. Ships loaded cargo from the mill at this landing.

Mill Mountain, e Haywood County between Big Branch and Crabtree Creek. Alt. 3,459.

Mill Mountain, e Stanly County on the w bank of Pee Dee River in Morrow Mountain State Park.

Mill Neck, community in n Hertford County on Buckhorn Creek.

Mill Point, ne Carteret County extending into the mouth of Styron Bay.

Mill Point extends from s Pasquotank County into Little River.

Mill Point, n Tyrrell County, extends from River Neck into the mouth of Scuppernong River.

Mill Point. See Elon College.

Mill Pond Branch rises in n Nash County and flows ne into Flat Rock Branch.

Mill Pond Creek rises in central Henderson County and flows nw into French Broad River.

Mill Pond Creek rises in n Pasquotank County and flows nw into Newland Drainage Canal.

Mill Ridge, s Avery County.

Mill Ridge, n Madison County between Little Hurricane Creek and Big Laurel Creek. Alt. 2,763.

Mill Run rises in central Greene County and flows se into Contentnea Creek. Early settlers built a gristmill and later a sawmill on this stream. Evidence of the old mill dam is still visible in the woods about three miles upstream from its mouth in Contentnea Creek.

Mill Run rises in central Jones County and flows ne into Trent River.

Mill Run rises in central Onslow County and flows ne into Southwest Creek. See also Troublesome Creek.

Millsaps. See Santeetlah.

Mills Bay, a bay in the n end of Church Island in Currituck Sound in central Currituck County.

Mills Creek rises in se Brunswick County and flows n into Prices Creek.

Mills Creek rises in w Transylvania County and flows e into Toxaway River.

Millseat Branch rises in ne Cherokee County and flows sw into Valley River.

Mills Gap, on Point Lookout Mountain, e Henderson County. Named because it was used by William Mills, first known white settler of Henderson County, when he crossed the mountains after being wounded at the Battle of Kings Mountain.

Mill Shoal Ridge, w Avery County.

Millshoal Township, ne Macon County.

Mills Mountain, between McDowell Creek and Foster Creek in n Henderson County. Alt. 2,761.

Mills Pond, lake in sw Wake County on Basal Creek. Originally named Norris Pond. Renamed in 1925 for the owner. Covers 58 acres and has a maximum depth of 20 ft. Open to the public for recreation; also used for irrigation.

Mill Spring, town in central Polk County. Inc. 1885 as Mills Spring, but long inactive in municipal affairs. Named for a son of William Mills, pioneer settler. Alt. 1,017.

Mills Ridge, a strip of high ground in n Tyrrell County extending east-west s of Big Savanna from near the community of Levels and supporting a road on its surface.

Mills River is formed in nw Henderson County by the junction of South Fork and North Fork and flows ne into French Broad River.

Mills River, community on Mills River in w Henderson County. Alt. 2,077. A post office was established here as early 1828.

Mills River Township, nw Henderson County.

Mill Station Creek rises in nw Transylvania County and flows se into Court House Creek.

Millstone Creek rises in ne Franklin County and flows ne into Richland Creek.

Mill Stone Creek rises in n Richmond County and flows sw into Rocky Fork Creek.

Millstone Creek rises in nw Wilson County and flows e aprox. 5 mi. to join Juniper Creek in forming Bloomery Swamp. Named prior to 1783 from the fact that millstones were made from a type of stone found here.

Millstone Creek. See Austin Creek.

Millstone Creek. See Big Governors Creek.

Millstone Mountain, e Haywood County between the head of Rice Cove Creek and Thickety Creek.

Millstone Mountain, n Montgomery County on Barnes Creek.

Mill Swamp rises in se Bertie County and flows ne into Roquist Creek.

Mill Swamp rises in s Duplin County and flows s into Little Rockfish Creek.

Mill Swamp Branch rises in sw Johnston County and flows se into Mill Creek.

Mill Swamp rises in nw Onslow County and flows se into New River.

Mill Swamp rises in ne Sampson County and flows sw into Six Runs Creek.

Mill Swamp rises in se Sampson County and flows ne along the Duplin-Sampson County line and into Doctors Creek on the Duplin-Pender County line.

Mill Swamp rises in w Sampson County and flows sw into Little Coharie Creek.

Mill Swamp Creek rises in e Robeson County and flows se into Lumber River.

Mill Tail Creek rises in w Dare County and flows n and w into Alligator River. Appears on the Collet map, 1770, as Mill Creek.

Mill Timber Creek rises in central Avery County and flows sw into Linville River.

Milltown, community in central Graham County on Long Creek.

Mill Town. See Shiloh.

Millville. See Rockwell.

Millwood. See Gilkey.

Milray Knob, s Watauga County e of Boone Fork and nw of Cannon Branch.

Milton, town in ne Caswell County on Dan River. Site settled by 1728; inc. 1796. Named for (a) Robert Milton, Virginian, who settled on the Dan River nearby; (b) Thomas Milton, who operated a mill where planters held community meetings; or, (c) the mills operated in the community. Originally known as Thomas Mill, then as Mill Town until 1796. It was an important town in antebellum days, at one time having two newspapers, a branch of the State Bank, and considerable traffic on Dan River.

Milton. See Hamilton.

Milton Township, ne Caswell County.

Milwaukee, town in e Northampton County. Inc. 1915. Settled about 1889 and known first as Bethany. Said to have been named by Hezekiah Lasker, railroad conductor, for the city in Wisconsin. Alt. 85.

Mimosa. See Melrose.

Mimosa Shores, community in w Beaufort County on Pamlico River.

Mince Branch rises in w Jackson County and flows sw into Long Branch.

Mine Branch rises in w Haywood County and flows n into Jonathans Creek.

Mine Branch rises in e Yancey County and flows sw into South Toe River.

Mine Creek rises in nw Alamance County and flows se into Stony Creek.

Mine Creek rises in e Mitchell County and flows nw into Cane Creek.

Mine Creek rises in n Wake County and flows s into Crabtree Creek.

Mine Fork rises in n central Yancey County and flows ne into Jacks Creek.

Mine Fork Branch rises in e Mitchell County and flows nw into Right Fork [Cane Creek].

Mine Fork Ridge, e Mitchell County between Bee Branch and Mine Fork Branch.

Mine Gap, s Henderson County between King Mountain and Butt Mountain.

Mine Hill, e Mitchell County between Buchanan Hollow and Cane Creek.

Minehole Gap, s Buncombe County between Chestnut Mountain and Cedar Cliff. Alt. 2,555. Named because in the first quarter of the nineteenth century very crude iron ore was mined nearby.

Mine Knob, e Yancey County near the head of Shoal Creek.

Mine Mountain, se Henderson County on Pacolet River.

Mine Mountain, central Swain County, between Peachtree Creek and Middle Peachtree Creek.

Mine Mountain, n Transylvania County extends s beside North Prong Turkey Creek.

Mineola, community in nw Beaufort County, formerly known as Old Ford.

Mineral Creek rises in ne Buncombe County and flows nw to join Carter Creek in forming Stony Creek.

Mineral Gap, Great Smoky Mountains National Park, Swain County, N. C.-Blount County, Tenn., line, near the head of Roaring Creek, lat. 35° 34' 08" N., long. 83° 40' 55" W. Alt. approx. 5,280.

Mineral Springs, located approx. 4 mi. e of Hookerton, on Contentnea Creek, in e Greene County on the old Jim Smith plantation. There is a high ridge on the s side of the creek and the springs are on the slope of this hill. They formerly were quite popular as a source of supposedly healthful waters. Several acres of adjacent lowlands are covered with laurel which blooms beautifully every spring.

Mineral Springs, town in w Union County. Inc. 1905. Post office est. as Potters between 1880-1885. Name changed to Mineral Springs in 1900. Alt. 631.

Mineral Springs Township, sw Moore County. Named for the spring at Jackson Springs.

Mineral Springs Township, n Richmond County.

Mine Ridge, n Haywood County extends s from Wildcat Spring to Skiffley Creek.

Mine Ridge, w Madison County between Grassy Creek and Shut-in Creek.

Mine Ridge, Great Smoky Mountains National Park, ne Swain County, a spur extending sw from Hughes Ridge, lat. 35° 36' 20" N., long. 83° 18' 38" W.

Mines Creek rises in nw Bladen County and flows e into Cape Fear River.

Mingo, community in nw Sampson County. A post office was est. here in 1875. Takes its name from East Mingo Branch (or Mingo Swamp). Mingo was an Indian word for a treacherous person.

Mingo Creek rises in ne Swain County and flows nw into Raven Fork.

Mingo Mill. See Burnt Mill Creek.

Mingo Swamp. See East Mingo Branch.

Mingo Township, nw Sampson County.

Mingus Creek, Great Smoky Mountains National Park, rises in ne Swain County and flows s and e into Oconaluftee River.

Mingus Ridge, w Haywood County extends se between Winchester Creek and Little Branch.

Mining Branch rises in n central Transylvania County and flows se into King Creek.

Mining Ridge, nw Henderson County, extends se from Big Knob to Queen Creek.

Mink Neck, community in se Hertford County.

Minneapolis, community in central Avery County. Post office est. 1892, named for the city in Minnesota. Inc. 1911, charter repealed 1915. An extensive deposit of asbestos was mined here at one time.

Minneapolis Ridge, central Avery Cour

Minnesott Beach, resort area in s Pamlico County on Neuse River. Developed by Hardison family, largely under the direction of Naaman Hardison, after World War I. Named for an Indian word said to mean "land of sky blue water."

Minpro, community in s Mitchell County on North Toe River.

Mint Branch rises in central Macon County and flows sw into Mill Creek.

Mint Hill, town in se Mecklenburg County. Site of Philadelphia Presbyterian Church, organized 1770. Inc. 1899, but long inactive in municipal affairs.

Minton, former community in s Wilkes County near Smithies Creek. Named for Meridy Minton, eighteenth century settler. The Smitheys Creek Public Use Area on W. Kerr Scott Reservoir is here.

Mintons. See Mintonsville.

Mintons Store, community in sw Hertford County.

Mintonsville, community in s Gates County. Post office in 1828 was Minton's, but by 1830 known as Mintonsville.

Mintonsville Township, s Gates County.

Mintz, community in w Sampson County. Named for Wm. Ashe Mintz. Daughter Mittie, first postmaster, 1900.

Mirey Branch rises in ne Hertford County and flows e into Chowan River.

Mirey Branch rises in se Onslow County and flows ne into Turpentine Creek.

Mirror Lake, se Macon County on Cullasaja River. Area approx. 50 acres; maximum depth 40 feet.

Miry Branch rises in ne Bladen County and flows e into South River.

Miry Branch rises in s Johnston County and flows e into Neuse River. Mentioned in local records as early as 1795.

Miry Branch rises in w Nash County and flows e into Tar River.

Miry Gut, n central Carteret County flows e into South River.

Misenheimer, community in nw Stanly County. Alt. 675. Former resort in the 1880's and 1890's known as Misenheimer Springs, which is still the name of the railroad station. Home of Pfeiffer College, a four-year coeducational institution. Inc. 1903 as Gladstone, but the charter was repealed in 1909, and the name later changed to Misenheimer.

Misenheimer Springs. See Misenheimer.

Miser Creek rises in w Transylvania County and flows se into Parker Creek.

Miss Creek rises in se Polk County and flows ne into Whiteoak Creek.

Mission, community in e Cherokee County near the mouth of Calhoun Creek.

Mission, community in w Stanly County. Named for a local church.

Mission Branch rises in e Cherokee County and flows sw into Hiwassee River.

Mission Mountain, e Cherokee County extends ne from the headwaters of Sud-

dereth Branch to the mouth of Moody Branch.

Mistletoe Creek rises in n Cherokee County and flows sw into Tellicoe River.

Mitchell, community in s Carteret County on Bogue Sound near the mouth of Spooners Creek.

Mitchell Branch rises in nw Beaufort County and flows sw into Tranters Creek.

Mitchell Branch rises in central Yancey County and flows se into Little Crabtree Creek.

Mitchell County was formed in 1861 from Yancey, Watauga, Caldwell, Burke, and McDowell counties. Located in the w section of the state, it is bounded by the state of Tennessee and by Avery, Mc-Dowell, and Yancey counties. It was named for Elisha Mitchell (1793-1857), professor at the University of North Carolina who was killed while exploring the peak which now bears his name—the highest point east of the Mississippi. Area: 220 sq. mi. County seat: Bakersville with an elevation of 2,550 ft. Townships are Bakersville, Bradshaw, Cane Creek, Fork Mountain, Grassy Creek, Harrell, Little Rock Creek, Poplar, Red Hill, and Snow Creek. Produces tobacco, apples, corn, dairy products, livestock, textiles, apparel, hosiery, lumber, mica, feldspar, kaolin, and quartz.

Mitchell Cove, w Haywood County on the head of Mitchell Cove Branch.

Mitchell Cove Branch rises in w Haywood County and flows se into Jonathans Creek.

Mitchell Creek rises in se Craven County and flows ne into Clubfoot Creek.

Mitchell Creek rises in n Person County and flows nw into Marlowe Creek.

Mitchell Creek rises in s Yancey County and flows ne into Timber Creek. See also Mitchell Falls.

Mitchell Falls, s Yancey County, on Mitchell Creek. It was here that Dr. Elisha Mitchell fell to his death in June, 1857.

Mitchell Lick, on Chreokee-Graham County

line approx. ½ mi. from Tenn. state line, on the headwaters of Snowbird Creek. It is a site at which early settlers salted stock and to which wild animals also came for salt.

Mitchell Mountain, ne Henderson County.

Mitchell Ridge, s Yancey County between Mitchell and Timber creeks.

Mitchell River rises in se Alleghany County and flows e into Surry County where it enters Yadkin River. Appears on the Collet map, 1770.

Mitchells Fork, community in s Gates County.

Mitchell's Island, w Craven County, in Trent River. 361 acres, partly culti- vated, the remainder is swamp.

Mitchells Township, n central Bertie Coun- ty.

Mitchell Swamp rises in w Robeson County and flows s into South Carolina.

Mitchiners Crossroads, community in nw Franklin County.

Mitcheners Pond, w Franklin County on Buffalo Creek. Formed in 1907. Covers 50 acres with a max. depth of 12 ft.

Mitchenor's Station. See Selma.

Mixon Bay, e Beaufort County, e of Bay- view opening into Pamlico River.

Mizell, community in nw Washington County.

Moadam's Creek rises in e Alamance Coun- ty and flows w into Back Creek.

Mobley Point extends from w Carteret County into White Oak River.

Moccasin Canal, e Washington County, drains from the n shore of Lake Phelps ne to Scuppernong River. Approx. 4.2 mi. long.

Moccasin Creek rises in n central Alleghany County and flows se into Little River.

Moccasin Creek rises in s Cherokee County and flows nw into Nottely River.

Moccasin Creek rises in sw Franklin Coun- ty and flows se on the Franklin-Wake County line, the Johnston-Nash County line, and the Johnston-Wilson County line until it joins Turkey Creek to form Contentnea Creek

Moccasin Creek rises in w Johnston County and flows se into Neuse River.

Moccasin Creek rises in w Wilson County and flows s and se into Contentnea Creek.

Moccasin Gap, s Cherokee County at the se end of Moccasin Mountain near the headwaters of Moccasin Creek.

Moccasin Gap, w Madison County between Partridge Gap Ridge and Hopis Branch.

Moccasin Mountain, s Cherokee County extends se from Sheep Knob to the Clay County line.

Moccasin River, a name sometimes ap- plied to the lower part of Contentnea Creek after it has been joined by Little Contentnea Creek. This portion lies on the Lenoir-Pitt County line.

Moccasin Swamp rises in e Johnston County and w Wayne County and flows s on the Johnston-Wayne County line into Neuse River.

Mocksville, town and county seat, central Davie County. Named for the Mock family, owners of the land on which the town was founded. Inc. 1839. Post office est. here 1810 as Mock's Old Field Post Office; name changed to Mocksville be- tween 1823 and 1826. Produces apparel, furniture, chemicals. Alt. 866.

Mocksville Township, central Davie Coun- ty.

Moffet Branch rises in s Clay County and flows n into Shooting Creek.

Moffitt, community in se Randolph County on Richland Creek. Named for Hugh Moffitt who operated the first flour and feed mill here. A post office est. prior to 1828 was known as Moffitt's Mills.

Moffitt Hill, community in sw McDowell County.

Moffitt Mountain, e Jackson County be- tween Chastine Creek and Coward Mountain.

Moffitt's Mill. See Moffitt.

Mojoson, community in nw Guilford Coun- ty.

Molasses Creek, a tidal creek in se Bruns- wick County, rises in the swampy ne part of Oak Island and flows e into Eliza- beth River.

Mollie, community in s Columbus County.

Mollie Branch rises in w Avery County and flow e into Roaring Creek.

Mollie Ridge, w Avery County.

Molly Fork rises in ne Rutherford County and flows se and ne into First Broad River.

Moltonville, community in e Sampson County.

Momeyer, community in w central Nash County. Est. about 1910 and named for Thomas Momeyer, local resident who established a sawmill here. Previously the community had been known as Bass's Crossroads. Alt. 190.

Monbo, community in e Catawba County on Catawba River. Named Mont Beau by the owner of a local cotton mill but residents of the area soon corrupted the name into its present form. *See also* East Monbo.

Moncure, community in se Chatham County on Deep River. A post office est. here in 1871. Inc. 1905; charter repealed, 1935. Named for Thomas Jefferson Moncure, civil engineer, who built the railroad station. The old town of Haywood is immediately se of Moncure.

Mondine Branch rises in s Jones County and flows s into White Oak River. Probably named for the Mundine family, early settlers.

Money. *See* Etowah.

Money Island, s central Carteret County, near the e end of Bogue Banks in Bogue Sound.

Money Island, e New Hanover County in Greenville Sound w of Wrightsville Beach. Several acres in area, it is the traditional hiding place of pirate treasure.

Money Island Bay in Bogue Sound, s Carteret County, between Atlantic Beach and Tar Landing Bay, opposite Morehead City.

Money Island Swamp rises in central Carteret County and flows sw into Black Creek.

Monger Creek rises in se Macon County and flows ne into Lake Sequoyah.

Monie Swamp is formed in s Columbus County by Gum Swamp and Beaverdam Swamp. It flows s to join Big Cypress Swamp in forming Seven Creeks.

Monkey Island in Currituck Sound, n Currituck County, 4 mi. e of Church Island. Approx. ½ mi. square. Site of an old hunting lodge. Appears on the Collet map, 1770.

Monkey Junction. *See* Fort Fisher Junction.

Monks Crossroads, community in n Sampson County between Mill and Craddock Swamps.

Monroe, city and county seat, central Union County. Named for President James Monroe (1758-1831). Inc. 1844. Merged with town of Benton Heights *(which see)* in 1945, and with town of West Monroe *(which see)* in 1949. William Henry Belk opened the first of his department stores here in 1888. Produces textiles, apparel, bricks, processed meat, industrial machinery, fabricated metals, and wood products. Alt. 576.

Monroe, former community in ne Warren County on Roanoke River. Grew up about Robinson's Ferry after Clack Robinson laid out a town on his lands near the ferry in 1818, named it for President James Monroe, and sold lots to prospective citizens; a post office, tavern, racetrack, tobacco warehouse, and stores soon sprang up. It was shown on the MacRae map, 1833, as a well established community. In 1840, when the Raleigh and Gaston Railroad was completed, it began a rapid decline.

Monroe Mountain, n Cherokee County between Allen Branch and Davis Creek. Alt. 3,171.

Monroes Millpond, n Scotland County on Jordans Creek. Formed about 1825; known in the 1850's as McWilliams Pond. Covers 70 acres; maximum depth 14 ft. Owned by Fayetteville Presbytery and used as a recreation area.

Monroeton, community in s Rockingham County between Troublesome Creek and Haw River. Est. prior to 1832; probably named for James Monroe (1758-1831), president of the United States. Cunningham Mill nearby built by James Patrick, Sr., in 1818 still stands. Patrick cemetery has graves dating from 1771. Cotton gin est. 1835.

Monroetown, a Negro community in s Moore County approx. 4 mi. n of Pinehurst. Named for John Monroe who est. the settlement about 1915.

Monroe Township, n central Guilford County.

Monroe Township, central Union County.

Mon Swamp, in se Tyrrell County.

Montague, community in sw Pender County. Alt. 39. Named for a local resident.

Mont Beau. *See* Monbo; East Monbo.

Monteith Branch rises in n Jackson County and flows se into Scott Creek.

Montezuma, community in central Avery County. Known first as Bull Scrape *(see* Bullscrape Gap). Post office est. here in 1883 as Aaron; name changed to Montezuma in 1891 when it was inc. Named for Aztec chief of ancient Mexico (1479-1520). Long inactive in municipal affairs. Alt. 3,797.

Montford, former town in central Buncombe County. Inc. 1893; became a part of Asheville, 1905.

Montford Cove Church. *See* Whitehouse.

Montford Cove Township, s central McDowell County.

Montford Point. *See* Mount Pleasant Point.

Montgomery. *See* Graham.

Montgomery Corner, a point on the North Carolina-Georgia state line at the se end of Sharptop Ridge, se Clay County, due s of 30 Mile Point, *which see*. From this point the state line runs w to the junction of the North Carolina-Georgia-Tennessee state lines.

Montgomery County was formed in 1779 from Anson County. Located in the s central section of the state, it is bounded by Moore, Richmond, Stanly, Davidson, and Randolph counties. It was named for General Richard Montgomery (1736-75), Revolutionary leader who was killed in the Battle of Quebec. Area: 499 sq. mi. County seat: Troy with an elevation of 664 ft. Townships are Biscoe, Cheek Creek, Eldorado, Little River, Mount Gilead, Ophir, Peedee, Rocky Springs, Troy, and Uwharrie. Produces peaches, oats, wheat, corn, cotton, poultry, hogs, livestock, cantaloupes, watermelons, textiles, furniture, carpets, mobile homes, lumber, apparel, clay, slate, pyrophyllite, and sand.

Montgomery Slough, a tidal waterway in se Brunswick County located just inside Long Beach and extending for 2½ mi. w to Eastern Chanel.

Monticello, community in n Guilford County. Named for Thomas Jefferson's home near Charlottesville, Virginia. Formerly known as Lambeth for a boarding academy operated here by one Reverend Mr. Lambeth.

Monticello, community in w Harnett County.

Monticello, community in central Iredell County which grew up around a school of the same name established here in the 1920's.

Monticello, former community and post office in sw Washington County approx.

1½ mi. n of the Tare-over. Settled prior to 1886; post office 1893-96.

Montpelier. *See* Wagram.

Montreat, town in ne Buncombe County on Flat Creek. Alt. 2,500. Est. by Mountain Retreat Association, chartered 1897. Montreat is derived from the words "Mountain Retreat." Later acquired by Presbyterian Church and now operated as its Assembly Grounds (4,500 acres). Historical Foundation (library and museum) and Montreat-Anderson College are here. Inc. 1967.

Montrose, community in w Hoke County. Alt. 483.

Montvale, community in sw Transylvania County.

Moody Branch rises in n Buncombe County near Moody Gap and flows s into Poverty Branch.

Moody Branch rises in ne Cherokee County and flows s into Webb Creek.

Moody Branch rises in e Cherokee County and flows s into Peachtree Creek.

Moody Branch rises in central Haywood County and flows ne into Cove Creek.

Moody Branch rises in ne Swain County and flows n into Bunches Creek.

Moody Cove, n Buncombe County, w of Pine Mountain.

Moody Gap, on the Buncombe-Madison County line, e of Moody Knob.

Moody Knob, on the Buncombe-Madison County line.

Moody Knob, nw Jackson County between Camp Creek and Hyatt Cove.

Moody Mountain, s Yancey County between Bowlens and Cattail creeks.

Moodys Mill Creek rises in sw Watauga County and flows ne into Spice Bottom Creek.

Moody Stamp, ne Cherokee County in the Snowbird Mountains.

Moody Top, w Haywood County between Fie Top and Hemphill Creek. Alt. 5,320.

Moon Creek rises in w Caswell County and flows ne into Dan River.

Mooney Branch rises in s Macon County and flows se into Hemp Patch Branch.

Mooney Gap, at the head of Mooney Branch in s Macon County.

Moore Branch rises in e Swain County and flows ne into Connelly Creek.

Moore Branch rises in s Watauga County and flows nw into Middle Fork [South Fork New River].

Moore County was formed in 1784 from Cumberland County. Located in the s central section of the state, it is bounded by Cumberland, Harnett, Hoke, Scotland, Richmond, Montgomery, Randolph, Chatham, and Lee counties. It was named for Captain Alfred Moore (1755-1810), of Brunswick County, a Revolutionary soldier and afterwards a judge of the United States Supreme Court. Area: 760 sq. mi. County seat: Carthage with an elevation of 575 ft. Townships are Carthage, Bensalem, Sheffields, Ritters, Deep River, Greenwood, McNeills, Sandhills, Mineral Springs, Little River. Produces corn, wheat, oats, poultry, eggs, livestock, hogs, carpets, hosiery, textiles, canned foods, furniture, pyrophyllite, sand, clay, and gravel.

Moore Cove, between Bear Branch and Seniard Mountain in nw Henderson County.

Moore Creek rises in sw Buncombe County near Stony Knob and flows se into Hominy Creek.

Moore Creek rises in sw Macon County and flows sw into Nantahala River. Also known locally as Jarrett Creek.

Moore Gap, on the Madison-Yancey County line near the head of Possumtrot Creek. Alt. approx. 3,100.

Moore Inlet, ne New Hanover County between Mason Inlet on the n and Masonboro Inlet on the s. The waters of Middle Sound enter the Atlantic Ocean through this inlet. Sometimes known as Wrightsville Inlet.

Moore Knob, e Macon County between Ellijay Creek and North Prong Ellijay Creek.

Moore Mountain, central Avery County.

Moores Beach, community in e Beaufort County on the n shore of Pamlico River, 35° 23' 51" N., 76° 37' 15" W. Formerly known also as Wade Point and Wades Point.

Mooresboro, community in w Cleveland County. Alt. 970. Settled in 1780's; inc.

1885. Charter repealed 1943. Named for Lem Moore, an early settler.

Moores Branch rises in central Clay County between Church Branch and Moss Branch and flows s into Tusquitee Creek.

Moores Corner, community in s Pamlico County.

Moores Creek rises in se Brunswick County and flows e into Orton Creek.

Moores Creek rises in w Guilford County and flows ne into Reedy Fork Creek.

Moores Creek rises in nw Pender County and flows s into Black River. Sometimes referred to as Widow Moores Creek in the eighteenth century, and probably named for the "Widow Eliz Moore" who owned land adjacent as early as 1735. It was on this stream that the Battle of Moores Creek Bridge was fought, February 27, 1776, the first battle of the Revolution in North Carolina. See also Currie.

Moores Creek rises in ne Pender County and flows sw into Holly Shelter Creek.

Moores Crossroads, community in ne Johnston County.

Moores Crossroads, community in w Wilson County near the head of Lee Swamp.

Moores Knob, in the Sauratown Mountain range, w Stokes County, in Hanging Rock State Park. See also, Tories Den.

Moore's Lake, central Anson County. Formed 1948. Fed by two springs. Covers 11 acres; max. depth 24 ft. Fishing, boating. Owned by Bernard W. Moore.

Moores Pond, s Franklin County on Little River. Covers 100 acres with a maximum depth of 10 ft.

Moore Springs Branch, Great Smoky Mountains National Park, rises in nw Swain County and flows sw into Twentymile Creek.

Moores Spring, former community and resort in w Stokes County on Cascade Creek, flourished from about 1870 until the early twentieth century. The hotel burned about 1935 and the site is now a popular camp ground. Bottled water from the spring was sold throughout a large area.

Mooresville, town in s Iredell County near Lake Norman. Inc. 1873. Named for John F. Moore, first mayor and donor of land for railroad depot in 1857. Construction of the railroad began in 1860. Alt. 910. Produces apparel, textiles, and milling products.

Moose Cove, central Cherokee County.

Mooshaunee, community in n Moore County.

Moratock, community in w Montgomery County.

Moratuc, village of the Moratuc Indian tribe on the Roanoke River near the present junction of Bertie-Martin-Washington counties. Appears on the John White map, 1585; Velasco, 1611; and John Smith, 1624. See also Roanoke River.

Moravian Creek rises in s Wilkes County and flows ne into Yadkin River. Named from the fact that Moravians had a grant from Earl Granville (see Granville District) here in the eighteenth century.

Moravian Falls, s Wilkes County on Moravian Creek. Water falls from 30 to 35 ft. over broad, steep rock between wooded hills. Named because of the discovery by Moravian surveyors in 1752. Fishing, swimming, picnicking.

Moravian Falls, community in s Wilkes County between Moravian and Cub creeks. Alt. 1,206. Est. in the late eighteenth century and named for the nearby waterfalls.

Moravian Falls Township, s Wilkes County.

Morehead. See Rudd.

Morehead Bluffs. See Edgewater.

Morehead City, town in s central Carteret County on Bogue Sound and Newport River. Summer resort and the only deep-sea port in the state n of Wilmington; state port facilities are here. Inc. 1861 and named for John Motley Morehead (1796-1866), governor of North Carolina, who had bought land here in 1853 as the terminus of a newly inc. railroad. Ships are built here; produces asphalt and apparel. The site was formerly known as Shepherds' Point, which see. Alt. 16.

Morehead Township, s Carteret County. Known for a time as township number 2.

Morehead Township, central Guilford County. Named for Governor John Motley Morehead (1796-1866) of Greensboro. Covers most of the western half of Greensboro.

Moretz, community in ne Watauga County on Meat Camp Creek. A post office was est. here by 1886.

Morgan Bay, in central Onslow County in New River.

Morgan Branch rises in n Buncombe County and flows n into McKinney Branch.

Morgan Branch rises in ne Buncombe County and flows sw into Right Fork.

Morgan Branch rises in sw Buncombe County near Smathers Mountain and flows se into South Hominy Creek.

Morgan Branch rises in e central Brunswick County and flows s into Town Creek.

Morgan Branch rises in central Clay County and flows nw then sw into Cold Branch.

Morgan Cove, sw Buncombe County, sw of Luthers.

Morgan Creek rises in central Cherokee County and flows se and sw into Valley River.

Morgan Creek rises in n Haywood County and flows se into Fines Creek.

Morgan Creek rises in sw Orange County and flows e into w Durham County where it turns s into Chatham County and enters New Hope River. Formerly known as Mark Creek. Named for Mark Morgan who owned land in the area as early as 1753.

Morgan Creek rises in s Pender County and flows sw into Long Creek.

Morgan District at the time of the 1790 census was composed of Burke, Lincoln, Rutherford, and Wilkes counties.

Morgan Hill, community in n Buncombe County.

Morgan Hill, peak in s Transylvania County near the mouth of Cherryfield Creek.

Morgan Mill Creek rises in s Transylvania County and flows se then ne into French Broad River.

Morgan Mills Ford, n Union County on Rocky River. Site of a large grist mill dating from the middle of the nineteenth century. The building and machinery still stand, but the mill is no longer operated.

Morgan Ridge, n Buncombe County, an extension of Bill Cole Mountain.

Morgan's Branch rises in n Wilson County and flows se into Cattail Swamp.

Morgan's Mills, community in ne Union County.

Morganton, town and county seat, central Burke County. Est. 1777; inc. 1784. Alt. 1,182. Named for General Daniel Morgan (1736?-1802), Revolutionary leader. Western Piedmont Community College, est. 1966, is located here. Produces furniture, electronics components, hosiery, apparel, textiles, and dairy products.

Morganton Township, s central Burke County.

Morgantown, community in e Carteret County near the nw limits of Newport.

Morgan Township, se Rowan County.

Morgan Township, nw Rutherford County.

Moriah, community in se Person County.

Morlin Mountain, n Rutherford County between Cane Creek and the head of South Creek. Alt. approx. 2,100.

Morning Star, community in e Haywood County on the head of Allens Creek.

Morning Star Township, former township in se Mecklenburg County, now township number 13.

Morattico River. See Roanoke River.

Morris Creek rises in e Caldwell County and flows s into Cedar Creek.

Morris Creek rises in ne Cherokee County and flows se and sw into Valley River.

Morris Field Air Base, Charlotte, central Mecklenburg County, was dedicated April 21, 1941, and used to train combat pilots during World War II. Named in honor of Major William C. Morris, Cabarrus County, distinguished World War I flyer. Property returned to City of Charlottee in 1946 for use as municipal airport.

Morris Knob, s Wilkes County at the sw end of Gill Mountain.

Morris Landing, community in sw Onslow County on Stump Sound.

Morris Mountain, n Montgomery County between Bundle Mountain and Barnes Creek.

Morrison, community in s Richmond County.

Morrison, former community in w Iredell County on Fourth Creek near the present community of Loray. William Morrison (1704-71) settled here in 1750 and by 1752 was operating a gristmill. In an Indian attack all buildings were burned except the mill, which was saved by an Indian superstition of evil which would befall them if they burned a mill. Appears on the Collet map, 1770, and as Morrisons Mill as recently as 1901 on a map of the county. A cemetery with eighteenth-century tombstones marks the site.

Morrison Creek, rises in w Iredell County and flows e into Fourth Creek. Formerly known as Middle Fourth Creek.

Morris Pond, on Juniper Creek, se Lee County. Formed about 1865. Covers 25 acres; max. depth 8 ft. Formerly a mill pond, now used for fishing, swimming, and boating.

Morris Run rises in sw Beaufort County and flows nw into Chocowinity Creek.

Morristown. See Asheville.

Morrisville, town in w Wake County on Crabtree Creek. Settled 1840; chartered in 1875 and named for Jerry Morris who owned the town site. Charter repealed in 1933. Reincorporated in 1947. Alt. 304.

Morrow Branch rises in central Haywood County and flows se into Jonathans Creek.

Morrow Branch rises in s Madison County and flows s into Little Sandymush Creek.

Morrow Creek rises in s Rutherford County and flows ne into Second Broad River.

Morrow Gap, w Cherokee County between Shuler and Sular creeks.

Morrow Mountain State Park, e Stanly County on Yadkin and Pee Dee rivers. 4,135 acres. Est. 1935 on land given in large part by James McKnight Morrow. Former Naked Mountain (which see) renamed Morrow Mountain. Scenic, recreational area; picnicking, swimming, fishing, tent and trailer camping, boating, hiking, nature study, museum. Restaurant, recreation lodge. There are several peaks (Mill Mountain, Sugarloaf Mountain, and Tater Top Mountain) in the park, none of which is over 1,050.

Morse Point, a neck of land extending from Virginia into the mouth of North Landing River in ne Currituck County.

Mortimer, town in w Caldwell County. Inc. 1907, but long inactive in municipal affairs. Alt. 1,502. Largely a ghost town. Established in connection with a lumber mill.

Morton Creek rises in w Transylvania County and flows se into South Fork Flat Creek.

Morton Township, former township in nw Alamance County, now township number 4.

Morven, town in se Anson County. Inc. 1883. Post office est. here in 1823 and named for Morven, Scotland, home of the mother of Hugh McKenzie, first postmaster. Alt. 341.

Morven Township, se Anson County.

Moseley County. About 1907 an unsigned petition was presented to the General Assembly proposing that a county be created from portions of Lenoir, Wayne, and Greene counties with the county seat at LaGrange. It was to be named for William D. Moseley (1795-1863) who was born near LaGrange and who was governor of Florida, 1845-49.

Moseley Creek rises in Great Dover Swamp, w Craven County, and flows nw into Neuse River. For a part of its course it forms the Craven-Lenoir County line.

Moseley Creek rises in nw Lenoir County and flows se into Falling Creek. Named for Matthew Moseley who settled here about 1770.

Moseley Hall. See LaGrange.

Moseley Hall Township, nw Lenoir County. Named for plantation house of Moseley family.

Moseley's Cove, s Pender County on Northeast Cape Fear River. Adjacent land once was owned by Edward Moseley (1682-1749), colonial surveyor general and member of the governor's council.

Moseley's Creek. See Parrotts Creek.

Moseleys Point. See Hornblower Point.

Moses Branch rises in e Macon County and flows nw into Elijay Creek.

Moses Branch rises in n Yancey County and flows e into Jacks Creek.

Moses Creek formed by junction of East Fork and West Fork in n Jackson County and flows sw into Caney Fork.

Moses H. Cone Memorial Park, s Watauga County on Blue Ridge Parkway, nw of Blowing Rock. Est. 1950. Former estate of Moses H. Cone (1857-1908); 3,517 acres. Flat Top Manor is now a museum and craft center at which mountain handicrafts are sold. Trails for hiking and horseback riding and lakes for fishing are here. See also Bass Lake.

Moses Knob, on the Jackson-Macon County line.

Moses Knob, e Caldwell County. Probably named for Capt. Moses Guest, Revolutionary soldier, who lived nearby on the Yadkin River.

Moss, community in n Cherokee County.

Moss, community in ne Stanly County.

Moss Branch rises in central Anson County and flows e into Brush Fork Creek.

Moss Branch rises in n Cherokee County on Hanging Dog Mountain and flows se into Slickrock Branch.

Moss Branch rises in central Clay County and flows s into Tusquitee Creek.

Moss Branch rises in e Macon County and flows s into Little Buck Creek.

Mossey Islands in Currituck Sound off the w shore of Currituck Banks, se Currituck County.

Moss Gap, on the Jackson-Macon County line.

Moss Knob on the Jackson-Macon County line. Alt. 4,500.

Moss Neck, community in w central Robeson County.

Mossy Back Gap, sw Macon County on Clear Branch.

Mossy Branch rises in w Haywood County and flows se into Cataloochee Creek.

Motes Creek rises in se Alamance County and flows s into Haw River.

Mott Creek rises in e Onslow County and flows nw into Northeast Creek.

Motts Creek. See Todds Creek.

Motts Falls, rapids in the Yadkin River, s Davidson County near the mouth of Riles and Ellis creeks. The rapids extend approx. ⁹/₁₀ of a mile and drop a total of 13½ ft., having six nearly vertical falls of from 6 in. to 2 ft. each.

Mott Swamp rises in e Lenoir County and flows n into Southwest Creek.

Moulder Branch rises in s Alamance County in the Cane Creek Mountains and flows se into Cane Creek. Also known as Foust's Creek.

Moulton, community in n Franklin County.

Mountain Branch rises in n Stokes County and flows e into Snow Creek.

Mountain Canal, e Washington County extends ne from Lake Phelps to Scuppernong River.

Mountain Creek rises in s Alexander County and flows s into Catawba River.

Mountain Creek is formed by the junction of its North and South Forks in se Catawba County. It flows se into Catawba River.

Mountain Creek rises in nw Durham County and flows se into Little River.

Mountain Creek rises in w Gaston County and flows sw into Long Creek.

Mountain Creek rises in central Graham County and flows sw into Santeetlah Lake.

Mountain Creek rises in n Granville County and flows ne into Grassy Creek.

Mountain Creek rises in w Hoke County and flows sw into Lumber River.

Mountain Creek rises in s Orange County and flows ne into New Hope Creek.

Mountain Creek rises in n Rutherford County and flows s into Broad River. Fort McFadden was located on this creek, near the present site of Rutherfordton, in the mid-18th century.

Mountain Creek rises in n Stanly County and flows se into Pee Dee River.

Mountain Creek, community in se Catawba County.

Mountain Creek Township, se Catawba County.

Mountain Home, community in n Henderson County.

Mountain Island, town in ne Gaston County on Catawba River at Mountain Island Lake. Inc. 1891, but long inactive in municipal affairs. See also Mountain Island Lake.

Mountain Island Branch rises in w Madison County and flows ne into French Broad River.

Mountain Island Lake on the Catawba River, Gaston and Mecklenburg counties. Formed 1922-1924. Covers 3,235 acres with a shore line of 61 mi. Owned by Duke Power Co. and site of hydroelectric power plant. See also, Mount Heckler.

Mountain Park, community in w Surry County, est. 1913 and named for its mountain location in a park-like setting.

Mountain Region, Mountain Section, or simply The Mountains, are terms applied to the mountainous section of w North Carolina. The e limit of the region runs generally through Surry, Wilkes, Caldwell, Burke, Rutherford, and Polk counties. The Indians referred to this area as Ottaray, "Highlands." The English sometimes rendered the word into English as Otaré which they translated "Over Hills." See also Appalachian Mountains.

Mountain Run rises in e Caldwell County and flows s into Upper Little River.

Mountainside Branch rises in s Macon County and flows nw into Big Mooney Branch.

Mountainside Grove, community on Falls Branch in e Macon County.

Mountain Tea Branch rises near Henry Mountain in s Transylvania County and flows s into East Fork French Broad River. Named for the abundance of wintergreen which grows near the branch, the herb from which "mountain tea" is made.

Mountain Township, sw Jackson County.

Mountain View, community in s Stokes County between the head of Danbury Creek and Town Fork Creek.

Mountain View, former community in e Warren County. A post office was est. here in 1879, but was discontinued in 1929.

Mount Airy, town in ne Surry County. Alt. 1,104. Settled about 1850; inc. 1869. In the early nineteenth century this vicinity seems to have been called the Hollow or Hallow. See also Perkinsville.

Mount Airy Township, n Surry County.

Mount Ararat. See Pilot Mountain.

Mount Bolus, hill in se Orange County near Bolin Creek, ½ mi. n of Chapel Hill. An extinct volcano. Said to have been named by University students after their nickname, "Old Diabolus" (devil), for Joseph Caldwell, President of the University, 1796-1835. Appears as Gander Mountain in local records as late as 1792.

Mount Buckley, the southernmost of three knobs, the central one of which is Clingmans Dome and the northern Mount Love, Great Smoky Mountains, on the border of Swain County, N. C.-Sevier County, Tenn., lat. 35° 33' 15" N., long. 83° 30' W. Named by Prof. Arnold H. Guyot prior to 1860 in honor of S. B. Buckley (1809-1884), naturalist, friend, and sometime co-laborer. Alt. 6,500.

Mt. Calvert. See Grimesland.

Mount Cammerer on the Haywood County, N. C.- Cocke County, Tenn., line in the Great Smoky Mountains National Park, on Cammerer Ridge about lat. 35° 45' 50" N., long. 83° 09' 40" W. Named in honor of A. B. Cammerer, formerly of the U. S. Department of the Interior, who was active in promoting the park. Alt. approx. 4,928.

Mount Carmel, community in s Vance County on Sandy Creek. Named for a local church in turn named for the Biblical mountain in nw Palestine from which Elijah called down fire from heaven.

Mount Chapman, Great Smoky Mountains National Park, on Swain County, N. C.-Sevier County, Tenn., line, lat. 35° 41' N., long. 83° 17' W. Named for David Carpenter Chapman (1876-1938?), of Knoxville, Tenn., whose initiative and persistent activity over many years was largely responsible for the establishment of the Great Smoky Mountains National Park by the act of Congress approved May 22, 1926. Alt. 6,425. Formerly known as Black, Old Black, and The Black.

Mount Collier, s Orange County at ne end of Grampian Hills.

Mount Collins, Great Smoky Mountains National Park, on the Swain County, N. C.-Sevier County, Tenn., line, lat. 35° 35' N., long. 83° 28' W. Named for Robert Collins (1806-63), one of the first settlers in the area and a guide for Arnold Guyot and other explorers. Mount Collins was renamed Mount Kephart in 1928 but that name was later given to another peak. Alt. 6,255.

Mount Craig, peak in Mount Mitchell State Park, s Yancey County, near lat. 35° 46' 40" N., lat. 82° 15' 40" W. Alt. 6,663. Second highest peak in the state. One of two peaks known as Black Brothers until 1947 when renamed in honor of Governor Locke Craig (1860-1924), who was largely responsible for the establishment of Mount Mitchell State Park. Known earlier as Balsam Cone.

Mount Davis, on the Swain County, N. C.-Sevier County, Tenn., line in Great Smoky Mountains National Park. Alt. approx. 5,000. Formerly named Greenbrier Knob, renamed about 1950 for Willis P. Davis of Knoxville, Tenn. who started the movement for the establishment of the park. Located at lat. 35° 34' 15" N., long. 83° 38' 03" W.

Mount Energy, community in s Granville County.

Mount Gallant, elevation in nw Northampton County. Alt. 250. Plantation here was owned by William Maule, and called by this name, in 1723. Gov. William Tryon visited Mount Gallant in 1765 and remarked upon the fine view from its summit. Appears on the Collet map, 1770, and on the MacRae map, 1833. *See also* Chowan Beach for another reference to this name at another site.

Mount Gibbes, s Yancey County in Black Mountains between Clingmans Dome and Stepps Gap. Alt. 6,600. Named about 1852 for Dr. Robert Wilson Gibbes (1809-66) of Columbia, S. C., the first to measure its altitude.

Mount Gilead, community in n Cabarrus County.

Mount Gilead, town in sw Montgomery County. Settled by 1830 when a post office was est. here. Inc. 1899. Named for the Biblical mountain. Alt. 421. Produces shoes, hosiery, textiles, and apparel.

Mount Gilead Township, former township in n Carbarrus County, now township number 5. In 1945 a part of this township was annexed to Concord.

Mount Gilead Township, sw Montgomery County.

Mount Glory, Great Smoky Mountains National Park, n Swain County on Welch Ridge near the head of White Mans Glory Creek, lat. 35° 31' 22" N., long. 83° 36' 08" W. Alt. 4,965.

Mt. Golland. *See* Mt. Gould.

Mt. Gould, community in e central Bertie County. Developed at the site of a plantation first known as Mt. Golland and later Mt. Gould after George Gould, a surveyor, came into possession of it. Littledals Ferry on the Chowan River nearby appears on the Collet map, 1770.

Mount Guyot, on Haywood County, N. C.,-Sevier County, Tenn., line, Great Smoky Mountains National Park, near lat. 35° 42' 20" N., long. 83° 15' 30" W. Alt. 6,621. Named by Prof. S. B. Buckley, prior to 1859, in honor of Arnold Guyot, geographer, who made the first comprehensive survey of this region and did much to stimulate public interest in these mountains. Known by the Cherokee Indians as *Sornook.*

Mount Hardison, Great Smoky Mountains National Park, ne Swain County at the n end of Dashoga Ridge. Alt. 6,148. Named for James Archibald Hardison (1867-1930), of Anson County, an original member of the N. C. State Park Commission.

Mount Hardy, s Haywood County, near lat. 35° 18' 15" N., long. 82° 55' 38" W. Named 1957-58 for Dr. James F. E. Hardy of Asheville, N. C., who, in the 1850's in cooperation with Arnold Guyot, explored and named many of the mountains of Western North Carolina. Formerly known as Black Mountain. Alt. 6,110.

Mount Hardy Gap, s Haywood County near lat. 35° 17' 55" N., long. 82° 55' 30" W. Formerly known as Black Mountain Gap.

Mount Heckler, former mountain in ne Gaston County. Following the construction of the dam on the Catawba River at this point it was almost covered by water. Its peak now forms an island in Mountain Island Lake. Named for Mt. Hecla Mills in Greensboro. In 1848 a cotton mill was transplanted near here from Greensboro by the son-in-law of the owner of Mt. Hecla Mills. *See also* Mountain Island Lake.

Mt. Hermon, community in s Caldwell County. Named for Mt. Hermon Church.

Mount Hermon Township, w central Pasquotank County.

Mount Holly, town in e Gaston County. Post office est. as Huntersville in 1801, named for the Rev. Humphrey Hunter, postmaster. Name changed to Woodlawn in 1836. Inc. 1879 as Mount Holly, named for the town in New Jersey where fine yarns were manufactured. **Produces**

textiles and hosiery. Alt. 621. *See also*
Nims.

Mount Ida, central McDowell County at
the s limits of the town of Marion. Alt.
approx. 2,000. Named for Ida Neal.

Mount Jefferson, se of and named for Jefferson in central Ashe County. State Park
of 474 acres is maintained here for sight-
seeing and picnicking; created 1956. Appears in local records as Nigger Mountain
as early as 1810; name changed at the
creation of the park. Original name given
because of the black appearance of the
weathered granite of which much of the
mountain is composed. A cave near the
top is said to have been used by Negro
slaves fleeing to the Ohio country before
the Civil War. Alt. 4,683.

Mount Junaluska. *See* Jones Knob.

Mount Kephart, Great Smoky Mountains
National Park, on the Swain County,
N. C.-Sevier County, Tenn., line, lat. 35°
38′ N., long 83° 24′ W. Named in 1928
for Horace Kephart (1862-1931), explorer, naturalist, and authority on campcraft who lived in the area for many
years. Alt. 6,400. Mount Collins, nearby,
bore the name Mount Kephart for a
short while. The Jump Off, on the
Tennessee side of Mount Kephart, was
formerly believed to be in North Carolina. A cliff here drops vertically for almost 500 ft., and then nearly vertically
for an additional 1,000 ft.

Mount Love, Great Smoky Mountains National Park, on the Swain County, N. C.-
Sevier County, Tenn., line, lat. 35° 33′
30″ N., long. 83° 30′ W. Named by
Arnold Guyot before 1860 for Dr. S. L.
Love (1828-87) who accompanied General Clingman and Professor Buckley in
1858 when Clingmans Dome was first
measured. Alt. approx. 6,500.

Mount Misery appears on the Collet map,
1770, as a large sandhill north of Eagle
Island in w New Hanover County. A
ferry across the Cape Fear River was
operated here from as early as 1754 and
possibly through the Revolution.

Mount Mitchell, community in s Mitchell
County on East Fork Grassy Creek.

Mount Mitchell, s Yancey County in Black
Mountains. Alt. 6,684, the highest peak
in Eastern America. Formerly known as
Black Dome, but renamed for Professor
Elisha Mitchell (1793-1857) of the University of North Carolina who fell to his
death nearby while trying to establish his

claim that it was the highest mountain
east of the Mississippi. Known by the
Cherokee Indians as Attakulla. *See also,*
Mitchell Falls.

Mount Mitchell State Park, s Yancey County. 1,224 acres. Est. 1915 as the first
state park in North Carolina. Scenic
area; tent camping, picnicking, hiking,
nature study; museum, recreation lodge,
lookout tower.

Mount Mourne, town in s Iredell County.
Inc. 1875 but long inactive in municipal
affairs. Settled prior to the American
Revolution and took its name from the
home of Rufus Reid which he had named
Mount Mourne for the mountain in Ireland. At Torrence's Tavern here Lt. Col.
Tarleton's British cavalry routed a force
of American militia, February 2, 1781.
Crowfield Academy, an early classical
school about a mile s was est. 1760 and
closed by the Revolution.

Mount Nebo. *See* Nebo.

Mount Night. *See* Pores Knob.

Mount Noble, Great Smoky Mountains National Park, e Swain County, lat. 35° 30′
20″ N., long. 83° 20′ 15″ W.

Mount Olive, community in n Columbus
County.

Mount Olive, community in s Stokes County, named for a church.

Mount Olive, town in s Wayne County.
Inc. 1870. Named by Benjamin Oliver,
local resident, for Biblical **Mount of**
Olives. Town limits now encompass
former community of Enterprise (*which
see*). Center for marketing produce—
vegetables, strawberries, and grapes;
location of a large cucumber pickle processing plant. Mount Olive Junior College is here.

Mount Pisgah on the Buncombe-Haywood
County line nw of Little Pisgah Mountain. Alt. 5,721. Also sometimes known
as Big Pisgah and Great Pisgah. View
from its top includes points in North
Carolina, South Carolina, Georgia, Tennessee, and Virginia. Reached by Forest
Service trail from the Blue Ridge Parkway at Pisgah Inn. Named for the
Biblical mountain from which Moses saw
the Promised Land. Known by the
Indians as *El-see-toss.*

Mount Pisgah, community in ne Alexander
County.

Mount Pisgah, community in n Rutherford
County on Little Camp Creek.

Mt. Pleasant, community in central **Avery**

County.

Mount Pleasant, town in e Cabarrus County. Alt. 630. Settled about 1750 by Germans from Pennsylvania. Inc. 1859. Took its name from its elevated site between Buffalo Creek and Adams Creek. Former home of two Lutheran Synod church schools: Mount Pleasant Collegiate Institute (boys), and Mount Amoena Seminary (girls).

Mount Pleasant, community in se Moore County between Crains Creek and Buffalo Creek.

Mount Pleasant, community in sw Nash County.

Mount Pleasant, community in n Yadkin County near the head of Forbush Creek.

Mount Pleasant. See Elliott.

Mount Pleasant. See Johnsonville.

Mount Pleasant Creek rises in e Randolph County and flows sw into Sandy Creek.

Mount Pleasant Point extends from e Onslow County into White Oak River, about 20 feet above the water. Named for the pre-Revolutionary plantation of Emanuel Jones. Also known as Montford Point in recent years.

Mount Pleasant Township, former township in e Cabarrus County, now township number 8.

Mount Prospect. See Waynesville.

Mount Regis. See Norlina.

Mount Sequoyah, Great Smoky Mountains National Park, on the Swain County, N. C.-Sevier County, Tenn., line, lat. 35° 40′ N., long. 83° 18′ 15″ W. Alt. approx. 6,000. Named for Sequoyah (1770?-1843), Indian who devised a Cherokee alphabet used in teaching thousands of his people to read and write.

Mount Squires, on the Swain County, N. C.-Blount County, Tenn., line in the Great Smoky Mountains National Park between McCampbell Knob and Rocky Top near lat. 35° 33′ 47″ N., long. 83° 44′ 30″ W. Alt. 5,042. Named for State Senator Mark Squires (1878-1938), a leader in the movement to establish the Park. Formerly known as Little Bald.

Mount Sterling, w Haywood County, Great Smoky Mountains National Park, near lat. 35° 42′ 10″ N., long. 83° 07′ 20″ W. Alt. 5,835. Said to have been named by a woodcutter and logger from the town of Sterling, Ky.

Mount Sterling, community in w Haywood County, on Big Creek, near lat. 35° 45′ 42″ N., long. 83° 06′ 15″ W.

Mount Sterling Creek rises in w Haywood County and flows ne into Pigeon River.

Mount Sterling Gap, w Haywood County, Great Smoky Mountains National Park, near lat. 35° 42′ N., long. 83° 05′ 59″ W. Alt. 3,887.

Mount Sterling Ridge, w Haywood County, Great Smoky Mountains National Park, from Balsam Mountain extending ne from lat. 35° 40′ 17″ N., long. 83° 10′ 55″ W., forming the watershed between Big Creek and Cataloochee Creek.

Mount Tirzah, community in s Person County. Said to have been named in 1783 by Colonel Stephen Moore, Revolutionary soldier. A post office as early as 1822.

Mount Tirzah Township, se Person County.

Mount Ulla, community in w Rowan County. Said to have been named for "a place in Ireland," probably the village of Oola. Wood Grove post office est. here in 1830; named for plantation home of Capt. Thomas Cowan which still stands. Named changed to Mount Ulla in 1842, and to Rowan for a few months in 1900. Alt. 839.

Mount Ulla Township, w central Rowan County.

Mount Vernon, community in nw Rowan County on Fourth Creek. A post office as early as 1819 and as recent as 1882.

Mount Vernon, crossroads community in central Rutherford County between Catheys Creek and Second Broad River.

Mount Vernon Springs, community in w Chatham County. The Springs, a popular resort area in the early and middle nineteenth century are approx. 1 mi. west; known earlier as Hickory Springs. The present community was inc. as Ore Hill in 1907, but the charter was repealed in 1913. Named for the home of George Washington. Alt. 500. See also Wilcox Iron Works.

Mount Willing, w Orange County on the head of Toms Creek.

Mount Yonaguska, on the Haywood-Swain County line between Tricorner Knob and Luftee Knob in Great Smoky Mountains National Park, near lat. 35° 41′ 40″ N., long. 83° 14′ 53″ W. Alt. 6,150. Named for Yonaguska, the last great chief of the Cherokee Indians.

Mount Zion, community in w Wilkes County on Stony Fork Creek. Named for a

Baptist church which was organized here in 1849.

Mount Zion. *See* Chowan Beach.

Mouse Creek, w Haywood County, Great Smoky Mountains National Park, rises near lat. 35° 42′ 22″ N., long. 83° 07′ 17″ W., and flows nw into Big Creek. The name is an Indian one.

Mouse Harbor, bay on the e side of Goose Creek Island, ne Pamlico County, in the waters of Pamlico Sound. The shape of the bay on a map vaguely suggests the shape of a mouse.

Mouse Knob, sw Graham County on Snowbird Creek. The name is a translation of the Indian name.

Mouse Mountain, n Macon County between Rickman Creek and Bradley Creek.

Moxley, community in n Wilkes County on Middle Prong Roaring River.

Moyes Run rises in e Pitt County and flows se into Broad Run.

Moyock, community in nw Currituck County. Name appears in local records as early as 1753. Alt. 5. The Rev. Thomas Coke in 1785 recorded that he visited and preached at "Mowyock."

Moyock Creek. *See* Shingle Landing Creek.

Moyock Township, nw Currituck County.

Moyton. *See* Stantonsburg.

Mucky Branch rises in n Durham County and flows ne into Little River.

Mud Castle, community in w Northampton County. Named for a pre-Revolutionary plantation here.

Mud Creek rises in sw Durham County and flows se into New Hope Creek. Formerly known as Bakers Creek.

Mud Creek rises in w Gates County and flows se into Chowan River.

Mud Creek rises in sw Henderson County and flows ne and nw into French Broad River. The Indian name was *Ochlawaha,* "Muddy Waters." *See also* Naples.

Mud Creek rises in n Wake County and flows s into Horse Creek. Known previously as Mutton Creek, as shown on several nineteenth-century maps.

Mudcut Branch rises in sw Swain County and flows se into Nantahala River.

Muddy Branch rises in Green Swamp in w central Brunswick County and flows ne and n into Juniper Creek.

Muddy Creek rises in se Beaufort County and flows nw into Bond Creek.

Muddy Creek rises in the s tip of Cabarrus County and flows se into Rocky River.

Muddy Creek rises in central Catawba County and flows se and sw into Henry Fork.

Muddy Creek rises in e Duplin County and flows sw into Northeast Cape Fear River.

Muddy Creek rises in nw Forsyth County and flows s into Davidson County where it enters Yadkin River. Appears to have been called Charles Creek on the Collet map, 1770.

Muddy Creek, formed in ne McDowell County by the junction of North Muddy Creek and South Muddy Creek, and flows ne into the Catawba River in w Burke County.

Muddy Creek rises in s Onslow County and flows se into Stones Bay.

Muddy Creek rises in nw Randolph County and flows se into Deep River. Appears on the Collet map, 1770.

Muddy Creek rises in n Scotland County and flows ne into Lumber River.

Muddy Creek rises in sw Stokes County and flows s through w Forsyth County and into nw Davidson County where it enters Yadkin River. Appears as Gargals Creek on the Fry-Jefferson map, 1755, and as Gargales Creek on the Collet map, 1770. The uppermost branch is shown on the Collet map as Dorithea Creek, named for Dorothea, Countess Zinzendorf, whose husband was a patron of the Moravians. Known as Dorithea Creek as early as 1756, but some time after 1770 the entire creek became known as Muddy Creek.

Muddy Creek, community in sw Forsyth County near the Davidson County line. Alt. 726.

Muddy Cross, community in s Gates County.

Muddy Fork rises in e Cleveland County and flows sw into Buffalo Creek.

Muddy Fork Creek rises in n central Alexander County and flows sw into Lower Little River.

Muddy Slue, a slough in the tidal marsh islands in the Cape Fear River opposite Southport, se Brunswick County.

Mud Gap, Great Smoky Mountains National Park, on Swain County, N. C.-Blount County, Tenn., line, lat. 35° 31′ 18″ N., long. 83° 48′ 24″ W.

Mulatto Branch rises in s Lee County and flows se into Little Juniper Creek.

Mulatto Mountain, s Ashe County. Alt. 4,680.

Mulberry, community in n central Wilkes

County at the head of Lousy Creek.

Mulberry Bay, sw Carteret County in Bogue Sound, between Banks Channel and Bogue Inlet.

Mulberry Branch rises in Green Swamp, sw Brunswick County and flows sw into Shallotte River.

Mulberry Creek is formed in se Ashe County by the junction of Meadow Fork and Laurel Fork creeks and flows n and w to join Piney Fork Creek in forming Cranberry Creek.

Mulberry Creek rises in n Caldwell County about 2½ mi. se of Blowing Rock in Pisgah National Forest and flows approx. 12 mi. south into Johns River.

Mulberry Creek rises in n central Carteret County, and flows s into South River.

Mulberry Creek rises in s Macon County and flows se into Little Tennessee River.

Mulberry Creek rises in ne Onslow County and flows se into White Oak River.

Mulberry Creek rises in n Wilkes County and flows se into Yadkin River. Appears as Mulberryfield on the Collet map, 1770.

Mulberry Fields. See North Wilkesboro.

Mulberry Gap on the Alleghany-Wilkes County line.

Mulberry Gap, at the head of Howard Branch in s Macon County.

Mulberry Point, on the s shore of the Neuse River about 5 mi. upstream from its mouth, between Cedar Bay and Turnagain Bay in n Carteret County.

Mulberry Township, n central Caldwell County.

Mulcahy. See Peachland.

Mule Gap, Great Smoky Mountains National Park, n Swain County on Welch Ridge, lat. 35° 33' 02" N., long. 83° 34' 15" W. Alt. approx. 5,000.

Mull Creek rises in n Catawba County and flows ne into Lyle Creek.

Mull Creek rises in e Jackson County and flows sw into Caney Fork.

Mullet Gut, a stream which rises in w Carteret County and flows se into Starkey Creek.

Mullet Pond, a bay on the extreme w end of Shackleford Banks, s Carteret County.

Mull Grove, community in sw Catawba County. Named for Mull family.

Mullin Hill, mountain in sw Avery County.

Mumblehead Top, e Cherokee County between the headwaters of Rattler Branch and Brooks Creek.

Mumford Point, central Onslow County, about 2 mi. s of the city of Jacksonville,

the point of land between the junction of New River and Northeast Branch. Now within the Camp Lejeune reservation.

Munday Cove, central Buncombe County, extends nw from Iron Ore Ridge to Reems Creek.

Murchison, community in s Yancey County on Cane River. Alt. 2,930.

Murfreesboro, town in w Hertford County on Meherrin River. Settled around 1707 and known as Murfree's Landing for William Murfree, colonial and Revolutionary leader and owner of the town site. Known as Murfree's Ferry by 1770. Inc. as Murfreesboro 1787. Chowan College founded here in 1848. Alt. 75. Produces wooden containers, tobacco, peanuts, cotton, corn, and pork. See also Princeton.

Murfreesboro Township, nw Hertford County.

Murfree's Ferry, Murfree's Landing. See Murfreesboro.

Murphey, community in s Duplin County.

Murphy, town and county seat, central Cherokee County at the junction of Hiwassee and Valley rivers. Alt. 1,535. Site known first as Christie Ford for an Indian named Christie who lived here. Later called Huntersville for Col. A. R. S. Hunter who est. a trading post here with the Cherokee Indians about 1830. Inc. as Murphy, 1851, and named for Archibald Debow Murphey (1758-1832), leader for internal improvements in North Carolina. Fort Butler, site ¼ mi. sw, was one of those used by Gen. Winfield Scott in 1838 to gather Cherokees before moving them west. The fort served as a site for the first courts until a suitable building was erected in Murphy. Produces textiles and lumber.

Murphy Bay, a swamp in e Bladen County se of Black Lake. See also Carolina Bays.

Murphy Branch rises in s Mitchell County and flows w into Crabtree Creek.

Murphy Branch rises in e Yancey County and flows w into South Toe River.

Murphy Falls on Big Crabtree Creek on the Mitchell-Yancey County line.

Murphy Gap, ne Graham County.

Murphy Township, central Cherokee County.

Murray Branch rises in e Haywood County in Buckeye Cove and flows s into Pigeon River.

Murray Branch rises in nw Henderson

County and flows s into Boylston Creek.

Murray Branch rises in w Madison County and flows sw into French Broad River.

Murray Cove, s Haywood County on a tributary of Little East Fork Pigeon River.

Murray Creek rises in s central Henderson County and flows n into Greer Creek.

Murray Gap, w Haywood County between Huckleberry Knob and Winding Knob.

Murray Gap, e Madison County at the head of California Creek.

Murraysville, community in n New Hanover County.

Murrayville, former community on Cane Creek in n Henderson County (then Buncombe County), named for William Murray whose home was here. Buncombe Turnpike ran nearby. A post office operated here for a brief time around 1822. The Catawba grape was discovered growing in this vicinity.

Mush Island, a sandy formation about 2¼ mi. long and 1¼ mi. wide, surrounded by silty clay, on the banks of the Roanoke River se of Weldon, ne Halifax County. The Collet map, 1770, shows Raglins Ferry at this point; called Prides Ferry on the Price map, 1808.

Musketo Inlet, through present Currituck Banks, e Currituck County, opened prior to 1657 and closed in the 1670's. Appears on the Ogilby map, 1671. *See also* Denniss Island.

Muskrat Branch rises in se Clay County and flows nw into Shooting Creek.

Muskrat Creek rises in central Macon County and flows e into Cartoogechaye Creek.

Mussel Run rises in e Greene County and flows sw into Contentnea Creek.

Musselshell Creek rises in ne Jones County and flows sw into Trent River.

Muttenz, community in w Caldwell County on Johns River.

Mutton Creek. See Mud Creek.

Myatt's Mills, community in s Wake County.

Myatts Pond, s Wake County on Black Creek. Covers 44 acres and has maximum depth of 12 ft. Used for recreation and power source.

Myers, community in n Wilkes County near Middle Prong Roaring River.

Myers. *See* South Gastonia.

Myers Branch rises in nw Swain County and flows sw into Fontana Lake.

Myra Lake, se Wake County on Marks Creek. Formed in 1900. Covers 50 acres and has maximum depth of 15 ft. Used for recreation.

Myrtle. *See* Elah.

Myrtle Grove, community in se New Hanover County on Myrtle Sound.

Myrtle Grove Island, tidal marsh island in se Onslow County just inside Bear Inlet.

Myrtle Grove Sound. *See* Myrtle Sound.

Myrtle Island in Bogue Sound, w Carteret County, s of Burthen Channel.

Myrtle Lawn, a family seat in s Warren County near the community of Inez. Built by the Williams family in 1790 and still standing.

Myrtle Sound, se New Hanover County. Also known as Myrtle Grove Sound. *See also* Snows Cut.

Myrtle Swamp. *See* Merkle Swamp.

N

Nags Head, town on n Bodie Island facing the Atlantic Ocean, e Dare County. A popular summer resort since the 1830's. Inc. 1923; charter repealed 1949; inc. again in 1961. Numerous legends exist explaining the origin of the name. One on the most popular tells of natives who tied lanterns around the necks of ponies ("nags") which were driven up and down the beach at night. The motion of the lanterns resembled that of a vessel and lured ships at sea into the shore where

they were wrecked and easily robbed. The name appears on maps of the area as early as 1738. Nags Head as a place name appears in various parts of England, the Channel Islands, and the West Indies.

Nags Head Coast Guard Station, central Bodie Island in e Dare County. First est. in 1874 as a lifesaving station. Lifesaving Service and Revenue Cutter Service joined to form United States Coast Guard in 1915.

Nags Head Township, e Dare County. Includes all of Roanoke Island and the town of Nags Head.

Nahunga Creek rises in w Duplin County and flows ne into Goshen Swamp.

Nahunta Swamp rises in e Johnston County and flows e across ne Wayne County and ne into Contentnea Creek in w Greene County. It is mentioned under various spellings as early as 1711—Norhanty, Norrihunta, No Honey. Appears on the Collet map, 1770, as Beaverdam Swamp in n Wayne County. It is not shown as such on subsequent maps. The name is either originally or in corrupted form a Tuscacora Indian word, perhaps from Kahunshe Wakena, "Black Creek."

Nahunta. See Fremont.

Nahunta, community in nw Wayne County south of Nahunta Creek from which it takes its name. Called Academy Crossroads as recently as 1915.

Nahunta Township, ne Wayne County.

Naked Creek rises in central Ashe County and flows e into South Fork New River.

Naked Creek rises in n Catawba County and flows n into Catawba River.

Naked Creek rises in se Montgomery County and flows se into Richmond County. At the Moore-Richmond County line it joins Drowning Creek to form Lumber River.

Naked Creek rises in sw Wilkes County and flows e into Lewis Fork Creek.

Naked Mountain, now Morrow Mountain State Park (which see), in e Stanly County. Named after a tornado stripped timber off and left it naked; renamed to honor donor of site and adjacent land for a state park in 1935.

Naked Place Mountain, ne Haywood County between Bear Wallow Gap and Fines Creek.

Nakina, community in s Columbus County. Formerly known as Wattsville.

Namonda. See Table Rock Mountain.

Nancy Hawkins Branch rises in ne Cherokee County and flows nw into Graybeard Creek. Named for an Indian woman.

Nancy Mountain, s Transylvania County between the headwaters of Toxaway Creek and Shoal Creek. Alt. 3,013.

Nancys Mountain, s Randolph County between Kies Mountain and Little River.

Nane Branch rises in central Clay County and flows nw into Cold Branch.

Nanito. See Shingle Hollow.

Nanny Mountain, se Buncombe County near the Rutherford County line.

Nansemond Indian Town appears on the Moseley map, 1733, near the forks of Nottoway River and Blackwater River where they form the Chowan River. The site is now in ne Hertford County.

Nantahala, community in sw Swain County. A post office was opened here by 1882. Alt. 1,942.

Nantahala Balds, grassy areas in the Nantahala Mountain Range (which see) of w Macon County. Wayah Bald is the most prominent of these areas. Named for the Cherokee word Nan-toh-ee-yah-heh-lih, "Sun in the Middle," that is noonday as Indian runners between Valley River crossed it at mid-day on their way to Oconaluftee or Soco in Swain County.

Nantahala Gorge, ne Graham and sw Swain counties, a canyon of the Nantahala River with such depth and such sheer sides that the Cherokee Indians named it "Land of the Middle Sun," believing that only the noonday sun could penetrate its depths.

One of the several Cherokee legends told of it is that the gorge was the haunt of the Uktena (keen eyed), a huge horned serpent. The bright gem blazing from between his horns was called ulstitlu (it is on his head), and meant death to the family of any Indian who beheld it. However, when detached it became the ulunsuti (transparent), the great talisman which revealed the future to the possessor. When a wary hunter encased himself in leather, surprised the monster, killed him, and tore the great jewel from his head, the snake writhed from one side of the gorge to the other, shutting out the radiance of the sun and causing the perpetual twilight. The great jewel was said to be the rutile quartz, so rare that there was only one specimen among the eastern Cherokee in 1890.

In the gorge, on the left bank of the river, are caves claimed by some to have been occupied by a race which preceded the Cherokee.

Nantahala Lake, in Clay and Macon counties on the headwaters of Nantahala River. Dam completed in 1942. Area 1,605 acres; maximum depth 225 ft.; shoreline 30 mi. Owned by Nantahala Power and Light Company and used for the generation of electricity. Nantahala is an Indian word meaning "land of the noonday sun," and was applied to the gorge through which the river runs.

Nantahala Mountain Range lies between the Great Smoky Mountains on the n and the Blue Ridge on the s. It extends about 50 mi. across Macon County from the junction of Nantahala and Little Tennessee rivers in Swain County to Tallulah Falls, Georgia.

Nantahala National Forest in portions of Cherokee, Clay, Graham, Jackson, Macon, Swain, and Transylvania counties was est. in 1911 and includes 1,366,027 acres. Nature trails, mountain climbing, picnicking, and other recreational uses. See also Joyce Kilmer Memorial Forest.

Nantahala River rises in sw Macon County and flows nw to the Clay-Macon County line which it forms for a part of its course and into Graham County where it enters Little Tennessee River. See also Camp Branch Falls.

Nantahala Township, nw Macon County.

Nantahala Township, s Swain County.

Naomi Falls. See Randleman.

Naples, community in n Henderson County. Alt. 2,080. Post office for Mountain Sanatorium and Asheville Agricultural School. A cooperative school, dairy, bakery, and hospital are maintained here by Seventh Day Adventists. Named about 1905 when a post office was est. here because Mud Creek in the valley below often flooded, reminding a local resident of the Bay of Naples.

Narassa, community in ne Brunswick County. Produces lumber and fertilizers.

Narrow Ridge, ne Yancey County between Green Mountain and Brush Creek.

The Narrows, the final mile and a half of Newport River confined within banks before it approaches the estuary, central Carteret County.

Narrows, boat channel through the narrow part of Currituck Sound near Poplar Branch. Tidal marsh islands lie on either side of the channel in s Currituck County. Appears on the Comberford map, 1657.

The Narrows. See Croatan Sound.

Narrows of the Yadkin, formerly a portion of Yadkin River in Montgomery and Stanly counties constricted by the Uwharrie Mountains through which the river passes at this point. With the construction of Badin Dam in 1917, the Narrows of the Yadkin were submerged by Badin Lake. Appears on the Price

map, 1808, and the MacRae map, 1833. Sometimes referred to as Yadkin Narrows.

Narrows Reservoir. See Badin Lake.

Nash County was formed in 1777 from Edgecombe County. Located in the ne section of the state, it is bounded by Edgecombe, Wilson, Johnston, Franklin, and Halifax counties. It was named for General Francis Nash (1742-77), of Hillsborough, mortally wounded at the Battle of Germantown while fighting under Washington. Area: 552 sq. mi. County seat: Nashville with an elevation of 180 ft. Townships are Bailey, Castalia, Coopers, Dry Wells, Ferrells, Griffins, Jackson, Mannings, Nashville, North Whitakers, Oak Level, Red Oak, Rocky Mount, South Whitakers, and Stony Creek. Produces tobacco, corn, wheat, oats, peanuts, cotton, poultry, hogs, livestock, bakery products, textiles, furniture, lumber, apparel.

Nash District, one of the districts into which Caswell County was divided at the time of the 1790 census. It contained 118 heads of families.

Nash Mine, e Cabarrus County, 1½ mi. nw of Phoenix Mine Village, which see. Known as Faggart Mine in the mid-nineteenth century when gold was mined here. Uranium was discovered here in 1954.

Nashville, town and county seat, central Nash County. Authorized to be laid out and inc., 1815. Named for General Francis Nash (1742-77), brilliant young Revolutionary officer who fell at Germantown. Produces lumber and apparel. Alt. 180.

Nashville Township, central Nash County.

Nathans Creek rises in e Ashe County and flows e into South Fork New River.

Nathans Creek, community in e central Ashe County. Alt. approx. 2,800.

Nations Creek rises in w Jackson County and flows ne into Tuckasegee River.

Nattie Branch rises in s Clay County and flows n into Giesky Creek.

Nausegoc, a name appearing on the White map, 1590, in Pamlico Sound, e Dare County, approx. between the present communities of Rodanthe and Salvo on Bodie Island. The name is believed to have been an Alqonquian Indian word for "take a breathing-spell," hence a resting place for those on a long canoe journey.

Navassa, community in ne Burnswick County on Cape Fear River.

Navy Yard Lake, e Anson County, se of Lilesville. Covers approx. 10 acres; max. depth 15 ft. Formed early in the twentieth century when gravel was removed from the site.

Naylors Knob, central Caldwell County. Named for James Nailor, an early settler.

Nazareth, community in central Wake County s of Raleigh. Settled 1898. Named for the town in Palestine by the Rev. Thomas Price who est. a Roman Catholic orphanage here. Alt. 325.

Neal Branch rises in sw Mecklenburg County and flows nw into Stowe Branch.

Neal Branch rises in s Wake County and flows e into Swift Creek.

Neal Creek, short stream in n central Carteret County which flows ne into South River.

Neal Gut, a narrow water-filled defile in central Franklin County which empties into Tar River.

Neals Creek rises in se Yancey County and flows nw into Big Lost Cove Creek.

Nealsville. See Glenwood.

Neatman, community in s central Stokes County. A post office in the late nineteenth century.

Neatman Creek rises in s central Stokes County and flows s into Town Fork Creek.

Nebo, community in e McDowell County. Inc. 1909; charter repealed 1943. Alt. 1,282. A popular Methodist campground here was known before the Civil War as Nebo for the Biblical mountain. When the North Carolina Railroad was constructed the station here took the name of the campground.

Nebo, community in n central Yadkin County. Once known as Mount Nebo.

Nebo Township, e McDowell County.

Nebraska, town in e Hyde County. Inc. 1855, but long inactive in municipal affairs. Probably named due to the impor-

tance of the Kansas-Nebraska Act of 1854 which repealed the Missouri Compromise.

Ned Branch rises in central Haywood County and flows se into Hemphill Creek.

Neddie Creek rises in e Jackson County and flows se into Tuckasegee River.

Neddie Knob on the ne end of Neddie Mountain in e Jackson County.

Neddie Mountain in e Jackson County extends ne between Dismal Mountain and Neddie Knob.

Ned Gap in sw Jackson County between Rich Mountain and West Fork [Dicks Creek].

Neds Creek rises in w Carteret County and flows w into Koonces Bay of White Oak River.

Neds Lick Gap, w Haywood County on the head of Hemphill Creek.

Neds Marsh, central Duplin County.

Needhams Mountain, s Randolph County near the head of Fork Creek.

Needmore, community in s Caldwell County between Lower and Smoky creeks.

Needmore, community in nw Franklin County. Also known as Wilder.

Needmore, community in nw Rowan County.

Needmore, former community in s Swain County, est. about 1880 on property of Allison McHan. A thriving trading center until after about 1912 when the site was purchased by Nantahala Power Company for a right of way for a proposed power project. Population in 1950 was 75 but by 1960 only one house was occupied. Post office named Needmore because of the habit of the people constantly complaining that they "needed more of this and that." Alt. 1,830.

Needmore Branch rises in s Clay County and flows n into Shooting Creek.

Neely Gap, sw Cherokee County near the headwaters of Persimmon Creek.

Nee-oh-la. See Pigeon River; West Fork Pigeon River.

Negro Hammocks, formerly two islands in s Hyde County in Pamlico Sound ne of Ocracoke Island, but now submerged. Known by this name as early as 1795. One of the islands was above water as late as 1910 and was called Negro Island.

Negro Island. See Negro Hammocks.

Negro Prong rises in w Transylvania County and flows ne into Catheys Creek.

Neil Gap in n central Transylvania County on the head of Lamb Creek.

Neills Creek rises in s Wake County and flows sw in n Harnett County into Cape Fear River. Named for Red Neill Mc-Neill who settled along its banks in 1740.

Neills Creek Township, central Harnett County.

Nella. See Husk.

Nellie, former community in w Haywood County on Cataloochee Creek near the mouth of Palmer Creek, near lat. 35° 37' 40" N., long. 83° 06' 10" W. Settled about 1848. Named for Nellie Palmer, who in 1907 at the age of one year, won first prize in a baby contest. Site now is in the Great Smoky Mountains National Park and is abandoned except for families of three employees of the Park.

Nellie Ridge, w Haywood County, Great Smoky Mountains National Park, a short spur of Big Fork Ridge, near lat. 35° 37' 10" N., long. 83° 06' 50" W. Named for nearby community of Nellie.

Nelms, community in s Pamlico County.

Nelson, community in se Durham County.

Nelson Bay, a bay formed by waters of Core Sound in ne Carteret County.

Nelson Branch rises in central Haywood County and flows ne into Jonathans Creek.

Nelson Branch rises in e central Union County and flows ne into Rays Fork.

Nelson Branch rises in n Haywood County and flows se into Whiteoak Branch.

Nelson Branch rises in w Haywood County and flows ne into Cataloochee Creek.

Nelson Cove extends se from Sassafras Ridge to Snowbird Creek in s Graham County.

Nelson Creek. See East Nelson Creek; West Nelson Creek.

Nelson Ridge, central Clay County between Vineyard Mountain and Tusquitee Creek.

Nelsons Old Ferry. See Graves Ferry.

Nelsonville. See Grimesland.

Nero, community in nw Wake County.

Ness Creek rises in n New Hanover County and flows sw into Cape Fear River.

Nettle Branch rises in s Burke County and flows n into Jacob Fork.

Nettle Creek, Great Smoky Mountains National Park, rises in n Swain County and flows sw into Deep Creek.

Nettle Creek rises in nw Haywood County and flows ne into Big Creek.

Nettle Creek Bald, Great Smoky Mountains National Park, n Swain County, lat. 35° 34' 02" N., long. 83° 22' 55" W. Alt. 5,172.

Nettle Knob in central Watauga County n of Howard Creek. Alt. 4,000.

Nettle Knob, community in se Ashe County.

Nettle Patch, mountain near the Blue Ridge Parkway on the McDowell-Mitchell-Yancey County line. Alt. approx. 3,950.

Nettles Cove, n Buncombe County, ne of Snowball Gap.

Neuse. See Neuse Crossroads.

Neuse Crossroads, community in n central Wake County. Named for nearby Neuse River. Formerly known as Dunnsville and as Neuse. Produces textiles. Alt. 234.

Neuse Forest, community in e Craven County.

Neuseoco Lake, e central Wake County on Beaverdam Creek. Covers 75 acres and has max. depth of 20 ft. Owned by a club and used for recreation.

Neuse River is formed in w Durham County by the junction of Eno and Flat rivers. It flows se forming in part the Durham-Granville and Durham-Wake County lines; through Wake, Johnston, Wayne, Lenoir and Craven counties and forming in part the line between Craven and Pamlico, and Carteret and Pamlico counties before entering Pamlico Sound Named in 1584 by Arthur Barlowe for the Neusiok Indians. The Tuscaror. Indians called the river Gow-ta-no, "pine in water."

Neuse River Township, central Wake County.

Neuse Township, central Lenoir County.

Never Mountain, an almost perfect cone, w Alexander County.

Neverson, community in nw Wilson County. Named for Neverson Williams. Post office, 1908-1911.

Nevil Creek rises in central Beaufort County and flows n into Pamlico River. Appears as Turners Creek on the Collet map, 1770, but by 1833 MacRae's map called it Nevil Creek.

Neville Creek rises in n Chatham County and flows n into Orange County where it enters University Lake.

Newasiwac, an Indian village of the Neusiok tribe, located in what is now the s tip of Craven County on the Neuse River estuary, appears on the White map, 1585. Called Neuustooc on the De Bry map, 1590, and Nustoc on Smith, 1624.

New began Creek. See New Begun Creek.

New Begun Creek rises in s Pasquotank

County and flows se into Pasquotank
River. Mentioned in records of the area
as early as 1660. The name Newbiggin
is a common place name in the north of
England, but in this case it may represent
an attempt to spell in English the Indian
name. Appears as New began Creek on
the Collet map, 1770, and New Beggin
Creek on the Price map, 1808, and the
MacRae map, 1833. See also Weeksville.

New Belden, community in e central Pitt
County.

New Berlin. See Delco.

New Bern, city and county seat, central
Craven County at the junction of Neuse
and Trent rivers. Settled in 1710; inc.
1723. Took its name from Bern, Switzerland, capital of the homeland of its
founder, Baron Christoph de Graffenried.
Alt. 12. New Bern was the colonial and
state capital from 1746 until the est. of
Raleigh in 1792, although during this
period the general assembly met in various places from time to time. It met here
in 1738-40, 1744-46, 1747-51, 1754-59,
1760, 1762, 1765-78, 1784-85, 1791-93,
and 1794. Produces boats, lumber, apparel, dairy products, fertilizer, and
processed meat. See also Tryon Palace;
Drysborough.

Newbern District at the time of the 1790
census was composed of Beaufort,
Carteret, Craven, Dobbs, Hyde, Johnston,
Jones, Pitt, and Wayne counties.

Newberry Creek rises in w McDowell
County and flows se into Curtis Creek.

Newbes Bridge. See Belvidere.

New Bethel, community in ne Orange
County. Developed around New Bethel
Methodist Church, est. 1859.

New Bethel Township, sw Rockingham
County.

New Biggin Creek. See New Begun Creek.

New Branch rises in n Avery County and
flows ne into Buckeye Creek.

Newby's Bridge. See Belvidere.

New Carthage. See Wilmington.

New Castle, community in se Wilkes County between Osborne and Hunting creeks.
Named for the plantation of James Clemmons Hunt (1804-47), local merchant and
planter. The town of Denneysville was
authorized to be laid out at this site in
1817 on land then owned by George
Denny, but it apparently did not develop.
Known as Hunt's Store by 1847 and by
its present name by the 1850's.

New Castle Township, e Wilkes County.

New Currituck Inlet from the Atlantic
Ocean into Currituck Sound through
Currituck Banks opened in the 1730's
and closed in 1828. The site is now in
e Currituck County.

Newdale, community in e Yancey County
on Long Branch. Flinty, former post office serving the area, is considered to be
a part of Newdale.

Newell, community in e Mecklenburg County. Settled about 1880 and named for
John A. Newell, local resident, in whose
home the first post office was est. Alt.
756.

New Exeter. See Exeter.

Newfound, community in w Buncombe
County on Newfound Creek.

Newfound Creek rises on the Buncombe-
Haywood County line near Newfound
Gap and flows ne into French Broad
River.

Newfound Gap, Great Smoky Mountains
National Park, on Swain County, N.C.,-
Sevier County, Tenn., line, lat. 35° 37',
N., long. 83° 26' W. Alt. 5,045.

Newfound Gap, on the Buncombe-Haywood
County line at the s end of Newfound
Mountain. Alt. approx. 3,000.

Newfoundland, community in n Tyrrell
County at the head of Alligator Creek.
Former post office, Gudger, located here.

Newfoundland. See Horseshoe.

Newfound Mountain on the Buncombe-Haywood County line. The peak of this
mountain is known as Big Butt Mountain.

New Garden. See Guilford College.

New Hanover County was formed in 1729
from Craven County. Located in the se
section of the state, it is bounded by
the Atlantic Ocean, Cape Fear River,
and Brunswick and Pender counties. It
was named in honor of the royal family
of England, members of the House of
Hanover. Area: 225 sq. mi. County seat:
Wilmington with an elevation of 38 ft.
Townships are Cape Fear, Federal Point,
Harnett, Masonboro, and Wilmington.

Produces miscellaneous fruits and vegetables, bulbs and flowers, corn, soybeans, hogs, dairy products, poultry, bakery products, fabricated metals, lumber, wooden containers, textiles, apparel, paper boxes, chemicals, refrigeration machinery, sand, and limestone.

New Hill, community in sw Wake County. Post office est. in 1832. Inc. 1907; charter repealed 1917. Alt. 356.

New Holland, community on the s shore of Lake Mattamuskeet in central Hyde County. Alt. 3. Settled 1910 and named by a development company which attempted to drain the lake for farm land but finally gave up in 1934 when the lake was allowed to refill. Their activity suggested the Netherlands' continuous efforts to drain farm land.

New Hope, community in s Franklin County.

New Hope, community in nw Iredell County.

New Hope, community in se Randolph County. Post office here in late nineteenth century was New Hope Academy, named for a local school; the building still stands but is used as a residence.

New Hope, community in e Wayne County. A post office was located here by 1828.

New Hope, community in nw Wilson County s of Silver Lake. Named for a local Baptist church.

New Hope. See Durants Neck.

New Hope Creek rises in central Orange County and flows e into w Durham County. There it turns se and flows into Chatham County where it becomes New Hope River, *which see.* Appears as New River on the Moseley map, 1733, but by 1770 (Collet map) appears as New-hope Creek.

New Hope River, the name applied to New Hope Creek in e Chatham County from the mouth of Whiteoak Creek to its confluence with Haw River, a distance of approx. 8 mi. *See also* New Hope Creek.

New Hope Township, e Chatham County.

New Hope Township, nw Iredell County. Named for a Civil War muster ground.

New Hope Township, se Perquimans County.

New Hope Township, sw Randolph County.

New Hope Township, e Wayne County. First listed in county tax records in 1838.

New House, community in w Cleveland County.

New Inlet from the Atlantic Ocean into Pamlico Sound south of Pea Island, se Dare County. It opened probably in the late 1720's and has closed periodically, the most recent closing being in the 1930's. Also known as Chickinacommock and as such appears on the Moll map, 1729.

New Inlet gave access from Onslow Bay and the Atlantic Ocean into the Basin at the s tip of New Hanover County. Used extensively by blockade runners under the guns of Fort Fisher. Closed by The Rocks, a great sea-wall constructed 1879-95.

New Institute. See Olin.

New Kirk Pond, on Rockfish Creek in w Duplin County. Built by slave labor long before the Civil War.

New Lake. See Alligator Lake.

New Lake Fork flows se from the s shore of Alligator Lake in n Hyde County and along the Hyde-Tyrrell County line to empty into Alligator River. N section also known as Squyars Canal.

Newland, town and county seat, central Avery County on Linville and North Toe rivers. Site selected by commissioners for county seat. Inc. 1913. Named for William Calhoun Newland (1860-1938), lieutenant governor 1909-1913. Site had been early muster ground in campaign against Indians and before the Battle of Kings Mountain; called Old Fields of Toe, for Toe River. Alt. 3,589. Produces textiles.

Newland Drainage Canal in Newland Township in nw Pasquotank County drains e into Pasquotank River.

New Lands, community in w Tyrrell County e of White Oak Island.

New Lands, in e Washington County, area at the ne boundary of East Dismal Swamp *(which see).* Name appears in county records as early as 1868.

Newland Township, n Pasquotank County.

New Lebanon. See South Mills.

Newlife, community in n Wilkes County near North Prong Roaring River. The former community of Ink is now a part of Newlife.

New Light Creek rises in se Granville County and flows sw into n Wake County where it enters Neuse River. Shown on Collet map, 1770, as Newlight Creek.

New Light, community in n Wake County.

New Light Township, n Wake County.

Newlin Township, former township in s central Alamance County, now township number 8.

New Liverpool. See Wilmington.

New London, town in n Stanly County. Alt. 697. Prior to incorporation in 1891 it was known as Bilesville.

Newman, community in nw Warren County. A post office was located here between 1892-1906.

Newmarket, town authorized in 1801 to be est. in Orange County at or near Woody's Ferry on Haw River. This was a project of the Deep and Haw River Company designed to improve river navigation but apparently the town was never laid out.

New Market, town in n Randolph County. Inc. 1813, but long inactive in municipal affairs.

New Market Township, nw Randolph County.

New Mattamuskeet Creek. See Juniper Bay.

Newport, town in w Carteret County on Newport River. Inc. 1866. Alt. 20 ft. First known as Bells Corners but Quakers from Rhode Island settled here and changed the name to Newport for the city in their native state.

Newport, chartered 1789 to be county seat of Tyrrell County. On sw side of Scuppernong River at Back Landing. The town was never built.

Newport Marshes, a marshy island in Newport River about 1 mi. ne of Morehead City, between the channel of the Intracoastal Waterway and Crab Point Thorofare in central Carteret County. Formerly Haystack Marshes.

Newport News Point, in se Tyrrell County, extends from the mainland into Alligator River. Appears on the Collet map, 1770, as Nupernuse Point.

Newport River rises in w Carteret County and flows about 23 mi. e and se into the central part of the county where it enteres Bogue Sound. Appears as Coranine River on the Lawson map, 1709, but as Newport River on the Moseley map, 1733.

Newport Township, on Newport River and Broad Creek in ne Carteret County. For a time called township number 3.

New River is formed on the Ashe-Alleghany County line by the junction of North Fork and South Fork New River. It flows ne and nw into Virginia and West

Virginia and enters Kanawha River at Charleston, W. Va. In its meanderings it crosses the North Carolina-Virginia line into Alleghany County several times. This is said to be the only large river in the United States to flow north. Named because of the discovery of the river in 1749 when the boundary between North Carolina and Virginia was extended 90 miles. The surveyors crossed what they thought was "a large branch of the Mississippi which runs between the ledges of the mountains," and which, in the words of Governor Gabriel Johnston, "Nobody ever drempt of before."

New River rises in nw Onslow County near the Jones County line and flows se across the county into Onslow Bay of the Atlantic Ocean. Appears as Corani River on the Moll map, 1729, and as New River on the Moseley map, 1733. Tradition says that this was originally a long lake in a swampy area, but after an extended period of torrential rain the lake overflowed into the Atlantic Ocean and became a new river. Camp Lejeune Marine Base is near the mouth of New River.

New River Inlet, s Onslow County between Stump Sound and Onslow Beach. Appears on the Moseley map, 1733.

New River Marine Base. See Camp Lejeune.

New River Township, central Watauga County.

New Salem, community in ne Union County. Named for a local school by the State Highway Commission when it took over maintenance of local roads and a name was entered on a road map of the county. The crossroads community here was originally called Euto by returning veterans of the Battle of Eutaw Springs, S.C., during the Revolution.

New Salem. See Salem.

New Salem Township, ne Union County.

Newsom, community in s Davidson County on Yadkin River. Alt. 558. Named for the family from whom land was acquired for the railroad station.

Newsome, community in e Wayne County between Walnut Creek and West Bear Creek.

Newsome Store, community in se Hertford County.

New Stirling, community in w central Iredell County.

Newstump Point, ne Carteret County, e extension of Piney Island into West Bay.

Newton, city and county seat, in central

Catawba County. Alt. 996. Authorized to be laid out in 1845, inc. 1855. Named for Isaac Newton Wilson, son of Nathaniel Wilson, and member of the General Assembly in 1842. He introduced the bill to create Catawba County. Produces textiles, furniture, hosiery, apparel, and paper boxes.

Newton. See Wilmington.

Newton Bald, Great Smoky Mountains National Park, n Swain County, lat. 35° 32' 39" N., long. 83° 21' 32" W. Alt. 5,142.

Newton Grove, town in n Sampson County. Alt. 185. A post office, Coxe's Store, est. in the vicinity in 1825. Inc. as Newton Grove, 1879; reincorporated, 1935. Said to have been named for Sir Isaac Newton (1642-1727), English scientist.

Newton Grove Township, n Sampson County.

Newtons Crossroads, community in se Sampson County.

Newton Township, central Catawba County.

New Topsail Beach. See Topsail Beach.

New Topsail Inlet, s Pender County through which waters of Topsail Sound flow into the Atlantic Ocean, between Old Topsail Inlet and the Onslow-Pender County line. Appears on the Moseley map, 1733.

Newtown, community in e Northampton County. Known first as Miami, later as Liverman, and finally by its present name.

New Town. See Charles Town.

New Town. See Farmville.

New Town. See Swansboro.

New Town. See Wadesboro.

New Town. See Wilmington.

New Years Creek rises in s Watauga County on the w limits of the town of Blowing Rock and flows s into n Caldwell County where it enters Thunderhole Creek.

Niagara, community in se Moore County est. about 1904 by Northern interests. Alt. 402.

Nibb's Knob. See Big Cataloochee Mountain.

Nicanon, community in n Perquimans County.

Nichols Branch rises in s Macon County and flows ne into Tessentee Creek.

Nichols Branch rises in sw Macon County and flows ne into Nantahala River.

Nicholson Creek rises in central Transylvania County and flows se into French Broad River.

Nicholsons Creek rises in n Hoke County and flows s into Rockfish Creek.

Nickajack Creek rises in e Macon County and flows ne into Cullasaja River.

Nickajack Gap, at the head of Nickajack Creek in e Macon County.

Nick Bottom, loamy section in e Swain County on Oconaluftee River near the mouth of Goose Creek.

Nick Branch rises in ne Cherokee County and flows n into Radder Creek.

Nick Creek rises in s Haywood County and flows se into West Fork Pigeon River.

Nick Gap, central Haywood County on the head of Messer Branch.

Nicks Creek rises in s McDowell County and flows ne into Catawba River.

Nicks Creek rises in w Moore County and flows ne into Little River. Named for Nicholas Smith, who settled here about 1768.

Nicks Creek. See Pheasant Creek.

Nicks Knob, s Cherokee County near the headwaters of Moccasin Creek.

Nigger Bay between Swan Island and Currituck Banks in ne Currituck County.

Nigger Head, mountain on the Clay-Macon County line. Alt. approx. 4,900.

Niggerhead Creek rises in e Union County and flows nw into Richardson Creek.

Nigger Mountain. See Mount Jefferson.

Niggerskull Creek rises in central Jackson County and flows sw into Tuckasegee River.

Nigger Skull Mountain, w Haywood County on the head of East Fork.

Niggerskull Mountain, in central Jackson County between Niggerskull Creek and Gladie Creek. Alt. 3,500.

Nigger Spring, s Haywood County. A spring on the head of Little East Fork Pigeon River.

Nigh Inlet, a point of land on Ocracoke Island about 3½ mi. from the s end of the island, se Hyde County. This may be the site of Port Grenvil, which see, shown on the White map, 1590, but long closed.

Nikwasi. See Franklin.

Nims, formerly a community in e Gaston County, but now a part of the town of Mount Holly, (which see).

Nine Mile Creek. See Ninemile Swamp.

Ninemile Swamp rises in w Onslow County and flows sw into Duplin County (where the name becomes Nine Mile Creek) where it enters Back Swamp. Named for its distance from Rich Lands Chapel, an early center of settlement.

Ninive, community in w Transylvania County.

Nin Ridge, nw Cherokee County in the Unicoi Mountains, bounded on four sides by Bryson Lead, Groundhog Ridge, Copper Ridge, and Chestnut Orchard Ridge.

Nit Top, on the Cherokee County, N.C.-Monroe County, Tenn., line in the Unicoi Mountains.

Nix Creek rises in s Jackson County on n slopes of Sassafras Mountain and flows ne into Sapphire Lake.

Nix Mountain, s Jackson County between Nix Creek and Horsepasture River.

Nixon's. See Columbus.

Nixons Mill Creek flows se from Old Topsail Creek into Topsail Sound, s Pender County.

Nixon's town. See Nixonton.

Nixonton, town in w Pasquotank County on Little River. The site was originally known as Windmill Point. Laid out in 1746, settled then or soon afterwards and inc. 1758 as Nixon's town. Named for Zachariah Nixon, an early settler. Appears on the Collet map, 1770; county seat 1785-1800. Reincorporated 1818 and 1951, but not now active in municipal affairs.

Nixonton Township, s Pasquotank County.

No Ache Bay on the w shore of Hatteras Island in the waters of Pamlico Sound, s Dare County, s of the community of Salvo.

No Ache Island, a small island in No Ache Bay on the w shore of Hatteras Island in the waters of Pamlico Sound, s Dare County.

Noah Branch rises in se Buncombe County and flows se into Rutherford County where it enters Cedar Creek.

Noah's Mountain, in the Cane Creek Mountains, s Alamance County.

Nobles Crossroads, community in s Lenoir County.

Nobles Mill Pond, on tributary of Cokey Swamp in central Edgecombe County. Est. by Nobles family for furnishing water power for mill. Has maximum depth of 15 feet and area of 37 acres. Now used for fishing, swimming and boating. Open to the public.

Nobles Mill Pond, in s Lenoir County on Trent River. Formed prior to 1802 by William Williams or his son, Evan, and known as Williams Pond until 1852 when it was acquired by the Nobles family. Covers 125 acres. Maximum depth 8 feet.

Nobreeches Ridge, se Haywood County on the head of East Fork Pigeon River.

No Business Creek rises in nw Cleveland County and flows sw into First Broad River.

No Business Mountain, nw Cleveland County near the headwaters of Cox Creek. Said to be too rough to be surveyed. Local residents claim they have "no business" on it. Alt. 1,760.

Nocona, community in s Madison County. Alt. 1,585.

No Creek rises in s Davie County and flows s 4 mi. into Dutchmans Creek. It is said that an early settler bought land here and the deed called for a creek. He complained the he found no creek on his land, but later when he discovered one it came to be called No Creek.

Nofat Mountain on the Buncombe-Madison County line w of Pleasant Gap.

No Grease, riverside site in e central Hertford County on Chowan River approx. ¼ mi. n of Winton. A fishery here in the nineteenth century departed from custom when it kept no grease on hand which meant that customers could not cook green fish at the site.

No Honey Swamp. See Nahunta Swamp.

Nokassa. See Hawksbill Mountain.

Noland, former community in w central Swain County on Tuckasegee River. Alt. 1,622. Named for Andrew Noland, one of the first settlers in the area. Site now under the waters of Fontana Lake.

Noland Creek rises in e Davie County and flows approx. 1½ mi. sw into Dutchmans Creek.

Noland Creek, Great Smoky Mountains National Park, rises in n Swain County on Noland Divide, and flows se then sw into Tuckasegee River. Named for Andrew Noland, first settler along its banks.

Noland Divide, mountain ridge, Great Smoky Mountains National Park, central Swain County, extending from the Tennessee state line s to Bryson City. Roundtop Knob (which see), a peak on this ridge, has an elevation of 5,120 ft.

Noland Gap, w Haywood County, Great Smoky Mountains National Park, between Noland Mountain and Canadian Top, near lat. 35° 39' 10" N., long. 83° 06' W.

Noland Mountain, w Haywood County, Great Smoky Mountains National Park, near lat. 35° 39' 35" N., long. 83° 05' 18" W. Alt. 3,951.

Nolen Creek rises in w Haywood County and flows se into Richland Creek.

Nolichucky River is formed on the Mitchell-Yancey County line by the junction of Toe River and Cane River. It flows n and w along the county line and into Tennessee where it enters the French Broad River.

Nolton Ridge, se Graham County in the Snowbird Mountains.

Noratake River. See Roanoke River.

Norfleet, community in se Halifax County. Norfleet Ferry appears on the Collet map, 1770, ne of the present community. This ferry across the Roanoke River was operated as late as 1886 but discontinued in 1888 when the railroad bridge was built here.

Norfolk, County of. See County of Norfolk.

Norhanty Swamp. See Nahunta Swamp.

Norlina, town in w Warren County. Inc. in 1913. Alt. 438. Originally known as Mount Regis, but the name was changed after a post office was est. here in 1900 as Norlina, a contraction of "North Carolina."

Norman, town in n Richmond County. Known first as Sprawls Old Field. Post office est. about 1910 and named for Flim Norman, local lumber merchant. Inc. 1913. Long inactive in municipal affairs. Processes lumber.

Norrihunta Swamp. See Nahunta Swamp.

Norrington's Falls, in Cape Fear River, in n central Harnett County. In an 1819 survey of the rivers of North Carolina, the northern end, near the confluence of Hector Creek with the river, is called Norrington's Upper Falls; the southern end, near the confluence of Neals Creek with the river, is called Norrington's Lower Falls.

Norris Branch rises in w Wake County and flows sw into Cary Branch.

Norris Branch rises in central Watauga County and flows se and ne into Howard Creek.

Norris Branch rises in n Yancey County and flows n into Nolichucky River.

Norris Creek rises in s Franklin County and flows se and ne into Crooked Creek.

Norris Fork rises in n Watauga County on Rich Mountain and flows se into Meat Camp Creek.

Norris Pond. See Mills Pond.

Norris, community in e Watauga County.

North Albemarle Township, e central Stanly County.

Northampton County was formed in 1741 from Bertie County. Located in the ne section of the state, it is bounded by the state of Virginia and by Hertford, Bertie, Halifax, and Warren counties. It was named for James Compton, Earl of Northampton (1687-1754). Area: 544 sq. mi. County seat: Jackson with an elevation of 131 ft. Townships are Gaston, Jackson, Kirby, Oconeechee, Pleasant Hill, Rich Square, Roanoke, Seaboard, and Wiccacanee. Produces peanuts, corn, soybeans, cotton, hogs, livestock, lumber, apparel, sand, and gravel.

Northampton Court House. See Jackson.

North Asheboro. See Balfours.

North Banks. See Currituck Banks.

North Bay, in the n end of Cedar Island in ne Carteret County, adjacent to West Bay.

North Bay, in n Piney Island n of Rattan Bay, ne Carteret County. Approx. ½ mi. long and ½ mi. wide.

North Belmont, community in e Gaston County on the outskirts of the city of Belmont.

North Brook, community in nw Lincoln County.

North Brook Township, w Lincoln County.

North Buffalo Creek rises in central Guilford County flows ne through the city of Greensboro to join South Buffalo Creek in forming Buffalo Creek in ne Guilford County.

North Carolina is bounded on the e and se by the Atlantic Ocean, on the n by Virginia, on the w by Tennessee, and on the s by Georgia and South Carolina. It is 52,712 sq. mi. in area, of which 49,067 are land and 3,645 are water. Elevation ranges from sea level in the east to 6,684 ft. at Mount Mitchell, the highest peak e of the Mississippi River. Raleigh is the state capital. The largest cities are

Charlotte, Greensboro, Winston-Salem, Raleigh, Durham, High Point, Asheville, Fayetteville, Wilmington, and Gastonia.
Nickname: Tar Heel State, or Old North State
Colors: Blue and red
Bird: Cardinal
Flower: Dogwood
Tree: Pine
Shell: Scotch bonnet
Motto: *Esse Quam Videri*, "To Be Rather Than to Seem"
There are one hundred counties in the state:

County	County Seat
Alamance	Graham
Alexander	Taylorsville
Alleghany	Sparta
Anson	Wadesboro
Ashe	Jefferson
Avery	Newland
Beaufort	Washington
Bertie	Windsor
Bladen	Elizabethtown
Brunswick	Southport
Buncombe	Asheville
Burke	Morganton
Cabarrus	Concord
Caldwell	Lenoir
Camden	Camden
Carteret	Beaufort
Caswell	Yanceyville
Catawba	Newton
Chatham	Pittsboro
Cherokee	Murphy
Chowan	Edenton
Clay	Hayesville
Cleveland	Shelby
Columbus	Whiteville
Craven	New Bern
Cumberland	Fayetteville
Currituck	Currituck
Dare	Manteo
Davidson	Lexington
Davie	Mocksville
Duplin	Kenansville
Durham	Durham
Edgecombe	Tarboro
Forsyth	Winston-Salem
Franklin	Louisburg
Gaston	Gastonia
Gates	Gatesville
Graham	Robbinsville
Granville	Oxford
Greene	Snow Hill
Guilford	Greensboro
Halifax	Halifax
Harnett	Lillington
Haywood	Waynesville
Henderson	Hendersonville
Hertford	Winton
Hoke	Raeford
Hyde	Swan Quarter
Iredell	Statesville
Jackson	Sylva
Johnston	Smithfield
Jones	Trenton
Lee	Sanford
Lenoir	Kinston
Lincoln	Lincolnton
McDowell	Marion
Macon	Franklin
Madison	Marshall
Martin	Williamston
Mecklenburg	Charlotte
Mitchell	Bakersville
Montgomery	Troy
Moore	Carthage
Nash	Nashville
New Hanover	Wilmington
Northampton	Jackson
Onslow	Jacksonville
Orange	Hillsborough
Pamlico	Bayboro
Pasquotank	Elizabeth City
Pender	Burgaw
Perquimans	Hertford
Person	Roxboro
Pitt	Greenville
Polk	Columbus
Randolph	Asheboro
Richmond	Rockingham
Robeson	Lumberton
Rockingham	Wentworth
Rowan	Salisbury
Rutherford	Rutherfordton
Sampson	Clinton
Scotland	Laurinburg
Stanly	Albemarle
Stokes	Danbury
Surry	Dobson
Swain	Bryson City
Transylvania	Brevard
Tyrrell	Columbia
Union	Monroe
Vance	Henderson
Wake	Raleigh
Warren	Warrenton
Washington	Plymouth
Watauga	Boone
Wayne	Goldsboro
Wilkes	Wilkesboro
Wilson	Wilson
Yadkin	Yadkinville
Yancey	Burnsville

North Catawba Township, s central Caldwell County.

North Clinton Township, central Sampson County.

North Cove, community in n McDowell County on North Fork [Catawba River]. Former post office named Pitts served this community. Alt. 1,469.

North Cove Township, n McDowell County.

North Cox Creek rises in n Yancey County and flows nw into Cane Creek.

North Creek rises near Ransomville, e Beaufort County and flows se into Pamlico River. Appears as North Dividing Creek on the Collet map, 1770.

North Deep Creek, rises in n Yadkin County and flows se to join South Deep Creek in forming Deep Creek.

North Dividing Creek. See North Creek.

North Double Creek rises in w Stokes County and flows e into Dan River.

North Durham, former town in central Durham County at the n limits of the city of Durham. Inc. 1891. Now wholly within the limits of the city of Durham.

North Eaglenest Mountain. See Junaluska Mountain.

Northeast Branch [Newport River] rises in e Carteret County and flows s into Newport River e of the town of Newport.

Northeast Branch of New River. See Northeast Creek.

Northeast Cape Fear River rises in nw Duplin County about 2 mi. s of Mount Olive and flows se to form a part of the Duplin-Wayne County line, s through Duplin and Pender counties, turning slightly w to form a part of the New Hanover-Pender County line, and s in New Hanover where it enters Cape Fear River at Wilmington. Appears as Northeast Fork and North East River on the Collet map, 1770.

Northeast Creek rises in sw Durham County and flows sw into Chatham County where it enters New Hope River.

Northeast Creek rises in n Onslow County and flows sw into Morgan Bay. Also known as Northeast Branch of New River. Name appears in local records as early as 1744.

Northeast Fork. See Northeast Cape Fear River.

Northeast Hamlet. See Longwood Park.

Northeast Prong [of South Lake], central Dare County.

Northeast River. See Northeast Cape Fear River.

North Edenton, former town in s Chowan County adjacent to Edenton. Inc. 1911; charter repealed 1917.

North Fayetteville, community in central Cumberland County on the outskirts of the city of Fayetteville.

North Flat River rises in central Person County and flows sw into Flat River.

North Fork rises in s Clay County and flows e into Blair Creek.

North Fork rises in central Forsyth County and flows sw into Muddy Creek.

North Fork, rises in s Haywood County and flows se into Shining Creek.

North Fork rises in w Henderson County and flows w into Willow Creek.

North Fork is formed in nw Henderson County by the junction of Big and Fletcher creeks. It flows se to join South Fork in forming Mills River. Sometimes also known as North Fork Mills River.

North Fork rises in s Jones County and flows se into White Oak River.

North Fork rises in ne Madison County and flows s into Big Laurel Creek.

North Fork rises in ne Rutherford County and flows sw into First Broad River.

North Fork [Big Pine Creek] rises in s Madison County on the w side of Fork Mountain and flows ne to join South Fork in forming Big Pine Creek.

North Fork [Carvers Branch] rises in s Mitchell County and flows sw into Carvers Branch.

North Fork [Catawba River] rises in ne McDowell County and flows s into Lake James on Catawba River.

North Fork Cattail Creek rises in s Yancey County and flows sw to join South Fork Cattail Creek in forming Cattail Creek.

North Fork [Chambers Creek] rises in w Swain County and flows se into Chambers Creek.

North Fork [Cove Creek] rises in n Watauga County and flows se into Cove Creek.

North Fork Coweeta Creek rises in s Macon County and flows se into Coweeta Creek.

North Fork Crains Creek. See Whiteoak Creek.

North Fork Crooked Creek rises in se Mecklenburg County and flows e into n Union County where it joins South Fork Crooked Creek to form Crooked Creek.

North Fork [Duck Creek] rises in nw Alexander County and flows s into Duck Creek. Known locally as White Creek.

North Fork Flat Creek rises in w Transylvania County and flows se into Flat Creek.

North Fork French Broad River is formed in w Transylvania County by the junction of Indian and Shoal creeks and flows se to join West Fork French Broad River in forming French Broad River.

North Fork [Grassy Creek] rises in s Mitchell County and flows se into Middle Fork Grassy Creek.

North Fork Hawk Branch rises in n Yancey County and flows sw into Hawk Branch.

North Fork Ivy Creek rises in ne Buncombe County and flows sw to join Dillingham Creek in forming Ivy Creek. Known also as Big Ivy Creek.

North Fork Jones Creek rises in sw Anson County and flows e to join South Fork Jones Creek in forming Jones Creek.

North Fork Little River rises in n Orange County and flows se into nw Durham County where it joins South Fork Little River in forming Little River.

North Fork Mitchell River rises in nw Surry County and flows se into Mitchell River.

North Fork Mountain Creek rises in e Catawba County and flows se to join South Fork in forming Mountain Creek.

North Fork Nahunga Creek rises in w Duplin County and flows se into Nahunga Creek.

North Fork New River rises in n Watagua County and flows ne into Ashe County where it joins South Fork New River on the Ashe-Alleghany County line to form New River.

North Fork of Rattle Snake Creek rises in central Caswell County and flows ne to join South Fork of Rattle Snake Creek in forming Rattle Snake Creek.

North Fork Reddies River rises in nw Wilkes County and flows se to join Middle Fork Reddies River to form Reddies River.

North Fork Rock Creek rises in s Yancey County and flows se to join Middle Fork Rock Creek in forming Rock Creek.

North Fork Sawyer Creek rises in n Watauga County and flows sw into Sawyer Creek.

North Fork [Scott Creek] rises in n Jackson County and flows sw into Scott Creek.

North Fork [Skeenah Creek] rises in s Macon County near Blaine Knob and flows se to join South Fork [Skeenah Creek] in forming Skeenah Creek.

North Fork [Swannanoa River] rises in ne Buncombe County near Balsam Gap and flows s into Swannanoa River. Part of the Asheville watershed.

North Fork Tar River rises in central Granville County and flows sw into Tar River. Appears as Heartline Creek on the Collet map, 1770.

North Fork Tucker Creek rises in w Transylvania County and flows se into Tucker Creek.

North Fork [Whitewater River] rises in s Jackson County and flows se into South Carolina where it enters Whitewater River.

North Fork, community in n Watauga County on North Fork [Cove Creek].

North Fork. See Creston.

North Fork Township, n Watauga County.

North Fork Township, sw Ashe County.

North Harlowe, community in se Craven County.

North Harper Creek rises in se Avery County in Boone Wildlife Management Area and flows se to join South Harper Creek near the Caldwell County line in forming Harper Creek.

North Henderson, community in central Vance County on the outskirts of the city of Henderson.

North Hominy Creek rises in e Haywood County in Worley Cove and flows sw into Hominy Creek.

North Hunting Creek. See Flat Rock Creek.

North Hyco Creek rises in s Caswell County and flows ne into Person County where it joins South Hyco Creek to form Hyco River.

North Knob, n Buncombe County, ne of Windy Gap.

North Landing River rises in Princess Anne County, Va., and flows s into Currituck County where it enters Currituck Sound. The Intracoastal Waterway connects James River and North Landing River.

North Leopard Creek rises in e Carteret County and flows nw into North River.

North Lumberton, former town in e central Robeson County. Inc. 1911. Charter repealed 1953. Now a part of Lumberton. Was a mill-owned village (Jennings Cotton Mills) until 1949-1950 when houses were sold to individuals.

North Muddy Creek rises in central McDowell County and flows ne to join South Muddy Creek near the Burke County line to form Muddy Creek.

North Pacolet River. *See* Pacolet River.

North Point. *See* Eagleton Point.

North Prong [Clarks Creek] rises in n Mecklenburg County and flows se to join South Prong in forming Clarks Creek.

North Prong. *See* Correll Branch.

North Prong Creek rises in se Guilford County and flows ne into Alamance County where it enters Stinking Quarter Creek.

North Prong Ellijay Creek rises in e Macon County and flows sw into Ellijay Creek.

North Prong Horse Branch rises in central Duplin County and flows se into Northeast Cape Fear River.

North Prong Lewis Fork Creek rises in w Wilkes County and flows se approx. 9 mi. to join South Prong Lewis Fork Creek in forming Lewis Fork Creek. Yates Mountain lies between the two prongs.

North Prong Roaring River rises in n Wilkes County and flows se to join Middle Prong Roaring River in forming Roaring River. On recent State Highway Commission maps North Prong Roaring River has been called West Prong Roaring River.

North Prong Turkey Creek rises in n Transylvania County and flows s to join South Prong Turkey Creek in forming Turkey Creek.

North River rises in Dismal Swamp, e Camden County and flows s approx. 18 mi. into Albemarle Sound. For a part of its course it forms the boundary between Camden and Currituck counties. Above Thoroughfare Island it is sometimes known as Indiantown Creek. Shown as Potaskike River on the Comberford map, 1657, but as North River on Ogilby, 1671, and subsequent maps.

North River, about 10 mi. long, rises in central Carteret County and flows s into Back Sound and The Straits in se Carteret County. Appears on the Moseley map, 1733.

North River Pocosin, along the w shore of North River in s Camden County.

North River Point is the tip of s Camden Point which extends into the mouth of North River.

North River Thorofare, between two groups of tidal marsh islands in s Carteret County.

North Rock, island in Pamlico Sound, ne Carteret County n of Portsmouth Island. In 1795 the middle section of the island was submerged; the w end was called

Great Shell Rock, and the e end, Little Shell Rock.

North Rocky Creek rises in s Wilkes County and flows s into Rocky Creek.

North Rodanthe. *See* Rodanthe.

North Second Creek is formed in nw Rowan County by the junction of Back and Withrow creeks, and flows ne into Yadkin River. Appears as Second Creek on the Collet map, 1770. Named because it was the second creek reached by settlers moving west from Salisbury, Grants Creek being first. *See also* Withrow Creek.

North Shores, community on Pamlico River, w Beaufort County.

Northside, community in sw Ganville County.

North Slope Ridge, n Transylvania County extends e between Joel Branch and Davidson River.

North Stinking Quarter Creek rises in se Guilford County and flows ne into Alamance County where it enters Stinking Quarter Creek, *which see.*

North Toe River rises in n Avery County and flows s, e, and s again across Avery into Mitchell County. It flows sw across Mitchell to the Mitchell-Yancey County line where it joins South Toe River to form Toe River. The last elk shot in North Carolina is said to have been killed on this river in 1781.

North Turkey Creek rises in sw Buncombe County near Newfound Mountain and flows ne to join South Turkey Creek in forming Turkey Creek.

Northview, community in n Lee County.

Northwest, community in ne Brunswick County.

Northwest Creek rises in e Craven County and flows s into Neuse River.

Northwest Ditch drains water from nw Camden County (Dismal Swamp) to the se into Cross Canal.

Northwest Fork [Alligator River] rises in s central Tyrrell County and flows se into Alligator River.

Northwest Parish, Church of England, Bertie County and later Northampton County, was established in 1727 by the division of Society Parish in the nw part of the county. In 1741 the parish became Northampton County and, except for a part of the parish in the east, was renamed St. George's Parish in 1758. The following year the remaining part of Northwest Parish became a part of Hertford County and St. Barnabas' Parish. Northwest Parish, therefore, ceased to exist.

Northwest Point, the nw tip of Roanoke Island, central Dare County, which extends into Croatan Sound.

Northwest Prong Creek rises in nw Carteret County and flows s into Newport River.

Northwest River rises in Norfolk County, Va., and flows se into Currituck County where it empties into Tull Bay and North Landing River. Prior to the digging of the Dismal Swamp Canal Northwest River flowed from Lake Drummond, Virginia, to Currituck Sound. Appears on the Ogilby map, 1671.

Northwest Township, n Brunswick County.

North Whitakers Township, ne Nash County.

North Wilkesboro, town in s central Wilkes County on Yadkin River. Alt. 1,016. Inc. 1891, and named for the county seat, Wilkesboro, across the Yadkin River to the s. The site was described as Mulberry Fields, a former Cherokee Indian area, in a report of Moravian surveyors in 1752. Appears as Mulberry Fields on the Collet map, 1770. Produces furniture, mirrors, textiles, apparel, hosiery, processed poultry, and dairy products.

North Wilkesboro Township, central Wilkes County.

Norton, community on Grassy Camp Creek and Norton Creek in sw Jackson County.

Norton, community on Little Tennessee River in s Macon County. Also called Tryphosa.

Norton Branch rises in s Macon County near Downs Mountain and flows ne into Little Tennessee River.

Norton Branch rises in s Macon County near Plass Gap and flows w into Little Tennessee River.

Norton Branch rises in se Macon County and flows sw into Big Creek.

Norton Creek rises in sw Jackson County and flows ne into Lake Thorpe.

Norton Fork Creek rises in sw Madison County and flows nw into Spring Creek.

Norton Fork Gap, on the Buncombe-Madison County line between Chestnut Gap and Robinison Rough.

Norton Prong rises in e Macon County and flows s into Big Creek.

Norwood, town in se Stanly County on Lake Tillery. Alt. 365. Post office est. here in 1826 and named for William C. Norwood, first postmaster. Inc. 1881.

Norwood Lake. See Lake Tillery.

Notla Township, s central Cherokee County.

Nottely River rises in Georgia and flows n into Cherokee County through which it flows n, w, and ne into Hiwassee River about 2 mi. w of Murphy.

Nottoway River rises in Virginia and flows se into Hertford County where it joins Blackwater River on the Gates-Hertford County line to form Chowan River. Nottoway was a name applied by Algonquian neighbors to Indians in this area meaning "adders" or "rattlesnakes." The name Nataway River appears on the Ogilby map, 1671, intended for this river but mistakenly applied to the present Wiccacon River. See also Weyanoke Creek.

Notts Island. See Mackay Island.

Nova Scotia Branch rises in sw Macon County and flows nw into Nantahala River.

Nubbinscuffle Creek rises in w Yancey County and flows s into Bald Creek.

Nuna Ridge, Great Smoky Mountains National Park, nw Swain County between Tub-Mill Creek and Gunna Creek.

Nunda Branch, Great Smoky Mountains National Park, rises in nw Swain County and flows se into Bone Valley Creek.

Nunn Mountain, se Orange County on the head of Booker Creek.

Nupernuse Point. See Newport News Point.

Nutbush. See Williamsboro.

Nutbush Creek rises in city of Henderson in central Vance County and flows n into Kerr Reservoir. Shown on the Moseley map, 1733.

Nutbush Creek Fishing Access Area, operated by N. C. Wildlife Resources Commission on Kerr Reservoir in n central Vance County. Controlled by Kerr Reservoir Commission which has provided a paved access road to a boat launching ramp. Area located about 5 mi. north of the city of Henderson.

Nutbush Township. See Middleburg-Nutbush Township.

O

Oakanoahs. *See* South Mountains.

Oakboro, town in sw Stanly County. Inc. 1915. Known as Furr City until about 1905. Post office est. here 1915 with the coming of the railroad and when Big Lick post office was closed.

Oak City, town in nw Martin County. Site given the name Goose Nest by a Union soldier on a raid here. Inc. as Conoho 1891. Name changed to Oak City 1905, because of confusion with Conetoe; name selected from a calendar advertising Oak City Laundry in Raleigh.

Oakdale, community on Deep River in sw Guilford County.

Oakdale, community in sw Wilkes County between Beaver Creek and Yadkin River.

Oakes Ridge. *See* Oak Knob.

Oakey Mountain, ne Rutherford County between North Fork and Collins Creek. Alt. approx. 2,200.

Oak Forest, community in e Iredell County, settled prior to 1800. Store here operated by James Gay, author of *A Collection of Various Pieces of Poetry, Chiefly Patriotic* (Raleigh, 1810). Thriving business community around 1900, now dying.

Oak Grove, community in sw Brunswick County.

Oakgrove, community in e Cleveland County.

Oak Grove, community in central Davie County between Elisha and Dutchmans creeks. Est. prior to 1879. Also known as Maine.

Oak Grove, community on Little Lick Creek in e Durham County.

Oak Grove, community in s Jones County.

Oak Grove, community in n Macon County between Caler Cove Branch and Lakey Creek.

Oak Grove, community in nw Northampton County. The post office here, now discontinued, was known as Stancell.

Oak Grove, community in n Surry County between Wood Fork Branch and Little Fisher River.

Oakgrove, community in nw Union County.

Oak Grove, community in w Yadkin County, n of Flat Rock Creek.

Oak Grove Township, e central Durham County.

Oak Hill, community in n central Burke County about 4 mi. n of Morganton.

Oak Hill, community in e Caldwell County.

Oak Hill, community in n Granville County. A post office est. here as early as 1822 was called Young's Store but by 1830 the present name was being used.

Oak Hill, community in central Macon County between Crawford Branch and Wallace Branch.

Oak Hill Mountain, peak in the Cane Creek Mountains, s Alamance County.

Oak Hill Township, nw Granville County.

Oak Island, a peninsula between Elizabeth River and the Atlantic Ocean at the mouth of the Cape Fear in se Brunswick County. Site of Fort Caswell, Long Beach and Yaupon Beach. Appears as an island on the Collet map, 1770.

Oak Knob on the Buncombe-Madison County line. Alt. approx. 4,400. Also appears on maps as Oakes Knob and as Oak Ridge.

Oak Knob, e Haywood County on James Branch.

Oakland, community in s central Rutherford County near the head of Floyds Creek. Formerly known as Frog Level. A post office est. here in 1853 was known as Butler.

Oakland, community in sw Transylvania County n of Round Mountain. Alt. 3,104.

Oakland Township, s central Chatham County.

Oak Level Township, se Nash County.

Oakley, former community se of Asheville, central Buncombe County, now within the limits of Asheville.

Oakley, town in n Pitt County. Inc. 1903.

Oak Lodge, community in e Guilford County.

Oaklog Gap, on the Haywood-Transylvania County line.

Oak Park, community in s Buncombe County.

Oak Park, community in w Cherokee County on Shoal Creek s of Hiwassee River.

Oak Ridge, town in nw Guilford County. Alt. 885. Est. in 1852 and inc. in 1897. Named for its location on an oak-grown ridge. Oak Ridge Military Institute, oldest military preparatory school in North Carolina, founded here in 1854.

Oak Ridge, community in n Stokes County.

Oak Ridge. See Oak Knob.

Oak Ridge Creek rises in e Jackson County and flows sw into Piney Mountain Creek.

Oak Ridge Township, nw Guilford County.

Oaks, community in sw Orange County on Cane Creek. Site of an academy as early as 1829. The Bingham School operated here from 1844 until 1865.

Oaks Knob, w Avery County.

Oak Spring, community in central Rutherford County on Catheys Creek. A post office was here 1855-1907.

Oak Swamp rises in e Robeson County and flows ne into Big Swamp.

Oakview, community in sw Guilford County adjacent to High Point. A portion of High Point was formerly a part of the Oakview community.

Oak Villa, community in e Hertford County. It developed on the old post road from Norfolk, Virginia, to Wilmington and was a point from which mail was rerouted.

Oakville, community in n Franklin County.

Oakville, community in n Warren County between Hawtree Creek and Sixpound Creek. A post office est. here in 1872 was discontinued in 1907.

Oakwood Acres, community in s Davidson County on High Rock Lake.

Oakwoods, community in s Wilkes County between Cub Creek and East Prong Cub Creek. Settled by several Scottish families.

Oaky Mountain, ne Chatham County.

Obadiah Cove, w Graham County between Fork Ridge and Hooper Mill Creek.

Obadiah Gap, on Horse Cove Ridge in w Graham County.

Oberlin, formerly a community in central Wake County nw of Raleigh, but now a part of the city of Raleigh.

Obids, community in s Ashe County. Alt. approx. 2,800.

Obids Creek rises in se Ashe county and flows n into South Fork New River.

Obids Township, se Ashe County.

Obies Creek rises in n Chatham County and flows ne into Orange County where it enters Morgan Creek.

Ocala, community in s Jackson County on Fowler Creek.

Occacock. See Ocracoke.

Occam. See Croatan Sound.

Occoneechee Creek rises in w Northampton County and flows s into Roanoke River. The name is probably from the Tutelo Indian word yuhkañ, "man."

Occoneechee Mountain, central Orange County s of the town of Hillsborough. Named for an Indian tribe mentioned frequently in seventeenth and eighteenth century records. The mountain is referred to in a letter of January 31, 1767 by Governor Tryon. Appears but not named on the Collet map, 1770. Called Occaneeche Hills on the Kerr map, 1882. Alt. approx. 700. Since 1960 a mining company has been cutting away the top of the mountain, and its appearance is rapidly being changed.

Occoneechee Neck, the w neck of Northampton County, formed by a large bend in Roanoke River.

Occoneechee Township, sw Northampton County.

Ocean Isle Beach, town on the Atlantic Ocean, s Brunswick County. Inc. 1959.

Ochlawaha. See Mud Creek.

Ochre Creek rises in n Jackson County and flows w into Scott Creek.

Oconaluftee River is formed in the Great Smoky Mountains in ne Swain County by the junction of Beech Flats Prong and Kephart Prong. For a part of its course it forms the Jackson-Swain County line. It flows se into Tuckasegee River. The name, long written as two words (Ocona Luftee), is from the Cherokee word Egwanulti, Egwani, "river," and nulati or nuti, "near" or "beside." The Cherokee town of Oconalufte mentioned by explorer-naturalist William Bartram about 1775 was probably on the lower course of the river at the present Birdtown.

Oconalufty Township, formerly in e Swain County, but incorporated into the limits of Charleston Township when it was enlarged between 1934-1940 with the establishment of Great Smoky Mountains National Park.

Ocracoke, community on Ocracoke Island, se Hyde County. Settled in the seventeenth century. The name Ocracoke seems originally to have been Wococon which appeared first on the White map of 1585. The Indian word apparently was waxkahikani, meaning "enclosed place," "fort," or "stockade," and it is believed that a fortified Indian village existed at the site. By 1676 the name Okok was used, and by 1709 it had developed into Occacock. *See also* Wococon Island.

Ocracoke Inlet, from the Atlantic Ocean into Pamlico Sound, lies between Ocracoke Island (Hyde County) on the n and Portsmouth Island (Carteret County) on the s. The pirate, Blackbeard, was killed in this vicinity in 1718. Once chief trade inlet for North Carolina.

Ocracoke Island, se Hyde County, one of the Outer Banks. Approx. 17 mi. long. *See also* Croatoan Island; Wococon Island.

Ocracoke Township, se Hyde County on the Outer Banks.

Odam Millpond, sw Wayne County on Thoroughfare Swamp.

Odamsville. *See* Faisons Old Tavern.

Odear Cove, e Swain County on the head of Wesser Creek.

O'Dear Creek rises in nw McDowell County and flows e on the n side of Pompey Ridge into Threemile Creek.

Odell, community in e Warren County s of Little Fishing Creek. Post office est. here in 1892, but discontinued in 1915.

Odell Mill. *See* Forest Hill.

Odell School Township, former township in nw Cabarrus County, now township number 3. Once known as Deweese Township.

Offen, community in n Wilkes County near Middle Prong Roaring River.

Off Island, approx. ½ mi. in diameter, lying off s Bodie Island in Roanoke Sound, e Dare County. Separated from Bodie Island by Blossie Creek.

Ogburn, community in w Johnston County. Formerly spelled Aughburn.

Ogburn's Crossroads, community in nw Guilford County.

Ogburntown, community in central Forsyth County within the urban extension of the city of Winston-Salem.

Ogden, community in sw Clay County on Crawford Creek.

Ogle Branch rises in ne Buncombe County and flows s into North Fork Ivy Creek. Named for a pioneer family.

Ogle Creek rises in s Yancey County and flows sw to join Timber Creek in forming Sugar Camp Creek.

Ogle Gap, s Yancey County at the nw end of Ogle Ridge.

Ogle Knob, s central Swain County between the head of Bucknor Branch and Davis Branch.

Ogle Meadow Knob on the Buncombe-Yancey County line. Alt. 5,384. A grassy bald known locally simply as Ogle Meadows.

Ogle Ridge, s Yancey County near the head of Ogle Creek.

Ogreeta, community in w Cherokee County on Hiwassee Lake between the mouth of Chambers Creek and Grape Creek.

Ohanoak or **Ohaunoock,** an Indian village visited by Ralph Lane, 1585-86, on the w bank of Chowan River in what is now ne Bertie County, s of Colerain. Appears on the DeBry map, 1590. On the Comberford map, 1657, it appears as Wohanoke. Modern Tuscarora Indians say the name means "old village."

Ohlanto. *See* Blowing Rock.

Oine, community in nw Warren County. Post office est. here in 1886 but discontinued in 1904.

Okeewemee, community in n Montgomery County.

Okie Branch rises in s Duplin County and flows se into Northeast Cape Fear River.

Okisko, community in w Pasquotank County. Settled prior to 1890. Named for a king of the Yeopim Indians. Alt. 12.

Okok. *See* Ocracoke.

Ola, former community in w Haywood County near lat. 35° 36' 15" N., long. 83° 08' 00". This site is now within the Great Smoky Mountains National Park and abandoned.

Old Apalachia, former community in nw Cherokee County below and n of Apalachia Dam near the junction of Shuler Creek with Hiwassee River.

Old Bald Creek rises in s Haywood County and flows ne into Allen Creek.

Old Bald Mountain on Haywood-Jackson County line. Alt. 5,800. Named for bald appearance from the Jackson County side.

Old Bald Ridge, extends from Chastine Creek in e central Jackson County n and ne to Allen Creek in sw Haywood County. Named for Old Bald Mountain, one of its peaks.

Old Barfields. *See* Tuscarora Beach.

The Old Bear, point of land off e Pamlico County extending into Jones Bay.

Old Bethlehem, community in se Warren County near the Halifax-Warren County line.

Old Billy Top, on the Cherokee-Graham County line in the Snowbird Mountains.

Old Black Mountain, at the junction of the lines of Haywood County, N. C., and Cocke and Sevier counties, Tenn., Great Smoky Mountains National Park, near lat. 35° 42′ 44″ N., long. 83° 15′ 18″ W. Alt. 6,430.

Old Black. *See* Mount Chapman.

Old Catawba River rises at the Çatawba River Dam on Lake James and flows se and ne into Catawba River about 1 mi. se of Linville Dam in w Burke County.

Old Cove, n Swain County on Chambers Creek.

Old Dock, community in se Columbus County on Waccamaw River, 1 mi. se of Schulkens Pond. Settled about 1800. Alt. 40.

Old field, an area in what is now Beaufort County, between Pungo and Pamlico rivers, shown on the Ogilby map, 1671.

Old Field Bald Mountain, on Ashe-Watauga County line. Alt. 4,939. Named for muster ground and drill field used by Benjamin Cleveland during the Revolution.

Old Field Branch rises in ne Ashe County and flows se into Poison Branch.

Old Field Creek rises in n Caldwell County and flows ne into Buffalo Creek.

Old Field Creek rises in e Orange County and flows ne into New Hope Creek.

Oldfield Creek. *See* Redbank Creek.

Oldfield Gap, n Graham County between Yellow Creek Mountains and Fork Ridge.

Oldfield Gap on the Madison-Yancey County line near Indian Creek.

Old Fields of Toe. *See* Newland.

Oldfields Township, sw Ashe County. Named for muster ground and drill field used by Benjamin Cleveland during the Revolution.

Old Fields Township, w Wilson County.

Oldfield Swamp rises in s Robeson County and flows se into Hog Swamp.

Old Field Top Mountain, w Haywood County between Plott Balsams and Mingus Ridge. Alt. 5,820. Sometimes called Plott's Old Field Mountain.

Old Ford. *See* Mineola.

Old Ford Swamp rises in nw Beaufort County and flows w to join Snoad Branch in forming Aggie Run.

Old Fort, town in w McDowell County on Catawba River. Alt. 1,438. Inc. 1872 as Catawba Vale by a northern land com-

pany which expected to develop a city on the Davidson plantation which it had purchased the previous year. Name changed in 1873 to Old Fort, the name by which the community had been known since 1828 or earlier when a post office existed here. Named for Davidson's Fort erected in 1776 by troops under the command of Griffith Rutherford to protect settlers from Cherokee Indians.

Old Fort Township, sw McDowell County.

Old Gilreath, community in s Wilkes County 3 mi. nw of Gilreath.

Old House Branch rises in se Watauga County and flows ne into Dugger Creek.

Old House Channel, a slough in the waters of Pamlico Sound immediately w of and leading to Oregon Inlet, e Dare County. Also known as Old House Slough.

Old House Creek, a short stream in n central Carteret County flowing n into South River.

Old Hundred, community in w Scotland County. Named because the 100-mile post was here when the railroad from Wilmington was built. Alt. 318.

Old Lanesboro. *See* Lanesboro.

Old Mattie Ridge, ne Cherokee County in the Snowbird Mountains.

Old Mattie Top, on the Cherokee-Graham County line in the Snowbird Mountains.

Old Mill Creek rises in n central Washington County in East Dismal Swamp, ne of the town of Roper, and flows nw into Kendricks Creek.

Old Mill Swamp rises in n Sampson County and flows se into Great Coharie Creek.

Old Paddy Creek, about 7/10 mi. long, rises at Paddy Creek Dam on Lake James and flows e into Old Catawba River in w Burke County about 9 mi. west of Morganton.

Old Richmond Township, nw Forsyth County. Named for the former town of Richmond, *which see,* seat of Surry County from 1774 to 1789.

Old Road Gap, on the Cherokee-Macon County line.

Old Road Ridge, n Mitchell County between Spring Creek and Greasy Creek.

Old Rock. *See* Shell Castle.

Old Rocky Mountain, e Macon County between the head of Ellijay Creek and the head of Little Salt Rock Creek. Alt. 4,825.

Olds, community in s Currituck County. Known locally as Olds Hill for a sandhill nearby.

Old Salem. *See* Salem.

Old Shatter. *See* Axtell.

Old Sheep Knob, n Cleveland County. Alt. 1,497.

Old Skinnersville. *See* Skinnersville.

Old Sneedsborough, abandoned town in se Anson County on Pee Dee River. Laid out in 1795 to be at the head of navigation on the Pee Dee River and named for Honora Sneyd, stepmother of Richard Lovell Edgeworth, founder of the town. Navigation was not developed sufficiently and the town declined after about thirty years. Post office est. in the early nineteenth century closed in 1883. Sneedsborough was famous for its inn. John J. McRae, governor of Mississippi, 1854-58, and a member of United States and Confederate Congresses, born here. *See also* McFarlan.

The Old Sow, tidal marsh island in Pamlico Sound off the se tip of Goose Creek Island, ne Pamlico Sound.

Old Sparta, town in s Edgecombe County on Tar River. Inc. as Sparta, 1876, and reinc. as Old Sparta, 1903. No longer active in municipal affairs. Was a post office as early as 1830; probably came to be called Old Sparta after Sparta, county seat of Alleghany County est. 1859, began to thrive.

Old Stanhope. *See* Spring Hope.

Old Station Gap, central Madison County between Brush Creek and Walnut Creek.

Olds Township, e central Greene County. Named for the Olds family whose members moved here after 1779.

Old Topsail Creek rises in s Pender County and flows s into Topsail Sound.

Old Topsail Inlet, s Pender County, through which waters of Topsail Sound enter the Atlantic Ocean. It lies between New Topsail Inlet on the n and Rich Inlet on the s.

Old Topsail Inlet. *See* Beaufort Inlet.

Old Town, community in central Forsyth County. Settled 1753 by first Moravians to arrive at the Wachovia tract from Pennsylvania. First named Bethabara, or House of Passage, since it was intended to be a temporary settlement. After 1766, when Salem was begun, Bethabara declined. The post office ceased to be called Bethabara in 1835 and was changed to Old Town.

Old Town Creek. *See* Town Creek.

Old Town Township, w central Forsyth County.

Old Trap, community in s Camden County probably settled as early as the 1650's. In the eighteenth century it was the cente: of much maritime activity and a grog shop here supplied the local trade with West India rum. Tradition says that men carrying grain to a local windmill tarried long at the grog shop—a trap. By the end of the Revolution the name "The Trap" was being used and after 1800 "Old Trap" came into use.

Old Tree Swamp rises in w Hertford County and flows se into Potecasi Creek.

Old Weeksville. *See* Weeksville.

Oldwoman Branch rises in w Pitt County and flows se into Little Contentnea Creek.

Old Woman's Swamp. *See* Gilletts Creek.

Olin, town in n central Iredell County. Est. and inc. 1855 as New Institute when Brantley York and Baxter Clegg opened an academy here. Reincorporated 1857 as Olin in honor of Stephen Olin, Methodist educator. Inc. again in 1905, but long inactive in municipal affairs.

Olin Creek rises in nw Iredell County and flows se into Patterson Creek. Formerly known as Little Rocky Creek.

Olin Township, n central Iredell County.

Olive Branch, community in ne Union County east of Gourdvine Creek.

Olive Grove, community in n Cleveland County.

Olive Hill, community in central Macon County on Iotla Creek.

Olive Hill, community in w Person County.

Olive Hill Township, w central Person County.

Olive Hollow, w Watauga County extends northward, w of Laurel Creek.

Oliver Reef, s Dare and e Hyde counties, in the waters of Pamlico Sound n of Hatteras Inlet. Presented by the state to the United States government in 1874 for use in naval target practice. Returned to the state in 1965.

Olivers, community in central Jones County.

Olivers Crossroads, community in s Catawba County.

Oliver's Crossroads, community in central Jones County.

Olivet, community in nw Caldwell County on Mulberry Creek. Named for Olivet Methodist Church, in turn named for Biblical Mount Olivet or Mount of Olives.

Olivia, community in w Harnett County.

Settled about 1865. Known as Rock Branch until 1913 when it was renamed to honor W. J. Olive who, in 1912, introduced the growing of flue-cured tobacco here.

Ollie Branch rises in central Graham County and flows sw into East Buffalo Creek.

Olympia, community in w Pamlico County. Named for Mount Olympus when a post office, now discontinued, was est. here.

O'Neals Township, n Johnston County.

Onetree Point, shown on Moseley map, 1733, extending from the mainland of what is now se Brunswick County into Cape Fear River between Elizabeth River and Walden Creek. Located n of and adjacent to Deep Water Point. Not shown on modern maps.

Onion Falls in West Fork Tuckasegee River at the n end of Thorpe Reservoir in w Jackson County.

Onion Knob, Alexander-Wilkes County line.

Onion Mountain, e Macon County between the head of Cat Creek and Laurel Creek. Alt. 3,500.

Onitalooga Lake. See Ela Lake.

Onslow Bay in the Atlantic Ocean off the se coast from Cape Fear on the s to Cape Lookout on the n.

Onslow Beach, se Onslow County between New River Inlet and Browns Inlet. Known earlier as Hurst Beach. Now a part of the Camp Lejeune Marine Base and used for training for amphibious landings.

Onslow County was formed in 1734 from New Hanover County. Located in the se section of the state, it is bounded by the Atlantic Ocean and by Pender, Duplin, Jones, and Carteret counties. It was named for Arthur Onslow (1691-1768), member of Parliament and Speaker of the House of Commons, 1728-61. Area: 806 sq. mi (756, land; 50, water). County seat: Jacksonville with an elevation of 23 ft. Townships are Jacksonville, Richlands, Stump Sound, Swansboro, and White Oak. Produces tobacco, corn, soy-

beans, hogs, livestock, lumber, apparel, crushed limestone, sand, and gravel.

Onslow Court House. See Jacksonville.

Onvil, community in central Montgomery County near the head of Thickety Creek.

Ooneroy, a Tuscarora Indian village on the Roanoke River in Bertie County shown on the Moseley map, 1733. This was a chief town of the Tuscarora and the name meant "gathered together."

Open Branch rises in n Jackson County and flows nw into Hornbuckle Creek.

The Opening, a clay and swamp area in e Pitt County between the head of Clayroot Swamp and Chicod Creek.

Open Land or Open Ground, a shrub bog area of approximately 50,000 acres in Carteret County, about 12 mi. ne of Beaufort. An attempt to reclaim the area in 1926 was abandoned, but much of it is now included in a large experimental farm.

Open Ridge, s Yancey County between Rock Creek and South Toe River.

Ophir, community in n Montgomery County. Settled shortly after the middle of the nineteenth century in the midst of a gold producing area and named for the land furnshing gold for King Solomon's Temple in Biblical days. Now an agricultural and timber producing community.

Ophir Township, nw Montgomery County.

Oporauck, an otherwise unidentified designation appearing on the Comberford map, 1657, shown parallel with what is now Scuppernong River in Washington and Tyrrell counties.

Opossum Swamp rises in w Sampson County and flows s into Little Coharie Creek.

Orange, community in w Sampson County between Caesar Swamp and Little Coharie Creek.

Orange County was formed in 1752 from Johnston, Bladen, and Granville counties. Located in the central section of the state, it is bounded by Durham, Chatham, Alamance, Caswell, and Person counties. It has long been said that the county was named for William III (1650-1702) of the House of Orange, who ruled England from 1689 to 1702. However, in 1752 when the county was formed, the infant William V (1748-1806) of Orange was Stadholder, and his mother, Anne, daughter of George II of England, controlled affairs of state. It seems reasonable to assume that Orange County was named in honor of William V of Orange (and perhaps also to flatter his grandfather, George II of England) instead of for William III who had been dead for fifty years. Area: 398 sq. mi. County seat: Hillsborough with an elevation of 543 ft. Townships are Bingham, Cedar Grove, Chapel Hill, Cheeks, Eno, Hillsborough, and Little River. Produces corn, tobacco, wheat, oats, dairy products, poultry, livestock, hogs, textiles, furniture, pyrophyllite, and crushed stone.

Orange Factory, community on Little River in n Durham County formerly known as Laura Cotton Mill. Once operated by Willard Manufacturing Company.

Orange Grove, community in sw Orange County between Cane Creek and Bear Creek.

Orange Point, in e Tyrrell County, extends from the mainland into Alligator River s of the mouth of The Frying Pan.

Orapeake. See Corapeake.

Orapeake Creek. See Corapeake Swamp.

Orapeake Swamp. See Corapeake Swamp.

Orchard Branch rises in e Haywood County and flows se into Fines Creek.

Orchard Branch rises in n central Transylvania County and flows s into King Creek.

Orchard Creek rises in e Pamlico County and flows se into Neuse River. Appears on the Moseley map, 1733.

Orchard Creek. See Craborchard Creek.

Orchard Ridge, n Madison County between Big Laurel Creek and Little Foster Creek.

Oregon. See South Creek.

Oregon Hill, community in n Rockingham County between the heads of Quaqua and Lovelace creeks. It is said that a man stopped here early in the nineteenth century on his way to Oregon, but he never got any farther so he called the site Oregonville. From this the present name evolved. Nearby Guerrant Springs was a popular resort later in the century and into the early 1900's.

Oregon Inlet, e Dare County, from Pamlico Sound into the Atlantic Ocean between s tip of Bodie Island and n tip of Pea Island. Formed by a hurricane on Sept. 7, 1846. Named for the first vessel to pass through, the side-wheeler Oregon. State-operated free ferry across the inlet now replaced by the Herbert C. Bonner Bridge, approx. 2½ mi. long and opened in Dec., 1963; named for N. C. Congressman Herbert C. Bonner (1891-1965).

Oregon Inlet Coast Guard Station, e Dare County on Pea Island near Oregon Inlet. First est. as Bodie's Island Lifesaving Station in 1874; name later changed. The Lifesaving Service and Revenue Cutter Service joined in 1915 to form United States Coast Guard.

Ore Hill. See Mount Vernon Springs.

Ore Knob, former town in se Ashe County. Inc. 1875. Copper mine here once employed 250 men; closed in 1886. Little evidence of buildings remains. Alt. 3,150.

Ore Knob, n Haywood County between Fall Branch and Hurricane Creek.

Orenburg. See Harris.

Orfords Pond. See Sunset Lake.

Oriental, town in s Pamlico County on Neuse River at the mouth of Smith Creek. First settled about 1870 by "Uncle Lou" Midgett and known as Smith's Creek. Later renamed for the Federal transport, Oriental, which sank in 1862 near Bodie Island. The ship's nameplate had been found by Rebecca Midgett, wife of the town's first settler.

Orion, community in se Ashe County.

Orlando, community in s Macon County.

Ormonds Township, se Greene County. Named for the Ormond family which settled in the Ormondsville community prior to 1769.

Ormondsville, community in e Greene County. Developed from a country crossroads store at the Ormond family plantation.

Orris's Run, swampy stream rises in n central Beaufort County and flows se into Pungo Creek. Named for Orris Waters who lived nearby.

Orrum, town in s Robeson County. Settled as early as 1832 as a community around Big Branch Church. Inc. 1903. Orton was the first choice for a name in 1903 when a post office was about to be established, but as the name was already in use in Columbus County it was rejected. Orrum was coined as a near approach to Orton.

Orrum Township, se Robeson County.

Orton, community in e central Brunswick County on Cape Fear River.

Orton Branch rises in s Buncombe County and flows ne into French Broad River.

Orton Creek rises in se Brunswick County and flows e into Cape Fear River.

Orton Plantation, e central Brunswick County overlooking Cape Fear River. House built about 1725 by Roger Moore, later the home of Governor Benjamin Smith, is now a handsome showplace with extensive azalea gardens. The gardens are open to the public. The old town of Brunswick, *which see,* was nearby.

Orton Point, point of land s of mouth of Lilliput Creek in e Brunswick County extending into Cape Fear River.

Orton Pond, artificial pond on Orton Creek in e Brunswick County. Built about 1810. Maximum depth of 12 feet. Surface area 500 acres.

Osage Mountain, s Macon County between West Fork Overflow Creek and Watkins Creek.

Osborn Branch rises in ne Transylvania County and flows se into Boylston Creek.

Osborne, community in s Richmond County.

Osborne Creek rises in se Wilkes County and flows s into Iredell County where it enters Hunting Creek.

Osborn Mountain, e Watauga County between Elk Creek and Southwest Stony Fork Creek.

Osbornville, community in se Wilkes County on Osborne Creek.

Osburn Ford, shallows in Pigeon River just ne of the town of Clyde in central Haywood County.

Osceola, crossroads community in ne Guilford County.

Osceola Lake in central Henderson County is fed by Findley, Perry, and Tonys creeks and drained by Shephard Creek. It was formed about 1914 and named for an Indian chief in the area. Covers 12 acres; maximum depth 20 feet. Owned by a resort hotel which is operated on its shores.

Osgood, community in n Lee County. Inc. 1889; charter repealed 1891. Named for local family. Early known as Shakerag, traditionally because two prominent men fought here until their clothes were torn off. Alt. 242.

Osmond, community in ne Caswell County.

A post office was operated here during the approx. period 1880-1920.

Os-quee-ha-ha. *See* Clear Creek.

Ossipee, community in w Alamance County on the s side of Altamahaw. Developed after 1890 when a mill was established here.

Osteen, community in sw Henderson County on Crab Creek.

Ostin Creek rises in w central Polk County at the base of Chimney Top, and flows ne into Lake Adger on Green River.

Ostin Knob, se Macon County between Brown Gap and East Fork Overflow Creek.

Ostwalt, community in s Iredell County. Known as Cambridge, for an Associate Reformed Presbyterian Church, from the early nineteenth century until just prior to 1900 when it took its present name from J. K. Ostwalt's store when it became a post office.

Otaré. *See* Mountain Region.

Oteen, community in central Buncombe County near the eastern limits of Asheville. Site of a Veterans Hospital established during World War I for tubercular soldiers. Name said to be an Indian word meaning "chief aim," and descriptive of the hospital's efforts to restore health to the disabled.

Othello, community in se Ashe County.

Ottanola, community in ne Henderson County.

Ottaray. *See* Mountain Region.

Otter Creek rises in e Alamance County and flows s into Quaker Scrub Creek.

Otter Creek rises in e Craven County and flows n into Neuse River.

Otter Creek rises in nw Macon County and flows sw into Whiteoak Creek.

Otter Creek rises in n Rutherford County and flows se into Cove Creek.

Otter Creek rises in e Wilson County and flows e across s Edgecombe County into w Pitt County where it enters Tar River

Otter Creek, community in n Rutherford County on Cove Creek. A post office was here 1854-1915.

Otter Creek Township, former township in s Edgecombe County, now township number 9. Earlier known as Autreys Creek Township.

Otter Gap, nw Macon County between Long Branch and Otter Creek.

Otter Mountain, nw Macon County between Cold Spring Creek and the head of Jane Otter Branch.

Otters Knob. *See* Arturs Knob.

Otto, town in s Macon County. Alt. 2,060. Inc. 1909, but long inactive in municipal affairs.

Otway, community in e Carteret County near the mouth of Ward Creek. Settled about 1800. Named for Otway Burns (1775-1848), captain of a privateer vessel in the War of 1812. Alt. 5.

Ouaniche. *See* Wananish.

Outer Banks are a string of low, narrow, sandy islands extending for more than 175 mi. from the Virginia state line to below Cape Lookout. They are separated from the mainland of North Carolina by broad, shallow sounds. Narrow inlets through the Outer Banks provide access to the Atlantic Ocean from the sounds. The Outer Banks, from n to s, are Currituck Banks, Bodie Island, Pea Island, Hatteras Island, Ocracoke Island, Portsmouth Island, Core Banks, Shackleford Banks, and Bogue Banks. In 1709 John Lawson wrote of the "Sand Banks." In 1713 the term "Sea Banks" was used in describing them (*See* Shackleford Banks). *See also* Carolarns Islands; Croatoan Island.

Outer Diamond Shoal. *See* Diamond Shoals.

Outlaws Bridge, community in ne Duplin County.

Outlaws Pond, on Halls Marsh Branch in n Duplin County.

Outlook, community in e Madison County.

Outz Creek rises in e Alexander County and flows e into Iredell County.

Overcup Creek rises in ne Chatham County and flows se into New Hope Creek.

Overflow Creek is formed in s Macon County by the junction of East Fork Overflow Creek and West Fork Overflow Creek and flows southeast into Rabun County, Georgia, where it enters Chattooga River.

Over Hills. *See* Mountain Region.

Overhills, community in sw Harnett County. Approx. 20,000 acres developed by the Rockefeller family as a hunting and timber-growing preserve.

Overlook Ridge, Great Smoky Mountains National Park, ne Swain County, lat. 35° 33' 37" N., long. 83° 10' 50" W.

Owenby Branch rises in central Macon County and flows ne into Little Tennessee River.

Owenby Cove, central Buncombe County between Little Cedar Mountain and Gashes Creek.

Owen Creek rises in central Granville

Owen Hill Landing, nw Bladen County on Cape Fear River at the site of Owen Hill plantation, home and birthplace of Governor John Owen (1787-1841), only governor from Bladen County. Foundation and basement of original house are still here on a bluff above the landing.

Owen Jones Tar Landing. *See* Tar Landing.

Owens, community in central Cumberland County.

Owens Branch rises in s Clay County and flows nw into Shooting Creek.

Owens Cove, s Buncombe County n of Face Rock.

Owen's Creek rises in ne Alamance County and flows sw into Jordan Creek.

Owens Creek rises in w Warren County and flows sw into Fishing Creek. Appears on the MacRae map, 1833.

Owens Gap on the Jackson-Transylvania County line n of the head of West Fork French Broad River. Alt. 3,590.

Owens Knob, s Wilkes County at the ne end of Gill Mountain. Alt. 1,350. The W. Kerr Scott Dam on Yadkin River is nearby. Named for one Owen who lived here in 1752 when Moravian surveyors arrived.

Owens Point extends from e Onslow County into White Oak River. Named probably for one of two early settlers here: Thomas Owens or Benjamin Owens.

Owen Store. *See* Grove Hill.

Owensville. *See* Roseboro.

Owl Branch rises in e Swain County near Rattlesnake Mountain and flows sw parallel to Adams Creek into Oconaluftee River.

Owl Creek rises in n Cherokee County and flows sw into Hiwassee River.

Owl Creek Gap, n Cherokee County on Hanging Dog Mountain near the headwaters of Owl Creek.

Owl Knob, on the Jackson-Swain County line sw of Rattlesnake Mountain.

Owl Knob, n Macon County on Matlock Creek.

Owltown, community in sw Buncombe County, n of Hooker Gap.

Ox Creek rises in central Buncombe County and flows nw into Reems Creek.

Oxear Cove, w Haywood County on the head of Hyatt Creek.

Oxford, town authorized to be laid off on the lands of Robert Fields, 1806. The Oxford Academy was to be established there. Said to have been located on

Cedar Creek, present Davie County. No evidence that the town ever existed.

Oxford, town and county seat, central Granville County. Authorized to be laid off in 1811 and inc. 1816. The land on which the town was est. had been a part of Samuel Benton's plantation, "Oxford," hence the name. See also Harris Burgh. Produces tobacco and textiles. Appears on the Price map, 1808. Alt. 476.

Oxford District, a section of Granville County, perhaps in the central part of the county in which Samuel Benton's plantation, "Oxford," was located. In 1790 there were 65 heads of families in the District.

Oxford Lake. See Lake Hickory.

Oxford Township, central Granville County.

Ox Pen Branch rises in s central Brunswick County and flows sw into Skipper Branch.

Oyama. See Few.

Oyster Creek rises in central Carteret County and flows s into Newport River. Appears on the Moseley map, 1733. Approx. ¾ mi. long.

Oyster Creek rises in e Carteret County and flows se into Core Sound. Approx. 2 mi. long.

Oyster Creek, a channel among the tidal marsh islands on the sw shore of Roanoke Island, e Dare County, in the waters of Croatan Sound. Approx. 1 mi. w of community of Wanchese.

Oyster Creek rises on nw Goose Creek Island, ne Pamlico County, and flows ne into Pamlico River.

Oyster Creek Landing, community in s Hyde County on Swanquarter Bay.

P

Pace Branch rises in central Cherokee County and flows sw into Rogers Creek.

Pacific. See Youngsville.

Pack Gap, sw Cherokee County on Pack Mountain.

Pack Mountain, sw Cherokee County extends se from Pack Gap near the Polk County, Tenn., line to Signal Pole Hill. In Nantahala National Forest. Named peaks include Harris Top, Pack Top, and Signal Pole Hill.

Packs Creek rises in s Jackson County and flows nw into Robinson Creek.

Pack Top, sw Cherokee County at the nw end of Pack Mountain near the Tenn. state line; in the Nantahala National Forest. Alt. approx. 2,415.

Pacolet Fall, on Pacolet River in se Henderson County.

Pacolet River rises in se Henderson County near the South Carolina state line and flows ne into Polk County where it turns se to flow into South Carolina. There it enters Broad River. Sometimes also known as North Pacolet River.

Pactolus, town in e Pitt County. Inc. 1887. Named for the ancient river in Asia Minor. Alt. 22.

Pactolus Township, e Pitt County.

Paddy Creek rises in w Burke County and flows se approx. 6½ mi. into Lake James.

Paddy Mountain, central Ashe County, west of West Jefferson.

Paddys Delight Creek rises in n Northampton County and flows se into Potecasi Creek.

Padgett, community in w Onslow County on Sandy Run Swamp.

Padgett Branch rises in n Buncombe County and flows se into White Branch.

Padgett Swamp rises in w Onslow County and flows se into Sandy Run Swamp.

Page's Branch rises in e Wilson County and flows n into Cattail Swamp. Named for Thomas Page prior to 1786.

Pages Creek rises in ne New Hanover County and flows se into Topsail Sound.

Pages Lake, nw Bladen County, formed about 1925 by a dam on Mines Creek. Maximum depth 18 feet. Formerly known as Davis Mill Pond.

Page's Mill, community on East Prong Moon Creek, w Caswell County. Earlier known as Jones Mill for Richard Jones who established a water mill here about 1840.

Page's Siding. See Cary.

Page's Tavern. See Cary.

Page's Turnout. See Cary.

Paget Branch rises in s Duplin County and flows s into Boney Mill Pond.

Pailin Creek rises in e Pasquotank County and flows se into New Begun Creek.

Paine Mountain, nw Cleveland County. Alt. approx. 1,975.

Pains Bay, s Dare County in the mouth of Long Shoal River.

Paint Creek. *See* Paint Fork.

Painted Rock. *See* Paint Rock.

Painter. *See* Cullowhee.

Painter Branch rises in e Cherokee County and flows nw into Peachtree Creek.

Painter Branch rises in n Haywood County and flows sw into Pigeon River.

Painter Branch rises in w Swain County and flows se into Little Tennessee River.

Painter Knob, n Cleveland County. Alt. 2,323.

Painters Gap, n Rutherford County on the ne side of Chalk Mountain. Perhaps originally Panthers Gap.

Painter Swamp, rises in w Hertford County and flows se into Potecasi Creek.

Paint Fork rises in n Buncombe County near Paint Fork Gap and flows n into Dillingham Creek. Also known as Paint Creek.

Paint Fork rises in e Madison County and flows se to join California Creek in forming Little Ivy Creek.

Paint Fork, community in n Buncombe County on the stream of the same name. Alt. 2,455.

Paint Fork, community in e Madison County on Paint Fork.

Paint Fork Gap, n Buncombe County near the headwaters of Paint Fork.

Paint Gap on the Madison-Yancey County line.

Paint Gap, w Yancey County on Horton Creek.

Paint Gap, community in w Yancey County on Indian Creek at the mouth of Horton Creek. Alt. 2,676.

Paint Hill, se Moore County. Indians made red paint from stones found at this site, hence the name. Alt. 640.

Paint Mountain, sw Swain County between Big Creek and Right Fork [Wesser Creek].

Paint Rock, community in w Madison County on French Broad River. Inc. 1891; charter repealed 1895. Early landmark, site of a blockhouse to protect settlers from Indians, 1793. Figures on a rock cliff here appeared to early settlers to be paintings. Appears as Painted Rock on the Price map, 1808. Alt. 1,265.

Palestine, community in n Stanly County. Alt. 582.

Palmer Branch rises in e Cherokee County and flows sw into Valley River.

Palmer Branch rises in w Haywood County and flows nw into Caldwell Fork.

Palmer Camp Branch rises in e central Madison County and flows se into Big Laurel Creek.

Palmer Creek, w Haywood County, Great Smoky Mountains National Park, is formed by the junction of Beech Creek and Falling Rock Creek, near lat. 35° 38' 05" N., long. 83° 09' 17" W. Flows e to join Caldwell Fork in forming Cataloochee Creek. Named for "Turkey" George Palmer who lived on its banks. Sheriff of Haywood County, he acquired the nickname, "Turkey," because he killed so many wild turkeys.

Palmer Mountain, ne Stanly County on a peninsula in Badin Lake.

Palmerville, community in ne Stanly County.

Palmetto Point extends from the mainland into Albemarle Sound in n Tyrrell County. Appears as Hoskins Point on the Tanner map, 1829.

Palmetto Swamp rises in n Craven County and flows sw into Swift Creek.

Palmyra, town in se Halifax County. Inc. 1883. A post office was est. here in 1811. Alt. 96.

Palmyra Township, se Halifax County.

Pamlico, town in e Pamlico County on Broad Creek near Neuse River. Founded by Joshua Dean, first postmaster, who was a native of Fall River, Mass., and engaged in the lumber business here as well as in his native town. Known earlier as Broad Creek. Inc. 1913, but long inactive in municipal affairs.

Pamlico Beach, resort community in e Beaufort County on the n side of Pamlico River.

Pamlico County was formed in 1872 from Craven and Beaufort counties. Located in the e section of the state, it is bounded by Pamlico Sound, Neuse River, and by Craven and Beaufort counties. It was named for Pamlico Sound. Area: 576 sq. mi. (341, land; 235 water). County seat: Bayboro with an elevation of 8.5 ft. Townships are Nos. 1-5. Produces corn, soybeans, Irish potatoes, turkeys, hogs, and processed seafood.

Pamlico Point, peninsula off Goose Creek Island, ne Pamlico County, extending into Pamlico River.

Pamlico River is the lower course of Tar River after it enters Beaufort County. It flows se for 33 mi. before emptying into Pamlico Sound. Explored in 1584 by Arthur Barlowe and called Cipo River, for *sipowi,* the local Indian word for "river." Appears as Pamptico River on the Comberford map, 1657, and as Pamticough River on the Moll map, 1729. Named for the Pamlico Indians in the area. Bonds Ferry appears on the Collet map, 1770, as crossing the Pamlico River on the road from Bath to New Bern.

Pamlico Sound, ne and e North Carolina, separated from the Atlantic Ocean by a part of the Outer Banks. Approx. 80 mi. long and 15 to 30 mi. wide. Shallow in the north, max. depth 21 ft. in the south. Sea level, fresh water, not affected by the tide. Waters from Albemarle Sound and Pamlico and Neuse rivers enter the Sound, and it drains into the Atlantic Ocean through Hatteras and Ocracoke Inlets. Named for the Pamlico Indians who lived along its shores. Shown but not named on early maps; appears simply as The Sound on the Ogilby map, 1671, but as Pamticoe Sound on the Moseley map, 1733. The White map, 1590, labels the central part of the Sound as Mentso, *which see,* and the northern part as Nausegoc, *which see.* The largest sound on the e coast of the United States and often said locally to be the largest in the world. *See also* Paquiac.

Pamptecough Precinct was created in Bath County on December 3, 1705. It took its name from Pamptecough (Pamlico) River. About 1712 the name was changed to Beaufort County, *which see.* The town of Bath was the county seat from its inc. in 1705 until 1785 when Washington became the county seat.

Pamticoe Sound. *See* Pamlico Sound.

Panacea, community in e Warren County and nw Halifax County on Bens Creek.

Named for Panacea Springs, a famous resort here in early 1900's with a large hotel near mineral springs supposedly curative, and a lake. Water is still bottled and sold, although the hotel, lake, and cottages are gone.

Panacea Springs. *See* Panacea.

Panauuaioc, Indian village site shown on the DeBry map, 1590, in what is now Beaufort County near the head of Pamlico River, on its s bank.

Pancake Branch rises in w Avery County and flows nw into North Toe River.

Panhandle Creek rises in s Madison County and flows nw into French Broad River.

Pantego, town in ne Beaufort County on Pantego Creek. Alt. 7. A post office as early as 1828. Inc. 1881.

Pantego Creek rises in Dismal Swamp, e Beaufort County and flows s and e into Pungo River. It is also fed by several canals draining from the Swamp. Appears on the Moseley map, 1733.

Pantego Swamp, e Beaufort County.

Pantego Township, ne Beaufort County.

Panther Branch rises in n Buncombe County and flows sw into French Broad River.

Panther Branch rises in se Caswell County and flows n into North Hyco Creek.

Panther Branch rises in e Cherokee County and flows nw into Peachtree Creek.

Panther Branch rises in s Haywood County and flows sw into Little East Fork Pigeon River.

Panther Branch rises in w Madison County and flows e into Meadow Fork.

Panther Branch rises in s Wake County and flows s into Middle Creek.

Panther Branch Township, se Wake County.

Panther Cove, s Graham County between Little Snowbird Creek and Old Mattie Top.

Panther Creek rises in e Duplin County and flows w into Northeast Cape Fear River.

Panther Creek rises in e Durham County and flows ne into Neuse River.

Panther Creek rises in w Forsyth County and flows se into Yadkin River.

Panther Creek rises in e Graham County and flows ne into Little Tennessee River.

Panther Creek rises in central Haywood County and flows w into Pigeon River.

Panther Creek rises in w Lenoir County and flows n into Dailys Creek.

Panther Creek rises in e Pitt County and flows se into Tar River.

Panther Creek rises in e Rowan County and

flows ne about 6 mi. into High Rock Lake.

Panther Creek rises in ne Sampson County and flows ne into Duplin County where it enters Goshen Swamp.

Panther Creek rises in w Wake County and flows sw into Chatham County where it turns nw to flow into Northeast Creek.

Panther Den Falls on Britton Creek in ne Cherokee County. A picnic area, est. by ·the U. S. Forest Service, is nearby.

Panther Flat Top, mountain on Cherokee-Graham County line.

Panther Gap, s Macon County between Sheep Knob and Panther Knob.

Panther Knob between Savannah Ridge and East Fork [Savannah Creek] in w Jackson County. Alt. 4,010.

Panther Knob, s Macon County at the head of Nickajack Creek. Alt. approx. 3,450.

Panther Knob, se of Cope Knob on the Jackson-Macon County line. Alt. 4,376.

Panther Knob, w Macon County between heads of Bryson Branch and Poplar Cove Creek. Alt. 4,621.

Panther Knob, w Madison County between Hogback Mountain and Meadow Fork.

Panther Mountain, se Macon County between Buck Creek and Deep Gap. Alt. approx. 4,600.

Panther Mountain, s Transylvania County between Eby Creek and Cannon Creek.

Panther Ridge, ne Macon County between Beasley Creek and Mica City Creek.

Panthers Gap. See Painters Gap.

Panther Spring Gap, w Haywood County, Great Smoky Mountains National Park, near lat. 35° 36′ 35″ N., long. 83° 03′ 50″ W.

Panther Swamp, e Moore County on Turkey Creek.

Panther Swamp, a sandy loam area approx. 1 mi. square in e Northampton County on the headwaters of Canal Swamp.

Panther Swamp Creek rises in central Greene County and flows sw into Contentnea Creek.

Panthertail Mountain, w Transylvania County n of Toxaway River. Alt. 4,516.

Panther Top, s Cherokee County between Beech Creek and Nottely River. Alt. 2,287.

Panthertown Creek rises in se Jackson County and flows nw then ne to join Greenland Creek in forming Tuckasegee River.

Paquiac, name given by White on his maps of 1585 and 1590, to the section of Hat-

teras Island s of Cape Kenrick and extending almost to modern Cape Hatteras, se Dare County. This section lay between present Chicamacomico Banks and Kinnakeet Banks. The name Paquiac appears to be an Algonquian Indian term for "it is shallow," describing the adjacent Pamlico Sound.

Paquike Lake. See Lake Mattamuskeet.

Paquinouc. See Perquimans River.

Paquippe. See Lake Mattamuskeet.

Paradise Point, on the e side of New River in central Onslow County. Named for a former owner of the area. Now within the Camp Lejeune Marine Base. Local tradition says that the home of David Simmons was here and that he had several daughters widely known for their charms and beauty. Lovesick beaux called the place Paradise Point.

Parched Corn Bay in the waters of Pamlico Sound off the se shore of the mainland of Dare County.

Parched Corn Point, land on the se mainland of Dare County extending into Pamlico Sound.

Park Creek rises in sw Macon County and flows ne into Nantahala River.

Parker, community in w Ashe County. Alt. 3,950.

Parker Branch rises in nw Buncombe County and flows se into Newfound Creek.

Parker Branch rises in ne Cherokee County on Brushy Head Mountain and flows nw into Valley River.

Parker Creek rises in central Currituck County on s Piney Island and flows se into Currituck Sound near community of Barco. Approx. ¾ mi. long.

Parker Creek rises in central Pitt County and flows se into Tar River.

Parker Creek rises in w Transylvania County and flows se into West Fork French Broad River.

Parker Gap between Neddie Knob and Cub Branch in e Jackson County. Alt. 4,038.

Parker Knob, central Jackson County between Wayehutta Creek and Moses Creek. Alt. 4,187.

Parker Knob, on the Jackson-Haywood County line. Alt. 5,420.

Parker Mountain, w Cherokee County near Bearpaw Creek.

Parker Ridge, n Cherokee County in the Snowbird Mountains.

Parkersborough. See The Borough.

Parkers Branch rises in e Union County and flows e into Lanes Creek.

Parkersburg, town in w Sampson County. Settled about 1888; inc. 1891, but long inactive in municipal affairs. Named for William J. Parker, an early subscriber of stock in the railroad on which the town was located. Alt. 118.

Parkers Creek rises in e Chatham County and flows se into New Hope River.

Parkers Creek rises in n Harnett County and flows sw into Cape Fear River. Named by Peter Parker when he settled along its banks prior to 1746.

Parker's Ferry. *See* Meherrin River.

Parkers Fork, community in ne Gates County.

Park Gap, se Clay County between Marbleyard Ridge and Little Buck Creek.

Parks Branch rises in central Haywood County and flows nw into Jonathans Creek.

Parks Mountain, nw tip of Burke County. Alt. 4,066.

Park Springs, lake on Moon Creek in w Caswell County. Formerly a health resort and mineral spring. Lake, covering 8 acres, is owned by the Danville, Va., Kiwanis Club and is used for fishing and swimming.

Parkstown, community in e Wayne County near the coincident boundaries of Greene, Lenoir, and Wayne counties.

Parkton, town in ne Robeson County. Settled about 1884. Inc. 1901. Known first as Gillis Station for Mrs. John Gillis who sold land for a railroad station. When the railroad was completed the name was changed to Parkton, probably from the fact that farmers of the surrounding area "parked" teams at the station to take the train to Fayetteville.

Parkton Township, n Robeson County.

Parktown, community in s Warren County between Fishing Creek and Shocco Creek.

Parkville, community in nw Pasquotank County.

Parkville, community in e Perquimans County.

Parkville Township, e central Perquimans County.

Parkwood, community in s Durham County a few miles w of Lowes Grove. Name derived from the Research Triangle Park. Developed in the early 1960's.

Parkwood, formerly an industrial community in n Moore County. Est. before the Civil War when William Donnelly, stonemason, began making millstones here. A sawmill, brick kiln, flour mill and other businesses developed. Bankruptcy in the 1880's forced the closing of the businesses and the community began to decline. During World War II the remaining buildings were dismantled and removed. In 1953 the community of Hallison about 1¼ mi. n changed its name to Parkwood. Hallison had been named by Major W. C. Petty, a railroad man, from the given names of his deceased son, Hall Jefferson. Alt. 450.

Park Yarn, community in se Cleveland County s of the town of Kings Mountain. Park Yarn mills are here.

Parmele, town in w Martin County. Settled about 1885; inc. 1893. Named for a partner in the Parmele-Eccleston Lumber Company operating at the site. Alt. 76.

Parrish Creek rises in central Macon County and flows nw into Burningtown Creek.

Parrish's Pond, formed approx. 1890 on Redbud Creek in e Franklin County. Covers 20 acres with a max. depth of 15 ft. Known first as Babbit's Pond and then as Woods Pond.

Parrotts, community in n Lenoir County. Named for the Parrott family which settled in the vicinity in the 1760's. Alt. 54.

Parrotts Creek rises in e Onslow County and flows e into Queens Creek. Named for John Parrott. Generally known locally as Parrotts Swamp but also called Moseley's Creek.

Parrotts Swamp. *See* Parrotts Creek.

Parson Bald, Great Smoky Mountains National Park, on Swain County, N. C.,- Blount County, Tenn., line, lat. 35° 31' 25" N., long. 83° 53' W. Alt. 4,730.

Parson Branch rises in n Yancey County and flows se into Peterson Branch.

Parsons Branch rises in ne Cherokee County on Brushy Head Mountain and flows w into Valley River.

Parsonville, community in w Wilkes County on North Prong Lewis Fork Creek.

Partee. *See* Tuttles Store.

Partins Millpond in s Wake County on Black Creek.

Partridge Creek rises in n Macon County and flows sw into Whiteoak Creek.

Partridge Gap Ridge, w Madison County between Bluff Mountain and Pine Mountain.

Partridge's Bluff. *See* Gabourel's Bluff.

Paschall, community in n Warren County. Alt. 311. Formerly known as Merrymount, its post office name from 1847-1929.

Paschalls. See Ridgeway.

Pasley, community in s Duplin County.

Pasley Cove, se Watauga County extends se on the head of Dugger Creek.

Pasleys Ridge, s Watauga County extends se between Hog Camp Branch and Joe Creek.

Pasour (PAY-sewer) Mountain, a ridge approx. 4 mi. long extending ne from Long Creek to Sulphur Branch in n Gaston County. Alt. 1,100.

Pasquotank, community in w Pasquotank County.

Pasquotank County was formed by 1681 as a precinct of Albemarle County. Located in the ne section of the state, it is bounded by Albemarle Sound and by Perquimans, Gates, and Camden counties. The name of the county is from the Indian word *păsk-e'tan-ki,* "where the current [of the stream] divides or forks." Area: 290 sq. mi. (229, land; 61 water). County seat: Elizabeth City with an elevation of 12 ft. Townships are Elizabeth City, Mount Hermon, Newland, Nixonton, Providence, and Salem. Produces corn, soybeans, potatoes, miscellaneous vegetables, cotton, hogs, livestock, textiles, ships, lumber, hosiery, apparel, paper boxes, and industrial machinery.

Pasquotank River rises in nw Camden County and flows se to form the Camden-Pasquotank County line until it enters Albemarle Sound. An Indian village, Pasquenoke, is shown in this area on the DeBry map, 1590. Appears as Pacequenock on the Blaeu map, 1640, and as Prascantanck River on the Comberford map, 1657. The Intracoastal Waterway enters Pasquotank River through Dismal Swamp Canal. See also Shipyard.

Passmore Branch rises in ne Clay County and flows sw into Perry Creek.

Passmore Knob, e Macon County between Jack Knob and Brown Gap.

Pasture Branch rises in s Duplin County and flows se into Northeast Cape Fear River.

Pasture Creek, stream in Nelson Bay which cuts nw into the mainland in ne Carteret County. Approx. ¼ mi. long.

Patchet Creek rises in e Lee County and flows s into Little River.

Pate Creek rises in nw Mitchell County and flows s into Pigeonroost Creek.

Pates, community in w Robeson County. Inc. 1883, but long inactive in municipal affairs. Named for Ed Pate, a section boss on the railroad.

Pate Store, community in e Wayne County s of the community of Cherry and n of The Slough.

Patetown, town in e Wayne County near The Slough. Inc. 1907, but not now active in municipal affairs. Named for the Pate family living in the area.

Pat Knob, n Macon County between Sawmill Ridge and Shepherd Creek.

Patrick, community in w Cherokee County near Camp Creek.

Pat Stable Branch rises in sw Macon County and flows ne into Nantahala River.

Pat Stable Ridge, sw Macon County between Kimsey Bald and Pat Stable Branch.

Patsy Creek rises in nw Yancey County and flows se into Roaring Fork.

Patterson, town in central Caldwell County. Founded in 1851 as the site of a textile mill. Inc. 1905 but long inactive in municipal affairs. Named for Samuel Finley Patterson (1799-1874), local resident and state official. Alt. 1,253. Patterson School for boys is operated here by the Episcopal Church.

Patterson Branch rises in ne Cherokee County and flows nw into Junaluska Creek.

Patterson Branch rises in central Franklin County and flows se into Fox Creek.

Patterson Branch rises in e Hoke County and flows sw into Puppy Creek.

Patterson Branch rises in n Yancey County and flows se into Jacks Creek.

Patterson Creek rises in nw Iredell County and flows e into Rocky Creek. Formerly known as Big Rocky Creek.

Patterson Creek rises in w Lee County and flows nw into Deep River.

Patterson Creek rises in s central Transylvania County and flows se into French Broad River.

Pattersons Mill. See Roberta.

Patterson Springs, community in s Cleveland

County. Alt. 904. Settled in the 1880's. Named for Arthur Patterson, Sr., who lived near Kings Mountain at the time of the battle.

Patterson Top, w Cherokee County n of Hiwassee Dam and e of Anderson Creek.

Patterson Township, former township in sw Alamance County, now township number 1.

Patterson Township, n central Caldwell County.

Patterson Township, former township in sw Durham County, now combined with Cedar Fork Township to form Triangle Township.

Patton Cove, nw Buncombe County e of Hanlon Mountain.

Patton Cove, the valley through which Patton Cove Creek flows in se Buncombe County.

Patton Cove Creek rises near Patton Gap in se Buncombe County and flows n through Patton Cove into Swannanoa River.

Patton Gap, se Buncombe County between Big Flats and High Hickory Knob in the Swannanoa Mountains.

Patton Mountain, central Buncombe County near the headwaters of Ross Creek.

Patton Mountain, central Macon County at the head of Blaine Branch.

Patton Ridge, community in w Wilkes County near the head of South Prong Lewis Fork Creek.

Pattonsville, former community in s Vance County 3 mi. w of the mouth of Tabb Creek on Tar River. Appears on the McRae map, 1833, but not on later maps.

Paul Gamiels Hill Coast Guard Station, located at Paul Gamiels Hill on n end of Bodie Island in e Dare County. Active until after World War II. Est. as lifesaving station in 1878-79. Lifesaving Service and Revenue Cutter Service joined to form United States Coast Guard in 1915.

Pauls Creek rises in Virginia and flows s into Surry County where it enters Stewarts Creek. Approx. 14 mi. long.

Pauls Gap, on the Haywood-Swain County line between Cataloochee Balsam and Sugar Tree Licks. Alt. approx. 5,100.

Paw Creek rises in w Mecklenburg County and flows sw into Catawba River.

Paw Creek, community in w Mecklenburg County. Name of the railroad depot is Thrift.

Paw Creek Township, former township in w central Mecklenburg County, now township number 12.

Pawpaw Creek rises in s Madison County and flows ne into French Broad River.

Pawpaw Creek rises in nw Rockingham County and flows sw into Mayo River.

Pawpaw Creek rises in nw Swain County and flows sw into Eagle Creek.

Paw Paw Ridge, Great Smoky Mountains National Park, nw Swain County, extends sw from Cherry Knob on Jenkins Trail Ridge, lat. 35° 30' 50" N., long. 83° 44' 52" W.

Paxton Creek rises in central McDowell County and flows se approx. 2 mi. into Clear Creek. Formerly known as Poplar Cove Creek.

Paxton Creek rises in s Transylvania County and flows ne into French Broad River.

Payne Branch rises in nw Swain County and flows se into Fontana Lake.

Payne Branch rises in s Watauga County and flows ne into Middle Fork [of South Fork New River].

Payne Mountain, sw Cherokee County extends ne from Wolf Pen Gap to Harris Top.

Paynes Branch rises in sw Clay County and flows ne into Brasstown Creek.

Paynes Knob, central Buncombe County ne of Rocky Knob.

Paynes Store, community in se Alexander County.

Paynes Tavern, community in s Person County near North Flat River. Cornwallis spent a night here in 1781 during the Revolution. The Tavern has long since ceased to exist.

Pea Branch rises in e Pitt County and flows e into Tranters Creek.

Peace, community in sw Wake County.

Peach, community in n Perquimans County.

Peach Bottom Mountains, a range of high, grass-covered mountains extending across most of Alleghany County from sw to n central. Among the named peaks are Cheek, Fender, and Doughton mountains and Bald Knob.

Peach Knob, central Buncombe County, sw of Craven Gap in Elk Mountains.

Peachland, town in w Anson County. Originally known as Mulcahy; name changed in 1888 for a large peach orchard nearby. Inc. 1895. Alt. 446.

Peach Orchard, mountain in the Cane Creek Mountains, s Alamance County.

Peach Orchard Creek rises in ne Buncombe County and flows w into Carter Creek.

Peachtree, community in e Cherokee County.

Peachtree Branch rises in se Duplin County and flows w into Mill Branch.

Peachtree Creek rises in ne Cherokee County and flows sw into Hiwassee River in the central part of the county.

Peachtree Creek rises in central Swain County and flows sw into Tuckasegee River.

Peachtree Creek rises in e central Wake County and flows w into Neuse River near Milburnie.

Peachtree Creek. See White Oak Swamp.

Peachtree Gap, on Graham-Swain County line between Broke-Yoke Gap and Round Top.

Peachtree Knob, on the Cherokee-Clay County line. Alt. 4,200.

Peacocks, community in n Columbus County. Earlier known as Peacocks Store.

Peacock's Bridge, se Wilson County over Contentnea Creek approx. 1½ mi. se of Stantonsburg. A bridge existed here by 1751 and is shown on the Price map, 1808, and on the MacRae map, 1833. Here Lt. Col. Banastre Tarleton's British dragoons and Col. James Gorhams militia engaged in a skirmish, May, 1781. Known for a time as Ruffin's Bridge.

Peacocks Crossroads, community in sw Johnston County.

Pea Hill Creek rises in s Virginia and flows s into Northampton County where it enters Roanoke River. Appears on the map of the North Carolina-Virginia line run by William Byrd and others, 1728.

Pea Island, part of the Outer Banks in e Dare County bounded on the n by Oregon Inlet and on the s by Hatteras Island. Also known as Chicamacomico Banks, which see.

Pea Island Migratory Waterfowl Refuge, a national bird sanctuary covering all of Pea Island and the n end of Hatteras Island to Chicamacomico Coast Guard Station.

The Peak, mountain in e Ashe County between Peak Creek and South Fork New River. Alt. approx. 3,950.

The Peak, mountain in sw Ashe County. Alt. 5,195.

The Peak, sw Mitchell County between Crabtree Creek and North Toe River. Alt. 3,866.

Peak Creek rises on the Ashe-Wilkes County line near Mulberry Gap and flows nw into South Fork New River.

Peak Creek Township, e Ashe County.

Peaked Knob, on the Haywood County, N.C.-Cocke County, Tenn., line. Alt. 3,370.

Peaked Top, central Caldwell County near the headwaters of Abingdon Creek.

Peak Knob, e Macon County between Grindstone Knob and the head of Moses Branch.

Peak Mountain, ne Avery County.

Peaks Bald, on the Macon-Swain County line between Davis Bald and Low Gap.

Pea Landing. See Calabash.

Pearce Crossroads, community in s Franklin County.

Pearce's Creek rises in n Burke County and flows e into Carroll's Creek.

Pearces Mill Township, central Cumberland County.

Pearceville, community in nw Camden County. Named for Pearce family from New England which settled here following the Revolution. Often appears on maps as Pierceville.

Pea Ridge, elevated sandy area in n Washington County on Albemarle Sound extending ne from Leonards Point.

Pea Ridge, community in e Polk County. Alt. 1,050.

Pea Ridge. See Cycle.

Pea Ridge. See Ridgeville.

Pearsall, community in n Duplin County.

Pearson Knob, mountain in nw Alexander County. Alt. 1,898.

Pearson's Falls, sw Polk County between town of Saluda and city of Tryon on Colt Creek. Named for Charles William Pearson, former owner of the site. The falls tumble over 75 ft. of rugged rock. The surrounding 308 acres contain a wild flower sanctuary and herbarium maintained by the Tryon Garden Club. There are more than 200 different varieties of flowers and woodland growth here, described by Donald Culross Peattie in his book, A Natural History of Pearson's Falls.

Peartree Point extends from the mainland into the mouth of Alligator River in ne Tyrrell County.

Peckerwood Creek rises in n Cherokee County and flows sw into Tellicoe River.

Peckerwood Creek rises in central Clay County and flows nw into Tusquitee

Creek. Named for an Indian, Jim Peckerwood, who lived near its head.

Peckerwood Ridge, n Cherokee County.

Pecks Corner, mountain, on the Swain County, N.C.-Sevier County, Tenn., line at the head of Enloe Creek. Alt. approx. 5,700. Also known as Pecks Peak.

Pecks Peak. *See* Pecks Corner.

Pedlars Hill. *See* Pleasant Hill.

Peebles Tavern. *See* Garysburg.

Pee Dee, community in e Anson County.

Pee Dee, community in w Montgomery County. Produces hosiery and lumber.

Pee Dee River is formed by the junction of the Yadkin and Uwharrie rivers in Montgomery County. It flows s along the Stanly-Montgomery and Anson-Richmond County lines into South Carolina where it empties into Winyah Bay. Also known as Great Pee Dee River. The name may be a Catawba Indian word *pi'ri,* "something good," or *pfhere,* "smart," "expert," or "capable."

Peedee Township, w Montgomery County.

Peek, community in e Madison County.

Peeks Creek rises in s Macon County and flows ne into Cullasaja River.

Peele Branch rises in ne Bertie County and flows sw into Chinkapin Swamp.

Peeler Creek rises in s Davie County and flows se approx. 2 mi. into Yadkin River.

Peels Top, nw Cherokee County in the Unicoi Mountains.

Peewee Branch rises in w Jackson County and flows s into Greens Creek.

Peggy Gap on the head of Camp Creek in nw Jackson County.

Peggy Knob, s Macon County between Tessentee Creek and Bennies Branch.

Peggy Peak, sw Buncombe County at the e end of Smathers View Mountain.

Pekin, community in s Montgomery County. A post office, Chisholm's Store, existed here as early as 1828; the name had been changed by 1882 to Pekin.

Peletier, community in w Carteret County. Named for family of same name.

Peletier Creek rises in s Carteret County and flows s into Bogue Sound. Probably named for Gerome (or Jerome) Peletier, first of the family to settle in the vicinity.

Pelham, community in nw Caswell County. Est. during the Civil War as a station on the Piedmont Railroad; named for Major John Pelham, Alabamian, killed in action during the war. Alt. 740.

Pelham Precinct appears on the Wimble

map, 1738, between the Cape Fear and the Northeast Cape Fear rivers at approx. what is now Pender County. Wimble's map was dedicated to Thomas Hollis Pelham, Duke of Newcastle (1693-1768), Secretary of State for the Southern Department. Pelham County appears at the same location on the Mouzon map, 1775. Since there appears to be no reference to such a precinct or county in the records of North Carolina it is possible that Wimble was simply flattering his patron and that Mouzon followed Wimble's map in making his own.

Pelham Township, nw Caswell County.

Pell Mell Pocosin, n central Bertie County.

Pembroke, town in w central Robeson County. Alt. 172. Inc. 1895. Originally called Campbell's Mill on Waterhole Swamp; later, Scuffletown, after Scoville Town in England, or because it was a good place to get into a fight. Today, it is center of Lumbee Indian business and social life. Named for Pembroke Jones (1825-1910), an official of the Wilmington and Weldon Railroad which intersected the Wilmington, Charlotte, and Rutherford Railroad here. Home of Pembroke State College, founded in 1887. Produces apparel.

Pembroke Creek rises in Pollock Swamp, e Chowan County, and flows s and se into the w side of the head of Edenton Bay. Formerly known as the w branch of Mattacomack Creek and later of Queen Anne's Creek. Took its present name from Thomas Barker's plantation, Pembroke, which was named for his birthplace, Pembroke, Massachusetts. Barker bought his property from Edmund Gale about 1751. *See also* Ramushawn River.

Pembroke Township, central Robeson County.

Pender, community immediately s of the town of Halifax, e Halifax County.

Pender County was formed in 1875 from New Hanover County. Located in the se section of the state, it is bounded by the Atlantic Ocean, and by New Hanover, Brunswick, Columbus, Bladen, Sampson, Duplin, and Onslow counties. It was named for General William D. Pender (1834-63), a Confederate officer killed at Gettysburg. Area: 869 sq. mi. (857, land; 12, water). County seat: Burgaw with an elevation of 49 ft. Townships are Burgaw, Canetuck, Caswell, Columbia, Grady, Holly, Long Creek, Rocky Point, Topsail, and Union. Produces corn, oats, soybeans, miscellaneous fruits and vegetables, peanuts, poultry, eggs, hogs, dairy products, livestock, and lumber. See also, Pelham Precinct; Lillington County.

Pendergrass Mountain, central Macon County between Blaine Branch and the heads of Battle Branch and Salser Branch.

Penderlea, community in nw Pender County. Beginning in 1934 the U. S. government purchased a total of 10,500 acres which was subdivided into tracts of about 30 acres each. Houses and other buildings were erected and farmers, removed from submarginal land taken out of cultivation by the government, were moved into this area. A total of 142 farm units were established, and a school, community center, and lake were built. The farms were later sold to those who lived on them. Approximately the same land in Penderlea had been purchased after the Civil War by a carpetbagger, E. R. Brink. He subdivided it, prepared an attractive map, and sold about 50 farms to people in New York City. His mortgage with a Wilmington bank was foreclosed, and the New Yorkers lost their farms and money.

Pender's Crossroads, community in e Wilson County near White Swamp and Town Creek. Confederate Major General William Dorsey Pender (1834-63) born nearby.

Pendleton, town in ne Northampton County. Est. about 1887; inc. 1893. Known as Woodward's Crossroads until renamed to honor an employee of the railroad on the first train to pass through. Alt. 84.

Penelo, community in central Edgecombe County.

Penelope. See Longview.

Penland, community in s Mitchell County on North Toe River. Alt. 2,462. Named for Milton P. Penland, pioneer settler and businessman. Penland School for Handi-

crafts has grown out of a school est. here in 1910.

Penland Bald, on the Clay-Macon County line at the head of Park Creek. Alt. approx. 5,000.

Penland Cove, se Cherokee County at the ne end of Poor House Mountain.

Penland Gap, on Middle Ridge in sw Macon County.

Penland Yellow. See Big Bald.

Penley, community in se Watauga County.

Penley Branch rises in s Watauga County and flows se into Middle Fork [of South Fork New River].

Penly Cove, central Buncombe County e of Bee Ridge.

Pennix Cove, n Buncombe County, e of Hemphill Mountain.

Penn Point, in central Carteret County extending into Newport River.

Penny Hill, town on the Edgecombe-Pitt County line on Tar River. Inc. 1875 but no longer active in municipal affairs.

Pennys Hill, a large sand hill at the present community of Seagull on Currituck Banks, e Currituck County, has been an outstanding landmark since the early eighteenth century.

Penrose, community in e Transylvania County between Lydia Creek and French Broad River. Alt. 2,087.

Pensacola, community in s Yancey County on Cane River. Alt. 2,858. Named from an Indian word probably meaning "hair people," for those who wore their hair long.

Pensacola Township, s central Yancey County.

Penson Knob, s Macon County between Dover Knob and the Georgia state line.

Penson Mountain, s Macon County between Middle Creek and Norton Branch.

Peoria, community in nw Watauga County on the head of Stone Mountain Branch.

Pepper Creek rises in ne McDowell County and flows s into North Fork [Catawba River] near North Cove.

Peppers, community in w Mitchell County on Bee Creek.

Perfection, community in w Craven County.

Perkins Branch rises in central Watauga County and flows s into Hardin Creek.

Perkinsville, community in n Burke County on John's River.

Perkinsville, town authorized in 1819 to be laid off on the land of Constantine Perkins "on the main Hallow road" in the

vicinity of modern Mount Airy, ne Surry
County. There is no evidence that any
building activity took place before 1848,
after which the town of Mount Airy
began to develop.

Perkinsville, community in central Watauga County on Perkins Branch and
Hardin Creek.

Permetter Creek rises in n central Anson
County and flows s into Brown Creek.
Named for the Permenter family, early
settlers.

Permudas Island, s Onslow County in Stump
Sound, approx. 1½ mi. long.

Perquimans County was formed by 1679 as
Berkeley precinct in Albemarle County.
Located in the ne section of the state, it
is bounded by Albemarle Sound and by
Chowan, Gates, and Pasquotank counties.
It was named for Indians in the vicinity.
The legislature met here, 1707-16. Area:
324 sq. mi. (261 land, 63 water). County
seat: Hertford with an alt. of 15 ft.
Townships are Belvidere, Bethel, Hertford, New Hope, and Parkville. Produces
corn, soybeans, peanuts, cotton, hogs,
livestock, apparel, and sand.

Perquimans River rises in the Dismal
Swamp in n Perquimans County and
flows se into Albemarle Sound. Appears
as Pequaimings River on the Comberford
map, 1657; as Wiquemans on the Ogilby
map, 1671; and as Paquinous on the
Hack map, 1684.

Perrishoes Creek. See Raccoon Creek.

Perry, community in nw Gaston County.

Perry Creek rises in e Clay County and
flows w through Joe Cove into Tusquitee
Creek.

Perry Creek rises in central Henderson
County and flows ne into Osceola Lake.

Perry Creek rises in e Wake County and
flows se into Little River. Formerly
known as Middle Prong of Little River.

Perry Creek rises in n central Wake County
and flows e, through Gresham's Lake and
into Neuse River. Shown as Simes Creek
on Bevers map, 1870.

Perry Gap, e Clay County between the
headwaters of Perry and Barnett creeks.

Perry Knob, n Graham County between
Cables Cove Creek and Tuskegee Creek.

Perry Knob. See Perry Top.

Perry Ridge, central Avery County.

Perrys Pond in ne Wake County on Buffalo
Creek. Formed in 1910, covers 20 acres
with a max. depth of 10 ft. Open to the
public; used for recreation.

Perry Store, community in n Wake County.

Perry Top, peak in Plott Balsams in n
Jackson County on the head of Monteith
Branch. Also called Perry Knob. Alt.
5,080.

Perrytown, community in ne Bertie County.

Pershing. See Delco.

Persimmon Branch rises in central Duplin
County and flows se and ne into Northeast Cape Fear River.

Persimmon Branch rises in ne Washington
County and flows n and ne into Deep
Creek.

Persimmon Creek rises in sw Cherokee
County and flows ne into Hiwassee River.
A fixed level impoundment of Persimmon
Creek covers an area of 100 acres and
overflows into Hiwassee Lake. It is main-
tained by the National Forest Service.

Persimmon Creek rises in e Cleveland
County and flows sw into Muddy Fork.

Persimmon Creek rises in central Lee County and flows n into Big Buffalo Creek.

Persimmon Creek, community in w Cherokee County.

Persimmon Ridge, se Avery County.

Persimmon Swamp rises in sw Brunswick
County and flows n into Shingletree
Swamp.

Person Branch rises in n Franklin County
and flows sw into Sandy Creek.

Person County was formed in 1791 from
Caswell County. Located in the n cen-
tral section of the state, it is bounded
by the state of Virginia, and by Granville,
Durham, Orange, and Caswell counties.
It was named for General Thomas
Person (1733-1800), Revolutionary patriot,

member of the Council of Safety, and benefactor of the University of North Carolina. Area: 400 sq. mi. County seat: Roxboro with an elevation of 671 ft. Townships are Allensville, Busby Fork, Cunningham, Flat River, Holloway, Mount Tirzah, Olive Hill, Roxboro, and Woodsdale. Produces tobacco, corn, wheat, oats, poultry, eggs, dairy products, livestock, hogs, textiles, lumber, and fabricated metals. Copper was formerly mined in the county.

Person Ordinary. See Littleton.

Perth, community in nw Bladen County.

Peru, community in s Onslow County on New River.

Pescud. See Thermal City.

Petche Gap, s central Burke County.

Peter Cove, s Haywood County on the head of Peter Cove Branch.

Peter Cove Branch rises in s Haywood County and flows se into Bird Creek.

Peter Cove Creek rises in ne Madison County and flows sw into Foster Creek.

Peter Cove Mountain, e Madison County between Foster Creek and Roaring Fork.

Peter Dick Gap, central Cherokee County near the head of Cook Creek and n of Flea Mountain. Named for an early settler.

Peter Mashoes Creek, a bay off the mainland of central Dare County in the waters of Croatan Sound. The community of Mashoes is located on this creek. For a legend concerning Peter Mashoes see Mashoes.

Petersburg, community in s Madison County on Bull Creek. Alt. 1,972.

Petersburg, community on Jenkins Swamp in n Onslow County.

Petersburg Crossing, a crossroads community in e Duplin County.

Peters Creek rises in ne Bladen County and flows ne across se tip of Cumberland County, then back into Bladen County where it enters South River.

Peters Creek rises in central Forsyth County in Winston-Salem and flows sw and s through the city into Middle Fork. Probably named for 28-year-old Hans Petersen who was among the first settlers at Bethabara, 1753.

Peters Creek rises in Virginia and flows s into Stokes County where it enters Dan River. This was the w limit of William Byrd's survey of the North Carolina-Virginia boundary in 1728.

Peters Creek, community in n central Stokes County on the Virginia line. Peters post office in the late nineteenth century was here.

Peters Creek Township, n central Stokes County.

Peters Ferry. See Grifton.

Peterson, community in se Bertie County.

Peterson, community in w Mitchell County on Nolichucky River. Also known as Warrick.

Peterson Branch rises in n Yancey County and flows s into Jacks Creek.

Peterson Gap, n Mitchell County on Fork Mountain.

Peterson Inn. See Littleton.

Peterson Ridge, n Yancey County between Cooper Gap and Bee Branch.

Peters Point, point of land 1 mi. nw of Fort Fisher in s New Hanover County extending into the Cape Fear River near its mouth. See also Point Peter.

Peter Swamp rises at the se shore of Warwick Bay in e Robeson County and flows e into Big Swamp.

Peter Weaver Creek rises in s Jackson County and flows se then ne into Morgan Mill Creek.

Petra Mills, a small farming community in se Caldwell County.

Pett, community in e central Wake County

Pettifords Creek. See Pettivers Creek.

Pettigrew State Park, e Washington and w Tyrrell counties, 9 mi. s of Creswell. Contains 16,828 acres, including 16,600-acre Lake Phelps. Est. 1939. Address: Route 1, Creswell. Scenic, recreational, historical; fishing. Somerset House, antebellum mansion, included in area. See also Somerset.

Pettivers Bay at the mouth of Pettivers Creek in White Oak River, w Carteret County. Also known as Hampton Bay.

Pettivers Creek rises in w Carteret County and flows sw approx. 8 mi. into White Oak River. Named for John Pettiver who owned land in the vicinity as early as 1728. Sometimes also called Pettifords Creek.

Petty Gulf Creek rises in e Anson County and flows s into Blewett Falls Lake.

Petty Point, peninsula extending from ne Pamlico County into Bay River.

Pettys Shore, community in e Hertford County on Chowan River at the site of an earlier Indian village. A large fishery once was operated here.

Pfafftown, community in w Forsyth County.

Named for Peter Pfaff who arrived in the Wachovia settlement in 1771.

Pharisee Swamp rises in se Sampson County and flows ne into Bulltail Swamp.

Pheasant Creek in the tidal marsh islands of Bear Banks, se Onslow County. Named for the pheasants formerly found here. Known also as Nicks Creek for Nick Moore.

Phelps Point. See Hertford.

Philadelphus, community in n Robeson County on Richland Swamp. Settled 1796-1799 and site of an early private academy.

Philadelphus Township, w central Robeson County.

Phillip Knob, s Swain County between Yalaka Creek and Little Yalaka Creek.

Phillips' Branch rises in w Caldwell County and flows e into Wilson's Creek.

Phillips Branch rises in e Haywood County and flows e into Fines Creek.

Phillips Branch rises in n central Henderson County and flows se into Clear Creek.

Phillips Branch rises in w Watauga County and flows se into East Fork [Cove Creek].

Phillips Creek rises in nw Bladen County and flows s into Cape Fear River.

Phillips Creek rises in ne Cherokee County and flows ne into Tatham Creek.

Phillips Creek rises in s Transylvania County and flows nw into Hogshead Creek.

Phillips Crossroads, community in n Jones County.

Phillips Gap, on the Ashe-Wilkes County line.

Phillips Knob, n Alexander County.

Phillips Knob, n central Yancey County on the head of Guilders Creek, 1½ mi. n of town of Burnsville. Alt. 4,390.

Phillipsville, community in e Haywood County on the w outskirts of Canton.

Phils Creek rises in s Orange County and flows se into University Lake.

Phin's Island, in the e end of Brown's Sound in s Onslow County. Probably named for Phineas Stephens, an early landholder on Bear Creek.

Phipps Branch rises in e Yancey County and flows w into South Toe River. Named for Sidney Phipps, an early settler.

Phipps Cove, w Swain County between Yalaka Creek and Stevenson Branch, almost entirely submerged by the backwaters of Fontana Lake.

Phipps Creek rises in w Yancey County and flows nw into Cane River.

Phipps Gap, w Yancey County between Indian and Price creeks.

Phoebes Creek rises in w Warren County and flows ne into Fishing Creek.

Phoenix, community in ne Brunswick County. A post office by this name est. by 1882; named for the mythical bird which, after death, rises again from its own ashes. Alt. 40.

Phoenix Creek rises on the e side of Phoenix Mountain central Ashe County, and flows n into North Fork New River.

Phoenix Mine Village, former community in e Cabarrus County at site of Phoenix Mine. Period of greatest activity was from 1870-1907, when the chlorination process for treatment of gold ores was perfected here by Captain Adolph Thies. At the time, this was a notable step forward in metallurgy. The mine shafts were de-watered in 1955 for further ore-deposit appraisals.

Phoenix Mountain, central Ashe County. Alt. 4,673-4,700.

Pickards Mountain, sw Orange County on the head of Morgan Creek.

Pick Breeches Creek rises in ne Watauga County and flows se into Rube Creek.

Pickens Gap, nw Swain County on the s end of Jenkins Trail Ridge.

Pickens Nose, mountain in s Macon County between Betty Creek and Dryman Fork. Alt. approx. 4,900.

Picket Branch rises in ne Cherokee County and flows se and sw into Valley River.

Picketts Bay, an arm of White Oak River n of Swansboro, se Onslow County, between Muddy Creek and Mount Pleasant Point.

Picks. See Somerset.

Pick's Sliding. See Somerset.

Picture Creek rises in sw Granville County and flows sw into Knap of Reeds Creek.

Piedmont or Piedmont Plateau extends from the fall line (see Coastal Plain) on the e to the Blue Ridge. In elevation the area ranges from approx. 500 ft. above sea level on the e to 1,500 ft. on the w. Rolling hills and stiff clay soil are characteristic of the Piedmont. The Indians knew this region as Tar-ko-ee, "Catawba Land," or "Under Hills."

Piedmont, community in central Mecklenburg County, e of Charlotte.

Piedmont Crescent is an extended area in the Piedmont section of the state from Wake County on the e through Durham, Orange, Alamance, Guilford, Randolph,

Forsyth, Davidson, Rowan, Cabarrus, Mecklenburg, Gaston, and Lincoln counties. It contains numerous rapidly growing urban and industrial areas most of which had their beginning along the route of the old North Carolina Railroad.

Piedmont Lake in se Transylvania County near Panther Mountain drains s into Little River. Covers 5 acres with a max. depth of 12 ft.

Piedmont Springs, former resort in nw Burke County. Now abandoned.

Piedmont Springs, community in central Stokes County on Dan River. A popular resort from about 1900 to 1930, when the hotel burned. Some cottages still in use.

The Piedmont Triad, a term used for the Greensboro, High Point, Winston-Salem area.

Pierce Creek rises in nw Macon County and flows ne into Nantahala River.

Pierce Creek rises in se Pamlico County and flows se into Neuse River. Named for Edmond Pierce who settled here in 1708.

Pierces Crossroads, community in n Halifax County. Named for the Pierce family which settled here in 1812.

Pierceville. *See* Pearceville.

Pig Basket Creek rises in nw Nash County and flows se into Stony Creek. Legend says that an early settler, going home with a basket of newborn pigs, dropped them into the water as he tried to cross this stream when it was swollen after a storm.

Pigeon Branch rises in n Transylvania County near Pigeon Gap and flows se into South Fork Mills River.

Pigeon Creek rises in ne Swain County and flows nw into Raven Fork.

Pigeon Creek rises in s Swain County and flows sw into Yalaka Creek.

Pigeon Flats Bay, a sand filled bay in s Sampson County. *See also* Carolina Bays.

Pigeon Gap, s Haywood County on the head of Bird Creek.

Pigeon Gap on the Haywood-Transylvainia County line on Pisgah Ridge between Green Knob and Wagon Road Ridge.

Pigeon House Branch rises in central Wake County within the city limits of Raleigh. It rises in what is now Cameron Village and flows e into Crabtree Creek.

Pigeon Ledge, on the Haywood-Buncombe County Line.

Pigeon River is formed in se Haywood County by the junction of East Fork Pigeon River and West Fork Pigeon River. It flows nw into Tennessee where it ent..rs French Broad River. Known by the Cherokee Indians as *Nee-oh-la. See also* Canton.

Pigeonroost, community in w Mitchell County on Pigeonroost Creek. Named when carrier pigeons, now extinct, were common in this area.

Pigeonroost Creek rises in nw Mitchell County and flows sw into Toe River.

Pigeonroost Creek rises in w Watauga County and flows ne into Dutch Creek. *See also* Dutch Creek Falls.

Pigeon Township, s central Haywood County.

Pigpen Bluff, ne Yancey County at the s end of Green Mountain.

Pigpen Cove, ne Buncombe County between Pinnacle Mountain and Cedar Cliff Knob.

Pigpen Creek rises in ne Yancey County and flows nw into Toe River.

Pigpen Flats, se Swain County on the head of Connelly Creek.

Pigpen Knob, ne Buncombe County between High Knob and Sheepwallow Knob.

Pigpen Knob, s Watauga County between Buck Ridge and Fall Ridge.

Pig Point, extends into s waters of Currituck Sound in s Currituck County.

Pigtail, community in central Caldwell County near Hulme Hill.

Pike Creek rises in central Pender County and flows se into Northeast Cape Fear River.

Pike Crossroads, community in w Wayne County between Little River and Nahunta Swamp. Named for Quaker family which settled in the area prior to 1758.

Pike Road, community in n Beaufort County.

Pikeville, town in n Wayne County in a region first settled by Quakers and on land originally granted to Samuel Pike in 1763. Land transferred in 1785 to Nathan Pike, for whom the town was named. Inc. in 1891. Alt. 142.

Pikeville Township, n central Wayne County.

Pilands Crossroads, community in se Hertford County.

Pile Creek rises in ne Cherokee County and flows s into Valley River.

Pilkey Creek rises in w Swain County and flows sw into Fontana Lake.

Pilot, community in s Franklin County.

Pilot Cove, n Transylvania County, extends se from Slate Rock Ridge to Bradley Creek.

Pilot Creek rises in e Surry County and flows sw into Ararat River.

Pilot Gap, w Swain County on Pilot Ridge.

Pilot Knob, on Avery-Caldwell County line.

Pilot Knob, s Madison County at the head of Bailey Branch.

Pilot Knob, Great Smoky Mountains National Park, w Swain County, at the se end of Pilot Ridge, lat. 35° 27′ 53″ N., long. 83° 34′ 22″ W. Alt. 2,967.

Pilot Mountain, on Burke-McDowell County line. Alt. 2,050.

Pilot Mountain, se Caldwell County. Alt. 1,486.

Pilot Mountain, on Lewis Creek in e Henderson County. Alt. 2,608.

Pilot Mountain in central Jackson County between Stoal Creek and Betsy Branch. Alt. 4,059.

Pilot Mountain, e Randolph County.

Pilot Mountain, se Surry County. Alt. 2,700. The mountain is an isolated peak surviving from ancient mountains which have eroded away. The peak stands 1,500 ft. above the surrounding countryside and served as a landmark for Indians and pioneer white settlers of the area. Appears as "Mount Ararat or the Stonehead" on the Fry-Jefferson map, 1753, and as Mount Ararat on the Collet map, 1770. Price's map, 1808, and subsequent maps show it with the present name. Called "Jomeokee" by the Indians, meaning "The Great Guide." The Devil's Den on Pilot Mountain is a small grotto from which a steady breeze blows at all times. See also Brushy Mountains.

Pilot Mountain, w Transylvania County s of Deep Gap. Alt. 5,151.

Pilot Mountain, s Wilkes County s of Hunting Creek.

Pilot Mountain, town in e Surry County. Alt. 1,100. Inc. 1889. Named for the nearby mountain.

Pilot Ridge, central Madison County parallel to Teat Branch. Walnut Knob is on the s end of this ridge.

Pilot Ridge, Great Smoky Mountains National Park, w Swain County, a spur of Welch Ridge extending se from Cherry Gap to Pilot Knob, lat. 35° 28′ 18″ N., long. 83° 35′ 37″ W.

Pilot Rock, n Transylvania County between Dividing Ridge and Pilot Cove.

Pilot Township, e Surry County.

Pilot View, community in central Yadkin County between North Deep and Forbush creeks. Formerly known as Sugartown.

Pinchback's Tavern. See Clarksville.

Pinchgut Branch rises in s Duplin County and flows s into Island Creek.

Pinch Gut Branch rises in e Surry County and flows se into Stokes County where it enters Big Creek. Said to have been named by Saura Indians who almost starved in the vicinity because of the scarcity of game.

Pinch Gut Creek rises in w Anson County and flows n into Brown Creek.

Pinch Gut Creek rises in e central Brunswick County and flows s to join Red Run in forming Lockwoods Folly River.

Pinchgut Creek rises in nw Caldwell County and flows e into Johns River. See also, Coldass Creek.

Pinch Gut Creek rises in s Catawba County and flows sw into Maiden Creek.

Pinckton, community in nw Ashe County. Alt. approx. 3,498.

Pine. See Stokesdale.

Pine Barrens. See Sandhills.

Pinebluff, town in s Moore County. Settled approx. 1890. Inc. in 1899. Named for the longleaf pine in the vicinity. Alt. 307.

Pine Branch rises in central Avery County and flows n into Plumtree Creek.

Pine Branch rises in w Macon County and flows ne into Dicks Creek.

Pine Branch rises in e central Madison County and flows n into Big Laurel Creek.

Pine Branch rises in e Mitchell County and flows sw into North Toe River.

Pine Branch rises in n Mitchell County and flows sw into Right Fork Bean Creek.

Pine Branch rises in w Surry County and flows sw into Mitchell River.

Pine Cabbin. See Weaverville.

Pine Camp Branch rises in n Avery County and flows w into Tennessee where it enters Elk River.

Pine Creek rises in w Jackson County and flows ne into Lake Thorpe.

Pinedene, community in s Moore County, s of town of Southern Pines.

Pine Gap Branch rises in w Swain County and flows nw into Hazel Creek.

Pine Grove, community in se Craven County on Tucker Creek. Alt. 23.

Pine Hall, community in se Stokes County. Named for the pine trees growing here.

Pine Hammock, a tidal marsh island approx. 1¼ mi. long in n Pamlico County.

Pine Hill, mountain in the Cane Creek Mountains, s Alamance County.

Pinehurst, town in s Moore County. Settled 1895. Inc. 1949. Named for its location in a pine forest. A popular winter resort with five 18-hole golf courses. Alt. 536.

Pine Knob, on the Avery-Mitchell County line.

Pine Knob, central Buncombe County between Rocky Knob and Jack Gap.

Pine Knob, n Cherokee County.

Pine Knob, se Clay County at n end of Sharptop Ridge. Alt. approx. 3,650.

Pine Knob, on Cash Creek in w Henderson County.

Pine Knob, nw Jackson County between Gibbs Branch and Oconaluftee River.

Pine Knob, s Macon County between Plass Gap and High Top.

Pine Knob, w Mitchell County between Pigeonroost Creek and Brummett Creek.

Pine Knob, n Rutherford County between two unnamed branches which are the headwaters of Mountain Creek. Alt. approx. 1,555. Sometimes known as Piney Knob.

Pine Knob, se Watauga County n of Bens Ridge.

Pine Knob Branch rises in se Watauga County and flows ne into Laurel Fork.

Pine Level, town in e Johnston County. Settled about 1868; inc. 1874. Named for pine forest and level land of the area. Alt. 155. Produces cottonseed oil.

Pine Level Township, e central Johnston County.

Pinelog, community in sw Clay County on Pinelog Creek.

Pinelog, community in central Columbus County.

Pinelog Branch rises in nw Beaufort County and flows w into Tranters Creek.

Pine Log Branch rises in n Nash County and flows ne into Beaverdam Swamp.

Pinelog Branch rises in w Pitt County and flows sw into Little Contentnea Creek.

Pine Log Creek rises in w Anson County and flows n into Richardson Creek.

Pinelog Creek rises in sw Clay County and flows ne into Brasstown Creek.

Pinelog Swamp, rises in n Columbus County and flows s into Soules Swamp.

Pine Mountain, n Buncombe County between Moody Cove and Maney Branch.

Pine Mountain on the Buncombe-Henderson County line between Double Head and Cold Knob.

Pine Mountain, in the South Mountains in se Burke County. Alt. 1,821.

Pine Mountain, s Macon County between Jones Creek and South Fork [Skeenah Creek].

Pine Mountain, sw Macon County between Park Creek and Nantahala River.

Pine Mountain, sw Madison County between Norton Fork Creek and Friezeland Creek.

Pine Mountain, w Madison County between Partridge Gap Ridge and Spring Creek.

Pine Mountain, s Mitchell County between Brushy Creek and North Toe River.

Pine Mountain, ne Transylvania County between Sitton Creek and Osborn Branch.

Pine Mountain, n central Transylvania County on the head of Allison Creek.

Pine Mountain, e Transylvania County between Blythe Branch and Ballard Gap.

Pineola, community in s Avery County on Linville River. Alt. 3,538. Post office est. here in 1899 as Saginaw. Name changed to Pineola in 1914, for the pine trees growing in the vicinity and for Ola Penland, daughter of a local hotel-keeper.

Pine Orchard Mountain, n Watauga County extends ne from the head of Riddle Fork.

Pine Plains. See Cape Fear Section.

Pine Ridge, central Avery County.

Pine Ridge, s Buncombe County between Laurel Branch and Boyd Branch.

Pine Ridge extends from nw Burke County into w Caldwell County.

Pine Ridge, w Graham County between Cold Branch and Johns Branch.

Pine Ridge, w Jackson County between Brush Fork and Sugar Fork.

Pine Ridge, along the n bank of the Tuckasegee River opposite Barkers Creek community in w Jackson County.

Pine Ridge, s Macon County between South Fork [Skeenah Creek] and North Fork [Skeenah Creek].

Pine Ridge, e Mitchell County between Dry Branch and Left Fork [Cane Creek].

Pine Ridge, n Mitchell County between Hughes Branch and Bean Creek.

Pine Ridge, s Watauga County extends sw parallel with Flannery Fork [South Fork New River].

Pine Ridge, se Yancey County extends ne between South Toe River and Pine Ridge Branch.

Pine Ridge, community in e Mecklenburg County.

Pine Ridge, community in n Surry County between Little Fisher River and Stewart Creek. Alt. 1,347.

Pine Ridge Branch rises in se Yancey County and flows s into Three Forks Creek.

Pineroot Branch rises in n Mitchell County and flows w into Big Rock Creek.

Pine Run rises in e Watauga County and flows ne into South Fork New River.

Pine Stand Ridge, n Cherokee County, extends se from Copper Ridge to the junction of Beaverdam and Garreck creeks.

Pine Station, community in s Wake County.

Pine Swamp rises in s Ashe County and flows n into South Fork New River.

Pine Swamp Branch rises in central Yancey County and flows sw into Cane River.

Pine Swamp Creek rises in s Alleghany County and flows n into Little River.

Pine Swamp Township, se Ashe County.

Pine Top, peak in w Surry County near the head of South Fork.

Pinetops, town in s Edgecombe County. Inc. 1903. Named by Henry Clark Bridgers (1876-1951), founder of the East Carolina Railway which was completed between Tarboro and Hookerton in 1900. On the first run of the new railroad, Bridgers noticed that he could see only the tops of pine trees from the train here. Produces furniture. Alt. 100.

Pinetown, town in n central Beaufort County. Alt. 43. Inc. 1907.

Pine Tree Cove, w Haywood County on Pine Tree Cove Creek.

Pine Tree Cove Creek rises in w Haywood County and flows ne into Jonathans Creek.

Pinetree Creek, a channel of water separated from the main body of Neuse River by two small islands, in central Craven County.

Pine Tree Gap, w Haywood County, Great Smoky Mountains National Park, near lat. 35° 33' 23" N., long. 83° 06' 37" W., between Little Bald Knob and Hemphill Bald. Alt. 5,270.

Pine Tree Mountain, s Buncombe County e of the Biltmore Estate.

Pine Tree Swamp rises in ne Craven County and flows nw into Little Swift Creek.

Pineview, community in w Harnett County. Formerly the center of a large area devoted to dewberry culture. Alt. 320.

Pineville, town in s Mecklenburg County. Inc. 1873. James K. Polk, eleventh President of the United States, was born one

mi. e, 1795. Produces textiles. Alt. 575.

Pineville Township, former township in central Mecklenburg County, now township number 14.

Piney, community in sw Caldwell County, formerly known as Hobart. Alt. 1,309.

Piney Bottom Creek rises on the Fort Bragg Military Reservation, nw Hoke County, and flows sw into Rockfish Creek.

Piney Branch rises in ne Brunswick County and flows e into Jackeye Creek.

Piney Branch rises in n Mitchell County and flows s into Little Rock Creek.

Piney Creek rises in nw Alleghany County and flows n into Virginia where it enters New River.

Piney Creek rises in n central Ashe County and flows se into North Fork New River.

Piney Creek, an inlet on the sound side of Bogue Banks in sw Carteret County.

Piney Creek, community in nw Alleghany County.

Piney Creek Township, nw Alleghany County.

Piney Creek Township, n central Ashe County.

Piney Field Top, e Haywood County between Pisgah Creek and Hungry Creek.

Piney Fork Creek rises in sw Alleghany County and flows sw into e Ashe County where it joins Mulberry Creek to form Cranberry Creek.

Piney Forks Creek rises in s Rockingham County and flows se into Troublesome Creek.

Piney Green, community in central Onslow County between Wallace and Mott creeks near the main gate of Camp Lejeune Marine Base. An early post office, and on the stage route from New Bern to Wilmington. Takes its name from the last eighteenth-century plantation of Joseph Marshall.

Piney Green, community in n Sampson County.

Piney Grove, community in ne Caldwell County.

Piney Grove, community in e Wayne County near the mouth of Walnut Creek in Neuse River. Named for a local church.

Piney Grove. See Pino.

Piney Grove Landing on Pungo River, e Beaufort County.

Piney Grove Run rises in e Beaufort County and flows n into Pungo River.

Piney Grove Township, ne Sampson County.

Piney Island, ne Carteret County, bounded

by Neuse River on the w, Long Bay and West Bay on the e, and Pamlico Sound on the n. Approx. 8 mi. n to s, and 3 mi. e to w.

Piney Island, a small island in Bogue Sound, sw Carteret County.

Piney Island, w portion of Church Island (which see), peninsula in central Currituck County extending into Currituck Sound. Coinjock Bay lies between the w shore and the mainland. Shown as a separate island, Pine Island, on the Mac-Rae map, 1833.

Piney Island Bay, central Currituck County between Coinjock Bay and the sw coast of Piney Island.

Piney Knob. See Pine Knob.

Piney Knob Fork rises in s Macon County and flows ne into Turtle Pond Creek.

Piney Marsh, n Tyrrell County, an area of swampland on Scuppernong River opposite the town of Columbia.

Piney Mountain, sw Buncombe County, e of Bent Mountain.

Piney Mountain, sw Buncombe County s of Peggy Peak.

Piney Mountain, central Buncombe County se of Cisco Mountain.

Piney Mountain, e Davidson County between the headwaters of Fourmile Branch and Flat Swamp Creek.

Piney Mountain, n Haywood County between Stevens Creek and Whiteoak Creek.

Piney Mountain, on Tumble Bug Creek in e Henderson County.

Piney Mountain, n Henderson County between Green Mountain and Clear Creek.

Piney Mountain, on the head of Whiterock Creek in w Jackson County.

Piney Mountain, ridge across w central Polk County. Alt. approx. 1,920.

Piney Mountain, sw Polk County, w of town of Tryon. Alt. 1,550.

Piney Mountain, e Rutherford County between Puzzle Creek and the head of Brushy Creek.

Piney Mountain Creek rises in e Jackson County and flows se to join Rough Butt Creek in forming Caney Fork.

Piney Mountain Ridge, e Jackson County extends ne from Rich Gap to Richland Balsam.

Piney Point, a point extending from mainland in ne Carteret County into Core Sound. See also Stacy.

Piney Point, site of early settlement on e end of Bogue Banks, s Carteret County.

Storms drove out early settlers until the settlement of Salter Path, which see.

Piney Point, sw Carteret County, extends from the w side of Bogue Banks into Bogue Sound. Located near the mouth of Piney Creek. Appears on the Moseley map, 1733.

Piney Point, peninsula in e Pamlico County extending into Pamlico Sound. Appears on the Moseley map, 1733.

Piney Prospect. See Point Prospect.

Piney Ridge, Great Smoky Mountains National Park, nw Swain County, a short spur extending w from Paw Paw Ridge, lat. 35° 31′ 30″ N., long. 83° 45′ 22″ W.

Piney Top, central Clay County at the n end of Big Pine Ridge.

Piney Wood Creek rises in e Swain County and flows sw into Una Creek.

Pin Gap, s Macon County between Foster Knob and the head of Jones Creek.

Pin Hook, community in se Duplin County.

Pin Hook, community in central Northampton County.

Pinhook Gap on the Jackson-Transylvania County line at the head of Bee Tree Fork. Alt. 4,175.

Pink Beds, plateau area in n Transylvania County in Pisgah National Forest. Used extensively as a recreation area. Name comes from the color of rhododendron which once covered the area. Alt. 3,280.

Pink Fox Cove, n Buncombe County between Hemphill and Brank Mountains.

Pink Hill, town in se Lenoir County. A post office est. here in 1849. Inc. 1907. Named for a nearby plantation.

Pink Hill Township, s Lenoir County.

Pinkney, community in nw Wayne County n of Nahunta Swamp.

Pinkney. See South Gastonia.

Pink Ridge, s Avery County.

Pinkston, community in central Anson County. Named about 1911 when railroad construction reached this point on the land of John Pinkston.

The Pinnacle, peak of Holland Mountain in sw Buncombe County. Alt. approx. 4,000.

Pinnacle, mountain at the intersection of the Buncombe-McDowell-Yancey County lines. Alt. 5,665. Sometimes referred to as Blue Ridge Pinnacle to distinguish it from other mountains named Pinnacle.

The Pinnacle, a peak on Kings Mountain (which see) on the Cleveland-Gaston County line. Alt. 1,705.

The Pinnacle, mountain at the head of Dismal Creek in sw Henderson County.

The **Pinnacle**, on the Jackson-Transylvania County line at the head of Miser Creek. Alt. approx. 4,145. Part of Tennessee Ridge, *which see*.

The **Pinnacle**, mountain in s Macon County between Hickory Knoll Creek and Gray Gap.

Pinnacle, peak in nw Swain County on the ne end of Pinnacle Ridge.

Pinnacle, community in sw Stokes County. Alt. 1,085. Inc. 1901; charter repealed 1903. Originally known as Culler, for Emanuel W. Culler who owned part of the land on which a railroad station was built. The railroad began operation in 1888 and the post office here in the late nineteenth century was known as Culler. The present name was adopted about 1894.

Pinnacle Branch rises in s Macon County and flows e into Shope Fork.

Pinnacle Creek rises in nw Swain County on Jenkins Trail Ridge and flows sw into Eagle Creek.

Pinnacle Gap, ne Buncombe County near Craggy Pinnacle in Great Craggy Mountains.

Pinnacle Knob at the junction of Buncombe-McDowell-Yancey County lines. Alt. 5,665.

Pinnacle Knob, central Graham County between Sweetwater Creek and Mountain Creek.

Pinnacle Knob, sw Haywood County on the ne end of Pinnacle Ridge.

Pinnacle Knob, on Macon-Swain County line s of Brush Creek.

Pinnacle Mountain, ne Buncombe County between Town Branch and Corner Rock Creek.

Pinnacle Mountain, central Henderson County, overlooking Kanuga Lake. Alt. 3,662.

Pinnacle Mountain, n Jackson County between Dills Creek and Fisher Creek.

Pinnacle Mountain on the McDowell-Rutherford County line. Alt. 3,832.

Pinnacle Mountain, s Macon County at the head of Pinnacle Branch. Alt. 5,020.

Pinnacle Ridge, sw Haywood County, extends ne from Wesner Bald to Pinnacle Knob.

Pinnacle Ridge, nw Swain County extends ne from Eagle Creek to Pinnacle [peak].

Pinnacle Ridge, w Watauga County extends ne between Bear Branch and Brassy Gap Branch.

Pinnacle Spring, s Yancey County, the source of Left Prong South Toe River.

Pinner Cove, the valley through which Robinson Creek flows in s Buncombe County, w of Merrill Mountain.

Pinner Creek rises in s Buncombe County and flows se into Henderson County where it enters Cane Creek.

Pino, community in nw Davie County. First known as Piney Grove, but changed to Pino in 1890 when a post office was est.

Pin Oak Gap, on Haywood-Swain County line on the head of Ledge Creek in Great Smoky Mountains National Park. Alt. 4,428. A prominent Indian trail passed through this gap before the coming of white men.

Pinson, sw Randolph County.

Pinson Creek rises in s Caswell County and flows se into South Country Line Creek.

Pioneer Mills, community in s Cabarrus County. Gold and copper mines operated here from the 1850's until 1931.

Piper Gap. *See* Lambsburg.

Piper Hill, se Currituck County, former sand hill on s Currituck Banks. Erosion has now almost worn the hill down to beach level.

Pipes Branch rises in e Cherokee County in the Valley River Mountains and flows s of Tibb Ridge into Peachtree Creek.

Pipetrack Gap, s Macon County between Thomas Knob and the Georgia state line.

Pipkins Crossroads. *See* Savages Crossroads.

Pireway, town in s Columbus County near Waccamaw River. Inc. 1883, but long inactive in municipal affairs. Nineteenth century post office name was Pireway Ferry.

Pisgah, community in s Randolph County. Named for nearby Pisgah Church. A post office est. here in the nineteenth century but no longer operated.

Pisgah Creek rises in e Haywood County and flows nw into East Fork Pigeon River.

Pisgah Forest, community in e central Transylvania County near the confluence of Davidson and French Broad rivers. Now includes the old communities of Davidson River and Ecusta. Produces lumber, chemicals, and paper products.

Pisgah Mountain, e Mitchell County parallel to the head of Green Cove Creek.

Pisgah National Forest in portions of Avery, Buncombe, Burke, Caldwell, Haywood, Henderson, Madison, McDowell, Mitchell, Transylvania, Watauga, and Yancey counties was est. in 1911 and includes 1,177,303 acres. Nature trails, mountain climbing, picnicking, and other recreational uses.

Pisgah Ridge extends the length of the Haywood-Transylvania County line. The Blue Ridge Parkway traverses its length.

Pit Branch rises in n Yancey County and flows ne into Big Creek.

Pitch Landing, former community on Chinkapin Creek in s Hertford County. Appears on the Price map, 1808; was a post office by 1822, and is shown on maps as recently as 1916.

Pitch Landing. See Princeton.

Pitman Creek rises in n Carteret County and flows n into Turnagain Bay.

Pitt County was formed in 1760 from Beaufort County. Located in the e section of the state, it is bounded by Beaufort, Craven, Lenoir, Greene, Wilson, Edgecombe, and Martin counties. It was named for William Pitt, Earl of Chatham (1708-78), Secretary of State in England and virtual prime minister whose vigorous war policies resulted in the defeat of the French in America by the British. Area: 656 sq. mi. County seat: Greenville with an elevation of 64 ft. Townships are Arthur, Ayden, Belvoir, Bethel, Carolina, Chicod, Falkland, Farmville, Fountain, Greenville, Grifton, Grimesland, Pactolus, Swift Creek, and Winterville. Produces tobacco, corn, soybeans, oats, peanuts, cotton, poultry, hogs, livestock, lumber, textiles, batteries, baked goods, boats, canned foods, and apparel. See also Chatham County.

Pitt Crossroads, community in s Edgecombe County.

Pittman Creek rises in e Pamlico County and flows s into Broad Creek.

Pittmans Island, in White Oak River in se Onslow County. Known first as Bell Island for Ross Bell, owner from 1717 until about 1746; later as Jones Island for Emanuel Jones who purchased it about

1746 from Bell. Present name from John A. Pittman, a later owner.

Pittmans Store. See Hickory.

Pitts. See North Cove.

Pittsboro, town and county seat, central Chatham County. Inc. 1778 as Chatham, site of the courthouse. Pittsboro authorized to be laid out on land adjacent to the courthouse in 1785, but owners would not sell the desired land. In 1787 land on another site was acquired. Named for William Pitt, Earl of Chatham (1708-78), defender of American rights in the British Parliament. Alt. 409. Produces textiles, hosiery, poultry.

Pitts Creek rises in e Chatham County and flows sw into Whiteoak Creek.

Pitt's Creek rises in e Onslow County and flows e into White Oak River. Named for Richard Pitts.

Pivers Island, s Carteret County, w of the town of Beaufort. Named for the Piver family. Site of a United States marine biological station. Museum open to the public.

Pix Head Rock, a jutting mass of stone towering 30 ft., sw Alamance County. Located on a farm off the Kimesville road, sw of the community of Alamance, it is near the junction of Stinking Quarter and North Stinking Quarter creeks. Also known as Indian Rock and Indian Rock Tomb. According to legend, the tomb in which the cleansed, polished, and rejointed bones of Indian chieftains were kept is located in this rock. A small cave extends a short distance into it. Nearby are 2 rectangular stone pits, approx. 7 ft. long and 3 ft. deep, which may have been graves hewn for lesser Indians.

Pixie Mountain, central Avery County.

Plain View, community in n Richmond County.

Plainview, community in w Robeson County on the nw outskirts of Rowland, which see. McQueen's Store, a post office as early as 1822, was in this vicinity.

Plain View Township, nw Sampson County.

Plank Bridge. See Camden.

Plank Ford, n Union County across Rocky River.

Plass Gap, s Macon County between Norton Branch and Middle Creek.

Plateau, town in sw Catawba County. Inc. 1885 as Keeversville. Name changed, 1893. Long inactive in municipal affairs.

Player, community in e Pender County between Shaken Creek and Northeast Cape Fear River.

Players Swamp rises in s Pender County and flows sw into Merricks Creek.

Play Rock Hill, elevation in s Henderson County on Mud Creek.

Pleasant Branch rises in ne Swain County and flows nw into Bunches Creek.

Pleasant Gap on the Buncombe-Madison County line between Nofat and Carter Mountains.

Pleasant Garden, community in s Guilford County. Alt. 805. Known first as Fentress for local family; renamed Pleasant Garden about 1879.

Pleasant Gardens, community in central McDowell County. Named for the home of Joseph McDowell, Indian fighter and hero of the Battle of Kings Mountain (1780). At one time a post office named Garden City existed nearby.

Pleasant Grove, community in ne Alamance County. A post office est. here as early as 1822 operated as late as 1882.

Pleasant Grove, community in e central Caswell County.

Pleasant Grove, community in w Northampton County.

Pleasant Grove, community in n Washington County e of Kendricks Creek.

Pleasant Grove Township, former township in ne Alamance County, now township number 11.

Pleasant Grove Township, w Johnston County.

Pleasant Grove Township, se Randolph County.

Pleasant Hill, community in se Chatham County. A post office here in the early nineteenth century was known as Pedlars Hill.

Pleasant Hill, community in w Cherokee County between the headwaters of Little Shoal Creek and Hiwassee River.

Pleasant Hill, community in w Jones County on Trent River.

Pleasant Hill, community in n Northampton County. Alt. 118. A post office as early as 1828.

Pleasant Hill, home of William Hawkins, governor, 1811-14, stands about eight miles n of Henderson in e Vance County.

Pleasant Hill Township, n central Northampton County.

Pleasant Knob, central Buncombe County w of Beaver Lake.

Pleasant Plains, community in central Hertford County. A free Negro Baptist

church said to have existed here as early as 1845.

Pleasant Ridge. See South Gastonia.

Pleasant View, crossroads community in n central Tyrrell County about 1½ mi. sw of community of Levels on s side of Riders Creek.

Pleasantville, community in w Rockingham County. A post office est. here as early as 1830.

Pledger Landing, n Tyrrell County on Albemarle Sound e of Lewis Point.

Plot Knob, sw Clay County between the headwaters of Suddawig and Rocky branches. Alt. 2,390.

Plott Balsam, a knob in w Haywood County on the ne end of Plott Balsams (ridge). Alt. 6,088. Named for Amos Plott, pioneer settler. Nearby Enos Plotts Balsam Mountain was named for his brother.

Plott Balsams, a ridge extending ne from Tuckasegee River in w Jackson County to Plott Balsam (knob) in w Haywood County. Known by the Cherokee Indians as Tunn Ensleas.

Plott Creek rises in w Haywood County and flows se into Richland Creek.

Plotts. See Eufola.

Plott's Old Field Mountain. See Old Field Top Mountain.

Plum Branch rises in se Cabarrus County and flows w into Hamby's Branch.

Plum Branch rises in e Yancey County and flows s into Little Crabtree Creek.

Plum Creek rises in nw Alamance County and flows sw into Ridge Creek.

Plummers Creek rises in e Davidson County and flows ne into Randolph County where it enters Little Uwharrie River.

Plumtree, community on North Toe River, sw Avery County. Named for Plumtree Creek which enters North Toe River nearby. Alt. 2,830. Mica has been mined here since 1891.

Plumtree Creek rises in central Avery County and flows s and w into North Toe River. Named for plum orchards set out here by Avery and Connelly families.

Plyler, community in w Stanly County.

Plymouth, town and county seat, w Washington County on Roanoke River. Settled by 1727. Inc. 1807, named for Plymouth, Mass. Important as a shipping center and as a producer of lumber products, veneer, plywood, also the location of a paper mill and a center of grains mills. Alt. 21. Battle of Plymouth fought here in 1863 during the Civil War.

Plymouth Township, w Washington County, formed in 1868, but a voting precinct before that date.

Pocahuntas, community in sw Swain County on Nantahala River.

Pochike River. See Meherrin River.

The Pocket. See Pocket Township.

Pocket Creek rises in w Lee County and flows n into Deep River.

Pocket Township, former township in w Lee County, now township number 7. A post office named The Pocket was est. here by 1830 and it continued as late as 1882. Named from the fact that it was isolated from the remainder of the county by a bend in Deep River, hence a pocket.

Pocomoke, community in w Franklin County.

Pocosin Branch rises in s Jones County and flows n into Trent River.

Pocosin Branch rises in e Pitt County and flows se into Tranters Creek.

Pocosin Point. See Poquoson Point.

Poe-li-co. See French Broad River.

Poga or Pogey Mountain, n Avery County at the n end of Beech Mountain. Alt. 3,790. Local tradition is that a man was lost on this mountain for several days, and when he returned home he explained to his friends that he had "been to Pogey." He may have been using the English dialect word poggy meaning "boggy" or "sloppy" as a field in wet weather.

Pogey Mountain. See Poga Mountain.

Poindexter. See Smithtown.

Poindexter Branch rises in central Macon County and flows ne into Iotla Creek.

Point Bacon appears on the Smith map, 1624, as the n portion of present Currituck Banks in e Currituck County. It was shown as extending s from Cape Henry, Va., to Currituck Inlet. Undoubtedly named for Sir Francis Bacon whose favor Smith sought to win.

Point Caswell, community in w Pender County on Black River. Named for Richard Caswell (1729-1789), Governor of North Carolina. Settled prior to the Civil War. Inc. in 1883 as Caswell; charter repealed, 1901. Formerly a thriving shipping point on the river; now only a church and a few houses remain.

Point Corbett appears on the Smith map, 1624, as the area of ne North Carolina

presently included in Camden and Currituck counties.

Point Durant. See Durants Neck.

Point Harbor, community at the extreme s tip of Currituck County at Powells Point. Settled prior to 1667. Post office est. in 1907 as Marvin but changed a few years later to Point Harbor.

Point Hezel appears on the Collet map, 1770, as a point of land in se New Hanover County between Hewlets and Bradley creeks on the mainland behind modern Wrightsville Beach. Probably named for James Hasell (d. 1786), Chief Justice of the colony.

Point Lookout, e Haywood County on Glade Mountain. Alt. approx. 4,530.

Point Lookout Mountain, e Henderson County, extends ne from the w side of Hungry River. William Mills built a crude fort here soon after moving to the area, and it served as a haven for pioneer settlers in time of threat from the Indians. It was here that Polly Stepp, firing through a porthole, struck an Indian and gave her oft-quoted cry: "I've hit the Big Chief, darned if I ain't hit the Big Chief." Remains of the old foundation logs of this fort can still be seen.

Point Misery, mountain peak on the Buncombe-Yancey County line at the e end of Big Andy Ridge. Alt. 5,715.

Point of Grass, nw point of Cedar Island in ne Carteret County, between West Bay and Pamlico Sound.

Point of Grass Creek, a tidal creek on the Core Sound side of Core Banks near Drum Inlet, ne Carteret County.

Point of Marsh, a point of land extending into the mouth of Neuse River in the most northerly part of Carteret County.

Point of Woods. See Archie's Point.

Point Peter, point of land extending into Cape Fear River at its junction with Northeast Cape Fear River opposite Wilmington, w New Hanover County. Before the Civil War this was a terminal for river traffic to and from Fayetteville and Averasboro. Named for Peter Mallett (b. 1744), Revolutionary leader. See also Peters Point.

Point Prospect, s Orange County in the town of Chapel Hill about one half mile e of the University of North Carolina campus, a very high ridge below which, as William R. Davie wrote in 1793, "the flat country spreads off . . . like the ocean, giving an immense hemisphere, in which the eye seems to be lost in the extent of space." The peak was owned by the University until 1894 when the U.S. Circuit Court ordered it to be sold to pay University debts. Sometimes known as Piney Prospect for the pines in the vicinity and because Point was often pronounced "Pint" which evolved into Piney.

Poison Branch rises in ne Ashe County and flows ne into North Fork New River.

Poison Branch rises in n Graham County and flows nw into Fontana Lake.

Poison Cove, e Haywood County on the head of Poison Cove Branch.

Poison Cove Branch rises in ne Buncombe County and flows nw into North Fork Ivy Creek.

Poison Cove Branch rises in e Haywood County and flows nw into Pigeon River.

Poison Cove Top, e Haywood County near the head of Poison Cove Branch.

Poison Fork rises in s Randolph County and flows sw into Montgomery County where it enters Barnes Creek.

Poison Springs. See Barium Springs.

Pokeberry Creek rises in n Chatham County and flows sw into Haw River.

Pole Branch rises in w Johnston County and flows se into Black Creek.

Pole Bridge Branch rises in central Cherokee County and flows nw into Valley River.

Pole Bridge Branch rises in nw Swain County and flows s into Lake Cheoah.

Pole Bridge Branch rises in s Swain County and flows w into Little Tennessee River.

Pole Bridge Branch rises in s Transylvania County and flows ne into Little River.

Pole Bridge Creek rises in w Stanly County and flows ne into Big Bear Creek.

Pole Bridge Gap, n Wilkes County at the n end of Greenstreet Mountain.

Polecat Branch rises in ne Cherokee County and flows n into McClellan Creek.

Polecat Branch rises in ne Cherokee County and flows sw into Junaluska Creek.

Polecat Branch rises in e Greene County and flows sw into Contentnea Creek.

Polecat Branch rises in n Jackson County and flows sw into Hornbuckle Creek.

Polecat Branch rises in central Johnston County and flows sw into Neuse River.

Polecat Branch rises in n Macon County and flows sw into Lakey Creek.

Polecat Creek rises in s Guilford County and flows se into Randolph County where it enters Deep River. The name appears in local records as early as 1762.

Polecat Creek rises in s Union County and flows se into South Carolina where it enters Wildcat Creek.

Polecat Hollow, w Madison County on an unnamed tributary of French Broad River.

Polecat Ridge, n Macon County between Bradley Creek and Lakey Creek.

Pole Creek rises in sw Buncombe County from 2 branches, each rising on the s slopes of Holland Mountain. One flows se through Milksick Cove; the other flows se through Herren Cove; they join to flow se into Hominy Creek.

Pole Mountain, s Wilkes County near the head of Fishing Creek.

Pole Road Creek, Great Smoky Mountains National Park, rises in n Swain County and flows se into Deep Creek.

Poley Branch rises in n Duplin County and flows s into Back Marsh.

Poley Branch rises in ne Pitt County and flows e into Tranters Creek.

Poley Branch rises in se Richmond County and flows s into Joes Creek.

Poley Swamp rises in n Duplin County and flows n from Whitfields Pond into Deavers Mill Pond. Also known as Polly Run Creek.

Polk County was formed in 1855 from Rutherford and Henderson counties. Located in the sw section of the state, it is bounded by the state of South Carolina, and by Henderson and Rutherford counties. It was named for Col. William Polk (1758-1834), Revolutionary officer who was, before his death, the last surviving field officer of the North Carolina line. Area: 235 sq. mi. County seat: Columbus, with an elevation of 1,145 ft. Townships are Columbus, Cooper Gap, Greens Creek, Saluda, Tryon, and White Oak. Produces corn, wheat, oats, cotton, livestock, hogs, textiles, and apparel.

Polk Ditch rises in sw Mecklenburg County and flows se into Walker Branch.

Polk Mountain. *See* Gibraltar.

Polkton, town in w Anson County. With the coming of the railroad the town was laid out on the lands of and named for Leonidas L. Polk (1837-92), state agricultural leader. He first proposed that it be called Luneville. Inc. 1875. Alt. 320.

Polkville, community in w Cleveland County.

Polkville Township, former township in w Cleveland County, now township number 8.

Pollard Swamp rises in sw Beaufort County and flows sw into Creeping Swamp.

Pollock Mill Creek rises in w Duplin County and flows se into Stewarts Creek.

Pollock's Ferry. *See* Bridgers Creek.

Pollocksville, town in s Jones County on Trent River. Known as Trent Bridge as early as 1779 and a post office by this name was est. prior to 1828. Inc. 1834 as Pollocksville, but a municipal government was not formed at that time. Reinc. 1849. The name Pollock appears at this location on the Collet map, 1770, and others into the nineteenth century when Trent Bridge is shown across the river and Pollocksville at the site of the town. Produces lumber. Alt. 13.

Pollocksville Township, e Jones County.

Pollock Swamp, a marshy stream, rises in Bear Swamp, e Chowan County, and flows sw into Pembroke Creek. Pollock Swamp watershed, approx. 17 mi. long, is in this area.

Polls Gap, w Haywood County, Great Smoky Mountains National Park, on Balsam Mountain, near lat. 35° 33' 48" N., long. 83° 09' 42" W. Alt. 5,090. Named after Aunt Polly Moody's family milch cow, Poll, died and her bones were left here bleaching in the sun for many years.

Polly Hollow, e Mitchell County parallel to Laurel Branch.

Polly Middleton Gap in central Jackson County between Double Top Mountain and Horneyhead Mountain.

Polly Mountain, s Jackson County, bordered on the e by Scotsman Creek and on the s by Chattooga River. Alt. approx. 3,150.

Polly Run Creek. *See* Poley Swamp.

Polycarp, community in s Alexander County. Alt. approx. 1,000. Named for the Rev. Polycarp Henkle, Lutheran minister in the vicinity in the nineteenth century.

Pomeiooc appears on the White map, 1585, as an enclosed Indian village in present Hyde County between Lake Mattamuskeet and Wyesocking Bay.

Pomona, former community in central Guilford County now within Greensboro city limits. Alt. 868. Named for the Italian goddess of the fruit of trees; a nursery was once located here. Clay pipe and electrical goods are produced here.

Pompey Ridge, nw McDowell County. Average alt. approx. 2,600. Locust Knob is on this ridge.

Pond Branch rises in s Buncombe County near Stradley Mountain and flows ne into Hominy Creek.

Pond Branch rises in e Moore County and flows s into Little River.

Pond Branch rises in w Watauga County and flows n into Beech Creek.

Ponder Branch rises in se Madison County and flows n into French Broad River.

Ponder Creek rises in e Madison County and flows sw into Middle Fork.

Pond Knob, Great Smoky Mountains National Park, nw Swain County, on Big Grill Ridge, lat. 35° 32' N., long. 83° 46' 23" W. Alt. 4,148.

Pond Mountain, nw Ashe County. Alt. approx. 5,000. The top of the mountain is a large level plateau covered with bluegrass and containing several small ponds. Said to have been named by Peter Jefferson in 1749.

Pond Mountain, e McDowell County.

Pond Mountain, s Randolph County between Bachelor Creek and Fork Creek.

Pond Mountain Township, nw Ashe County.

Pond Ridge, in most w part of Burke County. Alt. 3,546.

Pony Ridge, s Mitchell County at the head of Brushy Creek.

Ponzer, community in nw Hyde County on Pungo River.

Pool Creek rises in w Rutherford County and flows ne into Lake Lure. The Bottomless Pools, *which see*, are on this creek.

Pooletown, community in e Rowan County between Cedar and Panther creeks. A post office named Pool was est. here in 1872.

Pool Point extends from e Pasquotank County into Pasquotank River at the mouth of New Begun Creek.

Poolville, community in se Pasquotank County on Pasquotank River.

Poor House Mountain, s Cherokee County, extends ne from Martin Creek.

Poorhouse Run, rises in s Greene County and flows ne, by the County Home, into Contentnea Creek. Earlier called Caswells Branch.

Poorlith, community in w Union County.

Poors Knob, e Watauga County between Chestnut Branch and Elk Creek. Alt. approx. 2,350.

Poor Town, community in s Hertford County.

Pop Castle, w Vance County approx. one mi. w of the town of Kittrell. Popecastle Inn was est. here approx. 1734, and local usage changed the name to Pop Castle. Racetrack, cock-pit, and tavern were adjuncts of the inn; the racetrack grew up during the Revolution, and the main building of the inn was dismantled after the Civil War. Site now marked by an old oak.

Pope Air Force Base, Fort Bragg Military Reservation, nw Cumberland County, was est. during World War I and named in honor of Lt. Harley Halbert Pope, who died in an aircraft accident on the Cape Fear River near Fayetteville, January 7, 1919.

Pope Branch rises in w Halifax County and flows s into Fishing Creek.

Popecastle Inn. *See* Pop Castle.

Popes Pond, slightly less than ½ mi. long, on Black River, se Harnett County.

Poplar, community in w Mitchell County on Nolichucky River. Alt. 1,993. A post office here in the late nineteenth century was called Hollow Poplar.

Poplar Branch rises in s Cleveland County and flows se into Beaverdam Creek.

Poplar Branch rises in central Guilford County and flows ne into Reedy Fork Creek. Appears on the Collet map, 1770.

Poplar Branch rises in s Haywood County and flows se into West Fork Pigeon River.

Poplar Branch rises in n Johnston County and flows se into Neuse River. Mentioned in local records as early as 1780.

Poplar Branch rises in s Jones County and flows nw into Trent River.

Poplar Branch rises in s Lee County and flows s into Little River.

Poplar Branch rises in n Rockingham County and flows sw into Matrimony Creek.

Poplar Branch rises in e central Wilson County and flows s into Whiteoak Swamp.

Poplar Branch rises in sw Wilson County and flows ne into Black Creek.

Poplar Branch, community on the w shore of Currituck Sound in s Currituck County. Known first as Currituck Narrows. Post office as early as 1822. *See also* Narrows.

Poplar Branch Bay, s central Currituck County, formed in Currituck Sound by the mainland, Rattle Snake Island, and Long Point.

Poplar Branch Township, s Currituck County.

Poplar Cove, w Graham County between Horse Cove Ridge and Little Santeetlah Creek.

Poplar Cove, e Haywood County between Turkey Cove and Bill Cove.

Poplar Cove, nw Haywood County between Rough Mountain and Big Branch.

Poplar Cove, central Macon County at the head of Mill Creek.

Poplar Cove, n Macon County, extends n to the junction of Right Fork [Wesser Creek] and Wesser Creek in s Swain County.

Poplar Cove, on a tributary of Hickory Knoll Creek in s Macon County.

Poplar Cove, s Swain County extends sw from Little Tennessee River.

Poplar Cove Branch rises in sw Macon County and flows ne into Poplar Cove Creek.

Poplar Cove Creek rises in w Macon County se of Panther Knob and flows ne into Cartoogechaye Creek.

Poplar Cove Creek. *See* Paxton Creek.

Poplar Cove Gap, central Macon County between the head of Mill Creek and Trimont Ridge.

Poplar Cove Knob, w Jackson County between Big Cove and Savannah Creek.

Poplar Cove Knob, s Macon County between Commissioner Creek and the Georgia state line.

Poplar Creek rises in n Onslow County and flows s into Little Northeast Creek. Mentioned in local records as early as 1744 as Poplar Swamp.

Poplar Creek rises in n Transylvania County s of Fryingpan Gap, and flows se into South Fork Mills River.

Poplar Creek rises in w Vance County and flows sw into e Granville County where it enters Tabbs Creek.

Poplar Creek rises in e Wake County and flows s into Neuse River.

Poplar Gap, e Haywood County between Sheep Mountain and Glade Mountain.

Poplar Grove, community in n Polk County. A post office was est. here prior to 1882.

Poplar Grove, community in ne Sampson County.

Poplar Hollow Branch rises in ne Swain County and flows s into Raven Fork.

Poplar Lick Gap, n Transylvania County on the head of Sitton Creek.

Poplar Point, a bluff on the Roanoke River, n Martin County. Appears on the Collet map, 1770. A steamboat landing was here at one time; Poplar Point Church and a rural community are nearby. Roanoke, a post office, existed at or near this point in 1846.

Poplar Point Township, n central Martin County.

Poplar Spring Top, on the Cherokee-Graham County line in the Snowbird Mountains.

Poplar Springs, community in s Stokes County.

Poplar Swamp. See Poplar Creek.

Poplar Tent Township, former township in w Cabarrus County, now township number 2.

Poplar Township, nw Mitchell County.

Poppaw Creek rises in sw Alamance County and flows n into Stinking Quarter Creek.

Poquoson Point, s Camden County in the mouth of Pasquotank River. Also sometimes called Camden Point. Named from an Algonquian word, pequessen, meaning a swamp or a dismal.

Porcelain. See Linville.

Pores Knob, s Wilkes County, the highest peak in the Brushy Mountains. Alt. 2,680. Named for Moses Poore, an eighteenth century resident. Appears on the Collet map, 1770, as Mount Night. See also Brushy Mountains.

Pores Knob, community in s Wilkes County near the peak of the same name. Name changed at one time to Fruitland and to East Fruitland, but the original name was soon restored.

Pork Creek. See Fork Creek.

Porpoise Point, ne Pamlico County on the e side of Goose Creek Island between Big Porpoise Bay and Little Porpoise Bay.

P[ort] Box appears on the Smith map, 1624, in Pamlico Sound but the feature for which this name is intended is uncertain.

Porter, community in se Stanly County. Named for an official of the railroad.

Porter Cove, central Buncombe County near Azalea.

Porter Cove, on a tributary of Cullasaja River in s Macon County.

Porter Creek rises in se Beaufort County and flows n into Durham Creek.

Porterfield Gap, on the Cherokee-Graham County line. Alt. 3,462.

Porters Gap, Great Smoky Mountains National Park, on Swain County, N. C.-Sevier County, Tenn., line, lat. 35° 38′ 55″ N., long. 83° 21′ 28″ W. Alt. approx. 5,500.

Portersville. See Emerson.

Porter Swamp rises in w Columbus County and flows nw and sw into Lumber River.

Port Fernando. See Hatorask Inlet.

Port Grenvil appears on the White map, 1590, as an inlet through Ocracoke Island a short distance n of the community of Ocracoke, se Hyde County. Named for Sir Richard Grenville. Appears as Greenevills rode on the Smith map, 1624. There is some doubt that such an inlet actually existed, though it may have been at what is now known as Nigh Inlet, which see.

Portia inc. as a town in McDowell County, 1891; charter repealed 1893. It apparently was never laid out and the proposed site is unknown.

Portis Gold Mine, now abandoned, ne Franklin County. Shown on a map as recently as 1931.

Port Landing. See Fort Landing.

Port Lane, an inlet from the Atlantic Ocean into Roanoke Sound through Bodie Island opposite the se shore of Roanoke Island, e Dare County. Opened prior to 1585 and closed prior to 1657.

Portohonk Creek rises in sw Camden County and flows s into Pasquotank County. See also Jones Mill.

Portsmouth, formerly a thriving town in ne Carteret County at the tip of Core Banks. Settled in the early 1700's; inc. 1753, and probably named for the city in England. Long inactive in municipal affairs. Alt. 8. See also, Portsmouth Island.

Portsmouth Island, ne Carteret County, is the name applied to the ne end of Core Banks. Appears as Wococon (which see) on the White map, 1585. May have been a part of Croatoan Island. See also Portsmouth; Core Banks; Cape Lookout National Seashore Recreational Area.

Portsmouth Township, e Carteret County, is made up of Core Banks extending from Cape Lookout to Ocracoke Inlet. See also Portsmouth Island.

P[ort] Vaughn appears on the Smith map, 1624, in Pamlico Sound but the feature for which this name is intended is uncertain.

Possum Branch rises in s Macon County and flows n into Tessentee Creek. Approx. one mi. long.

Possum Branch rises in s Macon County and flows nw into Hickory Knoll Creek. Approx. ½ mi. long.

Possum Creek. See Possumquarter Creek.

Possum Hollow, nw Swain County extends se from Pinnacle Ridge to Hazel Creek.

Possum Hollow, community on the n side of Yadkin River, n central Caldwell County.

Possum Hollow, s Haywood County on the e side of Bearpen Gap. An unnamed stream rises here and flows e into Haywood Gap Stream.

Possum Neck Swamp, rises in s Craven County and flows nw into Brice Creek.

Possumquarter Creek rises in w central Warren County and flows s into Fishing Creek. Probably named for the plantation of Gov. Gabriel Johnston, Possum Quarter, mentioned in his will, dated 1751. Appears on the Price map, 1808, as Possum Creek.

Possumtown. See Bethany.

Possumtrot, community in w Yancey County on Possumtrot Creek. Named by an early settler who was riding down a trail on horseback when a lone 'possum entered the path ahead of him and trotted along in front of the horse for some distance.

Possumtrot Creek rises in w Yancey County and flows ne into Bald Creek.

Postell, community in w Cherokee County on Shoal Creek. Alt. 1,900. Named for Thomas Postell, an early settler.

Post Oak. See Blaine.

Potaskike River. See North River.

Potato Branch rises in sw Buncombe County near Potato Gap and flows nw into South Turkey Creek.

Potato Creek rises in nw Alleghany County and flows n into Virginia where it enters New River.

Potato Creek rises in sw Cherokee County and flows w into Polk County, Tenn., where it turns sw and flows into Ocoee River.

Potato Field Gap, ne Buncombe County s of Snowball Mountain. The Blue Ridge Parkway passes through this gap.

Potato Gap, sw Buncombe County near the headwaters of Potato Branch.

Potato Gap, n Madison County at the sw end of Sugarloaf Mountain.

Potato Hill, s Henderson County on Mud Creek.

Potato Hill, on Jackson Line Mountain in s central Swain County between the head of Laurel Branch and the head of Davis Branch. Alt. 3,306.

Potato Hill, s Yancey County between Cattail Peak and the head of Colbert Creek.

Potato Hill. See Tater Hill.

Potato Hill Bald, Great Smoky Mountains National Park, ne Swain County, on Chiltoskie Ridge near the se end of Ravens Roost Ridge, lat. 35° 35' 42" N., long. 83° 12' 33" W. Alt. 5,209.

Potato Hill Lake, artificial lake in central Watauga County on Howard Creek between Rich Mountain and Harmon Knob. Formed in 1947; max. depth 25 ft.; covers 9 acres. Open to public. Also known as Tater Hill Lake.

Potato Hill Mountain, w Randolph County on Little Caraway Creek.

Potato Knob, at the head of Brooks Branch in sw Buncombe County, ne of Potato Gap.

Potato Knob, on the Buncombe-Yancey County line, between Rainbow Gap and Swannanoa Gap. Alt. approx. 6,400, the highest point in Buncombe County. Known earlier as Potato Top.

Potato Knob, e Haywood County between Dutch Cove Creek and Doubletop Mountain.

Potato Lump Mountain, sw Madison County between Johns Branch and Spring Creek.

Potato Mountain, nw Buncombe County, between Willow and Sandy Mush creeks.

Potato Patch, mountain in w Haywood County on the head of a tributary of Hemphill Creek.

Potato Top. See Potato Knob.

Pot Branch rises in s McDowell County and flows se into Rutherford County where it enters Briar Creek. Erosion in rocks over which it flows has made pot-like holes.

Pot Cove Gap, on the Buncombe-McDowell County line near the headwaters of Flat Creek.

Potecase Bridge. See Jackson.

Potecasi (potty-casey), community in e Northampton County. Named for its location near Potecase Creek, an Indian word meaning "parting of the waters." A post office was est. here about 1839.

Potecasi Creek rises in central Northampton County and flows e into Hertford County where it enters Meherrin River. Appears as Weyanok Creek on the Ogilby map, 1671. The upper portion of Potecasi Creek is marked Catawhisky on the Moseley map, 1733. Appears as Meherrin Creek on the Collet map, 1770.

Potoskite, appears on the Moseley map, 1733, in s Currituck Precinct (now County), possibly representing an Indian village.

Potrock Bald, a peak in n Clay County near the headwaters of Potrock Branch and Compass Creek. Alt. 5,200-5,250. Named for a large rock on top of the mountain which was hollowed out by an Indian medicine man and used to steep his medicinal herbs.

Potrock Branch rises in n Clay County and flows sw into Fires Creek.

Pott Creek rises in s Catawba County and flows s into Lincoln County where it enters South Fork Catawba River.

Potters. See Mineral Springs.

Potters Hill, community in e Duplin County.

Potter's Hill, community in s central Lenoir County. So called for the Potter family which early settled here.

Pottertown. See Tamarack.

Potts Branch rises in n Macon County and flows sw into Little Tennessee River.

Potts Creek rises in se Cleveland County and flows nw into Buffalo Creek.

Potts Creek rises in central Macon County and flows ne into Cartoogechaye Creek.

Potts Creek. See First Potts Creek; Second Potts Creek.

Pounding Creek rises in central Clay County and flows s into Shooting Creek.

Pounding Mill Branch rises in n Cherokee County in the Snowbird Mountains and flows se into Hyatt Creek.

Pounding Mill Branch rises in n Haywood County and flows se into Cold Springs Creek.

Pounding Mill Branch rises in n Madison County and flows sw into Little Laurel Creek.

Pounding Mill Branch rises in n Transylvania County near Green Knob and flows se into Looking-glass Creek.

Pounding Mill Branch rises in n Transylvania County near Poundingstone Mountain and flows se into South Fork Mills River.

Pounding Mill Branch rises in s Watauga County and flows ne into Elk Creek.

Pounding Mill Cove, n Yancey County on Pounding Mill Creek.

Poundingmill Creek rises in ne Cleveland County and flows s into Knob Creek.

Pounding Mill Creek rises in n Yancey County and flows nw into Cane River.

Poundingstone Mountain, n Transylvania County between Pounding Mill Branch and Jumping Branch. Alt. approx. 3,450.

Pound Mill Gap, w Macon County between Burningtown Creek and Deweese Creek.

Pousville, community in n Franklin County.

Poverty Branch rises in n Buncombe County and flows sw into North Fork Ivy Creek.

Powder Burnt Creek rises in ne Cherokee County and flows nw into Valley River.

Powdermill Creek rises in w Avery County and flows se into North Toe River. Said to have been named because Lodawick and Dora Oakes, who lived along its banks, burned willow switches to make enough gunpowder to buy a Negro man.

Powder Springs. See Eupeptic Springs.

Powell Creek rises in s Buncombe County and flows w into French Broad River. Skyland Lake, which see, is on this stream.

Powell Creek rises in Virginia and flows sw into Northampton County where it enters Meherrin River.

Powell Creek rises in e Wake County and flows sw into Hodges Mill Creek.

Powell Crossroads, community in s Gates County.

Powell Knob, Great Smoky Mountains National Park, on Swain County, N. C.-Blount County, Tenn., line between Buck Gap and Ekaneetlee Gap. Lat. 35° 32′ 24″ N., long. 83° 49′ 19″ W.

Powells Creek rises in w Halifax County and flows se into Little Fishing Creek.

Powells Creek. See Whitaker Creek.

Powells Pocosin, nw Bertie County.

Powells Point, tip of the peninsula of s Currituck County in Albemarle Sound. Appears in local records as early as 1665 and on the Ogilby map, 1671. The community (and post office) of Powells Point is 6½ mi. north.

Powellsville, town in n central Bertie County. Post office est. 1879; inc. 1887. Named for a local family and originally known as Powell's Crossroads. Alt. 67.

Powellton, community in sw Montgomery

County. A post office est. here as early as 1830. Named for Pleasant M. Powell.

Powelltown, community on the outskirts of Lenoir, central Caldwell County. Named for a British soldier, Elias Powell (d. 1831), who remained in the area following the Battle of Kings Mountain, 1780. Known earlier as Powellton.

Powelltown, community in s Transylvania County near the mouth of East Fork French Broad River.

Powel's Creek. See Greens Creek.

Powers Branch rises in e Mitchell County and flows se into Fall Creek.

Powhatan, community in n Johnston County. Alt. 294.

Poyner Hill, formerly a sand hill on s Currituck Banks, e Currituck County. Erosion has now almost obliterated the hill. During World War II a temporary Coast Guard base was located here.

Prather Gap, w Yancey County between Possumtrot and Price creeks.

Prathers Creek rises in sw Alleghany County and flows nw into South Fork New River.

Prathers Creek Township, w central Alleghany County.

Prattsburg, former community in central Durham County approx. 2 mi. e of the original railroad station for Durham. In the 1850's, William Pratt refused to give a right-of-way or land for station at Prattsburg. The railroad avoided his property and as a result, Durham was est.

Prentiss, community in s Macon County.

Prescott, community in s central Beaufort County.

Presley Branch rises in n Transylvania County and flows sw into Avery Creek.

Presley Creek rises in w Jackson County and flows ne into Tilley Creek.

Press Cove, n Jackson County on the head of East Fork [Dicks Creek].

Pressley Gap, at the head of Rose Creek in n Macon County.

Pressly Mountain, e Haywood County on the head of Conner Mill Branch and Stamey Cove Branch.

Press Prong rises in w Nash County and flows se into Murrays Mill Pond on Turkey Creek.

Prestonville, community in ne Stokes County.

Pretty Hollow Creek, w Haywood County, Great Smoky Mountains National Park, rises near lat. 35° 40' 55" N., long. 83° 08' 17" W., on Mount Sterling Ridge and flows s into Palmer Creek.

Pretty Hollow Gap, w Haywood County, Great Smoky Mountains National Park, on Mount Sterling Ridge, near lat. 35° 41' 10" N., long. 83° 08' 26" W. Alt. 5,176 at the head of Pretty Hollow Creek.

Pretty Pine Branch rises in nw Cherokee County and flows se into Shuler Creek.

Pretty Pond, a natural lake in se Brunswick County. Max. depth 8 feet. Surface area, 150 acres.

Price, community in nw Rockingham County. Est. 1868. Named for John Price on whose plantation a store and post office were built. The post office for a time was known as Price's Store.

Price Creek rises in se Brunswick County and flows e into the Cape Fear River.

Price Creek rises in s Orange County and flows ne into Neville Creek.

Price Creek rises in sw Yancey County and flows n into Cane River.

Price Creek Township, w Yancey County.

Price's Mill, community in w Union County.

Price Township, nw Rockingham County.

Prickly Ash Ridge, w Jackson County between Tarcamp Branch and Hunter Jim Creek.

Prickly Pear Mountain, w Randolph County just w of Caraway Mountain in a close group with Black Jack, Slick Rock, and Vineyard mountains.

Prides Ferry. See Mush Island.

Prince George Creek rises in n New Hanover County and flows nw into Northeast Cape Fear River. Appears in local records as early as 1744, hence probably named for Prince George (1738-1820), who became George III in 1760.

Prince's Bridge, former community in ne Chatham County on New Hope Creek. A post office existed here in the early nineteenth century. See also Cyprett's Bridge.

Princess Anne, town in se Robeson County. Inc. in 1796 "on lands of Mary Griffin and William Ashley on Drowning Creek," now Lumber River. Long inactive in municipal affairs. Site approx. 2½ mi. se of the community of Barnesville.

Princeton, town in e Johnston County. Inc. 1861 as Boon Hill for the name of the Boon family plantation in the vicinity. Named changed to Princeton in 1873. Alt. 152.

Princeton, town inc. 1787 on Meherrin

River in ne Northampton County. Previously known as Pitch Landing. Streets were laid off and some homes built, but it soon declined as nearby Murfreesboro (inc. at the same time) grew. A plantation on the site continues to be called Princeton. Washington Ferry crossed the river here and is shown on the Collet map, 1770.

Princeville, town in central Edgecombe County just s of the Tar River from Tarboro. Settled 1865 by former slaves and called Freedom Hill. Inc. 1885 and named for Turner Prince, a resident. Alt. 58.

Print, community in n Halifax County.

Priscilla. See Ranlo-Rex-Priscilla.

Prissy Bay, sand filled bay in se Sampson County at the head of Wildcat Swamp. See also Carolina Bays.

[Pritchard Tavern]. See Buena Vista.

Privett, community in s Franklin County.

Procks Point extends into Jarrett Bay se of community of Davis, se Carteret County.

Proctor, former town in w Swain County on Hazel Creek. Alt. 1,735. Inc. 1911, but the site is now in the Great Smoky Mountains National Park. Named for William Proctor who was instrumental in having a post office est. here in 1887.

Proctor Branch rises in nw Swain County on Twentymile Ridge and flows sw into Twentymile Creek.

Proctor Creek, Great Smoky Mountains National Park, rises in w Swain County and flows s into Hazel Creek.

Proctor Ridge, Great Smoky Mountains National Park, n Swain County between Proctor Creek and Long Cove, lat. 35° 33′ 18″ N., long. 83° 35′ 46″ W.

Proctor Sang Branch rises in nw Swain County and flows east into Ekaneetlee Creek. See also Seng Branch.

Proctorville, town in s Robeson County. Alt. 120. Settled about 1870. Inc. 1913. Named for Edward Knox Proctor, Jr. (1862-1902), promoter of the Raleigh and Charleston Railroad.

Proffits Knob, n Watauga County sw of Laurel Branch.

Progress, community in nw Randolph County. Formerly known as Fraziers for a local storekeeper.

Promontorium tremendum. See Cape Fear.

Prophet Branch rises in nw Haywood County and flows se into Big Branch. Named

for a prominent mountain family who lived in the area.

Propst's Knob, sw Burke County. Alt. 3,022.

Prospect, community in w central Caswell County.

Prospect, community in nw Robeson County.

Prospect Hill, community in se Caswell County, named for the site on the former Warren family plantation because of the elevated view. A post office was est. here about 1820.

Prospect Knob, nw Iredell County.

Prospect Ridge, a narrow loam and sandy ridge traversing Green Swamp from se to nw. A road between the communities of Supply and Makatoka follows this ridge.

Prospect Ridge, se Burke County, between Laurel Creek and Henry Fork.

Prosperity. See High Falls.

Protection, community in ne Madison County.

Providence, community in nw Caswell County, sometimes known locally as "Hell's Half Acre." Post office est. here in 1953.

Providence, community in central Granville County. A former post office here was known as Hargrove. Alt. 431.

Providence, community in s McDowell County on the head of Nicks Creek.

Providence, community in s Mecklenburg County, grew up around Providence Presbyterian Church organized in 1767.

Providence Township, former township in s Mecklenburg County, now township number 5.

Providence Township, ne Pasquotank County.

Providence Township, ne Randolph County.

Providence Township, se Rowan County. Named traditionally because an act of Providence enabled Gen. Nathanael Greene to cross Yadkin River in 1781 to escape Cornwallis. See Trading Ford.

Proximity, formerly a cotton mill community in central Guilford County, now a part of Greensboro. Camp for Overseas Replacement Depot located here during World War II.

Pruetts Fork. See Jones Creek.

Public Creek rises in the highlands of Indian Island, se Camden County, and flows e into North River.

Puett Cove, ne Cherokee County in the Valley River Mountains.

Puett Creek rises in central Cherokee County and flows n into Vengeance Creek. *See also* Will Puett Cove.

Pughs, community in n Franklin County.

Pughs Island. *See* Tucker Island.

Pug Knob, on Haywood-Madison County line. Alt. 4,245.

Pulham Creek rises w Polk County and flows sw into Green River.

Pulhams Ferry. *See* Bridgers Creek.

Pump, community in ne Madison County.

Pump Branch rises in n Madison County and flows se into French Broad River.

Pump Branch rises in n Mitchell County and flows w into Big Rock Creek.

Pumpkin Center, community in n Lincoln County.

Pumpkin Center, community in central Onslow County.

Pumpkin Creek rises in sw Wilkes County and flows e into Warrior Creek. Publicity and maps of the W. Kerr Scott Reservoir show this as Punkin Creek.

Pumpkin Patch Gap, n Mitchell County between Pumpkin Patch Mountain and Meadlock Mountain.

Pumpkin Patch Mountain, central Mitchell County between Cub Creek and Little Rock Creek. Alt. 4,263.

Pumpkintown, community in w Jackson County on Savannah Creek.

Pump Mountain, n Jackson County between Cope Creek and Scott Creek. Named for the fact that the first running water in the area was run through log pipes from the mountains to the home of Thaddeus Clingman Bryson, in which the first court in Jackson County was held.

Punch Bowl, community in a small valley in s Macon County between Bates Mountain and the head of Bates Branch.

Punch Bowl Creek rises in s Alexander County and flows se into Catawba River.

Puncheon Branch rises in ne Cherokee County and flows nw into Valley River. Fortified Indian villages were protected by "wooden puncheons," high stakes driven into the ground, and this may be the source of the name.

Puncheon Camp Branch rises in w Madison County and flows nw into Spring Creek.

Puncheon Camp Creek rises in e Henderson County and flows ne into Clear Creek.

Puncheon Creek rises in se Transylvania County near Standingstone Mountain and flows nw into Reasonover Creek.

Puncheon Fork Creek rises in e Madison County and flows sw into Big Laurel Creek.

Pungo, community in ne Beaufort County on Indian Run near its junction with Pungo River. Alt. approx. 5.

Pungo Creek rises in Great Swamp, n central Beaufort County and flows se into Pungo River. Appears as Machapunga Creek on Moseley's map, 1733.

Pungo Lake, natural lake in s Washington and nw Hyde counties, in East Dismal Swamp. Inaccessible except through private property; not open to the public; owned by Roper Lumber County. Covers 2,700 acres with a maximum depth of five feet. Name is shortened from name for the Machapunga Indians.

Pungo River rises in East Dismal Swamp, Washington County and flows generally se forming the Beaufort-Hyde County line into Pamlico River near its mouth. Appears as Machapounga River on the Comberford map, 1657; as Machaponga on the Moseley map, 1733, and others until 1807 when it appears, apparently for the first time, as Pungo River on the William Tatham map. Named for the Machapunga Indians whose name is said to have meant "bad dust" or "much dust."

Punkin Creek. *See* Pumpkin Creek.

Puppy Creek rises in e Hoke County and flows s into Rockfish Creek.

Pups Branch rises in nw McDowell County and flows se into Armstrong Creek.

Pups Branch Ridge. *See* Pups Ridge.

Pups Ridge, nw McDowell County, approx. 2 mi. long. Located in Pisgah National Forest. Formerly known as Big Ridge and as Pups Branch Ridge.

Purchace Islands, the name given on the Smith map, 1624, to the nine islands in Roanoke and Cashie rivers at the conjunction of Bertie, Martin, and Washington counties. Apparently one of the islands is unnamed, but the other eight are known as Louse Island, Rice Island, Goodmans Island, Wood Island, Great Island, Huff Island, Conine Island, and Tabor Island. Smith is thought to have named the islands in honor of Samuel Purchas (1575?-1626), an English compiler of travel books.

Purchase Knob in central Haywood County between Sugar Cove and the head of Cove Creek. Named for its commanding position. It overlooks a large section of the old North Carolina Land and Lumber Co. tract and prospective buyers were taken here to get a good view of the property. Alt. 5,086.

Purgatory Mountain, central Randolph County, site of state zoo.

Purgatory Pocosin, a sandy loam filled pocosin in sw Jones and nw Onslow counties, at the head of Mill Swamp.

Purlear, community in w central Wilkes County on Cole Creek. Named for Isaac Parlier who settled on nearby Purlear Creek.

Purlear Creek rises in w Wilkes County on the w side of Rendezvous Mountain and flows s into North Prong Lewis Fork Creek. Once known as Isaac Parlier's Creek.

Purley, community in n central Caswell County. Named probably for Miss Purley Cobb, local resident. A post office was operated here during the approx. period 1860-1920. Alt. 524. Bright leaf tobacco was first produced about 1852 on the Slade farm here.

Purnell, community in n Wake County on the head of Mud Creek formerly known as Purnell Crossroads.

Purnell Crossroads. *See* Purnell.

Purviance Creek rises in e New Hanover County and flows e into Masonboro Sound.

Purvis, community in w Robeson County.

Push, community in s Person County near Aldridge Creek.

Putnam, community in n Moore County. Called Johnson City for Harvell Johnson, local resident, until renamed for Israel Putnam (1718-90), Revolutionary War General, leader and ancestor of local residents. Alt. 442.

Puzzle Creek rises in e Rutherford County and flows sw into Second Broad River. Quicksand in the creek made it a "puzzle" to early settlers who wondered whether their horses could cross it.

Pyatt Creek rises in sw Avery County and flows e into North Toe River.

Pyatte, community in central Avery County.

Q

Quail Roost, community in n Durham County. Named for a former hunting club here acquired in 1925 by George Watts Hill of Durham who turned it into a dairy farm. In 1963 the farm was given to the State of North Carolina by Hill. The large handsome house is used as a conference center by the University of North Carolina, and North Carolina State University makes use of the surrounding land.

Quaker Creek rises in ne Alamance County and flows s into Quaker Scrub Creek.

Quaker Gap Township, w central Stokes County.

Quaker Meadows, a grassy region in w central Burke County, 1 mi. ne of Morganton, lying between Canoe and Upper creeks. Settled as early as 1752; appears on the Collet map, 1770. A frontier rendezvous, built here about 1812, was called McDowell House. It was the home of Joseph and Charles McDowell, officers in the Kings Mountain campaign (1780) and later public leaders. Zebulon B. Vance and his first wife, Harriet Espy, were married here. The area is now owned by Duke Power Company.

Quaker Neck, w central Wayne County, is formed by a crook in Neuse River. Location of a Quaker settlement prior to 1758. *See also* Goldsboro Cooling Pond.

Quaker Meadows Township, central Burke County.

Quaker Scrub Creek rises in ne Alamance County and flows s into Back Creek.

Qualla, community in nw Jackson County on Shoal Creek. The name is from the Cherokee word *kwalli,* "old woman," because an old Cherokee woman, Polly, lived here. Also called Quallatown. Alt. 2,250.

Qualla Reservation, home of the Eastern Band of Cherokee Indians in the Great Smoky Mountains, Swain, Jackson, and Haywood counties. Est. by the United States after the Cherokee removal of 1838. Covers 63,000 acres and is the largest Indian reservation e of the Mississippi. The reservation is divided into Big Cove Town, Wolf Town, Yellow Hill Town, Paint Town, and Bird Town townships. In addition approx. 256 Cherokee living in Cheoah Township, Graham County, off the reservation, are under tribal jurisdiction. Land is held in common and assigned on a tenant system.

Quallatown. *See* Qualla.

Qualla Township, n Jackson County.

Qualls Creek rises in s Clay County and flows ne into Hiwassee River approx. ¾ mi. n of town of Hayesville. Named for an Indian woman.

Quankey Creek rises in n Halifax County and flows se into Roanoke River. Appears as Quountka Creek on the Moseley map, 1733; does not appear on the Collet map, 1770, or the Price map of 1808. Appears next on the MacRae map, 1833, with its present name. A Tuscarora Indian name. Numerous Indian relics have been found along its lower course.

Quaqua Creek rises in n Rockingham County and flows e into Wolf Island Creek.

Quarry Branch rises in n Alamance County and flows se into Tom's Creek.

Quarter Swamp rises in central Northampton County and flows se into Urahaw Swamp.

Quebec, community in s Transylvania County between Blue Ridge and West Fork French Board River. Alt. 2,530.

Queen. *See* Love Joy.

Queen Anne's Creek rises in s Chowan County and flows sw into the e side of Edenton Bay. Prior to about 1712 known as Mattacomack Creek. The present name appears in local records as early as 1712. *See also* Pembroke Creek.

Queen Anne's Town. *See* Edenton.

Queen Branch rises in n Macon County and flows sw into Little Tennessee River.

Queen Creek rises in nw Henderson County and flows se into South Fork.

Queen Creek rises in s Haywood County and flows e into West Fork Pigeon River.

Queen Creek Mountain, nw Henderson County extends se from Yellow Gap to Buttermilk Mountain. Alt. 3,650.

Queen Inlet. *See* Mason Inlet.

Queen Mountain, se Macon County between Sassafras Gap and Big Creek.

Queen Ridge extends ne between Snowbird and Squally creeks in w Graham County.

Queens Creek rises in nw Macon County and flows w and n into Swain County where it enters Nantahala River. Queens Falls on this stream obliterated when Nantahala Power and Light Company diverted the water for a hydroelectric project.

Queens Creek rises in e Onslow County and flows se into White Oak River. Named for Queen Anne (1665-1714). Name occurs in local records as early as 1713. Appears on the Moseley map, 1733. Otway Burns (1775-1848), Privateer in the War of 1812, was born on the w side of Queens Creek.

Queens Creek Reservoir, formed in 1948 on Queens Creek in nw Macon County. Covers 37 acres with a max. depth of 68 ft. Owned by Nantahala Power and Light Company to generate electricity.

Queens Falls. *See* Queens Creek.

Quhele. *See* Maxton.

Quewhiffle Creek rises in w Hoke County and flows s into Lumber River. The name may be derived through faulty pronunciation from the Gaelic *Culmhutar* (*pron.* kulvutar), "smuggler" or "mutineer." *See also* Cuwhiffle.

Quewhiffle Township, w Hoke County.

Quick, community in w Caswell County, originally known as Kill Quick. Post office est. here in 1898 closed about 1909.

Quillaree Branch rises in ne Swain County and flows se into Straight Fork.

Quillen Mountain on the Transylvania County, N. C.-Greenville County, S. C., line near the head of Pole Ridge Branch.

Quinerly, community in s Pitt County.

Quinine Swamp rises in nw Bertie County and flows se into Roanoke River.

Quinn Creek rises in w Cherokee County and flows nw into Shoal Creek.

Quinn's Ferry. *See* Irvinsville.

Quioccosin Swamp rises in n central Bertie County and flows nw into Stony Creek.

Quitsna, community in sw Bertie County. Name formerly spelled Quitonoi, a Tuscarora Indian word meaning "strong and mighty."

Quonutka Creek. *See* Quankey Creek.

Quoracks River. *See* Trent River.

Quotankney Creek. *See* Contentnea Creek.

R

Rabbit Creek rises in e Macon County and flows sw into Lake Emory.

Rabbit Mountain, e Macon County between Cat Creek and Rabbit Creek.

Rabbit Mountain, w Montgomery County between Lick Mountain and Cedar Creek.

Rabbit Ridge, w Haywood County on Caldwell Fork.

Rabbits Crossroads, community in sw Chatham County approx. 3¼ mi. w of Bonlee.

Rabbit Shuffle, community in central Caswell County, named because the land was said to be so poor that "a rabbit had to shuffle to get his rations."

Rabbitskin Branch rises in central Haywood County and flows n into Pigeon River.

Raby Bend, in Little Tennessee River in n Macon County.

Raccoon Bay in Currituck Sound off the w shore of Currituck Banks, e Currituck County.

Raccoon Branch rises in w Madison County and flows ne into French Broad River.

Raccoon Branch rises in s Watauga County and flows n into East Fork [of South Fork New River].

Raccoon Creek rises in s Haywood County and flows n into Richland Creek.

Raccoon Creek rises in w Lee County and flows nw into Pocket Creek.

Raccoon Creek rises in n Pamlico County and flows se into Bay River.

Raccoon Creek rises in sw Perquimans County in Bear Swamp and flows ne into Perquimans River. Until early in the twentieth century it was known as Skinners Creek. In colonial days it was known as Castletons Creek (for George Castleton, a landowner here prior to 1688). Two small streams, now without names, which form the headwaters of Raccoon Creek were known in the seventeenth and eighteenth centuries as Lakers Creek (for Benjamin Laker who owned land here in 1686) and Perrishoes Creek (for James Perishoe who lived on the creek prior to 1688). Lakers Creek appears on the Moseley map, 1733.

Raccoon Creek rises in n Stokes County and flows sw into Snow Creek.

Raccoon Creek rises in w Mitchell County and flows sw into Toe River.

Raccoon Key, an island in Pamlico Sound in n end of Carteret County.

Raccoon Mountain, w Polk County. Alt. approx. 2,000.

Raccoon Ridge, w Avery County.

Raccoon Swamp rises in se Bladen County and flows w into Colly Creek.

Raccoon Swamp rises in se Johnston County and flows s into Neuse River.

Race Prong rises in ne Nash County and flows se into Beaverdam Swamp.

Rackley Mill Pond. See McLamb Mill Pond.

Radder Creek rises in ne Cherokee County and flows ne into Worm Creek.

Radford Crossroads, community in e Johnston County.

Radical, community in n Wilkes County between Chestnut and Herald Mountains.

Raeford, town and county seat, central Hoke County. Settled 1867; inc. 1901. Took its name from the last syllables of two of the town's founders, J. A. MacRae and A. A. Williford. Produces textiles, lumber, concrete, rubber; processes poultry, and cotton. Alt. 262.

Raeford Township, central Hoke County.

Raft Swamp rises in s Hoke County and flows se into central Robeson County where it enters Lumber River. Much Tory activity during the Revolution was centered here, and the name is frequently mentioned in records of the time.

Raft Swamp Township, central Robeson County.

Rag Creek rises in n McDowell County and flows approx. 2 mi. se into Cox Creek.

Ragged Point, in central Onslow County, extends into n Morgan Bay.

Raglins Ferry. See Mush Island.

Ragsdale Creek rises in central Buncombe County and flows se into Hominy Creek.

Raider Camp Creek rises in se Avery County and flows se into Caldwell County where it enters Harper Creek.

Raider Camp Ridge, se Avery County.

Rail Cove, ne Cherokee County at the head of Rail Cove Branch.

Rail Cove Branch rises in ne Cherokee

County and flows sw and ne into Ingram Branch.

Railroad Pond, e Anson County, se of Lilesville. Covers approx. 4 acres; max. depth 12 ft. Formed early in the twentieth century when gravel was removed from the site.

Rainbow Banks, steep bank of the Roanoke River, n Martin County between Poplar Point on the e and town of Hamilton on the w. Mentioned in an act of the General Assembly in 1729 and appears on the Collet map, 1770.

Rainbow Creek rises in s Greene County and flows ne into Contentnea Creek. The name appears in local records as early as 1730.

Rainbow Falls in sw Transylvania County on Horsepasture River. Height of falls is 200 ft.

Rainbow Gap, ne Buncombe County between Lookout Mountain and Montreat. Alt. approx. 3,250.

Rainbow Gap on the Buncombe-Yancey County line between Blackstock and Potato Knobs. Alt. approx. 5,860.

Rainbow Islands, areas of fine, sandy loam surrounded by swamp in e Washington County sw of the community of Scuppernong.

Rainbow Lake in s Transylvania County on Middle Creek near its junction with East Fork French Broad River. Covers two acres and has a max. depth of 20 ft. Used for recreation.

Rainbow Springs, community in sw Macon County on Pat Stable Branch.

Raines Crossroads, community in e Johnston County.

Raines Mountain, Transylvania County between Carson Creek and Dunn Creek.

Rainey Knob, sw Transylvania County between Thompson River and Horsepasture River.

Rakahak. See Rockyhock Creek.

Raleigh, city, county seat, and state capital, central Wake County on Neuse River. Made county seat in 1771 and known as Wake Court House until the site was selected as the state capital in 1792 and named for Sir Walter Raleigh (1552?-1618), English statesman who sent the first English colonists to Roanoke Island. Inc. 1794. The legislature met at Wake Court House in 1781 and has met in Raleigh since 1794. Alt. 363. Now includes former communities of Oberlin and Caraleigh, which see; and West Raleigh.

Home of North Carolina State University, Meredith College, Peace College, St. Mary's Junior College, Shaw University, and St. Augustine's College. Produces farm machinery, bakery products, processed meat, paper products, fabricated metals, textiles, dairy products, and cottonseed oil; printing and publishing.

Raleigh Bay in the Atlantic Ocean off the central coast of North Carolina from Cape Lookout on the s to Cape Hatteras on the n.

Raleigh Township, central Wake County.

Ramah Creek rises in n Mecklenburg County and flows se into Clarks Creek.

Ram Branch rises in central Buncombe County and flows nw into Swannanoa River.

Ramey Creek rises in nw Surry County and flows e into Roaring Fork.

Raminger Creek rises in s Cherokee County and flows ne into Nottely River.

Ramoth, former town in central Buncombe County. Inc. 1889; name changed to Woolsey in 1903; became a part of Asheville in 1905.

Ramp Branch rises in n central Avery County and flows ne into Elk River.

Ramp Cove, ne Cherokee County in the Valley River Mountains. Named because ramps grow abundantly here.

Ramp Cove Branch rises in ne Cherokee County and flows nw through Ramp Cove and Big Cove into Vengeance Creek.

Ramsaytown, community in n Yancey County on Cane River s of Sugarloaf Mountain. Alt. 2,141.

Ramseur, town in e Randolph County on Deep River. Known as Allen's Fall prior to 1878; named Columbia after 1878 when Deep River Mills est. Inc. 1895 as Ramseur in honor of Stephen D. Ramseur (1837-64), Confederate Major General with whom William H. Watkins, one of the local mill owners, had been associated during the Civil War. Alt. 442.

Ramsey, community in s tip of Burke County on headwaters of Jacob Fork.

Ramsey Bend, in the Hiwassee River in central Cherokee County.

Ramsey Creek rises in s Iredell County and flows w into Catawba River.

Ramsey Creek rises in nw Northampton County and flows se into Potecasi Creek.

Ramsey Gap, n Madison County at the head of Cascade Branch.

Ramsey Mountain, n Buncombe County, n of Wolfpen Gap.

Ramsey's Mill. See Lockport.

Ramseytown Township, n Yancey County.

Ramsour's Mill. See Lincolnton.

Ramushawn River appears on the Comberford map, 1657, in what is now Chowan County. Its identity is uncertain but it lay between Yeopim River and Chowan River and may have been intended for the present Pembroke Creek.

Randall Gap, central Buncombe County near the headwaters of Ross Creek.

Randall Lake, on Big Creek in se Macon County.

Randleman, town in n Randolph County on Deep River. First known as Dicks for Peter Dicks who built a grist mill here approx. 1830; in 1848, a cotton mill was built here and the name changed to Union Factory. In 1866 the name was changed to Randleman for John B. Randleman, one of the owners of the mill. Inc. in 1880 as Randleman Mills; name changed to Randleman in 1889. Naomi Falls, low natural falls in Deep River, was here but now under the water behind a 25 ft. dam. Falls named for Naomi Wise who was drowned here by Jonathan Lewis in 1808.

Randleman Township, nw Randolph County.

Randolph. See Hinshaw.

Randolph County was formed in 1779 from Guilford County. Located in the central section of the state, it is bounded by Chatham, Moore, Montgomery, Davidson, Guilford, and Alamance counties. It was named for Peyton Randolph (1721?-75), president of the Continental Congress. Area: 801 sq. mi. County seat: Asheboro with an elevation of 879 ft. Townships are Asheboro, Back Creek, Brower, Cedar Grove, Coleridge, Columbia, Concord, Franklinville, Grant, Level Cross, Liberty, New Hope, New Market, Pleasant Grove, Providence, Randleman, Seagrove, and Trinity. Produces wheat, corn, oats,

poultry, dairy products, hogs, livestock, hosiery, apparel, textiles, batteries, toys, furniture, shoes, and electric blankets.

Randolph Mill. See Forest Hill.

Rands Mill, community in e Wake County near Swift Creek.

Rands Mill Pond. See Lake Benson.

Randys Store, community in n Montgomery County on Barnes Creek.

Ranger, community in s Cherokee County on Walker Mill Creek near Nottely River. Alt. approx. 1,565.

Ranlo-Rex-Priscilla and Smyre Mills, an industrial community in e Gaston County between Lowell and East Gastonia. Textile manufacturing plants and a large warehouse of the Burlington Industries are here.

Ranns Falls, rapids in Cape Fear River in central Harnett County e of the town of Lillington. Mentioned as early as 1819 in a survey of the rivers of North Carolina.

Ransom's Bridge, community at the junction of Nash, Franklin, Warren, and Halifax counties, formerly thriving, but now sparsely settled. There is a bridge here over Fishing Creek. A post office by this name existed as early as 1822 and as recently as 1882. Was the center of gold mining activity before the Civil War.

Ransomville, community in e Beaufort County at the head of North Creek. Named for the Confederate general, Matthew W. Ransom (1826-1904).

Ranson Township, e Columbus County.

Rantersville. See LaGrange.

Raoul Branch rises in s Buncombe County near the Biltmore Estate and flows sw into Fourmile Branch.

Rapid Creek Ridge, Great Smoky Mountains National Park, ne Swain County, a short spur extending s from Dashoga Ridge, lat. 35° 39' 10" N., long. 83° 15' W.

Rapier Mill Creek rises in sw Cherokee County and flows se and ne into Nottely River.

Ratcliff Cove, in central Haywood County, forms a semicircle on the head of a tributary of Raccoon Creek, w of Ratcliff Mountain.

Ratcliff Mountain, central Haywood County between Bird Creek and Ratcliff Cove.

Rattan Bay, w Piney Island in ne Carteret County bounded by Neuse River and North, East, and South bays. Approx. 1 mi. wide and ¾ mi. long.

Rattan Ridge, a strip of higher ground in the Dismal Swamp in se Gates County.

Rattler Branch rises in e Cherokee County and flows nw into Valley River.

Rattler Ford, across Santeetlah Creek in w Graham County.

Rattle Shoal Creek rises in n Gaston County and flows ne into South Fork Catawba River.

Rattlesnake Branch rises in e central Brunswick County and flows e to join Lewis Swamp in forming Town Creek.

Rattlesnake Branch rises in se Brunswick County and flows sw into River Swamp.

Rattlesnake Branch rises in nw Columbus County and flows w then n into Horsepen Creek.

Rattlesnake Branch rises in n Duplin County and flows e into Northeast Cape Fear River.

Rattlesnake Branch rises in n Jones County and flows se into Beaver Creek.

Rattlesnake Branch rises in nw McDowell County on the s slope of Woods Mountain and flows se, approx. 1 mi., into Little Buck Creek.

Rattlesnake Branch rises in e Macon County and flows nw into Brush Creek.

Rattlesnake Cliff, mountain in e Swain County between Hayes Ridge and Hickorynut Knob. Alt. 4,950.

Rattle Snake Creek is formed in n Caswell County by the junction of North Fork of Rattle Snake Creek and South Fork of Rattle Snake Creek and flows n into Dan River.

Rattlesnake Creek rises in n Macon County and flows ne into Swain County where it enters Little Tennessee River.

Rattlesnake Creek rises in w Pender County and flows se into Whiteoak Creek.

Rattle Snake Island, a small tidal marsh island in Currituck Sound off the se shore of the mainland of Currituck County.

Rattlesnake Knob, se Buncombe County, nw of Lake Charles.

Rattlesnake Knob, on the Buncombe-Haywood County line.

Rattlesnake Knob, ne Cherokee County in the Valley River Mountains.

Rattlesnake Knob, w Haywood County on the w end of Eaglenest Ridge.

Rattlesnake Knob, n Henderson County at the head of Harper Creek.

Rattlesnake Knob, at the head of Younce Creek in n Macon County.

Rattlesnake Knob, in se Macon County between Rich Mountain and Houston Branch.

Rattlesnake Knob on the Jackson-Macon County line.

Rattlesnake Knob between Glassy Rock Ridge and Glenville Lake in s Jackson County.

Rattlesnake Knob on the se end of Rattlesnake Ridge in n Jackson County.

Rattlesnake Knob, nw Macon County between Pierce Creek and Rowlin Creek.

Rattlesnake Knob, sw Macon County between Bryson Branch and Moore Creek.

Rattlesnake Knob, Great Smoky Mountains National Park, n Swain County, on the sw end of Long Drive Ridge, lat. 35° 33' 07" N., long. 83° 23' 50" W. Alt. 4,311.

Rattlesnake Mountain, on Jackson-Swain County line near the head of Owl Branch.

Rattlesnake Pocosin, s Duplin County on Island Creek.

Rattlesnake Ridge, n Buncombe County between Greenfield Ridge and Snowball Gap.

Rattlesnake Ridge, n Jackson County between Rocky Face and North Fork.

Rattlesnake Ridge, s Macon County parallel to Shoal Creek.

Rattlesnake Ridge, e Mitchell County between Young Cove and Rock Creek Gap.

Rattlesnake Ridge, Great Smoky Mountains National Park, n Swain County, a short spur extending nw from Welch Ridge, lat. 35° 30' 55" N., long. 83° 37' W.

Raven Cliff Branch rises in n Haywood County and flows nw into Cold Springs Creek.

Ravencliff Mountain, e Haywood County between Crab Orchard Fields and Rush Fork Gap.

Raven Cliff Ridge, se Haywood County between Bell Collar Cove and Little Buckeye Cove.

Raven Cliffs, on the Avery-Mitchell County line.

Raven Den, peak in n Swain County on Locust Ridge near the head of Bee Gum Branch. Alt. 4,247.

Ravenel Lake, se Macon County in the e edge of the town of Highlands on Mill Creek. Approx. ½ mi. long.

Ravenel Lake, se Macon County near the head of Cullasaja River, 2 mi. nw of Highlands. Approx. 2 mi. long. This is probably the Stewart's Pond visited by Bradford Torrey and described in *The Atlantic Monthly*, September, 1897.

Raven Fork [Oconaluftee River], ne Swain County in Great Smoky Mountains National Park, is formed by the junction of Left Fork [Raven Fork] and Right Fork [Raven Fork] and flows sw into Oconaluftee River. *See also* Straight Fork.

Raven Fork rises in sw Yancey County and flows ne into Cane River.

Raven Hollow, s Haywood County between Beartrap Knob and Beartrap Ridge.

Raven Knob, n Buncombe County between Ingles Gap and Paint Fork Gap.

Raven Knob, nw Surry County.

Raven Knob. *See* Raven Mountain.

Raven Knob Pond, nw Surry County on an unnamed tributary of Fisher River. Covers 15 acres; max. depth 20 ft. Formed in 1950. Fishing, boating, swimming. Owned by Old Hickory Council, Boy Scouts of America.

Raven Mountain, on the Macon-Swain County line near the head of Cold Spring Branch. Alt. approx. 4,700. Sometimes also known as Raven Knob.

Raven Ridge, Great Smoky Mountains National Park, ne Swain County, lat. 35° 40' N., long. 83° 17' W.

Raven Rock, mountain in ne Henderson County.

Raven Rock, ne Swain County at the s end of Hyatt Ridge between Raven Fork and Straight Fork.

Ravenrock Ridge, se Clay County between Left Fork and Right Fork [of Eagle Creek].

Raven Rocks, peak in s Watauga County on the head of China Creek, approx. 2 mi. nw of town of Blowing Rock. Alt. 3,913.

Raven Roost Ridge, Great Smoky Mountains National Park, ne Swain County, a short spur extending nw from Chiltoskie Ridge, lat. 35° 36' 08" N., long. 83° 12' 55" W.

Ravensford, community in Great Smoky Mountains National Park, e Swain County, on Raven Fork near where it enters Oconaluftee River. Alt. 2,100.

Ravenswood, community in s Jones County.

Rawls, community in n Harnett County.

Ray Branch rises in w Macon County and flows ne into Deweese Branch.

Ray Cove, n Buncombe County between Ray Knob and Reems Creek.

Ray Knob, n Buncombe County between Horse Gap and Vance Knob.

Raymond Island, off of w side of Currituck Banks in Currituck Sound s of South Channel, ne Currituck County.

Raymond's Creek rises in s Camden County and flows sw into Pasquotank River. Named for William Raymond who was granted land bordering the creek on February 25, 1696. Earlier called Fleming's Creek for George Fleming who owned a small tract along the creek and who died there in 1694.

Rayner Millpond, w Wayne County on a tributary of Beaverdam Creek.

Raynham, community in s Robeson County. Alt. 125. Settled about 1884. Named for the parish in Norfolk, England, from which the local Townsend family had come.

Raynor, community in s Franklin County.

Raynor Pond, on Mingo Swamp in sw Johnston County and e Harnett County.

Raynors Lake, a crescent-shaped lake on Cypress Creek in se Duplin County.

Raynor Swamp rises in s Gates County and flows nw to join Harrell Swamp and Duke Swamp in forming Bennetts Creek. Originally known as Meherrin Swamp.

Ray's Branch rises in ne Wake County near the Franklin County line and flows s into Neuse River.

Rays Creek rises in w Franklin County and flows ne into Cedar Creek.

Rays Fork rises in e Union County and flows nw into Richardson Creek.

Ray's Mill Creek rises at the town of Southern Pines in s Moore County and flows sw into Aberdeen Creek at the town of Aberdeen.

Razo Creek. *See* Resoe Creek.

Razorback Ridge, w Avery County.

Razor Mountain, n Buncombe County between Poverty Branch and Martin Creek.

Reading. *See* Elizabeth City.

Ready Branch rises in s Jones County and flows n into Trent River.

Ready Branch rises in s Martin County and flows se into Statons Pond on Sweetwater Creek.

Readybranch, community in sw Wilkes County near the head of Naked Creek. A post office was est. here prior to 1882.

Reas Beach. *See* Albemarle Beach.

Reasonover Creek rises in se Transylvania County and flows ne then n into Little River.

Reasonover Lake in se Transylvania County in Reasonover Creek. Covers 16 acres and has a max. depth of 22 ft.

Reatkin River. *See* Yadkin River.

Reaves, community in n Cumberland County.

Reba, community in s central Transylvania County.

Reba. *See* Fountain.

Rebels Creek rises in central Mitchell County and flows sw into North Toe River.

Rector Branch rises in w Madison County and flows ne into Big Pine Creek.

Rector Butte, w Madison County near the head of Rector Branch.

Rector Knob, e central Burke County. Alt. 2,153.

Rector Knob, s Macon County between Cadon Branch and Cadon Gap.

Redallia, community in s Pitt County.

Redbank Branch rises in w Haywood County and flows nw into Richland Creek.

Redbank Creek rises in n Forsyth County and flows ne into s Stokes County where it enters Town Fork Creek. Called Old-field Creek on the Collet map, 1770, and on subsequent maps through the Kerr map, 1882. Apparently the soil survey map of 1913 was the first to use the present name. A Redbanks Church near the creek has been in existence since 1859.

Redbank Creek rises in n Stokes County and flows s into Dan River.

Redbanks, community in w Robeson County. Alt. 179. Pembroke Farms here est. 1938 by the Farm Security Administration as a cooperative under a 99-year lease. Fifteen families, members of the cooperative, still operate the farms here. Redbanks is named for the relatively high clay banks of nearby Lumber River.

Red Branch rises in e Cabarrus County and flows e into Dutch Buffalo Creek.

Redbud Creek rises in ne Franklin County and flows e into Nash County where it enters Sandy Creek. Formerly known as Redbud Swamp.

Redbud Creek rises in w Vance County and flows sw into Ruin Creek. Named for the abundance of redbud trees (*Cercis canadensis*) in the area.

Red Bug, community in sw Brunswick County.

Redbug, community in central Columbus County.

Redcross, community in n Randolph County.

Red Cross, community in sw Stanly County.

Red Creek. *See* Clear Creek.

Reddick Branch. *See* Reddix Branch.

Reddies River is formed in w Wilkes County by the junction of North Fork Reddies River and Middle Fork Reddies River. It flows se into Yadkin River.

Reddies River, community in w Wilkes County on Reddies River. The area was settled prior to the Revolutionary War.

Reddies River Township, central Wilkes County.

Redding. *See* Elizabeth City.

Redding Mountain, e Wilkes County n of Flat Rock Creek.

Reddix Branch rises in s Mitchell County near Swafford Gap and flows w into East Fork Grassy Creek. Said to have been named for the Reddix family which camped near its head. While here two of their children died of colic and were buried at the head of the stream. Recent maps have used the form Reddick.

Reddy Branch rises in nw Madison County and flows s into Shelton Laurel Creek.

Red Hill, community in n Duplin County.

Red Hill, community in n Edgecombe County. In 1855, when Wilson County was formed in part from Edgecombe, Red Hill was described as "Henry Horn's old place."

Red Hill, community in w Mitchell County.

Red Hill, community in n Sampson County between Merkle Swamp and Great Coharie Creek.

Red Hill Creek rises in w Surry County and flows se and ne into Fisher River.

Red Hill Knob, central Madison County. Alt. 3,180.

Red Hill Swamp, the lower course of Brown Marsh Swamp (*which see*). The name is applied at the Bladen-Columbus County line and it flows s across Columbus County. At the junction with Western Prong the name is changed to White Marsh, (*which see*).

Red Hill Township, w central Mitchell County.

Red Horse Creek. *See* Worley Cove Branch.

Red House, community in ne Caswell County. Post office from about 1820 to about 1850. Named for Red House Presbyterian Church where the Rev. Hugh McAden, eighteenth-century missionary, preached and is buried.

Redland, community in n Davie County. Originally known as Bethlehem community for a Methodist Church (on the site of Old Timber Ridge Meeting House where Moravian ministers preached as early as 1773). When a post office was est. here in 1892 the name Bethlehem could not be used as it was already in use elsewhere in the state. Redland was chosen as descriptive of the soil hereabout. Alt. 875.

Red Log Gap, n Cherokee County at the sw end of State Ridge. Alt. 3,697.

Redman Creek is formed in ne Swain County by the confluence of Left Fork and Right Fork and flows sw into Bunches Creek.

Redman Ridge, Great Smoky Mountains National Park, ne Swain County, a spur extending sw from Balsam Mountain, lat. 35° 34' 15" N., long. 83° 12' W.

Redmans Cove, s Buncombe County sw of Hogback Ridge.

Redmans Old Field, appears on the Collet map, 1770, as open ground on the n side of Cokey Swamp, which see, w central Edgecombe County, s of Tarboro.

Red Marble Gap, ne Cherokee County. Alt. 2,750. See also Topton.

Red Marble Gap, at the head of Rowlin Creek on the Graham-Macon County line. Alt. approx. 2,750.

Redmon, community in se Madison County. Inc. 1897; charter repealed 1899. Alt. 1,603.

Redmond Creek, a tidal stream on the w side of Eagles Island in the Cape Fear River, ne Brunswick County.

Red Mountain, n Durham County.

Red Mountain. See Rougemont.

Red Oak, town in n Nash County. Settled about 1880 and named for a grove of red oaks at the site. Inc. 1961. Alt. 225.

Red Oak Cove, nw Haywood County on the head of Low Gap Branch in the Great Smoky Mountains National Park.

Red Oak Knob, n Buncombe County near the Madison County line.

Red Oak Township, n central Nash County.

Red Ridge, Great Smoky Mountains National Park, nw Swain County, a short spur extending e from Twentymile Ridge, lat. 35° 29' 40" N., long. 83° 48' 10" W.

Red Ridge Gap, Great Smoky Mountains National Park, nw Swain County, on Twentymile Ridge between Lost Cove Creek and Coldspring Branch, lat. 35° 29' 52" N., long. 83° 48' 47" W.

Red Rock Ridge, n Avery County.

Red Run rises in e central Brunswick County and flows se to join Pinch Gut Creek in forming Lockwoods Folly River.

Red Shoal, community in e central Stokes County. A post office est. here as early as 1822 continued through 1882.

Red Sour, mountain in nw Cleveland County.

Red Springs, town in n Robeson County. Alt. 204. Inc. 1896 but settled much earlier. At the site of former Flora MacDonald College here, Vardell Hall, a school for girls, was est. in 1964. The town was named for the color of spring and well water here—red because of iron oxides. Known first as Dora but changed to Red Springs in 1885. Formerly a popular health resort. Produces textiles, fertilizer, and lumber products.

Red Springs Township, nw Robeson County.

Redstone Point, on the mainland of n Dare County extending into Croatan Sound. The William B. Umstead Bridge, approx. 3 mi. long and opened on Dec. 22, 1956, extends from this point to Weir Point on nw Roanoke Island; named for Governor William B. Umstead (1895-1954).

Red Store Crossroads, community in w Duplin County.

Red Town. See Deep Run.

Redwood, community in e Durham County on Neuse River. Est. 1890. Named for red oaks growing in the vicinity. Flourished 1895-1917. Following the removal of a lumber mill during World War I the community declined.

Reece Mountain, e Lincoln County near Killian Creek.

Reed Branch rises in se Buncombe County and flows sw into Ashworth Creek.

Reed Branch rises in w Jackson County and flows ne into Savannah Creek.

Reed Cove, s Buncombe County e of Fannie Ridge.

Reed Cove, e Haywood County on n side of Fork Mountain. Reed Creek flows w through this cove.

Reed Creek rises in s Buncombe County and flows se into Gap Creek.

Reed Creek rises in central Buncombe County nw of Asheville near Patton Mountain and flows w through Asheville into French Broad River.

Reed Creek rises in se Catawba County and flows se into Mountain Creek.

Reed Creek rises in e Haywood County and flows w into Pisgah Creek.

Reed Creek rises in n Lincoln County and flows s into Leepers Creek.

Reed Creek rises in e Randolph County and flows sw into Deep River.

Reed Creek rises in s Randolph County and flows se into Little River.

Reed Creek rises in e Stokes County and flows e into Rockingham County.

Reeders Creek rises in s Greene County and flows e into Tyson Marsh.

Reed Marsh, rises in s Nash County and flows sw into Haw Branch.

Reed Mine, former gold mine in e central Cabarrus County w of community of Georgeville. Gold was discovered here in 1799, and the finding of a 28-lb. nugget set off a gold rush. This was the site of the first authentic discovery of gold in the state. Named for John Reed on whose farm the discovery was made.

Reed Misenheimers Township. See Earnhardt's township.

Reeds Creek rises in s Iredell County and flows s into Mecklenburg County where it enters Davidson Creek.

Reeds Crossroads, community in w Davidson County at the head of Beaverdam Creek.

Reeds Hammock, an island in Pamlico River, se Beaufort County, approx. ½ mi. long and ²/₁₀ mi. wide. See also The Ditch.

Reed's Landing. See Great Neck Landing.

Reeds Point, a point extending from the mainland of ne Dare County into Croatan Sound.

Reedy Branch rises in s Alamance County and flows ne into Cane Creek.

Reedy Branch rises in ne Caldwell County and flows n into Yadkin River.

Reedy Branch rises in nw Duplin County and flows ne into Goshen Swamp.

Reedy Branch rises in se Duplin County and flows se into Back Swamp.

Reedy Branch rises in ne Franklin County and flows ne into Little Shocco Creek.

Reedy Branch rises in n Johnston County and flows sw into Little Branch.

Reedy Branch rises in w Johnston County and flows se into Black Creek.

Reedy Branch rises on the Jones-Craven County line and flows nw into Trent River.

Reedy Branch rises in s Lee County and flows n into Thoroughfare Branch.

Reedy Branch rises in ne Northampton County and flows ne into Kirbys Creek.

Reedy Branch rises in s Robeson County and flows se into Oldfield Swamp.

Reedy Branch rises in e Wake County and flows sw into Little River.

Reedy Branch rises in s Wake County and flows s into Buck Branch.

Reedy Branch rises in w Wake County and flows sw into Beaver Creek.

Reedy Creek rises in sw Burke County and flows nw into Old Catawba River approx. 8 mi. w of town of Morganton.

Reedy Creek rises in sw Cabarrus County and flows ne into Rocky River.

Reedy Creek rises in n Davidson County and flows sw into Yadkin River. Appears on the Collet map, 1770.

Reedy Creek rises in e Mecklenburg County and flows ne into Cabarrus County where it enters Rocky River.

Reedy Creek rises in s Rowan County and flows ne approx. 4 mi. into South Second Creek. Mentioned in local records as early as 1762 as Reedy Fork.

Reedy Creek rises in central Warren County and flows se into w Halifax County where it enters Little Fishing Creek. Appears on the Price map, 1808.

Reedy Creek, community in nw Davidson County.

Reedy Creek Bay, an arm of Big Colly Bay in ne Bladen County.

Reedy Creek State Park, former park in nw Wake County est. 1943 for Negroes on 1,234 acres. Consolidated in 1965 with William B. Umstead State Park, which see.

Reedy Creek Township, nw Davidson County.

Reedy Fork rises in e Forsyth County and flows e into w Guilford County, ne across Guilford County and into nw Alamance County where it enters Haw River. Mentioned in local records as early as 1755.

Reedy Fork. See Reedy Creek.

Reedy Fork Creek rises in central Anson County and flows s into North Fork Jones Creek.

Reedy Fork Creek rises in e Caswell County and flows ne into North Hyco Creek.

Reedy Glade, a branch, rises in e Craven County and flows e into Broad Creek.

Reedy Island, an elevated sand and loam area approx. ¼ mi. wide and ¼ mi. long in e Duplin County approx. 2 mi. se of community of Hadley.

Reedy Meadow Creek rises in w Bladen County and flows w into Bryants Pond on Black Swamp.

Reedy Patch Creek rises in e Henderson County and flows ne into Broad River.

Reedy Patch Gap, e Henderson County

near the head of Reedy Patch Creek. Alt.
2,242.

Reedy Pocosin, the nw section of Big Pocosin, sw Beaufort County.

Reedy Swamp rises in e Robeson County
and flows s into Ten Mile Swamp.

Reedy Swamp rises from several small
branches in w Harnett County and flows
se to join McLeod Creek in forming
Jumping Run Creek. Approx. 3½ mi.
long.

Reelsboro, community in w Pamlico County. Named for the local Reel family.

Reems Branch rises in s Madison County
and flows se into Ponder Branch.

Reems Creek rises in ne Buncombe County
near Snowball Mountain and flows w into
French Broad River. Probably named for
a pioneer settler named Reems who was
killed by Indians near present Weaverville about 1785. The name also appears
in local records as Rims, Reams, and
Rheims Creek. See also Lane Pinnacle.

Reems Creek. See Weaverville.

Reems Creek Township, n central Buncombe County.

Reepsville, community in w central Lincoln
County.

Reese, community in nw Watauga County
on Little Beaverdam Creek. Est. before
1900. Alt. 3,320.

Reese Creek rises in e Cumberland County
and flows sw into Lords Creek.

Reeves, community in s Columbus County.

Regal Station, a stop on the Southern Railway in central Cherokee County.

Regans Crossroads, community in w Brunswick County.

Registers Creek rises in s Guilford County
and flows se into Hickory Creek.

Rehoboth, community in s Northampton
County on Quarter Swamp. Grew up
around Rehoboth Methodist Church, est.
1798.

Reid, community in sw Transylvania County near the head of South Fork Flat
Creek. Alt. 2,725.

Reids Mountain, se Rowan County near
Yadkin River at the mouth of Flat Creek.

Reid's Springs. See Catawba Springs.

Reidsville, town in s Rockingham County.
Grew out of a settlement begun in 1815
by Reuben Reid on his farm. A post
office est. as early as 1829. Inc. 1873. Alt.
841. Appears on the Colton map, 1861.

Reidsville Township, se Rockingham County.

Reinhardt Gap, on the Haywood-Jackson
County line. Alt. 5,440.

Reinhart Knob, on the Haywood-Jackson
County line. Alt. 6,100.

Relief, community in w Mitchell County on
Toe River. Alt. 2,092. Named for the
patent medicine, Hart's Relief, a popular
product with a high alcoholic content
sold at John Peterson's store here after
about 1870.

Rena, community in w Yadkin County on
South Deep Creek.

Rendezvous Mountain, w central Wilkes
County between the heads of Purlear and
Cole creeks. Alt. 2,450. Named from the
fact that militiamen from the area are
believed to have gathered here to drill
and that it is the traditional rendezvous
site for some troops which assembled before marching to the Battle of Kings
Mountain, October 7, 1780. In 1926
Judge and Mrs. Thomas B. Finley gave
the state 142 acres here for a state park.
In 1956 it was voted by the Board of the
Department of Conservation and Development to return this property to the
donors or their heirs-at-law since it lacked certain qualities and characteristics for
a state historic park. This action is still
pending, and the property remains under
state control.

Renfro Knob, w Yancey County between
Hardscrabble Branch and Nubbinscuffle
Creek.

Rennert, community in n Robeson County.
Inc. 1895; charter repealed 1947. Known
as McAlpin's Grove until the Atlantic
Coast Line Railroad was constructed
when the name was changed, probably
to honor someone connected with the
railroad. James McAlpin, for whom the
community was first named, is said to
have been a Scottish officer in the British
Army during the American Revolution.
After the war he remained in North Carolina, taking an oath of allegiance to the
United States and becoming a school
teacher in the comunity which came to
bear his name.

Rennert Township, n Robeson County.

Rennys Creek rises in s Craven County and
flows ne into Neuse River.

Renston, community in sw Pitt County.
Alt. 67.

Reps Martin Island, 14-acre sandy island in
Yadkin River, ne Yadkin County.

Republican, community in w central Bertie
County. Named for the Republican Baptist Church here. The name derived from

the fact that the church was a public meeting place for the neighborhood.

Resaca, community in ne Duplin County.

Research Park, a 5,000-acre tract in se Durham and w Wake counties near the center of the Research Triangle, *which see.* Many industrial and governmental research facilities have been est. here in a campus-like setting. The site began to be occupied in 1959 although several years of planning had preceded that event.

Research Triangle, a term applied to that part of Durham, Orange, and Wake counties between Duke University, the University of North Carolina, and North Carolina State University. The name was applied by mid-1954. The Research Park, *which see,* lies near the center of the triangle formed by these three universities. Named from the fact that much scientific and other research is carried on in the area by persons associated with the institutions in Durham, Chapel Hill, and Raleigh.

Reservoir Branch rises in nw Madison County and flows e into Spring Creek.

Resoe Creek rises in central Pender County and flows s into Rileys Creek. Also known as Razo and Rizzo Creek.

Resolution Branch rises in n Jones County and flows s into Trent River.

Resootskeh, a Tuscarora Indian village in Bertie County on Indian Creek which appears on the Moseley map, 1733. This was the town of "King Blount," the friendly Indian chief who aided the whites during the Tuscarora Indian War, 1711-13. The modern Tuscarora spelling of the word is Resootska, and it means "to our grandfather."

Retreat, community in s Haywood County between Inman Branch and West Fork Pigeon River. Also known as Riverside, the name of the local Baptist Church.

Reuben, community in ne Union County.

Reuben Creek rises in e Mitchell County and flows sw into Little Rock Creek.

Reuben Mountain, w Stokes County at the head of East Prong Little Yadkin River.

Revere, community in central Madison County on Revere Creek.

Revere Creek rises in central Madison County and flows nw into Big Laurel Creek.

Revis Branch rises in n Buncombe County and flows nw into s Madison County where it enters Ivy River.

Revolution, former community in central Guilford County. Est. 1899. Named because the textile plant est. here was expected to revolutionize the cotton manufacturing industry. Now within Greensboro city limits.

Rex, community in ne Robeson County.

Rex. *See* Ranlo-Rex-Priscilla.

Reynolda Lake, semi-natural lake on Silas Creek on Reynolda Estate near the Wake Forest College campus in central Forsyth County. Covers 25 acres with a max. depth of 15 ft. Used for fishing, boating, swimming, and irrigation. Not open to the public.

Reynolds Cove, nw Buncombe County ne of Rocky Knob.

Reynolds Gap, s Buncombe County between Lancy Mountain and Grassy Knob.

Reynolds Gap, s Macon County between the head of Ball Creek and the head of Dryman Fork.

Reynoldson, community in n Gates County. Reynoldson School operated here prior to the Civil War to prepare boys for Wake Forest College. The school was opened in 1856 and operated into the twentieth century.

Reynoldson Township, nw Gates County.

Rhea Branch rises in n Cherokee County in Rhea Cove and flows se and s into Valley River.

Rhea Cove, n Cherokee County at the head of Rhea Branch.

Rheasville, community in n Halifax County on Quankey Creek.

Rhems, community in w Craven County. Alt. 38. Est. prior to 1900 as Debruhls, named for a local family. When a post office was est. in 1913 the name was changed to honor Dr. Joseph Rhem (1871-1924) of New Bern.

Rhinehardt Creek rises in n Macon County and flows ne into Little Tennessee River.

Rhoades Academy, community in s Wayne County between Thoroughfare Swamp and Beaverdam Creek.

Rhodarme Cove, e Haywood County on the head of Kems Branch.

Rhode Branch rises in w Jackson County and flows se into Savannah Creek.

Rhodes, community in nw Bertie County.

Rhodes, community in central Duplin County.

Rhodes Creek rises in e Orange County and flows ne into Eno River.

Rhodes Mill Creek rises in s Catawba County and flows se into Pott Creek.

Rhodes Point, central Onslow County in Farnell Bay, in Camp Lejeune Marine Base.

Rhodestown, community in e Onslow County.

Rhodhiss, town on Burke-Caldwell County line near the e extremity of Burke County. Settled 1875. Inc. 1903. Alt. 965. Named in 1902 for John Rhodes and George Hiss who est. a cotton mill here. The town is divided by the Catawba River and at one time the portion in Burke County was known as Cliffs. Produces textiles.

Rhodhiss Lake on the Catawba River, Burke and Caldwell counties. Formed 1924-1925. Covers 3,515 acres with a shore line of 90 mi. Owned by Duke Power Co. and site of hydroelectric power plant.

Rhodo, community in n Cherokee County. According to local tradition it was named for the "raw dough" biscuits once served at a local boarding house.

Rhody Franklin Mountain, n Madison County between Shelton Laurel Creek and the head of Martin Branch.

Rhyne. See Daniels-Rhyne.

Rhynes Crossroads, community in w central Pender County.

Ricahokene, a village of Weapemeoc Indian tribe in what is now s Perquimans County on Perquimans River, shown on the White map, 1585. Appears as Rickahock on the Comberford map, 1657. The name survives in adjoining Chowan County as Rockyhock, which see.

Rice Branch rises in central Buncombe County and flows nw into Beaverdam Creek. Named for a pioneer settler.

Rice Branch rises in central Madison County and flows sw into Ammons Branch.

Rice Cove, e Haywood County on the head of Rice Cove Creek.

Rice Cove Creek rises in e Haywood County in Rice Cove and flows se into Beaverdam Creek.

Rice Cove Creek rises in n central Madison County and flows n into Big Laurel Creek.

Rice Creek rises in sw Beaufort County and flows n into Chocowinity Bay of Pamlico River.

Rice Gap, n central Transylvania County between Shutin Ridge and Lamb Creek.

Rice Island, in se Bertie County between Roanoke River and Eastmost River. A large swampy island, it measures almost

2½ mi. from tip to tip and is approx. 1 mi. wide at its greatest width. See also Purchace Islands.

Rice Knob, central Buncombe County between Craven Gap and Roaring Gap.

Rice Path, site of early settlement on e end of Bogue Banks in s Carteret County. A vessel went aground here once, laden with a cargo of rice. The people on the sound side made a path across the banks to the ocean side to get the rice, and so they called it Rice Path. Storms drove out early settlers until settlement of Salter Path, which see.

Rice Pinnacle, s Buncombe County at the n end of Stradley Mountain.

Rices Creek rises in se Brunswick County and flows n into Town Creek.

Rices Pocosin, a swamp in central Greene County.

Riceville, community in n Buncombe County on Bull Creek, which see. Named for family of pioneer settlers. Formerly a post office.

Richards. See Crown Stream.

Richards Mill, on the Collet map, 1770, was located on a tributary of the Pasquotank River in what is now n Pasquotank County. The stream was located approx. 12 to 15 mi. nw of the present Knobbs Creek but has long since left its stream bed to become a part of the surrounding marsh.

Richardson, community in sw Bladen County.

Richardson Creek rises in s Rutherford County and flows s into Broad River. P. H. Richardson operated a very fine gold mine on this creek in the 1830's.

Richardson Creek rises in s Union County and flows ne into nw Anson County and enters Rocky River on the Stanly County line.

Richardson Creek, community in n Union County on the e side of Richardson Creek.

Rich Branch rises in s Buncombe County and flows ne into Bent Creek.

Rich Branch rises in n Mitchell County and flows e into Spring Creek.

Rich Cove, between Laurel Mountain and Big Creek in nw Henderson County.

Richey Gap, s Macon County between Buck Knob and Richey Knob.

Richey Knob, s Macon County between Sheep Hollow and Middle Creek.

Richfield, community in n Stanly County.

Alt. 661. Inc. 1899. Named for local Ritchie family.

Rich Fork Creek rises in ne Davidson County and flows sw into Abbotts Creek.

Rich Gap, se Macon County between Fodderstack Mountain and Rich Mountain.

Rich Gap, Great Smoky Mountains National Park, on the Swain County, N. C.,-Blount County, Tenn., line between Gregory Bald and Forge Knob, lat. 35° 31' 45" N., long. 83° 51' 14" W.

Rich Gap Mountain, nw Henderson County on Laurel Mountain between Johnson Knob and Black Mountain.

Rich Hammock, a name applied on the Moseley map, 1733, to a neck of land (apparently especially suitable for cultivation) extending into North River, s Carteret County, e of present town of Beaufort.

Rich Hill, peak on the Alleghany-Surry County line. Alt. 3,260.

Rich Hill, community in e Alleghany County.

Rich Hill Creek rises in w Ashe County and flows se into North Fork New River.

Rich Inlet, se Pender County, from Topsail Sound into Atlantic Ocean. Appears on the Moseley map, 1733.

Rich Island Gut in n central Carteret County flows n into South River.

Rich Knob, central Buncombe County ne of Randall Gap. Alt. 3,535.

Rich Knob, sw Buncombe County, between Green Top and Long Gap.

Rich Knob, n Buncombe County at the se end of Richland Mountain in Pisgah National Forest.

Rich Knob, on the Cherokee-Macon County line between Junaluska Gap and Wolf Creek Gap.

Rich Knob on the Haywood-Madison County line.

Rich Knob, s Macon County between Commissioner Gap and Doubletop Mountain.

Rich Knob, s Mitchell County between South Fork [Carvers Branch] and North Fork [Grassy Creek].

Richland Balsam, a peak on the Haywood-Jackson County line, 8 mi. s of town of Waynesville. Alt. 6,540, the highest point on Balsam Mountain, which see.

Richland Creek rises in n Franklin County and flows ne into Sandy Creek.

Richland Creek rises in w Franklin County and flows sw into Wake County where it enters Neuse River. Appears on the Collet map, 1770, although somewhat mis-placed. The name Richmond Creek is applied on the Mouzon map, 1775.

Richland Creek rises in n central Guilford County and flows ne into Reedy Fork Creek. Appears on the Collet map, 1770.

Richland Creek rises in w Haywood County and flows ne into Pigeon River.

Richland Creek rises in w Moore County and flows ne into McLendon Creek.

Richland Creek rises in w Person County and flows nw into South Hyco Creek.

Richland Creek rises in s Randolph County and flows se into Deep River.

Richland Creek rises in s Rutherford County s of Oakland and flows se into Broad River.

Richland Creek rises in w Transylvania County and flows ne into West Fork French Broad River.

Richland Creek rises in w central Wake County near Asbury and flows n into Crabtree Creek.

Richland Gap, s Haywood County on the head of Shiny Creek.

Richland Gap at the sw end of Piney Mountain Ridge in e Jackson County.

Richland Knob, n Buncombe County on Richland Mountain, in Pisgah National Forest.

Richland Lake, central Guilford County formed by dam on Richland Creek. Built in 1943 by Cone Mills and used for industrial and municipal purposes.

Richland Mountain, n Buncombe County between Courthouse Knob and Rich Knob.

Richland Mountain, Great Smoky Mountains National Park, n Swain County, a ridge extending se from Charlies Bunion between Kephart Prong and Bradley Fork, lat. 35° 36' 47" N., long. 83° 20' 30" W. Alt. approx. 5,600.

Richland Mountains, ne Rutherford County along Sally Queen Creek. There are several named peaks in these mountains.

Richlands, town in nw Onslow County between New River and Mill Swamp. Alt. 64. Settled approx. 1775; inc. 1880. Named for fertile soil of the region. Former home of Richlands Academy (1848-1904), founded by Randolph Macon College; it served as the educational center of Jones and Onslow counties. Produces lumber. Known as Upper Richlands until it was inc. in 1880.

Richlands Township, nw Onslow County.

Richland Swamp rises in s Hoke County

and flows se into Robeson County where it enters Big Raft Swamp.

Richland Township, se Beaufort County.

Richland Township, s central Randolph County.

Richmond, former seat of Surry County, 1774-1789. Inc. 1779. Site now in nw Forsyth County near the community of Donnoha. Town completely destroyed by a cyclone in or soon after August, 1830, and the site abandoned. A history of the courthouse is in *Records of the Moravians*, II, 642-49.

Richmond. *See* Bear Creek.

Richmond County was formed in 1779 from Anson County. Located in the s central section of the state, it is bounded by the state of South Carolina, and by Anson, Stanly, Montgomery, Moore, and Scotland counties. It was named for Charles Lennox (1735-1806), third Duke of Richmond, military officer, ambassador, and Secretary of State who denounced British policy toward the American colonies. Area. 483 sq. mi. County seat: Rockingham with an elevation of 211 ft. Townships are Beaverdam, Black Jack, Marks Creek, Mineral Springs, Rockingham, Steeles, and Wolf Pit. Produces cotton, corn, wheat, oats, peaches, poultry, hogs, livestock, textiles, paper, furniture, hosiery, and lumber.

Richmond Creek. *See* Richland Creek.

Richmond District, one of the districts into which Caswell County was divided at the time of the 1790 census. It contained 253 heads of families.

Richmond Hill, community on the outskirts of Burlington, central Alamance County.

Richmond Hill, community n Yadkin County. Home of Richmond Pearson (1805-78), chief justice of North Caroline Supreme Court, who conducted a famous law school at his home, "Richmond Hill," which still stands.

Richmond Millpond, nw Scotland County on Gum Swamp Creek. Formed prior to 1800 and known, until 1893, as Malloys

Pond for Charles Malloy, original owner. Covers 75 acres; max. depth 18 ft. Named because it was located in Richmond County when it was formed.

Richmond Mills, community in w Scotland County on Gum Swamp Creek.

Rich Mountain on the Alleghany-Wilkes County line. Alt. 3,500.

Rich Mountain, se Davidson County on headwaters of Beaverdam Creek.

Rich Mountain, n Henderson County between Couch Mountain and Baldwin Gap.

Rich Mountain, on the Henderson-Polk County line. Alt. 2,542.

Rich Mountain extends ne from Johns Creek to the Haywood-Jackson County line in e Jackson County.

Rich Mountain in nw Jackson County between Dicks Creek and Camp Creek.

Rich Mountain on the McDowell-Rutherford County line.

Rich Mountain extends sw in w Mitchell County along the course of Pigeonroost Creek.

Rich Mountain, e Macon County between Keener Mountain and Rattlesnake Knob.

Rich Mountain, in se Macon County between Big Creek and Rich Gap.

Rich Mountain, s Madison County at the head of Little Sandymush Creek.

Rich Mountain on the Madison County, N. C.-Greene County, Tenn., line.

Rich Mountain, s Swain County on the head of Pigeon Creek. Alt. 3,865.

Rich Mountain, n Transylvania County, extends ne from Club Gap to Soapstone Ridge. Alt. approx. 4,100.

Rich Mountain, n Transylvania County between Sunfish Cove and Laurel Gap. Alt. 3,952.

Rich Mountain, s Transylvania County between the head of Steel Creek and the head of Cannon Creek. Alt. 3,779.

Rich Mountain, peak on Brushy Mountain se of Gloucester Gap in w Transylvania County. Alt. approx. 3,580.

Rich Mountain, an extended ridge beginning at town of Boone in central Watauga County and running nw to head of Sharp Creek in n Watauga County, then ne to its highest point, Rich Mountain Bald *(which see),* ending at Rich Mountain Gap. Named for its unusually fertile though rugged slopes.

Rich Mountain, s Wilkes County between Pole Mountain and Hunting Creek.

Rich Mountain, community on n side of

mountain of same name in e Jackson
County where Sugar Creek enters Caney
Fork.

Rich Mountain Bald, a peak on Rich Mountain near the head of Charley Creek in e
Jackson County.

Rich Mountain Bald, n Watauga County on
Rich Mountain. Alt. 5,372.

Rich Mountain Creek rises in s Alleghany
County and flows w into Bullhead Creek
on the Alleghany-Wilkes County line.

Rich Mountain Gap on the head of Johns
Creek in central Jackson County.

Rich Mountain Gap, n Watauga County between Rich Mountain and Snake Mountain. Cove Creek rises on its w slope and
Meat Camp Creek rises on its e slope.
Alt. 4,420.

Rich Neck. *See* Wilkinson Point.

Richneck Creek rises in sw Warren County
and flows e into Fishing Creek.

Rich Ridge, w Madison County near the
head of Jones Branch.

Richs Gap, w Avery County.

Rich Square, town in s Northampton County. Inc. 1869. Alt. 78. Settled about 1750
by Quakers from Virginia. Meeting organized in 1753 and Meeting House completed in 1760. A deed of 1761 to Thomas
Hunter refers to "a tract of land called
rich square," probably referring to the
fertility of the soil. Appears as Richsquare
on the Price map, 1808. Produces apparel.

Rich Square Township, se Northampton
County.

Rich Top, mountain in e Haywood County
between Harbon Cove and Silvers Cove
Creek.

Rickman Creek rises in n Macon County
and flows se into Matlock Creek.

Ricks Branch rises in se Cherokee County
and flows se into Little Brasstown Creek.

Ricks Creek rises in nw Duplin County
and flows sw into Goshen Swamp.

Ricky Knob, central Haywood County between Ned Branch and the head of
Hemphill Creek.

Rico, community in n Columbus County.

Riddick Crossroads, community in w Gates
County.

Riddicksville, community in ne Hertford
County near Chowan River. Known as
Maney's Ferry until 1825 for the Maney
family which had lived here since about
1750. The site acquired by Adam Riddick in 1825 and the present name adopted soon afterward.

Riddie Cove, w Haywood County on Big
Spring Branch.

Riddle, community in s Camden County. A
post office operated here 1907-18 as Bray
for Dempsey Bray, first postmaster who
removed to another community after two
years. Renamed for Charles Riddle (1862-
89), local schoolmaster.

Riddle Branch rises in nw Yancey County
and flows se into Bald Mountain Creek.

Riddle Creek rises in n Watauga County
and flows s into Meat Camp Creek.

Riddles Creek rises in se Rutherford County and flows s into Broad River.

Ridenhour Township, nw Stanly County.

Riders Creek rises in n central Tyrrell
County near community of Levels and
flows sw and nw into Scuppernong River.

Riders Creek Community. *See* Levels.

Ridge. *See* South Gastonia.

Ridge Creek rises in nw Alamance County
and flows se into Haw River.

Ridgecrest, community in se Buncombe
County. Alt. 2,530. Southern Baptist summer assembly grounds are here.

Ridgepole Mountain, s Macon County between Little Ridgepole Mountain and
Gulf Branch. Alt. 5,008.

Ridge's Mountain, w Randolph County between Uwharrie River and Caraway
Creek, a long rather low ridge.

Ridge Spring. *See* Scuffletown.

Ridgeville, community in se Caswell County. Known as Pea Ridge until 1875
when the present name was adopted for
the ridge on which it is located. Alt. 750.

Ridgeway, community in w Warren County.
Alt. 422. Inc. 1869; charter repealed
1879. Grew up around a series of inns
on the site, the first of which was Colers
Ordinary, shown on the Collet map,
1770. By 1800 Charles Marshall had a
tavern here; portions of the original
building still exist in a local dwelling. In
1816 John Paschall operated a tavern
here, and the community was known as
Paschalls, the name under which it appears on the MacRae map, 1833. The
present name was used when a post
office was est. here in 1839, and is said to
be derived from the ridge on the n edge
of the community on which a railway
was built. After the Civil War, a development company induced immigrants from
Germany, Alsace, France, Switzerland,
and England to settle here.

Riegelwood, community in ne Columbus
County near the Cape Fear River. Devel-

oped around the Riegel Paper Corporation after it began production in 1951.

Right Fork rises on the s slopes of Potato Knob in ne Buncombe County near the Yancey County line and flows sw into North Fork [Swannanoa River]. Often referred to locally as Right Hand Fork. Part of the Asheville watershed.

Right Fork rises in ne Buncombe County on s slopes of Craggy Knob and flows sw into Beetree Creek.

Right Fork rises in ne Cherokee County in the Valley River Mountains and flows n into Bear Branch.

Right Fork Bean Creek rises in n Mitchell County and flows s to join Left Fork Bean Creek in forming Bean Creek.

Right Fork Belews Creek. See East Belews Creek.

Right Fork [Cane Creek] is formed in e Mitchell County by the junction of Mine Fork Branch and Stagger Weed Creek and flows nw to join Left Fork [Cane Creek] in forming Cane Creek.

Right Fork [Cold Spring Branch] rises in w Swain County and flows nw into Cold Spring Branch near its confluence with Hazel Creek.

Right Fork Cove Creek rises in central Haywood County and flows se into Cove Creek.

Right Fork Davidson River rises in nw Transylvania County and flows se into Davidson River.

Right Fork [Eagle Creek] rises in se Clay County and flows nw to join Left Fork [Eagle Creek] in forming Eagle Creek. Known also as Dave Barrett Creek.

Right Fork [Indian Creek] rises in n Swain County and flows sw to join Left Fork [Indian Creek] in forming Indian Creek.

Right Fork [Pigeonroost Creek] rises in w Mitchell County and flows sw into Pigeonroost Creek.

Right Fork [of Raven Fork] rises in ne Swain County in Great Smoky Mountains National Park and flows sw to join Left Fork and Middle Fork to form Raven Fork [of Oconaluftee River]. See also McGee Spring.

Right Fork [Redman Creek] rises in ne Swain County and flows sw to join Left Fork [Redman Creek] in forming Redman Creek.

Right Fork Webb Creek rises in ne Cherokee County near Old Billy Top and flows sw and s to join Left Fork Webb Creek in forming Webb Creek.

Right Fork [Wesser Creek] rises in n Macon County and flows ne into Swain County where it enters Wesser Creek.

Right Hand Fork. See Right Fork.

Right Hand Prong [of Pigeon River] rises in s Haywood County and flows ne into Middle Prong.

Right Prong Bent Creek rises in n Yancey County and flows se to join Left Prong Bent Creek in forming Bent Creek.

Right Prong [Ledge Creek] rises in ne Swain County and flows nw into Ledge Creek.

Right Prong Martin Creek rises in s Cherokee County and flows e into Martin Creek.

Right Prong South Toe River rises in s Yancey County and flows e to join Left Prong South Toe River in forming South Toe River.

Right Prong Three Forks Creek rises in se Yancey County and flows w to join Left Prong Three Forks Creek in forming Three Forks Creek.

Riles Creek rises in se Rowan County and flows se into Stanly where it turns ne back into Rowan County in which it enters Yadkin River. The Kerr map, 1882, shows this stream as Loyal Creek.

Riley, community in s Franklin County. Post office here in 1882 known as Rileys Cross Roads.

Riley Cove, e Clay County between Chunky Gal Mountain and Buck Creek.

Riley Knob, e Clay County between Riley Cove and Glade Gap.

Riley Knob, e Macon County between Higdon Mountain and Ledford Branch.

Rileys Creek rises in central Pender County and flows sw into Long Creek.

Rileys Cross Roads. See Riley.

Rimer, community in n Cabarrus County, known also as Rimertown.

Ring Fire Knob, se Wilkes County between Little Hunting Creek and Osborne Creek. Alt. approx. 1,300.

Ringstaff Mountains, range in the Cane Creek Mountains, s Alamance County.

Ringwood, town in sw Halifax County. Inc. 1877, but long inactive in municipal affairs. A number of old homes here date from the early nineteenth century.

Rio, community in s central Transylvania County.

Rio Jordan. See Cape Fear River.

Ripley, former town on the w outskirts of Hendersonville in central Henderson County. Inc. 1909; charter repealed 1917.

Rippetoe Mountain, s Caldwell County.

Alt. 1,298. Named for William Rippetoe who received the mountain in a land grant.

Rippys Township, former township in s Cleveland County, now township number 3.

Ripshin Mountain, sw Buncombe County n of Mount Pisgah.

Rip Shin Mountain, n Caldwell County. Alt. 2,200.

Ripshin Ridge, nw Burke County, extends from se to nw between Steels Creek and Upper Creek. Alt. 2,875.

Risden. See Rufus.

Ritter, former community in w Swain County on Tuckasegee River. Site now under the waters of Fontana Lake.

Ritters Township, n central Moore County.

River Acres, community in central Beaufort County on the n shore of Pamlico River.

River Bend, community in ne Gaston County near Mountain Island Lake at the steam power generating plant of the Duke Power Co.

River Bend Township, ne Gaston County.

Riverdale, community in e Craven County. Settled 1878 and named because of its location near Neuse River.

River Neck, community in nw Tyrrell County near the mouth of Scuppernong River. Alt. 2. Formerly called Devenport.

River Neck Landing, nw Tyrrell County on the e side of mouth of Scuppernong River.

River Side, community on South Fork New River in sw Ashe County. Alt. approx. 2,950.

Riverside, community in s Macon County on Little Tennessee River.

Riverside, community in w central Yancey County on Cane River.

Riverside. See Retreat.

Riverside Park, community in central Beaufort County on the n shore of Pamlico River.

River Swamp rises in se Brunswick County and flows nw into Lockwoods Folly River.

Riverton, community in e Scotland County on Lumber River. A summer resort used by residents of nearby towns. Subject of some of John Charles McNeill's poetry.

River Township, former township in sw Cleveland County, now township number 1.

River Township, central Jackson County.

River Township, ne Warren County.

River View Community, se Columbus

County, formerly known as Crusoe Island. Renamed by resolution of the General Assembly, 1961. A marshy and sandy section between the Waccamaw River and the Columbus-Brunswick County line, it lies on the edge of Green Swamp, which see. It was named Crusoe Island by outsiders because of its isolation. French political refugees, who first settled in Haiti, are said to have arrived here in 1806, where their descendants still live. Roads now penetrate the area.

Rizzo Creek. See Resoe Creek.

Roach Creek rises in central Rockingham County and flows nw into Dan River.

Road Ridge, e Mitchell County at the head of Bear Creek.

Roan Creek rises in e Ashe County and flows nw into South Fork New River.

Roan High Bluff, ne Mitchell County on Roan Mountain. Alt. 6,267.

Roan High Knob, on the Mitchell County, N. C.-Carter County, Tenn., line. Alt. 6,286.

Roan Island, a silt island in s Pender County, approx. 4 mi. long and 1½ mi. wide, surrounded by Cape Fear River, Thoroughfare, and Black River.

Roan Mountain, ne Mitchell County, extends ne into Tennessee. Alt. approx. 6,200. Probably named for its roan color when seen from a distance in the rhododendron blooming season. Site of Rhododendron Festival each June.

Roanoac, an Indian village the site of which is now submerged in the waters of Albemarle Sound, formerly near the n tip of Roanoke Island, e Dare County. Appears on the White maps of 1585 and 1590.

Roanoak Town. See Carteret.

Roanoke. See Poplar Point.

Roanoke Canal, constructed between 1817 and 1823 and extended between 1824 and 1834 to bypass the Upper and Lower Falls of Roanoke River in n Halifax County. The canal, built by the Roanoke Navigation Company, provided a series of locks which made uninterrupted navigation of the river possible. The locks raised and lowered vessels 44 ft. from the basin to the river, and could accommodate boats of from 30 to 50 tons. With the completion of Raleigh and Gaston Railroad, and its junction with Seaboard Railroad about 1841, the canal began a decline, and was no longer used by 1865.

Roanoke County was proposed as the name

for the se portion of Halifax County in
1868 when there was a move to divide
the county. A manuscript map of Roanoke County made by M. L. Venable is
in the North Carolina Collection in
Chapel Hill.

Roanoke Inlet, former inlet from the Atlantic Ocean into Roanoke Sound, through
Bodie Island s of the present location of
Nags Head, ne Dare County. This was
the original n boundary of Bodie Island.
Opened prior to 1657 and closed in 1795,
according to a note on the Kerr map,
1882. Appears on the Ogilby map, 1671.

Roanoke Island, approx. 11 mi. long and
2¼ mi. wide, e Dare County, separated
by Roanoke Sound from Bodie Island
(Outer Banks) on the e, and by Croatan
Sound from the mainland on the w. Site
of Fort Raleigh, center of English exploration and settlement, 1584-87. Name
believed to be of Algonquian Indian
origin signifying "northern people" or
"northerners," referring to the fact that
(1) the Indians lived on the n end of the
island, or (2) that they had earlier migrated from an ancestral home in the n.
The name Roanoke also came to be applied to shell beads. Fort Raleigh National Historic Site is on the n end of
the island. *See also* Manteo; Carteret.

Roanoke Marshes, extensive string of low
marsh islands in Croatan Sound, e central Dare County, stretching from sw end
of Roanoke Island to a large marshy area
on the mainland. Site of a beacon est.
approx. 1875; last of man-tended lights
along the coast replaced by automatic
beacon in 1955. The islands for the most
part have washed away. Shown on the
Collet map, 1770, as Daniels Marshes.
Unnamed but shown prominently on the
Moseley map, 1733.

Roanoke Rapids, city in n Halifax County
on the Roanoke River. Founded in 1893
by John Armstrong Chaloner (1862-1935)
as a cotton mill site and named for the
rapids in the river. Inc. 1897. Originally
known as Great Falls. Produces paper
and textiles. Alt. 169.

Roanoke Rapids Dam. *See* Gaston Lake.

Roanoke Rapids Lake, formed by a dam
near the city of Roanoke Rapids in ne
Halifax County on Roanoke River. The
lake extends nw along the Halifax-Northampton County line to Gaston dam. The
dam here was completed in 1955 and the
lake covers 4,900 acres with a shore line

of 47 mi. and a max. depth of 90 ft.
Built by Virginia Electric and Power
Company to generate hydroelectric
power, the lake is also used for recreation. *See also* Gaston Lake.

Roanoke Rapids Township, n Halifax County.

Roanoke River is formed in Montgomery
County, Va., by the junction of North
Fork and South Fork and flows se into
North Carolina in ne Warren County. It
flows across a corner of Warren, along
the Halifax-Northampton, Halifax-Bertie,
Bertie-Martin, and Bertie-Washington
County lines into Batchelor Bay of Albe-
marle Sound. The John H. Kerr Dam on
Roanoke River in Virginia creates Kerr
Lake, a part of which is in Granville,
Vance, and Warren counties. Appears as
Morattico River on the Comberford map,
1657, and as Noratake River on the
Ogilby map, 1671. The Moseley map,
1733, has Roanoke River.

Roanoke Sea. *See* Albemarle Sound.

Roanoke Sound, between Roanoke Island
and the Outer Banks in e Dare County.
Known in the eighteenth century as
Sanderson's Channel for Richard Sanderson, local landowner. The name Walter
Rawleigh appears here on the Collet
map, 1770, though it is uncertain whether
it was intended to represent the name of
the sound. *See also* Albemarle Sound.

Roanoke Township, e central Northampton
County.

Roanoke Township, ne Warren County.

Roan Valley, parallel to Fall Creek in e
Mitchell County.

Roaring Branch rises in s Mitchell County
and flows nw into Crabtree Creek.

Roaring Creek rises in w Avery County and
flows s into North Toe River.

Roaring Creek rises in nw Swain County in
Great Smoky Mountains National Park
and flows se to join Defeat Branch in
forming Bone Valley Creek.

Roaring Creek (community). *See* Valley.

Roaring Creek Township, sw Avery County.

Roaring Fork rises in nw Ashe County and
flows sw into Big Laurel Creek.

Roaring Fork rises in nw McDowell County on the n slope of Woods Mountain
and flows n into Armstrong Creek.

Roaring Fork rises in w Madison County
and flows ne into Meadow Fork.

Roaring Fork rises in e Madison County
and flows s into Big Laurel Creek.

Roaring Fork rises in nw Surry County and flows sw into Fisher River.

Roaring Fork rises in se Yancey County and flows n into Three Forks Creek.

Roaring Fork rises in nw Yancey County and flows se into Bald Mountain Creek.

Roaring Fork Creek rises in w Macon County and flows sw into Nantahala River.

Roaring Fork Mountain, w Madison County parallel to Roaring Fork.

Roaring Fork Ridge, sw Macon County between Roaring Fork Creek and the head of Rough Fork.

Roaring Gap, central Buncombe County, n of Rice Knob in Elk Mountains.

Roaring Gap at the junction of the Alleghany-Surry-Wilkes County lines. Alt. 2,914.

Roaring Gap, community in se Alleghany County. Est. in 1890 as a summer resort by Alexander Chatham of Elkin who bought land here and built the first house. Named from the fact that wind is said to rush with a roar through a gap here. Alt. 3,800. There are now more than 200 summer homes here.

Roaring River is formed in central Wilkes County by the junction of Middle Prong Roaring River and North Prong Roaring River and flows se into Yadkin River. Named because of an early description of the river which said that it "comes rushing and roaring" out of the Blue Ridge Mountains.

Roaring River, community in e central Wilkes County on Yadkin River at the mouth of Roaring River. Alt. 934. Settled about 1770. Inc. 1905; charter repealed 1907. A post office est. here prior to 1882.

Roaring Spout Creek rises in e Yancey County and flows e into Browns Creek.

Roaring Spout Falls on Roaring Spout Creek, e Yancey County.

Robbins, town in n Moore County on Bear Creek. Known as early as 1828 as Mechanicks Hill and Mechanicsville for David Kennedy, local mechanic and gunsmith. Later known as Elise, and inc. 1935 as Hemp. Name changed in 1943 to Robbins for Karl Robbins, owner of a local mill. Produces textiles, minerals, and processed poultry. Alt. 424.

Robbinsville, town and county seat, central Graham County. Alt. 2,150. Post office est. 1843 as Cheoah Valley. Town authorized to be laid out in 1872 as Robbinsville for local Robbins family. Inc. in 1893 as Robinsville; name changed in 1897 to Robbinsville. Produces carpets and lumber.

Roberdel, town in central Richmond County on Hitchcock Creek. Settled approx. 1850; inc. 1889. Named for Robert L. Steele, textile manufacturer. Alt. 246.

Roberdo, community in s Montgomery County.

Roberson Ridge, s Haywood County between Bearpen Branch and Deep Gap Creek.

Roberson Store, community in se Martin County on Harrison Mill Creek. Settled about 1898 and known as Amherst until after 1920. Alt. 75.

Robersonville, town in w Martin County. Settled before the Civil War. Inc. 1870 and named for Henry D. Roberson, local landowner and Confederate veteran. Alt. 78. Produces processed poultry and apparel.

Robersonville Township, sw Martin County.

Roberta, community in w Cabarrus County which grew up around Pattersons Mill, a name by which it was once known.

Robert Branch rises in s Madison County and flows n into French Broad River.

Robert Gap on the Haywood-Madison County line.

Roberts Branch rises in s Cleveland County and flows e into Buffalo Creek. Named for "Squire Billy" Roberts through whose land it ran.

Roberts Branch rises in n Cherokee County and flows nw into Farner Branch.

Roberts Cove, in e Haywood County on the head of Rush Fork.

Roberts Creek rises in n Lee County and flows ne into Hughes Creek.

Roberts Crossroads, community in w Franklin County.

Robertson Creek rises in s central Granville County and flows s into Beaverdam Creek near the Granville-Wake County line.

Robertson Mountain, n Jackson County between Locust Creek and Mill Creek.

Robertsons Pond, e Wake County on Buffalo Creek. Formed in 1900. Covers 65 acres with a max. depth of 15 ft. Used for recreation and as power source.

Robeson (ROB-he-s'n) County was formed
in 1787 from Bladen County. Located
in the se section of the state, it is
bounded by the state of South Carolina,
and by Scotland, Hoke, Cumberland,
Bladen, and Columbus counties. It was
named for Colonel Thomas Robeson
(1740-85), Revolutionary officer. Area:
948 sq. mi. County seat: Lumberton
with an elevation of 137 ft. Townships
are Alfordsville, Black Swamp, Britts,
Burnt Swamp, East Howellsville, Fairmont, Gaddy, Lumber Bridge, Lumberton, Marietta, Maxton, Orrum, Parkton,
Pembroke, Philadelphus, Raft Swamp,
Red Springs, Rennert, Rowland, Saddletree, St. Pauls, Shannon, Smiths, Smyrna,
Sterlings, Thompson, Union, West
Howellsville, and Wishart. Produces
tobacco, corn, soybeans, wheat, oats,
cotton, poultry, eggs, livestock, onions,
tomatoes, lumber, textiles, and apparel.

Robeson Creek rises in central Chatham
County and flows e into Haw River.

Robeson Point. See Robinson Point.

Robey's Camp Ground. See Rock Springs.

Robin Branch rises in w Macon County and
flows sw into Jarrett Creek.

Robin Branch rises in w Wilson County
and flows ne and n into Black Creek.

Robinson Cove, the valley through which
Robinson Creek flows in nw Buncombe
County.

Robinson Creek rises in nw Buncombe
County and flows sw into Sandy Mush
Creek.

Robinson Creek rises in s Buncombe County near Busbee Mountain and flows se
into Cane Creek. See also Pinner Cove.

Robinson Creek rises in s Jackson County
and flows ne into Bear Creek Lake on
the Tuckasegee River.

Robinson Creek rises in e Rutherford County and flows sw into Second Broad River.

Robinson Gap, s central Swain County between Bucknor Branch and Cochran
Branch.

Robinson Mountain, nw Buncombe County,
between Earlies Gap and High Knob.

Robinson Point extends from e Onslow
County into White Oak River. Sometimes known as Robeson Point.

Robinson Point. See Cedar Island Point.

Robinson Rough, mountain on the Buncombe-Madison County line between
Norton Fork Gap and Davidson Gap.

Robinson's Ferry. See Monroe.

Robinwood Lake, se Gaston County on
Anthony Creek. Formed 1947. Covers
35 acres. Max. depth 25 ft. Swimming,
fishing, boating. Owned by Elbert S.
Robinson and L. L. Alexander.

Robson Branch rises in central Avery County and flows s into Plumtree Creek.

Roby Creek, rises in Yadkin County and
flows e into Turner Creek.

Rochdale, town authorized to be laid out in
Richmond County (now w Scotland
County) in 1816, on the land of John
Marine and others, on or near Joes
Creek. Apparently the town was never
laid out.

Rock Branch rises in e Alamance County
and flows s into Haw Creek.

Rock Branch rises in s Macon County and
flows sw into Betty Creek.

Rock Branch rises in n Madison County
and flows sw into Shelton Laurel Creek.

Rock Branch. See Olivia.

Rockbrook Camp Branch rises in s central
Transylvania County and flows nw
through Rockbrook Camp into French
Broad River.

Rock Camp Branch rises in nw Swain County and flows e into Roaring Creek.

Rock Camp Branch rises in ne Swain County and flows nw into Bunches Creek.

Rock Camp Run rises in ne Swain County
and flows nw into Straight Fork.

Rock Creek rises in sw Alamance County
and flows n into Stinking Quarter Creek.

Rock Creek rises in w Alleghany County
and flows n into New River.

Rock Creek rises in w Ashe County and
flows se into North Fork New River.

Rock Creek rises in se Buncombe County
and flows se into w Rutherford County
where it enters Lake Lure.

Rock Creek rises in s Burke County and
flows se into Catawba County where it
enters Jacob Fork.

Rock Creek rises in se Caldwell County
and flows e into Upper Little River.

Rock Creek rises in central Graham County
and flows ne into Atoah Creek.

Rock Creek rises in e Graham County and flows ne into Panther Creek.

Rock Creek rises in w Graham County and flows ne into Cheoah River.

Rock Creek rises in e Guilford County and flows s into Alamance Creek.

Rock Creek rises in sw Henderson County and flows se into Green River.

Rock Creek rises in central Montgomery County and flows s into Little River.

Rock Creek rises in n central Rutherford County and flows se into Second Broad River.

Rock Creek rises in e central Wilkes County and flows s into Yadkin River.

Rock Creek is formed in s Yancey County by the junction of North Fork Rock Creek and Middle Fork Rock Creek and flows ne and se into South Toe River.

Rock Creek, community in sw Alamance County. A post office est. here as early as 1828 operated as late as 1882.

Rock Creek. See Greens Mill Run.

Rock Creek Gap, e Mitchell County on Rock Creek Mountain.

Rock Creek Knob, w Graham County between Deep Creek and Rock Creek.

Rock Creek Mountain, e Mitchell County at the head of Little Rock Creek.

Rock Creek Township, e Guilford County.

Rock Creek Township, e central Wilkes County.

Rockdale, community in ne Cleveland County.

Rockdam Creek rises in s Lincoln County and flows ne into Howards Creek.

Rockett, community in ne Catawba County. Est. 1886 as Roseman, but the name was changed in 1902 when a post office was est. here. Post office discontinued in 1903. Both names were for local families.

Rockfield Creek rises in central Graham County and flows sw into Santeetlah Lake.

Rockfish, community in e Hoke County. Settled about 1900 and named for nearby creek. Alt. 218.

Rockfish. See Hope Mills.

Rockfish Creek rises in sw Duplin County and flows s and e into Northeast Cape Fear River on the Duplin-Pender County line. Appears on the Moseley map, 1733.

Rockfish Creek rises in se Moore County e of town of Aberdeen and flows se across Hoke County into Upchurch Pond on the w Cumberland County line. From the w pond, it flows e across Cumberland County to enter Cape Fear River 1½ mi.

e of community of Grays Creek. Appears on the Moseley map, 1733.

Rockfish Township, w Cumberland County.

Rockfish Township, sw Duplin County.

Rockford, town in s Surry County on Yadkin River. Est. 1790 as the county seat and so remained until 1851 when the county was divided and the county seat removed to Dobson. Alt. 838. Inc. 1819 but long inactive in muncipal affairs.

Rockford Township, s central Surry County.

Rock Fork rises in n Swain County and flows se into Right Fork [Deep Creek].

Rock Fork Branch rises in se Person County and flows sw into Deep Creek.

Rock Gap, sw Macon County at the head of Little Rock Branch.

Rock Hole Creek rises in sw Stanly County and flows se into Rocky River. Called Cucumber Creek on the Kerr map, 1882.

Rock Hollow, e Haywood County between Soapstone Gap and Sheep Mountain.

Rock Hollow Branch rises in Rock Hollow in e Haywood County and flows nw into Crabtree Creek.

Rock House. See Sweezy Mountain.

Rockhouse Branch rises in sw Madison County and flows e into Sugar Camp Branch.

Rockhouse Creek rises in e Avery County and flows se into Caldwell County where it enters Wilsons Creek.

Rock House Creek rises in n Clay County and flows sw into Fires Creek.

Rockhouse Creek rises in s Mitchell County and flows ne into Grassy Creek.

Rock House Creek rises in s Rockingham County and flows n into Dan River. Mentioned in local records as early as 1767.

Rockhouse Creek rises on Seniard Ridge in n Transylvania County and flows s into Davidson River.

Rockhouse Creek rises in s Watauga County and flows se into Caldwell County.

Rockhouse Knob, s Macon County between Long Ridge and Wolfpen Gap. Alt. 3,100. A weather station here has recorded in various years the greatest amount of rainfall e of the Rocky Mountains.

Rocking Chair Branch rises in s Clay County and flows s into Shooting Creek.

Rockingham, town and county seat, w Richmond County. Courthouse est, at site, 1779, and known as Richmond Court House until 1784 when it was named for

Charles Watson-Wentworth (1730-82), second Marquis of Rockingham, British advocate of American independence. Manufactures textiles, paper, apparel, and processes poultry. *See also* East Rockingham; West Rockingham. Alt. 211.

Rockingham County was formed in 1785 from Guilford County. Located in the n central section of the state, it is bounded by the state of Virginia, and by Caswell, Guilford, and Stokes counties. It was named for Charles Watson-Wentworth (1730-82), second Marquis of Rockingham, Prime Minister at the time of the repeal of the stamp act and supporter of proposals to grant independence to the American colonies. Area: 572 sq. mi. County seat: Wentworth with an elevation of approx. 900 ft. Townships are Huntsville, Leaksville, Madison, Mayo, New Bethel, Price, Reidsville, Ruffin, Simpsonville, Wentworth, and Williamsburg. Produces tobacco, corn, wheat, oats, dairy products, hogs, livestock, apparel, textiles, furniture, hosiery, bricks, electric blankets, carpets, cigarettes, and other tobacco products.

Rockingham Township, w central Richmond County.

Rock Landing, formerly a landing and supply point on Roanoke River in n Halifax County constructed before 1818 for the purpose of landing stone and building supplies to be used in the construction of Roanoke Canal (*which see*).

Rock Point, s Carteret County, extends n from central Bogue Banks w of community of Salter Path.

Rockrace Branch rises in e Transylvania County and flows ne into Cascade Lake (Little River).

Rock Ridge, community in w Wilson County near Marsh Swamp. Post office, named Taylor, served the community, 1882-1914; named for J. M. Taylor.

Rock Run. *See* Telfairs Creek.

The Rocks, a great sea-wall constructed by the United States government, 1879-1885, to close off New Inlet between the Atlantic Ocean and the Cape Fear River, s New Hanover County.

Rock Springs, community in central Craven County on Trent River.

Rock Springs, community and camp meeting ground, ne Lincoln County near Denver. Camp meetings held annually in August since 1830. This camp, 45 acres in area, succeeded an older one, Robey's, near Catawba Springs.

Rock Springs, community in n Polk County.

Rockstack, a mountain on the Graham County, N. C.-Monroe County, Tenn., line.

Rockview, community in n Buncombe County near the junction of Martin Creek and North Fork Ivey Creek. Alt. 2,394.

Rockville. *See* Rockwell.

Rockwell, town in s Rowan County. Early travelers from Salisbury to Cheraw and Camden, S. C., enjoyed good water from a rock well here, hence the name. A post office est. here 1838 as Millville, changed to Rockville in 1839 and to Rockwell in 1872. Inc. 1911. Alt. 785.

Rocky Bald, w Macon County between the head of Holloway Branch and Wine Spring Creek. Alt. 5,333.

Rocky Branch rises in s Chatham County and flows se into Deep River.

Rocky Branch rises in w Clay County and flows n into Hiwassee River.

Rocky Branch rises in e Durham County and flows ne into Neuse River.

Rocky Branch rises in se Durham County and flows ne into Lick Creek.

Rocky Branch rises in nw Guilford County and flows se into Haw River.

Rocky Branch rises in central Haywood County and flows ne into Pigeon River.

Rocky Branch rises in nw Haywood County and flows s into Big Creek.

Rocky Branch rises in s Haywood County and flows nw into West Fork Pigeon River.

Rocky Branch rises in sw Haywood County and flows ne into Allen Creek.

Rocky Branch rises in w Jackson County and flows ne into Tuckasegee River.

Rocky Branch rises in central Macon County and flows ne into Little Tennessee River.

Rocky Branch rises in w Macon County and flows w into Nantahala Lake.

Rocky Branch rises in w Madison County and flows ne into Doe Branch.

Rocky Branch rises in n Madison County
and flows e into Little Laurel Creek.

Rocky Branch rises in s Mecklenburg County and flows w into Fourmile Creek.

Rocky Branch rises in e Vance County and
flows ne into w Warren County where it
enters Matthews Creek.

Rocky Branch rises in n Wake County and
flows sw into Neuse River.

Rocky Branch rises in e Wake County and
flows e into Little River.

Rocky Branch rises in e Watauga County
and flows nw into South Fork New River.

Rocky Branch Ridge, sw Haywood County
parallel to Rocky Branch.

Rocky Broad River. See Broad River.

Rocky Butte Mountain, e Jackson County
near the head of Chastine Creek.

Rocky Cove, s Buncombe County.

Rocky Cove, e Haywood County on Hominy
Creek.

Rocky Cove, se Haywood County on East
Prong Pigeon River.

Rocky Cove, sw Macon County on a tributary of Poplar Cove Creek.

Rocky Cove, w Macon County on a tributary of Nantahala River.

Rocky Cove Branch rises in e Haywood
County and flows sw into Hominy Creek.

Rocky Cove Knob, sw Macon County at
the sw end of Rocky Cove.

Rocky Creek rises in s Iredell County between Troutman and Oswalt and flows
sw into Catawba River.

Rocky Creek rises in s Transylvania County and flows sw into Toxaway River.

Rocky Creek rises in w Warren County and
flows se into Fishing Creek.

Rocky Creek rises near Pores Knob in se
Wilkes County and flows se across the
nw corner of Alexander County and into
Iredell County where it enters South
Yadkin River.

Rocky Creek rises in s Wilkes County and
flows ne into Hunting Creek n of Pilot
Mountain. Approx. 4 mi. long.

Rocky Creek. See Stoney Creek.

Rocky Face, mountain in ne Alexander
County. Alt. 1,851. Extensive quarry
operated here early in the twentieth
century.

Rocky Face, exposed rock surface on Angel-
co Mountain, sw Cherokee County.

Rocky Face, n Jackson County between
Rocky Face Branch and Cane Creek. Alt.
approx. 3,575.

Rocky Face, n Jackson County between

Cut-off Ridge and Whiterock Ridge. Alt.
approx. 4,600.

Rocky Face Branch rises in n Jackson County on se slopes of Rocky Face and flows
s into Wayehutta Creek.

Rocky Face Knob on the Jackson-Macon
County line.

Rocky Face Mountain, e Haywood County
between the head of Harley Branch and
Long Branch. Alt. approx. 4,600.

Rockyface Mountain, on the Jackson-Transylvania County line between Bald Rock
and Bald Knob. Part of Tennessee Ridge.
Alt. approx. 4,700.

Rockyface Mountain, s Macon County between Lee Creek and Jones Creek. Alt.
approx. 4,500.

Rocky Face Mountain, n Rutherford County between Second Broad River and Box
Creek.

Rocky Face Mountain, s Swain County extends ne from the head of Jenkins
Branch to the forks of Kirkland Creek.

Rocky Face Ridge, n Jackson County between Wayehutta Creek and Cane Creek.

Rocky Ford, community in n Franklin
County.

Rocky Ford Branch rises in nw Wilson
County and flows e and ne into Town
Creek.

Rocky Ford Creek rises in central Anson
County and flows n into Goulds Fork.

Rocky Ford Creek rises in sw Cherokee
County and flows nw into Polk County,
Tenn., where it enters Ocoee River.

Rocky Fork rises in se Buncombe County
near Jesses High Top and flows sw into
Cane Creek.

Rocky Fork rises in sw Henderson County
and flows e into North Fork.

Rocky Fork rises in s Lee County and flows
w into Crane Creek.

Rocky Fork Creek rises in n Richmond
County and flows sw into Falling Creek.

Rocky Fork Ridge, Great Smoky Mountains
National Park, n Swain County, lat. 35°
35' 20" N., long. 83° 25' 55" W.

Rocky Glen. See Catawba Falls.

Rocky Hill. See Medoc Mountain.

Rockyhock, community in central Chowan
County. Alt. 28. For a possible origin of
the name, see Rockyhock Creek.

Rockyhock Creek rises in central Chowan
County and flows sw into Chowan River.
Appears as Rakahak on the Ogilby map,
1671, and as Rockyhock on the Moseley
map, 1733. Name may be derived from
an Indian village, Ricahokene, on the e

side of Perquimans River at Albemarle Sound. It may have meant "where combs [rakes?] are made."

Rocky Hollow, w Watauga County between Laurel Creek and Watauga River.

Rocky Knob, central Buncombe County in Pisgah National Forest between Paynes Knob and Pine Knob. Alt. approx. 3,950.

Rocky Knob, n Buncombe County approx. 1 mi. s of Richland Knob. Named by early settlers because the peak is crowned by a mass of rock.

Rocky Knob, se Buncombe County between Sand Branch and Rush Branch.

Rocky Knob on Newfound Mountain on the Buncombe-Haywood County line n of Haywood Gap.

Rocky Knob, on the Buncombe-McDowell County line between Graybeard Mountain and Pinnacle.

Rocky Knob, on the Buncombe-Yancey County line between Campground Gap and Coxcomb Mountain.

Rocky Knob, nw Caldwell County between head of Amos Creek and head of Anthony Bolick Branch. Alt. 3,280.

Rocky Knob, w Caldwell County between Franklin Branch and Coffey Creek. Alt. approx. 1,960.

Rocky Knob, n Cherokee County in the Unicoi Mountains. Alt. approx. 4,250.

Rocky Knob, n Cherokee County on Hanging Dog Mountain. Alt. 3,830.

Rocky Knob, central Haywood County between Rogers Cove Creek and Big Branch. Alt. approx. 3,840.

Rocky Knob, e Haywood County between Rough Creek and Laurel Gap, approx. 4 mi. n of town of Canton. Alt. approx. 4,175.

Rocky Knob, s central Haywood County on the head of Peter Cove Branch.

Rocky Knob on the Jackson-Transylvania County line n of Pinhook Gap. Part of Tennessee Ridge, which see. Alt. approx. 4,000.

Rocky Knob on the head of Charley Creek in e Jackson County.

Rocky Knob, n Macon County between the head of Wildes Creek and Younce Creek.

Rocky Knob, s Macon County between Watkins Creek and Jake Branch.

Rocky Knob, s Macon County at the head of Peeks Creek.

Rocky Knob, e Madison County at the head of East Fork [Bull Creek].

Rocky Knob, n Madison County between Sapling Mountain and Spillcorn Creek.

Rocky Knob, e Swain County in Whiteoak Flats on the head of Adams Creek.

Rocky Knob, se Watauga County between Ben Ridge and Swift Ford Branch.

Rocky Knob, w Watauga County between Watauga River and School House Branch.

Rocky Knob, n central Yancey County on the head of Guilders Creek, 1½ mi. n of town of Burnsville. Alt. approx. 4,100.

Rocky Knob, w Yancey County between Elk Wallow Creek and Lickskillet Branch. Alt. approx. 3,880.

Rocky Knob, w Yancey County between Possumtrot and Horton creeks. Alt. approx. 3,960.

Rocky Knob. See Haw Knob.

Rocky Knob Creek rises in e Watauga County and flows nw into South Fork New River.

Rocky Knob Gap between Wolf Creek and Tanasee Creek in e Jackson County.

Rockyknob Mountain, w Yancey County between Dryspring Branch and Slickrock Mountain.

Rocky Knob Ridge, s Haywood County on the head of Mauney Cove Branch.

Rocky Knob Ridge, e Macon County between Dalton Creek and Tippet Creek.

Rocky Knobs, sw Transylvania County; two knobs s of Horsepasture River.

Rocky Mount, city in e Nash and w Edgecombe counties. Est. 1816, inc. 1867. Named for the rocky mounds and ledges on the site near the falls of the Tar River. Home of North Carolina Wesleyan College. Produces tobacco, furniture, and fabricated metals. Alt. 121.

Rocky Mount. See Bear Poplar.

Rocky Mountain, s Jackson County between Chimneytop and Horsepasture River. Alt. 4,427.

Rocky Mountain, between Featherston Creek and Harper Creek in n Henderson County.

Rocky Mountain, s Transylvania County between Laurel Branch and Bradley Creek.

Rocky Mountain, s Transylvania County between Woodruff Branch and Browns Mill Creek.

Rocky Mountain, w Transylvania County between Morton Creek and Indian Creek. Alt. 3,527.

Rocky Mountain, e central Watauga County between Rocky Branch and Rocky Knob Creek.

Rocky Mount Township, se Nash County.

Rocky Mount Township, former township in

w central Edgecombe County, now township number 12.

Rocky Pen Ridge, central Cherokee County, extends ne from Nottely River to Hiwassee River near Murphy.

Rocky Point, community in s Pender County. Alt. 39. Inc. 1905; charter repealed 1945. Name applied to this area by Barbadian explorers in 1663 for an unusual outcropping of rock near Lane's Ferry in this otherwise flat country. This particular community was settled in the late eighteenth century. Clayton Hall, home of Francis Clayton, native of Scotland and member of the Wilmington Safety Committee, 1774, was here. Produces lumber. *See also* Lillington County.

Rocky Point Township, s central Pender County.

Rocky Ridge, between Jim Creek and The Flatwoods in sw Henderson County.

Rocky Ridge, s Madison County parallel to Little Pine Creek.

Rocky River rises in se Iredell County near Mooresville and flows s along the Cabarrus-Mecklenburg County line for a short distance, then across Cabarrus to the Cabarrus-Stanly County line which it forms for a short distance, to the Stanly-Union and Anson-Stanly County lines which it forms, before entering Pee Dee River. Appears on the Collet map, 1770.

Rocky River rises in ne Randolph County and flows sw across Chatham County into Deep River.

Rocky River Springs, community and former resort in s Stanly County. Mineral springs here said to have been known to Indians as the "place of healing waters." Hotel and places of amusement in operation from the 1830's until 1920's.

Rocky River Township, former township in sw Cabarrus County, now township number 1.

Rocky Run rises in se Alamance County and flows sw into Hobby Branch.

Rocky Run rises in w Craven County and flows ne into Hayward Creek.

Rocky Run rises in e Onslow County and flows nw into Little Northeast Creek.

Rocky Shoal Branch rises in s Ashe County and flows se into South Fork New River.

Rocky Springs, community in ne Alexander County. Alt. approx. 1,150. York Collegiate Institute operated here 1856-1858 by Brantley York, one of the founders of Trinity College in Randolph County, later Duke University.

Rocky Springs, community in sw Rockingham County. A post office est. here as early as 1822.

Rocky Spring Top, on the Cherokee-Graham County line in the Snowbird Mountains.

Rocky Springs Township, se Montgomery County.

Rocky Swamp rises in w Halifax County and flows se into Fishing Creek. Appears on the Collet map, 1770.

Rocky Top, on the Cherokee County, N.C.-Monroe County, Tenn., line.

Rocky Top, on the Swain County, N.C.-Blount County, Tenn., line in the Great Smoky Mountains National Park between Mount Squires and Thunderhead Mountain.

Rocquis Creek. *See* Roquist.

Rodanthe, community in e Dare County on Hatteras Island. Formerly known as North Rodanthe. A post office was est. here by 1864.

Rodman's Creek rises in w Beaufort County and flows e into Pamlico River.

Rodman's Point, near the mouth of Rodman's Creek, w Beaufort County on the s side of Pamlico River.

Roduco, community in w Gates County near Flat Branch in Jones Swamp. Alt. 35.

Roe, community on Cedar Island in ne Carteret County. Alt. 12.

Rogers Branch rises in central Haywood County and flows nw into Pigeon River.

Rogers Cove, central Haywood County on a tributary of Richland Creek.

Rogers Cove, e Haywood County on the head of Rogers Cove Creek.

Rogers Cove Creek rises in e Haywood County and flows nw into Crabtree Creek.

Rogers Creek rises in central Cherokee County and flows nw into Valley River.

Rogers Creek. *See* Beech Swamp.

Rogers Crossroads, community in e Wake County n of Powell Creek.

Rogers Gap, nw Buncombe County in Fodderstack Mountain near Greasy Cove.

Rogers Gap, w Cherokee County between Wehutty Mountain and Shoal Creek.

Rogers Mountain, w Yancey County between Indian and Price creeks.

Rogers or **Rogers Quarter,** community in n Northampton County.

Rogers Ridge, s Avery County.

Rogers Store, community in n central Wake County. Settled prior to 1840 and named for Colonel Ransome Rogers, first store-keeper. Alt. 300.

Rogers Swamp rises in n Northampton County and flows se to join Corduroy Swamp in forming Kirbys Creek.

Rogues Creek rises in nw Clay County and flows sw and se into Rock House Creek.

Roland Creek Canal rises in nw Currituck County and flows e into Guinea Mill Run.

Roland Branch rises in w central Yancey County and flows se into Cane River. Believed to have been named for a Negro settler. See also Roland Hollow; Roland Knob.

Roland Hollow, w central Yancey County on w side of Cane Mountain. Contains a tributary of Higgins Creek.

Roland Knob, w central Yancey County between head of Roland Branch and head of Bailey Branch, approx. 2 mi. w of town of Burnsville. Alt. approx. 3,620.

Roland Ridge, e Haywood County parallel to Ugly Creek.

Rolesville, town in e Wake County near the head of Cedar Fork. Settled in the early nineteenth century and named for William Roles, original settler. Inc. 1837; reinc. 1941.

Rollins, community in s Madison County on French Broad River.

Rollinson Channel, se Dare County, provides access through Pamlico Sound from Hatteras Inlet to the town of Hatteras. Dredged to a depth of 10 ft.; 10 ft. wide.

Rollover Creek rises in Great Dover Swamp in w Craven County and flows se into Bachelor Creek.

Rominger, community in w Watauga County on Laurel Creek. Named for the Rev. W. Smith Rominger, a Methodist minister in whose home the first post office was est. in early 1900's.

Ronda, town in e Wilkes County on Yadkin River. Alt. 934. Inc. 1907. Est. on Col. Benjamin Cleveland's estate, "Round-about," named for a sharp bend in Yadkin River here. The town's name is a shortened form of the plantation name. Produces furniture.

Rooks, community in w Pender County.

Roosevelt, community in ne Henderson County between Whiteside Mountain and Chicasaw Knob. Named for Theodore Roosevelt (1858-1919).

Rooty Branch rises in e Craven County and flows e into Broad Creek.

Roper, town in n central Washington County on Kendricks Creek. Alt. 13. Settled in 1706 by Thomas Blount who built a dam here. Upon his death, his widow married Col. Thomas Lee who built a mill at the site, and the designations S. Lee, Saw Mills, appears on the Moseley map, 1733. The mill, which began operation in 1709, was destroyed in an explosion in 1921. The town served as county seat from 1800-1823 (see also Cabin Ridge Plantation). Post office est. 1822; post office name changed to Union in 1851. In 1820, the town of Duckettsville was authorized to be laid out here but never developed. Lees Mills was renamed Roper in 1889 for John L. Roper who est. a lumber industry here, and the town was inc. under this name in 1907.

Roper Knob, n Macon County between the head of Rose Creek and Little Tennessee River.

Roper's Knob, s Burke County. Alt. 2,200.

Roper Springs, community in nw Halifax County. A mineral spring here was the site of an Indian camp before the arrival of white settlers. A man named Roper later operated a tavern here, hence the name.

Roquist Creek rises in w Bertie County and flows se into Cashie River. Many spellings (Rocquis, Rakwis, Rocquist, Roquewhist, etc.) have been used in the past, but Roquist is the accepted spelling. The word is Tuscarora for "turtle." Mentioned in local records as early as 1723.

Roquist Pocosin, sw Bertie County.

Rose. See Rosewood.

Rose Bay in Pamlico Sound w of Bell Island in s Hyde County. See also Cecils Harbor.

Rose Bay, community in s Hyde County at the head of Rose Bay.

Roseboro, town in w Sampson County. Inc. 1891 and named for George McNeil Rose (1846-1924), chief counsel of the Cape Fear & Yadkin Valley Railroad. Alt. 137. Owensville (Owenville post office), est. prior to 1839 on Little Coharie Creek a short distance w of the site of Roseboro, declined with the growth of Roseboro.

Roseborough, community in se Avery County.

Rose Branch rises in central Mitchell County near Burns Mountain and flows w into North Toe River.

Rose Branch rises in w Nash County and flows s into Sapony Creek.

Rosebud, community in se Stokes County.

Rosebud, community in n Wilson County

between the head of White Swamp and
Cattail Swamp.

Rose Creek rises in nw Burke County on
Rose Mountain and flows se into Irish
Creek. Named for pioneer Rose family.

Rose Creek rises in central Cherokee County and flows se into Dockery Creek.

Rose Creek rises in se Mitchell County and
flows s and nw into North Toe River.

Rose Creek rises in ne Yancey County near
Chestnut Mountain and flows n into
North Toe River.

Rosedale, community in ne Pasquotank
County. Settled prior to 1890.

Rose Hill, town in sw Duplin County. Alt.
89. Settled approx. 1847; inc. 1875.
Named for wild roses growing in the
vicinity. Produces lumber and poultry.

Rose Hill Township, sw Duplin County.

Roseland, community in sw Moore County.
Est. approx. 1896 as a rival resort to
Southern Pines and Pinehurst. At one
time there were a number of homes here,
a hotel, lake, and stores as well as a
weekly newspaper, but now it is only a
rural community.

Roseman. See Rockett.

Rosemary, former community in n Halifax
County, now within the limits of Roanoke Rapids.

Rosemead, community in ne Bertie County.

Rosemont. See Bertie.

Rose Mountain, extends along nw Burke
County. Alt. 2,600.

Roseneath, community in s Halifax County.

Roseneath Township, se Halifax County.

Rose Ridge, a spur of Big Yellow Mountain
in w Avery County. Named for Rose
family. Also called Hurricane Ridge.

Roses Branch rises in central Mitchell County and flows w into Toe River.

Roses Branch rises in ne Swain County and
flows se into Straight Fork.

Roses Branch rises in ne Yancey County
and flows ne into Toe River.

Roses Branch, community in central Mitchell County on Toe River.

Roses Creek rises in nw Burke County and
flows se into Irish Creek.

Roses Creek rises in nw McDowell County
and flows se between Pompey Ridge and
Pups Ridge into Armstrong Creek.

Roses Gap, ne Swain County between
Thicket Branch and Roses Branch in the
Great Smoky Mountains National Park
near lat. 35° 39′ 34″ N., long. 83° 13′
29″ W.

Roseville, community in sw Person County.

Named for Duncan Rose, local Tory
leader during the Revolutionary War.

Rosewood, community in w central Wayne
County. Formerly known as Rose. Alt.
133.

Rosindale, community in se Bladen County.
Alt. 120. Settled in 1866 by George C.
McDougald who produced turpentine
and rosin (from which the name was
taken).

Rosin Hill, community in n Sampson County on Sevenmile Swamp. Named from
the fact that rosin was produced in the
pine forests here.

Roslin, community in s Cumberland County. Alt. 179.

Rosman, town in s ˙Transylvania County
on French Broad River between its junction with East Fork and North Fork.
Named by an industrialist, J. S. Silver-
stern, who compounded the word from
the names of two associates, Rosenthal
and Ormansky. Inc. 1901 as Toxaway;
name changed to Estatoe [sic] in 1903;
and changed from Eastatoe to Rosman in
1905. A NASA satellite tracking station
was built nearby in 1962. Produces lumber. Alt. 2,188.

Ross Creek rises in central Buncombe County near Patton Mountain and flows s into
Swannanoa River. Named for an early
settler. Often called Chunn Cove Creek.

Rosser, community in ne Lee County.

Ross Falls, former waterfalls (8.1 ft. drop in
a distance of 0.9 mi.) in Catawba River a
short distance n of the South Carolina
state line in sw Mecklenburg and se
Gaston counties. The site is now under
the waters of Lake Wylie.

Rosy, community in s central Transylvania
County.

Roten, community in w Ashe County. Alt.
approx. 3,050.

Rougemont, community in nw Durham
County. Named for nearby Red Mountain. French rouge, "red," and mont,
"mountain." Alt. 561.

Rough Branch rises in n Jackson County
and flows nw into Hornbuckle Creek.

Rough Butt Bald on the Jackson-Haywood
County line. Alt. 6,010.

Rough Butt Creek rises in e Jackson County
and flows nw to join Piney Mountain
Creek in forming Caney Fork.

Rough Creek rises in e Haywood County
and flows se into Beaverdam Creek.

Rough Fork, w Haywood County, Great
Smoky Mountains National Park, is

formed by the junction of Bear Branch and Horse Creek, near lat. 35° 36' 10" N., long. 83° 09' 43" W., and flows ne into Palmer Creek.

Rough Fork rises in s Macon County and flows ne into Wayah Creek.

Rough-hew Ridge, n Swain County between Bee Gum Branch and Board Camp Creek in the Great Smoky Mountains National Park near lat. 35° 30' 18" N., long. 83° 32' 30" W. It is a short spur extending w from Forney Ridge.

Rough Knob on the Haywood-Madison County line.

Rough Knob, e Macon County between Burgoin Gap and Riley Knob.

Rough Mountain, w Haywood County, Great Smoky Mountains National Park, between Low Gap Branch and Big Branch, center near lat. 35° 44' 27" N., long. 83° 10' W.

Rough Ridge, e Avery County.

Rough Ridge, w Haywood County, Great Smoky Mountains National Park, a short spur extending se from Mount Sterling Ridge between Andy Branch and Woody Branch, center near lat. 35° 40' 55" N., long. 83° 07' 10" W.

Rough Run rises in w Jackson County and flows se into West Fork Tuckasegee River.

Rough Run Falls, just above the mouth of Rough Run in w Jackson County.

The Roundabout. See Goldsboro Cooling Pond.

Roundabout. See Ronda.

Roundabout Creek rises in w Ashe County and flows se into North Fork New River.

Round Bald, on the Mitchell County, N. C.-Carter County, Tenn., line.

Round Bottom Creek rises in ne Swain County and flows nw into Straight Fork.

Round Cove, ne Cherokee County in the Valley River Mountains.

Round Hill, w central Swain County near the head of Greasy Branch.

Round Hill Branch rises in nw Buncombe County and flows ne through Green Valley into Newfound Creek.

Round Knob, s Haywood County between Sam Branch and Inman Branch. Alt. 4,265.

Round Knob, sw McDowell County. Alt. approx. 3,500. The Southern Railway winds around this mountain.

Round Mountain, on the Buncombe-Haywood County line se of Twelve O'clock Top.

Round Mountain, sw Caldwell County. Alt. approx. 1,800.

Round Mountain, n Cherokee County in the Unicoi Mountains.

Round Mountain, se corner of Jackson County between East Fork [Chattooga River] and Whitewater River. Alt. approx. 3,700.

Round Mountain on the Jackson-Transylvania County line n of head of West Fork French Broad River and approx. 1½ mi. e of Tuckasegee River. Alt. approx. 4,220. Most southerly peak of Tennessee Ridge, which see.

Round Mountain, e Macon County between Deep Gap and Brush Creek.

Round Mountain, ne Mitchell County between Charles Creek and Roan Valley.

Round Mountain, sw Polk County, e of Tryon. Site of Battle of Round Mountain between Rangers from both Carolinas under Capt. Thomas Howard, and Cherokee Indians under Big Wayah in the spring of 1776. Alt. 1,831. See also Skyuka Creek; Skyuka Mountain.

Round Mountain, a ridge in nw Swain County in Great Smoky Mountains National Park. It is a spur extending se in an arc from Twentymile Ridge to Lost Creek with its center near lat. 35° 30' 57" N., long. 83° 47' 20" W.

Round Mountain, e central Wilkes County between Camp Branch and the head of Rock Creek.

Round Mountain, community in e central Wilkes County.

Round Mountain. See Roundtop.

Round Mountain Knob, nw Swain County in Great Smoky Mountains National Park at the se end of Round Mountain Ridge near lat. 35° 29' 43" N., long. 83° 46' 38" W. Alt. 3,033.

Round Peak Mountain, n Surry County between Camp Branch and the head of Little Fisher River. Alt. 2,094.

Round Top, mountain in ne Alexander County, an almost perfect cone. Alt. 1,750.

Round Top, on the Buncombe-Henderson County line.

Round Top, w Cherokee County w of Shoal Creek. Alt. approx. 2,130.

Round Top, on the Cherokee County, N. C.-Monroe County, Tenn., line. Alt. approx. 3,700.

Round Top, on the Graham-Swain County line near the head of Ammons Branch. Alt. 3,080.

Roundtop, mountain in sw Transylvania County n of Horsepasture River. Also known as Round Mountain. Alt. approx. 3,500.

Roundtop Knob, n Swain County in the Great Smoky Mountains National Park on Noland Divide. Alt. 5,120.

Round Top Mountain, central Chatham County.

Round Top Mountain, se Clay County n of Sharptop Ridge near the Towns County, Ga., line. Alt. approx. 3,560.

Round Top Mountain, n Madison County between Silvermine Branch and Cascade Branch.

Round Top Mountain, w Rutherford County s of Rumbling Bald Mountain.

Roundtree, community in sw Pitt County. Named for Jesse Roundtree (1765-1831), Irish immigrant and soldier in the Revolutionary War who settled here after the war. He served as sheriff from 1818 to 1820.

Rouse Pond, on the head of Grape Branch in n Duplin County.

Rowan. See Mount Ulla.

Rowan Branch rises in e Sampson County and flows e into Six Runs Creek.

Rowan Branch rises in w Swain County and flows ne into Hazel Creek.

Rowan (ROW-an) County was formed in 1753 from Anson county. Located in the central section of the state, it is bounded by Davidson, Stanly, Cabarrus, Iredell, and Davie counties. It was named for Matthew Rowan (d. 1760), acting governor at the time the county was formed. Area: 527 sq. mi. County seat: Salisbury with an elevation of 764 ft. Townships are Atwell, China Grove, Cleveland, Franklin, Gold Hill, Litaker, Locke, Morgan, Mount Ulla, Providence, Salisbury, Scotch Irish, Steele, and Unity. Produces corn, wheat, oats, cotton, poultry, dairy products, livestock, hogs, refrigeration equipment, bakery products, textiles, rubber products, chemicals, furniture, apparel, industrial machinery, millstones, concrete products, and crushed stone.

Rowan Creek rises in se Bladen County and flows se into Black River.

Rowan Mills, community on the sw outskirts of city of Salisbury, e central Rowan County.

Row Branch rises in central Avery County and flows n into North Toe River.

Rowland, town in w Robeson County. Alt. 150. Inc. 1889. Named for Colonel Alfred Rowland, II, a Confederate officer. Ashpole Presbyterian Church here organized, 1796. See also, Plainview.

Rowland Branch rises in w Macon County and flows nw into Nantahala River.

Rowland Township, sw Robeson County.

Rowlin Creek rises in nw Macon County and flows ne into Nantahala River.

Roxboro, town and county seat, central Person County. Est. as county seat, 1793. Named for Roxburgh, Scotland. Inc. 1855. Produces lumber, fabricated metals, textiles, processed poultry, and tobacco. Alt. 671.

Roxboro Lake. See Carolina Power Lake.

Roxboro Township, central Person County.

Roxobel, town in nw Bertie County. Settled about 1800; inc. 1895. The early settlement was known as Cotten's Cross Roads; around 1808 the name was change to Granberrys Cross Roads; and by 1833 a post office here was called Brittons Cross Roads or Store. Roxobel appears as the post office name in 1847. The name was selected by Miss Frances Norfleet for the popular 3-volume novel, Roxobel, by Mrs. Mary Martha Sherwood. The final change was reportedly necessary to avoid confusion with Britton's Neck, S. C.

Roxobel Township, nw Bertie County.

Royal, community in se Beaufort County, est. 1908 and known first as Dublin for the city in Ireland. Renamed for George E. Royal, a railroad official.

Royal, community in s Franklin County.

Royal Cotton Mills, community in ne Wake County. Named for the mills est. here. Chartered 1907; charter repealed 1943.

Royal Creek, a short stream in n central Carteret County flowing e into South River.

Royal Oak appears on the Price map, 1808, and on the MacRae map, 1833, on the Jones-Onslow County line where a slight change in direction is made. Said to have been named after a British soldier, found hiding in its top to spy on Americans, was hanged from a limb of the tree. The decayed stump of the tree was removed about 1916 when the road from Richlands to Comfort was widened.

Royal Oak Swamp rises in Green Swamp in central Brunswick County and flows e into Lockwoods Folly River.

Royal Point, on the Pamlico Sound side of Portsmouth Island, approx. 3 mi. from Drum Inlet, e Carteret County.

Royal Shoal, in Pamlico Sound in ne Carteret and se Hyde counties. Extends nw in an arc from Beacon Island, and obstructs the passage through Ocracoke Inlet. Appears as Ryals Shoal on the Moseley map, 1733, but by present name on the Collet map, 1770.

Rube Creek rises in n Watauga County and flows sw into Beaverdam Creek.

Rube Green Top, e Mitchell County between Middle Mountain and the Avery County line.

Rube Rock Branch, rises in n Haywood County and flows sw into Pigeon River.

Rudd, community in n Guilford County. Alt. 826. Est. 1898 as Sippanaw; later named Morehead. Because of a delay in shipment of merchandise consigned to Morehead City, railroad officials renamed the community to avoid confusion and to honor Senaca and Cicero Rudd, local residents.

Rufe, former town in w Greene County near the head of Fort Run. Inc. 1887 and name changed from Shine. No longer in existence. Shine family prominent in the vicinity as early as 1750. A public school at or near the site is known as Shine School.

Ruffin, community in e Rockingham County. Settled prior to 1860 and known first as Stubblefield for a local family. Name changed to honor Thomas Ruffin (1787-1870), Chief Justice of the North Carolina Supreme Court. Inc. 1887; new charter issued 1891; charter repealed 1897. Alt. 712.

Ruffin's Bridge. See Peacock's Bridge.

Ruffin Township, ne Rockingham County.

Rufus, community in nw Caldwell County on Mulberry Creek in Pisgah National Forest. Formerly known as Risden, the present name honors W. Rufus Coffey, a nineteenth-century merchant here.

Rugby, community in n Henderson County on Mill Pond Creek.

Ruggles, community in e Halifax County.

Ruin Creek rises in w Vance County and flows s into Tabbs Creek. Appears on the Collet map, 1770.

Rumbling Bald Mountain, nw Rutherford County on a ridge extending se from Shumont Mountain. Alt. approx. 3,020. There are numerous caves in the mountain, and boulders sometimes fall in them, making a rumbling noise. Known by the Cherokee Indians as Sokassa. See also The Caves. A series of earthquakes occurred here from February 10 until April 17, 1874. There were between 50 and 75 shocks.

Rumley Bay, a small bay in se Cedar Island, ne Carteret County. Named for the Rumley family.

Rumley Marsh, a tidal marsh peninsula approx. 1¾ mi. long and ¾ mi. wide on the n shore of Pamlico River s of Jackson Swamp, e Beaufort County. Appears as Rumneys Marsh on the Collet map, 1770.

Rumneys Marsh. See Rumley Marsh.

Runaway Knob, on the se end of Runaway Ridge in sw Macon County.

Runaway Ridge, sw Macon County between the head of Allison Creek and the head of Ash Flat Branch.

Run Branch rises in s Lee County and flows ne into Thoroughfare Branch.

Runion, community in w Madison County on French Broad River approx. 3 mi. e of town of Hot Springs.

Running Creek rises in w Stanly County and flows ne into Big Bear Creek.

Runnymede, former town in central Edgecombe County. Inc. 1907 as the site of the county fair; charter repealed 1909. The site is now within the limits of the town of Tarboro, and the name survives only as the name of a mill.

Run of Swamp, a canal which drains the Big Pocosin in sw Gates County and empties into Chowan River.

Run of the Mill Pond, a stream which rises in se Duplin County and flows n into Jump and Run Branch.

Run Swamp Canal rises in w Currituck County and flows se into Indiantown Creek. It forms a part of the boundary between Camden and Currituck counties.

Runyon Creek is formed by the junction of several small unnamed streams ne of Washington, w Beaufort County, and flows s into Pamlico River.

Runyon Creek rises in n Haywood County and flows sw into Pigeon River.

Runyon Gap, n Haywood County on Snowbird Creek.

Runyon Ridge, n Haywood County parallel
to Snowbird Creek.

Rural Hall, community in n Forsyth County. Earliest settler apparently was Ludwig
Bitting, former German soldier in General Nathanael Greene's army who liked
the area when passing through and returned after the Revolution to settle. His
descendants still live in the county. Rural
Hall, however, developed after the Cape
Fear and Yadkin Valley Railroad erected
a station here in 1887. Produces furniture and lumber. Alt. 1,002.

Rush Branch rises in ne Buncombe County
and flows se into Broad River.

Rush Branch rises in nw Henderson County and flows ne into North Fork Mills
River.

Rush Branch rises in w Watauga County
and flows sw into Watauga River.

Rush Creek rises in nw Caldwell County
and flows sw into Mulberry Creek.

Rush Fork rises in e Haywood County and
flows sw into Crabtree Creek.

Rush Fork Gap, e Haywood County on the
head of James Branch.

Rushing, community in se Union County.

Rush Mountain, s Henderson County between Huckleberry Ridge and McAlpine
Mountain.

Rush Mountain, s Lincoln County. Named
for a local family.

Rush. See Burch.

Ruskin, community in nw Bladen County.

Russell Branch rises in Union County,
Georgia, and flows ne into Clay County
where it enters Pinelog Creek.

Russell Gap on the Alexander-Wilkes County line. Alt. 1,650.

Russellborough, se Brunswick County on
the Cape Fear River just n of the site of
the town of Brunswick, site of the home
of royal governors Arthur Dobbs and
William Tryon. A house here, begun by
Capt. John Russell of His Majesty's Sloop
Scorpion, was purchased in 1758 by
Dobbs; renamed Castle Dobbs after his
marriage in 1762. At Dobb's death in
1765 Tryon occupied the house and
named it Castle Tryon. When Tryon left
the house in 1770 it was purchased by
William Dry and renamed Bellfont. It
burned in 1776. The site was excavated
in 1967 by the State Department of
Archives and History and many eighteenth century artifacts discovered, many

of which are on display at the museum
at Brunswick State Historic Site.

Russell Gap, w Clay County near the headwaters of Trout Cove Branch.

Russell Gap on the Alexander-Wilkes County line. Alt. 1,550.

Russells Creek rises in e central Brunswick
County and flows e and n into Town
Creek.

Russells Creek rises in central Carteret
County and flows s into Newport River.

Russtown, community in sw Brunswick
County.

Ruth, town in w central Rutherford County. Inc. 1893 as Hampton. Named for
S. D. Hampton, first mayor. Name
changed to Ruth (first part of the county
name) in 1906.

Rutherford College, former town and college in e Burke County. The school was
founded by Dr. R. L. Abernathy in 1853
and the 400 acre site was inc. as village
of Excelsior in 1872; inc. as town of
Rutherford College in 1881. Alt. 1,210.
The school merged with Weaver College
in 1932 and was moved to Brevard,
which see, and renamed Brevard College.
Town charter repealed in 1933. Now a
residential community approx. 2 mi. e
of town of Valdese. Named for John
Rutherford who donated the land for
the school in 1853. Original post office
was named Happy Home; it also served
Connelly Springs, which see.

Rutherford County was formed in 1779
from Tryon County when it was divided
to form Rutherford and Lincoln counties.
Located in the sw section of the state,
it is bounded by the state of South Carolina, and by Polk, Henderson, Buncombe,
McDowell, Burke, and Cleveland counties. It was named for Griffith Rutherford
(1731-1800), Indian fighter, member of
the Provincial Congress, and Revolutionary general. Area: 568 sq. mi. County
seat: Rutherfordton with an elevation of
1,096 ft. Townships are Camp Creek,
Chimney Rock, Colfax, Cool Spring,

Duncans Creek, Gilkey, Golden Valley, Green Hill, High Shoals, Logan Store, Morgan, Rutherfordton, Sulphur Springs, and Union. Produces corn, wheat, oats, cotton, dairy products, livestock, hogs, textiles, apparel, lumber, sand, and gravel.

Rutherfords Mill. See Exeter.

Rutherfordton, town and county seat, w central Rutherford County. Inc. 1787. Alt. 1,096. Town and county named for Gen. Griffith Rutherford (1731-1800), Revolutionary leader. See also Gilbert Town; Mountain Creek.

Rutherfordton Township, central Rutherford County.

Rutherwood, community in e Watauga County s of South Fork New River.

Rutledge Creek rises in ne Surry County and flows se into Ararat River.

Ryders Pond, e Warren County on Little Fishing Creek. Covers approx. 10 acres with a max. depth of 4 ft.

Rye Mountain, e Jackson County on the head of Flat Creek. Alt. 4,542.

Rye Patch Branch rises in nw Swain County and flows se into Twentymile Creek.

Rye Ridge, w Avery County.

Ryes, community in w Harnett County.

Rye Swamp rises in w Sampson County and flows sw into Little Coharie Creek.

Ryland, community in n Chowan County. Site of an early Quaker settlement. Post office est. here in 1888 said to have been named for a railroad official.

S

Saddleback, ridge in nw Swain County in Great Smoky Mountains National Park between Roaring Creek and Desolation Branch. Its center is near lat. 35° 33' 26" N., long. 83° 40' 48" W.

Saddle Gap, n Transylvania County between Lookingglass Creek and Avery Creek.

Saddle Mountain on the Alleghany-Surry County line.

Saddle Mountain Creek rises in w Surry County and flows se into Mitchell River.

Saddle Tree Gap, w Graham County between the headwaters of Hangover Creek and Deep Creek.

Saddletree Swamp rises in n Robeson County and flows s into Lumber River.

Saddletree Township, central Robeson County.

Safe, community in sw Duplin County.

Sag Branch rises in w Haywood County and flows nw into Caldwell Fork.

Sage Path, site of early settlement on the e end of Bogue Banks, s Carteret County. Storms drove out early settlers until the settlement of Salter Path, which see.

Sage Rock, peak in w Yancey County on Sevenmile Ridge near the head of Murphy Branch.

Sages Ordinary. See Holly Ridge.

Saginaw. See Pineola.

Sahara of North Carolina. See Sandhills.

Sahlee Creek rises in n Swain County and flows se into Deep Creek.

St. Andrew's Parish, Church of England, Tyrrell County, est. 1729 with the formation of the county and coextensive with it. Previous to the formation of the county the territory had been South Shore Parish (est. 1722), Chowan County. In 1767 St. Andrew's Parish had 594 white taxables.° See also St. Paul's Parish.

St. Asaph's District, one of the districts into which Orange County was divided at the time of the 1790 census. It contained 199 heads of families.

St. Barnabas' Parish, Church of England, Hertford County, est. 1759 with the formation of the county and coextensive with it. The parish in 1767 had 900 white taxables.°

St. Bartholomew's Parish, Church of England, Chatham County, est. with the formation of the county in 1770. Coextensive with the county.° St. Bartholomew's Parish of the Episcopal Church, still functions in Pittsboro.

St. Clair Creek rises in Jackson Swamp, e

°The parish as a unit of local administration was abolished in 1776 with the adoption of the state constitution and the disestablishment of the Church of England.

Beaufort County, and flows se into Pamlico River.

St. Colomb Parish. See Donegal County.

St. David's District, one of the districts into which Caswell County was divided at
the time of the 1790 census. It contained
166 heads of families.

St. David's Parish, Church of England,
Cumberland County, est. 1754 with the
formation of the county and co-extensive
with it. In 1767 the parish had 899
white taxables described as "mostly
Scotch—Support a Presbyterian Minister."°

St. Gabriel's Parish, Church of England,
Duplin County, est. 1750 with the formation of the county and coextensive
with the county. In 1767 there were 1,071
white taxables in the parish.° St. Gabriel's
Parish of the Episcopal Church functions
in Faison at the present, though there is
some question of its unbroken descent
from the colonial Parish.

St. George's Parish, Church of England,
Anson County, est. in 1750 when the
county was formed and coextensive with
it. Composed of 969 white taxable inhabitants in 1767 who were described as
"in general poor & incapable to support
a Minister."°

St. George's Parish, Church of England,
Northampton County, est. 1758 when
Northwest Parish was divided. The western part became St. George's and after
1759 when the eastern part of Northampton became a part of Hertford County,
the parish was coextensive with the county. In 1767 there were 1,600 white taxables living in the parish.° Records of
St. George's Parish, 1773-1814, are in
the State Department of Archives and
History, Raleigh.

St. George's Parish. See Hyde Parish.

Saint Helena, community in central Pender
County. Alt. 55. Settled 1908 by a colony
of Italian farmers. Saint Helena (d. about
330) was the mother of Constantine the
Great, Roman emperor. Hugh MacRae,
Wilmington realtor, developed this as the
first of several agricultural colonies for
immigrants.

St. James District, one of the districts into
which Caswell County was divided at

the time of the 1790 census. It contained
111 heads of families.

St. James' Parish, Church of England, New
Hanover County, probably est. in 1729
with the creation of the county and co-
extensive with it. The parish is men-
tioned as early as 1734. In 1741 St.
James' Parish was divided to form St.
Philip's Parish on the south side of the
Cape Fear River. With the creation of
Brunswick County in 1764 St. Philip's
Parish became coextensive with it, and
St. James' Parish with New Hanover.°
St. James' Parish of the Episcopal Church
still functions in Wilmington.

St. Johns, community in sw Hertford County at the head of Chapel Branch. Mentioned in local records as early as 1722.
Douglas Ordinary appears on the Collet
map, 1770, at this site.

St. Johns, community in s Pitt County.

St. John's Parish, Church of England, Carteret County, probably was est. with the
formation of the county in 1722. It is
mentioned as early as 1724. Coextensive
with the county. In 1767 there were 470
white taxables in the parish.° The ves-
try book of St. John's Parish, 1742-1743,
in three volumes, is in the Department
of Archives and History, Raleigh.

St. John's Parish, Church of England, Granville, later Bute County, est. in 1746
with the formation of Granville County.
Coextensive with the county. In 1758
the parish was divided creating Granville Parish in the west; St. John's was
in the east. Bute County, created in 1764,
and the parish were coextensive. In 1767
there were 1,299 white taxables in St.
John's Parish. Warren and Franklin counties were formed from Bute County in
1779.°

St. John's Parish, Church of England, Onslow County, was est. in 1734 with the
formation of the county and coextensive
with it. In 1767 the parish had 716 white
taxables described as "willing to receive
tho' hardly capable of making provisions
for Minister."°

St. John's Parish, Church of England, Pasquotank County, est. in 1701. In 1715
the parish was divided leaving St. John's
on the sw side of the Pasquotank River
and creating St. Peter's Parish on the ne
side. In 1756 the two parishes were consolidated to form St. John's Parish. In
1767 the parish had 433 white taxables
and was described as a "weak parish."°

°The parish as a unit of local administration was abolished in 1776 with the
adoption of the state constitution and the
disestablishment of the Church of England.

St. Johns Township, sw Hertford County.

St. Jude's Parish, Church of England, Surry County, est. 1771 with the formation of the county and coextensive with it.°

St. Lawrence District, one of the districts into which Caswell County was divided at the time of the 1790 census. It contained 215 heads of families.

St. Lewis, town in s Edgecombe County. Inc. 1895 but not now active in municipal affairs. Named for first postmaster, John I. Lewis.

St. Lukes District, one of the districts into which Caswell County was divided at the time of the 1790 census. It contained 137 heads of families.

St. Luke's Parish, Church of England, Rowan County, est. 1753 with the formation of the county and coextensive with it. In 1767 the parish had 3,000 white taxables. Dobbs Parish, organized by the Moravians in the Wachovia settlement, was created from St. Luke's Parish in 1755.° St. Luke's Parish of the Episcopal Church still functions in Salisbury.

St. Margaret's Parish, Church of England, Wake County, est. with the formation of the county in 1770 and coextensive with it.° (This parish probably was named for St. Margaret because the county was named for Margaret Wake, wife of Governor William Tryon.)

St. Mark's District, one of the districts into which Orange County was divided at the time of the 1790 census. It contained 138 heads of families.

Saint Martin, community in s Stanly County between Big Bear Creek and Little Bear Creek. Named for a local Lutheran Church.

St. Martin's Parish, Church of England, Bladen County, est. in 1734 when the county was formed, coextensive with the county. The parish had 791 white taxables in 1767, described as "in midling circumstances."°

St. Martin's Parish, Church of England, Mecklenburg County, est. 1762 with the formation of the county and coextensive with it. The parish in 1767 had 1,600 white taxables, described as "mostly Presbyterians."° St. Martin's Episcopal Church still exists in Charlotte.

St. Martin's Parish, Church of England,

Martin County, est. 1774 with the formation of the county and coextensive with it.°

St. Mary's District, one of the districts into which Orange County was divided at the time of the 1790 census. It contained 237 heads of families.

St. Mary's Parish, Church of England, Edgecombe County, est. 1756 by the division of the Parish of Edgecombe. St. Mary's Parish was in the south, the Parish of Edgecombe in the north. With the creation of Halifax County from Edgecombe County in 1758, the Parish of Edgecombe (est. 1741 with the formation of Edgecombe County) became coextensive with the new county. St. Mary's Parish then became coextensive with Edgecombe County. In 1767 St. Mary's Parish had 1,200 white taxables.°

St. Marys Township, e Wake County.

St. Matthew's Parish, Church of England, Orange County, est. in 1752 with the formation of the county and coextensive with it. In 1767 the parish had 3,573 white taxables—the most populous in the colony.° Reestablished in 1824, St. Matthew's Parish of the Episcopal Church continues to function in Hillsborough.

St. Matthews Township, e central Wake County.

St. Michael's Parish, Church of England, Pitt County, est. 1760 with the formation of the county and coextensive with it. In 1767 the parish had 775 white taxables and was described as a "small county—willing to make provision for a Minister."°

St. Patrick's Parish, Church of England, Johnston County, later Dobbs County, est. 1746 with the formation of Johnston County. It was coextensive with the county, but divided in 1756 to form St. Stephen's Parish in the western part of the county. St. Patrick's was in the east. With the creation of Dobbs County in 1758, St. Patrick's Parish became coextensive with that county. In 1767 the parish had 1,268 white taxables.° The present counties of Wayne, Lenoir, and Greene are made up wholly or in part of territory which was once St. Patrick's Parish.

St. Pauls, town in ne Robeson County. Inc. 1909. Named for local Presbyterian Church. Post office est. here in 1832 was named Tuton; changed to St. Pauls about four years later. Originally the settlement

°The parish as a unit of local administration was abolished in 1776 with the adoption of the state constitution and the disestablishment of the Church of England.

centered about a stage depot on the Fayetteville-Lumberton road, about 3 mi. from present site. When the railroad came through, about 1900, the settlement drifted south to center about the depot. Produces textiles.

St. Paul's Parish, Church of England, Chowan County, est. in 1701. In 1715 the parish was divided to create South West Parish in the w part of the county. The area became Bertie County in 1722 and coextensive with it was Society Parish. In 1722 St. Paul's Parish was further divided to create South Shore Parish in the southern part of the county on the south shore of Albemarle Sound. With the creation of Tyrrell County in 1729 South Shore Parish became St. Andrew's Parish, coextensive with the county. In 1767 St. Paul's Parish had 900 white taxables.° St. Paul's Parish of the Episcopal Church, however, still functions in Edenton. St. Paul's Church there was begun in 1736.

St. Pauls Township, ne Robeson County.

St. Peter's Parish. See St. John's Parish.

St. Philip's Parish, Church of England, New Hanover, later Brunswick County, established in 1741 when St. James' Parish (which see) was divided. St. Philip's Parish was that part of the county s of the Cape Fear River. With the creation of Brunswick County in 1764, St. Philip's Parish became coextensive with the new county. The parish had 224 white taxable inhabitants in 1767, described as being "mostly Gentlemen."° The ruins of St. Philip's Church, completed in 1765, begun a number of years earlier, still stand near Orton Plantation, Brunswick County, at the site of the old town of Brunswick.

St. Stephen's Parish, Church of England, Johnston County, est. 1756 in the western part of the county upon the division of St. Patrick's Parish. When Dobbs County was formed from Johnston in 1758 St. Patrick's became coextensive with the new county. St. Stephen's Parish then was coextensive with Johnston County. In 1767 the parish had 1,229 white taxables, described as "able to make provision for a minister."°

°The parish as a unit of local administration was abolished in 1776 with the adoption of the state constitution and the disestablishment of the Church of England.

St. Thomas District, one of the districts into which Orange County was divided at the time of the 1790 census. It contained 139 heads of families.

St. Thomas' Parish, Church of England, Beaufort County, organized 1701. St. Thomas' Church, Bath, (oldest church building in North Carolina) constructed in 1734. The parish had 110 white taxables in 1767.° St. Thomas' Parish of the Episcopal Church still functions in Bath.

St. Thomas Parish, Church of England, Tryon County, est. 1768 with the formation of the county and coextensive with it. In 1767 the parish was described as "too unsettled to make provision for a Minister."°

Sa-koh-na-gas. See Blue Ridge.

Saldeer Gap, n Macon County between Burningtown Creek and Rose Creek.

Salem, community in se Burke County.

Salem, formerly an independent city in central Forsyth County, inc. 1856, but since 1913 consolidated with Winston as Winston-Salem, which see. Salem was laid out and settled in 1766 by Moravians; its name, meaning "peace," is said to have been selected by Count Nikolaus Zinzendorf, patron and leader of the Moravian Church, prior to his death in 1760. Records of the Moravians from 1752 to 1851 have been published in ten volumes. Old Salem has been largely restored as a museum with shops, homes, a tavern (in which Washington was entertained in 1791), and other buildings open to the public.

Salem, community in s Lincoln County.

Salem, community in n Randolph County. Authorized to be laid off as New Salem, 1818; inc. 1831 but long inactive in municipal affairs. Came to be known as Salem after 1882. Long the site of a popular camp meeting in the summer.

Salem, community in n Surry County between Lovills Creek and Ararat River.

Salemburg, town in w Sampson County. Settled about 1870. Inc. 1905 and took its name from Salem Academy est. here by the Rev. Isham Royal in 1874. The academy developed into Pineland College and Edwards Military Institute which merged in 1965 to form Southwood College.

Salem Chapel. See Dennis.

Salem Chapel Township, ne Forsyth County.

Salem Creek rises in e Forsyth County and flows sw through the city of Winston-Salem into Muddy Creek in the sw corner of the county. Appears as Wack Creek on the Collet map, 1770; as "Middle Watch Creek" on the Price map, 1808; and finally as Middle Fork on the MacRae map, 1833. Known as Middle Fork or Middle Fork Muddy Creek until 1966 when the present name was adopted. Wack and Watch undoubtedly are derived from the name Wachovia, *which see.*

Salem Lake, ne Forsyth County, fed by Lowery Mill Creek, Kerners Mill Creek, and other streams. Formed 1942. Covers 400 acres with a max. depth of 35 ft. Source of water for Winston-Salem.

Salem Township, e central Granville County.

Salem Township, s Pasquotank County.

Sales Branch rises in central Cherokee County and flows nw into Valley River.

Sales Ford, community in central Cherokee County on Valley River.

Salisbury, city and county seat, e central Rowan County. Est. 1755. Presumably named for the town in England, but possibly for the town in Maryland, the origin of some of the earliest settlers in Rowan County. Catawba and Livingstone Colleges are here. Produces textiles, processed food, corrugated boxes, furniture, chemicals, machinery, structural steel, wire cloth. Alt. 764.

Salisbury District at the time of the 1790 Census was composed of Guilford, Iredell, Mecklenburg, Montgomery, Rockingham, Rowan, Stokes, and Surry counties.

Salisbury Township, e Rowan County.

Salisbury West, uninc. outskirts of city of Salisbury, e central Rowan County.

Sally Branch rises in e Franklin County and flows n into Lick Meadow Branch.

Sally Branch rises in e Haywood County and flows sw into Fines Creek.

Sally Cove Branch rises in nw Macon County and flows n into Whiteoak Creek.

Sally Gap, s Swain County between Yalaka Creek and Little Yalaka Creek.

Sally Haines Branch rises in e Haywood County and flows n into Pigeon River.

Sally Mountain, e Madison County between Middle Fork and Ponder Creek.

Sally Queen Creek rises in ne Rutherford County near the Burke County line and flows sw into North Fork.

Sally's Creek rises in w Caldwell County and flows se into Johns River.

Salmon Creek rises in e Bertie County and flows se into Chowan River. Appears as Flatt's Creek on the Comberford map, 1657, but as Salmon Creek on the Ogilby map, 1671. Probably named for an early settler.

Salmon Creek. *See* Southwest Creek.

Salola. *See* Sugarloaf Mountain.

Salola Branch rises in n Swain County s of Clingmans Dome and flows se into Noland Creek. Salola was the Cherokee Indian word for squirrel.

Sal Patch Gap, w Haywood County. Great Smoky Mountains National Park, near lat. 35° 38′ 24″ N., long. 83° 03′ 28″ W.

Sals Creek rises in s Transylvania County and flows ne into Glady Fork.

Sal's Creek rises in central Wake County and flows ne into Crabtree Creek.

Salser Branch rises in central Macon County and flows e into McDowell Branch.

Salt Branch rises in s Onslow County and flows e into Chadwick Bay.

Salter Creek rises in ne Carteret County and flows se into Nelson Bay.

Salter Path, community near the center of Bogue Banks, s Carteret County. Settlement begun about 1900 on property owned by John A. Royall of Boston, Massachusetts. A court judgment in 1923 restricted the settlement to 84 acres and declared that only persons then resident at Salter Path and their descendants could occupy the land. *See also* Rice Path.

Salters Lake, a natural lake in central Bladen County on Ellis Creek, 6 mi. n of Elizabethtown. Covers 315 acres with a max. depth of 10 ft. State-owned and open to the public. Fishing, swimming, and boating. Part of Jones Lake State Park, *which see.*

Salters Lumps, two small islands in Brett Bay off Piney Point, ne Carteret County.

Salton Gap, n Buncombe County between North Knob and Grassy Knob.

Saltrock Branch rises in ne Buncombe County and flows se into North Fork [Swannanoa River].

Saltrock Branch rises in se Macon County and flows nw into Cullasaja River.

Saltrock Gap, s Macon County on Tennessee Valley Divide.

Salt Rock Gap, s Yancey County on Buncombe Horse Range Ridge.

Saluda, town in sw Polk County. Settled

1878 after the construction of the railroad. Inc. 1881. Took its name from the Indian word *salutah*, which means "corn river." Alt. 2,097.

Saluda Mountain, s Henderson County along the South Carolina state line. Approx. 5 mi. long.

Saluda Township, sw Polk County.

Salvage Island. *See* Core Banks.

Salvo, community on Hatteras Island, e Dare County. Formerly known as Clarks or Clarksville.

Salyer's Bay. *See* Sulliers's Bay.

Samarcand, community in w Moore County. Named in 1916 by Raphael W. Pumpelly, Jr., for the town in Asia Minor which he had visited in his travels. A state home and industrial school for girls was opened here in 1918. Alt. 698.

Samaria, community in sw Nash County. Named for local Baptist Church.

Sam Branch rises in central Cherokee County and flows nw into Valley River.

Sam Branch rises in s Haywood County and flows se into Nick Creek.

Sam Branch rises in s Haywood County and flows nw into West Fork Pigeon River.

Sam Cove, nw Graham County on Deep Creek.

Sam Doane Mountain on Madison-Yancey County line between Moore Gap and Paint Gap. Named for an early settler.

Sam Gap, se Buncombe County between Flint Knob and Round Mountain.

Sam Knob, s Haywood County between Sam Branch and Flat Laurel Creek. Alt. 6,030.

Sam Newton Branch rises in central Cherokee County and flows nw into Valley River.

Sampson, community in n central Caldwell County on the headwaters of the Yadkin River near Blowing Rock.

Sampson Branch rises in n Yancey County and flows se into Jacks Creek. Named for Sampson Honeycutt, an early settler who died and was buried nearby about 1891.

Sampson County was formed in 1784 from Duplin County. Located in the e section of the state, it is bounded by Wayne, Duplin, Pender, Bladen, Cumberland, Johnston, and Harnett counties. It was named for Colonel John Sampson (d. 1784), member of the House of Commons and of the governor's council under royal governors Dobbs, Tryon, and Martin. Area: 963 sq. mi. County seat: Clinton with an elevation of 158 ft. Townships are Belvoir, Dismal, Franklin, Hales, Herrings, Honeycutts, Lisbon, Little Coharie, McDaniels, Mingo, Newton Grove, North Clinton, Piney Grove, Plain View, South Clinton, South River, Taylors Bridge, Turkey, and Westbrook. Produces corn, soybeans, wheat, oats, tobacco, cotton, cucumbers, pepper, miscellaneous vegetables and fruit, poultry, hogs, livestock, lumber, processed meat, electronics, apparel, and textiles.

Sampson Creek rises in s Catawba County and flows ne into Pott Creek.

Sampson Gap, ne Transylvania County ne of Sharpy Mountain near the Haywood County line.

Sampson Gap, w Yancey County on Sampson Mountain near the head of Simms Fork.

Sampson Mountain, se Watauga County. Alt. 4,716.

Sampson Mountain, w Yancey County extends se from the head of Simms Fork to Slickrock Knob. Alt. 4,826 at Sampson Peak on the mountain.

Sampson Point, s Currituck County e of community of Point Harbor, extends into Albemarle Sound. Shown on U.S. Coast Survey map, 1865. Ferry between this point and Currituck Banks was replaced in 1930 by the Wright Memorial Bridge, a 3 mi. long wooden bridge named for Wilbur and Orville Wright, pioneers in aviation. This bridge was replaced by a new bridge opened in the summer of 1966.

Sampson's Chimney, rock formation on Howard Knob, central Watauga County.

Sams Branch rises in sw Buncombe County near Twelve O'clock Top and flows w into South Hominy Creek.

Sams Branch rises in w Mitchell County and flows sw into Nolichucky River.

Sams Branch rises in w Pitt County and flows ne into Tar River.

Sams Gap on the Madison County, N. C.- Unicoi County, Tenn., line.

Sams Gap, on the Swain County, N. C.,-
Sevier County, Tenn., line in the Great
Smoky Mountains National Park near lat.
35° 34' 02" N., long. 83° 38' 12" W.

Samuel Creek. See Hayward Creek.

Sanatorium. See McCain.

Sandbank Creek rises in w Avery County
and flows sw into Roaring Creek.

Sandbank Ridge, w Avery County.

Sandbluff, community in central Bladen
County.

Sand Branch rises in se Buncombe County
and flows s into Broad River.

Sand Creek rises in se Granville County
and flows n into Tar River.

Sanders Creek rises in w Carteret County
and flows s into Goose Creek. Appears as
Smiths Creek on the Moseley map, 1733.

Sanders Creek, a tidal inlet on the n side
of Bogue Sound approx. 2 mi. w of Broad
Creek, w Carteret County. It is formed
by the junction of Sikes Branch and East
Prong.

Sanders Creek, e Onslow County, flows
from the n of Queens Creek sw into the
mouth of Bear Creek. Mentioned in local
records as early as 1744.

Sanders Island, e Onslow County in
Brown's Sound, between the mouths of
Bear and Sanders creeks.

Sanders Knob, on McDowell Branch in
central Macon County.

Sanders Knob, s Macon County between
Shope Fork and North Fork Coweeta
Creek.

Sanders Point, w Carteret County, extends
into Bogue Sound w of the mouth of
Goose Creek.

Sanderson Fish Pond, on a tributary of
Cabin Creek in e central Duplin County.

Sanderson's Channel. See Roanoke Sound.

Sand Flat Mountain, n Henderson County
between Garren Mountain and Hooper
Creek.

Sand Hill, community in central Buncombe
County.

Sandhill, community in n Pamlico County.

Sand Hill Cove, e Pender County on Northeast Cape Fear River.

Sand Hill Creek rises in e central Brunswick County and flows ne into Cape Fear
River.

Sandhills, a series of rolling hills between
the Cape Fear and Pee Dee rivers covering portions of Richmond, Scotland,
Moore, Cumberland, and Harnett counties. Includes approx. 1,110 sq. mi. The
surrounding area is approx. 600 ft. above

sea level, but within the Sandhills there
are ridges rising to 300 to 400 ft. higher.
Little River, Drowning Creek, and Rockfish Creek are the principal streams.
Coarse sandy soil is characteristic of the
area. The Basset map, 1676, marks the
area "Deserta Arenosa." It has also been
called Deserta Montana, Sandy Barrens,
Pine Barrens, and the Sahara of North
Carolina. William Hooper, in a letter of
June 15, 1779, to James Iredell, used
the term sandhills. The climate of the
region has been classed as "Humid Sub-
tropical," and it has an average annual
temperature of approx. 61.5°. The area
was settled by Scotttish Highlanders beginning about 1740. They found the
region covered by a magnificent stand of
long leaf pine, ranging in height from
100 to 120 ft., with diameters up to 36
inches. Beneath the pines wire grass
covered the ground. Most of the pines
were cut between 1875 and 1895 (for an
exception see Weymouth Woods Sandhills Nature Preserve), and the region is
now covered with smaller long leaf pines,
scrub oak (chiefly Turkey and Black
Jack), and wire grass. Extensive peach
orchards have flourished in the Sandhills
since 1892. The resort towns of Pinehurst
and Southern Pines (which see) have
developed here.

Sandhills Township, s Moore County.

Sand Hill Township, e Lenoir County.

Sand Mountain, w Caldwell County. Alt.
1,500.

Sand Point, ne Carteret County, extends
from w side of central Cedar Island into West Bay.

Sand Point, on nw shore of Roanoke Island,
extends w into Croatan Sound, ne Dare
County.

Sands, community in e central Watauga
County between Howard Creek and
Meat Camp Creek.

Sandy Barrens. See Sandhills.

Sandy Bay in the waters of Pamlico Sound
off the se mainland of Dare County between Sandy Point on the n and Parched
Corn Point on the s.

Sandy Bay, a bay in the waters of Pamlico
Sound, off the coast of Hatteras Island,
se Dare County. It lies between Durant
Point, near the town of Hatteras, and
Frisco.

Sandy Bottom, a sandy strip approx. ½ mi.
long along the w bank of French Broad

River in s Buncombe County between Bent Creek and Orton Branch.

Sandy Bottom, community in w Lenoir County. The site is mentioned by name in local records beginning in the 1760's. In December 1862 invading Union forces gave the more sophisticated name Sandy Foundation to the community, and a post office here for a short time bore this name. Also known as Sandy Ridge during the Civil War.

Sandy Bottom, community in w Madison County on French Broad River.

Sandy Branch rises in e Mitchell County and flows se into Cane Creek.

Sandy Branch rises in s Stokes County and flows se into Town Fork Creek.

Sandy Creek rises near Buckingham Mountain in sw Alamance County and flows n into Rock Creek.

Sandy Creek rises in e Cumberland County and flows e into South River.

Sandy Creek rises in w Davidson County and flows nw into Hartleys Creek.

Sandy Creek rises in central Durham County and flows sw into New Hope Creek.

Sandy Creek rises in ne Randolph County and flows sw into Deep River.

Sandy Creek rises in se Vance County and flows se across Warren and Franklin counties and into Nash County where, in Hilliardston community, the name is changed to Swift Creek, which see.

Sandy Creek, community in ne Randolph County. Sandy Creek Baptist Church here founded, 1755. Here, in 1766, the first attempt was made to organize the Regulators.

Sandy Creek Township, former township in n Franklin County, now township number 6.

Sandy Creek Township, se Vance County.

Sandy Creek Township, sw Warren County.

Sandycross, community in se Gates County.

Sandy Cross, crossroads community in s Nash County. Named because of sandy soil in the vicinity.

Sandy Cross, community in s Rockingham County, the center of good tobacco-producing country.

Sandy Foundation. See Sandy Bottom.

Sandy Gap, ne Cherokee County in the Snowbird Mountains.

Sandy Gap, central Cherokee County between West Prong Grape Creek and Rose Creek.

Sandy Gap, nw Cherokee County in the Unicoi Mountains.

Sandy Gap, sw Cherokee County near the headwaters of Buck Creek.

Sandy Gap, on the McDowell-Mitchell County line.

Sandy Gap, n Transylvania County near the head of Cedar Rock Creek.

Sandy Gap Branch rises in w Swain County on Welch Ridge and flows nw into Hazel Creek.

Sandy Grove, community in se Hoke County.

Sandy Tuss Creek rises in n Carteret County and flows approx. 1 mi. sw into Adams Creek on the Craven County line. Perhaps named for the fish, amiatus calva, a dogfish sometimes also known as huss.

Sandy Inlet, former inlet between Topsail Sound and Atlantic Ocean, se Pender County. Appears on the Moseley map, 1733; closed soon after 1775.

Sandy John Ridge, n Haywood County between Big Creek and Pigeon River.

Sandy Landing, se Beaufort County, on the w side of South Creek.

Sandy Mush, community in nw Buncombe County near the junction of Clark Branch and Sandy Mush Creek. Took its name from the creek.

Sandy Mush, community in s Rutherford County near the head of Holland Creek.

Sandy Mush Bald, on Newfound Mountain at the junction of Buncombe, Haywood, and Madison County lines. Alt. 5,152. Took its name from the nearby creek.

Sandy Mush Creek rises near Wade Gap in nw Buncombe County and flows ne into French Broad River, forming a part of the Buncombe-Madison County line. Named by an early hunting party when sand from the creek water got into the mush they were cooking for supper.

Sandy Mush Township, w Buncombe County.

Sandy Mush Township, former township in sw Madison County, now township number 6.

Sandy Plains, community in s Polk County.

Sandy Point appears on the Gascoyne map, 1682, as the point of land presently in se Bertie County between Salmon Creek and Roanoke River. It also appears on the Hack map, 1684.

Sandy Point, extends from the n mainland of Carteret County into Neuse River.

Sandy Point, point of s Chowan County extending into Albemarle Sound. Appears on the Hack map, 1684, and on the Moseley map, 1733.

Sandy Point extends from the mainland of s Dare County into Pamlico Sound. It separates Sandy Bay on the s from Stumpy Point Bay on the n. Appears on the Moseley map, 1733.

Sandy Point extends e from the mainland of ne Tyrrell County into Alligator River. Shown on the Price map, 1808. State-operated free ferry from this point to East Lake Landing in nw Dare County now replaced by the Lindsay C. Warren Bridge, 2.83 mi. long and opened in May, 1962; named for Lindsay C. Warren (b. 1889), former U.S. Congressman and Comptroller-General.

Sandy Point, community on Morse Point in ne Currituck County.

Sandy Ridge, community in n Stokes County near Buffalo Creek.

Sandy Ridge. See Sandy Bottom.

Sandy Ridge Township, w Union County.

Sandy River. See First Broad River.

Sandy Run rises in s Cumberland County and flows se into Rockfish Creek.

Sandy Run rises in ne Duplin County and flows se on the Duplin-Wayne County line until it enters Northeast Cape Fear River.

Sandy Run rises in n Greene County and flows se into Middle Swamp. Appears on the Collet map, 1770. Known as Horn Swamp until some time between 1760 and 1767.

Sandy Run, rises in s Moore County and flows sw into Deep Creek.

Sandy Run rises in se Northampton County and flows se into Roanoke River. For a part of its course it forms the boundary between Northampton and Bertie counties. Mentioned in local records as early as 1722.

Sandy Run Branch rises in n Duplin County and flows sw into Northeast Cape Fear River.

Sandy Run Creek rises in central Burke County and flows n into Hunting Creek.

Sandy Run Creek rises in e Rutherford County and flows se into Cleveland County where it enters Broad River.

Sandy Run Swamp rises in w Onslow County and flows sw into Pender County where it enters Holly Shelter Creek.

Sandy Run Township, former township in sw Cleveland County, now township number 7.

Sandy Springs, community in sw Rutherford and se Polk counties. A post office est. here as early as 1882.

Sanford, city and county seat, central Lee County. Laid out about 1872. Inc. 1874. Said to have been named for Colonel C. O. Sanford, locating engineer for the Chatham Railroad. Jonesboro, (which see), merged with Sanford in 1947. Produces bricks, pottery, lumber, electrical parts, primary metals, sheet metal working, apparel, industrial machinery, furniture, insecticides, and cosmetics. Alt. 375.

Sans Souci, community in se Bertie County. The name of an early plantation which in French means "without care or worry."

Santeetlah, community in central Graham County on Santeetlah Lake. The former post office here was called Millsaps.

Santeetlah Creek rises in w Graham County and flows e into Santeetlah Lake. Name said to have meant "blue waters" in Cherokee, but Mooney's glossary says the Indians did not recognize or understand the name, insisting it was given to the creek by white men. They called this creek Nayuhi geyuni, or "sandplace stream," and Little Santeetlah Creek was known by them as Tsundaniltiyi.

Santeetlah Gap, w central Graham County approx. ¾ mi. w of Funnel Top.

Santeetlah Lake, central Graham County, was formed in 1928 by a dam on Cheoah River. Covers 2,580 acres with a shore line of 105 mi. Max. depth, 240 ft. Alt. 1,940. Owned by Aluminum Company of America. Used for power, fishing, and boating.

Santeetlah Wildlife Management Area in w Graham County. 37,168 acres, operated by the State of North Carolina on United States Forest Service Lands. Principal wildlife: bear, boar, deer, raccoon, trout.

Sapling Mountain, n Madison County between Shelton Laurel Creek and Spillcorn Creek.

Sapona River. See Yadkin River.

Sapony Creek rises in w Nash County and flows se into Tar River. Probably named from a stopping place of the Saponi Indians as they moved from the Yadkin River area in the w soon after 1701 to join the Tuscarora in the e.

Sapphire, community in sw Transylvania County s of Horsepasture River. Named (a) because sapphires are found in the vicinity, (b) the vivid blue of the sky and water.

Sapphire Country, a descriptive name applied to the area around Fairfield, Sapphire, and Toxaway lakes in s Jackson and w Transylvania counties. It probably came into use in commercial promotion of Mountain Lodge, Fairfield Inn, and Sapphire Inn, about 1898. Named for the blue of the mountains as well as for sapphire gems found in the area.

Sapphire Lake, s Jackson County on Horsepasture River and Nix Creek. Formed by 1916; covers 50 acres with a max. depth of 20 ft. Part of "Sapphire Country" (which see). Used for fishing, swimming, and boating; not open to the public. See also Lake Sapphire.

Sapsucker Branch rises in central Clay County and flows nw into Peckerwood Branch.

Saratoga, town in se Wilson County between White Oak Swamp and Goss Swamp. Settled prior to 1839; inc. 1874.

Saratoga Township, se Wilson County.

Sardis, community in s Mecklenburg County. Sardis Associate Reformed Presbyterian Church here was organized in 1790.

Sardis. See Hudson.

Sarecta, town in central Duplin County on Northeast Cape Fear River. Settled about 1736 under the direction of Henry McCulloch of London. Inc. 1787 as Sarecto; long inactive in muncipal affairs. Alt. 67. Named for Soracte Mountain in Italy, near Rome, on which a temple to Apollo stood in ancient times. Town often referred to as Soracte in early colonial records.

Sarem, community in w central Gates County, named for the ancient name of Salisbury, England. Alt. 34. A school for Indians was in operation here in 1712, and it was a preaching station for the Rev. Clement Hall, of Edenton, in the 1750's.

Sarem Creek rises in s Gates County and flows se into Chowan River. Appears on the Collet map, 1770, where the modern Cole Creek is also shown with this name.

Sarvis Gap, ne Mitchell County between Wiles Creek and Lyddies Creek.

Sarvis Ridge, ne Mitchell County between Wiles Creek and Lyddies Creek.

Sasnett Mill Branch rises in central Edgecombe County and flows sw into Cokey Swamp.

Sassafras Branch rises in central Cherokee County and flows se into Colvard Creek.

Sassafras Branch rises in se Clay County and flows se into Tallulah River.

Sassafras Branch rises in w Jackson County and flows n into Savannah Creek.

Sassafras Creek rises in e central Avery County and flows s into Lost Cove Creek.

Sassafras Creek rises in sw Graham County in the Snowbird Mountains and flows ne into Snowbird Creek.

Sassafras Falls, in Sassafras Creek, sw Graham County. Water drops approx. 70 ft.

Sassafras Fork. See Stovall.

Sassafras Fork Township, ne Granville County.

Sassafras Gap, central Buncombe County e of Buzzard Rock.

Sassafras Gap, on Graham-Swain County line between Cheoah Bald and Swim Bald; in Nantahala National Forest. Alt. approx. 4,380.

Sassafras Gap, on Laurel Mountain w of Johnson Knob in nw Henderson County near the Transylvania County line. Alt. approx. 4,060.

Sassafras Gap in e Jackson County on Old Bald Ridge.

Sassafras Gap, on the Jackson-Macon County line. Alt. approx. 4,100.

Sassafras Gap, se Macon County between Clear Creek and Queen Mountain. Alt. approx. 2,860.

Sassafras Gap, on the North Carolina-South Carolina line at the junction of Transylvania County, N. C., and Greenville and Pickens counties, S. C. Alt. 2,774.

Sassafras Gap, nw Swain County on Twentymile Ridge in Great Smoky Mountains National Park near lat. 35° 29' 22" N., long. 83° 48' 55" W. Alt. approx. 3,650.

Sassafras Knob on the Cherokee-Clay County line in the Valley River Mountains.

Sassafras Knob, e Haywood County on the n end of Sassafras Ridge.

Sassafras Knob, se Macon County between Brushy Face and Monger Creek.

Sassafras Knob, on Noland Divide, n Swain County in Great Smoky Mountains National Park between Lower and Upper Sassafras Gaps near lat. 35° 32' 03" N., long. 83° 27' 10" W. Alt. 4,665.

Sassafras Knob, nw Transylvania County s of Farlow Gap.

Sassafras Mountain on the Jackson-Transylvania County line sw of Bearpen Mountain. Alt. 4,347.

Sassafras Mountain on the Transylvania County, N. C.-Pickens County, S. C., line s of the head of South Prong [of Glady Fork]. Alt. 3,554.

Sassafras Ridge extends ne from Bee Gap to Willie Knob in sw Graham County.

Sassafras Ridge, e Haywood County between Buckeye Cove and Beaverdam Creek.

Sassafras Ridge, s Macon County between Nantahala River and Nantahala Mountains.

Sassafras Ridge, elevated ground in e Washington County, sw of the community of Scuppernong. The name appears in county records as early as 1868.

Sassarixa Swamp rises in w Johnston County and flows se into Black Creek.

Sasseenohla. See Big Bald.

Sassers Mill, community in nw Jones County on Heath Mill Run.

Sassers Millpond. See Aycock Millpond.

Satterfield Creek rises in w Person County and flows ne into Storys Creek.

Satterthwaite Creek rises in e Beaufort County and flows e into Pungo River. See also Chappel Creek.

Satterwhite, community in n Granville County, formerly known as Locust Grove for the home of the Satterwhite family.

Satterwhite Creek rises in sw Burke County and flows n into Silver Creek.

Satulah Branch rises in se Macon County and flows n into Mill Creek.

Satulah Falls, se Macon County near the head of Clear Creek.

Satulah Mountain, se Macon County between Satulah Falls and Little Fodderstack Mountain. Alt. 4,490.

Saucepan Creek rises in sw Brunswick County and flows e into Shallotte River.

Sauls Creek rises in n Warren County and flows ne into Hawtree Creek.

Sauls Crossroads. See Eureka.

Saulston, community in e Wayne County s of The Slough and n of the head of West Bear Creek.

Saulston Township, e Wayne County.

Saunders Bay in Currituck Sound off the w shore of Currituck Banks and n of Mossey Islands, se Currituck County.

Saunders Point, peninsula extending from ne Pamlico County into Bay River.

Saunders' Store, community in sw Caswell County.

Saunook, community in w Haywood County. Alt. 3,206. Said to have been named for a Cherokee Indian who lived in the vicinity.

Saurat. See Upper Saura Town.

Sauratown, former community in se Stokes County near the mouth of Town Fork Creek on Dan River. A post office existed here as late as 1882.

Saura Town. See Lower Saura Town; Upper Saura Town.

Sauratown Mountain, a range extending from w Stokes County into the center of the county. Alt. 2,465. Appears on the Collet map, 1770. Named for the Saura Indians who once lived in the area. These Indians were mentioned by William Byrd in 1728.

Sauratown Township, se Stokes County.

Savage, community in e Gates County. Alt. 33. Settled prior to Civil War and named for G. W. Savage, local landowner.

Savages Crossroads, community in n Gates County. Known first as Pipkin's Crossroads, then as Brickhouse.

Savannah, community on Savannah Creek in w Jackson County.

Savannah Creek rises in e Anson County and flows ne into Blewett Falls Lake.

Savannah Creek rises in w Jackson County and flows n into Tuckasegee River.

Savannah Ridge in w Jackson County between Little Savannah Creek and Savannah Creek.

Savannah Township, w Jackson County.

Saw Branch rises in sw Buncombe County near Saw Mountain and flows nw into South Hominy Creek.

Sawbrier Ridge, n Swain County in Great Smoky Mountains National Park, a short spur extending nw from High Rocks on Welch Ridge. Its center is near lat. 35° 31' N., long. 83° 38' 02" W.

Saw Mill, community in s Caldwell County.

Sawmill Branch rises in ne Buncombe County and flows n into Carter Creek.

Sawmill Branch rises in central Cherokee County and flows se into Colvard Creek.

Saw Mill Branch rises in n Davie County and flows s into Dutchmans Creek.

Sawmill Creek rises in n Lincoln County and flows se to join Lippard Creek in forming Leepers Creek.

Sawmill Creek rises in s Swain County and flows nw and then sw into Little Tennessee River.

Sawmill Creek rises in w Transylvania County and flows se into Cherryfield Creek.

Sawmill Ridge, n Macon County between Shepherd Creek and Matlock Creek.

Saw Mountain, sw Buncombe County between Saw Branch and Stony Fork.

Sawpit Branch 'rises in s Watauga County and flows se into East Fork [of South Fork New River].

The Sawteeth, broken, pointed summits along the Swain County, N. C.,-Sevier County, Tenn., line in the Great Smoky Mountains National Park near lat. 35° 38′ 30″ N., long. 83° 21′ 50″ W. Alt. approx. 5,450.

Sawyer Cove, n Buncombe County e of Ingles Ridge.

Sawyer Creek rises in n central Graham County and flows ne into Little Tennessee River.

Sawyer Creek rises in n Watauga County and flows w into Cove Creek.

Sawyers Creek rises in n central Camden County and flows s into Pasquotank River. Settlements existed at its mouth prior to 1677. See also Grays Mill.

Sawyers Creek rises in n Pender County and flows n into Rockfish Creek.

Sawyers Ferry appears on the Moseley map, 1733, on Pasquotank River in what is now Camden County n.of Sawyers Creek. This was in Pasquotank Precinct of Albemarle County. Later Shipyard Ferry was operated near the site. See also Shipyard.

Sawyers Landing, e Beaufort County, on Pungo River.

Saxapahaw, community in se Alamance County on Haw River. Named for the Sissipahaw Indians who once lived in the area. A yarn mill was est. here in 1849.

Saxapahaw River. See Haw River.

Scale Creek rises in ne Onslow County and flows sw into Northeast Creek.

Scalesville, community in n Guilford County. Named for the Scales family of Guilford and Rockingham counties.

Scaly Mountain, s Macon County between the head of Middle Creek and the head of Piney Knob Fork. Alt. 4,804.

Scaly Mountain, community in s Macon County on Middle Creek.

Scaly Ridge, se Clay County between Tallulah River and Beech Creek.

Scapecat Branch rises in s Haywood County and flows w into Little East Fork Pigeon River.

Scarlet Ridge, n Swain County in Great Smoky Mountains National Park extending se from Welch Ridge to Forney Creek. Near lat. 35° 31′ 54″ N., long. 83° 34′ 40″ W.

Scarlet Ridge Creek rises in n Swain County in Great Smoky Mountains National Park and flows se into Jonas Creek.

Schenck Forest. See Carl Alwin Schenck Forest.

Schene Wolf Creek rises near Organ and Lower Stone churches approx. 5 mi. sw of town of Rockwell, se Rowan County, and flows s into ne Cabarrus County where it enters Dutch Buffalo Creek. Probably named by early German settlers, Schene being derived from schön, "beautiful." Sometimes also called Jennie Wolf Creek.

Schlosstown, community in n Franklin County. Known locally as "Slosh."

Scholl, community .in w Scotland County.

School House Branch rises in w Carteret County and flows sw into Hadnot Creek.

Schoolhouse Branch rises in central Cherokee County and flows se into Marble Creek.

Schoolhouse Branch rises in ne Cherokee County and flows se into Junaluska Creek.

Schoolhouse Branch rises in s Haywood County and flows sw into Little East Fork Pigeon River.

Schoolhouse Branch rises in central Pitt County and flows ne into Tar River.

School House Branch rises in w Watauga County and flows sw into Watauga River.

Schoolhouse Flats, e Haywood County on Glade Mountain.

Schoolpath Branch rises in s central Transylvania County and flows ne into West Fork French Broad River.

Schooner Creek rises in se Beaufort County and flows n into South Creek.

Schooners Bay. See Spooners Bay.

Schuler Cove. See Jack Cove.

Schulkens Pond, a natural lake in se Columbus County, approx. 7 mi. sw of Lake Waccamaw, and one mile w of Waccamaw River. Bear Branch drains Schulkens Pond into Waccamaw River.

Scippco Swamp rises in Cawcaw Bay, sw Brunswick County and flows w into Waccamaw River.

Scotch Grove, community in n central Scotland County.

Scotch Hall. See Bonarva.

Scotch-Irish Township, n Rowan County.

Scotia, community in n central Tyrrell County at the head of Second Creek.

Scotland County was formed in 1899 from Richmond County. Located in the se section of the state, it is bounded by the state of South Carolina, and by Richmond, Moore, Hoke, and Robeson counties. It was named for Scotland in the British Isles from which many of the early settlers of the region came. Area: 317 sq. mi. County seat: Laurinburg with an elevation of 227 ft. Townships are Laurel Hill, Spring Hill, Stewartsville, and Williamsons. Produces cotton, corn, soybeans, oats, watermelons, cantaloupes, hogs, livestock, processed meat, textiles, clocks, lumber, and mobile homes.

Scotland Neck, a name formerly applied to a tract of land approx. 40 sq. mi. in area in se Halifax County. It lay e of Kehukee Swamp, w of Roanoke River and extended s through the present Buzzard Point. It was settled in 1722 by Scottish colonists. Appears on the Collet map, 1770, and on the Price map, 1808.

Scotland Neck, town in se Halifax County. Named for region settled 1722 by Scottish colonists. Inc. 1867. Produces textiles. Alt. 103.

Scotland Neck Township, se Halifax County.

Scotland Village. See East Laurinburg.

Scotsman Creek rises in s Jackson County and flows sw into Chattooga River.

Scott Branch rises in e Macon County and flows sw into Cullasaja River.

Scott Creek rises in central Alexander County and flows w into Glade Creek.

Scott Creek rises in e Beaufort County and flows se into Pungo Creek.

Scott Creek rises in central Craven County and flows n into Neuse River at James City.

Scott Creek rises in ne Jackson County n of Judaculla Mountain and flows sw through the towns of Sylva and Dillsboro to empty into Tuckasegee River just w of Dillsboro.

Scott Creek rises in e Jones County and flows e into Trent River.

Scott Creek Township, ne Jackson County. Named for John Scott, a trader among the Cherokees.

Scottish Mountain, w Haywood County, Great Smoky Mountains National Park, near lat. 35° 41′ 34″ N., long. 83° 05′ 08″ W. Named for Scottish Mountain Lumber Co. which operated in the area in the 1920's. Alt. 4,290.

Scott Knob, s Swain County between the head of Welch Branch and Yalaka Creek.

Scott Mountain, s Buncombe County e of Enka Lake.

Scott Reservoir. See W. Kerr Scott Reservoir.

Scotts, community in w central Iredell County.

Scott's, formerly Scott's Store, community in w Wilson County s of Contentnea Creek. Named for S. H. Scott.

Scotts Creek rises in nw Rutherford County and flows se into Cove Creek.

Scotts Hill, community in se Pender County. Alt. 50.

Scott's Pond, w Wilson County on Robin Branch. Formed 1954 and named for Exum Scott, owner. Covers 10 acres; max. depth 12 ft. Fishing, swimming, boating, irrigation.

Scotts Store, community in w Pamlico County.

Scottsville. See Belfast.

Scottville, community on Alleghany-Ashe County line. Alt. approx. 2,950. Settled about 1830 and known first as Flint Hill. Post office est. 1855 as Scottville; believed to have been named for Mrs. Elizabeth Scott (1799-1856), highly respected local citizen.

Scranton, community in w Hyde County on Scranton Creek near Pungo River. Alt. 3. Originally known as Clark for the owner of a lumber mill here. Later renamed Scranton for another lumber mill which moved here from Scranton, Pennsylvania. Near the site of an old Indian village, Aquascogoc, which see.

Scranton Creek rises in w Hyde County and flows w approx. 3.3 mi. into Pungo River. Formerly known as Broad Creek.

Scratch Hall Swamp rises in w Gates County and flows w into Chowan River.

Scratch Hall Township. See Hall Township.

Scream Ridge, s Macon County parallel to Yellow Patch Creek.

Scrougetown, community in s Clay County.

This site is now partially covered by the waters of Chatuge Lake.

Scuffletown, town in e Greene County on Little Contentnea Creek. Inc. 1885, but long inactive in municipal affairs. Settled priod to 1756; a post office as early as 1837. Name said to be derived from disagreement among members of the local Free Will Baptist Church. In recent years generally known as Ridge Spring.

Scuffletown. See Pembroke.

Scuppernong, community in e Washington County. Post office est. in 1882, but discontinued in 1908.

Scuppernong Lake. See Lake Phelps.

Scuppernong River rises in e Washington County in East Dismal Swamp, and flows e into w Tyrrell County where it turns to flow nw into Albemarle Sound. Appears on the Moseley map, 1733, as Cascoponung River. It appears as Cuscopang River on a 1788 map. Approx. 22 mi. long.

Scuppernong Township, nw Tyrrell County.

Scuppernong Township, se Washington County, formed in 1868 and incorporates within its limits the old voting precinct of Cool Springs.

Scull Camp. See Skull Camp.

Sea Banks. See Outer Banks; Shackleford Banks.

Seaboard, town in n Northampton County. Alt. 126. Settled about 1750 and known first as Concord. Inc. 1877. Named for the Seaboard Air Line Railroad.

Seaboard Township, n central Northampton County.

Sea Breeze, community in s New Hanover County near the s end of Myrtle Sound. Developed by Negroes.

Sea Cattle. See Middle Ground.

Seaforth, community in e Chatham County. The site will be covered by the lake formed by New Hope Dam.

Seagate, community in e New Hanover County on the s side of Bradleys Creek. Alt. 10. Settled about 1890. Named from the fact that it is located on an inlet of Wrightsville Sound with access thereby to the sea.

Seago's Lake, e Anson County, se of Lilesville. Covers approx. 10 acres; max. depth 20 ft. Formed early in the twentieth century when gravel was removed from the site. Named for owner.

Seagrove, town in s Randolph County. Inc.

1913. Named for a railroad official. Alt. 716.

Seagull, community on Currituck Banks, e Currituck County. A Lifesaving Station here was originally called Old Currituck Inlet. A Coast Guard Station here was decommissioned following World War II. The Seagull post office operated from 1908 to 1924.

Sealevel, community in ne Carteret County on Core Sound.

Sea Level Township, ne Carteret County on Nelson Bay and Core Sound.

Sealeys Creek. See Celia Creek.

Sea of Rawnocke. See Albemarle Sound.

Searcy Creek rises in w central Transylvania County and flows ne into Davidson River.

Seaside, community in sw Brunswick County.

Seay Mountain, central Haywood County between Jonathans Creek and Pigeon River. Alt. 3,358.

Secession, community in sw Brunswick County.

Seco, an Indian village shown on John White's map of 1585 located in what is now central Beaufort County. The name is associated with American discoveries dating from 1536, though located on different maps from the Chesapeake Bay s to Florida. De Bry's version of White's map, printed in 1590, changes Seco to Cotan. See also Secotan.

Second Broad River rises in s McDowell County and flows se into Rutherford County which it crosses to the Cleveland County line where it enters Broad River.

Second Creek rises in w Randolph County and flows e into Uwharrie River.

Second Creek rises in e Tyrrell County and flows se into Alligator River. Called Third Creek on the Collet map, 1770. Approx. 4½ mi. long and ¾ mi. wide at its mouth.

Second Creek rises in n central Tyrrell County s of community of Pleasant View and flows w into Scuppernong River approx. 2¼ mi. s of town of Columbia. An old Indian village of uncertain tribal affiliation, Mequopen, is shown at the mouth of this creek on the De Bry map, 1590. Name means "red tribes," or "where there are red tribes."

Second Creek, community on the creek of the same name, in n central Tyrrell County.

Second Creek. See North Second Creek; South Second Creek; Back Creek.

Second Creek Bluff, at the mouth of Second Creek in e Tyrrell County.

Second Creek Point, e Tyrrell County, extends from the mainland into Alligator River near the mouth of Second Creek.

Second Falls, the middle of a series of three waterfalls on Yellowstone Prong, s Haywood County.

Second Hurricane Branch rises in e Swain County and flows sw into Yalaka Creek.

Second Potts Creek rises in w Davidson County and flows s into High Rock Lake on Yadkin River. Appears on the Collet map, 1770, as Potts Creek.

Secotan, an Indian village once located on the s side of Pamlico River in what is now e Beaufort County in the vicinity of Hobucken; visited by John White and other explorers based on Roanoke Island in the sixteenth century. The name meant "town at the bend of a river." Appears as Secoton on the White map, 1585; as Secota on De Bry, 1590; and as Secotan on Velasco, 1611. *See also* Seco.

Sedalia, community in e Guilford County. The Alice Freeman Palmer Memorial Institute, a junior college and high school for Negroes, est. 1901, is here.

Sedgefield, resort community in w central Guilford County in a 3,600-acre woodland park. Contains an English-style inn, tennis courts, golf course, and riding stables. Opened 1927.

Sedges Garden, community in n central Forsyth County.

Seed Cane Creek rises in e Surry County and flows sw into Ararat River.

See-noh-ya. *See* Black Mountains.

Seeoff, community in se Transylvania County.

See Off Mountain, s central Transylvania County between Dunn Creek and Haunty Branch. Alt. 3,080.

Seeshore, community in s Transylvania County on a tributary of Carson Creek.

Sega Lake in central Transylvania County on Graham Creek. Covers ¼ acre with a max. depth of 10 ft.

Seibold Branch rises in e Cherokee County and flows se into Fall Branch.

Seigle Creek rises in ne Lincoln County and flows s into Forney Creek.

Selena. *See* Center.

Selica, community in w central Transylvania County between Wilson Mill Creek and Catheys Creek. Alt. 2,179.

Selma, town in central Johnston County. Known first as Mitchenor's Station for John Mitchenor. Inc. as Selma, 1873; named for the town of the same name in Alabama. The town of Selma Cotton Mills, inc. 1915 and long inactive in municipal affairs, is now within the w section of Selma. Alt. 179. Produces textiles, furniture, milled grain, and chemicals.

Selma Cotton Mills. *See* Selma.

Selma Creek rises in ne Swain County and flows sw into Bunches Creek.

Selma Township, central Johnston County.

Selwin, community in s Gates County.

Seminole, community in w Harnett County.

Semora, community in ne Caswell County. Settled prior to the Revolution and known as Campbell's Crossroads. Post office est. 1877, named Semora for the daughter of the first postmaster, James M. McAden.

Seng Branch rises in nw Yancey County and flows nw into Cane River. Named for the herb ginseng which was gathered in large quantities in this vicinity beginning about 1837.

Seng Gap, n Madison County at the head of Little Laurel Creek.

Seng Ridge, nw Madison County between Alum Ridge and Camp Creek Bald.

Senia, community in w Avery County. Named for a local resident, Senia Pritchard.

Seniard Creek rises in nw Henderson County and flows s into North Fork in Pisgah National Forest.

Seniard Mountain on the Haywood-Transylvania County line at the n end of Lanning Ridge. Alt. 5,025.

Seniard Ridge in n Transylvania County extends se from Seniard Mountain to Looking Glass Rock.

Service Ridge, w Haywood County, Great Smoky Mountains National Park, a spur extending nw from Cataloochee Divide, center near lat. 35° 33′ 27″ N., long. 83° 07′ 15″ W., between Big Bald Branch and Little Bald Branch.

Servis Creek rises in central Alamance County and flows e into Haw River.

Sessoms Mill Pond, approx. ½ mi. long, on Chinkapin Creek in se Hertford County.

Setrock Creek rises in s Yancey County and flows se into South Toe River.

Settle, community in ne Iredell County. Alt. 700. A weather station from the 1880's until recently.

Setzer Mountain, w Haywood County parallel to Campbell Creek. Named for a prominent family of early settlers. Maggie Setzer, for whom the community of Maggie was named, was a descendant of this family. The highest peak of this 2½ mi. long ridge is 4,810 ft. in elevation.

Setzer's Creek rises in n central Caldwell County and flows se into Warrior Creek. Named for John Setzer who settled nearby about 1830.

Setzers Depot. *See* Claremont.

Setzers Gap, central Caldwell County. Alt. 1,342.

Seven Bridges, community in w Robeson County.

Seven Creeks is formed in s Columbus County by Big Cypress Swamp and Monie Swamp. It flows se into Waccamaw River.

Seven Devils, commercially developed recreation area in e Avery and w Watauga counties on a 1,288 acre tract. Opened 1966.

Seven Mile Creek rises in e Orange County and flows se into w Durham County where it enters Eno River.

Sevenmile Creek rises in w Orange County and flows ne into Eno River w of town of Hillsborough.

Seven Mile Ridge, n Haywood County extends n parallel to McGinty Creek.

Seven Mile Ridge extends from e Madison County into the s part of the county and is parallel to Bull Creek and West Fork [Bull Creek]. Named for its length.

Sevenmile Ridge, e Yancey County, extends ne from Stones Knob to Crabtree Creek near Cox Knob. Alt. approx. 4,400.

Sevenmile Swamp rises in nw Sampson County and flows se into Great Coharie Creek.

Seven Paths, community in e Franklin County.

Seven Sisters, sand dunes a short distance s of Nags Head on Bodie Island, e Dare County.

Seven Springs, town in se Wayne County on Neuse River. Inc. 1855 as Whitehall; reinc. as White Hall, 1881; named for the plantation home of William Whitefield who built here about 1741. Name changed to Seven Springs in 1951, although it had generally been so called for many years. Named for seven mineral springs around which a resort operated from 1881 until 1944. The hotel and spring house still stand. The Confederate ironclad, *Neuse*, was built here. A Civil War skirmish occurred here in December, 1862. Alt. 75.

Seven Springs Gap, w Graham County between Hooper Mill Creek and Wright Creek, in Nantahala National Forest. Alt. approx. 3,700.

Seventy-First Township, w Cumberland County. Named for the 71st Highland Scots Regiment.

Severn, town in ne Northampton County. Alt. 59. Settled about 1833 and known first as Meherrin for an Indian tribe which had lived in the vicinity. Inc. 1919. Named for Severn Ayers, a stockholder in the Seaboard Air Line Railroad.

Sevier, community in n McDowell County on North Fork [Catawba River]. Alt. 1,401.

Seward, community in w Forsyth County.

Sexton, community in s Madison County on Bull Creek.

Sexton's Branch rises in ne Wake County and flows se into Upper Bartons Creek.

Seymour Johnson Air Base, central Wayne County at Goldsboro: est. 1941 as an Army Air Forces Technical Training School and named for Lt. Seymour Johnson (1904-41), Navy test pilot of Goldsboro. Now an Air Force Base.

Shackelfoot Island. *See* Brown's Island.

Shackleford Banks, one of the Outer Banks, se Carteret County, approx. 8½ mi. long. Named for John Shackleford, who, with Col. Enoch Ward, purchased the "Sea Banks" in 1713. *See also* Cape Lookout National Seashore Recreational Area.

Shackleford Point, the w tip of Shackleford Banks, se Carteret County, extending into Beaufort Inlet. The community of Shackleford formerly existed near the Point.

Shacktown, community in se Yadkin County between North Deep Creek and South Deep Creek. Named for B. G. "Shack" Colvard, local businessman. Produces tobacco baskets.

Shad Cove, central Craven County in se end of Hog Island adjacent to Neuse River. Approx. ¼ mi. wide.

Shaddock's Creek is formed in se Moore County by the junction of McDeeds and Mill creeks. It flows e through Crystal Lake into Little River. This name was originally also applied to the present McDeeds Creek. Named for Thomas Shaddock, an eighteenth-century settler.

Shaddox Creek rises in se Chatham County and flows s into Cape Fear River.

Shade Branch rises in n Madison County and flows sw into Martin Branch.

Shadepen Branch rises in nw Buncombe

County and flows se into North Fork [Swannanoa River].

Shad Point on the ne mainland of Hyde County extending into the mouth of Long Shoal Bay.

Shadrick Creek rises in e McDowell County and flows e approx. 5 mi. into Old Catawba River in sw Burke County.

Shady Banks, community in central Beaufort County on the n bank of Pamlico River.

Shady Grove, community in nw Caswell County.

Shadygrove, community in nw Sampson County.

Shady Grove, community in n Yadkin County. Named for a Baptist church.

Shady Grove. See Advance.

Shady Grove Township, e Davie County. Named for Shady Grove Methodist Church, est. prior to or in 1816.

Shaftesbury Precinct was formed by 1668 as a division of Albemarle County. It was named for Anthony Ashley Cooper, Earl of Shaftesbury (1621-83), one of the original Lords Proprietors ot Carolina. Renamed Chowan Precinct about 1681. *See also* Chowan County.

Shaken, community in ne Pender County on Shaken Creek e of its junction with Holly Shelter Creek.

Shaken Creek rises in e Pender County and flows nw into Holly Shelter Creek.

Shakerag. See Osgood.

Shaleville, community in w Madison County on Ferry Branch.

Shallop's Landing. See Columbia.

Shallotte, town in sw Brunswick County. Appears on the Morse-Breese map, 1843. Inc. 1899. Named for Shallotte River on which it is located. Alt. 33.

Shallotte Creek rises in s Brunswick County and flows w into Shallotte River.

Shallotte Inlet, sw Brunswick County between Big Beach and Hales Beach connecting Long Bay in the Atlantic Ocean with the mouths of Shallotte River, Shallotte Creek, and Saucepan Creek. Also provides access to the Intracoastal Waterway from the Atlantic Ocean.

Shallotte River rises in sw Brunswick County and flows ne and s into the Atlantic Ocean through Shallotte Inlet. Appears on the Moseley map, 1733. May have been named for shallot, an onion-like plant growing in the vicinity.

Shallotte Sound, sw Brunswick County between Brantley Island on the mainland

and Hales Beach, running parallel to and s of the Intracoastal Waterway. Narrow and approx. 1½ mi. long.

Shallotte Township, sw Brunswick County.

Shallowbag Bay, a bay in Roanoke Sound off the ne shore of Roanoke Island, e Dare County. The Bay forms the harbor at the town of Manteo. In the late eighteenth century it was referred to as Shalon-bas Bay (French *chalon-bas,* "low trawl net").

Shallow Ford, in Little Tennessee River in n Macon County.

Shallow Ford, passage through the Yadkin River, se Yadkin County-sw Forsyth County. The main w road from the early Moravian settlements crossed here and it is mentioned in their records as early as 1767. Site of military encounters in both Revolutionary and Civil Wars.

Shalon-bas Bay. See Shallowbag Bay.

Shanghai, community in se Sampson County.

Shankle Mountain, se Stanly County. Named for local family.

Shannon, community in n Robeson County on Big Raft Swamp.

Shannon Township, n Robeson County.

Shanty Cove, e Cherokee County on the headwaters of Seibold Branch.

Shanty Gap, in central Graham County between Mountain Creek and Sweetwater Creek.

Shanty Mountain, w Haywood County, Great Smoky Mountains National Park, a spur extending ne from Balsam Mountain between Sugar Fork and Palmer Creek, centers near lat. 35° 37′ 15″ N., long. 83° 09′ 35″ W. Alt. 4,812.

Shanty Spring Branch rises in e Avery County and flows n into Watauga County where it enters Watauga River.

Shark Shoal, in the waters of Pamlico Sound, n of Hatteras Inlet, s Dare County.

Sharon, community in nw Camden County. Named for a Methodist Church erected here in 1894. Previously known as Slab Ridge. Alt. 18.

Sharon, community in s Cleveland County.

Sharon, community in w Iredell County.

Sharon. See Iron Station.

Sharon Township, former township in s central Mecklenburg County, now township number 4.

Sharp Branch rises in ne Cherokee County and flows nw into Valley River.

Sharp Creek rises in n Watauga County and flows w into Cove Creek.

Sharper Mountain, w Wilkes County near the head of Cole Creek.

Sharpesburg Township, nw Iredell County. Named for the Sharpe family.

Sharpes Township, se Alexander County.

Sharp Point, community in w Pitt County.

Sharps, community in w Rockingham County.

Sharpsburg, town at the coincident corners of Edgecombe, Nash, and Wilson counties. Inc. 1883. Settled about 1851. Named for John Jay Sharp who moved here in 1844 and was later representative for Nash, Wilson and Franklin counties in the General Assembly. Alt. 143.

Sharp Top, mountain in central Swain County in Great Smoky Mountains National Park, on Noland Divide near lat. 35° 28′ 05″ N., long. 83° 27′ 27″ W. Alt. 3,430.

Sharptop, peak in s Yancey County n of Little Creek. Alt. approx. 5,500.

Sharptop Ridge, se Clay County, nw of Hightower Bald, Ga. See also Montgomery Corner.

Sharpy Mountain, n Transylvania County between Sandy Gap and Sampson Gap in Pisgah National Forest. Alt. 3,383.

Sharron Branch rise in s central Brunswick County and flows sw into Sharron Creek.

Sharron Creek rises in s central Brunswick County and flows sw into Shallotte River.

Shate Gap, s Yancey County near Cane River.

Shateen Branch rises in sw Yancey County and flows e into Cane River.

Shatley Springs, community in e Ashe County.

Shatter Muster Ground. See Axtell.

Shaw, community in central Cumberland County. Alt. 227.

Shawano Ridge, ne Swain County in Great Smoky Mountains National Park extending sw from Balsam Mountain near lat. 35° 40′ N., long. 83° 12′ 33″ W.

Shawboro, community in w Currituck County. Settled about 1775 and first known as Bayley. Perhaps to avoid confusion with Bailey in Nash County, was renamed Shaw's Corner after the Civil War, in honor of Col. Henry Shaw, Confederate officer. Name later changed to Shawboro by the Norfolk and Southern Railroad. Alt. 15.

Shaw Creek rises in sw Anson County and flows s into Deadfall Creek.

Shaw Creek rises in central Henderson County and flows nw into French Broad River.

Shawnee. See Long Island.

Shawneehaw Creek rises in w Watauga County and flows sw into ne Avery County where it enters Elk River.

Shawneehaw. See Banner Elk.

Shawneehaw Township, sw Watauga County.

Shaws, community in e Scotland County.

Shaw's Corner. See Shawboro.

Shearer Creek rises in n Clay County and flows sw into Johnson Mill Creek.

Shearer's Hill, a low ridge on the n side of Yadkin River, ne Caldwell County. Named for John Shearer who settled here about the end of the Revolution. A Negro cemetery here has been in use since before the Civil War when the slaves of a number of wealthy planters in the neighborhood were buried there.

Shear Knob, w Swain County between Yalaka Creek and a bend in Little Tennessee River.

Sheehan Creek rises in nw McDowell County and flows se into Little Buck Creek.

Sheepback Knob, w Haywood County, Great Smoky Mountains National Park, on Cataloochee Divide, near lat. 35° 33′ 10″ N., long. 83° 07′ 33″ W., between Little Bald Knob and Little Spruce Ridge. Alt. 5,520.

Sheepback Mountain, n Jackson County between Rich Mountain and Plott Balsams. Alt. 4,700.

Sheep Cliffs Creek rises in s Jackson County and flows n into Webb Lake.

Sheep Cliffs Mountain between Little Sheep Cliffs and Sheep Cliffs Creek in s Jackson County. Alt. 4,681.

Sheep Hollow, s Macon County between Richey Knob and Richey Gap.

Sheep Island, a tidal marsh island just inside Lockwoods Folly Inlet, s central Brunswick County.

Sheep Island in Pamlico Sound off Portsmouth Island and separated from it by Baymarsh Thorofare, e Carteret County.

Sheep Knob, n Buncombe County nw of Courthouse Knob.

Sheep Knob, s Cherokee County on the nw end of Mocassin Mountain.

Sheep Knob, n Cleveland County.

Sheep Knob, w Jackson County near the head of East Fork [Savannah Creek]. Alt. 4,784.

Sheep Knob, e Macon County between Caler Fork and Cowee Creek.

Sheep Knob, s Macon County at the head of Rough Fork.

Sheep Knob, nw Swain County in Great Smoky Mountains National Park on Twentymile Ridge near lat. 35° 28' 50" N., long. 83° 49' 30" W. Alt. 3,852.

Sheep Mountain, e Haywood County between Rock Hollow and Jordan Branch.

Sheep Mountain, n Jackson County between Black Mountain and Moses Creek.

Sheep Mountain, e Transylvania County between Laurel Creek and Little River.

Sheep Pen Gap on Swain County, N. C.-Sevier County, Tenn., line in Great Smoky Mountains National Park near lat. 35° 31' 13" N., long. 83° 52' 27" W.

Sheep Ridge, se Buncombe County in the Blue Ridge Mountains, extends n from High Top to Swannanoa River, s of town of Black Mountain.

Sheep Rock, mountain in sw Buncombe County s of Browns Knob.

Sheepwallow Knob, ne Buncombe County between Cedar Cliff Knob and Pigpen Knob.

Sheep Wallow Knob, on the Swain County, N. C.-Blount County, Tenn., line at the nw end of Dalton Ridge.

Sheffield, community in nw Davie County. Named by Thomas M. Smith, postmaster, in whose store the post office was est. in 1893.

Sheffields Township, nw Moore County.

Shehan, community in n Henderson County.

Shehan Crossroads, community in ne Polk County at the Rutherford County line.

Shelby, city and county seat in central Cleveland County. Alt. 853. Inc. 1843; charter repealed 1847. Reinc. 1849. Named for Colonel Isaac Shelby (1750-1826), Revolutionary commander. Produces textiles, bakery products, hosiery, apparel, fiberglass, chemicals, and glass products.

Shelby Township, former township in s central Cleveland County, now township number 6.

Shellback Island, a tidal marsh island in the Cape Fear River opposite Southport, se Brunswick County.

Shellbank Point, peninsula extending from the w shore of n Bodie Island into Kitty Hawk Bay and Currituck Sound, nw

Dare County. Named for an old mound of shells found at the site by early settlers.

Shell Branch rises in w Jackson County and flows sw into Savannah Creek.

Shell Castle, ne Carteret County, an island in Pamlico Sound between Casey Island and North Rock near the tip of Portsmouth Island at Ocracoke Inlet. Built by John Gray Blount and John Wallace in 1790 on an earlier island known as Old Rock. At one time a dwelling house, tavern, warehouses, lumber yard, wharf, and a notary public's office were here. Appears on the Price map, 1808.

Shelley Branch rises in nw Nash County and flows se into Sandy Creek.

Shell Island, ne Carteret County in Core Sound between Wainwright Island and Core Banks. Named as early as the Moseley map, 1733. See also Hunting Quarter Sound.

Shell Knob, on the Buncombe-Henderson County line ne of Glady Fork Gap. Alt. approx. 4,020.

Shell Point, the se point of Harkers Island in se Carteret County. Mound of shells, apparently left by Indians, gives the point its name. Indian remains have been found here.

Shell Point, community in sw Brunswick County on e side of Shallotte River.

Shell Ridge, ne Mitchell County between Blevins Branch and Broad Branch.

Shell Rock Channel, se Onslow County, flows s out of Bear Inlet.

Shell Stand Creek rises in e Graham County and flows ne into Panther Creek.

Shelly Point extends from the mainland of sw Carteret County into Bogue Sound.

Shelly Point, se Onslow County on The Hammock, extends into White Oak River.

Shelmerdine, town in s Pitt County.

Shelter Mountain, w Montgomery County between Clark's Creek and Pee Dee River.

Shelter Neck, community in n central Pender County on the e side of Northeast Cape Fear River near DeRossett Creek.

Shelter River. See Holly Shelter Creek.

Shelter Swamp rises in s Onslow County and flows w into Pender County where it enters Holly Shelter Creek.

Shelton Branch rises in n Buncombe County and flows nw into Paint Fork. See also Anderson Cove.

Shelton Branch rises in s Haywood County and flows ne into Richland Creek.

Shelton Creek rises in w Granville County and flows se into Tar River. Appears as Charlone Creek on the Collet map, 1770.

Shelton Laurel, community in n Madison County. Alt. 1,849. Settled by Martin and David Shelton about 1790, near the junction of Shelton Laurel Creek and Big Laurel Creek. Here on January 19, 1863, thirteen Union supporters (12 men and a boy) were shot by a detail of Confederate soldiers. This has become known as the Shelton Laurel Massacre. White Rock, once a post office, is in the center of the Shelton Laurel community.

Shelton Laurel Creek rises in n Madison County and flows sw into Big Laurel Creek.

Shelton Laurel Township, former township in n Madison County, now township number 2.

Shelton Store, community in n Stokes County.

Shelton Town, community in ne Surry County between Rutledge Creek and Ararat River.

Shepards Mill, community in central Stokes County on Snow Creek. A mill, still standing, operated here as early as 1819 and as recently as 1957. Snow Creek Ironworks started here in 1770 by Col. James Martin. Limestone for ironworks at Danbury mined here.

Shephard Creek drains Osceola Lake in central Henderson County and flows w into Mud Creek.

Shephard Ditch, nw Pasquotank County drains ne into Pasquotank River.

Shepherd Bald, on Macon-Swain County line between Davis Bald and Leatherman Knob.

Shepherd Branch rises in n Buncombe County and flows sw into Flat Creek.

Shepherd Branch rises in w Yancey County and flows se into Bald Creek.

Shepherd Creek rises in n Macon County and flows s into Cowee Creek.

Shepherd Creek rises in e Swain County and flows nw into Kirkland Creek.

Shepherd Knob, n Mitchell County on Shepherd Mountain.

Shepherd Millpond, on Briery Swamp in ne Pitt County.

Shepherd Mountain, w Henderson County on South Fork.

Shepherd Mountain, n Mitchell County between Bean Creek and Spring Creek.

Shepherd Mountain, w Randolph County

between Little Caraway Creek and Uwharrie River. Alt. 1,390.

Shepherd Run rises in s Greene County and flows ne into Contentnea Creek. It was named for the Sheppard family which has lived in the vicinity since the colonial period.

Shepherds, community in s Iredell County. Known as Shepherds Cross Roads in the early and middle nineteenth century.

Shepherd's Branch rises in w central Wilson County and flows se into Contentnea Creek.

Shepherdsburgh. See Snow Hill.

Shepherd's Point, a name formerly applied to the point of land on the w side of Newport River on which Morehead City now stands. Appears on the Moseley map, 1733.

Sherard. See Cherry.

Sherards Crossroads. See Cherry.

Sheridan Mountains, e Madison County between California Creek and Bailey Branch.

Sherman, community in nw Wilkes County near the head of Middle Fork Reddies River.

Sherrars Gap in Kings Mountain, sw Gaston County. The Gap is s of The Pinnacle. See also Kings Mountain.

Sherrill Cove Branch rises in e Swain County and flows n into Raven Fork.

Sherrill Gap, central Swain County between Bryson Branch and Lands Creek.

Sherrill Gap, s Swain County between Rich Mountain and Will Knob.

Sherrills Ford, across Catawba River between Catawba and Iredell counties. Named for Adam Sherrill, trail blazer in the settlement of w North Carolina, who crossed the Catawba River here in 1747. This passage over the river was used by troops during the Revolutionary War. The site is now under the waters of Lake Norman. The name appears on various maps dating from the eighteenth-century through 1963.

Sherrills Ford, community in se Catawba County; known earlier as Sherrills Mill. Named for Adam Sherrill, a pioneer settler who crossed the Catawba River at Sherrills Ford, which see, a short distance e. A post office was est. here in 1831.

Sherrill's Gap. See Hickorynut Gap.

Sherrills Mill. See Sherrills Ford.

Sherrills Springs, community in s Cabarrus County. Mineral springs here still used

by some people. Also known as Sossamon's Spring.

Sherron Acres, community in central Durham County approx. one mi. se of the
city of Durham.

Sherwood, community in w Watauga Coun-
ty at the junction of Vanderpool and
Cove creeks. Post office est. in 1913 as
Doughton to honor Congressman Robert
L. Doughton. Name changed at his re-
quest to Sherwood.

Shewbird Mountain, s Clay County near
the sw end of Cherry Mountain.

Shields, community in sw Cherokee County.

Shields Ridge, n Yancey County between
Charlie Creek and Cove Branch.

Shiloh, town in sw Camden County inc.
1883 but no long active in municipal
affairs. Daniel Billet settled here before
1694 and the name "Billet's Bridge" is
still known locally at the site of a bridge
which he built. Named Danson's Manor
after 1696 when 3,640 acres were granted John Danson, son-in-law of Governor
John Archdale. Danson never lived here
but his heirs held the property until
1739. In the middle of the eighteenth
century the place came to be called Mill
Town from a group of watermills erected
on a bluff overlooking the Pasquotank
River. Shortly after 1800 the local Baptist Church (organized 1729) changed its
name to Shiloh and the name came to be
applied to the community.

Shiloh, community in nw Rockingham
County. Named for Shiloh Primitive Baptist Church.

Shiloh, community in sw Rutherford County near the headwaters of Jarretts Creek.

Shiloh Mills, community in e Edgecombe
County.

Shiloh Township, s Camden County.

Shiloh Township, se Iredell County. Named
for Shiloh Presbyterian Church near its
center.

Shinbone Creek rises in nw Mitchell County and flows se into Hollow Poplar Creek.

Shinbone Ridge, n Clay County between
Fires Creek and Long Branch.

Shinbone Ridge, n Madison County between Wolf Branch and Orchard Ridge.

Shine. See Rufe.

Shine Township, w central Greene County.
Named for the Shine family. See also
Rufe.

Shines Crossroads, community in w Greene
County. See also Rufe.

Shingle Cove, s Haywood County on Richland Creek.

Shingle Creek, a tidal creek in the waters
of Pamlico Sound on n Ocracoke Island,
se Hyde County.

Shingle Hollow, community in w central
Rutherford County s of Toms Mountain.
A late nineteenth-century post office
serving this community was named
Nanito.

Shingle Landing Creek rises in Norfolk
County, Virginia, and flows se through
nw Currituck County and into Northwest
River. Appears on the Moseley map,
1733, and others as recent as MacRae,
1833, as Moyock Creek. Apparently
named Shingle Landing about 1800.

Shingle Pile Creek rises in e Yancey County
and flows w into Little Whiteoak Creek.

Shingle Point, the w side of an unnamed
island off Core Banks in Core Sound, e
Carteret County. This island is between
Goose Island on the s and Duges Island
on the n.

Shingle Top, s Cherokee County between
Cane, Martin, and Moccasin creeks.

Shingletree Branch rises in central Macon
County and flows s into Wayah Creek.

Shingletree Swamp rises in sw Brunswick
County and flows nw into Cawcaw
Swamp on w edge of Thomas Bay.

Shining Creek rises in s Haywood County
and flows e into East Fork Pigeon River.

Shining Creek Gap, se Haywood County
on the mouth of Shining Creek.

Shining Rock Creek rises in s Haywood
County and flows w into Little East
Fork Pigeon River.

Shining Rock Gap, s Haywood County on
the head of North Fork.

Shining Rock Ledge, s Haywood County,
extends n from Black Balsam Knob to
Cold Mountain.

Shining Rock Mountain, s Haywood County between Shining Rock Gap and Buck
Spring Gap. Alt. 5,940.

Shinnville. See Georgeville.

Shinnsville, community in se Iredell County.

Shiny Creek rises in s Haywood County e
of Spruce Ridge and flows n and then
nw into Allen Creek.

Ship Channel. See Blair Channel.

Ship Point, n Tyrrell County, extends from
the mainland into Albemarle Sound.

Shipyard, community on the Pasquotank
River in w Camden County. In the
eighteenth century this was a center for
the building of small commercial sailing

vessels. The river here is straight and narrow for more than a mile and it is now a popular spot for motor boat races.

Shit-Britches Creek rises in se Buncombe County on Burney Mountain and flows nw into Cane Creek. Named by early settlers who saw an Indian washing himself in the stream after an "accident" in his britches. The name appears frequently in early deeds but is coming to'be called Dirty Britches Creek.

Shoal Creek rises in se Buncombe County and flows nw into Cane Creek.

Shoal Creek rises in ne Burke County and flows n into Catawba River.

Shoal Creek rises in w Cherokee County between Signal Pole Hill and Arp Gap and flows ne into Apalachia Lake on Hiwassee River. Sometimes known as South Shoal Creek.

Shoal Creek rises in s Cleveland County and flows w into First Broad River.

Shoal Creek rises in sw Henderson County and flows nw into Crab Creek.

Shoal Creek rises in nw Jackson County and flows nw into Soco Creek.

Shoal Creek rises in s Jackson County and flows nw into West Fork Tuckasegee River.

Shoal Creek rises in s Macon County and flows sw into Middle Creek.

Shoal Creek rises in s Transylvania County and flows ne into Middle Fork French Broad River.

Shoal Creek rises in w Transylvania County and flows sw to join Indian Creek in forming North Fork French Broad River.

Shoal Creek rises in e Yancey County and flows s into Little Crabtree Creek.

Shoal Creek Falls, on Shoal Creek in sw Henderson County.

Shoal Creek Gap, e Yancey County near the head of Shoal Creek.

Shoal Creek Township, w central Cherokee County.

Shoal Inlet. See Masonboro Inlet.

Shoal Mountain, w Jackson County between Thorpe Reservoir and Shoal Creek.

Shoal Mountain, ne Rutherford County near the head of Hardbargain Branch. Alt. 2,340.

Shoals, community in se Surry County between Grassy Creek and Yadkin River. Named for Bean Shoals in Yadkin River.

Shoals Township, se Surry County.

Shocco Creek rises in e Vance County and flows se through Warren County onto the Franklin-Warren County line where it enters Fishing Creek. Shown on the Price map, 1808. Named for the Shoccoree Indian tribe.

Shocco Springs, former health resort in s Warren County on Shocco Creek. Located approx. 9 mi. s of the city of Warrenton, it was famous in the nineteenth century as a social, recreational, and health resort built around mineral springs. Shocco Male Academy was located here. Neither is in existance any longer. Shocco Springs had a post office from 1832 until 1866, and was shown on the Price map, 1808.

Shocco Township, s Warren County.

Shoe, community in w Wilkes County between North Prong Lewis Fork Creek and South Fork Reddies River.

Shoe Branch rises in n central Carteret County and flows s into Newport River.

Shoe Heel. See Maxton.

Shoeheel Creek rises in e Scotland County and flows s into Big Shoeheel Creek. See also Maxton for an explanation of the name Shoeheel.

Sholars Crossroads, community in s Duplin County.

Shole Inlet. See Masonboro Inlet.

Sholes of Hatteras. See Diamond Shoals.

Shoofly, community in w Granville County between Culbreth and Stem.

Shoofly. See Maribel.

Shook Branch rises in e central Madison County and flows w into Big Laurel Creek.

Shook Brook rises in s Catawba County and flows se into Rhodes Mill Creek.

Shook Gap, central Haywood County between Colman Gap and Cansadie Top. Alt. 2,800.

Shookville, community on Little Buck Creek in e Macon County.

Shooting Creek rises in se Clay County and flows w into Lake Chatuge on the Hiwassee River. The name is believed to be a translation of the Cherokee *du-stagalan'yi,* "where it made a great noise," applied to the stream.

Shooting Creek, community in s Clay County on Shooting Creek.

Shooting Creek Bald, s central Clay County. Alt. 5,010.

Shooting Creek Township, e Clay County.

Shooting Ridge, n Transylvania County extends ne from Funneltop Mountain to Bradley Creek.

Shop Branch rises in ne Cherokee County and flows nw into Worm Creek.

Shop Branch rises in w Johnston County and flows se into Middle Creek.

Shop Branch rises in w Mitchell County and flows nw into Nolichucky River.

Shop Cove, on the Beaufort-Pitt County line at the confluence of Tar River and Tranters Creek.

Shop Creek rises in w Macon County and flows s into Little Choga Creek.

Shope Branch rises in s Macon County and flows se into North Fork [Skennah Creek].

Shope Cove, n Macon County on a tributary of Burningtown Creek.

Shope Creek rises in n Buncombe County and flows se into Bull Creek.

Shope Fork rises in s Macon County and flows ne into Coweeta Creek.

Shope Knob, s Swain County between Cullasaja Branch and Jones Creek.

Shopton, community in w Mecklenburg County on the head of Steel Creek.

Shore. See Flint Hill.

Shore Ridge Mountain, ne Rutherford County between Lump and Chalk Mountains.

Short Bunk, ridge in w Haywood County between Conrad Branch and Coggins Branch.

Short Creek rises in se Beaufort County and flows n into South Creek.

Short Off, peak in nw Clay County near the Cherokee-Clay County line. Probably named for C. W. Short (1794-1863), American botanist.

Short Off, community in se Macon County near the mountain of the same name.

Shortoff Gap, on the Jackson-Macon County line.

Shortoff Mountain, w Burke County. Alt. approx. 3,115.

Shortoff Mountain on the Jackson-Macon County line. Alt. 5,054.

Short Swamp Branch rises in nw Nash County and flows s into Sandy Creek.

Shorty Top, central Cherokee County near the headwaters of Dockery and Rose Creeks.

Shot Beech Ridge, n Swain County in Great Smoky Mountains National Park extending s from Thomas Ridge near lat. 35° 35' N., long. 83° 25' W.

Shot Pouch Creek rises in w Macon County and flows se into Wayah Creek.

Shot Pouch Knob, on the Jackson-Haywood County line.

Shotwell, community in e Wake County between Marks and Poplar creeks. Named

for Randolph Abbott Shotwell (1844-85), Confederate soldier, Democratic editor, and victim of unfair federal court trial in 1871. Apparently first appears on a map of 1893.

Shoups Ford in s Burke County crosses Jacob Fork.

Shuckpen Gap on the Buncombe-Haywood County line between Doubletop Mountain and Thompson Knob.

Shuck Ridge Creek rises in nw Transylvania County and flows se into Daniel Ridge Creek.

Shuckstack Mountain, w Swain County in Great Smoky Mountains National Park on Twentymile Ridge near lat. 35° 29' 08" N., long. 83° 48' 55" W. Alt. 4,100.

Shuckstack Ridge, nw Swain County extends se from Shuckstack Mountain to Fontana Lake.

Shuford Creek rises in e Yancey County and flows se into Whiteoak Creek.

Shuford Mountain, e Transylvania County near the head of McCall Branch.

Shufordsville. See Arden.

Shugan Creek. See Little Sugar Creek.

Shular Gap, s Swain County n of Little Yalaka Creek.

Shuler Creek rises in nw Cherokee County and flows sw into Hiwassee River on the Polk County, Tenn., line.

Shuler Mountain, sw Cherokee County near the headwaters of Dickey Branch.

Shulls Mill, community in s Watauga County on Watauga River. Est. as a post office in 1878; named for Joseph Shulls, settler, whose daughter eloped with the local sheriff, Cobb McCandless. The couple went to the West where McCandless joined the Jesse James gang and was killed by a member of the Jones gang, a rival group.

Shumaker Mountain. See Fox's Mountain.

Shumont, community in se Buncombe County.

Shumont Mountain on the Buncombe-Rutherford County line, approx. 2 mi. n of the community of Chimney Rock. Alt. approx. 3,839. Formerly known also as Harris Mountain and Leaventhorps View.

Shunkawakan Falls, on Whiteoak Creek, central Polk County. Water originally fell for a total of 500 ft. but recent blasting for road construction has broken the falls into two sections.

Shute, community in central Union County nw of the city of Monroe.

Shute Branch rises in ne Buncombe County

and flows se into North Fork [Swannanoa River].

Shutin Branch rises in n central Transylvania County and flows ne into Davidson River.

Shut-in Creek rises in n Jackson County on n slopes of Bald Mountain and flows n into Soco Creek.

Shut-in Creek, formed in w Madison County by the junction of West Fork Shut-in Creek and East Fork Shut-in Creek and flows ne into French Broad River.

Shut-in Ridge, s Buncombe County between Bent Creek and French Broad River.

Shutin Ridge, n central Transylvania County, extends e along the course of Joel Branch.

Sid Hill, n Yancey County between Peterson Branch and Whitson Branch.

Sidney, community in e Beaufort County.

Sidney, town in sw Columbus County. Inc. 1881, but long inactive in municipal affairs.

Sigmonsburg See Glen Alpine.

Signal Bald, peak on the Clay-Macon County line. Alt. 5,275.

Signal Pole Hill, sw Cherokee County on se end of Pack Mountain. Alt. 3,459.

Sikes Branch rises in w Carteret County and flows approx. 2 mi. s and e to join East Prong in forming Sanders Creek.

Silas Creek rises in nw Ashe County and flows se into North Fork New River.

Silas Creek rises in sw Beaufort County and flows n into Chocowinity Bay, Pamlico River.

Silas Creek rises in nw Forsyth County and flows sw into Muddy Creek. Known earlier as Spangenberg Creek for Bishop August G. Spangenberg, who led a surveying party from Edenton to the Blue Ridge Mountains in 1752 in search of a suitable site for a Moravian settlement. Spangenberg Creek appears as Strangenbergs Creek on the Collet map, 1770, and as Spanking Back on the Price map, 1808. By 1833, when the MacRae map appeared, it was called Silas Creek. Reynolda Lake is on Silas Creek.

Silas Creek, community in n Ashe County. Alt. approx. 2,740.

Siler Bald, sw Macon County at the head of Roaring Fork Creek, approx. one mi. s of Wayah Gap. Alt. 5,216. Part of Nantahala Mountain Range. Named for Jesse Richardson Siler, pioneer settler in the area. See also Silers Bald.

Siler Bald Branch rises on the s side of Siler Bald in sw Macon County and flows se into Bryson Branch.

Siler City, town in w Chatham County. Known first as Matthews Cross Roads, at the junction of the Raleigh-Salisbury and Fayetteville-Greensboro plank roads. Later known as Siler's Store and Siler's Station. Post office est. here in 1880 as Energy, changed to Siler City in 1884. Inc. 1887. Alt. 598. Produces furniture, textiles, processed grain, and poultry.

Silers Bald, mountain on the Swain County, N. C.-Sevier County, Tenn., line in Great Smoky Mountains National Park on Welch Ridge near lat. 35° 33' 58" N., long. 83° 33' 56" W. Alt. 5,620. Named for Jesse Richardson Siler (1793-1876) of Franklin, who owned this mountain and kept large herds of cattle on it.

Siles Branch rises in w Swain County and flows nw into Nantahala River.

Siles Gap, s Swain County between the head of Tarkiln Branch and the head of Siles Branch.

Silk Hope, community in nw Chatham County. Probably named in antebellum period at a time when there was an interest in producing home-grown silk.

Sills Creek rises in n Pender County and flows ne into Sawyers Creek.

Sills Creek rises in w Rowan County and flows ne into Back Creek. Named for John Sill who settled here in 1749.

Siloam, community in s Surry County on Yadkin River. Alt. 811. Halls Ferry across the river was operated here as late as the 1930's.

Siloam Township, se Surry County.

Silver Bluff, community in s Haywood County on Pigeon River.

Silverboro. See Boyette.

Silver City, community in central Hoke County n of town of Raeford.

Silver Creek rises in sw Burke County and flows ne into Catawba River.

Silver Creek rises in nw Burke County and flows se into Rose Creek.

Silver Creek rises in se Caldwell County and flows se into Gunpowder Creek.

Silver Creek rises in central Polk County and flows n into Lake Adger on Green River.

Silver Creek rises in n Transylvania County and flows se into Turkey Creek.

Silver Creek Gap in n Transylvania County on Sitton Mountain.

Silver Creek Knob, on the Burke-Rutherford County line. Alt. 2,838.

Silver Creek Township, sw Burke County.

Silverdale, community in e Onslow County between Freemans Creek and Webb Creek.

Silver Hill, community in s central Davidson County between Fourmile Branch and head of Battle Branch. A mine operated here almost continuously from about 1838 until 1860; produced lead, gold, and silver.

Silver Hill, community in w Pamlico County. Named for local Silver family.

Silver Hill, community in n Scotland County near Monroes Millpond.

Silver Hill Pocosin, a muck-filled area approx. 4 mi. by 4½ mi. in nw Pamlico County.

Silver Hill Township, central Davidson County.

Silver Knob, nw McDowell County near Limekiln Creek.

Silver Lake, tidal basin or boat harbor, 700 yds. long, at the community of Ocracoke on Ocracoke Island, se Hyde County.

Silver Lake, a natural lake fed by springs, sw New Hanover County, between Todds and Barnards creeks near the Cape Fear River. Covers approx. 16 acres; max. depth 30 ft. Owned by Allied-Kennecott Corp.

Silver Lake, nw Wilson County on Toisnot Swamp. Covers 175 acres; max. depth 12 ft. Fishing, swimming, boating, municipal water supply. Formed 1785 by John Dew and known as Dew's Mill until about 1847. Called by the name of various owners until about 1922 when present name applied.

Silvermine Bald on the Haywood-Transylvania County line ne of Chestnut Bald.

Silvermine Branch rises in ne Cherokee County and flows se into Valley River.

Silvermine Branch rises in n Madison County and flows sw into French Broad River.

Silvermine Branch rises in central Swain County and flows sw into Lands Creek.

Silvermine Creek rises in sw Swain County and flows ne into Nantahala River.

Silvermine Gap, sw Swain County on the head of Silvermine Creek.

Silver Run rises in e Cumberland County and flows nw into Cape Fear River.

Silver Run rises in s Mitchell County and flows e into Grassy Creek.

Silver Run Creek rises in s Jackson County on the se slope of Chimneytop Mountain and flows sw 3 mi. to join Little Whitewater Creek in forming Whitewater River.

Silver Run Creek rises in w Randolph County and flows sw into Uwharrie River.

Silver Run Falls, in Cape Fear River at its junction with Silver Run approx. 3 mi. s of the mouth of Little River, ne Cumberland County. A series of small falls or rapids drop approx. 5 ft. in 300 yards. Mentioned in Fulton's survey of North Carolina rivers in 1819 and appears on the MacRae map, 1833.

Silvers Cove, e Haywood County on the head of Silvers Cove Creek.

Silvers Cove Creek rises in e Haywood County in Silvers Cove and flows sw into Rush Fork.

Silver Springs, community in central Gates County on the s side of Merchants Millpond. Named for an artesian spring. Formerly a popular spot for picnics.

Silverstone, community in n Watauga County on Sharp Creek.

Silver Town, community in sw Brunswick County.

Silver Valley, community in e Davidson County.

Simes Creek. See Perry Creek.

Simmons Branch rises in s Madison County and flows se into Sandy Mush Creek.

Simmons Branch rises in ne Swain County and flows se into Raven Fork.

Simmons Branch rises in w Wilkes County and flows e into Dugger Creek.

Simmons Cove, n Buncombe County w of Paint Fork community.

Simmons Knob, e Yancey County between the head of Mine Branch and Crabtree Creek.

Simmons Landing, nw Tyrrell County on Scuppernong River.

Simmons Ridge, se Avery County.

Simms Fork rises in w Yancey County and flows s into Elk Wallow Creek.

Simon Branch rises in central Cherokee County and flows se into Morgan Creek.

Simon Branch rises in n Macon County and flows sw into Little Tennessee River.

Simpson, town in e Pitt County. Inc. 1923; post office est. 1912 as Chicod. Alt. 63.

Simpson Branch rises in sw Union County and flows s into South Carolina where it enters Cane Creek.

Simpsonville Township, s Rockingham County.

Sims, town in nw Wilson County, settled

before 1908 when a post office was est. Inc. 1913 as Simms; named for W. W. Simms. Reinc. in 1923 as Sims. A large stone quarry is nearby.

Sims Creek rises in s Watauga County and flows sw into Boone Fork.

Sincerity, community in ne Union County on Richardson Creek.

Singecat Ridge, nw McDowell County near the head of Buck Creek.

Singletary Lake, e Bladen County, a 572-acre natural lake with a max. depth of 11 ft. 8 in. Named for Richard Singletary who received a grant of land in Bladen County in 1729. Part of Singletary Lake Group Camp. Fishing, boating, swimming, and camping. See also Carolina Bays.

Singletary Lake Group Camp (of state park system) in e Bladen County, 10 mi. se of Elizabethtown. 1,287 acres. Est. 1939. Address, Elizabethtown. Organized camp.

Singletons Bay, loam-filled bay in se Hoke County between Big Marsh Swamp and Little Marsh Swamp.

Singleton Swamp rises in nw Beaufort County and flows nw and w into Old Ford Swamp.

Sings Creek rises in w Moore County and flows ne into Wet Creek.

Sinking Creek rises in nw Haywood County and flows ne into Big Creek.

Sioux, community in n Yancey County on Big Creek. Alt. 2,109.

Sippanaw. See Rudd.

Sites, community in s Bladen County in Carvers Creek Township.

Sitting Bear Mountain, nw Burke County. Alt. approx. 4,100.

Sitton, community in nw Henderson County on South Fork.

Sitton Creek rises in nw Henderson County and flows sw into Seniard Creek.

Sitton Creek rises in n Transylvania County and flows se into Boylston Creek.

Sitton Knob, n Transylvania County at the se end of Sitton Mountain.

Sitton Mountain, n Transylvania County extends se between North Prong Turkey Creek and Sitton Creek.

Six Forks, community in n Wake County near the head of Mine Creek where 6 roads come together; formerly called Tippers Crossroads.

Sixmile Creek rises in se Mecklenburg County and flows sw on the Mecklenburg-Union County line into South Carolina where it enters Sugar Creek.

Sixpound Creek rises in n central Warren County and flows n then ne into Gaston Lake. Appears on the Moseley map, 1733.

Sixpound Township, n Warren County.

Six Runs, community in e Sampson County.

Six Runs Creek rises in ne Sampson County and flows s and sw to join Coharie River in forming Black River. Appears on the Collet map, 1770.

Skalley Branch rises in n Avery County and flows w into Elk River.

Skalley Knob, n Avery County.

Skeenah Creek is formed in s Macon County by the junction of North Fork [Skeenah Creek] and South Fork [Skeenah Creek] and flows e into Little Tennessee River. The name is said to be an Indian word meaning "the abode of satan."

Skeenah Gap, s Macon County between Black Mountain Branch and Jones Creek.

Skewarky. See Williamston.

Skibo or Skibow (Sky-bow), community in central Cumberland County. Alt. 221.

Skidder Branch rises in ne Swain County and flows se into Straight Fork.

Skiffley Creek rises in n Haywood County and flows se into Pigeon River.

Skiffly Branch rises in w Madison County and flows s into Roaring Fork.

Skin Cabin Creek rises in s Surry County and flows se into Ararat River.

Skinner Canal, in n Washington County drains n from East Dismal Swamp to Kendricks Creek. Known in 1868 as McRae Canal.

Skinner's Point. See Hornblower Point.

Skinnersville, community in n Washington County. Post office est. in 1808, and had a post office variously in 1822, 1828, 1849, 1850, 1878, and 1886-1908. In 1850 the post office name was changed to Leo; sometime after 1908 the site of the community began moving to the ne, and the old site is still known locally as Old Skinnersville.

Skinnersville Township, ne Washington County, formed in 1868.

Skipper Branch rises in s central Brunswick County and flows s into Shallotte Creek.

Skitty Creek rises in e Macon County and flows s into Cullasaja River.

Skull Camp Mountain, nw Surry County. Alt. 2,082. A post office, Scull Camp, served this area about 1822 and this name appears on the U. S. Coast Survey map, 1865.

Skunk Creek rises in central Lee County

and flows nw into Big Buffalo Creek.

Skyco, former community and steamboat landing on the sw shore of Roanoke Island, e Dare County. It was on Ashbee Harbor. Named for Skiko, son of the Chief of the Choanoke Indians, who was taken prisoner by Ralph Lane in 1586. Skyco was a post office from 1892 until 1913.

Skyland, community in s Buncombe County. Alt. 2,257. Est. 1888 by Otis A. Miller as a resort. Produces electronic components and glass products.

Skyland Lake, s Buncombe County on Powell Creek, was formed in 1963 by Carolina Power and Light Company with the construction of an eastern dam and concrete spillway. It covers 320 acres with a max. depth of 100 ft. and a shoreline of 9 mi. Used to condense turbine exhaust steam at a steam electric generating plant and for public recreation.

Skyuka Creek rises in s Polk County e of Tryon Mountain and flows s into Pacolet River. Named for the Cherokee who, about 1774, showed his friendship for the whites by revealing to them an unknown route through the mountains. Knowledge of this route enabled Captain Thomas Howard to defeat the Indians at Round Mountain, *(which see).*

Skyuka Mountain, sw Polk County rising above the town of Tryon. Said to be named for Skyuka, son of a Cherokee chief. Skyuka was thrown from his horse and broke his leg when the horse became frightened by a snake. Captain Thomas Howard found Skyuka, set his leg, and the two became friends. Betraying his own tribe, Skyuka showed Howard the pass which now bears his name. *See also* Howard Gap.

Sky View Pond, spring-fed lake in ne Iredell County. Formed in 1950, covers 38 acres; 35 ft. max. depth. Fishing, swimming, boating. Owned by Claude and Moody White.

Slab Camp Branch rises in n Swain County in the Great Smoky Mountains National Park and flows e into Forney Creek.

Slab Ridge. *See* Sharon.

Slade Creek rises in sw Hyde County and flows nw and sw into Pungo River. Appears on the Collet map, 1770.

Slade Creek. *See* Blounts Creek.

Slades Swamp rises in s Bladen County and flows nw along the Bladen-Columbus County line into Brown Marsh Swamp.

Sladesville, town in sw Hyde County on Slade Creek. Inc. 1849, but long inactive in municipal affairs.

Slap Swamp rises in n Columbus County and flows se into Friar Swamp.

The Slashes, a large marsh approx. 4 mi. wide, in e Halifax County between Conoconnara Swamp and Roanoke River.

Slate Creek rises in nw Cherokee County and flows se into Shuler Creek.

Slate Mountain, ne Surry County between Ararat River and Archies Creek.

Slate Rock Creek rises between Laurel Mountain and Slate Rock Ridge in w Transylvania County and flows se into Henderson County where it enters Bradley Creek in Pisgah National Forest.

Slate Rock Ridge in n Transylvania County extends se from the nw end of Dividing Ridge to the nw end of Pilot Cove.

Slatestone, community in n central Beaufort County. Alt. 40.

Slatten Creek rises in central Jackson County and flows se into Robinson Creek.

Slaty Branch rises in ne Buncombe County and flows se into Flat Creek.

Slaty Knob, w Madison County between Rector Branch and French Broad River. Alt. 2,790.

Sled Runner Gap, in the Unicoi Mountains on the Cherokee County, N. C.-Monroe County, Tenn., line near the headwaters of Garreck Creek. Alt. approx. 3,850.

Sleepy Creek rises in se Carteret County between the communities of Gloucester and Marshallberg and flows s approx. 1½ mi. into The Straits. Appears on the Collet map, 1770.

Sleepy Creek rises in s Wayne County and flows ne into Neuse River. Saponi Indians lived along its banks and many arrow heads and artifacts have been found here. Tradition says that the Indians believed the waters of the creek had medicinal values. Sick Indians came to drink the water and later would lie along the creek banks to sleep, hence the name.

Sleepy Gap, s Buncombe County between Grassy Knob and Truckwheel Mountain.

Slek Creek. *See* Town Fork Creek.

Slickens Creek rises in e Jackson County and flows ne into Tuckasegee River.

Slicking Gap, on the Transylvania County, N. C.-Greenville County, S. C., line in the Blue Ridge Mountains near the head of Bursted Rock Creek. Sometimes known as Slick Gap or Slicken Gap. Alt. 2,873.

Slick Rock, elevation between the head of

Norton Branch and the head of Cane Creek in se Macon County approx. 3 mi. se of town of Highlands. Alt. approx. 3,340.

Slick Rock, elevation in s Macon County between Stephens Creek and Gold Mine Branch. Alt. approx. 3,860.

Slickrock Branch rises in n Cherokee County near Bearpen Gap and flows ne into Hyatt Creek.

Slickrock Branch rises in n Haywood County and flows se into Pigeon River.

Slickrock Branch rises in ne Henderson County approx. 2 mi. sw of Bat Cave community and flows approx. one mi. se into Reedy Patch Creek. Named for the appearance of rocks in the stream.

Slickrock Creek rises in nw Graham County and flows ne to the Graham County, N. C.-Monroe County, Tenn., line which it follows into Little Tennessee River.

Slick Rock Falls, n Transylvania County in a branch of Rockhouse Creek.

Slickrock Knob, w Yancey County at the s end of Sampson Mountain.

Slick Rock Mountain, w Randolph County w of Caraway Mountain and in close proximity with Black Jack, Vineyard, and Prickly Pear Mountains.

Slickrock Mountain, w central Yancey County between Phipps and Baker creeks.

Slide Branch rises in nw Haywood County and flows n into Big Creek.

Sliding Knob Creek rises in sw Madison County and flows w into Spring Creek.

Sligo, community in n Currituck County on the w side of Tull Creek. Named by a Methodist circuit rider from Sligo, Ireland, who visited the area in 1783.

Slim Creek rises in n McDowell County on the w slope of Betsy Ridge and flows s into Little Buck Creek.

Slipoff Branch rises in e Swain County and flows ne into Connelly Creek.

Slipoff Knob, e Swain County between the head of Connelly Creek and the head of Slipoff Branch.

Slippery Hill Ridge, w Avery County.

Sloan, community in se Duplin County. Alt. 50.

Sloan, Sloans Station. See Stony Point.

Sloans Creek rises in w Rowan County and flows n aprox. 3 mi. into Kerr Creek, which see. Known first as South Fork of James Cathey's Mill Creek and later as Marlins Creek.

Sloan's Crossing. See Garland.

Slocomb, community in n Cumberland County.

Slocomb Crossroads. See Turlington.

Slocum Creek rises in se Craven County and flows n into Neuse River. Appears on the Moseley map, 1733, as Slocumbs Creek.

Sloop Point extends from the mainland of s Pender County into Virginia Creek estuary in Topsail Sound. Named from the fact that sloops entering the sound moored here. Sloop Point post office was located at what is now Barlowes, which see.

Slosh. See Schlosstown.

The Slough, stream, rises in n Wayne County and flows e into Nahunta Swamp.

Slow Creek rises in e Cherokee County and flows sw into Peachtree Creek.

Sluder Branch rises in nw Buncombe County on e slopes of Hanlon Mountain and flows ne and then se into Newfound Creek.

Sluice Gap, on the Swain County, N. C.,-Sevier County, Tenn., line between Mt. Kephart and The Sawteeth.

Sly, community in w Ashe County.

Small, community in s central Beaufort County.

Smallwood Island, a silty clay-loam island approx. 1¼ mi. long in Roanoke River, w Northampton County.

Smart Branch rises in s Macon County and flows sw into Middle Creek.

Smathers View Mountain, extends e from Thompson Knob, which see, to Peggy Peak in sw Buncombe County.

Smethport, community in central Ashe County. Named for the town in Pennsylvania from which a local tanning extract plant had moved.

Smileys Falls, s Harnett County in Cape Fear River at the mouth of Upper Little River. A succession of ledges of rock here drops the water from 6 to 18 inches in most cases, but there is one fall of 4 ft. and another of 5 ft. Mentioned in Fulton's survey of North Carolina rivers in 1819.

Smith Branch rises in s central Carbarrus County and flows ne into Coddle Creek.

Smith Branch rises in e Madison County and flows s into Little Creek.

Smith Branch rises in se Mitchell County and flows n into Rose Creek.

Smith Branch rises in n Swain County and flows sw into Oconaluftee River.

Smith Creek rises in e Anson County near

the town of Lilesville and flows ne into Blewett Falls Lake.

Smith Creek rises in e Beaufort County and flows se into Pungo Creek.

Smith Creek rises in central Buncombe County and flows ne into French Broad River.

Smith Creek rises in se Granville County and flows w 7 mi. into Beaverdam Creek at the Granville-Wake County line.

Smith Creek rises in w Hyde County and flows n into Pungo River. Appears as Smiths Creek on the Collet map, 1770.

Smith Creek rises in n Pamlico County and flows se into Bay River.

Smith Creek rises in se Pamlico County and flows s into the Greens Creek estuary at Neuse River. Appears on the Moseley map, 1733.

Smith Creek rises in w Warren County and flows ne into Mecklenburg County, Virginia, where it enters Roanoke River. Shown on the Moseley map, 1733, as Great Creek, but appears by the present name on the Price map, 1808.

Smith Creek Township, nw Warren County.

Smitheys Creek rises in w Wilkes County and flows s into W. Kerr Scott Reservoir. Prior to 1962, the spelling was Smithies Creek.

Smithfield, town and county seat, central Johnston County on Neuse River. County court first held at this site in August, 1771, when it became the county seat. Known as Johnston Court House until 1777 when it was inc. as Smithfield. Named for John Smith, owner of land on which the town developed. The legislature met here in 1779. Produces textiles, apparel, lumber, electronic components, and processed meat. Alt. 155. *See also* Hinton's Quarter.

Smithfield Township, central Johnston County.

Smith Gap, e Haywood County between Big Branch and Crabtree Creek.

Smith Grove, community in central Davie County, approx. 6 mi. ne of town of Mocksville. Named for a Methodist camp ground est. here in 1826. Post office est. 1834. Alt. 824.

Smithies Creek. *See* Smitheys Creek.

Smith Island, se Brunswick County at the mouth of Cape Fear River and bounded on the n by Corncake Inlet. The se tip is Cape Fear, and the sw portion is known as Bald Head because of its round, sandy

surface. The island is approx. 17,000 acres in area and contains palmetto trees and other interesting vegetation and wildlife. Except for a caretaker, it is unoccupied. Named for Landgrave Thomas Smith who acquired it in 1690. Appears as Landgrave Thomas Smith's Island on the Moseley map, 1733, on which the present Bald Head is marked Barren Head. The Collet map, 1770, shows only "Bald Head." When Thomas Smith willed the island to his four sons in 1738, he said that its old name was Cedar Island.

Smith Mill Creek rises in central Buncombe County near Deaver View Mountain and flows w through the city of Asheville into French Broad River.

Smith Millpond, s Wayne County on Sleepy Creek.

Smith Mountain, e Burke County. Alt. approx. 2,000.

Smith River rises in w Virginia and flows ne to a point approx. three mi. n of the North Carolina-Virginia state line where it turns s and flows se into n Rockingham County. It enters Dan River at Leaksville. Called Irvin River by William Byrd in 1728 and appears as Irvine River on the Moseley map, 1733. Named for Alexander Irvine, professor of mathematics at the College of William and Mary and a member of Byrd's survey party of the North Carolina-Virginia line. Appears as Smith River on the Price map, 1808.

Smiths, community in s central Brunswick County.

Smiths Bridge Township, sw Macon County.

Smith's Corner, community in s central Camden County. Named for a physician who practiced here about 1840-70. Alt. 10.

Smiths Corner. *See* Smyrna.

Smiths Creek rises in ne Davie County and flows e approx. 6 mi. into Carters Creek.

Smiths Creek rises in w Lee County and flows n into Deep River.

Smiths Creek rises in n New Hanover County and flows sw into Cape Fear River.

Smiths Creek rises in ne Wake County and flows sw into Neuse River.

Smith's Creek. *See* Oriental.

Smith's Creek. *See* Sanders Creek.

Smith's Ferry. *See* Hinton's Quarter.

Smiths Mill Creek. *See* Mill Creek.

Smiths Mill Pond, e Robeson County on Oak Swamp. Covers 50 acres; max. depth 8 ft.

Smith's Point. See Mauls Point.

Smiths Pond, an artificial pond in ne Bladen County built about 1883. Max. depth approx. 10 ft. Fishing.

Smiths Store, community in e Alexander County.

Smiths Store, community in nw Cabarrus County.

Smiths Store, community in s Lincoln County.

Smith's Store. See Albemarle.

Smiths Township, former township in e Cabarrus County, now township number 9.

Smiths Township, w Robeson County.

Smithtown, town in n Yadkin County, inc. 1924 and named for Columbus Smith who settled here about 1894 to operate a cabinet shop and small furniture factory. Post office named Poindexter served the community until about 1909. No longer active in muncipal affairs.

Smith Township, e central Duplin County.

Smithville. See Southport.

Smithville Township, s Brunswick County.

Smith Walker Mountain, sw Wilkes County between Warrior and Beaver creeks. Named for a nineteenth century resident of the area.

Smithwick, community in s Martin County on Long Creek.

Smithwick Creek rises in s Martin County and flows n into Statons Pond on Sweetwater Creek.

Smokemont, community in ne Swain county in Great Smoky Mountains National Park on Oconaluftee River. Alt. 2,188.

Smokey Gap, n central Avery County.

Smoky. See Bald Mountains.

Smoky Cove, s Haywood County on Dix Creek.

Smoky Creek rises in s Caldwell County and flows s into n Burke County where it enters Catawba River.

Smoky Creek Township, n central Burke County.

Smoky Dome. See Clingmans Dome.

Smoky Mountain, se Henderson County between Butler and Blake mountains.

Smoky Mountains. See Great Smoky Mountains.

Smyre Creek rises in central Catawba County and flows w and then s into Clark Creek.

Smyre Mills. See Ranlo-Rex-Priscilla.

Smyrna, community in e Carteret County on Middens Creek. First called Wit and later Smiths Corner.

Smyrna Creek rises in e Carteret County and flows se into Jarrett Bay.

Smyrna Township, on Core Sound and Jarrett Bay in e Carteret County. At one time parts of Smyrna made up Carteret and number 6 and 7 townships.

Smyrna Township, se Robeson County.

Smyth. See Balfour.

Snaggy Bald, e Jackson County between Thunder Struck Mountain and Deep Gap. Alt. 5,538.

Snaggy Point, peak in w Madison County between Hogback Mountain and Meadow Fork.

Snaggy Ridge, s Haywood County between Cold Spring Branch and Deep Gap Branch.

Snake Bite Township, central Bertie County.

Snake Branch rises in w Haywood County and flows nw into Caldwell Fork.

Snake Branch rises in s Hertford County and flows ne into Ahoskie Swamp.

Snakeden Knob, s Macon County between Dryman Fork and Ball Creek.

Snakeden Mountain, s central Avery County.

Snake Den Mountain, ne Madison County between Little Foster Creek and Foster Creek.

Snakeden Ridge, w Swain County, extends e from Pinnacle Creek to Pinnacle Ridge.

Snakeden Ridge, w Swain County, extends se between Birchfield Branch and Lost Cove Creek from Shuckstack Mountain to Eagle Creek.

Snakeden Top, central Haywood County on the e end of Goatrock Ridge.

Snake Island, a long, narrow tidal marsh island in sw Carteret County in Bogue Sound.

Snake Knob, n central Avery County.

Snake Knob, n Yancey County between Little Creek and Bald Mountain Creek.

Snake Knob. See Inadu Knob.

Snake Mountain, n Watauga County extends n from Rich Mountain. Alt. 5,574.

Snake Ridge, w Haywood County, Great Smoky Mountains National Park, a short spur extending nw from Cataloochee Divide, center near lat. 35° 36' 10" N., 83° 04' 54" W.

Snapp, community in w Gaston County.

Snead Branch rises in e Cherokee County and flows se into Slow Creek.

Sneads Creek rises in s Onslow County and flows se into New River.

Sneads Ferry, community in s Onslow County on New River. Alt. 10. Originally named Lower Ferry on New River when first ferry licensed and operated here by Edmund Ennett in 1725. Robert W. Snead settled here about 1760, and operated the ferry and a tavern. The name of the community wa then changed to Sneads Ferry. Sneaa died about 1799. The ferry ceased to operate in 1939 when a bridge was opened a short distance up the river. Appears on the Collet map, 1770. See also Fulcher Landing.

Sneads Grove, community in central Scotland County. Known earlier as Sneads Grove Church.

Sneed Branch rises in central Cherokee County and flows sw parallel to Rocky Pen Ridge into Nottely River.

Sneedsborough. See Old Sneedsborough.

Sneeky Creek formerly rose in s Clay County and flowed ne into Hiwassee River. Its course is now covered by the waters of Chatuge Lake.

Snider, community in s Davidson County.

Snipe Creek rises in w Person County and flows nw into Mill Creek.

Snoad Branch rises in nw Beaufort County and flows se to join Old Ford Swamp in forming Aggie Run.

Snodes Creek rises in se Beaufort County and flows e into Goose Creek.

Snowball Gap, n Buncombe County se of Little Snowball Mountain.

Snowball Mountain, ne Buncombe County at the s end of Little Fork Ridge. Also known as Big Snowball Mountain. Alt. 5,494. Named from the fact that in winter the peak is frequently covered at its crest by rime or frozen fog giving the appearance of a large snowball.

Snowbird Creek rises in sw Graham County and flows se and ne into Santeetlah Lake. Called by the Indians *Titiyi*, "snowbird place."

Snowbird Creek rises in n Haywood County and flows sw into Pigeon River.

Snowbird Gap, central Graham County between Snowbird Creek and Atoah Creek.

Snowbird Mountain, on the Jackson-Macon County line.

Snowbird Mountains extend across the e half of the Cherokee-Graham County

line between Hawk Knob and Nantahala River. Max. alt. 4,743 at Teyahalee Bald.

Snowbird Top, on the Cherokee-Graham County line in the Snowbird Mountains. Alt. 3,882.

Snow Camp, community in sw Alamance County on Cane Creek. Dixon's Mill here dates from 1753. An iron foundry was est. here about 1800 and as late as 1879 was still in operation. Legend says the name Snow Camp was given the community by Cornwallis' soldiers who camped here after the Battle of Guilford Courthouse during a heavy snow.

Snow Creek rises on Asbury Mountain, ne Alexander County, and flows se into w central Iredell County where it enters South Yadkin River.

Snow Creek rises in n Catawba County and flows ne into Catawba River.

Snow Creek rises in central Mitchell County and flows sw into North Toe River. Named for snow white rocks in its bed.

Snow Creek rises in n Stokes County and flows se into Dan River.

Snow Creek rises in w Surry County and flows se and s into Mitchell River.

Snow Creek, community in n central Iredell County. Developed around a Methodist Church founded here in 1802 at a graveyard begun in the 1780's.

Snow Creek, community in sw Mitchell County. Alt. approx. 2,600.

Snow Creek Township, s central Mitchell County.

Snow Creek Township, ne Stokes County.

Snowden, community in n Currituck County. Post office est. 1881; named for first postmaster, Milton Snowden. Alt. 9.

Snow Hill, community in n Chowan County.

Snow Hill, county seat and town, central Greene County. Alt. 74. Authorized to be laid off, 1811; inc. 1828. Named for a nearby plantation of the same name which probably was named for a hill of white sand. John Becton in 1753 willed lands "called the Snow Hills" in this county to his son Michael. Shortly after the Revolution the Shepherd family tried without success to promote a town to be called Shepherdsburgh at this site. The ancient Tuscarora Indian town, Cotechney, was located near the site of Snow Hill. Today the town produces lumber, milling, and textile products.

Snow Hill Crossroads, community in n Duplin County.

Snow Hill Township, central Greene County.

Snow Marsh, a series of small tidal marshes, se Brunswick County, in the Cape Fear River below Sunny Point.

Snow Mountain, n Avery County. Alt. 5,332.

Snow Point, se Brunswick County, extends se from the mainland into Cape Fear River at the mouth of Walden Creek and on the w side of Snow Marsh. Appears on the Collet map, 1770.

Snows Cut, a canal in s New Hanover County approx. 1⅝ mi. long, connecting Myrtle Sound with Cape Fear River. It forms a part of the Intracoastal Waterway.

Snyder Creek rises in ne Cherokee County and flows nw into Tatham Creek.

Snyder Creek rises in n Lincoln County and flows se into Anderson Creek.

Soakas Creek rises in n Davidson County and flows w into s Forsyth County where it enters South Fork Muddy Creek.

Soapstone Branch rises in nw Henderson County in Pisgah National Forest and flows e into McDowell Creek.

Soapstone Branch rises in e Mitchell County and flows w into Left Fork [Cane Creek].

Soapstone Branch rises in nw Swain County and flows sw into Eagle Creek at Horseshoe Bend.

Soapstone Creek rises in n Jackson County and flows n into Scott Creek.

Soapstone Gap, e Haywood County between Mary Gray Knob and Wines Top. Alt. 3,640.

Soapstone Gap, n Jackson County on the ne end of Rocky Face Ridge.

Soapstone Knob, s Swain County near Marr Branch and Brush Creek.

Soapstone Mount, formerly a large pyrophyllite formation in ne Randolph County; for a number of years it was mined, crushed at nearby Staley, and shipped away for refining and use in talc products. A post office by this name existed here in 1882.

Soapstone Ridge extends se from Three Forks Mountain in w Transylvania County to Catheys Creek in w central Transylvania County.

Soapstone Ridge, n Transylvania County extends ne from Rich Mountain to South Fork Mills River.

Society Parish, Church of England, Bertie County, est. with the formation of the county in 1722 and coextensive with it. Named for the Society for the Propagation of the Gospel. Previously this territory had been in South-West Parish, Chowan County, est. 1715. The parish had 930 white taxable inhabitants in 1767, described as "capable to maintain & willing to receive a Minister." Divided in 1727 to form Northwest Parish which became Northampton County in 1741. The church for Society Parish was in the Merry Hill section of the county on Duckenfield land. The parish as a unit of local administration was abolished in 1776 with the adoption of the state constitution and the disestablishment of the Church of England.

Soco Bald, on the Jackson-Swain County line near the head of Madcap Branch.

Soco Creek rises near Soco Gap, w Haywood County and flows ne into Jonathans Creek.

Soco Creek rises in n Jackson County and flows sw into Oconaluftee River on Jackson-Swain County line.

Soco Falls on Soco Creek, w Haywood County. Water falls in a double stream over a series of rocky ledges for about 60 ft. into a cup-like basin. Said to have been named by the Cherokees for their word Sog-wah, "one," when they threw one of De Soto's men over the falls.

Soco Falls in the head of Soco Creek in n Jackson County.

Soco Gap on the Haywood-Jackson County line. Alt. 4,344. The most important passageway through Balsam Mountain for the Indians before the arrival of the white man.

Soco Ridge, s Macon County between North Fork Coweeta Creek and the head of Hoglot Branch.

Soda Hill, community in ne Watauga County.

Sodom Branch rises in nw Madison County near Sodom Mountain and flows n into Big Laurel Creek.

Sodom Branch rises in sw Yancey County and flows nw into Indian Creek. Named for an early sawmill camp at which prostitution, violence of all kinds, and drunkeness were common. Nearby settlers drew upon the Bible for an appropriate name for the camp.

Sodom Hollow, central Buncombe County, the valley through which French Broad River flows nw of Asheville toward Dryman Mountain. Named by a very early circuit rider who compared the rough pioneers living here with the inhabitants of Sodom and Gomorrah.

Sodom Mountain, central Madison County between Walnut Gap and Lumptown.

Soggy Hill Branch rises in ne Swain County and flows s into Raven Fork.

Sokassa. See Rumbling Bald Mountain.

Solitude. See Ashland.

Solola Valley, community in n central Swain County on Noland Creek. The name comes from *salola*, the Cherokee Indian word for squirrel.

Solomons Creek rises in s Richmond County and flows w into Pee Dee River.

Solray Gap, central Haywood County between Little Pine Mountain and Pigeon River.

Sols Creek rises in e Jackson County and flows sw into Bear Creek Lake on the Tuckasegee River.

Somerset, community in central Person County. Est. 1895-1900 as Pick's or Pick's Siding where lumber was brought by tramroad to be transferred to the railroad.

Somerset, plantation of Josiah Collins on Lake Phelps in Washington and Tyrrell counties, developed between 1780 and 1788. At one time the plantation comprised more than 100,000 acres, and about 20 buildings. The main house, Somerset House, was built about 1830. The estate was abandoned and ruined before the end of the Civil War, and the property passed through various owners before it was sold at public auction in 1946. The state had previously purchased the mansion house and 16,628 acres in 1939. Somerset House has been restored and is the main attraction in Pettigrew State Park, *which see*.

Somerset Canal, in se Washington County, drains the waters of Lake Phelps into Scuppernong River, and forms a portion of the Washington-Tyrrell County line. The canal was built by slave labor in 1787 at a cost of $30,000 and was 20 ft. wide, 6 ft. deep, and 6 mi. long. Known for almost a century as Collins Canal for the builder, Josiah Collins.

Somers Township, se Wilkes County.

Somerton Creek rises in Virginia and flows sw into nw Gates County where it enters Chowan River.

Somey Creek. See Sumey Creek.

Sommey Creek. See Sumey Creek.

Sophia, community in n Randolph County. Settled prior to 1779. Probably named for Sophia Clement, local resident. Alt. 801.

Soracte. See Sarecta.

Sornook. See Mount Guyot.

Sorrell Creek rises in s Haywood County and flows nw into Little East Fork Pigeon River.

Sorrells Cove, e Haywood County between Brown Cove and Thickety Creek.

Sorrell's Creek rises in w Wake County and flows nw into Black Creek.

Sorrow Creek appears on the Collet map, 1770, apparently rising in what is now n Davidson County and flowing w into South Fork in s Forsyth County. It cannot presently be identified with any known stream in that vicinity.

Sossamon's Spring. See Sherrills Spring.

Soules Swamp, rises in n Columbus County and flows ne then se into White Marsh.

The Sound. See Pamlico Sound.

Sound, community in ne Washington County.

Sound Side, community in n Tyrrell County on the s side of Albemarle Sound.

Sourwood Gap on the Buncombe-McDowell County line ne of Montreat.

South Albemarle Township, e central Stanly County.

South Bay, in n Piney Island s of Rattan Bay, ne Carteret County. Approx. 1¾ mi. long and ½ mi. wide.

South Belmont, uninc. outskirts of city of Belmont, se Gaston County.

South Biltmore, former town in central Buncombe County, inc. 1895, but now within the corporate limits of Asheville. See also Biltmore.

South Branch Cartledges Creek rises in n Richmond County and flows sw into Cartledges Creek.

South Buffalo Creek rises in s central Guilford County and flows ne joining North Buffalo Creek in ne Guilford County to form Buffalo Creek.

South Channel, ne Currituck County.

South Clinton Township, central Sampson County.

South Country Line Creek rises in s Caswell County and flows nw into Country Line Creek.

South Cox Creek rises in n Yancey County and flows se into Jacks Creek.

South Creek rises in se Beaufort County and flows n and e into Pamlico River. Appears as Chickorack River on the Com-

berford map, 1657, and as South Dividing
Creek on the Collet map, 1770.

South Creek rises in e Chatham County and
flows e and s into Wake County where it
enters Big White Oak Creek near the
Chatham County line.

South Creek rises in ne Rutherford County
and flows ne into First Broad River.

South Creek, town in se Beaufort County on
a peninsula formed by the mouths of
Bond and Muddy creeks as they enter
Pamlico River. Settled prior to 1794
when it was known as Stanton-Harrold
for two men who operated a saw mill
here. Apparently known as Harold in the
early nineteenth century and as Oregon
(for the first steamboat to come up the
Pamlico River—see Oregon Inlet) about
the middle of the century. Inc. 1883 as
Stanton. Inc. 1925 as South Creek, but
no longer active in municipal affairs.

South Crowders Creek rises in s Gaston
County and flows se into Crowders
Creek.

South Deep Creek rises in w Yadkin County and flows se and e to join North Deep
Creek in forming Deep Creek.

South Dividing Creek. See South Creek.

South Double Creek rises in w Stokes County and flows ne into Dan River.

Southeast Muddy Creek rises in se Mc-
Dowell County and flows ne into South
Muddy Creek.

Southerland Millpond, in e Vance County
on Sandy Creek. Area, 30 acres; maximum depth, 10 ft. Now used by the
city of Henderson as a reservoir. See also
Millford.

Southern City. See East Spencer.

Southerne Virginia Sea appears on the
Comberford map, 1657, as the area of
the Atlantic Ocean off the Outer Banks
of modern North Carolina, roughly between the coast and the Gulf Stream.

Southern Mountain, central Transylvania
County between Brushy Creek and Burl
Mountain.

Southern Pines, town in s Moore County.
Inc. 1887. Known earlier as Vineland,
but the Post Office Department would not
accept the name because of possible
confusion with the town of the same
name in New Jersey. Named from its
location on the edge of the long leaf pine
belt. A popular winter resort. West
Southern Pines, inc. 1923, became a part
of Southern Pines in 1931. Produces

furniture. Alt. 516. Sandhills Community
College, est. 1965, is located here.

Southern Plantation. See South Virginia.

Southern Shores, resort community in ne
Dare County on the s coast of North
Banks between Kitty Hawk and Duck.
The 1963 General Assembly passed an
act under which, by a vote of the residents, Southern Shores may be inc. as a
town by a resolution of the county commissioners.

South Fayetteville, uninc. outskirts of city
of Fayetteville in central Cumberland
County.

South Flat River rises in sw Person County
and flows se into Flat River.

South Fork, rises in s Forsyth County and
flows sw into Davidson County where it
enters Muddy Creek a short distance s of
the county line. Early Moravian settlers
called this Ens Creek and it appears as
such on the Collet map, 1770. On the
Price map, 1808, it is marked "Ens or
South Fork."

South Fork rises in s Henderson County
and flows nw into Willow Creek. Also
known locally as Greer Creek.

South Fork rises in n McDowell County
near Betsy and Hensley ridges and flows
se into Toms Creek.

South Fork rises in nw McDowell County
on the n slope of Pups Ridge and flows se
into Roses Creek.

South Fork rises in w Surry County and
flows se into Mitchell River.

South Fork rises in e Transylvania County
and flows se into w Henderson County
where it flows ne to join North Fork to
form Mills River. Sometimes also known
as South Fork Mills River.

South Fork. See South Fork Catawba River.

South Fork Beech Creek rises in e Graham
County and flows nw into Beech Creek.

South Fork [Big Pine Creek] rises in s
Madison County and flows n to join
North Fork to form Big Pine Creek.

South Fork [Cane Creek] rises in n Chat-
ham County and flows ne into s Alamance
County where it enters Cane Creek.
Known also as South Fork Creek.

South Fork [Carvers Branch] rises in s
Mitchell County and flows sw into Carvers
Branch.

South Fork Catawba River is formed in
central Catawba County by the junction
of Jacob Fork and Henry Fork. It flows
s through Catawba County, s across central Lincoln County, and se through

central Gaston County to enter Catawba River in se Gaston County. Also known locally in various places as South Fork, South Fork River, Little Catawba River. Appears as South Fork of the Catawba River on the Collet map, 1770.

South Fork Cattail Creek rises in s Yancey County and flows nw to join North Fork Cattail Creek in forming Cattail Creek.

South Fork Creek rises in w Tyrrell County and flows n into Scuppernong River.

South Fork Creek. See South Fork [Cane Creek].

South Fork Crooked Creek rises in w Union County and flows ne to join North Fork Crooked Creek in forming Crooked Creek.

South Fork Flat Creek rises in s Transylvania County and flows ne into Flat Creek.

South Fork Hawk Branch rises in n Yancey County and flows w to join Middle Fork Hawk Branch to form Hawk Branch.

South Fork Jones Creek rises in sw Anson County and flows ne to join North Fork Jones Creek to form Jones Creek.

South Fork Little Horse Creek rises near Apple Grove in nw Ashe County and flows e into Little Horse Creek.

South Fork Little River rises in n Orange County and flows se into nw Durham County where it joins North Fork Little River to form Little River.

South Fork Mountain Creek rises in e Catawba County and flows e to join North Fork Mountain Creek in forming Mountain Creek.

South Fork New River is formed in s Watauga County approx. 2 mi. se of town of Boone by the confluence of East Fork, Flannery Fork, and Middle Fork. It meanders ne to join North Fork New River in forming New River on the Ashe-Alleghany County line. See also East Fork [of South Fork New River]; Flannery Fork [of South Fork New River]; Middle Fork [of South Fork New River].

South Fork of James Cathey's Mill Creek. See Sloans Creek.

South Fork of Rattle Snake Creek rises in central Caswell County and flows nw to join North Fork of Ratttle Snake Creek in forming Rattle Snake Creek.

South Fork Rapier Mill Creek rises in sw Cherokee County and flows se and ne into Rapier Mill Creek after dipping in Fanin County, Ga.

South Fork Reddies River rises in western Wilkes County and flows se into Middle Fork Reddies River.

South Fork River. See South Fork Catawba River.

South Fork Rock Creek rises in s Yancey County and flows ne into Rock Creek.

South Fork [Second Creek]. See Back Creek.

South Fork [Skeenah Creek] rises in s Macon County and flows ne to join North Fork [Skeenah Creek] to form Skeenah Creek.

South Fork Township, s Forsyth County.

South Fork Township, w Tyrrell County.

South Fork Upper Creek rises in s Yancey County and flows se to join Middle Fork Upper Creek in forming Upper Creek.

South Fork Yadkin River. See Mill Fork; South Yadkin River.

South Gaston, former town in nw Halifax County on Roanoke River. Chartered 1895; charter repealed 1907. Appears as So. Gaston on the Colton map, 1861, but as Gaston on the Kerr map, 1882. It was at this point that passengers on the Raleigh and Gaston Railroad took a ferry across the Roanoke River to the town of Gaston before a railroad bridge spanned the river. The community of Thelma is now at this site.

South Gastonia, community in s Gaston County adjacent to the city of Gastonia. The former communities of Myers, Pinkney, and Ridge (originally Pleasant Ridge) are now considered to be parts of South Gastonia. Alt. 772.

South Harper Creek rises in se Avery County in Boone Wildlife Management Area and flows se to join North Harper Creek near the Caldwell County line to form Harper Creek.

South Henderson, uninc. outskirts of city of Henderson in s central Vance County.

South Hominy, community in sw Buncombe County near the junction of Glady Fork and South Hominy Creek.

South Hominy Creek rises in sw Buncombe County near Brooks Gap and flows ne into Hominy Creek.

South Hyco Creek rises in n Orange and se Caswell counties and flows ne into Person County where it joins North Hyco Creek to form Hyco River. That part of South Hyco Creek which lies in Caswell County is sometimes called Sugartree Creek.

South Lake, nw mainland of Dare County. It drains into Alligator River.

South Lake, artificial pond on Long Creek in s Vance County. Covers 14 acres with maximum depth of 15 ft. Originally named Beckham Millpond, and was formed sometime in the nineteenth century. Name was change in early 1940's when the lake was bought by South Lake, Inc., a social club. The mill is still standing; lake is used for recreation (fishing, swimming, boating). The name appeared on the soil survey map of 1913 as Beckon Mill.

South Leopard Creek, an inlet of North River into the mainland s of North Leopard Creek in e Carteret County.

South Lowell, community in nw Durham County between Buffalo and Horse creeks on the n side of North Fork Little River.

South Mills, town in nw Camden County, inc. 1883 but not active in municipal affairs. Prior to 1800 the community was known as New Lebanon because the stately junipers which formerly grew in this area adjacent to the Dismal Swamp suggested the Biblical reference to the tall cedars of Lebanon. Post office was New Lebanon from 1815 until 1839 when the name was changed to South Mills because waters from a spillway at the s end of the Dismal Swamp Canal were used to turn wheels of mills there.

South Mills Township, n Camden County.

Southmont, community in s Davidson County on High Rock Lake and the Winston-Salem Southbound Railroad. Post office here from about 1878 to 1905 was known as Fairmont. Re-est. as Southmont in 1910; probably named for the new Winston-Salem Southbound Railroad. Alt. 669.

South Mountains, a range of mountains extending from ne Rutherford into sw Burke and n Cleveland counties. Known by the Cherokee Indians as Oakanoahs.

South Mountains Wildlife Management Area, in se Burke County. 17,700 acres. Jointly owned by private interests and the town of Morganton. Est. 1952-1953.

South Muddy Creek rises in se McDowell County and flows ne to join North Muddy Creek near the Burke County line to form Muddy Creek.

South Point, n extremity of Pea Island in e Dare County. Lies at junction of Oregon Inlet and Atlantic Ocean.

South Point Township, se Gaston County.

Southport, town, se Brunswick County, on Cape Fear River. Fort Johnston, which

see, built here 1748-64. The town began to develop by 1792 and was named Smithville for General Benjamin Smith (1751-1826). Inc. 1805 and made county seat, 1808, until a new government center opened near Bolivia, 1978. Name changed to Southport in 1889 because it was the most southerly seaport in the state. Alt. 26.

South Prong, stream, rises in s Haywood County and flows ne into Shining Creek.

South Prong rises in s Transylvania County and flows ne into Little River.

South Prong [Clarks Creek] rises in n Mecklenburg County and flows e to join North Prong to form Clarks Creek.

South Prong Creek rises in e Guilford County and flows ne into sw Alamance County where it enters Stinking Quarter Creek.

South Prong [Glady Fork] rises in s Transylvania County on n slopes of Sassafras Mountain and flows ne and then nw to join West Prong [of Glady Fork] in forming Glady Fork. Also known as Kirkendall Creek.

South Prong Lewis Fork Creek rises in w Wilkes County and flows se approx. 9 mi. to join North Prong Lewis Fork Creek to form Lewis Fork Creek. Yates Mountain lies between the two prongs.

South Prong Stanley Creek rises in ne Gaston County and flows se into Dutchmans Creek.

South Prong Turkey Creek rises in n Transylvania County and flows se to join North Prong Turkey Creek in forming Turkey Creek.

South Prong West Branch rises in n Mecklenburg County and flows se into Rocky River.

South Prong [Wet Ash Swamp] rises in Green Swamp, w Brunswick County and flows nw into Wet Ash Swamp.

South River rises in n Carteret County and flows n approx. 9½ mi. into Neuse River. Appears on the Moseley map, 1733.

South River is formed on the Cumberland-Sampson County line by the junction of Black River and East Mingo Branch. It flows se along the Cumberland-Sampson and the Bladen-Sampson County lines into Black River near the Pender County line.

South River, community on the w side of South River, near its mouth, n Carteret County.

South River, community in n Rowan County on South Fork Yadkin River. Settled about 1800.

South River Township, sw Sampson County.

South Rocky Mount, the s part of Rocky Mount in w Edgecombe County.

South Rodanthe. *See* Waves.

South Salisbury, uninc. outskirts of city of Salisbury, e central Rowan County.

South Second Creek rises in s Rowan County and flows ne into High Rock Lake. Appears as Lower Second Creek on the Collet map, 1770; as Dutch Second Creek on the Price map, 1808, and the MacRae map, 1833; as Second Creek on the Kerr map, 1882; and as South Second Creek on recent maps.

South Shoal Creek. *See* Shoal Creek.

South Shore Parish. *See* St. Andrew's Parish; St. Paul's Parish.

Southside, community in central Lincoln County. Named for a mill built on the s side of Lincolnton in 1891. Alt. 753.

South Skitty Branch rises in e Macon County and flows sw into Cliffside Lake.

South Spring Top, on the Haywood-Transylvania County line.

South Stony Fork Creek rises in e Watauga County and flows se into Wilkes County and into Stony Fork Creek.

South Sunbury, community in central Gates County on Raynor Swamp.

South Toe River is formed in s Yancey County by the junction of Left Prong South Toe River and Right Prong South Toe River. It flows n to join North Toe River on the Mitchell-Yancey County line to form Toe River.

South Toe Township, s Yancey County.

South Tunis, community in e Hertford County.

South Turkey Creek rises on the Buncombe-Haywood County line near Turkey Creek Gap and flows ne to join North Turkey Creek in forming Turkey Creek.

South Virginia, a name frequently applied from about 1612 until about 1663 to the area which subsequently became the County of Albemarle in the colony of Carolina. William Strachey's *The Historie of Travell into Virginia Britannia* (1612) contains a brief description of South Virginia. After this region began to be settled (1650?-onward) it was also referred to as the Southern Plantation. In 1662 Samuel Stephens was made commander of the Southern Plantation by the Virginia Council.

South Wadesboro, town in central Anson County. Wadesboro Cotton Mill built here in 1892. Town inc. in 1893, but long inactive in municipal affairs.

South Washington, former town in n central Pender County on Washington Creek near its mouth in Northeast Cape Fear River. Laid out about 1740 by Malatiah Hamilton as the center of trade for the Welsh Tract, *which see.* Inc. 1791 as South Washington. About 1840 moved approx. 1½ mi. sw to a site on the newly completed railroad and came to be called Hiawatha, corrupted into Watha, *which see.*

Southwest Creek rises in n Carteret County and flows ne into South River.

Southwest Creek rises in sw Lenoir County and flows ne into Neuse River. Appears as Salmon Creek on the Moseley map, 1733; called Canterbury Creek by Governor Arthur Dobbs; and appears as Southwest Creek on the Collet map, 1770.

Southwest Creek rises in w Onslow County and flows se into New River. Appears on the Collet map, 1770.

South Westfield Township, e Surry County.

Southwest Fork [Alligator River] rises in s Tyrrell County near Alligator Lake and flows ne into Northwest Fork [Alligator River.]

South West Parish. *See* St. Paul's Parish; Society Parish.

Southwest Prong Branch rises in w central Carteret County and flows n into Moon Creek.

Southwest Stony Fork Creek rises in e Watauga County and flows se into w Wilkes County to enter Stony Fork Creek.

South West Township, e Lenoir County.

South Whitakers Township, ne Nash County.

South Williams Township, s Columbus County.

South Wilmington, uninc. outskirts of the city of Wilmington, w New Hanover County on the Cape Fear River.

Southwood, community in s Bladen County in Carvers Creek Township.

South Yadkin River rises in ne Alexander County and flows se across Iredell County and to the Davie-Rowan County line which it forms to its junction with Yadkin River. Also sometimes known as South Fork Yadkin River. *See also* Cedar Run Creek; Mill Fork. Appears as "Sapona or Yatkin River" on the Moseley map, 1733.

Sowell Run rises in s Greene County and

flows ne into Rainbow Creek. Named for the Sowell family which settled in the vicinity before the Revolution.

Sowell's Mill Creek. See Mill Creek.

Spaightville, a town inc. 1802 and authorized to be laid out on the "ne side of French Broad River . . . opposite, or a little above the upper Warm Springs" to accommodate visitors to the springs. It is not known whether this town ever existed, but it is reasonable to assume that the present Hot Springs (which see) in w Madison County is its "descendant." Spaightville was undoubtedly named for former governor Richard Dobbs Spaight (1758-1802), who died approx. two months before this act was passed.

Spain Branch rises in s Buncombe County and flows se into Avery Creek.

Spainhour Creek rises in central Caldwell County and flows sw approx. 4 mi. into Lower Creek.

Spains Creek rises in se Onslow County and flows sw into Sulliers Bay.

Spangenberg Creek. See Silas Creek.

Spanish Oak Branch rises in w central Transylvania County and flows s into Catheys Creek.

Spanish Oak Branch rises in n Watauga County and flows s into Buffalo Branch.

Spanish Oak Gap, s Haywood County on Shining Creek.

Spanish Oak Hill, sw Alamance County.

Spanish Oak Mountain, central Avery County.

Spanking Back Creek. See Silas Creek.

Sparkling Catawba Springs. See Catawba Springs.

Sparkman, community in w Onslow County.

Sparks Creek appears on the Collet map, 1770, in nw Davidson County n of Fryes Creek. It flows w into Muddy Creek. Not now identified.

Sparks Gap, central Mitchell County on Pumpkin Patch Mountain.

Sparks Ridge, e Mitchell County between Bear Creek and Bailey Meadows.

Sparta, town and county seat, central Alleghany County. Post office est. here as Bower's Store, 1825; name changed to Gap Civil, 1846, and to Sparta, 1879. Inc. 1879. Named for the ancient city in Greece. Alt. 2,939. Produces apparel and textiles. See also Gap Civil Township.

Sparta. See Old Sparta.

Sparta Mill Pond, central Alleghany County on Little River. Formed in 1920. Covers 8 acres; max. depth 10 ft. Fishing and swimming.

Sparta Township, former township in se Edgecombe County, now township number 8.

Spear, community in w Avery County, settled 1815-1830. Named for nearby Spear Tops Mountain.

Spear Tops Mountain on Avery-Mitchell County line. Named because of its two spear-shaped peaks.

Speed, town in e Edgecombe County, inc. 1901. Named for E. T. Speed.

Speedwell, community in w Jackson County on Tilley Creek.

Speights Bridge, former community in n Greene County on Contentnea Creek. Settled about 1751 by Speight family, some of whom operated a toll bridge here. Civil War muster grounds a short distance n. When Fieldsboro (now Walstonburg) developed during the 1880-1890 decade, Speights Bridge declined.

Speights Bridge Township, n Greene County.

Spence Field, bald spot on the Swain County, N. C.-Sevier County, Tenn., line in Great Smoky Mountains National Park near lat. 35° 33' 48" N., long. 83° 43' 58" W. Alt. 4,886.

Spencer, town in e Rowan County. Construction of shops for the Southern Railway begun here in 1896. Inc. in 1901 and named for Samuel Spencer (1847-1906), president of Southern Railway. Whiteheads Mill appears on Grants Creek near present site of Spencer on the Collet map, 1770. Alt. 747.

Spencer Mountain, e central Gaston County. WBTV (Charlotte) transmitting towers are here. Named for Zachariah Spencer, local Revolutionary Loyalist (Tory) who was captured during Revolution, tried and condemned to be shot. He turned "Whig" promising allegiance to the new republic; having no Bible, he took an oath on an almanac, and was released. Alt. 1,304.

Spencer Mountain, community immediately n of the mountain, e central Gaston County. Inc. 1895 as town of Spencer Mountain Mills. Charter repealed, 1909.

Spencers Fork, rises in ne Caldwell County and flows sw into Brumleys Creek.

Spences Corner, community in w Camden County, named for a pioneer family in the area and dates from about 1700.

Spero. See Balfours.

Spewmarrow Creek rises in n Granville

County and flows nw into Grassy Creek.

Spice Bottom Creek rises in sw Watauga County and flows ne into Watauga River.

Spice Cove, the valley through which Spice Cove Branch flows in n Buncombe County.

Spice Cove Branch rises near Louis Ray Knob in ne Buncombe County and flows nw through Spice Cove into North Fork Ivy Creek.

Spice Cove Branch rises in w Transylvania County and flows se into North Fork French Broad River.

Spice Creek rises in w Watauga County and flows ne into Laurel Creek.

Spicers Bay, s Onslow County in Stump Sound. Named for John Spicer.

Spices Cove, ne Buncombe County between Pinnacle Mountain and Dillingham Creek.

Spies (speece), community in nw Moore County.

Spikes Creek rises in sw Gates County and flows se into Chowan River.

Spillcorn Creek rises in n Madison County and flows sw into Big Laurel Creek. Said to have been named because an early settler spilled a load of corn in the creek.

Spindale, town in central Rutherford County. Est. 1916 by K. S. Tanner and named by him from its location in a valley where cotton mills were est. Inc. 1923. Isothermal Community College, est. 1966, is located here.

Spit Bay, between Davis Island and Davis Shore in Core Sound in e Carteret County.

Spivey Creek rises in nw Yancey County and flows nw into Tennessee where it enters Indian Creek.

Spivey Gap, central Buncombe County between Spivey and Miller Mountains.

Spivey Mountain, central Buncombe County n of Deaver View Mountain. Alt. 3,317.

Spiveys Corner, community in n Sampson County near Little Coharie Creek. Formerly known also as West Crossroads.

Spiveys Pond. See Lake Tabor.

Splash Dam Lake in e Transylvania County drains sw into Cascade Lake. Covers five acres and has a maximum depth of 30 ft.

Splashy. See Spray.

Split Mountain, e Haywood County between Fines Creek and the county line.

Split Whiteoak Ridge, w Macon County between Whiteoak Creek and Gold Pit Creek.

Spooks Branch rises in central Buncombe County near Lewis Gap and flows nw into Beaverdam Creek.

Spooners Bay, in Brown's Sound, s Onslow County. Probably named for Jabez Spooner, landowner in the vicinity by 1743. Sometimes mistakenly called Schooners Bay.

Spooners Creek rises in s Carteret County and flows s into Bogue Sound.

Spoonwater Creek rises in ne Person County and flows nw into Maho Creek. Said to have received its name because it is so shallow that anyone wanting water from it would have to use a spoon to dip it up.

Spot, community on Currituck Sound, s Currituck County. Formerly Hog Quarter but renamed, for the fish which is caught locally, when a post office was est. here about 1920.

Spot Knob, on Haywood-Jackson County line. Alt. 5,900-6,000.

Spout Branch rises in w Avery County and flows e into Roaring Creek.

Spout Branch rises in sw Madison County and flows se into Little Creek.

Spout Springs, community in sw Harnett County. Once the center of a great lumber and naval stores industry. Alt. approx. 330.

Sprawls Old Field. See Norman.

Spray, former town in n Rockingham County on Smith River. Settled about 1813 and known first as Splashy from the water thrown up by a water wheel at a local mill; name later changed to the more sophisticated Spray. Inc. 1951; merged with Leaksville and Draper in 1967 to form Eden, which see. Alt. 625.

Spread Branch rises in ne Swain County and flows n into Bunches Creek.

Spread Eagle Branch rises in ne Cherokee County and flows sw into Pile Creek.

Spring Bank, former plantation and ferry, central Wayne County on Neuse River midway between the mouths of Stoney and Sleepy creeks. Owned by Joseph Green, Sr., largest slaveowner in the county in 1790 and a member of the General Assembly. In 1784 Spring Bank was designated as a location for the receipt and inspection of tobacco. The Price map, 1808, shows only Green's Ferry at this location; a post office was in existence here in 1828.

Spring Branch rises in e Craven County and flows se into Broad Creek.

Spring Branch rises in w Franklin County and flows se into Little River.

Spring Branch rises in s Greene County and flows e into Tyson Marsh.

Spring Branch rises in e Johnston County and flows sw into Little River.

Spring Branch rises in s Lenoir County and flows nw into Southwest Creek.

Spring Branch rises in ne Onslow County and flows ne into Grants Creek.

Spring Branch rises in central Wake County and flows nw into House Creek.

Spring Branch rises in sw Wilson County and flows se into Black Creek.

Spring Creek rises in w Alexander County and flows sw into Lower Little River.

Spring Creek rises in se Brunswick County and flows se into Walden Creek.

Spring Creek rises in nw Columbus County near the Bladen County line and flows ne into Horsepen Creek.

Spring Creek rises in sw Madison County and flows ne into French Broad River.

Spring Creek rises in n Mitchell County and flows se into Big Rock Creek.

Spring Creek rises in e Pamlico County and flows ne into Bonner Bay.

Spring Creek, community in se Beaufort County.

Spring Creek, community in w Madison County on Spring Creek.

Spring Creek. See Florence.

Spring Creek Gap, on the Haywood-Madison County line.

Spring Creek Mountain extends ne from Friezeland Creek in s Madison County to Rector Branch. Hop Mountain with an alt. of 4,072 ft. is a peak on this mountain.

Spring Creek Township, former township in sw Madison County, now township number 8.

Springers Point, point of land from Ocracoke Island, near community of Ocracoke, extending into Pamlico Sound, se Hyde County.

Springfield, community in w Scotland County on Gum Swamp Creek.

Springfield, community in n Wilkes County on North Prong Roaring River.

Spring Garden, community in nw Craven County on Neuse River. A farming area which has retained the name of the plantation of Gov. Richard Dobbs Spaight.

Spring Garden. See Castle Hayne.

Spring Hill, community in e Halifax County. Alt. 70.

Spring Hill, community in e Haywood County on Garden Creek.

Spring Hill Plantation. See East Spencer.

Spring Hill Township, ne Scotland County.

Springhill Township, sw Wilson County.

Spring Hope, community in e Craven County.

Spring Hope, town in w Nash County. Inc. 1889. Previously located approx. 4 mi. se, but moved here after a railroad was constructed in 1886-87. Said to have been named by early settlers who hoped a spring nearby would always provide water for the community. Produces lumber and apparel. Alt. 261.

Springhouse Ridge, e Clay County between Arch and Bruce ridges.

Spring Lake, town in nw Cumberland County near e limits of Fort Bragg Military Reservation. Inc. 1951. See also Manchester.

Spring Mountain, ne Alexander County. Alt. 1,620.

Spring Mountain, se Buncombe County between Laughter Cove and Cane Creek.

Spring Mountain, sw Buncombe County ne of Twelve O'Clock Top.

Spring Mountain on the Madison County, N. C.-Greene County, Tenn., line.

Spring Mountain Branch rises in se Buncombe County and flows sw into Cane Creek.

Spring Point, central Onslow County in Farnell Bay of New River.

Spring Shoals. See McAdenville.

Sprinkle Branch rises in central Madison County on the w slope of High Rock Ridge and flows se 1½ mi. to empty into Walnut Creek at the community of Walnut Creek.

Sprinkle Cove, ne Buncombe County near the junction of Walker and Dillingham creeks.

Sprinkle Creek rises in e Madison County and flows se into California Creek.

Spruce Fork rises in ne Buncombe County and flows sw into Beetree Creek.

Spruce Knob, s Watauga County nw of White Rock Ridge.

Spruce Mountain, Haywood and Swain counties, Great Smoky Mountains National Park, on Balsam Mountain, near lat. 35° 36' 48" N., long. 83° 10' 34" W. Alt. 5,590.

Spruce Mountain Ridge, western Haywood County, Great Smoky Mountains National Park, a spur extending e from Spruce Mountain on Balsam Mountain, center near lat. 35° 36' 40" N., long. 83° 09' 05" W.

Spruce Pine, town in s Mitchell County on North Toe River. Alt. 2,620. Inc. 1907. Named for a large Carolina hemlock, locally called spruce pine, which grew near a tavern operated by Isaac English. Produces apparel, hosiery, textiles, minerals, and lumber.

Spruce Pine Cove, n Buncombe County between Wiley Mountain and Coles Cove.

Spruce Pine Mountain, sw Avery County.

Spruce Pine Ridge, ne Buncombe County between Waterfall and Carter creeks.

Spruce Pinnacle, ne Buncombe County on Big Fork Ridge.

Spruce Ridge, s Haywood County between Cherry Cove Creek and Shiny Creek.

Spruills Bridge, e Washington County, se of Creswell. First known as Samuel Spruills Landing; designated by the General Assembly in 1740 as a point for a warehouse for receipt and shipping of crown quitrents. Called Spruills Landing as late as 1812.

Spurgeon, community in s Wilkes County near Hunting Creek.

Spurgeon Creek rises in ne Davidson County and flows s into Abbotts Creek.

Spur Ridge, e Mitchell County parallel to Green Cove Creek.

Spurrier, community in w Mecklenburg County.

Squally Creek rises in w Graham County and flows e into West Buffalo Creek.

Squhawky. See Williamston.

Squirrel Branch rises in sw Gaston County and flows ne into Crowders Creek.

Squirrel Branch rises in n Guilford County and flows e into Reedy Fork Creek.

Squirrel Branch rises in w Madison County near Squirrels Gap and flows w into Spring Creek.

Squirrel Creek rises in central Avery County and flows w into North Toe River.

Squirrel Creek rises in w Lenoir County and flows n into Neuse River.

Squirrel Gap, n Transylvania County between Laurel Brook and South Fork Mills River.

Squirrels Gap, w Madison County on the sw end of Hot Springs Mountain.

Squyars Canal. See New Lake Fork.

Stacey Creek rises in se Avery County and flows nw into Linville River.

Staceyville. See Stacy.

Stackhouse, community in n Madison County on French Broad River at the mouth of Woolsey Branch. Alt. 1,418.

Stacy, community in ne Carteret County on a point of land extending into Core Sound from the mainland. Was called Piney Point prior to 1888.

Stacy, community in e Rockingham County. Named for a local family. Appears as Staceyville on an 1860 map.

Stafford Hill, peak in the Cane Creek Mountains, s Alamance County.

Staffords Creek rises in s Caldwell County and flows s into Catawba River on the Burke-Caldwell County line. Formerly also known as James Mill Creek and McCalls Mill Creek.

Staffords Mill, community in nw Guilford County near Oak Ridge. Called Saunders Mill during the American Revolution. Cornwallis' troops ground corn here.

Stag Creek rises in ne Alamance County and flows s into Back Creek.

Stagg Creek rises in nw Ashe County and flows se into North Fork New River.

Stagger Weed Creek rises in e Mitchell County and flows nw to join Mine Fork Branch to form Right Fork [Cane Creek].

Stag Park, community and former plantation, central Pender County on the Northeast Cape Fear River. Named in 1663 by Barbadian explorers for park-like terrain on which they saw deer feeding. Appears on the Ogilby map, 1671. Gov. George Burrington, about 1730, acquired 10,000 acres here where he built a summer home.

Stagville. See Fairntosh.

Staircase Mountain, nw Caldwell County near Maple Grove.

Staire Branch rises in ne Buncombe County and flows nw into Walker Branch.

Stairs Mountain, s Haywood County on the head of Crawford Creek. Alt. 5,869.

Stairwalk Ridge, se Buncombe County e of Potato Knob.

Stairway Falls, sw Transylvania County in Horsepasture River downstream from High Falls.

Stalcup Top, s Cherokee County near the headwaters of Little Brasstown Creek.

Staley, town in e Randolph County. Post office est. here in 1883 as Staleyville. Inc. 1901 as Staley. Named for Colonel John W. Staley, Confederate soldier. Alt. 725.

Staley Creek rises in central Alamance County and flows ne into Servis Creek.

Staleyville. See Staley.

Stallings, community in e Franklin County. Alt. 347. Est. 1880. Named for J. M.

Stallings, who established a cotton gin
and sawmill here.

Stallings, community in nw Union County.

Stallings Crossroads, community in nw
Beaufort County.

Stallings Station. See Clayton.

Stamey Cove, e Haywood County on the
head of Stamey Cove Branch.

Stamey Cove Branch rises in e Haywood
County and flows se into Pigeon River.

Stamey Cove Gap, e Haywood County on
the sw end of Anderson Mountain.

Stamper, community in s Halifax County.

Stamy Knob, central Clay County between
Peckerwood Creek and Cold Branch.

Stancell. See Oak Grove.

Standard, community in w Pitt County.
Alt. 74.

Standhill Mountain, sw Buncombe County
n of Buzzard Knob.

Standing Indian, peak on the Clay-Macon
County line. The Indian name was
Yunwitsulenunyi, "where the man stood."
Alt. 5,500. The peak has been called
"the grandstand of the southern Appa-
lachians."

Standing Indian Wildlife Management Area,
se Clay County.

Standingstone Mountain, at the junction of
the lines of Henderson and Transylvania
counties, N. C., and Greenville County,
S. C.

Stanfield, town in sw Stanly County. Inc.
1955.

Stanfield Branch rises in n Buncombe County and flows w into Dick Branch.

Stanford. See Burgaw.

Stanhope, community in s Nash County.
Was site of pre-Civil War Stanhope
Academy. Community of Old Stanhope,
about 2 mi. w, was a stop on the Raleigh-
Tarboro stage line. Named for Stanhope
Crenshaw who operated the old stage
line prior to 1896.

Stanley, town in n Gaston County. Inc.
1897 as Brevard Station and named for
Robert Alexander Brevard who gave land
in 1861 for railroad station. Renamed
Stanley Creek, 1893, and Stanley in 1911.
Produces zippers and textiles. Alt. 852.

Stanley Branch rises in n Buncombe County near Lankford Mountain and flows
w into Dick Branch.

Stanley Creek rises in ne Gaston County
and flows se into Dutchmans Creek.

Stanley Creek. See Stanley.

Stanleyville, community in n central Forsyth County.

Stanly County was formed in 1841 from
Montgomery County. Located in the central section of the state, it is bounded
by Montgomery, Richmond, Anson, Union,
Cabarrus, and Rowan counties. It was
named for John Stanly (1774-1834), member of the General Assembly, several
times speaker of the House of Commons,
and member of Congress. Area: 406 sq.
mi. County seat: Albemarle with an elevation of 505 ft. Townships are Almond,
Big Lick, Center, Endy, Furr, Harris,
North Albemarle, Ridenhour, South Albemarle, and Tyson. Produces wheat, oats,
corn, lespedeza, poultry, eggs, dairy products, hogs, livestock, textiles, bakery
products, furniture, aluminum, lumber,
brick, and crushed stone.

Stansbury, community in s central Brunswick County.

Stansfield Branch rises in e Macon County
and flows n into Cullasaja River.

Stanton. See South Creek.

Stanton-Harrold. See South Creek.

Stantonsburg, town in se Wilson County on
Contentnea Creek. Alt. 92. Inc. 1817.
Post office name in 1828 was Stanton-
burgh. Named for Willie J. Stanton, one
on the first commissioners, or James
Stanton, first mayor. The former community of Moyton, named for Francis
M. Moye, on the e outskirts of the town
is now considered to be a part of Stantonsburg.

Stantonsburg Township, s Wilson County.

Stanton's Gut, begins in se Wilson County
at the ne outskirts of Stantonsburg and
runs sw into Contentnea Creek after a
course of approx. 2 mi.

Stanton Township, w Wilkes County.

Star, town in e Montgomery County. Inc.
1897. Named by Angus Leach, local merchant, because of the high elevation of
the site, visible from all directions. Known
first as Hunsucker's Store. Alt. 637. Produces textiles and hosiery.

Star Branch rises near Oaks Knob, w Avery
County, and flows ne into Roaring Creek.

Star Branch rises in n central Yancey County and flows nw into Jacks Creek.

Star Hollow, valley of Star Branch, w Avery County.

Starkey Gap, on the Swain County, N. C.,-Sevier County, Tenn., line in the Great Smoky Mountains National Park near lat. 35° 34' 12" N., long. 83° 40' 15" W.

Starkey Ridge, n Swain County in Great Smoky Mountains National Park, near lat. 35° 32' 58" N., long. 83° 37' 47" W.

Starkeys Creek rises in w Carteret County and flows s approx. 3 mi. into Pettivers Creek. Named for John Starkey, colonial treasurer and member of the Assembly.

Starkeys Creek rises in ne Onslow County and flows se into White Oak River. Formerly called Great Swamp. Probably named for John Starkey, pioneer settler.

Starkey's Hammock. See The Hammock.

Starling, community in se Onslow County near the head of Queens Creek. Named for Sam Starling.

Starling's Bridge. See Falcon.

Starnes Branch rises in central Transylvania County and flows s into Davidson River.

Starnes Cove, central Buncombe County nw of Starnes Ridge.

Starnes Ridge, central Buncombe County w of Ragsdale Creek.

Star Peak, See Fox Knob.

Starretts Meadows, e Onslow County between the head of Wallace Creek and the head of Bear Creek.

Startown, community in central Catawba County. Named for pioneer Starr family. Earlier known as Danville.

State Line Gap, on the Watauga County, N. C.-Johnson County, Tenn., line near the head of Little Beaverdam Creek. Alt. 3,738.

State Line Ridge on the Watauga County, N. C.-Johnson County, Tenn., line extends se from State Line Gap to the head of Cove Creek.

State Ridge in the n tip of Cherokee County along the North Carolina-Tennessee state line.

State Road, community in w Surry County near the head of Camp Creek. Said to have taken its name from a "state road camp" established here temporarily during the construction of a highway.

Statesville, city and county seat central Iredell County. Authorized to be laid out in 1789 and probably named in honor of the fact that North Carolina had approved the Federal Constitution a few

weeks previously and thus become a State. Inc. 1847. Settlement grew up around Fourth Creek Presbyterian Church organized here in 1753. Home of Mitchell College. Produces textiles, apparel, fabricated metals, furniture, flour, lumber, and machinery. Alt. 925. See also Fourth Creek.

Statesville Township, central Iredell County.

Staton, community in n Pitt County. Alt. 42.

Statons Pond, central Martin County, is fed by the waters of several streams: Hardison Mill Creek, Ready Branch, and Smithwick Creek. It is drained by Sweetwater Creek. The pond is approx. 2 mi. long.

Stauken's Quarter Creek. See Stinking Quarter Creek.

Staunton, community in w Wilkes County on North Prong Lewis Fork Creek.

Staunton. See Kittrell.

Steadmans Creek rises in central Stokes County and flows n into Dan River.

Steadmans Lake, formed by a dam across Steadmans Creek, central Stokes County. Covers about 15 acres; max. depth 30 ft. Owned by Izaak Walton League of America.

Stearns, community in w central Polk County.

Stecoah, community in e Graham County on Stecoah Creek. Alt. 2,030. Name derived from Cherokee word stika'yi, the meaning of which Mooney believed to be lost though thought by local residents to mean "lean" in the sense of "no game."

Stecoah Creek rises in e Graham County and flows ne into Little Tennessee River.

Stecoah Gap, e Graham County between the headwaters of Sweetwater Creek and Stecoah Creek.

Stecoah Township, ne Graham County.

Stedman, town in e Cumberland County. Inc. 1913. Named for Major Charles M. Stedman (1841-1930), president of the North Carolina Railroad and member of Congress. The nineteenth-century community (with a post office) of Blocker's or Blockersville was at or near the site of Stedman.

Steeds, community in ne Montgomery County. Named in 1898 for J. W. Steeds, local merchant. Alt. 662.

Steel Creek rises in s Transylvania County and flows sw into Little River.

Steele Creek, community in sw Mecklenburg County. Steele Creek Presbyterian

Church here was organized in 1760. A post office was established here as early as 1828.

Steele Creek rises in w Mecklenburg County and flows s into South Carolina where it enters Catawba River. The name appears on the Collet map, 1770, but applied to the head of present Kings Branch. Named for Moses Steele.

Steele Creek Township, former township in sw Mecklenburg County, now township number 3.

Steele Township, w central Rowan County. Named for Gen. John Steele (176.-1815).

Steeles Mill. See Cordova.

Steeles Township, nw Richmond County.

Steelman Creek rises in s Yadkin County and flows se into n Davie County where it enters Dutchmans Creek.

Steels Creek rises in nw Burke County and flows se into Upper Creek. Flows between Tettered Rock Ridge and Rip Skin Ridge.

Steeltrap Creek rises in n Swain County in Great Smoky Mountains National Park and flows sw into Forney Creek.

Steeltrap Knob, in s Macon County between Bearpen Mountain and Mooney Branch.

Steel Trap Ridge extends from central Cherokee County ne to n Cherokee County between Bald and Hanging Dog creeks.

Steep Hill Branch rises in w Carteret County and flows w approx. 3 mi. into White Oak River.

Steep Hill Branch rises in w Johnston County and flows se into Middle Creek. Mentioned in local records as early as 1770.

Steep Point extends from the mainland of ne Carteret County into Core Sound.

Steep Rock Mountain, peak in w Randolph County.

Steer Gap, e Haywood County between Hungry Creek and Pisgah Creek.

Steestachee Bald, on the Haywood-Jackson County line. Alt. 5,700. Named for the Indian word for rats or nest of rats. Indian hunters are said to have found and destroyed a nest of rats here.

Steestachee Branch rises near Steestachee Bald in sw Haywood County and flows e into Allen Creek.

Stella, community in w Carteret County on White Oak River. Alt. 30, the highest point in the county. Originally named Barkers Bridge in honor of a local doctor, but when a post office was est. the Post Office Department declined to accept the name.

Stem, town in s Granville County. Inc. 1911. Named for a local family. The area was first served by the Tally Ho post office, one mi. ne. In 1889, however, the post office was moved here and the name changed. Alt. 470. See also Tally Ho.

Stephens Creek rises in s Macon County and flows ne into Cullasaja River.

Stephens Crossroads, community in n Rockingham County.

Stephenson's Lake, a spring-fed lake covering 35 acres, 2 mi. e of Garysburg, w Northampton County. Numerous wild ducks and geese winter here each year.

Stephens Swamp rises in e Duplin County and flows sw into Muddy Creek.

Stepp Branch rises in se Buncombe County and flows nw into Swannanoa River.

Stepp's Cove, on the s side of Point Lookout in ne Henderson County about 1½ mi. e of community of Edneyville. Named for Fannie Stepp, who, according to legend, was scalped here by Cherokee warriors in 1779. They then burned her son while she watched, and the heat from that fire is still supposed to keep the cove warm.

Stepps Gap, on Kings Mountain on Cleveland-Gaston County line. Alt. 1,040.

Stepps Gap, s Yancey County in the Black Mountains between Mount Gibbes and Mount Mitchell. Named for Jesse Stepp who guided the geographer Arnold Guyot through the area when he mapped it in 1860.

Sterlings Township, se Robeson County.

Steve Branch rises in n Clay County and flows se into Tuni Creek.

Steve Branch rises in w Madison County and flows se into Spring Creek.

Stevens. See Stevens Mill.

Stevens Branch rises in ne Clay County and flows e into Clear Creek.

Stevens Cove, s Madison County at the head of Little Pine Creek.

Stevens Creek rises in n Haywood County and flows ne into Pigeon River.

Stevens Creek rises in se Mecklenburg County and flows s into Union County where it enters Duck Creek.

Stevens Creek rises in e Onslow County and flows se into White Oak River.

Stevens Mill, community in nw Union

County on Goose Creek. Formerly called Stevens.

Stevens Mill, community in w Wayne County on Thoroughfare Swamp.

Stevenson Branch rises in w central Swain County on Cooper Mountain and flows sw into Greasy Branch.

Steward Millpond in nw Union County in Goose Creek.

Stewards Creek. See Stewart Creek.

Stewart Branch rises in ne Cherokee County and flows sw into Valley River.

Stewart Cove, e Macon County between Buck Creek and Little Buck Creek.

Stewart Creek rises se of the town of Warsaw in w Duplin County and flows sw into Six Runs Creek in e Sampson County. Appears as Stewards Creek on the Collet map, 1770.

Stewart Creek rises in n Mecklenburg County and flows s to join Taggart Creek to form Sugar Creek.

Stewart Creek rises in Virginia and flows se into Surry County where it enters Ararat River.

Stewart Mountain, sw Cherokee County, extends se into Fannin County, Ga.

Stewart Ridge, ne Cherokee County in the Snowbird Mountains.

Stewarts Creek rises in w Cumberland County and flows se into Beaver Creek.

Stewarts Creek rises in w Forsyth County and flows se into Muddy Creek. Until some time prior to 1762 it was known as Tomahawk Branch. In that year Joseph Stewart settled near its banks and it presumably took his name. It appears as Stewarts Creek on the Collet map, 1770, but small streams flowing into it are still known as Tomahawk Creek and Little Tomahawk Creek.

Stewarts Creek rises in s Harnett County and flows se into Little River.

Stewarts Creek rises in e Hoke County and flows se onto Cumberland-Hoke County line and into Rockfish Creek.

Stewarts Creek rises in n central Union County and flows se and ne into Richardson Creek.

Stewarts Creek Township, s Harnett County.

Stewarts Creek Township, n Surry County.

Stewarts Ferry. See Hickory Grove Crossroads.

Stewart's Pond. See Ravenel Lake.

Stewart's Town, town inc. in 1799 "between Peedee and Markees's Creek" in Richmond County to encourage navigation on the Pee Dee River. Apparently it was never laid out but there may have been some relationship between plans for it and the Stewartsville of a somewhat later date in adjoining Scotland County.

Stewartsville, former community in se Scotland County. A post office by this name existed as early as 1833. In the 1890's Stewart was a station on what is now the Seaboard Coast Line Railroad. A cemetery called "Stewartsville" in the vicinity bears the inscription "Founded 1785." See also Stewart's Town.

Stewartsville Township, se Scotland County.

Stice Dam, on Broad River, s Cleveland County, provides power for mills in Shelby. Stice's Shoal community was here in the late nineteenth century.

Stice's Shoal. See Stice Dam.

Stiff Knee Knob, sw Madison County at the head of Sugar Camp Branch.

Stiles, community in n Macon County between Bird Branch and Burningtown Creek.

Still Bluff, community in sw Pender County on a bluff overlooking Black River. Named from the fact that it is a still (quiet) spot on a bluff.

Still Branch rises in se Yancey County and flows ne into Roaring Fork.

Still Creek rises in w Carteret County and flows w into White Oak River. Named because a whiskey still was once located on the creek.

Stilley, community s Beaufort County.

Stillhouse Branch rises in s Avery County and flows nw into Whiteoak Branch.

Stillhouse Branch rises in central Cherokee County and flows se into Valley River.

Stillhouse Branch rises in n Macon County and flows w into Rose Creek.

Stillhouse Branch rises in s Macon County and flows sw into Tessentee Creek.

Stillhouse Branch rises in s Madison County and flows s into Ivy River.

Stillhouse Creek rises in central McDowell County and flows s into Paxton Creek.

Stillwater Branch in w central Transylvania County and flows n into Davidson River.

Stillwater Creek. See Island Creek.

Stillwell Creek rises in ne Swain County in Great Smoky Mountains National Park and flows sw into Straight Fork of Raven Fork Creek.

Stinking Creek rises in s Chatham County and flows se into Haw River.

Stinking Quarter Creek rises in s Guilford County and flows ne into Alamance County where it enters Great Alamance Creek. Appears on the Collet map, 1770. Name said to have been derived from the fact that Indians cleaned animals here and left quarters of meat to spoil. Caruthers, writing in 1856, said it was formerly known as Stauken's Quarter Creek, presumably, therefore, named for a grant of land to a pioneer settler.

Stirewalt Creek rises in central Alexander County a short distance s of Taylorsville and flows s into Lower Little River.

Stirrup Iron Creek rises in se Durham County and flows se into w Wake County where it enters Crabtree Creek.

Stockade Mountain, sw Cherokee County along the Nottely River se of Die Bend.

Stocking Head Creek rises in central Duplin County and flows se into Northeast Cape Fear River.

Stokes, town in n Pitt County. Settled about 1880. Inc. 1903. Named for William G. Stokes, local landowner. Alt. 56.

Stokesbury. See Walnut Cove.

Stokes County was formed in 1789 from Surry County. Located in the n central section of the state, it is bounded by the state of Virginia, and by Rockingham, Forsyth, and Surry counties. It was named for Captain John Stokes (1756-90), Revolutionary officer, member of the House of Commons and of the Convention of 1789. Area: 458 sq. mi. County seat: Danbury with an elevation of 825 ft. Townships are Beaver Island, Big Creek, Danbury, Meadows, Peters Creek, Quaker Gap, Sauratown, Snow Creek, and Yadkin. Produces tobacco, corn, wheat, oats, poultry, eggs, dairy products, hogs, livestock, motor vehicle parts, brick, and crushed stone.

Stokesdale, town in nw Guilford County. Alt. 950. Inc. 1907. Known earlier as Pine; renamed probably for Governor Montford Stokes (1762-1842).

Stokes Mill Run rises in e Sampson County and flows e into Duplin County where it enters Stewart Creek.

Stocksville, community in n Buncombe County. A post office existed here as early as 1882; closed 1958.

Stockton Cove, n Buncombe County between Morgan Ridge and Morgan Branch.

Stone Creek rises in sw Henderson County and flows se into Rock Creek.

Stone Creek rises in sw Johnston County and flows e into Mill Creek.

Stonecutter Creek rises in central Rutherford County and flows sw into Cleghorn Creek. Named for a stonecutter who lived along its banks and cut millstones.

Stonehead. See Pilot Mountain.

Stonehouse, home of William Person, member of the Provincial Congress, in ne Warren County on Stonehouse Creek. The house, which is still standing, dates from 1746.

Stonehouse Creek rises in e Warren County near the town of Vaughn and flows ne into Gaston Lake. Appears on the Price map, 1808, and the MacRae map, 1833. Sometimes referred to locally as Big Stonehouse Creek.

Stone Mountain on the Alleghany-Wilkes County line. Alt. 3,879.

Stone Mountain, se Buncombe County n of Jarvis Mountain. Alt. 3,700.

Stone Mountain, at the head of Jim Creek in sw Henderson County. Alt. 3,647.

Stone Mountain, w Transylvania County s of Butter Gap. Alt. 3,698.

Stone Mountain, ne Watauga County e of Grassy Creek.

Stone Mountain Bald, on the Watauga County, N. C.-Johnson County, Tenn., line at the n end of Stone Mountains, which see. Alt. 4,657.

Stone Mountain Branch rises in nw Watauga County in the Stone Mountains and flows sw into Watauga River.

Stone Mountain Creek rises in s Alleghany County and flows sw into northern Wilkes County where it enters Bullhead Creek.

Stone Mountain Gap, se Buncombe County between Stone and Round Mountains.

Stone Mountains, a chain of mountains in w Ashe and Watauga counties and in Johnson County, Tennessee, from the Watauga River near lat. 36° 17′ 30″ N., long. 81° 55′ W., to the nw corner of North Carolina and thence in Virginia to Whitetop Mountain. They form the common boundary line of North Carolina and Tennessee. The name dates from as early as 1795.

Stones Bay, in New River in s Onslow County. Mentioned in local records as early as 1748 as Stones Creek Bay. Named for William Stone, an early surveyor in the county.

Stones Creek rises in s Onslow County and flows ne approx. 10 mi. into Stones Bay. Mentioned in local records as early as 1744. Named for William Stone, an early surveyor in the county.

Stones Creek Bay. *See* Stones Bay.

Stones Island. *See* Huggins Island.

Stones Knob, se Yancey County between Clear and Crabtree creeks.

Stoneville, town in w Rockingham County. Said to have been founded in 1857 by the Rev. Frank J. Stone and Pinckney M. Stone, the latter operator of a general store at the site. Inc. 1877. Alt. 823.

Stonewall, town in central Pamlico County on Bay River, Inc. 1857 as Jackson and apparently named for the owner of a local mill. Name changed to Stonewall, 1871, to honor General T. J. ("Stonewall") Jackson (1824-63). Long inactive in municipal affairs. Alt. 10.

Stonewall Township, se Hoke County.

Stoney Creek rises in ne Mecklenburg County and flows se into Mallard Creek.

Stoney Mountain, central Henderson County between Mill Pond Creek and Mud Creek. Alt. 2,843.

Stoney Run rises in w Cleveland County and flows se into First Broad River.

Stoney Town Creek. *See* Stonyton Creek.

Stonington Creek. *See* Stonyton Creek.

Stony Bald on the Buncombe-Henderson County line ne of Cutthroat Gap. Alt. 4,563.

Stony Creek rises in n central Bertie County and flows n into Hertford County where it enters Ahoskie Creek.

Stony Creek is formed in ne Buncombe County by the junction of Carter and Mineral creeks. It flows n into Dillingham Creek.

Stony Creek rises in s Caswell County and flows s into Alamance County where it enters Haw River. Appears as Marrow Bone River on the Moseley map, 1733.

Stoney Creek rises in s Hertford County and flows in an inverted arc into Ahoskie Swamp. Stony Bridge appears on the Moseley map, 1733, as spanning this stream s of the present town of Ahoskie. Appears as Stony Creek Bridge on the Collet map, 1770; as Bonner Bridge on MacRae, 1833; and as Jernigan's Bridge on soil survey map, 1916.

Stony Creek rises in e Lee County and flows nw into Lick Creek.

Stony Creek, formed in w Nash County by the junction of Big and Little Peachtree creeks, flows se into Tar River. Appears on the Collet map, 1770.

Stony Creek rises in e Orange County and flows ne into Eno River.

Stony Creek rises in e Surry County and flows sw into Ararat River.

Stony Creek rises in central Wayne County and flows sw into Neuse River. Named in local records as early as 1756. The name appears as Rocky Creek on the Price map, 1808.

Stony Creek, community in s Caswell County. A post office was operated here during the approx. period 1820-1905.

Stony Creek. *See* Stony Fork Creek.

Stony Creek Lake. *See* Lake Burlington.

Stony Creek Mountain, high grounds on the Caswell-Alamance County line.

Stony Creek Township, sw Caswell County.

Stony Creek Township, e Nash County.

Stony Creek Township, central Wayne County.

Stony Fork rises in sw Buncombe County near Little Pisgah Mountain and flows n into Warren Creek.

Stony Fork, community in sw Buncombe County on Stony Fork near the mouth of McKinney Creek. Alt. 2,368.

Stony Fork rises in w Johnston County and flows se into Hannah Creek.

Stony Fork, community in e Watauga County near the head of Stony Fork Creek.

Stony Fork Branch rises in ne Buncombe County and flows sw into North Fork [Swannanoa River].

Stony Fork Creek rises in e Watauga County and flows se into w Wilkes County to enter Yadkin River. Also known as Stony Creek.

Stony Fork Township, e Watauga County.

Stony Hill, community in nw Wilkes County on North Prong Lewis Fork Creek.

Stony Knob, n Buncombe County between Wagner Branch and Reems Creek.

Stony Knob, on the Buncombe-Henderson County line between High Top and Luther Gap.

Stony Knob, on the McDowell-Mitchell County line between Gillespie Gap and Little Switzerland. Alt. approx. 3,330.

Stony Knoll, community in s Surry County

between Fisher River and West Double
Creek. Alt. 1,194.

Stony Mountain, e Madison County between Chandler Creek and the head of
California Creek.

Stony Mountain, range about 1½ mi. long
in e Stanly County on w bank of Pee
Dee River.

Stony Mountain Ridge, ne Swain County in
the shape of an inverted "S" between
Poplar Hollow Branch and a bend in
Raven Fork.

Stony Point, community in se Alexander
County. Site settled 1789. Stony Point
post office est. 1826 but operated in different homes, stores, etc., within a radi-
ous of about two mi. In 1887 a railroad
station, Sloan or Sloans Station, was
opened, but the community soon came to
be known by the official post office name,
Stony Point. Named for rocky formation
at the site. Alt. 1,090. Produces textiles.

Stony Point, community in e Cleveland
County.

Stony Ridge, se Surry County, extends ne
between Yadkin River and Grassy Creek.

Stony Run rises in w Stanly County and
flows se into Big Bear Creek.

Stony Spur, w Madison County between
Little Bottom Branch and John Taylor
Branch.

Stonyton Creek rises in n Lenoir County
and flows se into Neuse River. Now frequently appears as Stonington Creek but
first called the Stoney Town Creek in the
1730's because it was near an Indian
town on a hill with outcroppings of slate
and sandstone.

Stony Valley, in e Mitchell County between
Bee Ridge and Middle Mountain.

Store Point, peninsula extending off the w
side of Goose Creek Island into Goose
Creek, ne Pamlico County.

Storey Branch rises in s Watauga County
and flows nw into Days Creek.

Story Mountain, n Caldwell County. Named
for the Storie family, local residents.

Storys, community in w Gates County,
formerly known as Storys Crossroads.

Storys Creek rises in central Person County
and flows ne into Marlowe Creek.

Storys Crossroads. *See* Storys.

Stott Knob, central Surry County between
Turner Mountain and Beaver Creek. Alt.
1,550.

Stotts Crossroads, community in nw Wilson
County e of Marsh Swamp. Named for
Godfrey Stott.

Stouts, community in w Union County, 2

mi. se of town of Indian Trail. Inc. 1907;
charter repealed 1917. Alt. 658.

Stovall, town in ne Granville County. Inc.
1883 as Sassafras Fork, named for large
sassafras trees at the crossroads. Name
changed in 1889 for John W. Stovall who
gave land for the railroad station. Alt.
478. Produces lumber.

Stover Ridge, mountain in central Avery
County.

Stowe's Hills. *See* Frisco.

Strabane, community in w Lenoir County.
Named for home in Ireland of early
settler.

Stradley Mountain, s Buncombe County,
extends from Little Hickory Top to Rice
Pinnacle.

Straight Creek rises in ne Buncombe County and flows nw into North Fork Ivy
Creek.

Straight Creek, w Haywood County, Great
Smoky Mountains National Park, rises
near lat. 35° 34' 37" N., long. 83° 09'
36" W., and flows e into Caldwell Fork.

Straight Fork rises in ne Swain County in
Great Smoky Mountain National Park
and flows s and sw into Raven Fork.

The Straits, straits in the waters between
North River and Core Sound in se Carteret County, between Harkers Island
and the mainland.

Straits, community in se Carteret County
on a point of land extending into the
mouth of North River.

Straits Township, on The Straits in central
Carteret County. At one time a portion
of Straits was called number 5 township.
From Straits were formed Carteret and
number 9 townships (both now abolished)
and Merrimon.

Strange Branch rises in ne Cherokee County and flows se into Big Cove Branch.

Strangenbergs Creek. *See* Silas Creek.

Stratford, community in w central Alleghany County.

Stratton Bald, w Graham County at nw end
of Horse Cove Ridge. Alt. approx. 5,380.

Stratton Branch rises in nw Swain County
and flows se into Lake Cheoah.

Straw, community in s Wilkes County near
East Prong Cub Creek.

Strawberry Branch rises in e Lenoir County in the n part of Ball Pocosin and flows
n into Southwest Creek.

Strawberry Knob, on the Graham County,
N. C.-Monroe County, Tenn., line.

Strawberry Knob, on the Haywood-Swain
County line, Great Smoky Mountains
National Park, near lat. 35° 32' 54" N.,
long. 83° 09' 35" W., between Whim

Knob and Black Camp Gap. Alt. 5,340.

Street Gap, on the Madison County, N. C.-Unicoi County, Tenn., line.

Streets Ferry, est. over the Neuse River by Richard Graves before 1730, 7 mi. s of Vanceboro, central Craven County. Ceased operation, 1962.

Strickland Crossroads, community in s Johnston County.

Stricklandsville. See Magnolia.

Strieby, community in sw Randolph County. Named for a philanthropist who helped est. a church and school for Negroes here in 1880.

Striking Island, a tidal marsh island in the Cape Fear River opposite Southport, se Brunswick County.

Stringfellow Branch rises in s Watauga County in Moses H. Cone Memorial Park and flows e through Bass Lake and into Chetola Lake on Middle Fork [of South Fork New River].

Strouds Creek rises in n Orange County and flows se into Eno River.

Strouph Gap, on the sw end of Burney Mountain on the Buncombe-Henderson County line.

Stuards Reach appears on the Smith map, 1624, in what is now the Roanoke River between Halifax and Northampton counties.

Stuart Creek rises in nw Henderson County in Pisgah National Forest and flows ne into North Fork.

Stubblefield, community in nw Caswell County. Named for a local family.

Stubblefield. See Ruffin.

Stubbs, community in e Cleveland County on Buffalo Creek. Alt. 950. Settled about 1885. Named for Colonel Seth W. Stubbs who made the clock for the Lincoln County courthouse, 1856.

Stump Inlet or Stumpy Inlet, former inlet from the Atlantic Ocean to Stump Sound, se Onslow County. Appears on the Moseley map, 1733, and on other maps through 1882. Apparently closed by 1912.

Stump Sound skirts the s edge of Onslow County between the Onslow-Pender County line and Alligator Bay in s Onslow County. The sound is filled with tidal marsh islands and is separated from the Atlantic Ocean by a barrier beach.

Stump Sound Township, sw Onslow County.

Stumpy Creek rises in s Iredell County and flows sw into Cornelius Creek.

Stumpy Inlet. See Stump Inlet.

Stumpy Point, peninsula extending s from the e mainland of Dare County into Pamlico Sound and Stumpy Point Bay. Appears on the Moseley map, 1733.

Stumpy Point, community on the e mainland of Dare County on Stumpy Point Bay. Alt. 3.

Stumpy Point Bay, an almost round bay on the e mainland of Dare County. It has a narrow entrance into Pamlico Sound on the se side. Formerly a lake, it appears as Stumpy Point Lake on the Moseley map, 1733. Erosion opened the lake into Pamlico Sound.

Stumpy Point Lake. See Stumpy Point Bay.

Sturdivants Cross Roads, community in se Union County s of Lanes Creek.

Sturgeon Creek rises in ne Brunswick County and flows e into Mill Creek.

Sturgeons Point on Mosely map, 1733, was what is now se Brunswick County between Elizabeth River and Walden Creek.

Sturgills, community in n Ashe County. Named for Sheriff B. Sturgills who helped to obtain a post office which has now been discontinued.

Styron Bay on the w side of Core Sound about 1.3 mi. sw of the town of Atlantic and e of Nelson Bay, ne Carteret County. Named for a local family.

Suddawig Branch rises in sw Clay County and flows nw into Hiwassee River.

Suddereth Branch rises in e Cherokee County on Mission Mountain and flows se into Hiwassee River.

Sugar Branch rises in w Jackson County and flows se then ne into Savannah Creek.

Sugar Camp Branch rises in sw Madison County and flows ne into Spring Creek.

Sugar Camp Creek is formed in s Yancey County by the junction of Ogle and Timber creeks and flows sw and nw into Cane River.

Sugarcamp Fork rises in n Buncombe County and flows nw into Main Creek.

Sugarcamp Ridge, mountain in w Avery County.

Sugar Cove, n Buncombe County w of Ingles Ridge.

Sugar Cove, se Clay County.

Sugar Cove, s Haywood County on the head of Right Hand Prong [of Pigeon River].

Sugar Cove, sw Macon County between Firescald Ridge and Nantahala River.

Sugar Cove Branch rises in s Haywood County and flows nw into Sorrell Creek.

Sugar Cove Creek rises near Tellico Bald in n Macon County and flows ne into Tellico Creek.

Sugar Cove Creek rises in se Yancey County and flows sw into Three Forks Creek.

Sugar Cove Gap on the Haywood-Madison County line.

Sugar Cove Gap, se Yancey County near the head of Sugar Cove Creek.

Sugar Creek rises in nw Buncombe County near Newfound Mountain and flows ne into Sandy Mush Creek.

Sugar Creek rises in n Buncombe County near Watershed Ridge and flows n into Ivy Creek.

Sugar Creek rises in ne Davie County and flows se 2 mi. into Cedar Creek w of Smith Grove. Referred to in early local records as Sugar Tree Creek.

Sugar Creek rises in e Jackson County and flows ne into Caney Fork.

Sugar Creek rises in s Lee County and flows nw into Pocket Creek.

Sugar Creek is formed in central Mecklenburg County by the junction of Stewart and Taggart creeks and flows sw into South Carolina where it enters Catawba River. Appears on the Collet map, 1770. Name derived from an Indian word apparently meaning "group of huts."

Sugar Creek Ridge, e Jackson County between Sugar Creek and Rough Butt Creek.

Sugar Fork rises in ne Buncombe County and flows se into North Fork [Swannanoa River].

Sugar Fork rises in w Jackson County and flows ne into Greens Creek.

Sugar Fork rises in the Great Smoky Mountains National Park, nw Swain County, and flows 1.5 mi. se into Haw Gap Branch.

Sugar Fork. See Messer Creek.

Sugar Fork Township, se Macon County.

Sugar Gap, central Avery County.

Sugar Grove, community in w Watauga County on Cove Creek. Settled 1837; named for sugar maple trees in vicinity. Alt. 2,775.

Sugar Hill, community in s McDowell County on Cove Creek.

Sugar Hollow, se Buncombe County between Ashworth Creek and Reed Branch.

Sugar Hollow, e central Yancey County between Jim Ray Branch and Three Quarters Creek. Named for sugar maples growing here.

Sugarhouse Cove, ne Buncombe County between Glassmine Ridge and Locust Gap.

Sugar Loaf, mountain in n Alexander County. Named from its resemblance to an old-fashion loaf of sugar.

Sugarloaf, community in n central Watauga County.

Sugar Loaf. See Carolina Beach.

Sugarloaf Bluff on Cape Fear River in central Bladen County. Probably named for the beautiful white sandy beach across the river from the bluff. The river makes a 45° turn at this point.

Sugarloaf Creek rises in e Henderson County and flows n into Reedy Patch Creek.

Sugarloaf Creek rises in n Jackson County and flows nw into Scott Creek.

Sugar Loaf Island in Bogue Sound off Morehead City in s Carteret County.

Sugarloaf Knob, n Madison County at the ne end of Sugarloaf Mountain. Alt. 4,540.

Sugarloaf Mountain, on the Henderson-Rutherford County line about 1 mi. nw from the coincident corners of Henderson, Polk, and Rutherford counties. Alt. 3,965. The Indian name for this mountain was Salola, "squirrel."

Sugarloaf Mountain on the head of Sugarloaf Creek in n Jackson County.

Sugarloaf Mountain, n Madison County between Shelton Laurel Creek and Colvin Creek.

Sugarloaf Mountain, e Stanly County in Morrow Mountain State Park.

Sugar Loaf Mountain, central Transylvania County between curves in the French Broad River.

Sugarloaf Mountain, central Watauga County extends nw from Howard Creek. Alt. 4,705.

Sugarloaf Mountain, n Yancey County, extends se parallel to and s of Big Creek. Alt. 3,202.

Sugarloaf Ridge, n Jackson County, extends se from Blanton Branch to Black Mountain.

Sugar Loaf Township, n Alexander County.

Sugar Mountain, central Avery County. Alt. 5,240.

Sugar Springs Cove, ne Buncombe County between Little Craggy Knob and North Fork [Swannanoa River].

Sugar Top, mountain in e Haywood County near the head of Garden Creek. Alt. 4,400.

Sugar Town. See Cullasaja.

Sugartown. See Pilot View.

Sugar Town Creek. *See* Cullasaja River.

Sugar Tree Branch rises in nw Ashe County and flows s into North Fork New River.

Sugartree Branch rises in e Mitchell County and flows nw into Mine Fork Branch.

Sugartree Creek. *See* South Hyco Creek.

Sugar Tree Creek. *See* Sugar Creek.

Sugartree Gap, on the Buncombe-Madison County line w of Campground Knob.

Sugartree Gap, on the Swain County, N. C.-Sevier County, Tenn., line in the Great Smoky Mountains National Park near lat. 35° 34' 12" N., long. 83° 39' 28" W.

Sugartree Gap, on the Haywood-Swain County line.

Sugartree Licks, on the Haywood-Swain County line, Great Smoky Mountains National Park, on Balsam Mountain near lat. 35° 33' 23" N., long. 83° 09' 28" W. Alt. approx. 5,160. The name comes from the days of cattle ranging in the area and a salting place. Salt for cattle was spread on the roots of a sugar maple tree.

Sugartree Ridge, e Mitchell County between Mine Fork Branch and Dobson Branch.

Sugartree Ridge, n Watauga County, extends se from Cove Creek to Snake Mountain.

Suggs Mill Pond, a natural pond in n Bladen County. Named for Aligood Suggs. Has decreased in size considerably since 1914. This is one of the Carolina Bays, *which see.*

Suggs Creek rises in se Edgecombe County and flows s, forming the Edgecombe-Pitt County line, until it flows into the Tar River.

Suggs Creek rises in ne Montgomery County and flows se into Little River.

Suggs Landing, s Edgecombe County, on Tar River.

Suit, community in sw Cherokee County on the headwaters of Bearpaw Creek.

Sukey Young Crossroads, community in n Franklin County.

Sular Creek rises in nw Cherokee County and flows sw into Hiwassee River between Apalachia and Hiwassee Dams.

Suli Knob, n Swain County in Great Smoky Mountains National Park near lat. 35° 33' 13" N., long. 83° 33' 02" W. Alt. 4,920.

Suli Ridge, n Swain County in the Great Smoky Mountains National Park between Jonas and Huggins Creeks near lat. 35° 32' 53" N., long. 83° 32' 50" W.

Sulliers Bay, se Onslow County between Howards Bay and Craigs Point. Appears in early county records as Salyer's Bay.

Sullins Branch rises in e Mitchell County and flows sw into North Toe River.

Sullivan County, now in Tennessee, was created in 1779 and named in honor of General John Sullivan (1740-95). Blountsville became the county seat. This was a part of the territory ceded by North Carolina in 1789 to the Federal government. For further information *see* D. L. Corbitt, *The Formation of North Carolina Counties.*

Sulphur Branch rises in n central Gaston County, just nw of Pasour Mountain, and flows ne to empty into South Fork River near the community of High Shoals.

Sulphur Springs, community in central Buncombe County between Acton and Boswell.

Sulphur Springs, community in n Surry County on Ararat River. Formerly a popular resort.

Sulphur Springs. *See* Davis White Sulphur Springs.

Sulphur Springs Township, s Rutherford County.

Sumey Creek rises in ne Rutherford County and flows s into First Broad River. The name is variously spelled: Summy, Somey, and Sommey. Named for the Sumey family, early settlers.

Summerfield, community in n Guilford County. Alt. 881. Settled about 1769 by Charles Bruce, later Revolutionary patriot, and known as Bruce's Crossroads until 1812 when a post office was est. and the community renamed in honor of the evangelist, John Summerfield (1798-1825). Site of Revolutionary skirmish between Lee and Tarleton; campsite of British army under General Charles O'Hara of the Coldstream Guards, February 12, 1781.

Summer Haven, community in central Beaufort County on the n shore of Pamlico River.

Summerhaven, community in ne Buncombe County on Spruce Fork Creek.

Summerlins Crossroads, community in n Duplin County.

Summerville, community in central Harnett County. The law creating Harnett County in 1855 directed that the first courts were to be held here until a county seat could be est. Continued as seat of government until 1860. First called Toomer for Judge J. D. Toomer (1784-1856).

Summit, community in nw Halifax County. Since the elevation here is considerably higher than that of the surrounding region, Easter sunrise services are frequently held here. Alt. 312.

Summit, community in w Wilkes County between Lewis Fork Creek and North Prong Lewis Fork Creek.

Summit. See Elliott.

Summy Creek. See Sumey Creek.

Sumner, community in s Rowan County.

Sumner Township, s central Guilford Countw. Named for General Jethro Sumner (1733-85).

Sumpter Cabin Branch rises in s Watauga County and flows s into Middle Fork [of South Fork New River].

Sun, community in e Wilson County between Toisnot Swamp and Whiteoak Swamp.

Sunburst, community in s Haywood County on Lake Logan. Named because the sun rises suddenly from behind a mountain ridge.

Sunbury, community in e central Gates County. Alt. 39. Had its origin at nearby site of Costens Mill which appears as Constants Mill on the Collet map, 1770. Owner of the mill moved to present site of Sunbury when the road was changed. Probably named for the city in Pennsylvania.

Sunday Branch rises in e central Clay County and flows nw into Tusquitee Creek.

Sunfish Cove in n Transylvania County just s of Shooting Ridge.

Sunk Branch rises in ne Cherokee County and flows se into Dan Holland Creek.

Sunkoto Ridge, n Swain County in Great Smoky Mountains National Park, a long spur extending sw from Thomas Ridge with its center near lat. 35° 31' 40" N., long. 83° 24' 28" W.

Sunnatee. See Great Craggy Mountains.

Sunneehaw. See Enos Plotts Balsam Mountain.

Sunny Point, on the w bank of Cape Fear River in se Brunswick County. Now an ammunition loading depot.

Sunnyside, community in nw Cabarrus County.

Sunnyside, community in w Gaston County.

Sunnyside, community in nw Pender County.

Sunny Vale, community in nw McDowell County on Buck Creek.

Sunny View, community in n Polk County on Walnut Creek.

Sunset, community in central Granville County.

Sunset Beach, town in sw Brunswick County. Inc. in 1963.

Sunset Lake, s Wake County on Middle Creek at the junction of Basal Creek, formerly known as Orfords Pond. Covers 100 acres; max. depth 20 ft. Used for fishing and boating.

Sunset Mountain, central Buncombe County ne of Asheville.

Sunset Park, former town in central Buncombe County, now wholly within the corporate limits of Asheville. Inc. 1891; charter repealed 1897. It lay n of the town limits and w of Charlotte Street extension.

Sunset Rock, on Satulah Branch in se Macon County.

Sunshine, community in ne Rutherford County on Robinson Creek. Named prior to 1881 by J. W. Biggerstaff who had a store here. The site is shaded in the early morning by Cherry Mountain but it acquired its name because local residents could see the sunshine on the top of the mountain.

Sunup Knob on Haywood County, N. C., and Cocke County, Tenn., line, Great Smoky Mountains National Park, near lat. 35° 44' 45" N., long. 83° 10' 14" W. Alt. 5,050-5,100.

Supply, community in s central Brunswick County on Lockwoods Folly River. From 1805 until 1810 the county courthouse was at this site.

Surf City, town in se Pender County on the Atlantic Ocean. Inc. 1949.

Surl, community in e Person County.

Surry. See White Post.

Surry County was formed in 1771 from Rowan County. Located in the n central section of the state, it is bounded by the state of Virginia, and by Stokes, Yadkin,

Wilkes, and Alleghany counties. Long said to have been named for "Lord Surry" or the "Earl of Surrey," but this title and others was held then by the Duke of Norfolk, Edward Howard (1686-1777), who used his ranking title of Norfolk. The county actually was named for the County of Surrey in England, birthplace of incumbent governor William Tryon. The fact that the name is similar to Saura, the Indian tribe which had recently inhabited the region, may have had some influence in the choice. Area: 538 sq. mi. County seat: Dobson with an alt. of 1,265 ft. Townships are Bryan, Dobson, Eldora, Elkin, Franklin, Long Hill, Marsh, Mount Airy, Pilot, Rockford, Shoals, Siloam, South Westfield, Stewarts, and Westfield. Produces tobacco, corn, wheat, poultry, dairy products, hogs, livestock, textiles, hosiery, apparel, furniture, granite, and crushed stone.

Sussex, community in n Ashe County.

Sutherland, community in w Ashe County. Alt. approx. 3,150.

Sutphin, community in s Alamance County. *See also* Lindley's Mill.

Sutton, community in s Duplin County.

Sutton, community in s Franklin County on Norris Creek.

Sutton Branch rises in w Jackson County and flows se into Savannah Creek.

Suttons Creek rises in e Perquimans County and flows s into Perquimans River. Named for the Sutton family which owned land here before 1700.

Suttons Mill Pond, approx. ½ mi. long, on Bear Creek in w Lenoir County.

Suttontown, community in ne Sampson County near Goshen Swamp.

Swafford Gap, on the MacDowell-Mitchell County line. The Blue Ridge Parkway passes through the gap. Alt. 2,852. Named for Marcus Swafford (1856-1943), who lived here.

Swag Cove, ne Cherokee County on Buckhorn Ridge in the Valley River Mountains.

Swain, community in n Washington County near the head of Bakers Swamp.

Swain County was formed in 1871 from Jackson and Macon counties. Located in the sw section of the state, it is bounded by the state of Tennessee and by Graham, Cherokee, Macon, Jackson, and Haywood counties. It was named for David L. Swain (1801-68), governor of the state and president of the University of North Carolina. Area: 544 sq. mi. County seat: Bryson City with an elevation of 1,736 ft. Townships are Charleston, Forneys Creek, and Nantahala. Qualla Cherokee Indian Reservation, Great Smoky Mountains National Park, Nantahala National Forest, and Fontana Lake occupy much of Swain County. Produces corn, poultry, livestock, furniture, textiles, apparel, leather goods, crushed stone, and feldspar.

Swains Mill Pond, approx. 2 mi. long on Deep Swamp Branch just before it enters the Chowan River in se Hertford County. Formerly Taylor Pond. Est. *ca.* 1720.

Swallow Fork, w Haywood County, Great Smoky Mountains National Park, rises near lat. 35° 42′ 11″ N., long. 83° 07′ 47″ W., and flows nw into Big Creek.

Swamp Creek rises in se Bertie County and flows ne into Cashie River.

Swamp Creek rises in sw Dare County and flows sw into Alligator River. Appears on the Collet map, 1770.

Swampy River. *See* Black River.

Swan Corner, community in n Pamlico County on Chapel Creek. Named for local Swan family.

Swan Creek rises in e Pamlico County and flows se into Pamlico Sound.

Swan Creek is formed in e Wilkes County by the junction of East Swan Creek and West Swan Creek and flows n into Yadkin River.

Swancreek, community in w Yadkin County. Named from the fact that wild geese, erroneously called swans, once lived on nearby streams.

Swan Island, ne Currituck Sound, 2 mi. s of Knotts Island, n Currituck County. Approx. ½ x ¼ mi. in size. Site of Swan Island Club, noted old duck and goose shooting club owned by wealthy Bostonians.

Swan Island, tidal marsh island in the mouth of Swan Creek, e Pamlico County.

Swan Islands, three islands in Pamlico Sound, in n end of Carteret County.

Swan Mountain, central Buncombe County, extends from the junction of Swope and Bull creeks to High Swan peak.

Swann, town in se Lee County. Inc. 1875 as Swann's Station; charter repealed 1877. Reinc. as Swann's, 1911, but long inactive in municipal affairs. Named for Frederick Jones Swann who settled here about 1815. Alt. 278.

Swannanoa, community in se Buncombe County. Named for the river of the same name on which it is located. Known first as Cooper for A. D. Cooper, owner of the land on which it developed. Produces textiles and wearing apparel. Warren Wilson Junior College is here. Alt. 2,220.

Swannanoa Creek rises in w McDowell County and flows e into Mill Creek.

Swannanoa Gap in the Blue Ridge Mountains, on the Buncombe-McDowell County line, at the w end of Youngs Ridge. Lat. 35° 37' 20" N., long. 82° 16' 20" W. One of the two gaps (the other being Hickory Nut Gap) through which early settlers and travellers from the e reached the Asheville plateau. See also Black Mountain Gap.

Swannanoa Gap on the Buncombe-Yancey County line between Potato Knob and Bald Knob.

Swannanoa Mountains, range of mountains in se Buncombe County s of the community of Swannanoa and parallel to the Swannanoa River.

Swannanoa River rises near Swannanoa Gap on the Buncombe-McDowell County line and flows w into French Broad River s of Asheville. Name is a corruption of Suwali-Nunna, the Cherokee word for "trail of the Suwali tribe."

Swannanoa Township, e central Buncombe County.

Swannanoa Tunnel on the Southern Railway, se Buncombe County near Ridge-

crest. Cut in 1879 at a cost of $600,000 and 120 lives, the tunnel marked the completion of this section of the railroad. An early use of nitroglycerine in engineering occurred here.

Swanner, community in nw Alexander County.

Swann Point. See Swan Point.

Swann's. See Swann.

Swannsborough. See Swansboro.

Swann's Station. See Swann.

Swan Point, the nw point of Cedar Island in ne Carteret County.

Swan Point extends from Bell Island in s Hyde County into Rose Bay.

Swan Point, in s Onslow County, extends into n Chadwick Bay. Appears as Swann Point in early county records.

Swan Pond, a natural pond about 1½ mi. long in the Neuse River lowgrounds of se Johnston County.

Swan Quarter, former town and present county seat, s Hyde County. Alt. 10. Settled prior to 1836 when it was made the county seat. Inc. 1903; charter repealed 1929. Believed to have been named for Samuel F. Swann, an early owner of the site.

Swan Quarter Bay in Pamlico Sound e of Bell Island in s Hyde County. See also Cecils Harbor.

Swan Quarter Island, a marsh island, in Pamlico Sound, s Hyde County. Approx. 10 to 15 acres in area. See also Abigails Islands.

Swan Quarter Township, se Hyde County.

Swansboro, town in se Onslow County on White Oak River. Earlier names had been Bogue, Weeks Point, The Wharf, and New Town. Inc. as Swannsborough in 1783, named for Samuel Swann (1704-72) who represented the county in the Assembly (1739-62). Inc. in 1877 as Swansboro.

Swansboro Township, se Onslow County.

Swansee Gap, w Cherokee County between an arm of Hiwassee River and Sular Creek.

The Swash, a narrow channel between Horse Island and Core Banks, ne Carteret County.

Swayney, community in ne Swain County at the junction of Straight Fork with Raven Fork in Qualla Reservation.

Swearing Creek rises in n Davidson County and flows sw into Yadkin River. Named for Swearingen family. Appears on the Collet map, 1770, as Swaring Creek.

Sweet Branch rises in nw Swain County and flows s into Lake Cheoah.

Sweet Branch rises in w Yancey County and flows nw into Cane River.

Sweet Creek rises in central Mitchell County and flows se into Cub Creek.

Sweet Creek. See Frost Mill Creek.

Sweeten Creek rises in s Buncombe County and flows nw into Swannanoa River. Named for the Sweiton family, early settlers. Name later changed to Foster's Mill Creek and then back to Sweeten Creek again.

Sweetgum, community in s Graham County.

Sweetwater, community in w Watauga County on Beaverdam Creek.

Sweetwater Branch rises in n central Henderson County and flows se into North Fork.

Sweetwater Branch rises in s Madison County and flows se into French Broad River.

Sweetwater Branch rises near Black Mountain in n Transylvania County and flows ne into South Fork Mills.

Sweetwater Branch rises in n Yancey County and flows se into Sampson Branch.

Sweetwater Creek rises in w Clay County and flows sw and nw into Hiwassee River.

Sweetwater Creek rises in e Graham County and flows sw and nw where it joins Tulula Creek to form Cheoah River.

Sweetwater Creek drains Statons Pond, which see, in central Martin County, and flows n into Roanoke River. Appears as Flat Branch on the Collet map, 1770.

Sweetwater Gap, s Clay County between Kimsey Ridge and Ivy Top.

Sweetwater Gap, in e Graham County at the head of Sweetwater Creek.

Sweetwater Spring, in the headwaters of Haywood Gap Stream in s Haywood County.

Sweetwater Township, w Clay County.

Sweezy Mountain, a peak on Cherry Mountain, e Rutherford County. A large pile of rocks on the w side is known as the Rock House.

Swepsonville, community in central Alamance County. Named for George W. Swepson (1811-83) who built a cotton mill here in 1868. Inc. 1887; charter repealed 1901. Produces textiles.

Swift Creek, name given Sandy Creek in Hilliardston community, n Nash County. Sandy Creek, which see, rises in se Vance County. As Swift Creek it flows se across

Nash County and into Edgecombe County where it enters Tar River. Swift Creek appears on the Moseley map, 1733.

Swift Creek rises in s central Pitt County and flows se into n Craven County where it enters Neuse River. Appears on the Moseley map, 1733.

Swift Creek rises in s Wake County and flows se into Johnston County where it enters Neuse River. Appears on the Collet map, 1770.

Swift Creek. See Vanceboro.

Swift Creek Township, former township in nw Edgecombe County, now township number 7.

Swift Creek Township, s Pitt County.

Swift Creek Township, s central Wake County.

Swift Fork Branch rises in se Watauga County and flows se into Elk Creek.

Swim Bald, on the Graham-Swain County line between Sassafras Gap and The Jump-up.

Swimmer Branch rises in n Jackson County and flows s into Wrights Creek.

Swindell, community in s Hyde County. A post office was est. here as early as 1830.

Swindell Fork, community in central Hyde County.

Swinging Lick Gap, sw Macon County between Winding Stair Gap and Bryson Branch.

Swiss, community in w Yancey County on Bald Creek. Alt. 2,681. Named because the surrounding countryside suggested that of Switzerland.

Swopes Branch rises in e Cabarrus County and flows se into Little Buffalo Creek.

Sycamore Creek rises in nw Wake County and flows w and s along the Durham-Wake County line for a part of its course and then se in Wake County into Turkey Creek.

Sycamore Creek rises in central Franklin County and flows sw into Tar River.

Sylva, town and county seat in central Jackson County. Inc. 1889. Settled in 1861; named for William D. Sylva, a Dane employed as a carpenter by General E. R. Hampton, who constructed buildings at the site. Produces paper, electronics, and textiles. Alt. 2,047. See also Webster, which was the county seat until 1913.

Sylvasla, community in central Wake County.

Sylva Township, n central Jackson County.

Symonds Creek rises in s Pasquotank County and flows s into Little River.

T

Tabbs Creek rises in e Granville County
and flows se across sw Vance County into
Tar River on the Vance-Franklin County
line. Appears on the Collet map, 1770,
as Tans Creek, probably as an engraver's
error. For a time prior to 1764 the Granville County courthouse was located on
Tabbs Creek. A Tabb's Creek District
had 57 heads of families at the time of
the 1790 census.

Tabernacle, community in se Guilford
County.

Tabernacle Township, w central Randolph
County.

Tablerock, community in nw Burke County.

Table Rock Branch rises in ne Swain County and flows sw into Straight Fork.

Table Rock Mountain, nw Burke County in
Pisgah National Forest. Alt. 3,918. Sum-
mit accessible by foot trail. Appears on
the Collet map, 1770, as Table Mountain.
Known by the Cherokee Indians as
Namonda.

Tabor Branch rises in n Swain County and
flows se into Bradley Fork.

Tabor City, town in sw Columbus County.
Settled 1886. Inc. 1905 as Tabor; name
changed to Tabor City, 1935. Named for
Mount Tabor Presbyterian Church. Produces lumber, processed food. Alt. 50.

Tabor Island, in Roanoke River in se Bertie
County at the sw end of Bluff Island.
Known by this name since the mid-
nineteenth century. Measures approx. ¾
mi. long and ⅛ mi. wide. See also Purchace Islands.

Tackett Branch rises in n Rockingham
County and flows se into Smith River.

Tadmore, community in the nw tip of Pasquotank County.

Taggart Creek rises in central Mecklenburg
County and flows se to join Stewart
Creek to form Sugar Creek.

Tah-kee-os-tee. See French Broad River.

Talbot, community in w Wilson County.
Post office est. here 1892 but moved a
few years later to another nearby community and discontinued in 1902.

Talc Mountain, community in sw Swain
County on Nantahala River.

Talc Mountain Branch risees in sw Swain
County and flows se into Nantahala River.

Tali Gap, in nw Swain County between
Pickens Gap and Haw Gap Branch.

Talley Mill Creek rises in se Macon County
and flows se into Rabun County, Georgia,
where it enters Big Creek.

Talleys Crossing, community in e Forsyth
County.

Tallulah River rises in se Clay County and
flows se into Towns County, Georgia,
where it enters Tugaloo River.

Tally Ho, community in w Granville County. A post office est. here as early as 1830
was moved to Stem in 1889 and the
name changed. Alt. 500. Named for the
traditional call of fox hunters when the
quarry is sighted. Fox hunting was a popular sport in this area in the eighteenth
and early nineteenth centuries.

Tally Ho Township, w central Granville
County.

Ta-loh-na. See Yellow Mountain.

Tamarack, community in n Watauga County on Hoskin Fork. Post Office est. 1936
by this name; surrounding community
generally known as Pottertown. Named
for tamarisk tree.

Tamban Branch rises in central Duplin
County and flows w into Northeast Cape
Fear River.

Tanawha. See Grandfather Mountain.

Tanasee Bald, mountain peak on the Haywood-Transylvania County line at the
junction of Pisgah Ridge and Tanasee
Ridge in Pisgah National Forest. Alt.
5,560. 35° 17′ 30″ N., 82° 55′ 03″ W.
The Cherokee name for this peak was
Tsul-ka-lu-tsu-na-gun-yi.

Tanasee Creek rises in e Jackson County
at Mount Hardy Gap and flows approx.
9 mi. sw to enter Tuckasegee River.

Tanasee Gap, in Tanasee Ridge on the
Jackson-Transylvania County line in Pisgah and Nantahala National Forests.

Tanasee Ridge, on the Jackson-Transylvania
County line, forming the boundary between Nantahala and Pisgah National
Forests. It is approx. 11 mi. long and
extends nnw from the Blue Ridge.

Tanbark Gap, sw Cherokee County between Pack Top and Potato Creek.

Tanbark Ridge, central Buncombe County between Jones Cove and Bull Creek.

Tandaquomuc, an Indian village of either the Weapemoc or Chowanoac tribes located in what is now se Bertie County between the mouths of Chowan and Roanoke rivers. Appears on the DeBry map, 1590. The name may have meant "where the road goes by the big evergreens."

Tank Creek rises in nw Cumberland County and flows ne into Little River.

Tantram Branch rises in se Buncombe County near Patton Gap in the Swannanoa Mountains and flows s into Trantham Creek.

Tantroft Branch. See Tantrough Branch.

Tantrough Branch rises in e central Yancey County and flows n into Little Crabtree Creek. Named for the wooden trough used in tanning hides which an early settler had here. The form Tantroft is also sometimes used.

Tanyard Branch rises in central Rutherford County nw of Rutherfordton and flows se into Cleghorn Creek. At one time it was known as Milk House Branch.

Tanyard Creek rises in n Yadkin County and flows ne into Yadkin River.

Tanyard Gap, n Madison County at the head of Silvermine Branch.

Tapoco, resort community in nw Graham County on Cheoah River. Est. about 1930. Alt. 1,110. Name coined by the Tallassee Power Company, using the first two letters of the three words in the company name.

Tarawa Terrace, residential area of Camp Lejeune Marine Base, central Onslow County. Named for the Pacific Island on which an important battle was fought, Nov. 21-24, 1943.

Tarboro, town and county seat in central Edgecombe County, settled in 1732 and inc. 1760. Named for Tar River on which it is situated. Town commons, created by legislative act of 1760 is still maintained. The legislature met here in 1787. Produces textiles, lumber, machinery, toys, and paper products. In early records the name sometimes appears as Tawboro. Alt. 58. See also Runnymeade and West Tarboro.

Tarboro Township, former township in central Edgecombe County, now township number 1.

Tarcamp Branch rises in w Jackson County

and flows e into West Fork Tuckasegee River.

Tar Corner, community in ne Camden County. Name said to derive from a barn painted with tar which stood at intersection of two roads.

Tar Creek rises in e Pamlico County and flows n into Broad Creek.

Tare-over, in sw Washington County, a bridge and straight stretch of the road from Plymouth to Leachville crossing the headwaters of Flat Swamp at the ne end of Van Swamp. The name appears on the Price map, 1808, and is thought to have originated as the name for the grassy, swampy depression which cuts into Long Acre (which see) at this point.

Tar Heel, a town in nw Bladen County. Settled 1875. Inc. in 1963. Alt. 100. Named (a) for the appelation said to have been given North Carolinians by Cornwallis' troops who emerged from a river with tar adhering to their heels, (b) tar produced in this vicinity was taken to the Cape Fear River, thence by raft to Wilmington; along the river front the ground was covered with tar, and so were the feet that passed over it.

Tarkiln Branch rises in w Swain County and flows se into Little Tennessee River.

Tarkiln Branch rises in w Transylvania County and flows ne into Catheys Creek.

Tar Kiln Creek rises in s Pamlico County and flows s into Dawson Creek.

Tarkiln Gap, ne Cherokee County in the Valley River Mountains.

Tarkiln Mountain, peak on Forge Mountain in w Henderson County.

Tarkiln Mountain in w Transylvania County between Tarkiln Branch and King Mountain.

Tarkiln Neck, peninsula at the junction of Pamlico and Pungo rivers, e Beaufort County.

Tar Kiln Ridge, nw Clay County, extends from Short Off to the Tusquitee Mountains.

Tarkiln Ridge, central Macon County parallel to Poplar Cove.

Tar-ko-ee. See Piedmont.

Tar Landing, community in n Onslow County between Blue Creek and New River. Early deeds refer to the landing on New River as Owen Jones' Tar Landing.

Tar Landing Bay in the extreme e end of Bogue Banks, on the sound side, s Carteret County.

Tarpleys Pond, se Wake County on Little

River. Covers 50 acres and has a maximum depth of 15 ft. Used for irrigation
and recreation.

Tar Ridge, s Watauga County extends se
from the head of Days Creek.

Tar River rises in w central Person County
and flows se through Granville, Franklin,
Nash, Edgecombe, and Pitt counties to
Beaufort County where it becomes the
Pamlico River. It is 179 mi. long. Appears
on the Moseley map, 1733, apparently
for the first time; previously known as
Pampticough and other spellings of the
modern Pamlico. There are many explanations of the origin of the name: that it
is from an Indian word, "Tau," meaning
"river of health"; named for the Taw
River in Devonshire, England; or named
because of the tar produced in the counties through which it flows.

Tar River, community in s Granville County.

Tarts Store, community in s Johnston
County.

Tartt Path, pre-Civil War path still in use
in e central Wilson County. It runs n
from the community of Sun to the vicinity of modern state highway 42 e of
Wilson. Enos Tartt operated Tartt's Mill
on Bear Branch in the mid-nineteenth
century.

Tate, community in n Rutherford County
on Second Broad River.

Tate Branch rises in ne Clay County and
flows ne into Nantahala River.

Tate Gap, e Clay County, between the
headwaters of Passmore Branch and Fishprong Branch.

Tater Hill, in s Macon County between
Poplar Cove and Rocky Knob.

Tater Hill, in s Macon County between
Rattlesnake Ridge and Licklog Gap.

Tater Hill, peak in n Watauga County on
Rich Mountain, approx. ¾ mi. s of Rich
Mountain Bald. Also known in recent
years as Potato Hill. Named because it
resembles a large storage hill for potatoes. Alt. 5,194.

Tater Hill Lake. See Potato Hill Lake.

Tater Top Mountain, in Morrow Mountain
State Park, e Stanly County.

Tate's Knob, a small, sharp-top mountain in
ne Caldwell County. Named for Andrew
Tate, eighteenth-century settler.

Tatham Creek rises in ne Cherokee County
and flows nw through Andrews into
Valley River.

Tatham Creek rises in w Jackson County
and flows nw into Savannah Creek.

Tatham Gap on the Cherokee-Graham
County line in the Snowbird Mountains.
Alt. 3,500-3,639.

Tatter Knob, se Buncombe County nw of
Hickorynut Gap.

Tatums Township, nw Columbus County.

Tava Cove, n Cherokee County in the
Snowbird Mountains.

Taylor. See Rock Ridge.

Taylor Bay in Bogue Sound, w Carteret
County s of community of Bogue.

Taylor Bay, central Currituck County at s
tip of Great Swamp.

Taylor Creek, a waterway separating Carrot
Island from the mainland in s central
Carteret County, flowing from Lenox
Point on the e to the mouth of Newport
River on the w.

Taylor Creek rises in ne Cherokee County
and flows nw into Valley River.

Taylor Creek rises in n Craven County and
flows se into Neuse River.

Taylor Crossroads, community in s Nash
County.

Taylor Millpond, in sw Gates County, receives waters of a number of small
streams and flows se into Big Pocosin.

Taylor Pond. See Swains Mill Pond.

Taylor Township, n Wilson County.

Taylors Branch rises in ne Columbus County and flows ne into Livingston Creek.

Taylors Bridge, community in se Sampson
County on Cuwhiffle Swamp.

Taylors Bridge Township, se Sampson
County.

Taylors Corner, community in w Jones
County.

Taylors Creek rises in the w tip of Carteret County and flows sw approx. 1 mi.
into White Oak River.

Taylors Creek rises in sw Duplin County
and flows se into Duffs Creek.

Taylors Creek rises in nw Franklin County
and flows n into Tar River.

Taylors Creek rises in e Gaston County and
flows se into Dutchmans Creek.

Taylors Creek rises in s central Randolph
County and flows w into Caraway Creek.

Taylors Ferry, operated across the Roanoke
River between Bertie County and Martin
County. Appears on the Collet map, 1770,
and known to have been in operation as
late as 1833.

Taylors Mill. See Tippets Mill.

Taylors Mill Pond, approx. ¾ mi. long, on
the head of Corduroy Swamp in central
Northampton County.

Taylors Pond, on the head of Reedy Branch in nw Duplin County.

Taylors Store, community in nw Nash County.

Taylorsville, town and county seat, central Alexander County. Settled 1847; inc. 1851. Probably named for Zachary Taylor (1784-1850), whose defeat of Santa Anna early in 1847 ended the war in n Mexico; Taylor was President of the U.S., 1849-50. Alt. 1,247. Produces textiles, furniture, and paper boxes.

Taylorsville, a Negro community in s Moore County. Named for Robert L. Taylor, a Negro educator of note, who founded a store and a school here in 1908.

Taylorsville, town authorized in 1818 to be laid off on the lands of George Taylor on Black River in Sampson County. Probably never developed and the exact site is unknown.

Taylorsville Township, central Alexander County.

Taywa Creek rises in ne Swain County in Great Smoky Mountains National Park on Hughes Ridge and flows sw into Bradley Fork. Named for a Cherokee Indian chief.

Teaberry Ridge, central Haywood County between Right Fork Cove Creek and Wright Branch.

Teaches Hole, se Hyde County, a navigable channel running ne and sw from Ocracoke Inlet. Traditionally named for Edward Teach or Blackbeard, the notorious pirate said to have been killed here in 1718. Appears as Thatches Hole on the Moseley map, 1733, and shown as being closed at the ne end.

Teachey, town in se Duplin County. Inc. 1874; charter repealed, 1897; reinc. 1903. Alt. 71.

Teague Branch rises in central Haywood County and flows nw into Pigeon River.

Teague Branch rises in s Macon County on the n side of Turkey Knob and flows n into Tellico Creek.

Teagues Ridge, mountain in w Avery County.

Teaguetown, community in ne Davidson County between the headwaters of Spurgeon and Abbotts creeks. Named for a local family.

Tearshirt. See Dunn.

Tea Swamp rises in central Duplin County and flows ne into Grove Creek.

Teat Branch rises in central Madison County and flows nw into Big Laurel Creek.

Teds Branch rises in ne Swain County and flows s into Straight Fork.

Teer, community in sw Orange County on Cane Creek.

Teeseteska Ridge, s Graham County extends n from Atoah Gap.

Telfairs Creek rises in s New Hanover County and flows se into Cape Fear River. Called Rock Run on a coastal survey map made in 1851-53.

Tellico Bald, n Macon County at the head of Cold Spring Creek. Alt. 5,130.

Tellico Creek rises in n Macon County and flows ne into Little Tennessee River.

Tellico River rises in n Cherokee County and flows w into Monroe County, Tenn., where it turns n to flow into Tennessee River.

Tempa Mountain, s Mitchell County between Beaver Creek and North Toe River.

Temples Creek rises in n Davidson County and flows n into Reedy Creek.

Teneriffe Mountain, on Mud Creek in central Henderson County.

Ten Mile Fork, community in e Jones County.

Tenmile Swamp rises in w Onslow County and flows nw into Ninemile Swamp. Named for its distance from Rich Lands Chapel, an early center of settlement.

Ten Mile Swamp rises in n Robeson County and flows se and ne into Big Swamp.

Tenmile Swamp rises in e Sampson County and flows sw into Six Runs Creek.

Tennelina, community in w Madison County. The name is a combination of parts of the words Tennessee and Carolina.

Tennent Mountain, se Haywood County, in Pisgah National Forest, near lat. 35° 20' 15" N., long. 82° 52' 10" W. Named for Dr. Gaillard Stoney Tennent (1872-1953) in recognition of his lifelong interest in studying and preserving the beauty of the w North Carolina mountains. Alt. over 6,040.

Tennessee, a state formed from w territory formerly a part of North Carolina which was ceded to the Federal government in 1789. See also Watauga Settlement; District of Washington; Franklin; Davidson County; Greene County; Hawkins County; Sullivan County; Tennessee County; Washington County.

Tennessee. See also Tanasee.

Tennessee Bald, most n peak on Tennessee Ridge, on Haywood-Transylvania County line near Jackson County line. Alt. approx. 5,575.

Tennessee Branch rises in n Swain County and flows se into Bradley Fork.

Tennessee County, former county in what is now the state of Tennessee, was formed in 1788 and named for a Cherokee Indian word whose meaning is not now known. Clarksville became the county seat, but the county was divided into Montgomery and Robertson counties in 1796 when Tennessee County gave its name to the new state. This was a part of the territory ceded by North Carolina in 1789 to the Federal government. For further information *see* D. L. Corbitt, *The Formation of North Carolina Counties.*

Tennessee Ridge, extends from n to s along the Jackson-Transylvania County line between Haywood County line and head of West Fork French Broad River. Named peaks include Balk Knob, Bald Rock, The Pinnacle, Rockyface Mountain, Round Mountain, and Tennessee Bald.

Terebinthe. *See* Cedar Creek.

Teresita, community in s Macon County on Jones Creek.

Terrace Fork. *See* Terris Fork.

Terra Ceia, community in n central Beaufort County. Alt. 16. Settled in the early 1920's by Dutch bulb growers, the community's name means "heavenly land."

Terra Cotta, former community in central Guilford County, now within the bounds of Greensboro. Alt. 889. Named for the hard-baked clay (Latin, "cooked earth").

Terrapin Creek rises in e Catawba County and flows e into Catawba River.

Terrapin Creek rises in w Warren County and flows n into Blue Mud Creek.

Terrapin Island, tidal marsh island in Pamlico Sound, ne Pamlico County.

Terrapin Mountain in s Jackson County between Chattooga Ridge and Chattooga River. Also known as Fodderstack Mountain. Alt. 4,510. Known by the Cherokee Indians as *Klansoona*, "terrapin."

Terrapin Point, in se Bertie County extending into Batchelor Bay at the n side of Cashie River.

Terrapin Point, community in w Halifax County.

Terrapin Run, a bay in White Oak River, w Carteret County, which empties into Croaker Channel. Named from the fact that fishermen catch numerous terrapins here.

Terrazzo Switch, community in Nantahala National Forest, ne Cherokee County, on Southern Railway. The Columbia Marble Co. has a plant here. Named for terrazzo flooring made from marble chips.

Terrell, community in se Catawba County. Named for an early Methodist minister in the vicinity.

Terrell Creek rises in n Chatham County and flows ne into Haw River.

Terrell Gap, in e Swain County on Williams Branch.

Terrell Mountain, n Chatham County, 7 mi. sw of town of Chapel Hill. Alt. 849. Transmitting station and tower of the University of North Carolina's WUNC-TV and WUNC-FM are atop this mountain.

Terrible Creek rises in sw Wake County n of town of Fuquay-Varina, and flows e through Johnsons Pond and into Middle Creek.

Terris Fork rises in e Madison County and flows w into Paint Fork. Appears as Terry Fork and Terrace Fork on various maps.

Terry Branch rises in nw Nash County and flows e into Tumbling Run.

Terry Creek rises in s Henderson County and flows n into Green River.

Terry Fork. *See* Terris Fork.

Terry Gap, in n Henderson County at the head of Kyles Creek.

Tessentee Creek rises in s Macon County and flows w into Little Tennessee River.

Texana, community in central Cherokee County n of Murphy.

Teyahalee Bald on the Cherokee-Graham County line in the Snowbird Mountains. Alt. 4,743.

Thagards Pond on Little River in e Moore County. Covers approx. 100 acres. Named for William C. Thagard who owned it from 1854 until about 1900. Was the site of Nicholas Smith's mill from as early as 1769. A residential community, Whispering Pines, and a golf course were developed here about 1901.

Thanksgiving, community in n Johnston County, named for Baptist Church founded here on Thanksgiving Day, 1899.

Tharon, community in e Duplin County on the head of Limestone Creek.

Tharp Mountain, ne Buncombe County between Martin and North Fork Ivy creeks.

Thatches Hole. *See* Teaches Hole.

Thaxton, community in nw Ashe County. Alt. approx. 3,700.

Thelma, community in nw Halifax County

near Roanoke River and s of the site of the old town of Gaston, *which see.* The town of South Gaston, *which see,* at this site, was chartered in 1895 but the charter was repealed in 1907. Alt. 224.

Theoff Point, projection from s Bodie Island into Roanoke Sound, e Dare County. Approx. ½ mi. n of Cedar Island.

Thermal Belts (also Isothermal Belt), verdant zones largely in Polk and Rutherford counties, though to a lesser extent also in Caldwell, Mitchell, and other mountain counties, in which on certain cool nights the temperature may be 20° or more higher on the slope of a mountain than at the base. In these areas fruit growing is a successful undertaking, and at Tryon (Polk County) the thermal belt has contributed to resort prosperity. The thermal belt was first described here by Silas McDowell in 1858.

Thermal City, community in n Rutherford County on Second Broad River. A post office est. here in 1888 was named Pescud; name changed to Thermal City for the Thermal Belt, *which see,* in 1891. Post office discontinued 1926.

Thermo Knob, w Haywood County, Great Smoky Mountains National Park, on Balsam Mountain, near lat. 35° 41′ 39″ N., long. 83° 13′ 34″ W. Alt. 6,120. Formerly known as Thermometer Knob.

Thicket Branch rises in ne Swain County and flows sw into Right Fork [Raven Fork].

Thickety Creek rises in e Haywood County and flows s into Pigeon River.

Thickety Creek rises in s Montgomery County and flows sw into Little River.

Third Creek rises in e Alexander County and flows se across Iredell County and into Rowan County where it enters Fourth Creek. It is the third creek in a series of creeks crossed by early settlers moving w from Salisbury. Appears on the Collet map, 1770.

Third Creek. *See* Cleveland.

Third Creek. *See* Second Creek.

Third Fork Creek rises in s Durham County and flows sw into Newhope Creek.

Thirty Foot Canal, in e Washington County extends ne between Lake Phelps and Scuppernong River.

30 Mile Post, marked corner on the North Carolina-Georgia state line, se Clay County, 30 mi. w of Ellicott Rock, *which see.* Survey completed to this point in 1819. Here the state line turns due s for

1,983 ft. to Montgomery Corner, *which see.*

Thomas Bay, s extension of Cawcaw Swamp in sw Brunswick County between its junctions with Little Cawcaw Swamp and Shingletree Swamp.

Thomasboro, community in sw Brunswick County. Named for Cornelius Thomas (1889-1961).

Thomas Branch rises in sw Macon County and flows nw into Nantahala River.

Thomas Branch rises in central Madison County and flows sw into Hopewell Branch.

Thomas Creek rises in w Wake County and flows se into Little Whiteoak Creek.

Thomas Knob, s Macon County between Pipetrack Gap and Watkins Creek.

Thomas Landing, community in s Onslow County on Spicers Bay.

Thomas Peak, nw Jackson County between Camp Creek and Shoal Creek.

Thomas Ridge, n Swain County in Great Smoky Mountains National Park, extends in a semi-circle from Deep Creek n following the general curve of Oconaluftee River with its center near lat. 35° 32′ 30″ N., long. 83° 22′ 03″ W. Named for Col. William Holland Thomas (1805-93), native of Haywood County, and chief of the Cherokee Indians.

Thomasville, city in ne Davidson County. Founded 1852; inc. 1857. Named for John Warwick Thomas (1800-71), founder. Produces furniture, textiles, hosiery, apparel, lumber, and concrete pipe.

Thomasville Township, ne Davidson County.

Thompkins Knob at the junction of the Ashe-Watauga-Wilkes County lines in the Blue Ridge Mountains. Alt. 4,100. Also spelled Tomkins Knob.

Thompson. *See* Westover.

Thompson Branch rises in w Cherokee County on Ghormley Mountain and flows nw into Shoal Creek.

Thompson Branch rises in e Macon County and flows s into Watauga Creek.

Thompson Branch rises in s Swain County and flows n into Sawmill Creek.

Thompson Creek rises in n Transylvania County and flows s into South Fork Mills River.

Thompson Knob, n of Shuckpen Gap on the Buncombe-Haywood County line on Smathers View Mountain. Alt. 4,192.

Thompson River rises in sw Transylvania

County and flows se into Oconee County, S. C., where it enters Whitewater River.

Thompson's Branch rises in n Greene County and flows e into Sandy Run. Named for a pioneer family.

Thompson's Bromine-Arsenic Springs. See Crumpler.

Thompsons Gap, e Alleghany County.

Thompsons Gut rises in w Bertie County and flows w into Roanoke River.

Thompsons Millpond, n Wake County in Horse Creek.

Thompson Store, community in ne Mecklenburg County.

Thompson Township, former township in se Alamance County, now township number 9.

Thompson Township, sw Robeson County.

Thompsonville. See Williamsburg.

Thorn Mountain, sw Macon County between Siler Bald Branch and Bryson Branch.

Thorntons Creek rises in e Harnett County and flows sw into Cape Fear River.

Thoroughfare, portion of Pee Dee River flowing s of Youngs Island, n Anson County.

Thoroughfare, a waterway approx. 2 mi. long in se Bertie County connecting the Cashie and the Roanoke rivers.

Thorofare, channel in ne Carteret County connecting Thorofare Bay with West Thorofare Bay and forming the s boundary of Cedar Island.

Thoroughfare, a waterway connecting Black River and Cape Fear River, sw Pender County.

Thorofare Bay, on the s side of Cedar Island emptying into Core Sound, ne Carteret County.

Thoroughfare Branch rises in s Lee County and flows ne into Juniper Creek.

Thoroughfare Island, a small island in North River, w Currituck County. Above this point the river is sometimes known as Indiantown Creek.

Thorofare Swamp rises in e Pitt County and flows se into Clayroot Swamp.

Thoroughfare Swamp rises in sw Wayne County and flows ne and n into Neuse River. Formerly known as Falling Creek, and so designated on the Price map, 1808, and by Dr. Elisha Mitchell in his journal for 1827.

Thorpe Reservoir. See Lake Thorpe.

Thrash Branch rises in central Transylvania

County and flows sw into French Broad River.

Thrash Creek rises in ne Cherokee County on Old Mattie Ridge and flows se and sw into Valley River. See also Wood Lake.

Three Forks Creek, formed in se Yancey County by the junction of Left Prong and Right Prong and flows nw into South Toe River.

Three Forks Mountain, w central Transylvania County at the nw end of Big Mountain Ridge and at the w end of Soapstone Ridge. Alt. 3,774.

Three Forks. See Busick.

Three Hat Mountain, e Davidson County on the headwaters of Flat Swamp Creek.

Three Knobs, s Avery County.

Three Knobs on the McDowell-Yancey County line.

Three Mile, community in s Avery County.

Three Mile Branch rises in n Cabarrus County and flows se into Cold Water Creek.

Three Mile Creek rises in s Avery County and flows sw into North Toe River.

Threemile Creek rises in nw . McDowell County near Little Switzerland and flows s into Armstrong Creek.

Threemile Creek rises in w Orange County and flows se into Sevenmile Creek.

Three Point Gap, nw Cherokee County below Hazel Knob and near Bryson Lead.

Three Quarters Creek rises in e central Yancey County and flows s into Little Crabtree Creek.

Three Top Creek rises in s central Ashe County and flows n into North Fork New River.

Three Top Mountain, w Ashe County. Alt. 5,029.

Three Top Ridge, in s Haywood County between Nick Creek and McClure Creek.

Thrift, railroad depot name for the community of Paw Creek, which see.

Thrift Cove Branch rises in n Transylvania County and flows s into Davidson River.

Thumb Swamp, ne Bladen County, approx. 2 mi, long, drains w into Turnbull Creek.

Thumb Swamp rises in se Bladen County and flows e into Colly Creek approx. 5 mi. se of Singletary Lake.

Thumping Branch rises in se Clay County on Little Mountain and flows sw into Eagle Creek.

Thunderbolt Landing on Cashie River, se Bertie County.

Thunderhead Mountain, on the Swain County, N. C.-Blount County, Tenn., line in the Great Smoky Mountains National Park near lat. 35° 34' 08" N., long. 83° 42' 24" W. Alt. 5,530.

Thunder Hill, s Watauga County near the head of Groundhog Branch.

Thunderhole Creek rises in s Watauga County approx. 2 mi. w of the town of Blowing Rock, and flows s into n Caldwell County where it enters Johns River.

Thunderstruck Knob in e Yancey County at the e end of Bee Ridge.

Thunderstruck Knob in nw Yancey County at the s end of Fork Ridge between Hensley Branch and Cane River.

Thunder Struck Mountain, e Jackson County between Snaggy Bald and Mayapple Gap.

Thunderstruck Ridge, n Jackson County between Polecat Branch and Soco Creek.

Thunder Swamp rises in s Wayne County and flows nw into Thoroughfare Swamp.

Thundertontrenck. See Lenox Castle.

Thurman, community in e Craven County on Neuse River. Alt. 26. Settled about 1850 and named for Allen G. Thurman (1813-95), member of Congress (1845-47) and later a Senator from Ohio. His mother was the daughter of Nathaniel Allen, nephew and adopted son of Joseph Hewes of Edenton.

Thurmond, community in ne Wilkes County at the Surry County line.

Thurz Mountain, n Buncombe County nw of Wiley Mountain.

Tiancok, an Indian village of the Chawanoac tribe; appears on the Comberford map, 1657, located in what is now n Hertford County between Potecasi Creek and Meherrin River near the Chowan River. See also Cokey Swamp.

Tibb Ridge, e Cherokee County in the Valley River Mountains.

Tibbs Run rises in e Randolph County and flows se into Richland Creek.

Ticer Branch rises in w Mecklenburg County and flows sw into Paw Creek.

Tick Creek rises in w Chatham County and flows ne into Rocky River.

Tickle Creek rises in e Guilford County and flows se into Alamance County where it enters Traverse Creek.

Tidewater Area, a portion of the Coastal Plain, which see, from 30 to 80 mi. wide on the mainland side of the sounds in e North Carolina. Much of the area is swampland, known locally as "dismals" and "pocosins." There also are a number of natural lakes here and many areas of savanna with a thick growth of grass and many wild flowers.

Tiger, community in nw Rutherford County on Buffalo Creek.

Tilden. See Maxton.

Tillery, town in e Halifax County. Inc. 1889, but long inactive in municipal affairs. Named for Tillery family who settled here before 1790. Alt. 64.

Tillery Branch rises in s Madison County and flows w into French Broad River.

Tilley Creek rises in w Jackson County and flows ne into Cullowhee Creek.

Tillis's Mill Creek. See Mill Creek.

Timber Creek rises in s Yancey County and flows w to join Ogle Creek in forming Sugar Camp Creek.

Timbered Ridge, mountain in se Avery County.

Timberlake, community in s Person County. Settled about 1890. Named for William Timberlake, Sr., first postmaster. The railroad station here is known as Helena, named for the wife of an official of the railroad. Alt. 570.

Timberland, community in w Hoke County.

Timber Ridge, mountain in e central Avery County.

Timber Ridge, sw Jackson County between Cashier Valley and Chattooga River.

Timber Ridge, nw McDowell County near the head of Armstrong Creek.

Timber Ridge, s Macon County parallel to Gulf Branch.

Timber Ridge, s Yancey County between Timber and Ogle creeks.

Timothy, community in n Sampson County on Sevenmile Swamp.

Timothy Knob, s Watauga County on the head of Clark Creek.

Tim Creek rises in n Cleveland County and flows sw into Ward Creek.

Tims Creek rises in se Burke County near Smith Mountain and flows se into Henry Fork.

Tin Cap Knob, w Macon County between Tyler Branch and Nantahala River.

Tin City, community in s Duplin County.

Tincoco. See Cokey Swamp.

Tindallsville, former town in e Stanly County on Pee Dee River in what is now Morrow Mountain State Park. Inc. 1795. Served as a county seat of Montgomery County for a brief time.

Site long since abandoned. *See also* Henderson.

Tinoco Creek. *See* Cokey Swamp.

Tinsley Creek rises in n central Transylvania County and flows se into King Creek.

Tippers Crossroads. *See* Six Forks.

Tippet Branch rises in e Macon County and flows sw into Little Tennessee River.

Tippet Creek rises in e Macon County and flows nw into Caler Fork.

Tippetts Mill Pond on Moccasin Creek at the Johnston-Nash County line. Approx. ½ mi. long. Formed before the Civil War and known first as Taylor's Mill, later as Hilliard's Mill, and since about 1949 as Tippetts Mill. In the past a saw mill, cotton gin, and corn and wheat mills have been operated here. Wagons known as Moccasin Wagons were made here.

Tipton Branch rises in ne Clay County and flows ne into Nantahala River.

Tipton Creek rises in n Cherokee County in the Unicoi Mountains and flows nw through Tipton Gap into Tellico River.

Tipton Gap, n Cherokee County in the Unicoi Mountains.

Tipton Hill, community in w Mitchell County on Raccoon Creek.

Tipton Knob, n Cherokee County in the Unicoi Mountains.

Titepano appears on White's map, 1585, in what is now Currituck Sound, e Currituck County. The name may have applied to the sound and seems to have been *tetep-anwi-wi*, "there is a swirling current," or "it swirls around."

Titus Point. *See* Lenox Point.

Toast, community in n Surry County.

Tobacco Branch rises in ne Graham County and flows ne into Wolf Creek.

Tobacco Branch rises in n central Union County and flows se into Chinkapin Creek.

Tobaccoville, community in n Forsyth County. Post office est. before 1887, named for a chewing tobacco factory built here in the 1880's. Alt. 994.

Tobermory, community in nw Bladen County. Named for the village in w Scotland.

Tobie's Branch rises in ne Wilson County and flows se into Town Creek.

Todd, town on the Ashe-Watauga County line at the junction of Big Elk Creek with South Fork New River. Inc. 1915 in Ashe County but that same year the county line was changed so that the town came to lie partially in Watauga County. No longer active in municipal affairs. A post office est. here as Elk X Roads in the nineteenth century but changed to Todd after 1882. Alt. approx. 3,000.

Todds Creek rises in s New Hanover County and flows sw into Cape Fear River. Called Motts Creek on a coastal survey map made in 1851-53.

Todds Crossroads, community in e central Bertie County.

Toddy, community in w Pitt County. The community was known as Tugwell and the railroad name was Toddy Station in the early twentieth century. Named for the fact that a drink of whiskey could be had at a local store.

Toecane, community in central Mitchell County at the junction of Toe River and Cane Creek. Alt. 2,058.

Toe River is formed on the Mitchell-Yancey County line near Boonford by the junction of North Toe and South Toe rivers. It flows nw along the line to join Cane River to form Nolichucky River. Tradition says the name is derived from Estatoe, the name of an Indian princess who drowned herself in the river when her lover was killed by her kinsmen.

Toe River Township, s Avery County.

Togo. *See* Genlee.

Toisnot. *See* Elm City.

Toisnot Swamp rises in s Nash County and flows se into s Wilson County. It flows across the county and enters Contentnea Creek in s Wilson County. Name derived from Tosneoc, a Tuscarora Indian town near the confluence of Buck Branch and Toisnot Swamp. Until about the 1850's the name was spelled Tosneot and so appears in local records dating from 1741 and on the Collet map of 1770.

Toisnot Township, n Wilson County.

Tokay, community just outside the n limits of the city of Fayetteville, central Cumberland County.

Tolar Landing, United States Lock Number 3, on Cape Fear River in nw Bladen County.

Tolarsville, community in e Robeson County.

Toledo, community in ne Yancey County.

Toliver, community in sw Ashe County.

Toluca, community in ne Cleveland County at the Lincoln County line.

Tomahawk, community in s Sampson County. Settled about 1888. Alt. 99.

Tomahawk Branch rises in ne Buncombe

County and flows s into Lake Tomahawk then sw into Swannanoa River.

Tomahawk Branch. *See* Stewarts Creek.

Tomahawk Creek rises in w Forsyth County and flows se into Stewarts Creek, *which see.*

Tomahawk Creek is formed in s Sampson County by the junction of Little Tomahawk and Big Tomahawk creeks and it flows w into South River.

Tomblin Branch rises in e central Brunswick County and flows ne into Lewis Swamp.

Tom Branch rises in ne Cherokee County and flows ne into Taylor Creek.

Tom Branch rises in se Macon County and flows sw into Brooks Creek.

Tom Bryan Cove, n Macon County between Miller Hollow and Fall Branch.

Tom Creek rises in se Buncombe County and flows se into Broad River.

Tom Creek rises in s Haywood County and flows n into West Fork Pigeon River.

Tom Creek rises in n Mitchell County and flows s into Spring Creek.

Tom Creek rises in e Transylvania County and flows s then abruptly ne into Little River.

Tom Hall Branch rises in n Haywood County and flows w into Pigeon River.

Tom Jack Creek rises in s Wake County and flows s into ne Lee County where it joins Whiteoak Creek.

Tomkins Knob. *See* Thompkins Knob.

Tom Knob, w Watauga County near the head of Spice Creek. Alt. 4,293.

Tom Mann Creek, a bay on the n shore of Durant Island, central Dare County.

Tommy Branch rises in s Macon County and flows ne into Wayah Creek.

Tommy Knob, n Graham County between the headwaters of Yellow Creek and Cables Cove Creek.

Tomotla, community in central Cherokee County. Alt. 1,575.

Toms Branch rises in n Haywood County and flows s into Fines Creek.

Tom's Creek rises in s Caswell County and flows s into Alamance County where it enters Stony Creek.

Toms Creek rises in ne Henderson County and flows se into Mill Creek.

Toms Creek rises in w McDowell County and flows se into Catawba River. Toms Creek Falls are n of Marion.

Toms Creek rises in w Orange County and flows se into Cane Creek.

Toms Creek rises in w Randolph County and flows ne and se into Uwharrie River.

Toms Creek rises in e Surry County and flows sw into Ararat River.

Toms Creek rises in e Wake County and flows w into Neuse River.

Toms Creek. *See* Westfield.

Toms Devil Knob, se Alleghany County between Bullhead and Stone Mountains.

Toms Fork, stream rises in s Columbus County and flows n into Grissett Swamp.

Toms Mountain, a double-topped peak in nw Rutherford County near the headwaters of Cove Creek. Alt. approx. 1,920. Sometimes known as Chalk Mountain.

Toms Top, central Haywood County between Snakeden Top and Colman Gap.

Tom Thumb Creek rises on s slopes of High Peak in the Snowbird Mountains, ne Cherokee County, and flows sw and se into Valley River approx. 3 mi. ne of Andrews.

Tony, community in s Caswell County. A post office was operated here during the approx. period 1890-1909.

Tonys Branch rises in se Watauga County and flows se into Joes Creek.

Toodies Creek rises in s Yancey County and flows ne into Cane River.

Tooles Creek rises in n Franklin County and flows sw into Lynch Creek.

Tooleys Creek rises in se Beaufort County and flows s into South Creek.

Tooleys Point, point of land in e Beaufort County, on the n side of Pungo River at the mouth of Pantego Creek, se limits of Belhaven.

Tools Ford, former passage across Catawba River between Gaston and Mecklenburg counties e of the present site of Mount Holly. Named for Matthew Tool who had a grant of land in the vicinity in 1750. This ford was used by troops crossing the Catawba River during the Revolutionary War.

Toomer. *See* Summerville.

Toot Hollow Branch rises in central Swain County and flows s through Bryson City into Tuckasegee River.

Topnot, community in central Caswell County. A post office was operated here during the approx. period 1900-1930.

Topsail, community in s Pender County. Alt. 40.

Topsail Beach, town in se Pender County on the Atlantic Ocean side of Topsail Island. Inc. 1963. Known prior to this date as New Topsail Beach.

Topsail Inlet. *See* Beaufort Inlet.

Topsail Island, e Pender County. Barrier beach lying between Topsail Sound and the Atlantic Ocean. Approx. 8½ mi. in length.

Topsail Sound, extends ne from Mason Inlet in ne New Hanover County, across Pender County, to Stump Inlet on the Onslow-Pender County line. It is separated from the Atlantic Ocean by a barrier beach. The sound, about 17 miles in length, is filled with tidal marsh islands. Named from the fact that local residents watched from here for the appearance of top sails of approaching vessels.

Topsail Township, se Pender County.

Topsy, community in w Gates County. Alt. 33. Settled about 1870.

Topton, community in ne Cherokee County. Alt. 2,599. Named because it is at the top of a pass, Red Marble Gap. It is located very near the junction of Cherokee, Graham, and Macon counties, and residents of all three counties consider themselves citizens of the community.

Torhunta Fort, a village of the Tuscarora Indian tribe appears on the Moseley map, 1733, at the head of Contentnea Creek in what is now w Wilson County.

Tories Den, cave beneath Moores Knob on Sauratown Mountain, w Stokes County. Entrance 12 ft. high and 10 ft. wide; cave about 25 ft. deep. Said to have been occupied by a band of Tories during the Revolutionary War. In Hanging Rock State Park.

Torrence Creek rises in n Mecklenburg County and flows w into McDowells Creek.

Tory Hole. See Elizabethtown.

Tosneoc. See Toisnot.

Tosnot Depot. See Wilson.

Totero Fork appears on the Moseley map, 1733, as being between Uwharrie and Caraway Creek in what is now w Randolph County. Named for Totero or Tutelo Indians who lived in the foothills of the Blue Ridge in the seventeenth century but who subsequently migrated to e Virginia and later to Pennsylvania and elsewhere.

Totherrow Branch rises in ne Cherokee County and flows sw into Valley River.

Tottering Bridge, w central Washington County, is over Skinner Canal near the community of Basnight. Known by this name as early as 1868.

Tough Ridge, w Haywood County, Great Smoky Mountains National Park, a spur extending nw from Cataloochee Divide, center near lat. 35° 35' 05" N., long. 83° 05' 54" W., between Clontz Branch and McKee Branch.

Tower Hill, former plantation of Governor Arthur Dobbs in what is now ne Lenoir County. He purchased 850 acres here in 1755 as a possible site for a provincial capital. By an act of the assembly in 1758 the site was purchased for a capital to be named George City in honor of King George II. The capital was not approved by authorities in London and the property was eventually sold by the state in 1799. Tower Hill appears on the Collet map, 1770. The name apparently originated because an "old redoubt tower" remained here from a fort constructed during the Tuscarora War, 1711-13. See also George City.

Tower Hill Branch rises in ne Lenoir County near Georgetown and flows n into Jericho Run.

Town Branch rises in ne Buncombe County and flows sw into Dillingham Creek.

Town Branch rises in ne Cherokee County and flows nw through Andrews into Valley River.

Town Branch, rises in s central Yadkin County and flows se, just s of Yadkinville, into North Deep Creek.

Town Creek is formed in e central Brunswick County by the junction of Rattlesnake Branch and Lewis Swamp and flows se into Cape Fear River just above Campbell Island. Named Indian Creek by William Hilton in 1663 but appears as Old Town Creek on the Moseley map, 1733. See also Charles Town.

Town Creek rises in s central Carteret County and flows w into Newport River. It forms the n limits of the town of Beaufort.

Town Creek rises in central Catawba County and flows sw into Clark Creek.

Town Creek rises in s Clay County and flows se and ne into Hiwassee River.

Town Creek rises in s Montgomery County and flows se into Little River.

Town Creek rises in se Nash County, flows sw across Wilson County into sw Edgecombe County where it flows ne and se into Tar River. Called Mallard Creek on Moseley map, 1733, but appears as Town Creek on Collet map, 1770.

Town Creek rises in central Onslow County and flows ne into Farnell Bay. Land taken up along this river beginning about 1706.

Town Creek rises in n central Rockingham County and flows n into Dan River. Named from the fact that Lower Saura Town *(which see)*, an Indian village, was near its mouth.

Town Creek rises in n Stanly County and flows s into Long Creek.

Town Creek, town in ne Wilson County near the stream of the same name. Inc. 1899, but long inactive in municipal affairs. A Baptist Church here was est. in 1802.

Town Creek. *See also* Crane Creek.

Town Creek Indian Mound, state historic site, s Montgomery County. Area: 53 acres. Est. 1937. Contains excavated and restored Indian mound dating from early sixteenth century and a museum.

Town Creek Township, central Brunswick County.

Town Fork Creek rises in w Stokes County and flows se and then ne across the s part of the county, entering Forsyth County for a short distance, and into Dan River. The headwaters are labeled Slek Creek on the Collet map, 1770, and the lower course simply Town Fork. An iron forge was operated along the banks of this creek by 1796.

Townhouse Branch rises in sw Swain County and flows se into Nantahala River.

Townhouse Creek rises in ne Cherokee County below Old Mattie Ridge and flows s into Welch Mill Creek.

Townhouse Ridge, ne Cherokee County between Welch Mill Creek and Townhouse Creek. Alt. 2,523.

Town Marsh, a tidal marsh island sw of Beaufort in s Carteret County.

Town Mountain Gap, central Buncombe County in the Elk Mountains.

Town Point, central Onslow County at the n end of Farnell Bay and the s end of Morgan Bay. Now within the Camp Lejeune Marine Base.

Townsend, community in sw Watauga County.

Townsend Gap, s Watauga County near the head of Clark Creek.

Townsville, town in n Vance County between Little Island Creek and se prong of Kerr Reservoir. Alt. 421. James Lyne operated a store here about 1780, and the surrounding community was named Lynesville, the name by which it appears on the MacRae map, 1833. Inc. in 1857 and named for Edmund Towne who donated land for a railway station.

Townsville Lake. *See* Kerr Reservoir.

Townsville Township, n Vance County.

Town Swamp, sw Bertie County, a part of the larger Broadneck Swamp. Probably named for a Tuscarora Indian town in the vicinity, abandoned before 1800.

Tow String Creek rises in ne Swain County and flows sw into Oconaluftee River. Named because an old woman who lived on the creek made tow strings for the settlers.

Toxaway. *See* Lake Toxaway; Rosman.

Toxaway Creek rises in s Transylvania County and flows sw into Toxaway River.

Toxaway Falls, sw Transylvania County on Toxaway River, s of community of Lake Toxaway. The falls, which cascade 123 ft., are crossed by a highway bridge.

Toxaway Mountain on the Jackson-Transylvania County line n of Horsepasture River.

Toxaway River rises in sw Transylvania County and flows n for a short distance then se and sw into South Carolina where it joins Whitewater River in forming Keowee River. The name is derived from the Cherokee word *Tor-tzoo-whah*, "redbird."

Tracadia. *See* Baltimore.

Trace Branch rises in n Jones County and flows s into Beaver Creek.

Trace Ridge extends se from Beaverdam Gap in nw Henderson County to the junction of Wash Creek and North Fork Mills River.

Tracey Swamp rises in n Jones County and flows n along the Craven-Lenoir County line into Neuse River. *See also* Gum Swamp.

Tracy, community in n Watauga County on North Fork New River.

Trading Ford, former ford across the Yadkin River, Rowan-Davidson counties. The e end of Big Island was one terminus of the ford. John Lawson visited this site in 1701 which was on a trading path maintained by the Indians across central North Carolina. General Nathanael Greene's American army made a miraculous crossing here February 1, 1781, when almost caught by Cornwallis. High water prevented the British from overtaking the exhausted Americans. A Confederate fort and earthworks nearby protected the railroad and a toll bridge during the Civil War.

Trading Path, a colonial trading route dating from the seventeenth century from Petersburg, Va., to the Catawba and Waxhaw Indians. One branch entered North Carolina in Granville County and another in Warren County. They converged near the present site of Oxford and followed a sw route through Granville, Durham, Orange, Alamance, Guilford, Randolph, Davidson, Rowan and Cabarrus counties. At about the present site of Concord the road split with a w branch leading through present Charlotte to the Catawba Indians. The e branch led almost directly s through Union County to the Waxhaw Indians. The Trading Path appears on the Collet map, 1770, and the Mouzon map, 1775. It is traced on a modern map in the *North Carolina Historical Review*, VIII, 404.

Trafalgar, Cabo de. *See* Cape Fear.

Trail Branch rises in ne Cherokee County and flows nw into McClellan Creek.

Trailbranch, community in se Madison County. A nineteenth century post office here was Trail Branch.

Trail Ridge, a twisting mountain ridge in n Clay County extending n from Tusquitee Ridge to Wolf Ridge.

Trail Ridge, w Haywood County extends e from the county line to Palmer Creek.

Trail Ridge, nw Macon County between Long Branch and Otter Creek.

Trail Ridge, s Macon County between Cunningham Creek and Henson Creek.

Tramaskecooc, Indian village, appears on the White map, 1585, at or near the present location of Cherry Ridge Landing, *which see*, s Tyrrell or n Hyde County near the head of Alligator River. The tribal affiliation of the Indians here is uncertain although the Secotan Indians were active in the area. The name of the village is said to have meant either "beavers" or "people of the white-cedar swamps."

Tramble Gap, se Henderson County near the South Carolina line.

Tramway, community in w Lee County. Named because it was the terminal of a tramroad from Cameron. A Civil War drillground was located approx. 1 mi. s of Tramway.

Transou, community in e Ashe County. Alt. 3,300.

Transportation Canal. *See* Old Canal.

Transylvania County was formed in 1861 from Henderson and Jackson counties. Located in the w section of the state, it is bounded by the state of South Carolina, and by Jackson, Haywood, and Henderson counties. Its name is a combination of two Latin words, *trans*, "across," and *sylva*, "woods." Area: 379 sq. mi. County seat: Brevard with an elevation of 2,230 ft. Townships are Boyd, Brevard, Catheys Creek, Dunns Rock, Eastatoe, Gloucester, Hogback, and Little River. Produces corn, apples and other fruits and vegetables, poultry, dairy products, livestock, hogs, lumber, paper products, chemicals, textiles, crushed stone, asbestos, sand, and mica.

Tranters Creek rises in sw Martin County and flows se on the Pitt-Martin County line and s on the Pitt-Beaufort County line into Tar River near the point at which the Tar becomes the Pamlico River. Appears on the Moseley map, 1733. Site of a battle June 5, 1862, during the Civil War.

Trantham Creek rises in se Buncombe County near Flat Top Mountain and flows sw into Cane Creek.

Trap, community in ne Bertie County. Named because a local tavern about 1860 "trapped" men of the community, according to their wives.

Trap Branch rises in ne Swain County and flows w into Straight Fork.

Traphill, community in n Wilkes County e of Little Sandy Creek. Area settled by 1775. In 1833 a town to be named Johnsonville (for an invalid Revolutionary War veteran wounded at Kings Mountain, Captain Samuel Johnson, who died the next year) was authorized to be laid out at Trap Hill but never developed. A post office to serve the community was est. here in 1837 and named Trap Hill for hunter William Blackburn's railpen snare which he frequently set on a nearby hill to catch wild turkeys.

Trap Hill Township, ne Wilkes County.

Traps Bay, s Onslow County on the e side of New River nears its mouth. Named for Capt. Cornelius Trap who was living in the county in 1746.

Traps Creek rises in se Onslow County and flows sw into Traps Bay.

Traverse Creek rises in e Guilford County and flows ne into Alamance County where it enters Haw River.

Travis, community in nw Tyrrell County n of Scuppernong River.

Trays Island Creek rises in s Jackson County on the n slope of Bald Rock Mountain. It flows n and w around the mountain and then s through Fairfield Lake into Horsepasture River.

Treeland. See Whitnel.

Treetop, community in central Ashe County.

Trenholm Mountain, central Henderson County on Memminger Creek. Named for the family of George H. Trenholm of Flat Rock. Trenholm became Confederate Secretary of the Treasury after C. G. Memminger in 1864.

Trent. See Frisco; Merritt; Trenton.

Trent Branch rises in central Buncombe County and flows ne into Hominy Creek.

Trent Branch rises in n Madison County and flows sw into French Broad River.

Trent Bridge. See Pollocksville.

Trent River rises in s Lenoir County and flows se across Jones County and into Craven County where it enters Neuse River at New Bern. Appears as Quoracks River on the Comberford map, 1657; apparently first called Trent River by John Lawson, 1709, probably for the river of that name in England. Appears as Trent River on the Moseley map, 1733.

Trent River rises in central Pamlico County and flows n into Bay River. Often known locally as Trent Creek.

Trenton, town and county seat, central Jones County. Courthouse apparently est. at this site in or soon after 1779 when the county was formed. Apparently known as Trent until 1784 when a town to be known as Trenton was authorized to be laid off at the site of the courthouse. Inc. 1874. Took its name from the Trent River on which it is located. Alt. 28.

Trenton Township, central Jones County.

Trent Township, sw Lenoir County.

Trent Woods, town in central Craven County on Trent River s of New Bern. Inc. 1959.

Triangle, community in e Lincoln County.

Settled 1902. Named for triangle formed by roads at the site.

Triangle Township, se Durham County. Named for Research Triangle, *which see.*

Trickum Creek rises in n Forsyth County and flows n into Buffalo Creek.

Tricorner Knob, on the Haywood-Swain County, N. C.-Sevier County, Tenn., line. Alt. more than 6,100. Named for its location at the coincidence of three counties

Trilby. See Allensville.

Trim Cove, ne Cherokee County through which an unnamed stream flows se into Valley River.

Trimont Branch rises in central Macon County and flows se into Wallace Branch.

Trimont Mountain, central Macon County at the head of Jacob Branch. Alt. approx. 3,700.

Trimont Ridge extends from White Oak Ridge in w Macon County to Jacob Branch in central Macon County.

Trinity, town in nw Randolph County. Union Institute, a school, was est. here in 1838. Located midway between the neighborhoods of Hopewell on the s and Springfield on the n, it took its name from the fact that it was expected to serve to unite the two. Twelve years later the school was reorganized as Trinity College, and the town took its name from the college. Inc. 1869. In 1892 the college moved to Durham and later became Duke University.

Trinity, community in s Union County on Buffalo Creek, named for a local church. Former Hope community was located just e of here.

Trinity Harbor, a former inlet from the Atlantic Ocean into Albemarle Sound through North Banks, s of the present community of Duck. It opened prior to 1585 and closed prior to 1657. Appears on the White map, 1590. The Smith map, 1624, labels it Worcester Inlet. Probably named because it was discovered on one of the Sundays after Trinity (either the 1st or 8th of August, 1585). The site is now in ne Dare County.

Trinity Township, nw Randolph County.

Triple Falls, e Transylvania County in Little River between the mouth of Hooker Creek and the mouth of Grassy Creek. Height of the falls is 50 ft.

Triplett, community in e Watauga County.

Triplett Creek rises in s Watauga County and flows sw into Joes Creek.

Tritt Knob, central Haywood County on Jonathans Creek. Alt. 3,600.

Trollinger's Crossing or **Ford.** *See* Haw River.

Trotman Creek rises in s Gates County and flows w and s into Warwick Creek to form Catherine Creek.

Trotters Creek rises in w Lenoir County and flows nw then n into Dailys Creek. Davis Mill Pond, *which see,* is on this creek.

Trotville, community in s Gates County. Alt. 39.

Troublefield Run Creek rises in w Northampton County and flows s into Roanoke River.

Troublesome Creek rises in n Guilford County and flows ne into Rockingham County where it enters Haw River. Sometimes also known as Big Troublesome Creek.

Troublesome Creek appears on the Kerr map, 1882, and on the 1865 coastal survey map as rising in w Onslow County and flowing ne into New River or into Southwcst Creek. The name Troublesome Run is applied to this stream on the Price map, 1808, and on the MacRae map, 1833. It is no longer shown on modern maps but might be identified with Mill Run, although this stream is much shorter than Troublesome Creek.

Troublesome Iron Works, used during Revolutionary War, built on Troublesome Creek, sw Rockingham County, by William Patrick, 1770. Nathanael Greene camped here, 1781; George Washington had breakfast here, June 3, 1791.

Troublesome Point, extends into the mouth of the North Landing River in ne Currituck County.

Trout, community in w central Ashe County. Alt. approx. 2,900.

Trout Cove Branch rises in sw Clay County and flows sw into Brasstown Creek.

Trout Creek, a slough in the w end of Bogue Sound, sw Carteret County. Named by fishermen for the trout caught here.

Trout Creek rises in central Jackson County and flows w into West Fork Tuckasegee River.

Trout Creek rises in s Watauga County and flows ne into Elk Creek.

Trout Lake, artificial lake in central Watauga County on Flannery Fork. Formed in 1954, it has a max. depth of 20 ft. and an area of approx. 13 acres. Open to the public.

Troutman, town in s Iredell County. Settled about 1859 and inc. 1905. Named for Mrs. Annie Troutman and her sons, Sydney and Jacob, who settled here and operated a wagon shop. Produces apparel and furniture. Alt. 955.

Troutman Mine, former gold mine in ne Cabarrus County.

Troy, town and county seat in central Montgomery County. Laid out as the county seat in 1843 and inc. 1852. Alt. 664. May have been named for Robert Troy, member of the House of Commons in 1802 and 1806 from Anson County, and Trustee of the University of North Carolina, 1804-07, who died on April 25, 1807; or for John B. Troy, member of the General Assembly from Randolph County who died before 1837; or for the ancient city of Troy. Produces furniture, carpets, textiles, mobile homes, and lumber.

Troy's Store, community in ne Randolph County. A post office was est. here as eary as 1828 and continued in operation as recently as 1882. John B. Troy operated a school here in 1837.

Troy Township, central Montgomery County.

Troyville. *See* Coats.

Truckwheel Mountain, s Buncombe County between Chestnŭt Cove and Sleepy Gap.

Truebloods Point in w Pasquotank County extends into Little River just s of Nixonton.

Truett Branch rises in ne Cherokee County and flows se into Morris Creek.

Trull Cove, e Cherokee County through which a short tributary of Slow Creek flows.

Trumpet Branch rises in n central Iredell County and flows s into Rocky Creek just n of Olin. Before the Civil War, Joseph Weisner had an iron foundry here known as Trumpet Branch Iron Foundry. It is believed that machinery for antebellum cotton factories in this section of the country was made here.

Trumpeters Swamp rises in s Pender County and flows nw into Merricks Creek.

Trust, community in sw Madison County on Spring Creek. Alt. 2,411.

Truth, community in se Chatham County.

Tryon, town in sw Polk County. Inc. 1885 as Tryon City. Named for nearby Tryon Mountain, *(which see).* Post office, est.

as early as 1882 known as Tryon City. Alt 1,075.

Tryon City. *See* Tryon.

Tryon County, named in honor of William Tryon (1729-88), governor of North Carolina, 1765-71, was formed from Mecklenburg County in 1769. The county was abolished in 1779 when it was divided into Lincoln and Rutherford counties, *which see.*

Tryon Mountain, w Polk County above the town of Tryon between Skuka Creek and Little Cove Creek. Named for William Tryon (1729-88), governor of North Carolina, 1765-71. Named by the Cherokees for the governor in 1767 when a boundary was being est. between white and Cherokee lands. Appears on the Collet map, 1770. Alt. 3,231.

Tryon Palace, state historic site in New Bern, central Craven County. 6 acres. Est. 1952. Contains restored and reconstructed "Tryon's Palace" completed 1770 for royal Governor William Tryon. Partly burned 1798. First capitol of state of North Carolina. Reconstruction begun 1952; palace opened to public 1959.

Tryon Township, sw Polk County.

Tsiyahi. *See* Cheoah.

Tubbs Inlet, a tidal waterway in sw Brunswick County between Bald Beach and Hales Beach.

Tub-Mill Creek rises in nw Swain County and flows s to join Gunna Creek in Great Smoky Mountains National Park to form Eagle Creek.

Tuckahoe, community in w Jones County. Mentioned in a letter from James Iredell to his wife, May 17, 1782. Named for a plant (*Peltandra virginica* or *Orontium aquaticum*) whose roots were cooked and eaten by the Indians.

Tuckahoe Creek rises in nw Hoke County and flows nw into James Creek.

Tuckahoe Creek, rises from Tuckahoe Swamp in w Jones County and flows e into Trent River. Appears on the Collet map, 1770.

Tuckahoe Creek rises in w Pender County and flows ne into Moores Creek.

Tuckahoe Swamp rises in s Lenoir County and flows se into w Jones County where it becomes less well defined and more nearly a true swamp. The swamp is drained to the e by Tuckahoe Creek.

Tuckahoe Township, w Jones County.

Tuckasege, community in e Gaston County on Catawba River. Tuckasege Ford over

the river was nearby. It is mentioned in local records as early as 1780 and appears on the Price map, 1808. Tuckasege Ferry here was in operation in the early years of the twentieth century.

Tuckasegee, community in central Jackson County at junction of West Fork Tuckasegee River with Tuckasegee River. Named for Cherokee Indian word meaning "crawling terrapin." Alt. 2,184.

Tuckasegee Falls, w Jackson County on West Fork Tuckasegee River. The construction of Lake Thorpe stopped the flow of water and the falls are no longer noticeable. Formerly the water plunged 60 ft. and then split into two 25 ft. cataracts. Also known as High Falls of the Tuckasegee.

Tuckasegee Lake in central Jackson County on West Fork Tuckasegee River. Formed in 1950; covers 2 acres and has max. depth of 90 ft. Used for fishing, boating and as a power source. Open to the public.

Tuckasegee River is formed in se Jackson County by the junction of Panthertown and Greenland creeks and flows nw through central Jackson County and into Swain County where it enters Little Tennessee River. Named for the Cherokee Indian town which stood beside the river, *Tsiksitsi,* which means "crawling terrapin," after the sluggish movement of the water.

Tuck Creek rises in sw Cleveland County and flows n into Broad River.

Tucker Creek rises in s Craven County and flows ne into mouth of Slocum Creek.

Tucker Creek rises near Brevard in central Transylvania County and flows se into Nicholson Creek.

Tucker Creek rises in w Transylvania County and flows se into North Fork French Broad River.

Tuckerdale, community in nw Ashe County.

Tucker Gap, central Graham County between Mountain Creek and Sweetwater Creek.

Tucker Hollow, mountain valley in n central Avery County.

Tucker Island, a silty clay and loam island in Roanoke River, nw Northampton County. Formerly approx. 2 mi. long, but now largely covered by the waters of Roanoke Rapids Lake. Appears as Pughs Island on the Price map, 1808, and as a part of Hamlins Shoals on the MacRae map, 1833.

Tucker's Barn. *See* Lenoir.

Tuckertown, former community in nw Montgomery County. Site now covered by waters of Tuckertown Lake, a reservoir for Carolina Aluminum Company completed in 1962. Originally named Milledgeville; renamed about 1900 for an official of a Northern firm which operated a rope manufacturing plant here. The mill was abandoned and houses moved from the site when construction of the dam for the lake began.

Tuckertown Lake on Yadkin River in Davidson, Montgomery, Rowan, and Stanly counties. Covers 3,000 acres with a shore line of 40 mi. Max. depth 50 ft. Named for a former community in Montgomery County whose site it now covers. Completed in 1962 by Carolina Aluminum Company as a reservoir, to generate hydroelectric power, and for recreation.

Tugman Mountain, w Wilkes County between Stony Fork Creek and Yadkin River.

Tugwell. *See* Toddy.

Tulin, community in nw Cabarrus County.

Tull Bay, an inland bay in n Currituck County in the mouth of the Northwest River.

Tull Creek rises in e Onslow County and flows e into Bear Creek.

Tull Creek rises in central and e Currituck County and flows nw and ne into Tull Bay. Appears on the Collet map, 1770. Named for the Tull family livng here by 1710.

Tull Creek, community in n Currituck County. A post office was est. here as early as 1828.

Tull Mill Pond, on the head of Southwest Creek in sw Lenoir County. Formed approx. 1875. Covers 180 acres; max. depth 14 ft.

Tully Gap, ne Yancey County at the sw end of Buck Ridge.

Tulula, community in s Graham County on Tulula Creek, *which see.*

Tulula Creek rises in se Graham County and flows nw where it joins Sweetwater Creek to form Cheoah River. Named for the Cherokee word for the cry of the frog, *talula.*

Tumble Bug Creek rises in e Henderson County and flows sw into Hungry River.

Tumblerville, community in s Macon County s of Bristle Ridge.

Tumbling Run rises in nw Nash County and flows ne into Sandy Creek.

Tump Island, ne Carteret County, in West Bay off Tump Point on Cedar Island. A tump is defined as a low hill or mound or as a clump of grass, especially one forming a dry spot in a swamp.

Tump Point, ne Carteret County, on w side of Cedar Island extending into West Bay.

Tuneigh Branch rises in ne Swain County and flows sw into Bunches Creek.

Tungsten, community in n Vance County near Little Island Creek. Named for the nearby tungsten deposits, reputedly the second largest in the world.

Tuni Creek rises in n Clay County and flows e and sw into Tusquitee Creek.

Tuni Gap on the Clay-Macon County line e of Bearpen Gap at the head of Little Tuni Creek. Alt. 3,526.

Tunis, community in e Hertford County. Inc. 1909. Charter repealed 1935. Alt. 17.

Tunnel Branch rises in w Swain County and flows w into Goldmine Branch.

Tunnel Falls, se Haywood County on West Fork of Pigeon River. Water drops approx. 50 ft. Named because a small hole goes into the rock behind the falls suggesting the entrance to a tunnel.

Tunnel Gap, se Haywood County on the head of East Fork Pigeon River.

Tunnel Ridge, w Swain County extends se from Forney Ridge to Tunnel Branch.

Tunn Ensleas. *See* Plott Balsams.

Turkey, town in e Sampson County. Settled about 1847; inc. 1913. Named for Turkey Creek which flows a short distance n of the town. Alt. 153.

Turkey Branch rises in w central Halifax County and flows e approx. 1½ mi. into Jacket Swamp.

Turkey Branch rises in central Jackson County and flows ne into Tuckasegee River.

Turkey Branch rises in w Scotland County and flows s into Gum Swamp Creek.

Turkey-Buzzard River. *See* Hyco River.

Turkey Cock Mountain. *See* Hibriten Mountain; Hen Mountain.

Turkey Cove, e Haywood County on the head of Cove Creek.

Turkey Cove, nw McDowell County.

Turkey Cove, nw Swain County between Twentymile Creek and Twentymile Ridge.

Turkey Cove Branch rises in w Madison County and flows se into Spring Creek.

Turkey Cove Gap, w Madison County between Turkey Cove Branch and East Fork Shut-in Creek.

Turkey Cove Gap, nw Swain County on Twentymile Ridge in Great Smoky Mountains National Park near lat. 35° 28' 09" N., long. 83° 50' 07" W.

Turkey Creek rises in nw Bertie County and flows nw into Hertford County and into Ahoskie Creek.

Turkey Creek is formed in nw Buncombe County by the junction of North and South Turkey creeks and flows ne and n into Sandy Mush Creek on the Madison County line.

Turkey Creek rises in w Duplin County and flows sw into Sampson County where it enters Six Runs Creek. Appears as Turkey Branch on the Collet map, 1770. Called Turkey Swamp on the 1959 Duplin County soil survey map.

Turkey Creek rises in e Haywood County and flows sw into Fines Creek.

Turkey Creek is formed on the Hertford-Northampton County line by the junction of Maple Fork Branch and a small unnamed stream which rises in Hertford County. It flows n along the county line into Kirbys Creek.

Turkey Creek rises in se Moore County and flows s into Little River.

Turkey Creek rises in sw Nash County and flows s into Wilson County where it joins Moccasin Creek to form Contentnea Creek.

Turkey Creek rises in s Onslow County and flows s into Spicers Bay.

Turkey Creek rises in s Pender County and flows sw into Northeast Cape Fear River.

Turkey Creek rises in w Swain County and flows ne into Nantahala River.

Turkey Creek is formed in n Transylvania County by the junction of South Prong Turkey Creek and North Prong Turkey Creek, and flows sw into Davidson River.

Turkey Creek rises in nw Wake County and flows s into Crabtree Creek.

Turkey Creek Gap, on the Buncombe-Haywood County line n of Big Butt Mountain near the headwaters of South Turkey Creek.

Turkey Gap, on the Haywood County, N. C.-Cocke County, Tenn., line.

Turkey Hen Mountain. See Hen Mountain.

Turkey Hill Creek rises in w Orange County and flows se into Cane Creek.

The Turkey Hole, a deep slough on the e side of Contentnea Creek, e Greene

County. So called from early times, probably from the abundance of wild turkeys in the vicinity.

Turkey Knob, n Henderson County near the head of Laurel Branch. Alt. approx. 3,600.

Turkey Knob, on Slickens Creek in e Jackson County.

Turkey Knob, on the Jackson-Macon County line. Alt. 4,540.

Turkey Knob, s Macon County between Board Gap and Wolf Gap.

Turkey Mountain, se McDowell County. Alt. approx. 1,900.

Turkey Mountain, w Madison County between Baltimore Branch and Spring Creek.

Turkey Pen, community in sw Cherokee County between Wolfe and Hot House creeks.

Turkeypen Branch rises in ne Cherokee County and flows s into Pile Creek.

Turkeypen Branch rises in s Watauga County and flows ne into Trout Creek.

Turkey Pen Cove, w Macon County between Pierce Creek and Nantahala River.

Turkey Pen Gap, on Forge Mountain in w Henderson County.

Turkey Pen Hollow, nw Cherokee County through which an unnamed stream flows se into Copper Creek.

Turkeypen Ridge, e Madison County at the head of West Fork [Bull Creek].

Turkey Point, s Onslow County at the mouth of Turkey Creek. Appears in local records as early as 1734.

Turkey Quarter Creek, nw Craven County, a channel of water separated from the main body of Neuse River by a large swampy island.

Turkey Quarters, name applied to a portion of what is now Pender County by Barbadian explorers in 1663 because of the many turkeys killed here. Appears on the Ogilby map, 1671, but otherwise no longer used.

Turkey Ridge, se Buncombe County between Johnson Cove and Briar Branch.

Turkey Swamp rises in s Martin County and flows s into Tranters Creek.

Turkey Swamp. See Turkey Creek.

Turkey Tail. See Glen Alpine.

Turkey Township, e Sampson County.

Turlington, community in e Harnett County. Slocomb Crossroads, formerly recognized as a separate community, is now a part of the Turlington community.

Turnagain Bay, ne Carteret County emptying into Neuse River. Known as The Bay until about 1775.

Turnagain Creek, ne Carteret County flows n to empty into Turnagain Bay. Known as The Bay Creek until around 1775. Said to have been named by Joseph Pittman who ran an Indian out of his sweet potato patch. The Indian fled, swam the creek and emerged on the opposite shore where he turned to make an insulting remark to Pittman. Pittman told him to "turn again" and repeat what he had said. This the Indian did, and Pittman shot him.

Turnage, community in s Edgecombe County.

Turnbull Creek rises in White Pond Bay in s Cumberland County and flows se into ne Bladen County where it enters Cape Fear River in central Bladen County. Named for Thomas Turnbull, an early colonial resident.

Turnbull Township in ne Bladen County.

Turner Branch rises in w Haywood County and flows nw into Jonathans Creek.

Turner Creek rises in s central Carteret County a short distance e of Beaufort and flows e approx. 1 mi. into Cheny Bay and North River.

Turner Creek rises in s Yadkin County and flows se into Yadkin River.

Turner Crossroads, community in e Cleveland County. Alt. 985.

Turner Crossroads, community in n Northampton County n of Cypress Creek.

Turner Crossroads, community in s central Northampton County s of Bear Swamp.

Turner Mountain, central Surry County. Alt. approx. 2,100.

Turners, community in n Polk County between Green River and Walnut Creek.

Turnersburg, community in ne Iredell County on Rocky Creek. Settled 1849 and named for Wilford Turner, local landowner. A nineteenth-century textile mill on Rocky Creek here was the first in the county; it was burned before 1900 but rebuilt and is still in operation. Alt. 791.

Turnersburg Township, ne Iredell County.

Turners Creek. See Neville Creek.

Turner's Crossroads. See Lewiston.

Turners Cut, an extension of the Dismal Swamp Canal, w Camden County. This is an extension of the canal from near its former mouth in the Pasquotank River to a point farther downstream bypassing a very narrow section of the river. The

Intracoastal Waterway passes through Turners Cut.

Turners Lake. See Lake Adger.

Turner Swamp rises in ne Wayne County and flows n into Wilson County where it enters Black Creek.

Turner Top, nw Cherokee County between Copper and Sular creeks.

Turnout, community in w Robeson County.

Turnpike, community in sw Buncombe County near the Haywood County line. Named from the fact that it was the site of the first tollgate w of Asheville on the old turnpike between Asheville and Murphy. In the early 1860's a tavern for the accommodation of stagecoach passengers was opened here by John C. Smathers; with the coming of the railroad in 1882 he enlarged his building and served meals to railway passengers and took in summer tourists. A post office existed here as early as 1882.

Turnpike Branch rises in e Hertford County and flows se into Hoggard Swamp.

Turnpike Creek rises in ne Cherokee County and flows nw into Valley River.

Turnpike Creek rises in s Haywood County and flows sw into West Fork Pigeon River.

Turpentine Creek rises in se Onslow County and flows se through tidal marsh into the Atlantic Ocean through Browns Inlet.

Turtle Pond Creek rises in s Macon County and flows n into Cullasaja River.

Turtletown, community in w Cherokee County on the Tennessee line, near Copperhill, Tenn.

Tuscarora, community in w Craven County. Settled 1825. Named for the Indians who formerly lived in the area. Alt. 39.

Tuscarora Beach, summer resort in e Hertford County near the town of Winton on Chowan River. Originally a Tuscarora Indian village; settled about 1710 by John Cotton of Virginia and known as Cotton's Crossing as late as 1759 when it was authorized to be laid out as the county seat. Later known as Old Barfields and Barfields.

Tuscola. See Lake Junaluska.

Tusk Creek, a tidal creek about 1 mi. n of Marshallberg in the waters of Core Sound, e Carteret County. Formerly known also as Wolfert Creek.

Tuskee Gap, n Swain County on Thomas Ridge in Great Smoky Mountains National Park near lat. 35° 33' 32" N., long. 83° 22' 25" W.

Tuskeegee, community in n Graham County on Tuskeegee Creek.

Tuskeegee Creek rises in n Graham County and flows ne into Little Tennessee River.

Tusquitee, community in central Clay County on Johnson Mill Creek. Alt. 2,050.

Tusquitee Bald, n Clay County near the headwaters of Compass Creek. Alt. 5,200-5,250.

Tusquitee Creek rises in ne Clay County and flows sw into Hiwassee River.

Tusquitee Gap, n Clay County near the headwaters of Clear Creek. Alt. approx. 3,800.

Tusquitee Mountains, nw Clay County extending ne from Leatherwood Branch to the Clay-Macon County line. Named for the Cherokee word Tusquittee or Tusquitta, "rafters," because the spurs of the range suggest the rafters of a roof.

Tusquitee Township, n Clay County.

Tussock Bay in e Bladen County.

Tuton. *See* St. Pauls.

Tuttles Cross Roads. *See* Hartland.

Tuttles Store, community in w Alexander County. Alt. approx. 1,100. A former post office, Partee, once served this community.

Tuxedo, community in s Henderson County on Lake Summit. Alt. 2,187. Post office est. 1908 as Lakewood, but name later changed to avoid confusion with another Lakewood in North Carolina. Tuxedo chosen simply because it was considered euphonious. Produces textiles.

Tweed Branch rises in se Cherokee County and flows se into Little Brasstown Creek.

Tweed Creek rises in s Buncombe County and flows s into Cane Creek.

Twelve O'Clock Top, knob on the Buncombe-Haywood County line between the head of Dutch Cove Creek and Rocky Face Mountain. Alt. approx. 4,640.

Twelvemile Creek formed in w Union County by the confluence of East Fork Twelvemile Creek and West Fork Twelvemile Creek, and flows sw into Catawba River in South Carolina.

Twentymile Creek rises in nw Swain County in Great Smoky Mountains National Park and flows sw into Little Tennessee River. Named because it is twenty miles from the junction of Tuckasegee and Little Tennessee Rivers.

Twentymile Ridge, nw Swain County in Great Smoky Mountains National Park. Its center is near lat. 35° 28' 50" N., long. 83° 50' 15" W.

Twin Falls in s Jackson County on Long Branch, ⅓ mi. n of Fairfield Lake. Alt. approx. 3,420.

Twin Knobs, n Wilkes County between East Prong Roaring River and Little Sandy Creek.

Twin Oaks, community in n central Alleghany County. Alt. 2,624.

Twin Poplars, mound and trees 4 mi. n of Lenoir central Caldwell County. According to local tradition, the Cherokee and Catawba Indians fought here for almost a week, until exhausted. They then made a pact declaring that thereafter the two tribes would live in peace. As a token of this, they constructed a mound of rocks and tied two young poplar trees together. These trees, now giants of the forest, stand approx. 12 ft. apart at the base, and approx. 20 ft. above the ground they join to form a single tree.

Twin Springs, springs near Cedar Knob in se Buncombe County, the source of a small unnamed stream which flows nw into Grassy Creek.

Twomile Creek rises in sw Guilford County and flows e into Deep River. Appears as Third Creek on the Collet map, 1770.

Twomile Swamp rises in w Sampson County and flows se into Caesar Swamp.

Tyancoka Creek. *See* Cokey Swamp.

Tyler Branch rises in w Macon County and flows sw into Nantahala River.

Tynch Town. *See* Harris Landing.

Tyndall Point, se Beaufort County, extends into Goose Creek.

Tyner. *See* Centre Hill.

Tyre Knob, on the Graham-Swain County line between Grassy Gap and Broke Yoke Gap. Named for the Biblical city on the Mediterranean Sea, famous throughout the classical world for its costly, royal purple. Called Tyre Top on some maps.

Tyre Top. *See* Tyre Knob.

Tyro, community in w Davidson County.

Tyro Township, w central Davidson County.

Tyrrell (TIR-ehl) County was formed in

1729 from Chowan, Bertie, Currituck, and Pasquotank counties. Located in the e section of the state, it is bounded by Albemarle Sound, and by Dare, Hyde, and Washington counties. It was named for Sir John Tyrrell (1685-1729), one of the Lords Proprietors of North Carolina. Area: 583 sq. mi. County seat: Columbia with an elevation of 10 ft. Townships are Alligator, Columbia, Gum Neck, Scuppernong, and South Fork. Produces soy-beans, corn, peanuts, hogs, livestock, and lumber.

Tyson Creek rises in w Pitt County and flows ne into Tar River.

Tyson Marsh, stream, rises in s Greene County and flows ne into Contentnea Creek.

Tyson's Mill. *See* Jefferson.

Tyson Township, s central Stanly County.

Tysonville, community in central Wake County named for Tyson's Chapel and long known by that name.

U

U-Alta Lake, w Randolph County, formed by a dam on Caraway Creek. Covers 20-25 acres. Named for Eula Alta Farlow, wife of Arthur Farlow who developed the lake. A boys' camp operated by the Baptist Church is here.

Ucohnerunt, a Tuscarora Indian town shown on the Moseley map, 1733, as situated on the mouth of Town Creek in what is now central Edgecombe County. Also called King Blount's Town for the chief under whom the Tuscarora Indians began their removal to the Roanoke River in 1732.

Ugly Creek rises in s Stanly County and flows se into Hardy Creek.

Ugly Fork, rises in w Haywood County near the Swain County line on the n side of Big Fork Ridge and flows e and ne into Rough Fork.

Ulah, community in s Randolph County. Originally Uhla; probably named for the daughter of M. R. Moffitt, first postmaster.

Umstead Bridge. *See* Redstone Point; Weir Point.

Umstead State Park. *See* William B. Umstead State Park.

Una Creek rises in se Swain County and flows w into Yalaka Creek.

Una Gap, se Swain County on Una Mountain near the head of Mason Branch.

Unahala, community in s Swain County on Yalaka Creek and Una Creek.

Unaka, community in nw Cherokee County near the junction of Copper and Beaverdam creeks.

Unaka Mountain on the Mitchell County, N. C.-Unicoi County, Tenn., line. Alt. approx. 5,190. *See also* Unicoi Mountains.

Unaka Mountains, Avery and Mitchell counties, N. C., and Unicoi and Carter counties, Tenn., forming the common boundary line between the two states from the Nolichucky River to the Doe River (in Tenn.). Of 40 miscellaneous maps, dating from 1795 to 1930, 22 called this ridge, in whole or in part, Iron Mountains; others divide between Iron and Yellow Mountains, and 5 call them Unaka the entire distance. Unaka is a corruption of Unega meaning "white," and was used in the act of 1789 passed by the General Assembly of North Carolina ceding what is now the state of Tennessee to the U.S. government.

Una Mountain, se Swain County on the head of Una Creek.

"Underground railroad." *See* Glassy Rock; Mount Jefferson.

Under Hills. *See* Piedmont.

Underwood Branch rises in ne Cherokee County and flows se into Webb Creek.

Underwood Mountain, w Henderson County, extends e in an arc between Little Willow Creek and South Fork. Alt. approx. 3,250.

Unicoi Gap, on the Cherokee County, N. C.-Monroe County, Tenn., line in the Unicoi Mountains.

Unicoi Mountains, Cherokee and Graham counties, N. C., and Monroe and Polk counties, Tenn., forming in part the common boundary line of the two states between the Little Tennessee River and Hiwassee River. The name is one of those in common use and was suggested by Horace Kephart and approved by the Nomenclature Committees of the Great

Smoky Mountains Park Commissions of N. C. and Tenn. This name, which, like Unaka, is a corruption of "Unega," meaning "white," is used in the act of 1789, passed by the Assembly of N. C. ceding what is now the state of Tennessee to the Federal Government: ". . . where it is called Unicoy or Unaka Mountain between the Indian towns of Cowee and Old Chota."

Union, community in s Hertford County. Inc. 1889; charter repealed 1939. Brittle Ordinary appears at this location on the Collet map, 1770; in 1808 it was called Brickle Inn; by 1833 a post office had been est. with the name Union.

Union, community in s Macon County on Dowdle Branch.

Union City. See Fairmont.

Union Copper Mine, former mine in ne Cabarrus County operated extensively from the early 1900's until 1914. Further explorations made in 1960, but mine not reopened for work.

Union County was formed in 1842 from Anson and Mecklenburg counties. Located in the s central section of the state, it is bounded by the state of South Carolina, and by Mecklenburg, Cabarrus, Stanly, and Anson counties. At the time the county was formed there was a dispute between local Whigs and Democrats as to whether it should be named Clay or Jackson. The name Union was suggested and adopted as a compromise and because the new county was created from parts of two others. Area: 643 sq. mi. County seat: Monroe with an elevation of 576 ft. Townships are Buford, Goose Creek, Jackson, Lanes Creek, Marshville, Monroe, New Salem, Sandy Ridge, and Vance. Produces oats, wheat, corn, cotton, lespedeza, poultry, turkeys, hogs, dairy products, livestock, textiles, apparel, bricks, processed meat, industrial machinery, wood products, asbestos, and crushed stone.

Union Cross, community in se Forsyth County.

Union Cross, community in central Yadkin County. Named for Union Cross Friends Meeting, organized in 1883.

Union Factory. See Randleman.

Union Grove, community in n Iredell County. Settled prior to 1847 when a Methodist Church was built. Named for a grove of trees in which union camp meetings were held. Alt. 850.

Union Grove, community in n Yadkin County near the head of Fall Creek.

Union Grove Township, n central Iredell County.

Union Hill, community in w Surry County between Little Mountain and South Fork.

Union Hill, community in ne Yadkin County.

Union Hope, community in sw Nash County.

Union Mills, community in n Rutherford County. Est. 1892. Inc. 1907; charter repealed 1924. Named from the consolidation of several small sawmills in the period 1885-1890.

Union Ridge, community in n Alamance County. Named for an old church which stood on the ridge here between Tom's Creek and Jordan Creek.

Union Ridge, community in s Forsyth County now within the urban extension of the city of Winston-Salem.

Union Township, n Pender County.

Union Township, s central Randolph County.

Union Township, sw Robeson County.

Union Township, sw Rutherford County.

Union Township, w Wilkes County.

Unionville, town in n Union County at the head of Chinkapin Creek. Inc. 1911.

Unity Parish, Church of England, Guilford County, est. 1771 with the formation of the county and coextensive with it. The parish as a unit of local administration was abolished in 1776 with the adoption of the state constitution and the disestablishment of the Church of England.

Unity Township, n Rowan County. Named for local Presbyterian Church.

University, community in e Orange County on Southern Railway approx. 9 mi. n of Chapel Hill, and former station serving the University of North Carolina. Railroad name for the station is Glenn. Alt. 471.

University Lake on Morgan Creek in s Orange County. Formed 1932 as a municipal water supply for Chapel Hill-

Carrboro. Covers 219 acres; max. depth 30 ft. Owned by the University of North Carolina.

Uno, community in central Henderson County on Clear Creek.

"Unorganized territory," the designation for most of the area formerly in Mattamuskeet Township, central Hyde County. Owned by the Federal government and used as a fish and wildlife reservation. Residents vote and list taxes in Lake Landing Township.

Upchurch, community in w Wake County. Named for William B. Upchurch around whose farm the community grew after a railway station was built here. Upchurch is said to have built first flue cure tobacco barn in Wake County.

Upchurch Pond on Rockfish Creek, e Hoke and w Cumberland counties. Approx. 5 mi. long.

Upper Bartons Creek rises in nw Wake County, nw of community of Leesville, and flows ne into Neuse River, w of mouth of Lower Bartons Creek. Formerly called Great Elliby and Little Elliby.

Upper Beaverdam Creek rises in w Scotland County and flows se into Richmond Millpond (Gum Swamp Creek).

Upper Broad Creek rises in ne Craven County on the Craven-Pamlico County line and flows sw along the line into Neuse River. Appears as Broad Creek on the Moseley map, 1733; mentioned in local records as early as 1723. Sometimes referred to in eighteenth century local records as Ashes Creek.

Upper Campbellton. See Fayetteville.

Upper Conetoe Township, former township in e Edgecombe County, now township number 3.

Upper Creek rises in nw Burke County and flows s and se to join Irish Creek in forming Warrior Fork [Catawba River].

Upper Creek rises in s Transylvania County and flows sw into East Fork French Broad River.

Upper Creek is formed in s Yancey County by the junction of Middle Fork Upper Creek and South Fork Upper Creek. It flows ne into South Toe River.

Upper Creek Township, n Burke County.

Upper Dowry Creek rises in e Beaufort County and flows approx. 1½ mi. s into Pungo River.

Upper Falls, in Snowbird Creek in sw Graham County. Water pours over a steep rock for 75 to 100 ft.

Upper Falls, the first of a series of three waterfalls on Yellowstone Prong, s Haywood County.

Upper Falls in sw Transylvania County in Laurel Creek. Height of the falls is 40 ft.

Upper Falls, se Yancey County near the head of Crabtree Creek. Water falls approx. 75 ft.

Upper Fishing Creek Township, former township in n Edgecombe County, now township number 6.

Upper Flat Creek. See Flat Creek.

Upper Flats, area of stony loam in nw Swain County on Greer Branch covering approx. 1.45 sq. mi., level except the e end which is hilly from n to s.

Upper Fork Township, sw Burke County.

Upper Goose Creek rises in central Beaufort County and flows s into Pamlico River.

Upper Haw Knob on the Madison-Yancey County line in the Walnut Mountains.

Upper Hominy Township, sw Buncombe County.

Upper Laurel Township, former township in ne Madison County, now township number 11.

Upper Little River is formed in se Caldwell County by a number of small streams. It flows se, forming a part of the Alexander-Caldwell County line, into Catawba River. Formerly known as Clarks Little River.

Upper Little River rises in s Lee County and flows se into Harnett County where it enters Cape Fear River. Scottish Highlanders settled the fertile lands along its banks during the period 1740-60. Appears on the Collet map, 1770.

Upper Little River Township, nw Harnett County.

Upper Long Creek rises in se Swain County and flows sw into Yalaka Creek.

Upper Pigeonroost, community on Right Fork [Pigeonroost Creek] in w Mitchell County.

Upper Poplar, community on Hollow Poplar Creek in nw Mitchell County.

Upper Richlands. See Richlands.

Upper Sassafras Gap, n Swain County in Great Smoky Mountains National Park on Noland Divide near lat. 35° 31' 56" N., long. 83° 27' 15" W.

Upper Saura Town, former Indian village in w Rockingham County on Dan River. Site approx. 4 mi. e of Madison. Probably occupied by Saura Indians by the middle of the seventeenth century and abandoned in the early eighteenth century. *Saura* or *Sara* meant "a place of tall grass or weeds." The site, occupied by whites, was still known as Sauratown as late as 1894. Appears on the Collet map, 1770, as Upper Sawra and on the Price map, 1808, as Saurat, but does not appear on later maps.

Upper Spring Creek rises in nw Goose Creek Island, nw Pamlico County and flows n to join Campbell Creek at the Beaufort-Pamlico County line in forming Goose Creek.

Upper Town Creek Township, former township in w Edgecombe County, now township number 11.

Upper Township, former township in n Chowan County, now township number 3.

Upper Trail Ridge, sw Macon County between Nichols Branch and Big Shoal Branch.

Upton, community in nw Caldwell County. Alt. 1,420.

Upward, community in e Henderson County. Took its name from a local estate of a South Carolina summer resident.

Urahaw Swamp rises in s Northampton County and flows ne into Potecasi Creek. The name appears in local records as early as 1719.

Uree, community in nw Rutherford County on Broad River.

Utah Mountain, central Haywood County between Snakeden Top and Fulbright Cove. Named from the fact that a band of Mormons lived here in the 1880's and 1890's. Their practicing polygamy made them unpopular with their neighbors and the Mormons were forced to leave North Carolina. Their houses, barns, fences, and other property were abandoned and the ruins still exist. Orchards and vineyards as well as ornamental flowering shurbs are now growing wild in the vicinity.

Utley's Creek rises in s Wake County near Holly Springs and flows sw into Big White Oak Creek.

Uwharrie (u-whar-e), community in nw Montgomery County.

Uwharrie Mountains extend ne-sw across Montgomery, Randolph, and Stanly counties. The Yadkin River flows through their sw end. Geologists describe them as isolated, residual knobs which have resisted erosion and weathering better than the surrounding countryside. They were probably formed several hundred million years ago by a number of explosive-type volcanoes. The name may be derived from Suala, a name applied by De Soto to the Indians he found on the s border of what is now North Carolina. Lawson visited the area in 1701 and used the name Heighwaree. Morrow Mountain State Park and Town Creek Indian Mound Historic Site are here. There are many named peaks, particularly in Montgomery and Randolph counties. Alts. are not over 1,800 ft.

Uwharrie National Forest, largely in w Montgomery County but also in sw Randolph County, se Davidson County, and nw Stanly County. Covers 204,682 acres with headquarters in Troy. Originally laid out as a purchase unit in 1934 and made a National Forest in 1961.

Uwharrie River rises in nw Randolph County and flows s into Montgomery County, thence sw to join the Yadkin River in forming the Pee Dee River. The source of the Uwharrie River is approx. 840 ft. above sea level, and the elevation at the junction of the Uwharrie and Yadkin rivers is approx. 280 ft. Appears as Uharie River on the Moseley map, 1733, but is incorrectly placed and out of proportion. The Collet map, 1770, makes the necessary corrections but calls it Voharee Creek.

Uwharrie Township, w Montgomery County.

V

Vade Mecum, former resort and present Episcopal Church summer camp, at the junction of Vade Mecum Creek and South Double Creek in w Stokes County. Alt. 1,800. Local mineral springs ac-

credited with curative powers by Saura Indians; about 1860 the site was acquired by Sparks family, circus operators, who built a resort hotel; later acquired by Episcopal Church. Name from Latin,

go *with me*, attributed to an Indian
legend involving a planned elopement.

Vade Mecum Creek rises in w Stokes County and flows ne into South Double Creek.

Valda. See Val Dor.

Valdese, town in e central Burke County.
Alt. 1,203. Settled in 1893 by a group of
Waldensians from n Italy. Inc. 1920.
Name is Italian for "Valley of Our Lord."
Produces hosiery, textiles, furniture, and
bakery products.

Val Dor (or **Valda**), former rural post office
located in a country store on the headwaters of Silver Creek, sw Burke County.
Operated for approx. 2 years around
1900. Probably named for a gold mine
on the Hodge plantation approx. 1 mi.
away.

Vale, community in central Avery County.

Vale, community in nw Lincoln County.
Noted for the apple orchards in the
vicinity. Post office est. in 1924.

Valhalla, community in central Chowan
County. Alt. 39.

Valhalla, community in sw Polk County.
Settled about 1885. Named for the
Norse mythological hall of Odin where
the souls of heroes slain in battle were
received; the name is said to have been
applied in commemoration of the battle
at Round Mountain, *which see*, in 1776.

Valhalla Dome, peak on the ne end of Rich
Mountain, w Mitchell County. Alt. over
4,060 ft.

Valle Crucis, community in central Watauga County near the junction of Dutch
Creek and Watauga River. Est. in 1842
as an Episcopal mission. The name is
Latin for "Valley of the Cross," because
of the shape of the Watauga River valley
here. The valley is approx. 600 acres in
extent. Alt. 3,000.

Valley, community on Roaring Creek in w
Avery County. Sometimes also called
Roaring Creek.

Valley Creek rises in sw Watauga County
and flows e in an arc into Watauga River.

Valley River rises in ne Cherokee County
and flows sw into Hiwassee River at
Murphy.

Valley River Mountains extend along the
Cherokee-Clay County line to Macon
County.

Valley Springs, community in s Buncombe
County.

Valley Squirrel Gap, ne Cherokee County
between Andrews and Rhodo.

Valley Town, community in ne Cherokee

County on the outskirts of Andrews,
which see. A post office existed here as
early as 1882.

Valley Town Township, ne Cherokee
County.

Valmead, community in central Caldwell
County. A large part of the community
was annexed to the city of Lenoir prior
to 1960. Named for its location in a
valley meadow. Alt. 1,131.

Vanceboro, town in n Craven County on
Swift Creek. Settled about 1750, known
as Durgantown. Name changed in 1845-
50 to Swift Creek. Inc. 1877 as Vanceboro in honor of Governor Z. B. Vance
(1830-94) after he made a campaign
speech here in 1876, running for second
term as governor. Alt. 24.

Vance County was formed in 1881 from
Granville, Warren, and Franklin counties.
Located in the ne section of the state,
it is bounded by Warren, Franklin, and
Granville counties, and by the state of
Virginia. It was named for Zebulon Baird
Vance (1830-94), governor of North
Carolina, Congressman, and Senator.
Area. 268 sq. mi. County seat: Hender-
son with an elevation of 513 ft. Town-
ships are Dabney, Henderson, Kittrell,
Middleburg, Nutbush, Sandy Creek,
Townsville, Watkins, and Williamsboro.
Produces tobacco, corn, wheat, oats, cot-
ton, poultry, hogs, dairy products, live-
stock, cantaloupes, textiles, hosiery, glass
products, pickles, tungsten, crushed stone,
and sand.

Vance Knob, n Buncombe County between
Ray Knob and the junction of Ox and
Reems creeks.

Vance Mountain, sw Cherokee County be-
tween Hot House and Rapier Mill creeks.
Probably named for Governor Zebulon
B. Vance (1830-94).

Vance Mountain, on the Henderson County, N. C.-Greenville County, S. C., line.
Named for Governor Z. B. Vance (1830-
94). The scene of the Vance-Carson duel.

Vance Township, w Union County.

Vandalia, former community in s Guilford County, now within the Greensboro city limits.

Vandemere, town in n Pamlico County on Bay River. A Dr. Abbott, former Union army surgeon, settled here in the 1870's, and his wife gave the community its name—a Dutch word meaning "from the sea." Inc. 1874; charter repealed in 1893 but renewed two years later. From the formation of Pamlico County in 1872 until 1876 Vandemere served as the county seat. Alt. 4.

Vandemere Creek rises in n Pamlico County and flows se into Bay River.

Vander, community in central Cumberland County. Alt. 151.

Vanderpool Creek rises in central Watauga County and flows nw into Cove Creek.

Van Eden, community in n Pender County. Est. on land purchased in 1909 by Frederik van Eeden (1860-1932) and Hugh MacRae for a colony of Dutch farmers. In 1939 the remaining land was purchased by a New York corporation as a refuge for Jews fleeing Germany. The last Dutch family left in 1949.

Vannoy, community in nw Wilkes County on North Fork Reddies River.

Van Noy Branch rises in ne McDowell County and flows e into Long Branch.

Van Swamp, extends ne from n Beaufort County into sw Washington County. Area, approx. 12,000 acres.

Vanteen, community in n central Wake County.

Varina, former town in sw Wake County. Settled about 1890, and named for first postmaster's wife, who used the fanciful name, Varina, in her courtship correspondence. Alt. 426. Merged with Fuquay Springs to become part of Fuquay-Varina in 1963.

Varnals Creek rises in the Cane Creek Mountains, s Alamance County, and flows ne into Haw River.

Varnum, community in s central Brunswick County on Lockwoods Folly River.

Vashti, community in ne Alexander County. Known as Cedar Run in the 1880's when Cedar Academy was operated here. Alt. approx. 1,240.

Vass, town in e Moore County. Known as Winder, for an official of the Raleigh and Augusta Air Line Railroad, prior to 1907 when it was inc. with its present name. Named for William Worrell Vass (1820-96), treasurer of the Raleigh and Gaston Railroad, 1845-90. Produces textiles. Alt. 320.

Vaughan, town in e central Warren County. Alt. 353. Founded in 1851 as Brown's Siding or Brown's Turnout by Dr. Ridley Browne. Name changed to Vaughn in 1881 in honor of John F. Vaughn, local merchant and first postmaster. Inc. 1893.

Vaughan Creek rises in South Carolina and flows n into Polk County where it enters Lake Lanier.

Vaughan Hill, an elevation on the Fort Bragg Military Reservation, nw Cumberland County.

Vaughan's Springs, se Surry County, mineral springs resort developed by the Gid Y. Vaughan family in the early twentieth century and in recent years the site of Camp Wilson, a private summer camp for boys.

Vaught Gap, w Watauga County in Stone Mountains near the head of Beaverdam Creek.

Veecaune Creek. See Wiccacon River.

Vein Mountain, community in s McDowell County. Named from the fact that it lies in a former gold mining area.

Venable. See Carrboro.

Vengeance Creek rises in ne Cherokee County and flows nw into Valley River.

Venters, community in s Pitt County.

Vera Cruz Shoal, ne Carteret County, obstructing in part Ocracoke Inlet. Known during the eighteenth century as Dry Sand Shoal for the fact that it was never covered by water except during a gale.

Verd, community in sw Madison County.

Verona, community in central Onslow County. Named as a means of honoring Vera McIntyre whose husband was one of the builders of the Wilmington and Onslow Railroad. A post office, Aman's Store, was est. nearby as early as 1862. With the construction of the railroad and the establishment of Verona the post office was moved here and the name changed. Alt. 49.

Vests, community in w Cherokee County sw of Hiwassee Lake.

Viands, community in central Wilkes County s of the junction of Middle and North Prongs Roaring River. The name means "food" or "provisions."

Vicksboro, community in e Vance and w Warren counties. Known prior to 1885, and until after 1913, as Coleys Cross-roads.

Victoria, former town in central Buncombe County. Inc. 1887; became a part of Asheville, 1905.

Vienna, town in w Forsyth County, inc. 1794, but not now active in municipal affairs.

Vienna Township, w Forsyth County.

Vilas, community in w central Watauga County on Linville Creek. Alt. 2,811.

Village Creek rises in n Craven County and flows ne into Neuse River.

Villanow. *See* White Hill.

Vinegar Hill, community in se Beaufort County.

Vineland. *See* Southern Pines; Whiteville.

Vine Swamp rises in e Lenoir County and flows e into Jones County where it enters Beaver Creek. Named prior to the Revolution for the Vine family which settled nearby.

Vineyard Creek rises in e Clay County and flows s into Shooting Creek.

Vineyard Mountain, s Clay County. Alt. approx. 4,900. An Englishman is said to have covered the mountain with grape vines, but his vineyard failed to prosper and he returned to England.

Vineyard Mountain, w Randolph County just w of Caraway Mountain in a close group with Black Jack, Slick Rock, and Prickly Pear Mountains.

Vinson Store, former community in e Wayne County near West Bear Creek.

Violet, community in w Cherokee County on Sular Creek between Swansee and Morrow Gaps.

Virgil, community in e Watauga County.

Virgilina, town in nw Granville County on the Virginia-North Carolina border,

hence its name. Inc. 1899 in North Carolina and 1900 in Virginia.

Virginia, the name applied to the American territory granted by Queen Elizabeth to Walter Raleigh and explored in 1584 by Philip Amadas and Arthur Barlowe. The earliest evidence of the use of the name occurs before March 25, 1585, in Raleigh's seal as Lord and Governor of Virginia which is now in the British Museum. The name honored Elizabeth, "The Virgin Queen," and was applied in the sixteenth century to the area explored from bases on Roanoke Island. In the seventeenth century it came to be applied to the permanent settlement around Jamestown, and after the granting of the Carolina charter in 1663 it no longer was applied correctly to the territory which was soon to become North Carolina. *See also* South Virginia.

Virginia Creek rises in se Pender County and flows se into Topsail Sound.

Virgin's Inlet, apparently a short-lived inlet in se Onslow County from Brown's Sound into the Atlantic Ocean. It was described in records of 1784-1785 as being near Gillets Creek.

Vista, community in s Pender County on Virginia Creek.

Vivian, community in s Gates County.

Vixen, community central Yancey County. Alt. 2,278.

Voharee Creek. *See* Uwharrie River.

Volga, community in s Madison County on French Broad River. Alt. 1,721.

Vosses Creek. *See* Mill Creek.

Vultare, community in nw Northampton County.

W

Waccamaw River rises in Lake Waccamaw, ne Columbus County, and flows s and sw in part along the Brunswick-Columbus County line into South Carolina where it enters Winyah Bay. Appears on the Collet map, 1770.

Waccamaw Township, w Brunswick County.

Waccamaw Township, n Columbus County.

Wach. *See* Wachovia; Salem Creek.

Wachovia, a tract of land laid off by the General Assembly in 1755, in ne Rowan

County (now Forsyth) as an area for settlement by Moravians. The Parish of Dobbs was est. at the same time, coextensive with Wachovia. Wachovia or Wachau-the-Aue (meadow land) along the Wach or Wack (principal stream) received its name from the fact that it bore some resemblance from its water course and meadow land to a valley in Austria of the same name which formerly belonged to the Zinzendorf family, prominent Moravian leaders. The parish was named Dobbs in honor of Governor Arthur Dobbs. *See also* Dobbs Parish.

Wack. *See* Wachovia; Salem Creek.

Waco, town in e Cleveland County. Alt. 916. settled 1857. Inc. 1887. Named by George W. Hendrick for Waco, Texas.

Wade, town in ne Cumberland County. Settled about 1886. Inc. 1889; reinc. 1913, but long inactive in municipal affairs. Named for N. G. Wade who donated the railroad right-of-way. Alt. 141.

Wade Creek rises in e Carteret County and flows s approx. 1 mi. into Jarrett Bay. Formerly also known as Willis Creek.

Wade Gap, in Newfound Mountain on Buncombe-Haywood County line near the headwaters of Sandy Mush Creek.

Wade Point extends from s Pasquotank County into Albemarle Sound. Appears as Wades Point on the Moseley map, 1733. It lies between Big Flatty Creek and the Pasquotank River.

Wadesboro, town and county seat, central Anson County. Authorized to be est. 1783 as county seat. Called New Town until 1787 when it was changed to Wadesboro to honor Col. Thomas Wade, Revolutionary patriot and brother-in-law of Patrick Boggan, pioneer settler. Alt. 423. Scientists from all over the United States and Europe gathered here in 1900 to view a total eclipse of the sun. Produces hosiery, textiles, wooden boxes.

Wadesboro City Pond, s central Anson County on Jones Creek. Formed 1938. Covers 75 acres with a max. depth of 25 ft. Municipal water supply, fishing, boating.

Wadesboro Township, central Anson County.

Wades Point, point of land in e Beaufort County on the n side of Pamlico River at the w side of the mouth of Pungo River, lat. 35° 23′ 18″ N., long. 76° 34′ 35″ W. *See also* Moores Beach. Appears as Battis Point on the Comberford map, 1657.

Wade's Shore, a bay on the n side of Shackleford Banks, s Carteret County. A former whaling settlement by the same name existed here.

Wadeville, community in s Montgomery County. Est. 1872 and named for Wade brothers who operated a store here in

which the first post office was est. Alt. 558.

Wading Branch Ridge, n Haywood County parallel to Dicks Branch.

Wading Place Creek rises in e central Bertie County and flows s into Cashie River.

Wads Creek rises in central Moore County and flows se into Little River. Named for William Wadsworth who settled on its banks in 1756.

Wagner Branch rises in central Buncombe County near Beard Mountain and flows nw into Reems Creek.

Wagoner, community in e central Ashe County.

Wagoner, community in w Yadkin County near South Deep Creek.

Wagon Road Gap on the Haywood-Transylvania County line at the nw tip of Wagon Road Ridge. Began as a foot trail for man and horse on way to Brevard; later widened for 2-wheeled wagons to haul salt and other provisions and eventually for large, 4-wheeled wagons hence the name. The Blue Ridge Parkway now crosses the Wagon Road at this point. Alt. 4,535.

Wagon Road Gap in nw Transylvania County between Poplar Lick Gap and Sandy Gap n of Pine Mountain.

Wagon Road Ridge extends se in n Transylvania County from Pisgah Ridge on the Haywood-Transylvania County line to the confluence of the forks of Bearwallow Brook.

Wagon Timber Branch rises in central Cherokee County and flows se into Colvard Creek.

Wagram, town in e Scotland County. Known first as Montpelier, then (around 1900) as Fontcal. Inc. 1911 as Wagram. Probably named for the Austrian town where a battle was fought in 1809 during Napoleonic Wars. Alt. 250.

Wagstaff Store, community in w Person County.

Wahoo, community in nw Alexander County on Middle Little River.

Wahtom Pocosin, nw Bertie County.

Wahtom Swamp rises in nw Bertie County and flows se into Cashie River.

Wainwright Island, approx. ⅔ mi. long, in Core Sound, ne Carteret County. Probably· named for James Winwright or Wainwright.

Wake County was formed in 1771 from Johnston, Cumberland, and Orange counties. Located in the e central section of the state, it is bounded by Johnston, Harnett, Chatham, Durham, Granville, and Franklin counties. It was named for Margaret Wake (1733-1819), wife of Governor William Tryon. Area: 867 sq. mi. County seat: Raleigh is also state capital and has an elevation of 363 ft. Townships are Barton Creek, Buckhorn, Cary, Cedar Fork, Holly Springs, House Creek, Leesville, Little River, Marks Creek, Meredith, Middle Creek, Neuse River, New Light, Panther Branch, Raleigh, St. Marys, St. Matthews, Swift Creek, Wake Forest, and White Oak. Produces tobacco, corn, wheat, oats, cotton, poultry, dairy products, hogs, livestock, farm machinery, concrete products, baked goods, textiles, cottonseed oil, apparel, furniture, crushed stone, and fabricated metals.

Wake County Court House. *See* Raleigh.

Wakefield, community in e Wake County, 1 mi. n of Zebulon. Inc. 1899; charter repealed 1913. Named for its location on a field in Wake County. The failure of local citizens to sell land for a right-of-way resulted in the location of a railroad a short distance south where the town of Zebulon soon developed. Alt. 338.

Wake Forest, town in ne Wake County between Hatters Branch and Richland Creek. Settled 1823. Inc. 1880 as "town of Wake Forest College," but referred to after the turn of the century as Wake Forest. Named for large wooded areas of n Wake County. Home of Wake Forest College (1834-1956) until it was moved to Winston-Salem. Home of Southeastern Baptist Theological Seminary since 1951. Produces textiles. Alt. 400.

Wake Forest Township, ne Wake County.

Wakelon, community in ne Bertie County.

Wakulla, community in nw Robeson County. Alt. 208. Settled about 1860. Named by Colonel Peter P. Smith for the Indian word meaning "clear water" because of numerous springs in the vicinity.

Walden Creek rises in se Brunswick County and flows e into Cape Fear River.

Waldrop Branch rises in ne Cherokee County and flows s into Valley River.

Walker, community in w Polk County on Harm Creek.

Walker Bald, w Haywood County se of Potato Patch. Alt. 5,420. Named for Felix Walker (1753-1828), land speculator and member of Congress, whose cabin dwelling was at its base on upper Jonathan Creek.

Walker Branch rises in ne Buncombe County and flows w to join Corner Rock Creek to form Dillingham Creek. Walker Falls are on this stream.

Walker Branch rises in ne Buncombe County near Brushy Knob and flows w through Walkertown into North Fork [Swannanoa River].

Walker Branch rises in central Lincoln and flows sw into Clark Creek.

Walker Branch rises in sw Mecklenburg County and flows se into Steele Creek.

Walker Creek rises in sw Brunswick County, Virginia, and flows s into ne Warren County, N. C., where it enters Gaston Lake.

Walker Creek rises in s Transylvania County and flows nw into Little River.

Walker Falls, waterfalls in ne Buncombe County on Walker Branch.

Walker Gap, in Yellow Creek Mountains in n Graham County.

Walker Gap, w Swain County between the head of Mill Branch and Rowan Branch.

Walker Knob, ne Buncombe County near Balsam Gap in the Great Craggy Mountains.

Walker Knob, mountain in sw Burke County. Alt. 2,919.

Walker Low Gap, e Haywood County on Glades Mountain.

Walker Mill Creek rises in sw Cherokee County and flows se into Nottely River.

Walker Mountain, w Montgomery County between Woodrun Creek and Dennis Mountain.

Walker Ridge, ne Buncombe County w of Walker Knob.

Walkers, community in e central Pender County on Burgaw Creek. Formerly known as Walkers Store.

Walkers Bluff, on Cape Fear River in e Bladen County, 5 mi. above White Hall Landing.

Walkers Branch rises in sw Yadkin County and flows e into North Hunting Creek.

Walkersburg, town in se Brunswick County at Deep Water Point. Inc. 1784 on lands of John Walker for whom it was named. Courthouse and other public buildings were to be est. here, but apparently this was never done.

Walkers Creek rises in n Swain County in Great Smoky Mountains National Park on the s slope of Mount Davis and flows s on the e side of Locust Ridge into Hazel Creek.

Walkers Creek rises in central Warren County and flows se to join Big Branch in forming Little Fishing Creek.

Walkersville, community in s central Union County on the e side of Cane Creek. Formerly known as Wilson's Old Store community. Shown on maps as Walkersville as early as 1886.

Walker Top, on the Buncombe-Haywood County line.

Walkertown, community in ne Buncombe County.

Walkertown, community in e Forsyth County. Dr. Robert Walker was living here as early as 1771 and the community was named for him. Love's Meeting House (Methodist) built here in 1797 was visited by Bishop Francis Asbury in 1799. He was greatly impressed by its glass windows. Alt. 980.

Walkeys, community in sw Union County.

The Walks, series of immovable natural stepping stones below Flat Shoals of Watauga River, near the Tennessee line in nw Watauga County. They are regularly placed across the river and one may walk over even when stream is swollen, hence the name.

Wallace, town in s Duplin County. Alt. 51. Inc. 1873 as Duplin Roads. Name changed to Wallace in honor of Stephen D. Wallace, vice president of the Atlantic Coast Line Railroad, prior to 1899, in which year the town was reinc. Produces textiles.

Wallace Branch rises in central Lee County and flows ne into Lick Creek.

Wallace Branch rises in central Macon County and flows se into Cartoogechaye Creek.

Wallace Branch rises in se Union County and flows ne into Little Brown Creek.

Wallace Channel, ne Carteret County, a navigable lane in Ocarcoke Inlet running nw and se. Appears by this name on the Price survey of Ocracoke Inlet, 1795. Named for David Wallace, Jr., whose house on Portsmouth Island was used as a sighting point by pilots using the channel entering the Atlantic Ocean. Sometimes referred to as Beacon Island Road in the eighteenth century.

Wallace Creek rises in ne Alexander County and flows s in Greasy Creek. Probably named for Richard Wallace, pioneer Baptist minister.

Wallace Creek rises in ne Mecklenburg County and flows ne into Cabarrus County where it enters Reedy Creek.

Wallace Creek rises in e Onslow County and flows se into Morgan Bay. Named in local records as early as 1744 as Wallace's Creek.

Wallace Gap, sw Macon County between the head of Allison Creek and Nantahala River.

Wallace Gap, s Transylvania County between the head of Boring Creek and the head of West Prong [of Glady Fork].

Wallace Mountain, ne Buncombe County near Walkertown.

Wallace's Creek. See Wallace Creek.

Walla Watta, community in n central Beaufort County, lat. 35° 35' N., long. 76° 52' 15" W. Named by Surry Parker, local lumberman, for Wallace and Waters families who lived here. Alt. 34.

Wallburg, community in ne Davidson County. Named for Sam. W. Wall, state Senator in 1895.

Wallnut-Tree Creek. See Walnut Creek.

Walnut, community in central Madison County between Brush Creek and Hopewell Branch. Inc. 1905; charter repealed 1917. Named for walnut trees in the vicinity. See also Marshall.

Walnut Bottom in nw Haywood County on Big Creek in the Great Smoky Mountains National Park. Named from the fact that numerous walnut trees formerly grew in the narrow bottom land here.

Walnut Branch rises in w Alleghany County and flows e into Elk Creek.

Walnut Cove, w Macon County on a tributary of Nantahala River.

Walnut Cove, town in s Stokes County. Settled 1883 and know as Lash until 1889 when it was inc. under its present name. Named for a grove of walnut trees. Alt. 634. Stokesbury, formerly a separate community just s of Walnut Cove, is now within the corporate limits.

Walnut Cove Branch rises in s Madison County and flows se into Little Sandymush Creek.

Walnut Cove Branch rises in w central Transylvania County and flows s into Catheys Creek.

Walnut Creek rises in e Macon County and flows sw into Cullasaja River.

Walnut Creek rises in central Madison County and flows sw into French Broad River.

Walnut Creek rises in n Polk County and flows se into Green River.

Walnut Creek rises in w Wake County on the e edge of the town of Cary and flows e, s of the city of Raleigh, into Neuse River. Appears as Wallnut-Tree Creek on the Collet map, 1770.

Walnut Creek rises in e Wayne County and flows se then sw into Neuse River. (As location of Dobbs County courthouse, see Bizzell Millpond.)

Walnut Creek, community in central Madison County on Walnut Creek.

Walnut Creek Gap, between Walnut Creek and the head of Moss Branch in e Macon County.

Walnut Creek Township, former township in central Edgecombe County, now township number 11.

Walnut Gap, on the Macon-Jackson County line. Alt. 4,150.

Walnut Gap, n Madison County at the head of Walnut Creek.

Walnut Gap, n Madison County at the head of Woolsey Branch.

Walnut Grove Township, w central Granville County.

Walnut Grove Township, n Wilkes County.

Walnut Hill, mountain in ne Ashe County. Alt. approx. 2,700.

Walnut Hill Township, ne Ashe County.

Walnut Hollow Gap, in n Graham County on Tuskeegee Creek.

Walnut Knob, on the Alexander-Wilkes County line. Alt. approx. 1,990.

Walnut Knob, central Madison County on the s end of Pilot Ridge.

Walnut Knob, n Madison County between Big Laurel Creek and Walnut Gap.

Walnut Mountains extend e through central Madison County from French Broad River into w Yancey County. Alt. 4,335.

Walsh, community in w Wilkes County on North Prong Lewis Fork Creek.

Walstonburg, town in n Greene County. Lands here acquired after 1775 by John Chester whose plantation house,

"Chesterfield," still stands. His son-in-law, Bennett Fields, after 1845 changed the name to Fieldsboro. The latter name was, and is still, used as the name of the railroad station. Fields' cousin, Seth Walston, acquired the property after the Civil War and the name Walstonburg came to be applied. Inc. in 1908 as Walstonburg.

Walter Rawleigh. See Roanoke Sound.

Walter Slough in the waters of Pamlico Sound nw of Oregon Inlet, e Dare County.

Walters Mill, community in nw Caswell County named for the mill on Hogans Creek.

Walters Mill Pond, nw Lenoir County, originally formed about 1755; rebuilt about 1900. Fed by springs and wells and drains into nearby Moseley Creek. Covers 32 acres; max. depth 12 feet.

Walthall. See Wilbon.

Walton County was created by the State of Georgia in part in territory claimed by that state but which a subsequent survey made in 1807 revealed to be in Buncombe County, North Carolina. Riots and bloodshed occurred during the "Georgia War" over disputed land grants made by the two states in the area. For further information see F. A. Sondley, *A History of Buncombe County*, II, 685-87.

Walton Crossroads, community in s Gates County.

Walton Pond, a swamp, rises in s Gates County and drains se into Trotman Creek. Watton Mill appears on this stream on the Collet map, 1770, and the name is derived from the mill which existed as late as 1833 but had disappeared by 1862.

Wampler. See Elk Shoal.

Wananish, former community in n Columbus County. Now within the limits of the town of Lake Wacamaw but still with its own post office. It was to have been named Ouaniche for the Indian word meaning "land-locked salmon," but the spelling Wananish was preferred for the post office name.

Wanchese, community on the s end of Roanoke Island, e Dare County. Named for one of the two Indians taken to England by Amadas and Barlowe in 1584. Produces packaged sea food. Alt. 10.

Wantland's Ferry. See Jacksonville.

Warbler, former community in s Tyrrell

County between Kilkenny and Kilkenny Landing but now absorbed into the community of Kilkenny. Warbler was the post office for the region.

Ward Creek rises in e Carteret County and flows s into North River. Appears on the Moseley map, 1733.

Ward Creek rises in n Cleveland County and flows sw into First Broad River.

Ward Gap, on the Burke-Cleveland County line.

Ward Gap, w Watauga County on the head of Phillips Branch.

Ward Hollow, w Watauga County, extends sw from Love Gap to Watauga River.

Ward Mine, a gold mine in e Davidson County, worked as early as 1842 and shown on maps as recently as 1915. Ward Gold-Mine Co., chartered 1852, purchased 400-acre tract from John Ward.

Ward Mountain, n Henderson County on Featherston Creek.

Ward Run rises in se Wilson County and flows se into Pitt County where it turns sw and enters Little Contentnea Creek.

Wards, community in central Columbus County.

Wards Corner, community in w Pender County at the intersection of two highways.

Wards Creek. See Hawkins Slough.

Wards Mountain, n Avery County.

Wards Mountain, sw Orange County between Toms Creek and Cane Creek.

Wards Store, community in se Randolph County.

Ward Swamp rises in n Sampson County and flows sw into Great Coharie Creek.

Wardville, community in e Gates County. Name changed from Bosley about 1936.

Ware Creek rises in central Carteret County and flows sw into the mouth of Newport River.

Wareiock. See Beaufort.

Warington. See Fort Landing.

Warlick Township, former township in e Cleveland County, now township number 5.

Warm Cove Branch rises in w Haywood County in the Great Smoky Mountains National Park and flows se into Caldwell Fork.

Warm Springs. See Hot Springs.

Warne, community in s Clay County between Crawford and Brasstown creeks. Alt. 1,800. Named for the Warrens, an

English family who mined gold here; the name was corrupted to Warne by the Indians.

Warowtani appears on the White map, 1585, as a village of the Weapemeoc Indians, located in what is now s Chowan County on Albemarle Sound near Edenton.

Warren, community in n Craven County. Settled after 1910. Named for James and Ben Warren, local residents. Alt. 11.

Warren Bridge. See East Lake Landing; Sandy Point.

Warren County was formed in 1779 from Bute County when it was divided to form Warren and Franklin counties. Located in the ne section of the state, it is bounded by Northampton, Halifax, Franklin, and Vance counties. It was named for General Joseph Warren (1741-75), Revolutionary patriot and physician, killed at Bunker Hill. Area: 445 sq. mi. County seat: Warrenton with an elevation of 451 ft. Townships are Fishing Creek, Fork, Hawtree, Judkins, Nutbush, River, Roanoke, Sandy Creek, Shocco, Sixpound, Smith Creek, and Warrenton. Produces tobacco, corn, wheat, oats, cotton, poultry, dairy products, hogs, livestock, lumber products, textiles.

Warren Creek rises in sw Buncombe County near the Haywood County line and flows nw into South Hominy Creek.

Warren Hollow, n Watauga County, extends sw from State Line Ridge to North Fork of Cove Creek.

Warren Plains, community in central Warren County. Alt. 450. The site of a post office since 1857.

Warren Ridge, sw Buncombe County between Warren and Curtis creeks.

Warren's Station. See Conetoe.

Warrensville, town in central Ashe County. Inc. 1931 but not now active in municipal affairs. Settled about 1826 and known as Buffalo Creek until renamed for the builder of first grist and sawmill.

Warrenton, city and county seat, in w central Warren County. Inc. 1779. Alt.

451. Named for the county, in turn named for Joseph Warren, killed at Bunker Hill. Produces lumber products, textiles.

Warrenton Township, central Warren County.

Warrick. See Peterson.

Warrick Branch rises in w Mitchell County and flows s into Toe River.

Warrington. See Fort Landing.

Warrior, Negro community in central Caldwell County.

Warrior Creek rises in central Caldwell County and flows ne into Yadkin River in w end of Happy Valley.

Warrior Creek rises in s Wilkes County and flows n into W. Kerr Scott Reservoir. Originally known as Bear Creek. Daniel Boone's wilderness trail into Kentucky passed nearby.

Warrior Creek. See Boomer.

Warrior Fork [Catawba River] is formed in w central Burke County by the junction of Irish and Upper creeks and flows se into Catawba River.

Warrior Gap, central Caldwell County.

Warrior Mountain, central Caldwell County. Alt. approx. 2,000.

Warrior Mountain, s Polk County. See Big Warrior Mountain and Little Warrior Mountain.

Warrior Mountain, nw Surry County. Alt. 1,805.

Warsaw, town in w Duplin County. Alt. 160. Settled about 1825. Inc. 1855. Named by the conductor of the first train to run through the then crossroads community because he was reading a popular novel, *Thaddeus of Warsaw* by Jane Porter (1776-1850). Produces apparel.

Warsaw Township, w central Duplin County.

Warwick Bay, a natural lake, one of the Carolina Bays, *which see,* in e Robeson County. Approx. 1¾ mi. long and 1 mi. wide. Drained from the se by Peter Swamp. Known also as Lennon's Marsh and Lennon's Mill Pond. Now a privately owned wildfowl refuge with ducks, egrets, and cranes.

Warwick County. On December 4, 1771, in the General Assembly, a bill for erecting the n part of Orange County into Warwick County and St. Stephens Parish was read for the second time and rejected.

Warwick Creek rises on the Chowan-Gates County line and flows sw through Welsh Pond where it joins Trotman Creek to form Catherine Creek. Appears on the Collet map, 1770. A brick house, still standing, built on this creek in 1746 was an early trading center.

Warwick Mill Pond, e Robeson County on Jacob Swamp. Covers 10 acres; max. depth 10 ft.

Washburn, community in w Cleveland County. Alt. 960. Settled 1875. Named for W. W. Washburn, a county commissioner.

Washburn Creek rises in s Rutherford County and flows sw into Cleghorn Creek.

Washburns Store, community in e Rutherford County between Puzzle and Heaveners creeks. Formerly known as Green's Grove and, when a post office from 1901 to 1905, as Lexine—named for Lexine Pruett, daughter of Greenbury Pruett, a member of the General Assembly.

Wash Creek rises in central Henderson County and flows se into Mud Creek.

Wash Creek rises in nw Henderson County and flows se into North Fork.

Wash Hollow, s Haywood County on Sam Branch.

Washington, city and county seat, w Beaufort County on Pamlico River. Alt. 11. Inc. 1782. Known originally as Forks of Tar River but called Washington as early as 1776. Named by Col. James Bonner, founder of the town and friend of George Washington. Produces lumber, tobacco, textiles, and apparel.

Washington County was formed in 1799 from Tyrrell County. Located in the e section of the state, it is bounded by Tyrrell, Hyde, Beaufort, Martin, and Bertie counties, and by Albemarle Sound. It was named for George Washington (1732-99). Area: 420 sq. mi. (336, land; 84, water). County seat: Plymouth with an elevation of 21 ft. Townships are Lees Mills, Plymouth, Scuppernong, and Skinnersville. Produces tobacco, peanuts, corn, soybeans, hogs, livestock, lumber, and paper.

Washington County, now in Tennessee, was created from the District of Washington, *which see,* in 1777. North Carolina ceded her w territory to the Federal Government in 1789. For further information, see D. L. Corbitt, *The Formation of North Carolina Counties.*

Washington Creek rises in n Jackson County and flows n into Soco Creek.

Washington Creek rises in n Pender County and flows ne into Northeast Cape Fear River. First known as Hamilton Creek for Malatiah Hamilton who laid out a town near its mouth about 1740; this town became South Washington, *which see.*

Washington, District of See District of Washington.

Washington Ferry. See Princeton.

Washington Forks, community in central Craven County.

Washington Heights, community in w Beaufort County adjacent to and ne of the city of Washington.

Washington Park, town in w Beaufort County. Inc. 1923. Adjoins the city of Washington on the e.

Washington Township, nw Beaufort County.

Washington Township, ne Guilford County. Named for George Washington.

Wash Ridge, w Haywood County, Great Smoky Mountains National Park, a short spur extending se from Shanty Mountain, center near lat. 35° 37' 07" N., long. 83° 08' 15" W.

Wash Woods, community and former Life Saving Station, 4 mi. s of the Virginia line on Currituck Banks, ne Currituck County. Named for hundreds of old stumps which are exposed at low tide. A post office operated here, 1907-1917, was named Deals.

Wasulu Ridge, n Swain County in Great Smoky Mountains National Park, a short spur extending nw from Welch Ridge near lat. 35° 29' 22" N., long. 83° 38' 32" W.

Watauga (wah-TAW-guh) County was formed in 1849 from Ashe, Wilkes, Caldwell, and Yancey counties. Located in the nw section of the state, it is bounded by the state of Tennessee, and by Ashe, Wilkes, Caldwell, and Avery counties. It was named for Watauga River. Area: 320 sq. mi. County seat: Boone with an elevation of 3,266 ft. Townships are Bald Mountain, Beaverdam, Blowing Rock, Blue Ridge, Boone, Brushy Fork, Cove Creek, Elk, Laurel Creek, Meat Camp, New River, North Fork, Shawneehaw, Stony Fork, and Watauga. Produces tobacco, corn, dairy products, livestock, electronics, apparel, and gravel.

Watauga Creek rises in e Macon County and flows sw into Lake Emory.

Watauga Falls on Watauga River in w Watauga County (near Laurel Creek Falls) at mouth of Laurel Creek.

Watauga Falls, community in w Watauga County on Laurel Creek near its confluence with Watauga River.

Watauga Gap, on the Jackson-Macon County line. Alt. 3,280.

Watauga River rises in sw Watauga County near Grandfather Mountain and flows n forming a short portion of the Avery-Watauga County line before flowing into Tennessee where it enters Holston River. Took its name from an Indian word meaning "beautiful water."

Watauga Settlement began to develop in 1769 in what was then w North Carolina but is now Tennessee with the arrival of settlers on the Watauga and Nolichucky rivers. A government was formed in 1772 and in 1776 its leaders asked to be annexed to North Carolina. The District of Washington, *which see,* was formed to include the Watauga Settlement. *See also* Franklin.

Watauga Township, sw Watauga County.

Watch Knob, central Buncombe County near the junction of Beetree Creek and Swannanoa River.

Water Creek rises in s Scotland County and flows sw into Gum Swamp Creek.

Waterfall Branch rises in n Mitchell County and flows s into Right Fork Bean Creek.

Waterfall Creek rises in ne Buncombe County and flows nw into Carter Creek.

Water Fork rises in w Orange County and flows s into Bear Creek.

Water Fork rises in n Wake County and flows s into Horse Creek.

Water Gap, central Graham County between Mountain Creek and Sweetwater Creek.

Waterhole Mine, mica and feldspar mine, sw Avery County.

Watering Hole Swamp rises in w Robeson County and flows s into Wilkinson Swamp. Also sometimes known as Waterhole Swamp.

Waterlily, community on the s end of Church Island, e Currituck County. Settled about 1750. Named for water lilies growing in ponds and ditches here.

Waterloo, community in s Union County near the present Prospect School between the head of Cane Creek and Polecat Creek.

Waterloo Branch rises in s Macon County and flows se into Little Tennessee River.

Watermelon Branch rises in n central Madison County and flows ne into Big Laurel Creek.

Wateroak Creek rises in se Clay County and flows se into Tallulah River.

Wateroak Gap, se Clay County between Chunky Gal and Yellow Mountains.

Water Oak Gap, n Swain County in Great Smoky Mountains National Park on Welch Ridge near lat. 35° 30′ 32″ N., long. 83° 36′ 21″ W.

Waterrock Knob, on the Haywood-Jackson County line. Alt. 6,292. Named Amos Plott Balsam in 1858 by Arnold Guyot for a pioneer settler at its base. Wood cutters and loggers knew it as Waterrock Knob because there was a good spring running out over a smooth rock near its top. The Blue Ridge Parkway officials have now accepted this name for the peak. Also written as Water Rock Knob.

Waters, community in n Burke County.

Watershed Mountain, central Madison County between Walnut and Hunter creeks. Alt. approx. 3,100.

Watershed Ridge, n Buncombe County between North Knob and Wildcat Mountain.

Water Tank Branch rises in ne Cherokee County and flows se into Valley River. Named because the Southern Railway used it as a source of water for its steam locomotives.

Waterville, community in n Haywood County on Big Creek. Alt. 1,440. Named for the lake and dam built here in 1929. *See* Waterville Lake.

Waterville Lake, on Pigeon River in n Haywood County, in Pisgah National Forest. Alt. 2,258. Constructed in 1929 for hydroelectric power. Covers 340 acres; max. depth 180 ft. Owned by Carolina Power and Light Co.

Watery Branch rises in w Johnston County and flows e into Juniper Swamp.

Watery Branch rises in n Scotland County and flows ne into Lumber River.

Watery Branch rises in ne Wayne County near the town of Eureka and flows ne into Greene County where it enters Contentnea Creek.

Watery Branch, community in ne Wayne County. Settled as early as 1887.

Watery Swamp rises in central Gates County and flows s into Bennetts Creek.

Watha, town in n central Pender County. Alt. 60. Inc. 1909. About 1840, with the construction of the railroad, the old town of South Washington, *which see,* moved to this site from a point approx. 1½ mi. ne. The railroad station was originally named Hiawatha from which the present name was corrupted. For about two years after the formation of Pender County this served as a temporary county seat. *See also* Welsh Tract.

Watia Creek rises in w Swain County and flows e into Nantahala River.

Watkins, community in w Vance County on Little Ruin Creek.

Watkins Branch rises in ne Cherokee County and flows nw into Valley River.

Watkins Creek rises in s Macon County and flows nw into Middle Creek.

Watkins Township, w Vance County.

Watson Creek rises in n Union County and flows se into Richardson Creek.

Watson Crossroads, community in nw Wayne County near a tributary of Great Swamp.

Watson Gap, w Jackson County on Cox Branch.

Watson Gap, se Watauga County on the head of Dugger Creek.

Watson's Mill. See Worrell Mill Pond.

Watsons Pond, s Hoke County on Little Raft Swamp. Formed 1865 and known first as Edens and later as Johnsons Pond. Covers 50 acres. Max. depth 7 ft.

Watsonville, community in w central Rowan County.

Watts Creek rises in se Stokes County and flows se into Town Fork Creek.

Watts Cross Roads, community in ne Cabarrus County.

Watts Cross Roads Township, former township in n Cabarrus County, now township number 6.

Watts Landing, community in se Pender County on Intracoastal Waterway.

Wattsville. See Nakina.

Wauchecha Bald, central Graham County in Cheoah Mountains at the head of Bee Creek. Alt. 4,400.

Waughtown, former town in s Forsyth County, inc. 1891. First called Charlestown or Charleston for Charles Bagge who first settled here and opened a store. When the store was sold to James Waugh the scattered settlement surrounding it came to be called Waugh's store or Waughtown. Post office was Waughtown by 1828. Now within the corporate limits of Winston-Salem.

Waumans Creek rises in ne Columbus County and flows ne into Cape Fear River.

Waverly, community in e Madison County on Paint Fork.

Waves, community on Hatteras Island, e Dare County, formerly known as South Rodanthe.

Waxhaw, town in w Union County between East Fork Twelvemile Creek and Waxhaw Creek. Inc. 1889. Named for Waxhaw settlements made by Scotch-Irish and Germans in 1740. The name Waxhaw comes from the Waxhaw Indians who once claimed the region between Rocky River and Catawba River. President Andrew Jackson born somewhere nearby. Produces textiles.

Waxhaw Creek rises in w Union County and flows sw into Catawba River in South Carolina.

The Waxhaws, an area generally recognized as including much of Anson, Mecklenburg, and Union counties, North Carolina, and Chester, Lancaster, and York counties in South Carolina. Catawba River forms the w limits. Waxhaw Creek flows through the area forming what has been called "a rich oasis in a region of pine barrens." President Andrew Jackson was born here in 1767. The name came from the Waxhaw Indians of the area whose chief village, Wisacky, was visited in 1670 by John Lederer.

Wayah Bald, w Macon County at the head of Camp Branch. Alt. 5,385. Named for a Cherokee youth who, according to legend, visited this mountain with his grandfather to listen to the message of the stars. Young Wayah's name meant "wolf."

Wayah Branch rises in sw Buncombe County and flows ne into Stony Fork.

Wayah Creek rises in w Macon County and flows se into Cartoogechaye Creek.

Wayah Gap, w Macon County at the head of Wayah Creek.

Wayanock. See Meherrin River.

Waycross, community in e Sampson County.

Wayehutta Creek rises in central Jackson County and flows sw into Tuckasegee River.

Wayne County was formed in 1779 from Dobbs County. Located in the e section of the state, it is bounded by Greene, Lenoir, Duplin, Sampson, Johnston, and Wilson counties. It was named for General Anthony Wayne (1745-96), Revolutionary leader. Area: 555 sq. mi. County seat: Goldsboro with an elevation of 111 ft. Townships are Brogden, Buck Swamp, Fork, Goldsboro, Grantham, Great Swamp, Indian Springs, Nahunta, New Hope, Pikeville, Saulston, and Stony Creek. Produces tobacco, corn, soybeans, wheat, oats, cotton, poultry, dairy products, hogs, livestock, and cucumbers. See also St. Patrick's Parish.

Waynesboro, first county seat of Wayne

County, inc. 1787. The town died after
the county seat was moved to Goldsboro
in 1850. Waynesboro was located on
land formerly owned by Dr. Andrew
Bass, delegate to the Provincial Congress
of 1775, at the sw edge of the present
county seat on Neuse River. After 1847
many houses were removed from the old
town to the new. The old courthouse,
built by Col. William McKinne, was
destroyed prior to 1917.

Waynesville, town and county seat, s Haywood County. Settled about 1800 and
known first as Mount Prospect. Inc. 1810.
Said to have been named by Col. Robert
Love (1760-1845), one of the founders
and owner of part of the site, for General Anthony Wayne whom he knew
during the Revolution. Produces rubber,
shoes, and paper products. In 1953 the
adjacent town of Hazelwood (which see)
was inc. into the limits of Waynesville.
Alt. 2,635.

Waynesville Township, sw Haywood
County.

Wayside, community in central Hoke County between Beaver Creek and Black
Branch.

Wayside, former community in w Swain
County on Little Tennessee River. A
post office as early as 1882. Site now
submerged by Fontana Lake.

Weapemeoc, the principal town of the
Weapemeoc Indians, visited by Ralph
Lane and his explorers in 1585-86, was
near present-day Edenton, s Chowan
County. This was also the Indian name
for Albemarle Sound and may be an
Algonquian word for "where shelter
from the wind is sought."

Weasel, community in nw Ashe County.
Alt. 2,790.

Wease Mountain, ne Rutherford County
between the head of South Creek and
Molly Fork. Alt. approx. 2,100.

Weatherman Bald, on the Cherokee-Clay
County line in the Valley River Mountains. Alt. 4,700. Known by the Indians
as *Kolasko.*

Weatherspoon Cooling Pond, in e Robeson
County at the junction of Lumber River
and Jacob Swamp. Approx. 3 mi. se of
city of Lumberton. Formed in 1955 to
cover 231 acres with a max. depth of 5
ft.; shoreline is 4 mi. Named for W.
Herbert Weatherspoon, longtime official
of Carolina Power and Light Company.
Used to cool steam condensers for near-

by W. H. Weatherspoon Steam Electric
Generating Plant.

Weaver Branch rises in ne Cherokee County and flows sw into Junaluska Creek.

Weaver Branch rises in ne Swain County
and flows se into Breedlove Branch.

Weaver Creek rises in e Chatham County
and flows nw into Beaver Creek.

Weaver Creek rises in e Vance County and
flows s into Southerland Millpond on
Sandy Creek.

Weaversford, community in ne Ashe County.
Alt. approx. 2,500.

Weaverville, town in n central Buncombe
County. The site was referred to as Pine
Cabbin in eighteenth-century records of
the county and a little later as Salem
Camp Ground. A post office est. here in
1850 was named Reems Creek and
changed to Weaverville in 1873. Inc.
1875. Named for the Rev. Montraville
Weaver who gave land and money in
1872 to est. Weaver College (closed in
1933). From 1919 until 1921 the town
was named Elkwood. Alt. 2,300. Produces textiles.

Weaverville Reservoir, n Buncombe County on Ox Creek near Bull Mountain.

Webb, community in w Mitchell County
on Brummett Creek.

Webb Branch rises in sw Buncombe County near Holland Mountain and flows sw
into Hominy Creek.

Webb Branch rises in s Macon County and
flows ne into West Fork Overflow Creek.

Webb Cove, the valley through which
Webb Cove Creek flows in central Buncombe County.

Webb Cove Creek rises in the Elk Mountains in central Buncombe County and
flows sw to join Linn Cove Creek in
forming Beaverdam Creek.

Webb Creek rises in e central Avery County and flows se into Gragg Prong.

Webb Creek rises in s Buncombe County
and flows sw into Gap Creek.

Webb Creek is formed in ne Cherokee
County by the junction of Left Fork
Webb Creek and Right Fork Webb
Creek and flows se into Valley River.

Webb Creek rises in s Clay County and
flows sw into Crawford Creek.

Webb Creek rises in e Onslow County and
flows e into White Oak River. Named
for Thomas Webb.

Webb Lake, s Jackson County on Cedar
Creek. Formed before 1946, covers 5

acres and has max. depth of 12 ft. Used for fishing. Not open to the public.

Webbs, community in s Edgecombe County near headwaters of Otter Creek.

Webbs, community in ne Lincoln County.

Webbs Creek rises in e Rutherford County and flows s into Second Broad River.

Webbs Mill Branch rises in se Halifax County and flows se into Kehukee Swamp.

Webster, town in central Jackson County just n of Tuckasegee River, 2 mi. s of town of Sylva. Inc. 1859. Named for Daniel Webster. Alt. 2,203. This was the county seat from its establishment as such in 1852 until 1913.

Webster Creek rises in central Jackson County and flows n into Tuckasegee River.

Webster Creek, short tidal creek and inlet, rises on the w side of the mainland of s Currituck County and flows e into Currituck Sound.

Webster Station. See Dillsboro.

Webster Township, central Jackson County.

Weddington, community in w Union County between Sixmile Creek and West Fork Twelvemile Creek.

Weecaunse Creek. See Wiccacon River.

Weed Patch Mountain, on the Henderson-Rutherford County line.

Weedy Mountain, se Buncombe County near the Rutherford County line se of Jarvis Mountain.

Weeks Point. See Swansboro.

Weeksville, community in s Pasquotank County on New Begun Creek. Named for families of James and Charles Weeks, local landowners. Known as New Begun Creek until about 1890. Older w section of the community is sometimes known as Old Weeksville.

Wehutty, community in w Cherokee County on Rocky Ford Creek.

Wehutty Mountain, w Cherokee County between Rocky Ford and Shoal creeks.

Weightman Branch rises in central Davidson County and flows s into Swearing Creek.

Weil, former community in central Wayne County near the junction of Little and Neuse rivers. This was the site of a brick yard and a railroad station near the site of the old county seat of Waynesboro.

Weir Point, point of land on nw end of Roanoke Island, ne Dare County. The William B. Umstead Bridge, approx. 3 mi. long and opened on Dec. 22, 1956,

extends from this point to Redstone Point on the n Dare County mainland; named for N. C. Governor William B. Umstead (1895-1954).

Weitock River. See White Oak River.

Weitzel's Mill, site on Reedy Fork Creek, n central Guilford County. A skirmish occurred here on March 6, 1781, between American and British forces.

Welch Bald, n Swain County on Welch Ridge near the ne end of Big Fork Ridge. Alt. 5,087.

Welch Branch rises in n Swain County and flows se into Bear Creek.

Welch Branch rises in s Swain County and flows nw into Yalaka Creek.

Welch Branch rises in w Swain County and flows se into Fontana Lake.

Welch Cove, n Graham County w of Fontana, follows the ne course of a stream that empties into Little Tennessee River. Formerly known as Brooks Cove. See also Fontana Village.

Welch Creek rises in n Beaufort County and flows ne on the Martin-Washington County line into Roanoke River. Name appears as Welches Creek throughout the nineteenth century.

Welch Creek Township, n Columbus County.

Welches Creek. See Welch Creek.

Welch Mill Creek rises in ne Cherokee County and flows se into Valley River.

Welch Ridge, n Swain County in Great Smoky Mountains Natonal Park extends sw from Silers Bald to Little Tennessee River. Its center is near lat. 35° 31' 40" N., long. 83° 35' 30" W.

Welch's Bluff appears on the Moseley map, 1733, on the w side of Cape Fear River in present Brunswick County, between the mouth of Indian Creek and Eagle Island, Possibly named for James Welch who owned land in the vicinity.

Welch's Millpond, formed by a dam across Warwick Creek on the Chowan-Gates County line.

Welcome, community in n Davidson County. Alt. 860. Formerly called Hinklesville for the Hinkle family residing here. Disagreement arose over selection of a name for the new railroad depot and brought about the selection of Welcome because of (1) "Welcome" sign over the door of the community store. or (2) because, in the dispute over the name, one man declared, "everybody's welcome here."

Weldon, town in n Halifax County on Roanoke River. Inc. 1843. The Collet map, 1770, shows "Weldans" at approx. this site, perhaps referring to the family name of the owner of the land. Town site settled prior to 1830 when it was known as Weldon's Orchard or Weldon's Place for Daniel Weldon, owner. In 1834, it became the terminus of a railroad from Virginia. Lumber and apparel produced here. Alt. 81. *See also* Blakely.

Weldons Millpond, on Sandy Creek in e Vance County. Covers 10 acres with max. depth of 6 ft. Named for owner, Obed W. Weldon. Known prior to 1913 as Amos Millpond. The mill here is still used for grinding corn; the pond is used for fishing, swimming, and boating.

Weldon's Orchard; Weldon's Place. *See* Weldon.

Weldon Township, ne Halifax County.

Wellington, name given the former Jacocks Landing on Cashie River, se Bertie County, for a brief time when it was the s terminus of a short railroad. Wellington is shown on the 1892 Rand McNally map as well as on the 1897 North Carolina Railroad Commission map. The Carolina Southern Railroad was inc. as the Wellington and Powellsville Railroad in 1893.

Wells Bay, in Currituck Sound off Mossey Islands, se Currituck County.

Wells Creek rises in s Alamance County and flows sw into Cane Creek.

Wells Creek, a channel between Currituck Banks and several small tidal marsh islands in Currituck Sound, e Currituck County.

Wells Creek rises in e Vance County and flows s into w Warren County where it enters Sandy Creek.

Wells Knob, ne Wilkes County between Little Elkin River and Elkin River. Alt. 1,810.

Wells Mineral Spring, s Nash County on a tributary of Sapony Creek. A popular recreation spot in the early 1900's; water thought to have curative qualities. Now almost abandoned.

Wells Mountain, on the Cherokee-Clay County line from Coleman Gap to the mouth of Little Brasstown Creek.

Welsh Pond, on Warwick Creek on the Chowan-Gates County line covers approx. 75 acres and is from 2 to 15 ft.

in depth. Named for Welch family who owned it.

Welsh Tract, an area between the Northeast Cape Fear and Cape Fear rivers, now largerly in central Pender County, on which a number of Welsh families from Pennsylvania settled in 1730 and shortly afterwards. The first grant was made in 1731 to David Evans for 640 acres. Apparently no single large block of land was granted to the Welsh; instead individuals acquired their own land. Appears on the Moseley map, 1733, as Welch Settlement. The Rev. Hugh McAden mentioned the Welsh Tract during his visit to the area in 1755, and the name was still in use in 1775. Persons other than those of Welsh descent soon moved into the area and the Tract lost its identity. About 1740 the Welsh laid out a town which became South Washington, *which see*.

Wendell (win-DELL), town in e Wake County. Settled 1895. Inc. 1903. Named for Oliver Wendell Holmes (1809-94), American writer. Produces tobacco, apparel, and furniture.

Wenona, community in s Washington County on the n shoulder of Dogwood Ridge in East Dismal Swamp. Est. after A. E. Rice purchased 160 acres of land here and built a house in 1912. Other settlers then purchased land from Roper Lumber Company and settled; by 1914 a school was built. A post office was est. here in 1913. Settlers came here from Pennsylvania, West Virginia, Illinois, and Ohio.

Wentworth, unincorporated county seat, central Rockingham County. Courthouse authorized to be est. here. 1787; first court held here, 1799. Named for Charles Watson-Wentworth, Duke of Rockingham, prime minister of England when the Stamp Act was repealed, and who, on March 9 and 17, 1778, declared for immediate recognition of the independence of the American colonies. Rockingham Community College, est. 1966, is located here. Alt. approx. 900.

Wentworth Township, central Rockingham County.

Wesley Chapel, community in w central Union County.

Wesley Creek rises in s Buncombe County and flows se into Bent Creek.

Wesley Creek rises in ne Haywood County and flows s into Fines Creek.

Wesley Martin Branch rises in e Cherokee County and flows nw into Valley River.

Wesner Bald on Haywood-Jackson County line. Alt. 5,600. Named for David Wesner, of Cabarrus County, who obtained a grant for 100 acres in the vicinity in 1808. Wesner froze to death while hunting deer about 1812 on the mountain which now bears his name.

Wesser, community in sw Swain County near Nantahala Gorge. Alt. 1,714. Named for the nearby Wesser Creek.

Wesser Bald, n Macon County at head of Tellico Creek. Alt. 4,800.

Wesser Creek rises in n Macon County and flows nw into Swain County where it enters Nantahala River. Named for an old hunter who lived on its banks.

Wesser Creek rises in e Swain County and flows ne into Connelly Creek.

Wesser Gap, se Swain County on the head of Connelly Creek.

West Alliance. See Alliance.

West Asheville, former town in central Buncombe County on the w side of the French Broad River. Inc. 1889; became a part of Asheville, 1897.

West Bald, peak in the Tusquitee Mountains, n Clay County.

West Bay, s extension of Pamlico Sound between Piney Island and Cedar Island in ne Carteret County.

West Bear Creek rises in e Wayne County and flows se into Bear Creek.

West Beaver Creek rises in s Ashe County and flows se into Beaver Creek.

West Belews Creek rises in e Forsyth County and flows ne into s Stokes County and into Belews Creek. Also known as Left Fork Belews Creek and in Stokes County as Little Belews Creek.

West Bend, community in w Forsyth County in a bend of Yadkin River.

West Bladenboro, town in sw Bladen County, adjacent to Bladenboro, which see. Inc. 1913. No longer active in municipal affairs.

West Bluff Bay in Pamlico Sound w of Bluff Point in s Hyde County.

West Branch rises in central Madison County and flows se into Walnut Creek.

West Branch rises in n Mecklenburg County and flows se into Rocky River.

West Branch rises in w Warren County and flows n into Malones Creek.

Westbrook, community in se Bladen County. Named for early colonial family of Westbrook.

Westbrooks Township, n Sampson County.

West Buffalo Creek rises in sw Graham County and flows ne into Hooper Mill Creek. Also known as Little Buffalo Creek.

West Buies Creek rises in n Harnett County and flows s and se into Buies Creek.

West Canton, suburban area of the city of Canton in e Haywood County.

West Concord, uninc. outskirts of city of Concord, central Cabarrus County.

West Cove extends sw in e Haywood County between Wilson Cove and Long Branch.

West Crossroads. See Spiveys Corner.

West Double Creek rises in s Surry County and flows se to join East Double Creek in forming Double Creek.

West End, community in s Moore County. Named from the fact that it was the w terminus of a railroad from Aberdeen (about 1890-1898) which later became a part of the Norfolk and Southern Railway. Alt. 604.

Western Branch of Queen Anne's Creek. See Pembroke Creek.

Western Cliffs, e Macon County between Houston Branch and the head of Brush Creek.

Western Point, ne Carteret County, nw point of Cedar Island extending into West Bay.

Western Prong rises in n Columbus County and flows ne and se into Red Hill Swamp after which it is known as White Marsh.

Western Prong Township, n Columbus County.

Westfield, community in ne Surry County. Grew up around a Quarker mission est. here in 1760 and known first as Tom's Creek. Renamed for the fact that it was a w missionary field for the New Garden [Guilford County] Quakers.

Westfield Township, ne Surry County.

West Fork rises in central Avery County and flows s into Linville River.

West Fork [Barkers Creek] rises in w Jackson County and flows ne to join Middle Fork [Barkers Creek] in forming Barkers Creek.

West Fork [Bull Creek] rises in n Madison County near Bull Creek Gap and flows s to join East Fork [Bull Creek] in forming Bull Creek.

West Fork Campbell Creek rises in w Haywood County and flows ne into Campbell Creek.

West Fork Deep River rises in w central Guilford County and flows se into High Point Lake where it joins East Fork Deep River.

West Fork [Dicks Creek] rises in n Jackson County and flows s to join East Fork [Dicks Creek] in forming Dicks Creek.

West Fork French Broad River rises in w Transylvania County and flows se to join North Fork French Broad River to form French Broad River.

West Fork [Goose Creek] rises in nw Pamlico County and flows se into Goose Creek.

West Fork [Jenkins Creek] rises in n Jackson County and flows s to join East Fork [Jenkins Creek] in forming Jenkins Creek.

West Fork [Kirkland Creek] rises in s Swain County and flows n to join East Fork [Kirkland Creek] in forming Kirkland Creek.

West Fork Little River rises in s Randolph County and flows se into Montgomery County where it enters Little River.

West Fork [Moses Creek] rises in n Jackson County and flows sw to join East Fork [Moses Creek] in forming Moses Creek.

West Fork of Ivy Township, former township in e Madison County, now township number 5.

West Fork Overflow Creek rises in s Macon County and flows se to join East Fork Overflow Creek to form Overflow Creek.

West Fork Pigeon River rises in s Haywood County near the Jackson-Transylvania County line and flows ne to join East Fork Pigeon River to form Pigeon River. Known by the Cherokee Indians as Nee-oh-la, the name which they applied to the main river formed by the junction of East and West Forks Pigeon River.

West Fork Rocky River rises in s Iredell County and flows se into Mecklenburg County where it enters Rocky River on the Mecklenburg-Cabarrus County line.

West Fork [Rube Creek], rises in nw Watauga County and flows se into Rube Creek.

West Fork Sandy Branch rises in s Stokes County and flows s into Sandy Branch.

West Fork Shut-in Creek rises in w Madison County and flows ne to join East Fork Shut-in Creek to form Shut-in Creek.

West Fork [South River], a short stream at the headwaters of South River in n central Carteret County.

West Fork Tuckasegee River rises in w Jackson County at n end of Thorpe Lake and meanders ne to enter Tuckasegee River, approx. 8 mi. away at the community of Tuckasegee.

West Fork Twelvemile Creek rises in w Union County and flows se to join East Fork Twelvemile Creek in forming Twelvemile Creek.

West Haven, community in s Buncombe County on the e limit of Pisgah National Forest.

West Hillsborough, uninc. outskirts of town of Hillsborough, central Orange County.

West Howellsville Township, e Robeson County.

West Jefferson, town in central Ashe County. Inc. 1915. Named from its location with reference to Jefferson, the county seat. Produces hosiery and furniture.

West Jefferson Township, central Ashe County.

West Knob, on the Buncombe-Henderson County line between Double Knob and Graham Mountain.

West Littleton Branch rises in e Warren County near the town of Littleton and flows nw into Little Stonehouse Creek.

Westminster, community in n central Rutherford County which grew up around Fort McGaughey, built approx. 1765 and used through the Revolution. Sometimes known also as Brittain for Little Brittain Presbyterian Church est. here in 1768. Present name is taken from Westminster School founded here in 1901 by ten Presbyterian churches in Cleveland, Polk, and Rutherford counties; the school closed in 1923.

West Monroe, former town in central Union County. Inc. 1909 as Icemorlee, a mill village, named for three major stockholders. Iceman, Morrow, and Lee. Later renamed. Merged with the city of Monroe in 1949.

West Mountain, w Cherokee County between Camp and Shoal creeks.

Westmouth Bay between Browns and Harkers island in The Straits, se Carteret County.

West Nelson Creek rises in ne Cherokee County and flows se into Valley River.

Weston Knob, s Buncombe County s of Merrill Mountain.

Westover, community in w central Wake County, formerly the site of Thompson, a railroad station. Settled 1917 and named for Westover, Maryland. Alt. 325.

Westover, community in nw Washington County. Alt. 17. A post office, White Marsh, was est. here in 1878 and continued at least until 1882. A 450-acre tract of land here owned by Surveyor-General Edward Moseley (1682-1749) was known as White Marsh, a name which appears on the Moseley map, 1733.

Westover, community in ne Wilson County. A post office operated here in the early years of the twentieth century.

West Point, former plantation, tavern, and ferry in w Wayne County at the junction of Thoroughfare Swamp with Neuse River, owned by Dr. Andrew Bass, delegate to the Provincial Congress of 1775, whose lands included site of Waynesboro (which see). Wayne County court met here during 1785. Later known as Bass Ferry. West Point was location for receipt and inspection of tobacco in 1784.

West Prong [Glady Fork] rises in s Tansylvania County and flows se and then ne to join South Prong [of Glady Fork] in forming Glady Fork. Also known as Galloway Creek.

West Prong Grape Creek rises in central Cherokee County and flows se and sw into Grape Creek.

West Prong [Hickory Fork] rises in n Madison County and flows se into Hickory Fork.

West Prong Horse Branch rises in central Duplin County and flows se into Northeast Cape Fear River.

West Prong Little Yadkin River rises in w Stokes County and flows se to join East Prong Little Yadkin River to form Little Yadkin River.

West Prong Roaring River. See North Prong Roaring River.

West Ridge Branch rises in n Transylvania County and flows sw into South Fork Mills River.

West Rockingham, uninc. outskirts of town of Rockingham, w Richmond County.

Westry, town in e central Nash County. Settled about 1880; inc. 1909. Named for an early settler. Alt. 125.

West Sanford Township, former township in w central Lee County, now township number 6.

Wests Branch rises in n Macon County and flows s into Matlock Creek.

Wests Cove, on a tributary of Cowee Creek in n Macon County.

Wests Crossroads, community in e Lenoir County.

Wests Mill, community on Cowee Creek in n Macon County. In 1767, Thomas Griffiths, a South Carolina planter, shipped several tons of fine white clay taken from a nearby pit, to the Wedgwood potteries in England.

West Swan Creek rises in e Wilkes County and flows ne to join East Swan Creek to form Swan Creek.

West Tarboro, former town in central Edgecome County on the nw limits of Tarboro. Inc. 1903. Charter repealed in 1909 when it became a part of Tarboro. A former West Tarboro community on the sw limits of Tarboro was inc. in 1893 and the name changed to Hilma. See also Farrar.

West Thorofare Bay, ne Carteret County w of Cedar Island and adjacent to Long Bay. Connected with Thorofare Bay via Thorofare, a channel forming the s boundary of Cedar Island.

Wet Ash Swamp rises in Green Swamp in w Brunswick County and flows w into Waccamaw River.

Wet Creek rises in w Moore County and flows n into Cabin Creek.

Wethero Mountain, between Cox Creek and Clear Creek in n Henderson County.

Wet Hollow, s Cherokee County, a mountain valley sw of Rocky Pen Ridge near the mouth of Crane Creek.

Weyanok Creek. See Potecasi Creek.

Weyanoke Creek is mentioned in the Carolina charter of 1665 in which the n boundary of the province is describd as lying "within or about the degrees of 36 and 30 minutes northern latitude." It is shown on one version of the Comberford map, 1657, as Weyanoke River and on the other as Wepanoke River, one of several [Nottoway?] flowing into Chowan River. Before white settlements reached the point, tradition no longer located a creek by this name. Virginians thought it was intended to refer to Wiccacon River, while North Carolinians thought it was Nottoway River. Because of this, a strip 15 mi. wide was long in dispute.

Weymouth Woods Sandhills Nature Preserve, a 403-acre tract of forest land se of Southern Pines, se Moore County. Administered by the Division of State Parks. Reverter clause held by the Nature Conservancy, Washington, D. C.

Vegetation varies from dense hardwood swamp forest to open stands of longleaf pine. Given to the State of North Carolina by Mrs. James Boyd, April 23, 1963. Alt. 350 to 500 ft.

Whalebone, commercial intersection on Bodie Island, e Dare County, about 2½ mi. s of the town of Nags Head. Begun around 1930 as intersection of then existing sand trails and roads. Originally important commercial center. Named for whalebones in front of service station originally located here.

Whalebone Inlet. See Drum Inlet; Hog Island.

Whale Camp Point. See Camp Point.

Whale Head Bay in Currituck Sound off the w shore of Currituck Banks, e Currituck County, a short distance s of Corolla.

Whaley, community in n Avery County. Said to have been named for one Whaley who became frightened by a screech owl and hid in a hollow log until morning.

Whaley Branch rises in w Haywood County near the Tennessee state line and flows sw into Big Creek.

The Wharf. See Swansboro.

Wharton, community in nw Beaufort County. Alt. 19. Named for Lt. Col. Rufus W. Wharton, Washington resident and Confederate officer.

Wheat Creek rises in e Polk County and flows se into Green River.

Wheatfield Branch rises in s Macon County and flows sw into Tessentee Creek.

Wheat Swamp rises in n Lenoir County and flows ne on the Lenoir-Greene County line into Contentnea Creek. Named for John Wheat who had an early grant of land here.

Wheat Swamp rises in sw Wilson County and flows se into Wayne County where it enters Great Swamp.

Wheeler Creek is fomed in w Northampton County by the junction of Gumberry Swamp and Lily Pond Creek and flows s into Roanoke River. The Collet map, 1770, shows Baker Mill at the mouth of this creek.

Wheeler's Mill. See Barrows Mill Pond.

Whetstone, community in n Granville County.

Whetstone Branch rises in s Davie County and flows e into Peeler Creek.

Whetstone Creek rises in n Rockingham County and flows ne into Dan River. Traditionally named from the fact that

early white settlers found the Indians used stones from this stream to whet their knives.

Whetstone Ridge, s Transylvania County extends ne from Blue Ridge to West Fork French Broad River.

Whichard, community in ne Pitt County.

Whigg Branch rises in w Graham County and flows ne into Santeetlah Creek.

Whim Knob on the Haywood-Swain County line between Sugar Tree Lick and Strawberry Knob. Alt. approx. 5,400. Named from the fact that a whim, a horsepowered winch used to draw logs out of the valley, was operated on its top for several years.

Whipping Creek rises in sw Dare County and flows sw into Long Shoal River. Appears as Aquascog River on the Comberford map, 1657, and under its present name on the Collet map, 1770. Aquoscogoc was an Algonquian Indian village near the head of the Pungo River estuary; the name is believed to have meant "where a place for disembarking exists."

Whispering Pines, residential community on Thagards Pond, e Moore County, developed about 1962. See also, Thagards Pond.

Whistling Gap, nw Yancey County between Chestnut Ridge and the head of Whistling Gap Branch.

Whistling Gap Branch rises in nw Yancey County and flows se into Little Creek.

Whitaker Branch rises in w Avery County and flows se into North Toe River.

Whitaker Branch rises in ne Buncombe County and flows s into Town Branch.

Whitaker Branch rises in ne Cherokee County and flows nw into Valley River.

Whitaker Creek rises in e Cleveland County and flows s into Buffalo Creek.

Whitaker Creek rises in se Pamlico County between Smith Creek and Pierce Creek and flows se into Neuse River. First named Powells Creek for William Powell who settled here in 1703. Appears as Powells Creek on the Lawson map, 1709.

Whitaker Crossroads, community in s Surry County near the head of Hagan Creek.

Whitaker Mountain, s Cleveland County.

Whitaker. See Grover.

Whitakers, town on the Edgecombe-Nash County line. Settled approx. 1840; post office est. 1869. Post office name changed to Mayonia for approx. 3 months in 1886. Inc. 1872. Named for Richard and Henry Whitaker, local landowners who supplied wood to the railroad when it was being built. Known first as Whitaker's Turnout. Alt. 134.

Whitaker's Mills. *See* Gold Rock.

White Branch rises in n Buncombe County and flows sw into Flat Creek.

White Branch rises in ne Cherokee County and flows s into Junaluska Creek.

White Branch rises in n Franklin County and flows ne into Little Shocco Creek.

White Creek rises in s central Avery County and flows se into Linville River.

White Creek rises in s Buncombe County and flows ne into French Broad River.

White Creek. *See* North Fork [of Duck Creek].

White Creek Township in s Bladen County.

White Cross, community in s Orange County. A post office here in the nineteenth century was known as Gath.

Whiteface Mountain at the junction of the Caldwell-Watauga-Wilkes County lines. Alt. 2,450.

White Hall, community in central Cabarrus County.

Whitehall. *See* Seven Springs.

White Hall Landing in se Bladen County on the Cape Fear River. An important early trading center.

Whitehead, community in central Alleghany County. Named for D. C. Whithead, early settler. Alt. 3,026.

Whitehead Creek rises in n central Avery County and flows s, joining Hickory Branch before flowing into Elk River.

Whiteheads Mill. *See* Spencer.

Whitehead Township, s central Alleghany County.

White Hill, community in sw Lee County at the Moore County line. Took its name from a Presbyterian Church here on a small knoll of very white sand. A former post office here was known as Villanow. The community has also been known as Caviness Crossroads.

Whitehouse, community in n Rutherford County between Cove and Otter creeks. A stockade for the protection of settlers against Indians was erected in the vicinity of nearby Montford Cove Church in the eighteenth century.

White Horse Branch rises in s Lee County and flows s into Little River.

White Hurricane Knob, on the Buncombe-Yancey County line se of Cane River Gap. Appears on recent State Highway Commission maps as Mahogany Knob.

Whitehurst, community in n Pitt County.

Settled about 1890 and known as Grindool until early in the twentieth century when the name was changed to honor S. C. Whitehurst, local farmer. Alt. 68.

Whitehurst Creek rises in se Beaufort County and flows e into South Creek.

Whitehurst Creek rises in central Onslow County and flows e into New River.

Whitelace Creek rises in w Lenoir County and flows n into Neuse River.

White Lake, a natural lake in e central Bladen County. Covers 1,068 acres; max. depth 10½ ft. Appears as Granston Lake on the Collet map, 1770; later known as Bartrams Lake for William Bartram who owned adjacent property and operated a grist mill near the lake. Apparently appears first as White Lake on the Shaffer township map of 1886; named for the white sandy bottom and the clear water. It first attracted outside interest about 1922 after roads made it accessible. Boating, fishing, and swimming. *See also* Carolina Bays.

White Lake, town in e central Bladen County. Originally chartered in 1923 charter, repealed in 1925. Chartered again in 1951.

White Mans Glory Creek rises in n Swain County in Great Smoky Mountains National Park on Welch Ridge and flows se into Forney Creek.

White Marsh, stream in the lower course of Red Hill Swamp after it is joined by Western Prong, n Columbus County. It flows se into Waccamaw River. Appears on the Moseley map, 1733, as Great White Marsh in the vicinity of Waccamaw River. *See also* Brown Meadow.

White Marsh rises in s Pender County and flows w into Godfrey Creek.

White Marsh. *See* Westover.

Whitener Creek rises in s Burke County and flows s into Rock Creek.

White Oak, community in nw Bladen County. Alt. 46. Settled 1890. Named for John Whiteoak, a colonial resident. Once called Winnie for Jefferson Davis' daughter.

White Oak, community in w central Gates County.

White Oak, former community in central Guilford County, now a part of Greensboro.

White Oak, community in sw Halifax County.

White Oak, community in s Wake County.

Settled 1900 and named for the white oaks in the vicinity. Alt. 300.

Whiteoak Bald, ne Cherokee County in the Valley River Mountains.

Whiteoak Bottoms, sw Macon County between Kimsey Creek and Nantahala River.

Whiteoak Branch rises in s Avery County and flows w into North Toe River.

Whiteoak Branch rises in e Duplin County and flows s into Little Limestone Creek.

Whiteoak Branch rises in nw Duplin County and flows s into Goshen Swamp.

Whiteoak Branch rises in n Haywood County and flows ne into Pigeon River.

Whiteoak Branch rises in s Johnston County and flows se into Stone Creek.

Whiteoak Branch rises in s Macon County and flows sw into Tessentee Creek.

Whiteoak Branch rises in e Montgomery County and flows e into Little River.

Whiteoak Branch rises in n Swain County and flows sw into Forney Creek.

Whiteoak Creek rises in central Avery County and flows s into Fall Branch.

White Oak Creek rises in sw Avery County and flows se into North Toe River.

Whiteoak Creek rises in s tip of Burke County and flows ne into Jacob Fork.

Whiteoak Creek rises in w Macon County and flows nw into Nantahala River.

Whiteoak Creek rises in s Madison County and flows sw into Ivy River.

Whiteoak Creek rises in central Mitchell County and flows nw into Cane Creek.

Whiteoak Creek is formed in e Moore County by the junction of Crains Creek and Dry Fork Branch, both of which rise in Lee County. Whiteoak Creek flows s into Crains Creek (the lower course of Dunhams Creek). It formerly was known as North Fork Crains Creek and as Little Crains Creek.

Whiteoak Creek rises in w Pender County and flows e into Moores Creek.

Whiteoak Creek rises in central Polk County and flows e into Green River.

Whiteoak Creek rises in n Rockingham County and flows ne into Virginia where it enters Dan River.

Whiteoak Creek rises in e Wake County and flows s into Johnston County where it enters Swift Creek.

Whiteoak Creek rises in sw Wake County and flows sw into Chatham County where it enters Buckhorn Creek.

Whiteoak Creek rises in w Wake County and flows sw into Chatham County where it enters New Hope River.

Whiteoak Creek rises in e Yancey County and flows e into South Toe River.

Whiteoak Creek rises in n Yancey County and flows se into Nolichucky River.

Whiteoak Creek Falls, more accurately a cascade, near the mouth of Whiteoak Creek at Nantahala River, nw Macon County.

Whiteoak Flats, an area of stony loam in e Swain County n of Rocky Knob near the head of Adams Creek.

Whiteoak Flats, n Yancey County near the head of Whiteoak Creek.

Whiteoak Flats, community in n Yancey County on Whiteoak Creek.

Whiteoak Gap, n Madison County at the head of East Prong [Hickory Fork].

White Oak Island, in w Tyrrell County, is a loamy section surrounded by swampland. Famous for deer and bear hunting.

Whiteoak Knob, on the Cherokee-Clay County line.

White Oak Knob, w Graham County in the Snowbird Mountains. Alt. 4,301.

White Oak Landing on the Cape Fear River in nw Bladen County.

Whiteoak Limb Ridge, s Graham County in the Snowbird Mountains between Rocky Spring Top and Poplar Spring Top.

Whiteoak Mountain, in n Haywood County extends ne along the course of Whiteoak Branch.

Whiteoak Mountain, w central Polk County. Alt. 3,102.

White Oak Mountain on the Transylvania County, N. C.-Greenville County, S. C. line e of Sassafras Gap.

Whiteoak Pocosin, w Gates County. Alt. from 26 to 38.

Whiteoak Ridge, w Macon County parallel to Big Laurel Creek.

Whiteoak Ridge, n Swain County in Great Smoky Mountains National Park, a short spur extending w from Forney Ridge and forming an arc between Bee Gum Branch and Whiteoak Branch. Its center is near lat. 35° 28' 38" N., long. 83° 33' 12" W.

White Oak River rises in n Onslow and s Jones counties and flows se on the Jones-Onslow County line to the Carteret-Onslow County line and into the Atlantic Ocean through Bogue Inlet. It is approx. 20 mi. long. Name derived from the Weetock Indian tribe. Appears as Weetock on the Lawson map, 1709, as Weitock River on the Moseley map, 1733, and as White Oak River on the Collet map, 1770.

Whiteoak Spring, ne Haywood County, on the head of Raven Cliff Branch.

White Oak Spring Canal. *See* Hamburg Ditch.

White Oak Stamp, a peak in se Clay County at the se end of Little Mountain.

Whiteoak Swamp rises in central Bertie County and flows s into Cashie River.

White Oak Swamp rises in se Bladen County and flows se into Cape Fear River.

White Oak Swamp rises in ne Edgecombe County near the town of Whitakers and flows se into Swift Creek. Appears on the Collet map, 1770, as Peachtree Creek.

White Oak Swamp rises in ne Franklin County and flows se into Nash County where it turns ne to flow into Fishing Creek.

Whiteoak Swamp rises in the town of Ahoskie, s Hertford County, and flows e into Bear Swamp.

White Oak Swamp rises in s Nash County and flows ne into Toisnot Swamp.

Whiteoak Swamp rises in w central Sampson County and flows sw into Great Coharie Creek.

Whiteoak Swamp rises in e Wilson County and flows sw into Toisnot Swamp. Mentioned in local records as early as 1740.

White Oak Township, n Bladen County.

White Oak Township, w Carteret County on White Oak River and Bogue Sound. For a time called township number 1.

White Oak Township, n central Haywood County.

White Oak Township, se Jones County.

White Oak Township, ne Onslow County.

White Oak Township, central Polk County.

White Oak Township, w Wake County.

White Owl Falls, sw Transylvania County in Thompson River. Height of falls is 80 ft.

White Plains, community in n central Surry County. Alt. 1,150. Settled in the 1850's and named for the white sandy loam soil in the vicinity. Eng and Chang Bunker (1811-74), Siamese twins, moved here in 1854 and are buried in a local churchyard.

White Plains. *See* Hiddenite.

White Point extends from the mainland of ne Carteret County into Core Sound.

White Pond, community in s Robeson County.

White Pond Bay, a sand filled bay in s Cumberland and n Bladen counties.

White Post, community in central Beaufort County. Formerly known as Surry.

White Rock, mountain on Haywood County, N. C.-Cocke County, Tenn., line, near lat. 35° 45' 30" N., long. 83° 10' W. Known in Tennessee as Sharp Top from its appearance from that state. A white appearance on the North Carolina side gives it its name which has been accepted by the Great Smoky Mountains National Park officials. Alt. 5,025.

White Rock, peak in s Watauga County between Pigeonroost and Dutch creeks.

White Rock. *See* Hill's Rock.

White Rock. *See* Shelton Laurel.

White Rock Branch rises in sw Buncombe County near White Rock Mountain and flows ne into Warren Creek.

White Rock Branch rises in n Madison County and flows s into Hickory Fork.

White Rock Cliffs, n Madison County at the head of White Rock Branch.

Whiterock Creek rises in w Jackson County and flows se into Dodgen Creek.

Whiterock Gap, s Macon County between Jones Knob and the head of Crow Creek.

White Rock Mountain, sw Buncombe County se of Spring Mountain.

Whiterock Mountain, s Macon County between Whiterock Gap and Conley Ridge.

Whiterock Ridge, n Jackson County near the headwaters of Buff Creek.

Whiterock Ridge, w Jackson County between Wilson and Whiterock creeks.

White Rock Ridge, e Mitchell County between Stagger Weed Creek and Sugartree Branch.

White Rock Ridge, s Watauga County extends nw from Hillside Branch w of Buffalo Creek.

White Rocks, mountain on the Avery-Mitchell County line.

White Rocks, sw Watauga County between Bench Mountain and the head of Boone Fork.

Whites Branch rises in n Mecklenburg County and flows ne into Clarks Creek.

Whites Creek rises in s central Bladen County and flows n into Hammonds Creek.

Whites Creek rises in n Washington County in Chappel Swamp and flows nw and ne into Albemarle Sound.

Whites Creek rises in sw Wilkes County and flows nw into W. Kerr Scott Reservoir.

Whites Crossroads, community in ne Bertie County.

Whites Fork, community in sw Pasquotank County.

Whiteside Branch rises in s Yancey County and flows se into South Toe River.

Whiteside Cove, e Swain County between East Fork [Kirkland Creek] and Shepherd Creek.

Whiteside Cove, community near Whiteside Mountain in sw Jackson County.

Whiteside Creek rises in w Swain County on Welch Ridge and flows sw into Fontana Lake.

Whiteside Mountain, on Clear Creek in n Henderson County.

Whiteside Mountain, sw Jackson County, 3½ mi. ne of the town of Highlands in the Blue Ridge. Ne slopes are head of Chattooga River. Near the top is a sheer rock precipice 1,800 ft. high from which the mountain takes its name. Called *Sanigilagi* by the Cherokee Indians, but the meaning is unknown. In 1950 a Spanish inscription, apparently left by De Soto's expedition in 1540 was discovered here. A connected peak on the n is known as Devil's Court House.

Whiteside Ridge, s Yancey County between Camp Creek and Whiteside Branch.

Whites Island. *See* Church Island.

Whites Knob, sw Burke County. Alt. approx. 1,800.

Whites Mill Creek. *See* Bristol's Mill Creek.

Whites Point, se Onslow County, on the w side of Queens Creek.

White's Spring. *See* Kelsey.

White's Store. *See* Hominy Heights.

White Store, community in sw Anson County. Est. about 1770 and named for Col. Joseph White, Jr., who owned and operated a store here. A post office in the late nineteenth century.

White Store Township, sw Anson County.

Whites Township, e central Bertie County.

White Sulphur Springs, former popular resort in ne Surry County. Ceased operation about 1935.

White Sulphur Springs. *See* Catawba Springs.

White Swamp rises in central Wilson County and flows ne into Cattail Swamp.

Whiteville, town and county seat, central Columbus County. Authorized to be laid out in 1810 on the lands of James B. White. Originally known as White's Crossing; inc. 1832 as Whiteville, but ap-

peared on many maps as Whitesville. Named for the man on whose land it was est. and who was a state senator, 1809-10. The former community of Vineland is now included in the s part of the town. Southeastern Community College, est. 1966, is located here. Produces lumber, apparel, tobacco, textiles. Alt. 59.

Whiteville Township, central Columbus County.

White Walnut Branch rises in n Swain County and flows sw into Bone Valley Creek.

Whitewater Falls located on Whitewater River along the Jackson-Transylvania County line near the South Carolina line. These falls, among the highest in the e United States, cascade 411 ft. from an alt. of approx. 2,560. Known as *Contara* or *Contaroga* (meaning unknown) by the Cherokee Indians.

Whitewater River is formed in s Jackson County by the junction of Silver Run and Little Whitewater creeks, and flows se on the Jackson-Transylvania County line into South Carolina where it is joined by Toxaway River to form Keowee River.

Whitfields Crossroads, community in e Lenoir County. Named for a prominent family which settled here before the Revolution.

Whitfields Pond, on the headwaters of Poley Swamp in n Duplin County. Alt. 118.

Whitford, community in e Jones County. Named for local Whitford family.

Whiting Spur, mountain on the McDowell-Mitchell County line.

Whitleys Crossroads, community in sw Nash County.

Whitnel, community in central Caldwell County. Named for two local mill owners, J. O. White and J. L. Nelson. Formerly known as Treeland. Produces textiles.

Whitney, community in ne Stanly County on Badin Lake. Alt. 516.

Whitney Mines, former gold mine in ne Cabarrus County on Little Buffalo Creek.

Whitsett, community in e Guilford County. Est. 1884. Named for Whitsett Institute, successor of Fairview Academy, of which W. T. Whitsett was prinicpal in 1888.

Whitson Branch rises in w Mitchell County and flows sw into Toe River.

Whitson Branch rises in n Yancey County and flows se into Jacks Creek.

Whitted Knob, n Buncombe County between Brittain Cove and Charlie Ridge.

Whittemore Creek rises in n Buncombe County near the Madison County line and flows sw into Ivy Creek.

Whittier, town in e Swain and nw Jackson counties on Tuckasegee River. Alt. 1,839. Est. 1885 by Dr. Clarke Whittier of California who purchased 60,000 arces including the town site. Chartered 1887; charter repealed, 1895. Rechartered 1897, 1899, and 1907.

Whittier Branch rises in n Buncombe County and flows ne into French Broad River.

Whittier Creek rises in s Surry County and flows ne into Bull Run Creek.

Whittington, community in w Wilkes County on Reddies River.

Whittle Creek rises in nw Alamance County and flows w into Buttermilk Creek.

Whortleberry Creek rises in se Anson County and flows se into Pee Dee River.

Whortleberry Mountain. See Huckleberry Ridge.

Whortonsville, community in e Pamlico County on Brown Creek. Called Bethel until a post office was est. when the name of the first postmaster was adopted (pronounced as if written Hortonsville).

Whynot, community in s Randolph County, est. late in the nineteenth century. A group of local citizens, meeting to select a name for the post office about to be est. here, heard many suggestions, "Why not name it for so-and-so?" Finally someone, in desperation said, "Why not name it Whynot?" The group thought this was as good a name as any that had been suggested and, since it removed any element of further controversy, the place was so named.

Wiccacanee Township, n central Northampton County.

Wiccacon River is formed by the junction of several small streams in Hoggard Swamp in s Hertford County. It flows e into Chowan River. Approx. 17 mi. long. Appears as Weecaunse Creek on the Moseley map, 1733; Veecaune Creek on the Collet map, 1770; and as Wiccacon Creek on the Richardson map, 1808. See also Weyanoke Creek.

Wickham Precinct, formed on Dec. 3, 1705, from Bath County, was named for the manor of Temple Wycombe, the home of the Archdale family in Buckinghamshire, England. John Archdale had been governor in 1694-96. In 1712, Wick-

ham Precinct became Hyde County, which see.

Wide Bay, swamp in w central Brunswick County, a part of Green Swamp.

Widow Moores Creek. See Moores Creek.

Widow Mountain, n Wilkes County between Cane Creek and North Prong Roaring River.

Wiel, community in s Onslow County on the n side of the mouth of Duck Creek.

Wiggins Branch rises in n Swain County and flows se into Cooper Creek.

Wiggins Cove, e Mitchell County at the head of Beaver Creek.

Wiggins Creek rises in w Swain County and flows ne into Little Tennessee River.

Wiggins Crossroads, community in s Edgecombe County.

Wiggins Crossroads, community in ne Gates County. Alt. 30. Settled in the eighteenth century and named for a local family.

Wiggins Lake, w Edgecombe County, formed in 1953 by a dam on Deloach Branch. Covers 52 acres with a max. depth of 15 ft. Fishing, swimming, boating, and irrigation. Open to the public.

Wiggins Pond. See Contentnea Lake.

Wiggins Top, sw Clay County at the ne end of Chasteen Mountain.

Wilbanks, community in e Wilson County. A post office operated here 1895-1906.

Wilbar, community in w Wilkes County on South Fork Reddies River. Alt. 2,000. Named for Henry T. Wilbar, nineteenth century resident.

Wilbon, community in s Wake County. Also called Walthall.

Wilcox Iron Works, remains of large stone blast furnace located at the foot of Ore Hill near Mt. Vernon Springs, w central Chatham County. One of at least 3 iron works built in this area by John Wilcox (1728-93), ironmaster and landowner, during the Revolutionary era.

Wild Boar Creek formerly rose near the e shore of the mainland of Dare County s of Stumpy Point Bay and flowed e into Pamlico Sound. Erosion which opened Stumpy Point Lake into the Sound also removed all evidence of this creek. Appears on the Moseley map, 1733, and on the Collet map, 1770.

Wild Branch rises in central Madison County and flows ¾ mi. se into Hunter Creek.

Wild Branch rises in n central Madison County and flows s into Big Laurel Creek.

Wildcat Branch rises in e Franklin County and flows e into Big Peachtree Creek.

Wildcat Branch rises in s Macon County and flows se into Betty Creek.

Widcat Branch rises in s Swain County and flows s into Brush Creek.

Wildcat Branch rises in se Transylvania County and flows nw into Reasonover Creek.

Wildcat Branch rises in central Wake County, in Raleigh, and flows n into Walnut Creek.

Wildcat Cliffs, on the Jackson-Macon County line, se of Whiteside Mountain.

Wild Cat Cove, on the Cherokee County, N. C.-Polk County, Tenn., line betweeen Angelica Mountain and Hays Knob.

Wildcat Creek rises in n central Avery County and flows n into Elk River.

Wildcat Creek rises in e Macon County and flows sw into North Prong Ellijay Creek.

Wildcat Gap, n Graham County at the ne end of Hogback Mountain between Sawyer Creek and Stecoah Creek.

Wildcat Gap, on the Jackson-Macon County line.

Wildcat Hollow, n Yancey County between Seng Branch and Cane River.

Wildcat Knob, n Buncombe County between Haw Knob and Carson Mountain.

Wildcat Knob, on Sassafras Ridge in s Graham County.

Wildcat Knob, on the Jackson-Macon County line.

Wildcat Knob, sw McDowell County. Alt. approx. 2,600.

Wildcat Knob, central Macon County between Tarkiln Ridge and Trimont Ridge.

Wildcat Lake, n Avery County on the campus of Lees-McRae College, Banner Elk, on Wildcat Creek. Covers 3 acres with a max. depth of 12 ft. Fishing, swimming, boating.

Wildcat Pond, a marsh in se Duplin County.

Wild Cat Rock, a rugged precipice in sw Alleghany County near Doughton Park.

Wildcat Mountain, n Buncombe County n of Watershed Ridge between Sugar Creek and Paint Fork.

Wildcat Mountain, s Cherokee County e of Cane Creek. Almost right-angled in shape, it extends n and ne.

Wild Cat Mountain, e Davidson County between Flat Swamp Creek and Lick Creek.

Wildcat Rock, w Henderson County at the head of South Fork.

Wildcat Spur, peak in nw Polk County at the head of Brights Creek.

Wildcat Spring, n Haywood County on the head of Holly Bottom Branch.

Wildcat Swamp rises in central Bertie County and flows nw into Loosing Swamp.

Wildcat Swamp rises in central Northampton County and flows se into Potecasi Creek.

Wildcat Swamp rises in se Sampson County and flows nw into Black River.

Wildcat Top, peak on the Haywood County, N. C.-Cocke County, Tenn., line. Alt. 4,201. The Appalachian Trail passes here.

Wild Cherry Creek rises in n Swain County and flows ne into Beech Flats Prong.

Wild Cherry Ridge, n Swain County in Great Smoky Mountains National Park, a short spur of Loggy Ridge near lat. 35° 32' 35" N., long. 83° 31' 25" W.

Wilder. See Needmore.

Wilders Grove, community in e central Wake County n of Crabtree Creek.

Wilders Township, n Johnston County.

Wildes Creek rises in n Macon County and flows se into Burningtown Creek.

Wildes Knob, n Macon County at the head of Wildes Creek.

Wild Rock Mountain, se Watauga County between Joes Creek and Old House Branch.

The Wild Side. See Big Pocosin.

Wildwood, community in w central Carteret County, between Morehead Bluffs and Newport. Alt. 19 ft.

Wiles Creek rises in n Mitchell County and flows nw into Big Rock Creek.

Wiley Knob, s Madison County at the head of Robert Branch.

Wiley Mountain, n Buncombe County between Thurz Mountain and Chestnut Knob.

Wilgrove, community in e Mecklenburg County.

Wilkerson Creek rises in w Hyde County and flows nw approx. 1½ mi. into Pungo River. Its lower course forms part of the channel of the Intracoastal Waterway.

Wilkerson Crossroads, community in w Wilson County n of Contentnea Creek.

Wilkesboro, town and county seat in s central Wilkes County on Yadkin River. North Wilkesboro (which see) lies just across the river. Laid out by 1801; inc. 1847. Took its name from the county. Wilkes Community College, est. 1967, is located here. Alt. 1,042.

Wilkesboro Reservoir. See W. Kerr Scott Reservoir.

Wilkesboro Township, central Wilkes County.

Wilkes County was formed in 1778 from Surry County and the District of Washington. Located in the nw section of the state, it is bounded by Yadkin, Iredell, Alexander, Caldwell, Watauga, Ashe, Alleghany, and Surry counties. It was named for John Wilkes (1727-97), English political leader who championed American rights at the time of the Revolution. Area: 765 sq. mi. County seat: Wilkesboro with an elevation of 1,042 ft. Townships are Antioch, Beaver Creek, Boomer, Brushy Mountains, Edwards, Elk, Jobs Cabin, Lewis Fork, Lovelace, Moravian Falls, Mulberry, New Castle, North Wilkesboro, Reddies River, Rock Creek, Somers. Stanton, Trap Hill, Union, Walnut Grove, and Wilkesboro. Produces corn, wheat, oats, tobacco, apples, poultry, livestock, hogs, furniture, mirrors, textiles, apparel, hosiery, and crushed stone.

Wilkes Gap, central Macon County at the head of Iotla Creek.

Wilkes Cove, at the head of Iotla Creek in central Macon County.

Wilkes Mill Pond in e Richmond County drains into Gum Swamp Creek.

Wilkie Gap, s Swain County on Licklog Creek.

Wilkin, community in sw Granville County. Named for L. A. Wilkins, donor of right-of-way for railroad and land for the station. Alt. 360.

Wilkins Bluff, s Onslow County, extends into New River.

Wilkins Creek rises in n Haywood County and flows sw into Pigeon River.

Wilkinson, community in e Beaufort County.

Wilkinson Creek rises in n Chatham County and flows sw into Haw River.

Wilkinson Point, the s tip of Pamlico County extending into Neuse River. Appears on the Lawson map, 1709; called Rich Neck in local records of 1706.

Wilkinson's Lake. See Bakers Lake.

Wilkinson Swamp rises in w Robeson County and flows sw into South Carolina, where it enters Little Pee Dee River.

Willard, community in n Pender County. Alt. 50. Settled about 1890. Known first as Leesburg until renamed for the Willard family, local lumber dealers.

Willardville, community in n Durham County. Alt. 438.

Will Branch rises in n Swain County and flows sw into Oconaluftee River.

Will Creek rises in n Cherokee County in the Snowbird Mountains and flows s into Hanging Dog Creek.

Will Gap, s Swain County between Will Knob and the head of Little Yalaka Creek.

William B. Umstead Bridge. See Redstone Point; Weir Point.

William B. Umstead State Park, w Wake County, 10 mi. nw of Raleigh. Est. 1943 as Crabtree Creek State Park; name changed 1955 to honor the late Governor William B. Umstead (1895-1954). Contains 5,080 acres. Nature trail; camping, fishing, boating. See also Reedy Creek State Park.

Williams, community in s Wayne County near Williams Millpond.

Williams, formerly an inc. town in e Yadkin County, the site now being in w Forsyth County. A whiskey distillery was operated at the site by the Williams family (who settled here about 1765) from shortly after the Revolution until 1908. On Feb. 26, 1903, the General Assembly passed a bill prohibiting the operation of whiskey distilleries outside inc. towns. On March 3, 1903, the town of Williams was inc. With the coming of state-wide prohibition in 1908 the Williams distillery closed and the "town" ceased to exist.

Williamsboro, town in n Vance County near the head of Little Island Creek. It was authorized to be laid out in 1786 and inc. 1808. Long inactive in municipal affairs. The place was first called The Lick for a salt lick in the vicinity. It was later known as Nutbush from the creek of that name which was named by William Byrd's dividing line party in 1728 because of the profusion of hazelnuts there. Williamsboro was named in honor of Judge John Williams (1732-99). St. John's Episcopal Church here, dating from 1757, has been restored to its original condition.

Willamsboro Township, nw Vance County.

Willams Branch rises in ne Buncombe County near Ingraham Mountain and flows sw into Dillingham Creek.

Williams Branch rises in e Swain County and flows e into Wesser Creek.

Williamsburg, former town in ne Iredell County. Commissioners appointed and town laid out 1815. Long inactive in municipal affairs.

Williamsburg, community in se Rockingham County. Known first as Thompsonville and a post office by that name existed 1848-1907 when the name was changed to McIver because of confusion with Thomasville. The community name remained unchanged, however, until 1960 when it became Williamsburg. In January, 1840, Williamsburg School, the first public school in the state, opened here.

Willamsburg Township, se Rockingham County.

Williams Creek rises in central Cleveland County and flows sw into First Broad River.

Williams Creek rises in ne Montgomery County and flows se into Moore County where it enters Wolf Creek.

Williams Creek rises in w Wake County and flows se into Swift Creek.

Williams Crossroads, community in s Wake County near the head of Neal Branch.

Williams Lake, nw Sampson County on Caesar Swamp. Formed about 1855 as a millpond. Covers 30 acres; max. depth 12 ft. First owned by Joel Jackson and known as Joel Jackson Pond; acquired by his daughter who married a Williams, hence the present name.

Williams Mill Creek rises in e Anson County and flows se into Jones Creek.

Williams Millpond, s Wayne County on a tributary of Northeast Cape Fear River. Dam and corn mill built here prior to 1915 by Robert Williams, for whom it is named. Max. depth, 10 ft.; area, 25 acres. Fishing, boating; open to the public. Owned by grandaughter of builder, Elizabeth Wooten Holmes.

Williams Millpond. See Merchants Millpond.

Williams Mountain, e Haywood County extends ne from Beaverdam Creek to Big Butte Mountain.

Williams Mountain, s Polk County. Alt. approx. 1,450.

Williams Old Mill Branch rises in central Sampson County and flows sw into Great Coharie Creek.

Williamson Branch rises in ne Wilson County and flows se into Edgecombe County where it enters Town Creek.

Williamson Creek rises in ne Rockingham County and flows ne into Virginia where it enters Dan River.

Williamson Creek rises in e Transylvania County and flows nw into French Broad River.

Williamson Crossroads, community in nw Columbus County.

Williamsons Township, sw Scotland County.

Williams Pond. See Nobles Mill Pond.

Williams Store, community in w Halifax County.

Williamston, town and county seat in n central Martin County, on the Roanoke River. Inc. 1779 as Williamstown on Thomas Hunter's plantation, Skewarky (also commonly spelled Squhawky). Named in honor of William Williams, colonel in the Revolution. Produces canned foods, chemicals, tobacco, lumber, and apparel. Alt. 60.

Williamston Township, central Martin County.

Williamstown. See Williamston.

Williams Township, ne Chatham County.

Williams Township, s central Columbus County.

Williams Township, ne Martin County.

Willie Knob, s Graham County between Snowbird Creek and Little Snowbird Creek.

Willis Branch rises in sw Cleveland County and flows n into Broad River.

Willis Cove, e Haywood County. An unnamed stream which rises at Big Butte Mountain flows se through the cove into North Hominy Creek.

Willis Cove, on a tributary of Iotla Creek in central Macon County.

Willis Creek, a tidal creek approx. 1 mi. long, flowing e into Nelson Bay, e Carteret County.

Willis Creek. See Wade Creek.

Williston, a community in e Carteret County on Williston Creek. Named for a local family, possibly that of John Williston who settled here in 1745.

Williston Creek rises in e Carteret County and flows se approx. 2½ mi. into Jarrett Bay.

Willits, community on Scott Creek in n Jackson County.

Will King Gap, ne Cherokee County in the Valley River Mountains near the Clay County line.

Will Mason Branch rises in sw Clay County

and flows ne into Brasstown Creek. Named for a farmer who lived nearby.

Will Mason Gap, sw Clay County in Wells Mountain.

Willow, community in s Gates County on a branch of Trotman Creek. Post office here prior to 1912 was known as Willow Branch.

Willowbies Island. See Bell Island.

Willow Branch rises in e Bertie County and flows se into Chowan River.

Willow Branch. See Willow.

Willow Creek rises on the Buncombe-Haywood County line and flows ne across Buncombe County into Sandy Mush Creek.

Willow Creek rises in w Henderson County and flows nw into French Broad River.

Willow Falls, rapids in Cape Fear River in central Harnett County ne of the town of Lillington. Mentioned as early as 1819 in a survey of the rivers of North Carolina.

Willow Green, community in e Greene County. Settled prior to 1890.

Willow Point extends from the s mainland of Hyde County into Bell Bay.

Willow Spring, community in s Wake County. Settled about 1800; named for weeping willows in the vicinity. Alt. 275.

Will Puett Cove, central Cherokee County near the headwaters of Puett Creek. Named for Will Puett who lived in the cove in the 1860's.

Will Scott Creek rises in central Cherokee County and flows s and sw into Hiwassee River.

Will Scott Mountain, central Cherokee County, extends ne from Murphy.

Wills Creek rises in s Cumberland County and flows se into Cape Fear River.

Will Quarter Creek. See Hoggard Mill Creek.

Willy Knob, n central Alleghany County between Doughton and Black (formerly Carson) Mountains.

Wilmar, community in sw Beaufort and nw Craven counties. Alt. 57.

Wilmer Branch rises in se Richmond County and flows se into Poley Branch.

Wilmet, community in nw Jackson County. Alt. 1,866.

Wilmington, city and county seat, w New Hanover County on Cape Fear River. A port for ocean-going vessels, it is approx. 30 mi. from the Atlantic Ocean. Inc. 1739/40. The town enjoyed a succession of names in its earliest years. Apparently settled and first known as New Carthage about 1733. New Liverpool seems to have been used briefly, followed by New Town or Newton, the name by which it was chartered in 1739/40, and finally Wilmington. Named for Spencer Compton (1673?-1743), Earl of Wilmington, patron of Governor Gabriel Johnston during whose administration the town was chartered. The legislature met here 1741, 1746, 1754, 1759-60, 1760-61, 1764. Alt. 38. Produces baked goods, fabricated metals, lumber, wooden containers, textiles, apparel, dairy products, paper boxes, chemicals, and refrigeration machinery. Wilmington College is here.

Wilmington Beach, s New Hanover County on the Atlantic Ocean. Est. approx. 1913.

Wilmington District at the time of the 1790 census was composed of Bladen, Brunswick, Duplin, New Hanover, and Onslow counties.

Wilmington Township, w central New Hanover County, coextensive with the city of Wilmington.

Wilson, city and county seat, central Wilson County. Alt. 147. An early community at this site which developed around Toisnot Baptist Church (est. 1803) was known as Hickory Grove. Tosnot Depot est. on the railroad here about 1840 became the post office name. In 1849 Tosnot Depot and Hickory Grove were inc. as Wilson, named in honor of Capt. Louis D. Wilson (1789-1847) who died at Vera Cruz during the War with Mexico. Atlantic Christian College is here. Large tobacco market. Produces textiles, apparel, concrete pipe, lumber products, processed meat, and grain. See also Hominy Heights.

Wilson, community in central Buncombe County.

Wilson. See Yadkinville.

Wilson Branch rises in central Cherokee County and flows se into Morgan Creek.

Wilson Branch rises in e Madison County and flows s into Big Laurel Creek.

Wilson County was formed in 1855 from Edgecombe, Nash, Johnston, and Wayne counties. Located in the e central section of the state, it is bounded by Pitt, Greene, Wayne, Johnston, Nash, and Edgecombe counties. It was named for Louis Dicken Wilson (1789-1847), delegate to the Constitutional Convention of 1835 and an officer in the War with Mexico where he died. Area: 373 sq. mi. County seat: Wilson with an elevation of 147 ft. Townships are Black Creek, Cross Roads, Gardner, Old Fields, Saratoga, Springhill, Stantonsburg, Taylor, Toisnot, and Wilson. Produces tobacco, corn, wheat, oats, soybeans, cotton, poultry, tobacco products, textiles, apparel, concrete pipe, motor vehicle parts, lumber products, and processed meat.

Wilson Creek rises in e Avery County near Grandfather Mountain and flows se into Caldwell County where it enters Johns River at the Burke County line.

Wilson Creek rises in central Craven County and flows s into Trent River.

Wilson Creek rises in w Jackson County and flows e into Cullowhee Creek.

Wilson Creek Township, w Caldwell County.

Wilson Gap, se Macon County between Clear Creek and Little Creek.

Wilson Hollow, nw Watauga County extends e from Little Beaverdam Creek.

Wilson Knob, e Mitchell County at the head of Bear Creek.

Wilson Knob Mountain. See Big Butte.

Wilson Mill Creek rises in w central Transylvania County and flows se into Catheys Creek.

Wilson Mountain extends ne in n Watauga County n of North Fork River.

Wilson Ridge, n Avery County.

Wilson Ridge extends from se Avery County in nw Caldwell County. Alt. varies from 2,500 to 2,696.

Wilson Ridge, s Yancey County near the head of Big Poplar Creek and the head of Beech Nursery Creek.

Wilsons Bay, central Onslow County in New River s of the city of Jacksonville.

Wilsons Creek Township, e Avery County.

Wilson's Factory, town inc. 1883 to be laid out on the bank of the South Fork of Catawba River in Gaston County. There is no evidence that it ever existed as a town.

Wilson's Mills, town in n Johnston County. Settled about 1868; inc. 1927 and named for local family. Alt. 228.

Wilson's Mills Township, n central Johnston County.

Wilson's Old Store. See Walkersville.

Wilson's Pond, nw Wilson County on Marsh Swamp. Formed about 1900. Covers 15 acres; max. depth 12 ft. Named for Sanford Wilson, owner. Used for fishing, swimming, boating, and irrigation.

Wilsons Store, community in ne Orange County.

Wilson Township, central Wilson County.

Wilsonville, community in e central Chatham County. Named for Cecil Wilson, owner of a store here.

Wilton, community in se Granville County at the head of Sand Creek. A post office was est. here as early as 1828.

Wilton, town authorized by the General Assembly in 1818 to be est. on the lands of Sias Billingsby, Sr., at the mouth of Clarks Creek, sw Montgomery County. There is no evidence that the town was ever laid out.

Wimberly. See Coniott Landing.

Wimble Shoals in the Atlantic Ocean off the community of Salvo on Hatteras Island, e Dare County. The Shoals are at the approx. site of the former Cape Kenrick, which see. They were charted and given their present name by James Wimble in, or shortly prior to, 1738.

Wimberly. See Coniott Landing.

Winchester, former community in w Union County between West Fork Twelvemile Creek and East Fork Twelvemile Creek.

Winchester Cove, central Clay County near the headwaters of Greasy Creek.

Winchester Creek rises in Towns County, Georgia, and flows nw into Clay County where it enters Brasstown Creek.

Winchester Creek rises in w Haywood County and flows se into Richland Creek.

Wind Blow, community in se Montgomery County. Named about 1920 by S. R. Gaddy because it was believed that the wind would blow here if it blew anywhere in the area.

Winder. See Vass.

Winders Crossroads, community in sw Yadkin County.

Windfall Creek rises in n Ashe County and flows se into Horse Creek.

Winding Knob, w Haywood County on the e end of Balsam Ridge.

Winding Stair Branch in w Haywood County, Great Smoky Mountains National Park, rises near lat. 35° 38′ 13″ N., long. 83° 02′ 55″ W., and flows nw into Cataloochee Creek.

Winding Stair Gap, at the head of Poplar Cove Branch in sw Macon County.

Windingstair Knob, nw Burke County. Alt. 3,473.

Winding Stairs, section of road in nw Macon County between Queens Creek and the Macon-Swain County line, winding about 5 mi. down a ½ mi. drop and giving the appearance of winding stairs. Present road laid out about 1923 along a pioneer or Indian trail which, before the Civil War, was sometimes referred to as the Cat's Stairs.

Wind Mill Creek. *See* Jacks Creek.

Windmill Point extends from w Carteret County into White Oak River. Named from the fact that a wind-powered gristmill was once operated here. Also known as Hatchell's Point for Armistead Hatchell who settled here in the eighteenth century.

Windmill Point, point of land at the entrance to Silver Lake, Ocracoke Island, se Hyde County.

Windmill Point, extends into Bay River in n Pamlico County.

Windmill Point. *See* Nixonton.

Windom, community in e central Yancey County on Little Crabtree Creek.

Windsor, town and county seat in central Bertie County. Settled 1722; inc. 1766; became county seat in 1774. Built on the family estate of William Gray and was known originally as Gray's Landing. Windsor was named for the royal castle near London, England. In 1959 Windsor annexed Bertie, a small town across the Cashie River. This site is head of navigation for the Cashie River. Alt. 10. *See also* Hoggard's Mill.

Windsor Township, s central Bertie County.

Windy Gap, n Buncombe County between North Knob and Chestnut Knob.

Windy Gap, e Haywood County on the e end of Chestnut Mountain.

Windy Gap, w Jackson County on the head of Tatham Creek.

Windy Gap, at the head of Rocky Branch in central Macon County.

Windy Gap, on the Madison-Yancey County line in the Walnut Mountains.

Windy Gap, s Swain County s of Licklog Creek near Little Tennessee River.

Windy Gap, community in se Wilkes County on Little Hunting Creek.

Windy Point, on the n side of Pettivers Creek at its junction with White Oak River.

Wine Spring Bald, w Macon County between Middle Ridge and Rocky Bald. Alt. 5,445.

Wine Spring Creek rises on McDonald Ridge, w Macon County, and flows nw into Nantahala Lake.

Wines Top, peak at sw end of Glade Mountain in e Haywood County. Alt. approx. 4,375.

Winfall, town in central Perquimans County. Inc. 1887. Alt. 16.

Winfrey Gap, on the Cherokee-Clay County line. Alt. 3,493.

Wing, community in w central Mitchell County on Snow Creek. Named for Charles Hallet Wing (1836-1915), professor at Massachusetts Institute of Technology, who settled nearby and in 1887 opened a lending library of some 15,000 volumes. This was the first free public library in the state and the third county library in the United States. *See also* Ledger.

Wingate, town in e central Union County. Formerly known as Ames Turnout. Inc. 1901 as Wingate. Home of Wingate Junior College. Produces wood products. Alt. 575.

Winkler Creek rises in s Watauga County and flows ne into Flannery Fork [of South Fork New River].

Winklertown, community in ne Caldwell County on Donahues Creek.

Winnabow, community in e central Brunswick County. Named for the plantation of the Russell family which, in turn, had an Indian name of unknown meaning. Called Evans Store Crossroads during the Civil War. Alt. 40.

Winnie. *See* White Oak.

Winstead Crossroads, community in s Nash County.

Winstead Mills, community in w central Person County.

Winsteadville, community in e Beaufort County.

Winston, formerly an independent city in central Forsyth County, authorized by act of 1849 creating Forsyth County and named the county seat in 1851. Since 1913 it has been consolidated with Salem as Winston-Salem, *which see*. Named for Major Joseph Winston (1746-1814), Revolutionary leader.

Winston Lake, central Forsyth County on Brushy Fork Branch. Known earlier as City Lake. Covers 100 acres with a max. depth of 20 ft. Used for fishing and municipal water supply. Owned by the city of Winston-Salem; open to the public.

Winston-Salem, city and county seat, central Forsyth County, formed in 1913 by the consolidation of Winston and Salem, previously independent towns, *which also see*. Winston-Salem Teachers College, Salem College, Wake Forest University, Piedmont Bible College, and North Carolina School of the Arts are here. Produces tobacco, textiles, hosiery, bakery products, machinery, fabricated metals, furniture, corrugated boxes, apparel, aluminum foil, and processed meat. Alt. 858.

Winston Township, central Forsyth County, coextensive with the city of Winston-Salem.

Winter Park, community on the e outskirts of the city of Wilmington, w New Hanover County. Alt. 45.

Winter Star Ridge, s Yancey County between South Fork Cattail Creek and North Fork Cattail Creek.

Winterville, town in s Pitt County. Inc. 1897. Alt. 72.

Winterville Township, s central Pitt County, formerly Contentnea Township.

Winton, town and county seat, e Hertford County on Chowan River. Authorized to be laid out and inc. 1766 on the land of Benjamin Wynns for whom it undoubtedly was named. Appears as Wynnton in eighteenth century records and as recently as on the Tanner map, 1827. Produces aluminum castings. Alt. 45.

Winton Township, e Hertford County.

Wiquemans. *See* Perquimans River.

Wise, community in n Warren County between Malones Creek and Sauls Creek. Alt. 392. Settled in 1890's and named for Henry Wise, local resident. A post office was est. here in 1891 but was discontinued in 1951.

Wise Branch rises in sw Buncombe County and flows ne into Bill Moore Creek.

Wise Forks, community in nw Jones County. Named for local family. Known as Wise's Crossroads in 1863 when a Civil War engagement took place here on April 28. The battle is referred to variously as Wise's Crossroads, Dover Crossroads, and First Gum Swamp. *See also* Gum Swamp.

Wise Knob, sw Buncombe County near the headwaters of Bill Moore Creek.

Wiseman's View, nw Burke County, overlook for Linville Gorge. Named for William Wiseman, early settler who came from London in the eighteenth century.

Wise's Crossroads. *See* Gum Swamp; Wise Forks.

Wishart Township, se Robeson County.

Wis's Creek. *See* Long Creek.

Wit. *See* Smyrna.

Withrow Creek rises in s Iredell County and flows ne into Rowan County where it joins Back Creek to form North Second Creek. Appears as North Fork [Second Creek] on the Collet Map, 1770.

Witness Rock Ridge, n McDowell County on the s side of Armstrong Creek.

Wittenburg, community in s Alexander County. Named for Daniel Wittenburg who settled in the vicinity about 1830. A post office in the late nineteenth century.

Wittenberg Township, sw Alexander County.

Wittys Crossroads, community in s Rockingham County. Aspen Grove was a nearby post office in the mid-nineteenth century.

W. Kerr Scott Reservoir, sw Wilkes County on Yadkin River. Formed by a dam completed in 1962. Covers 1,470 acres with a shoreline of 55 mi. Alt. 1,030. Named for William Kerr Scott (1896-1958), Governor of North Carolina and U.S. Senator. Constructed for flood control and public recreation.

Wococon Inlet. *See* Wococon Island.

Wococon Island appears on the White map, 1585, as composed of parts of the present Ocracoke and Portsmouth Islands in Hyde and Carteret counties. Port Grenvil, *which see*, formed its n limit and Wococon Inlet (an inlet, now closed, in Portsmouth Island) the s. Probably named from the Indian word *wahkahikani*, "enclosed place," or "stockade." Appears as Gordens Island on the Smith map, 1624. *See also* Portsmouth Island.

Wohanoke. *See* Ohanoak.

Wolf Bald, on the Haywood-Jackson County line.

Wolf Branch rises in se Alamance County and flows sw into Motes Creek.

Wolf Branch rises in s central Alleghany County and flows e into Glade Creek.

Wolf Branch rises in central Buncombe County near Wolf Knob and flows se into Shope Creek.

Wolf Branch rises in ne Buncombe County and flows w into Beetree Creek.

Wolf Branch rises in s Cleveland County and flows nw into Long Branch.

Wolf Branch rises in n Madison County and flows s into Big Laurel Creek.

Wolf Branch rises in s Montgomery County and flows se into Little Hamer Creek.

Wolf Branch rises in w Yancey County and flows s into Fox Creek.

Wolf Cove, the valley through which Wolf Cove Branch flows in central Buncombe County.

Wolf Cove Branch rises in central Buncombe County near Asheville and flows nw into Beaverdam Creek.

Wolf Creek rises in s Buncombe County near Stradley Mountain and flows se into Bent Creek.

Wolf Creek rises in se Cherokee County and flows sw into Fannin County, Ga., where it enters Ocoee River.

Wolf Creek rises in ne Graham County and flows ne into Little Tennessee River.

Wolf Creek rises in e Jackson County and flows sw into Tuckasegee River.

Wolf Creek rises in w Jackson County and flows nw into Cullowhee Creek.

Wolf Creek rises in w Macon County and flows se into Nantahala Lake.

Wolf Creek rises in ne Montgomery County near the town of Star and flows e into n Moore County where it enters Bear Creek.

Wolf Creek rises in e Surry County and flows n into Chinquapin Creek.

Wolf Creek, community in sw Cherokee County on Wolf Creek.

Wolf Creek Falls in Canada Township of e Jackson County, on Wolf Creek. Consists of a series of five separate falls, one being approx. 85 ft. high, and the others aver-* aging 35 ft. Located above Wolf Creek Lake.

Wolf Creek Gap, on the Cherokee-Macon County line.

Wolf Creek Lake in central Jackson County on Wolf Creek. Formed in 1955 as a reservoir for Nantahala Power and Light Co. Covers 183 acres with a max. depth of 170 ft. Shoreline is 6.9 mi. Used for generation of hydroelectric power. Named for Wolf Creek. See also East Fork Lake.

Wolfden Branch rises in s Watauga County and flows sw into Buffalo Creek.

Wolfden Knob, n Buncombe County between Rich Knob and Lane Pinnacle.

Wolfden Ridge, e Mitchell County at the head of Little Bear Creek.

Wolfert Creek. See Tusk Creek.

Wolf Gap, s Macon County between Turkey Knob and Buck Knob.

Wolfharbor Branch rises in s Franklin County and flows se into Nash County where it enters Turkey Creek.

Wolf House Point, neck of land extending into waters of Currituck Sound on the w side of Church Island in e Currituck County.

Wolfington. See Hoggard's Mill.

Wolf Island Creek rises in s central Rockingham County and flows ne into nw Caswell County where it turns n to flow into Dan River.

Wolf Knob, central Buncombe County ne of Swan Mountain.

Wolf Knob, central Cherokee County near the head of Rose Creek.

Wolf Knob, on Jackson-Swain County line near the head of Yalaka Creek. Alt. approx. 4,900.

Wolf Knob, on the Jackson-Macon County line.

Wolf Knob, on the Watauga-Wilkes County line e of the head of Stony Fork Creek.

Wolf Laurel Basin, depression between Fork Ridge and nw end of Horse Cove Ridge in w Graham County.

Wolf Laurel Branch rises in w central Haywood County and flows e into Jonathan's Creek.

Wolf Mountain, s Henderson County at the head of South Fork.

Wolf Mountain extends ne in e Jackson County between Wolf Creek and Tanasee Creek.

Wolf Mountain, n Madison County between Lewis Branch and Wolf Branch.

Wolf Mountain, community in e Jackson County on Tanasee Creek.

Wolf Pen Branch rises in central Franklin County and flows se into Tar River. Now generally called Wolf Pit Branch.

Wolfpen Creek rises in central Henderson County and flows nw into Clear Creek. Also known locally as Bengle Creek.

Wolfpen Gap, n Buncombe County between Ramsey Mountain and Bruce Knob.

Wolf Pen Gap, sw Cherokee County on the headwaters of Persimmon Creek.

Wolfpen Gap, s Haywood County in Wolfpen Mountain.

Wolfpen Gap, n Jackson County between Black Mountain and West Fork [Moses Creek].

Wolfpen Gap, n Jackson County between East Fork [Dicks Creek] and Dills Creek.

Wolfpen Gap, central Macon County between Willis Cove and Trimont Ridge.

Wolfpen Gap, s Macon County between Rockhouse Knob and Dryman Fork.

Wolf Pen Mountain, e Caldwell County. Alt. 2,137.

Wolfpen Mountain, s Haywood County on the head of Farmer Branch and the head of Camp Branch. Alt. approx. 3,200.

Wolfpit Branch rises in se Buncombe County and flows nw into Swannanoa River.

Wolf Pit Branch. *See* Wolf Pen Branch.

Wolf Pit Creek rises on the Fort Bragg Military Reservation in w Hoke County and flows ne into Rockfish Creek.

Wolf Pit Gap, e Haywood County between Millstone Mountain and Buck Cove Mountain.

Wolfpit Gap, w central Yancey County near the head of Jacks Creek.

Wolf Pit Township, sw Richmond County. In colonial times, it is said, this area was overrun with wolves. A trap was constructed for them, but the first animal to fall into it was a mule owned by a prominent farmer. Scottish settlers were so amused they gave the region the name of Wolf Pit.

Wolf Pond, community in s Union County.

Wolf Ridge, nw Cherokee County, extends ne between Gowans Cove and Hipps Ridge.

Wolf Ridge, n Clay County extends ne from Tar Kiln Ridge to Trail Ridge.

Wolf Ridge, e Mitchell County between Charlies Ridge and Rube Green Top.

Wolf Ridge, n Mitchell County between the forks of Gouges Creek.

Wolf Ridge, nw Swain County in Great Smoky Mountains National Park, a spur extending se from Parson Bald.

Wolf Ridge in central Watauga County extends ne from Rich Mountain to Howard Creek.

Wolf Rock, peak in s Macon County between Fishhawk Mountain and Tater Hill.

Wolfscrape Township, nw Duplin County.

Wolfsville, community in s Union County.

Wolf Swamp rises in n Onslow County and flows se into Northeast Creek.

Womacks Mill, community in central Caswell County, named for the mill on Country Line Creek.

Wood, community in ne Franklin County. Alt. 350. Settled about 1893 and known as Woods Store until 1913. Inc. as Wood in 1917; charter repealed 1961.

Woodard, community in se Bertie County.

Woodard Mountains, e Madison County between California Creek and Middle Fork.

Woodard's Pond, e Wilson County, formed in 1954 by the construction of a dam across a natural hollow between two hills. Covers 12 acres; max. depth 14 ft. Named for W. D. Woodard, owner. Used for fishing, swimming, boating, and irrigation.

Woodburn, commuity in ne Brunswick County.

Woodburn. *See* McGehees Mill.

Woodby Gap, n Yancey County between Hawk Branch and Byrds Branch.

Woodcock Knob, w Caldwell County. Alt. approx. 2,500.

Wood Cove, swamp in central Pender County on Northeast Cape Fear River.

Woodenton. *See* Woodington.

Woodfin, community in central Buncombe County on the e bank of French Broad River nw of Asheville.

Woodford, community in nw Ashe County.

Wood Fork Branch rises in n Surry County and flows se into Beaverdam Creek.

Wood Grove. *See* Mount Ulla.

Woodington, community in s Lenoir County. Named by Richard Caswell when he acquired a plantation here about 1767, before he became governor. Name sometimes appears as Woodenton in nineteenth-century records.

Woodington Township, se Lenoir County.

Wood Island, in the mouth of Cashie River in se Bertie County. Approx. 2,000 ft. long and 200 ft. wide. *See also* Purchace Islands.

Wood Island, a small island in sw Carteret County in Bogue Sound.

Wood Lake, ne Cherokee County, formed by a dam on Thrash Creek. Covers approx. 8 acres with a max. depth of 35 ft.

Woodland, town in e Northampton County. Alt. 72. Inc. 1883. Settled about 1835. Named for the Wood family, early Quaker settlers. *See also* George. Produces lumber and zippers.

Woodlawn, community in nw McDowell

County in Turkey Cove and on Limekiln Creek. This was the site of Cathey's Fort, a rendezvous for the North Carolina militia led by Gen. Griffith Rutherford against the Cherokee Indians in 1776.

Woodlawn. See Mount Holly.

Woodleaf, town in n Rowan County. Inc. 1909, but long inactive in municipal affairs. A post office est. here in 1855 with Daniel Wood as first postmaster. Alt. 711. A large gravel pit is worked here.

Woodleigh, community on Knotts Island in ne Currituck County.

Woodley, community in nw Tyrrell County between Scuppernong River and the Tyrrell-Washington County line. Originated as a depot, but tracks and depot no longer in use.

Wood Mountain, between Mill Creek and Pine Creek in sw Jackson County.

Woodpin Creek rises in n Jackson County and flows sw into Scott Creek.

Woodpin Falls in the headwaters of Woodpin Creek in n Jackson County.

Woodrow, community in s Haywood County. Alt. 2,700. Named for President Woodrow Wilson.

Woodruff Branch rises in s Transylvania County and flows ne into West Fork French Broad River.

Woodrun Creek rises in w Montgomery County and flows sw into Pee Dee River.

Woods Branch rises in central Jackson County and flows sw into Tuckasegee River.

Woodsdale, community in n Person County. Settled about 1800. Named for the Hugh Woods family, early residents. Alt. 482.

Woodsdale Township, n central Person County.

Wood's Ferry formerly crossed the Haw River in se Alamance County approx. 2 mi. below Saxapahaw. Mentioned in local records prior to the Revolution.

Woods Gap, ne Rutherford County at the ne end of the Richland Mountains.

Woodside, community in s Pender County.

Woodside. See Granite Quarry.

Woods Knob, s Mitchell County between Pony Ridge and South Fork [Carvers Branch]. Alt. 2,248.

Woods Millpond, e Wayne County on a Tributary of West Bear Creek.

Woods Mountain, nw McDowell County, a series of small peaks. Max. alt. 3,646.

Woodson Branch rises in w central Madison

County and flows n into Big Laurel Creek.

Woods Pond. See Parrish's Pond.

Woodstock Point, e Beaufort County on Pungo River. In 1738 a town named Woodstock was laid out here to serve as the county seat of Hyde County. The courthouse burned in 1789 and the following year the county seat was moved. Remains of the old courthouse may still be seen at low tide off Woodstock Point. A post office at Woodstock operated as late as 1822.

Woodstock Savanna, e Beaufort County between Pungo Creek and Pamlico River.

Woods Store. See Wood.

Wood Swamp. See Hood Swamp.

Woodville, community in ne Cherokee County in Nantahala National Forest.

Woodville, community in e Parquimans County on Little River. An early Quaker settlement. A post office was est. here by 1822.

Woodville, community in ne Surry County near Big Creek.

Woodville, town in nw Bertie County. Appears as Hotel on the MacRae map, 1833 and this was the post office name from 1840 through 1865. Inc. as Woodville, 1911, taking the name of the home of Whitmell Hill Pugh which had been named for an estate in England. Adjacent to Lewiston (which see) and Lewiston is the railroad name for Woodville.

Woodville Township, w Bertie County.

Woodward Knob, nw Swain County in Great Smoky Mountains National Park on Jenkins Trail Ridge near lat. 35° 31' N., long. 83° 43' 02" W. Alt. 3,939.

Woodward's Crossroads. See Pendleton.

Woodworth, community in n Vance County.

Woody Branch rises in n Cherokee County in the Snowbird Mountains and flows sw into Will Creek.

Woody Branch rises in nw Haywood County at n end of Fork Mountain, and flows 1½ mi. se to join Conrad Creek to form Little Cataloochee Creek.

Woody Branch rises in n central Henderson County and flows se into Boylston Creek.

Woody Creek, w Haywood County, Great Smoky Mountains National Park, rises near lat. 35° 35' N., long. 83° 10' 20" W., and flows ne into Ugly Fork.

Woody Ridge, w Haywood County, Great Smoky Mountains National Park; a short spur extending ne from Balsam Mountain, center near lat. 35° 35' 30" N., long. 83° 10' W.

Woody's Ferry. See Newmarket.

Woolard Crossroads, community in nw Beaufort County.

Wooleyshot Branch rises in sw Madison County w of Hap Mountain and flows s and w into Spring Creek.

Woolly Ridge, nw Swain County in Great Smoky Mountains National Park, a short spur extending se from Blockhouse Ridge. Its center is near lat. 35° 32' 58" N., long. 83° 41' 37" W.

Wooly Ridge Branch rises in w Swain County in Great Smoky Mountains National Park and flows se into Nunda Branch.

Woolsey See Ramoth.

Woolsey Branch rises in n Madison County on the s slope of Walnut Knob and flows s and w into French Broad River at Stackhouse.

Wooten Millpond, e Wayne County on Walnut Creek. Named for Ensign Shadrach Wooten, Revolutionary War soldier, who moved to Columbus County in 1805. Relatives still live in the area.

Wooten Mountain, e Macon County between Cat Creek and Rabbit Creek.

Wootens Creek rises in n Wilkes County and flows se into Mulberry Creek.

Wootens Crossroads, community in n central Greene County. Named for the Wooten family which ran a store here in the 1920's and 1930's.

Wootens Crossroads, community in n Lenoir County. Named for a family which has operated a store here for more than fifty years.

Wootentown, community in central Beaufort County, 1 mi. e of Washington Park. Alt. 14. Misspelled Hootentown frequently because that is the way the name is pronounced locally. This is a Negro community on land originally owned by Harkness Wooten, a well-known free Negro of the early nineteenth century. Most of the inhabitants are descended from him.

Wootonton. See Fair Bluff.

Worcester Inlet. See Trinity Harbor.

Worlds Edge, high bluff s of Chinquapin Gap, nw Polk County.

Worley, community in s Madison County on Big Pine Creek.

Worley Branch rises in e Swain County and flows se into Galbreath Creek.

Worley Cove, nw Buncombe County near the Madison County line.

Worley Cove, e Haywood County on the head of North Hominy Creek.

Worley Cove Branch rises in s Madison County and flows se into Sandy Mush Creek. Recent State Highway Commission maps of the county apply the name Red Horse Creek to this stream.

Worley Knob, e Swain County on the head of Worley Branch.

Worm Creek rises in ne Cherokee County and flows sw and nw into Valley River.

Worrell Mill Pond, ne Northampton County on Kirbys Creek. Prior to about 1916 when M. E. Worrell purchased the mill it was known as Watson's Mill. For a time a generator here produced electricity for the town of Murfreesboro, 3 mi. s. A marl cliff near the millrace has yielded evidence of at least ten species of marine life.

Worrells Mill Pond, w Hertford County at the junction of Hares and Institute branches. Formed prior to 1842 and known first as Griffith's Mill Pond. Covers 75 acres with a max. depth of 17 ft.

Worry, community in n central Burke County, about 6 mi. nw of town of Morganton. Named by Jane Elizabeth Caldwell who, according to local legend, had submitted several names which were rejected, and troubled by this dilemma, she proposed Worry, which was approved.

Worsley Creek. See Chocowinity Creek.

Worth. See Hardin.

Worth's Mill. See Worthville.

Worthville, community in n Randolph County on Deep River. Settled approx. 1810 and known as Hopper's Ford for Charles Hopper, local resident. With the est. of a cotton mill by J. M. and Hal M. Worth about 1881, it came to be called Worth's Mill. Inc. 1895 as Worthville; charter repealed 1920.

Wrendale, community in n Edgecombe County.

Wright Branch rises in central Haywood County and flows se into Jonathan Creek.

Wright Brothers National Memorial, located on n Bodie Island, e Dare County. Includes the Kill Devil Hills Monument National Memorial, the reconstructed Wright hangar and work shop, and Visitor Center. Occupies 314 acres.

Wright Cove, s Buncombe County sw of Ballard Gap.

Wright Cove, the valley through which Crawford Creek flows in s Clay County.

Wright Creek rises in e Beaufort County and flows n into Pungo River near Pamlico Beach.

Wright Creek rises in ne Cherokee County and flows se into Valley River.

Wright Creek rises in w Graham County and flows ne into Santeetlah Creek.

Wright Knob, central Haywood County between Morrow Branch and Wright Branch.

Wright Memorial Bridge. See Sampson Point.

Wright Nature Preserves. See Harry M. Wright Nature Preserves.

Wrightsboro, community in n New Hanover County. Alt. approx. 35.

Wrights Creek rises in n Jackson County and flows sw into Soco Creek.

Wrights Island, s Onslow County on the ne side of New River Inlet.

Wrights Station. See Lowell.

Wrightsville, community on the mainland of e New Hanover County near the mouth of Bradleys Creek and Middle Sound. Settled about 1780. Known at one time as Wrightsville Sound. Named for Joshua G. Wright (1840-94), of Wilmington, organizer of a real estate agency.

Wrightsville, former community in nw Duplin County near the present site of Faison, which see. Appears on the MacRae map, 1833, but apparently declined after the est. of Faison.

Wrightsville Beach, island approx. 4 mi. long, e New Hanover County between Atlantic Ocean and Wrightsville Sound.

Wrightsville Beach, town in e New Hanover County on Wrightsville Beach island between the Atlantic Ocean and Wrightsville Sound. Settled about 1889; inc. 1899. Alt. 5. Summer resort.

Wrightsville Inlet. See Moore Inlet.

Wrightsville Sound, e New Hanover County behind Wrightsville Beach island. See also Wrightsville.

Wriston, community in w Mecklenburg County.

Wyanoke, community in nw Gates County on Chowan River.

Wyant Branch rises in sw Macon County and flows sw into Long Branch.

Wyatt, community in n Wake County near Smiths Creek.

Wycle Creek rises in w central Haywood County and flows e into Jonathans Creek.

Wye, community in e Harnett County 1 mi. ne of Erwin where the railroad has a "Y" connection with one line leading to Erwin and the other to Dunn.

Wyesocking Bay in Pamlico Sound, e Hyde County, bounded by Long Point on the ne and by Hog Island Point on the sw. The Collet map, 1770, shows Yesocking Creek flowing into this bay, unnamed on the map. The creek named by Collet no longer exists since a canal has been dug at or near its course. The Indian word from which Wyesocking has developed is believed to have been *wayáci* which, in combination with another word, meant "directly" or "straightaway" referring to a landing place.

Wykle Hill, n Macon County between the head of Hampton Branch and Queens Creek.

Wynn Creek rises in se Alamance County and flows w into Haw Creek.

Wynn Ferry, formerly in n Tyrrell County on Scuppernong River s of Columbia.

Wynnton. See Winton.

Wyo, community on the Davie-Yadkin County line. Named for local church.

Wysner Mountain, n Montgomery County near Barnes Creek.

X

X-Way. See Exway.

Y

Yadkin, community in e Rowan County at Yadkin River. A large textile mill is here.

Yadkin College, town in w Davidson County on Yadkin River. Inc. 1875, but long inactive in municipal affairs. Named for the Methodist Protestant college opened here in 1865, closed in 1924. One college building and the ruins of another remain.

Yadkin College Township, w central Davidson County.

Yadkin County was formed in 1850 from Surry County. Located in the n central section of the state, it is bounded by Forsyth, Davie. Iredell, Wilkes, and Surry counties. It was named for Yadkin River, *which see*. Area: 335 sq. mi. County seat: Yadkinville with an elevation of 960 ft. Townships are Boonville, Buck Shoal, Deep Creek, East Bend, Fall Creek, Forbush, Knobs, and Liberty. Produces tobacco, corn, wheat, oats, poultry, textiles, crushed granite, and limestone.

Yadkin Creek rises in s Watauga County and flows s into Caldwell County.

Yadkin Narrows. *See* Narrows of the Yadkin.

Yadkin River rises in s Watauga County near Blowing Rock and flows se into Caldwell where it turns ne to flow through Wilkes, on the Surry-Yadkin, Yadkin-Forsyth, Davie-Forsyth, Davie-Davidson, Davidson-Rowan, and a part of the Montgomery-Stanly County lines. It is joined by the Uwharrie River to form the Pee Dee River. Called Sapona River by John Lawson in 1709. Appears as "Sapona or Yadkin River" on the Moseley map, 1733. The Sapona Indians lived in the area, but the origin or meaning of Yadkin is uncertain. It was also spelled Yatkin, Atkin, Reatkin, and other ways in the eighteenth century.

Yadkin Township, sw Stokes County.

Yadkin Valley, community in ne Caldwell County.

Yadkin Valley, community in ne Davie County.

Yadkin Valley Township, ne Caldwell County.

Yadkinville, town and county seat, central Yadkin County. Commissioners in 1850 authorized to select site and lay off county seat to be named Wilson. Name changed to Yadkinville, 1852, town chartered 1857. Alt. 960.

Yalaka Creek rises in se Swain County and flows nw into Little Tennessee River. Sometimes also called Alarka Creek.

Yalaka Mountains extend se from the head of East Fork [Kirkland Creek] in s Swain County to the head of Upper Long Creek in se Swain County. Sometimes also called Alarka Mountains.

Yale, community in w Henderson County. Alt. 2,104.

Yamacraw, community in w Pender County.

Yancey Branch rises in s Cleveland County and flows se into First Broad River.

Yancey County was formed in 1833 from Burke and Buncombe counties. Located in the w section of the state, it is bounded by the state of Tennessee, and by Mitchell, McDowell, Buncombe, and Madision counties. It was named for Bartlett Yancey (1785-1828), member of the General Assembly and of Congress. Area: 311 sq. mi. County seat: Burnsville with an elevation of 2,817 ft. Townships are Brush Creek, Burnsville, Cane River, Crabtree, Egypt, Green Mountain, Jacks Creek, Pensacola, Price Creek, Ramseytown, and South Toe. Produces corn, oats, poultry, dairy products, livestock, hogs, hosiery, carpets, textiles, mica, feldspar, olivine, sand, and gravel.

Yancey Ridge, e Avery County.

Yanceyville, community and county seat in central Caswell County. Est. 1791 as Caswell Court House; name changed to Yanceyville in 1833 to honor Bartlett Yancey (1785-1828), Congressman and presiding officer of the State Senate. Inc. 1877; charter repealed 1915. Produces textiles and lumber. Alt. 619.

Yanceyville Township, central Caswell County.

Yanu Ridge, n Swain County in Great Smoky Mountains National Park, a short spur extending se from Welch Ridge with its center near lat. 35° 32′ N., long. 83° 34′ 40″ W.

Yarbro, community in ne Caswell County. Named for Captain Joseph Yarbrough, superintendent of ammunition manufacturing in Salisbury during the Civil War. A post office was operated here during the approx. period 1880-1905.

Yarnall Knob, s Watauga County n of Goldmine Branch. Alt. approx. 3,900.

Yates Cove, central Haywood County between Fincher Mountain and McElroy Cove.

Yates Mill Pond. See Lake Trojan.

Yates Mountain, w Wilkes County, extends from e to w between North and South Prongs Lewis Fork Creek.

Yates Top, s Cherokee County s of Shingle Top and between Cane, Martin, and Moccasin creeks.

Yaupon Beach, town in se Brunswick County. Inc. 1955. Named from a species of holly which grows in the area.

Yaupon Creek, a bay in e Pamlico County in the waters of Bay River.

Yawpim appears on the Moseley map, 1733, as a community in e Pasquotank Precinct, now Camden County, on North River. The name survives elsewhere as Yeopim, which see.

Yeates Knob. See Big Butte.

Yeatesville, town in e Beaufort County on Pungo Creek. Inc. 1881, but long inactive in municipal affairs. Named for Jesse J. Yeates (1829-92), Confederate officer and member of Congress.

Yellow Bald, s Macon County between Hurricane Creek and Bearpen Creek.

Yellow Branch rises in ne Swain County and flows se into Raven Fork.

Yellow Buck Ridge, n Caldwell County. Named by Bryson Coffey for a large

yellow buck which he killed here. Alt. approx. 1,500.

Yellow Creek rises in n Graham County and flows w into Cheoah River.

Yellow Creek rises in nw Haywood County and flows se into Big Creek.

Yellowcreek, community in n Graham County on Yellow Creek. Alt. 1,800.

Yellow Creek Gap, n Graham County between the headwaters of Yellow Creek and Tuskeegee Creek.

Yellow Creek Mountains extend from Cheoah River in nw Graham County e along the course of Yellow Creek to the headwaters of Mountain Creek.

Yellow Creek Township, nw Graham County.

Yellow Face, peak in n Jackson County on Plott Balsams. Alt. 6,032.

Yellow Gap, sw Buncombe County between Green Top and Billy Cove Knob.

Yellow Gap, s central Burke County.

Yellow Gap, nw Henderson County on the se end of Laurel Mountain. Alt. approx. 3,202.

Yellowhammer Branch rises in nw Graham County and flows e into Cheoah River.

Yellowhammer Gap, nw Graham County between Hangover Lead and Little Tennessee River.

Yellow Hill, mountain in w Wilkes County between Lewis Fork Creek and North Prong Lewis Fork Creek. Alt. approx. 1,300.

Yellow Jacket Lake, s Wilkes County on Moravian Creek. Covers approx. 2 acres; max. depth 15 ft. Built by R. Don Laws and named for his newspaper, The Yellow Jacket, which was est. in Moravian Falls in 1895.

Yellow Mountain, w Avery County near the Tennessee state line. Alt. 5,269.

Yellow Mountain, nw Buncombe County se of Davidson Gap.

Yellow Mountain, se Clay County, between the forks of Little Buck and Buck creeks to Water Oak Gap. Alt. 5,000-5,050.

Yellow Mountain, on the Jackson-Macon County line. Alt. 5,145. Known by the Indians as Ta-loh-na or Da-loh-no-geh, "yellow."

Yellow Mountains. See Unaka Mountains.

Yellow Patch Branch rises in e Jackson County and flows sw into Wolf Creek.

Yellow Patch Branch rises in s Macon County and flows nw into Hemp Patch Branch.

Yellow Spot, mountain in n Mitchell County. Alt. 5,112.

Yellowstone Falls, the final of a series of three waterfalls on Yellowstone Prong, s Haywood County.

Yellowstone Prong rises in s Haywood County on the s slope of Black Balsam Knob and flows e into East Fork Pigeon River. Named because of the yellow color of mosses growing on stones in the stream. Upper Falls, Second Falls, and Yellowstone Falls are located on this stream.

Yellow Swamp rises in s Wayne County and flows w into Thoroughfare Swamp.

Yeopim, community in sw Perquimans County. Named for the Yeopim Indian tribe which inhabited the region in the seventeenth century. Alt. 15.

Yeopim Creek rises in s Prequimans County and flows se into the mouth of Yeopim River. Appears as Clargeons Creek on the Collet map, 1770.

Yeopim River rises in Bear Swamp on the Chowan-Perquimans County line and flows se along the line into Albemarle Sound. Named for a tribe of Indians. Appears on the Comberford map, 1657, at the location of present Little River on the Pasquotank-Perquimans County line, an error which was corrected on the Ogilby map, 1671. Appears as Yeopim Creek on the Collet map, 1770.

Yeopim Township, former township in se Chowan County, now township number 4.

Yerger, community in n central Watauga County.

Yesocking Creek. See Wyesocking Bay.

Yonah-wayah. See Hanging Rock.

Yorick, community in central Bladen County.

York, former community in nw Warren County. A post office was est. here in 1902 but discontinued in 1905.

York County. On December 7, 1771, in the General Assembly, a bill for dividing the w part of Rowan County and erecting York County and St. James Parish read the second time and passed. Rejected on December 10 by the Council. Iredell County, which see, was created from western Rowan County in 1788. St.

James Episcopal Church in the s part of Iredell County, was est. about 1800.

York Creek rises in sw Carteret County and flows w into White Oak River.

Yorkville, community in nw Bladen County.

Younce Creek rises in n Macon County and flows se into Burningtown Creek.

Young Cove, sw Buncombe County e of Peggy Peak.

Young Cove, e Macon County on a tributary of Watauga Creek.

Young Cove, at the head of Young Cove Creek in e Mitchell County.

Young Cove Creek rises in e Mitchell County and flows sw into Cane Creek.

Young Gap, on the ne end of Burney Mountain on the Buncombe-Henderson County line.

Young Mountain, w Cherokee County between Camp and Shoal creeks.

Young Mountain, w Rowan County between Third and Withrow creeks. Alt. 1,092.

Young Pisgah Mountain, sw Buncombe County between Hogpen Gap and Berrys Gap. Alt. 4,017.

Youngs Creek rises in s Iredell County s of Troutman and flows sw into Rocky Creek. Now largely covered by Lake Norman.

Youngs Creek rises in nw Rutherford County and flows e into Cedar Creek.

Youngs Cross Roads. See Maysville.

Youngs Island, a loam island approx. 2 mi. long and ¾ mi. wide, in Pee Dee River, n Anson County.

Youngs Mountain, nw Rutherford County. extends ne parallel to Buffalo Creek. Alt. approx. 2,700.

Young's Store. See Oak Hill.

Youngs Swamp rises in ne Sampson County and flows ne into Goshen Swamp.

Youngsville, town in w Franklin County. Railroad name is Youngville. Alt. 449. Settled about 1839 and first known as Pacific. Inc. 1875. Named for John Young, local land owner. Produces apparel and furniture.

Youngsville Township, former township in sw Franklin County, now township number 3. Earlier called Freemans Township.

Youngville. See Youngsville.

Yuma. See Deep Gap.

Z

Zachary's, community in s Transylvania County near Rosman.

Zacks Fork Creek rises in ne Caldwell County and flows sw approx. 10 mi. into Lower Creek.

Zade Knob, n Madison County between Bull Creek Gap and Arington Branch.

Zara, community in se Bladen County.

Zebra, community in n Wilkes County near East Prong Roaring River.

Zebulon, town in e Wake County. Inc. 1907. Named for Zebulon B. Vance (1830-94), governor of North Carolina and U.S. Senator. Produces apparel, lumber products. Alt. 323.

Zeke Island, sandy island in the Cape Fear River opposite Snow Marsh, se Brunswick County.

Zephyr, community in w Surry County between Mitchell River and Little Creek.

Zillicoah. See French Broad River.

Zilphy Creek rises in s central Stokes County and flows e into Dan River.

Zion, community in sw Yadkin County.

Zionville, community in n Watauga County on Cove Creek. Alt. 3,159.

Zircon Mountain, s Henderson County near Freeman Creek.

Zirconia, community in s Henderson County. Alt. 2,084. Named for zircon mines operated here in the 1880's. Zircon discovered here in 1869.

Zoar, community in se Union County near Lar es Creek.

INDEX